The Pragmatics Encyclopedia

This single-volume encyclopedia covers the growing area of pragmatics: the analysis of language in context. Pragmatics has increasingly become a catch-all area for linguists and so has seen very rapid growth in recent years. It is probably the biggest sub-field of language and linguistics at research level.

A key aspect of this encyclopedia is that it seeks to re-establish the identity of pragmatics, by focussing on what is at the core of the discipline. However, the encyclopedia also demonstrates how pragmatics interacts with neighbouring disciplines and so has a multidisciplinary outlook. It aims to both reflect the field and help shape the future of the discipline.

An A–Z list of entries of varying lengths covers terms and concepts, theories, approaches, significant figures, issues and related disciplines. Including extensive cross-referencing, and graded further reading, *The Pragmatics Encyclopedia* aims to be the most compact and user-friendly volume available.

Louise Cummings is a Reader in Linguistics at Nottingham Trent University, where she teaches advanced level modules in pragmatics and clinical linguistics. She is the author of *Pragmatics: A Multidisciplinary Perspective* (Edinburgh University Press, 2005), *Clinical Linguistics* (also EUP, 2008) and *Clinical Pragmatics* (Cambridge University Press, 2009). She was a Visiting Fellow at Harvard University (1996/97) and at Cambridge University (2006).

The
Pragmatics
Encyclopedia

Edited by
Louise Cummings

 Routledge
Taylor & Francis Group

LONDON AND NEW YORK

First published 2010
by Routledge
2 Park Square, Milton Park, Abingdon, OX14 4RN

Simultaneously published in the USA and Canada
by Routledge
270 Madison Ave, New York, NY 10016

Routledge is an imprint of the Taylor & Francis Group, an informa business

© 2010 Louise Cummings

Typeset in Baskerville by Taylor & Francis Books
Printed and bound in Great Britain by CPI Antony Rowe, Chippenham, Wiltshire

British Library Cataloguing in Publication Data
A catalogue record for this book is available from the British Library

Library of Congress Cataloging in Publication Data
The pragmatics encyclopedia / edited by Louise Cummings.
p. cm.
ISBN 978-0-415-43096-8 (hardback : alk. paper) –
ISBN 978-0-203-87306-9 (ebk)
1. Pragmatics–Encyclopedias. I. Cummings, Louise.

P99.4.P72P7395 2009
306.44–dc22
2009004669

ISBN10: 0-415-43096-8 (hbk)
ISBN10: 0-203-87306-9 (ebk)

ISBN13: 978-0-415-43096-8 (hbk)
ISBN13: 978-0-203-87306-8 (ebk)

Contents

Board of consultants

Contributors

Barbara Abbott taught linguistics and philosophy at Michigan State University from 1976 to 2006. Her main areas of specialization fall within semantics, pragmatics, and philosophy of language. Specific topics of interest include definiteness and indefiniteness, referential opacity, presuppositions, natural kind terms, and conditionals. Among her published articles are 'Nondescriptionality and natural kind terms', 'Models, truth, and semantics', 'Water = H₂O', 'Presuppositions as nonassertions', 'Donkey demonstratives', and 'Conditionals in English and First Order Predicate Logic'.

Asif Agha is Professor of Anthropology, Linguistics, History and Sociology of Science, Folklore, South Asia Studies, International Studies, and Education at the University of Pennsylvania, where he is also Chair of the Department of Anthropology. He is the author of many articles and books, including *Language and Social Relations* (Cambridge University Press, 2007), which won the Edward Sapir Prize in 2008.

Romina Angeleri is a postdoctoral fellow in the Centre for Cognitive Science at the University of Turin. She received her Ph.D. in cognitive science from the same institution, studying communicative disorders in patients with unilateral brain injury. Her current research interests include clinical assessment of pragmatic abilities in patients affected by cerebral lesions, communicative rehabilitation, and early linguistic development, particularly cross-linguistic variation in children's speech and gesture. She has published a number of articles including a recent paper in *Brain and Language*.

Salvatore Attardo is Professor of Linguistics and Head of the Department of Literature and Languages at Texas A&M University–Commerce. He has published two books on the linguistics of

humour (*Linguistic Theories of Humor*, 1994; *Humorous Texts*, 2001, both with Mouton de Gruyter) and co-authored with Steve Brown an introduction to linguistics (*Understanding Language Structure, Interaction, and Variation*, Michigan University Press, 1999; second edition, 2005). He is the Editor of *HUMOR: International Journal of Humor Research*.

Dare Baldwin is Professor of Psychology at the University of Oregon and a former fellow at the Center for Advanced Study in the Behavioral Sciences. Her current research pursues two trajectories: examining the foundational role that early-emerging social understanding plays in language development, and investigating action-processing mechanisms that support the emergence of social understanding. She is a recipient of the American Psychological Association's Distinguished Scientific Award for Early Career Contribution, the Boyd McCandless Award, the John Merck Scholars Award, the James McKeen Cattell Sabbatical Award, and the John Simon Guggenheim Junior Memorial Award.

Bruno G. Bara, M.D., has a Ph.D. in Medical Psychology from Milan University. He trained at the Medical Research Council in Cambridge, UK, and at the International Computer Science Institute at Berkeley, California. Presently, he is full Professor of Psychology of Communication at the University of Turin and Director of the Centre for Cognitive Science. His research interests are in the fields of reasoning, pragmatics of communication, with attention to developmental and neuroscientific aspects, and cognitive psychotherapy. He is the author of *Cognitive Science* (LEA, 1995) and *Cognitive Pragmatics* (MIT Press, to appear).

Lavinia Merlini Barbaresi is Professor of English Linguistics and Director of the Ph.D. School in Linguistics at the University of Pisa. Her scientific interests are in text linguistics, language and discourse varieties, pragmatics and semiotics, with focus on the pragmatic effects of morphology, markedness and text complexity. She has published in national and international journals and collections, authored volumes such as *Markedness in English Discourse* (Edizioni Zara, 1988) and (with W. Dressler) *Morphopragmatics* (Mouton de Gruyter, 1994) and edited *Complexity in Language and Text* (Edizioni Plus, 2003).

Francesca Bargiela-Chiappini is a Senior Research Fellow at Nottingham Trent University, UK. She has published widely in the field of business discourse. Her recent and forthcoming publications include the co-authored book *Business Discourse* (Palgrave Macmillan, 2007) with C. Nickerson and B. Planken and the edited volume *The Handbook of Business Discourse* (Edinburgh University Press, 2009). She is also co-editor of the *Journal of Politeness Research* and has edited with M. Haugh a volume on *Face, Communication and Social Interaction* (Equinox, 2009).

Avner Baz is an Assistant Professor of Philosophy at Tufts University. He has published papers on ethics, aesthetics, perception, and epistemology. He is currently working on a book manuscript in which he argues that, widespread rumours to the contrary notwithstanding, ordinary language philosophy – as exemplified, however differently, in the writings of Wittgenstein and Austin – still constitutes a well motivated and viable alternative to the philosophical work that is currently carried out within the mainstream of analytic philosophy.

Cristina Becchio is currently a researcher in the Centre for Cognitive Science at the University and Polytechnic of Turin. She graduated in Philosophy from the University of Turin. After completing her Ph.D. in Cognitive Science, she went on to carry out postdoctoral research on spatial reasoning. Her current research interests include social cognition, temporal cognition and intentionality. Her work on these topics has appeared in scientific peer-reviewed journals including *Cognition*, *Brain* and *Trends in Cognitive Sciences*.

Cesare Bertone is a philosopher and philosophy teacher. He is a member of the Centre for Cognitive Science at the University and Polytechnic of Turin and collaborates with the Centre for Theoretical and Applied Ontology. His main research interests are at the border between philosophy and neuroscience, and span from social ontology and

collective intentionality to object processing and time. He is author or co-author of a number of articles published in scientific peer-reviewed journals.

Anne Bezuidenhout received her doctorate in philosophy from the University of Michigan, Ann Arbor in 1990. She has been teaching ever since at the University of South Carolina, where she is a member of the Philosophy Department and the Linguistics Program. She works in the philosophy of language on issues at the semantics-pragmatics interface, as well as in psycholinguistics. She is editor (with M. Reimer) of *Descriptions and Beyond* (Oxford University Press, 2004) and has published articles in *Mind and Language*, *Philosophical Perspectives* and *Midwest Studies in Philosophy*.

Reinhard Blutner is Privatdozent at the Humboldt University in Berlin. He began his scientific career in theoretical physics and shifted later to artificial intelligence, cognitive psychology and theoretical linguistics. In his work he integrates insights from connectionist psychology, logics, computer science and cognitive linguistics. Currently, he is a lecturer in Artificial Intelligence and Cognitive Philosophy at the University of Amsterdam.

Emma Borg is Professor of Philosophy at the University of Reading, UK. She works on the philosophy of language and mind and is the author of *Minimal Semantics* (Oxford University Press, 2004), together with numerous articles. Her recent research topics include minimalism, referential intentions, and mirror neurons. In 2006, she was awarded a Philip Leverhulme Prize for outstanding young researchers.

Francesca M. Bosco has a Ph.D. in Cognitive Science from the University of Turin. She is currently a researcher of General Psychology and a member of the Centre for Cognitive Science at the same institution. Her studies are concerned with the development of pragmatic ability, its decay and rehabilitation in brain damaged and schizophrenic patients, the normal development of theory of mind and theory of mind deficits in schizophrenic patients. She has published a number of articles including co-authored papers in the *Journal of Pragmatics*, *Cognitive Development* and *Brain and Language*.

Philippe De Brabanter is a Lecturer in English Linguistics at Paris 4–Sorbonne and a member of Institut Jean Nicod. He wrote his Ph.D. on the semantics and pragmatics of quotation (Brussels, 2002) and in 2005 edited an issue of the *Belgian*

Journal of Linguistics on 'Hybrid Quotation'. His current research interests are theories of quotation, the semantics-pragmatics interface, semantic deference, metalinguistic anaphora, speaker commitment and the 'intrusion' of non-linguistic communication into linguistic utterances.

Richard Breheny is Reader in Linguistics in the Division of Psychology and Language Sciences, University College London. His research interests include semantics, pragmatics, experimental and developmental pragmatics and the philosophy of psychology. He is currently the editor of the Palgrave series *Palgrave Studies in Pragmatics, Language and Cognition*. He is the author of articles in formal semantics, pragmatics, psycholinguistics and developmental pragmatics.

Penelope Brown is a linguistic anthropologist whose research focuses on the relationship between language, culture and cognition. The central concern of her work is the study of language usage in its sociocultural context. She has worked for many years in a Tzeltal Mayan community in Mexico and more recently in Rossel Island in Papua New Guinea. She has authored papers in a number of volumes including *Person Reference in Interaction* (Cambridge University Press, 2007) and is the editor with M. Bowerman of *Crosslinguistic Perspectives on Argument Structure* (Lawrence Erlbaum, 2008).

Elisabeth Camp is an Assistant Professor of Philosophy at the University of Pennsylvania, USA. Her research focuses on non-literal language (metaphor, sarcasm, and fiction) and on non-propositional and non-sentential thought (perception, cognitive 'perspectives', and non-human animal cognition). Publications include 'Contextualism, metaphor, and what is said', 'Metaphor and that certain "Je ne sais quoi"', and 'The generality constraint, nonsense, and categorial restrictions'.

Malinda Carpenter is a Senior Scientist in the Department of Developmental and Comparative Psychology at the Max Planck Institute for Evolutionary Anthropology in Leipzig, Germany. Her research interests include prelinguistic communication, imitation, joint attention, joint action and theory of mind in infants, apes and children with autism. She is co-author of two Society for Research in Child Development monographs on communication and social cognition, as well as numerous research articles and theory papers in developmental and other journals.

Robyn Carston is Professor of Linguistics at University College London. Her research focuses on the semantics/pragmatics distinction and the explicit/implicit distinction. Her approach is interdisciplinary, integrating insights from philosophy of language and cognitive science. The main framework she employs is Sperber and Wilson's Relevance Theory, with Grice's ideas on communication an important influence. She has published *Thoughts and Utterances* (Blackwell, 2002) and is preparing a volume of papers *Pragmatics and Semantic Content* (Oxford University Press, 2009).

Maud Champagne-Lavau is an Adjunct Professor at the University of Montreal. Her research interests focus on pragmatic deficits and their relation to social cognition deficits in right-brain damaged individuals and in schizophrenia. She is the author of several articles in reputed journals including *Brain*, *Brain and Language* and *Brain and Cognition*. In 2002 she received a partnership award in health research (Focus on stroke) from the Canadian Institute of Health Research for her project on pragmatic deficits in right-brain damaged individuals.

Winnie Cheng is a Professor and the Director of the Research Centre for Professional Communication in English in the Department of English at The Hong Kong Polytechnic University. Her main research interests include corpus linguistics, phraseology, intercultural professional communication, discourse analysis, discourse intonation and intercultural pragmatics. Recent publications include *Intercultural Conversation* (John Benjamins, 2003); (with C. Greaves and M. Warren) *A Corpus-Driven Study of Discourse Intonation* (John Benjamins, 2008); and (co-edited with K.C.C. Kong) *Professional Communication: Collaboration between Academics and Practitioners* (Hong Kong University Press, 2008).

Chris Christie is a lecturer in the Department of English and Drama at Loughborough University, UK. Her research and publications have focused primarily on the exploration of gender through the application of pragmatic theories, in particular focusing on methodologies that engage with relevance theory and politeness theories. Her publications include *Gender and Language: Towards a Feminist Pragmatics* (Edinburgh University Press, 2000). She is Editor-in-Chief of *The Journal of Politeness Research*.

Carl Coelho, Ph.D., is a speech-language pathologist who has worked clinically and conducted research in the area of neurogenic communication disorders for over thirty years. He is currently Professor and Head of the Communication Sciences Department at the University of Connecticut. Coelho is also an Associate Investigator on the Vietnam Head Injury Study. He is a Fellow of the American Speech-Language-Hearing Association, and President of the Academy of Neurologic Communication Disorders and Sciences.

Herbert L. Colston is a Professor of Psychology at the University of Wisconsin-Parkside. He received a B.S. (Psychology) at Purdue University and M.S. and Ph.D. degrees (Cognitive Psychology) from the University of California–Santa Cruz. His research investigates comprehension and use of figurative and indirect language, non-verbal communication, embodiment and cognitive linguistics. He edited with A.N. Katz *Figurative Language Comprehension* (Routledge, 2005) and with R.W. Gibbs *Irony in Language and Thought* (Lawrence Erlbaum, 2007).

David Crystal has been Honorary Professor of Linguistics at the University of Bangor, Wales, since 1985. The author of a wide range of books on language study, recent publications relating to the subject of his paper include *A Glossary of Netspeak and Textspeak* (Edinburgh University Press, 2004), *Language and the Internet* (Cambridge University Press, 2nd edition, 2006), *Txtng: the Gr8 Db8* (Oxford University Press, 2008), and *The Cambridge Encyclopedia of Language* (Cambridge University Press, 3rd edition, 2010).

Jonathan Culpeper is a Senior Lecturer in the Department of Linguistics and English Language at Lancaster University, UK. Spanning pragmatics, stylistics and the history of English, his publications include *History of English* (2nd edition, 2005), *Cognitive Stylistics* (2002, edited with Elena Semino), *Exploring the Language of Drama* (1998, co-edited with Mick Short and Peter Verdonk) and *Language and Characterisation in Plays and Other Texts* (2001). He is currently completing a three-year research fellowship investigating impoliteness.

Louise Cummings is Reader in Linguistics at Nottingham Trent University, UK. Her research interests include philosophical and cognitive aspects of pragmatics and pragmatic disorders. She is author of *Pragmatics: A Multidisciplinary Perspective* (Edinburgh University Press, 2005), *Clinical Linguistics* (also EUP, 2008) and *Clinical Pragmatics* (Cambridge University Press, 2009). She has been a Visiting Fellow in the Department of Philosophy at Harvard University and the Centre for Research in the Arts, Social Sciences and Humanities at Cambridge University.

Ilaria Cutica has been a Researcher in General Psychology at the Faculty of Psychology of the University of Turin since 2005. She received her Ph.D. in Cognitive Science from the same institution in 2001. She is a member of the Centre for Cognitive Science of Turin University and of the Teaching Committee of the Doctoral School in Neuroscience, Turin. Her research interests include communication in brain injured patients and gestural communication. She has co-authored articles in a number of publications including the journals *Brain and Language* and *Cognitive Science*.

Marcel Danesi is full Professor of Semiotics and Anthropology at the University of Toronto. His main research interests include semiotic theory and practice and youth culture. Among his recent publications are *The Puzzle Instinct* (Indiana University Press, 2004), *Brands* (Routledge, 2006), *The Quest for Meaning* (University of Toronto Press, 2007), and *Popular Culture* (Rowman and Littlefield, 2007). He is currently Editor-in-Chief of *Semiotica*, the official journal of the International Association of Semiotics Studies.

Nicole Dehé received her doctorate in 2002 from Leipzig University, Germany. Since then, she has held research and teaching positions at universities in Germany and the UK. She is currently a member of the English Department at the Freie Universität Berlin. Her main research interests lie in intonational phonology, prosody and the syntax-prosody interface. Her publications include a monograph on *Particle Verbs in English* (Benjamins, 2002) and an edited volume on *Parentheticals* (Benjamins, 2007).

Wolfgang U. Dressler was born in Vienna in December 1939. He has studied in Vienna, Rome and Paris and has taught at various American and European universities. He was Professor of Linguistics at the University of Vienna up to 2008 and is head of the Department of Linguistics of the Austrian Academy of Sciences. His current major research areas are morphology in linguistic theory, language acquisition and aphasia, morphopragmatics and morphonology. He has also done research on historical linguistics, text linguistics and text pragmatics, phonology and language death.

Vyvyan Evans is Professor of Linguistics at Bangor University, UK. His research relates to lexical and compositional semantics, figurative language and thought, and conceptual structure. He is a specialist in cognitive linguistics and is President of the UK Cognitive Linguistics Association. His published work includes *A Glossary of Cognitive Linguistics* (Edinburgh University Press, 2007), with Melanie Green *Cognitive Linguistics: An Introduction* (Edinburgh University Press, 2006), *The Structure of Time* (Benjamins, 2004) and with Andrea Tyler *The Semantics of English Prepositions* (Cambridge University Press, 2003).

Jane Evison is a University Teacher in TESOL at the School of Education, University of Nottingham, UK. Her research interests include the corpus linguistic analysis of the pragmatics of turn taking. She is co-author of 'Looking out for love and all the rest of it: vague category markers as shared social space' in the edited volume *Vague Language Explored* (Palgrave, 2007) and author of 'What are the basics of analysing a corpus?' in *The Routledge Handbook of Corpus Linguistics* (to appear).

Katalin Farkas is Associate Professor in the Philosophy Department of the Central European University. She studied mathematics and philosophy at the Eötvös Loránd University in Budapest. She is interested in the philosophy of mind, metaphysics, scepticism, and Descartes. She is the author of *The Subject's Point of View* which was published by Oxford University Press in 2008.

John Field teaches psycholinguistics and child language development at the University of Reading and cognitive approaches to second language acquisition at Cambridge University. He has written several books with a view to making psycholinguistics more accessible, including the standard reference guide *Psycholinguistics: The Key Concepts* (Routledge, 2004). His main research interests lie in second language listening processes, on which he has published widely. His most recent book in this area is *Listening in the Language Classroom* (Cambridge University Press, 2009).

Bruce Fraser is Professor of Linguistics and Education at Boston University. His research interests lie in pragmatics, forensic linguistics, and political linguistics. His recent work includes 'Hedging in Political Linguistics: The 2007 Bush News Conferences and the Discourse Marker /but/ in English'. He is currently working on a book entitled *Contrastive Discourse Markers in English*.

Raymond W. Gibbs, Jr is Professor of Psychology at the University of California–Santa Cruz. He is author of *The Poetics of Mind: Figurative Thought, Language, and Understanding* (Cambridge University Press, 1994), *Intentions in the Experience of Meaning* (CUP, 1999) and *Embodiment and Cognitive Science* (CUP, 2006) and is editor of *The Cambridge Handbook of Metaphor and Thought* (2008) and the journal *Metaphor and Symbol*. His research interests include psycholinguistics, figurative language, and pragmatics.

Steven Gimbel is an Associate Professor of Philosophy at Gettysburg College in Pennsylvania in the United States. His research ranges from the philosophy of language to the philosophy of physics. He is the co-editor with Anke Walz of *Defending Einstein: Hans Reichenbach's Early Writings on Space, Time, and Motion* (Cambridge University Press, 2006). His work on the pragmatics of tautologies with Johannes Bulhof has appeared in the *Journal of Pragmatics* and *Pragmatics and Cognition*. Other articles have appeared in *The British Journal for the Philosophy of Science*, *Erkenntnis*, *Philosophy of Science*, *Studies in History and Philosophy of Modern Physics*, and the *Journal of Applied Philosophy*.

Rachel Giora is Professor of Linguistics at Tel Aviv University. Her research areas include discourse coherence, relevance, cognitive pragmatics, language and ideology, and women and language. Her recent work focuses on the psycholinguistics and neurolinguistics of figurative language (irony, jokes, and metaphor), context effects, optimal innovation and aesthetic pleasure, discourse negation, and the notion of salience. Her book *On Our Mind: Salience, Context, and Figurative Language* was published by Oxford University Press in 2003.

Cliff Goddard is Professor of Linguistics at the University of New England, Australia. His research interests lie at the intersection of language, meaning and culture. He is a proponent of the NSM (Natural Semantic Metalanguage) approach and a close collaborator with its originator, Anna Wierzbicka. His recent books include the edited volumes *Ethnopragmatics* (de Gruyter, 2006) and *Cross-Linguistic Semantics* (Benjamins, 2008), and the textbook *The Languages of East and Southeast Asia* (Oxford University Press, 2005).

Helen Goodluck is Anniversary Professor of Linguistics at the University of York, UK. She joined the faculty at York in 2004, having previously taught at the University of Ottawa, Canada. Her main research interests are in language acquisition by children and sentence processing, and the relation between these two areas. She has contributed papers to a number of volumes including *The Blackwell Handbook of Language Development* (Blackwell, 2007) and *UG and External Systems* (Benjamins, 2005). Her recent publications include articles in the *Journal of Linguistics, Language, Journal of Child Language* and *Journal of Psycholinguistic Research*.

Sarah Grandage is a Teaching Fellow at the University of Nottingham, UK. She completed her doctoral thesis on Shakespearean intertextuality in contemporary newspapers discourse at the same institution. Her linguistic research interests include literary linguistics, discourse analysis and pragmatics, which intersect with interests in drama, particularly Shakespeare and Early Modern drama. Publications include 'Imagining England: contemporary encodings of "this sceptred isle"', in W. Maley and M. Tudeau-Clayton (eds) *This England, That Shakespeare: New Angles on Englishness and the Bard* (Ashgate, 2009).

Georgia M. Green is Professor Emeritus of Linguistics at the University of Illinois at Urbana-Champaign. She received her Ph.D. from the University of Chicago in 1971. Her work is concerned with the nature of syntactic constraints and the nature and analysis of implicated meaning in natural language understanding. Her book *Pragmatics and Natural Language Understanding* (Lawrence Erlbaum, 1989, 1996) is now in its second edition and has been translated into at least three languages.

Jeanette Gundel is Professor of Linguistics at the University of Minnesota. Her research interests include semantics and pragmatics, information structure, and the relation between language and other cognitive systems. She is author of *The Role of Topic and Comment in Linguistic Theory* (Garland, 1988) and co-author of *Reference and Referent Accessibility* (Benjamins, 1996) and *Reference: Interdisciplinary Perspectives* (Oxford University Press, 2008). She has taught at the LSA Summer Institutes at Michigan State (2003) and Stanford (2007).

Dean Hardman is Lecturer in Linguistics at Nottingham Trent University, UK. His research interests are in the fields of discourse analysis and sociolinguistics. He is particularly interested in critical discourse analysis and media discourse. His recent research work has examined a diachronic corpus of British print media texts by utilizing a mixed analytical framework that combined sociolinguistic insights with critical discourse analysis.

Sandra Harris is Professor Emeritus at Nottingham Trent University, UK. She has a longstanding interest in institutional, particularly courtroom, discourse, and is the author of two books on business discourse, both with Francesca Bargiela, *Managing Language: The Discourse of Corporate Meetings* (Benjamins, 1997) and *The Languages of Business: An International Perspective* (Edinburgh University Press, 1997). She has contributed a large number of articles to a wide range of international journals and edited collections. Her current research interest is in linguistic (im)politeness in institutional and political contexts, and she is one of the editors of the *Journal of Politeness Research*.

Kevin Harvey is Lecturer in Sociolinguistics at the University of Nottingham, UK. He is interested in multi-modal approaches to language use and particularly discourse produced in the context of healthcare. His current research involves a corpus linguistics analysis of medical problems posted to a website dedicated to providing evidence-based health advice and information for young people. He has co-authored articles in *Social Science and Medicine, Journal of Adolescent Health, Journal of Pastoral Counselling* and *The International Journal of Pharmacy Practice*.

Paul ten Have was, until his retirement in 2002, Associate Professor in the Department of Sociology and Anthropology of the University of Amsterdam. He has written numerous articles and several books on qualitative research, ethnomethodology and conversation analysis. Recent publications include *Understanding Qualitative Research and Ethnomethodology* (Sage, 2004), 'On the interactive constitution of medical encounters', *Revue Française de Linguistique Appliquée* (2006) and *Doing Conversation Analysis: A Practical Guide*, second edition (Sage, 2007).

Leo Hickey holds the degrees of B.A., M.A. and LL.B. from the National University of Ireland, Licenciado and Doctor en Filosofía y Letras from the Universidad Complutense, Madrid. He is a barrister with a Diploma in Public Service Interpreting. Until 2001, he was Professor of Spanish at the University of Salford, UK. He has over 100 publications in areas including translation theory and practice, linguistics, stylistics and pragmatics. He is the editor of *The Pragmatics of Translation* (Multilingual Matters, 1998). He now works as a legal translator and interpreter.

Janet Holmes is Professor of Linguistics at Victoria University of Wellington. She is also Director of the Language in the Workplace Project and teaches sociolinguistics from first year to Ph.D.

level. She has published on politeness in discourse, pragmatic particles, New Zealand English, language and gender, sexist language, and many aspects of workplace discourse. Her most recent book is the third edition of *An Introduction to Sociolinguistics* (Pearson, 2008).

Paul J. Hopper has published books and articles on language change, historical linguistics, and discourse analysis. He has served as the Collitz Memorial Professor at the Linguistic Society of America Linguistics Institute, as Directeur d'Études at the École Pratique des Hautes Études in Paris, and as lecturer at the Collège de France. He is the Paul Mellon Distinguished Professor of Humanities at Carnegie Mellon University.

Laurence Horn, Ph.D. UCLA, 1972, is Professor of Linguistics at Yale University. He is the author of *A Natural History of Negation* (Chicago 1989/CSLI 2001), the co-editor with Gregory Ward of *The Handbook of Pragmatics* (Blackwell, 2004) and with Yasuhiko Kato of *Negation and Polarity* (Oxford, 2000), and has published numerous articles on implicature, presupposition, negative polarity, lexical semantics, logical operators, and the semantics/pragmatics interface. He is a Fellow of the Linguistic Society of America.

Kate Howarth has a Ph.D. on police interview discourse and its roles in the criminal justice process from the University of Nottingham, UK. She is a (non-practising) barrister. Her research interests include all aspects of language and the law and forensic linguistics, especially language as evidence. She has recently published an article in the journal *Discourse and Society* and is the author of a paper in the edited volume *Routledge Handbook of Forensic Linguistics* (Routledge, 2010).

Yan Huang, Ph.D. Cambridge, D.Phil. Oxford, is Professor of Linguistics at the University of Auckland. He has previously taught linguistics at the universities of Cambridge, Oxford, and Reading, where he was Professor of Theoretical Linguistics. His books include internationally acclaimed *The Syntax and Pragmatics of Anaphora* (Cambridge University Press, 1994; reissued in 2007), *Anaphora: A Cross-Linguistic Study* (Oxford University Press, 2000), and *Pragmatics* (Oxford University Press, 2007).

Elly Ifantidou is Assistant Professor of Linguistics in the Faculty of English Studies at the University of Athens. Her research interests are in pragmatics, semantics, cognitive and linguistic development,

academic discourse and media discourse. Her publications include *Evidentials and Relevance* (John Benjamins, 2001) and articles in edited volumes and journals such as the *Journal of Pragmatics*, *Pragmatics and Cognition* and *Pragmatics*.

Cornelia Ilie is Professor of English Linguistics at Örebro University, Sweden. Her research covers three main areas – pragmatics, institutional discourse analysis, and rhetoric and argumentation – on which she has published extensively. Apart from the rhetorical study of question-response patterns, her recent publications have focused on pragma-rhetorical strategies in political and media discourse, academic discourse and cross-cultural communication. She has initiated and coordinated international research projects and is on the editorial board of several journals.

Tania Ionin is an Assistant Professor of Linguistics at the University of Illinois at Urbana-Champaign. Her research interests include second language acquisition and the syntax-semantics interface. Her recent publications include 'Sources of linguistic knowledge in the second language acquisition of English articles' (with M.L. Zubizarreta and S. Bautista-Maldonado, *Lingua*), 'Progressive aspect in child L2-English' (*Current Trends in Child Second Language Acquisition*, John Benjamins, 2008) and 'This is definitely specific: specificity and definiteness in article systems' (*Natural Language Semantics*).

Terry Janzen is Associate Professor in the Department of Linguistics at the University of Manitoba. He has a Ph.D. in linguistics from the University of New Mexico. His research interests include ASL morpho-syntax, clause structure and topicality issues within the context of discourse, the grammatical coding of signer perspective in ASL discourse, and grammaticization in signed languages. He is the author of recent articles in the journal *Cognitive Linguistics* and the edited volume *Verbal and Signed Languages* (Mouton de Gruyter, 2007).

Kasia M. Jaszczolt is Reader in Linguistics and Philosophy of Language, University of Cambridge and Fellow of Newnham College, Cambridge. She is the author of four books (*Discourse, Beliefs and Intentions*, Elsevier, 1999; *Semantics and Pragmatics*, Longman, 2002; *Default Semantics*, Oxford University Press, 2005; *Representing Time*, Oxford University Press, 2009) and many articles on various topics in semantics and pragmatics. She has edited several books and a book series *Current Research in the Semantics/Pragmatics Interface* (Elsevier).

Phillip Johnson-Laird left school early and spent ten years in various occupations before going to University College, London, to read psychology. Subsequently, he has held appointments at UCL, the Institute for Advanced Study, Sussex University, the MRC's Applied Psychology Unit Cambridge, and Princeton. He has published many papers and books. He is a fellow of the Royal Society, the British Academy, and the American Philosophical Society, and is a member of the National Academy of Sciences.

Asa Kasher is Professor Emeritus of Philosophy at Tel Aviv University, where he held different chairs. He has had visiting positions at UCLA, Amsterdam, Berlin, Ghent, and Oxford amongst other institutions. His research interests include theoretical studies in philosophical pragmatics and empirical studies in neuropsychological pragmatics, as well as professional ethics. He is the editor of *Pragmatics: Critical Concepts*, volumes I–VI (Routledge, 1998) and volumes VII–X (to appear). He won the National Prize of Israel for general philosophy in 2000.

Gabriele Kasper is Professor of Second Language Studies at the University of Hawai'i at Manoa. Her research interests include second language pragmatics, discourse and, formerly, psycholinguistics. Currently she is working on conversation analysis as an approach to second language interaction and learning and qualitative research methodology in applied linguistics. She is a co-author of *Pragmatic Development in a Second Language* (Blackwell, 2002) and has edited with K.R. Rose *Pragmatics in Language Teaching* (Cambridge University Press, 2001).

Friederike Kern, Dr. phil., currently holds a position as a Visiting Professor in the German department at the Freie Universität Berlin, Germany. Her research interests are in the area of interactional linguistics, first language acquisition and language development, culture and language, grammar of spoken language, and prosody. Her publications include work on rhythm in Turkish German, the use and function of intonation contours in children's instructions, and the development of story telling in young schoolchildren.

Leung Chi Kong conducts research in linguistics at The Hong Kong Polytechnic University. He

obtained his Doctor of Business Administration degree and master's degree in Professional English from the same institution. He has more than thirty years of practical experience in the banking industry. Currently, he is a compliance officer with a specific focus on the recent developments of rules and regulations of the financial regulators.

Dennis Kurzon is Professor of Linguistics in the English Department of the University of Haifa, Israel. His fields of research include speech act theory, the pragmatics and semiotics of legal discourse, and of silence, as well as the sociolinguistics of India, adpositions, writing systems and linguistic landscape. He has recently published articles on silence and on diacritics. His book *Where East Looks West: Success in English in Goa and on the Konkan Coast* was published in 2003 by Multilingual Matters, and he has recently edited a second book on adpositions (published by John Benjamins).

Cristina Lafont is Professor of Philosophy at Northwestern University. She specializes in German philosophy, particularly hermeneutics and critical theory. She is author of *The Linguistic Turn in Hermeneutic Philosophy* (MIT Press, 1999) and *Heidegger, Language, and World-Disclosure* (Cambridge University Press, 2000). Some of her recent articles include 'Meaning and interpretation. Can Brandomian scorekeepers be Gadamerian hermeneuts?' in *Philosophy Compass* (2007) and 'Alternative visions of a new global order' in *Ethics and Global Politics* (2008).

Karen Le conducts research in the Communication Sciences Department at the University of Connecticut. She has been a speech-language pathologist for six years and has a Certificate of Clinical Competency from the American Speech-Language-Hearing Association. Her research interests include the study of discourse deficits following traumatic brain injury, the development of sensitive and reliable discourse measures for clinical use, the examination of the effect of cognitive impairments on discourse ability and social interactions, and the role of the frontal lobes in social communication and discourse processing.

Stephen Levinson has been Director of the Max Planck Institute for Psycholinguistics since 1994. His research interests include linguistic semantics and pragmatics, cognitive anthropology, language, culture, cognition and comparative linguistics. He is the author of *Presumptive Meanings* (MIT Press, 2000), *Space in Language and Cognition* (Cambridge

University Press, 2003), and has edited (with P. Jaisson) *Evolution and Culture* (MIT Press, 2006), (with D. Wilkins) *Grammars of Space* (Cambridge University Press, 2006), and (with N.J. Enfield) *Roots of Human Sociality* (Berg Publishers, 2006).

Kirk Ludwig is Professor of Philosophy at the University of Florida. He has published numerous articles in the philosophy of language, philosophy of mind and action, and epistemology. He is editor of *Donald Davidson* (Cambridge University Press, 2003) and co-author (with Ernie Lepore) of *Donald Davidson: Meaning, Language, Truth and Reality* (Oxford University Press, 2005) and *Donald Davidson's Truth-theoretic Semantics* (Oxford University Press, 2007).

Didier Maillat received his Ph.D. from Oxford University. He currently works as Associate Professor of English Linguistics at the University of Fribourg, Switzerland. His research focuses on pragmatic models at various interfaces. He has published several articles on the pragmatics of spatial reference frames including a paper in *Meaning through Language Contrast* (John Benjamins, 2003). More recently, his publications have investigated the pragmatics of second language acquisition in connection with bilingual education. In his latest project, he develops a pragmatic account of manipulative discourse.

Valeria Manera has a Ph.D. in cognitive science from the University of Turin, Italy. She currently works in the Centre for Cognitive Science in the Psychology Department of the same institution. Her current research interests include emotion recognition, the emergence of social abilities in neonates and infants, and the attribution of communicative intention from biological motion. Since 2007, she has been collaborating with the Psychology Department of the University of Leuven, Belgium. She has published articles in leading developmental journals such as *Developmental Science* and *Developmental Review*.

Sophia Marmaridou is Professor of Linguistics at the University of Athens. Her academic interests lie in the areas of semantics, pragmatics, cognitive linguistics and lexicography. Her recent publications include *Pragmatic Meaning and Cognition* (John Benjamins, 2000), 'On the conceptual, cultural and discursive motivation of Greek pain lexicalizations' (*Cognitive Linguistics*, 2006) and with K. Nikiforidou and E. Antonopoulou as editors, *Reviewing Linguistic Thought: Converging Trends for the 21st Century* (Mouton de Gruyter, 2005).

Bilyana Martinovski is an Assistant Professor and a University Lecturer at the University College of Boras and Göteborg University. She received her Ph.D. in linguistics from the University of Gothenburg, Sweden in 2000. Between 2001 and 2007 she worked at the Institute for Creative Technologies, University of Southern California, investigating multi-modal cross-cultural communication among humans and virtual agents and the communicative manifestation of emotion. She has published articles in the *Journal of Pragmatics* and the *Journal of Group Decision and Negotiation*.

Davide Mate has a degree in Psychology and a Ph.D. in Cognitive Science from the University of Turin. He is currently a postdoctoral researcher at the same institution. His research interests include theoretical psychology, the study of communication and mindreading, the adult learning process, clinical psychology, and brain mapping studies of motor rehabilitation. He has co-authored articles in international journals, including *Neuroimage*, and has published papers in a number of conference proceedings.

Tomoko Matsui is Associate Professor at Kyoto University, Japan. Her research interests include the inferential mechanisms that are involved in utterance interpretation, which is the topic of her book *Bridging and Relevance* (John Benjamins, 2000). More recently, she has been working on how acquisition of epistemic vocabulary contributes to children's overall understanding of the speaker's mental states. Part of this work has been reported in a co-authored paper in the journal *Cognitive Development* (2006).

Michael McTear is Professor of Knowledge Engineering at the University of Ulster. He has been researching in the field of spoken dialogue systems for more than ten years and has delivered keynote addresses and tutorials at several recent conferences and workshops. Other research interests include natural language processing, user modelling, and language acquisition. His most recent book *Spoken Dialogue Technology: Toward the Conversational User Interface* was published by Springer Verlag in 2004.

Sara Meilijson is the Chairperson of the Communication Disorders Department at Hadassah Academic College in Jerusalem. Her research examines the pragmatics of language in different clinical populations including autism, schizophrenia, hearing impairment and fluency disorders. She conducts supervision in clinical education and curriculum development. Her publications include (with A. Kasher and A. Elizur) 'Language performance in chronic schizophrenia: a pragmatic approach' (*Journal of Speech, Language and Hearing Research*) and (with A. Kasher) 'Autism and pragmatics of language' (*Incontri*).

Cristina Meini is a Researcher at the University of Eastern Piedmont, Italy, where she teaches Cognitive Psychology. Her research areas are philosophy of psychology (the nature of naïve psychology, modularity of mind, Darwinian psychology, communication) and experimental psychology (pathologies of naïve psychology, psychology of aesthetic experience). She is the author of several books including *Psicologi Per Natura* (Carocci, 2007) and (with M. Marraffa) *La Mente Sociale* (Bollati-Boringhieri, 2005). She has contributed a paper to the edited collection *Cartographies of the Mind* (Springer, 2007) and has a forthcoming article in the journal *Philosophical Psychology*.

Jacob L. Mey is Professor Emeritus of Linguistics at the University of Southern Denmark, and Senior Research Associate of the University of Brasilia. He has taught and undertaken research at the Universities of Oslo, Texas (Austin), Hong Kong (City), Yale and Northwestern. He holds honorary doctorates from several universities. In 2008, his own university honoured him with a lifetime achievement award. His publications include *Pragmatics: An Introduction* (2nd edn, Blackwell, 2001) and *When Voices Clash: A Study in Literary Pragmatics* (Walter de Gruyter, 1998). He is the founder and chief editor of the *Journal of Pragmatics*.

Meredith Meyer conducts research in developmental psychology at the University of Oregon. She researches child language acquisition and is particularly interested in how language and gesture function together to contribute to children's early category knowledge. She is co-author with Dare Baldwin of articles in the *Blackwell Handbook of Language Development* (Blackwell, 2007), *Cognition* (Elsevier, 2008), and the *Proceedings of the 30th Annual Conference of the Cognitive Science Society* (Cognitive Science Society, 2008).

Laura Monetta is an Assistant Professor at Laval University in Quebec. After completing a Ph.D. at the University of Montreal, Laura was awarded a postdoctoral fellowship from the Canadian Institute of Health Research, Institute of Aging, to conduct research on Parkinson's disease and pragmatics at McGill University. Today, her research focuses on pragmatic communication disorders in the brain-damaged population. She has published several articles in international journals including *Brain and Language* and the *Journal of Speech-Language Pathology*.

Liz Morrish is Subject Leader of Linguistics at Nottingham Trent University, UK. Her research interests lie in the areas of language and sexual identity, and language and gender. She is the co-author, with Helen Sauntson, of *Language and Sexual Identity*, published in 2007 by Palgrave. The work focuses on ways in which lesbian or gay identities are performed linguistically. She is currently working on neoliberal discourse and its impact on gendered subjectivity in the academy.

Jennifer Mozeiko conducts research in the Communication Sciences Department at the University of Connecticut. She has been a speech-language pathologist for three years and has a Certificate of Clinical Competency from the American Speech-Language-Hearing Association. Her research interests include the study of discourse deficits following traumatic brain injury, auditory processing deficits following cerebral vascular accidents, and the role of the frontal lobes in social communication, particularly as this relates to discourse processing.

Brigitte Nerlich is Professor of Science, Language, and Society at the Institute for Science and Society, University of Nottingham, UK. She studied French and philosophy in Germany. Her current research focuses on the cultural and political contexts in which metaphors are used in science and the media. She has written books and articles on the history of linguistics, semantic change, metaphor, metonymy, polysemy and the linguistic and cultural framing of science in society.

Neal R. Norrick holds the chair of English Linguistics at Saarland University in Saarbrücken, Germany. His research specializations include verbal humour, conversation, narrative and formulaicity. In recent years, he has focused his research on spoken language. Professor Norrick serves on the editorial staff of the *Journal of Pragmatics* (Special Issues editor) and the advisory boards of the journals *Text and Talk*, *Discourse Processes*, and *Humor: International Journal of Humor Research*.

Ira Noveck received his Ph.D. in Cognitive Psychology from New York University in 1992. He has since held research or teaching positions in France and North America. He is currently Director of the

Laboratoire sur le Langage, le Cerveau et la Cognition (L2C2) in Lyon, France. There, he heads a team that focuses on the role of pragmatics in reasoning and comprehension. He has edited with D. Sperber *Experimental Pragmatics* (Palgrave Macmillan, 2004) and has authored articles in *Cortex, Brain and Language, Trends in Cognitive Sciences* and *Cognition*.

Joseph B. Orange is Associate Professor and Director of the School of Communication Sciences and Disorders at the University of Western Ontario, London, Canada. His current research includes analyses of discourse, conversation and functional communication of individuals with various types of dementia, including Alzheimer's disease and frontotemporal lobe dementia, and those with amyotrophic lateral sclerosis. Other ongoing studies include developing and testing communication enhancement education and training programmes for family caregivers of individuals with dementia.

Maryann Overstreet is an Associate Professor and Chair of the German Program at the University of Hawai'i at Manoa. Her research interests include pragmatics, discourse analysis, second language teaching and learning, and psycho-sociolinguistic perspectives on linguistic categorization. Her publications include *Whales, Candlelight, and Stuff Like That: General Extenders in English Discourse* (Oxford University Press, 1999) and articles in the *Journal of Pragmatics, Journal of English Linguistics* and *Discourse Processes*.

Ruth Page is a Reader in the School of English at Birmingham City University. Her research interests focus on the intersections between narrative theory, language and gender and digital media. Her publications include *Literary and Linguistic Approaches to Feminist Narratology* (Palgrave, 2006) and the edited collections *New Perspectives on Narrative and Multimodality* (Routledge, 2009) and (with B. Thomas) *New Narratives: Theory and Practice* (University of Nebraska Press, 2009).

Jaroslav Peregrin is a researcher at the Institute of Philosophy of the Academy of Sciences of the Czech Republic and a professor of logic at the Faculty of Arts and Philosophy of the Charles University in Prague. His research is located at the intersection of logic, analytic philosophy and semantics. He is the author of *Doing Worlds with Words* (Kluwer, 1995) and *Meaning and Structure* (Ashgate, 2001). As a Visiting Scholar, he worked at the University of Konstanz in Germany and the University of Pittsburgh in the USA.

Adrian Pilkington, formerly of the London University Institute in Paris, is the author of *Poetic Effects: A Relevance Theory Perspective* (Benjamins, 2000). He has published articles in several journals including *Language and Literature* and has contributed papers to a number of volumes, most recently *Linguistic Approaches to Poetry* (Belgian Journal of Linguistics, Benjamins, 2003). His research interests lie mainly in the areas of the pragmatics of literary style and metaphor.

Diana de Souza Pinto is an Associate Professor at the Federal University of the Estate of Rio de Janeiro (UNIRIO) where she is a researcher in the Graduate Program in Social Memory. She has a MA in Applied Linguistics and a Ph.D. in Mental Health at the Federal University of Rio de Janeiro (UFRJ). Dr Pinto has published on the interface between discourse analysis and mental health and on the fields of transcultural psychiatry and narrative studies.

Christopher Potts received his doctorate from the University of California–Santa Cruz in 2003. He has published widely on topics in semantics and pragmatics, including the book *The Logic of Conventional Implicatures* (Oxford University Press, 2005). His research on expressive content has been supported by the National Science Foundation. He serves on the editorial boards of *The Journal of Semantics, Linguistics and Philosophy, Natural Language Semantics*, and the LSA eLanguage journal *Semantics and Pragmatics*. He is currently Associate Professor of Linguistics at the University of Massachusetts–Amherst.

Stefano Predelli is Professor of Philosophy at the University of Nottingham. He has written on indexicals and contextual dependence, and is the author of *Contexts: Meaning, Truth, and the Use of Language* (Oxford University Press, 2005). His recent publications include 'Modal monsters and talk about fiction' (*The Journal of Philosophical Logic*, 2008), 'I exist' (*American Philosophical Quarterly*, 2008), and 'Vocatives' (*Analysis*, 2008).

Branca Telles Ribeiro directs a research project in language and communication in psychiatry at the Federal University of Rio de Janeiro (Brazil). She is Associate Professor at Lesley University (M. A., USA). Her current research explores intercultural communication and access to health care for Brazilian immigrants in the Boston area. Her major publications are *Coherence in Psychotic Discourse* (Oxford University Press, 1994), *Sociolinguistica Interacional* (São Paulo, Loyola, 2002), and 'Medical

Discourse, Psychiatric Interview' in *The Encyclopedia of Language and Linguistics* (Elsevier, 2005).

Nicky Riddiford is the coordinator and teacher of a workplace communication programme for skilled migrants at Victoria University of Wellington. She is also a member of the Language in the Workplace Project (LWP) research team. She is currently developing pragmatic training resources that draw heavily on LWP research, and is involved in a research study that is tracking the development of pragmatic competence of a group of skilled migrants in New Zealand.

Celia Roberts is Professor of Applied Linguistics at King's College London. Her research interests are in language, ethnicity and institutional discourse, particularly in health communication and selection interviewing and the impact of linguistic diversity on minority ethnic group life chances. She also has a particular interest in research methodology. Her publications include (with M. Bryam, A. Barro, S. Jordan and B. Street) *Language Learners as Ethnographers* (Multilingual Matters, 2001) and (with S. Sarangi as editors) *Talk, Work and Institutional Order* (Mouton, 1999).

Douglas Robinson is Professor of English and director of first-year writing at the University of Mississippi. He is author of *Performative Linguistics*, *Introducing Performative Pragmatics*, and several books on translation (*The Translator's Turn, Translation and Taboo, What Is Translation?, Who Translates?*), comparative literary theory (*Estrangement and the Somatics of Literature: Tolstoy, Shklovsky, Brecht*), and American literature and culture (*American Apocalypses, Ring Lardner and the Other*, and *No Less a Man*).

Pamela Rosenthal Rollins is an Associate Professor at the University of Texas in the Dallas/Callier Center for Communication Disorders. She is director of Early Services for Children with Autism Spectrum Disorders at Callier and a member of the Texas Council for Autism and Pervasive Developmental Disorders. Her research focuses on the continuity between early social-pragmatic skills and the acquisition of language in children with and without disorders. Of particular interest is the co-construction of joint attention within infant-caregiver dyads.

Nuala Ryder is a Research Fellow in Developmental Psychology at the University of Hertfordshire, UK. Her research interests include specific language impairment, the cognitive processes of pragmatic language impairment and the interactional nature of communication. She has co-authored articles in a number of journals including 'Use of context in question answering by 3-, 4- and 5-year-old children' (*International Journal of Psycholinguistic Research*, 2003) and 'A cognitive approach to assessing pragmatic language comprehension in children with specific language impairment' (*International Journal of Language and Communication Disorders*, 2008).

John Saeed is a Fellow of Trinity College Dublin and Associate Professor of Linguistics. His research interests include semantics and African linguistics. He is author of *Semantics* (3rd edn, Blackwell, 2009) and *Somali* (John Benjamins, 1999). He has been a Visiting Fellow in the Department of the Languages and Cultures of Africa, School of Oriental and African Studies, London and in the Research Centre for Linguistic Typology, LaTrobe University, Melbourne.

Helen Sauntson is Lecturer in English Language and Linguistics at the University of Birmingham, UK. Her research interests include classroom discourse, language and gender, and language and sexuality. She is the author (with Liz Morrish) of *New Perspectives on Language and Sexual Identity* (Palgrave, 2007), co-editor (with Sakis Kyratzis) of *Language, Sexualities and Desires: Cross-Cultural Perspectives* (Palgrave, 2007) and co-editor (with Kate Harrington, Lia Litosseliti and Jane Sunderland) of *Gender and Language Research Methodologies* (Palgrave, 2008).

Marina Sbisà is Professor of Philosophy of Language at the University of Trieste, Italy. Her research interests include speech act theory, presupposition and implicature, contextualism, discourse analysis, and gender studies. She has published two volumes in Italian (*Linguaggio, Ragione, Interazione*, Il Mulino, 1989; *Detto Non Detto*, Laterza, 2007) and papers in international journals and collections. She collaborated with J.O. Urmson on the revised edition of J.L. Austin's *How To Do Things With Words* (Oxford University Press, 1975).

Thomas C. Scott-Phillips undertook his Ph.D. in the Language Evolution and Computation Research Unit at the University of Edinburgh, and currently holds a postdoctoral position in the same group. His research focuses on the origins and evolution of language, and in particular on the relationship between pragmatics and social evolution theory, the branch of the biological

sciences that addresses organisms' social behaviour. He has published articles in the *Journal of
Evolutionary Biology* and *Evolutionary Psychology*.

Peter Sells is Professor of Linguistics at the
School of Oriental and African Studies, University
of London. His research interests include the mor-
phology, syntax and semantics of Japanese and
Korean, and more broadly the architecture of
grammar. He is co-author with Jong-Bok Kim of
English Syntax (CSLI Publications, 2008) and co-
editor with Yoshiko Matsumoto, David Y. Oshima,
and Orrin W. Robinson of *Diversity in Language*
(CSLI Publications, 2007). He taught at Stanford
University for over twenty years before moving to
London in 2007.

Elena Semino is a Senior Lecturer in the
Department of Linguistics and English Language at
Lancaster University, UK. She is interested in sty-
listics, corpus linguistics and metaphor research.
Her books include *Cognitive Stylistics: Language and
Cognition in Text Analysis* (John Benjamins, 2002, co-
edited with Jonathan Culpeper), *Corpus Stylistics:
Speech, Writing and Thought Presentation in a Corpus of
English Writing* (Routledge, 2004, with Mick Short)
and *Metaphor in Discourse* (Cambridge University
Press, 2008).

John Shook is Vice President and Senior
Research Fellow at the Center for Inquiry in
Amherst, NY, and also Research Professor in Philosophy at the University at Buffalo. Shook focuses
on American philosophy, philosophy of science,
and philosophy of mind. He authored *Dewey's
Empirical Theory of Knowledge and Reality*, co-authored
Dewey's Philosophy of Spirit, and edited the *Dictionary
of Modern American Philosophers*. He is also a co-editor
of *Contemporary Pragmatism*, *Philo*, and *The Pluralist*.

Maria Sifianou is Professor in the Faculty of
English Studies, University of Athens. Her publications include *Politeness Phenomena in England and
Greece* (Oxford University Press, 1992), *Discourse
Analysis* (Hillside Press, 2006) and a number of
articles in books and journals. She has co-edited
Themes in Greek Linguistics (Benjamins, 1994) and
Linguistic Politeness across Boundaries (Benjamins,
2001), among others. Her main research interests
include politeness phenomena and discourse analysis
in an intercultural perspective.

Stef Slembrouck is Professor of English Linguistics and Discourse Analysis at Ghent University,
Belgium. He has published mainly on the role of

language use, communication and discursive processes in the construction of institutional identities
(bureaucracy, child protection and health), including the impact of migration-connected multilingualism. Publications include (with S. Sarangi)
Language, Bureaucracy and Social Control (Longman,
1996), (with C. Hall and S. Sarangi) *Language Practices in Social Work* (Routledge, 2006) and (with J.
Collins and M. Baynham) *Globalization and Languages
in Contact* (Continuum, 2009).

Robert J. Stainton completed his Ph.D. in Linguistics and Philosophy at the Massachusetts Institute of Technology in 1993. Since then, he has
authored or edited numerous books at the intersection of these two fields, with particular emphasis
on the pragmatics of subsentential speech. His most
recent research focuses on pragmatic abilities
in autism spectrum disorder. Currently, he is
Professor of Philosophy and Associate Dean
(Research) at the University of Western Ontario,
London, Canada.

Kenneth Taylor is Henry Waldgrave Stuart
Professor of Philosophy at Stanford University. His
research interests include Gricean and neo-Gricean
pragmatics, the semantics-pragmatics interface,
formal semantics, formal pragmatics, the theory of
reference, the philosophy of mind, and the nature
of normativity. He is author of *Truth and Meaning*
(Blackwell, 1998) and *Reference and the Rational Mind*
(CSLI Publications, 2004). He is also co-host, with
John Perry, of the nationally syndicated radio programme *Philosophy Talk*.

Marina Terkourafi holds a Ph.D. from the
University of Cambridge, UK, and is currently
Assistant Professor of Linguistics at the University
of Illinois, Urbana-Champaign. Her research
interests focus on theories of (im)politeness, post-
Gricean pragmatics, the sociolinguistics of Greece
and Cyprus, cognitive linguistics, computational
pragmatics and language change. She has published on these topics in the *Journal of Pragmatics*,
Journal of Historical Pragmatics, *Journal of Politeness
Research*, *Journal of Greek Linguistics* and *Diachronica*
among others.

J. Robert Thompson teaches philosophy at
Mississippi State University. His research focuses
on two interrelated issues – the manner in which
semantic theories should deal with expressions with
context-dependent meanings, and the ability that
humans use in understanding the minds of others.
He explores theories that allow semantics to accom-

modate a modest number of context-dependent expressions and examines how communicative intentions fix the meaning of these context-dependent expressions. He has published articles in *Synthese* and *Teorema*.

Christopher W. Tindale is Professor of Philosophy at the University of Windsor, Ontario, Canada, and a fellow of the Centre for Research in Reasoning, Argumentation and Rhetoric. His publications are principally in argumentation and rhetoric and include the books *Fallacies and Argument Appraisal* (Cambridge University Press, 2007), *Rhetorical Argumentation* (Sage, 2004), *Acts of Arguing* (SUNY, 1999) and with L. Groarke *Good Reasoning Matters! A Constructive Approach to Critical Thinking* (Oxford University Press, 4th edn, 2008).

Maurizio Tirassa has a degree in Medicine and a Ph.D. in Psychology. He is currently full Professor of General Psychology at the University of Turin. His research interests include theoretical psychology, the study of communication and mindreading, their ontogeny, their disturbances after neuropsychological or psychiatric damage, and their rehabilitation. He has authored or co-authored several articles in international journals (including *Brain and Language*, *Consciousness and Cognition*, and *Cognitive Systems Research*), conference proceedings, and book chapters.

John Todman is an Emeritus Professor in the School of Psychology, University of Dundee. From 2005 to 2007, he edited *Augmentative and Alternative Communication* (*AAC*). He was recently awarded a Fellowship of the International Society of Augmentative Communication for outstanding and distinguished achievement in the field of AAC. He is lead author of *Whole Utterance Approaches in AAC* in the September 2008 special issue of *AAC*, celebrating ISAAC's 25th birthday.

Mark Dietrich Tschaepe is the 2008–9 postdoctoral Naturalism Research Fellow at the Center for Inquiry–Transnational, which is located in Amherst, NY. His research interests include pragmatics and pragmatic considerations, especially as they pertain to mechanistic and folk explanations of behaviour. He is author of 'Pragmatics and pragmatic considerations in explanation' (*Contemporary Pragmatism*, 2009) and 'Halo of identity: the significance of first names and naming' (*Janus Head: Journal of Interdisciplinary Studies in Literature, Continental Philosophy, Phenomenological Psychology, and the Arts*, 2003).

Ken Turner is Senior Lecturer in Linguistics with special reference to Analytic Philosophy of Language at the University of Brighton, UK. He has previously held appointments at the University of Lancaster and the University of Sussex. His research interests include semantics, pragmatics, the philosophy of language and minority languages in China. He is co-editor, with Klaus von Heusinger (University of Stuttgart), of the series *Current Research in the Semantics/Pragmatics Interface* (Emerald) and serves on the editorial board of the *Journal of Pragmatics*.

Marianna Vallana has a degree in Psychology and a Ph.D. in Cognitive Science from the University of Turin. Her main research area is cognitive science, in particular pragmatics. Her studies in pragmatics are concerned with the normal development and decay of mental processes underlying pragmatic competence. She has recently co-authored the paper 'Communicative ability in schizophrenic patients: executive function, theory of mind and mental representations' in the *Proceedings of the 29th Annual Conference of the Cognitive Science Society* (Cognitive Science Society, 2007).

Jessica de Villiers is an Associate Professor in the Department of English at the University of British Columbia. Her areas of research interest are pragmatics, discourse analysis, clinical linguistics, philosophy of language and autism spectrum disorders. She is the author of several papers including 'Discourse analysis in autism spectrum disorders' (*Linguistics and the Human Sciences*, 2006) and has co-authored 'Brief report: a scale for rating conversational impairment in autism spectrum disorder' (*Journal of Autism and Developmental Disorders*, 2007).

Tim Wharton is a cognitive pragmatist. His research focuses on 'natural' communicative behaviours – such as facial expressions, gesture, tone of voice – and how these might be integrated within a pragmatic theory using the notions of 'showing' and 'meaning'. His main theses are outlined in a forthcoming book entitled *Pragmatics and Non-Verbal Communication* (Cambridge University Press). Other interests include relevance theory and lexical pragmatics, the evolution of language and communication and the philosophy of Paul Grice.

Anne Wichmann is Emeritus Professor of Speech and Language at the University of Central Lancashire, UK. Her main area of research is intonation in spoken discourse. She is particularly interested in the prosodic expression of attitude, and in the prosodic cues to grammaticalization processes. Her work is based mainly on spoken corpora. Publications include *Intonation in Text and Discourse* (Pearson Education, 2000) and editorship in 2006 of a special issue of the *Journal of Pragmatics* on Prosody and Pragmatics.

Anna Wierzbicka is Professor of Linguistics at the Australian National University. She is the author of numerous books, including *Cross-Cultural Pragmatics* (Mouton de Gruyter, 1991; 2nd edn, 2003), *Semantics: Primes and Universals* (Oxford University Press, 1996), *Understanding Cultures Through Their Keywords* (Oxford University Press, 1997), *Emotions Across Languages and Cultures: Diversity and Universals* (Cambridge University Press, 1999), *What Did Jesus Mean? Explaining the Sermon on the Mount and the Parables in Simple and Universal Human Concepts* (Oxford University Press, 2001) and *English: Meaning and Culture* (Oxford University Press, 2006).

Lynne J. Williams received her Ph.D. from the University of Texas at Dallas. Her research interests include cognitive linguistics and psycholinguistics including the conceptual mapping of meaning and how that is expressed in everyday interactions. She is currently a post-doctoral fellow in the School of Communication Sciences and Disorders at the University of Western Ontario, London, Canada.

Deirdre Wilson is Professor Emeritus in the Department of Linguistics at University College London and research professor and co-director of the Linguistic Agency project at the Centre for the Study of Mind in Nature, University of Oslo. Her main research interests are in theoretical pragmatics. Her book *Relevance: Communication and Cognition* (Blackwell, 1986, 1995), written jointly with Dan Sperber, has been translated into eleven languages. She was awarded an honorary doctorate from the University of Geneva in 2007.

Ruth Wodak is Distinguished Professor of Discourse Studies in the Linguistics Department at Lancaster University, UK. Besides various other prizes, she was awarded the Wittgenstein Prize for Elite Researchers in 1996 and is also head of the Wittgenstein Research Centre 'Discourse, Politics, and Identity' at the University of Vienna. Recent book publications include *Politics as Usual* (Palgrave, 2009), *Migration, Identity and Belonging* (Liverpool University Press, 2008), and *The Politics of Exclusion* (Transaction Press, 2008).

Lynsey Wolter is an Assistant Professor at the University of Wisconsin, Eau Claire. After receiving her Ph.D. from the University of California–Santa Cruz, she was a postdoctoral fellow at the University of Rochester. Her research focuses on the interface of formal semantics and pragmatics. Specific research interests include the semantics of definite noun phrases, particularly demonstratives; the nature of identification in natural language; the lexical semantics of attitude verbs; and experimental approaches to pragmatics.

John Woods is Director of the Abductive Systems Group, University of British Columbia, and Charles S. Peirce Professor of Logic, Group on Logic and Computation, King's College London. His books include *Fallacies* (1989/2007), *The Death of Argument* (2004), *Agenda Relevance* (2003), and *The Reach of Abduction* (2005). He is Fellow of the Royal Society of Canada, recipient of the International Society for Studies in Argumentation Research Prize and the Queen's Golden Jubilee Medal, and President Emeritus, University of Lethbridge.

Henk Zeevat is a Senior Lecturer in Computational Linguistics at the University of Amsterdam. His research interests include discourse particles, discourse semantics, discourse structure, various aspects of pragmatics and formal models of grammar. He is the author of articles in a number of journals including the *Journal of Semantics* and *Linguistics*. He has edited with R. Blutner *Optimality Theory and Pragmatics* (Palgrave Macmillan, 2003).

Vladimir Žegarac is a Reader in Language and Communication at the University of Bedfordshire, UK. His primary research interest is in the field of pragmatics. He works within the cognitive framework provided by relevance theory, but is also interested in social approaches to communication and culture. His publications include articles in *Journal of Linguistics* (co-authored), *Lingua* and *Second Language Research*, as well as chapters in a number of books.

Preface

Few disciplines have experienced the degree of expansion that has been witnessed in pragmatics. In the relatively short history of this field, pragmatics has moved well beyond its early philosophical roots to connect with a large number of concerns in linguistics and other disciplines. Pragmatics continues to examine central concepts such as implicature but its contexts for doing so have enlarged considerably. So as well as examining the philosophical and linguistic features of implicature, investigators are increasingly concerned to address questions such as the following: How do young children acquire the pragmatic competence needed to use and understand implicatures? How are implicatures disrupted in child and adult clients with communication disorders? What are the cognitive processes that enable someone to recover the implicature of an utterance? These questions, and others like them, require investigators to engage with disciplines such as child language acquisition, language pathology and cognitive psychology. It emerges that the pragmatist can no longer operate with a tightly circumscribed set of key pragmatic concepts and theories. Indeed, the pragmatist who believes he can will find that he has already been overtaken by developments in the field.

The *Pragmatics Encyclopedia* aims to capture the multidisciplinary influences that have shaped and continue to shape the field of pragmatics. As one would expect, core concepts and theories are represented in entries on implicature, deixis, presupposition, speech act theory and relevance theory. Important theoretical work at the interfaces of pragmatics and other language levels is discussed in entries on morphopragmatics, the semantics-pragmatics, syntax-pragmatics and prosody-pragmatics interfaces. However, there is much else besides. This encyclopedia gives recognition to areas that have tended to exist in parallel to pragmatics in the absence of proper interdisciplinary integration. Work in disordered pragmatics is a case in point. Entries reflect the very latest developments in the field, such as the recent emergence of experimental pragmatics. Scholars who have had a formative influence on pragmatics, as well as those who have been deeply influenced by key pragmatic ideas are represented in entries on Grice, Austin, Searle and Habermas. In short, this encyclopedia aims to convey to the reader the historical, intellectual and disciplinary influences that have shaped the modern discipline of pragmatics.

The entries in this encyclopedia were carefully crafted by experts with a diverse readership in mind. Each entry is designed to engage students of pragmatics and junior academics, while at the same time challenging more advanced scholars in the field. To guide the reader who wants to explore a particular topic in more depth, each entry is accompanied by a number of suggestions for further reading. At the end of each entry, '*see also*' items direct the reader to other related entries. Bold type indicates where a word or term appears as another entry in the encyclopedia. Finally, a bibliography is included that contains a wide range of texts that represent all the main topics, approaches and theories in pragmatics. I hope the reader gains some sense of the large and vibrant field of study that is pragmatics from reading the entries in this encyclopedia.

Louise Cummings
Editor

Acknowledgements

There are a number of people whose contribution to this volume I would like to acknowledge. I want to thank Louisa Semlyen (Senior Commissioning Editor), Ursula Mallows (Development Editor) and Samantha Vale Noya (Editorial Assistant) at Routledge for their important roles in the realization of this encyclopedia. The idea for the *Pragmatics Encyclopedia* was entirely Louisa's. I'm grateful to her for considering me as the editor of this work and for her steadfast support during the completion of this project. This encyclopedia has been a huge undertaking and I received Ursula's assistance throughout most of its preparation and Samantha's contribution in the final stage of its development. I acknowledge their efforts with

gratitude. My sister, Judith Heaney, has assisted me throughout with the collation of entries and the preparation of the final manuscript. I cannot thank her enough for the diligence she has shown and the time she has committed to this project.

I owe an enormous debt of gratitude to the consultants who have worked alongside me and to the authors of the individual entries that appear in this volume. The professionalism and commitment shown by these academics has been truly gratifying. I have gained intellectually and personally from the experience of working with them. This volume simply would not have been possible without their combined expertise and collaboration.

Abduction

Widely understood as **inference** to the best explanation, abduction may be conceived of even more generously as a form of backwards-chaining **reasoning**, with or without explanatory force as the case may be. Adumbrated in remarks of Aristotle (*Prior Analytics* 2, 69ᵃ 20–36), today's notion of abduction is more commonly associated with the American pragmatist, Charles Sanders **Peirce** (1839–1914), who schematized it as follows:

> The surprising fact C is observed. But if A were true, C would be a matter of course. Hence there is reason to suspect that A is true.
>
> (Peirce 1931–58: 5.189)

In some contexts, it is clear that 'C would be a matter of course' can be interpreted as 'C would be explained'. From the fact that, if true, A would explain C, it is conjectured that A might be true. In this form, successful abduction is understood as 'inference to an explanation', but it is more faithful to Peirce's schema to say 'inference *from* an explanation'. Where there is more than one explanation, abduction opts for the best, that is, the most explanative of them. Some commentators are of the view that 'C would be a matter of course' also admits of non-explanationist interpretation. Consider, for example, Newton's celestial mechanics, in which gravitational force acts instantaneously over arbitrary distances. Newton regarded this as a conceptual impossibility, but he tied his acceptance of it to the extraordinary accuracy of the relevant equations. '*Hypothesis non fingo*', as he famously said. By this Newton meant that he regarded the action-at-a-distance claim as inexplicable. Abductions such as these may be thought of as having instrumental rather than explanatory value. More recent examples of instrumental abduction are Planck's conjecture of quanta and Gell-Mason's conjecture of quarks.

Peirce himself was careful to emphasize the highly conjectural nature of abduction. He holds that abduction is a form of guessing (Peirce 1931–58: 5.172); that a successful abduction lacks probative value, that is, it provides no grounds for believing the abduced **proposition** to be true (Peirce 1992a: 178); that, rather than believing them, the proper thing to do with abduced hypotheses is to submit them to experimental trial (1931–58: 5. 599, 6. 469–6. 473, 7. 202–19); that the connection between an abduced hypothesis and the observed fact is subjunctive (1931–58: 5. 189); that the inference licensed by abduction is not to the proposition A, but rather to the proposition that A's truth might plausibly be conjectured; and that the inference itself is defeasible (1931–58: 5. 189). As with many of his better ideas, Peirce has nothing like a fully developed account of abduction. But these remarks are telling all the same. It is interesting to speculate on what Peirce's rather bare-bones schema would look like had these six observations been incorporated into it.

It is possible to construe Peirce's notion of surprise not as a psychological shock, but as the kind of cognitive irritation that attends one's failure to hit an epistemic target with resources presently at hand. There are two standard responses to this kind of ignorance problem. One is to acquire some new **knowledge**. The other is to abandon or suspend the epistemic target in question. The first way, one overcomes one's ignorance. The second way, one's ignorance overcomes one. Sometimes there is a third response. This is the abductive response, intermediate between the other two. Like the first, abduction furnishes the basis for new action (albeit defeasibly). Like the second, it fails to remove the ignorance that occasioned the irritation to which it is a response. It is, in other words, an action-enabling but ignorance-preserving form of inference. For generality, let T be an agent's epistemic target at a time, and K the agent's knowledge base at that time. Let R be an attainment relation for T and R^{subj} a subjunctive attainment relation for it. Let H be a hypothesis. Then K(H) is the revision of K upon the addition of H. C(H) denotes the conjecture of H, and H^c denotes its activation. With these parameters at hand, the expanded Peircean schema would look something like this (Gabbay and Woods 2005):

(1) Target T is set by an agent.
(2) K does not attain T.   [fact]
(3) H is a proposition not in K.   [fact]
(4) K(H) does not attain T.
(5) But K(H) does subjunctively attain T. [fact]
      ('If H were true then K(H) would attain T.')
(6) So, C(H).   [sub-conclusion]
(7) So, H^c.

Step (6) says that conjecturing H is justified by the foregoing facts, and (7) denotes the permissibility of acting on H in a certain way, namely by making it a 'working' hypothesis. This is done by releasing it for provisional premissory work in the domain of **discourse** that gave rise to the agent's ignorance problem.

The Peircean element of surprise is represented here as the cognitive irritation inherent in an ignorance problem. Since abduction is ignorance-preserving, the 'so' of the schema is meant defeasibly. The schema is also expressly subjunctive about the attainment relation between K(H) and T. So the further elements of non-probativity and conjecture-only are clearly present. Step (7) of the schema takes abduction further than Peirce himself wanted to go. For

him, the only thing to do with an abduced hypothesis is to submit it to experimental test. On the face of it, Peirce's caution is sensible. Given that abduction is a kind of guessing, it would seem imprudent to place any cognitively serious weight on it. Against this, (7) proposes a suitably constrained relaxation of Peirce's diffidence. This it does by generalizing the notion of test in a way that recognizes that there are classes of apparently reasonable abductions for which experimental testing is not presently (or ever) available. Accordingly, (7) allows for the indirect testing of an H by dint of its contribution to a successful practice or theory. A well-known example is Bertrand Russell's embrace of the 'axiom' of infinity, whose postulation he sought to justify by its contribution to a type-theoretic treatment of classes. Russell's employment of the postulate is precisely the kind of action mandated by step (7).

If the present schema deviates from the Peircean paradigm by 'over-playing' step (7), other approaches deviate by 'under-playing' this and other Peircean elements. The following is a format for the 'stripped-down' schema (Josephson and Josephson 1994; Magnani 2001; Aliseda 2006). In it E is a sentence reporting some event, K is a knowledge base, H a hypothesis and → an implication relation:

(1) E   [fact]
(2) It is not the case that K → E   [fact]
(3) It is not the case that H → E   [fact]
(4) It is the case that K(H) → E   [fact]
(5) So, H.   [conclusion]

Peircean elements are not to be found here. The standard schema imposes no requirement that E be surprising, or that successful abduction be non-probative, or that the sentence 'K(H) → E' be in the subjunctive mood, or that H be merely conjectured, or that the 'so' of line (5) marks the inference as defeasible. It is possible, of course, that some proponents of the present schema take it that some or all of these features are 'understood'.

Both schemata are somewhat over-simplified. Neither makes express provision for the requirement that if more than one hypothesis is available for a given abduction problem, a hypothesis-selection procedure is activated. Various criteria for bestness have been proposed. Among them are that H be consistent, minimal, simplest, most coherent with K, most relevant, and most plausible. It is a matter of contention as to whether all these are necessary for bestness, still less sufficient.

A further point of contention is the claim that abduction is inherently ignorance-preserving. There is no space to give this full consideration here. But two observations can be made briefly. One is that among philosophers of science there is some disagreement as to whether explanation is probative. If it is, explanative abduction will not rest easily with the Peircean insistence that the successful abduction of H is no reason to believe that it is true, with obviously negative consequences for the ignorance-preservation claim. A second point is that ignorance preservation does not preclude there being some antecedent reason to believe an abductively successful H. But it does preclude that its abductive success provides *additional* reason to believe it. Accordingly, a winning H may enjoy a degree of evidential support, provided that the evidence in question is not sufficiently strong or abundant to reach the epistemic bar embedded in the target with respect to which the abduction-creating ignorance-problem arose in the first place.

JOHN WOODS

See also: Inference; Peirce, C.S.; reasoning

Suggestions for further reading

Flach, P.A. and Kakas, A.C. (eds) (2000) *Abduction and Induction: Essays on Their Relation and Interpretation*, Dordrecht and Boston, MA: Kluwer.
Gabbay, D.M. and Woods, J. (2006) 'Advice on abductive logic', *Logic Journal of IGPL*, 14: 189–219.

Academic Discourse

The range of **communication** which comprises academic discourse is wide and ever expanding. Although published academic writing such as research articles and textbooks has been seen as the mainstay of communication

between academics, there is growing emphasis on the importance of academic talk (e.g. lectures, seminars and conference presentations) and computer mediated academic communication such as podcasts and online discussion fora. English remains the global language of academia, and for this reason the necessity of providing English for Academic Purposes (EAP) instruction and testing for those whose first language is not English is a driving force behind much research into academic discourse. This field of endeavour has expanded dramatically over the past three decades, and with it, interest in the role that **pragmatics** plays in academic communication.

One important area of research into the pragmatics of academic discourse focuses on the role of metadiscourse, or text about text. Research into writing has concentrated on defining the scope of metadiscourse (Vande Kopple 1985; Crismore and Farnsworth 1990; Mauranen 1993; Bunton 1999; Hyland 1999), classifying metadiscursive elements (Hyland and Tse 2004; Hyland 2005) and contrasting the metadiscourse of different languages (Mauranen 1993; Hyland and Milton 1997). The pragmatic importance of metadiscourse is explored particularly in relation to two of Halliday's metafunctions, the textual and the interpersonal (e.g. Halliday 1985). Textual metadiscourse is connected with **discourse coherence** and **discourse cohesion**. Interestingly, Hyland and Tse (2004: 164) question the usefulness of distinguishing between the textual and the interpersonal in metadiscourse, arguing that the distinction is 'unhelpful and misleading', because what is often labeled textual metadiscourse in fact 'contributes to the interpersonal features of a text'. Hyland's work is particularly influential in this area and highlights the fact that metadiscourse is a critical pragmatic feature which cannot be separated from its overall social and rhetorical **context** (*see* Hyland 2005 for a collection of his research).

In respect of academic speech, Coulthard and Montgomery (1981a: 35) in their seminal work characterize metadiscourse as playing a 'subsidiary' but crucial role in lecture talk: 'monitoring, reflecting upon and commenting on the main thrust of the discourse'. In another key work, Mauranen (2001) discusses the importance of discourse reflexivity, which she connects with two sets of tutor–student relationships (expert/ novice and client/server). Her conclusion is that the tutors' role as servers means that they are obliged to mitigate the discourse authority that their expert status brings. **Discourse markers** (e.g. *right, now, so*) are well researched meta-discursive items. Whilst studies carried out during the 1980s and 1990s tended to focus on the roles that discourse markers play in lecture compre-hension and information recall (Chaudron and Richards 1986; DeCarrico and Nattinger 1988; Dunkel and Davis 1994; Flowerdew and Tauroza 1995), subsequent research has highlighted the fact that discourse markers are multifunctional interpersonal and organizational resources avail-able to academic speakers (Swales and Malczewski 2001; Biber 2006; Fung and Carter 2007).

Interactiveness is a key characteristic of spoken academic discourse in particular. Its centrality can be associated with the shift from reading style lecture delivery to less scripted forms of talk (Flowerdew 1994) and a greater emphasis on interactive lectures, seminars and small group teaching. The importance of inter-action between tutors and students is linked to what Fairclough (1992) observes as the growing democratization of universities and the related conversationalization of their discourse practices. A number of studies have shown the interactive nature of academic monologue (Coulthard and Montgomery 1981a; Rounds 1987; Northcott 2001; Crawford Camiciottoli 2004; Simpson and Mendis 2003; Bamford 2004; Morell 2004), suggesting that academics choose to use linguis-tic features associated with interactivity (e.g. third person pronouns, inclusive *we* structures, **deixis**, idiomatic language) in order to project interpersonal closeness. Academic writing too is increasingly identified as 'an account of social interactions' (Hyland 2004: x), and whilst studies of academic talk have tended to highlight the relationship between tutors and students, research into writing has foregrounded the ways in which established academics from particular disciplines collaborate and interact with each other.

Disciplinary differences are just one example of linguistic variation that has been investigated through the analysis of the distribution of prag-matic features in academic discourse. Many of the most influential studies have been based on

the collection of authentically occurring samples of language or corpora. **Corpus linguistics** has proved a fruitful approach to the study of academic discourse, because it allows the auto-matic comparison of pragmatic features across texts or groups of texts. Hinkel (1997) contrasts indirectness strategies such as **rhetorical questions** and **ambiguity** in Anglo-American first language writers and second language wri-ters from Confucian, Taoist and Buddhist socie-ties. Hyland (2004) compares pragmatic features such as boosters and **hedges** across eight dis-ciplines and five genres (research articles, book reviews, scientific letters, textbooks and abstracts) using a corpus of 1.5 million words of English academic writing in conjunction with interviews with academics. He argues that choices of prag-matic features give insights into 'how writers from different disciplines typically position themselves and their work in relation to other members of their professional communities' (Hyland 2004: x). Biber (2006) uses corpus ana-lytical techniques to compare a range of aca-demic registers including classroom talk, study groups, office hours and textbooks. He analyzes a total of 3 million words. Like Hyland, Biber concludes that there are significant differences in the distribution of pragmatic features across academic speech and writing, with the commu-nicative demands of classroom interaction favouring the use of stance markers especially (e.g. *you might want to*).

Differences across academic level have also been investigated. Csomay (2002) compares the distribution of pragmatic features across 1.4 million words of undergraduate and post-graduate talk. She concludes that both discipline and level of instruction influence linguistic choi-ces and that the higher proportion of stance-marking interactive features in graduate classes results in 'a more collegial atmosphere' (Csomay 2002: 220). American and British academic talk has also been contrasted. Using a corpus of 1.2 million words, Nesi and Basturkmen (2006) report similarities between discourse marking patterns in American and British academic spoken English. All these large-scale studies highlight the importance of academic context to prag-matic choices. Hyland sums this up by observing that 'successful writing and speaking means pro-jecting a shared context' (2004: 39), and that 'disciplinary novices' are required to 'write themselves into their disciplines' (2004: x).

There is growing research interest in how the pragmatic choices of academic writers and speakers reflect their membership of a variety of groups within academia, not simply those defined along disciplinary lines. Such groupings have been conceptualized as discourse communities (Swales 1990), communities of practice (Lave and Wenger 1991) and in-groups (Cutting 2001). Cutting (2001), who investigates informal group-ings of students in her longitudinal study of uni-versity common room chat, finds that the use of **vagueness** and non-neutral **speech acts** increases over time, and stresses the interactional nature of **conversation** and its solidarity-building function. Understanding the pragmatic norms of in-groups and other kinds of commu-nities is of particular importance to the increas-ing numbers of international students studying at English-medium universities, and to their tutors. This has resulted in increasing research focus on various aspects of **cross-cultural pragmatics** related to EAP provision (Hinkel 1997; Crandall and Basturkmen 2004; Hyland 2006). This research is being carried out against the backdrop of a 'repositioning of education as a commodity in global markets' (Blackmore 2004: 385).

JANE EVISON

See also: Classroom discourse; competence, pragmatic; conversation; corpus linguistics; cross-cultural pragmatics; discourse markers; sociolinguistics

Suggestions for further reading

Biber, D. (2006) *University Language: A Corpus-based Study of Spoken and Written Registers*, Amster-dam: John Benjamins.

Flowerdew, J. (ed.) (2002) *Academic Discourse*, Harlow: Longman.

Hyland, K. (2006) *English for Academic Purposes: An Advanced Resource Book*, London: Routledge.

Advertising, Pragmatics of

Sometimes a headline can make no sense at all on its own. And the picture on its own can be a mystery. When the two come together, however, the whole story is revealed – with punch and originality.

> (Crompton 1987: 62; quoted in
> Tanaka 1994: 58)

The concepts and insights of **pragmatics** can be applied to the study of advertising language and design. The first major linguistic survey of advertising language is Leech (1966). Pragmatic concepts as such are the foundations of only two books – Geis (1982) and Tanaka (1994). Geis (1982) primarily focuses on **presupposition** and other less logical **inferences** in his analysis of television advertisements (he refers to pre-supposition as 'conventional implicature'). He also discusses the analytical role that **Grice**'s **maxims of conversation** (Grice 1975) can play in such analysis, although they have never been formally used in much published work. However, the notion of relevance as used in **relevance theory** (Sperber and Wilson 1995) has been quite influential in the analysis of advertising, and is the foundation of Tanaka (1994). As implied by the quote above from Crompton, it is possible to use the same pragmatic concepts to analyze text advertise-ments in printed media with regard to the text, the images, and the relationships between the two.

Cook (2001) and Vestergaard and Schrøder (1986) present analyses framed in part on the Hallidayan notions of cohesion and coherence. Vestergaard and Schrøder also briefly mention 'implicit and explicit content', by which they refer to **entailment**, presupposition, and less strictly logical inferences (*see also* Geis 1982).

Cohesion refers to overt linkages within texts, such as the use of connectives and anaphoric pronouns. Coherence refers to the overall infer-red interpretation of a text, to which cohesive devices may provide some pointers. An example from Leech (1966: 180) illustrates these linguistic properties as well as the relation that must be inferred between the text and the visuals – from a television advertisement in this case:

(1) (video of boy playing with train set)
His first toy train is a Hornby train. Big, strong engine. Bright, shiny coaches. His Hornby clockwork set – at only 27/6.

The pronoun *his* clearly links from the boy in the video to the text. The second and third parts of the text are determinerless noun phrases, which have to be coherently inferred to refer to the train and the (visually presented) train set. And the last part of the advertisement presents a presupposition that the boy has a Hornby train set.

Advertising copy typically uses few cohesive devices, preferring 'punchy' presentation, and leaving the coherence of the text to be inferred. Leech (1966: 150) also discusses (2):

(2) Nimble bread. Delicious, light as a feather.

He observes that this does not have the same communicative force as:

(3) Nimble bread is delicious and (it is) light as a feather.

In particular, (2) 'has no interrogative equivalent ... by which its truth or falsity can be questioned'. In other words, although the description in (2) may or may not be actually asserted, it is not in fact challengeable.

In a discussion of more creative uses of language, Leech (1966: 182) discusses the following example:

(4) (toothpaste advertisement)
What does the tingle taste like?

Although Leech does not use the term, the phrase *the tingle* induces a presupposition that toothpaste has 'tingle'. In doing so, it provides an association to the product that may not have been there for the consumer before encountering this advertisement.

The concepts of given and new information are also important in the analysis of advertising, with given information partly represented using presuppositions of the kind just mentioned (these concepts are briefly mentioned in Cook 2001 and Goddard 2002). Every advertisement presents some new information, and one might initially presume that this is main point of an advertisement. While this was true in the early stages of advertising in the late nineteenth century, modern-day advertising has taken on different communicative functions. Typically in the modern age, the new information will concern enhanced technological properties, claimed greater effectiveness with regard to the product's purpose, and so on, although sometimes the new information is literally quite trivial. For example:

(5) (a picture of a lady's razor)
Choose your Venus. Now Venus comes in two colours.

The reader infers that 'Venus' refers to the pictured razor, while the advertisement presupposes that the reader has such a razor. Hence, the new information – that the Venus razor now comes in different colours – must come later. This information is indeed rather trivial. However, this is not a failing or an oddity but an interesting property of advertisements. As long as there is any new information presented, it must be presented against the background of given information, and having the reader access this given information is a key design property of the advertisement. Geis (1982) presents many different kinds of example of the ways that presuppositions are used in advertisements.

Relevance is a key concept in understanding advertisements, because it concerns a primary component of all aspects of human **communication**. Tanaka (1994) presents a very thorough analysis of advertising based on the concept of relevance. Pateman (1983) mentions the role of relevance in the sense given by Sperber and Wilson (1986/1995) as generating extra **propositions** based on an advertisement's core content – a process which can in principle continue for as long as the reader or hearer is willing to try to generate implications from what has been presented. An important observation of Pateman's is that there is no such thing as 'the' **meaning** of an advertisement, and relevance theory provides a good model of this point. Whatever the reader can extract is effectively successful communication as far as the advertiser is concerned, for the advertisement has caused some cognitive activity in the reader (in the famous quote from Brendan Behan, 'There is no such thing as bad publicity'). Coleman (1990) also draws attention to the fact that an advertisement has no single intended message – it merely needs to communicate something. In a discussion of what kind of benefit an advertisement might offer to a consumer, Aitchison (1999) provides the following quote from Gary Goldsmith of Lowe and Partners, New York. The question posed is 'Is advertising more powerful if it offers a rational benefit?'. Here is Goldsmith's answer: "'I don't think you need to offer a rational benefit. I think you need to offer a benefit that a rational person can understand"' (Aitchison 1999: 49).

The concept of relevance is particularly important in understanding how advertisements work for two reasons. First, it uncovers the cognitive links between parts of the advertisement which are necessary for any interpretation to arise. Second, it provides a means for considering any number of the 'open-ended' implications that an advertisement might have for a given reader. A striking example of these points is provided by the following text which accompanies a picture of a luxurious-looking armchair:

(6) Surprisingly well-behaved considering all the studs and leather.

This description has to apply to the armchair, as there is nothing else in the advertisement. This in turn leads to rather whimsical interpretation, as the description in (6) would typically be assumed to apply to a person. From this point on, there may be no necessary coherent interpretation for a reader, and it is unlikely that one was intended. (One possible implication is that the chair is comfortable despite having a rugged exterior.) The **intention** behind the advertisement is simply to call attention to the chair, and to have the reader expend some cognitive activity. The reader is guided by relevance to take the text to be about the chair, and then considers that there might be some benefit associated with the chair.

Finally, in (7), several concepts from pragmatics can be applied, in addition to some iconic and semiological properties of the style and layout of the text that are not considered here. The text is shown here close to its original style and layout, to the right of a head-to-toe picture of a woman wearing jeans:

(7) JEANS SHOULD
flatter the leg line.
Accentuate the curves.
INCREASE
the compliments.

RIDERS
Jeans that fit.
Beautifully.

The basic interpretation of this advertisement requires the reader to presuppose that there are leg lines, curves, and **compliments**. This is how advertising creates the ideology and **context** within which products are presented as 'needed'. The almost trivial consequence of relevance is that the woman's jeans are RIDERS jeans (in actuality, they may not be). It is not clear if the main text is spoken by the character in the advertisement to the reader, or is a more general statement assented to by the reader with the character in the advertisement as an exemplar. Although the text is not obviously asserted by anyone, the form of the last three lines renders them 'unchallengeable', in the way noted above with regard to example (2). The information that RIDERS jeans fit beautifully is therefore presented as new information in the advertisement.

PETER SELLS

See also: Discourse coherence; discourse cohesion; entailment; given/new distinction; Grice, H.P.; implicature; presupposition; relevance theory

Suggestions for further reading

Geis, M. (1982) *The Language of Television Advertising*, New York: Academic Press. Chapter 2.

Tanaka, K. (1994) *Advertising Language: A Pragmatic Approach to Advertising in Britain and Japan*, London and New York: Routledge. Chapters 2 and 3.

Ambiguity

Traditionally, the term 'ambiguity' is used when a linguistic expression can give rise to more than one specific interpretation. Typical examples include syntactic ambiguity as in (1), scope ambiguity as in (2) and lexical ambiguity as in (3):

(1) He watched the sailor with the telescope.
(2) All interviewees wanted to see one film.
(3) She held the note.

The ambiguity in (1) depends on whether the prepositional phrase *with the telescope* is interpreted as modifying the verb *watch* or the noun phrase *the sailor*. Both interpretations are possible but describe different situations. In (2), the ambiguity derives from interpretations of the relative scope of the quantifiers *all* and *one*. If *all* is given wide scope over *one*, then there may be as many films as interviewees. If *one* has scope over *all*, then they all want to see the one film. In (3), the noun *note* can of course be a musical sound or a written message.

We can characterize lexical ambiguity as cases where the same phonological shape is shared by two or more distinct semantic units (or lexemes). A distinction is often made between homonymy, like *bat* 'the flying mammal' and *bat* 'club used in sports', where the semantic units are clearly distinct, and polysemy, where different but related senses are involved, like *free* in 'I'm free on Tuesdays' and 'This gum is sugar-free'. The decisions about relatedness are, however, not without difficulty (Lyons 1977: 550–69).

A major challenge in identifying ambiguity is to distinguish cases like these from others where a lack of **specificity** allows varying interpretations. There are two important types. The first type is deictic expressions, also called **indexical** expressions. These are abbreviatory forms the interpretation of which depends on participants employing contextual information. Perhaps the simplest examples of these are personal pronouns like *I*, *you* and *she*, whose denotation is only determinable in **context**. Clearly, we don't want to say that *I* is ambiguous in as many ways as it has possible referents. Spatial and temporal expressions like *here* and *now* share this behaviour.

The second type is **vagueness**, where expressions display a degree of indeterminacy. One parameter here is degree of generality. Some words in English, for example, are not specified for gender. Linguists would not want to say that *sibling* is ambiguous because it can be

used to refer to both types of individual identified by *brother* and *sister*; similarly, *parent* with *mother* and *father*. Here, the function of the more general term is to allow the speaker to refer to the larger set. Some writers have included this type of lexical generality under the term vagueness (Kempson 1977). Another type of underspecification is shown by gradable adjectives (Kennedy 2007), for example, like *tall*, *expensive*, and *fast*, which require contextual 'fill in' to be interpreted. This is clear in implicit comparison uses like:

(4) Alexander is tall.
(5) Rents in Tokyo are expensive.

Participants have to access contextually determined standards to interpret such examples: Alexander might be tall for an eight year old child, for example. Context update models (Kyburg and Morreau 2000; Barker 2002) provide a presuppositional account of this process.

A related phenomenon is loose talk, argued by Lasersohn (1999) to be distinct from vagueness. This is where speakers employ a pragmatically licensed degree of approximation in their use of words. Thus, a speaker might in casual **conversation** say (6) below:

(6) I've a five a.m. flight tomorrow.

even if the flight is actually at 5.05am. If the context is right, the inaccuracy is treated as pragmatically irrelevant. This process allows contextually variable meanings of the same word, for example, *round* in 'George has a round head' and 'Gaelic football is played with a round ball'.

In examining the contextual plasticity of words, what remains an open question in the literature is the relationship and balance between the processes of resolving ambiguity, determining the **reference** of **indexicals**, sometimes described as 'saturation', and the incorporation of contextual **knowledge**, often termed enrichment. Carston (2002), for example, adopts a **relevance theory** approach that proposes a unified account of these processes as contextually derived **inferences**, subject to the principle of relevance and leading to the level of explicit content that relevance theorists term 'explicature'.

JOHN SAEED

See also: Context; deixis; demonstratives; disambiguation; formal pragmatics; indexicals; lexical pragmatics; meaning; presupposition; relevance theory; specificity; vagueness

Suggestions for further reading

Cruse, D.A. (1986) *Lexical Semantics*, Cambridge: Cambridge University Press.

Keefe, R. and Smith, P. (eds) (1996) *Vagueness: A Reader*, Cambridge, MA: MIT Press.

Anaphora, Pragmatics of

For the last two decades, anaphora has been one of the most important and vibrant topics of research in theoretical linguistics. But what, then, is anaphora? In contemporary linguistics, the term 'anaphora/anaphor/anaphoric' has three distinct senses. In the first sense, it can be used to refer to a relation between two or more linguistic elements, in which the interpretation of one element (called an anaphor or anaphoric expression) is in some way determined by the interpretation of another element (called an antecedent) (e.g. Huang 1991a, 1994: 1, 2000a: 1, 2004a, 2007: 245). Linguistic elements that can be employed to encode an anaphoric relation in this general sense range from phonetically unrealized gaps/zero anaphora/empty categories through pronouns and reflexives to various reference-tracking systems like gender/class, switch-function, and switch-reference. For example, in (1), *he* is the anaphoric expression and on one interpretation, *Newton* is its antecedent. The relation between *he* and *Newton* is then called anaphoric.

(1) Newton knew that he had laid down the laws of mechanics and universal gravitation.

In the second sense, the term can be used in Chomsky's (e.g. 1981, 1995a) generative syntax for reference to a NP with the features [+anaphor, -pronominal] versus pronominal as a NP with the features [-anaphor, +pronominal]. Thus, the reflexive in (2) is treated as an anaphor, and the pronoun in (3) as a pronominal in the Chomskyan sense.

(2) Einstein$_1$ admired himself$_1$.
(3) Einstein$_1$ admired him$_2$.

In the third sense, the term can be used to refer to an anaphoric expression whose antecedent comes earlier, as in (4); as opposed to 'cataphora/cataphor/cataphoric', whereby the antecedent comes later, as in (5).

(4) After John$_1$ was diagnosed with diabetes, he$_1$ gave up smoking.
(5) After he$_1$ was diagnosed with diabetes, John$_1$ gave up smoking.

Anaphora can be (intra-)sentential, in which case the anaphoric expression and its antecedent occur within a single simplex or complex sentence. It can also be discoursal, in which case the anaphoric expression and its antecedent cross sentence boundaries.

Finally, in terms of syntactic category, anaphora can be divided into two categories: (i) NP-anaphora and (ii) VP-anaphora. But in this essay, I shall focus on NP-anaphora (see, for example, Huang 2000a: 131–56 and Huang 2006 for detailed discussion of VP-ellipsis).

The pragmatic nature of anaphora

Anaphora is essentially a pragmatic phenomenon. As pointed out by Levinson (2000: 272), there are at least three reasons why this is the case. First, although anaphora can be (intra-)sentential, its basic use is discoursal. As such, it is expected to be subject to pragmatic factors. In fact, a parallel pattern of interpretation can be established between (intra)-sentential and discourse anaphora. Consider (6) and (7).

(6) a. Einstein $_1$ likes his$_{1/2}$ theory.
    b. He$_1$ likes Einstein$_2$'s theory.
(7) a. John$_1$ went to a bookshop. He$_{1/2}$ bought a novel.
    b. He$_1$ went to a bookshop. John$_2$ bought a novel.

There is a clear pattern here: the use of a reduced, semantically general anaphoric expression like a pronoun tends to favour local co-referential interpretation, whereas the use of a full, semantically specific anaphoric expression like a proper name tends to encourage a locally non-co-referential reading. As (6) and (7) show, +this pattern applies both intra- and inter-sententially. Following Levinson (1987b, 1991, 2000) and Huang (1994: 16, 2000a: 214), let us dub this the general pattern of anaphora. Second, anaphoric expressions are semantically general, and thus require pragmatic specification to achieve **reference**. Third, the selection of one out of a number of structurally possible, potential antecedents for an anaphoric expression can only be achieved pragmatically. As an illustrating example, take (8).

(8) a. The metropolitan authorities₁ barred the anti-globalization demonstrators₂ because they₂ advocated violence.
   b. The metropolitan authorities₁ barred the anti-globalization demonstrators₂ because they₁ feared violence.

The choice of the antecedent for the pronoun *they* in (8) depends crucially on our background assumption about who would most likely be advocating or fearing violence. This extra-linguistic information is responsible for the two opposing readings: namely, *they* being linked to *anti-globalization demonstrators* in (8a) and to *the metropolitan authorities* in (8b).

Further, as I argued in Huang (1994, 2000a), the extent to which anaphora is pragmatic varies typologically. There is a class of languages (such as Chinese, Japanese, and Korean) where **pragmatics** plays a central role which in familiar European languages (such as English, French, and German) has hitherto been alleged to be played by grammar. In these pragmatic languages, many of the constraints on the allegedly grammatical processes of (intra-)sentential anaphora are in fact primarily due to principles of language use rather than rules of grammatical structure. What, then, are the benchmarks for the pragmatic nature of anaphora in a pragmatic language? First, there is massive occurrence of gaps/zero anaphora despite the absence of a rich inflectional morphology. This occurrence of zero anaphora is much more widespread than that observed in either an English-style, paradigmatic, non-pro-drop language or an Italian-type, paradigmatic, pro-drop language (*see also* Huang 1995). Second, somewhat

related is that in a pragmatic language, there exists a class of zero anaphora that can be determined only pragmatically. Put differently, this class of zero anaphora is simply ambiguous; it can fit in simultaneously with more than one type of empty category in the standard Chomskyan inventory (e.g. Chomsky 1981, 1995a). Consequently, it cannot be determined syntactically but only pragmatically (*see also* Huang 1992). Third, in such a language, control enjoys a great freedom in interpretation. For one thing, such a language allows – rather freely – remote or long-distance control, that is, control by a controller in a non-immediate, higher clause or even from **discourse**. For another, sometimes, even obligatory control has to be determined pragmatically. This is the case with the Chinese example in (9), taken from Huang (1994: 63) (3SG = third-person singular pronoun).

(9) a. bingren   shuofu   yisheng   ø mingtian
       patient   persuade   doctor   tomorrow
       gei   ta   kaidao.
       for   3SG   operate
       'The patient₁ persuades the surgeon₂ that (he₂ …) will operate on him₁ tomorrow.'
   b. yisheng   shuofu   bingren   ø mingtian
       doctor   persuade   patient   tomorrow
       gei   ta   kaidao.
       for   3SG   operate
       'The surgeon₁ persuades the patient ₂ that (he₁ …) will operate on him₂ tomorrow.'

In unmarked cases, *shuofu* in Chinese, like *persuade* in English, is a verb of object control, as in (9a). But this unmarked reading is merely a preferred one; it can be overridden in the face of inconsistency with, say, real-world knowledge. This is exactly what happens in (9b). In (9b), there is a shift of preference for the choice of controller: the subject control reading becomes the favoured one. Therefore, an obligatory control construction like (9) in a pragmatic language such as Chinese is allowed to have (at least) two possible interpretations, in accord with the number of potential controllers in it (*see* Huang 1991b; *see also* Huang 2000a: 265 for a parallel Japanese example). The selection of one of them as the preferred controller is determined pragmatically in keeping with real-world knowledge.

There are thus some grounds for believing that in a pragmatic language, when syntax and real-world knowledge clash, real-world knowledge frequently wins. By contrast, in a syntactic language like English, when there is a clash between **syntax** and real-world knowledge, syntax usually takes the upper hand, as can be seen by the ungrammaticality of the English control construction parallel to (9b) under the indicated indexing, namely, *The surgeon₁ persuades the patient₂ PRO₁ to operate on him₂ tomorrow*. Finally, in a pragmatic language, a reflexive can be long-distance bound, that is, it can be co-indexed with an antecedent outside its local syntactic domain, and even across sentence boundaries into discourse (Huang 1996; *see also* Huang 2000a: 261–77 for more exemplification and detailed discussion of the pragmatic nature of anaphora in a pragmatic language).

A pragmatic approach to anaphora

We turn next to a neo-Gricean pragmatic approach to (intra-)sentential anaphora. In the last two decades, one of the most encouraging advances in the study of (intra-)sentential anaphora has been the development of pragmatic accounts, as an alternative to syntactic (e.g. Chomsky 1981, 1995a) and semantic ones (e.g. Reinhart and Reuland 1993). Of these pragmatic analyses, the most influential is the neo-Gricean pragmatic theory of anaphora developed by Levinson (1987b, 1991, 2000) and Huang (1991a, 1994, 2000a, 2000b, 2004a, 2007). Central to this theory is the assumption that anaphora is fundamentally pragmatic in nature, though the extent to which anaphora is pragmatic varies typologically. Consequently, anaphora can largely be determined by the systematic interaction of some general neo-Gricean pragmatic principles such as Levinson's (1987b, 1991, 2000) Q-, I- and M-principles (10), à la Grice (1989), depending on the language user's **knowledge** of the range of options available in the grammar, and of the systematic use or avoidance of particular anaphoric expressions or structures on particular occasions.

(10) Levinson's Q-, I- and M-principles (simplified)
  a. The Q-principle

Speaker: Do not say less than is required (bearing I in mind).
Recipient: What is not said is not the case.
  b. The I-principle
Speaker: Do not say more than is required (bearing Q in mind).
Recipient: What is generally said is stereotypically and specifically exemplified.
  c. The M-principle
Speaker: Do not use a marked expression without reason.
Recipient: What is said in a marked way conveys a marked message.

Applying the Q-, I-, and M-principles to the domain of anaphoric reference, we can derive a general, revised neo-Gricean pragmatic apparatus for the interpretation of various types of anaphoric expression in (11) (Huang 2000a: 215, 2004a, 2007: 260).

(11) Huang's revised neo-Gricean pragmatic apparatus for anaphora (simplified)
  (i) The use of an anaphoric expression x I-implicates a local co-referential interpretation, unless (ii) or (iii).
  (ii) There is an anaphoric Q-scale $<x, y>$, in which case the use of y Q-implicates the complement of the I-implicature associated with the use of x in terms of reference.
  (iii) There is an anaphoric M-scale $\{x, y\}$, in which case the use of y M-implicates the complement of the I-implicature associated with the use of x, in terms of either reference or expectedness.

Needless to say, any interpretation generated by (11) is subject to the general consistency constraints applicable to Gricean conversational **implicatures**. These constraints include world knowledge, contextual information, and semantic **entailments**.

In Huang (2000a, 2004a, 2007) and Levinson (2000), substantial cross-linguistic evidence has been presented to show that the revised neo-Gricean pragmatic theory of anaphora is empirically more adequate than both a syntactic and a semantic approach. Consider, for example, Chomsky's (1981, 1995a) binding conditions, as in (12) and its paradigmatic illustrations, as in (13).

(12) Chomsky's binding conditions
    A. An anaphor is bound in a local domain.
    B. A pronominal is free in a local domain.
    C. An r-expression is free.
(13) a. $Einstein_1$ admired $himself_1$.
    b. $Einstein_1$ admired him_2.
    c. $Einstein_1$ admired $Einstein_2$.

On the neo-Gricean account, Chomsky's binding conditions B and C can be reduced to pragmatics. In somewhat simplified terms, this can be achieved in the following way. If binding condition A is taken to be either grammatically constructed (as in the English-type, syntactic languages) or pragmatically specified (as in the Chinese-type, pragmatic languages), then binding condition B is the direct result of the application of the Q-principle. Given this principle, the use of a semantically weaker pronoun where a semantically stronger reflexive could occur gives rise to a conversational implicature which conveys the negation of the more informative, co-referential interpretation associated with the use of the reflexive, as in (13b). By the same reasoning, binding condition C can also be eliminated. Wherever a reflexive could occur, the use of a semantically weaker proper name Q-implicates the non-applicability of the more informative, co-referential interpretation associated with the use of the reflexive. This is exactly what has happened in (13c). Further, the revised neo-Gricean pragmatic theory can provide an elegant account of many of the anaphoric patterns that have embarrassed a generative analysis such as the cases where a pronoun is bound in its local domain. It can also accommodate examples like (1) and (8), which falls outside the scope of Chomsky's binding theory. In the case of long-distance reflexivization, the concept of logophoricity can be invoked to explain why such a marked anaphoric expression is used. By logophoricity is meant the phenomenon whereby the 'point of view' of an internal protagonist of a sentence or discourse, as opposed to that of the current, external speaker, is being reported using some morphological and/or syntactic means. The expression 'point of view' is employed here in a technical sense and is intended to encompass words, thoughts, knowledge, emotion and perception (e.g. Huang 2000a: 172–204, 225–29, 2002, 2006; *see*

also Hagège 1974, Clements 1975). This use of long-distance reflexives is accountable in terms of the M-principle. Since the grammar allows the unmarked regular pronoun to be employed to encode co-reference, the speaker will use it if such a reading is intended, as in the Icelandic example (14a) (cited in Huang 2000a: 227) (INDIC = indicative mood, SBJV = subjunctive mood). On the other hand, if the unmarked regular pronoun is not used, but the marked long-distance reflexive is employed instead, then an M-implicature will be licensed. The implicature is that not only co-reference but logophoricity as well is intended by the speaker. This is the case with the Icelandic example (14b) (cited in Huang 2000a: 227).

(14) a. Jon   veit   að   Maria
       John   knows-INDIC that   Mary
       elskar   hann.
       loves-INDIC him
       '$John_1$ knows that Mary loves him_1.'
    b. Jon   segir   að   Maria
       John   says-INDIC   that   Mary
       elski   sig.
       loves-SBJV   self
       '$John_1$ says that Mary loves $self_1$.'

Notice another correlation here. If relevant, the choice between regular pronouns on the one hand and logophoric long-distance reflexives on the other hand is correlated with that between indicative and subjunctive mood in the embedded clause. The use of a regular pronoun tends to go with that of indicative mood, as in (14a); the employment of a logophoric long-distance reflexive tends to go with subjunctive mood, as in (14b). This correlation is a reflection of a semantic/pragmatic choice made by the external speaker about the responsibility he or she assumes for the truthfulness of what he or she is reporting. If a regular pronoun and indicative mood are used, it indicates that the speaker asserts that the report is true. However, if a logophoric long-distance reflexive and subjunctive mood are deployed, it shows that the speaker does not take responsibility for the truth of the report (*see* e.g. Huang 2000a, 227–28, 2002, 2006 for further discussion). Finally, the revised neo-Gricean pragmatic theory can also be extended to provide an account of discourse anaphora in naturally occurring **conversations** (see, for example, Huang 1994, 2000a, 2000b) and has made a significant contribution to the current debate about universals, innateness, and learnability.

YAN HUANG

See also: Context; Grice, H.P.; implicature; neo-Gricean pragmatics; pragmatics

Suggestions for further reading

Chomsky, N. (1995) *The Minimalist Program*, Cambridge, MA: MIT Press.

Huang, Y. (2000) *Anaphora: A Cross-linguistic Study*, Oxford: Oxford University Press.

Levinson, S.C. (2000) *Presumptive Meanings: The Theory of Generalized Conversational Implicature*, Cambridge, MA: MIT Press.

Anglo-American and European Continental Traditions

In contemporary **pragmatics**, there are two main schools of thought: the Anglo-American tradition and the (European) Continental tradition (Levinson 1983; Huang 2001, 2007: 4–5). Alternatively, the two traditions are also called the component and perspective views of pragmatics, respectively.

The Anglo-American tradition

Within the Anglo-American conception of linguistics and the **philosophy of language**, pragmatics may be defined as the systematic study of **meaning** by virtue of, or dependent on, language use. The central topics of inquiry include **implicature, presupposition, speech acts, deixis**, and **reference**, all of which originate in twentieth-century analytical philosophy (Huang 2007: 2; Levinson 2000; but *see also* Levinson 1983, who added **conversation analysis** to the above list). This is known as the component or 'pigeon-hole' view of pragmatics. From this view, a linguistic theory consists of a number of core components: phonetics (the study of speech sounds), phonology (the study of sound systems), morphology (the study of the grammatical structure of words), **syntax** (the study of the grammatical relation between, or

distribution of, words and other units within the sentence), and **semantics** (the study of (certain aspects of) meaning). Each of these core components has a relatively properly demarcated domain of inquiry. Pragmatics, then, is just another core component placed in the same contrast set within a linguistic theory. By contrast, other 'hyphenated' branches of linguistics such as anthropological linguistics, educational linguistics, and **sociolinguistics** lie outside this contrast set of core components. The component view of pragmatics is to some extent a reflection of the modular conception of the human mind, namely, the claim that the mental architecture of *homo sapiens* is divided roughly into a basic dichotomy between a central processor and a number of distinctive, specialized mental systems known as modules (Fodor 1983; *see also* Cummings 2005: 140–60; Huang 2007: 198–201).

The European Continental tradition

Within the Continental tradition of linguistics and the philosophy of language, the view that pragmatics should be treated as a core component of a linguistic theory, in conjunction with phonetics, phonology, morphology, syntax, and semantics, is rejected. Instead, pragmatics is taken to present a functional perspective on all core components and 'hyphenated' areas of linguistics and beyond. As early as 1977, in their editorial of the first issue of the *Journal of Pragmatics*, Haberland and Mey (1977: 5) remarked: 'Linguistic pragmatics … can be said to characterize a new way of looking at things linguistic, rather than marking off clear borderlines to other disciplines'. By 'a new way of looking at things linguistic', Haberland and Mey meant that pragmatics should offer a perspective on all core components and 'hyphenated' branches of linguistics (Mey 2001: 8). This position is made explicit by Jef Verschueren, another leading proponent of the Continental school. According to him, pragmatics constitutes 'a general functional (i.e. cognitive, social and cultural) perspective on linguistic phenomena in relation to their usage in forms of behaviour' (Verschueren 1999: 7, 11). Elsewhere, he declared: 'Pragmatics should be seen … as a specific perspective … on whatever phonologists, morphologists, syntacticians, semanticists, psycholinguists, sociolinguists, etc. deal with' (Verschueren 1995: 12). Consequently, within the wider Continental tradition, the empirical orbit of pragmatics has been considerably widened, encompassing not only much that goes under the rubric of those non-core branches of linguistics such as sociolinguistics, **psycholinguistics**, and **discourse analysis**, but also some that falls in the province of certain neighboring social sciences. This represents the perspective view of pragmatics. Furthermore, Verschueren argued that language use involves essentially a continuous making of linguistic choices. As such, the functional perspective can be determined in terms of three, hierarchically related notions. The first notion is variability. It refers to the property of language that defines the range of possibilities from which choices can be made. The second notion is negotiability. This is the language property which explains why choices are made on the basis of highly flexible principles and strategies, rather than mechanically or in accordance with strict form–function relationships. The third notion is adaptability. By adaptability is meant the property of language which enables people to make negotiable choices from a variable range of options in such a way as to approach points of satisfaction for communicative needs (Verschueren 1999: 55–69).

This broader Continental demarcation of pragmatics is similar to the definition of pragmatics provided within the former Soviet and East European tradition. Under this approach, pragmatics (called pragmalinguistics) is in general conceived of as a theory of linguistic **communication**, including how to influence people through verbal messages, i.e. political propaganda (see, for example, Prucha 1983).

Which of the two schools of thought, then, is conceptually more coherent and methodologically sounder? Interestingly enough, the Continental version is more faithful to the view of pragmatics originally expressed by Charles **Morris**, the founding father of modern pragmatics. As is well known, pragmatics as a modern branch of linguistic inquiry has its origin in the philosophy of language. Its philosophical roots can be traced back to the work of the philosophers Charles Morris, Rudolf Carnap, and Charles **Peirce** in the 1930s. Influenced by Peirce, Morris (1938: 6–7), for example, presented a threefold division into syntax, semantics, and

pragmatics within **semiotics** – a general science of signs. According to this semiotic trichotomy, syntax is the study of the formal relation of one sign to another, semantics deals with the relation of signs to what they denote, and pragmatics addresses the relation of signs to their users and interpreters (Levinson 1983: 1; Horn and Ward 2004; Huang 2007: 2–4). This trichotomy was taken up by Carnap (1942), who following Morris's (1938: 33) insight that syntax, semantics, and pragmatics are ranked hierarchically, posited a similar order of degree of abstractness for the three branches of linguistic inquiry: syntax is the most abstract, and pragmatics the least abstract, with semantics lying somewhere in between. Consequently, syntax provides input to semantics, which provides input to pragmatics (Recanati 2004a; Huang 2007: 2). Returning to Morris, while he took the view that pragmatics constitutes a component – 'Syntactics, semantics, and pragmatics are the components of a single science of semiotic but mutually irreducible components' (Morris 1938: 54) – he did conclude that '[s]ince most, if not all, signs have as their interpreters living organisms, it is a sufficiently accurate characterization of pragmatics to say that it deals with the biotic aspects of semiosis, that is, with all the psychological, biological, and sociological phenomena which occur in the functioning of signs' (Morris 1938: 30).

In keeping with this broader Morrisian approach, the Continental branch of pragmatics takes its cue not only from analytical philosophy, but also from a variety of research traditions as diverse as Prague school functionalism, Firthian linguistics, early pragmatic research conducted by German, Dutch and Scandinavian scholars, the Paris-Geneva school of pragmatics, **Habermas**'s universal pragmatics, Apel's transcendental pragmatics, and Rehbein's and Ehlich's functional pragmatics. Consequently, it adopts a much wider conception of pragmatics, 'perspectivizing' not only all the core components and 'hyphenated' areas of linguistics but also some fields of inquiry from certain neighboring social sciences, with its research interests ranging from speech acts through **politeness** to medical communication (Verschueren 1999; Mey 2005; *see also* issues of the *Journal of Pragmatics*, *Pragmatics*, and *Intercultural Pragmatics*, and entries in

Verschueren *et al.*'s (1995) *Handbook of Pragmatics* and its periodic updates). Thus, pragmatics in the Continental sense appears to be a study of 'everything'. But a study of 'everything' is hardly a viable academic enterprise. Given the degree of overlap with the phenomena dealt with in other relatively well established interdisciplinary fields of linguistics such as sociolinguistics, psycholinguistics, and neurolinguistics, it is rather difficult to see how a coherent theory of pragmatics can be built up within the broader Continental tradition. 'Everything is pragmatics' seems to amount to saying that 'nothing is pragmatics'. Pragmatics delineated within such a conception seems too inclusive to be of much theoretical significance. It can at best serve as a flag of convenience under which divergent branches of linguistic inquiry and beyond can momentarily find a common front in an intellectual coalition (*see also* Levinson 1987a). By way of contrast, the narrower Anglo-American, component view of pragmatics has a much more restricted research agenda. It focuses on topics emerging from the principal concerns of twentieth-century analytical philosophy, some of which stem from work done by such eminent philosophers as Gottlob Frege, J.L. **Austin**, H.P. **Grice**, Peter Strawson, John **Searle**, and Ludwig **Wittgenstein**. While it may be too restrictive, the Anglo-American school of pragmatics seems to delimit the scope of the discipline in a slightly more coherent, systematic, and principled way than the Continental tradition (Huang 2007: 4–5; *see also* the rather heated exchanges between Mey 2005 and Horn and Ward 2006).

Finally, two points should be noted. First, there has recently been some convergence between the two camps. On the one hand, interesting work has been done on topics such as implicature, speech acts, and presupposition from a Continental, perspective point of view. On the other hand, research in the Anglo-American tradition has recently been extended to certain 'hyphenated' domains of linguistics such as computational linguistics, historical linguistics, and discourse analysis. The same is also true in relation to **cognitive science** (see, for example, the articles collected in Horn and Ward 2004, Marmaridou 2000 and Cummings 2005). One case in point is Sperber and Wilson's (1986/1995) **relevance theory** – a reductionist

revision of the Gricean programme – which has taken many insights from **cognitive psychology**. Another case is the recent emergence of **experimental pragmatics** (e.g. Noveck and Sperber 2004). Second, each side of the divide complements, and has much to learn from, the other side. Whereas the strength of the Anglo-American branch lies mainly in theory, and philosophical, cognitive, and **formal pragmatics**, the Continental tradition has much to offer in empirical work, and socio- (or societal), (cross- or inter-) cultural, and **interlanguage pragmatics**, to mention just a few examples. Consequently, a cross-fertilization in pragmatics of theory and empirical work on the one hand, and different approaches and methodologies on the other hand, is highly desirable. Furthermore, as an old saying goes in ancient China (during the Spring and Autumn and Warring States period 770–221 B.C.): '*baijia zhengming* (Let a hundred schools of thought contend)'. Looking at issues from different angles may not be a bad thing. Therefore, we should not only encourage both schools of thought to exist side-by-side peacefully, but more importantly, we should also promote dialogue and cooperation between them. Only in this way can the entire field of pragmatics, broadly construed, continue to flourish.

YAN HUANG

See also: Conversation analysis; deixis; history of pragmatics; implicature; indexicals; Morris, C.; pragmatics; presupposition; reference; speech act theory

Suggestions for further reading

Horn, L.R. and Ward, G. (eds) (2004) *The Handbook of Pragmatics*, Oxford: Blackwell.
Mey, J.L. (2001) *Pragmatics: An Introduction*, 2nd edn, Oxford: Blackwell.
Verschueren, J. (1999) *Understanding Pragmatics*, London: Arnold.

Animal Communication, Pragmatics of

Human communication is ostensive-inferential in nature. As such, it is based on the recognition of **intentions** (Grice 1975). Yet, since it is at best unclear whether or not it is even coherent to talk about the intentions of non-human animals (with the possible exception of some non-human primates (see later)), it is not immediately apparent how we can coherently talk about the pragmatics of animal communication. However, if, following Austin (1962), we take a more general perspective of **pragmatics** and conceive of **communication** as something that we *do* to others, then ostension and **inference** reveal themselves to be simply the particular way in which our own species achieves such ends.

Indeed, evolutionary biologists *define* signalling as something that organisms *do* to each other (Maynard Smith and Harper 2003). The general characterization is that signals are selected to initiate a response that is itself also the product of design by natural selection (Scott-Phillips 2008). As such, the signals achieve their goals by virtue of an evolved response whose function is to exploit the presence of the signal. This account has non-coincidental echoes of Grice's analysis of **meaning**, whereby speakers have an intention that an utterance will produce an effect in the audience 'by means of the recognition of this intention' (Grice 1971: 21).

What is general to both human and animal communication, then, is an interdependency of signal and response. One is the act of doing, the other the fact of being done to, and neither can properly exist without the other. This is a reasonable characterization of animal communication, but it is also a feature of human communication, a fact that has been recognized by **psycholinguistics** for some time (e.g. Clark 1996). It is also inherent in many neo- and post-Gricean approaches to pragmatics (e.g. Sperber and Wilson 1995). What will vary from species to species is the source of this synergy. In many cases we will be happy to say that the source is natural selection. Whilst human brains are also ultimately the product of the same evolutionary process as animal brains are, it may be more explanatorily satisfactory to say that the source of our utterances is our capacity to reason about intentions, and our ability to understand others in such terms, i.e. to have a **theory of mind**.

We should not, however, be too quick to dismiss the intentional skills of other animals out of hand, and in particular those of non-human primates. Indeed, exactly what our phylogenetic cousins can and cannot do with respect to the detection of intentions is a topic of considerable controversy in psychology. Whilst it is clear that non-human primates adjust their communicative efforts according to their interlocutors' behaviour (Tomasello and Call 1997), interpretations of this fact vary. At one end there are those, typically laboratory-based experimentalists, who insist that if any purported evidence can be explained in terms of 'associative learning or inferences based on nonmental categories' (Heyes 1998: 101), then it should be. At the other end there are researchers, often those with a background in fieldwork, who complain that this places the bar impossibly high: '[S]hould one prefer an implausible, complicated, non-mentalistic account, over a simple mentalistic one?' (Byrne 1998: 117). Although the issue is far from settled, the consensus tends towards the latter position. As more results come in, for example that apes can differentiate between cooperative and uncooperative behaviour even when the two are minimally different in form and consequence (Call *et al.* 2004), and that not just apes but also Old- and New-world monkeys are able to differentiate between the accidental and goal-directed behaviour of a human experimenter (Wood *et al.* 2007) (to pick two pretty much at random), it is becoming increasingly difficult to defend the position that the denial of mental states to non-human primates, and apes in particular, is the most parsimonious conclusion (but *see* Povinelli and Vonk 2003 for a different view).

In that case, it may be that what differentiates humans and primates is not the understanding of others as goal-directed agents, but rather what is known as shared **intentionality** (Tomasello *et al.* 2005): the motivation and ability to participate in *collaborative* activities with shared goals and intentions. To do this requires not just reasonably sophisticated mind-reading abilities, which some primates arguably possess, but also a willingness to share psychological states with others, and the cognitive capacity to conceive of a mutually shared goal. These traits all appear to be uniquely human (Tomasello *et al.* 2005), and their foundations may lie in our propensity for group living: it is thought that our ability to reason, often in quite complex ways, about the behaviours of others, both in Machiavellian and collaborative terms, may be a specific adaptation to the demands of living in large social groups (Humphrey 1976; Dunbar 1998b).

Moreover, these skills are not simply a function of an increase in cognitive power. Apes are the equal of 30-month-old human infants in tests of general intelligence but not in tests of social intelligence (Herrmann *et al.* 2007). This capacity for social **reasoning**, which enables the pursuit of joint goals, may well be crucial. It is often emphasized that natural language is an inherently mutual activity in at least two senses. First, linguistic symbols are by their very nature collaborative: they are coordination devices that are useful only in so far as one's interlocutor is prepared to recognize their significance (Clark 1996). Second, interlocutors use **conversation** to orient themselves to others' perspectives and thus converge upon mutual understanding (Pickering and Garrod 2004). This may, then, be how we can best characterize the difference between the pragmatics of animal and human communication: the former can be seen as an intellectually solitary act, albeit one that is designed to influence the future behaviour of others, while the latter is a joint activity, in which the shared goal is the alignment of perspectives.

THOMAS C. SCOTT-PHILLIPS

See also: Cognitive anthropology; cognitive science; communication; gestural communication; inference; intention; intentionality; language evolution; metarepresentation; psycholinguistics; relevance theory; theory of mind

Suggestions for further reading

Hurford, J.R. (2007) *Origins of Meaning*, Oxford: Oxford University Press.

Apologies

Over the past three decades or so, the apology has probably generated more research over a wide range of disciplines than any other **speech act** except the **request**. Much of this work can usefully be categorized, in a general sense, as being within the field of **pragmatics**. In a

helpful survey article, Meier (1998) reviews insightfully some of the goals and results of 'apology research'. This research is focussed primarily on describing the strategies which speakers use to make an apology and on identifying the contextual factors that inform such choices, whether the setting is an intra- or an intercultural one (Meier 1998: 216). Much of the early work in linguistics and pragmatics on apologies (Blum-Kulka and Olshtain 1984; Cohen and Olshtain 1981; Olshtain and Cohen 1983, for example) attempted to identify a speech act set of semantic formulas for apologizing. In this way, Olshtain and Cohen (1983) characterized the apology as (i) an illocutionary force indicating device (IFID) and (ii) an expression of responsibility/blame, which are both general strategies. Three further situation-specific strategies that attend the apology involve (iii) an explanation or account; (iv) an offer of repair; and (v) a promise of forbearance (Olshtain and Cohen 1983). This work was later extended to setting out a speech-act specific 'sociopragmatic set' of social and contextual factors (Olshtain 1989; Olshtain and Weinback 1987). Meier further maintains that only rarely have researchers working on the apology as a speech act attempted to approach its form and strategic functions by means of underlying cultural attitudes, though some more recent work has set out to do this (Luke 1997; Marquez Reiter 2000; Meyerhoff 1999; Obeng 1999; Okamura and Wei 2000; Suszczynska 1999; Wouk 2006). However, taxonomies such as the one above provide a convenient starting point for anyone interested in apology research.

Defining an apology has also proved problematic, and following Goffman (1971: 140), Holmes (1998a: 204) offers what is probably one of the most often quoted definitions: 'an apology is a speech act addressed to B's face-needs and intended to remedy an offence for which A takes responsibility, and thus to restore equilibrium between A and B (where A is the apologizer, and B is the person offended)'. Clearly, definitions along these lines necessarily assume that it is two individuals who are involved in the process of apologizing and that addressing the face-needs of the 'person offended' is the primary motive for the apology, with the restoration of the equilibrium between the apologizer and the offended as the main goal. Brown and Levinson (1987), whose work on apologies has also been influential, similarly stress the primary importance of 'face' in the performance of such speech acts as the apology.

A further important issue when assessing previous research on the apology as a speech act has been the nature of the data on which the research is based. As Meier's review contends, although there are a range of elicitation methods represented in the various studies, many, if not most of these, involve some kind of simulated data that is obtained by means of discourse-completion tests, questionnaires based on specified hypothetical encounters, retrospective self-reports, written or oral closed role-play, more open role-play, intuition and informal observation. Recorded **discourse**, which involves natural language, is 'conceded to be preferable' (Meier 1998: 225), but is difficult to obtain (but *see* Holmes 1995, 1998a; Jaworski 1994; Obeng 1999). What is also often left unconsidered and implicit in such work is the extent to which methods of data collection on apologies constrain and influence the results of the various studies. Tanaka *et al.* (2000) argue that the fact that the results of their research on Japanese and English apologizing behaviour did not conform to conventional cultural stereotypes suggests that the findings of certain other studies may be an unintended artefact of the research procedures. Obeng (1999) too, basing his work on natural language data collected among the Akan communities in Ghana, argues convincingly that much of the research on the apology underestimates its complexity as a speech act and that future work should be more ethnographically and culturally grounded.

Importantly, it is also the case that much of the research on apologies has been strongly influenced by **politeness** theory and, indeed, Holmes (1998a: 217) states unequivocally that 'the apology is quintessentially a politeness strategy'. A useful source of some recent work from this perspective, which involves a variety of **cultures**, languages and methodologies, is the recent special issue of the *Journal of Politeness Research* on the 'apology', edited by Grainger and Harris (2007). All of the articles included in the volume attempt to move on in different ways from Brown and Levinson's canonical but limited

treatment of the apology as a speech act, and the authors attempt to bring together a group of both multilingual and multidisciplinary studies of the apology. Other recent work, such as Mills (2003: 222), goes further and contends that 'apologies cannot be considered to be a formal linguistic entity … since they can be made using a wide range of different linguistic strategies'. They are instead 'a judgement made about someone's linguistic performance: whether the right amount of effort and work has been expended and whether sufficient commitment and sincerity have been expressed' (2003: 112). This takes us more directly into the realm of recent politeness theory and a decided shift of perspective into a post-modern linguistic world, in which the main characteristics of a theory of politeness are argued to be its 'variability, evaluativity, argumentativity, and discursiveness' (Eelen 2001: 240). The recent emphasis on the apology as a politeness strategy that no longer represents a normative set of prescripts but is rather a contested concept emerging dynamically from discursive struggles, is particularly relevant to the field of pragmatics.

Looking to the future, one of the most interesting and challenging areas of apology research is to examine more closely the nature and significance of public apologies. In the past, apology research has been almost entirely focussed on the interpersonal and interactive behaviour of individuals in mainly informal situations. There has been relatively little work on 'public' apologies within either institutional or other professional contexts, despite their increasing social and political importance. As Luke (1997: 344) argues, the 'apology has become a form of political speech with increasing significance and **power**'. These 'speeches' are often the result of some kind of publicly voiced 'demand' and, as a consequence, they frequently generate a considerable amount of controversy, conflict and public debate, at least in Western countries. The tendency of current politicians across the political spectrum and across the globe, in particular, to issue public apologies for serious past events for which they cannot be held personally responsible has prompted an Editorial (2005: 24) in *The Times* in the UK to declare that 'the currency of the word [apology] has been devalued beyond recognition'.

At the same time, the reluctance of those same politicians to apologize for 'serious' events for which they are accountable has been a source of public distress and anger.

Given their apparent cultural as well as political significance, it is perhaps surprising that there has been relatively little interest in political apologies in **sociolinguistics** and pragmatics, until fairly recently (Harris *et al.* 2006; Lakoff 2000, 2003; Langley 2006; Meier 2004). (Both Harris *et al.* (2006) and Jeffries (2007) explore in some detail the response of Tony Blair to public demands that he apologize for the consequences of UK involvement in the Iraq War, as mediated through various media in the UK.) Also of increasing interest and importance are the types of political apologies which constitute a response to the demands of one nation by another when an 'incident' or a dispute has occurred (Tian 2007; Yamayaki 2004; Zhang 2001). Public apologies provide a rich database of increasing importance. They also challenge current definitions of what constitutes an apology, not only in terms of earlier 'canonical' politeness research but also in relation to more recent 'post-modern' perspectives.

SANDRA HARRIS

See also: Context; conversation; discourse; gender; institutional and professional discourse; politeness; political discourse; pragmatics; request; societal pragmatics; sociolinguistics; speech act theory; speech act type

Suggestions for further reading

Liebersohn, Y., Neuman, Y. and Bekerman, Z. (2004) 'Oh baby, it's hard for me to say I'm sorry: public apologetic speech and cultural rhetorical resources', *Journal of Pragmatics*, 36: 921–44.

Robinson, J. (2004) 'The sequential organisation of "explicit" apologies in naturally occurring English', *Research in Language and Social Interaction*, 37: 291–330.

Applied Linguistics

The definition of applied linguistics varies within the broad field of **pragmatics**. Applied linguistics is still seen by some to be primarily engaged in devising a 'coherent model of linguistic description ... relevant to language teaching' (Widdowson 1984: 1). This view still persists, but many others see applied linguistics as enhancing the understanding of the role of language so that applied linguists can supply this knowledge to those 'taking language related decisions in the classroom, the workplace, the law court, or the laboratory' (Wilkins 1994: 7). Importantly, the latter view emphasizes the fact that knowledge generated within applied linguistics can be put to good use beyond language learning and teaching. Relatively new applications, such as forensic discourse analysis (e.g. Svartvik 1968; Coulthard and Johnson 2007) and author identification (e.g. Woolls and Coulthard 1998; Woolls 2003), are constantly being added to applied linguistics, thus confirming its broad reach. The fact that applied linguistics seeks to be relevant and useful in many areas of society, and that applied linguists are dealing with issues and concepts involving language function, means that pragmatics has a role to play in almost every area of applied linguistics.

An increasingly important field within applied linguistics, which has revolutionized both how language is studied and our understanding of how **meaning** is created, is **corpus linguistics** (e.g. Sinclair *et al.* 1970; Sinclair 1991, 1996, 1998, 2004a; Svartvik 1992; Biber *et al.* 1999; Biber *et al.* 2004; Carter and McCarthy 2006; Scott and Tribble 2006; Sinclair and Mauranen 2006). The first major impact of corpus linguistics was on lexicography. The *Collins Cobuild English Language Dictionary* (Sinclair 1987a), based on a study of many instances of actual usage, led to an increased emphasis on pragmatic meaning and, most importantly, on phraseology in recognition of the fact that meaning resides not in one word but in the co-selection of words by speakers and writers. This phraseological tendency is termed the 'idiom principle' (Sinclair 1987b) and has become a major focus for corpus linguists.

Since **context** plays a major role in the **communication** process, so the relationship between the participants, the nature of the message (degree of face threat), and the nature of the communicative activity has meant that the notion of pragmatic **politeness** (Brown and

Levinson 1987) is often adopted and used by applied linguists. The notion of pragmatic transfer (*see* Žegarac and Pennington 2000), whereby speakers of one language transfer characteristics of the language into a second language, a process which is a product of cultural differences, is also important in applied linguistics. The distinctions between pragmalinguistic differences (i.e. differences in linguistic strategies to convey pragmatic meaning) and sociopragmatic differences (i.e. differences in cultural behaviours and beliefs that influence language use) (Thomas 1983) are important considerations for language teachers (Schmitt 2002). The latter has led to an increasing appreciation of the importance in applied linguistics of **interlanguage pragmatics** (e.g. Kasper and Rose 2001), which seeks to compare how speech acts are performed across **cultures**.

Another field of pragmatics, which has been taken up by applied linguists, is **speech act theory**. Speech act theory influenced the functional approach to language learning in the 1970s (e.g. Wilkins 1976; Munby 1978) and still influences the language functions covered in many language-learning textbooks. The field of **discourse analysis** within applied linguistics, and especially the analysis of spoken **discourse** (e.g. Sinclair and Coulthard 1975; Stubbs 1983b; Coulthard 1985; Stenström 1994), while different in key respects from speech act theory, draws on the work of **Austin** and **Searle** in foregrounding the function of an utterance: 'we are interested in the function of an utterance … and thus the sorts of question we ask about an utterance are whether it is intended to evoke a response, whether it is a response itself, whether it is intended to mark a boundary in the discourse and so on' (Sinclair and Coulthard 1975: 14).

This attention to functionality, context and the analysis of actual language use, all important components of pragmatic studies, has influenced a subfield of applied linguistics, i.e. genre analysis (e.g. Swales 1990, 2004; Bhatia 1993a, 2004). However, another field, critical discourse analysis (e.g. Fairclough 2001, 2003; Wodak and Chilton 2005), specifically rejects pragmatics on the grounds that pragmatics 'takes a prediscoursal theory of the subject and of context … subjects and contexts are not constituted in dis-course, they are constituted before and outside the discourse – subjects use contexts to interpret discourse'. For many discourse analysts and for critical discourse analysts, language is 'part of the social whole' and they seek to explore 'the socially and culturally constitutive effects of discourse' (Fairclough 1996: 54).

Speech act theory has also influenced **stylistics**. There has been a move away from the study of linguistic form to an interest in pragmatics which is sometimes termed 'pragma-stylistics' (Davies 1999: 104). This approach extends beyond speech acts and sets out to explain 'how the style of a communication varies as the speaker aids the hearer to identify the thought behind an utterance, and the implicit interchanges with the explicit' (Hickey 1989: 9).

A relatively new field in applied linguistics is forensic discourse analysis (Coulthard 1992, 1993; Shuy 1993, 1998; Coulthard and Johnson 2007). The influence of pragmatics can be seen in expert witness reports and related research papers. For example, Grice's (1975) maxim of quantity has successfully been used to illustrate the over-explicitness (i.e. too much information) of some supposed witness statements which have been fabricated by the police (e.g. Coulthard 1994). Conversely, Tiersma and Solan (2002) cited the lack of information in a case in which smokers were suing a tobacco company over a cigarette packet warning that simply stated 'cigarette smoke contains carbon monoxide'. The smokers successfully argued that the warning gave insufficient information to the consumer who is unlikely to fully understand the implications of the warning. The use of corpora to establish the 'lay meaning' of words has also been employed in expert reports submitted to courts, as in the case of whether or not 'visa' permits entry to the issuing country or whether it is 'a permit to request leave to enter' (Sinclair, cited in Coulthard and Johnson 2007: 126). By examining its collocates in a large corpus of general English, Sinclair was able to show that for the lay person 'visa' is understood to mean the former.

WINNIE CHENG

See also: Complaints; context; corpus linguistics; culture; discourse; discourse analysis; interlanguage pragmatics; politeness; pragmatics; refusals; second language acquisition; sociolinguistics; speech act theory; stylistics

Suggestion for further reading

Seidlhofer, B. (2003) *Controversies in Applied Linguistics*, Oxford: Oxford University Press.

Argumentation Theory

Argumentation experienced a revival of interest in 1958 when Chaïm Perelman and Lucie Olbrechts-Tyteca published their seminal work in the area entitled *La Nouvelle Rhétorique* (the English translation of this work was published in 1969). The achievement of this study was the rediscovery of 'a part of Aristotelian logic that had been long forgotten or, at any rate, ignored and despised. It was the part dealing with dialectical reasoning, as distinguished from demonstrative reasoning – called by Aristotle analytics – which is analyzed at length in the *Rhetoric*, *Topics*, and *On Sophistical Refutations*' (Perelman 1979: 9). This 'new rhetoric', as it was called, was motivated by the search for 'an ideal of practical reason, that is, the establishment of rules and models for reasonable action' (1979: 8), a search which Perelman had previously conducted from 'within the limits of logical empiricism', but with unsatisfactory results. This new-found interest in argumentation brought with it an emphasis on audience adherence, the attributes of speakers and listeners, rules of discussion, **communication** and a juridical, as opposed to a mathematical, model of **reasoning** with its focus on opinion as the starting point of argumentation and its rejection of the 'unicity of truth'. Specifically, this 'new rhetoric' was to challenge the traditionally dominant position of formal logic in the study of argument:

> Formal logic essentially studies proof through calculation, i.e., formally correct demonstrative reasoning. But, the way we reason in a discussion, or in an intimate deliberation, when we give reasons pro or contra, when we criticize or justify a certain thesis, when we present an argument, e.g., in drawing up a preamble for a legal draft or the justification of a judgment, all the techniques utilized in these situations have escaped the modern logician's attention to the extent that he has limited himself to the analysis of purely formal reasoning. It is doubtless that in all these situations we reason, and the nature of these reasonings did not escape Aristotle, considered by everyone to be the father of formal logic.
>
> (Perelman 1979: 56)

Also in 1958, Stephen Toulmin published a book that was to erode yet further the dominance of formal logic in the study of argument. Entitled *The Uses of Argument*, this book was to give prominence to the actual procedures used by arguers in different fields of argument:

> The statements of our assertions, and the statements of the facts adduced in their support, are, as philosophers would say, of many different 'logical types' – reports of present and past events, predictions about the future, verdicts of criminal guilt, aesthetic commendations, geometrical axioms and so on. The arguments which we put forward, and the steps which occur in them, will be correspondingly various.
>
> (Toulmin 1958: 13)

These procedures had hitherto been neglected by philosophers and logicians whose preoccupation had been with logico-mathematical ideals of argument. Jurisprudence, not mathematics, Toulmin argued, should be the logician's model in analysing rational procedures: 'If we are to set our arguments out with complete logical candour, and understand properly the nature of "the logical process", surely we shall need to employ a pattern of argument no less sophisticated than is required in the law' (1958: 96). This 'pattern of argument' sets out with a conclusion or claim (C), which must be established if challenged. The facts that we use to support this claim form our data (D). The **proposition** that carries us from the data to the conclusion is described as the warrant (W) and may confer 'different degrees of force on the conclusions they justify' (1958: 100). Some warrants lead us 'necessarily' from the supporting data to the conclusion of an argument. In other arguments, the warrant authorizes a more tentative or qualified step between data and conclusion. The strength that a particular warrant confers on the step between data and conclusion is indicated by the qualifier (Q) beside the conclusion in the model. The 'general authority' of a warrant may be set aside if certain conditions of exception or rebuttal (R) obtain. As well as specifying the conditions under which a warrant may be presumed to hold, we may also be required to state for a challenger why a particular warrant should be accepted. To satisfy this challenger's demand, we will be required to reveal the grounds we have for a particular warrant – what Toulmin calls the backing (B) of a warrant. Toulmin's model for the pattern of an argument thus has the following form (Figure 1):

The 'new rhetoric' of Perelman and Olbrechts-Tyteca had more impact initially on communication and rhetorical studies than on philosophy, particularly in North America (Gilbert 1997). Although the impact of Toulmin's monograph has probably been wider than that of the 'new rhetoric', his work certainly attracted its detractors (*see* Cowan 1964). Notwithstanding the unfavourable reaction to the ideas of these early argumentation theorists in some quarters, it is clear that Perelman's and Toulmin's work marked a significant pragmatic turn in the study of argument (Cummings 2005). This pragmatic turn emphasized the study of arguments in a range of different contexts. Arguers were no longer irrelevant to the study of argument, as they had been for formal logicians. Argument was now not a static phenomenon, but was con-

ceived in terms of a process of argumentation that arose between two or more participants who were concerned to debate the rational merits of different positions and standpoints. Notions such as *context, arguer, standpoint* and *argumentation*, which had been driven out of the study of argument by formal logic, began to find their place within pragmatic frameworks such as the **pragma-dialectics** of Frans van Eemeren and Rob Grootendorst. From today's pragmatically informed perspective on argument, it may seem that pragmatic concepts such as **context** have always been central to the study of argument. Yet, without the pioneering work of Perelman and Toulmin in the latter half of the twentieth century, it is difficult to imagine how the rapid development of pragmatic frameworks for the analysis and evaluation of argument could have occurred. Perelman's and Toulmin's criticisms of formal logic and their ideas for a new conception of argument prepared the way for the emergence of the informal logic movement in North America during the 1970s (van Eemeren and Grootendorst 1996) and have influenced the thinking of later theorists such as Jürgen **Habermas** (*see* Habermas 1984 for discussion of Toulmin's analysis of argument structure).

Shortly after argumentation theorists began to loosen the grip of formal logic on argument, fallacy theorists started to question its relevance to their own attempts to evaluate arguments. Formal logic with its emphasis on deductive validity had long been the presumed ideal of argument and any argument which failed to conform to this ideal was consigned to the category of fallacy. In his 1970 book *Fallacies,*

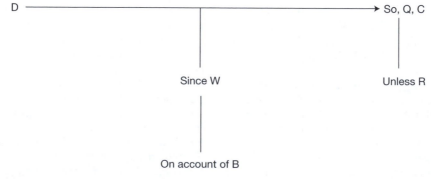

Figure 1 Toulmin's model.

Charles Hamblin directly challenged formal logic's relevance to the study of argument evaluation:

> The point is … that … there are various criteria of worth of arguments; that they may conflict, and that arguments may conflict; that when criteria conflict some are more dispensable than others, and that when arguments conflict a decision needs to be made to give weight to one rather than another. All this sets the theory of *arguments* apart from Formal Logic and gives it an additional dimension.
>
> (1970: 231; italics in original)

Hamblin rejects alethic criteria of argument evaluation ('an argument is a good one if the premises are true and the conclusion immediately follows from it') in favour of dialectical criteria that are based on acceptance: 'acceptance by the person the argument is aimed at – the person for whom the argument is an argument – is the appropriate basis of a set of criteria' (1970: 242). While an argument that proceeds from accepted premises using an accepted **inference** process may not be judged to be a good argument 'in the full, alethic sense', it is, Hamblin claims, 'a good one in some other sense which is much more germane to the practical application of logical principles' (1970: 241).

It is significant that in advancing dialectical criteria, Hamblin draws on concepts that are pragmatic in nature. Our criteria of good argument, he argues, would be 'less than adequate' if they could not account for the *purposes* for which we advance arguments. Assessed against the contexts in which they occur and the purposes for which they are advanced, many previously fallacious arguments began to be described as having non-fallacious variants. Douglas Walton and John Woods have made a particularly important contribution to this area of **fallacy theory**. In a large number of books and journal articles, these theorists have described non-fallacious forms of *petitio principii* (begging the question), *argumentum ad ignorantiam* (the argument from ignorance), and *argumentum ad baculum* (the argument from the stick or appeal to force), amongst others (Walton 1985, 1992; Woods 1995). Non-fallacious forms of three informal

fallacies – *petitio principii*, arguments from analogy and *argumentum ad ignorantiam* – have been analysed as reasoning **heuristics** that facilitate the progress of scientific inquiry under conditions of epistemic uncertainty (Cummings 2000, 2002, 2004). A pragmatic reorientation in argument evaluation of the type set in motion by Hamblin has been a central impetus in enquiries of this type.

LOUISE CUMMINGS

See also: Fallacy theory; inference; pragma-dialectics; reasoning; rhetoric

Suggestions for further reading

Hitchcock, D. and Verheij, B. (eds) (2006) *Arguing on the Toulmin Model: New Essays in Argument Analysis and Evaluation*, Dordrecht: Springer-Verlag.

Tindale, C.W. (2007) *Fallacies and Argument Appraisal*, New York: Cambridge University Press.

Walton, D. (2006) *Fundamentals of Critical Argumentation*, New York: Cambridge University Press.

Artificial Intelligence

Defined by McCarthy (2007) as 'the science and engineering of making intelligent machines', artificial intelligence (AI) is a branch of computer science whose origins can be traced back to a model of artificial neurons developed by McCulloch and Pitts (1943). However, it was not until 1955 that the term 'artificial intelligence' was coined by McCarthy at a workshop at Dartmouth College. Two different directions can be distinguished in early AI research: the symbolic, logic-based approach, which dominated from the 1970s through to the mid-1980s, and the sub-symbolic (or neural networks) approach, which declined after 1970, then was revived in the mid-1980s and has continued to flourish since that time.

According to Russell and Norvig (2003), the main topics within AI are: problem solving using search; **knowledge** and **reasoning**; planning; reasoning with uncertain knowledge; learning; communicating, perceiving, and acting.

Problem solving can often be viewed as searching through a space of possible states to find a solution. A search problem is defined in terms of an initial state, a goal state, and a set of legal moves for transforming one state to another state. Simple games and puzzles are often used to develop new search algorithms, while real world applications include route finding and robot navigation. Uninformed (or blind) search strategies are applicable when no additional information is available to guide the search, while informed (or **heuristic**) search involves the use of problem-specific knowledge to guide the selection of the most promising solution. Games such as Go and chess present a more complex challenge for search algorithms because of the uncertainty of the opponent's moves and the large state space to be explored.

Knowledge and reasoning involve the formal **representation** of knowledge and mechanisms for deriving new knowledge through **inference**. Logic has been used widely for knowledge representation – propositional logic to represent facts, and first-order predicate calculus to represent objects, relations, properties, and functions (McCarthy 1968). Temporal logics are used to represent events, states and their relation to time and change (Galton 2008), while modal logic is used for reasoning about beliefs and knowledge (Hintikka 1962). A logic-based system provides a mathematically rigorous procedure for automated reasoning.

Reasoning based on knowledge represented in the form of rules has been used widely in expert systems. An expert system solves problems by building a chain of rules leading to a solution or by applying all rules that match the given facts until a solution is found. An example of the latter approach is the XCON expert system which was used to configure DEC's VAX computer systems (McDermott 1982). Other commonly used formalisms for knowledge representation and reasoning include semantic networks and frames, which are used to represent relations between objects within a structured taxonomy (Quillian 1968; Minsky 1975).

Planning is a type of problem solving which focuses on the actions required to achieve a given set of goals. In the STRIPS language (Fikes and Nilsson 1971), actions are represented in terms of an action description, preconditions that must be true before the action can be executed, and the effects of executing the action. A plan consists of a sequence of actions in which the effect of each action is either a precondition of another action in the sequence or a goal to be achieved. Early work on planning focused on simple domains such as the blocks world using the STRIPS language. More recently, richer representations and more advanced planning algorithms have been used in planners that operate in more realistic domains such as systems developed at NASA to guide their missions before and after landing (Barrett 2005).

A major limitation of logic-based and planning approaches is that they are unable to support decision making in the face of uncertain and/or incomplete information. Making an optimal decision involves reasoning about the likelihood of a goal as well as considering its desirability (or utility). Probability theory is used to model uncertainty (or degrees of belief) using representations such as belief networks, while utility theory computes the expected utility of an action given the available evidence. Decision networks can be used to represent and solve simple decision problems (Pearl 1988). More complex sequential decision problems require more complex models, such as a Markov Decision Process (MDP), and a method for determining the optimal sequence of decisions (or policy) based on the model (Bellman 1957).

Machine learning is an important branch of AI that focuses on enabling systems to learn from experience since handcrafting knowledge is tedious and even impossible in some cases (Mitchell 1997). In supervised learning the system learns by mapping inputs to desired outputs. A typical example is classification, in which the system learns the category of objects based on seeing examples of objects from different categories. In unsupervised learning the system learns relationships among its input experiences (or percepts) without any information about the correct outputs. Reinforcement learning involves exploring an unknown environment and learning the best choices to take (the optimal policy) on the basis of positive and negative rewards. Learning in complex networks, such as neural networks and Bayesian belief networks, is currently an important topic in machine learning with applications such as biomedical and business analysis (Neal 1991).

Communicating, perceiving and acting involve interaction with other agents and with the environment. Natural language processing (NLP) is a major application of AI (Allen 1995). Until the early 1990s, NLP was dominated by the symbolic approach, with a major focus on grammars and parsing strategies. However, most computational work on natural language understanding currently uses statistical methods (Manning and Schütze 1999). Practical applications of NLP include machine translation, database access, information retrieval, text categorization, spelling and grammar correction, and dialogue modelling. Perceiving involves senses such as vision, hearing, and touch that are modelled computationally. Examples include computer vision for image processing and object recognition (Forsyth and Ponce 2003), and speech recognition (Jurafsky and Martin 2000). Acting with an environment is the subject matter of robotics, which studies both the hardware required (sensors and effectors) as well as tasks involving navigation and object manipulation (Canny 1988).

MICHAEL MCTEAR

See also: Abduction; cognitive science; communication; computational pragmatics; heuristic; inference; knowledge; logical form; reasoning

Suggestions for further reading

Luger, G.F. (2004) *Artificial Intelligence: Structure and Strategies for Complex Problem Solving*, Reading, MA: Addison Wesley.

Russell, S. and Norvig, P. (2003) *Artificial Intelligence: A Modern Approach*, Upper Saddle River, NJ: Prentice Hall.

Scientific American (2002) *Understanding Artificial Intelligence (Science made Accessible)*, New York: Grand Central Publishing.

Assertion

An assertion is a speech act of a certain type. Speech acts are intentional and rule governed. A speech act is performed in order to achieve a certain end. The nature of the end and the nature of the means for its achievement are specified by the rules that govern the **speech act type**.

The end of making an assertion is claiming about a represented state of affairs that it fits the facts. One can describe a speech act of assertion as involving (a) a **representation** of a state of affairs, and (b) a claim that this representation fits the facts. In terms used by many philosophers of language, the former is the propositional content of the speech act, while the latter is its force as an assertion.

The means of making an assertion are also rule governed, but this time the rules are of assertion in a certain natural language rather than of assertion in general. The reason is clear: representations of a state of affairs are made by using sentences of certain types. Commonly, sentences that can be used for making representations have certain linguistic properties, such as having the syntactic structure of the indicative (that of *The book is open*, not that of *Is the book open?* or *Open the book, please*.) A specification of such linguistic properties depends on the natural language in use.

Speech acts are performed in appropriate contexts of utterance and the latter are also among the means of making assertions. Consider a speaker who utters the sentence 'He is my son' in the presence of a son of the speaker, while pointing at him. The **context** of utterance, which includes the gesture of pointing at the son and his presence, is an integral part of the speech act event. Thus, a speech act of assertion consists of an utterance of an appropriate sentence in a certain natural language in an appropriate context of utterance. Within the framework of the context, the sentence is a representation of a state of affairs. The utterance of the sentence in the context counts as claiming that the represented **proposition** fits the facts.

Assertions involve not only the propositions that are claimed to fit the facts, but possibly propositions of two additional kinds. First, there are **presuppositions**, which are propositions that have to fit the facts, for the asserted proposition to fit or fail to fit the facts. The proposition that there is a king of Sweden is a presupposition of an assertion that the king of Sweden is tall. Second, there are **implicatures**, which are propositions that have to fit the facts for the speech act to be appropriate under the circumstances. The assertion that Mary has three children implicates, under ordinary circumstances, that she does not have four children.

The conceptual relationships between the speech act type of assertion and the notions of truth, belief and **knowledge** are debated. According to one theory, to assert is to claim that the represented proposition is true (Austin 1962). According to another theory, a proposition is true in a context of utterance if the rules of the speech act of assertion allow it to be asserted in that context (Dummett 1976). According to some theories, the rules require that the speaker believes that the represented proposition fits the facts (Searle 1969). According to other theories, the rules require knowledge rather than belief (Williamson 2000).

ASA KASHER

See also: Implicature; presupposition; speech act theory; speech act type

Suggestion for further reading

Greimann, D. and Siegwart, G. (eds) (2007) *Truth and Speech Acts*, London: Routledge.

Assessment, Pragmatic

Assessment is a necessary first step in the management of any communication disorder. Clinicians have long recognized that standardized tests (so-called formal tools), such as those used to assess the syntax and **semantics** of language, are particularly poorly suited to an assessment of pragmatic language skills. Although such tests exist for the assessment of **pragmatics**, most clinical and research effort has been directed towards the development of informal methods of assessment. These methods include a diverse array of techniques, ranging from **conversation analysis** and narrative assessment to the use of communication checklists and pragmatics profiles. The assessment procedures that are used by clinicians (principally, speech and language therapists) to assess disordered pragmatics in children and adults will be examined below.

Not all clinicians and researchers subscribe to the view that pragmatic aspects of language cannot be assessed using formal techniques. Adams (2002: 973), for example, believes that some aspects of pragmatics can be formally assessed: 'Formal testing of pragmatics has limited potential to reveal the typical pragmatic abnormalities in interaction but has a significant role to play in the assessment of comprehension of pragmatic intent.' That comprehension of pragmatic intent is more readily assessed than interactional aspects of pragmatics is demonstrated by the large range of studies that have examined the uptake of **speech acts** and the recovery of conversational **implicatures** in children and adults across different clinical groups. Studies have examined the understanding of indirect **requests** and indirect **refusals** in subjects with left- and **right-hemisphere damage** (Hatta *et al.* 2004), the understanding of **irony** in schizophrenia (Langdon *et al.* 2002a) and the recognition of communicative **intentions** in children with epilepsy and autistic features (Parkinson 2006). Recently, Young *et al.* (2005) investigated if two formal assessment tools could be used to differentiate pragmatic language disorders in children with **autism spectrum disorders** (ASDs) from controls matched on verbal IQ and language fundamentals. The tests in question – the Test of Pragmatic Language (TOPL; Phelps-Terasaki and Phelps-Gunn 1992) and the Strong Narrative Assessment Procedure (SNAP; Strong 1998) – were administered to thirty-four matched ASD subjects. Results showed that ASD subjects obtained significantly poorer scores than controls on the TOPL. On the SNAP, children with ASDs performed similarly to controls in the areas of syntax, cohesion, story grammar and completeness of episodes. On the ability to answer inferential **questions**, controls performed significantly better than ASD subjects. Young *et al.* concluded that while the TOPL was effective in differentiating pragmatic language disorders in children with autism spectrum disorders, the SNAP was not effective in differentiating these disorders in the two groups in this study.

Notwithstanding the clinical utility of formal assessments such as TOPL, it remains the case that few formal tests of pragmatics exist. Moreover, such tests as do exist must be supplemented by a range of informal techniques in order to obtain a reliable picture of an individual's pragmatic functioning. Adams (2002: 976) remarks that '[i]n practice there are ... no really satisfactory single tests of language pragmatics which cover all the aspects one would wish to assess with an individual child. Tests will always need to be supplemented by observations and elicitation procedures.' Many of these informal procedures are structured according to categories set out in communication checklists and pragmatics profiles. Now in its second edition, the *Children's Communication Checklist* (Bishop 2003a) has 'rapidly become the instrument of choice for the identification of pragmatic language impairment' (Adams 2002: 976). This 70-item questionnaire is intended for use with children aged 4 to 16 years and may be completed by a caregiver. As well as identifying pragmatic impairment in children, the checklist may also be used to screen children who may have a language impairment and to identify children who may merit further assessment for an autistic spectrum disorder. The *Pragmatics Profile* (Dewart and Summers 1995) places pragmatics at the centre of an investigation of children's language and communication skills. Through a structured interview, which is conducted informally with a parent, teacher or other carer, investigators can glean information on the following broad communicative areas: communicative functions, response to **communication**, interaction and **conversation**, and contextual variation. The profile is intended for use with school-age children between 5 and 10 years of age, although other versions are available for use with pre-school children up to approximately 4 years of age and for use with adults. For a critical discussion of pragmatics profiles and checklists, *see* Cummings (2007b).

Conversation and discourse analytic techniques were once treated as an adjunct in the assessment of language. Today, these techniques are integral to the communication assessment of a diverse range of client groups. Two assessment tools that have been devised in the UK for use with aphasic clients and which are based on the methodology of conversation analysis are the *Conversation Analysis Profile for People with Aphasia* (CAPPA; Whitworth *et al.* 1997) and *Supporting Partners of People with Aphasia in Relationships and Conversation* (SPPARC; Lock *et al.* 2001). The

CAPPA can be used to assess the effectiveness of the conversational strategies of the aphasic person and his or her partner, identify changes in pre-morbid communication styles and establish areas of greater conversational opportunity for the aphasic person (Beeke *et al.* 2007). The SPPARC assesses three main areas of conversation (trouble and repair; turns and sequences; topic and overall conversation) and is also an intervention programme. Disruption of **discourse** is widely reported in the child and adult schizophrenia literature. Deficits in **discourse coherence and cohesion** are particularly common (Caplan *et al.* 1992; Barch and Berenbaum 1997; Vallance *et al.* 1999). Discourse coherence disturbances in schizophrenia are characterized by tangential responses, loss of goal, derailments, non-sequitur responses, distractible speech and incompetent references (Barch and Berenbaum 1997). As well as being disrupted in schizophrenia, cohesion variables (e.g. anaphoric references) have been found to be sensitive to changes in the psychiatric state of schizophrenic patients who have undergone drug treatment (Abu-Akel 1999). Discourse measures including productivity, efficiency, content accuracy and organization, story grammar, coherence and topic management have been used to characterize the discourse deficits of clients with **traumatic brain injury** (TBI). Notwithstanding the value of **discourse analysis** as an assessment procedure in TBI, time and training constraints have served to limit its widespread use (for further discussion of discourse analysis in TBI, *see* Coelho 2007).

LOUISE CUMMINGS

See also: Autism spectrum disorders; clinical pragmatics; communication aids, pragmatics of; dementia and conversation; pragmatic language impairment; psychotic discourse; rehabilitation, communication; right-hemisphere damage and pragmatics; schizophrenic language; sign language, pragmatics of; traumatic brain injury and discourse

Suggestions for further reading

Coelho, C.A., Ylvisaker, M. and Turkstra, L.S. (2005) 'Nonstandardised assessment approaches for individuals with traumatic brain injuries', *Seminars in Speech and Language*, 26: 223–41.

Farmer, M. and Oliver, A. (2005) 'Assessment of pragmatic difficulties and socio-emotional adjustment in practice', *International Journal of Language and Communication Disorders*, 40: 403–29.

Penn, C. (1999) 'Pragmatic assessment and therapy for persons with brain damage: what have clinicians gleaned in two decades?', *Brain and Language*, 68: 535–52.

Austin, J.L.

John L. Austin (1911–60) started as a brilliant student of classics and then turned to philosophy. His thinking developed in the 1930s in the climate created by neo-positivism and by **Wittgenstein**'s teaching in Cambridge. However, he was also influenced by the Oxford philosophers of the preceding generation (among whom was H. Prichard) and by the tradition of Oxford Aristotelian studies. During the Second World War he served in the Intelligence Corps of the British Army. Back at Oxford University, he conducted weekly meetings known as 'Saturday mornings' in which a linguistic approach to philosophy was cultivated (Warnock 1973). Austin qualified as the most central representative of **ordinary language philosophy**. In his lifetime, he published only a handful of papers, and a translation (from German) of Frege's *Foundations of Arithmetic*. Two books were edited from two of his sets of lecture notes after his premature death from cancer.

Like Wittgenstein, Austin believed that the investigation of ordinary language could prevent philosophical mistakes from arising. He also maintained it can provide substantial contributions to philosophical issues, since the distinctions embodied in ordinary linguistic usage, as products of a selection which has been made for centuries by the community using that language, are more likely to have a real point than those a philosopher can invent by him or herself alone in one afternoon (Passmore 1966: 431–75; Hanfling 2001). His approach to the analysis of ordinary linguistic usage can be synthetized in the question 'what we should say when' (Austin 1979: 181). He imagined contextualized **discourse** sequences and considered whether the use of a certain word or phrase in any of them was appropriate. He recommended resort to the dictionary in order not to miss the richness of actual linguistic usage. He believed that philosophy, practised this way, could become a cooperative enterprise and lead to discoveries. According to Austin's critics, the subtle distinctions that he set such great store by were not always pertinent to philosophy (Graham 1977; Grice 1989: 376). He was also charged with conservativism (Gellner 1959), since his approach would appear to favour the plain man's views over the philosopher's conceptual innovations. However, the outcomes of his investigations, being far from trivially commonsensical, should suffice to vindicate him. Beyond the commitment to the analysis of ordinary linguistic usage, Austin adopts other characteristic procedures such as rejection of philosophical oversimplifications, deconstruction of alleged conceptual dichotomies, the focusing on marginal as opposed to default cases, and contextualization of objects of enquiry.

Austin discussed various problems in epistemology, the philosophy of action, and the **philosophy of language**.

He argued for a divide between **knowledge** and belief, not admitting of belief-based definitions of knowledge. Discussing perception, he took sides against those theories that describe it as involving **inferences** from sense data to material objects (e.g. Ayer 1940), defending a view that vindicates the plain man's 'natural realism' (*see* Putnam 1994). He claimed that the sense data versus material objects dichotomy is spurious. He argued (coming close to what was later called 'disjunctivism', *see* e.g. Snowdon 1990) that it is not necessary to introduce sense data as what is common between a veridical perceptual experience and an experience which is illusory or delusive but indistinguishable from it, since the two experiences belong to different kinds. According to him, moreover, if we consider experiences in their contexts, indistinguishability between the two kinds can hardly arise. Although he had a vivid sense of human situatedness and fallibility, Austin rejected scepticism (*see* Kaplan 2000; Soames 2003a: 171–92): when a person is in the best possible position to know how things are, he or she is entitled to have complete confidence in his or her own judgement.

Austin also investigated various issues in the philosophy of action, among which were freedom and responsibility. He attacked compatibilism, that is, the view that free will is compatible with determinism, and argued that belief in determinism does not fit the way in which we ordinarily speak (Austin 1956a). Most famous is his paper entitled 'A Plea for Excuses' (Austin 1956b), in which he attempts to throw light on the structure or the 'stages' of action by examining 'non-normal' cases such as those which require the offering of excuses or justifications. Austin was aware that many descriptions may be true of the behaviour of an agent at a time (what has been later called the 'accordion effect'; see Feinberg 1964: 146) and he inclined towards a non-reductionist approach, counting each description as the description of a different action. His conception of action involved the idea of bringing about a change in a state of affairs and the practice of ascribing responsibility for it to an agent.

Austin's contributions to the philosophy of language include the notion of performative utterance, an analysis of **assertion** and truth, and the outline of a **speech act theory**.

Austin introduced the notion of performative utterance in a paper on epistemological issues (Austin 1946). He proposed a comparison between the use of 'I promise' not to report, but to perform a promise, and the use of 'I know' not to report a mental state but to give the hearer the guarantee that things are indeed in a certain way. He claimed that utterances such as 'I promise ... ' in the first person singular, present indicative tense, occurring in the appropriate circumstances, do not report or describe an action of the speaker's, but function as ritual phrases by which the speaker performs an action of the specified kind (e.g. a promise). He took such utterances to be neither true nor false, since truth and falsity pertain, for him, only to the assertive uses of language. Austin elaborated upon the notion of performative utterance in his book *How to Do Things with Words*. Here, he argued that while performative utterances comprising an action verb in the first person singular, present indicative tense are explicitly performative, utterances not displaying this form may also be said to perform an action, provided they are 'reducible, or expandible, or analysable

into a form, or reproducible in a form' (Austin 1975: 61–62) which makes explicit the action the speaker performs in issuing them. The **ambiguity** between a view of performatives as 'doing' something and as 'making explicit' that something is being done has been criticized by Urmson (1977). Subsequent literature on performatives has also questioned the idea that they fail to be true or false and attempted to explain how it is that they count as performances of actions (see Hornsby and Longworth 2006).

As for assertion, Austin argued that statements are made in 'historic events' and are demonstratively connected to 'historic situations' in the world, while the sentences used in making them are descriptively connected to types of situations. A statement can be said to be true when the pertinent historic situation belongs to the type that the sentence used is designed to describe (Austin 1950). In his elaboration upon the intuitive idea that statements are true when they 'correspond to the facts', Austin does not posit structural similarity between language and the world. However, according to him, 'true' is not (as others have argued) semantically superfluous: saying that a statement is true is saying something about that statement, and is therefore saying something more than what is said in making the statement. Truth/falsity assessments are (at least to some extent) a matter of degree, as is shown by the use of other words besides 'true' and 'false', such as 'rough', 'general', and 'exaggerated', in assessments about words–world correspondence. Moreover, these assessments are influenced by **context** (Austin 1950, 1975: 143–45). Austin's views about truth have been criticized by P.F. Strawson (1950b) and a lengthy debate has ensued (Pitcher 1964).

In *How to Do Things with Words*, Austin (1975) put forward the outline of a speech act theory. He developed his notion of the performative utterance into a more general conception of speech as action. Austin starts from a restatement of the contrast between performative utterances and assertions (here, also called 'constatives'). He discusses at length the 'felicity conditions' of performatives (those socially accepted conditions which speakers and circumstances must satisfy in order for the utterance to succeed in performing the action) and the criteria for recognizing a performative utterance. He observes intermediate cases between performatives and constatives as well as analogies, and concludes that the dichotomy has to be abandoned. He then proceeds to formulate a new framework for the study of language which is based on the notion of a speech act. Critics have initially misunderstood Austin's intent and have taken him as actually seeking to isolate the performative utterance from the constative, but failing to do so (Black 1969). More correctly, Warnock (1989: 106–7) has pointed out that Austin explored the hypothesis of a performative/constative dichotomy in order to show why a new start on the problem, i.e. speech act theory, was needed.

Austin distinguished three main levels in the total speech act, that is, three main ways in which an utterance can be described as 'doing' something (Austin 1975: 91–120): (i) the act of saying something or locutionary act, to be further analyzed into the act of uttering certain noises (phonetic act), the act of uttering noises of certain types, conforming to and as conforming to certain rules (phatic act), and the act of using the words uttered with a certain **meaning** (rhetic act); (ii) the act of doing something 'in' saying something or illocutionary act, which may be exemplified by such acts as promising, ordering, warning, asking, thanking, and stating, all performed, according to Austin, on the basis of conventions and taking effect in conventional ways; (iii) the act of doing something 'by' saying something or perlocutionary act, which may be exemplified by such acts as persuading, alerting, getting someone to do something, all consisting of the production of psychological or behavioural consequences by means of an utterance. This threefold analysis of the speech act has been taken up, but also discussed and transformed, in the ample literature on speech act theory stemming from **Searle** (1969).

The kind of action that is explicitly performed in performative utterances is used by Austin as a model for the illocutionary level of the speech act. Austin uses a list of verbs that admit of performative use to single out kinds of illocutionary acts and group them in classes or types. His classes highlight prototypes of speech action (judgement as to fact or value, exercise of authority or influence, the undertaking of commitments or espousals, reaction to events or lines

of conduct in the social context, the organization of exposition or **discourse**) and admit of marginal cases and overlaps, yielding a dynamic, but hardly ever exploited, set of tools for **discourse analysis** (Sbisà 2006: 164–67).

Austin wanted to separate the issue of the internal structure of the total speech act from the issue of those uses of language that suspend or shift some of the default features of the speech situation. He called such uses 'aetiolations' or 'non-serious uses': they comprise **quotation**, play-acting, poetry and joke. This separation was criticized by Derrida (1977a) and a debate between Derrida and Searle ensued (Searle 1977; Derrida 1977b; *see* Cavell 1995).

Extremely influential in his lifetime, Austin was soon put aside after his death. The time of ordinary language philosophy was already coming to an end. During the 1960s and early 1970s, the philosophies of Quine and Davidson, the developments of formal semantics, the increasing import of the **philosophy of mind** and of mentalist approaches to language, and last but not least, **Grice**'s way of distinguishing **pragmatics** from **semantics** deeply changed the scene. When, in the 1970s, Austin became renowned as the initiator of speech act theory in the framework of the new interdisciplinary interest for pragmatics, his ideas were often conflated with those of John Searle. At present, Austin is recognized as the proponent of an original perspective on speech as action and as one of the inspirations for **contextualism** both in epistemology and in the philosophy of language (*see* e.g. Preyer and Peter 2005). Austin has also been influential on the American philosopher and literary critic Stanley Cavell (whose work has paid attention to the philosophical role of the ordinary; *see* Cavell 2002) and on the historian Quentin Skinner (who has developed an approach to historical research that is particularly attentive to context; *see* Tully 1988).

MARINA SBISÀ

See also: Assertion; context; contextualism; Grice, H.P.; knowledge; ordinary language philosophy; philosophy of language; philosophy of mind; pragmatics; Searle, J.; semantics; semantics-pragmatics interface; speech act theory; speech act type; Wittgenstein, L.

Suggestions for further reading

Fann, K.T. (ed.) (1969) *Symposium on Austin*, London: Routledge.

Sbisà, M. (2007) 'How to read Austin', *Pragmatics*, 17: 461–73.

Warnock, G. (1989) *J.L. Austin*, London: Routledge.

Autism Spectrum Disorders

Since it was first described in 1943 (Kanner 1943), autism has come to be regarded as a spectrum disorder, with a range of severity and variable expression of features. *Autism Spectrum Disorder* is now recognized as an umbrella term for several associated neurodevelopmental disorders, including autism, Asperger Syndrome and pervasive developmental disorder not otherwise specified (PDD-NOS). Autism spectrum disorders (ASDs) are among the most prevalent of childhood developmental disorders, affecting an estimated 1 in 165 children (Fombonne *et al.* 2006). While each individual with an autism spectrum disorder is unique, diagnoses along the spectrum share a common set of characteristics: problems with social relationships and interactions; impairments in language and **communication**; and a preference for repetitive behaviours and activities over imaginative play (American Psychiatric Association 1994). The causes of ASDs are not known.

Autism spectrum disorders affect language development and social interaction in that many people with an ASD never achieve functional verbal communication. Those who do acquire functional language nevertheless exhibit linguistic problems and have difficulty with social communication. Speech difficulties noted in the literature include pronoun reversal, atypical intonation (de Villiers *et al.* 2007), neologisms (Volden and Lord 1991), and stereotyped, repetitive language and echolalia (Prizant and Duchan 1981). The most pronounced difficulties, however, are in **pragmatics** – the ability to deploy knowledge of language effectively in communication. People with an ASD often omit necessary information, which their interlocutors do not know (Kanner 1946; Baltaxe 1977; Tager-Flusberg 1981; Baron-Cohen 1988; Lord and Paul 1997) and have problems connecting their speech with previous **discourse** (i.e. cohesion) (Fine *et al.* 1994). Some investigations have found that people with ASDs have trouble understanding **irony** and **humour** in jokes and stories (Ozonoff and Miller 1996; Martin and McDonald 2004). Others have noted a tendency to be literal (Happé 1993; Ozonoff and Miller 1996; Szatmari 2004), which some researchers have interpreted in terms of a lack of cognitive flexibility (Ozonoff and Miller 1996). In studies looking at speakers' abilities to interpret or disambiguate discourse, where the content of what is being communicated must be found pragmatically, speakers with ASDs also invariably have difficulty (Happé 1993; Szatmari 2004).

A growing body of evidence suggests that in inferential reasoning, people with ASDs have trouble incorporating information from instances to make interpretations, using general knowledge rather than salient information supplied in **context**. For example, Happé (1997) found that children who had autism made more errors than others on a homograph task, in which the resolution of a sentence containing a potentially ambiguous word required integration of sentence context. Dennis *et al.* (2001a) found that children with autism had problems with **presupposition** on tasks involving inferencing in discourse. Jolliffe and Baron-Cohen (1999) observed incorrect **inferences** in tasks where interpretation required participants with high-functioning autism and Asperger Syndrome to make bridging inferences. Norbury and Bishop (2002) showed that in answering **questions** about a story, children with autism relied on general information to make inferences, rather than using information supplied in the story. Another fairly robust finding in the pragmatic communication of people with ASDs is difficulty with Gricean **maxims**, particularly those of quantity and relevance (Bishop and Adams 1989; Surian *et al.* 1996; de Villiers *et al.* 2007). Speakers with ASDs often provide too little information, in the form of minimal or polar responses, or too much information for the interactive context (de Villiers *et al.* 2007). Surian *et al.* (1996) observed that children with autism had difficulty identifying violations of conversational maxims in a structured pragmatic task. Problems in relevance have also been found in tasks requiring relevant answers to questions

(Happé 1993; Loukusa *et al.* 2007a). In Loukusa *et al.* (2007a), speakers with high-functioning autism and Asperger Syndrome responded to questions relevantly, but then added information that violated the maxim of quantity. Loukusa *et al.* suggest this pattern may relate to processing difficulties, with speakers failing to stop processing after giving a response.

Given these pragmatic difficulties, it is perhaps not surprising that people with ASDs find **conversation** very difficult. In unstructured contexts, conversational discourse is unconstrained and dynamic and builds upon contributions of interlocutors. Even individuals with ASDs who have comparatively strong language skills have trouble creating reciprocal conversations. They often have difficulty initiating and sustaining conversation, and for many, collaborating in **topic** development is also a challenge: topics of special interest may be introduced repeatedly, while others go undeveloped. Thus, an active area of investigation in ASD communication is the capacity for conversation, both for its potential to provide insight into the causes of ASDs and for informing interventions.

An area of pragmatic communication that appears to be unique to ASDs is pedantic speech (Ghaziuddin and Gerstein 1996; de Villiers 2006). In pedantic speaking, the language used often has a formal or 'wooden' quality. This may be characterized by grammatical and organizational features that resemble written text (Asperger 1944), and by the inclusion of more detail than would be expected for the situation (Baltaxe 1977). Speech may also have marked technical vocabulary and information as well as redundancies that do not appear cohesive (de Villiers *et al.* 2007). In addition, speakers may use stereotyped expressions, or vocabulary and clausal patterning associated with a register not matched to the immediate speech context, as though the syntactic structures are being recalled.

The pragmatic communication difficulties found in ASDs have generally been interpreted in terms of an inability to infer intentional states of others (the **Theory of Mind** hypothesis, Baron-Cohen *et al.* 1985; Baron-Cohen 1995). Increasingly, studies are also investigating communication difficulties in terms of other model-theoretic perspectives such as executive processes that enable integration, selection and inhibition of information in discourse processing (Executive Dysfunction hypothesis, Russell 1998 and the Theory of Underconnectivity, Just *et al.* 2004; Koshino *et al.* 2005) and differences in processing style leading to a reduced ability to pull together information from different sources to form an integrated whole (Weak Central Coherence Theory, Happé 1997; Happé and Frith 2006). To date, cognitive models have provided the most convincing explanations for pragmatic problems in ASDs, together with hypothesized neural bases of face processing (Baron-Cohen *et al.* 2000; Pierce *et al.* 2001). Research into functional (under)connectivity also shows potential for explaining pragmatic difficulties, since neural connectivity seems to support higher discourse processing (Just *et al.* 2007).

JESSICA DE VILLIERS

See also: Ambiguity; clinical pragmatics; communication; context; conversational failure; development, pragmatic; disambiguation; humour; inference; irony; maxims of conversation; pragmatics; presupposition; relevance theory; theory of mind

Suggestions for further reading

Asp, E. and de Villiers, J. (to appear) *When Language Breaks Down: Analysing Discourse in Clinical Contexts*, Cambridge: Cambridge University Press.

Frith, U. (2003) *Autism: Explaining the Enigma*, Oxford: Blackwell.

Saldaña, D. and Frith, U. (2007) 'Do readers with autism make bridging inferences from world knowledge?', *Journal of Experimental Child Psychology*, 96: 310–19.

B

Bar-Hillel, Y.

Yehoshua Bar-Hillel was an Israeli philosopher of language, science and information, and one of the founding fathers of **pragmatics** in the twentieth century. Bar-Hillel was born in Vienna in 1915, emigrated in 1933, and studied at the Hebrew University of Jerusalem. During World War II he served in the Jewish Brigade of the British Forces. He also participated in the 1948 Israel War of Independence, during which he was injured and lost an eye while trying to rescue comrades. Bar-Hillel died in Jerusalem in 1975.

From 1961 Bar-Hillel was Professor of Logic and Philosophy of Science at the Hebrew University of Jerusalem. He was a member of the Israel National Academy of Sciences and Humanities from 1963. Bar-Hillel was a visiting professor in various research institutes, including the Massachusetts Institute of Technology, where he met Noam Chomsky. At the University of Chicago he worked with Rudolf Carnap, one of the leaders of the highly influential philosophical movement of logical empiricism. Bar-Hillel became one of Carnap's major followers.

Bar-Hillel's scientific works included three significant novelties. First, he initiated the systematic study, both in **philosophy** and in linguistics, of pragmatics, the study of language use. His 1954 paper 'Indexical Expressions', published in the journal *Mind*, was one of the formative contributions to pragmatics. The paper drew attention to the ubiquity of indexical expressions in natural language and to the problems it creates for natural logic, the study of arguments in natural language. Logical relations were usually taken to hold between '**propositions**' which had constant **meanings**. Expressions that include an indexical element, such as 'I', 'here', 'now' or a verb of a certain tense, were argued by Bar-Hillel to be of a different nature that cannot be incorporated into classical logics. Later philosophical studies of the **semantics** and pragmatics of indexical expressions, by David Kaplan, Saul Kripke, Richard Montague and others, have shown the philosophical depth and pregnancy of the area to which Bar-Hillel had drawn attention.

Second, Bar-Hillel's work created an original and reasonable combination of conceptions that had developed in two separate philosophical traditions, commonly held to be alternatives to each other. One tradition is that of logical empiricism, as manifest in Carnap's works, from which Bar-Hillel adopted the conviction that science is the human device of **knowledge** and understanding of the world and the method of using formal systems for presentation of scientific theories. Another tradition is that of rationalism, as manifest in Chomsky's works, from which Bar-Hillel adopted the conception of language, its cognitive **representation** in the human mind/brain and its use in human life. Third, Bar-Hillel developed the notion of 'categorical grammar', which was later used in a variety of studies, including in **formal pragmatics**.

Among Bar-Hillel's books are *Foundations of Set Theory* (Fraenkel and Bar-Hillel 1958; Fraenkel *et al.* 1973), *Aspects of Language* (Bar-Hillel 1970), and *Pragmatics of Natural Languages* (Bar-Hillel 1971).

ASA KASHER

See also: Context; history of pragmatics; indexicals; philosophy of language; pragmatics

Suggestion for further reading

Kasher, A. (ed.) (1976) *Language in Focus: Foundations, Methods and Systems. Essays in Memory of Yehoshua Bar-Hillel*, Dordrecht: Reidel.

Business Discourse

'Business discourse' has been defined as the interaction which takes place between individuals whose main activities are located within business and whose contact is motivated by matters relating to their respective businesses (Bargiela-Chiappini and Nickerson 1999: 2). Thus, the status of the interactants is the decisive element in distinguishing business discourse from, for example, professional discourse (Gunnarsson *et al.* 1997), in that the latter, but not the former, would involve a lay person. Moreover, in business discourse, a 'business' identity would normally also imply a 'corporate' identity, i.e. membership of an organization devoted to the production and/or sale of goods or services (Gunnarsson *et al.*1997).

A possible chronology of business discourse would take us as far back as the 1960s. In the early days, Language for Specific Purposes (LSP) and later English for Specific Purposes (ESP) dominated the scene and have continued to attract a steady following alongside the other vocational stream of language needs analysis (Hagen 1999).

Concern for users' needs in industry had led to the formation of a strong body of LSP research, which concentrated on the analysis, composition and teaching of practical text-types as required in the workplace. The study of English as a lingua franca saw the emergence of ESP, a field that concentrates on the analysis of the linguistic features of specialist texts, at first through register analysis and later through genre analysis (Dudley-Evans and St John 1998).

In the 1980s, the 'linguistic turn' promoted pragmatic and sociolinguistic analyses of the language of work and a discursive approach to its social-psychological dimensions, as well as an interest in multi-method research and cross-disciplinary dialogue. Language needs analysis and a quantitative approach to language(s) in the workplace was slowly, though not completely, overtaken by analyses of situated business language by scholars from a range of disciplines, frequently collaborating with practitioners and professionals.

The late 1980s and early 1990s witnessed the emergence of a distinctive body of discourse-based scholarship. Various understandings of **discourse** led to further situated analysis of interactional exchanges but also to the re-conceptualization of work organizations as discursive constructions. These developments are illustrated in landmark publications such as, for example, Drew and Heritage (1992) and Boden (1994) on **conversation analysis** of work and organizational practices, and Firth's (1995) and Ehlich and Wagner's (1995) collections of mainly discourse analytic studies.

More recently, discourse analytic and ethnographic studies have enriched and expanded the original focus of the field. These studies rely on empirical data and growing interest in intercultural business interactions, especially negotiations and meetings. Also, advances in communication technology have transformed the communication landscape in the workplace, affecting interpersonal and inter-company communication (Gimenez 2009). At the same time, 'localization', a centripetal movement contrasting with globalization and its contested imposition of 'Americanization', has led to the re-evaluation of the role of indigenous languages and value systems and is challenging the long-established position of English as a neutral lingua franca (Nair-Venugopal 2009).

Since the 1990s, the interpretation of business discourse has been both contextual and inter-discursive, that is, both firmly situated in the **context** of production (be it a business meeting or a call service centre) and sensitive to the inherent hybridity of discursive formations in business organizations. It follows that the analysis of business discourse implies both a concern with language use above sentence level, whether spoken or written, and with the relevance of context beyond the boundaries of the text (Bhatia 1993b; Huckin 1997). The accompanying view of the social and dynamic nature of 'discourse' as situated action is quite distant from the narrow notion of professional language of some of the early (LSP-related) research (Johns 1986), and is in line with an evolution in the field that promises new horizons and fresh challenges (Swales 2000).

It is also worth noting that business discourse, though originating in Europe, has from its inception sought to engage with fields and disciplines in the USA which also study **communication** in business and corporate settings, though through different theoretical and methodological approaches (Bargiela-Chiappini and Nickerson 2002). The *Handbook of Business Discourse* (Bargiela-Chiappini 2009a) has sought to illustrate the variety of perspectives that pre-existed but also inspired business discourse. Through dialogue with management communication (Reinsch 2009), rhetorical analysis (Zachry 2009), organizational communication (Jian *et al.* 2009) and business communication (Louhiala-Salminen 2009) (the latter with a strong presence also in northern Europe), business discourse is seeking to establish a multidisciplinary scholarly base, which seeks to involve linguists and communication researchers operating beyond Europe.

A notable development of the contrastive studies of Japanese and American/Australian English of the 1990s is the growth of research in a number of other Asian languages (Bargiela-Chiappini and Gotti 2005; Bargiela-Chiappini 2005/2006), including Chinese (Zhu and Li 2009), Korean (Jung 2009), Vietnamese (Chew 2009), and Malay (Nair-Venugopal 2009). The enlargement of the original Anglophone basis of the field has led to a critique of Western, essentialist concepts of '**culture**' and 'nation' and to the engagement with indigenous psychologies and philosophies (Bargiela-Chiappini and Nickerson 2003; Bargiela-Chiappini and Harris 2006; Bargiela-Chiappini 2009b).

The concern for the relevance of academic research to professional practice (Candlin 2002, 2003) is one that business discourse shares with business communication on both sides of the Atlantic (Charles 2009; Dulek and Graham 2009) and in East Asia (Cheng 2009). Accordingly, researchers are increasingly called upon to collaborate with practitioners and professionals towards developing joint modes of interpretation and analysis of issues of practice which are often discursively constructed (Iedema and Sheeres 2009).

Influenced by critical studies (Deetz and McClellan 2009), business discourse has developed an increasingly self-reflexive and self-questioning orientation towards its objectives, modes of operation, research outcomes and applications (Bargiela-Chiappini 2009b). Given its eclectic constitution and its openness to influences from other fields, disciplines and 'cultural' traditions, business discourse is set to remain a fluid domain with a strong experimental character. In some respects, and against the expected evolution of a scholarly field (e.g. business communication, Baker Graham and Thralls 1998), the 'disturbing' and unsettling nature of business discourse research (Bargiela-Chiappini 2009b) is likely to slow down concerted efforts towards disciplinary consolidation and a unifying identity.

FRANCESCA BARGIELA-CHIAPPINI

See also: Communication; context; conversation analysis; cross-cultural pragmatics; culture; discourse; discourse analysis; institutional and professional discourse; intercultural communication; interlanguage pragmatics

Suggestions for further reading

Bargiela-Chiappini, F. (ed.) (2009) *The Handbook of Business Discourse*, Edinburgh: Edinburgh University Press.

Bargiela-Chiappini, F., Nickerson, C. and Planken, B. (2006) *Business Discourse*, Basingstoke: Palgrave Macmillan.

Chaney, L. and Martin, J. (2006) *Intercultural Business Communication*, 4th edn, Harlow: Pearson.

C

Child Language Acquistion

Children's pragmatic **knowledge** has been a relatively unstudied area of first language development, although there has been a welcome explosion of published research in the 2000s (*see* Krämer 2007 for a recent collection of papers). This discussion first summarizes results in a number of grammatical areas (article use, pronoun interpretation, **topic** and **focus** constructions and complementation) and then sketches critical areas for further research and debate.

Article use

Early studies of children's use of definite and indefinite articles (*the*, *a*) demonstrated a tendency on the part of preschool children to over-use the definite article, using it where a referent had not been established in the **discourse** (*see* Maratsos 1976 for a study of English and Karmiloff-Smith 1979 for a study of French). Maratsos discusses this finding in the context of the Piagetian construct of egocentricity and Karmiloff-Smith argues that children use definite articles deitically with reference to the child's memory store. Under these accounts, the child fails to compute the shared knowledge between speaker and hearer that is necessary for correct article use. In a more recent study, Krämer (2003) shows that 4- to 5-year-old children have difficulty using prior discourse to select a referent for an indefinite noun phrase (in contrast to their ability with definite pronouns, for which they have somewhat better ability to use discourse). Schaeffer and Matthewson (2005) put a cross-linguistic spin on children's problems with articles. They argue that English children's use of articles is parallel to the article system of St'at'imcets (a Salish language of British Columbia). In that language, article use is determined by whether a referent is believed to exist by the speaker. Schaeffer and Matthewson propose that English-speaking children are aware of the conditions on article use in English, but that they lack a principle that dictates that speaker and hearer assumptions are independent. If English-speaking children are using their own beliefs to determine article use, then the inappropriate use of the definite article comes to resemble the St'at'imcets system.

Pronoun interpretation

Chien and Wexler (1990) is an early example of the finding that children may misconstrue the **reference** of a definite pronoun such as English *him*, allowing the pronoun to refer to the subject *Dave* in a sentence such as 'Dave hit him', rather than to an entity not mentioned in the sentence, as normally required by the adult grammar. Following theoretical work by Reinhart (1983a), Chien and Wexler attribute this type of error to a lack of knowledge on the child's part of a pragmatic principle that permits coreference in sentences such as that just cited, under particular discourse conditions. Recent research has shown that children are not, however, insensitive to discourse **context** in their interpretation of pronouns. Song and Fisher (2007) demonstrate that children as young as 2.5 years pay attention to prominence in the discourse of potential antecedents for a pronoun, choosing more prominent antecedents, as do older children and adults.

Referentiality, topic and focus

Schaeffer (2000) initiated the study of children's sensitivity to referentiality of noun phrases and choice of syntactic structure. In Dutch, an indefinite direct object follows an element such as **negation** when the object does not refer to any specific entity. But when the direct object is an indefinite with a specific interpretation (the equivalent of English 'a *certain* X'), or when it is a proper name or definite noun phrase, it precedes negation. Using an elicited production technique, Schaeffer found that children aged three and older were sensitive to these word order restrictions. Two-year-olds, however, were not. Similar results were found with respect to clitic pronoun placement in Italian. Schaeffer proposes that children younger than three fail to mark referentiality on nouns, a failure rooted in an immature pragmatic system.

Also using an elicited production task, De Cat (2008) showed that French speaking children distinguished between elements that had been previously established in the discourse and those which had not. For previously established entities, the children selected a structure in which the noun phrase in question was dislocated to the front or end of the sentence, or in which the subject of the sentence was pronominalized. For elements new to the discourse, by contrast, canonical subject-verb order was used, or an existential construction. Unlike in Schaeffer's study of Dutch, the syntactic differentiation between topic (previously established) and focus (new) elements was observed by even the youngest (2-year-old) children.

Complementation

Sentences embedded as complements to verbs can express a variety of **propositions** concerning the subject's mental **representation** of the world, including false beliefs. 'He thought that the keys were in the box', for example, can be used in the circumstance where the keys are not in fact in the box. By contrast, 'he knew that the keys were in the box' entails that the proposition that the keys are in the box is true. The verb *know* (but not *think*) presupposes the truth of its complement. Work by Macnamara *et al.* (1976) and Johnson and Maratsos (1977) showed that

4-year-olds were aware of the presuppositional distinction between the two verbs, although this was not true of the 3-year-olds in Johnson and Maratsos' study. More recently, de Villiers and de Villiers have looked at the relationship between use of sentential complements and children's skill with **theory of mind** tests (*see* de Villiers and de Villiers 2003 for a summary). In classic theory of mind tests, preschool children have been shown to do poorly at computing the mental states of others, an essential skill for efficient pragmatic functioning. For example, when a person has placed a set of keys in a box, which are then removed (unbeknownst to the person), children will fail to say that the person will look for the keys in the box. De Villiers and de Villiers find that use of complement structures is a significant predictor of skill on theory of mind tasks, but not vice versa. This suggests that the development of complement structures may drive the development of ability to compute the mental states of others, and hence by extension syntactic skill may pave the way for pragmatic skill.

Lack of knowledge or failure to execute knowledge?

Some of the studies above claim that young children lack knowledge of pragmatic principles (Chien and Wexler 1990; Schaeffer 2000). Others show young children conforming to the pragmatically driven constraints. Is it really the case that pragmatic skills are acquired over time? A recent study by Unsworth (2007) provides data that support the view that some of children's failures with pragmatic principles may be rooted in performance (use of knowledge in production and comprehension) rather than in an absolute deficit. Unsworth, like Schaeffer, studied children's knowledge of object positioning in Dutch. She found that performance in a production task far outstripped performance in a comprehension task; in the latter task, performance was at a fairly low rate for children as old as eight years. This asymmetry between production and comprehension makes sense in the context of models of production and comprehension in which discourse and context is recruited early in the course of production, but late in the course of comprehension (*see* Goodluck 2007 for a discussion). On this type of approach the difficulty that the 2-year-olds in Schaeffer's study had with object placement may simply have been the result of an immature production mechanism. In addition, a comprehension mechanism in which context and discourse are late accessed may help explain errors with definite pronoun interpretation (*see* section on pronoun interpretation above; also *see* Goodluck 2007 and Foster-Cohen 1994). Reinhart (2004) also broaches processing explanations of children's deficits, with reference to focus constructions.

Theory of mind versus Gricean principles

We have already seen that recent research has examined the child's grasp of theory of mind constructs in relation to his or her syntactic development. A question that has not been addressed is the relationship between theory of mind and Gricean conversational principles (as formulated by Grice 1975, or as reworked by Sperber and Wilson 1995). Intuitively, it would seem that theory of mind skills would form a basis for skilful execution of Gricean principles, since the latter require the computation of the knowledge state of the hearer.

Universals of pragmatics

Work on syntactic development over the past twenty-five years has studied both syntactic phenomena that may be argued to be invariant across languages (such as c-command constraints on pronominal systems) and those that display cross-linguistic variation (such as whether a language permits phonetically null subjects). Can a similar distinction be drawn with respect to pragmatic knowledge? Von Fintel and Matthewson (2008) present data that strongly suggests that **pragmatics** may involve both universal and parameterized features. Aside from Schaeffer and Matthewson (2005) and Fragman *et al.* (2007), to the author's knowledge no child language work has tackled the universal versus particular at the **syntax-pragmatics interface**.

HELEN GOODLUCK

See also: Anaphora, pragmatics of; clinical pragmatics; competence, linguistic; definiteness; Grice, H.P.; post-Gricean pragmatics; presupposition; reference; relevance theory; second language acquisition; syntax-pragmatics interface; theory of mind; topic; word learning, the role of mindreading in

Suggestions for further reading

De Villiers, J. (2007) 'The interface of language and theory of mind', *Lingua*, 117: 1858–78.
Krämer, I. (ed.) (2007) 'Language acquisition between sentence and discourse', *Lingua*, 117: 1833–988.

Classroom Discourse

Classroom discourse has been studied within linguistics for almost forty years. Early studies focused on producing structural-functional descriptions of teacher–student interaction, while later and current work is more diverse and draws on a variety of approaches and analytic frameworks.

One of the earliest and still most influential studies on teacher–student interaction was by Sinclair and Coulthard (1975). Their work was informed by **discourse analysis** in which the descriptive labels used to classify utterances focus on the function each utterance performs within the **context** of other utterances, rather than on its form. In the following example, the pupil interprets the teacher's interrogative 'What are you laughing at?' as a **command** to stop laughing rather than as a **question**:

> T: What kind of person do you think he is? Do you – what are you laughing at?
> P: Nothing.
>   (Sinclair and Coulthard 1975: 10)

The system of analysis would, therefore, label the teacher's interrogative as a directive rather than a question. Discourse analysis arranges its descriptors into hierarchical units of analysis such as those found in structural-functional models of grammar. Sinclair and Coulthard's model consists of the following units: Interaction; Transaction; Exchange; Move; Act. Each unit of analysis is realized by the units below it. So transactions are realized by exchanges which, in turn, are realized by moves, and so on.

A key contribution of Sinclair and Coulthard's model is the identification of the three-part exchange which, they argue, is a key characteristic of classroom discourse. Traditional, teacher-led exchanges typically consist of three structurally linked moves: Teacher Initiation (I), Pupil Response (R) and a Teacher Follow-up or Feedback move (F). (Note that the alternative terminology Initiation-Response-Evaluation (IRE) is used more within American descriptions.) An example of an IRF exchange is shown below:

T: what sort of poems are they Paul   (I)
P: they're shape poems sir   (R)
T: shape poems   (F)

Although the (F) move is optional, it does occur frequently in classroom discourse, as teachers constantly evaluate students' responses to their questions. The dominance of this IRF exchange structure in classroom discourse is a key means through which teachers control the interaction. Since the publication of Sinclair and Coulthard's work, subsequent studies have developed the model to account for more diverse and complex types of classroom discourse, and to extend it to other interactional contexts (e.g. Coulthard and Brazil 1992; Coulthard and Montgomery 1981b; Francis and Hunston 1992; Hoey 1993; Sinclair and Brazil 1982; Stubbs 1976).

Some of the problems associated with a discourse-analytic approach include its multi-functionality. It is often difficult to identify accurately the functions being performed by acts and moves. Utterances may have a number of possible functions depending on their context. It has been argued, therefore, that discourse-analytic approaches involve a degree of simplification and reduction (Walsh 2006). Sinclair and Coulthard's model in particular has been criticized for the fact that it is based on analysis of 'traditional', teacher-fronted primary classrooms typical of the 1960s, which may not be relevant to contemporary classroom settings. These settings are more dynamic, contain more student–student interaction and often involve more than one teacher or adult.

What this kind of classroom discourse analysis does reveal, however, is that students are systematically denied access to certain kinds of language functions. For example, pupil initiation and follow-up moves are rare and when they do occur, they are largely procedural rather than relating to pedagogic content. By denying students access to certain moves and acts, their language use is restricted. As a result of this finding, there has been a growing body of work which examines the structures and pedagogic benefits of student–student classroom discourse (e.g. Edwards and Westgate 1994; Maybin 1991; Mercer 1995; Mercer *et al.* 2004; Sauntson 2007; Wells 1999).

The work of Barnes and his colleagues constituted an early body of work which examined interaction between students (Barnes 1976; Barnes *et al.* 1969; Barnes and Todd 1977). Barnes argues that students' language development runs parallel to their intellectual development. As they develop new linguistic processes through which they can express their experiences, those experiences become modified and broadened because they are being expressed in a new way. Barnes argues that student-centred talk is, therefore, more effective in enhancing learning, because students can start with their own familiar experiences and expand them into a new pedagogic context via processes of interaction.

Wells (1986) develops these arguments by proposing that it is this very process of negotiating and constructing **meanings** through interaction with others that not only enables learning to take place, but actually constitutes learning itself. When student-centred interaction is encouraged, it provides opportunities for students to co-construct their own meanings. Teacher-led interaction is usually more restrictive in terms of the meaning-making opportunities it affords. In later work, Wells (1999) argues that **knowledge** is co-constructed by classroom participants whilst they are engaged in dialogic activity. Therefore, opportunities for a wide variety of dialogic encounters, including student-student interaction as well as teacher-led discourse, are beneficial to students' learning. Edwards and Westgate (1994) and Nystrand *et al.* (1997) similarly argue that group discussion enables students to create their own meanings, which are limitless in terms of both quantity and quality.

Discourse analysis is not the only approach to investigating classroom talk. Some studies have drawn on the methods and analytical frame-works of **conversation analysis** (e.g. Seed-house 2004; Walsh 2006) and poststructuralist analysis (Baxter 2003). Edwards and Mercer (1987) draw on social constructivism to analyze **discourse** in primary classrooms. Rather than simply describing utterances in functional terms, they explore how teachers and students work together to co-create new meanings. Mercer (1995: 9) later describes this process as the 'guided construction of knowledge' and sub-sequent studies have developed this notion through further detailed analysis of classroom discourse (e.g. Edwards and Westgate 1994; Mercer *et al.* 2004).

Whilst many studies have focused upon monolingual classrooms, there is a body of work which examines interaction in EFL, other second language and bilingual classrooms (e.g. Boulima 1999; Cazden 1988; Seedhouse 2004; Tsui 1995; Walsh 2006; Willis 1992). There has also been a recognition that much classroom discourse analysis has concentrated upon English (either as a first or second language) classrooms. Some studies have analyzed the interaction in other subject classrooms such as Mathematics (Pirie 1997), Science (Lemke 1990; Mercer *et al.* 2004) and Design and Technology (Sauntson 2007). Other work has analyzed collaborative teacher–teacher interaction in classrooms where more than one adult is actively engaged in the lesson (Creese 2005).

It has also been recognized that, as language is a social phenomenon and social meanings are enacted through linguistic structures and pro-cesses, analysis can reveal how social identities are inscribed in and constructed through class-room discourse. Baxter (2002a, 2002b, 2003), for example, has analyzed the ways in which **gender** identities are negotiated and constructed through classroom interactions. By incorporat-ing elements of feminist and post-structuralist theory into descriptions of classroom interaction, Baxter proposes a feminist post-structuralist dis-course-analytic framework to account for the complex ways in which classroom participants are both positioned by, and actively construct their gender through, discourse. Other studies which explore constructions of gender through classroom discourse include Sunderland (2004) and Swann (1992). Other work has explored the construction of identities in students' informal talk in educational settings (e.g. Davies 1997; Maybin 1991, 1994).

HELEN SAUNTSON

See also: Command; communication; context; conversation; conversation analysis; discourse; discourse analysis; gender; institutional and pro-fessional discourse; power; question; speech act theory; speech act type

Suggestions for further reading

Coulthard, R.M. (ed.) (1992) *Advances in Spoken Discourse Analysis*, London: Routledge.
Sinclair, J.McH. and Coulthard, R.M. (1975) *Towards an Analysis of Discourse: The English Used by Teachers and Pupils*, Oxford: Oxford University Press.

Clinical Pragmatics

The concepts and insights of **pragmatics** have been applied to the study of language disorders for approximately thirty years. Early studies focused almost exclusively on pragmatic func-tions and impairments in language disordered, autistic and hearing impaired children. In this way, studies examined communicative intent in autistic children (Wetherby and Prutting 1984), the communicative functions of immediate and delayed echolalic behaviours in autistic children (Prizant and Duchan 1981; Prizant and Rydell 1984), the comprehension of **metaphor** by deaf children (Iran-Nejad *et al.* 1981), the marking of new and old information by language disordered children (Skarakis and Greenfield 1982) and the presuppositional and performative abilities (Rowan *et al.* 1983), and use of revision beha-viours (Gallagher and Darnton 1978) by lan-guage disordered children. Early investigations of pragmatic impairment in adults were less common and included studies of the compre-hension of indirect **requests** in adults with autistic disorders and mental retardation (Paul and Cohen 1985) and pragmatic functions in the expressive speech of adult aphasics (Guilford and O'Connor 1982). At the same time as clinical studies of pragmatics began to gather pace, investigators realized that little was known about the **development** of pragmatics in language intact children. An understanding of pragmatic norms against which findings of impairment could be compared gave impetus to the study of a range of pragmatic phenomena in normally developing children. Alongside investigations of pragmatic impairment in children, studies also emerged that examined the pragmatic functions of **questions** (James and Seebach 1982), the understanding of definite descriptions (Ackerman 1979), comprehension of indirect requests (Leonard *et al.* 1978), the acquisition of **idioms** (Lodge and Leach 1975) and topic manipulation skills (Brinton and Fujiki 1984) in normally developing children.

Today, our knowledge of pragmatic disorders in children and adults is at least as well developed as our understanding of impairments of structural levels of language. Present-day investigations of disordered pragmatics in children examine clinical populations that were neglected in earlier research. For example, pragmatic language impairment has recently been studied in children with conduct disorder (Gilmour *et al.* 2004), Williams syndrome (Laws and Bishop 2004), attention deficit hyperactivity disorder (Casas *et al.* 2004) and closed head injury (Dennis and Barnes 2001; Dennis *et al.* 2001b). These studies have shown that children with conduct disorder and Williams syndrome have pragmatic language impairments and other behavioural features which are similar to those of children with **autism**; that children with attention deficit hyperactivity disorder display pragmatic problems in the use of **discourse markers** and topic changes; and that children who have sustained mild or severe closed head injury have difficulty understanding inferential language and language that involves establishing mental states and **intentions** (specifically, **speech acts**, **irony** and deception). Since early clinical pragmatic studies of children were first undertaken, there has been considerable growth in the number and type of pragmatic phenomena examined. Almost every pragmatic feature of **conversation** and **discourse** has been the subject of investigation – conversation repair strategies (Volden 2004), Gricean **maxims** (Surian *et al.* 1996), request–response sequences (Befi-Lopes *et al.* 2004) and cohesion in narrative

sequencing (Casas *et al.* 2004) are cases in point. A capacity for **inference** is integral to pragmatic interpretation and has been the focus of several recent studies (Dennis *et al.* 2001a; Letts and Leinonen 2001; Norbury and Bishop 2002). For further discussion of pragmatic disorders in children, *see* Cummings (2008, 2009).

Increasingly, studies are attempting to relate pragmatic deficits in children to a range of cognitive impairments. Executive functions, **theory of mind** skills and central coherence abilities have all been investigated recently with a view to explaining the pragmatic deficits in autism. Bishop and Norbury (2005) assessed generativity (a component of executive function) in children with pragmatic language impairment who exhibited communication abnormalities that resembled those of autism. They found a significant relationship between these children's performance on two fluency tasks (a test of generativity) and measures of communicative abnormality. They concluded that 'difficulties in generating relevant ideas can be [a] cause of autistic-like communicative abnormalities' (Bishop and Norbury 2005: 7). Pragmatic impairments in autism have also been examined from within a theory of mind framework (Baron-Cohen *et al.* 1999; Surian *et al.* 1996). While this framework has proven useful in understanding the social communication deficits in autism, limited **intentionality** and symbol formation have been identified in more recent studies as core problems in autism (Noens and van Berckelaer-Onnes 2005). In particular, symbol formation 'might be better understood from the viewpoint of the central coherence hypothesis' (Noens and van Berckelaer-Onnes 2005: 123). In a study of inferential processing in children with specific language impairment (SLI), those with pragmatic language impairment and children with high-functioning autism, Norbury and Bishop (2002) argue that weak central coherence underlies deficits in inferencing.

The pragmatic turn in the study of language pathology has also brought about a major revision in the nosology of developmental language disorder. To reflect the disproportionately poor use of language by some children whose structural language skills were relatively intact, Rapin and Allen (1983) in the USA, and later Bishop and Rosenbloom (1987) in the UK, introduced the term 'semantic-pragmatic disorder' (SPD). Rapin (1996) characterizes the core pragmatic deficits of SPD as verbosity, inadequate conversational skills, speaking aloud to no one in particular, poor maintenance of **topic** and answering besides the point of a question in the presence of comprehension deficits for connected speech, word-finding deficits, atypical word choices and unimpaired phonology and syntax. Today, Dorothy Bishop takes the view that semantic-pragmatic disorder does not form a distinct syndrome. Rather, pragmatic difficulties that were previously identified with semantic-pragmatic disorder are more accurately a 'variable correlate' of SLI. In this way, it is possible to find pragmatic difficulties in children with structural language problems (the type of child that Rapin (1996) describes as having a phonologic-syntactic deficit disorder) and in fluent children who have good structural language skills (the type of child identified as having semantic-pragmatic disorder). Also, pragmatic difficulties do not co-occur with semantic problems, as the term 'semantic-pragmatic disorder' suggests, but can also be found in children who have no word-finding or vocabulary problems. To capture this pattern of pragmatic deficits across a range of other language impairments and competences, a pattern that cuts across earlier classificatory labels, Bishop proposes to institute the label 'pragmatic language impairment' as a more satisfactory successor to 'semantic-pragmatic disorder'. The debate about how best to classify pragmatic language impairments in children and their relation to SLI and autism is still ongoing (Bishop 2003b).

Pragmatic disorders in adults were somewhat neglected by early clinical studies. However, there is now a growing body of literature in this area of clinical pragmatics, with studies reporting pragmatic impairments in adults with left-hemisphere damage (LHD), **right-hemisphere damage**, schizophrenia, **traumatic brain injury** and neurodegenerative disorders (principally, Alzheimer's disease). The traditional view of aphasia – the language disorder that is caused by left-hemisphere damage – is that pragmatic skills are relatively well preserved in the presence of structural language impairments. However, the findings of studies indicate that pragmatic disorders do occur in this language disorder. Moreover, they are not merely the consequence

of structural language deficits in aphasia. While Chapman *et al.* (1997) relate the poor **proverb** processing of their fluent aphasic subjects to the linguistic demands of a spontaneous condition (subjects had to express verbally their interpretation of proverbs in this condition), other pragmatic impairments are less readily accounted for in terms of linguistic deficits. In this way, Kasher *et al.* (1999) found that LHD subjects were significantly impaired in the processing of verbal and nonverbal **implicatures** (linguistic deficits are unlikely to explain the poor performance on nonverbal implicatures). Borod *et al.* (2000) found that subjects with left brain damage were impaired on verbal pragmatic aspects of discourse production, only some of which (e.g. lexical selection) could be explained by linguistic deficits (problems with relevancy and topic maintenance would appear to be unrelated to any impairment of structural language). Finally, Coelho and Flewellyn (2003) found that local and global coherence in the story narratives of a subject with anomic aphasia failed to improve over a 12-month period, notwithstanding gains in this subject's microlinguistic skills. For a detailed discussion of pragmatic deficits in right hemisphere damage, schizophrenia, traumatic brain injury and neurodegenerative disorders, the reader is referred to Cummings (2007b).

Beyond the characterization of pragmatic impairments in adults, the emergence of pragmatics in language pathology has had a profound influence on how clinicians assess and treat acquired language disorders such as aphasia. Where language batteries such as the Boston Diagnostic Aphasia Examination (Goodglass *et al.* 2001) and the Western Aphasia Battery (Kertesz 2006) once dominated **assessment** of language in aphasic adults, a pragmatic emphasis on the actual use of language by clients in a range of communicative contexts has seen techniques such as **conversation analysis** assume greater significance in the assessment process. In this way, conversation analysis has been used to examine collaborative repair in aphasic conversation (Perkins *et al.* 1999), aphasic grammar within the context of turns at talk in conversation (Beeke 2003; Beeke *et al.* 2003), word search strategies in aphasia (Oelschlaeger and Damico 2000) and the distribution of turns at talk in aphasic participants' conversations with a relative (Perkins 1995). There are now a number of published resources that employ the methodology of conversation analysis to assess aphasia. One such resource is the *Conversation Analysis Profile for People with Aphasia* (Whitworth *et al.* 1997). A related profile – the *Conversation Analysis Profile for People with Cognitive Impairment* (Perkins *et al.* 1997) – is designed for use with clients who have generalized cognitive impairment, such as occurs in **dementia** or head injury. As well as encouraging more naturalistic assessments of language in aphasia, pragmatics has been instrumental in achieving a greater acknowledgement of factors such as the role of conversational partners during communication intervention in aphasic persons. Thus, programmes such as Supporting Partners of People with Aphasia in Relationships and Conversation (SPPARC; Lock *et al.* 2001) use conversation analytic techniques to help clinicians identify for the partners of aphasic individuals areas of **communication** that might be usefully addressed during intervention (SPPARC also contains a conversation assessment tool).

Theories in pragmatics are increasingly being applied to the study of children and adults with pragmatic impairments. These theories go beyond merely describing pragmatic deficits and can offer explanatory accounts of subjects' impairments (Leinonen and Kerbel 1999). Schelleter and Leinonen (2003) used the assumption of optimal relevance in **relevance theory** (Sperber and Wilson 1995) to explain SLI children's specification of referents. Loukusa *et al.* (2007b) used relevance theory in an investigation of the ability of children with Asperger syndrome and high-functioning autism to use **context** to answer questions and give explanations of those answers. Dipper *et al.* (1997) looked to relevance theory to explain bridging inference problems in subjects with right-hemisphere damage. As well as serving to explain the performance of pragmatically impaired children and adults, theories in pragmatics can receive much needed validation from the study of subjects with pragmatic disorders. The study of these subjects provides theories in pragmatics with 'a natural empirical test bed' (Bara and Tirassa 2000: 10). Bara *et al.* (2000), for example, have tested the predictions of **cognitive pragmatics** theory in patients with Alzheimer's disease. In a later study, Bara *et al.* (2001) used patients with closed head injury to test predictions of this theory. Cutica *et al.* (2006) used predictions from cognitive pragmatics theory in a study that compared extralinguistic communication (communication by means of gestures) in patients with right- or left-hemisphere damage. The results of these studies and others like them may cause theorists in pragmatics to revise or even reject certain theoretical proposals. Although a significant start has been made on the testing and validation of pragmatic theories in these studies of neuropragmatic populations, it is clear that further work remains to be done in this area (Bara and Tirassa 2000). Some conceptual issues raised by clinical pragmatics are also beginning to be addressed (Cummings 2007b).

LOUISE CUMMINGS

See also: Assessment, pragmatic; autism spectrum disorders; communication aids, pragmatics of; dementia and conversation; development, pragmatic; neuropragmatics; pragmatic language impairment; psychotic discourse; rehabilitation, communication; right-hemisphere damage and pragmatics; schizophrenic language; signed language, pragmatics of; theory of mind; traumatic brain injury and discourse

Suggestions for further reading

Cummings, L. (2007) 'Pragmatics and adult language disorders: past achievements and future directions', *Seminars in Speech and Language*, 28: 98–112.
——(2009) *Clinical Pragmatics*, Cambridge: Cambridge University Press.
Leinonen, E., Letts, C. and Rae Smith, B. (2000) *Children's Pragmatic Communication Difficulties*, London: Whurr Publishers.

Cognitive Anthropology

Cognitive anthropology can be broadly construed as the comparative study of the interrelations between language, thought and **culture**. It has a long history in Western thought, extending from Humboldt to the French structuralists (Durkheim, Mauss, Lévi-Bruhl, Lévi-Strauss) to

the early twentieth-century American anthropological linguists (Boas, Sapir, and Whorf).
These linguists articulated what has come to be
known as the 'linguistic relativity hypothesis',
which states that the language we speak constrains the way we think (Sapir 1921; Whorf
1956b).

Cognitive anthropology as a named sub-
discipline arose in North America as part of the
cognitive revolution in the late 1950s. Originally
known as 'the new ethnography', 'ethnographic
semantics', or 'ethnoscience', its proponents
argued that anthropology should move away
from studying 'culture' conceived in terms of
behaviour and artefacts to 'culture' as systems of
knowledge, or mental dispositions. The
anthropologist's job was to reconstruct a society's culture, which was understood to be 'whatever it is one has to know or believe in order to
operate in a manner acceptable to its members,
and do so in any role that they accept for any
one of themselves' (Goodenough 1964: 36). Such
knowledge, it was argued, could best be investigated through language, and especially through
formal structural **semantics** of particular
domains. The basic strategy was to focus on
the taxonomic and paradigmatic structure of
categorization systems as revealed through
semantic feature analysis, and later through
prototype semantics. This cognitive anthropological agenda was set initially by Goodenough, Lounsbury, Frake, Wallace, Conklin,
Romney, and D'Andrade (*see* papers in the
edited volumes by Hymes 1964b; Romney and
D'Andrade 1964; Tyler 1969; Spradley 1972;
Goodenough 1981 for classic statements).

This approach to language and culture lost its
impact on mainstream anthropology in the early
1970s. This was due in part to the contrast
between the grandeur of its goals and the limited
nature of the studies (lexical semantics of specific
domains, predominantly kinship, biological, and
colour terminologies), and in part to the impoverished view of cultural knowledge. Even
within the group of practitioners there was some
scepticism as to the 'psychological reality' of the
categories being discovered and their degree of
sharedness across speakers (Keesing 1972, 1987).
Yet, this early period produced some important
results, including fundamental insights into the
structure of kinship systems based on the work of

Lounsbury, Conklin, Goodenough, and others
on kinship terminologies (*see* Tyler 1969; Casson
1981), as well as the discovery by Berlin and Kay
(1969) of universals in colour terminology and in
ethnobiological classification (Berlin *et al.* 1974;
Berlin 1992).

Cognitive anthropology today is a much more
diffuse field, having been stimulated in a number
of different directions by developments in **cognitive science** and by our greatly increased
knowledge about the human mind. Within
American anthropology, one line of research
focuses on cultural models (Strauss and Quinn
1997), trying to capture the cultural knowledge
that underlies the understanding of **meaning** in
a particular domain, knowledge in the form of
'models of culturally constituted common sense'.
Such knowledge is organized as 'schemas', a
term borrowed from psychology, **cognitive
linguistics**, and **artificial intelligence** (e.g.
Schank and Abelson 1977) to characterize
internal **representations** of some part of the
world learned from experience and stored in
memory (Casson 1983: 430). A 'cultural model'
(or 'folk model', or 'ideational system') is a
schema of this kind that is shared among the
members of a cultural group (see, for example,
Holland and Quinn 1987; D'Andrade and
Strauss 1992; D'Andrade 1995). A second line of
research investigates everyday **reasoning** in its
cultural **context** (e.g. Hutchins 1980, 1995;
Rogoff and Lave 1984; Lave 1988).

Another major development crosses the disciplines of anthropology, psychology, and linguistics, where there is a renewed interest in
'Whorfian' questions. The core idea of linguistic
relativity (or the Sapir/Whorf hypothesis) is that
'culture, *through* language, affects the way we
think, especially perhaps our classification of the
experienced world' (Gumperz and Levinson
1996: 1). In its non-extreme form (not language
determines thought, but rather habitual language
patterns and ways of categorizing experience
influence thought), this idea was at the heart of the
ethnoscience programme (though it was not
always acknowledged to be), and it went out of
fashion in the 1970s with this programme's
demise. Its resuscitation is partly in response to
uninformed claims for linguistic and cognitive
universals from within the cognitive sciences, and
has been aided by the articulate championing of

John Lucy (1985, 1992a, 1992b, 1997; Lucy and Gaskins 2001, 2003). Lucy has reassessed the notion of linguistic relativity, clarified what Sapir and Whorf actually claimed about it, and formulated a rigorous programme for empirical investigation to which he himself has made major contributions.

The original idea – differently articulated by Humboldt, Boas, Sapir, and Whorf –

> was that the semantic structures of different languages might be fundamentally incommensurable, with consequences for the way in which speakers of specific languages might think and act. On this view, language, thought, and culture are deeply interlocked, so that each language might be claimed to have associated with it a distinctive world-view.
>
> (Gumperz and Levinson 1996: 2)

In this sweeping version which claims to extract a grandiose 'world view' from the observation of particular semantic patterns in a language, the idea was abandoned in the 1970s, with the rise of the cognitive sciences and the associated emphasis on cognitive universals based in human genes. But there has been a recent swing back in psychology, linguistics, and linguistic anthropology towards a position that views diversity in linguistic and cultural practice *within* what has been learned about universals (see, for example, Gumperz and Levinson 1996; Gentner and Goldin-Meadow 2003; Bowerman and Levinson 2001).

The new intellectual climate is informed by new views of meaning. Culture is brought back into meaning and is seen as instantiated in **communication** rather than located in individual minds, with meaning seen as arising in situated interactional contexts (Hanks 1995; Gumperz and Levinson 1996; Duranti 1997b). This provides the basis for a view of linguistic relativity based in cultural practices, social interaction, and the social distribution of knowledge and understanding (Gumperz and Levinson 1996: 8). There is a shift from theories of context-free lexical and grammatical meaning, which were at the heart of the classic Whorfian studies, to theories of situated language use, which distinguish universal principles from culture-specific characteristics of language use in context. Such universal principles (arguably) may include Gricean conversational '**maxims**', or the underlying principles of interactional **politeness**, or the principles governing the systematics of **conversational turn-taking**, repair, sequential organization, and **reference** to persons and places. (For examples of each of these principles, *see* Grice 1975; Brown and Levinson 1987; Sacks *et al.* 1974; Schegloff 2007; and Enfield and Stivers 2006, respectively.) But a great deal seems to be culture-specific, and worthy of investigation as to its effects on cognition.

The research work of the Max Planck Institute for Psycholinguistics has been a major player in this renewed programme. Levinson and his research group study cultural and linguistic diversity in a number of different domains. In a large comparative study of spatial language and cognition, they have identified three spatial frames of reference used differentially in different cultural groups, and have demonstrated that nonlinguistic cognition matches the linguistic system used by the group (Levinson 1996, 2003; Pederson *et al.* 1998; Levinson and Wilkins 2006). These findings show that Whorfian effects can be demonstrated not only at the grammatical level but also at the lexical level. Lexical distinctions that require speakers to notice and remember particular aspects of their experience may pervade thinking and memory even about aspects of thinking as fundamental as spatial relations.

A second focus of work at the Max Planck Institute has been on semantic categories in particular domains (e.g. object categories in verbs of 'cutting and breaking' (Majid and Bowerman 2007), and verbs of 'putting and taking', (Kopecka and Narasimhan, to appear). This has led to the identification of a new kind of lexical structure – a semplate – where the same categories (e.g. of body position, or object types) are expressed covertly through verbs of different form classes (Levinson and Burenhult, 2009). A third focus of study is social interaction in all its multimodal complexity (speech, gesture, gaze, kinesics). The emphasis now is on the human mind in relation to the demands of social interaction, especially interactive reflexive reasoning, the **pragmatics** of meaning in interaction, and the externalization of thought in social products and activities (*see*, for example, Goody 1995; Enfield and Levinson 2007).

Despite theoretical diversity, there are clearly common themes in recent cognitive anthropological work. The current trend is towards more integrated theories of mind and culture, along with an insistence on the role of culture (and thereby, of cultural difference) in cognition (*see*, for example, Sperber 1987, 1996b; Shore 1996; Levinson 1997, 1998; Bloch 1998; Brown 2002). The role of culture is explored not just in the content and structure of mental entities (meanings), but in cognitive processes such as memory, motivation, and reasoning. Work is increasingly interdisciplinary, with attention to the rapidly accumulating knowledge about human mental processes within the cognitive sciences, but with a (healthy) scepticism about exorbitant claims for universals based overwhelmingly on work in English-speaking societies. A further trend is attention to how children learn cultural knowledge, and how it affects their cognitive development (e.g. Ochs 1988; Schieffelin 1990; Brown and Levinson 2008). Current work reflects changing views of 'language' and 'culture', away from monolithic entities to cultural practices located and learned in interaction with others in one's social networks, as well as the deconstruction of culture, with different bases for cultural knowledge, 'common ground', which is seen as more fragmented, partially shared, and ideologically based (*see* Fox and King 2002 for a review). There is also a broadened view of language as social interaction, and a perspective on interpretation rather than on language production. This includes levels of linguistic patterning invoked by 'contextualization cues' (Gumperz 1992), complex transpositions, markers of stance, the cueing of context through subtle, subliminal cues reminiscent of Whorf's view of the subliminal nature of grammatical patterning. These can vary significantly across languages, networks, and cultural groups. These modern trends bring much work in cognitive anthropology squarely within the sphere of interest of students of linguistic pragmatics.

PENELOPE BROWN

See also: Cognitive linguistics; cognitive pragmatics;   cognitive psychology;   cognitive science; cultural scripts; culture; intercultural communication

Suggestions for further reading

Bloch, M. (1998) *How We Think They Think: Anthropological Approaches to Cognition, Memory, and Literacy*, Boulder, CO: Westview Press.
Levinson, S.C. (2003) *Space in Language and Cognition: Explorations in Cognitive Diversity*, Cambridge: Cambridge University Press.
Strauss, C. and Quinn, N. (1997) *A Cognitive Theory of Cultural Meaning*, Cambridge: Cambridge University Press.

Cognitive Linguistics

Cognitive linguistics is a modern school of linguistic thought and practice which is concerned with the relationship between human language, the mind and socio-physical experience. It emerged in the 1970s arising from rejection of the then dominant formal approaches to language in linguistics and philosophy. While its origins were, in part, philosophical in nature, cognitive linguistics has always been strongly influenced by theories and findings from other **cognitive science** disciplines, particularly **cognitive psychology**. This is particularly apparent in work relating to human categorization, as evidenced in work by Charles Fillmore in the 1970s (Fillmore 1975) and George Lakoff in the 1980s (Lakoff 1987). In addition, earlier traditions such as Gestalt psychology has been influential, as applied to the study of grammar by Leonard Talmy (Talmy 2000) and Ronald Langacker (Langacker 1987). Finally, the character of cognitive linguistic theories have been influenced by the neural underpinnings of language and cognition. This is evident both in early work on how visual perception constrains colour terms systems (Kay and McDaniel 1978) and more recent work on the neural theory of language (Gallese and Lakoff 2005).

Cognitive linguistics constitutes an 'enterprise' rather than a single, closely articulated theory. This follows as it is populated by a number of complementary, overlapping and, occasionally, competing theories. The cognitive linguistics enterprise derives its distinctive character from a number of guiding assumptions. In particular, cognitive linguists assume (1) that language is the outcome of general properties of cognition (the generalization commitment, Lakoff 1990); (2) that conceptual **representation** is the outcome of the nature of the bodies humans have and how they interact with the socio-physical world (the thesis of embodied cognition, Lakoff 1987; Johnson 1987); (3) that grammar is conceptual in nature (Langacker 1987; Talmy 2000); and (4) that **meaning**, as it emerges from language use, is a function of the activation of conceptual **knowledge** structures as guided by **context**; hence, there is no principled distinction between **semantics** and **pragmatics** (Fauconnier 1997).

Cognitive linguistic practice can be divided into two main areas: cognitive semantics and cognitive (approaches to) grammar. The area known as cognitive semantics is concerned with investigating the relationship between experience, the conceptual system and the semantic structure encoded by language. Specifically, scholars working in cognitive semantics investigate knowledge representation (conceptual structure) and meaning construction (conceptualization). Cognitive semanticists have employed language as the lens through which these cognitive phenomena can be investigated. Consequently, research in cognitive semantics tends to be interested in modelling the human mind as much as it is concerned with investigating linguistic semantics.

A cognitive approach to grammar, in contrast, is concerned with modelling the language system (the mental 'grammar'), rather than the nature of mind *per se*. However, it does so by taking as its starting point the conclusions of work in cognitive semantics. Meaning is central to cognitive approaches to grammar, which view linguistic organization and structure as having a conceptual basis. From this it follows that cognitive linguists reject the thesis of the autonomy of **syntax**, as advocated by the generative tradition in linguistics.

Cognitive approaches to grammar have also typically adopted one of two foci. Scholars such as Ronald Langacker (Langacker 1987, 1991a, 1991b) have emphasized the study of the cognitive principles that give rise to linguistic organization. In his theory of cognitive grammar, Langacker has attempted to delineate the principles that structure a grammar, and to relate these principles to aspects of general cognition.

The second avenue of investigation, pursued by researchers including Fillmore and Kay (Fillmore *et al.* 1988), Lakoff (Lakoff and Thompson 1975; Lakoff 1987) Goldberg (Goldberg 1995, 2006) and Croft (Croft 2002), aims to provide a more descriptively and formally detailed account of the linguistic units that comprise a particular language. These researchers attempt to provide an inventory of the units of language, from morphemes to words, **idioms** and phrasal patterns, and seek accounts of their structure, compositional possibilities and relations. Researchers who have pursued this line of investigation are developing a set of theories that are collectively known as construction grammars. This general approach takes its name from the view in cognitive linguistics that the basic unit of language is a form-meaning pairing known as a construction.

It is cognitive semantics, rather than cognitive approaches to grammar, which bear on the study of pragmatics. Hence, the remainder of this article considers some of the main theories and approaches in this area.

Encyclopaedic semantics

Approaches to the study of meaning within cognitive linguistics take an encyclopaedic approach to semantics. This contrasts with the received view which holds that meaning can be divided into a dictionary component and an encyclopaedic component. According to this view, which is associated with formal linguistics, it is only the dictionary component that properly constitutes the study of lexical semantics (the branch of semantics concerned with the study of word meaning). There are a number of assumptions associated with the encyclopaedic semantics perspective:

(i) There is no principled distinction between semantics and pragmatics

Cognitive semanticists reject the idea that there is a principled distinction between 'core' meaning on the one hand, and pragmatic, social or cultural meaning on the other hand. This means that cognitive semanticists do not make a sharp distinction between semantic and pragmatic knowledge. Knowledge of what words mean and knowledge about how words are used are both types of 'semantic' knowledge.

Cognitive semanticists do not posit an autonomous mental lexicon which contains semantic knowledge separately from other kinds of (linguistic or non-linguistic) knowledge. It follows that there is no distinction between dictionary knowledge and encyclopaedic knowledge: there is only encyclopaedic knowledge, which subsumes what we might think of as dictionary knowledge.

(ii) Encyclopaedic knowledge is structured

Cognitive semanticists view encyclopaedic knowledge as a structured system of knowledge which is organized as a network. Moreover, not all aspects of the knowledge that is, in principle, accessible by a single word, have equal standing.

(iii) Encyclopaedic meaning emerges in context

Encyclopaedic meaning arises in context(s) of use, so that the 'selection' of encyclopaedic meaning is informed by contextual factors. Compared with the dictionary view of meaning, which separates core meaning (semantics) from non-core meaning (pragmatics), the encyclopaedic view makes very different claims. Not only does semantics include encyclopaedic knowledge, but meaning is fundamentally 'guided' by context. From this perspective, fully specified, pre-assembled word meanings do not exist, but are selected and formed from encyclopaedic knowledge.

(iv) Lexical items are points of access to encyclopaedic knowledge

The encyclopaedic approach views lexical items as points of access to encyclopaedic knowledge (Langacker 1987). Accordingly, words are not containers that present neat pre-packaged bundles of information. Instead, they selectively provide access to particular parts of the vast network of encyclopaedic knowledge.

Specific theories in cognitive semantics which adopt the encyclopaedic approach include frame semantics (Fillmore 1982; Fillmore and Atkins 1992), the approach to domains in cognitive grammar (Langacker 1987), the approach to dynamic construal (Croft and Cruse 2004), and the theory of lexical concepts and cognitive

models – LCCM theory (Evans 2006, to appear).

Cognitive lexical semantics

Cognitive linguistic approaches to lexical semantics take the position that lexical items (words) are conceptual categories. A word represents a category of distinct yet related meanings organized with respect to a prototype, a central meaning component (Lakoff 1987). In particular, Lakoff argued that lexical items represent the type of complex categories he calls radial categories. A radial category is structured with respect to a prototype, and the various category members are related to the prototype by convention, rather than being 'generated' by predictable rules. As such, word meanings are stored in the mental lexicon as highly complex structured categories of meanings or senses.

This approach was developed in a well known case study on the English preposition *over*, developed by Claudia Brugman and George Lakoff (Brugman and Lakoff 1988). Their central insight was that a lexical item such as *over* constitutes a conceptual category of distinct but related (polysemous) senses. Furthermore, these senses, as part of a single category, can be judged as more prototypical (central) or less prototypical (peripheral). Hence, word senses exhibit typicality effects. For instance, the ABOVE sense of *over* – *The picture is over the mantelpiece* – would be judged by many native speakers of English as a 'better' example of *over* than the CONTROL sense, as in *Jane has a strange power over him*.

While the Brugman/Lakoff approach has been hugely influential, there nevertheless remain a number of outstanding problems that have attracted significant discussion. For instance, this view has been criticized as it entails a potentially vast proliferation of distinct senses for each lexical item (Sandra 1998). A proliferation of senses is not problematic *per se*, because cognitive linguists are not concerned with the issue of economy of representation. However, the absence of clear methodological principles for establishing the distinct senses is problematic. More recent work such as the principled polysemy model of Evans and Tyler (Evans 2004; Tyler and Evans 2003) has sought to address some of the difficulties inherent in Lakoff's approach by providing a methodology for examining senses associated with lexical categories. With the also quite recent use of empirical methods in cognitive linguistics (*see* Cuyckens *et al.* 1997), and particularly the use of corpora and statistical analysis (Gries 2005), cognitive lexical semantics has now begun to make serious progress in providing cognitively realistic analyses of lexical categories.

Conceptual metaphor theory

Conceptual metaphor theory (Lakoff and Johnson 1980, 1999) adopts the premise that **metaphor** is not simply a stylistic feature of language, but that thought itself is fundamentally metaphorical. According to this view, conceptual structure is organized by cross-domain mappings which inhere in long-term memory. Some of these mappings are caused by pre-conceptual embodied experiences, while others build on these experiences in order to form more complex conceptual structures. For instance, we can think and talk about QUANTITY in terms of VERTICAL ELEVATION, as in *She got a really high mark in the test*, where *high* relates not literally to physical height but to a good mark. According to conceptual metaphor theory, this is because the conceptual domain QUANTITY is conventionally structured and therefore understood in terms of the conceptual domain VERTICAL ELEVATION.

Mental spaces theory and conceptual blending theory

Mental spaces theory is a theory of meaning construction developed by Gilles Fauconnier (1994, 1997). More recently Fauconnier, in collaboration with Mark Turner (Fauconnier and Turner 2002), has extended this theory, which has given rise to a new framework called conceptual blending theory. Together these two theories attempt to provide an account of the often hidden conceptual aspects of meaning construction. From the perspective of mental spaces theory and blending theory, language provides underspecified prompts for the construction of meaning, which takes place at the conceptual level.

According to Fauconnier, meaning construction involves two processes: (1) the building of mental spaces, and (2) the establishment of mappings between those mental spaces. Moreover, the mapping relations are guided by the local **discourse** context, which means that meaning construction is always context-bound. The fundamental insight this theory provides is that mental spaces partition meaning into distinct conceptual regions or 'packets' when we think and talk.

From this perspective, linguistic expressions are seen as underdetermined prompts for processes of rich meaning construction: linguistic expressions have meaning potential. Rather than 'encoding' meaning, linguistic expressions represent partial 'building instructions', according to which mental spaces are constructed. Of course, the actual meaning prompted for by a given utterance will always be a function of the discourse context in which it occurs. This entails that the meaning potential of any given utterance will always be exploited in different ways dependent upon the discourse context.

The crucial insight of blending theory is that meaning construction typically involves integration of structure from across mental spaces. Such integration draws upon background (encyclopaedic) knowledge and contextually available information giving rise to emergent structure: structure which is more than the sum of its parts. Blending theorists argue that this process of conceptual integration or blending is a general and basic cognitive operation, which is central to the way we think.

VYVYAN EVANS

See also: Cognitive anthropology; cognitive pragmatics; cross-cultural pragmatics; cultural scripts; philosophy of language; philosophy of mind

Suggestions for further reading

Evans, V. (2007) *A Glossary of Cognitive Linguistics*, Edinburgh: Edinburgh University Press.

Evans, V. and Green, M. (2006) *Cognitive Linguistics: An Introduction*, Edinburgh: Edinburgh University Press.

Evans, V., Bergen, B. and Zinken, J. (2007) *The Cognitive Linguistics Reader*, London: Equinox.

Cognitive Pragmatics

Cognitive pragmatics can be defined as the study of mental processes of the agents involved in a communicative interaction. **Communication** is a social activity consisting of a combined effort of at least two participants, who consciously and intentionally cooperate to construct together the shared **meaning** of their interaction. In basing the analysis of communicative interactions on mental states, the proponent of cognitive pragmatics must first examine individual motivations, beliefs, goals and **intentions**. The next step in the analysis is to examine how these mental states are expressed. From the definition of communication as a process, it derives that communicating linguistically or extralinguistically means employing two different ways of processing data. The same input may thus be analyzed from a linguistic and an extralinguistic standpoint and, except in special cases, it will be processed in two parallel ways.

The study of cognitive pragmatics must respect a series of methodological constraints. Any type of data that may be cited in this kind of study, whether it be experimental or observational, refers, by definition, to performance, since it has been generated in a given **context**. The fact that a subject manages to do a certain thing is definite proof that that specific capacity forms part of their **competence**. For instance, if for once and once only in my life I manage to run very quickly, perhaps because I am being chased by an angry bull, this shows that running quickly is part of my potential capacities, that is, I possess that trait at the level of competence. Taking the opposite case, the fact that a subject has never been observed doing a given thing gives rise to doubt in the observer. Perhaps the subject is capable of performing that particular action, but she has never found herself in a situation requiring the activation of that capacity. In this case, the subject might possess the competence even though performance data are not available to confirm the fact. Alternatively, she might not possess the necessary competence, which means that the pertinent performance would never be observed. If I were being chased not by one, but by three angry bulls, I would be unable to take off the ground and fly, because I am incapable of flying. Flight not being part of my competence, I am unable to exhibit the performance of flying.

In conclusion, the sole proof of the existence of a given competence is an instance of the related performance. The non-detection of a performance has no intrinsic meaning. It might indicate a deficit in competence, a deficit in performance, or a defect in the support structures. Especially at the developmental stage, the non-detection of a performance might be due to the immaturity of the support structure. The situation is so complex that it warrants two comments. The first is an invitation to interpretational caution in attributing a deficit: the lack of observation of an expected performance may be understood to indicate a deficit only when a strong theory is available which predicts the deficit and explains it in terms of competence and performance. The second is an invitation to courageously eliminate any data, the collection of which is not based on a theory: these data are quite simply useless inasmuch as they are performance data not connected to competences.

The inability to comprehend a communication act may depend on the fact that the person does not possess the essential tools required to do so. Alternatively, the person might possess the necessary tools but might not have applied them for some reason: she was tired, distracted, overwrought. From an experimental standpoint, it is a question of distinguishing between a systematic failure in carrying out a task, which usually indicates the existence of a problem at the level of competence, and occasional failures which may be attributed to specific causes. These causes may be eliminated and are generally symptomatic of problems at the performance level. A chimpanzee does not have the competence necessary to comprehend a deceit: it does not possess the ability to attribute mental states which are different from its own to other living beings (Tomasello *et al.* 2005). Even a drunken person may be incapable of understanding that he is being lied to. However, such incapacity is temporary, since it is caused not by a lack of mental states, but by too high a level of alcohol in the blood. If the experiment is repeated a day later when the mind is clear, the subject will be capable of exhibiting the correct performance.

A fundamental methodological point is that a theory must not only explain what happens when the system has reached stability, but it must also account for its ontogenetic development: in line with developmental **cognitive science**, one important criterion to test the power of a theory is whether it manages to explain not only the phenomena under investigation but also how those phenomena have gradually been constructed (Bara 1995). Hence, explaining the development of communicative competence is a fundamental issue. Finally, starting from our awareness of the fact that our minds are biological, success in correlating mental processes employed in communication with the cerebral functions that realize those processes is a further step forward in demonstrating the validity of the theory itself.

The two main theories of the mental processes involved in communication are **relevance theory** (Sperber and Wilson 1995) and cognitive pragmatics theory (Bara, to appear). Relevance theory is based on an underlying principle, called the *cognitive principle*, since the theory attempts to explain cognition in general: 'Human cognition tends to be geared to the maximisation of relevance' (Sperber and Wilson 1995: 260). What this principle means is that cognitive resources tend to be allocated to the processing of the most relevant inputs available, whether they originate from internal or external sources. This first principle gives rise to a second principle, called the *communicative principle*, since it is specific to communication. It is usually referred to as the *principle of relevance*: 'Every act of ostensive communication communicates the presumption of its own optimal relevance' (1995: 158, 260). The essence of this second principle is that an actor is implicitly asserting that simply by communicating something, she has something pertinent to communicate. By *ostension*, the authors mean behaviour which makes manifest an intention to make something manifest. The second principle asserts that each communication act must guarantee its relevance, in the sense that the speaker must make it clear that her own contribution is sufficiently important to merit the listener's making a cognitive effort to understand what she is saying.

Relevance continues, even if with transfusions of fresh cognitive blood, the inferential approach pioneered by **Austin** (1962), **Grice** (1975, 1989), and the early **Searle** (1979b, 1983), who

is focused on the single individual. On the contrary, cognitive pragmatics (Bara, to appear) casts itself in the tradition of **Wittgenstein**'s language game, with his typical emphasis on the social aspects of mental activity (Wittgenstein 1953a). Other influential authors in this social approach are the late Searle (Searle 1995), and Pickering and Garrod (2004), with their interactive alignment account of dialogue processes.

In my definition of cognitive pragmatics, communication is a social activity that consists of the combined effort of an actor and a partner. The actor and partner consciously and intentionally cooperate to construct together the shared meaning of their interaction. To be able to discuss communication, the analyst must have among his tools the concepts of **sharedness**, consciousness and **intentionality**. The fundamental idea is that communication is an activity in which the agents active in the process take an equal share in the interaction, independently of the roles they play, roles which nevertheless may change in the course of the interaction. The meaning of what they are doing is constructed together, and it includes both the specific content of the communication and the way in which individual relationships are played out. The problem that the agents who wish to communicate amongst themselves must face is how to manage to progressively agree on what activity they are engaged in. This activity is attributed a meaning which is not purely individual, but which must in some way be shared. The efficacy of a communication is measured by the degree of satisfaction expressed by all the participants in relation to the shared component *after* the completion of the interaction, compared to what was considered to be the shared component *before* the interaction got under way. Viewed in this light, communication consists in constructing together an acceptable interpretation of the reciprocal communication acts, at all levels at which the participants consider it significant to do so.

Cognitive pragmatics offers a unified account of different pragmatic phenomena that are realized either through the linguistic or the gestural channel. The theory can be roughly summarized around three concepts: the definition provided for standard and non-standard communication, the notion of shared belief, and the concept of a behavioural game. Pragmatic phenomena can be identified both in standard and non-standard communication (Airenti *et al.* 1993a). Standard communication, which occurs in the form of direct and indirect communication acts, involves both the comprehension and production of communication acts through the use of default rules of **inference**, i.e. rules which are always valid unless their consequent is explicitly denied (Reiter 1980). The default rules of inference can be applied only when there is no contrast between the mental states overtly expressed by the agents, and the mental states that the partners assume they are privately entertaining. If there is no trace of conflicting **representations**, the default assumptions of sincerity, well informedness, capacity, etc., lead to the standard path of communication. On the contrary, if partners hold conflicting representations, they follow a non-standard path. Non-standard communication involves the comprehension and production of communication acts via the blocking of default inferences and the occurrence of classic inferential processes. Examples are deceit (private non-standard) and **irony** (shared as non-standard by both agents).

Airenti *et al.* (1993a) argue that communication requires shared belief, a concept derived from the notion of mutual **knowledge** (Lewis 1969; Schiffer 1972). Cognitive pragmatics adopts a subjective view of mutual belief by assuming that each actor has shared belief spaces containing all beliefs the actor assumes as shared with one or more specific partners, or with a group of people, or with all human beings. Thus, it may happen that A believes p to be shared by A and B, whereas B does not believe p to be shared by B and A. Shared belief is considered a primitive, i.e. a specific mental state not reducible to a conjunction of standard private beliefs. All the inferences drawn during the phases of understanding are drawn in the space of shared beliefs of A and B. Thus, communication requires that each agent maintain a shared belief space (Clark and Wilkes-Gibbs 1986).

In order to reconstruct the meaning intended by an actor, cognitive pragmatics claims that a partner has to recognize the behaviour game of which the communication act constitutes a move. Behaviour games can be thought of as action plans, i.e. trees of intentions whose leaves are specified either as terminal, precisely defined

actions, or as higher-level intentions to be worked out according to the context (Pollack 1990). In addition, a behaviour game specifies the typical situation in which it can be played. The actions prescribed by a behaviour game need not be logically necessary. Some of them may constitute a conventional, habitual part of the interaction, as is the case of the actions of greetings, typically prescribed by the games governing meetings between persons. The game represents what both agents believe they are engaged in and the meaning they are giving to the entire sequence of interactions. The sequence may be extremely short, as when asking the way to the station, or extremely long, as when two lovers are debating whether to leave each other or to get married. In both these examples, all the participants must be fully aware of what is happening, what social and personal obligations are involved, what one may legitimately expect from the other partner and what one may not expect.

The actual actions performed by the agents realize the moves of the behaviour game they are playing. The meaning of a communicative action (either linguistic or gestural or, more often, a mix of the two) is fully understood only when it is clear which move of the behaviour game it realizes. Thus, communication acts are moves of behaviour games; conversely, each move of a behaviour game has a communicative value, and can therefore be considered as a communication act. Consider, for instance, the communicative exchange:

A: Let's invite Charlie to the party.
B: Forget about it.

By this request, A proposes to B to play the behaviour game (ORGANIZING-A-PARTY), which requires A and B to advance and discuss reciprocal proposals. The recognition of the behaviour game bid by the actor does not bind the partner to play his or her role in the game. On the contrary, the partner can decide to accept or reject the proposed game, or try to negotiate a different one, or even let the **conversation** game be interrupted.

Communication acts find their shared meaning only within the context provided by the behavioural game played by the participants to the communicative exchange. Thus, the difficulty of comprehension of an act depends upon the complexity of the inferences necessary to link the communication act to a move of the game. It follows that there is no essential difference between a direct speech act (as defined by Searle 1979b), and a conventional indirect speech act: both of them are simple acts, immediately linking the move to the game. A difference is instead predicted between conventional indirect speech acts (simple indirects) and non-conventional indirect speech acts (complex indirects). Several experimental studies support this distinction (Bucciarelli *et al.* 2003; Bosco and Bucciarelli 2008). Moreover, in order to be able to speak of communication, all the agents must make their own conscious intention to take part in the interaction explicit. My argument is that it is not possible for A to communicate something to B if she has no intention of doing so; if this were to happen, then it is B who has autonomously inferred some information from A's behaviour without A's participation. Further, if A intends to communicate something to B, she must be aware of the fact: while unconscious intentions may exist, unconscious communicative intentions do not. Grice (1975) has justified the need for a fully conscious, and recursive, communicative intention.

As far as neuroscience can be used to investigate the brain correlates of the mental structures involved in communication, Walter *et al.* (2004) have launched a series of brain mapping experiments, with the purpose of distinguishing between merely individual aim-intention and social aim-intention. The most interesting result was a significant increase in brain activation associated with the condition of social interaction. Seeing two agents communicating resulted in significant activation in the medial prefrontal cortex, especially in the anterior paracingulate cortex. Walter *et al.* found no paracingulate activation during the reading of comic strips depicting either one agent acting or two agents acting independently. Indeed, the activation of the anterior paracingulate cortex requires two agents interacting socially. Moreover, the left temporo-parietal junction is activated only when a subset of social intentions are involved, namely communicative intentions. Ciaramidaro *et al.* (2007) propose a dynamic intentional network,

where four brain regions are progressively recruited depending on the nature of the intention processed, from individual intention to communicative intention.

In principle, it should be possible to falsify either cognitive pragmatics theory or relevance theory, or both, through developmental, clinical or neural data. And, in fact, developmental pragmatics, **clinical pragmatics** and **neuropragmatics** are the areas where the theories have been empirically tested. But if we consider relevance theory as focusing on the mental processes of single individuals while communicating, and cognitive pragmatics theory as the investigation of the agents' cooperative activity, we can understand why no evidence can be claimed to be conclusive. These theories assume perspectives which are more complementary than antithetical, and the reader remains free to privilege one approach over the other.

BRUNO G. BARA

See also: Clinical pragmatics; cognitive science; communication; communication failure; competence, communicative; competence, pragmatic; defaults in utterance interpretation; development, pragmatic; gestural communication; Grice, H.P.; intention; intentionality; knowledge; neuropragmatics; rehabilitation, communication; relevance theory; Searle, J.; sharedness; Wittgenstein, L.

Suggestions for further reading

Bara, B.G. (to appear) *Cognitive Pragmatics*, Cambridge, MA: MIT Press.
Grice, H.P. (1989) *Studies in the Way of Words*, Cambridge, MA: Harvard University Press.
Sperber, D. and Wilson, D. ([1986] 1995) *Relevance: Communication and Cognition*, Oxford: Blackwell.

Cognitive Psychology

As the scientific field devoted to the study of the mind, psychology has had several dominant frameworks since its birth at the end of the nineteenth century. Cognitive psychology has prevailed as the central approach to psychology since its introduction in the mid-1950s. At that time, it represented a break from behaviourism. Whereas behaviourism focussed almost exclusively on observable behaviours, such as a rat's bar presses in well controlled conditions, it eschewed concerns about the inner workings of the mind. Cognitive psychology, while maintaining an emphasis on systematic and well controlled experiments, was (and remains) expressly concerned with the way the mind engages non-observable **representations** that determine behaviours, including linguistic behaviours.

A confluence of two events, one intellectual and the other technological, is largely credited with the cognitive turn in psychology. One is that several pioneers ushered in arguments and data that showed that there were limits to behaviourism. Most notably, Noam Chomsky (1959) convincingly argued that notions such as *stimulus*, *response* and *reinforcement*, which were the currency of behaviourist models, simply could not capture fundamental linguistic phenomena, such as the extraordinary rate of language acquisition among children or grammaticality judgements among adults. A second influence is the advent of computers and the information processing models that were associated with them. As digital machines became more common, their inner workings served as a model for human cognition as did the ubiquitous flow chart, which would describe how information is transformed in any given cognitive system.

Cognitive psychologists can be classified into three main types (*see* Eysenck and Keane 1993). There are (1) experimentalists, who test and refine theories; (2) modellers, who aim to construct sophisticated models of a given behaviour; and (3) neuroscientists, who aim to uncover the neural substrates of behaviours. It is rare to find a single psychologist who does all three (though many will be comfortable with two).

A typical textbook in cognitive psychology will cover topics such as attention, perception, memory (working and long-term), language and language comprehension, concept formation, **reasoning**, problem solving and decision-making. Some generally held (though not always uncontroversial) facts to have come out of landmark studies in cognitive psychology are that an adult memory can hold 7±2 items (Miller 1956), that one can attend to more stimuli than one can report (Sperling 1960), that people generally

prefer to confirm, rather than falsify, a hypothesis (Wason 1966), that some exemplars are better representatives of a concept than others (*robin is a bird* is recognized as correct more quickly than *penguin is a bird*; Rips *et al.* 1973; *see* Rosch 1975), that we humans can fall prey to biases that, at times, predominate over valid **inference** making (Tversky and Kahneman 1974), that **metaphor** understanding does not require exceptional processing (Glucksberg *et al.* 1982), that visual context influences spoken word recognition and mediates syntactic processing (Tanenhaus *et al.* 1995), and that 6- to 10-month-old infants can detect whether an individual is helpful or not (Hamlin *et al.* 2007).

Central to cognitive psychology is its rigorous methodology. The findings described above and countless others are validated and replicated through experiments that aim to establish facts or test theories. Also, novel (and often clever) techniques are introduced in order to uncover the findings. Technological advances have also played a role in the advent of cognitive experiments by helping produce revealing measures, such as reaction times and eye movements to a millisecond level. Consider priming techniques that take advantage of associations between concepts in order to detect how features of a word are represented. For example, the homonym *bug* in English activates ('primes') the word *insect* as well as *microphone* when it first appears in a sentence, but only one of these remains active (about a second) later as a function of the sentence it is in and its **context**. These sorts of discoveries are then incorporated as dependent measures in order to test other theories. For example, priming techniques can be used to determine whether initial potential readings in 'garden path sentences' – sentences that lead to a single reading before a second, more grammatically supported, reading takes hold (e.g. *While Anna dressed the baby sat up on the bed*) – are activated in the course of **disambiguation** resolution (Christianson *et al.* 2001).

Paradigms and theories from cognitive psychology often serve as pioneering constructs. For example, as much as the medical sciences and the neurosciences aim to describe **autism**, it is cognitive theory that has arguably provided the most parsimonious and descriptive models of the exceptional behaviour associated with this disorder. Spearheaded by its investigations of **theory of mind** tasks, cognitive theorists have led the way in describing the phenotype of autistic behaviour, e.g. as a deficit of theory of mind (Leslie 1987) or as extreme male behaviour (Baron-Cohen 2004).

Since experimentation compels theories to make available specific empirical predictions, cognitive experiments have often been developed to test pragmatic claims and to evaluate how well pragmatic theories can account for cognitive phenomena. Consider how cognitive tasks have borne out claims based on **Grice**'s (modified) Occam's razor ('Senses are not to be multiplied beyond necessity') by showing that a term such as *Some* has essentially one **meaning** that is compatible with a *Some and perhaps all* reading. Studies based on cognitive development (Noveck 2001) and reading time (e.g. Breheny *et al.* 2006) show how *Some but not all* readings (which may intuitively appear as an alternative reading of *Some*) are the result of effortful enrichments to the lexical meaning. **Relevance theory**, which incorporates cognitive factors such as attention and theory of mind into its account of human **communication**, has been influential in informing these investigations. The influence of relevance theory on cognitive psychology has similarly been felt in other areas, such as reasoning (Sperber *et al.* 1995; Medin *et al.* 2003; Van der Henst *et al.* 2002a), metaphor (e.g. Noveck *et al.* 2001), and autism (Happé 1993).

IRA NOVECK

See also: Child language acquisition; development, pragmatic; experimental pragmatics; idiom; psycholinguistics; utterance interpretation

Suggestions for further reading

Eysenck, M.W. and Keane, M.T. (1993) *Cognitive Psychology*, London: Lawrence Erlbaum.
Pinker, S. (1999) *How the Mind Works*, New York: W.W. Norton.

Cognitive Science

Cognitive science is a multidisciplinary approach to the study of mind and intelligence. Its main goals are to draw the architecture of cognition and to understand how cognition enables an organism to interact with and to produce adaptive behaviour within its environment. Cognitive science has also been defined as the study of the different forms of intelligence that characterize the domains of humans, animals and machines (Von Eckardt 2001). As a result of the complexities intrinsic to the study of the mind and of the different levels and perspectives from which it may be studied, some theorists prefer to speak of 'cognitive sciences' in the plural (Miller 2003).

Some characteristics that were defining of cognitive science in the 1960s are now considered of doubtful utility, while others that were initially marginal occupy a central role in current theorizing. A consequence of the dynamic and multidisciplinary nature of cognitive science is that it is often unclear whether it should be defined based on its object of study (the mind) or on a particular epistemological and methodological approach to it (the simulative or computational one). The only way to avoid this question is to conflate ontology and methodology, an option that presents problems of its own. For these reasons, the nature of cognitive science is better understood from a historical perspective. The proximal intellectual roots of cognitive science may be situated around the middle of the twentieth century with the rise of cybernetics (Wiener 1948). This new science claimed that complex machines have to have control systems (that is, subcomponents of their architecture in charge of governing their inner functioning and their interactions with the external world), and that all such systems are to be considered instances of the same natural kind. Control systems began to be considered as machines in their turn and, because Turing machines (Turing 1936), of which digital computers practically are physical incarnations, were provably able to simulate the functioning of any other finite machine, digital computers began to be used to understand and duplicate control systems. The next step on this path was to view the mind as a control system in its turn (Miller *et al.* 1960) and to therefore claim that it is a machine (Chomsky 1957) and can be simulated by a digital computer. The final pillar of the burgeoning discipline was the reification of the analogy, that is, the claim that human minds – all minds, actually – are digital computers (Newell and Simon 1976).

These final steps took place in the mid-1950s when some disciplines began to view computer simulation as the unifying methodology for the study of the human mind and its cognitive processes (Bara 1995). A specific event, which is often taken to be the birth date of the new science, is a symposium on information science that was held at the Massachusetts Institute of Technology in Boston on 11 September 1956 (Gardner 1985). The converging disciplines were philosophy, psychology, computer science (later to become **artificial intelligence**), neuroscience, linguistics and anthropology (Keysers *et al.* 1978). The formalization of the enterprise as a properly recognized scientific discipline took place in 1977 when the journal *Cognitive Science* commenced publication, and was completed with the first conference of the Cognitive Science Society in 1979 at the University of California at San Diego.

The subcommunities within psychology that underwent the 'cognitive revolution' (Miller 2003) were thus able to abandon behaviourism, which had considered that mind and cognition were unamenable to scientific inquiry. The simulative methodology was based on the functionalistic assumption that the physical structure on which cognitive processes are built in the human body is substantially irrelevant. If, given an input, a computational model can reproduce the same output of a mental process, it may be claimed that such a model reproduces that process, and this is claimed to be all that needs to be understood about it (Turing 1950; Pylyshyn 1984).

This close relationship between artificial intelligence and psychology thus lies at the very heart of cognitive science. Human beings are conceived of as information processors with limited capacities and top-down architecture, capable of coding, elaborating, storing and retrieving symbolic structures that represent the objective external world (Neisser 1967; Lindsay and Norman 1977). **Knowledge** representation and organization (Collins and Quillian 1969; Pylyshyn 1973; Minsky 1974; Bobrow and Collins 1975; Schank and Abelson 1977; Kosslyn 1980) rapidly began to be viewed as the kernel of cognition and accordingly became the central topic of cognitive science. This was followed by **reasoning** and thought (Johnson-Laird 1983; Newell and Simon 1972; Wason and Evans 1975). Great attention was also devoted to the study of perception (Winston 1975; Marr 1982; Ellis and Young 1988), attention (Broadbent 1958; Deutsch and Deutsch 1963; Norman and Shallice 1980), memory (Atkinson and Shiffrin 1968; Shallice and Warrington 1970; Craik and Lockhart 1972; Schank 1980; Baddeley 1986), and language (Chomsky, 1957, 1965, 1980; Winograd 1972; Grosz *et al.* 1986; Ellis and Young 1988). In the 1980s, substantially the same cognitive functions also began to be studied through connectionist models, which rejected the top-down architecture of cognitive functions and used distributed models of cognition, with an emphasis on learning (McClelland *et al.* 1986; Rumelhart *et al.* 1986; Elman *et al.* 1996; but *see* Fodor and Pylyshyn 1988).

Beginning in the 1980s, both the simulative methodology and the identification of mind and computation began to be questioned (Searle 1980). A diversity of criticisms has since led to a matching variety of reactions and further developments. In terms of community size, the most successful of these criticism/development blocks is the substitution of the brain for the digital computer. Claims about the importance and the specificity of the neurological substrate on which cognitive processes rely, as well as the fast technological advancements in neuroimaging techniques, has led cognitive neuroscience with its methodology to be elected as the new core discipline of cognitive science (Gazzaniga 1999). Here, cognitive processes are claimed to be better (or only) understood if they are linked to the activity of specific brain regions or neural networks. The functionalistic assumption and the 'arrows-and-boxes' approach of classical cognitive science are recast in terms of the isomorphism principle (Eysenck and Keane 1990), which assumes that a correspondence exists between the cognitive architecture of the mind and the physical structure of the brain. This principle is commonly understood as the notion that cognitive processes are segregated in dedicated submachines called modules.

Assumptions about the **modularity of the mind** here tend to be cast in so-called 'Darwinian' rather than in strictly Fodorian terms. The main difference is that Fodor's (1975, 1983) modules are supposed to be unintelligent, non-inferential submechanisms that are in charge of feeding the central processes with the raw materials, starting from which they begin actual computations. However, Darwinian modules are supposed to be simple, domain-specific, locally intelligent mechanisms that operate within a completely distributed model of cognition (Minsky 1988), where the very existence of general-purpose central processes is claimed to be impossible from an evolutionary viewpoint (Barkow *et al.* 1992; Cosmides and Tooby 1994a, 1994b; Pinker 1997). Accordingly, the cognitive processes investigated and their modular physical counterparts are defined as types of organism/world interactions like **social cognition**, parenting and foraging rather than more abstract functions like memory or attention. The study of cognitive impairments and of their double dissociations in patients with specific brain damages, and the use of neuroimaging techniques to understand which brain regions are more active during the execution of specific cognitive tasks, have thus become crucial steps in the construction and the falsification of hypotheses about the architecture of human mind (McCarthy and Warrington 1990).

A second criticism/development block has been concerned with the allegedly too abstract and disembodied description of cognition given by classical cognitive science, and has worked from the assumption that only the empirical study of real organism/world interactions may yield a real understanding of cognition (Agre 1995). This claim has often been associated with the rejection of the notion that **representation** is the central property of cognition (Brooks 1991a, 1991b). Taken together, these claims have led to the development of autonomous robotics (Maes 1991), which is the material engineering of simple artificial agents that are able to move and to perform simple tasks in the real world. Robotics has thus become able to trade concepts and metaphors with biology and its subdisciplines.

A third criticism of classical cognitive science has been its alleged incapability of (or lack of interest in) dealing with topics such as **context** and **culture**, and with the social and ontogenic features of the mind in general. Classical cognitive science is taken to have preferred a supposedly universal, rational and rigidly innate idea of the mind. Here, scientific focus has been shifting from the mind and brain to the whole organism that is formed by a biological body with a biological mind, placed into an environment that includes language, culture, values, and the individual's personal history. The physical, interpersonal and sociocultural context in which cognition takes place, which was treated by early cognitive scientists as noise, has thus gained increasing importance (Bruner 1990; Westbury and Wilensky 1998), and studies of culture (Hutchins 1995; Cole 1996; Tomasello 1999), situated cognition and activity (Agre 1997; Clancey 1997b; Wenger 1998) and the bodily bases of cognition (Lakoff and Johnson 1980; Johnson 1987; Clark 1997) have begun to flourish.

The fourth and most radical departure from the classical perspective has been based on the re-evaluation of consciousness and subjectivity as the main, or only, feature of cognition. It has been argued that classical cognitive science's adoption of the 'view from nowhere' (Nagel 1986) is a fatal mistake and that no comprehension of the mind is possible while its subjective nature is neglected. This has led subcommunities of researchers to delve into studies of consciousness (Nagel 1974; Maturana and Varela 1980; Edelman 1992; Searle 1992; Chalmers 1996; Damasio 1999) and sometimes to even adopt views based on radical constructivism and phenomenology (Guidano 1987, 1991; Dreyfus 1992; Varela *et al.* 1991; Varela 1996). As discussed above, the extent to which works like these still pertain to cognitive science – and probably, therefore, the very future of the discipline – depends on whether the discipline itself is defined on ontological or methodological grounds.

VALERIA MANERA and MAURIZIO TIRASSA

See also: Artificial intelligence; cognitive anthropology; cognitive linguistics; cognitive pragmatics; cognitive psychology; computational pragmatics; inference; intentionality; knowledge; modularity of mind thesis; philosophy of language; philosophy of mind; psycholinguistics; rationality; reasoning; representation and computation

Suggestions for further reading

Boden, M.A. (2006) *Mind as Machine: A History of Cognitive Science*, Oxford: Oxford University Press.
Haugeland, J. (ed.) (1981) *Mind Design*, Cambridge, MA: MIT Press.
Wilson, R.A. and Keil, F.C. (eds) (1999) *The MIT Encyclopedia of Cognitive Sciences*, Cambridge, MA: MIT Press.

Command

Speech acts are governed by rules. Performing a speech act is similar to taking a particular step in a certain game. You throw a ball. It is a step in basketball play, say. The game of basketball is governed by rules. The rules of basketball determine the nature of the game: it involves two teams, the goal of each team is to gain victory, as defined by the rules, and so on. The rules of the game determine whether your act of throwing the ball, under certain circumstances, is appropriate or not. Similarly, the rules of a **speech act type**, such as command, determine the nature of it and regulate appropriate activity within its framework.

Naturally, speech acts of command are made by utterances of appropriate sentences under appropriate circumstances. The specification of the family of sentences by means of the utterance of which one can make a speech act of command is language specific. For example, in English it involves sentences of the imperative grammatical structure ('Open the door!'), while in modern Hebrew it involves a similar grammatical structure or a certain intonation on declaratives (literally presented, 'You-will-go from-here!').

The specification of the circumstances under which one can make a speech act of command is not language specific. A rule that governs speech acts of command requires that the speaker be in a position to order the addressee to act in a certain way or to avoid acting in a certain way. Usually, such a position involves a hierarchy in which the speaker is of a higher position than the addressee. Such a hierarchy can be natural, such as that of parents and babies, or societal, such as military or police commanders and their subordinates.

Accordingly, understanding a speech act of command involves more than understanding the literal **meaning** of the sentence used in its per-

formance. To use the game analogy again, think of the role played in football by a goalkeeper. The goalkeeper's actions are often considered appropriate even though they would not have been judged to be so if performed by other players. In order to understand a step made by a goalkeeper in a football play, one has to understand the goalkeeper's role in football. Similarly, in order to understand a speech act of command, one has to understand the role of the speaker in the **context** of utterance. To do that, one has to identify the hierarchy in which the speaker holds a position higher than that of the addressee. Quite often, the identity of the relevant hierarchy is not self evident.

Usually, it is assumed that the speaker of a speech act of command and the addressee are different persons. However, consider a driver who utters 'Enough!' just after one has crossed an intersection, while the traffic lights showed red in one's direction. To the extent that this is a speech act of command, how can the speaker and the addressee occupy different positions in the same hierarchy when they are one and the same person? If it isn't a speech act of command, does it mean that a seeming self-command is not a command? A theory of command is not sufficiently developed if it fails to solve such problems.

Speech acts of command have been investigated from a variety of perspectives, such as acquisition of the speech act type, its localization in the brain and its usage in some **culture** or a certain corpus (James 1978; Foldi 1987; Takahashi 1994; Myhill 1998; Soroker *et al.* 2005). Such investigations have broadened knowledge and understanding of language acquisition and culture parameters, but not the nature of command as a speech act type. Study of brain localization is an exception, since it discovered an intricate relationship between commands and **requests** (*see* Soroker *et al.* 2005).

ASA KASHER

See also: Speech act theory; speech act type

Suggestions for further reading

Hamblin, C.L. (1987) *Imperatives*, Oxford: Blackwell.
Searle, J.R. (1969) *Speech Acts*, Cambridge: Cambridge University Press.

Vanderveken, D. (2001) 'Universal grammar and speech act theory', in D. Vanderveken and S. Kubo (eds) *Essays in Speech Act Theory*, Amsterdam and Philadelphia, PA: John Benjamins.

Communication

Communication is a social process that requires the participation of two or more persons. It involves the human ability to use abstract concepts in order to affect the actions and thinking of other individuals. The term 'communication', which is from the Latin term 'communicare', literally means to make common, share, participate, or impart. Communication indicates a sense of commonness with others by sharing information, signals, and messages. Human beings are intrinsically communicative subjects. They are social beings that have evolved with the necessity to establish relationships with other members of their living group and, in order to make this possible, they have to share ideas, projects, desires, **knowledge,** and so forth (Tirassa *et al.* 2006a, 2006b; Tirassa and Bosco 2008).

Over the years, different approaches have attempted to delineate an inclusive definition of this pervasive human phenomenon. In the twentieth century, communication was studied mostly in terms of language and in connection with the philosophical definition of **meaning** and sense. The semiotic approach placed an emphasis on meaning, since it considered the construction of sense as the basis of the whole communication process. In this perspective, communication is essentially the ability to create new meanings (Ogden and Richards 1923). The key point was **reference**, which is the process that made it possible to establish a relation between objects, wherein one object (sign) designates, connects, or links to another object (referent). In linguistics, words and gestures were a perfect example of signs, since they referred to real entities without having any direct relation with them. This approach presents some problematic points regarding human communication, as was pointed out by Frege (1892). He argued that reference cannot be treated as identical with meaning. He used the famous example of 'Hesperus' (ancient Greek name for the eve-

ning star) and 'Phosphorus' (ancient Greek name for the morning star): both refer to Venus but with two functional and informative meanings. However, the key point was that it was definitely established that human beings use signs, which have a merely conventional relation with the represented object. The conventional meaning, in its double facet of a signifier and the signified, is only defined in a system of signs, since it is completely conventional regarding reality.

One of the most prominent American linguists of the twentieth century, Bloomfield (1933), developed a general and comprehensive theory of language by creating a formal procedure for the analysis of language and by providing a rigorous scientific methodology that was able to describe the communication process. For Bloomfield, the structure of language represents the central object of linguistic study and it is seen as a closed code that is bounded by formal rules that are applicable to every utterance. This rigorous methodology found concrete expression in the model of communication by Shannon and Weaver (1949). From this viewpoint, communication is seen as the transmission of information through a specific channel from an information source, which produces a message, to a receiver, who decodes the original message. To illustrate this model, consider Juliet in Shakespeare's romantic tragedy. An *information source* (Juliet) produces a *signal* (the sentence 'Romeo, Romeo, why do you have to be who you are?') by a *transmitter* (Juliet's voice). This signal is carried through a particular *channel* (the air through which sound propagation occurs) to a *receiver* (Romeo) who, thanks to his *receptor* (his acoustic apparatus), can finally receive the original signal. It is noteworthy that, in this model, the meaning of every communicative interaction is always established a priori. This means that, if any trouble occurs during the transmission of the information, the meaning of the message created by the source always corresponds to the meaning of the message the receiver obtains.

Starting in the 1960s, some philosophers of language (Austin 1962; Grice 1975, 1989; Searle 1979b) advanced criticisms of the information transmission model. These philosophers proposed a new model of the thought processes that are involved in human communication, the so-called inferential model. The starting point was the penetrating observation that language cannot always be seen merely as a code with specified symbols and meanings: human communication is not reducible to a simple coding/decoding process. By contrast, communication represents a complex phenomenon consisting of several aspects that are neglected by the information transmission model. Some of these aspects involve the previous knowledge of interlocutors, a speaker's communicative **intentions** in producing a message and the inferential processes which are activated for the comprehension of a **speech act**. In the inferential model, communication can be defined as a form of social cooperative interaction among people who would like to share, and make common, part of their knowledge with one or more individuals (Grice 1975). This theoretical perspective marks the onset of **pragmatics**, which is a discipline that is focused on the communicative meaning that an utterance can assume in the specific **context** in which it is proffered (Bosco *et al.* 2004). Communication is more than a simple sum of words that is transmitted by a source to a receiver: it is the combined effort of the interlocutors, who actively engage in a continuous co-construction of meanings.

Viewing human communication as the continuous co-construction and negotiation of meanings makes it rather different from **animal communication**, for example, in which a message corresponds necessarily to a pre-specified meaning. This important difference can perhaps be explained in the light of a human cognitive ability that is absent in animals, called **theory of mind**. This is the ability to ascribe mental states, such as beliefs, intentions and desires, to oneself and to others and to use knowledge of these states to predict and explain one's own and other people's behaviour (Premack and Woodruff 1978). Some authors (e.g. Hurford *et al.* 1998) have proposed continuity between the evolution of cognitive, social and communicative skills in humans and those of our primate relatives, even if many authors affirm that human beings are unique in their ability to develop a theory of mind (Premack and Premack 1994; Heyes 1998).

The relation between human communication and theory of mind represents a fundamental and still ongoing controversy. For some authors (e.g. Bloom 2002), pragmatic ability is part of a more general theory of mind skill, as when people communicate they have to actively attempt to figure out the meaning that they intend to express to another. This is particularly evident in children when they have to learn the names of things, not simply by associating the sounds of words with objects (Birch and Bloom 2002), but rather by making **inferences** about the speaker's intended meaning. Other perspectives (e.g. Sperber and Wilson 2002) argue that while pragmatics is similar to theory of mind in that it involves the attribution of mental states, it represents a distinct module at the cognitive level with its own peculiar principles and mechanisms that evolved as a specialization of a more general mind-reading module. The debate is still open but theory of mind, if it is considered alone, seems unable to explain people's ability to communicate (*see* Vallana *et al.* 2007; Tirassa and Bosco 2008).

Even though language is the most studied means of communication, it is only one of the multiple channels through which communication can be achieved. Alternative expressive means are represented by gestures, painting, and any other actions that are performed with communicative intention. In particular, the extra-linguistic modality represents the most ancient way of communicating from a phylogenetic perspective and the most precocious expressive means from an ontogenetic perspective in human beings. Traditionally, it has been proposed (Hinde 1972) that there is a clear distinction between verbal and nonverbal communication that is based on the different channels through which these forms of communication are realized. As Bara and Tirassa (1999) noted, this distinction is not comprehensive and contains many contradictions. For example, following the traditional distinction, the Braille system or sign language – languages totally structured and regulated by syntactic and semantic rules as in spoken language – have to be included in nonverbal communication. By contrast, aspects of communication such as **prosody**, which is something spoken but which does not involve any structure or rule, is seen as verbal communication. Thus, the traditional distinction seems to be focused on the more superficial aspects of communication and omits the most important differences between the two forms of communication. Bara and Tirassa (1999) proposed a different classification that is based not on the type of input (verbal versus nonverbal) but on the way through which humans elaborate communicative data. Linguistic communication is performed using a system of compositional symbols, whereas extralinguistic communication is the use of a set of associable symbols. Therefore, in this view, the Braille system and sign language are considered a linguistic form of communication because they comprise elementary units that can be combined in infinite ways, whereas body movements as well tone of voice are considered extralinguistic forms of communication.

During a communicative exchange, in both linguistic and extralinguistic modalities, paralinguistic aspects are also present. These aspects can be considered tributary communication structures, since they do not have an autonomous meaning but they are better understood as qualifiers of communicative actions. Paralinguistic communication includes all of those aspects that accompany, qualify, and structure linguistic and extralinguistic communication. For example, the utterance 'It's 5 o'clock' can have different communicative meanings based on the paralinguistic elements used. Uttered with an annoyed tone of voice, it would probably mean 'Unfortunately, it is still 5 o'clock, time never passes … ', whereas with an excited tone it would probably mean 'It is already 5 o'clock! We have to hurry up!'. Traditionally, the term 'paralinguistic' refers to tributary language structures and, in particular, to prosodic cues such as the intonation, rhythm, and voice quality (tone, pitch, and intensity) that accompany speech. However, it is also noteworthy that extralinguistic communication is often accompanied by paralinguistic modifiers, such as kinesics and proxemics. Kinesics includes, for instance, head signs, facial expressions, body movements, and ocular movements; proxemics refers to posture and interpersonal distance. Some authors (McNeill and Duncan 1999) have rejected the language/paralanguage distinction, theorizing that gestures, broadly construed to include prosodic and rhythmic phenomena, iconic gestures, non-representational movements of the hands and body, are intrinsic to language. In this view, language is an organized form of online, interactive, embodied, and contextualized human cognition.

To conclude, communication represents a complex activity that characterizes human beings and their method of conveying and sharing meanings. Communication is realized through linguistic, extralinguistic and paralinguistic modalities, which enable us to express beliefs, opinions, ideas, and desires to others. Moreover, the variety of communicative modalities and elements enables us to create an infinite number of new messages and to use the same utterance to convey very different meanings.

FRANCESCA M. BOSCO and ROMINA ANGELERI

See also: Cognitive pragmatics; competence, communicative; competence, pragmatic; context; conversation; cooperative principle; development, pragmatic; discourse; inference; inferential comprehension; intentionality; language evolution; rehabilitation, communication; sharedness; utterance interpretation

Suggestions for further reading

Bara, B.G. (to appear) *Cognitive Pragmatics*, Cambridge, MA: MIT Press.
Ellis, D.G. (1999) *From Language to Communication*, London and Mahwah, NJ: Lawrence Erlbaum Associates.
Tirassa, M. (1999) 'Communicative competence and the architecture of the mind/brain', *Brain and Language*, 68: 419–41.

Communication Aids, Pragmatics of

Communication aids are low- or high-tech systems that are designed to provide augmentative or alternative communication (AAC) possibilities for people with limited ability to use speech for **communication**. They include voice output communication aids (VOCAs). Initially, AAC systems were aimed at supporting **linguistic competence**, focussing on vocabulary, morphology and syntax (Gerber and Kraat 1992). This missed the point that communication goals typically extend beyond information transfer achieved by selecting appropriate words or constructing grammatical sentences. We need to continually work at presenting ourselves as competent social actors (Goffman 1959) and **communicative competence** eventually became the new watchword (Mathy-Laikko and Yoder 1986). **Conversation** was recognized as a mutually created event in which the participants performed illocutionary **speech acts** (Austin 1962) such as requesting, demanding and advising. These acts were driven by goals, such as projecting one's personality, that may bear little relationship to the ostensible meaning of the utterance (Lloyd *et al.* 1993). In this view, conversational competence involves the mutual effective enactment and understanding of speech acts. This, of course, concerns the **pragmatics** of conversation. Although the centre of gravity of AAC research shifted, the pragmatics label was little used to define the shift initially, except by a relatively few trail blazers (e.g. Alm *et al.* 1989; Calculator 1988; Kraat 1985; Newell 1984). Recently, however, the centrality of pragmatics in AAC research has been strongly asserted by some research groups (e.g. Iacono 2003; McCoy *et al.* 2003; Todman and Alm 2003).

People who use AAC generally experience exceptional difficulties in fulfilling the pragmatic requirements of conversation, and alleviation of their difficulties is a major goal of AAC research and system development. To build pragmatic help into AAC systems, there must first be an awareness of pragmatic features of unaided conversation; how things get done appropriately to make it 'work' (the pragmatics of execution). Then, the pragmatic skills that are compromised for aided conversationalists have to be identified, along with the goals that drive their attempts at communication. It then becomes possible to seek ways around their pragmatic limitations. A model linking pragmatic features, short- to long-term goals and approaches to the design and evaluation of AAC systems was proposed by Todman and Alm (2003).

Various pragmatic features of conversation, such as shared conversational management, maintenance of conversational momentum and repair of misunderstandings, are compromised by the long pauses that typically precede turns at speech by people using AAC. The limitations imposed by slow conversational rates interfere particularly with the achievement of immediate goals, such as creating a favourable impression,

mutual enjoyment of the interaction and projecting personality (Alm and Newell 1996). Indeed, conversational rate has been shown to be a powerful cause of negative attributions (Todman and Rzepecka 2003). Attempts to increase conversational rate by means of word prediction in the generation of utterances at the time they are required have met with limited success; around 2–15 words per minute (Beukelman and Mirenda 2005). With whole utterance approaches, however, in which potential utterances are pre-stored and retrieved whole when needed, it has proved possible to increase conversational rate to around 60 words per minute without loss of coherence (File and Todman 2002) and with aided and unaided partners sharing more or less equally in the management of the conversations (e.g. Todman 2000). This approach was predicated on the pragmatic reality that in much social conversation it is only necessary for an utterance to approximate an ideal formulation. This opened the way for the use of pragmatic features, such as use of *quick-fire* formulaic expressions (Wray 2002a, 2002b) for such functions as repair and feedback, along with navigational support for retrieval, modelled on the way in which natural conversation proceeds with small shifts in perspective, such as from me to you, or from present to past (Todman 2001).

Other pragmatic features, such as coping with the unexpected, uniqueness and precision are more related to medium-term goals, such as participation in activities, independence and the maintenance of close relationships. For such goals, accuracy of information transfer can be achieved with word-by-word phrase creation, albeit with a time penalty. Typically, such goals are concerned with transactional interactions – getting things done in the world – and tend, therefore, to be highly **context** specific. A group of researchers (Higginbotham and Wilkins 2006) has been using a frame approach (Minsky 1975) for the support of stereotypically situated conversations. Another group has been applying **Grice**'s (1975) **cooperative principle** and conversational **maxims** to investigate trade-off choices confronted by users of whole utterance-based systems (e.g. McCoy *et al.* 2007). There has also been interest in the application of Sperber and Wilson's (1995) **relevance theory** to an understanding of pragmatic language difficulties in children (Leinonen and Kerbel 1999). The theory has also been applied to trade-offs between information gained and effort expended by people using AAC devices (e.g. Clibbens 1997), which may provide insights into reasons for the abandonment of these devices (e.g. Johnson *et al.* 2006).

People using AAC often have limited ability to use conventional non-verbal means of finessing the pragmatic **intentions** behind their communications (Wetherby and Prizant 1998). The situation is exacerbated by an inability to express **meaning** through intonation. The issue of **prosody** is being tackled for VOCAs on a number of fronts. Pijper (1997) used concatenation of pre-recorded words, with prosody provided by a waveform manipulation technique. Murray and Arnott (1995) produced recognizable vocal emotions using rules to simulate in synthetic speech the features of emotion expressed in the human voice. Black (2003) has been investigating the potential of selection from large databases of natural speech and Zhang *et al.* (2004) have turned their attention to the generation of prosodic variation to match contexts that extend beyond the level of individual sentences. Most recently, Pullin (2006a, 2006b) has been exploring the possibilities for achieving prosodic variation by means of joystick control of timing and pitch in VOCAs. The next generation of VOCAs may be expected to show advances in terms of prosody, conversational rate and ease of use (e.g. http://blink-twice.com/tango/).

JOHN TODMAN

See also: Austin, J.; communication; competence, communicative; competence linguistic; context; conversation; cooperative principle; development, pragmatic; discourse coherence; gestural communication; Grice, H.P.; intention; maxims of conversation; meaning; perspective taking/ point of view; pragmatic language impairment; pragmatics; relevance theory; request; speech act theory; speech act type

Suggestions for further reading

Müller, N. (ed.) (2000) *Pragmatics in Speech and Language Pathology: Studies in Clinical Applications*, Amsterdam: John Benjamins.

Todman, J. (2003) 'Pragmatic aspects of communication', in S. von Tetzchner and M.H. Jenson (eds) *Proceedings of the Seventh Biennial Research Symposium of the International Society for Augmentative and Alternative Communication*, Toronto, Canada: ISAAC.

Communication Failure

Successful **communication** is to be defined in terms of the partner's recognition of a particular set of mental states of the speaker, in whom there is the intention to achieve such an effect on the partner (Grice 1989). Within this perspective, communication failure may be defined as an unsuccessful attempt on the part of the speaker to modify the partner's mental states in the desired way. Failure repair, then, is a new attempt to produce the intended communicative effect. Traditionally, a major research perspective on the topic has been **conversation analysis** (CA). However, communication failures have received little attention in recent years.

Within a CA perspective, Schegloff *et al.* (1977) showed that a structural-based preference for self- versus other-initiation of repair exists in turn-taking after a breakdown (*see also* Zahn 1984). Friedland and Miller (1998) also found that in brain-injured patients over 80 per cent of repairs were self-initiated. Fox and Jasperson (1995) classified self-repair into different types that include operations such as repeating or recycling, replacing or substituting, adding or inserting, and abandoning or restarting. Self-repair is preferably initiated in the same turn where the trouble has occurred or in the 'third turn to the trouble source turn', i.e. the turn subsequent to the one which follows the trouble source (Schegloff *et al.* 1977; but *see also* Schegloff 1992, 1997a). Self-repair may be carried out in response to other-initiation of repair (Schegloff 2004). When the repair is initiated by the partner, it is almost always initiated in the turn that follows the trouble source (Schegloff 1997b). Robinson (2006) has argued that the 'meaning' of other-initiated forms of repair can affect the speaker's response. For example, if the trouble-source speaker understands himself to be blameworthy for the breakdown, he is more likely to correct, rather than merely repeat, the trouble source, and to engage in other types of accounting behaviours, such as apologizing.

CA aims at a descriptive analysis of communication failures, which it views as breakdowns or trouble occurring during **conversation**. More recently, some authors have proposed that a specific case of communication failure, **misunderstanding**, be viewed as an integral part of the comprehension process rather than just a breakdown (Dascal 1985; Weigand 1999). In line with such a perspective Bosco *et al.* (2006) have claimed that all communication failures, not only misunderstanding, integrally belong to the cooperative process (Grice 1957) in which agents are involved during communication. Within a cooperative model of communication, the replies received from a partner provide the speaker with the grounds on which to realize that a communicative attempt has failed. Recognizing that a failure has occurred provides in its turn a starting point for repair. Focusing on the complexity of the cognitive processes involved in failure recognition and repair and following the assumptions of **cognitive pragmatics** theory (Airenti *et al.* 1993b; Bara, to appear), Bosco *et al.* (2006) have proposed a taxonomy of the types of failures that may occur in communicative interaction. These are failure of the literal meaning, failure of the speaker's meaning, and failure of the communicative effect (i.e. the partner's **refusal** to accept a partner's communication act). A failure may also involve a combination of two or all of these types. In order to achieve his or her communicative goal, and depending on the kind of failure that has occurred, a speaker may employ different repair strategies. A speaker may simply repeat what he or she said (in the case of failure of the expression act), reformulate what he or she said (in the case of failure of the speaker's meaning) or change the content of what he or she said (in the case of failure of the communicative effect). This taxonomy allowed Bosco *et al.* (2006) to generate empirical hypotheses about the relative difficulty of recognizing and repairing different kinds of failure that were confirmed by empirical evidence obtained from 3- to 8-year-old children. In particular, it was found that it was easier for children to repair a failure of literal meaning than a failure of speaker's meaning, whereas repair of communicative effect was the most difficult.

From a cognitive and developmental pragmatics perspective it is useful to keep in mind children's performance, since it can offer suggestions on the increasing difficulty in the production of a specific pragmatic task. Direct observations of children show that in the prelinguistic phase their recovery strategy is essentially to persist in repeating the failed communicative act (Alexander *et al.* 1997). Use of this strategy tends to decrease as the child gets older (Garvey 1984) and becomes capable of distinguishing different types of failure and of adopting a fitting repair strategy (Marcos 1991). During the second year of life children become able to perform two different kinds of verbal repair: repetition and modification. In particular, they just repeat their request when the adult replies with a neutral query. They give a more specific version of it in response to a specific query from the adult (Anselmi *et al.* 1986) and reformulate it when the adult replies with a simple declarative comment (Wilcox and Webster 1980). Children also appear to adopt a repair strategy suitable to the type of failure that has occurred. When their mother misunderstands a request (rather than refuses to comply with it), children try to clarify it rather than simply repeat it (Marcos and Kornhaber-le Chanu 1992). Thus, while repetition appears to be the easiest strategy for recovery, the use of more sophisticated and appropriate strategies appears to be an early acquisition.

A very early version of communication failure, rooted more in the failed realization of the infant's expectation of a certain action on the part of the mother than in the actual failure of a communicative attempt on the part of the infant, has been claimed to play a role in the development of **theory of mind** (ToM) and Gricean communication (Tirassa *et al.* 2006a). In general, the possible relation between ToM and the ability to recognize and repair communication failures appears to be a particularly interesting topic. It has been suggested that when an agent – be it a young child (Golinkoff 1986, 1993) or an adult (Feldman and Kalmar 1996) – repairs a communication failure, he or she usually adapts his or her strategy to take the partner's perspective into account. In line with this hypothesis, children with autism, a condition which has been claimed to be associated with an impaired ToM (Baron-Cohen *et al.* 1985), appear to experience communication failures more frequently than their typically developing peers (*see* Keen 2003). However, Volden's (2004) study of the problem yielded ambiguous results. On the one hand, children with **autism spectrum disorder** (ASD) performed similarly to controls in responding to requests for clarification. They used more flexible and increasingly complex repair strategies according to whether they had received a neutral request, a request for clarification, or a semistructured prompt ('Tell me in another way') from an interlocutor. On the other hand, ASD children also produced a greater number of inappropriate replies than the controls.

Also, the symptomatology of schizophrenia has been explained on the basis of a ToM impairment (Frith 1992). Children suffering from such a psychiatric disorder have been described as using self-initiated repair strategies like repetition, revision and fillers less frequently than normally developed children (Caplan *et al.* 1996). Adults suffering from the same disorder have been described as attempting to self-repair their messages inadequately during a referential communication task (Leudar *et al.* 1992). Docherty (2005) used the Communicative Disturbances Index (Docherty *et al.* 1996) to measure different kinds of failures during a natural conversation in a group of adult schizophrenic patients. These investigators found that these patients experienced more trouble than controls.

To conclude, notwithstanding the importance of understanding communication failure, recent literature on the topic does not abound. Further studies are needed to understand more deeply the nature and role of the various cognitive processes involved in the ability to recognize and recover communication failures. The study of recoveries in relation to the type of failure that occurs appears to be a promising perspective.

FRANCESCA M. BOSCO and MAURIZIO TIRASSA

See also: Autism spectrum disorders; clinical pragmatics; discourse; discourse analysis; gestural communication; inference; inferential comprehension; schizophrenic language

Suggestions for further reading

Bazzanella, C. (ed.) (1996) *Repetition in Dialogue*, Tübingen: Niemeyer.

Bosco, F.M., Bucciarelli, M. and Bara, B.G. (2006) 'Recognition and recovery of communicative failures: a developmental perspective', *Journal of Pragmatics*, 38: 1398–429.

Sche004, E.A. (1992) 'Repair after next turn: the last structurally provided defense of intersubjectivity in conversation', *American Journal of Sociology*, 97: 1295–345.

Competence, Communicative

The notion of communicative competence is central to an approach to the study of **communication** known as 'ethnography' (Hymes 1964a, 1972b, 1974; Gumperz 1964). In contrast to **ethnomethodology**, which developed out of sociological and sociolinguistic studies, ethnography (literally, 'picture of the people') has it roots in the anthropological work of Edward Sapir (1921).

The founder of modern ethnography is Dell Hymes. In the 1960s and 1970s, he argued (against the dominant position of the time) that linguistic theory should not only concern itself with explaining speakers' and hearers' **knowledge** of grammaticality or **linguistic competence**, but also their communicative competence: the tacit social, cultural (and linguistic) knowledge that governs appropriate use of language within a **culture**.

For Hymes, it was not enough to study grammatical differences such as those between 'he pushed me' and 'it was him that pushed me', or between 'it was me that was pushed by him' and 'it was me that he pushed'. Instead, he proposed, linguists should also explore the sociocultural factors that might influence a speaker to choose to utter one of these in preference over the others. As a result, he argued that the 'sentence' should be replaced as the basic unit of analysis by the 'speech event' or **speech act**.

Ethnographers have explored a range of questions that Hymes identified as relating to the broader issue of what might constitute the tacit sociocultural knowledge members of a speech community share. What is it that makes particular utterances appropriate and others inappropriate within a culture? Albert (1964) reports that differences in social status among the Burundi require a peasant farmer to make 'a rhetorical fool of himself' if in **conversation** with a herder, or a prince (i.e. a social 'superior'). What rules govern the appropriateness of certain behaviours? In some cultures, **silence** is considered to be undesirable, even hostile. In others, however, it is to be expected in many situations (*see* Basso's 1972 study of Western Apache culture). What are the cultural constraints that make some utterances feasible and others simply unfeasible? Hymes (1974) refers to an anthropologist working among the Cochiti of New Mexico (Fox 1967) who was unable to elicit from a single member of the tribe the first-person possessive of the noun 'wings'. Whilst the word existed, no-one would say it: people don't have wings and therefore the first-person possessive could not be uttered.

Those who take an ethnographic approach to language and communication focus on the cultural values and social roles that operate in particular communities. They are particularly concerned not to impose their own cultural presuppositions on other societies, but rather to undertake detailed study which reflects the patterns of custom and communication of the culture being studied.

TIM WHARTON

See also: Cognitive anthropology; communication; competence, linguistic; competence pragmatic; context; cross-cultural pragmatics; discourse analysis; ethnomethodology; intercultural communication; pragmatics; silence; sociolinguistics

Suggestions for further reading

Hymes, D. (1972) 'On communicative competence', in J. Pride and J. Holmes (eds) *Sociolinguistics*, Harmondsworth: Penguin.

Saville-Troike, M. (2003) *The Ethnography of Communication: An Introduction*, Oxford: Blackwell.

Schiffrin, D. (1994) *Approaches to Discourse*, Oxford: Blackwell. Chapter 5.

Competence, Linguistic

The notion of 'competence' has been used, particularly within the theoretical framework of Generative Linguistics, to mean a system of **knowledge** of a certain type. Such a system underlies our distinctions between sentences that are well formed and meaningful and series of words that are not well formed and are not meaningful. Another such system underlies our distinction, for any sentence, between appropriate and inappropriate **contexts** of its utterance. Those systems of knowledge involve rules of certain types. They have been argued to be determined partly by our genetic endowment and partly by our experience as children in the vicinity of speakers of a certain language.

In our daily life, we are familiar with two ordinary types of knowledge. Philosophers have called them 'knowledge how' and 'knowledge that'. A person makes perfect sense when one says, in a sincere assertoric manner, 'I know how to drive a car'. One is naturally understood to thus be ascribing to oneself an ability to perform the actions involved in driving a car in an ordinary and proper way. When we take a person to know a certain natural language, we do not ascribe to that person a 'knowledge how'. Knowing a language is not captured by any knowledge of how to perform certain actions. For example, although an essential part of knowing a language is being able to understand its sentences in ordinary contexts of utterance, no action is being performed in understanding what has been said. Knowledge of a natural language is, therefore, not a case of 'knowledge how'.

A person makes perfect sense when one says, in a sincere and assertoric manner, 'I know that the Great Blue Heron is a long-legged bird that hunts fish'. One is naturally understood to thus be ascribing to oneself awareness of some facts about certain birds. These facts are present in one's mind (and brain). They were incorporated into one's memory and can be retrieved from it. Even if one does not recall when exactly one became aware of these facts about the Great Blue Heron, there is no doubt in anyone's mind that there was such a first time, when the person watched such birds or was informed about them by someone else, a book or a programme. When we take a person to know a certain natural language, we do not ascribe to that person a 'knowledge that'. Knowing a language is not captured by any knowledge of facts that one is aware of since they were brought into one's awareness. A person knows a natural language only if one is able to produce and understand **speech acts** of certain types, such as **assertion**, **question**, and promise. However, at no point in time does a person become aware, and then remember, that each speech act consists of two parts: a 'force' and a '**proposition**'. Although the **meanings** of certain words are often brought into the awareness of children when they develop their knowledge of a language, such instances do not characterize that development. Knowledge of a natural language is, therefore, not a case of 'knowledge that'.

The notion of 'competence' is usually contrasted with the notion of 'performance'. Our linguistic performance manifests our linguistic competence, but not in a pure form, since it manifests other cognitive systems as well, such as memory, attention, and the physiology of speech and hearing. Linguistic competence is a useful, even necessary, abstraction, which enables us to understand knowledge of language independently of its interaction with other cognitive systems.

ASA KASHER

See also: Competence, pragmatic

Suggestion for further reading

Chomsky, N. (1965) *Aspects of the Theory of Syntax*, Cambridge, MA: MIT Press. Section 1.

Competence, Pragmatic

Competence in general is a system of **knowledge** of a certain nature. Linguistic competence is the system of knowledge that every normal person has as a speaker of one's native language. Pragmatic competence is part of that linguistic competence. It is the system of knowledge that a person has in order to be able to use linguistic means, which are utterances of expressions and sentences in **contexts** of utterance, for attaining linguistic ends, such as making a statement or asking a **question**.

Pragmatic competence is a system of knowledge that is neither a system of 'knowing how' nor a system of 'knowing that'. An element of pragmatic competence is the knowledge a person has, as a speaker of a certain natural language, to produce and understand questions under various circumstances. This element of knowledge is not a piece of 'knowing how', since the knowledge required for understanding a question in one's natural language does not involve an ability to perform any action. Nor is that element of knowledge a piece of 'knowing that', since native speakers of a natural language are not being taught rules that govern interrogative **speech acts**. The knowledge required for production and understanding of such speech acts is not acquired by becoming aware of certain facts.

Being a system of knowledge, pragmatic competence should be contrasted with pragmatic performance. The latter notion involves not only the system of knowledge of the pragmatic component of the linguistic competence, but also a variety of cognitive systems that are involved in the psychological and physiological processing of natural language in human minds and brains.

Pragmatic competence is the system of knowledge that governs use of language. There are two senses of 'use of language' that should be distinguished from each other. In the first, broad sense, everything done with words is a use of language. The system of knowledge that governs rhyming in writing poems is a system of knowledge that governs a use of language. A person who does not have that system of knowledge can still be a fully competent speaker of the same natural language. In the second, narrow sense of 'use of language' under consideration are only those uses of utterances in contexts, governed by parts of the language itself. Certain systems of knowledge that are parts of language itself govern questions, both in production and understanding, under various contexts of utterance. The latter sense is more interesting for the sake of understanding language itself and it constitutes pragmatic competence. The former sense is of interest for the sake of understanding social practices of doing things with words.

Generally speaking, the major components of pragmatic competence are systems of knowledge related to speech acts in general and speech acts of certain, basic types in particular, as well as systems of knowledge related to what is implicated in addition to **what is said**.

ASA KASHER

See also: Competence, linguistic; implicature; speech act theory; speech act type

Suggestion for further reading

Kasher, A. (1975) 'What is a theory of use?' in A. Margalit (ed.) *Meaning and Use*, Dordrecht: Reidel; reprinted in A. Kasher (ed.) (1998) *Pragmatics: Critical Concepts*, vol. I, London: Routledge.

Complaints

Pragmatics analyses the **meaning** of utterances in interaction. More specifically, many pragmatics researchers have focussed on developing criteria for identifying different **speech acts** such as **compliments**, compliment responses, **apologies**, **refusals**, and complaints, and describing the ways in which they are expressed in different languages (e.g. Olshtain and Weinbach 1987; Blum-Kulka *et al.* 1989; Ylanne-McEwen 1993; Nelson *et al.* 1996; Bardovi-Harlig *et al.* 2006). Like refusals, complaints provide interesting contrasts in preferred pragmatic choices of strategy across different **cultures**, as well as in preferred structures for expressing a complaint.

Definition

Complaints can be defined as 'speech acts in which disappointment or a grievance is expressed' (Clyne 1994: 49). Because they have different functions, it is useful to make a distinction between direct (or instrumental) complaints and 'whinges' (Clyne 1994), often labelled as indirect complaints (Alicke *et al.* 1992; Boxer 1993a, 1993b). A direct complaint involves an explicit or implicit accusation and at least one explicit or implicit directive (Clyne 1994: 54). An indirect complaint or whinge, by contrast, is a 'long or repeated expression of discontent not necessarily intended to change or improve the unsatisfactory

situation' (Clyne 1994: 49). Whinges do not hold the addressee responsible for the perceived offence (Boxer 1993a, 1993b). They can function to provide emotional release or to off-load negative affect. Whinges usually occur between people of equal or near equal status, and are often used to establish rapport and solidarity with others (Clyne *et al.* 1991; Clyne 1994; Daly *et al.* 2004).

Methodology

Much research on complaints uses some variant of the discourse completion task (DCT; Blum-Kulka *et al.* 1989) to elicit (usually written) data from student subjects. Subjects are presented with a scenario and asked to write down what they would say, e.g. *You have just paid for a newspaper. The shop assistant does not give you the correct change. What do you say?* This method has many advantages from the researcher's standpoint (Beebe and Cummings 1996). It is easy to administer to large groups, and the data is relatively straightforward to analyse. Social variables such as setting, social role, relative social status, social distance, and size of the imposition can be manipulated. However, written data elicited from well educated subjects responding to artificial scenarios also has obvious limitations (*see* Wolfson *et al.* 1989; Beebe and Cummings 1996; Miyuki 1998; Turnbull 2001). DCTs typically elicit only one response, whereas in authentic interaction speech acts such as complaints are typically negotiated between participants over several turns of talk. Moreover, people's intuitions about what they say are typically not accurate indications of what they actually say (e.g. Nunan 1992). In other words, DCTs provide information on 'the stereotypical shape of the speech act' (Beebe and Cummings 1996: 80–81). Student diaries recording people's recollections of complaints are scarcely more reliable regarding the form of complaints, although they can provide information on content and reasons for complaints (Alicke *et al.* 1992). Oral role plays offer the possibility of more extended, realistic, and even negotiated instances of complaints, with results closer to those produced in free speech (e.g. Cohen and Olshtain 1993; Arent 1996; Turnbull 2001; Morrison and Holmes 2003).

There is some research which focusses on naturally occurring 'authentic' complaints in a variety of settings, including factories (Daly *et al.* 2004), offices (Holmes and Stubbe 2003b), hospitals (Holmes and Major 2003), a university campus (Boxer 1996), a caregiver service company (Marquez Reiter 2005), and television programmes (Dersley and Wootton 2000), as well as complaint stories (i.e. whinges) in **conversations** (Boxer 1996, 2002; Günthner 1997; Edwards 2005). These studies demonstrate that expressing and interpreting complaints is typically a complex and dynamic process which may extend over several turns of talk (*see also* Stubbe *et al.* 2003).

Results

As well as describing their structure, researchers have identified different kinds of complaints (in terms of content, orientation to self or other), and different types and degrees of directness used in the expression of complaints (House and Kasper 1981; Olshtain and Weinbach 1987; Clyne *et al.* 1991; Boxer 1993a; Clyne 1994; Edwards 2005). Analysing four hundred role-played conversations, Trosborg (1995b), for example, provides a detailed description of four strategies and eight sub-categories used to express complaints, ranging from hint to explicit blame. Trosborg (1995b: 315) also describes ways of mitigating and up-grading complaints. Research on complaints by conversation analysts explores the role of complaints in ongoing conversational interaction (Coulter 1990; Garcia 1991; Sacks 1992; Drew 1998; Monzoni 2008). This research provides a detailed description of features of the sequencing of utterances in conversation and examines the range of different possible responses to complaints. Overall, research on responses to complaints (Alicke *et al.* 1992; Boxer 1993b, 2002) suggests that requests for direct action are often met with **silence** or change of **topic**. Complaints that require indirect action are more likely to elicit advice or a problem-solving response. Whinges commonly elicit agreement or commiseration.

A good deal of research on complaints has been concerned with the interpretation and expression of complaints by language learners compared to native speakers of English. Studies include Israeli, German, Danish, Chinese, Japanese, and Vietnamese learners of English. Overall, this research indicates that language learners tend to use less **mitigation** and to express complaints more directly than native speakers of English, and that their complaints are typically longer and less negotiated (Olshtain and Weinbach 1993; Nakabachi 1996; Kraft and Geluykens 2002; Li 2006). Murphy and Neu (1996), for instance, compared oral complaints by Americans and Koreans in response to a written scenario. While the preamble and follow-up were similar, the Koreans' complaint formulations tended to be less mitigated and more 'blaming'. They were also perceived by native speaker evaluators as aggressive, challenging, and lacking in credibility. The usual explanation for these differences is the learners' under-developed socio-pragmatic proficiency (inaccurate assessment of the relevant socio-cultural variables), and pragma-linguistic proficiency (fewer linguistic resources to express the complaint appropriately in **context**) (Trosborg 1995b; Arent 1996; Gershenson 2003). However, caution is necessary in making such generalizations, since in some cases they may be an artefact of the methodology. Beebe (1985a: 3, cited in Wolfson *et al.* 1989: 183), for instance, notes that 'written role plays [DCT] bias the response toward less negotiation, less hedging, less repetition, less elaboration, less variety and ultimately less talk'.

There is some research comparing the structure of complaints and responses to complaints in different cultures. Factors such as the length of the complaint and amount of mitigation vary in different cultures (e.g. Ouellette 2001). Cultural values also influence what is complained about as well as the content of justificatory material (Beebe and Takahashi 1989; Trosborg 1995b). Research on strategy choice confirms that this varies according to contextual, social and cultural variables, such as the relationship between interlocutors. Face threatening acts such as complaints in Chinese, for instance, were carried out in ways that emphasized common ground and constructive solutions (Du 1995). Comparing responses to complaints by Iranian speakers of Persian with American English speakers, Eslami-Rasekh (2004) found that the Iranians were more sensitive to contextual factors and varied their response strategies accordingly. The American English speakers mostly used one **apology** strategy and intensified it based on contextual factors. Another important factor is the broad cultural orientation to positive **politeness** (e.g. Held 2005 on Italian; Sifianou and Antonopoulou 2005 on Greek) versus negative politeness (e.g. Frescura 1995 on Canadians; Yli-Vakkuri 2005 on Finns).

Conclusion

Taking account of the importance of attending to potential methodological weaknesses in assessing the reliability of results and interpretations, information on the range of strategies and structures used to express complaints in different cultures makes a useful contribution to pragmatics. The structure of complaints, amount of mitigation, and preferred strategies for expressing complaints vary according to the socio-cultural background of participants. People from different socio-cultural groups may also perceive and assess the relevance of social variables, such as social roles, relative statuses and seriousness of the grievance, very differently from each other (*cf.* Nickels 2006).

JANET HOLMES and NICKY RIDDIFORD

See also: Apologies; applied linguistics; competence, pragmatic; context; conversation analysis; cross-cultural pragmatics; disagreement; discourse analysis; discourse markers; discourse particles; ethnomethodology; hedge; inference; intercultural communication; misunderstanding; politeness; power; refusals; request; sociolinguistics; speech act theory; stylistics

Suggestions for further reading

Boxer, D. (1993) *Complaining and Commiserating: A Speech Act View of Solidarity in Spoken American English*, New York: Peter Lang.

Clyne, M., Ball, M. and Neil, D. (1991) 'Intercultural communication at work in Australia: complaints and apologies in turns', *Multilingua*, 10: 251–73.

Trosborg, A. (1995) *Interlanguage Pragmatics: Requests, Complaints, Apologies*, Berlin: Mouton de Gruyter.

Compliments

The **speech act** of compliment is classified as an 'expressive' (Searle 1969). It functions to make known the speaker's psychological attitude towards a past act that was performed by the recipient and that was beneficial. It has a 'convivial' function and is therefore intrinsically polite (Leech 1983). It 'explicitly or implicitly attributes credit to someone other than the speaker, usually the person addressed, for some good (possession, characteristic, skill, etc.) that is positively valued by the speaker and the hearer' (Holmes 1986a: 485). The credit may be directed to the hearer or to a third person (Holmes 1988: 447).

Sociolinguistic and pragmatic studies on complimenting have mainly focused on 'fairly narrow linguistic contexts' and 'compliment-response sequences consisting of two- or three-part exchanges' (Johnson 1992: 67). They have also employed instruments that elicit hypothetical and contrived data. Compliments and compliment responses in film language seem to be most representative of naturally occurring speech pragmalinguistically, but not so much sociopragmatically (Rose 2001). Golato (2003: 90) argues that naturally occurring talk-in-interaction has the advantage of showing how compliment responses are organized and realized in natural settings, whereas elicited responses via a **discourse** completion task (DCT) 'indirectly reflect the sum of prior experience with language'. However, Spencer-Oatey and Ng (2001) acknowledge that questionnaire data including only a small selection of compliment response strategies from a full taxonomy are limited.

Compliments are sensitive to sociocultural values and assumptions, particularly those related to the notions of 'face' and '**politeness**' (Goffman 1967b; Brown and Levinson 1987; Wieland 1995; Yu 2003). The Persian cultural schema of *shekasteh-nafsi* 'modesty' is instantiated when Persian speakers respond to compliments (Sharifian 2005). Differences are found in the sex preference, compliment **topics**, syntactic structure, form, lexical choice or predictability, functions, response types, distribution, and intent in the complimenting behaviour (Brunner and You 1988; Chen 1993; Cheng 2003; Creese

1991; Farghal and Al-Khatib 2001; Gu 1990; Herbert 1986, 1989, 1990, 1991; Holmes 1986a, 1988; Hong 1985; Knapp *et al.* 1984; Loh 1993; Manes and Wolfson 1981; Nelson *et al.* 1993; Pomerantz 1978; Wieland 1995; Wolfson 1980, 1981, 1983, 1984, 1989; Ye 1995). Encoding and decoding compliments requires 'compliment competence' (Herbert 1989: 8), or 'complex cultural-linguistic skills' (Creese 1991: 47) of non-native speakers.

Cross-cultural similarities and differences are also evident in compliment responses (Lorenzo-Dus 2001; Yu 2003). Pomerantz (1978), in her classic study of compliment responses, finds a prevalence of rejections and disagreements in American English, whereas conflicting results are observed in New Zealand, British and American English (Holmes 1986a; Creese 1991; Nelson *et al.* 1996) and in Arabic (Nelson *et al.* 1996). Some studies conclude that compliments are rejected more frequently in Chinese than in English (Chen 1993; Yuan 1998; Loh 1993), while other studies suggest that acceptance and agreement are relatively common in Chinese (Rose and Ng 1999). In Korean interactions, Koreans tend to reject or deflect compliments in order to avoid self-praise. However, in English interactions, Koreans tend to accept compliments by saying 'Thank you', because they believe that Americans are direct and frank and always accept compliments upon receiving them (Han 1992).

WINNIE CHENG

See also: Competence, communicative; competence, linguistic; competence, pragmatic; context; cultural scripts; disagreement; discourse; politeness; Searle, J.; sequence organization; speech act type; topic

Suggestions for further reading

Farghal, M. and Haggan, M. (2006) 'Compliment behaviour in bilingual Kuwaiti college students', *International Journal of Bilingual Education and Bilingualism*, 9: 94–118.

Golato, A. (2005) *Compliments and Compliment Responses: Grammatical Structure and Sequential Organization*, Amsterdam and Philadelphia, PA: John Benjamins.

Huth, T. (2006) 'Negotiating structure and culture: L2 learners' realization of L2 compliment-response sequences in talk-in-interaction', *Journal of Pragmatics*, 38: 2025–50.

Computational Pragmatics

Computational pragmatics is concerned with relations between linguistic expressions and **context** that are relevant for language understanding and generation (Bunt 2000a). In computational pragmatics these relations are modelled formally using explicit **representations** and algorithms that can be implemented as a proof of concept in computer programs. Pragmatic phenomena that have been investigated in computational pragmatics include **reference** resolution, discourse structure, dialogue acts, context modelling, grounding, and rational agency.

Reference has been studied extensively within **pragmatics** and there are a number of computational models, particularly in the area of reference resolution. Lappin and Leass (1994) propose an algorithm that calculates a saliency value based on recency effects and syntactically based factors. An algorithm described by Hobbs (1978) examines the syntactic representations of sentences up to and including the current sentence within a tree-like structure and searches within the tree for a possible referent for the pronoun. A more elaborate approach involves the concept of centering, which states a preference for pronominalization of entities in the discourse history list that play a central role in a main clause over those in subordinate and adjunct clauses (Grosz *et al.* 1995). The centering algorithm uses an explicit discourse model representation in which there is a backward-looking centre that represents the entity currently in focus and a forward-looking centre containing a list of entities that are potential referents of the backward-looking centre. Entities are ordered according to their grammatical roles. Walker (1989) has compared the simpler use of history lists with analysis based on centering, while Walker *et al.* (1998) is a collection of recent papers on centering. Supervised learning is an alternative approach to reference resolution in which machine learning methods are used to train models from annotated corpora (Aone and Bennett 1995).

Discourse structure refers to the relations between sentences in a **discourse**. Local relations between sentences can be specified in terms of coherence relations such as explanation and elaboration (Hobbs 1979). Determining coherence relations involves a process of **inference** using logical **abduction**, which by **reasoning** backwards from an effect to potential causes allows for the generation of a range of inferences. Hobbs *et al.* (1993) apply this method to a range of problems in language interpretation, including **discourse coherence**, making use of domain and world **knowledge** to determine the most plausible coherence relations between utterances. Rhetorical Structure Theory (Mann and Thompson 1988), which proposes a set of twenty-three relations between stretches of text, has also been widely used to determine coherence relations.

The structure of longer stretches of discourse has been modelled in terms of hierarchical relations among discourse segments. Discourse Structure Theory (Grosz and Sidner 1986) is a widely used model in which discourse is represented in terms of three components: linguistic structure, discourse structure, and attentional state. Each segment within a discourse has a purpose that represents the **intentions** of a participant. Two relations are specified for discourse segments: dominance, which represents a hierarchical relationship, and satisfaction-precedence, which represents an ordering relationship. The segmentation of a discourse into its hierarchical structure has been used in reference resolution, inference, and the interpretation of tense and aspect (Allen 1995). Discourse structure has also been used widely in text generation to support message organization and for text summarization (Demberg and Moore 2006).

Dialogue acts represent the actions performed by a speaker in a dialogue (Bunt 1979). Other terms include speech act (Searle 1975b), communicative act (Allwood 1976), conversational move (Carletta *et al.* 1997), and dialogue move (Cooper *et al.* 1999). The DAMSL scheme is a widely used system for annotating dialogues on several different levels (Allen and Core 1997), while a scheme developed at Edinburgh, the HCRC Map Task Coding Scheme (Carletta

et al. 1997) codes not only the conversational moves but also how they can be combined into higher levels of analysis, such as games and transactions. The DIT++ coding scheme, based on studies in Dynamic Interpretation Theory, takes these and a number of other annotation schemes into account and provides a more solid basis for multidimensional coding than the original schemes (Bunt 2006). DIT++ is being used as a basis for a standard for dialogue act annotation in a project started by the International Organization for Standardization.

The earliest computational models of dialogue acts were applied in plan-based models of dialogue developed in the 1980s (Cohen and Perrault 1979; Allen and Perrault 1980). In these models dialogue acts were represented as operators in a planning system and described in terms of their preconditions and effects. For example, a precondition of a **request** is that the speaker should want the hearer to perform an action and an effect is that the hearer wants to perform the action. To achieve a communicative goal a speaker would chain together a series of dialogue acts that would lead from the current state to the goal. Allen (1995) provides a detailed account of the planning underlying a simple dialogue concerned with the purchase of a train ticket. Similarly, recognition of the intention behind an utterance involved matching this intention with some part of a plan that might achieve a particular goal (Allen and Perrault 1980). A cooperative system would adopt the user's goal, anticipate any obstacles to the plan, and produce a response that would promote the completion of the goal.

Two different approaches have been proposed in computational pragmatics for the automatic interpretation of dialogue acts. Such interpretation is a difficult problem, particularly in the case of indirect dialogue acts, where an utterance such as 'Can you tell me the way to the city centre?' can be interpreted either as a literal **question** about the hearer's ability or as a request for the hearer to provide directions (Jurafsky 2004). The first approach uses the methods developed in plan-based models of dialogue in which the hearer engages in a chain of reasoning based on the preconditions and effects of dialogue acts to determine the speaker's intentions (Allen and Perrault 1980). This inferential model of dialogue act interpretation, which has its theoretical foundations in earlier work in **speech act theory** by Gordon and Lakoff (1975) and **Searle** (1975b), has evolved into the BDI (belief, desire, intention) model of communicative agents (Allen 1995). The BDI model has been used as a basis for practical dialogue systems involving collaborative and incremental planning, such as the TRAINS (Traum and Allen 1994) and TRIPS (Allen *et al.* 2001) systems.

The second approach to dialogue act interpretation, which has been called the 'cue-based model of dialogue act interpretation' (Jurafsky 2004), uses cues in the input, such as words and collocations, **prosody**, and conversational structure to support the interpretation process. This approach uses probabilistic methods that have been used widely in speech recognition and statistical language understanding (Manning and Schütze 1999). The models are trained on a labelled corpus of dialogues and make use of supervised machine-learning algorithms to perform statistical classification of utterances as dialogue acts. A major strength of the BDI model is that it provides a sophisticated model of reasoning. However, there are practical limitations in terms of the effort required to develop plan-inferential algorithms as well as in terms of the computational resources required to run them. The cue-based approach, while providing a shallower interpretation, has the advantages of breadth and coverage afforded by data-driven methods.

Computational models of context are concerned with 'the totality of conditions that may influence the understanding and generation of communicative behaviour' (Bunt 2000a: 81–82). Context may refer to information from the preceding discourse, the physical environment, the domain of discourse, or the social situation. Bunt (2000a) argues that communicative behaviour does not depend on what a situation 'really' is, but on how participants view the situation. In other words, as modelled in Dynamic Interpretation Theory (DIT), context is not an objective notion, but rather a model of a participant's information state that guides the interpretation and production of dialogue acts (Bunt 2000b). Within DIT, dialogue acts are organized in a multidimensional taxonomy representing different aspects of the communicative process that they can address. Dialogue acts have a semantic

function, representing the content of the act, and a communicative function that specifies how the act changes the participant's information state. In other words, in DIT dialogue acts are defined as operators that dynamically update the context, and their interpretation and generation are modelled in terms of context change (Bunt *et al.* 2007).

Information State Theory (Traum and Larsson 2003) is a similar approach to context modelling that evolved out of the BDI model of communicative agents referred to earlier. In this theory the information state represents information about the dialogue history, what information is part of the common ground between the participants, and what obligations a participant has at a particular point in the dialogue. This information enables the dialogue manager – a central component of a dialogue system – to interpret the user's utterances and to decide what action to take next. Crucial elements in the theory are a set of dialogue moves (or acts) that trigger information state update and a set of update rules that specify how the information state is updated. The theory was implemented in a toolkit called TrindiKit which has been used in a number of prototype dialogue systems, such as GoDIS (Gothenburg Dialogue System) (Larsson *et al.* 2001).

Grounding describes the process by which participants in a dialogue achieve common ground (Stalnaker 1978). Clark and Schaefer (1989) proposed a collaborative theory of grounding in which participants coordinate their models of what has been mutually understood on a turn-by-turn basis. This theory was formalized and extended by Cahn and Brennan (1999). Traum (1994) developed a computational model of grounding. Paek and Horvitz (2000) implemented a formal model based on decision theory in which the system reasons about sources of **misunderstandings** and engages in a costs/benefits analysis to determine what actions to take to resolve them. Grounding plays a significant role in the context update model of Dynamic Interpretation Theory (Morante *et al.* 2007) and in Information State Theory (Matheson *et al.* 2000).

Rational agency refers to the view that dialogue can be seen as a special case of rational interaction. Rational agency evolved out of the plan-based approach to dialogue and is a central focus of Dynamic Interpretation Theory and the BDI model of **communication**. In this view dialogue structure emerges dynamically as a consequence of principles of rational cooperative interaction. The theoretical framework for rational agency is based on a set of logical axioms that formalize these principles and was developed by Cohen and Levesque (1990b) and extended and implemented as a dialogue management component of the ARTEMIS system (Sadek and de Mori 1998). In this system the dialogue manager includes a 'rational unit' that supports reasoning about knowledge and actions, and that enables the dialogue agent to produce rationally motivated plans of action. The model provides a theoretical motivation for why participants should wish to achieve mutual understanding and why in certain contexts they might provide more information than has been requested by the other participant. It also provides a more elaborate account of cooperation in communication. Whereas in plan-based approaches agents automatically adopt the other agent's goals in order to behave cooperatively, in the model of rational agency an agent attempts to achieve a rational balance between its own mental attitudes and those of other agents. This means that an agent does not necessarily have to adopt the other agent's goals, if there is a good reason not to. For example, an agent should not provide information that is confidential or assist in actions that it believes to be illegal or harmful.

The main practical applications of computational pragmatics are in natural language processing (Allen 1995) and spoken dialogue technology (McTear 2004). A wide range of pragmatic phenomena that have a bearing on the processes of language interpretation and language generation have been modelled in computational pragmatics, resulting in many cases in clearer and more explicit representations of these phenomena. Pragmatic phenomena such as indirect speech acts, reasoning, context-dependent interpretation, and cooperativeness, are relevant for the modelling of conversational agents in spoken dialogue systems and for explaining the processes of communicative interaction. Conversational interfaces for automated customer self-service applications are gradually replacing conventional touch-tone Interactive Voice Response (IVR) systems. Voice Search is a new application area in which services and products will become accessible using voice dialogues on small devices such as Personal Digital Assistants (PDAs) and mobile phones.

MICHAEL MCTEAR

See also: Abduction; anaphora, pragmatics of; artificial intelligence; communication; competence, communicative; competence, pragmatic; context; conversation; cooperative principle; definiteness; discourse; discourse analysis; discourse coherence; discourse cohesion; discourse markers; inference; information structure; intention; maxims of conversation; pragmatics; rationality; reasoning; reference; speech act theory; speech act type; telephone conversation; utterance interpretation

Suggestions for further reading

Bunt, H.C. and Black, W.J. (2000) (eds) *Abduction, Belief and Context in Dialogue: Studies in Computational Pragmatics*, Amsterdam: John Benjamins.
Jurafsky, D. (2004) 'Pragmatics and computational linguistics', in L.R. Horn and G.L. Ward (eds) *The Handbook of Pragmatics*, Oxford: Blackwell.
McTear, M. (2004) *Spoken Dialogue Technology: Toward the Conversational User Interface*, New York: Springer Verlag.

Context

Consider the utterance in (1) below:

> Mary: He's a banker.

In the absence of a context, our understanding of what Mary is saying remains incomplete. Before we can infer to whom the indexical 'he' is referring we need a context. Sometimes, this is provided by preceding **discourse**, such as in (2):

> Peter: What does John do for a living?
> Mary: He's a banker.

Sometimes, it is provided by other means. Consider the ambiguous utterance in (3):

Mary: The banks are collapsing.

If Mary utters (3) as she is standing with you near a river, pointing at the sides as they crumble into the rising water, then it will be the physical environment rather than any preceding discourse that ensures you arrive at the intended interpretation of the word 'bank'.

In **pragmatics**, context is everything. The distinction between context-dependent and context-*in*dependent **meaning** lies at the very heart of the distinction between pragmatics and **semantics** (with interesting complications: *see* Levinson 2000; Wilson and Sperber 2002; Carston 2002; Recanati 2004b; Horn 2006). Hearers need context in order to be able to assign **reference** to **indexicals** (such as in example (1)), resolve cases of **ambiguity** (example (2)), and much, much more.

Work within pragmatics tends to concentrate on those aspects of context illustrated above: *prior discourse*, which provides an evolving backdrop against which utterances are interpreted as **conversation** proceeds, and those features of the *physical environment* in which the conversation is taking place that may be relevant. However, these are far from the only aspects of context that play a role in **utterance interpretation**.

Context can be viewed from a much wider, sociolinguistic perspective, to include also the socio-cultural nature of the communicative event taking place, or the social status of those involved in it (*see* Brown and Yule 1983). And it could be argued that even this view of context is not broad enough. The set of beliefs or assumptions an individual uses in interpreting an utterance can be drawn from just about *any* piece of **knowledge** available to *both* speaker and hearer. Philosophers have called this 'common knowledge' (Lewis 1969) or 'mutual knowledge' (Schiffer 1972). Consider the example in (4):

Mary: John seems to be very tense and edgy at the moment. Is everything OK at work?
Peter: He's a banker.

Mary's (and, indeed, the reader's) successful understanding of the **implicature** conveyed by Peter's utterance of (4) – that things are very much *not* 'OK' for John at work – depends on shared background knowledge of the banking crisis in 2008. One attempt to view context in this broadest sense is to see it as a cognitive phenomenon. Thus construed, context is a 'psychological construct', 'a subset of the hearer's assumptions about the world' (Sperber and Wilson 1995: 15). Context is those beliefs or assumptions used by the hearer in the interpretation of an utterance whatever their source. This is the approach taken to context in **relevance theory** (Sperber and Wilson 1995; Carston 2002).

A potential problem with this view is that it leads potentially to one version of what is known in the literature on **artificial intelligence** as the 'frame' problem. How, from all the myriad pieces of information available from memory, perception and **inference**, do hearers manage to converge on the single set of assumptions that yield the interpretation the hearer intended? A pragmatic theory must constrain very tightly the number of plausible candidates for relevant assumptions if it is to rise to the challenge of explaining how this convergence takes place.

TIM WHARTON

See also: Ambiguity; artificial intelligence; communication; conversation; cultural scripts; discourse; implicature; indexicals; knowledge; semantics; sociolinguistics; utterance interpretation

Suggestions for further reading

Brown, G. and Yule, G. (1983) *Discourse Analysis*, Cambridge: Cambridge University Press. Chapter 2.
Clark, H. (1996) *Using Language*, Cambridge: Cambridge University Press. Chapter 2.
Sperber, D. and Wilson, D. ([1986] 1995) *Relevance: Communication and Cognition*, Oxford: Blackwell. Chapter 1.

Contextualism

A variety of distinct, but related philosophical doctrines go under the title contextualism. In epistemology, contextualism is the view that the sentences we use to ascribe **knowledge** to a subject – sentences of the form 'S knows that p' – may strictly and literally express different knowledge claims in different contexts of ascription (Lewis 1996; Cohen 1999). Moral contextualism makes similar claims about ought statements (Unger 1995; Brogaard 2008). More generally, contextualism about a class of expressions is the view that the semantic contents of expressions in that class vary with **context**. Contextualism is thus a semantic thesis that purports to explain contextual variations in semantic content by appeal primarily to facts about linguistic **meaning**, rather than by appeal to pragmatic factors.

Nonetheless, debates about contextualism also encompass many issues in **pragmatics**. For example, so-called radical contextualists deny that there is a neat separation between pragmatics and **semantics** (Searle 1978; Travis 1989; Sperber and Wilson 1995; Carston 2002; Recanati 2004b). They argue that pragmatic processes such as free enrichment play a central role in explaining contextual variation in semantic content. Moderate contextualists, by contrast, reject the idea of semantically unconstrained pragmatic intrusion into the determination of semantic content (Stanley 2000; Stanley and Szabo 2000; Taylor 2001). Moreover, there is considerable controversy over just which expressions, beyond certain paradigm or core cases, exhibit linguistically encoded context sensitivity. Some who reject contextualism about a given domain of **discourse** see only pragmatic variation where contextualists see variations in strict, literal semantic content. Settling such disputes requires some principled way of determining which aspects of the totality of contents communicated by an utterance on an occasion are properly called semantic and which aspects of that totality may properly be called pragmatic and not semantic.

It is uncontroversial that there are expressions the semantic contents of which vary with context and do so in virtue of linguistically encoded semantic properties of the relevant expressions. Paradigm examples are the various **demonstratives** and **indexicals** including (a) the personal pronouns 'I', 'he', 'she' and 'it', (b) the demonstrative pronouns 'this' and 'that', and (c) the demonstrative adverbs 'here', 'there', 'now', 'today', 'yesterday', 'tomorrow' and 'ago'. For example, depending on who is doing the talking,

where the talking is being done, and when it is being done, 'I' may denote different agents, 'here' may denote different locations, and 'now' may denote different times. Suppose that Pam, standing somewhere in Palo Alto at 5 p.m. on Wednesday, utters:

(1) I am here now.

Suppose that Michael, located somewhere in San Francisco at noon on Tuesday, utters the very same sentence. Pam and Michael have said different things. The **proposition** expressed by Pam is true just in case she, Pam, is in fact located somewhere in Palo Alto at 5 p.m. on Wednesday. What Michael says is true just in case he, Michael, is located somewhere in San Francisco on Tuesday at noon.

It is not the case that the entire linguistic significance of a context-sensitive expression varies with context. A context-sensitive expression will also have a fixed significance that is independent of context. For example, it is a consequence of facts about the fixed linguistic significance of (1) that *any* utterance of (1) as uttered by a speaker *s* at a location *l* and a time *t* will be true just in case the speaker, whoever she is, is standing at *l*, wherever *l* is, at *t*, whenever *t* is. In this vein, David Kaplan (1989a) draws a distinction between character and content. Character is that level of linguistic meaning that does not vary with context. Content is that level of linguistic meaning that does vary with context. Characters can be understood as functions from contexts of use to contents. Contents, in turn, can be understood as functions from what Kaplan calls circumstances of evaluation to extensions of various sorts. Intuitively, a context is a bundle of factors relevant to determining **what is said** by an utterance as used on an occasion. A circumstance of evaluation is a bundle of factors relevant to determining whether what is said by an utterance on a given occasion is true or false. The point to stress here is that there are two distinct semantic roles that factors like who is doing the speaking, when and where might be thought to play – either as contextual factors that go into determining what is said by an utterance on an occasion or as evaluative factors that go into determining whether what an utterance says is true or false. Kaplan has argued, for example, that factors like who is doing the talking and where the talking is being done are relevant to determining what is said by an utterance. But such factors are not, he claims, parameters relative to which the utterance should be evaluated for truth and falsity. As we shall see below, determining whether a given parameter is a contextual parameter (and thus relevant to determining what is said by an utterance as used on an occasion) or an evaluative parameter (and thus relevant to determining the truth value of what is said) is often a delicate matter subject to much dispute.

Now consider a less obvious, more controversial case of context sensitivity. Suppose that Janet remembers parking her car in the driveway. Suppose that she has no reason to doubt that the car is still there. Finally, suppose that the car is still there. Does Janet know where her car is? The answer would seem to be yes. For imagine that James, to whom Janet has given permission to borrow the car, asks Janet:

(2) Do you know where your car is?

Suppose that Janet responds:

(3) Yes, I know that the car is still parked in the driveway.

It seems intuitively obvious that Janet has said something true.

Now imagine a very slight change in the context. As before, Janet has parked the car in the driveway and Janet correctly remembers parking the car there. Unbeknownst to Janet, however, a gang of car thieves has been going around her neighbourhood stealing cars. James, however, is aware of this fact. And when he goes to get the keys from Janet, he again utters (2). When Janet responds as before, James tells her of the ring of car thieves victimizing her neighbourhood. Surprised and worried, Janet utters:

(4) No, I do not know whether the car is still parked in the driveway.

Has Janet spoken truly or falsely? Now it seems intuitively obvious that (4) is true and (3) false in the current context.

All that appears to differ between the two contexts is the salience of the mere possibility that Janet's car has been stolen. Suppose that the car thieves were prowling the neighbourhood in the first scenario, but that James and Janet were both unaware of that fact. It still seems true that (3) as uttered by Janet would express a truth, rather than a falsehood. It is not immediately obvious, however, why the salience or lack of salience of a mere possibility should affect the truth value of a claim to know. The first step toward a contextualist answer is the claim that the increased salience of the possibility that the car has been stolen renders a higher standard of knowledge operative in the relevant context. The crucial further claim is that contextually operative standards are additional elements of the context of utterance and are thus relevant to determining what is said by sentences containing the verb 'know' as uttered in the relevant context. In different contexts, with different operative standards, the same sentence containing 'know' will express different propositions with different truth conditions. When Janet claims to know in the first scenario she is making a different claim from the one she makes in claiming to know in the second scenario. In the first scenario, she is claiming to know by a relatively low standard. In the second scenario, she is claiming to know by a higher standard.

It is possible to grant that varying standards are semantically, rather than merely pragmatically, significant without endorsing contextualism. Again, contextualism is not merely the thesis that standards vary, but the stronger thesis that varying standards play a certain kind of semantic role, a role in determining what is said by an utterance. Recently, a number of thinkers have defended what is called semantic relativism as an alternative to contextualism (Richard 2004; MacFarlane 2005). Relativists grant that varying standards play a semantic role. But relativists insist that standards are not relevant to determining what is said by a sentence containing 'know' as a constituent, but to determining whether what is said is true or false. MacFarlane (2005), for example, distinguishes between what he calls contexts of use and contexts of assessment, and argues that epistemic standards are elements of contexts of assessment, rather than contexts of use. On MacFarlane's approach, the semantic content of a knowledge claim is standard neutral. That is, no reference to any particular standard is built into the very contents of our knowledge claims. But he insists that standard neutral knowledge claims can be evaluated for truth and falsity relative to different epistemic standards. Relativists have taken a similar approach to predicates of tastes (Lasersohn 2005) and epistemic modals (Egan *et al.* 2005; Egan 2007).

Consider a case of a different kind (Searle 1978; Travis 1989):

(5) Smith weighs 80kg.

Taken individually, none of the constituents of (5) would seem to be explicitly context-sensitive in the way that indexical expressions like 'I', 'here' or 'now' are widely acknowledged to be. Yet, utterances of (5) may appear to express different propositions in different contexts. Consider two different scenarios in which (5) might be uttered:

Scenario 1   Smith, who has been dieting for the last eight weeks, steps on the scale naked one morning before breakfast and it registers 80kg.

Scenario 2   Smith is wearing a heavy overcoat and carrying a briefcase full of books. He is about to step on an elevator with a capacity of no more than an extra 80kg.

In scenario 1, the speaker evidently communicates a proposition about the weight of Smith's naked body. In scenario 2, she communicates a different proposition, one about the combined weights of Smith's body, his clothing and his briefcase.

There is considerable disagreement over how to explain cases like the above. To appreciate the nature of these disagreements, it will help to distinguish between a minimal proposition and a pragmatically enriched proposition. A minimal proposition is a minimal projection from the semantic values of the semantically valued constituents of a given sentence. We arrive at a minimal proposition by taking the lexical meanings of the basic constituents of the sentence, the contextually determined values of any semantically

context-sensitive constituents of the sentence and combining them, in ways dictated by the syntactic structure of the sentence, to form a proposition. Every ingredient of a minimal proposition is in some way semantically 'called for' by some constituent of the relevant sentence. A pragmatically enriched proposition, by contrast, is a proposition that contains ingredients not semantically called for by any constituent of the relevant sentence. According to radical contextualists, pragmatically enriched propositions may sometimes be generated by a variety of different **primary pragmatic processes**, including what is called free enrichment.

Semantic minimalists believe that the strict, literal content of utterances of sentences like (5) will be a minimal proposition (Borg 2004a; Cappelen and Lepore 2005a). A minimalist about (5) would insist that our two utterances of (5) both express the minimal proposition that Smith weighs 80kg. Of course, the minimalist would allow that an utterance of (5) in the second scenario also conversationally implicates, or in some other way pragmatically conveys, an enriched proposition – in this case, the proposition that the combined weight of Smith, his briefcase, and his overcoat is 80kg. But the minimalist would insist that the enriched proposition is not *directly* asserted by the speaker. The enriched proposition is pragmatically conveyed in the course of or by asserting the minimal proposition but without itself being directly asserted.

By contrast, radical contextualists hold that an utterance of (5) may directly express a pragmatically enriched proposition and it can do so without the mediation of any minimal proposition (Searle 1978; Travis 1989; Sperber and Wilson 1995; Carston 2002; Recanati 2004b). Indeed, radical contextualists typically argue that the minimal propositions of the semantic minimalists either do not exist or are cognitively otiose, if they do exist. Such propositions play no role in driving either the speaker's linguistic production or the hearer's linguistic understanding. When we produce and/or understand an utterance of (5) in scenario two, for example, we do not first directly cognize the minimal proposition about the weight of Smith's body and then indirectly cognize the enriched proposition about the combined weight of Smith's body, briefcase and overcoat. Rather, the radical contextualist claims, we directly cognize the enriched propositions.

According to the radical contextualist, very few sentences express minimal propositions. That is because very few sentences linguistically encode fully determinate propositions in the first place, even when context does provide values that are semantically 'called for' by the semantically context-sensitive constituents of the sentence (Searle 1978; Travis 1989; Sperber and Wilson 1995; Bach 2001; Carston 2002; Recanati 2004b). Indeed, radical contextualists may fairly be said to take the direct expression of pragmatically enriched propositions to be the rule rather than the exception.

Semantic minimalism and radical contextualism represent two extremes. Moderate contextualists attempt to conform to a middle path between these two extremes (Stanley 2000; Stanley and Szabo 2000; Taylor 2001). Unlike minimalists, they deny that semantically encoded context sensitivity is restricted to a core set of uncontroversially context-sensitive expressions. Unlike radical contextualists, they deny that sentences may directly express pragmatically enriched, non-minimal propositions. Although the moderate contextualist agrees with the minimalist that a sentence directly expresses a proposition containing only constituents that are semantically 'called for' by its constituents, moderate contextualists differ from minimalists in holding that sentences semantically call for semantic values in more ways than the minimalist imagines. Moderate contextualists tend to believe, for example, that many context-sensitive expressions contain hidden or suppressed constituents that semantically call upon context to provide a value. While a moderate contextualist is likely to deny that (5) is genuinely context-sensitive, he is likely to grant that sentences like (6)–(8) are genuinely context-sensitive:

(6) John is tall. [for a what?]
(7) Susan is ready. [for what?]
(8) It is raining. [where?]

Clearly, the debates among semantic minimalists, semantic relativists, moderate contextualists, and radical contextualists are wide ranging. Adjudicating them requires attention to a variety of questions about the nature of lexical meaning, the nature of the **semantics-pragmatics interface**, the nature of **assertion**, and the nature of propositions. It also requires attention to syntactic questions about the nature of underlying **logical form** and to issues in **psycholinguistics** about linguistic processing. The ultimate resolution of these disputes will thus be a multidisciplinary task calling upon a wide variety of theoretical and empirical perspectives.

KENNETH TAYLOR

See also: Assertion; assessment, pragmatic; communication; context; conversation; cooperative principle; deixis; demonstratives; domain restriction; Grice, H.P.; implicature; impliciture; indexicals; knowledge; lexical pragmatics; logical form; maxims of conversation; meaning; modular pragmatics; neo-Gricean pragmatics; philosophy of language; post-Gricean pragmatics; pragmatics; primary pragmatic processes; proposition; psycholinguistics; radical pragmatics; relevance theory; Searle, J.; semantic minimalism; semantics; semantics-pragmatics interface; syntax-pragmatics interface; what is said

Suggestions for further reading

Cappelen, H. and Lepore, E. (2005) *Insensitive Semantics: A Defense of Semantic Minimalism and Speech Act Pluralism*, Oxford: Blackwell.
Recanati, F. (2004) *Literal Meaning*, Cambridge: Cambridge University Press.
Stanley, J. (2000) 'Context and logical form', *Linguistics and Philosophy*, 23: 391–434.

Conventionality

Etymologically originating from Latin *cum* + *venire* ('to come together'), conventionality in its most general sense refers to ways of doing things that rely on the existence of an agreement or contract between parties. This contract or agreement may be formalized and explicit, or it may be tacit and implicit, resembling what are most often called 'habits', 'preferences', or 'regularities'. Linguistic conventions are typically of the latter kind, though explicit regulation of language forms is also possible, as practised to different degrees within various institutionalized contexts (legal contracts, journalistic guidelines for good practice, language planning policies promoted by national governments or activist groups are cases in point). Recently, Millikan (1998) emphasized reproduction based on precedent – rather than on, say, coincidence or conscious **inference** – as central to natural conventionality, with which the conventionality of natural language is said to be continuous. In this way, conscious coordination (as the input to behaviour) or observed regularities (as the output of behaviour) are no longer required to define behaviour as conventional. Rather, defining behaviour as conventional relies on comparing it against previous instances of the same behaviour, which serve as its causes and models, thereby also circumscribing its **meaning**.

As a linguistic term, conventionality most commonly refers to a relationship between form and meaning that is established by virtue of a (tacit) agreement among speakers at a certain time and place rather than following from natural necessity (as in cases of onomatopoeia or, more generally, iconicity) or rational inference (as in cases of compositional or rule-based derivation). Conventionality is thus close to arbitrariness and idiomaticity, and contrasts with transparency and predictability. However, these notions are far from mutually exclusive and typically combine in various permutations. For instance, onomatopoeic forms, though motivated by an iconic relationship to their referent, are still subject to cultural conventions – witness the variation encountered across languages in, for example, forms representing animal sounds. Similarly, compositional interpretation builds on conventional (lexical) meanings. The limiting case is Nunberg *et al.*'s (1994) 'idiomatically combining expressions', where compositionality operates over idiomatic meanings of lexical items activated by their co-occurrence within a conventional pattern.

Conventional elements of language are learnt and stored in a repository of relevant items, rather than creatively generated on the fly based on language-specific rules or general principles of **rationality**. Adopting an acquisitionist perspective, Clark (2007: 12) distinguishes four such types of items: vocabulary items (words as conventional form-meaning associations par

excellence); syntactic constructions (lexically abstract yet conventional combinatorial patterns); pronunciation items (the phonological inventory of a community); and patterns of usage. Of these, the first three are akin to Morgan's (1978) 'conventions of language', while the fourth approximates his 'conventions of usage.' This expanded understanding of conventionality, which emphasizes arbitrariness at all levels of analysis as a result of differences in frequency emanating from societal preferences, lies at the heart of constructional and usage-based models of language (e.g. Tomasello 2003; Goldberg 2006). These models have recently mounted a powerful critique of generativist frameworks.

The question of whether the origin of linguistic meaning lies with natural necessity (Greek *physis*) or human convention (*nomos*) is raised in Plato's *Cratylus*. Here, Socrates expresses the view that linguistic meaning is a matter of habit, a view echoed in Aristotle's *De Interpretatione*. In modern times, conventionality is central to C.S. **Peirce**'s (1839–1914) definition of 'symbols' – which include words and sentences – as those signs that denote their objects not in virtue of some likeness or natural connection (as do 'icons' and 'indices'), but in virtue of habit. Conventionality is also acknowledged as a defining property of linguistic signs by Ferdinand de Saussure (1857–1913). Saussure emphasized the arbitrary association of signifier and signified as a necessary condition for this association to shift and change across languages and over time.

More recently, H.P. **Grice** (1913–88) explained linguistic meaning as a type of non-natural meaning. Contrary to other types of signs that are symptomatic of particular states of affairs and thus express **natural meaning**, the meaning of a linguistic sign is dependent on how speakers use it to bring about particular effects in an audience. Such use is in turn more or less constrained by the customary use of the sign by speakers in a community, i.e. by its conventional meaning. In Grice's theory of meaning, conventionality plays a part in defining both **what is said** (defined as 'closely related to the conventional meaning of the words (the sentence) [one] has uttered'; 1989: 25) and what is implicated (as a separate category of conventional **implicatures**; 1989: 25–26). Non-natural meaning thus encompasses both conventional (language-dependent) and intentional (speaker-dependent) aspects of meaning. The distinction between conventional meaning (what an expression means) and speaker's meaning (what a speaker means by using a particular expression) is sometimes used to draw the boundary between **semantics** and **pragmatics**.

The continuity between conventional and intentional aspects of meaning is the topic of Lewis's (1969) book *Convention*. Here, Lewis investigates the rational bases for conventions, explaining these as solutions to coordination problems. **Context** plays an important role in sustaining the transition from nonce to conventional, or coded, meaning (Traugott 1999). The related notions of conventionalization and standardization have been proposed to account for the gradual decontextualization of recurring meanings of linguistic expressions, such that these meanings eventually become part of an expression's conventional meaning (Bach 1998).

MARINA TERKOURAFI

See also: Context; Grice, H.P.; idiom; implicature; natural and non-natural meaning; Peirce, C.S.; pragmatics; rationality; semantics; semantics-pragmatics interface; what is said

Suggestions for further reading

Lewis, D. (1969) *Convention: A Philosophical Study*, Cambridge, MA: Harvard University Press.
Millikan, R.G. (1998) 'Language conventions made simple', *The Journal of Philosophy*, 95: 161–80.
Strawson, P. (1964) 'Intention and convention in speech acts', *Philosophical Review*, 73: 439–60.

Conversation

The study of conversation produced by English speakers was begun in the early 1970s by a group of sociologists, who looked at how participants manage the organizational and social aspects of conversation (*see*, for example, Duncan 1972; Sacks 1974; Sacks *et al.* 1974; Schegloff 1972; Schegloff and Sacks 1973). Since then, research studies have investigated an array of conversational features using the framework of

conversation analysis. Conversations have also been examined in a number of specific settings, including the family, the classroom and the workplace. This entry will examine some conversational research that has been undertaken in these settings.

Ng *et al.* (2000) compare conversations in European and Chinese families in New Zealand in terms of single- and multi-addressee turns. They find single-addressee turns are used more commonly in European (individualistic) than in Chinese (collectivistic) families, and vice versa for multi-addressee turns. Also examining family conversations, Tryggvason (2006) compares the amount of talk in Finnish, Swedish-Finnish, and Swedish families during mealtimes. She finds that Swedish families produce more talk and remarkably shorter and less frequent pauses. There is also a dominance of the mother across all the groups. Brumark (2006) analyzes dinner conversations and does not find any **gender** and age differences in the degree of non-observance of Gricean **maxims**. However, she finds quantitative differences in the distribution of different **contexts** in which maxims were not observed and in the types of non-observance.

Some studies focus on classroom talk (Seedhouse 2004). Richards (2006a: 51) concludes that 'conversation involving teacher and students in the classroom is indeed possible'. He observes different interactional patterns in teacher-fronted talk caused by shifts in the orientation to different aspects of identity. Huth and Taleghani-Nikazm (2006) argue in favour of using CA-informed instructional materials in **pragmatics** teaching, as they provide empirical evidence that captures pragmatics in its most natural locus: the conversational encounter. These materials describe 'systematic action sequences underlying verbal activities that display cross-cultural variation' (2006: 53).

Conversation analysis is also applied to other forms of interactive talk in, for example, 'professional and workplace settings', 'political speeches' and 'radio phone-in programmes' (Deborah 2001: 89). Holmes (2000) examines verbal **humour** in routine interactions within professional workplaces, using material recorded in four New Zealand government departments. Stubbe *et al.* (2003) examine a nine-minute audio recording of a spontaneous workplace interaction, and Vine (2004) explores the expression of **power** in a New Zealand workplace through examination of fifty-two everyday interactions between four women and their colleagues. Richards (2006b) analyzes how three different professional groups construct and reaffirm their group identities through the talk which constitutes their being at work. Mazeland (2004) examines telemarketers' telephone calls to solicit respondents' opinions about a product or service. Nevile (2004) studies transcriptions from video recordings of airline pilots at work on actual flights, and Nevile (2006) specifically examines some locations and the interactional significance of a feature of routine talk in the airline cockpit: *and*-prefaced turns. Based on tape recordings of the work of a London child counselling practice, Ian (2007) focuses on the increasing incitement to communicate in modern society, the growing recognition of children's social competence and agency, and the enablements and constraints of institutional forms of **discourse** participation.

WINNIE CHENG

See also: Context; conversation analysis; gender; humour; maxims of conversation; power; pragmatics; telephone conversation

Suggestions for further reading

Tsui, A.B.M. (1994) *English Conversation*, Oxford: Oxford University Press.
Warren, M. (2006) *Features of Naturalness in Conversation*, Amsterdam: John Benjamins.

Conversational Turn-Taking

Very early in the development of **conversation analysis** (CA) two analytic themes emerged as crucial in understanding the organization of spontaneous interactive talk: **sequence organization** and turn-taking. It was recognized that when people are 'in conversation' there is, most of the time, just one who is talking and that participants regularly take turns at speaking. In other words, **conversation** has two basic properties: 'one at a time' and 'speaker change recurs' (Sacks 1992, 2004). Episodes in which more than one person is speaking at a time are mostly brief, while transitions from one turn to the next tend to be smooth, with just a small gap or a slight overlap. To preserve these basic properties, participants in a conversation have to work continuously at it and demonstrate that they are oriented to these properties as normative requirements.

These early observations were elaborated analytically in what is probably the most influential and often quoted paper in CA, *A Simplest Systematics for the Organization of Turn Taking for Conversation* (Sacks *et al.* 1974). In order to study the distribution of 'turns', an economic problem of sorts, it was essential to conceptualize the 'unit' to be distributed, which Sacks *et al.* call a turn constructional unit (or TCU). TCUs can consist of various unit-types, such as a single word, a clause or a sentence. Right from their first word turns may offer clues as to when they may be possibly complete, for instance, by suggesting a type of constituent that is to follow later. In other words, turn completion is projectable, and at turn completion, the floor is open. Sacks *et al.* (1974) state that:

> As for the unit-types a speaker employs in starting the construction of a turn's talk, the speaker is initially entitled, in having a turn, to one such unit. The first possible completion of a first such unit constitutes an initial transition-relevance place. Transfer of speakership is coordinated by reference to such transition-relevance places, which any unit-type instance will reach.
>
> (1974: 703)

At each transition-relevance place (TRP), a change in speakership is possible, depending on what the participants decide to do. Sacks *et al.* suggest a hierarchy of possibilities, depending on the turn-allocation technique employed. If the present speaker has selected a next speaker, that speaker gets the turn. If that is not the case, any other participant may self-select by starting a next turn. And if that does not happen, the current speaker may continue. In other words, for conversation it is the case that who speaks next can be 'negotiated' by the participants at each TRP, at the end of each TCU. Of course, it is possible that in the course of a conversation, especially when there are more than three participants, the encounter is split into more than one conversation. When such a schism occurs, these rules apply to the separate conversations, not to the encounter as a whole (Egbert 1997a). Another kind of complication in turn-taking occurs when a participant needs more than one TCU to perform a conversational action, for instance, to tell a story or make a joke. Such an action may be prepared by a pre-sequence and closed by a punchline or conclusion which are all to be arranged locally (Houtkoop and Mazeland 1985; Sacks 1992, 1974; Goodwin 2002).

Turn-taking in conversation is, then, locally managed by the parties concerned on a turn-by-turn basis. In this respect, conversation is organized differently compared to many other speech exchange systems, in which turns or turn-types may be 'pre-allocated'. Sacks *et al.* (1974: 729) suggest that speech exchange systems could be 'with respect to their allocation arrangements, linearly arranged'. Conversation would represent one polar type of exchange system in which one turn is allocated at a time, while debates, for instance, might represent the other polar type in which there is full pre-allocation of turns. The general, although at times disputed, idea is that conversation represents a basic or 'original' system, while others are seen as more restricted variations on it. In any case, this contrast suggests a comparative analysis of speech exchange systems, which has indeed been taken up by later researchers. In interviews, for instance, the turn-type '**question**' is pre-allocated to one party, the interviewer, while the complementary type, 'answer', is reserved for the interviewee (Greatbatch 1988).

Returning to conversation, it should be clear that turn-taking negotiations can be quite complicated. The identification of a TRP is a disputable matter, both for participants and for analysts (Ford 2004). A speaker may add additional parts to an utterance that could already be heard as complete, so-called turn-increments (Schegloff 1996; Ford *et al.* 2002), leading to an overlap with the start of a next turn. A speaker may signal incompleteness of a turn by grammatical, intonational or pragmatic means – grammatical, by using an if-construction, for example; intonational, by avoiding a final

intonation; or pragmatic, by projecting an as yet incomplete conversational action (Ford and Thompson 1996).

As the original CA model of turn-taking 'predicts' the minimization of simultaneous speech, cases when it does occur provide an interesting challenge for the study of turn-taking. This challenge has been taken up by CA researchers, notably Gail Jefferson (1973, 1986, 2004a), Gene Lerner (1989, 1996b, 2002, 2004) and Emanuel Schegloff (1987, 2000). Not all occasions of simultaneous speech are problematic for the participants; that is, they are not all treated as serious deviations from the one-at-a-time rule or as 'interruptions'. And when they are problematic, the parties can use various ways of achieving 'overlap resolution' (Schegloff 2000).

The early work on turn-taking was based on data-sets that were limited in some respects. Charles Goodwin has started an extension of the study of the organization of face-to-face interaction, including turn-taking, by working with video recordings. This demonstrated the significance of visual cues, such as gaze direction or pointing, in the organization of turn transition (Goodwin 1979, 1980, 1981; Mondada 2007b). Another limitation of the early work was that it only discussed conversations in English. Later work on verbal interactions in other languages, such as Japanese, has demonstrated that different language systems provide their users with different possibilities to project TRPs (Tanaka 1999).

PAUL TEN HAVE

See also: Communication failure; conversation; conversation analysis; ethnomethodology; sequence organization; transcription

Suggestions for further reading

Ford, C.E. and Thompson, S.A. (1996) 'Interactional units in conversation: syntactic, intonational, and pragmatic resources for the management of turn', in E. Ochs, E.A. Schegloff and S.A. Thompson (eds) *Interaction and Grammar*, Cambridge: Cambridge University Press.

Sacks, H., Schegloff, E.A. and Jefferson, G. (1974) 'A simplest systematics for the organization of turn taking for conversation', *Language*, 50: 696–735.

Schegloff, E.A. (2000) 'Overlapping talk and the organization of turn-taking for conversation', *Language in Society*, 29: 1–63.

Conversation Analysis

The label 'conversation analysis' (CA) has become the usual way to indicate a quite specific approach to the analysis of interaction. It emerged in the 1960s in the work of Harvey Sacks (1935–75; *cf.* Sacks 1992) and his co-workers Emanuel Schegloff and Gail Jefferson. Their basic interest was sociological in nature and involved understanding social order. They were inspired by the sociological perspective of Erving Goffman and the **ethnomethodology** that was developed at the time by Harold Garfinkel. Conversation, or as it later came to be called 'talk-in-interaction', was chosen as a field to explore because the creation and maintenance of social order could be studied in detail by inspecting recordings of actual interactions. As it developed, CA was refined. It attracts a still growing number of practitioners, not only from sociology, but also from linguistics, anthropology, **communication** studies and psychology. Its original impetus and way of working has, however, remained essentially the same.

Although CA's interests can be formulated in general terms as procedural, it is essentially a data-driven endeavour. It starts with the collection of data. Researchers in CA work on audio or video recordings of interactions which are 'naturally occurring', which means that they are not arranged or provoked by the researcher, as in experiments or interviews. For 'pure CA', there are in principle, and often in practice, no further requirements or limitations. However, for specialized forms of 'applied CA' it makes sense to collect recordings of specific types of situations.

With repeated listening (and viewing in the case of video) the recordings are carefully transcribed, using a set of conventions developed by Gail Jefferson. Apart from representing the words-as-spoken, these **transcription** conventions allow the researcher to highlight a range of 'production details' such as timing and intonation, which have proven to be important for the organization of the interaction.

Listening to the recording and reading the transcript, the analyst tries to understand what the interactants are doing 'organizationally' when they speak and act as they do. They may, for instance, be requesting information, offering to tell a story or changing the **topic**. Such understandings will be based, at first, on the membership **knowledge** of the researcher who is, as one might say, a 'cultural colleague' of the speakers (ten Have 2002). The analyst will then check the sequential **context** and especially the uptake of the utterances in question in subsequent talk. This may be the utterance immediately following, which can be implying a particular understanding, or an action later in the **conversation**, such as granting a **request**. Such uptakes may prove or disprove an analyst's understanding (Sacks at al. 1974: 728).

Understanding the actions is not, however, the purpose of the research, but a prerequisite for the next step, which is to formulate the procedures used to accomplish (and understand) the actions-as-understood. The ultimate aim of CA research is to analyze what Schegloff (1992: 1338) has called the 'procedural infrastructure of interaction' and, in particular, the practices of talking in interaction. This means that conversational practices are not analyzed in terms of individual properties or institutional expectations, but as situated accomplishments.

It is often recommended that the researcher approaches data with an open mind, that is, without pre-formulated interests, questions or hypotheses (except the general organizational and procedural orientation). The idea is that inspecting the data in this way will raise an interest in the researcher's mind which can be used as a starting point for a more systematic exploration of an emerging analytic theme. The researcher searches the available data for instances that seem to be similar to the 'candidate phenomenon' that inspired the first formulation of the theme, as well as data that seem to point in a different direction, the so-called deviant case analysis. It may also be useful to collect new data to expand the analysis. In short, the researcher builds a collection of relevant cases in search of patterns that help to elucidate some procedural issues (ten Have 2007: 117–69).

The general idea is that participants, through the way in which they design their utterances, perform understandable actions, which show how they connect (or not) to what went before and/or what could go afterwards. In their utterance design, speakers project when their turn may be finished, so that another speaker may take a turn. This is known as **conversational turn taking** (Sacks *et al.* 1974). By indicating connections between turns, speakers create more or less coherent sequences of turns. This is called **sequence organization** and involves a pair-structure such as **questions** being followed by answers (technically known as 'adjacency pairs'), which through various extensions may be the building blocks of more complex sequential structures (Schegloff 2007). A particular type of sequence, known as a 'repair sequence', deals with problems of understanding that are created by a previous utterance (Schegloff 1992, 2007: 100–106). When designing their turns, speakers often have a choice between typical alternatives, for instance, between accepting or refusing an invitation. These alternatives are unequally valued, and are therefore constructed in a different manner. Turns that are somehow positive, for instance accepting the invitation (a 'preferred' response), tend to be constructed differently from negative, 'dispreferred' turns. Utterances of the first type tend to come fast and be relatively short, while the latter are mostly delayed and more elaborate, with various prefaces and explanations (Atkinson and Heritage 1984: 53–163; Schegloff 2007: 58–96).

On these and other matters, CA research has produced a range of insights into the organization of talk-in-interaction that can be 'applied' to an enormous variety of social situations in which talking together plays an essential role. A few of these situations that have been researched extensively include doctor–patient consultations, news interviews, police interrogations, court sessions, school settings, research interviews, the talk of pilots in airline cockpits, and emergency calls (Boden and Zimmerman 1991; Drew and Heritage 1992; ten Have 2007: 173–212). Researchers using video have extended the analysis of talk-in-interaction to include visual aspects such as gaze, gesture, body posture and the use of various material artefacts (Goodwin 2000b). This extension has been most fruitful in the study of work practices in technologically complex environments, so-called 'workplace studies' (Heath and Luff 2000). CA has also been used to elucidate problems and solutions in the interaction with communicatively impaired persons (Goodwin 2003). Linguists have used CA to throw new light on properties of language-as-spoken, in contrast to language-as-written, as well as on the ways in which properties of various languages have an impact on the way in which talk using such languages gets organized (Ochs *et al.* 1996; Ford *et al.* 2002). For some social psychologists, CA has become a major influence in what they call 'discursive psychology' (Wooffitt 2005).

In all these branches and applications, the original methods developed by Sacks and his co-workers in the 1960s are still being fruitfully used.

PAUL TEN HAVE

See also: Assessment, pragmatic; communication failure; conversation; conversational turn-taking; ethnomethodology; sequence organization; transcription

Suggestions for further reading

Hutchby, I. and Wooffitt, R. (1998) *Conversation Analysis: Principles, Practices and Applications*, Cambridge: Polity Press.
Sacks, H. (1992) *Lectures on Conversation*, I and II, ed. G. Jefferson, Oxford: Blackwell.
ten Have, P. (2007) *Doing Conversation Analysis: A Practical Guide*, 2nd edn, London: Sage.

Cooperative Principle

It is no exaggeration to say that the work of philosopher of language H. Paul **Grice** has been some of the most influential in the development of modern **pragmatics**. During his life, Grice explored a range of topics (*see* Grice 1989, 2001a, 2001b) but he is probably best remembered (certainly by those working within pragmatics) for his theory of **conversation** (*see* Neale 1992), first presented in the William James Lectures delivered at Harvard in 1967. The cooperative principle was central to this theory.

During his time at Oxford, Grice had become heavily influenced by a movement known as **ordinary language philosophy**, a movement led by **speech act** theorist John **Austin** (*see* Austin 1962). Ordinary language philosophers opposed the idealized language philosophy of 'formalists' (Grice 1967: lecture II, 1) such as Russell and Frege, and thought the two views could never be reconciled. Grice saw no reason why the two approaches could not co-exist. Whilst formalists were engaged in the study of linguistic meaning or **semantics**, Grice suggested that what 'informalists' (Grice 1967: lecture II, 1) were interested in was the study of speaker meaning or pragmatics. The semantics-pragmatics distinction as we know it today was born.

By way of introducing his cooperative principle, Grice began with a characterization of his notion of **implicature**. Cases of implicature are among the clearest cases of the **semantics-pragmatics interface** or **explicit/implicit distinction** in action, cases in which (in intuitive terms) a speaker *says* one thing, but *means* something over above and above the words they have said. Consider the exchange in (1) below. Peter, Mary and John share an apartment:

(1) Peter: Is John asleep yet?
    Mary: His light is on and I can hear music.

Mary's response to Peter's **question** is at best indirect. He has asked her a specific question about John, and rather than answer him directly with a yes or no, she has responded with information about the light in John's room and some music she can hear. However, most of us, even in the absence of any form of extended **context**, share an intuition that Mary has implied – or 'implicated', to use Grice's technical term – that John has not gone to bed yet. This would be the likely implicature Peter arrives at.

Grice wanted to explain how it is that such **inferences** are so frequently and easily made by hearers. This broader question devolves into two related questions: first, why does Peter assume that there *is* an extra layer of **meaning** to be inferred from Mary's utterance? Second, if there is an extra layer of meaning, how does he go about deriving it?

Grice's idea was this. **Communication** is a cooperative activity, and when two or more people are communicating, it is in both their interests to make the communication go as smoothly as possible in order to achieve their mutual aim. Because communication is cooperative, speakers behave in certain predictable ways. In general, for instance, a speaker is not going to say something that is totally irrelevant, or that will not tell the hearer what he wants to know. Grice put it like this:

> Our talk exchanges do not normally consist of a succession of disconnected remarks, and would not be rational if they did. They are characteristically, to some degree at least cooperative efforts; and each participant recognises in them, to some extent, a common purpose or set of purposes, or at least a mutually accepted direction. ... We might then formulate a rough general principle which participants will be expected (*ceteris paribus*) to observe, *viz*: 'Make your conversational contribution such as is required, at the stage at which it occurs, by the accepted purpose or direction of the talk-exchange in which you are engaged'. One might label this the Cooperative Principle.
> (Grice 1967: lecture II, 6; 1989: 26)

Returning to the exchange in (1), then, the answer to the first question (why does Peter go beyond what Mary has said?) is that if all Mary was trying to convey was that the light is still on in John's room, and that there is music coming from there, she would not be providing him with an answer to his question. It wouldn't be relevant to him because what he wants to know is whether or not John has gone to sleep yet. However, the assumption that speakers obey the cooperative principle when they speak is so strong that Peter just won't accept that Mary is being uncooperative. Instead, he will look around and see if there's any way he can reconcile what she has said with the assumption that she *is* being cooperative.

As far as the second question goes (how is the extra layer of meaning derived?), the search is again guided by the cooperative principle. Peter knows that a cooperative speaker would be saying something that was a response to his question, and he therefore asks himself how Mary's utterance might be understood as an answer to his question. He will put together what Mary has said with other pieces of information he has (and which Mary knows he has) and generate an inference along the following lines:

Mary has said: The light in John's room is still on, and she can hear music.

Peter knows that: If the lights are on in John's room, and there is music coming from his room too, the likelihood is that John hasn't gone to sleep yet.

Therefore: John hasn't gone to sleep yet.

(Implicature of Mary's utterance)

Hearers use Grice's cooperative principle as a basis for making the assumption that speakers are behaving cooperatively, and this is a key part of the process of **utterance interpretation**. They use it, in other words, as a premise in a process of logical **reasoning** or inference. Indeed, the model of communication Grice proposed was the first workable alternative to the code model of communication, which had been in place since the work of Aristotle (*see* Sperber and Wilson 1995). What Grice was suggesting was that human communication is a rational, inferential activity, rather than a simple process of coding and decoding.

But Grice's insight raises as many questions as it answers. What are these predictable ways in which cooperative speakers behave? What counts as being cooperative? Grice's answer to this question is that the cooperative principle can be broken down into a number of different **maxims of conversation**. These are the focus of a separate entry.

TIM WHARTON

See also: Austin, J.; conversation; explicit/implicit distinction; history of pragmatics; implicature; meaning; natural and non-natural meaning; neo-Gricean pragmatics; ordinary language philosophy; philosophy of language; post-Gricean pragmatics; pragmatics; radical pragmatics; rationality; reasoning; semantics-pragmatics interface; utterance interpretation; what is said

Suggestions for further reading

Grice, H.P. (1989) *Studies in the Way of Words*, Cambridge, MA: Harvard University Press. Chapter 2.

Neale, S. (1992) 'Paul Grice and the philosophy of language', *Linguistics and Philosophy*, 15: 509–59.

Corpus Linguistics

Different from traditional linguistics, corpus linguistics is the systematic study of authentic examples of language in use through observation of language evidence in corpora (Tognini-Bonelli 2001). As Sinclair (1991: 4) remarks, the 'ability to examine large text corpora in a systematic manner allows access to a quality of evidence that has not been available before'. Corpus linguistics, according to Halliday (1993), reunites the activities of data gathering and theorizing which leads to a qualitative change in our understanding of language. Corpus linguistics is about 'meaning, with symbolic content. People are not interested in grammatical constructions; they want to know the meaning of what has been said' (Teubert and Krishnamurthy 2007: 9). The two main approaches to corpus studies are the deductive, 'corpus-based' approach, i.e. 'a methodology that uses corpus evidence mainly as a repository of examples to expound, test or exemplify given theoretical statements' (Tognini-Bonelli 2001: 10), and the inductive, 'corpus-driven' approach, i.e. 'a "bottom-up" study of the language' (ibid.: 14).

Corpus linguistics dates back to the late nineteenth century with the compilation of the *Oxford English Dictionary* by means of the collection of an enormous number of slips containing authentic examples of language in use. The beginning of corpus linguistics proper was in the late 1950s and early 1960s when Randolph Quirk announced his plan to start a Survey of English Usage of both written and spoken English (Tognini-Bonelli 2001: 52). The corpus was, however, not computerized because 50 per cent of it is spoken language.

With the advent of new technologies such as digital computers, electronic databases can be scanned on CD-ROM and accessed remotely, and large amounts of data can be assembled from the Web, stored, processed and systematized in real time (Tognini-Bonelli 2001: 5–6). Software packages such as *WordSmith Tools* (Scott 2004), *ParaConc and Monoconc Pro* (Barlow 2000), *ConcApp* (Greaves 2000), *Concordance 3.2* (Watt 2004), *TextSTAT* (Hüning 2007), and *ConcGram* (Cheng *et al.* 2006) interrogate corpora and perform the main functions of selecting, sorting, matching, counting and calculating (Hunston and Francis 2000: 15). Main methods of corpus-based analysis are word lists, concordances, collocations and keywords, with keywords referring to those words 'whose frequency is unusually high in comparison with some norm' in a reference corpus, as defined by (Scott 2004) in the Wordsmith Tools program.

Sinclair (2005: 19) defines a corpus as 'a collection of pieces of language text in electronic form, selected according to external criteria to represent, as far as possible, a language or language variety as a source of data for linguistic research'. He describes ten basic principles of developing linguistic corpora: purpose and use of corpus, orientation, criteria, sampling, representativeness, balance, **topic**, size, and homogeneity (Sinclair 2005: 1–6).

Corpora come in many types, for example, specialized corpus, general-purpose corpus, multilingual corpora, comparable corpora, parallel corpora, free-translation corpus, learner corpus, pedagogic corpus, historical or diachronic corpus, monitor corpus, and the Internet as corpus (*see* Hunston 2002; Tognini-Bonelli 2001). The world's two largest monitor corpora in the United Kingdom are the Bank of English (over 550 million words) and the British National Corpus (BNC; 100 million words of which 90 per cent are written and 10 per cent are spoken). In America, the American National Corpus (ANC) is being developed to parallel the general structure of the BNC, while adding genres like blogging and instant messaging that did not exist when the BNC was created. The world's best known diachronic corpus is the Helsinki Corpus of English Texts, containing Old English 750–1150 AD (413,250 words), Middle English 1150–1500 AD (608,570 words)

and Early Modern English 1500–1710 AD (551,000 words). The one-million-word Hong Kong Corpus of Spoken English (prosodic) (Cheng *et al.* 2005) is the first prosodically transcribed corpus using Brazil's (1997) discourse intonation systems. Regarding the size of the World Wide Web as a 'corpus', Gulli and Signorini (2005) suggest that the indexable web is more than 11.5 billion pages.

Many electronic corpora are annotated with interpretative, linguistic information (Leech 1997: 2). Gu (2006: 148) discusses the 'objective versus subjective tension in any corpus segmentation and annotation'. Different ways of annotating a corpus include part-of-speech (POS) tagging, syntactic parsing (e.g. one-million-word Lancaster-Oslo/Bergen (LOB) Corpus 1961), semantic annotation (e.g. McEnery and Wilson 1996), pragmatic annotation, phonetic annotation, prosodic annotation (e.g. Cheng *et al.* 2005), sentence alignment in parallel corpora, and error annotation in learner corpora (e.g. Granger and Rayson 1998).

Corpora can be used in a number of ways. They include the tracking of changes in the target language, the production of dictionaries and other reference materials, the development of aids to translation, language teaching materials, the investigation of ideologies and cultural assumptions, the study of all aspects of linguistic behaviour (including vocabulary, grammar, **discourse**, **pragmatics** and discourse intonation), the study of register variation and natural language processing.

An increasing number of studies has explored the extent of phraseology in the English language, for instance, extended units of **meaning** or extended lexical items, pattern grammar, phraseology, lexical bundles, lexical phrases, clusters, and phrasal constructions (see, for example, Biber *et al.* 1998, 1999, 2004; Carter and McCarthy 2006; Cheng 2008; Clear 1993; Cowie 1998; Halliday *et al.* 2002; Hoey 2005; Hunston 2002; Hunston and Francis 2000; Partington 1998; Sinclair 1987c, 1996, 2004a, 2004b; Stubbs 1995, 2001, 2005; Teubert 2005).

This growth in corpus linguistics has resulted in the development of new language learning and teaching methodologies (e.g. Burnard and McEnery 2000; Ghadessy *et al.* 2001; Granger 1998; Hunston 1995, 2002), particularly the use of corpora in the learning and teaching of English as a second language (e.g. Cheng *et al.* 2005; Flowerdew 1998; Hunston 2002; Johns 1991, 2002; Thurstun and Candlin 1998). Leech (1997) discusses three relations between corpora and teaching: teach about corpora, exploit corpora to teach, and teach to exploit corpora. Nevertheless, as remarked by Tribble (2008: 214),

> although all the major ELT publishers have their state-of-the-art corpora, although the results of corpus research permeate every modern dictionary and grammar reference book, when it comes to the classroom, Sinclair's (1991) vision of most students and teachers happily interrogating the corpus to push learning forward has not yet been realized.

WINNIE CHENG

See also: Discourse; internet language; meaning; pragmatics; prosody and pragmatics; topic

Suggestions for further reading

O'Keefe, A., McCarthy, M. and Carter, R. (2007) *From Corpus to Classroom: Language Use and Language Teaching*, Cambridge: Cambridge University Press.

Thompson, G. and Hunston, S. (eds) (2006) *System and Corpus: Exploring Connections*, London and Oakville, CT: Equinox.

Tribble, C. and Scott, M. (2006) *Textual Patterns: Key Words and Corpus Analysis in Language Education*, Amsterdam and Philadelphia, PA: John Benjamins.

Cross-Cultural Pragmatics

Kraft and Geluykens (2007: 3) suggest viewing cross-cultural pragmatics (CCP) 'as a cover term delineating an independent field within pragmatic research'. The term subsumes four distinct research strands, namely, constrastive pragmatics (CoP), intercultural pragmatics (ICP), a combination of CoP and **interlanguage pragmatics** (ILP), and a combination of ICP and ILP (2007: 10). In the same volume, Geluykens (2007: 21) examines the methodology of CCP and suggests four ways of expanding the

scope and objectives of cross-cultural pragmatics: (a) defining more clearly the domain of operation of CCP and ILP; (b) broadening the scope of research objects in CCP beyond **speech acts** as realizations of face-threatening acts to include pragmalinguisitc phenomena such as the use of syntactic and prosodic resources 'in **discourse** organization, and interactional phenomena such as turn-taking and other patterns of conversational sequences'; (c) increasingly using authentic production and contextualized verbal exchanges while continuing with experimental and quasi-experimental, controlled elicitation through discourse completion tests (DCTs); and (d) integrating qualitative and quantitative methodologies within single research programmes.

More than twenty years ago, Tannen (1984b: 189) discussed and exemplified eight aspects of the **pragmatics** of cross-cultural communication which are 'the essence of language', namely, when to speak, what to say, pacing and pausing, listenership, intonation, formulaicity, indirectness, and cohesion and coherence. Following Fishman's (1972a) notion of 'domains' of day-to-day language use, Boxer (2002: 153) reviews research in the three domains that are most relevant to cross-cultural pragmatics, namely, 'the spheres of social interaction, educational encounters, and work life'. Cross-cultural pragmatics views cross-cultural communication as individuals from different societies or communities interacting according to their own pragmatic norms, often resulting in a clash of expectations and, typically, two-way misperceptions about each other (Boxer 2002: 150). Cross-cultural pragmatics research can help ameliorate stereotypes, prejudice, and discrimination that are commonplace consequences of increasing cross-cultural interaction (2002: 150).

Many studies of cross-cultural pragmatics have accounted for their results by drawing upon pragmatic **maxims**, e.g. **Grice**'s (1975) universal **cooperative principle** and its four conversational maxims, and culture-specific maxims such as Leech's (1983) **politeness** principle and six maxims and Gu's (1990) set of politeness maxims. As discussed by Spencer-Oatey and Jiang (2003: 11), Leech's (1983) politeness maxims are criticized because first, the formulation of maxims does not stipulate a motivated way of restricting the number of maxims (Brown and Levinson 1987; Fraser 1990; Thomas 1995); second, the politeness maxims function at a more superficial level than, and are therefore easily undermined by, the cooperative maxims (Brown and Levinson 1987); and third, the valences of the politeness maxims are indeed culture-specific (Spencer-Oatey 2000). Spencer-Oatey and Jiang (2003) argue that **culture**, rather than pragmatic maxims, should be used as an explanatory variable in cross-cultural pragmatics, and that the politeness maxims (Leech 1983) and 'interactive constraints' (Kim 1994; Kim *et al.* 1994: 119) should be reconceptualized as sociopragmatic interactional principles (SIPs). SIP is defined as 'socioculturally-based principles, scalar in nature, that guide or influence people's productive and interpretive use of language' (Spencer-Oatey and Jiang 2003: 11). Unlike maxims which stipulate desirable versus undesirable ends of a dimension, the 'scalar' characteristic of SIP concurs with House's (2000) dimensions of cultural differences and Wierzbicka's (1985) cultural values. Spencer-Oatey and Jiang (2003: 12) suggest that the fundamental SIPs help manage people's basic interactional motivations and include concerns about face, rights and obligations, and task achievement. The secondary SIPs reflect people's stylistic concerns, such as their concerns about directness/indirectness, cordiality/restraint, modesty/approbation, and routinization/novelty. In their study of the requesting behaviour of their Chinese and British university students, Spencer-Oatey and Jiang find that the relative importance of SIPs varies across interactional situations, and that SIPs are subject to cross-cultural variation, particularly the influential factor of 'national culture'. They also find that the motivating factor of 'sociality rights' (Spencer-Oatey 2000) underlies relations management.

Previous studies of cross-cultural pragmatics discuss communicative **misunderstanding** against the background of cultural differences expressed in rules of speaking, for example, thanking, requesting, complimenting, and so on. For instance, Kim (1994) compares the requesting behaviour among Korean, mainland US and Hawaiin US respondents, with reference to five conversational constraints that she proposes, drawing on theorizing in pragmatics and

communication studies. The constraints are concern to avoid hurting the hearer's feelings, concern to avoid imposition, concern to avoid negative evaluation by the hearer, concern for clarity, and concern for effectiveness. Kim's study is, nevertheless, criticized for not reporting factor analyses to show whether the five concerns were in operation (Spencer-Oatey and Jiang 2003: 11).

In cross-cultural speech act research, **requests** and **apologies** initiated in Blum-Kulka *et al.*'s (1989) cross-cultural speech act realization project (CCSARP) are considered the most frequently studied speech acts in the past two decades (Harris *et al.* 2006). For instance, Beebe *et al.* (1990) investigate cross-cultural variation in the speech acts of requests, **refusals** and apologies between Japanese and native English speakers. Other investigators have discussed cross-cultural variation in the form and strategic functions of apologies in terms of underlying cultural attitudes (e.g. Obeng 1999; Suszczynska 1999; Okamura and Wei 2000), and in requests in English e-mails written by Chinese English learners and native American English speakers (Chang and Hsu 1998). Chang and Hsu (1998) find that native American English speakers consider e-mail communication to be closer to written memos, and structure their e-mail request messages in a rather direct sequence. However, they employ more indirect linguistic forms to express their requests. The Chinese English learners are found to treat e-mail communication as either formal letters or **telephone conversations**. They structure their e-mail request messages in an indirect sequence, but they use more direct linguistic forms to express their requests (1998: 121).

Zhang (1995) shows that in modern Chinese **conversation**, direct requests may vary in degree of indirectness, and identifies nine request strategies that range from the most direct imperative to the most moderated. Contrary to Zhang's findings, Beamer (2003) illustrates how Chinese writers used directness in 115 extant English-language business letters to Jardine, Matheson & Company Ltd. in the nineteenth century. Beamer (2003: 201) suggests that 'indirectness in the organization of the message served to establish an informational **context** whereas directness served to signal a strong proximity dimension in the relationship between the correspondents'. Beamer also made a cursory examination of some letters written by British correspondents to the same company in the nineteenth century and finds 'much more indirectness through internal linguistic supporting moves than [in] Chinese-authored letters' (2003: 234).

Other cross-cultural speech act studies have focused on, for example, refusals, **compliments** and compliment responses, thanking, apologies (e.g. Ogiermann 2007), and **complaints** (Geluykens and Kraft 2007). Nelson *et al.* (2002) report on the study of strategy use in Egyptian and American English refusals. Nelson *et al.* (1996) investigated similarities and differences between Arabic Syrian and American English compliment responses. Results show that both Syrians and Americans are more likely to accept or mitigate the force of the compliment than to reject it. Both groups used similar response types, but the Americans employed more appreciation tokens and Syrians used 'acceptance + formula' which was not used by the Americans (1996: 411). An example of the Syrians' 'acceptance + formula' is *m'addame*, '[It is] presented [to you]' (Nelson *et al.* 1996: 425). Investigating the speech act of thanking, Aston (1995: 57) compares the use of thanks in the closings of English and Italian service encounters and finds that differences can be attributed both to preferred procedures of conversational management and to perceptions of the overall situation or cultural ethos. Similarly, on thanking, Hassall (2001: 97) finds that in interactive role-plays, Australian learners of Indonesian thank very consistently probably due to pragmatic transfer from their first language combined with influence from formal instruction, and that Indonesian native speakers also thank frequently showing a 'weakening of traditional cultural values'. Hassall concludes that changing values in developing countries may lead to the adoption of speech act behaviour that increasingly converges with Western pragmatic norms.

Cross-cultural pragmatics research has begun to explore the spheres of 'work life' (Boxer 2002: 153). Jiang (2006) examined the request and refusal strategies in the question-response sequences of interactions in routine press conferences held by the Ministry of Foreign Affairs of China

and the US Department of State on the **topic** of the North Korea nuclear crisis during a period of months. Jiang found that both US and Chinese press conferences adopted the strategy of making requests for specific information. However, the US press conferences used more clarification and confirmation **questions**, while the Chinese conferences asked more questions for comments. Also, the US conferences used more direct refusals and provided reasons for refusal, whereas the Chinese conferences evidenced a lot of avoidance and provided insufficient answers (2006: 237).

Apart from business and professional contexts, much cross-cultural pragmatics research has focused on teaching and learning. For example, Jones (1995) conducted pragmatic research into two small-group academic discussions, one between a group of Australian students and the other among a group of Vietnamese students who spoke English. Jones did not find many differences between these groups in terms of managing conversation and concluded that 'the international [Vietnamese] students have a potential for active and equal participation in small-group academic discussion' (1995: 44). LoCastro (1997) finds a noticeable absence of politeness in the learning materials Japanese students use in secondary school EFL, which has had a negative impact on their use of politeness markers in their expression of desires and wants in English. LoCastro observes that this absence has created discomfort among some native speakers of English. Takimoto (2006) finds that in teaching English polite requestive forms to Japanese learners, giving explicit reactive feedback after the structure input task enhances the students' pragmatic proficiency. Intachakra (2004: 37) investigated apologies and thanks in English and Thai, paying particular attention to the way in which cross-cultural pragmatics can contribute to language teaching and curriculum development.

Recently in Hong Kong, Cheng and Warren conducted a series of research studies that compared the teaching of various speech acts in the textbooks of senior forms, in the Hong Kong Corpus of Spoken English (HKCSE), and reference corpora such as the British National Corpus (BNC) and the Bank of English. The speech acts examined are **disagreement** (Cheng and Warren 2005), giving an opinion

(Cheng and Warren 2006), and checking understanding (Cheng and Warren 2007). Their studies recommend that both textbook writers and teachers need to employ authentic, naturally occurring spoken corpus data as a resource for both the forms and functions of speech acts. Other authors (e.g. Bardovi-Harlig and Hardford 1996; Bardovi-Harlig and Dörnyei 1998) conclude that it is essential to teach appropriate L2 pragmatic realization patterns of a speech act.

Ishida (2006: 1943) suggests that cross-cultural pragmatics research has tended to prefer 'the investigation of production strategies (i.e., what we say to whom in certain situations)' over 'receptive strategies (i.e., what we hear and how we interpret it)'. He investigates the receptive strategies, i.e. the perception and interpretation of contextualization cues (Gumperz 1982a), used by both the Japanese and English learners of Japanese in interpreting the back-channel cue 'uun' (*yeah, I see*). The study finds that the Japanese subjects interpret the use of brief cues such as 'uun', together with a distinct head nod, as 'sympathetic, attentive, kind' (Ishida 2006: 1972). This is not shared by the Japanese learners, who tend to make verbal comments to show their attentiveness. In addition, the Japanese back-channel cues, which are intended simply to signal listening or understanding, are often misinterpreted by English speakers as agreement (2006: 1972).

WINNIE CHENG

See also: Apologies; communication; complaints; compliments; context; conversation; cooperative principle; culture; disagreement; discourse; Grice, H.P.; interlanguage pragmatics; maxims of conversation; misunderstanding; politeness; pragmatics; question; refusals; request; speech act type; telephone conversation

Suggestions for further reading

Kraft, B. and Geluykens, R. (eds) (2007) *Cross-Cultural Pragmatics and Interlanguage English*, Munich: Lincom Europa.
Pütz, M. and Neff-van Aertselaer, J. (eds) (2008) *Developing Contrastive Pragmatics: Interlanguage and Cross-Cultural Perspectives*, Berlin and New York: Mouton de Gruyter.

Cultural Scripts
Cultural scripts and 'NSM' semantics

The theory of 'cultural scripts' is an offshoot of 'NSM' semantics. 'NSM' stands for 'Natural Semantic Metalanguage' – a metalanguage for explaining and comparing **meanings** and ideas across languages and **cultures**. NSM is a minilanguage which lies at the heart of all languages as their lexical and grammatical common core. Unlike full-blown natural languages, NSM is 'culture-free' and thus can be used as a neutral metalanguage for describing languages and cultures. Unlike formalisms used in many other contemporary approaches to **semantics** and **pragmatics**, NSM is based on natural languages and can be understood directly through natural language – any natural language.

The lexicon of NSM comprises 63 universal semantic primes, that is, elements which, evidence shows, surface as words or distinct word meanings in all languages and in terms of which all other meanings can be explained. A full list of these meanings (sometimes realized through bound morphemes rather than words) is given in Table 1. The grammar of these elements, which is described in detail in Goddard and Wierzbicka (2002), corresponds to the shared grammatical core of all natural languages.

Primes exist as the meanings of lexical units, not at the level of lexemes. Exponents of primes may be words, bound morphemes, or short phrases (e.g. A LONG TIME). They can be formally complex and can have different morphosyntactic properties, including word class, in different languages. They can have combinatorial variants (allolexes, e.g. SOMETHING/THING). Each prime has well specified syntactic (combinatorial) properties. Two or more primes can share the same lexical exponent with different syntactic properties.

Cultural norms and cultural scripts

The term 'cultural script', first introduced in Wierzbicka (1991), stands for a cultural norm articulated in the mini-language of universal human concepts, that is, in NSM. Both the term and analytical techniques associated with it have been used over the last two decades in a large body of works devoted to languages

Table 1 NSM's sixty-three universal semantic primes

Substantives:	I, YOU, SOMEONE, SOMETHING/THING, PEOPLE, BODY
Taxonomy, Partonomy:	KIND, PART
Determiners:	THIS, THE SAME, OTHER/ELSE
Quantifiers:	ONE, TWO, MUCH/MANY, SOME, ALL
Evaluators:	GOOD, BAD
Descriptors:	BIG, SMALL
Mental predicates:	THINK, KNOW, WANT, FEEL, SEE, HEAR
Speech:	SAY, WORDS, TRUE
Action, events, movement, contact:	DO, HAPPEN, MOVE, TOUCH
Location, existence, possession, specification:	BE (SOMEWHERE), THERE IS/EXIST, HAVE, BE (SOMEONE/SOMETHING)
Life and death:	LIVE, DIE
Time:	WHEN/TIME, NOW, BEFORE, AFTER, A LONG TIME, A SHORT TIME, FOR SOME TIME, MOMENT
Space:	WHERE/PLACE, HERE, ABOVE, BELOW, FAR, NEAR, SIDE, INSIDE
Logical concepts:	NOT, MAYBE, CAN, BECAUSE, IF
Augmentor, intensifier:	MORE, VERY
Similarity:	LIKE

[entry: Cultural Scripts, folio 203]

and cultures as diverse as English (in several varieties), Chinese, Ewe, French, German, Japanese, Korean, Malay, Polish, Russian, Spanish, Yankunytjatjara (*see*, inter alia, Goddard 1997, 2000; Goddard and Wierzbicka 2004; Wierzbicka 1996, 1998, 2002, 2006a, 2006b; Wong 2004).

The term 'cultural script' is used in a few of distinct but closely related senses. First, it is used to refer to cultural norms themselves, if these norms are seen from the point of view of cultural insiders and if they can be articulated in simple words familiar to native speakers and readily translatable into other languages. Second, it is used with reference to formulae which articulate such norms in the highly constrained mini-language of universal semantic primes (NSM). Third, the plural form 'cultural scripts' is used as the name of the technique for articulating cultural norms, values and practices using the natural semantic metalanguage of semantic primes as a medium of description.

Cultural scripts and cross-cultural communication

Cultural scripts exist at different levels of generality and may relate to different aspects of thinking, speaking, and behaviour. High-level scripts, which are sometimes called 'master scripts', are often closely associated with core cultural values. They articulate broad cultural themes which are typically played out in detail by way of whole families of related speech practices, which themselves can be captured by means of more specific scripts.

Script [A], which is regarded as a master script of Anglo culture, expresses a cultural preference for something like 'personal autonomy' (Wierzbicka 2003, 2006a; Goddard 2006):

> [A] *An Anglo script connected with 'personal autonomy'*
> people think like this:
> when someone does something it is good if this someone can think like this:
> 'I am doing this because I want to do it'

Two other scripts, also linked with the widespread Anglo distaste for abrupt directives, are scripts [B] and [C]:

> [B] *An Anglo cultural script against 'telling people what to do'*
> people think like this:
> when I want someone to do something I can't say something like this:
> 'I want you to do it, because of this you have to do it'

[C] *An Anglo cultural script for avoiding over-confident directives*
people think like this:
when I want someone to do something it will not be good if I say something like this to this someone:
'I want you to do it, I think that you will do it because of this'

The avoidance of direct or 'bare' imperatives ('Do this!') and the abundance of alternative strategies (such as so-called 'whimperatives', e.g. 'Could you/would you do X?') for conveying one's wishes flow directly from these cultural scripts. As argued in detail in Wierzbicka (2006a, 2006b), the avoidance of the imperative in modern English and the development of an extended class of interrogative directives is a linguistic phenomenon whose cultural and linguistic significance can hardly be overestimated. It is a phenomenon which should be the subject of the first lesson in acculturation taught to every migrant to an English-speaking country.

Other Anglo cultural scripts which can cause a great deal of friction and cultural miscommunication between 'Anglos' and immigrants from non-English-speaking societies have to do with Anglo values such as 'tact' and 'not hurting people's feelings', as against values such as *iskrennost* (Russian, roughly, 'frankness' and 'sincerity') which are central to Russian culture. They include scripts [D] and [E] (Wierzbicka 2002, 2008):

[D] *An Anglo cultural script against criticizing the addressee unnecessarily*
people think like this:
it will be bad if I say to someone something bad about this someone if I don't have to say it

[E] *An Anglo script against 'blurting out' one's negative thoughts about the addressee*
people think like this:
if I think something bad about someone when I am with this someone it will be bad if I say it to this someone if I haven't thought about it for some time before I say it

Such Anglo scripts clash with, for example, Russian and Ukrainian scripts such as [F] and [G] (Wierzbicka 2002, 2008):

[F] *A Russian cultural script for 'expressiveness'*
people think like this:
it is good if someone wants other people to know what this someone thinks
it is good if someone wants other people to know what this someone feels

[G] *A Ukrainian (and Russian) script for telling the addressee what one thinks about them*
people think like this:
if I think something bad about someone when I am with this someone it can be good if I say this to this someone

'Cultural scripts' as an alternative to 'universal pragmatics'

The theory of cultural scripts offers an alternative to the 'universal pragmatics' paradigm, the three leading branches of which are: (1) Gricean and **neo-Gricean pragmatics**, (2) the 'politeness theory' launched by Brown and Levinson (1978), and (3) the contrastive pragmatics of Blum-Kulka and colleagues (e.g. Blum-Kulka and Kasper 1993). All these approaches to pragmatics assume some universal models of communicative behaviour: universal principles and **maxims of conversation**, a universal model of positive and negative face need, and a universal inventory of **speech act types**.

According to NSM semantics, however, it is increasingly evident that all these universalist approaches to pragmatics are Anglocentric, because they adopt some Anglo practices and norms as baseline, and some English concepts (e.g. '**politeness**', 'relevance', 'face', '**request**', '**compliment**') as basic analytical and descriptive tools. This means, in effect, imposing on other cultures a perspective which is alien to the people concerned.

By contrast, the theory of cultural scripts allows the researcher to adopt the insider's perspective on a culture's values and norms, and to articulate them in a language that is accessible to the speakers themselves, rather than in a foreign language and a foreign conceptual system. At the same time, it enables the practitioner of the 'cultural scripts' pragmatics to build bridges between people from different linguistic and cultural backgrounds.

Conclusion

As discussed in detail in publications such as Goddard and Wierzbicka (2004), the accessibility and transparency of cultural scripts written in semantic primes gives them a huge advantage over technical modes of description when it comes to real-world situations of trying to bridge some kind of cultural gap with immigrants, language-learners, in international negotiations, or whatever. Because cultural scripts 'interface' more or less directly with simple ordinary language – in any language – they can not only throw a great deal of light on **social cognition** and cross-cultural differences in norms, values and practices, but they can also be practically useful for the purposes of cross-cultural education and **intercultural communication**.

ANNA WIERZBICKA

See also: Cross-cultural pragmatics; culture; interlanguage pragmatics; neo-Gricean pragmatics; politeness

Suggestions for further reading

Goddard, C. (ed.) (2006) *Ethnopragmatics: Understanding Discourse in Cultural Context*, Berlin: Mouton de Gruyter.
Goddard, C. and Wierzbicka, A. (eds) (2004) 'Cultural scripts', *Intercultural Pragmatics*, 1: 153–274.
Wierzbicka, A. (2003) *Cross-Cultural Pragmatics*, 2nd edn, Berlin: Mouton de Gruyter.

Culture
The culture concept: indispensable but contested

As Gerd Bauman (1996: 9) observes in his book *Contesting Culture*, '[n]o idea is as fundamental to an anthropological understanding of social life as the concept of culture'. Given that people's ways of speaking are often, if not always, culturally shaped, it would seem that the same must apply to linguistic **pragmatics**. Certainly cultural factors play a central part in the ethnography of **communication** (in anthropology) and in **cross-cultural pragmatics** (in linguistics). As suggested by Bauman's title, however, the

'culture concept' has lately been subject to sustained scrutiny and criticism for, among other things, its alleged essentialism, over-simplification, failure to accommodate variability and change, and under-estimation of human agency. Ironically though, as Bauman observes, '[a]t the same time, no anthropological term has spread into public parlance and **political discourse** as this word has done over the past twenty years'.

Four meanings of culture in ordinary English

The culture concept is largely an English-specific one. German *Kultur*, for example, differs significantly in **meaning**, and there are greater differences in concepts from more distant languages, such as Chinese *wénhuà* 'culture, cultivation'. Understanding the English folk concept of culture is important, first, because English is increasingly the global lingua franca of social science and, second, because the social science concepts of 'culture' have grown out of the everyday concept and, arguably, retain a dialectical relationship with it.

There are four main meanings of culture of relevance to pragmatics, typified by expressions such as (a) Chinese culture, Samoan culture, Aboriginal culture; (b) youth culture, gay culture; (c) police culture, beach culture, culture of the classroom; and (d) (Malaysia's) culture of deference, (the Department's) culture of secrecy. Though these meanings differ from one another in certain specifiable ways (Goddard 2005), they share some key conceptual components: the idea of a collectivity of people (living in a place or doing things together); the idea that these people behave in distinctive ways, think in distinctive ways and have distinctive values (attitudes about what is good and what is bad); and the idea that these people's distinctive ways of behaving, thinking and evaluating have been inherited or transmitted from their predecessors. One dimension of difference across the four meanings concerns the nature of the collectivity: whether it refers to a presumed 'people of one kind' or whether the principle of association is looser, being based on people engaging in common activities. Correlated with this is another difference: whether what is being indicated is a 'way of life' or, more selectively, a way of doing things in a particular occupational or activity-based

context. Uses like those in (a) correspond roughly with the classical anthropological concept of culture (see below), while those under (b) and (c) have been usefully referred to as 'small cultures' (Holliday 1999). In addition, two other meanings of culture are a semi-technical, generalized meaning referring to a generic attribute of the human species, and a quite separate meaning referring to artistic works and practices, as in expressions like *high culture* and *popular culture*.

Anthropological problems, linguistic solutions

The conceptual value of the culture concept derives from the nexus it posits between shared ideas and values, on the one hand, and shared practices and behaviours, on the other. A standard talking point in anthropology concerns the relative priority that should be accorded to these two aspects, both in terms of emphasis and in terms of causative efficacy. The symbolic and/or ideational approach, epitomized by Geertz's (1979: 89) classic formulation ('a historically transmitted pattern of meanings ... expressed in symbolic forms'), is often ranged against the practices approach (Bourdieu 1977), with its concept of habitus. In any case, most theorists agree that the culture concept subsumes both the mental and the behavioural, and that language and culture interpenetrate and help to co-constitute one another (Goddard 2002).

More potent objections – which have led some to speak of a 'crisis of confidence' in anthropology – are that the culture concept is unrealistically monolithic (unable or ill equipped to recognize variation, malleability, contact and change) and that it is deterministic or reductionist (in extreme formulations, implying that people are mere culture-bearers rather than active social agents). To the extent that these charges are valid, they largely spring from the 'nouniness' of the word *culture*, which tends to implicate the existence of a stable entity of some kind. They can be largely overcome by moving to a traits level of analysis, i.e. rather than speaking of whole cultures, one seeks to identify individual cultural traits which can be regarded as distributed in variable forms and in varying ways across populations. Such a trait-based, dynamic approach, sometimes described as an epidemiological model (Sperber 1996b), gets around any implication that there are essentialized and homogeneous social units underlying the culture concept.

A more insidious problem is what constitutes a suitable metalanguage (system of notation) for cultural description. On the one hand, the technical vocabulary of anthropology may be useful for social scientists, but it necessarily represents an 'outsider perspective' which can have only a tenuous claim to psychological reality for the speakers of any particular culture. On the other hand, the cultural key words and value concepts of any individual culture, while representing psychologically real ('experience-near') concepts to the people concerned, are by definition so heavily culture-specific that they cannot be rendered easily across languages. By default, culture-specific concepts from the English language are often imposed as inaccurate glosses upon indigenous concepts, with inevitably distorting results. Equally unfortunate, English-specific concepts such as '**politeness**', 'interaction', and 'imposition' can be employed as conceptual building blocks in theory construction, with the result that avowedly universalist frameworks can rest on Anglocentric foundations.

The most promising method for overcoming these problems is to employ a metalanguage of cultural description based on simple shared meanings (semantic primes) which appear to be present in all languages – meanings such as 'people', 'want', 'do', 'say', 'think', 'know', 'live', 'good' and 'bad' (Wierzbicka 1997). Such a metalanguage allows one to deconstruct the meaning content of complex culture-specific words into configurations of simple cross-translatable words. The same metalanguage has also been used in the development of a trait-based approach to cultural pragmatics – the **cultural scripts** approach.

Regardless of how the difficulties with the culture concept are dealt with, it seems clear that no account of **pragmatic competence** or politeness phenomena, for example, can be complete unless informed by a broad cross-cultural perspective on speech practices. Likewise, there can be little hope of developing an accurate understanding of the manifold relationships between language structure and language use if cultural factors are left out of the picture. In short, pragmatics must come to grips with culture, and with the links between ways of speaking and ways of thinking.

CLIFF GODDARD

See also: Competence, pragmatic; cross-cultural pragmatics; cultural scripts; intercultural communication; politeness

Suggestions for further reading

Geertz, C. ([1973] 1993) *The Interpretation of Cultures*, London: Fontana Press.

Shweder, R.A. (2001) 'Culture: contemporary views', in N.J. Smelser and P.B. Baltes (eds) *International Encyclopedia of the Social and Behavorial Sciences*, vol 5, Oxford: Pergamon.

Wierzbicka, A. (1992) *Semantics, Culture and Cognition*, Oxford: Oxford University Press.

D

Defaults in Utterance Interpretation

In the process of linguistic **communication**, not all of the intended **meanings** are uttered; some are assumed to go through unsaid. Among such pieces of information, there are salient, presumed, standard or default meanings that the addressee arrives at without the help of a conscious inferential process. For example, (1) and (2) normally communicate (1') and (2'), unless the **context** signals that this standard interpretation was not intended.

(1) John dropped a vase and it broke.
(1') John dropped a vase *and as a result* it broke.
(2) Dickens' novels often portray an unhappy Victorian childhood.
(2') *Novels written by Dickens* often portray an unhappy Victorian childhood.

Such salient, unmarked, presumed meanings arise independently of the particular context of utterance. In current pragmatic theory, approaches to default interpretations are often derived from **Grice**'s (1975) concept of the **generalized conversational implicature** (GCI), standing for context-independent pragmatic **inference**. Such interpretations are frequently considered to be automatic and non-inferential (e.g. Recanati 2004b). They are variously classified as implicatures (Levinson 2000), part of what is explicitly said (Recanati 2004b; Jaszczolt 2005) or as an intermediate level of what is implicit in **what is said** (Bach 1994b; Horn 2006).

The most influential post-Gricean approaches that acknowledge the presence of conversational defaults are as follows. According to Bach's (1984) default **reasoning**, in **utterance interpretation** we 'jump to conclusions', proceed to the first unchallenged interpretation, unless the context intervenes. According to Levinson's (1995, 2000) theory of generalized conversational implicature, default (presumptive) meanings are the result of rational, communicative behaviour and arise through three **heuristics**: 'What isn't said, isn't', 'What is expressed simply is stereotypically exemplified', and 'What's said in an abnormal way isn't normal'. Presumptive meanings arise at various stages in processing, are cancellable, and pertain to the social sphere of communication, being neither semantic nor pragmatic. **Optimality-theory pragmatics** (Blutner 2000; Blutner and Zeevat 2004a) recasts Grice's principle of rational communication as an optimization procedure that is realized as a series of constraints operating on the underspecified output of **syntax**. Neo-Gricean heuristics (Horn 1984; Levinson 2000) are formalized as, among others, strength, consistency, and faithful interpretation. In truth-conditional pragmatics (Recanati 2002a, 2003, 2004b), default interpretations are pragmatic enrichments to the output of syntactic processing. They are free; they are not controlled by the **logical form** of the sentence. Such interpretations are considered to be automatic and unreflective. For Recanati, they are defaults for the processing of an utterance in a particular context. They justify the label 'default' in view of their automatic, unreflective, subconscious nature rather than context-sensitivity. For example, (3) may be automatically enriched to (3') in a particular situation.

(3) I haven't eaten.

(3') The speaker hasn't eaten breakfast yet.

In *Default Semantics* (Jaszczolt 2005, 2006), sali-ent, unmarked interpretations are automatic and arise via two separate routes: the characteristics of human mental processes (cognitive defaults, CD) and the way the society and **culture** work (social and cultural defaults, SCD). The default, strong, referential interpretation of definite descriptions as in (4') is an example of a CD, and the culture-driven interpretation of (5) in (5') is an example of a SCD.

(4) The best British chef wrote this recipe book.

(4') The British chef whose identity the speaker knows wrote this recipe book.

(5) The Mona Lisa was stolen yesterday.

(5') The painting of Mona Lisa was stolen yesterday.

While they represent shortcuts through context-dependent, conscious pragmatic inference, there is no requirement that they be entirely independent of contextual information.

In more formal approaches to **discourse**, defaults derive from the research on non-monotonic reasoning in computational linguistics and can be traced back to Humboldt, Jespersen, Cassirer, and more recently to Reiter's (1980) default logic (*cf.* also Thomason 1997; Veltman 1996). In Segmented Discourse Representation Theory (SDRT; Asher and Lascarides 2003), defaults are probable interpretations of a sen-tence accounted for by rhetorical structure rules. The rules operate on the assumption that dis-course is coherent and provide the fully for-malized account of the logic of information structure.

Default interpretations are still the subject of heated debates in the **pragmatics** literature. The main differences between theorists arise on the following fronts:

(i) defaults have to or need not be context-independent;

(ii) defaults are or are not easily defeasible;

(iii) defaults are or are not automatic and subconscious;

(iv) defaults belong to the explicit or implicit content of the utterance;

(v) defaults are a semantic, pragmatic, psy-chological, or socio-cultural phenomenon;

(vi) defaults arise through one type of process or a variety of processes;

(vii) defaults come from one source or a variety of different sources;

(viii) defaults arise on the basis of a **proposi-tion** (are 'global') or arise incrementally as interpretation progresses (are 'local');

(ix) defaults do or do not necessarily arise quicker than non-default interpretations.

Different accounts of default meaning conform to different subsets of the above characteristics. Their common feature is that defaults constitute shortcuts in the communication process, exemplifying the rules of defeasible logic.

KASIA M. JASZCZOLT

See also: Abduction; generalized conversational implicature, theory of; impliciture; optimality-theory pragmatics; post-Gricean pragmatics; rationality; reasoning

Suggestions for further reading

Jaszczolt, K.M. (2005) *Default Semantics: Foundations of a Compositional Theory of Acts of Communication*, Oxford: Oxford University Press.

Levinson, S.C. (2000) *Presumptive Meanings: The Theory of Generalized Conversational Implicature*, Cambridge, MA: MIT Press.

Thomason, R.H. (1997) 'Nonmonotonicity in linguistics', in J. van Benthem and A. ter Meulen (eds) *Handbook of Logic and Language*, Oxford: Elsevier Science.

Definiteness

Definiteness is considered to be an attribute of Noun Phrases (NPs; sometimes also referred to as Determiner Phrases, or DPs), and is often associated with (singular) **reference**. This attri-bute has been most thoroughly studied with respect to English (though Lyons 1999 is one of several cross-linguistic studies). The definite arti-cle *the* is the most frequently used word of Eng-lish, and definite descriptions – NPs beginning with *the*, e.g. *the car dealer we met yesterday* – are the prototypical exemplars of definiteness. NPs with possessive determiners, like *my sister*, are usually considered to be a kind of definite description (but *see* Haspelmath 1999a). Other types of NP generally considered to be definite are **demonstrative** NPs (*this antique cupboard*), demonstrative and personal pronouns (e.g. *those, you, her*), and proper names (*Madonna, Melvin Douglas*). Intuitively, all of these kinds of NP are most typically used to pick out or refer to some particular entity (although as we will see below, they may have uses which are not definite).

We will start with definite descriptions, the most studied subcategory of definite NPs. Russell (1905) put forward the classic analysis, according to which definite descriptions differ from indefinite descriptions – like *a car dealer we met yesterday* – in requiring there to be a unique entity satisfying the descriptive content of the NP. This explains why the definite article is required when the descriptive content is such that only one entity could satisfy it – *the third house on the left, the present queen of England*. Russell's analysis needs to be modified to account for definite descriptions whose head nouns are plural (e.g. *cows*) or noncount (e.g. *corn*). Hawkins (1978, 1991) has proposed replacing Russell's uniqueness with a condition of maximality – the denotation of a definite description must constitute all of the entities or matter meeting the descriptive content of the NP. Thus *the cows/corn in farmer Jones's field* would denote all the cows or corn in his field (*see also* Sharvy 1980). Incomplete descriptions present another problem for Russell's analysis. NPs like *the book* do not imply that there is only one book in the universe. Proposals to solve this problem include the postulation of tacit descriptive or indexical material in the NP (Neale 1990; Stanley and Szabó 2000), and a narrowing of the domain of **discourse** to include only relevant entities (Barwise and Perry 1983; Westerståhl 1985; Hawkins 1984, 1991).

An alternative view holds that definite descriptions are distinctive in denoting entities which the speaker assumes that the addressee is familiar with. Christophersen (1939) is often cited as a progenitor of this view, which received a more recent boost with the work of Heim (1982, 1983a). Sometimes, familiarity relies on an **inference** from existing shared information. For utterances like *We got on a bus and the driver was yelling*, speakers rely on their addressees to

add a driver once a bus has been mentioned, a process referred to as 'bridging' (Clark 1977). Still, there remain examples that are difficult for the familiarity approach to account for. An utterance like *The new curling facility here, which you've probably never heard of, is the first of its kind* explicitly denies the assumption of addressee familiarity, yet is not anomalous. A compromise view proposes that definite descriptions require addressees in **context** to be able to determine a unique intended referent (Birner and Ward 1998; *see also* Roberts 2003).

We turn now to other types of definite NP. Pronouns have several uses which are illustrated in (1):

(1) a. A woman came in. *She* sat down.
   b. Tom jumped up and down. *That* was confusing.
   c. *Those* [pointing] are called 'woodchucks'.
   d. *He* [pointing] is the one I was thinking of.
   e. Most dogs want *their* owners to take them for a walk.

The pronouns in (1a) and (1b) most naturally have an anaphoric interpretation, referring respectively to the person and the event mentioned in the preceding utterance. In (1c) and (1d), the pronouns function as **indexicals**, to refer to entities in the utterance context. On the most natural interpretation of (1e), the pronoun is bound by the preceding quantified NP (*most dogs*), and is thus similar to a variable in logic. The first two of these uses of pronouns, the anaphoric and deictic uses, seem intuitively to be as definite as the uses of definite descriptions described above, and meet the criteria for definiteness we have looked at. In the third case, the bound variable type of reading of (1e), the pronoun is no more definite than its binder, *most dogs*. It is a bit of a strain to speak of reference at all in this kind of case, since the speaker apparently has no particular entities in mind with respect to the utterance.

Several facts about the grammar of proper names suggest that they behave as though they had a unique referent. In their ordinary uses they may not occur with a determiner (although other languages do allow, or even require, a determiner – typically a definite one), or with any kind of restrictive modification. Proper names may be used even when the speaker does not believe the addressee has prior **knowledge** of the individual named, although it is customary in such cases to provide additional identifying information in appositive or other nonrestrictive format, e.g. *Mark Penn, Hillary Clinton's chief strategist and pollster.*

Many linguists have used locating existential sentences, such as *There is a dog in the yard*, as a kind of test for definiteness. Definite and demonstrative descriptions, pronouns, and proper names do not occur naturally in such sentences, as shown in (2) (# is a common symbol indicating unnaturalness or anomaly):

(2) a. #There are the dogs in the yard.
    b. #There were those outside the house.
    c. #There will be Madonna in that movie.

Quantificational NPs are also anomalous in this type of existential:

(3) a. #There were all of the marbles in the bag.
    b. #There were most dog owners at the show.

Universal quantifiers (*all, every, each*) may plausibly be regarded as definite determiners, but *most* is not, which casts some doubt on the use of existential sentences as a test for definiteness. Following Milsark (1977), Barwise and Cooper (1981) have defined a category of strong NPs which includes definites plus NPs whose quantifier is a universal or *most*. Their criterion is based on a **presupposition** of existence (*see also* Keenan 1987).

'Definiteness' may ultimately turn out to be a cover term for an attribute that comes in degrees, as suggested by Bolinger (1977). Several current approaches look at NPs from the perspective of the cognitive state of the addressee, investigating the degree to which referents are accessible (Ariel 1988, 1990), or the addressee's assumed level of acquaintance (Gundel *et al.* 1993, 2001).

BARBARA ABBOTT

See also: Anaphora, pragmatics of; deixis; demonstratives; given/new distinction; indefiniteness; indexicals; presupposition; reference

Suggestions for further reading

Abbott, B. (2004) 'Definiteness and indefiniteness', in L.R. Horn and G. Ward (eds) *The Handbook of Pragmatics*, Malden, MA: Blackwell.
Lyons, C. (1999) *Definiteness*, Cambridge: Cambridge University Press.
Reimer, M. and Bezuidenhout, A. (eds) (2004) *Descriptions and Beyond*, Oxford: Clarendon Press.

Deixis

Given the broad definition of **pragmatics** as the study of the use of language in **context**, deixis has been considered as the most obvious and direct linguistic reflection of the relationship between language and context (Levinson 1983: 54). Deixis traditionally concerns the use of certain linguistic expressions to locate entities in spatio-temporal, social and discoursal context. In English, such deictic expressions typically include first and second person pronouns (I, you, we), **demonstratives** (this, that), certain place and time adverbials (here, there, now, then), some verbs (e.g. come, go) and tense. For example, the understanding of an expression like 'I'll see you there' requires **knowledge** of who the speaker and the addressee are, as well as the speaker's spatio-temporal whereabouts. Moreover, there are certain expressions whose understanding depends on stretches of surrounding **discourse**, as in 'Besides, he is a very good artist'. In this case, *besides* points to preceding discourse. Finally, there are uses of deictic elements which encode the social relationship between interlocutors, as when the second person plural pronoun is typically used in languages such as French and Greek to signal a socially distant interlocutor. Accordingly, five categories of deixis are typically identified: (1) person deixis, (2) place deixis, (3) time deixis, (4) discourse deixis, and (5) social deixis. These categories appear in all languages whose systems have been investigated so far. However, not all languages encode them in the same way.

Apparently, deictic categories constitute strong universals of language at the conceptual level, but their grammatical manifestations greatly vary (Levinson 2004: 112).

An important aspect of all categories of deixis in many languages appears to be their egocentricity, i.e. their organization relative to specific parameters of the communicative event that place the speaker as the deictic centre of the speech event. Bühler ([1934] 1982) claimed that deictic expressions refer to a deictic field of language, whose zero point – the *origo* – is fixed by the person who is speaking, the place and the time of the utterance (I, here, and now, respectively). By contrast, the symbolic field comprises naming words which function as symbols of **meaning**.

A parallel distinction concerns deixis as a pragmatic phenomenon and the particular uses of deictic expressions. Fillmore (1971a) has suggested that there are two kinds of deictic usages of deictic terms, namely gestural usage and symbolic usage. Gestural usage is fundamentally based on a kind of physical monitoring of the speech event. For example, an utterance such as 'I don't agree with you but with you' can be understood if the speaker physically indicates the identity of the intended addressee(s). The symbolic usage requires knowledge of the basic spatio-temporal parameters of the speech event, or its discourse, or social parameters, as in 'This room is badly lit'. For the understanding of this utterance, it is sufficient to know the general location of the speaker and no physical pointing is required, even though it may well coexist.

Moreover, there is a distinction to be made between deictic and non-deictic usages of deictic terms. For example, in the utterance 'Her mother walked in. This woman was the tallest female I had ever seen', the expression *this woman* is used anaphorically to refer to *her mother* in the first clause. Hence, there is no reliance on extra-linguistic context for the identification of the referent. This, then, is a non-deictic usage of the, typically deictic, demonstrative *this*. However, if reliance on extra-linguistic context is a criterion for deictic usages of terms, then discourse deixis should be out of the picture, since discourse deixis by definition makes reference to parts of text prior to, or following, the speaker's current utterance. This point remains relatively unresolved

(also *see* Levinson 2004: 107–11). Moreover, there are instances when a deictic expression can be used both deictically and anaphorically, as when one says 'I've been working at the university for thirty years now and I still love it here'. In this case, the adverbial *here* is used both anaphorically to refer to the university and deictically, if the speaker is in the premises at the time of the utterance.

Further, typically non-deictic expressions can also be used deictically. Third person **reference** is a case in point since, generally, it does not require reference to the speaker or addressee for its understanding, as in 'Melinda must go to bed'. However, the same utterance could be used in a child-caring context in which the proper name could actually refer to the addressee, rather than a third party, as, for example, when a mother asks her daughter to go to bed. Hence, there are uses of third person reference that pick out the addressee in some (probably socially marked) contexts (also *see* Marmaridou 2000: 71–73). As Levinson (2004: 101) points out, 'the property of indexicality is not exhausted by the study of inherently indexical expressions. For just about any referring expression can be used deictically.' In what follows, the five most discussed categories of deixis will be focused upon.

Person deixis is primarily concerned with the identification of participant roles in the speech event, i.e. the speaker, as the deictic centre, and the addressee. Given that these roles shift in the course of **conversational turn-taking**, the *origo* shifts with them (note Jespersen's (1922) term 'shifters'). In some languages, person deixis may also encode other participant roles, such as that of the bystander or hearer, who is other than the addressee, or that of the source, who is other than the speaker. Person deixis is typically expressed by first and second person pronouns in the singular and/or in the plural in many, but not all, languages. For example, in Southeast Asian languages titles are used in place of pronouns, such as *servant* for first person and *master* for second person (Levinson 2004: 112). Also, first person plural *we* does not identify more than one speaker, but rather both the speaker and the addressee, as in 'Why don't we take a break?'. Or, it might include the speaker and third parties, but exclude the addressee, as in 'We are going on strike next week' addressed to a non-participant of the strike. These uses have been termed addressee-inclusive and addressee-exclusive, respectively. Interestingly, there are also addressee-inclusive and speaker-exclusive uses, as in 'Now we are going to brush our teeth', whereby the mother invites the child to do something. In fact, such instances of 'pseudo-inclusive' deixis have been associated with the assertive or directive force of utterances, which they serve to soften or mitigate (Haverkate 1992). Person pronouns have also been associated with non-deictic uses, as in 'You beat the eggs until fluffy' from a recipe book or 'We vote for Parliament every four years' said by a speaker of non-voting age. In the former example, the pronoun picks out whoever is reading the recipe, whereas in the latter the pronoun invokes a quasi-generic addressee. Evidently, these uses are closely related to the particular discourse type and communicative interaction.

Apart from person deictic terms that belong to the arguments of a predicate, there are others that are used parenthetically in sentences, as in 'The exam, Mary, is tomorrow'. These are vocative uses, which are deictic *par excellence* and can be distinguished into calls or summonses (as in the above example), and addresses, which are by definition utterance initial, as in the famous example by Zwicky (1974) 'Hey lady, you dropped your piano.' Clearly, as Zwicky observes, vocatives are almost never neutral, since they locate the speaker and the discourse in a particular social world and directly concern the relationship between speaker and addressee. It is on such grounds that the claim has been made that person deixis cannot be effected independently of social deixis (Marmaridou 2000: 79). Supporting evidence for this view also comes from languages that make a distinction (usually termed the T/V distinction from French) between second person singular and plural pronouns to encode social distance between speaker and addressee.

Time deixis makes reference to temporal points and spans relative to the speaker's utterance time. Generally speaking, in many languages time is conceptualized unidirectionally and linearly, but it is measured in calendrical cycles that refer to the 24-hour day or larger units of socio-cultural significance (e.g. the 7-day week, the month, etc.). As Fillmore (1971a) has observed, these units either serve as measures relative to the deictic centre including utterance time, or they serve as absolute time indicators of events, as in 'She phoned yesterday' and 'She phoned on Thursday, 7th February 2008', respectively. Another distinction concerns the time an utterance is spoken as opposed to the time it is received by the addressee. In this case, reference is made to coding time (CT) and receiving time (RT), respectively. In case CT and RT coincide, then this is an instance of deictic simultaneity (Lyons 1977: 685). Time deixis is commonly grammaticalized in deictic adverbs of time, such as *now*, *then*, *today*, and *yesterday*, in demonstrative expressions combining *this* and *that* with time spans (e.g. this Monday, that year, this summer), or in combinations of the adjectives *last* and *next* with these time spans (e.g. last month, next year, etc.). In most languages, there is a complex interaction between systems of time measurement (e.g. calendrical units such as *Monday*) and deictic anchorage through demonstratives or the adjectives *next* and *last*. For example, *this week* typically refers to the week including CT, but *this Monday* does not. Also, *this December* does not necessarily include CT, but rather the December lying in the immediate future. To the extent that time is lexicalized and grammaticalized differently in different languages, time deictic expressions will also vary both in form and use cross-linguistically.

Time deixis is also expressed through tense marking on the verbs of utterances, but in some languages also on nouns (*see* Mithun 1999). Lyons (1977: 682) distinguishes between meta-linguistic tense (m-tense) and linguistic tense (l-tense), the former being a semantic category and the latter its linguistic realization. For example, both 'Whales are mammals' and 'The whales are ill' are l-tensed for simple present tense, but only the latter is m-tensed and deictic in that it refers to present time including the speaker's utterance. However, l-tense does not uniquely identify deictic time. For example, in 'The shop closes at 6' said to a customer, the present tense marking does not locate closing time in the time span including the speaker's utterance, but to a time span referring to the future and excluding the utterance. In many languages l-tense may also mark aspectual and modal elements, while the interpretation of tenses often involves

implicatures when no absolute deictic tenses are available (Levinson 2004: 115), or relies on temporal adverbials (Huang 2007: 148).

Importantly, the linear representation of time in many languages suggests that time is understood spatially, as the use of spatial demonstratives in temporal expressions suggests (e.g. this Monday, that year, etc.). Moreover, the use of time **metaphors** in terms of verbs of motion (as in *the coming year, the following Monday, the past month*), which are themselves specified spatially, suggests a close link between time and space deixis, if not the priority of the latter in accounting for the former (Marmaridou 2000: 102).

Place deixis prototypically concerns the specification of the location of objects relative to the participants in a speech event, i.e. the speaker and/or the addressee. Place deixis is expressed by adverbs such as *here* and *there*, arguably the most universal examples of the category (Levinson 2004: 116), to indicate a region including the speaker, or proximate to the speaker, and a region distal from, or excluding, the speaker, respectively. A parallel distinction seems to hold for the demonstratives *this* and *that*. However, objects that are marked by *that* do not necessarily encode distance from the speaker, as in 'Take that dog out of my sight' said of a salivating dog at the speaker's feet. This has been considered an instance of empathic deixis, indicating emotional distance from the object of reference or, in general, attitude, viewpoint, or evaluation (Mey 1993: 96). In fact, the study of demonstratives cross-linguistically shows that the distinctions made by them may not only relate to physical context, but to features of visibility, accessibility in memory, anticipation, perception, or prior discourse (*see* Enfield 2003a: 86; Hanks 2005: 197), or, generally, to coordinate the interlocutors' joint attentional focus (Diessel 2006: 472). Moreover, cross-linguistic research has shown that there are three linguistic frames of reference to express spatial relationships between an object, a perceiver and a location. One of them is the egocentric (deictic), relative frame, exemplified by 'The tree is to the left of the house', where the point of view is the speaker's. Another, the intrinsic frame, concerns inherent features of an object (e.g. the house) as in 'The tree is behind the house'. Finally, the absolute frame locates objects on the basis of absolute coordinates like north, south, east, and west, as in 'The tree is north of the house'. Languages vary with respect to which of these coordinate systems they use and the way they instantiate them (*see* Levinson 2003: 35–38).

Place deixis can also be related to the path taken by a moving object in relation to its source, or origin, and to its goal, or destination. It can be expressed in certain motion verbs such as *come* and *go*, or other verbs involving motion in their frames, such as *bring, take*, and *fetch* in English. As noted by Fillmore (1971b), *go* is the unmarked option indicating motion away from the speaker's location at the time of speaking (CT). The use of *come* is more complicated and may indicate that (i) the speaker is at the goal at CT, (ii) the speaker is at the goal at arrival time, (iii) the addressee is at the goal at CT, or (iv) the addressee is at the goal at arrival time. Therefore, the utterance 'Jane will come to the office tomorrow' is four ways ambiguous, while **Go here* is clearly ungrammatical. Verbs of coming and going vary cross-linguistically with respect to what they encode (see, for example, Antonopoulou and Nikiforidou 2002), whereas many languages do not have verbs encoding motion to or from the deictic centre (Levinson 2004: 117).

Discourse deixis concerns the use of linguistic expressions to point to the current, preceding, or following utterance(s) in the same text. A text, whether in its written or oral realization, is closely related to the concepts of space and time. Consequently, discourse deixis is expressed with terms that are primarily used in encoding space or time deixis as in 'Listen to this joke' and 'In the next chapter more will be said about dinosaurs'. Of particular interest is the distinction between discourse deixis and **anaphora** as a discourse cohesive device (Lyons 1977: 667). In 'Pat phoned and she's coming to dinner' both the proper name and the person pronoun refer to the same entity in the world. But in 'I know what a platypus is, but can you spell it for me please?', the pronoun *it* does not refer to the same object as *platypus*, bur rather to the word *platypus* itself in the text and therefore constitutes an example of discourse deixis. Undoubtedly, discourse deixis and text cohesion are interrelated, as is evidenced by the use of **discourse markers** such as *anyway, but, however*, etc. (*see* Blakemore 2004). These markers typically relate a current contribution to the prior utterance and do not affect the meaning of the **propositions** they conjoin. Finally, there are a number of East and Southeast Asian languages that grammatically mark the **information structure** of an utterance and **topic** (given information) in particular.

Social deixis concerns the marking of the social status of the speaker in respect of the addressee, an entity referred to in the discourse, a third party, or the relationship of the speaker to the setting of the speech event. Referent **honorifics** are linguistic forms that encode the speaker's respect towards a referent which can also be the addressee (e.g. titles of address). Addressee honorifics express the same respectful attitude of the speaker towards the addressee, but also when the speaker is talking about matters that do not directly relate to the addressee (Levinson 2004: 120; Huang 2007: 164). Southeast Asian honorifics systems typically combine these two parameters of social deixis. Bystander honorifics are used by the speaker to signal respect to a third party. This is, for example, the case with Australian aboriginal languages in which the speaker has to use a special register vocabulary when speaking in the presence of a mother-in-law with whom close social contact is taboo. Speaker-setting honorifics are again typical in some East and South Asian languages, but are also known as distinctions in formal versus informal style in many languages all over the world. Typical of speaker-setting social deixis are cases of diglossic variants with distinct morphology and vocabulary for formal, literary, and everyday styles of speech and writing.

Deictics are primarily described as establishing a relationship between the speaker and features of context. However, it has also been argued that they have attentional, intentional and subjective features in that they seek to draw and orient the interactants' subjective attention to aspects of the context and they can thus exhibit directive force. In these terms, the study of deixis becomes important in the investigation of interaction (see, for example, Enfield's (2003b) work on recognition deixis, Hindermarsh and Heath's (2000) work on deixis in workplace interaction, and Davidson's (2007) focus on political self-positioning in terms of temporal deixis). Moreover, emphasis on social aspects of

deixis has led to the embedding of the phenomenal context in a broader social one, which 'converts the [s]peaker and the [a]ddressee into social agents of certain kinds' (Hanks 2005: 210). In this context, 'speakers often engage in deictic practice not to position objects but to position themselves … the object functions as a landmark off which the [s]peaker can position himself' (Hanks 2005: 211). Finally, the insights from the study of deixis have fruitfully informed medical research on patients with Alzheimer's disease (March *et al.* 2006) and on patients who have sustained a right-hemisphere stroke (Talberg 2001), as well as research on the relation between language, perception and cognition (Kemmerer 2006).

SOPHIA MARMARIDOU

See also: Anaphora, pragmatics of; clinical pragmatics; context; conversational turn-taking; definiteness; demonstratives; discourse; discourse markers; honorific language; implicature; indexicals; information structure; interactional linguistics; metaphor; Peirce, C.S.; politeness; reference; speech act theory; topic

Suggestions for further reading

Huang, Y. (2007) *Pragmatics*, Oxford: Oxford University Press.
Levinson, S.C. (1983) *Pragmatics*, Cambridge: Cambridge University Press.
Marmaridou, S.S.A. (2000) *Pragmatic Meaning and Cognition*, Amsterdam and Philadelphia, PA: John Benjamins.

Dementia and Conversation

The term 'dementia' is derived from the Latin *de mens* ('out of mind') and historically has referred to a variety of mental state conditions. Dementia is often considered a condition associated with ageing (i.e. 65 years of age or older), though it does not manifest exclusively among older adults. Dementia prevalence worldwide is estimated at 26.6 million (Alzheimer's Association 2007).

Defined by the American Psychiatric Association's DSM-IV criteria (American Psychiatric Association 2000), dementia is a syndrome of progressive multiple cognitive deficits that include degeneration of memory plus one or more disturbances of (a) language, (b) the ability to carry out motor activities in the presence of intact motor function (i.e. apraxia), (c) the ability to recognize or to identify objects in the presence of intact sensory function (i.e. agnosia), and (d) planning, organizing, sequencing, and/or abstracting information (e.g. executive cognitive functions). These deficits have an adverse impact on everyday occupational or social functioning. There are many types of dementia all sharing the basic properties described above. Each type varies in its relative proportion of memory, language, motor, sensory, and organizational deficits.

Profiles of **conversation** vary with dementia type and clinical stage. These differing profiles enable researchers and clinicians to explore myriad relationships among cognitive ability, **linguistic competence**, sociolinguistic performance, neurolinguistic processes and psycholinguistic operations in the context of the associated medical, emotional and social aspects of caregiving. Conversation is one element of **pragmatics**. A comprehensive examination of pragmatics in all types of dementia is beyond the scope of the present discussion. For further detailed information on pragmatics in dementia, the reader is referred to Guendouzi and Müller (2006).

Conversation profiles of commonly occurring dementias

Alzheimer's Disease. Alzheimer's disease (AD) is the most common type of dementia. It is characterized primarily by memory problems. However, language and conversation changes emerge early. Individuals with AD produce more conversational troubles than their dyadic partners, with an increased need for repair with increased severity (Orange *et al.* 1996; Watson *et al.* 1999). These trouble sources arise from changes in turn-taking, **topic** maintenance, and cognitive and semantic impairments (Hamilton 1994; Small *et al.* 2000). Individuals with AD produce shorter conversational turns, show increased **reference** errors and increased use of non-specific terms (e.g. 'thing', 'that') (Ripich and Terrell 1988). Also, they experience difficulty maintaining and elaborating topics of conversation (Mentis and Briggs-Whittaker 1995). Frequent,

unexpected topic shifts are common and can occur due to perseveration (Garcia and Joanette 1997) or to difficulty tracking the thematic development of the conversation (Orange *et al.* 1996). Conversational partners use paraphrasing strategies to repair troubles successfully (Milroy and Perkins 1992; Small *et al.* 2000; Watson *et al.* 1999). Individuals with AD, in contrast, use a wide range of strategies that are not always successful in resolving troubles, such as elaboration of information (Müller and Guendouzi 2005; Orange *et al.* 1998b; Watson *et al.* 1999). The changes in turn-taking and topic maintenance affect the overall coherence of conversations between individuals with AD and their partners. Therefore, to maintain conversation throughout disease progression, conversational partners take increased responsibility for directing and for sustaining conversation (Hamilton 1994).

Frontotemporal Dementia – Behavioural Variant. Frontotemporal dementia is a frequently occurring form of dementia among the young–old cohort of adults (i.e. 55 to 65 years of age). The behavioural variant of frontotemporal dementia (FTD-b) is characterized by changes in personality and behaviour. The pragmatic profile of individuals with FTD-b is described as confabulatory, irrelevant, and insensitive to listener needs. Individuals with FTD-b also show reduced conversational initiation and social appropriateness (Barber *et al.* 1995; Gustafson 1993; Neary 1990; Neary *et al.* 1990). However, given appropriate contextual support in conversation, individuals with FTD-b show generally well-preserved topic maintenance and elaboration abilities despite reduced verbal output (Orange *et al.* 1998a). Despite these retained skills, family caregivers are concerned about the social inappropriateness of their relatives' conversations (Galvan 2005).

Frontotemporal Dementia – Linguistic Variant (Primary Progressive Aphasia). Individuals with the linguistic variant of FTD, primary progressive aphasia (PPA), exhibit a different pragmatic profile from subjects with FTD-b. Moreover, subtly different pragmatic profiles are evident between non-fluent (PPA-nf) and fluent (PPA-f) subtypes of PPA. However, the pragmatic differences between PPA-nf and PPA-f may be more a matter of degree than real differences in condition.

Individuals with PPA-nf show pragmatic performance characterized by inappropriate topic maintenance (i.e. poor reference, off-topic comments, poor response to **questions**, and limited elaboration of topic), whereas individuals with PPA-f show more subtle topic maintenance difficulties. The PPA-nf and PPA-f variants are dissociated not by overall pragmatic skills, but by the awareness of pragmatic and **communication** problems. Individuals with the PPA-f variant show better awareness of their pragmatic problems than do individuals with PPA-nf (Orange *et al.* 1998a).

Frontotemporal Dementia – Representational Variant (Semantic Dementia). In contrast with PPA, the semantic dementia (SD) variant of FTD differentially impairs memory for conceptual **knowledge**, including the semantic **representation** of words (Knibb and Hodges 2005; Snowden *et al.* 1989; Warrington 1975). Individuals with SD generally exhibit intact **syntax** and grammar with severe anomia and comprehension difficulties (Snowden *et al.* 1989). Individuals with SD also show better conceptual memory for recent personally salient information (Graham and Hodges 1997; Kertesz *et al.* 1998; Snowden *et al.* 1995, 1996). The loss of representation of concepts and subsequent word finding problems result in decreased conversational coherence. There is little published research on the conversational skills of individuals with semantic dementia. Further targeted and systematic investigations are thus warranted.

Dementia Associated with Lewy Body Disease and Parkinson's Disease Dementia. The dementia associated with Lewy body disease (DLB) and Parkinson's disease dementia (PDD) are characterized primarily by motor involvement. As such, much of their conversational interactions are characterized by inappropriate changes in speech production (e.g. dysprosodias), altered gestures and accuracy of gestures, and inappropriate facial expressions (McNamara and Durso 2003). Individuals with DLB and PDD also manifest deficits in high-level language and cognitive processing. The pragmatic profiles of individuals with DLB and PDD reveal difficulties processing information with metaphoric, implied, or ambiguous **meaning** (Berg *et al.* 2003; Hanes *et al.* 1995; McNamara and Durso 2003; Monetta and Pell 2007). Individuals with DLB and PDD show reduced information content (Bayles 1990) and problems with conversational appropriateness (McNamara and Durso 2003). In addition, individuals with DLB and PDD exhibit difficulties with topic initiation, topic maintenance, referencing, trouble-source repair, and turn-taking (Whitworth *et al.* 1999).

Optimizing conversation among individuals with dementia

Optimizing conversations among individuals with dementia should be paramount in any communication enhancement program. Optimizing conversations enhances social connectedness and has the potential to reduce dysfunctional and challenging behaviours (e.g. aggression, wandering, anxiety, etc.) and to minimize caregiver burden (Savundranayagam *et al.* 2005). This first requires an **assessment** of linguistic communication (Bayles and Tomoeda 1993), functional communication (Bayles and Tomoeda 1994), and conversational performance within the context of a comprehensive communication framework (Lubinski and Orange 2000). There are emerging measures of conversational performance in dementia that hold promise for scientifically based conversation enhancing interventions (Kuntz and Orange 2003; Perkins *et al.* 1997). Results from systematic analyses of language, pragmatics in general and conversation in particular, enable researchers and clinicans to develop and to test the clinical effectiveness and efficiencies of empirically derived conversation enhancing strategies.

Ripich and colleagues (Ripich and Terrell 1988; Ripich and Wykle 1996; Ripich *et al.* 1999), Santo Pietro and Ostuni (2003), Bourgeois *et al.* (2002), Small and Perry (2005) and Small *et al.* (2005), among others, all consider conversation as a keystone in their communication enhancement programs for individuals with dementia and their caregivers. The interventions they promote target supportive strategies for turn-taking, topic initiation, topic maintenance, topic changing, successful repair of **misunderstandings**, personhood affirming techniques, and the referential marking of relevant semantic content. In so doing, these researchers and clinicians elevate and reinforce the crucial importance of conversations for individuals with dementia and serve to advance levels of competent and compassionate care.

JOSEPH B. ORANGE and LYNNE J. WILLIAMS

See also: Ambiguity; anaphora, pragmatics of; assessment, pragmatic; communication; competence; context; conversation; deixis; discourse; explicit/implicit distinction; implicature; inference; neuropragmatics; pragmatic language impairment; pragmatics; reference; rehabilitation, communication

Suggestions for further reading

Davis, B.H. (ed.) (2005) *Alzheimer Talk, Text and Context: Enhancing Communication*, Houndmills: Palgrave Macmillan.
Guendouzi, J. and Müller, N. (2006) *Approaches to Discourse in Dementia*, Mahwah, NJ: Lawrence Erlbaum Associates.
Ramanathan, V. (1997) *Alzheimer Discourse: Some Sociolinguistic Dimensions*, Mahwah, NJ: Lawrence Erlbaum Associates.

Demonstratives

Demonstratives in English contain *this, that, these,* or *those*. Demonstratives belong to the class of definite noun phrases (Maclaran 1982; Roberts 2002; Wolter 2006). They pass diagnostic tests for **definiteness**: for example, they are unacceptable in the pivot of existential sentences like (1). Like other definites, a felicitous utterance of a demonstrative noun phrase has a uniquely identifiable referent.

(1) *There is *that/this unicorn* in the garden.

The interpretation of a demonstrative depends on elements of the **context** – that is, demonstratives belong to the class of **indexicals**. In particular, demonstratives in English and other languages are sensitive to the speaker's extralinguistic gestures. The nature of the relationship between demonstratives and the context has been the primary focus of research on demonstratives in **semantics**, **pragmatics** and philosophy.

The foundational work on demonstratives in the **philosophy of language** (Kaplan 1977) focuses on uses of demonstratives that are accompanied by pointing gestures. These demonstratives do not participate in scope ambiguities. For example, (2a) below, unlike (2b), is judged false, showing that it lacks a reading in which the demonstrative takes narrow scope under the modal.

(2) (Pointing at John) If John and Mary switched places ...
   a.   ... that person would be a woman. (*false*)
   b.   ... the person I'd be pointing at would be a woman. (*true*)

Kaplan (1977) argues that demonstratives differ from definite descriptions and personal pronouns in being interpreted by direct **reference**: a demonstrative contributes an entity – its referent – to the compositional semantics and does not interact with other elements of the sentence (*cf.* Kripke's 1982a treatment of proper names). On this view, the referent of a demonstrative is determined entirely by the context, suggesting that pragmatic factors play a role at a pre-propositional level. (For elaboration of the direct reference theory of demonstratives, *see also* Braun 1995b.)

A more recent line of research has focused on uses of demonstratives that do participate in scope **ambiguity**. For example, in the most salient reading of (3) the demonstrative takes narrow scope under the quantifier *every*:

(3) Every dog in the neighborhood has an owner who thinks that *that dog* is a sweetie. (Roberts 2002)

Researchers who wish to account for the existence of sentences like (3) have pursued indirect reference approaches on which the content of a demonstrative can in principle interact with other parts of the sentence (King 2001; Roberts 2002; Wolter 2006).

While many indexicals depend on well defined features of the context (for example, *I* refers to the speaker), the nature of the connection between demonstratives and the context is often less clear cut. One debate concerns whether demonstratives are sensitive to demonstrations, that is, extralinguistic gestures like pointing or nodding (Kaplan 1977; Reimer 1991) or to the speaker's referential **intentions** (Kaplan 1989b; Bach 1992). Another area of investigation concerns the distinctions that are encoded by systems of demonstratives in different languages. Spatial distinctions appear to be quite fundamental: one typological study of eighty-five languages found that the demonstratives of all languages made at least one distinction based on distance from the speaker (*cf.* proximal *this* and distal *that*), though some individual lexical items were not marked for such a contrast (Diessel 1999). In addition to distance from the speaker, some languages encode distance from the addressee, as well as more specific locative features such as distance uphill or downhill, upstream or downstream, movement toward or away from the speaker, and visibility to the interlocutors (Diessel 1999).

Demonstratives also encode a number of other relations to the context. Demonstratives that express discourse **deixis** depend on a relationship with previous or ongoing **discourse**. For example, French and German use proximal demonstratives to refer to recently mentioned entities and distal demonstratives to refer to entities mentioned less recently (*cf.* English *the former/the latter*) (Fillmore 1997). English demonstratives may express discourse deixis to a limited degree: distal demonstratives are exclusively anaphoric, while proximal demonstratives have a cataphoric use, as in (4).

(4) There are still these/*those candidates to interview: Lugton, Barnes, Airey, and Foster.
(Huddleston and Pullum 2001: 1509)

Demonstratives may also express temporal deixis when combined with time-denoting expressions. For example, in some dialects of English *this Tuesday* refers to the upcoming Tuesday in the same week as the time of utterance (Fillmore 1997). Some uses of demonstratives encode social deixis, or a dependency on the social relationships among the interlocutors. For instance, the expressive use of English demonstratives (*That John is quite a guy!*) evokes solidarity among the discourse participants (Lakoff 1974).

It should be noted that the basic proximal/distal distinction can be extended in ways that do not fit neatly into the above categories. Two cases in point are the English indefinite demonstrative exemplified in (5), which typically introduces a new **topic** (Prince 1981a), and the contrast in (6), showing that English proximal demonstratives prefer 'speaker activation' (Gundel *et al.* 1993):

(5) One time I went up to the roof ... and there's *this big black guy about six seven* on top of the stairs.

(Prince 1981a)

(6) a. Have you seen the neighbour's dog?
b. Yes, and ?this/that dog kept me awake all night.

(Gundel *et al.* 1993)

Both of these facts can be tied to a notion of proximity to the speaker (Fillmore 1997): in (5), only the speaker can identify the referent of the demonstrative, while in (6), the proximal demonstrative is degraded when the speaker did not introduce the referent into the discourse.

A final area of interest concerns the interaction of demonstratives with animacy. In particular, English demonstrative pronouns normally require a non-human referent (7), but this restriction is lifted in copular constructions (8) and perceptual similarity sentences (9) (Higgins 1973; Maclaran 1982).

(7) #I had lunch with that.
(8) That is Rosa.
(9) That looks like Rosa.

The contrast between (7) and (8) to (9) is not yet well understood, but it has inspired a growing literature that investigates the interaction of the contexts in which (8) and (9) are uttered with the interpretation of the demonstrative pronoun. Some researchers have argued that the demonstratives in (8) and (9) do not denote humans (Carlson 1991; Mikkelsen 2004), while others have argued that human-denoting demonstrative pronouns are licensed in certain special contexts (Ward 2004; Heller and Wolter 2008).

LYNSEY WOLTER

See also: Context; definiteness; deixis; indexicals; topic

Suggestions for further reading

Fillmore, C.J. (1997) *Lectures on Deixis*, Stanford, CA: CSLI Publications.

Kaplan, D. (1977) 'Demonstratives', in J. Almog, J. Perry and H. Wettstein (eds) (1989) *Themes from Kaplan*, Oxford: Oxford University Press.

King, J.C. (2001) *Complex Demonstratives: A Quantificational Account*, Cambridge, MA: MIT Press.

Development, Pragmatic

Developmental pragmatics is a heterogeneous field on a range of topics associated with the study of how young children develop the skills to use language effectively and appropriately in social interaction. Researchers have studied the development of communicative intentions, conversation skills, **discourse** rules, **politeness** rules, as well as the role of **culture** and caregiver behaviours needed for children to gain **communicative competencies** for successful interpersonal relations (*see* Ninio and Snow 1996 for a review). Others have focused on the relationship of pragmatic skills with other more formal areas of language acquisition such as children's early lexicon (Carpenter *et al.* 1998) and **syntax** (Rollins and Snow 1998). The main focus of this entry is on developmental trends of communicative acts and their relationship with social cognition.

The origins of pragmatic skills may be found in the intersection between social-cognition and language development. It is well established that infants are socially precocious from birth. They have a preference for human faces over other visual stimuli (Johnson and Morton 1991) and for previously experienced voice and speech stimuli over novel ones (DeCasper and Fifer 1980). By two months, infants engage in episodes of sustained mutual attention with caregivers. This interaction reflects consciousness and **intentionality** on the part of the infant (Trevarthen 1977, 1979). Within these early interactions the **intention** of each partner is reflected by their actions (Baldwin 2000) and a shared understanding evolves (Werner and Kaplan 1963).

Around 9–12 months, children begin to use gestures and vocalizations to initiate and respond with true communicative intent (Bates *et al.* 1979).

They regulate others' behaviours with **requests** or protests, and begin to share attention by pointing and showing (e.g. Bates *et al.* 1975; Wetherby *et al.* 1988). In addition, children learn to perform social moves embedded in speech games or routines such as wave bye-bye or peek-a-boo (Bruner 1983; Ninio and Bruner 1978; Wetherby *et al.* 1988). These early preverbal intentions can be ordered in terms of the degree they require children to integrate information about the social world (Rollins and Snow 1998). Regulating another's behaviour is the least social of these intentions, requiring little more than the attribution of agency to the interlocutor and attention to objects and events (Tomasello *et al.* 2005). Pointing and showing, in contrast, require the understanding of secondary intersubjectivity. This is a more advanced social competency that includes active sharing and understanding that others have attention and intention that is different from one's own (Ninio and Snow 1996; Rollins and Snow 1998; Tomasello *et al.* 2007; Trevarthen and Aitken 2001).

Developmental trends after 12 months of age, when children acquire verbal communicative repertoires, has historically been more difficult to chart. Although considerable attention was devoted to this area, several methodological inconsistencies obscured our understanding of how communicative repertoires change with age and with ever growing linguistic sophistication (Ninio *et al.* 1994; O'Neil 2007). Most notable obstacles have been the degree of disagreement among taxonomies in the extent to which they are (a) theoretically founded, (b) capture communicative intention distinct from other formal aspects of language, (c) allow for multiple levels of analyses and (d) capture the full range of intention that encompasses different types of social-cognitive and linguistic concepts (*see* Ninio *et al.* 1994 and Ninio and Snow 1996 for reviews).

The Inventory of Communicative Acts (INCA; Ninio and Wheeler 1984) as well as its shortened and abridged form INCA-A (Ninio *et al.* 1994) were developed to address many of these concerns. Ninio and Wheeler's system was based both on **speech act theory** (Austin 1962; Searle 1976) and on studies of events in face-to-face interaction (Goffman 1974; Streeck 1980) which emphasize the importance of socially constructed communicative interchanges. The system identifies and codes communicative intent at two different levels – the level of the social interchange and the level of the utterance – thus acknowledging the existence of an organization of talk at a level higher than the single utterance (*cf.* Dore and McDermott 1982; Streeck 1980). An interchange is defined as one or more rounds of talk, all of which serve a unitary interactive function implicitly agreed upon by the interlocutors. Within this social interchange, speakers express specific intents at the utterance level. Both of Ninio's systems consist of two subsystems, each of which codes for a different component of communicative intent. The system was designed to provide exhaustive coding of the communicative attempts expressed by children of varying ages (as well as their mothers) and to reflect development and continuity across a wide age range. In addition to its theoretical grounding, the ecological validity of the system was assured by distinguishing categories based on mothers' interpretations of their own and their children's intents.

Several longitudinal studies in Israel, the USA, China and Japan have been conducted using the INCA or INCA-A (Ninio 1983, 1984; Ninio and Goren 1993; Snow *et al.* 1996; Tsuji 2002; Zhou 2002). Although each of these studies varies slightly in their data collection technique, they have found similar results in the developmental unfolding of verbal communicative skills in the second and third year of life.

Early in the second year of life, a core set of communicative intentions begins to emerge. They consist of directing the other's attention, discussing a joint focus, and negotiating the immediate activity. These findings are consistent with preverbal intentions described previously (Bates *et al.* 1975; Bruner 1983). By 20 months of age, children continue to use previously established intentions. However, the proportion of acts used to direct the other's attention decreases, while those used to discuss a joint focus of attention increase. This finding indicates that children are able to join the adult's **topics** and maintain their own topics of **conversation** once initiated. Furthermore, communicative intentions that represent a decrease in **context** embeddedness are noted. Children can now discuss objects and events that are not in the environment but are somehow related to the environ-

ment and respond to clarification requests. The trend of incorporating discussions less embedded in the immediate context with greater perceptual distance from the here and now continues to 32 months when children are noted to discuss objects, events, thoughts and feelings all of which have no perceivable **reference** in the environment.

The developmental sequence, which emerges in the early verbal repertoires of young children, continues to reflect the understanding of the social world and specifically the unfolding of secondary intersubjectivity or the understanding of others as intentional agents. Children first must understand that others have attention and intentions that can be directed or shared. They begin to understand that **communication** is not just to get something done (as in the case of behavioural regulations) but is something to be done together (Baron-Cohen 1989; Camaioni 1993; Tomasello *et al.* 2005). Their pragmatic understanding is reflective of underlying motivations for cooperation and shared intentionality (Ninio and Snow 1996; Snow 1999; Tomasello *et al.* 2007). As children begin to understand others' mental states, they can take others' **perspectives** and understand what **knowledge** is shared and with whom (Baron-Cohen 1989; Ninio and Snow 1996). They move from joint perceptual focus to more decontextualized communicative intentions.

The work described here furthers our understanding of the early social-pragmatic relationship with an emphasis on the unfolding of joint attentional skills. This is especially relevant to our understanding of children with early social communication deficits, such as children with **autism spectrum disorders**.

PAMELA ROSENTHAL ROLLINS

See also: Autism spectrum disorders; child language acquisition; communication; competence, communicative; conversational turn-taking; culture; discourse; intention; intentionality; knowledge; politeness; reference; request; speech act theory; theory of mind

Suggestions for further reading

Ninio, A. and Snow, C.E. (1996) *Pragmatic Development*, Boulder, CO: Westview.

——(1999) 'The development of pragmatics: learning to use language appropriately', in T. Bhatia and W. Ritchie (eds) *Handbook of Language Acquisition*, New York: Academic Press.

Snow, C.E., Pan, B., Imbens-Bailey, A. and Herman, J. (1996) 'Learning how to say what one means: a longitudinal study of children's speech act use', *Social Development*, 5: 56–84.

Disagreement

Studies on disagreement have been conducted in different spoken genres and interactive contexts of **communication**, for example, in **conversation** in America, Britain, Hong Kong, Spain and Venezuela (Schegloff *et al.* 1977; Pomerantz 1984; Sacks 1987; Mori 1999; Moyer 2000; Georgakopoulou 2001; Cheng 2003; Edstrom 2004; Mortensen 2006; Ogden 2006), focus group discussions (Myers 1998), American television shows (Scott 2002), a television panel interview (Clayman 2002), committee meetings in Finland (Kangasharju 2002), workplace **discourses** (Kindler 1988, 1996, 2006; Holmes and Stubbe 2003a; Hugill 2004), network conferences in Sweden (Osvaldsson 2004), collaborative groups (Tocalli-Beller 2003), three generations of Greek-Australian women in interview-narratives (Petraki 2005), and **business discourses** and school textbooks in Hong Kong (Cheng and Warren 2005).

Many studies have described disagreement in terms of types, structures, patterns, (pragma-) linguistic realizations, strategies and functions. Pomerantz's (1984) notion of preference organization regards disagreements between interlocutors as dispreferred and marked in various ways. Myers (1998: 99) finds that participants manage disagreements by means of 'markers of dispreferred turns, hedges, concessions, and attributions'. Myers also observes that even for a direct disagreement between participants, the disagreement is often presented within a shared view, namely by agreeing with one aspect of the previous turn, using repetition, concessions, or repair. Similarly, Gardner (2000) observes that disagreements are delayed in the turn sequence and typically hedged or mitigated.

As Mey (2001: 166–67) states, 'the phenomenon of "(dis)preferred" response sequences is probably universal, the way (dis)preference is realized is not', and individual manifestations of this probably universal phenomenon of conversational organization are specific to the **context** of interaction. For instance, disagreement is considered a preferred response following self-deprecation, and may be a dispreferred response following assessment, or following a **question**, as in the case of a negative answer (Morgan and Krueger 1993; Myers 1998). In a study of conversations of English speakers in India, Valentine (1994) identifies four disagreement strategies: explicit statement of disagreement or stated disagreement components; softening of disagreement with softened negative statements, honorifics, **apologies**; delaying; and hedging. The effect of relative **power** in interpersonal relationships in disagreement has been investigated (Rees-Miller 2000; Holmes and Stubbe 2003a). Cheng (2003) finds that both Hong Kong Chinese (HKC) and native English speakers (NES) express disagreement in conversation, with the HKC disagreeing slightly more frequently. However, HKC use fewer bald, on-record strategies and more redressive language and mitigating devices. Petraki (2005: 269) identifies three disagreement strategies in intergenerational and cross-cultural interviews: 'the participants' questioning of opponent's arguments, appealing to logic, and calling for defense'. In network conferences, Osvaldsson (2004) examines the interactional upshots of participants' laughter in disagreements.

Paralinguistic features of disagreement have been studied, for example, vowel features in South Korean (Lin 2000) and phonetic resources in multiparty assessment talk (Ogden 2006). Cheng and Warren (2005) find that in many of the disagreements in business discourses, especially those that are less direct, the choice of high key and/or high termination (Brazil 1997) by speakers provides the hearer with additional situation-specific information confirming that the speaker is saying something contrary or against expectations.

WINNIE CHENG

See also: Apologies; assessment, pragmatic; business discourse; communication; context; conversation; conversational turn-taking; discourse; hedge; honorific language; power; question; sequence organization

Suggestions for further reading

Cheng, W. and Warren, M. (2005) '// → well I have a *DIF*ferent // ↘ *THIN*king you know //: a corpus-driven study of disagreement in Hong Kong business discourse', in F. Bargiela-Chiappini and M. Gotti (eds) *Asian Business Discourse(s)*, Frankfurt am Main: Peter Lang.

Kindler, H.S. (2006) *Conflict Management: Resolving Disagreements in the Workplace*, Boston, MA: Thomson/Course Technology.

Mortensen, C.D. (2006) *Human Conflict: Disagreement, Misunderstanding, and Problematic Talk*, Lanham, MD: Rowman and Littlefield.

Disambiguation

In a pre-theoretical sense disambiguation is needed in cases where a one-to-many correspondence between form and **meaning** occurs. From the early stages of pragmatic research disambiguation has figured in the essential processes governing language use. Incidentally, it also constitutes a key to some of the most hotly debated issues in the field (Blutner 2000, 2004; Carston 2002; Levinson 2000; Nunberg 1979, 2004; Recanati 2004b; Sperber and Wilson 1995; Wilson and Carston 2007a).

Disambiguation only crops up very indirectly in Grice's (1975) seminal account as it is intimately related to a fundamental property of utterances: **ambiguity** (*see* Hirst 1987). In **Grice**'s original, speaker-oriented account the avoidance of ambiguity is a key phenomenon in human **communication**. Although he takes it to be 'a matter of less urgency' than the other **maxims**, Grice's fourth maxim explicitly mentions ambiguity as one of the pitfalls from which a competent conversationalist must steer away: the speaker must 'avoid ambiguity' (Grice 1975: 308). Another sub-maxim also implicitly refers to a second form of ambiguity, at least from an intuitive point of view: the speaker must 'avoid obscurity of expression'. Nevertheless, the concept of disambiguation was shaped essentially through the various exegeses of Grice's proposal and came to refer to a different form of disambiguating which Grice exemplifies through (1):

(1) He is in the grip of a *vice*.

Here the homonymous noun *vice* can either denote a moral fault or a kind of tool. Weinreich (1964) refers to examples like (1) as instances of contrastive ambiguity. Thus, Grice distinguishes a deliberate form of ambiguity intended by the speaker from a presumably unintended form. Crucially, in the Gricean model the latter type of disambiguation focuses on the interpretative side of communication (i.e. the hearer) and lies outside the scope of the **cooperative principle** and of the maxims, as the disambiguation of (1) contributes to '**what is said**' and does not rely on **implicatures**.

Grice's followers soon pointed out some problems with his proposal. Atlas and Levinson (1981) and Levinson (2000) argue that 'what is said' also depends on some pragmatic **heuristics** – the original maxims or some more recent version. In (2), for example, disambiguation of the syntactic structure of B's reply relies on the relevance relationship with A's previous utterance (maxim of relation):

(2) A: i.   What are they doing in the kitchen?
       ii. What kind of apples are those?
     B: They are *cooking* apples.

Levinson (2000) claims that some disambiguating takes advantage of default pragmatic **inferences** (namely, **generalized conversational implicatures**). In this neo-Gricean model, two heuristics are more clearly connected to disambiguation processes: the I-heuristic, which states that what is simply described is stereotypically exemplified and the M-heuristic, which purports that what is said in an abnormal way is not normal. For instance, in (3) below the pyramid is taken to rest on its base, and not on one of its summits (by virtue of the I-heuristic):

(3) The blue pyramid is *on* the red cube.

Sperber and Wilson (1995: 168) agree with this and identify pragmatically calculated disambiguating processes in cases similar to (1) (e.g. *George has a big cat*), claiming that the right propositional form of an utterance is determined by applying their own heuristic, the principle of relevance: 'at every stage in disambiguation, **reference** assignment and enrichment, the hearer should choose the solution involving the least effort' (1995: 185). First-stage pragmatic inferences of this sort are categorized in **relevance theory** as explicatures (1995: 182). Bach (1994a, 1997, 1999a) also distinguishes propositional-level pragmatic inferences, calling them **implicitures**. With such claims, disambiguation is fully integrated in the domain of pragmatic inferential processes. This move, however, raises the question of the type of interface which should be entertained between **semantics** and **pragmatics**, as pragmatic heuristics appear to be necessary both in order to feed into the propositional form of an utterance, as well as to generate (standard) implicatures derived from it, i.e. a combination of pre- and post-semantic pragmatics. At the heart of disambiguation processes lies the evidence for 'pragmatic intrusion', as it has been dubbed. Moore (1986) emphasizes that in order to maintain a purely semantic propositional form independent of pragmatic inferences, it appears that some place-holding devices (indices) will have to be inserted in the **logical form** which will be saturated at a later stage (*see* Recanati's (2004b: 86) discussion of indexicalism). This corresponds to a line taken by Barwise and Perry (1983) in Situation Semantics, or by Stanley (2000, 2002). Alternatively, the interface between semantics and pragmatics can be regarded as much more permeable, as is the case in Discourse Representation Theory (Kamp and Reyle 1993) and in Segmented Discourse Representation Theory (Asher 1993; Asher and Lascarides 2003: 252), where the integration of both modules appears to allow reciprocal feeds. For instance, disambiguating polysemous words can depend on rhetorical (i.e. **discourse**) relations which hold across utterances as in (4):

(4) a. The judge asked where the defendant was.
   b. The barrister apologized, and said he was at the pub across the street.
   c. The court bailiff found him slumped beneath the *bar*.
   c'. But the court bailiff found him slumped beneath the *bar*.

The *Narration* relation which governs the interpretation of *c* in the discourse **context** of *a* and *b* is overridden by a different discourse relation,

namely *contrast*, when *a* and *b* combine with *c'*, which leads to a different disambiguation of the noun *bar* (pub bar in *c* and courtroom bar in *c'*).

Recanati (1989, 2002a, 2004b: 7) also writes in support of 'intrusive' pragmatics. He identifies utterances where 'what is said' needs to be disambiguated pragmatically through a mandatory 'saturation' process. He shows that there exists a class of expressions which denote a relation in their meaning that needs to be contextually instantiated; for instance between the *owner* and *author* meanings in the genitive nominal construction *Lucy's book* or in nominal compounds (*see also* Meyer 1993). Saturation belongs to a set of so-called **primary pragmatic processes** which derive 'what is said' from sentence meaning. According to Recanati (2004b: 131), disambiguation can also involve optional, pragmatic, 'top-down' inferences, such as modulation, to tease out the meaning of polysemous words as illustrated in the contrasting pair *light breeze/light package* where a co-compositional account à la Pustejovsky (1995) – whereby the meaning of *light* is co-constructed with the head it modifies – will not suffice. Thus, the meaning of *light* is dynamically, inferentially determined beyond the mere lexical collocation, allowing new, context-dependent readings.

The discussion of disambiguating processes has had important consequences for fundamental questions regarding the nature of the interface between semantics and pragmatics, as well as for other wider issues. An interesting claim made by some neo-Griceans (Horn 1984, 1989; Levinson 2000: 28) links the unavoidability of disambiguating interpretative processes to a 'design flaw' in the human communicative system: the physiological limitation of human articulation, which severely constrains the amount of information that can be coded in an utterance. Human speech rate constitutes a communication 'bottleneck' that needs to be circumvented. According to Levinson (2000), human communication combines underdeterminacy of the coded content (hence ambiguity) with specialized inferential heuristics to tease out more content of the restricted forms (*see* Zipf 1949; Horn 1984, 1989). Barsalou (1983, 1987, 1993), on the other hand, discusses the cognitive foundations which explain the need to posit the construction of ad hoc categories and concepts in normal, everyday uses of language: a line adopted in **lexical pragmatics** in an attempt to determine the kind of inferential work needed to construct such nonce categories (see below). Cummings (2005) demonstrates that the permeability and integration of pragmatic processes at all levels of the interpretative process, as seen in the case of disambiguation, puts into question the adequacy of a discrete pragmatic module, and more generally calls for a reassessment of the modular architecture of the brain (*see* Kasher 1984a).

While the neo-Gricean and relevance-theoretic enterprises seem to have resolutely brought disambiguation within the scope of mainstream pragmatics, other options have been considered in Pustejovsky (1995), Pustejovsky and Anick (1988) and Pustejovsky and Boguraev (1993, 1995). While these theorists recognize the pragmatic import in sorting out contrastive ambiguities (e.g. *bat, bank, vice*), they develop a rich lexical semantics – the Generative Lexicon – that can capture systematic ambiguities in cases of complementary polysemy, as illustrated in (5) and (6):

(5) Lucy finished/broke the *bottle*.
(6) Max slammed/walked through the *door*.

Interestingly, the ambiguity observed for the complement nouns in (5) and (6) instantiates a very productive property of relational nominals, i.e. complementary polysemy, that allows the exploitation of systematic conceptual contrasts, as for example here the Content/Container, and the Figure/Ground alternation, respectively. In these examples, it is claimed that disambiguation of the logically polysemous term is best captured in a bottom-up fashion through a combination of an underspecified lexical meta-entry with logical type-coercion mechanisms which then generate the different meanings of *bottle* and *door*. However, Nunberg (1995, 2004) and Recanati (2004b) illustrate how even this type of systematic polysemy does not undermine the pragmatic nature of the phenomenon as meaning alternations can be shown to be both a productive, context-dependent phenomenon, or the result of conventionalized (lexicalized) **knowledge**.

Experimental methodology has also been applied to disambiguation processes. Bezuidenhout

and Morris (2004), Murphy (1997), Peleg *et al.* (2004) and Vu *et al.* (1998, 2000) devised experimental designs to study the predictions made by several disambiguation models, as well as their cognitive underpinnings. In particular, Peleg *et al.* (2004: 179) have tried to decide whether contextually driven, top-down disambiguation takes place after, in parallel with, or instead of lexically driven, compositional, bottom-up construction of meaning in cases of contrastive ambiguity (e.g. *bulb* in carrier sentences like *The gardener dug a hole. The bulb was inserted.*). The results show that, in a lexical decision task, contextual information is more likely to override lexical salience in sentence final position (lexical salience is defined as the relative experiential frequency of the two senses; *see* Giora 1997). Their analysis suggests that both lexical disambiguation based on coded salience and contextual disambiguation based on some pragmatic heuristic run in parallel. Furthermore, they argue that both processes are encapsulated, as even in cases of strong contextual predictability the lexically salient (but contextually incompatible) reading gets activated and has a priming effect. Thus, a lexical salience effect only crops up in condition (a) in '*The gardener dug a hole. She inserted the* (a) *bulb* (b) *flower.*' The probe *light* is recognized faster in (a) than in (b) (Peleg *et al.* 2004: 181).

As we saw above, the place occupied by disambiguation in the architectural organization of pragmatic theory has become less and less marginal over the last forty years. A recent and promising development in theoretical pragmatic investigations – lexical pragmatics (Blutner 1998, 2000, 2004; Carston 1997, 2002; Wilson and Carston 2007a) – focuses most of its attention on disambiguating processes while re-defining considerably the original Gricean model. (Although the term 'disambiguation' is applied more restrictively by, for example, Wilson and Carston (2007a: 241), the range of phenomena covered by this approach certainly includes traditional cases of disambiguation.) A similar path is also followed by Nunberg (1979, 1995, 2004) through his observations on meaning transfers and deferred interpretation.

The relevance-theoretic approach entertains the view that 'lexical interpretation typically involves the construction of an ad hoc concept or occasion-specific sense, based on interaction among encoded concepts, contextual information and pragmatic expectations or principles' (Wilson and Carston 2007a: 230; *see* Barsalou 1987, 1993). With the generalized introduction of ad hoc concepts, lexical pragmatics looks at the sort of disambiguating processes illustrated in the examples cited above as the normal interpretative procedure that affects 'almost every word' (Wilson and Carston 2007a: 231). Such a procedure relies on two complementary concept-constructional processes, narrowing (e.g. *man* in *Churchill was a man* must be narrowed down to a context-dependent, restricted meaning such as 'an ideal man' or 'a typical man' in order to avoid a trivial statement) and broadening (e.g. *The bottle is empty* is broadened to denote an 'almost empty bottle'). This proposal brings together a variety of phenomena ranging from classical disambiguation examples and the interpretation of so-called non-literal uses of language typically found in tropes (**metaphors**, **hyperbole**, etc.) to loose uses (approximation, e.g. *The group formed a circle in the room*) under the heading of 'lexical adjustment'. Interestingly, this radical move posits that there is a continuum of inferential processes linking standard cases of disambiguation with, for example, creative neologisms as found in *The boy porched the newspaper*.

Within the growing framework of **optimality theory** (*see* Blutner 1998, 2000, 2004; Gärtner 2004), lexical pragmatics also extends the scope of phenomena covered by disambiguation processes as it offers a 'bi-directional' approach of the domain which includes the perspective of the speaker (production side). In the longer term, the importance and relevance of such unifying and extended accounts of disambiguating processes resides in their ability to bridge the gap with other domains of lexical investigation such as **child language acquisition** and language change (Blutner 2000, 2004; Levinson 2000; Nunberg 2004).

DIDIER MAILLAT

See also: Ambiguity; child language acquisition; cognitive science; contextualism; defaults in utterance interpretation; experimental pragmatics; explicit/implicit distinction; generalized conversational implicature, theory of; heuristic;

implicature; impliciture; inferential comprehension; lexical pragmatics; maxims of conversation; neo-Gricean pragmatics; optimality-theory pragmatics; primary pragmatic processes; radical pragmatics; relevance theory; semantics-pragmatics interface; vagueness; what is said

Suggestions for further reading

Carston, R. (2002) *Thoughts and Utterances: The Pragmatics of Explicit Communication*, Oxford: Blackwell. Chapters 2 and 5.
Levinson, S. (2000) *Presumptive Meanings: The Theory of Generalized Conversational Implicature*, Cambridge, MA: MIT Press. Chapter 3.
Peleg, O., Giora, R. and Fein, O. (2004) 'Contextual strength: the whens and hows of context effects', in I.A. Noveck and D. Sperber (eds) *Experimental Pragmatics*, London: Palgrave Macmillan.

Discourse
Three areas of definition

Most dictionary definitions of 'discourse' will describe the term's pre-scientific meaning as 'a long and serious treatment or discussion of a subject in speech or writing' (Hornby 2005: 434). This definition is echoed with an emphasis on public oral performance in *Le Petit Larousse Illustré* as a 'développement oratoire sur un sujet déterminé, prononcé en public' (2003: 328). The two dictionary entries also include a second meaning connected to the discipline of **discourse analysis**. This definition equally highlights the dimension of language-in-use, while identifying the naturally occurring utterance and meaningful language use as associated units of analysis: 'the use of language in speech and writing in order to produce meaning' (Hornby 2005: 434). The equivalent definition from *Larousse* is '[r]éalisation concrète, écrite ou orale, de la langue considerée comme un système abstrait' (2003: 328). By positing a contrast with 'language as an abstract system', de Saussure's concept of 'parole' is evoked as an alternative but displaced term. Whereas de Saussurean tradition had identified 'parole' in order to suppress its study as 'uninteresting' to the scholar of language because 'idiosyncratic' and the terrain of 'psychology', the term 'discourse' emerged with the promise that meaningful language use in a real situation is an area worthy of study. It opened a window on a range of phenomena which linguists thus far had not explored systematically in any great detail.

One way to throw light on the term and concept of 'discourse' is to examine how its use emerged and how it has been shaped historically, while recognizing that its appeal resided in the development of a particular agenda for language inquiry, sometimes complementary to and at other times in vehement opposition with prevailing practice at the time. This way, three defining areas can broadly be identified, which should not be discussed in strict in isolation from each other. First, viewed from within a linguistic project, 'discourse' emerged as a reference to specific language phenomena which are characteristic of running text and ongoing interaction. This area places stress on authentic language data and on pushing enquiry beyond both the bounds of the isolated grammatical sentence and the self-constructed language datum. Second, from within a sociolinguistic project, 'discourse' has been instrumental in developing a qualitative research agenda on the role of language use in social life. In the background is an interactional and a performative view in which language use is treated as **communication** and its complex manifestations as social action. Third, as it also surfaced in a social theoretical **context**, 'discourse' has become a metaphor for understanding processes of sociocultural **representation** (these are seen as permeated by **power** relationships, ideology and world view).

Attending to the first area of definition, the development of an analytical concept of 'discourse' resulted in a major breakthrough in linguists' efforts to study naturally occurring language use and to do so with specific reference to formal properties characteristic of running text and ongoing interaction. It also served to locate an area of **meaning** which is functionally relative to sequence, situation, purpose and user. It is worth reminding readers here that some instances of early discourse research prioritized the conversational domain of spoken exchanges, while other early developments focused more on the properties of written texts. Anglo-American work in particular interacted more directly with

speech act theory and **conversation analysis** and was quick to integrate their key concepts and taxonomies. At the same time, examples such as Sinclair *et al.* (1972), Labov and Fanschel (1977) and Brown and Yule (1983) were still very much bracketed by more traditional linguistic concerns, such as the detection of a hierarchical structure in speech events, which is akin to that which had been described earlier for the constituents of the sentence. In early continental European developments, which often identified themselves as 'text linguistics', the study of transsentential phenomena (e.g. aspects of crossreference, argumentative and rhetorical structure, connectivity and textual cohesion) and of the cognitive processing of textual units, provided key impetuses for pushing the linguistic project beyond the confines of the isolated sentence. Well-known examples include Harweg (1968), Werlich (1976), De Beaugrande and Dressler (1981) and Van Dijk and Kintsch (1983).

The second area in delineating the discursive has been tied up with the emergence of an integrated sociolinguistic project in the 1960s and 1970s, especially the more qualitative, 'interactional' sociolinguistic traditions which developed out of the work of Gumperz and Hymes (e.g. Gumperz and Hymes 1972). Not surprisingly, central insights on the nature of interaction and situated language use drew substantially on theoretical conversations with speech act theory, conversation analysis, **ethnomethodology** and Goffman's analysis of the interaction order. While for some (e.g. Fairclough 1989: 9), speech act theory's performative view on the language utterance (Austin 1962) counts as the primary point of departure for a generalized social actional view on language use, others also invoke the groundbreaking contributions in ethnomethodology and conversation analysis as primary loci for a view which connects the use of language with interaction and the in-course production of an operative situational and social context (e.g. Duranti and Goodwin 1992: 22). Interactional behaviour is, among other things, oriented to the display of participants' perspectives on the situation as it unfolds and is talked about. The latter is both profoundly instrumental and relational, and therefore social. Hymes's (1972a) formulation of the SPEAKING project can be interpreted as the formulation of a discourse perspective within **sociolinguistics** which takes the speech event and 'ways of speaking' as primary units of analysis. Like many other linguistic anthropologists he relies on the term 'discourse' to define such a project, but uses it in its countable form to refer to particular ways of interacting and communicating which are associated with a particular domain, setting or **topic**.

In relation to the third area, 'discourse' has surfaced in a social theoretical context where it has become a metaphor for understanding processes of sociocultural representation. This area of definition signals how the concept of discourse has been implicated in some of the theoretical and epistemological challenges to the human and social sciences by post-structuralist theory. In Foucault's version of this challenge (e.g. Foucault 1972b), the concept of discourse broadly covers what can be said about a particular topic as well as the rules which prescribe the ways of talking about topics (including who gets to speak about them in the first place). Discourse is seen as centrally connected to the production of truth and is located in a field of power relationships which produce social life in its various forms. It is particularly in this area that a discourse analytic perspective has spilled over into various other disciplines (law, social work, history, etc.), where it has given rise to a 'linguistic turn' which stresses that truth is relative to what is articulated in discourse, while highlighting the social, institutional and organizational conditions that enable its expression. The discourse perspective is central to understanding certain aspects of the crisis of legitimacy (a crisis of truth), which in recent years has been much discussed in the human and social sciences. For discourse theorists such as Laclau and Mouffe (1985), Howarth (2000) and Torfing (1999), discourse has subsequently become an epistemology for reading a societal state of hegemonic relationships vis-à-vis particular ideological formations. Discourse theory is a form of **political discourse** analysis, which does not come with specific text or language-oriented empirical imperatives.

A constructivist perspective in which language use, often in combination with other practices, is seen as constitutive of social reality is intrinsic to many traditions of discourse analysis. Critical discourse analysis (e.g. Fairclough 1992; Wodak

1996; Locke 2004) must be credited for seeking to link up textual analysis with the explanatory ambitions of social theory, societal critique and emancipatory goals. It has been agenda-setting for a discussion of the connections between situated language use, power and ideology and has acted as a broker for much social theoretical work on 'discourse'. In fairness, one must note that this development occurred alongside (and throughout the 1990s there has been growing interaction with) comparable programmes which originated in other traditions (e.g. Briggs 1996 in linguistic anthropology and Rampton 2006 in interactional sociolinguistics).

Finally, when the term 'discourse' is used in its countable form with a particular qualification which evokes the reality-creating capacities of forms of language use (e.g. capitalist discourses, sexist discourses, medical discourses, discourses of education), this sometimes counts as a reference to typical patterns of interaction and/or language use, and sometimes as a reference to ways of reading and 'coding' the world which are associated with a particular locus of social activity. In many cases, however, the reference has been to both and the underlying assumption is often that the full range of phenomena that can be addressed under the heading of discourse is imbued with value.

Remaining theoretical issues

A number of theoretical issues continue to stand out and have dominated debates and formulations of concepts. With varying emphases, these also foreground the problem of relevant contexts of interpretation. To begin with, the problem of understanding discourse practice takes the question of relevant meaning beyond the confines of linguistic meaning, more fully into the domain of social interpretation. Bourdieu's (1984: 94) understanding of discourse as 'practice' has been formative in this: situated speech is understood in terms of durably acquired dispositions in response to symbolic market conditions and it is viewed as imbued with value and power (especially the value of 'legitimacy'). Similarly, the concept of 'discursive practice' for Gumperz (2003: 112–14) requires a separate and more inclusive level of analysis. It is not tied to the specifics of linguistic analysis, but connects 'interpretation' to levels of discourse organization which are distinct from more commonly studied lexico-semantic signalling processes (he pays particular attention to the indexical functioning of so-called contextualization cues). In this view, discourse practice is viewed as constituted in the interplay of linguistic, sociocultural and ideological forces with organizational principles which are partly local and specific to the interaction and partly trans-situational (compare also with Hanks's (1996) concept of 'communicative practice').

A second set of issues can be captured as the debate of 'structure' versus 'agency' within discourse studies. This opposition is often articulated with reference to related pairs, such as the contrast between 'momentary' outcomes and 'longue durée' effects of communicative encounters. Expressed in slightly different terms, a contrast is noted between the flexibility and room for negotiation in 'micro' interactional behaviour and the stable directions of 'macro' units. The terms of this debate derive from the presence of simultaneously articulated versions of the reality-creating capacities of discourse processes (cf. Philips 2001). One such version reads that, especially in face-to-face interaction, interactants have the capacity to shape emerging realities through their participation in discourse and this is typically contrasted with a view which underlines the longer-term historical processes in which discourses are involved. The latter are often talked about in terms of sociocultural reproduction and accumulative transformation over time. It is also worth noting that, except in the context of new literacy studies (e.g. Street 2003), an interactional perspective on the 'momentary' is still in quite a number of respects ill developed with respect to written texts and texts with a one-to-many participation (e.g. mass **media discourse**). The challenge here is how to do justice to the in-course aspects of individual situated experiences of interpretation, while answering questions about the larger-scale impact on mass audiences. The risky assumption indeed has been that uniformity of textual artifact would warrant uniformity of interpretation (compare also with 'natural histories of discourse', Silverstein and Urban (1996)).

Discourse types (whether viewed as form-meaning complexes or as social-actional modes) have also been attributed an agentive role in societal orderings of discourse practices. This has been a specific theme in the work of Fairclough (1989), who draws for this on **Habermas**'s discussion of the historically shifting relationships between the social lifeworlds and the political and economic systems as well as on Foucault's postulate of the concept of an 'order of discourse' (Foucault 1971). Discourse types and formats can thus be thought of in terms of ordered relationships of inclusion/exclusion, with regulated boundaries, processes of meshing and relationships of intrusion, and this is an important form of social ordering. This line of discourse research has resulted in process-oriented analyses of macro socio-economic contexts as giving rise both to hybridity in discourse practices and to colonizing tendencies within a particular ordering of discourses (for example, Fairclough (1992) identifies the commodification and conversationalization of discourses of the public domain as two significant tendencies in contemporary neo-liberal Western democracies). Orderings of discourses are relevant at various levels of analysis, not just society-wide but also at the level of institutional procedure and interactional sequence (Sarangi and Slembrouck 1996). Other related concepts, such as that of communities of practice (Eckert 1999) have stressed the distribution of particular discourse practices over specific populations of users.

From a linguistic anthropological angle, the challenges posed by the ordering of discourses in a societal context have been addressed through the concept of orders of indexicality (Silverstein 2003). With this, the allocation of instances and conventions of language use to a particular level of contextual ordering, whether micro, meso or macro, has been represented as a problem of interpretation-in-discourse. Two further questions can thus be identified as running themes through the latter set of developments. There is the problem of space and time as contextual dimensions of discourse and, accompanying this problem, a crisis in the identification of stable units of analysis and interpretation. For Scollon and Wong-Scollon (2003) and associated researchers, geosemiotics engages with the study of spatially-distributed signs to address some of the challenges posed by place, while Collins et al. (to appear) and others have raised the relevance of spatial-temporal scales in the interpretation of enacted multilingual repertoires. Wortham (2006), drawing on Lemke (2000), critically raises the relevance of timescales within which to interpret interactional processes that result in the construction of institutional identities. Central here are questions of sample, unit, process and shift. In each of these cases, it is clear that contemporary processes (e.g. globalization) have destabilized received interpretations of time and space as stable backdrops to discourse. At the same time, the concept of discourse has been taken to a level of sophistication by taking on the full complexities in answering the question of what it means to use language in context.

STEF SLEMBROUCK

See also: Competence, communicative; context; conversation analysis; discourse analysis; discourse coherence; Habermas, J.; political discourse; sociolinguistics; speech act theory

Suggestions for further reading

Erickson, F. (2004) *Talk and Social Theory*, Malden, MA: Polity Press.
Fairclough, N. (2001) *Language and Power*, 2nd edn, London: Longman.

Discourse Analysis
A trans-disciplinary seminal project with key lenders and borrowers

Within linguistic circles, discourse analysis is typically defined as the study of naturally occurring and meaningful language use in its social context of occurrence and with particular reference to the real-time dimensions of ongoing interaction and running text. Historically, its emergence can be understood in terms of a number of quasi-simultaneous developments which originate in the late 1960s. These developments include a move away from the study of language through self-constructed examples, a move beyond the unit of the grammatical sentence and an undertaking to embrace the problem of **context** more fully than had hitherto been the case. Initially, this was achieved by understanding language use as social action and, later (referring here to developments from the mid-1980s onwards) by

recognizing its constructivist properties in bringing about, sustaining and transforming social realities and relations.

Attendant developments in the second half of the twentieth century which contributed substantially to the development of specific text-and-talk oriented perspectives within discourse analysis included **conversation analysis** (which originates in sociology and thematizes the study of aspects of turn-taking and sequential organization, e.g. Schegloff 2007), **speech act theory** and **pragmatics** (which originates in analytical philosophy and brought with it analytical foci such as indirect and implicit **communication**, information exchange and **politeness** phenomena, e.g. Grice 1975 and Brown and Levinson 1987), interactional **sociolinguistics** with its integrated focus on situated interpretation and practices of contextualization (e.g. Gumperz 1982a) and systemic-functional linguistics (especially Halliday 1978). The latter had amounted to linguistics' most explicit functionalist statement thus far. It came with a simultaneous focus on how aspects of language use contribute to the representation of actions and states, on interpersonal relationships and on text-connectedness as characteristic for specific registers and genres which are tied to specific situations of use.

At the same time, one can witness in the history of discourse analysis an accumulative dialogic engagement with social theoretical work on questions of language, **representation**, ideology, **power**, equity and identity. The works of **Habermas**, Foucault and Bourdieu have undoubtedly been central. The conversations with social theoretical work have also kept close to work that is on the pulse of the contemporary social era and its specific currents (e.g. Giddens 1991 on the reflexive individual as an aspect of late modernity; Harvey 1996 on globalization and neo-liberalism; Wernick 1991 on promotional **culture**; Anderson 1991 on nationalism). These conversations, in their turn, have shaped typical research questions addressed by discourse analysts.

The contemporary scene

While one can detect a gradual progression from an early, narrow, linguistic interest in the formal and functional mapping of various aspects of the situated utterance to a later, process-oriented research perspective which gives priority to social questions such as language and identity, it is probably more accurate to state that discourse analysis has crystallized within language studies in two directions. On the one hand, one can note a continuation of a linguistic use of the term in which **discourse** is viewed as the layer of **meaning** which is tied directly to situations of language use. The focus here is often on large collections of verbal material of a particular situation or activity type and the use of quantitative methods and techniques of **corpus linguistics**, selecting specific discourse-related themes for closer attention (e.g. Warren 2006 on aspects of naturalness in informal conversational language use). On the other hand, recent decades have witnessed the formulation of a broad project of discourse studies which views language use holistically, often in combination with other forms of semiotic behaviour, from the angle of what one can broadly refer to as 'social practices'. Much discourse research thus simultaneously attends to aspects of text and talk, processes of interpretation and cognition, social-actional dimensions of communicative behaviour, as well as its functioning at the level of ideological reproduction and socio-cultural transformation.

Within this second tradition, discourse analysis has often (if not mostly) stood in an applied relationship to the social, with discourse research being oriented to the identification, investigation and offering solutions for (here echoing Brumfitt's definition) real-world problems and issues in which language plays a central role (Brumfitt 2001). A quite arbitrary list which attempts to give an impression of the range of possible themes would probably include contextual complexity in the processing of cartoons by patients with unilateral lesions (Dagge and Hartje 1985), the effects of story sequencing on affective reactions to news broadcasts (Mundorf and Zillman 1991), self-commodification in dating advertisements (Coupland 2006), pedagogical focus in foreign language classrooms and the use of repair strategies (Kasper 1986), media coverage of the genetically modified food debate (Cook et al. 2006) and the communication of rights in contexts of police arrests and detention (Rock 2007), amongst others. Themes under the heading

of registering discourse change in response to shifts in socio-cultural values are also many and varied. One such theme is the interest in discourse technologies. This concept and the literature that has developed around it invite attention to the ways in which situation-specific forms of communication have become subject to explicit forms of teaching, training and monitoring. These forms have in recent decades given rise to a unrivalled battery of communication manuals (promoting the ideal of the self-regulating and self-reflexive individual). This line of research has also documented the salient role of particular discourse formats as having a colonizing appeal in the contemporary era, e.g. promotional talk, interviewing, counselling (Cameron 2000).

Specific fields of application have given rise to specialist offshoots such as professional discourse studies (e.g. Gunnarsson et al. 1997; Sarangi and Roberts 1999) with further subdivisions for medicine (e.g. Gotti and Salager-Meyer 2006), law and forensic science (e.g. Coulthard and Johnson 2007; Philips 1998) and social work (e.g. Hall et al. 2007). Discourse perspectives have been articulated for specific language-related interests. For instance, Hatim and Mason (1990) have done this for **translation** studies, Wadensjö (1998) and Roy (2000) for interpreting studies and Carter and Simpson (1989) for **stylistics**. While Barton (2007), Street (2003) and Collins and Blot (2003) have formulated a (critical) discourse analytical programme for literacy studies, Larsen-Freeman (1980) has broken comparable territory for **second language acquisition** research. Discourse analysis can thus be summed up as entailing a particular perspective on language use and social life and the themes of identities-in-discourse and identities-as-outcomes-of-discourse are undeniably among the most commonly addressed in research across fields of application.

Instances of discourse analysis will in many cases also draw seminally on various traditions in the study of language use or **semiotics**. For instance, whereas discursive psychology (e.g. Edwards and Potter 1992) has concentrated on themes from **cognitive psychology** such as everyday explanations, memory and attitude by bringing together a conversation-analytic perspective with social psychological constructivism, multimodal discourse analysis (e.g. Kress and Van Leeuwen

2001; O'Halloran 2004) has drawn substantially on a systemic-functional perspective on meaning making for the development of a discourse analysis which is not restricted by an exclusive interest in verbal modes of communication.

From the side of the borrowing disciplines, the term and methods of discourse analysis are sometimes used to refer to a 'linguistic turn' or a 'text analytical turn' within the social sciences, more generally. Examples include Dumolyn (2008) for medieval institutional history, Doty (1996) for North/South relations and Campbell and Dillon (1993) for international relations and narratives of war. Note that these studies are often culminations of longer lines of theoretical and empirical engagement with issues of situated language use in ways specific to these disciplines. Thus, milestone publications in a language-history debate include White (1973) on history as **narrative** and Stedman Jones (1983) on languages of class.

Recording, transcription and the relationship with fieldwork

It is hard to think of discourse analysis and not include a paragraph on the many advantages which audio, audio-visual, and later, digital recording have introduced, when it comes to producing reliable data in terms of potential for analyzing the social-in-the-interactional. Recording technology has in recent decades also been refined and its scope expanded with the advent of video and now various types of digital recording (think, for instance, of the use of radio microphones which register the sound within a person's aural range). Recording practices have also been debated. The debate has highlighted the importance of preparatory conditions of sustained observation before recording takes place, the issue of researcher presence during the recorded event, the effects of recording on the interaction which is being taped, as well as analyzing how recordings are selectively invested with viewpoint. Very recent discussions have swung the pendulum back in the direction of sustained direct observation and researcher field notes, as entailing both a wider and more comprehensive take on data events.

Typically, recordings are transcribed before analysis takes place. A **transcription** is a written re-rendering of a stretch of speech, often using a combination of conventions specific to writing together with other graphic devices which highlight the relevance of particular aspects of speech. The purpose of a transcription is to 'freeze' the spoken so that it becomes amenable to detailed scrutiny for purposes of analysis. Transcriptions come with varying degrees of sophistication and detail. Transcription practice has been described as posing particular challenges of authenticity/credibility, accuracy, accessibility/readability, translation and interpretative relevance (Bucholtz 2007), while also being 'coloured' by specific histories and traditions in the representation of orality in print (Jaffe 2000). Originally, transcription practice in discourse analysis tended to favour the representation of talk, but nowadays graphically aligned representations of paralinguistic, non-verbal and actional features of talk are increasingly included. Recent software developments in the context of digitized audio and video recordings have resulted in new possibilities, such as the use of integrative databases in which it is possible to read the transcription while the recording is being viewed or listened to. This has relieved transcription practice of some of the pressures of exhaustiveness, detailedness and authenticity.

STEF SLEMBROUCK

See also: Applied linguistics; context; conversation analysis; corpus linguistics; discourse; Grice, H.P.; Habermas, J.; implicature; inference; institutional and professional discourse; narrative discourse; politeness; power; sociolinguistics; transcription

Suggestions for further reading

Gee, J.P. (2005) *An Introduction to Discourse Analysis: Theory and Method*, 2nd edn, London: Routledge.
Scollon, R. and Wong Scollon, S. (2003) *Discourses in Place: Language in the Material World*, London: Routledge.

Discourse Coherence

There is no widely accepted definition of coherence or of what constitutes a coherent text, although 'an overwhelming consensus can be achieved for most naturally occurring texts' (Hoey 1991: 266). Discourse or textual coherence is termed the 'texture' of a text (Halliday and Hasan 1976: 2). It is 'a quality assigned to text by a reader or listener, and is a measure of the extent to which the reader or listener finds that the text holds together and makes sense as a unity' (Hoey 1991: 265–66). Sanders *et al.* (1993) advocate a cognitive theory of coherence relations and distinguish between 'semantic' and 'pragmatic' coherence relations and connectives. Semantic relations refer to the real world relation among the situations described in the successive utterances, and pragmatic relations describe relations among successive illocutions. Examining discourse 'connectedness' in students' academic writing, Todd *et al.* (2007) distinguish between 'cohesion', 'propositional coherence' and 'interactional coherence'. Maat (1998) argues for a classification of coherence relations supported by theoretical and psychological arguments, as well as linguistic evidence.

Different linguistic features that contribute to discourse coherence in written and spoken **discourse** have been examined. For instance, conversational coherence is organized by sequencing rules governing an adjacency pair, and these rules govern 'what is expected to occur' and 'what is allowed to occur in coherent discourse' (Tsui 1991: 111). Other features include referential coherence (Garnham *et al.* 1982), placement of discourse **topic** at the beginning of an informative text (Giora *et al.* 1996), global **discourse markers** placed at the beginning and at the end of topic digressions, and with topic shifts and drifts (Lenk 1998), the coherence-based formulation of the discourse marker *well* (Schiffrin 1987), micromarkers such as determiners, possessives, deictics, and conjunctions in publicity texts (Vivanco 2005), lexical repetition (Tyler 1994), the discourse markers of *you know, like, yeah* and *I mean* (Fuller 2003) and deictics (Grenoble and Riley 1996).

Lee (1998) describes a pedagogical framework of coherence, which comprises six elements: purpose, audience and **context** of situation; macrostructure; thematic development and topical development; propositional development and topical development; cohesion; and metadiscourse. First, purpose, audience and context of situation

refer to how explicitness of purpose and awareness of audience and context contribute to coherence. Second, macrostructure is the overall structure of texts which defines text types or genre. Third, thematic development and topical development are concerned with how information can be best organized (e.g. **given/new**) at various levels (sentence, paragraph) to contribute to overall topic development. Fourth, propositional development and modification mean how **propositions** can be made more explicit by means of elaboration, illustration, exemplification, etc. Fifth, cohesion is defined as connectivity of the surface text with the use of such cohesive devices as **reference**, substitution, conjunctions, **ellipsis**, and lexical cohesion (Halliday and Hasan 1976). Sixth, metadiscourse refers to the linguistic materials in texts that help the readers to organize, interpret, and evaluate the information given. Lee (1998) also describes Crismore *et al.*'s (1993) two types of metadiscourse found in persuasive writing, namely textual (textual and interpretive) and interpersonal markers.

WINNIE CHENG

See also: Cognitive pragmatics; deixis; discourse; discourse cohesion; discourse particles; ellipsis; reference; topic

Suggestions for further reading

Jurafsky, D.S. and Martin, J.H. (2000) *Speech and Language Processing: An Introduction to Natural Language Processing, Computational Linguistics, and Speech Recognition*, Upper Saddle River, NJ: Prentice Hall.

Louwerse, M.M. and Graesser, A.C. (2005) 'Coherence in discourse', in P. Strazny (ed.) *Encyclopedia of Linguistics*, Chicago, IL: Fitzroy Dearborn.

Ulatowska, H.K. and Olness, G.S. (2007) 'Pragmatics in discourse performance: insights from aphasiology', *Seminars in Speech and Language*, 28: 148–57.

Discourse Cohesion

Halliday and Hasan (1976: 2) define 'cohesion' as 'relations of meaning that exist within the text, and that define a text'. According to these authors, cohesion is an index of textual coherence. In different languages, discourse cohesion is achieved 'through different surface mechanisms, while following a similar underlying organization' (Morgan 2000: 279). Hoey (1991: 266) defines cohesion as 'a property of text whereby certain grammatical or lexical features of the sentences of the text connect them to other sentences in the text'. Hoey argues that cohesion is objective, whereas coherence is subjective. According to Hoey (1991: 10), lexical cohesion is the most common form of cohesive tie, accounting for 40 per cent of the cohesive ties cited in Halliday and Hasan (1976).

Halliday and Hasan (1976) discuss two types of cohesive relations in English: grammatical cohesion (**reference**, substitution, **ellipsis**, and conjunctions) and lexical cohesion (lexical reiteration and collocation). Reference is 'a relation on the semantic level' (1976: 89). The referent of a word or phrase may either be retrievable from the surrounding text (endophoric reference) or from the **context** of situation (exophoric reference). In English, there are personal (e.g. I, me), **demonstrative** (e.g. this, these), and comparative forms of reference (e.g. same, better) (1976: 37–39). Substitution refers to 'the replacement of one item by another' (1976: 88). It is a grammatical relation, i.e. 'a relation in the wording rather than in the meaning' (1976: 89), with the substitute item and the item for which it substitutes having the same structural function. In English, the substitute may function as a noun (e.g. one(s), the same), as a verb (e.g. do), or as a clause (e.g. so, not, assuming so, suppose not). Halliday and Hasan's third type of grammatical cohesion is ellipsis, which is the omission of elements required by grammatical rules. English has three main kinds

of ellipsis: nominal, verbal and clausal ellipsis. The following example is a verbal ellipsis (McCarthy 2002: 44):

> Will anyone be waiting?
> Jim will, I should think.

The last category of grammatical cohesion discussed by Halliday and Hasan is conjunction. Halliday (1985) offers a list of more than forty kinds of conjunction, which is simplified by McCarthy (2002: 47) into elaboration (apposition and clarification), extension (addition and variation), and enhancement (spatio-temporal and causal-conditional). Below is a simplified list (McCarthy 2002: 47) (Table 2).

Halliday and Hasan's (1976) second main category of cohesion – lexical cohesion – includes lexical reiteration and collocation. Lexical reiteration is divided into same word (repetition), synonym (or near-synonym), superordinate (a name for a more general class), and general word (general noun). The following show the different forms of lexical reiteration of 'I turned to the ascent of the peak':

> The ascent is perfectly easy. (repetition)
> The climb is perfectly easy. (synonym or near-synonym)
> The task is perfectly easy. (superordinate)
> The thing is perfectly easy. (general word)

Collocation is divided into pairs of words and long cohesive chains weaving in and out of successive sentences. Examples of pairs of words are synonyms and near-synonyms (disease ... illness), superordinates (elm ... tree; boy ... child; skip ... play), complementaries (boys ... girls), antonyms, converses (order ... obey), and same ordered series (Tuesday, Thursday) (1976: 285).

Table 2 McCarthy's simplified list of conjunctions

Type	*Sub-types*	*Examples*
Elaboration	apposition	*in other words*
	clarification	*or rather*
Extension	addition	*and / but*
	variation	*alternatively*
Enhancement	spatio-temporal	*there / previously*
	causal-conditional	*consequently / in that case*

Hasan (1984: 202) classifies lexical cohesion into general and instantial, with general lexical cohesion consisting of repetition, synonymy, antonymy, hyponymy, and meronymy and instantial lexical cohesion consisting of equivalence, naming, and semblance. The following examples are taken from Hasan (1984: 202):

A. General i. repetition   leave, leaving, left
            ii. synonymy   leave, depart
            iii. antonymy   leave, arrive
            iv. hyponymy   travel, leave
                            (including
                            co-hyponyms,
                            leave, arrive)
            v. meronymy   hand, finger
                            (including
                            co-meronyms,
                            finger, thumb)
B. Instantial i. equivalence the *sailor* was their
                              daddy; *you* be the
                              patient, *I'll* be the
                              Doctor
              ii. naming   the dog was called
                              Toto; they named
                              the *dog Fluffy*
              iii. semblance the *deck* was like a
                              pool; all my *pleasures*
                              are like *yesterdays*

WINNIE CHENG

See also: Context; demonstratives; discourse; ellipsis; meaning; reference

Suggestions for further reading

Cheng, W. (2006) 'Describing the extended meanings of lexical cohesion in a corpus of SARS spoken discourse', *International Journal of Corpus Linguistics*, 11: 325–44.
Hoey, M. (2005) *Lexical Priming: A New Theory of Words and Language*, London: Routledge.
Tanskanen, S.-K. (2006) *Collaborating Towards Coherence: Textual Cohesion in English Discourse*, Amsterdam and Philadelphia, PA: John Benjamins.

Discourse Markers

Discourse markers (DMs) are illustrated by the italicized expressions in (1):

(1) a. Three is a prime number *but* four is not.
    b. The water wouldn't boil *so* we couldn't make any tea.
    c. It rained at the picnic. *And* the beer was warm.

DMs are generally held to refer to a functional (as opposed to a grammatical) class of expressions. They do not contribute to the semantic meaning of the **discourse** segment (S2) which hosts them, but signal a relationship between this segment and the preceding one (S1). For example, in (1a), *but* signals that the relationship between S1 and S2 is one of contrast, while in (1b) *so* signals that it is one of implication.

DMs are researched under other names, such as discourse connectives, discourse operators, pragmatic connectives, cue phrases, and **discourse particles**, to name but a few. And, not surprisingly, there are disagreements among researchers employing the same term as to what expressions fall under it. This being said, the following discussion is intended to capture the sense of DMs that the majority of researchers use today.

Defining discourse markers

For an expression to fall into the semantic class of DMs, it must meet three necessary and sufficient conditions.

Condition 1: A DM is a lexical expression, for example, *but*, *so*, and *in addition*. This condition explicitly excludes syntactic structures, prosodic features such as stress, pauses, and intonation, and non-verbal expressions such as a grunt or a shrug. This narrowness is intended to provide a framework for a precise definition. It is not intended to suggest that phenomena other than a lexical expression cannot function analogously to DMs, for example, when a speaker utters 'It's raining. Ah, go anyway', with the 'Ah' playing the same role as *but*.

Condition 2: A DM must occur as a part of the second discourse segment, S2, and it may or may not have an intonation contour which separates it prosodically from the rest of the segment. This hosting by S2 occurs whether the segments are combined or there is a full stop after S1 as in 'We were late. *However*, no one seemed to mind.'

Condition 3: A DM does not contribute to the semantic meaning of the segment but signals a specific semantic relationship between two propositional segments, S1 and S2. This is in contrast to other pragmatic markers such as *frankly*, *allegedly*, and *stupidly* which, like DMs, are not part of the sentence meaning, but make a specific comment on S2 (*see* Fraser 1996). I shall say more below about the types of semantic relationship signaled by DMs.

A DM does not 'create' the relationship between two successive segments, since the relationship between S1 and S2 must already exist, independent of the presence of a DM. In many cases, it is unlikely that a relatively implausible relationship would be recognized, absent the appropriate DM, and by using a particular DM, the speaker signals (i.e. marks) the specific semantic relationship that is intended to be recognized as holding between S1 and S2. In (2), more than one semantic relationship exists between S1 and S2, and the DM utilized simply makes clear what the speaker of S2 intends:

(2) S1: This flight takes 5 hours.
    S2$_1$: There's a stopover in Paris.
    S2$_2$: *After all*, there's a stopover in Paris.
    S2$_3$: *Because* there's a stopover in Paris.
    S4$_4$: *So*, there's a stopover in Paris.

From the requirement that a DM signals a relationship between **propositions**, occurrences such as 'John likes Mary *but* not Susan', with the second segment elliptical, fit this condition, but cases such as 'All *but* one person passed the exam' do not.

Though not the canonical form of DM use, one or both of the discourse segments may be empty, the segment being replaced by an assumption derived from the **context**, both linguistic and situational:

(3) a. S1 absent
    Context: After spanking his son who hit his sister
    Father: *In addition*, you are grounded for a week.
    b. S2 absent
    Brother: I'll think I'll just take another piece of cake.
    Sister: *But* … [Protest intonation]

c. S1 and S2 absent
Context: John, seeing someone taking his bike
John: *But*!

The above definition excludes the following types of expressions, either because they do not represent a relationship between adjacent propositional segments, S1 and S2, as in (4):

(4) a. Interjections (*damn, hey, wow, gosh*, …)
    I like it here. *Damn!* I really like it here.
    b. Sentence adverbs (*certainly, surely, definitely*, …)
    John is very nice. *Definitely*, we should invite him over.
    c. Modal particles (Few in English. German: *doch, ja, eben*, …)
    She is pretty. *Indeed*, she is.
    d. Focus particles (*just, even, only*, …)
    Everybody is ready. *Even* Harriet is on time.
    e. Evidential adverbs (*allegedly, reportedly, according to*, …)
    People are angry. *Allegedly*, it's Bush.
    f. Attitudinal adverbs (*frankly, stupidly, cleverly*, …)
    The weather is lousy. *Frankly*, I don't care.

or the relationship is grammatical not semantic, as in (5):

(5) Complementizers (*that, in order that, so as, for*, …)
    I believe *that* John is right.

DMs are a heterogeneous syntactic group. They are drawn primarily from conjunctions (*and, but, although, since*, …), adverbs (*however, thus, afterwards*, …) and prepositional phrases (*in addition, as a result, on the other hand*, …), but seldom from nouns, adjectives, verbs, or prepositions.

There are a number of properties that DMs do or do not have, some of which have been suggested as playing a role in their definition. For example, some theorists have suggested that the fact that a DM does not contribute to the truth conditions of the host segment, S2, should be part of its definition (Schourup 1999). This condition is unnecessary, since DMs function as a relationship between two segments, not part of the **meaning** of either, and thus it follows that they do not contribute to the truth conditions. Other theorists have suggested that a defining property is that DMs are optional (Schiffrin 1987). That is, their absence doesn't change the possibility of interpreting S1-S2 as if the DM were present, it just makes the hearer less secure in the interpretation, given that there are other possible interpretations. However, there are cases like those in (6):

(6) a. Fred, a gentleman? *On the contrary*, he's a bastard.
    b. We didn't like Harry. *On the other hand*, he didn't seem to care.

In these cases, the DM must be present for acceptability for many native speakers. Since the requirement to be present varies amongst DMs, this feature must also be rejected as a defining property.

It is interesting that in some cases the meaning of a DM is exactly the same as the expression when it is used as, for example, an adverb, as in (7):

(7) a. He didn't brush his teeth. *As a result*, he got cavities.
    b. The substance suddenly hardened. This wasn't what we wanted *as a result* of our work.

In other cases, however, the meaning of the DM and its homophonous content expression is quite different:

(8) a. We stopped. *On the other hand*, there was little point in continuing.
    b. It doesn't feel right. Try it *on the other hand*.

There are a number of DMs which have no homophonous content form such as *nevertheless, on the contrary, moreover*, and *conversely*. There appear to be no cases of linguistic **ambiguity** with DMs, where an expression which can function both as a DM and a content constituent occurs in the same linguistic context.

The meaning of discourse markers

DMs naturally fall into three subclasses. The first expression in each subclass (*but, and, so*) is the primary – the most general – member of the subclass:

Contrastive markers (CDM) signal contrast of some type that exists between S1 and S2. For example: but, although, contrariwise, contrary to expectations, conversely, despite (this/that), however, in spite of, in comparison, in contrast, instead, nevertheless, notwithstanding, on the other hand, on the contrary, rather, still, though, whereas, yet

Elaborative markers (EDM) signal an elaboration or continuation of S1 by S2. For example: and, also, alternatively, besides, correspondingly, for example, for instance, further(more), in addition, in other words, in particular, more importantly, more to the point, moreover, on that basis, otherwise, rather, similarly

Inferential markers (IDM) signal a contextual implication S2 based on S1. For example: so, after all, as a conclusion, as a result, because, consequently, for this/that reason, hence, accordingly, in this/that/any case, on this/that condition, therefore, thus

Within each subclass there is occasional identity of meaning (for example, *nevertheless* and *notwithstanding*). But in general, each DM of the subclass carries a specific meaning – what it signals – different from the others. For example, the DM *however* can signal that the message which follows in S2 'conveys a message that is unexpected, given the message conveyed by S1':

(9) a. We arrived late. *However*, no one seemed to mind.
    b. Take your shoes off. *However*, leave your socks on for a little while.
    c. It's cold in here. *However*, don't shut the window.

Nevertheless, although closely associated with *however*, signals that the message that follows in S2 conveys 'a reasonable response in spite of the fact(s) represented in S1'. Only declarative sentences can be combined with *nevertheless*, and then, not all. In (10), S2 must be responsive to a fact in S1, not an opinion:

(10) a. I did not prepare to speak today. *Nevertheless*, I will say something
     b. A: I very much like your brother. B: **Nevertheless*, you know that she has been having a lot of trouble lately.

A major issue that is far from decided is how to account for the contribution of DMs in the interpretation of an utterance. Most researchers embrace the idea that **utterance interpretation** must contain a semantic **representation** capturing **what is said** which undergoes pragmatic **inference** to arrive at the utterance interpretation. Most would also agree that this process is not lock-step in nature, that the complete semantic meaning of an utterance requires pragmatic inference to resolve, for example, semantic ambiguity, and only then can further pragmatic inference occur to account for utterance interpretation.

One approach was suggested by Grice (1989), who noted that DMs such as *but*, *moreover*, and *on the other hand*, do not contribute to the propositional meaning of what is said, but seem to convey information about non-central or higher-level **speech acts**, which comment on the interpretation of the ground floor speech acts. For example, in (1a) 'Three is a prime number *but* four is not', the function of *but*, what Grice calls a conventional **implicature**, is to signal that there is a contrast between the interpretation of the two segments. It has been pointed out that this contrast notion of *but* would not cover all the uses, that this use of the term 'speech act' is very different from the usual uses.

Relevance theory (Blakemore 2005b; Hall 2007) suggests that there are two types of linguistic meaning, two types of information available to the hearer: conceptual meaning, which consists of concepts encoded into expressions and which gives rise to the semantic representation; and procedural meaning, which provides instructions to the pragmatic system regarding certain inferences it is to perform on these representations. Every expression has a procedural meaning, or it has a conceptual meaning, but not both. This approach to meaning maintains that DMs contain procedural meaning. Therefore, DMs such as *on the other hand*, *on the contrary*, *instead*, and *in spite of*, which clearly contain conceptual meaning, should not be treated as DMs. The emphasis of relevance theorists has been on a few cases, notably *but*, in an attempt to construct a purely procedural means of deriving the contribution of DMs in sequences which contain them.

A further approach is presented briefly in Fraser (2006), who proposes that every expression has both conceptual and procedural meaning, though not in equal proportions (*as a result* would have far more conceptual meaning than *so*). In this approach, these two aspects of meaning interact to arrive at the appropriate interpretation. For *but*, for example, there is a core meaning of simple contrast, with other, more nuanced uses of *but* being derived in terms of the core meaning, the linguistic/situational context, and specific pragmatic inferences.

Compounding the issue of DM meanings is the fact that some, though by no means all, DMs have more than one function. *But* is one of these. In the sequences below, each use of *but* arguably signals a different function, some greatly different, some only slightly. For example, in (11a) the two segments are in direct contrast, while in (11b) the second segment contradicts an implication of the first, namely, that people mind when you come late to a meeting. In (11d) the second segment provides an explanation for the fact expressed in the first segment:

(11) a. Water boils at 2112 degrees *but* mercury boils at a much higher temperature.
   b. I arrived late to the meeting. *But* no one seemed to mind.
   c. A: John is right here. B: *But* I just saw him on TV.
   d. John died. *But* he was very ill.
   e. A: Jake's a nice guy. B: *But* he's not a nice guy; he's a jerk.
   f. She's not my mother *but* my sister.
   g. A: The flowers are beautiful. B: *But* they're plastic.
   h. A: We had a very nice meal. B: *But* did you ask him about the money he owes us?

For a DM with multiple uses, such as *but* in (11), there is an important question of whether its various uses derive from a single form, with each interpretation derived pragmatically, or from several forms.

The issue of the meaning differences within a DM is different from the one where all uses of *but*, for example, are treated as being related to a basic or core form. Consider the different uses as well as the different syntactic categories in (12):

(12) a. I like you *but* I can't go out with you.
   b. Everyone *but* John was here.

c. I have *but* a moment.
d. You may think I'm crazy, *but* where is the dog?
e. He has all *but* clinched the championship.
f. A: I had dinner with Mary last night. B: *But* did you get the money she owed you?
g. I will get you *but* good.

These cases range from (12a), a DM which is a conjunction, syntactically, to (12f), a discourse management marker whose syntactic pedigree is unclear, to (12c), a qualifier which is an adverb. The issue is whether they should be treated as the same morpheme and combined into one 'class', with the task being one of explaining how they are related to each other.

Sequencing of discourse markers

A relatively unexplored yet very relevant area involves the sequencing of DMs. Typically, this occurs when two DMs occur as a part of S2, as in (13):

(13) a. John went swimming, *but, in contrast,* Mary went sailing.
b. John went swimming *and, in addition,* he rode his bicycle.
c. John went swimming, *so, as a result,* he won't be home for dinner.
d. We started late. *But,* we arrived on time *nevertheless*.

In these examples, the first DM in the sequence is one of the primary DMs (*and, but, so*), and the second DM, which doesn't necessarily follow directly, is one of the other members of the subclass (e.g. for the contrastive class *but* versus *however, nevertheless, on the contrary, instead, rather, in comparison, despite that* and so on). Subordinate conjunctions may not be a second DM in a sequence, and two ordinary members of the same subclass (e.g. the subclass of contrastive discourse markers) typically do not occur in a sequence although some combinations, when said a few times, don't seem too bad:

(14) a. John started late. *?Still/?However,* he arrived on time, *?nevertheless*.

b. We ordered ham. ?*Moreover*, we asked for it with lemon sauce, ?*furthermore*.

A second case is where a primary DM of one subclass occurs as the first in a sequence with an ordinary member of another subclass (e.g. *but* [CDM] + *as a result* [IDM]). The first DM signals the major relationship between S2 and S1 (contrast, elaboration, inference), while the second DM signals a more specific relation, not within the first relation's domain:

(15) a. He walked to town *but, as a result,* he caught a cold.
b. He was sick *and, thus,* he was unable to work.
c. He was home *and, yet,* he hadn't spoken to his wife.

Note that when there are different subclasses present in the DM sequence, the relationship signalled by each of the DMs must be satisfied.

Universality of discourse markers

There is no doubt that all languages have a variety of DMs. However, the extent to which they embrace the same semantic relationships is an interesting question. For example, the Spanish word *pero*, which translates into *but* in English, is not the functional equivalent of *but*, as the examples in (16) show, with *sino* replacing *pero* in the construction shown in (16d):

(16) a. Harry likes to ride *but/pero* John prefers walking.
b. We started late *but/pero* we arrived on time.
c. I hate to say this, *but/pero* you smell terrible.
d. Julia is not tall, *but/*pero/sino* short.

Differences such these, as well as languages which do not use the full inventory of DMs found in other languages, provide a new and potentially rich area of research.

BRUCE FRASER

See also: Discourse coherence; discourse particles; relevance theory; semantics; semantics-pragmatics interface

Suggestions for further reading

Fraser, B. (2006) 'Towards a theory of discourse markers', in K. Fischer (ed.) *Approaches to Discourse Particles*, Amsterdam: Elsevier.

Hall, A. (2007) 'Do discourse connectives encode procedures or concepts?', *Lingua*, 117: 149–74.

Discourse Particles

Discourse particles are a closed class of expressions. Schourup showed over twenty years ago that these particles do not occur randomly in **discourse** (Schourup 1985). Although they add nothing truth-conditional to the sentence they inhabit, they do convey something about the speaker's concerns about communicating with the addressee. They contrast with **discourse markers**, which convey information concerning the demarcation of boundaries of structural parts. Discourse particles can be either single words like *well*, *gosh* and *uh*, or collocations like *I mean* and *you know* which occur adjacent to an expression that is important in its **context**, as illustrated in (1). (Technically, expressions like *I mean* and *you know* are not phrases, as they lack a required object.)

1a. Well, there are 59 restaurants that meet that description.
1b. There are well, 59 restaurants that meet that description.
1c. #There well, are 59 restaurants that meet that description.
1d. There are 59 restaurants well, that meet that description.
1e. There are 59 restaurants that meet that well, description.
1f. There are 59 restaurants that well, meet that description.

Adverbials like *in fact*, *frankly* and *actually* fit this definition of discourse particles. However, adverbials like *thus* and *unfortunately* do not, because they convey non-truth-conditional information that is not about the discourse.

While there are constraints on where in a sentence a given discourse particle may occur (e.g. *you know* may occur in sentence-final position but *well* and *uh* never do), these constraints do not define particles as a coherent syntactic category,

either novel or familiar. Discourse particles are a little like punctuation in that: (1) they serve to help an interpreter integrate a bit of discourse they are adjacent to; (2) the bit of discourse can belong to practically any syntactic open class (N, V, A, P, NP, VP, AP, PP, S); and (3) the particle does not really form a syntactic constituent with that bit of discourse. If the police ask where the records are, the response 'in the commode' represents a full and complete answer. The alternative response, 'in the, uh, commode', indicates that the speaker is concerned about his word choice, but diagnostics do not reveal 'uh, commode' to be a syntactic constituent.

The bit of discourse that a discourse particle relates to may be anything from a word to a supra-textual unit like an entire argument that extends over several paragraphs. This is another reason to reject the notion that discourse particles might form a syntactic constituent with the bit of discourse to which they are adjacent. Indeed, particles are so widely understood as not being part of the utterance they occur in that they are frequently omitted from official transcripts (whether as a matter of policy or simply because they go under the radar of the transcribers) even when they are perfectly audible.

Although they have no truth-conditional content, discourse particles do reflect an attitude of the speaker toward what is being said (Lakoff 1973; Schourup 1985; Siegel 2002). Particles like *well*, *uh*, *like*, *gosh*, *oh*, *OK*, *I mean*, and *y'know* indicate something about how the speaker feels about what is being said, as illustrated in (2):

2a. Newsweek: If you had to start out today, would you write novels?
Vidal: Well, I don't know how I'd be brought up, you know.
(*Newsweek*, 25 September 2000: 70)

2b. 'The word was "goonya"' Franz says with a hearty laugh. 'It referred to … uh … a part of the female anatomy.'
(Interview with Dennis Franz, *USA Weekend*, 18–20 February 1994: 5)

In (2a) Vidal does not answer the interviewer's question directly, instead implicating that he doesn't know whether under different circumstances he'd make the same choices. The *well* that prefaces the evasion implies that some thought went into the non-answer response. (Compare how the response would sound without the *well* – like the interviewer should have known better than to ask the question.) In (2b), *uh* serves the purpose of indicating Franz's awareness that he is referring to an 'unmentionable' subject in an interview for a family magazine. The writer could have chosen to transcribe this sentence without the pauses and the *uh*, but this would not have given the readers the same impression of Franz as a human being like themselves. Some particles, like *gosh* and *oy*, are affective and convey an emotion that is evoked in the speaker by the content being expressed; others, which Schourup called evincive (like *well*, *uh*, and *like*), relate more to how the speaker feels about expressing the content which follows it.

In general, each attitudinal particle reflects a single attitude, but the effect of conveying that attitude varies widely, as Gricean principles would lead one to expect. One relevant factor is whether the particle appears in a sentence that provides information, or a sentence that **requests** information. Another factor is the nature of the relationship between speaker and addressee. A third variable is the degree to which the **speech act** in which the particle occurs can be considered to threaten the face of the addressee (Kose 1997; Dunn 1990).

For example, although *well* and *uh* are both used when the speaker is thinking (for any of a number of possible reasons) about how to say what must be said, and this fact invites the same **inferences** in both cases, using *well* indicates that the speaker is weighing how much to say, or deciding what **propositions** need to be articulated to convey an idea. As a consequence, *well* is unremarkable in the speech of mature and thoughtful adults. The conditions for *uh*, however, are less restrictive, and allow it to be used when the speaker is just searching for a word, or dealing with the logically prior task of determining the general strategy of a conversational turn. It is this latter condition that allows *uh* to be used as a vocalized pause. (*Um* is even more similar in effect to *uh*; they can be interchanged in every context without altering the effect. Still, two facts suggest that they have different communicative values: the same speaker may use both at separate points in the same discourse,

and in a given discourse, substituting the sequence *uh, um* for *um, uh* radically alters the effect.) *Well* is never used this way by native speakers; the effect of substituting *well* for *uh* in discourses like those in (3) is distinctly odd.

3a. Then you had two more justices, uh Souter and uh Ginsburg who took the position that because of a statute that Congress passed uh 30 years ago that says that no American citizen …

  … that was sufficient reason uh not to allow the detention of Mr. uh Hamdi as an enemy combatant

  … So they reached the same result as as uh uh Scalia and Stevens, but they did so on the basis of …

  … And therefore, they said, uh, the president had uh authority from Congress to detain American citizens as enemy combatants

  (Doug Cassell, Director of the Center for International Human Rights, Northwestern University School of Law, interviewed on *Focus 580* (radio call-in show) 3 August 2004)

3b. … deemed by the administration to be enemy combatants, being held uh, some of them being held at uh Guantanamo Bay in Cuba, and the others being held, the other two uh being held at uh a Navy prison in uh Charleston, S.C. Uh, questions welcome 333-9495 …

  (David Inge, host, *Focus 580* (radio call-in show) 3 August 2004)

Some speakers choose to 'fill' with some sort of low vowel the pauses that happen while they are putting the next words into the pipeline to be produced; others, at the risk of being interrupted before they are ready to relinquish the floor, and of producing choppy-sounding speech, do not. Even though *well* is a syllable of sonorants, capable of being prolonged as much as *uh*, it is not exploited in these contexts because of its non-truth-conditional baggage. The speaker who says 'they reached the same result as well, well Scalia and Stevens' may indicate that Scalia and Stevens are a considered choice from among a number of contemplated 'true' completions to the phrase. Or he may indicate that he is reluctant to acknowledge 'Scalia and Stevens' here as the standard to which others are being compared, or perhaps some other such thing. But 'well' will always convey more than that he just is having a hard time accessing their names. Most likely, it is from its use when the speaker is figuring out what content to convey that *uh* gets a reputation as a mark of ignorance, and that reputation is why it is a sore point with individuals concerned about usage standards. One consequence of this difference is that where *well* sounds thoughtful, *uh* may just sound embarrassed.

Another consequence is that because of the **vagueness** of the conditions for its use – the use of *uh* conveys only that the speaker is thinking about what s/he will say – *uh* can be used to soften the impact of a statement that implies some inadequacy on the part of the addressee, by inviting, or at least allowing, the inference that the speaker was concerned about what words to use in communicating the sentiment to the addressee. This is illustrated in (4), which is taken from an October 2000 David Letterman list of Top Ten Things You Don't Want to Hear at the Bottom of a World Series Pile-on:

4.   ... uh ... guys ... it's only the third inning.

With *uh*, this is a cautious approach to a delicate subject; with *well*, it would have been more of a rebuke because *well* would draw attention to the fact that the speaker had to put some thought into exactly how much to say, or how exactly to spin it.

5. Well, ... guys ... it's only the third inning.

This may be exactly what makes *uh* more suitable than *well* for an error message in an automated interface with pretensions to sounding like a helpful human, as illustrated in (6):

6a. Uh, you need to provide an email address.
6b. Well, you need to provide an email address.

In the context of a machine-generated error message, *uh* leaves room for interpretation as an attempt to spare the addressee's feelings, but *well*, intimating that there is even more the

speaker could criticize, has more the effect of rubbing the addressee's nose in the error.

The fact that writers consciously choose to use these particles is the strongest sort of evidence that they have communicative value and are much more than strategic space fillers (Shuy 1997) or meta-discourse about pauses (*cf.* Clark and Fox Tree 2002). Such examples can be found in virtually any newspaper on any day of the week; those in (7) are illustrative:

7a. Do you dare buy stocks? When the fed slashes rates aggressively, the market usually rises – um, eventually.
(Headline and subheading,
Newsweek, 2 April 2001: 61)

7b. So learn to keep it crisp and professional, and leave the theater for, well, the theater.
(Bob Rosner, Working Wounded column,
Champaign-Urbana News-Gazette,
18 December 2001: D-2)

Corroborating this evidentiary finding is the fact that these particles can be used in self-directed discourse, something that other performance-oriented theories of discourse particles are hard put to explain: 'holding the floor' (Shuy 1997) or alerting the addressee to an imminent pause (Clark and Fox Tree 2002) would not seem to be a relevant motivation when one is talking to oneself. And yet, one can use *well* with an utterance to oneself, out loud, e.g. uttering *well* with a strong expletive upon discovering that you have just done something outstandingly inappropriate. (It is not clear why self-directed discourse exists, but it clearly satisfies a human need, at the very least in the language-specific exclamation words that register pain, as well as in much more elaborate and creative grammatical constructions of indeterminate length that serve the same purpose.) The corresponding utterance with *uh* is so patently ridiculous that the mental states *uh* and *well* reflect must be very distinctly specified in our internal grammars. Precisely what they are remains a matter for further empirical research.

The investigation of discourse particles takes advantage of corpus research (to sample the variety of contexts in which a given particle appears), while controlled interactive techniques are more helpful for testing specific hypotheses about contexts and effects (Green 1995). Natural-language generators provide an additional test-bed for specific hypotheses. It is always instructive to get an algorithm to take a lexicon and a grammar (using grammar to apply to any consistent rule system that defines sentences) and output random sentences defined by that grammar, as it provides a healthy counterbalance to the temptation to confuse the content of a particle with the content of the sentence in which it occurs. When it's not practical to build an interface to test a pragmatic analysis, observing the effects of substituting one particle for another in the same natural context is also effective.

GEORGIA M. GREEN

See also: Discourse markers

Suggestion for further reading

Green, G.M. (1995) 'The right tool for the job: techniques for analysis of natural language use', in L.F. Bouton (ed.) *Pragmatics and Language Learning*, Monograph Series, volume 6, Urbana, IL: Division of English as an International Language, University of Illinois.

Domain Restriction

The term 'domain restriction' describes a cluster of phenomena involving the interaction of compositional **semantics** and the **context** in the interpretation of tripartite quantificational structures and referring expressions. Research on domain restriction has focused on the following questions: What constructions are associated with domains? What linguistic and contextual factors determine a particular domain of quantification or **reference**? And how may the contextual influences on domain restriction be modeled?

Constructions subject to domain restriction

Tripartite quantificational structures, consisting of a quantifier, domain, and nuclear scope, are subject to domain restriction. Tripartite quantificational analyses of nominal quantifiers date

back to Aristotle and are extremely common today (*see* Montague 1973; Barwise and Cooper 1981; McCawley 1981). For example, the interpretation of (1) has three parts: a universal quantifier; a domain of quantification consisting of the set of paintings in the Louvre; and a nuclear scope consisting of the set of things that have been catalogued. The sentence is true just in case every element of the domain is also an element of the nuclear scope:

(1) Every [painting in the Louvre] [has been catalogued].

Other items that have been analyzed as introducing tripartite quantification include modals (for example (2); *see* Kripke 1959; Kratzer 1977, 1989), adverbs of quantification (for example (3); Lewis 1975a; Kamp 1981; Heim 1982, 1990; Berman 1987; von Fintel 1994), focus-sensitive operators (for example (4); Rooth 1985; Partee 1991, 1995; Kadmon 2001) and focus-sensitive **negation** (for example (5); Kratzer 1989), and generic sentences (for example (6); Lewis 1975a; Farkas and Sugioka 1983; Schubert and Pelletier 1987, 1989; Partee 1991; Krifka *et al.* 1995):

(2) If it rains, the game *might* be cancelled.
(3) When it rains, Max *sometimes* takes a walk in the park.
(4) *Only* Rosa solved that mathematics problem.
(5) (I'm sure some of my friends are Parisian, but) PAULA *isn't* registered in Paris.
(6) a. An owl eats mice.
    b. Owls eat mice.

Referring expressions such as definite descriptions and **demonstratives** can be analyzed as denoting either quantifiers (7a) or entities (7b), as shown in the simplified logical translations below:

(7) The current president of the United States was born in Texas.
    a. $\exists x$ [president-of-US(x) & $\forall y$ [president-of-US(y) $\rightarrow$ x = y]] [born-in-Texas(x)]
                              (*cf.* Russell 1905)

    b. born-in-Texas (tx.president-of-US(x))
                              (*cf.* Strawson 1950a)

In the latter case, the referent is selected from a contextually determined domain of potential referents (*see* Barwise and Perry 1983 and Recanati 1996, 2004a on definite descriptions, and Wolter 2006 on demonstratives.) Similarly, the reference time for tense (Reichenbach 1947) is selected from a contextually determined domain of relevant times (Partee 1984; Roberts 1995).

Factors determining domains

The domain of a quantificational structure may be explicitly provided by an expression such as the italicized phrases in (8). The referent of a referring expression may also be determined entirely by its explicit linguistic content (9):

(8) a. *Every painting in the Louvre* has been catalogued.
b. *If John has spare change on Sundays*, he *sometimes* buys a newspaper.
c. *Out of all the students in my class, only* Mary wrote a term paper.
(9) a. *The current president of the United States* was born in Texas.
b. The mathematician chose *a prime number greater than 5*.

A domain of quantification may also be determined entirely by the context, as in (10), or by both explicit linguistic material and contextual factors. For example, the domain of *every* in (11) is most naturally understood as the set of paintings in the Louvre:

(10) a. The curators of the Louvre are very conscientious. *Everything* has been catalogued.
b. When Mary has spare change, she usually puts it in the bank. John *sometimes* buys a newspaper.
c. Most of the students in my class took the final exam. *Only* Mary wrote a term paper instead.
(11) The curators of the Louvre are very conscientious. *Every painting* has been catalogued.

The information from the context that influences domains of quantification and reference is quite rich. Recently, work in **experimental pragmatics** has begun to tease apart different

sources of this contextual information, including how the objects in a display may be manipulated (Chambers *et al.* 2002; Chambers *et al.* 2004), the presence or absence of contrasting objects in the context (Altmann and Steedman 1988; Britt 1994; Spivey and Tanenhaus 1998; Sedivy *et al.* 1999), the lexical semantics of verbs (Altmann and Kamide 1999), **prosody** (Dahan *et al.* 2002; Watson *et al.* 2006; Ito and Speer 2008), disfluencies (Arnold *et al.* 2004) and discrepancies between the speaker's and hearer's **knowledge** states (Keysar *et al.* 2000; Keysar and Barr 2005; Brown-Schmidt *et al.* 2008; Grodner and Sedivy, to appear; Heller *et al.*, to appear).

Some quantificational expressions are associated with special presumptions about the nature of the domain. For example, the domain of a generic sentence includes just the most relevant or stereotypical individuals or the most usual cases (*see* Krifka *et al.* 1995 and references therein), while *any* functions as a 'domain widener', indicating that the domain should include even exceptional individuals (Kadmon and Landman 1993). For example, the domain of quantification in (12a) includes only normal, healthy adult owls, while the domain of quantification in (12b) additionally includes sick owls:

(12) a. An owl eats mice.
b. Any owl eats mice.
(Kadmon and Landman 1993: 357)

Finally, some quantificational elements interact with a sentence's **focus** structure: the unfocused part of the sentence determines the domain and the focused part determines the nuclear scope (Partee 1991; Krifka 1992, 1995b; von Fintel 1994; Rooth 1995; Kadmon 2001). For example, the domain of *always* in (13a) consists of cases in which John is taken to the movies, while in (13b) the domain consists of cases in which Mary takes someone to the movies.

(13) a. MARY always takes John to the movies.
b. Mary always takes JOHN to the movies.
(Rooth 1985)

Modeling contextual influences on domains

Domain restriction has received the most attention in the formal semantics and **formal**

pragmatics literature, where two types of analyses model contextual influences on domains of quantification or reference. On one approach, quantificational or referential expressions introduce a free variable over sets whose value is set by the context (Westerståhl 1984; von Fintel 1994). For example, in (11) the domain of quantification might be determined by intersecting the set denoted by *painting* with the contextually provided set of things in the Louvre. On another approach, quantificational or referential expressions are interpreted relative to a contextually determined situation, or part of a possible world (Barwise and Perry 1983; Recanati 1996, 2004a; Cooper 1996). For example, in (11) *painting* might be relativized to the contextually provided minimal situation containing the Louvre, and therefore denote the set of paintings in the Louvre. In the **relevance theory** literature, domain restriction belongs to the more general process of pragmatic enrichment driven by **inferences** about relevance (Sperber and Wilson 1995; Wilson and Sperber 1998; Carston 2002). Domain restriction has received less attention in cognitive semantics. However, the structured domains in that tradition, which model the influence of lexical semantics on the salience of entities (Langacker 1987; Croft and Cruse 2004), may be relevant to a more fine-grained understanding of the information contributing to domain restriction.

LYNSEY WOLTER

See also: Anaphora, pragmatics of; context; definiteness; experimental pragmatics; focus; formal pragmatics; information structure; negation; relevance theory; semantics-pragmatics interface

Suggestions for further reading

Partee, B.H. (1995) 'Quantificational structures and compositionality', in E. Bach, E. Jelinek, A. Kratzer and B.H. Partee (eds) *Quantification in Natural Languages*, Dordrecht: Kluwer.
Roberts, C. (1995) 'Domain restriction in dynamic semantics', in E. Bach, E. Jelinek, A. Kratzer and B.H. Partee (eds) *Quantification in Natural Languages*, Dordrecht: Kluwer.
Westerståhl, D. (1984) 'Determiners and context sets', in J. van Benthem and A. ter Meulen (eds) *Generalized Quantifiers in Natural Language*, Dordrecht: Foris.

Dramatic Discourse

The term 'dramatic discourse' refers here to the linguistic component of a text written for performance, in which, in its archetypal form, a story develops through dialogue accompanied by extralinguistic elements such as physical action, costume, and staging. This linguistic component of play texts comprises not only the dialogic or monologic speech of characters, but also the framing aspects of the text such as stage directions (although this aspect has received little attention from linguists to date). Dramatic discourse often eludes straightforward study, characterized as it is by its apparently conversational exchanges and its embedded **discourse** levels, where the **communication** that takes place *between* characters is, in fact, communication between the author and the audience *about* the characters (*see* Short 1989a: 149). As such, Tan (1993: 50) argues that this layered aspect makes analysis of inter-character interaction somewhat unproductive, if not misleading. Nonetheless, the superficial similarities to naturally occurring speech events encourage much linguistic research to focus on dialogic exchanges between characters.

This is not necessarily an unproductive exercise, however. The hybridity or 'double life' of dramatic texts (Herman 1995:10), which is revealed in the layering of discourse conduits, engenders differing attitudes in literary, linguistic and performance research which can be mutually informative. Thus, whereas for theatre critics and practitioners, such texts are produced to be 'read' in performance, where linguistic, spatial and visual elements combine, for many literary scholars, dramatic texts are literary artefacts, studied on the page, and kept separate from the mundane aspects of the 'conversational' due to their literary texture. It is the 'conversational' aspect of dramatic dialogic interaction that has attracted the attention of linguists, many of whom have turned to the field of **discourse analysis** – particularly **pragmatics** – in order to 'account for reader and audience intuitions about dialogue in those texts' (Burton 1980: ix). Pragmatic approaches also reveal the dynamic process of **meaning** construction – and the exploitation of meaning potential – that involves the author, text and audience, to arrive at a sense of characterization and plot development. This has particular importance bearing in mind the performative role of language in drama, forming part of the action and creating characterization, often in the absence of a narratorial guide.

Growing out of developments in discourse analysis that began in the 1970s, linguists realized that an awareness of the norms of 'real' speech events allowed analysis of the way such rules are exploited by dramatists in fictional dialogic exchanges to communicate with the audience about the drama itself. The application of pragmatic approaches seemed particularly relevant as dramatic dialogue has the appearance of taking place within, and thus taking meaning from, a socially situated **context**. Initial approaches to dramatic dialogue focussed on two main areas of pragmatics: **conversation analysis**, to consider the 'architecture' of the dialogue, and applications of **Austin**'s and **Searle**'s speech act theories, **Grice**'s **cooperative principle** and conversational **implicature**, to consider the performative 'action' of the dialogue. Later developments in discourse analysis, such as **politeness** theories and cognitive approaches, have also been applied to dramatic discourse.

Speech act theory has been particularly influential. One of the earliest was Porter's (1979) study of Shakespeare's history plays *Richard II*, *1* and *2 Henry IV* and *Henry V*, which sought to apply a combination of Austin's (1962) and Searle's (1975a) speech act taxonomies to explore the linguistic 'worlds' of the plays. Porter's comparison of *Richard II* and *Henry V*, for example, suggests that where King Richard's speech is characterized by ceremonial performatives and 'self-expression' illocutionary acts (an overlap, Porter suggests, of Austin's 'behabitives' (Austin 1962: 151) and Searle's 'expressives' (Searle 1975a: 356–58)), creating a feeling of 'timeless … essences and necessities' (Porter 1979: 144), King Henry's speech is characterized by acts such as promising that are predicated on future action, creating a sense of dynamism in Henry's characterization. Similarly, Fish (1980) applies Searle's (1969) framework to what he refers to as Shakespeare's speech act play, *Coriolanus*. In doing so, he examines the consequences of the protagonist's illocutionary behaviour, which exposes an egocentricism and social disregard for his interlocutors at odds with his institutional role as leader. More recently, Lowe's (1994) examination of Arthur Miller's *The Crucible* and Worster's (1996) analysis of David Mamet's play *Glengarry Glen Ross* similarly employed speech act theory to explore notions of **power** and identity in the context of contemporary American drama.

In addition to these more singularly focussed approaches, many linguists have adopted a multifaceted approach, employing a variety of pragmatic concepts. One of the earliest and most influential was Burton's (1980) exploration of twentieth-century dramatic dialogue alongside naturally occurring **conversation**. She acknowledges that constructed dialogues, whilst apparently 'realistic', are 'tidied up' versions of naturally occurring speech events, having few, if any, of the hesitations, false starts, repetitions and so on which characterize everyday speech. Her analysis focusses first on the 'odd talk' (Simpson 1998) of Ionesco's absurdist drama *The Bald Prima Donna*, considering how it deviates from the 'rules' of linguistic interaction, thus defying the audience's ability to assume the use of Grice's cooperative principle and throwing the 'rules' into relief. Then, by analyzing the mundanely 'realistic' conversational small talk of Pinter's *The Dumb Waiter*, Burton reveals how the play's issues of social status and control are enacted through linguistic means such as **topic** control. This provides evidence for Quigley's (1976: 66) assertion that in Pinter's plays 'language is not so much a means of referring to structure in personal relationships, as a means of creating it'. Coulthard (1985: 184–92) similarly examines the manipulation of power in Shakespeare's *Othello*. This is achieved through the exploitation of turn management and topic control, along with Gricean **maxims** and the resulting implicatures.

Nash's (1989) eclectic approach to the opening lines of *Hamlet*, which combines aspects of exchange structure, speech acts and implicature, also shows the growing influence of politeness theory through a basic notion of 'face' to provide 'an instructive index to the general character of the scene as a complex of nervous interactive gestures, implying much yet conveying little' (1989: 33). Herman (1995) also combines approaches including conversation analysis, speech acts and politeness to explore power and control in a range of texts including Shakespeare and Pinter. She points out that although Austin and Searle expressed doubts about the status of the speech acts found in drama because of their inherent pretence, this issue has been overcome in much research by relying on the fact that audiences socially and cognitively frame their reception of dramatic discourse, thereby registering the fictionality of the speech acts. Fowler's (1996) multifaceted approach to exploring fictional dialogue, focussing on 'sequencing', i.e. conversational 'turn' construction/management, speech acts and implicature, is reminiscent of Nash's approach. Fowler (1996: 136) argues that 'flouting maxims and raising implicatures is central to dialogic structure in a good deal of elliptical, allusive modern drama'. However, he acknowledges the limitations of such an approach that, despite providing the impetus to explore certain anomalies of 'ordinary'-seeming dialogue, doesn't allow for the influence on the dialogue of the wider socio-historical context of the play's production and reception.

The 1990s and early part of this century showed a growing interest in the application of Brown and Levinson's politeness strategies to drama (see, for example, Short 1996; Bennison 1998; Abdesslem 2001). These studies assume, as does Brown and Levinson's original model, that politeness is a positive thing and that cooperation is sought at all times. However, as Jonathan Culpeper (1998: 86–87) points out, there are times – *particularly* in drama – when participants are seen to deliberately intensify the face-threatening act instead of trying to avoid or mitigate it. He argues that this intentional aggravation, or impoliteness, is a form of aggression, which has been a form of entertainment from the gladiatorial fights of Ancient Rome to *The Weakest Link*. He further argues that this explains, in part, the popularity of courtroom drama – this is a socially acceptable, legitimate form of verbal aggression where the prosecutors are licensed, and encouraged, to attack the witness's face. However, Culpeper (1998, 2001) argues that impoliteness in drama serves a more subtle purpose than simply providing voyeuristic pleasure for an audience. Being either the cause or result of social disharmony, it typically provokes tensions in the dramatic interaction between characters, leading to developments

in characterization and plot – particularly if, prototypically, a plot is considered to move from equilibrium to disequilibrium and back to equilibrium (*see* Culpeper 1998: 87).

Yet, despite the importance of impoliteness to the development of plot and character in drama, it was a relatively rare phenomenon in British drama, at least until the abolition of theatre censorship in 1968. However, late twentieth-century theatre saw the development of the 'in yer face' genre (Sierz 2001: 25) that deliberately maximizes the potential for conflict through language, seeking to unsettle and provoke both characters and audience alike. The ability of language to 'act' is taken to extremes in Steven Berkoff's verse play *Greek*, in a scene which begins as a 'normal' café service encounter but resolves through the protagonist Eddy abusing, 'fighting' and then 'killing' the manager with words. Birch (1991: 71) argues that the scene's overt deviation from the understood routines of a service encounter works to deconstruct ideas of societal 'cosy cooperation' and foregrounds the underlying conflictual nature of resistance and social control.

More recently, linguistic research into dramatic discourse has taken a cognitive turn. Culpeper's (2001) *Language and Characterisation* blends cognitive approaches, such as the notions derived from contextually driven schematic **knowledge**, with more traditionally recognized linguistic approaches to inferring characterization discussed previously. Similarly, McIntyre's (2004, 2006) work combines sociolinguistic approaches with the cognitive approach of deictic shift theory to explore the linguistic manifestation of point of view in dramatic texts.

With their move away from the focus on the conversational aspects of dramatic dialogue, both these approaches mirror the cognitive linguistic approaches being taken to stylistic analysis of other literary genres and pave the way for analysis that moves beyond analyzing dramatic discourse in purely 'conversational' terms. However, by bearing in mind an awareness of the layers and conduits of communication in a dramatic text written for performance, pragmatic approaches can continue to produce the insights into dramatic discourse that have not necessarily been accessible through other performance or literary approaches, and work continues to develop in the understanding of areas such as implicature, **deixis** and (im)politeness.

SARAH GRANDAGE

See also: Conversational turn-taking; conversation analysis; cooperative principle; deixis; discourse analysis; implicature; literary pragmatics; narrative discourse; politeness; speech act theory; stylistics

Suggestions for further reading

Culpeper, J. (2001) *Language and Characterisation: People in Plays and Other Texts*, London: Longman.

Culpeper, J., Short, M. and Verdonk, P. (eds) (1998) *Exploring the Language of Drama: From Text to Context*, London: Routledge.

Tan, P.K.W. (1993) *A Stylistics of Drama: With Special Focus on Stoppard's "Travesties"*, Singapore: Singapore University Press.

E

Echoic Use

Echoic use is a technical term developed in the framework of **relevance theory** (Sperber and Wilson 1981, 1990a, 1995, 1998a; Wilson and Sperber 1992; Wilson 2006). Echoic use was originally construed as part of the 'use-mention' distinction proposed by Sperber and Wilson (1981) to address verbal **irony**: how it is defined, how it can be explained and what the mechanism is for interpreting it. According to the use-mention distinction drawn in **philosophy** (Davidson 1979a), expressions may be 'used' to refer to entities and states of affairs, or expressions may be 'mentioned' to refer to the expressions themselves (Sperber and Wilson 1981: 303). Bank is 'used' in (1) to refer to the destination of a particular individual called Ian, while bank is 'mentioned' in (2) to refer to the word bank itself:

(1) Ian went to the bank.
(2) 'Bank' is an ambiguous word.

Ironical utterances were seen as cases of 'echoic mention', where another utterance (heard in, or familiar from, the near or remote past), or another **proposition** (thought or opinion), or one of their pragmatic **implicatures** is mentioned and rejected as 'ludicrously false, inappropriate, or irrelevant' (Sperber and Wilson 1981: 308). Recognition of irony requires the hearer's dual recognition of (a) the utterance as a case of 'mention' rather than 'use', and (b) the speaker's attitude of rejection to the proposition expressed. In (3), the speaker is claimed to echo a previous remark on the prospect of lovely

weather, or earlier expectations of good weather, while mockingly rejecting it at the same time. In (4), B echoes what he takes to be a pragmatic implication of A's utterance, while mockingly rejecting it at the same time:

(3) What lovely weather!
(4) A: This is a great car!
    B: And inexpensive too! (is what you're implying)

In the framework of relevance theory (Sperber and Wilson 1995; Wilson 2006), echoic use has been developed into a type of 'interpretive' use. An interpretively used utterance represents another **representation** (utterance or thought) which it resembles in content, whereas a descriptively used utterance represents a possible or actual state of affairs. It follows that interpretive uses require higher orders of meta-representational abilities than 'descriptive' uses, because the hearer has to identify that the speaker is considering another utterance or thought, rather than an actual state of affairs. Unless explicitly marked by means of linguistic expressions (e.g. *Chomsky says, I think*), the source of such an utterance or thought has to be pragmatically inferred. Free indirect speech and thought is a type of interpretive use the source of which may be up to the hearer to infer. The second utterance in (5) can be interpreted as a paraphrase or summary of the claim tacitly attributed to the registry clerk that the hearer is not eligible for the university grant. The second utterance in (6) can be interpreted as a thought tacitly attributed to Paul that unless he took the metro, he would have missed the performance:

(5) The registry was clear. You are not eligible for the university grant.
(6) Paul took the metro. Otherwise, he would have missed the performance.

Reporting another utterance or thought with a similar content is part of what determines echoic use as a (linguistic or cognitive) metarepresentational tool (Wilson 2000). Informing the hearer of the speaker's reaction to the metarepresented utterance (or thought) is the additional function echoic uses commonly fulfil, as illustrated in (8a–c):

(7) *Ian*: I am spending Christmas at the North Pole.
(8) a. *Ann*: You're spending Christmas at the North Pole! Fantastic!
   b. *Ann*: You're spending Christmas at the North Pole? It must be costing you a fortune.
   c. *Ann*: You're spending Christmas at the North Pole. Don't hold your breath.
   (adapted from Wilson 2006: 1730)

Clearly, Ann does not wish to remind Ian of what he has just said, but to convey her attitude to what he has just said: acceptance with pleasurable surprise in (8a), desire for information perhaps with discrete disbelief in (8b), blatant mockery and disbelief in (8c). From a range of attitudes that may be conveyed by echoic use – such as acceptance, doubt, **request** for confirmation, request for information, rejection – verbal irony is seen as a sub-type of echoic use whereby the speaker tacitly conveys a dissociative attitude to a tacitly attributed utterance or thought by suggesting that it is 'obviously false, irrelevant or under-informative' (Wilson 2006: 1731).

In typical cases of verbal irony, both the attribution of an utterance or thought and the speaker's attitude are tacitly expressed, and hence, have to be pragmatically inferred. In such cases, the speaker tacitly attributes to someone else, to herself at another time (e.g. hopes or expectations) or to cultural or moral norms, a conceptual representation which is intended to highlight an incongruity between the way it describes the world and the way the world actually is. In example (9), Jimmy is mockingly echoing Alison's 'prior utterance':

(9) *Alison*: All I want is a little peace.
   Jimmy: Peace! God! She wants peace! My heart is so full, I feel ill – and she wants peace!
   (Osborne 1983: 59)

whereas in (10), Cliff is mockingly echoing a 'pragmatic implication' conveyed by Jimmy's utterance:

(10) *Jimmy*: You're too ignorant.
   Cliff: Yes, and uneducated …
   (Osborne 1983: 59)

In (11), a mother is echoing her 'expectations' for consideration and cooperation in choosing a private school, or perhaps the cultural expectation or norm that people behave helpfully to each other, which have been clearly violated in this case:

(11) As I complained about the late pick-up hour, the school bus-driver politely shut the door in my face.
   (adapted from Wilson 2006: 1731)

In cases of free indirect speech or thought, the 'attribution' of an utterance or thought may be linguistically indicated, as in (12). The speaker's 'attitude' may be linguistically indicated, as in (13). Both attribution and speaker's attitude may be linguistically indicated, as in (14), or both may be pragmatically inferred on the basis of paralinguistic or contextual features, as in examples (5) and (6):

(12) He is clever, allegedly.
(13) He is clever. I don't think.
(14) He thinks he is clever. Huh!

In standard cases of metalinguistic **negation**, the attribution is covert while the attitude of dissociation is explicitly indicated by the use of the negation, as in (15) (from Carston 2002: 298; on metalinguistic and metaconceptual negation, *see also* Carston 1996; Noh 1998).

(15) A: She eats tom[eɪDouz]
   B: I don't eat tom[eɪDouz]; (I eat tom[a: touz])

ELLY IFANTIDOU

See also: Evidentials; inferential comprehension; irony; metarepresentation; quotation; relevance theory

Suggestions for further reading

Noh, E.-J. (2000) *Metarepresentation: A Relevance-Theoretic Approach*, Amsterdam: John Benjamins.
Sperber, D. (1984) 'Verbal irony: pretense or echoic mention?', *Journal of Experimental Psychology: General*, 113: 130–36.

Electronic Health Discourse

The rise of the **internet** has led to an upsurge in linguistic research aimed at describing computer-mediated discourse (e.g. Herring 1996; Baron 2000; Crystal 2006). Concomitant with the expansion of the World Wide Web has been an increase in websites dedicated to providing health advice and information. However, despite the proliferation of these online health forums, comparatively little is known about the discursive practices and exchanges that take place within them. Health communication research continues to be characterized by studies concerned with face-to-face encounters between health professionals and patients. In this discussion, we examine some of the communicative properties of electronic health discourse, focusing, in particular, on the relationship between the presentation of people's health concerns and the online **context** which helps to shape them.

Research into electronic health discourse has interrogated various modes of online interaction, including email or problem letters (Locher 2006; Harvey *et al.* 2007), health bulletin boards (Suzuki and Calzo 2004) and multi-user domains/web forums (Morrow 2006; Seale *et al.* 2006). Despite the uniqueness of each of these electronic platforms, a defining feature of many of these studies is the candid and personally exposing quality of the health concerns communicated by users online. For instance, Harvey *et al.* (2007) describe how problems submitted by patients to a virtual doctor were articulated without apparent inhibition, with the contributors typically eschewing euphemism in favour of more orthophemisitic terminology, that is language which, according to Allan and Burridge (2006), is

neither evasive nor overly polite (i.e. euphemistic) but direct or neutral. Thus, when articulating problems about psychological distress, such as self-destructive behaviour, the contributors expressly refer to the discursive object of 'suicide', rather than adopting implicit and euphemistic terms ('not worth living', 'no point to life', 'way out'), formulations which potentially impede establishing the likelihood of suicide or unambiguously expressing one's level of distress (Reeves *et al.* 2004).

The explicit and emotionally expressive nature of these online communiqués contrasts with the **discourse** described in much offline health communication. Research into face-to-face interaction, particularly in relation to delicate and taboo **topics**, such as sexual and mental health, has identified the communicative difficulties that participants (both patients and professionals alike) experience when discussing these sensitive topics (Weijts *et al.* 1993; Reeves *et al.* 2004; Stewart 2005; Pollock 2007; Emslie *et al.* 2007). For example, in a classic paper by Weijts *et al.* (1993) about discussions of sex in a clinical setting, it appeared that speaking about sexual issues was often conducted through vague language and omissions rather than through explicit references. Patients and professionals collaborated in substituting **demonstrative** pronouns and adverbs for more direct descriptions, referring to 'it', 'down there', 'that', and so forth. Terms like 'the event itself' and 'afterwards' were used to describe sex, without the nature of the 'event' being specified very precisely.

Given the consistently described contrast between online and face-to-face exchanges in terms of candour and emotional expressivity, the question arises as to the cause(s) of this communicative imbalance. Arguably, the most significant contextual factor that accounts for the increased levels of candour characteristic of electronic health discourse is anonymity – a factor which creates what Suler (2004: 321) refers to as the 'online disinhibition effect', the phenomenon whereby people self-disclose 'more frequently or intensely than they would in person'. Being anonymous involves altering one's identity or obscuring it altogether, allowing, in either instance, individuals to dissociate themselves from their own behaviours and thus, under this protective cloak of anonymity, 'express the way they truly feel and think' (McKenna and Bargh 2000: 62). As Suler (2004: 322) puts it, '[w]hen people have the opportunity to separate their actions online from their in-person lifestyle and identity, they feel less vulnerable about self-disclosing and acting out. Whatever they say or do can't be directly linked to the rest of their lives.'

Computer-mediated communication, then, constitutes a practical resource for eliciting emotionally rich and detailed disclosures from people who might otherwise be reluctant to seek health advice from professionals directly. The anonymous nature of much computer-mediated health care makes it an effective facility for discussing sensitive and taboo subjects, such as mental health. As Griffiths (2004: 157) observes, '[w]ords that are originated from within ourselves are received by the computer without contest or contempt' and so 'may produce the feelings that tell us we are being accommodated'. Consequently, electronic platforms are increasingly being harnessed to provide emotional support for individuals experiencing psychological distress.

The work of Barak and colleagues, for instance, reports on the efficacy of a dedicated online environment as a means of delivering psychological support to people experiencing suicidal ideation, while describing the written characteristics of the messages contributed to the forum (Barak and Miron 2005; Barak and Bloch 2006; Barak 2007). They show how, realized through the elevated use of first-person singular pronominal forms (e.g. 'I', 'me', 'mine', etc.), the writings of suicidal individuals on the internet are characterized by an intense linguistic self-attention (as compared with the language of non-suicidal individuals who were comparatively less self-focused). As with other research into the **communication** of self-destructive behaviour (e.g. Stirman and Pennebaker 2001; Rude *et al.* 2004), the authors' findings support the not uncontroversial idea that suicidal people can be characterized 'by distinctive textual verbalisations' (Barak and Miron 2005: 519). Thus, the online writing styles of distressed individuals can be potentially used for assessing the risk of suicide 'in that unique verbal characteristics are found that signify suicidal risk and sound an alarm for special attention' (Barak and Miron

2005: 519). However, despite online interaction being a proven effective source of emotional support, it remains to be seen whether **discourse analysis** alone can successfully anticipate, and so effectively prevent, suicidal behaviour.

Similar degrees of elevated self-focus have been identified in other discourse-based studies of electronic health communication. For instance, Morrow's (2006) research into the discourse features of postings to an internet discussion forum for depression reveals the common expression of intense personal emotion, typically, if not unsurprisingly, evinced through the verb 'feel'. Significantly, the verb was often followed by the preposition 'like' in order to construct metaphorical formulations that more vividly convey inner turmoil than would be otherwise afforded by more literal language (for example, to state 'I feel like screaming at everyone and everything' articulates personal feeling more vigorously than simply saying 'I feel frustrated').

Morrow (2006: 540) argues that the use of tropes in the online discussion of depressive experiences is not a matter of stylistic choice but arises from necessity: there are no ready-made linguistic formulae for describing mental states, with **metaphor** furnishing 'a means of talking about that which in nature is hard to put into words'. However, apart from the difficulty of literally rendering inner turmoil, the figurative and manneristic nature of the depressive postings are also inevitably influenced by the online context in which they are produced. Electronic health interaction typically allows users to communicate concerns in their own terms. Participants have space and time to formulate their problems and scope to prepare, if necessary, long and detailed texts which can be edited and then submitted without, crucially, the fear of being judged or stigmatized (Cotton and Gupta 2004).

Although online provision is not, and never can be, a substitute for face-to-face health intervention, it nevertheless constitutes a significant and practical therapeutic resource, giving rise to distinct forms of interaction that characteristically exhibit elevated levels of candour and self-disclosure. With the continuing expansion of the internet, and more and more people accessing online health services, it is ever important for discourse analysts to explore the rapidly evolving discursive landscape of electronic health care. Electronic health communication provides access to a rich seam of naturally-occurring discourse, the interrogation of which has the potential to further explicate the complex and intimate relationship between language and social life.

KEVIN HARVEY

See also: Internet language; institutional and professional discourse; psychotic discourse; rehabilitation, communication; schizophrenic language

Suggestions for further reading

Crystal, D. (2006) *Language and the Internet*, 2nd edn, Cambridge: Cambridge University Press.
Harvey, K., Churchill, D., Crawford, P., Brown, B., Mullany, L., Macfarlane, A. and McPherson, A. (2008) 'Health communication and adolescents: what do their emails tell us?', *Family Practice*, 25: 304–11.
Richardson, D. (2004) *Internet Discourse and Health Debates*, Basingstoke: Palgrave Macmillan.

Ellipsis

Ellipsis is a form of grammatical cohesion (the others being **reference**, substitution, and conjunction). It is classified into nominal, verbal and clausal ellipsis (Halliday and Hasan 1976: 200–202). Ellipsis means omitting a part of a sentence on the assumption that an earlier sentence or the **context** will make the **meaning** clear (Cook 1989: 20).

Quirk *et al.* (1985: 859–60) note that language users usually exhibit 'strong preferences' for using ellipsis in order to reduce their utterances as much as possible, while avoiding the possibility of **ambiguity**. They describe three main types of ellipsis: textual, situational and structural ellipsis. These types are based on the means by which the hearer or reader recovers the reduction (1985: 861–62). Quirk *et al.* also provide two reasons for ellipsis: clarity and economy. Situational ellipsis requires the hearer to recover the missing items from the immediate situation, and works by inserting a 'placeholding element' (Halliday 1994: 370) to replace a lexical

item. Carter and McCarthy (1995, 1997) suggest that ellipsis in spoken **discourse** is typically situational. Words are often omitted in informal spoken English when a speaker assumes the meaning will be clear to the hearer without them (Swan 1995; Stainton 1997).

Ellipsis, which is regarded as a form of inexplicitness, is non-specific when context-independent, but becomes specific when interpreted in the particular context in which it is used (Cheng and Warren 1999). In other words, ellipsis requires the hearer or reader to recover a part of the discourse, which the speaker or writer has chosen to omit, from the context. Cheng and Warren (1999) argue that the prevalence of ellipsis, especially situational ellipsis, in spoken language is further evidence of a difference in the grammars of spoken and written English. Ellipsis illustrates one of the means by which spoken language actively shapes context. When speakers converse they are engaged in what **Wittgenstein** (1953a: 10; Ring 1991) would term a different 'language-game' in which a higher level of inexplicitness is normally appropriate.

Foley and Van Valin (1984: 324) suggest that Southeast and East Asian languages are 'pragmatic **inference** languages', and so heavily utilize ellipsis, i.e. a pragmatic inference system for tracking referents. Nariyama (2001: 127) argues that Japanese actually utilizes all four reference-tracking systems proposed in Foley and Van Valin's (1984: 322ff.) typology: switch-function, switch-reference, noun class, and pragmatic inference. The first three of these systems are morphosyntactic and the fourth is discourse-oriented. Studying English, Nariyama (2004: 237) notes that subject ellipsis is common in **conversation** and casual letters, and that in conversational expressions subject ellipsis conveys 'specific implicated meanings' (2004: 247). They include implying an evasive and dismissive motive, an indeterminate state of mind, sounding more emphatic, sounding less directed/emphatic, implying trivial matters being described, and intimate relationship (2004: 247).

WINNIE CHENG

See also: Ambiguity; anaphora, pragmatics of; context; conversation; conversational turn-taking; deixis; discourse; inference; lexical pragmatics; meaning; reference; utterance interpretation; Wittgenstein, L.

Suggestions for further reading

Cheng, W. and Warren, M. (1999) 'Inexplicitness: what is it and should we be teaching it?', *Applied Linguistics*, 20: 293–315.
Cooper, R. and Ginzburg, J. (2004) 'Clarification, ellipsis, and the nature of contextual updates in dialogue', *Linguistics and Philosophy*, 27: 297–365.
McShane, M.J. (2005) *A Theory of Ellipsis*, New York: Oxford University Press.

Entailment

Entailment is a semantic relation associated with formal approaches that employ the notion of truth to characterize **meaning**. Entailment may be defined as follows:

(1) An expression A entails B if the truth of A guarantees the truth of B and the falsity of B guarantees the falsity of A.

So uttering a sentence like (2) is said to entail (3) because as (4) shows, asserting (2) and simultaneously denying (3) leads to a contradiction:

(2) The emperor was assassinated.
(3) The emperor is dead.
(4) The emperor was assassinated and is (in fact) not dead.

For many scholars the ability to recognize entailment and contradiction is fundamental to a speaker's semantic abilities.

Entailment is traditionally taken to be a semantic rather than pragmatic relation because it resists cancellation by contextual **knowledge**, or additional qualification. In this, it contrasts with other types of **inference**, such as Gricean **implicature**. So uttering sentence (5) might imply (6) but (5) does not entail (6) because (7) is not a contradiction:

(5) Some of my friends like football.
(6) Not all of my friends like football.
(7) Some of my friends like football, and (in fact) all of them do.

Sentence (6) is a natural or normal implication of (5), a **generalized conversational implicature** (Grice 1975, 1978; Levinson 2000), but is not entailed by it.

This freedom from contextual effects also distinguishes entailment from **presupposition**, which can be cancelled by conflicting contextual assumptions (Strawson 1950a, 1952). A further distinction between entailment and presupposition is that the latter survives under **negation**. Uttering (8) would normally give rise to the presupposition in (9):

(8) I regret buying this car.
(9) I bought this car.

However, negating (8) to form (10) can still give rise to the presupposition (9):

(10) I don't regret buying this car.

However, in contrast, negating an entailing sentence causes the entailment to fail. If we negate (2) earlier to form (11), then it no longer entails (3):

(11) The emperor wasn't assassinated.

Now we don't know automatically whether the emperor is alive or died in some manner other than assassination.

We have characterized entailment as less **context** sensitive than implicature and presupposition. However, in the wider sense all interpretation is context dependent, so entailment can only be understood relative to particular situations. Hence, trivially, *the emperor* has to denote the same individual in examples (2) and (3). Consequently, sentences are insufficiently specific, truth conditionally, to be related by entailment. As a result, some scholars view entailment as a relation between **propositions**, while others describe it as a relation between utterances.

In formal **semantics** entailment relations have been used to develop the theory of generalized quantifiers (Barwise and Cooper 1981; Keenan and Westerståhl 1997), which employs the notion of directional entailingness (also called monotonicity). This notion recognizes that different quantifiers affect entailment relations between sets and subsets in different ways.

Taking as an example the set *dogs* and the subset *poodles*, *all dogs* entails *all poodles* (but not vice versa), while *some poodles* entails *some dogs* (but not vice versa). The quantifier *all* in this construction is said to be downward entailing (also described as monotone decreasing, often represented as MON↓), while *some* is upward entailing (also described as monotone increasing, represented as MON↑). The notion has been applied elsewhere. The Fauconnier-Ladusaw proposal, for example, is that negative polarity items like English *any* and *ever*, which despite their name can occur in some non-overtly negative contexts, are in fact licensed by being in the scope of downward entailing operators. So we can see, for example, that the nominal with *everyone* in (12a) below is downward entailing because (12a) entails (12b):

(12) a. Everyone who owns dogs must pay the license fee.
b. Everyone who owns poodles must pay the license fee.

Sentence (13a) below shows that this is a possible context for the use of *any*, while in (13b) the same construction with *someone* is not possible:

(13) a. Everyone who owns any dogs must pay the license fee.
b. *Someone who owns any dogs must pay the license fee.

This proposal has produced a lively literature on this topic (Ladusaw 1979; Zwarts 1995; von Fintel 1999).

Entailment relations more generally have also been used to model how participants update **discourse** representations (Lascarides and Asher 1993; Asher and Lascarides 1998) and to investigate semantic relations in the lexicon (Fellbaum 1998a).

JOHN SAEED

See also: Abduction; assertion; context; formal pragmatics; generalized conversational implicature, theory of; Grice, H.P.; implicature; inference; logical form; negation, pragmatics of; philosophy of language; presupposition; reasoning; semantics

Suggestions for further reading

Bach, E., Jelinek, E., Kratzer, A. and Partee, B. (1995) *Quantification in Natural Languages*, Dordrecht: Kluwer.
Krifka, M. (1995) 'The semantics and pragmatics of polarity items', *Linguistic Analysis*, 25: 209–57.
Portner, P.H. (2005) *What is Meaning? Fundamentals of Formal Semantics*, Malden, MA: Blackwell.

Ethnomethodology

In the late 1950s and early 1960s, Harold Garfinkel (born 29 October 1917) developed a specific approach to the core problem of sociology 'how is social order possible?' He called this approach 'ethnomethodology'. The core idea was that members of collectivities continuously, as an essential part of their ordinary life together, use taken-for-granted 'methods' to create and maintain a local sense of social order. Ethnomethodology's mission is to study those methods, as actually used in social situations. It offers a re-specification of sociology as conceived by Talcott Parsons, inspired by the phenomenology of Edmund Husserl, Aron Gurwitsch and Alfred Schutz. Instead of analyzing social life in terms of abstract concepts like **power**, social structure and deviance, ethnomethodology studies the ordinariness of everyday life as a phenomenon 'in its own right', as a concerted achievement of participants' situated actions (Garfinkel 1967, 2002).

Therefore, ethnomethodological studies require a deep immersion in the details of members' practices in their local specifics through close observation, ethnographically and/or using audio or video recordings. At the same time, the researcher should 'bracket' pre-given conceptions and evaluations of the character of the activities to be studied. This is called ethnomethodological indifference. What people do is oriented to their particular purposes, in the situations in which they are acting, but at the same time it is oriented to others, fellow members, who have to understand the actions in order to react adequately. Intersubjective understanding is not achieved automatically; it often requires negotiation, in a turn-by-turn way. What is at stake is the local achievement of accountability. In anything they do, persons, as members of society, design their actions in such ways that their **meaning** is made available to other members. The empirical interest, then, is to explicate how this is achieved, how the sense of actions, their accountability, is made observable in situ.

Ethnomethodology has been a major influence in the emergence of **conversation analysis** (CA), while another offshoot, membership categorization analysis (MCA), is gaining more prominence. In CA, the concrete object of observation and analysis is talk-in-interaction, which is – as in ethnomethodology at large – approached in a procedural perspective. The question is how the exchange of verbal utterances (often accompanied by the use of other semiotic resources, such as visual cues) is organized. In MCA, the interest is in the ways in which 'membership categories', for instance referring to age, **gender**, ethnicity and profession, are used in talk or documents (Hester and Eglin 1997).

Ethnomethodology, then, studies practical action and practical **reasoning** (as embodied in actions) in an extremely wide array of settings and circumstances. These settings range from improvising at the piano (Sudnow 1978) to the coordination of activities in an airline cockpit (Nevile 2004), from high-level laboratory work (Lynch 1985) to playing with one's dog (Goode 2007), and from Tibetan philosophical debates (Liberman 2004) to making public announcements on the London Underground (Heath and Luff 2000: 88–124).

Because of its principled difference from other kinds of social science studies, ethnomethodology offers a major challenge to established traditions of theorizing and research in **pragmatics** as well as elsewhere.

PAUL TEN HAVE

See also: Conversation analysis

Suggestions for further reading

Francis, D. and Hester, S. (2004) *An Invitation to Ethnomethodology: Language, Society and Interaction*, London: Sage.

Hester, S. and Francis, D. (eds) (2007) *Orders of Ordinary Action: Respecifying Sociological Knowledge*, Aldershot: Ashgate.

ten Have, P. (2004) 'Ethnomethodology', in C. Seale, D. Silverman, J. Gubrium and G. Gobo (eds) *Qualitative Research Practice*, London: Sage.

Evidentials

The growing interest in linguistic evidentials during the last thirty years has nowadays spread to a variety of levels of analysis and research. Early studies were largely inspired by languages where evidentiality is obligatorily marked, either morphologically (e.g. by means of verbal affixes, particles) as in American Indian languages and languages in various parts of North and South America, or grammatically (e.g. by tense, aspect) as in Balkan Slavic, Turkish, Tibetan and Japanese (Chafe and Nichols 1986). The seminal collection edited by Chafe and Nichols (1986) also instigated the later concern with lexical evidentials in languages without grammaticalized evidentiality (e.g. English), where evidentiality is encoded by lexical expressions such as adverbials (*visibly, reportedly, apparently, allegedly*) or by verbs in main-clause or parenthetical types of construction (*I see, I hear, Chomsky says*) (Anderson 1986; Chafe 1986).

These early studies raised the central issue of whether evidentials should be examined in terms of (a) their function as markers indicating the 'source of speaker's **knowledge**' ('evidential' function) by observation (direct access), hearsay (indirect access) or **inference** (**reasoning**), or (b) as markers indicating the 'speaker's degree of certainty', and hence 'attitude' towards knowledge ('reliability'/'evaluative' function). A number of researchers have commonly, though not uncontroversially, opted for the latter, broader construal of the term, despite the overlap with other related classes of evidentials (e.g. epistemic modality, mental-state verbs) (Jakobson 1957; Barnes 1984; Palmer 1986; Anderson 1986; Ifantidou 2001; Rooryck 2001). From this perspective, a variety of evidentially driven sources of information can be considered, such as assumption, possibility, expectation, prediction, imagination, cultural knowledge, common knowledge, popular wisdom, desirability and intuition. These sources are encoded by a variety of linguistic phenomena, such as **propositional attitude** verbs (*I guess, I suppose, I realize, I* *remember, I feel, I imagine*), **speech act** verbs (*I swear, I promise, I predict*), mood (declarative versus interrogative), tense (present versus conditional) and adverbials (*clearly, supposedly, seemingly, certainly, presumably*). As a consequence, particularly in language typology studies (*see also* Johanson and Utas 2000), evidentials have often been examined in related and overlapping domains, such as epistemic modality (Halliday 1970; Lyons 1977; Palmer 1986, 1990), academic metadiscourse (Hyland 1998a; Hyland and Tse 2004; Ifantidou 2005), generative grammar (Rooryck 2001) and **parentheticals** (Urmson 1952; Emonds 1979; Hand 1993; Burton-Roberts 1999a). In relation to semantic analysis and pragmatic interpretation, evidentials have been considered with regard to three questions: (1) do they contribute to the **proposition** expressed by the utterance? (2) do they contribute to the explicit or implicit aspect of **communication**? and (3) do they contribute to conceptual or procedural information? (Ifantidou 2001; *see* Papafragou 2006 on truth conditions of epistemic modals).

The central issue of how 'evidentiality' cross-cuts 'speaker certainty' has resurged in work seeking to trace the conceptual origins of evidentiality. Developmental work shows that the two concepts may overlap, especially in languages such as Japanese, where the same linguistic forms – sentence final particles, adverbials and mental-state verbs – can convey degree of 'speaker (un)certainty' as well as 'source of evidence' (direct or hearsay) (*see* Matsui *et al.* 2006). Alternatively, speaker certainty has been separately examined by looking at mental-state verbs (e.g. English, *see* Bartsch and Wellman 1995) and evidentiality has been separately studied by looking at particles (e.g. Turkish, Korean, *see* Aksu-Koç 1988; Choi 1995).

This shift of interest over the last decade to **child language acquisition** informed the current concern with how the acquisition of evidentials is causally connected to the development of thought, specifically to the ability to monitor the origins of one's beliefs (source monitoring). Languages with obligatory, and hence systematic, grammaticalized evidentials were first to be investigated, with verb suffixes typically encoding different types of direct or indirect evidence. Pioneer experimental work on

language acquisition of Turkish and Korean (Aksu-Koç 1988, 2000; Aksu-Koç and Slobin 1986; Choi 1995) paved the way for research on the cognitive prerequisites for the emergence of evidentials. A large body of cognitive developmental data on children's ability to evaluate the evidence for their beliefs (Gopnik and Graf 1988; Pillow 1989; Pratt and Bryant 1990; Robinson *et al.* 1995; Mitchell *et al.* 1997; O'Neil and Chong 2001; Pillow 2002; Robinson and Whitcombe 2003), and on their ability to distinguish true information from misinformation (reality from deception) by means of false-belief tasks (Wimmer and Perner 1983; Perner *et al.* 1987; Flavell *et al.* 1990; Sullivan and Winner 1991; Saltmarsh and Mitchell 1998; Garnham and Perner 2001) has instigated the correlation between research separately pursued in language acquisition and cognitive development. A relevant strand of research on producing (and retrieving) evidential information for the purposes of improving child-witness expectations and interviewing procedures in forensic investigations seems to have been so far ignored (Poole and Lindsay 2002; Principe and Ceci 2002; Roberts 2002).

Ongoing research in **pragmatic development** seeks to address a number of intriguing issues: (1) to what extent does the acquisition of evidentials rely on mastering their complex cognitive prerequisites? (2) are learners of languages with grammaticalized evidential systems (e.g. Turkish, Korean, Japanese) privileged in accessing evidential concepts and, as a consequence, do they progress faster in source reasoning than learners of languages without systematic evidential contrasts (e.g. English, Greek)? (Whorf 1956a; *see* Bowerman and Levinson 2001), and (3) does understanding of knowledge states precede success in (fully representational understanding of) false-belief tasks?. Current experimental work focuses on explaining asymmetries in the early use and genuine understanding of evidentials and on clarifying the causal link between early understanding of others' states/ sources of knowledge and linguistic systems encoding source information. These goals are pursued by cross-linguistic studies of linguistic and non-linguistic aspects of evidentiality that draw on a diverse range of tasks and age groups (*see* Papafragou *et al.* 2007).

A related issue that has not been systematically explored so far refers to ranking evidential sources in terms of relative conceptual difficulty. Results obtained in developmental strands of research could be seen in a different light if there were empirical evidence on whether 'hearsay' is conceptually more demanding than 'inference', or whether 'inference' is the most sophisticated aspect of monitoring informational access, as it is standardly assumed.

ELLY IFANTIDOU

See also: Discourse coherence; discourse cohesion; discourse markers; discourse particles; echoic use; hedge; mitigation; parentheticals; propositional attitude

Suggestions for further reading

Ifantidou, E. (2005) 'Evidential particles and mind reading', *Pragmatics and Cognition*, 13: 253–95.

Mushin, I. (2001) *Evidentiality and Epistemological Stance: Narrative Retelling*, Amsterdam: John Benjamins.

Papafragou, A., Li, P., Choi, Y. and Han, C. (2007) 'Evidentiality in language and cognition', *Cognition*, 103: 253–99.

Experimental Pragmatics

The term 'experimental pragmatics' has recently been used by a group of British and European researchers to refer to work in **psycholinguistics** that uses traditional psycholinguistic methodologies but that is focused on investigating a particular set of issues at the **semantics-pragmatics interface**. These semantic-pragmatic issues have been hotly debated over the last twenty-five years or so by linguists and philosophers of language such as Bach (1994a), Carston (2002), Horn (1984, 1992), Levinson (1995, 2000), Recanati (1991, 1995, 2004b) and Sperber and Wilson (1995). It is precisely because this theoretical debate has threatened to result in a stalemate that experimental investigations have been launched with the aim of making progress in the theoretical debate. As Garrett and Harnish (2007: 65–66) write: 'In the

face of the intractability of some of these questions by the methodology of (pure) pragmatics, i.e., intuition and argument, some have suggested that it is time to turn to the experimental methodology of psycholinguistics for guidance.'

This experimental pragmatics movement began with the work of Gibbs and Moise (1997), which focused on the way in which readers understand utterances that convey Gricean **generalized conversational implicatures** (GCIs). For example, an utterance of 'Robert cut a finger' would normally be understood as communicating that Robert cut *his own* finger, even though in the special circumstance in which we know that Robert is a Mafia enforcer we might understand the utterance as communicating that Robert cut *someone else's* finger. Gibbs and Moise wanted to see whether listeners first access the semantically encoded **meaning** of the implicature-carrying words (in the example above this would be something like 'Robert cut *some finger or other*') and then use **context** to infer the GCI or whether the GCI is more directly accessed, bypassing the literal (encoded) meaning, as Gibbs (1994) argues happens in the processing of certain types of indirect speech acts, **idioms**, and **metaphors**.

Gibbs and Moise (1997), and to an even greater extent Nicolle and Clark (1999) and Bezuidenhout and Cutting (2002), cast this question as a debate between a Gricean-inspired and a relevance theory-inspired model of language understanding. Relevance theorists, such as Sperber and Wilson (1995) and Carston (1988, 2002), have challenged Grice's division between **what is said** and what is implicated, as well as Grice's assumption that pragmatic principles apply only to the understanding of what is implicated. Carston argues that GCIs are in fact explicatures ('explicature' is a technical term in **relevance theory** corresponding roughly to the intuitive notion of what is said).

Gibbs and Moise (1997) and Nicolle and Clark (1999) used forced-choice judgement tasks to investigate the degree to which readers are aware of explicatures, **implicatures**, and what Gibbs and Moise call minimal meanings – the non-enriched meanings that are semantically encoded in the implicature-/explicature-carrying words. After reading sentences containing such words (either in isolation or in context), readers were asked to choose the paraphrase that they felt most closely captured what was said by those sentences. The paraphrases offered corresponded to minimal meanings, explicatures, implicatures, or were unrelated in content. Minimal meanings were rarely chosen, which Gibbs and Moise took to show support for the view that enriched meanings are directly accessed. By contrast, Nicolle and Clark found that readers favoured implicature paraphrases. They offered a relevance theoretical explanation for this finding, arguing that readers chose the paraphrase that most closely matched the original in its degree of relevance (in the technical sense of Sperber and Wilson 1995: 153). Bezuidenhout and Cutting (2002) used online reading tasks to investigate the way in which sentences containing GCI-carrying words are processed in contexts that support either an enriched or a minimal meaning. The results of these investigations were taken to support a relevance theory-inspired context-based model over a Gricean literal-first serial model of processing, since people took longer to read sentences in contexts supporting their literal/minimal meaning than they took to read those same sentences in contexts supporting an enriched meaning.

Another closely related thread of research was initiated by Noveck (2001). It focused on children's **pragmatic competence**. Noveck compared the way in which children and adults understand sentences containing words that are triggers for **scalar implicatures**, which are one special subclass of generalized implicature. Scalar implicatures have been intensively studied from a theoretical perspective by neo-Griceans and others, such as Carston (1995, 1998b), Geurts (1998), Hirschberg (1991), Horn (1984, 1992, 2006), Levinson (1995, 2000), and Sauerland (2004). Scalar implicatures depend on so-called Horn or **entailment** scales. For instance, <all, some> forms a Horn scale with 'all' being the stronger element, since 'All S are P' entails 'Some S are P' but not vice versa. Given that a speaker is following Grice's maxim of quantity, when she utters a sentence containing a weaker element from a Horn scale, she will implicate that, as far as she knows, a statement using a stronger element from the scale is not true. Thus, an utterance of 'Some S are P' will scalar implicate that, as far as the speaker knows, not all S are P.

Noveck (2001) used a variety of tasks to elicit listeners' judgements about sentences containing scalar implicature-triggers. For example, one experiment examined the way in which children and adults differ in their understanding of modal statements such as 'There has to be a parrot in the box' and 'There might be a parrot in the box'. Participants saw various scenarios involving objects hidden in boxes and had to judge whether a puppet's statements about the hidden objects were true or false. This is a version of what has become known as the truth value judgement task. The crucial condition was the one in which the object, e.g. a parrot, *had* to be in the box but the puppet said that the parrot *might* be in the box. The puppet's statement would be logically true but pragmatically infelicitous: the weaker claim scalar implicates that the stronger statement is not true. As Noveck puts it, the puppet is being underinformative. Seventy-two per cent of 5-year-olds, 80 per cent of 7-year-olds and 69 per cent of 9-year-olds were prepared to accept the underinformative 'might' statement, whereas only 35 per cent of adults accepted it.

In another experiment that used a sentence evaluation task, Noveck found that children are more likely than adults to accept sentences such as 'Some elephants have trunks' as true, which logically it is, since it is entailed by the true 'All elephants have trunks'. Noveck concludes that children are more 'logical' than adults, since 89 per cent of children, as compared to only 41 per cent of adults, accepted such statements. Adults apparently derived the scalar implicature 'Not all elephants have trunks' and interpreted the statement as saying falsely that *some but not all* elephants have trunks. Moreover, older children fall somewhere between younger children and adults in the percentage of their 'pragmatic' as opposed to 'logical' responses. Thus, Noveck concludes that pragmatic abilities are a late development.

Subsequent studies by Papafragou and Musolino (2003), Feeney *et al.* (2004) and Guasti *et al.* (2005), using similar judgement tasks and/or materials, have found that children can respond 'pragmatically' when the context makes the pragmatic response relevant. These follow-up studies have found that when the conversational settings are more naturalistic and that when what can be known about the situation is carefully controlled, even 6- and 7-year-old children will derive the scalar implicatures and reject 'underinformative' statements at rates similar to those of adult participants. Contra Noveck (2001), it appears that young children do have pragmatic abilities. However, these abilities are often masked by factors such as task demands and unnaturalness of the experimental setup, which make it difficult for young children to understand the conversational goals of the experimenter's confederates, including the 'puppet' whose statements children are asked to evaluate.

Chierchia *et al.* (2001) found that their 5-year-old subjects did not respond pragmatically on a truth value judgement task that tested for sensitivity to the exclusive understanding of 'or' (which the authors assume is derived by means of incorporation of the scalar implicature 'Not both p and q' into the literal inclusive meaning of 'p or q'). These children accepted statements informationally weaker than the situation allowed for. That is, they accepted disjunctive statements of the form 'p or q' even in situations in which both p and q were true. In contrast, adults rejected disjunctive statements in such situations, presumably because they derived the scalar implicature and interpreted the disjunction in the exclusive sense. However, in a follow-up experiment in which children were presented with situations in which p and q were both true and they had to choose between two ways of describing the situation, children preferred the informationally stronger 'p and q' over the weaker 'p or q'. So children are aware that the informationally weaker 'p or q' is pragmatically infelicitous in situations in which both p and q are true. Thus, it may be working memory limitations that are responsible for the children's failure to derive the scalar implicature in the non-choice version of the task.

The initial trickle of experimental research on GCIs has since become a spate. This work received a boost with the organization of the first Experimental Pragmatics (XPRAG) Workshop, held in Lyons, France in 2003. Since then there have been two additional XPRAG workshops, one held in Cambridge, England in 2005 and a third held in Berlin, Germany in 2007. The first workshop resulted in an edited volume of papers, Noveck and Sperber (2004). A second volume of papers is forthcoming from the Berlin workshop, Sauerland and Yatsushiro (to appear).

Many of the initial questions that were addressed by Gibbs and Moise (1997) have become refined and sharpened. This has resulted in a narrowing of focus, since what was initially an interest in the entire class of Gricean GCIs, as well as in the issue of whether and when minimal meanings are accessed, has become an intense interest in scalar implicatures in particular, and moreover in just a few paradigm instances of those scalar implicatures, such as the **inference** 'Not all S are P' from 'Some S are P', the inference 'Not both p and q' from 'p or q', and the inference 'At most n S are P' from 'n S are P', where 'n' is a numeral word such as 'three'.

One major issue now being debated concerns whether or not scalar implicatures are default inferences that are automatically derived by a listener or reader on encountering scalar implicature-triggers (words such as 'some' or 'or'), or whether scalar implicatures will only be derived if the conversational context warrants it. More recently, a third contender has entered the theoretical arena. According to this view, the derivation of scalar implicatures depends heavily on structural or grammatical factors and such implicatures are generated preferentially in so-called upward-entailing (as opposed to downward-entailing) environments. The default inference theory is associated with the work of Levinson (2000). The contextual inference theory is associated with the work of relevance theorists such as Sperber and Wilson (1995) and Carston (2002). The structural inference theory is associated with the work of Crain and Pietroski (2002) and Chierchia (2004). Competing findings by experimentalists have often been cast as supporting one or another of these theoretical frameworks. For example, Bezuidenhout and Morris (2004), Bott and Noveck (2004), Breheny *et al.* (2006), Katsos *et al.* (2006), and Noveck and Posada (2003) have argued in favour of the contextual inference view. By contrast, Grodner *et al.* (2007) and Storto and Tanenhaus (2005) have argued in favour of the default inference view. Finally, Chierchia *et al.* (2006) and Panizza and Chierchia (2008) have argued in favour of the structural inference view.

This body of work cannot be described in detail here. The diverse materials and methodologies used defy any easy summary. For example, these studies have used a variety of methodologies, including event-related potential recordings, eye monitoring during reading, and the visual world paradigm, in which eye gaze to regions of a visual display are tracked over time while participants listen to sentences and follow directions to point to or otherwise act on objects in the display. Some experiments have used sentences containing scalar implicature-triggers presented in context, others presented such sentences in isolation. The type of trigger used varied across studies. Some experiments used materials with 'some', others used 'or', and others used numeral phrases such as 'three cars'. Some experiments used simple unembedded sentences, others used embedded sentences, especially those which aimed to test the claim made by Chierchia (2004) that scalar implicatures are blocked or cancelled whenever the local addition of the implicature fails to lead to a stronger statement, as would happen with local accommodation into a downward-entailing environment. (A statement p is stronger than q just in case p entails q but not vice versa.) Such environments include the antecedents of conditionals, the restriction clauses of universally quantified statements and environments within the scope of **negation**.

As mentioned, recent work in experimental pragmatics has focused rather narrowly on scalar implicatures and how they are processed both in and out of **discourse** contexts and with scalar implicature-triggers occurring in either embedded or unembedded sentences. This has led to some progress in understanding the factors involved in pragmatic processing and on the relative weight of semantic and pragmatic factors in language processing. By contrast, it is to be regretted that the broader class of GCIs has not received as much attention. However, as more people become attracted to work in this area, it is likely that the focus will once again widen. Judging by the variety of contributions to the XPRAG 2007 workshop in Berlin, this widening is already underway. Although work on scalar implicatures dominated, a variety of other work was presented as well. Work was presented on the role of context and common

ground in comprehension, on the distinction between saying and implicating, and on the processing of sentences containing negation, quantifiers, definites and indefinites, and negative polarity items.

Another sign of a broadening of focus is the recent work of Garrett and Harnish (2007), which returns to some of the issues investigated by Gibbs and Moise (1997). Their interest was not limited to scalar implicatures, but included the sorts of implicatures that Levinson (2000) argues are handled by his I(nformativeness)-principle. (Scalar implicatures, by contrast, fall under Levinson's Quantity-principle.) An example of an implicature falling under the I-principle is the implicature that Robert broke his own finger that follows from an utterance of 'Robert broke a finger'. Gibbs and Moise also investigated the comprehension of readers of utterances involving unarticulated constituents. For example, in utterances of 'It's raining' or 'I've eaten', the location of the rain and the time of the eating are not articulated and the hearer must infer this information from the context.

Bach (1995) invokes a notion of standardization to account for these cases. He argues that sometimes the literal meaning of a sentence will be bypassed in favour of a standardized interpretation, which involves an 'expansion' of what is said. He calls such expansions 'implicitures', since they are in some sense implicit in what is said. For example, when a speaker says 'I've had breakfast', her utterance will not be taken in its strict and literal sense, which according to Bach is that the speaker has had breakfast at some time in the past, but will be understood in its standardized sense as communicating the **impliciture** that the speaker has had breakfast on the day of utterance.

Garrett and Harnish (2007) focus on unarticulated constituent cases like 'It's raining' and 'I've had breakfast' (which they call 'location' and 'time' sentences, respectively) as well as cases that fall under Levinson's I-principle, such as 'Robert cut a finger' (which they call 'possession' sentences). They performed two experiments using impliciture-generating and non-impliciture-generating versions of such sentences. The first experiment used auditorily presented sentences followed by visually presented probe questions and pairs of words, and participants indicated their word choice by pressing a response key. For each of the three sentence types they investigated, Garrett and Harnish found that the impliciture interpretation was chosen significantly more often after presentation of an impliciture version than after a non-impliciture version. And even though the impliciture response was also the most frequent response chosen for the *non-*impliciture versions of location and possession sentences, the response times for these choices was longer than for the impliciture responses for *impliciture* versions of these two types of sentences. Garrett and Harnish (2007: 80) take their results to attest to 'the brute facts of standardization' and as a 'demonstration of a strong context free bias in favor of impliciture driven choices'.

Garrett and Harnish's second experiment was a self-paced reading experiment in which impliciture versions of time, location and possession sentences were presented as the final lines of stories that either favoured the impliciture interpretation or cancelled it. Probe questions with their two probe words followed the target sentences and participants indicated their choices orally. Response times for these answers were measured from presentation of probes to onset of voiced responses. Garrett and Harnish found that the difference in reading times for target sentences did not differ significantly across types of story context (enabling versus cancelling). Moreover, participants were accurate in their choices, in the sense that they chose the contextually appropriate answers – the impliciture response in enabling contexts and the non-impliciture (literal) response in cancelling contexts. However, participants took significantly longer to make the appropriate choice in cancelling as opposed to enabling contexts. Garrett and Harnish take this result to show that the impliciture response was derived even in cancelling contexts and thus was competing with the literal meaning, thereby causing longer answer response times in these cancelling contexts. They argue that this finding vindicates Bach's standardization view, since they construe this view as associating impliciture meanings with forms of words and hence as predicting such competition.

One final 'new' direction that bears mention is the recent work reported by Katsos (2007). This picks up on the thread of work initiated by Noveck (2001) on young children's pragmatic abilities. Noveck (2001) found that young children are willing to accept underinformative statements, whereas adults and older children reject them. Subsequent work by Feeney *et al.* (2004) and Papafragou and Musolino (2003) disputed these findings and showed that young children will reject underinformative statements, if the context makes the pragmatically enriched response relevant. As Katsos (2007) notes, these previous studies were focused on children's *comprehension*. He also notes that there has been some recent work looking at children's language *production*, e.g. by Schulz *et al.* (2005), which shows that there is a developmental trend when it comes to answering **questions** that call for exhaustive answers. Younger children tend to produce logically true but non-exhaustive answers whereas older children give exhaustive ones. This appears to show that, just as young children accept underinformative statements from others, they produce underinformative statements themselves.

However, these findings regarding young children's comprehension and production do not come from a single combined study. Thus, Katsos undertook to investigate both comprehension and production of 5-, 7-, 9- and 11-year-old children and adults in a single study. The material used involved both the Horn scale <all, some> and ad hoc scales constructed in specific story contexts. Katsos tested comprehension with a truth value judgement task, in which participants had to judge the acceptability of the statements of a fictional character, Mr Caveman. The crucial conditions were the ones in which Mr Caveman produced underinformative statements, such as 'The elephant pushed some of the trucks' when the elephant had pushed all of the trucks, or statements such as 'The dog painted the triangle' when the dog had painted both a triangle and a heart. To test production, participants were told that Mr Caveman did not know how to describe the situation and they were invited to answer on his behalf. The crucial conditions were ones in which an exhaustive answer would be appropriate, such as in answer to the question 'What did the dog paint?' in a situation in which the dog painted both the triangle and the heart.

Katsos (2007) found that even young children are informative speakers and are perfectly capable of giving exhaustive answers. However, somewhat surprisingly, they are underinformative comprehenders. That is, they accepted under-informative statements from Mr Caveman. By contrast, older children are both informative speakers and comprehenders. As to why pro-duction and comprehension are dissociated in younger children, Katsos suggests that this is the result of several factors. Some children seem to be operating with a principle of charity. The rate of rejection of underinformative statements by young children is also influenced by such things as whether the scale is a Horn scale or an ad hoc one and on how clear the **topic** under discussion is. In a follow-up experiment using a truth value judgement task, in which participants had privileged access to the situations and they were told that Mr Caveman's statements were mere guesses, children were more likely to accept underinformative statements from Mr Caveman than in the first experiment. This suggests that children take their interlocutor's epistemic situation into account and are not responding egocentrically, based on their own privileged epistemic position.

Although the term 'experimental pragmatics' has recently been used in this somewhat specia-lized way to refer to the work on the processing of generalized implicatures initiated by Gibbs and Moise (1997) and the related work on chil-dren's pragmatic abilities initiated by Noveck (2001), there is another sense in which the term could be used to refer to a rather broad class of investigations in experimental psychology that have been underway for several decades. In this broader sense, experimental pragmatics refers to any experimental investigation of any phenom-enon that is recognizably pragmatic, such as the investigation of Gricean conversational **maxims**, of Gricean conversational implicatures, of direct and indirect speech acts, and of non-literal lan-guage use. Such research can be classified into a number of distinct lines:

1 Research on indirect speech acts and Gri-cean conversational maxims (e.g. Clark 1979; Clark and Havilland 1977; Gibbs 1994).
2 Research on the processing of metapho-rical, metonymical, and ironical uses of language, of idioms, and of nonce uses of language (e.g. Cacciari and Glucksberg 1994; Cutting and Bock 1997; Frisson and Pickering 1999; Gerrig 1989; Gibbs 1994; Giora 2003; Glucksberg 2001; Katz 1996; Traxler *et al.* 2005; Winner 1988).
3 Research on **presupposition**, the **given/new distinction**, topic-focus structure, discourse-level processing, and ellipsis (e.g. Burkhardt 2005, 2006; Frazier 2006; Frazier and Clifton 2006; Frazier *et al.* 2007; Haviland and Clark 1974; Mauner *et al.* 1995; Schwarz 2005; Sussman *et al.* 2006).
4 Research on pragmatic competence and **theory of mind** abilities, including in children and impaired populations, such as **autism spectrum disorders** (e.g. Baron-Cohen *et al.* 1985; Happé 1993; Leslie 2000; de Villiers *et al.* 2007).

Each one of these lines could be the subject of its own entry and the cited work represents just a tiny fraction of four very large bodies of research. Thus, no attempt will be made here to say anything further about this research, except to observe that the trends in psycholinguistic research have more or less tracked those in lin-guistics and philosophy. For example, some of the most influential work being done when **pragmatics** was becoming a systematic sub-field of linguistics in the 1960s and 1970s was the work of the philosophers **Grice** and **Searle** on conversational maxims and **speech acts**, respectively. Psychologists soon became interested in studying these phenomena using traditional behavioural research methods. Similarly, Grice's work on conversational implicatures spurred an interest in the topic of metaphorical and non-literal language use. And soon psychologists fol-lowed suit and began to explore these issues experimentally. As linguists and philosophers have explored ever more of the pragmatic terrain, psycholinguists have never been far behind.

ANNE BEZUIDENHOUT

See also: Development, pragmatic; generalized conversational implicature, theory of; impli-cature; impliciture; inferential comprehension; neo-Gricean pragmatics; psycholinguistics; scalar implicature; semantics-pragmatics interface

Suggestions for further reading

Clark, H. (1992) *Arenas of Language Use*, Chicago, IL: University of Chicago Press.

Gibbs, R. (1994) *The Poetics of Mind*, Cambridge: Cambridge University Press.

Noveck, I. and Sperber, D. (2004) 'Introduction', in I. Noveck and D. Sperber (eds) *Experimental Pragmatics*, New York: Palgrave Macmillan.

Explicit/Implicit Distinction

Aspects of utterance meaning

It is widely accepted within **pragmatics** that there is a distinction to be made between the explicit content and the implicit import of an utterance. There is much less agreement about the precise nature of this distinction, how it is to be drawn, and whether any such two-way distinction can do justice to the levels and kinds of **meaning** involved in **utterance interpretation**. In order to approach these issues, let us consider the following conversational exchange:

(1) Alex: How was the party? Did it go well?
    Brit: There wasn't enough drink and everyone left early.

Focusing on Brit's utterance in response to Alex's **question**, it seems fairly clear that she is communicating that the party was not a great success. This is not something she says explicitly. Rather, it is an indirect or implied answer to the question – an **implicature**, as such implicitly communicated **propositions** are known. The hearer derives this implicated meaning by inferring it from the proposition which is directly and explicitly communicated by Brit, together with some contextual assumptions (concerning the characteristics of successful versus unsuccessful parties).

The question now is: what is the explicit content of Brit's utterance? One possibility is that it is simply the linguistically encoded meaning of the sentence that she uttered, so it is a conjunction of the meaning of the two simple sentences (a) 'there wasn't enough drink' and (b) 'everyone left early'. Certainly, that meaning is as explicit as any meaning can be, but what is it exactly? Consider, for instance, the noun 'drink', which

includes in its extension camomile tea, warm milk, and medicines in liquid form, to mention but a few of the many drinks which are unlikely to be relevant in the **context** of Brit's utterance. A similar sort of point applies to the linguistically encoded meaning of the bare quantifier 'everyone', whose extension includes vast numbers of people whom Brit has no **intention** of denoting. In the context of the dialogue above, it is clear that she intends to convey that everyone who came to the particular party that Alex asked her about left that party early. So, although the linguistic expression employed by Brit, the words she actually uttered, have a meaning and that meaning is, arguably, the most explicit meaning that her utterance provides, it seems to be somewhat remote from the proposition Alex is likely to take her to have directly communicated (to have said or asserted). That seems to be more like the content in (2) (where the italicized elements all go beyond the encoded meaning of the linguistic expressions uttered):

(2) There wasn't enough *alcoholic* drink *to satisfy the people at [the party]$_i$* and *so* everyone *who came to [the party]$_i$* left *[it]$_i$* early.

This is the proposition on the basis of which Brit's utterance would be judged as true or false, would be agreed or disagreed with ('Yes, there was so little beer that we all went off to the pub', or 'No, not everyone left early and those who did had an exam the next morning'). Notice too that it is this proposition (and not the very general encoded linguistic meaning) which plays the crucial role of premise in the **reasoning** process which leads to the implicated conclusion that the party didn't go well.

So we have two candidates for the explicit content of Brit's utterance: (a) the encoded linguistic meaning, which *is* fully explicit but which doesn't seem (on its own) to constitute a communicated proposition (part of the speaker's meaning), and (b) the richer content given in (2), which *is* communicated (part of the speaker's meaning) but which does not seem to be fully explicit, in that it includes elements of meaning that have no linguistic correlate in the utterance but arise from considerations of contextual relevance. Ultimately, I will argue in favour of the latter construal of explicit content and so for an explicit/implicit distinction which is a distinction between two kinds of communicated (speaker-meant) propositions; both are pragmatically derived by hearers, but with the difference that the 'explicit' one is a pragmatically inferred development of the linguistically encoded content while the implicit one(s) are wholly pragmatically inferred. However, there are other views to consider first, in particular Grice's saying/implicating distinction, which is not identical with either of the two positions so far discussed. And there is another distinction which is closely entwined with the explicit/implicit distinction, that is, the distinction between **semantics** and pragmatics. Any clarification of the former requires consideration of its relation to the latter.

Grice and the saying/implicating distinction

Grice made a distinction between **what is said** by a speaker and what is implicated, where what is said is taken to be the truth-conditional content of the utterance (the basis for judging the speaker as having spoken truly or falsely) and the implicature(s) of an utterance are additional communicated propositions which do not contribute to truth conditions. Implicated propositions may be either *conversational* (that is, dependent on the assumption that the speaker is following certain rational principles of conversational exchange) or *conventional* (that is, largely generated by the standing meaning of certain linguistic expressions, such as 'but' and 'moreover').

This truth-conditional/non-truth-conditional distinction was essential to **Grice** in his concern to defeat the 'illegitimate use' arguments of a certain group of ordinary language philosophers (Grice 1967: lecture 1). Those arguments won't be reviewed in detail here, but the utility of the distinction can be demonstrated by considering an utterance of the sentence in (3), where 'this' refers to a patently red pillar-box directly in front of the speaker and hearer:

(3) This looks red to me.

This utterance would be quite odd in a situation where lighting conditions are good and there is nothing impeding normal visual perception.

However, contrary to the claims of some philosophers, Grice's point was that this oddness need not militate against the use of such statements in a theory or analysis (in this case, of perception), because the statement made (the proposition expressed/said) by the utterance is perfectly true and that is all that matters for the theory or analysis. The oddness or infelicity lies outside the truth-conditional content of the utterance. It is caused (merely) by the conversational implicature that such an utterance would be likely to convey: that there is some doubt about the redness of the pillar-box, an implication which, in the given circumstances, is false. A similar story can be run for a case of conventional implicature which gives rise to some conversational infelicity:

(4) This looks red to me but it is red.

The use of 'but' carries a conventional implicature that there is some sort of contrast between the contents of the two **assertions** it conjoins, which, in the case of (4), is likely to be false in many contexts. However, according to Grice, this does not impinge on the truth-conditional content of the utterance (the statement explicitly made), which is equivalent to 'X looks red and X is red', a proposition that could well be true in those contexts. The general situation is summarized as follows:

(5) what is said   vs. what is implicated
     truth-conditional   non-truth-conditional
     if false, utterance   if false, utterance is
     is false   merely odd

According to the standard interpretation of the Gricean account, what is said (the truth-conditional content of the utterance) is very closely related to the conventional meaning of the sentence employed (excluding those expressions that give rise to conventional implicatures). It is not, however, identical to encoded or conventional linguistic content since the linguistic forms uttered may include ambiguous or indexical elements – Grice explicitly conceded that **disambiguation** and **reference** assignment might be required for a full identification of what the speaker has said (see his discussion of an utterance of 'he is in the grip of a vice', Grice 1975: 44–45). So, viewed as a candidate for the explicit/implicit distinction, Grice's saying/ implicating distinction is different from both of those discussed in the previous section. In particular, his conception of explicit content seems to fall between context-free encoded linguistic meaning and the considerably pragmatically-enriched content illustrated in (2). Many truth-conditional semanticists have found this an appealing notion of content since it appears to allow for an equation of what is said by uttering a sentence (explicit content) and the truth-conditional semantics of a sentence (albeit relativized to a context). The domain of pragmatics is then taken to be an account of how conversational implicatures arise, based on Grice's system of conversational **maxims** (quality, quantity, relevance and manner) and his overarching **cooperative principle**. On this view, then, the two distinctions, explicit/ implicit (saying/implicating) and semantics/ pragmatics effectively coincide.

However, when we look at particular examples of utterances, there seems to be a serious problem with the view that explicit utterance content is captured by the Gricean 'what is said':

(6) Mother (to child crying over a cut on his knee):
    You're not going to die. (example due to Bach 1994a)
    a. You (Billy) are not going to die from that cut.
    b. You (Billy) should stop making such a fuss about it.

What the mother means (what she intends to communicate to the child) is given in (a) and (b), where (b) is clearly an implicature and (a) seems to be what she explicitly communicates. But the proposition delivered by conventional linguistic meaning and the assignment of a referent to the pronoun 'you' (hence, the Gricean 'what is said') is 'Billy is not going to die', which seems to entail that Billy is immortal, something that the mother has no intention of conveying. Here's another example that makes the same point:

(7) Jim: Would you like some supper?
    Sue: I've eaten.

What Sue has said here, according to the strict Gricean construal, is 'Sue has eaten something at some past time'. But surely what she intends to express and what Jim will take her to have expressed is that she has eaten *a meal this evening*. It is this proposition that is needed as input to the pragmatic inferential process that delivers the implicated answer to Jim's question, namely that Sue is declining his offer of supper. The earlier discussion of 'drink' and 'everyone' in Brit's utterance in example (1) points in the same direction; that is, it looks as if there is quite a bit more to the recovery of what a speaker has said or asserted than just reference fixing and choice of the intended sense of an ambiguous form.

Grice wanted 'what is said' to have the following two properties: (a) to be an aspect of what the speaker meant (her 'm-intended' content), that is, like implicatures, it was to fall under what the speaker overtly intends her addressee to take from her utterance; (b) to be 'closely related to the conventional meaning of the words (the sentence) uttered', modulo disambiguation and reference assignment (Grice 1975: 44). What the examples indicate is that, for many utterances, it's just not possible to have it both ways. In other words, it is not generally the case that a single level of meaning can do double duty as both sentence semantics and explicitly communicated content. Broadly speaking, and setting aside many differences of detail, there have been two kinds of response to this situation among post-Griceans, each involving dropping one or the other of his favoured properties of 'what is said' (and some opting for a new terminology altogether).

Post-Gricean positions

On what we can call the 'semantic' or literalist view, the first of Grice's requirements on 'what is said' is dropped, so that 'what is said' need not be speaker-meant but, rather, may be used as an instrument for the **communication** of something else. It is this possibility that certain truth-conditional semanticists call on when they invoke a 'pragmatic' (= implicature-based) account for cases like the following:

(8) a. Everyone screamed.
    b. The door is locked.
    c. There is milk in the fridge.
    d. I've had breakfast.

The idea is that what is said by an utterance of (8a) is that everyone (in existence) screamed, but what is meant, hence implicated, on any given occasion of use will almost always be something more specific (e.g. everyone watching such and such a horror movie screamed). Similarly, for (8b), what is said is that there is one and only one door (in the universe) and it is locked, but what is meant, hence implicated, concerns the lockedness of some specific door in the context. In both cases, what is said directly reflects the (alleged) semantics of the construction and is so patently false that it cannot be part of what is meant. In both (8c) and (8d), a very weak general proposition is what is said: for (8c), that there is some presence of milk in the fridge (perhaps just a stale drip or two on a shelf); for (8d), that the speaker's life is not entirely break-fastless. Of course, something much more specific is understood in context, for instance, that there is milk usable for coffee in the fridge and that the speaker has had breakfast on the day of utterance. Arguably, it is only these latter that are speaker-meant and so, on this kind of account, these are implicatures (for advocates of this approach, *see* Kripke 1977 and Berg 2002).

An upshot of this view is that many utterances, including those in (8), do not communicate anything explicitly; that is, the speaker has not asserted anything since the proposition(s) that she intends to communicate are all merely implicated. This flies in the face of very strong intuitions that, in each instance, the speaker has asserted the proposition at issue and committed herself to its truth. For instance, in the case of (8d) the speaker may have communicated both (i) that she has had breakfast today, and (ii) that she is (therefore) not hungry. There seems to be a clear difference in the status of these two propositions: (i) is built directly out of the encoded linguistic meaning while (ii) is not, and (i) is the basis on which the speaker would be judged to have told the truth or not, and it provides the essential premise for inferring the further (impli-cated) proposition (ii). It seems that by treating (i) and (ii) as on a par, as both implicatures, not only do we ignore intuitions about asserted content, we also lose a distinction that does clear work within an account of communication.

The second response to the dilemma pre-sented by Grice's notion of 'what is said' is to retain the first requirement (that it is speaker-meant) while dropping the second one. On this view, it is acknowledged that the gap between encoded (conventional) linguistic meaning and explicit utterance content is much wider than Grice allowed and cannot be plugged simply by assigning referents to **indexicals** and selecting among the several senses of an ambiguous lin-guistic form. The claim that there is such a gap, requiring quite extensive processes of pragmatic enrichment, is sometimes known as the linguistic underdeterminacy thesis (Atlas 1989, 2005; Carston 1988, 2002) and the wide group of the-orists who hold to it in some form or other are known as contextualists (Bezuidenhout 1997, 2002; Elugardo and Stainton 2004; Recanati 2001c, 2004b, 2004c; Soames, to appear; Stain-ton 1994, 2005, 2006; Travis 1981, 1985) or as pragmatists (Carston 1988, 2002, 2004a, 2004b; Neale 2000, 2005a; Powell 2001, 2002; Sperber and Wilson 1995; Wilson and Sperber 2002, 2004). On this view, the truth-conditional con-tent of an utterance is taken to mesh with ordinary speaker-hearer intuitions about what a speaker has said or asserted. So, in the case of appropriately contextualized utterances of the sentences in (8), what the speaker meant and said (as opposed to merely implicated) could be as roughly shown in (9), albeit with a more fully determinate content replacing the instances of 'such and such' and the remaining indexicals:

(9) a. Everyone who was watching such and such a horror movie at such and such a time screamed.
   b. The door we are standing in front of is locked.
   c. There is milk suitable for using in coffee in the fridge.
   d. I've had breakfast this morning.

One particular manifestation of this approach, as developed within the framework of **rele-vance theory**, will be elaborated in more detail in the next section.

There is a third response, which encompasses both of the preceding approaches, by advocating a minimalist semantic notion of 'what is said' while also recognizing a level of pragmatically enriched content which is communicated (speaker-meant) but is distinct from, and logically prior, to implicature (Bach 1994a, 1997, 2001). Bach maintains a notion of what is said which is very close to encoded meaning, but includes the assigning of referents to pure indexicals such as 'I', 'you' and 'today', which allegedly do not require any consideration of speaker intentions (hence, are not a matter of pragmatics). He explicitly drops the requirement that what is said should be speaker-meant. Rather, it is a semantic notion which captures 'the linguistically determined input to the hearer's **inference** to what … the speaker intends to be conveyed in uttering the sentence' (Bach 2001: 15). One upshot of this is that, for Bach, there is no explicit communication. In his view, there are two distinct kinds of communicated proposition, but both are implicit: there are standard Gricean implicatures and there are what he calls '**implicitures**' which are communicated propositions that are 'implicit in what is said' (Bach 1994a). Here is an illustration of this three-way distinction applied to the example in (6) above:

(10) You're not going to die.
      What is said: Billy is not going to die.
      Impliciture: Billy is not going to die from the cut on his knee.
      Implicature: Billy should stop making such a fuss about the cut.

Setting aside the terminological issue here (that is, whether the second meaning level is to be thought of as explicit content or a kind of implicit meaning), there are various problems with this semantically-oriented notion of 'what is said'. First, demonstrative indexicals like 'she', 'that' and 'there' are not assigned a specific referent at this level since that would involve a fully pragmatic process (requiring consideration of speaker intentions). So this notion of 'what is said' is a mix of encoded constraints (for **demonstratives**) and contextually-provided content (for pure indexicals) and it is often subpropositional. Second, and more important, there doesn't seem to be any role for this conception of 'what is said' beyond that played by the linguistically encoded expression-type meaning of the sentence, e.g. the **logical form** of 'You're not going to die', which is the input to any further context-dependent pragmatic processes required to recover the intended utterance

meaning. If this is right, the move to this minimalist, not-speaker-meant construal renders the notion of 'what is said' redundant. For further discussion, *see* Carston (2002, 2008).

The explicature/implicature distinction

A well established pragmatic account of utterance interpretation which embraces the contextualist-pragmatist stance on the explicit/implicit distinction is that developed within the general cognitive framework of relevance theory (Sperber and Wilson 1995; Wilson and Sperber 2002, 2004). This account recognizes a level of explicit speaker meaning, labelled 'explicature' within the theory, which is defined as follows: 'A proposition communicated by an utterance U is *explicit* if and only if it is a development of a logical form encoded by U' (Sperber and Wilson 1995: 182). Any other communicated proposition is an implicature. Looking again at Brit's utterance in (1) above, repeated here in (11), the linguistically encoded meaning is a schema or template for pragmatically 'developing' the much richer content which is the proposition she has asserted (explicitly communicated), indicated here in (12):

(11) Alex: How was the party? Did it go well?
      Brit: There wasn't enough drink and everyone left early.
(12) There wasn't enough *alcoholic* drink *to satisfy the people at [the party]$_i$* and *so* everyone *who came to [the party]$_i$* left *[the party]$_i$* early.

Explicatures differ in their degree of explicitness depending on how much pragmatic inference is required in their recovery, but, in every instance, decoded linguistic content provides a crucial foundation and frame for the building of the asserted content. In practice, the content of an explicature is usually very similar to what Bach has called 'impliciture', but the term 'explicature' better reflects language users' intuitions that speakers communicate explicitly as well as implicitly.

On this view, the explicit/implicit distinction is quite distinct from the semantics/pragmatics distinction (where the latter equates with encoded expression-type meaning versus context-specific inferred meaning). In fact, the two distinctions cross-cut each other, since not only do pragmatic processes contribute to explicit utterance content (explicature), but also, it is claimed, the encoded semantics of certain words, such as 'but', 'moreover' and 'anyway' (cases of Gricean conventional implicature), constrains implicit content by providing indicators of the kinds of inferential processes to be performed by the hearer in deriving implicatures (*see* Blakemore 1987, 2000, 2002).

It's worth noting that this particular manifestation of **contextualism**-pragmatism comes with certain psychological commitments, arising from its close interface with work in generative linguistics, on the one hand, and evolutionary psychology, on the other. Sperber and Wilson (2002) take a modular view of human cognitive architecture, so that understanding verbal utterances involves two distinct modules: the linguistic decoder whose output is linguistic expression-type meaning (a logical form or 'semantic' **representation**, unaffected by extra-linguistic context) and a pragmatics module which is triggered into operation by verbal utterances and other overtly communicative acts. In the case of utterances, the pragmatics module takes the semantic representation (or logical form) which is the output of the language system and, in accordance with its own internal principles and operating procedures, it computes the speaker's meaning, that is, explicature(s) and implicatures. More philosophically oriented contextualist views are agnostic about the cognitive architecture involved or the nature of the psychological computations performed. Given a long tradition of thinking of semantics in truth-conditional terms, they are also less inclined to use the term 'semantics' for the rather meagre, often subpropositional, meaning encoded by linguistic expression types. For instance, when Travis (1985), Recanati (2004b) and others talk of 'contextualist semantics', they mean the pragmatics-dependent truth-conditional content that a speaker asserts, hence what is known as 'explicature' in relevance theory. (For discussion of different construals of 'semantics', hence of different ways of drawing the semantics/ pragmatics distinction, *see* Bach 1997; Carston 1999, 2008; King and Stanley 2005.)

There are two kinds of pragmatic process that relevance theorists (and contextualists more

generally) take to contribute to explicatures. The first of these, often known as 'saturation', involves finding the intended content (or 'value') for some linguistically indicated variable or slot. For instance, the occurrence of the pronoun 'she' in a particular syntactic position in an utterance overtly indicates that a specific female individual is to be identified and represented in the corresponding position in the developing propositional understanding. Saturation is generally thought to be a much more widely manifest process than simply finding values for overt indexicals. Arguably, it is involved in those pragmatic developments (of the decoded representations of the following utterances) which provide answers to the bracketed questions:

(13) a. Paracetamol is better. [than what?]
     b. It's the same. [as what?]
     c. He is too young. [for what?]
     d. It's hot enough. [to what?]
     e. I like Sally's portrait. [portrait in what relation to Sally?]

This 'completion' process is obligatory on every communicative use of these sentences, as without it there is no fully propositional form, nothing that can be understood as the explicit content of the utterance. So, although there is no overt pronounced constituent in these sentences which indicates the need for contextual instantiation, the claim is that there is a slot in their logical form, a kind of covert indexical, which marks the saturation requirement. The lexical items 'better', 'same', 'too' and 'enough' carry these imperceptible elements with them as part of their linguistic structure.

The second, and much more controversial, process is known as free enrichment, 'free' because it involves pragmatic enrichment of the decoded linguistic meaning in the absence of any indication (overt or covert) within the linguistic form that this is necessary. Consider utterances of the following sentences, whose interpretation, in many contexts, would include the bracketed element which is provided on pragmatic grounds alone:

(14) a. She has a brain. [a high-functioning brain]
     b. It's going to take time for these wounds to heal. [considerable time]

    c. I've had a shower. [today]
    d. It's snowing. [in location x]
    e. Mary gave John a pen and he wrote down her address. [and then] [with the pen Mary gave him]

Given disambiguation and saturation, each of these would, arguably, express a proposition (hence, be truth-evaluable) without the addition of the bracketed constituent, but in most contexts that minimal proposition would not be communicated (speaker-meant). One class of cases, represented here by (14a) and (14b), would express a trivial truth (every person has a brain as part of their anatomical make-up; any process takes place over some time span or other), and it is easy to set up cases of obvious falsehoods (the negations of (14a) and (14b), for instance). Others, such as (14c) and (14d), are so vague and general as to be very seldom what a speaker would intend to communicate (they would not be sufficiently relevant or informative). Across most contexts in which these sentences might be uttered, clear cases of implicatures of the utterance would depend on the enriched proposition; for instance, in (14a), the implicature that she is a good candidate for an academic job; in (14c), the implicature that the speaker doesn't need to take a shower at that moment. It is the enriched propositions that are communicated as explicatures and which function as premises in the derivation of implicatures. The uninformative, irrelevant, and sometimes truistic or patently false minimal propositions appear to play no role in the process of utterance understanding, which is geared to the recovery of just those propositional forms which the speaker intends to communicate. Unlike saturation cases, 'free' enrichments are optional, in that there could be contexts (somewhat unusual ones) in which they do not take place. For instance, consider an utterance of (14a) in a situation in which the removal of certain people's brains has become common practice; then, it could constitute a discovery of some interest that a particular woman (still) has a brain (no matter whether it is a good one or not).

In fact, there appear to be two kinds of free enrichment: (a) cases, such as those just discussed, where pragmatically supplied constituents of the explicature have no presence in the linguistic form used, so are known as 'unarticulated constituents' (*see* Recanati 2002b, 2004b), and (b) cases where the pragmatic process does not supply a whole new constituent of content but adjusts or modulates an existing element of linguistic meaning. The latter have recently become a major focus of investigation under the label '**lexical pragmatics**' (*see* Blutner 1998; Carston 1997, 2002; Recanati 1995, 2004b; Sperber and Wilson 1998b; Wilson and Carston 2006, 2007a). Consider utterances of the following, focusing on the meaning communicated by the italicized word:

(15) a. Boris is a *man*.
    b. Buying a house is easy if you've got *money*.
    c. Let's get rid of the *empty* bottles.
    d. This policy will *bankrupt* the farmers.

Reaching the intended interpretation of (15a) and (15b) is very likely to involve an optional pragmatic process of concept narrowing. In most contexts, the proposition that Boris is an adult male human will be trivially true and uninformative, so the lexically encoded concept MAN is likely to be strengthened to IDEAL MAN or TYPICAL MAN (where the notion of what constitutes a typical man or an ideal man will itself vary from context to context). Similar comments apply to (15b), since it is patently false that just any amount of money will do for buying a house. In these cases, the communicated concept picks out a subset of the denotation of the lexical concept. Arguably, (15c) and (15d) require an adjustment in the opposite direction, that is, a broadening of the encoded concept, so although 'bankrupt' *could* be taken literally, in certain contexts it would be understood as a loose use of the concept or even as a **hyperbole**, conveying that, as a result of the government's policy, the farmers will be substantially poorer than might have been expected or desired. In cases like this, the denotation of the concept communicated is broader than (and includes) the denotation of the encoded concept. Relevance theorists and other contextualists (in particular, Recanati and Travis) take the view that some degree of modulation of word meaning in context occurs across virtually all utterances and is essential in deriving the intended truth-conditional content (i.e. the explicit content of an utterance).

Looking back again to Brit's utterance in (11), it can be seen that recovering the proposition she explicitly communicated has involved the full range of pragmatic processes discussed here: saturation, e.g. 'left *the party*', and both kinds of free enrichment, e.g. the concept encoded by 'drink' is narrowed to the kinds of drink typical of parties, while the domain restriction on 'everyone' is arguably an unarticulated constituent, as is the cause-consequence relation taken to hold between the two states of affairs.

Challenges to the explicature/implicature distinction

The existence of the kind of 'free' pragmatic processes just outlined is vehemently denied by quite a number of semanticists who find it repugnant that pragmatics should have this kind of freedom to 'intrude' on the truth-conditional content (the 'semantics', as they construe it) of an utterance (King and Stanley 2005; Marti 2006; Stanley 2000, 2002; Stanley and Szabo 2000). In their view, the only pragmatic process (in addition to disambiguation) that can affect explicit utterance content is saturation. Any pragmatically derived meaning that has not been mandated by the linguistic form must, therefore, be a conversational implicature. The most important challenge here comes from Stanley (2002), who argues that the process of free enrichment is so unsystematic and unconstrained that it predicts constituents of explicit content that patently do not occur. For instance, given that in comprehending an utterance of (16a), free enrichment can provide the italicized constituent shown in (16b), what stops it from supplying the italicized constituent in (16d) in a context where it would be available and relevant in understanding an utterance of (16c)?

(16) a. Jane answered every question.
   b. Jane answered every question *on her syntax exam*.
   c. Bruce likes Sally.
   d. Bruce likes Sally *and his mother*.

This issue is currently being addressed within the relevance-theoretic framework by Hall (2008a,

2008b), who argues that the free enrichment of content is, in fact, quite tightly constrained by the nature of the relevance-driven inferential processes of interpretation and that these preclude the simple conjoining of components of content as in (16d).

A related question is how to tell with regard to some clearly pragmatically-derived element of utterance meaning whether it contributes to explicit content or is, rather, an implicated proposition. Take, for instance, the cause–consequence relation that is understood to hold in some cases of 'and'-conjunctions, such as Brit's utterance in (11) above. This is not a case of saturation (it is not mandated by an element of linguistic form), but while it is treated as an instance of free enrichment of explicit content by relevance theorists (Carston 1988, 2002, 2004b), neo-Gricean pragmatists assume that it is a conversational implicature (Horn 1984, 2004, 2006; King and Stanley 2005; Levinson 1987a, 2000). Another widely discussed and contentious sort of phenomenon is scalar pragmatic inference, as in the strengthening of the concepts lexically encoded by 'some' (semantically equivalent to 'some and perhaps all') and 'or' (equivalent to 'at least one of the disjuncts') to the upper-bounded meanings SOME BUT NOT ALL and EITHER BUT NOT BOTH, as in the following examples:

(17) a. Some of the children went swimming.
   b. I'll watch a video tonight or work on my essay.

Again, the standard neo-Gricean treatment of the upper-bound component of meaning is that it is a matter of (**scalar**) **implicature** (Horn 1985, 1992, 2004; Levinson 1987a, 2000), while relevance theorists claim that it is better thought of as a case of concept narrowing that contributes to the explicature (Carston 1995; Noveck and Sperber 2007). Some support for the latter position comes from ordinary speaker-hearer intuitions which take the strengthened meaning to affect truth conditions: people tend to judge utterances such as those in (17) as false when set beside real world facts that show that the upper bound does not hold, for instance, an utterance of (17a) given as a description of a scenario in which, in fact, all of the children went swimming (Noveck 2004).

A third contentious area concerns non-literal uses of language, such as hyperbole, **metaphor** and metonymy. Grice and those following him treat all instances of non-literalness as cases where the literal encoded concept is a component of what is said (so, in fact, the proposition at this level is not speaker-meant, not communicated) and the effects of the non-literal use emerge as implicatures (Grice 1975; Camp 2006). Relevance theorists and many contextualists, however, argue that certain figurative uses, including hyperbole and metaphor, are instances of lexical concept adjustment (involving both broadening and narrowing) and so they also affect the explicature (Carston 1997, 2002; Recanati 1995, 2004b; Wearing 2006; Wilson and Carston 2006, 2007a; Wilson and Sperber 2002, 2004).

Various tests and criteria have been proposed in an attempt to find a principled means of distinguishing between conversational implicatures and pragmatically derived meaning that contributes to explicitly communicated content (Carston 1988, 2002: Chapter 2; Recanati 1993: Chapters 13 and 14, 2004b). None of these has so far been found to be fully satisfactory, although they provide useful evidence in particular cases. It may well require the development of a fully explicit model of the pragmatic principles and processes at work in utterance interpretation before we can entirely grasp the different ways in which pragmatically derived meaning interacts with linguistic meaning in delivering explicatures and implicatures.

ROBYN CARSTON

See also: Contextualism; generalized conversational implicature, theory of; Grice, H.P.; implicature; impliciture; indexicals; inferential comprehension; lexical pragmatics; maxims of conversation; modularity of mind thesis; neo-Gricean pragmatics; ordinary language philosophy; post-Gricean pragmatics; pragmatics; primary pragmatic processes; radical pragmatics; relevance theory; scalar implicature; semantic minimalism; semantics; semantics-pragmatics interface; theory of mind; utterance interpretation; what is said

Suggestions for further reading

Carston, R. (2002) *Thoughts and Utterances: The Pragmatics of Explicit Communication*, Oxford: Blackwell. Chapter 2.

Grice, H.P. (1975) 'Logic and conversation', in P. Cole and J. Morgan (eds) *Syntax and Semantics 3: Speech Acts*, New York: Academic Press; reprinted in *Studies in the Way of Words* (1989), Cambridge, MA: Harvard University Press.

Recanati, F. (2001) 'What is said', *Synthese*, 128: 75–91.

F

Fallacy Theory

In 1970, the Australian logician C.L. Hamblin delivered a broadside to the logic community for having given up on the fallacies program and surrendering it to writers of introductory textbooks in which:

> [A] writer throws away logic and keeps the reader's attention, if at all, only by detailing the traditional puns, anecdotes, and witless examples of his forbears. 'Everything that runs has feet; the river runs; therefore the river has feet' {?} this is a medieval example, but the modern ones are no better.
>
> (Hamblin 1970: 12)

'There is', writes Hamblin, 'hardly a subject that dies harder or has changed so little over the years' (1970: 9). Contemporary fallacy theory is largely a response to Hamblin's criticism. Notwithstanding that Hamblin's rebuke was delivered to logicians, fallacy theory is now a multidisciplinary enterprise which engages the efforts of those who work in speech communication, critical thinking, informal logic and computer science.

Fallacy theory originated with the founding of systematic logic by Aristotle (384–322 BC). Aristotle wanted to develop a wholly general **argumentation theory** with which to discipline the vexing distinction between arguments that look good but aren't and arguments that actually are good, irrespective of how they look. Central to this account – indeed its theoretical core – was a theory of syllogistic **reasoning**.

Implicit in Aristotle's writings is a distinction between arguments in the broad sense and arguments in the narrow sense. Arguments in the narrow sense are typified by syllogisms. Syllogisms are finite sequences of context-insensitive **propositions** of which the terminal member is the conclusion and the others are premises (they must also fulfill various other conditions that need not concern us here). Arguments in the broad sense are social events. They are dialogues between two parties. Aristotle discusses four types of these arguments: refutation-arguments, instruction-arguments, examination-arguments and (scientific) demonstrations. Syllogisms can be exhaustively described by way of their syntactic and semantic properties. But refutations, indeed all arguments in the broad sense, also incorporate pragmatic factors that concern the roles of speakers and the forms and order of their utterances. In addition to the pragmaticization of logic (in the broad sense), we owe to Aristotle the introduction into logic (also in the broad sense) of expressly dialectical considerations. The definition of fallacy arises in the discussion of refutations, but it is clear that Aristotle does not think that fallacies are limited to refutation contexts.

In the writings in which he first introduces the concept of fallacy, Aristotle advances a pair of theses that pivot on the distinction between arguments in the narrow sense and arguments in the broad sense. The first thesis says that it is an error of logic in the narrow sense to mistake a non-syllogism for a syllogism. The second thesis says that there is an interesting class of cases for which the following holds true: if you make a mistake of logic in the narrow sense, you will also make a mistake of logic in the broad sense. In particular, if you mistake a non-syllogism for a syllogism you will wreck any refutation in which it is embedded. Mistakes of the first kind are called *fallacies*. Mistakes of the second kind are called *sophistical refutations*. Aristotle catalogues and briefly discusses thirteen ways in which refutations can go wrong, that is, ways in which they can be rendered sophistical by the commission of a fallacy. These are equivocation, amphiboly, combination of words, division of words, accent, *ignoratio elenchi* ('ignorance of what makes for a refutation'), forms of expression, accident, *secundum quid* ('in a certain respect'), consequent, non-cause as cause, begging the question, and many questions. Some of these ways (e.g. accent) are no longer seriously discussed. Others have a decidedly familiar ring to them, although in a number of cases it is the name that has survived, not the nominatum. Two examples are *secundum quid* and many questions. In modern treatments, *sequndum quid* is the fallacy of hasty generalization, whereas for Aristotle it is the fallacy of omitting a qualification, as in the **inference** of 'Ali is a white man' from 'Ali is a white-toothed-man'. Similarly, to modern ears, many questions is the fallacy of unconceded **presupposition**, as in 'Are you still drinking two bottles a day?' For Aristotle, it was the strictly technical mistake of asking a **question** whose answer is a compound statement, which is a violation of one of the defining conditions on syllogisms.

The last thing that one could claim for Aristotle was a comprehensive and unified theory of the thirteen items on his list. Put bluntly, there is no deep theory of fallacious inference to be found in Aristotle. Although over the centuries fallacies have remained part of the project of logic, this lack of theoretical depth has persisted, albeit with some rare exceptions. Although there was much logical sophistication in the Middle Ages, mediaeval logicians made comparatively little headway with the fallacies. John Locke (1690), who is much cited, devotes a scant few pages to arguments *ad hominem* ('to the man'), *ad verecundiam* (illicit authority) and *ad ignorantiam* ('from ignorance'), none of which he thought was a fallacy at all. The Port Royal *Logique* (Arnauld and Nicole 1662) has a fairly extensive treatment of what it calls 'sophisms', but here

too there is not much theoretical depth or sophistication. J.S. Mill's *A System of Logic* (1843) contains the most substantial and best treatment of the fallacies up to that time, and is surpassed, if at all, only by developments in the second half of the century to follow.

There is no strictly uniform understanding among modern theorists as to what counts as a fallacy. But most modern treatments recognize most of the following: arguments *ad baculum* (from threat), *ad hominem*, *ad ignorantiam*, *ad misericordiam* (appeal to pity), *ad populum* (appeal to popularity), affirming the consequent, denying the antecedent, biased statistics, composition and division, faulty analogy, equivocation, the gambler's fallacy, hasty generalization (or *secundum quid*), *ignoratio elenchi* (straw man, red herring), biased and insufficient statistics, many questions, *petitio principii* (begging the question), *post hoc ergo propter hoc* (false cause) and *tu quoque* ('look who's talking!'). In judging post-1970 developments, it is instructive to keep in mind Hamblin's own recommendations for the rehabilitation of fallacy theory: (1) fallacy theory should be guided by advances in modern logic; (2) fallacy theory should be agent-centred and contextually sensitive; (3) fallacy theory should be historically informed and (4) fallacy theory should minimize its attention to examples that are silly, punning, superficial or egregiously obvious.

Hamblin himself responds to proposal (1) with refinements of the mediaeval dialogue logics of disputation. Further advances in dialogue logic can be found in Barth and Krabbe (1982), and many other works. In what came to be called the Woods-Walton Approach, various fallacies were analyzed in adaptations of one or other nonstandard logic (Woods and Walton 2007). They include intuitionistic logic for *petitio principii*, dialogue logic for many questions, relatedness (or relevant) logic for the red herring fallacy, inductive logic for hasty generalization and the statistical fallacies, and modal logic for the causal fallacies. The idea that fallacy theory should be agent-centred – proposal (2) – is picked up on by most dialogue logics. A number of writers see fallacy theory as applied epistemology (Biro and Siegel 1997; Freeman 2005), and give concomitant attention to the cognitive constitution of human agency. Proposal (3) – that fallacy theorists acquaint themselves with the history of the subject – has fared less well, notwithstanding some notable exceptions (e.g. Hansen 2002). Proposal (4) – that fallacy theory should deal with real-life examples – has done reasonably well. Fallacy theorists now seek their data in contexts such as parliamentary debates, newspaper editorials, legal proceedings and advertising copy, as well as historically significant philosophical disputes.

The old idea that a fallacy is an argument (or argument move) that appears to be good (or legitimate) but is not so in fact continues to be the dominant idea. But it has a significant, and increasingly well received, rival in the so-called pragma-dialectical approach (PDA; van Eemeren and Grootendorst 1992). So conceived, a fallacy is simply a conversational move that violates a rule of critical discussion. It is sometimes the case that such violations are inadvertent and inapparent, but there is no necessary connection with inapparency. Critics of the traditional account raise what has been called the boundary question. What is it about the traditional twenty or so errors that justifies their classification as fallacies? Indeed, why isn't any type of argumentative or inferential error a fallacy? Implicit in the PDA is an answer to this question. It is that there is no particular reason to 'privilege' the traditional twenty. Any mistake of argument is properly regarded as fallacious. (A non-pragma-dialectical answer to the boundary question is developed in Woods 2004.)

But it remains the case that if the traditional conception of fallacy is to be persisted with, no theory of fallacy can count as deep until it offers systematic, precise and principled accounts of the two basic elements of the traditional conception. One element is that a fallacy is some kind of argumentative or inferential *error*. The other is that the error somehow *disguises* itself. This being so, fallacies must be distinguished from mechanical errors and what linguists call performance errors, that is, errors that arise from inattention, fatigue, intoxication and the like. The pragma-dialectical approach can claim two further advantages that the traditional approach cannot. First, since the account of fallacies is embedded in a theory of argument, then you automatically deepen the account of fallacies by deepening the theory of argument. The deeper the theory becomes, the clearer the

conditions under which a rule is breached. Second, since PDA-fallacies are not inherently deceptive, there is no obligation to develop an account of self-disguise. These putative advantages may also be claimed for Douglas Walton's voluminous contributions to fallacy theory (e.g. Walton 1995). Although Walton's work is much wider in scope, it has taken on a general sort of pragma-dialectical cast. Whether in van Eemeren and Grootendorst's way or Walton's way, fallacy theory is a sub-theory of argument, and fallacies are violations of dialogical rules. Some notable alternative theories of argument are Finocchiaro (2005) and Johnson (2000).

Given the advantages claimed, it is difficult to understand why theorists of pragma-dialectical leanings are so ready to include in their fallacies playbill traditional listings that aren't in the least dialectical in character. While fallacies such as begging the question and many questions would appear to be dialectical, most of the fallacies on the standard list are not. These include hasty generalization, the gambler's fallacy, biased and insufficient statistics, the fallacy of false cause, composition and division, and a number of others. All these fallacies can be committed in dialectical contexts, but all can also be committed in non-dialectical contexts. This holds true for both modern meanings of 'dialectical'. That is to say, these fallacies are not inherently mistakes of contention and are not inherently mistakes of dialogue. Since they are not dialectical mistakes, it can be argued that they shouldn't be counted as fallacies at all on any conception of them for which a fallacy is necessarily a dialectical misstep. Still, it remains the case that, whether they are called fallacies or not, hasty generalization and the gambler's fallacy amongst others appear to be errors that occur both with a disguised inadvertence and a certain frequency. They are legitimate candidates for theory. Here, too, such a theory would subsume two sub-theories, one a theory of error and the other a theory of self-disguise. Concerning the first sub-theory, the record to date is spotty. Although deductive and probabilistic error admits of well developed theoretical treatments, there is as yet no settled consensus about plausibilistic, presumptive, default and abductive error. Concerning the second sub-theory – an account of the self-disguising character of these errors – the fallacy theoretic track record to date is far from impressive.

JOHN WOODS

See also: Abduction; argumentation theory; inference; pragmatics; presupposition; proposition; reasoning

Suggestions for further reading

Fisher, A. (2004) *The Logic of Real Arguments*, 2nd edn, Cambridge: Cambridge University Press.
Hansen, H.V. and Pinto, R. (1995) *Fallacies: Classical and Contemporary Readings*, University Park, PA: Pennsylvania State University Press.
Tindale, C.W. (2007) *Fallacies and Argument Appraisal*, Cambridge and New York: Cambridge University Press.

Focus

The term 'focus' has been used in three distinct senses in the literature – psychological focus, semantic focus, and contrastive focus (Gundel 1999a). One of these senses corresponds to the psychological notion of focus of attention (Bosch 1988; Garrod and Sanford 1982; Grosz and Sidner 1986; Gundel *et al.* 1993, inter alia), what Hajičová (1987) calls 'focus AI'. This sense is correlated with appropriateness of null/zero and unstressed personal pronouns. For example, the use of *she* in *She looks more like her mother now* would be licensed if the preceding sentence were *Jane has changed* or if speaker and addressee were looking at a picture of a woman, as in both cases the speaker could assume the addressee's attention is focused on the intended referent. Psychological focus is also relevant for assigning **reference** to forms that Prince (1981b) calls inferrables, where interpretation involves a bridging **inference** (Clark and Havilland 1977) to a recently evoked entity. For example, consider the sentences in (1):

(1) We had drinks at the Hilton before going to the Thai restaurant. The waitress was from Thailand.

Most speakers associate the waitress with the Hilton, which is in focus, even though encyclo-pedic **knowledge** would favor the restaurant interpretation (Erkü and Gundel 1987). While syntactic structure is only one of a number of factors that can influence focus of attention (Gundel *et al.* 2003), an entity introduced in a main clause is more likely to be brought into focus than one introduced in a subordinate clause.

Whereas psychological focus is a property of entities that already have a high degree of salience/givenness, the other two senses of focus are associated with imposed linguistic salience (Mulkern 2003). One of these senses, semantic focus (Cutler and Fodor 1979; Gundel 1999a), refers to the new information asserted (questioned, etc.) in relation to what has variously been called the **topic** (e.g. Sgall *et al.* 1986; Gundel 1974, 1988), **presupposition** (e.g. Chomsky 1971; Jackendoff 1972), background (e.g. Jacobs 1991), or common ground/theme (Vallduví 1992). It is the part of the sentence that answers the relevant *wh*-question (implicit or explicit), depending on how the informational content of the sentence is structured and represented (Krifka 1993 inter alia). Thus, in the example in (2):

(2) Every time we get together, I'm the one who organizes things; but this time *BILL called the meeting*.

Bill represents the semantic focus. It instantiates the variable in the topic/theme/presupposition 'x called the meeting'. Semantic focus is most consistently marked across languages by prominent pitch accent, and the term 'focus' is sometimes used more narrowly to refer to such an accent. Semantic focus may also be marked by word order, focus particles, and by special syntactic structures, e.g. *It was Bill who called the meeting* as an alternative to the italicized clause in (2).

Semantic focus is always at least implicitly contrastive, in the sense that what is predicated about the topic is contrasted with all other things that could have been predicated (*see* Bolinger 1961). However, some semantic foci are explicitly contrasted with a limited set of alternatives in the discourse **context**. This kind of contrastive focus is not restricted to semantic focus, as topics, including topics that are already in psychological focus, may be contrasted, and thereby focused as well. For example, in *BILL ate the BEANS*, the topic, *Bill*, may receive a contrastive focus, e.g. in answer to a **question** like *What about BILL, what did HE eat?* Some authors (e.g. Rooth 1992) do not distinguish semantic focus and purely contrastive focus. However, many languages distinguish between them prosodically. Moreover, there is evidence that only semantic focus does not have truth-conditional effects (*see* Gundel 1999a).

JEANETTE GUNDEL

See also: Given/new distinction; information structure; presupposition; reference; topic

Suggestions for further reading

Bosch, P. and van der Sandt, R. (eds) (1999) *Focus: Linguistic, Cognitive and Computational Perspectives*, Cambridge: Cambridge University Press.

Gundel, J.K. and Fretheim, T. (2004) 'Topic and focus', in G. Ward and L. Horn (eds) *Handbook of Pragmatics*, London: Blackwell.

Lambrecht, K. (1994) *Information Structure and Sentence Form: Topic, Focus and the Mental Representation of Discourse Referents*, Cambridge: Cambridge University Press.

Formal Pragmatics

In the 1950s, Chomsky and his colleagues began attempts to reduce the complexity of natural language phonology and **syntax** to a few general principles. It wasn't long before philosophers, notably John **Searle** and H. Paul **Grice**, started looking for ways to do the same for rational **communication** (Chapman 2005). In his 1967 William James Lectures, Grice presented a loose optimization system based on his **maxims of conversation**. The resulting papers (especially Grice 1975) strike a fruitful balance between intuitive exploration and formal development. Though the work is not particularly formal, it marks the birth of modern formal pragmatics.

Pragmatics is central to the theory of linguistic meaning because, to paraphrase Levinson (2000), the encoded content of the sentences we utter is only the barest sketch of what we actually communicate with those utterances. **Utterance interpretation** involves complex interactions among (i) semantic content, (ii) the **context** of utterance, and (iii) general pragmatic pressures (of which Grice's maxims are one conception). The starting point for a formal pragmatics is the observation that speakers agree to a remarkable extent on the interpretations of the utterances they hear, suggesting that there are deep regularities across speakers, utterance contexts, and sentence types in how (i)–(iii) interact.

An overarching challenge for pragmatic theory is that semantic content and the context of utterance influence each other. It is common, for instance, to find that the **meaning** of a sentence is crucially incomplete without contextual information. **Indexicals** and **demonstratives** are paradigm cases: 'I am here now' doesn't have a fully specified denotation without information about who the speaker is, when he is speaking, and where he is speaking. Similarly, modal auxiliaries like *must* admit of a wide range of interpretations. The utterance 'Sam must be in his office' can be used to make a claim based on evidence (' … I see the light on'), or a claim based on the laws of the land (' … the boss has passed a new rule'), or any number of others. Sentence-internal features provide some clues, but the intended interpretation cannot generally be resolved without information from the utterance context. Other examples of this form are easy to find. Context dependency is ubiquitous in language, which means that essentially all semantic theories rest on particular views of how to model contexts.

Kaplan's (1989a) theory of indexicality is an early and influential approach to modelling how the context influences interpretation. For Kaplan, the context is modelled as a tuple of indices that identify the speaker, the time, the place, and so forth. These indices directly provide the meanings for indexical expressions like *me*, *now* and *here*. The methods are those of **semantics** (model-theoretic interpretation), but some interpretation happens in terms of these designated context tuples.

Kaplan's theoretical approach helps us to see how context helps determine semantic content. Its basic techniques have been used for a wide range of issues in context dependency. However, these theories have little to say about the reverse direction of influence, i.e. how the context is changed by the addition of new content. Dynamic theories of meaning attempt to model this aspect of context dependency as well. The earliest such systems in linguistics are those of Heim (1982) and Kamp (1981), who built on the insights of Karttunen (1976). The fundamental innovation of dynamic semantics is to ask, not what sentences mean, but rather how they affect, and are affected by, the flow of **discourse** information. For example, if I say 'A goat entered' with the force of an **assertion** then, with this utterance, I introduce a new discourse referent *d* into our context (this is the work of the indefinite), and I ascribe two properties to *d*: that of being a goat and that of entering. My language has thus changed the context. If I follow up with 'It looks hungry', the subject pronoun *it* gets its meaning from the recently introduced *d*. Dynamic theories provide systematic explanations for this language-context interplay. Historically, such theories have been developed to handle **presupposition** and discourse-mediated **anaphora** (Chierchia 1995; Beaver 2001), but they can be extended to many kinds of discourse information (Asher and Lascarides 2003).

The above phenomena and theoretical approaches largely concern using pragmatic information to obtain the basic content of a sentence. This is the area of pragmatics that has received the most formal attention to date, probably because it is amenable to treatment in terms of monotonic logics of the sort that have formed the backbone of semantic theory since Montague (1974) and Lewis (1976). However, this is not quite 'Gricean pragmatics' in the usual sense, which is concerned primarily with pragmatic enrichment. For example, even if we assume that we have a complete and accurate semantics of the sentence *Sam's work is satisfactory* (i.e. all context dependency has been resolved), we still need a theory of why some contexts invite us to infer from this that the speaker believes Sam's work is not great (not excellent, not outstanding), whereas other contexts permit us to conclude only that this stronger statement is irrelevant (or impolite, or false).

Gazdar (1979a, 1979b) is an early extended attempt to formalize the **reasoning** behind pragmatic enrichment of the sort that Grice concentrated on. Gazdar modelled a species of presupposition as well as a range of conversational **implicatures**. The system makes precise certain assumptions about speaker **knowledge** that are inherent in Grice's descriptions. It involves sentence/utterance comparison of the sort that runs through all of Grice's examples, and it is an early effort to handle default interpretations. The specific formal details did not have much influence, owing perhaps to their complexity, but the work remains a touchstone for present-day approaches to presuppositions and conversational implicatures. It is noteworthy also for being arguably more ambitious in its descriptive scope than the majority of work that has been attempted since.

The most heavily-trodden area of the original Gricean landscape is that of scalar conversational implicature (Horn 1972). Recall from above that saying 'Sam's work is satisfactory' is likely to have implications for alternative utterances of the form 'Sam's work is Adj', where Adj is a positive adjective like *great* or *excellent*. The basic dynamic is as follows: if $<A_1, ..., A_n>$ is a scale of adjectives (A_1 the lowest, A_n the highest), then picking A_i will convey that using A_j is pragmatically infelicitous in the current context (for some reason or other), for all $j > i$. Gazdar's system focused on such pragmatic **inferences**, and they have figured centrally in formal developments since then. They are of special interest for four central reasons. First, results concerning the nature of the scales are relatively accessible and broadly important (Sauerland 2004). Second, the principles governing inferences in terms of these scales are largely familiar from semantics. Third, one can identify scalar inferences without specifying their exact nature. We can study the inferences from 'Sam's work is satisfactory' without necessarily saying whether they are grounded in considerations of relevance, truthfulness, **politeness**, or some combination thereof. Fourth, **scalar implicatures** have been argued to indicate that pragmatic inference cannot be deferred to the utterance level, as Grice had it, but rather that they are an integral part of the compositional semantics (Chierchia 2004; *cf.* Geurts 2009).

As the above indicates, much work in formal pragmatics involves extending the basic tools and techniques of semantic theory. As a result, it inherits certain biases from that tradition, chief among them an emphasis on interpretation (over production) and a tendency to try to find single fixed solutions. Recent developments have begun to explore models that don't necessarily have these properties. The **optimality-theory pragmatics** of Blutner (1998) treats pragmatic inference as a joint effort on the part of both the speaker and the hearer. Roughly, the speaker tries to minimize his effort by using the least marked (shortest, least unusual) expressions he can, and the hearer tries to extract from it the most useful (informative, relevant) interpretation. It is an optimization system in virtue of the fact that both sides compromise in order to reach their point(s) of consensus. The basic dynamic is often credited to Horn (1984), and it echoes a fundamental information-theoretic insight of Zipf (1949).

In its emphasis on speaker and hearer working together to resolve the interpretation problem, optimality-theory pragmatics resembles the decision-theoretic and game-theoretic approaches that were developed at approximately the same time. The decision-theoretic approach regards discourse as structured and driven by abstract decision problems, with both production and interpretation guided by the discourse participants' shared desire to resolve those problems efficiently. This is strongly reminiscent of approaches that call upon abstract 'questions under discussion' to understand the dynamics of information exchange (Roberts 1996). Merin (1997) applies decision-theoretic ideas to presuppositional phenomena, Parikh (2001) uses a version of it to understand conversational implicatures and **speech acts**, and van Rooy (2003) studies the underspecification of interrogatives and declaratives in these terms.

Game-theoretic approaches are more explicit than decision-theoretic approaches about the fact that dialogue is multi-agent interaction. They seek to capitalize on the intuition that communication is a game, with its own strategies and measures of progress. The guiding idea is that the preferred pragmatic enrichments of the utterances we hear are equilibria in the game-theoretic sense. Linguists and logicians have explored a number of different solution concepts (and game structures) that might correspond to this pragmatic notion of preferences. These approaches trace to Lewis (1969), who developed signalling games and their associated solution concepts (for linguistic applications, *see* van Rooy 2004). Benz *et al.* (2005) is an influential and wide-ranging collection that opens with a useful tutorial on decision theory and game theory in linguistics.

All these more recent approaches are notable for their reliance on ideas from information theory, an extremely general mathematical framework for studying all kinds of communication and much more (Cover and Thomas 1991). Thus, they might be able to do justice to the fact that pragmatic inferences are not confined to linguistic interactions. Grice was careful to emphasize that they show up in nonlinguistic interactions as well, making them central not only in linguistics, but throughout **cognitive science** and **artificial intelligence**. This doesn't diminish the importance of pragmatics to linguistic exchanges, nor does it preclude finding phenomena that are unique to discourse, but it might suggest that these recent approaches are on the right track in their move to talking generally about agents and messages, rather than talking exclusively about people and natural language utterances.

To date, theories of formal pragmatics have been fairly limited in their descriptive scope. This can foster the incorrect, unfortunate impression that there is an interesting theoretical distinction between formal pragmatics and 'informal' pragmatics. The truth is that informal pragmaticists aspire to precision, and formal pragmaticists aspire to model as many pragmatic phenomena as possible. The strategies are different, but the communities share the common goal of understanding the methods by which utterance meanings are enhanced in virtue of their interaction with the particularities of the utterance context and the general pressures of rational communication.

CHRISTOPHER POTTS

See also: Anaphora, pragmatics of; artificial intelligence; assertion; competence, pragmatic; computational pragmatics; context; conventionality; conversation; conversation analysis; cooperative principle; defaults in utterance interpretation; definiteness; demonstratives;

domain restriction; generalized conversational implicature, theory of; Grice, H.P.; heuristic; implicature; impliciture; indefiniteness; indexicals; maxims of conversation; natural and non-natural meaning; neo-Gricean pragmatics; optimality-theory pragmatics; politeness; post-Gricean pragmatics; presupposition; scalar implicature; Searle, J.; semantics-pragmatics interface; utterance interpretation

Suggestions for further reading

Benz, A., Jäger, G. and van Rooij, R. (2005) 'An introduction to game theory for linguists', in A. Benz, G. Jäger and R. van Rooij (eds) *Game Theory and Pragmatics*, Houndsmills: Palgrave Macmillan.

Kadmon, N. (2001) *Formal Pragmatics*, Oxford: Blackwell.

Levinson, S.C. (2000) *Presumptive Meanings: The Theory of Generalized Conversational Implicature*, Cambridge, MA: MIT Press.

G

Gender

Scholarship on gender and on **pragmatics** overlaps in two ways. On the one hand, conceptual tools developed within pragmatics have traditionally informed two key trajectories of gender and language research: that which asks how males and females use and interpret linguistic resources, and that which asks how males and females are represented through linguistic resources. On the other hand, if we take the central question that pragmatics asks to be '[w]hy has this utterance been produced?' (Haberland and Mey 2002: 1672), then gender and language scholarship has, in turn, informed pragmatics: it has consistently provided evidence of the many different ways in which any explanation of an utterance requires a systematic engagement with socio-cultural phenomena. As Crawford (2003: 1417) argues, gender in current research is seen as 'a salient social and cognitive category through which information is filtered, [and] selectively processed'. The following account traces some of the key ways in which pragmatics has informed and has been informed by the two trajectories of gender and language research. It also charts developments in the theorization of gender. These developments have led to a blurring of these two trajectories as they have both moved away from a conceptualization of gender as a stable set of qualities that distinguish males and females in a given **culture** and towards the view that gendering is a dynamic process that is achieved through the repeated use of patterns of **discourse**.

The systematic study of differences in male and female uses of linguistic resources can be dated back to Lakoff's (1975) publication *Language and Woman's Place*. Although much of the research that was generated as a response to Lakoff's paper tended towards the sociolinguistic, in that it focused primarily on exploring her claims about gender-based differences in language use, for Lakoff herself it is the effect of the different linguistic choices made by men and women that give those choices significance, not the fact of the differences *per se*. Key to her argument that men and women use linguistic resources differently is an engagement with the function and **context** of utterances, and in this she draws on and develops pragmatics scholarship. In particular, she draws on **Grice**'s **maxims** (Grice 1968a), and her own account of **politeness** (Lakoff 1973). This account argues that if politeness norms are conceptualized as a set of culture-specific rules which differentially inform the choices made by men and women, then it is possible to explain what makes the use of a **speech act** acceptable in one context but not in another. Her aim is to show that, by conforming to these rules and learning to 'speak like a lady', women are, in effect, learning to use speech styles that lead them to be perceived by others, and by themselves, as powerless.

Although there are notable exceptions, studies of gender and language during the 1970s and 1980s tended to essentialize gender and, particularly in sociolinguistic studies, gender at this time is usually conceptualized as the cultural extension of biological sex. Seen as a set of qualities that are inculcated in individuals via various socialization practices, such qualities were assumed to remain a fixed aspect of an individual's identity after that process was complete.

Given that men and women within this paradigm were perceived as constituting two distinct, internally homogeneous groups of people, gender could be treated as an easily identifiable independent variable against which differences in language use might be measured. Holmes' early work represents one attempt to question claims that there is a direct link between speaker sex and language use by redirecting the study of men's and women's language use back towards the sorts of questions asked by pragmatics. In her work on the functions of stereotypically 'feminine' forms, Holmes (1984b) supports and characterizes her approach by citing Brown's claim that '[t]he analysis of communicative strategies provides an intervening variable allowing us to relate language and society in a direct and motivated way, rather than simply to correlate them' (Brown 1980: 133). Brown's (1990) own analysis of the speech of Tenejapan women shows clearly that the study of gender and language needs to address pragmatics by asking questions about who is using which communicative strategies, why they are using them and what specific contextual constraints on the generation of **meaning** obtain when such strategies are attempted. However, limited by the dominant models of gender at this time, Holmes' own early work, such as her *Women, Men and Politeness* (Holmes 1995), which develops her case for treating language use as strategic, still conflates sex and gender, treating speaker sex as a correlate (and by implication a determinant) of the range of effects generated by different utterance types.

However, what Holmes shares with both Lakoff and Brown is a concern to show that the same linguistic resources can produce different effects according to context of use and according to the sex of the speaker, and that it is the norms relating to what counts as gender-appropriate behaviour in a given culture that account for these differences. Given this variation, it is clear that a pragmatic framework is needed to account for the way in which these norms are activated as contextual assumptions in a given interaction. Cameron's (1998) paper 'Is there any ketchup, Vera?' puts forward one way in which pragmatics provides the analytical tools to address this issue. Locating her discussion in the claims, prevalent at the time, that differences in the way that men and women use language can lead to miscommunication between the sexes, Cameron argues that pragmatics, through its foregrounding of the inferential nature of **communication**, can better explain these supposed differences in **utterance interpretation**. Her claim is that rather than focusing on whether it is men's and women's differential use of language that leads to misinterpretation, the key issue is one of **power** and conflict. In her analysis she argues that data should be analyzed from a pragmatic perspective in that it should ask whether men and women 'make use of conflicting assumptions about the position a particular speaker in a given situation either is, or ought to be, speaking from; and thus hold conflicting beliefs about the rights and obligations that are normative in the speaker-hearer relationship' (Cameron 1998: 443).

Cameron's work contributes to a general move away from the conceptualization of gender as a way of accounting for differences in male and female behaviour by positing the existence of a stable set of qualities that pre-exist and indeed generate differences in the use and interpretation of language. This notion of gender has been questioned from a number of perspectives over the last two decades, and the re-theorization of gender that has resulted has followed a path that parallels one within pragmatics. Just as pragmatic accounts have increasingly taken on board the extent to which communication is achieved through the dynamic construction of meaning via context-specific uses of language, so current research in the field sees gender itself as a product of specific uses of linguistic and pragmatic resources, rather than a determinant of those uses. One of the earliest works to develop this argument is West and Zimmerman's (1987) paper, in which they argue that gender should be perceived as a verb rather than a noun: by engaging in particular linguistic and non-linguistic behaviours, individuals, they claim, are actively 'doing gender'. This is a radical departure from traditional notions of identity in that from this perspective, identity is fluid and unstable. Some versions of this approach are based loosely on **Austin**'s notion of **performativity**, and see gender as constantly having to be re-enacted, and that it is therefore open to challenge and change in a given culture (Butler 1990).

Eckert and McConnell-Ginet (1992) take the idea that gendering is at least in part a linguistic practice and develop it further by linking it with a model of context and community that has proved to be extremely influential in the study of how men and women use language. Lave and Wenger's (1991) notion of a 'community of practice' (CofP) provides a framework that explains variation in perceptions of what counts as gendered behaviour within a given culture, since it is premised on the assumption that the parameters of appropriate behaviour will differ from one CofP to another. For example, speaking assertively might in British culture be perceived as stereotypically masculine behaviour. However, in a CofP such as that made up of British Members of Parliament engaging in debate in the House of Commons, such behaviour is a requirement, and therefore in making strong **assertions**, a speaker is not necessarily 'doing gender', but simply 'doing being an MP' (*see* Christie 2002). A corollary of this approach is that speaker sex becomes a less reliable predictor of linguistic behaviour, and intervening variables become more relevant in the study of gender and language. A study that demonstrates this is described in Ostermann's (2003) paper, in which she analyzes differences in the way that two sets of women working in institutions in Brazil behaved when interviewing victims of domestic violence as part of their jobs. Her study shows that differences in the interactional behaviour of the women were primarily determined by the ethos of the CofP in which the interviews took place rather than speaker gender. Other examples that demonstrate intra-gender variation include Holmes' (2006) study of workplace interactions, which analyzes the way in which utterances that function as **humour** can be used to reinforce or to challenge traditional gender stereotypes.

These more recent developments in the theorization of gender are perceived as capable of providing a more nuanced and explanatory account of variation in language use since they provide a model for addressing differences related to the individual such as class, race, age, etc., as they emerge as relevant aspects of context in a given interaction. From this perspective, therefore, although studies of men and women's use of language still focus quite frequently on inter-group difference, there is an increasing recognition of intra-group difference. This alternative approach is premised on the assumption that neither individuals nor behaviours are intrinsically gendered, but that linguistic behaviours become gendered by being actively constructed as having some bearing on the general perception of males and females. It is in the study of the repeated gendering of behaviours by people engaged in a range of cultural practices that the strand of gender and language research that focuses on variation becomes relevant to the strand that typically focuses on representations of males and females. Studies of gender representations have included the analysis of both written and spoken texts, and are generally designed to make explicit unstated assumptions about gender that must be activated if a text is to be perceived as meaningful. They also aim to show how these assumptions, and the meanings generated by a text, contribute towards specific ideologies of gender that in turn inform the way that we perceive males and females in a given culture and our expectations about their behaviour.

Studies of the representation of gender tend to argue that cultural texts do not simply reflect an existing reality about the qualities and experiences of males and females, but that they function to construct gender-based differences. Del-Teso-Craviotto (2006: 2018) argues that analyses that demonstrate how these constructions are generated are important because 'the reiterative use of certain linguistic strategies, to the extent that we stop questioning the assumptions upon which the underlying ideologies are built, has a powerful 'naturalizing' effect'. Recent examples of such analyses that draw on pragmatics include Coupland's (2007) study of the gendered representation of ageing in skincare advertisements. Her analysis shows that advertisements directed at men and women are different in that they are predicated on distinct ideological **presuppositions** about what makes ageing a problem. Her argument is that, while those advertisements aimed at men use presuppositions to construct anti-ageing products as a form of grooming, the **implicatures** generated by the advertisements aimed at women pathologize ageing. Two further examples are del-Teso-Craviotto's (2006) analysis of the construction of gender ideologies through the deployment of different patterns of language use in magazines targeted at men and women, and Velasco-Sacristan and Fuertes-Olivera's (2006) relevance-theoretical analysis of **metaphors** in advertising. What makes such analyses relevant to the study of gender and pragmatics is summed up by Eckert and McConnell-Ginet's (2003: 6) definition of gender: 'Gender is, after all, a system of meaning – a way of construing notions of male and female – and language is the primary means through which we maintain or contest old meanings, and construct or resist new ones'.

CHRIS CHRISTIE

See also: Communication; context; cooperative principle; culture; discourse; humour; implicature; meaning; metaphor; misunderstanding; performativity; politeness; power; presupposition; relevance theory; societal pragmatics; sociolinguistics

Suggestions for further reading

Cameron, D. (1998) '"Is there any ketchup, Vera?" Gender, power and pragmatics', *Discourse and Society*, 9: 437–55.
Christie, C. (2000) *Gender and Language: Towards a Feminist Pragmatics*, Edinburgh: Edinburgh University Press.
Eckert, P. and McConnell-Ginet, S. (2003) *Language and Gender*, Cambridge: Cambridge University Press.

Generalized Conversational Implicature, Theory of

The philosopher H.P. **Grice** (1975, 1989) introduced the notion of conversational implicature for a philosophical purpose: he hoped to show that divergences between ordinary language understanding and the logical interpretation of connectives like *and*, *or* and *if* are due to certain pragmatic overlays on the underlying logical meanings that arise in conversational use. For example, if I say *Paul is a linguist or a philosopher*, I seem to imply that Paul is not both, and I don't know which. But that is not the interpretation of *p or q* from a logical point of view – *p or q* is true if either p, or q or both are true.

Grice put forward the idea that the difference is due to a rule of usage, which follows from the **cooperative principle**, namely that one shouldn't produce a weaker statement than one's **knowledge** of the situation allows. Thus, not having said *Paul is both a linguist and a philosopher*, I will have implicated (the term of art for this kind of **inference**) that Paul is one or the other but, as far as I know, not both. (It is implicated, or pragmatically suggested, rather than encoded because there is no contradiction in saying *Paul is a linguist or a philosopher, or possibly both*.) In this case, as in many others, we want to say that this inference will tend to go with the word *or* because speakers will always have had the opportunity to have used the stronger *and* if they knew it applied. Hence, Grice called this kind of inference a generalized conversational implicature (GCI for short), distinguishing this special kind of **implicature** from others that are tied to the details of the **context** and have no such generality, which he called particularized conversational implicatures (henceforth, PCI). For example, consider B's answer in two different contexts, represented by the alternative **questions** from A:

A: (i) "Is Paul a writer?"
    (ii) "We need someone with practical skills – would Paul be the man?"
B: "He's a linguist or a philosopher"
    GCI: He's either a linguist or a philosopher, and I don't know which.
    PCIs in context
    (i) Paul writes, but he is not perhaps what one normally means by a writer.
    (ii) Paul is not a practical man.

Here the two different questions set up alternative relevant answers, special to the contexts, and any inferences derived from the contextual specificities will be, by definition, PCIs. In contrast, regardless of the different contexts, B's utterance is likely to suggest that B is not in a position to say which is Paul's profession (the GCI).

From the point of view of linguistic theory, GCIs promise a wealth of generalizable insights into how inferential **meaning** is constructed around the basis of coded or lexical meaning. For example, the theory of GCIs suggests that any language that has a disjunction is likely to find it used in opposition to a conjunction, and thus its use will implicate that the conjunction does not hold. Alternatively, PCIs seem more interesting to **conversation** and **discourse analysis** and **rhetoric**.

Not all theorists think the contrast between GCIs and PCIs is theoretically useful (see, for example, Sperber and Wilson 1995), mostly on the grounds that all implicatures are context-bound, and that therefore there are no generalizations of the kind that GCIs are meant to capture. This is an empirical issue, and the onus is on GCI theorists to show that there are indeed useful generalizations to be collected, which have explanatory force within linguistic theory. A good case for GCIs can be made by considering the quantifiers, and more generally the sort of logical and sub-logical relations that were captured in the medieval 'square of oppositions' as in Figure 2 below (Horn 1989; Levinson 2000). Internal to the square are given the traditional names of the corners and the logical or sub-logical relations between them.

According to the theory of GCIs, the relation of the I and O corners, traditionally described as subcontraries, is in fact implicatural – there is a systematic GCI from 'Not all' to 'Some' and from 'Some' to 'Not all', as indicated in the example below:

(i) "Not all the boys came to class".
    GCI: Some of the boys came to class.

(ii) "Some of the boys came to class".
     GCI: Not all of the boys came to class.

The importance of this observation is that it generalizes to a wide range of logical operators. For example, the (alethic) modal *necessary* can fill the A corner, *impossible* the E corner, *possible* the I corner, *possible not* the O corner. The prediction then is that saying 'It's possible he'll come' implicates *It's possible he won't come*. One can even think of the A corner filled by *and*, the I corner by *or*, the E by *neither* and the O corner by *not both*. Then saying 'Paul is a linguist or a philosopher' implicates 'not both', as expected. So here are a wide range of predictions about GCIs based on the structure of the square. And a further prediction is of real interest to linguistic theory, namely that the O corner of the square resists lexicalization – we have 'not all', 'not both', etc., rather than a single word *nall or *noth (*cf. none* or *neither* at the E corner). The prediction is based on the observation that *some* implicates 'not all' by a general conversational principle, so having a lexicalized 'not all' would be unnecessary (for the full argument *see* Levinson 2000: 64–71). The challenge to those who do not want to subscribe to a theory of GCIs is, amongst other things, to account for these regular, cross-language patterns of implicature and lexicalization in terms of an entirely context-specific theory of PCIs.

To understand why GCIs play this systematic role in the square, consider Grice's **maxims of**

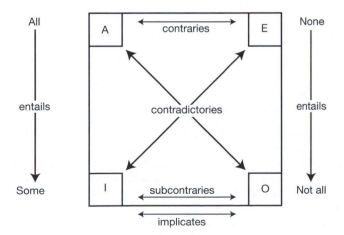

Figure 2 Square of oppositions with the quantifiers.

conversation, which describe working presumptions about the use of language. Grice posited a first maxim of quantity, 'make your contribution as informative as is required'. One way to fulfill the maxim is to choose carefully between the options your lexicon gives you. So in constructing the utterance 'Paul is a linguist or a philosopher', you ought to have considered the more informative 'Paul is a linguist and a philosopher' and rejected it, on the grounds you don't know it is true. The connectives *and, or* are in salient opposition, and in that way the structure of the lexicon forces a choice. The same goes for *all* and *some, necessary* and *possible*, and so on. Terms like these form scales, ordered pairs in these cases, such that the more informative member of the pair entails the less informative member in a neutral sentence frame (e.g. *p and q* entails *p or q*), and the **assertion** of the less informative member then carries a GCI to the effect that the more informative member could not have been substituted. GCIs thus ultimately depend on the structure of the lexicon for their general effect – it is because the lexicon is stable across contexts that GCIs are context independent.

There is now a large body of observations about GCIs and the kinds of words and constructions that give rise to them (*see* Levinson 2000). Together these give some account of the quite regular ways in which what we understand when we comprehend language always exceeds what is actually coded in the words and the grammar.

Another way to motivate the concept of a GCI is an argument from design. At up to four times slower than comprehension, language production is a bottleneck in the **communication** process. A design solution would be an information compression system, which uses simple **heuristics** to unpack a message. Heuristics have the advantage over some more mechanical 'zipping' solution that the information never has to be coded at all – the invoked information can be mutually presumed by speaker and addressee wherever it fits the news so far.

There do in fact seem to be such amplifying heuristics in language usage, of the following kind, more or less transparently related to Grice's two maxims of quantity and manner: (i) relevant things not mentioned can be assumed not to obtain (giving rise, for example, to **scalar implicatures**, so that *some* suggests 'not all'); (ii) simple descriptions suggest stereotypical exemplifications (giving rise to substantive enrichments of what was coded, so that, for example, *in the cup* suggests 'in the volume, not the wall' of the cup); (iii) marked messages suggest marked situations (giving rise, for example, to special inferences from periphrasis, as in *x caused the death of y* which suggests 'x didn't directly murder y'). GCI theory proposes that these sorts of heuristics are presumptively in force, so that GCIs are default inferences, which can nevertheless be cancelled by context and content where they do not fit.

STEPHEN LEVINSON

See also: Cooperative principle; Grice, H.P.; impliciture; maxims of conversation; post-Gricean pragmatics; radical pragmatics; scalar implicature; what is said

Suggestions for further reading

Horn, L. (2004) 'Implicature', in L.R. Horn and G. Ward (eds) *The Handbook of Pragmatics*, Oxford: Blackwell.
Huang, Y. (2007) *Pragmatics*, Oxford: Oxford University Press.
Levinson, S.C. (2000) *Presumptive Meanings: The Theory of Generalized Conversational Implicature*, Cambridge, MA: MIT Press.

Gestural Communication

Speech and gestures are almost always copresent during communicative actions (McNeill 1985) across all **cultures** (Cassell 1998). Gestures that accompany speech, called co-speech or speech-related gestures, are hand, head and arm movements produced by the speaker in a manner that is closely time-locked to the semantic and pragmatic properties of the corresponding speech. According to the relevant literature (Goodwin 1986; McNeill 1992), speech and gesture are aspects of a single communicative event arising from a common semantic **representation**. Before the **communication** unfolds, gesture and speech are part of a single idea. Then, as expression proceeds, the message is parsed into the two channels.

Speech-related gestures have a role in both the speech production (Hadar and Butterworth 1997; Krauss *et al.* 1996) and the speech comprehension process (Kendon 1994). For the speaker, co-speech gestures are used for the purposes of lexical access. They seem to facilitate speech both indirectly, by sustaining spatial representation in working memory, and directly, by activating embodied semantic representations involved in lexical search (Morsella and Krauss 2001). Furthermore, as co-speech gestures make it possible to easily represent ideas that are compatible with their mimetic and analog format, they also allow speakers to convey thoughts that may not fit straightforwardly into the categorical system of spoken language.

For the listener, co-speech gestures usually facilitate the comprehension of the spoken message (Alibali *et al.* 1997; Kelly and Church 1998). A possible reason is that gestures complete the **meaning** conveyed by the accompanying speech (McNeil *et al.* 2000): they carry symbolic and/or analogical information (Iverson and Goldin-Meadow 2001) that could reinforce, specify, add or simply mark some **discourse** content. The only exception is when co-speech gestures are discordant with speech (i.e. convey different information). In this case, they hinder the comprehension of that speech (Goldin-Meadow and Sandhofer 1999). Moreover, the facilitating function of co-speech gestures is dependent upon the quality of the speech they accompany. The more the verbal message is ambiguous (Thompson and Massaro 1986), highly complex (Graham and Heywood 1976; McNeil *et al.* 2000), or uttered in a soft voice (Berger and Popelka 1971), the more they help.

In the past, several different co-speech gesture classifications were proposed, each following a specific and unique taxonomic criterion (see, amongst others, Argyle 1975; Bavelas *et al.* 1995; Efron 1941; Ekman and Friesen 1969; Freedman and Hoffman 1967; Kendon 2004; McNeill and Levy 1982; Rosenfeld 1966). Although these gesture-type categorizations are not suitable for defining mutually exclusive categories, they do make it possible to establish some dimensions of gesture semiosis along which various types of gestures can be placed. There has been a general

acceptance of certain type designations in more recent literature. First, we may consider the traditional distinction between representational and non-representational gestures (McNeill and Levy 1982). Representational gestures pictorially represent semantic content related to speech, such as attributes, actions or relationships of objects or characters. They are referential and may appear in two forms: (1) *iconic gestures*, which depict concrete images of the speaker's thoughts; and (2) *metaphoric gestures*, which pictorially represent an abstract concept (also *see* Thompson *et al.* 1998). Representational gestures may be redundant with respect to the meaning of the spoken words, or may add meaning. However, information conveyed through representational gestures is incorporated in what listeners consider the intended meaning of the utterance to be, even when they are requested to recall only the spoken information (Goldin-Meadow and Butcher 2000). Conversely, non-representational gestures do not convey semantic content. Known as *beats*, or *batons* (*see* Ekman and Friesen 1969), they refer to the rhythm of speech and tend to have the same form regardless of the content of the accompanying speech. Instead of demonstrating parallels of propositional content between speech and gesture, beats demonstrate parallels of pragmatic function. The distinction between representational and beat gestures is supported by both theoretical analyses and empirical research (as summarized by Alibali *et al.* 2001). Finally, a third group of co-speech gestures are *deictic* gestures, which spatialize aspects of the story being narrated by locating them in the physical space in front of the narrator. They thus establish joint attention with the addressee.

Co-speech gestures also have a communicative effect for the listener when the speaker does not produce them for that purpose. Indeed, sometimes co-speech gestures seem to be produced more to facilitate language production than to communicate information to the addressee (Krauss *et al.* 1991). Moreover, speakers may produce co-speech gestures even when nobody is watching, for example, when speaking to a blind listener (Iverson and Goldin-Meadow 1997). However, especially in the case of representational gestures and deictics, these mostly appear to be produced with a communicative purpose. Indeed, they are usually modulated according to the characteristics of the communicative setting such as, respectively, visibility between speaker and listener (Alibali *et al.* 2001) and the location of shared space between speaker and listener (Ozyurek 2002).

The above discussion on gestural communication holds for gestures produced in communicative interactions as accompaniment to speech. A different type of gesture may be used as a substitute for speech. In this case, gestures carry the full burden of communication. Most of these gestures are symbolic, that is, they have an arbitrary socially defined relationship with their referent, knowledge of which must be learned and shared by those producing them and those seeing them (an example is the 'OK' gesture). These are called emblems (Efron 1941; Ekman and Friesen 1969) or conventional gestures (Argyle 1975). Emblems have standards of good form, a language-like property that co-speech gestures lack. However, they are not organized in a system of symbols, and therefore they are considered a fully non-linguistic communicative means. **Sign languages** used by non-hearing individuals (such as the American Sign Language) are also made up of symbolic gestures. They have linguistic properties such as compositionality, segmentation, a lexicon, a syntax, arbitrariness, and distinctiveness (see for instance Klima and Bellugi 1979). Thus, sign languages are considered linguistic forms of communication that use gestures.

ILARIA CUTICA

See also: Cognitive pragmatics; communication; conventionality; prelinguistic communication; signed language, pragmatics of

Suggestions for further reading

Goldin-Meadow, S. (1999) 'The role of gesture in communication and thinking', *Trends in Cognitive Science*, 3: 419–29.
McNeill, D. (1992) *Hand and Mind*, Chicago: University of Chicago Press.

Given/New Distinction

The given/new distinction is concerned broadly with the (relative) givenness or newness of parts of the conceptual content expressed by a sentence. The distinction has been used in at least two different senses, which have not always been carefully distinguished in the literature – referential givenness/newness and relational givenness/newness (*see* Gundel 1988; Gundel and Fretheim 2004).

Referential givenness/newness is typically encoded by the use of different referring forms (e.g. stressed and unstressed pronouns, **demonstratives**, definite descriptions). It involves the given/new status of the intended interpretation of a linguistic expression in the speaker's or hearer's mind, the discourse (model), or some real or possible world, depending on analysts' assumptions about where the referents or corresponding **meanings** of linguistic expressions reside. Some examples of referential givenness concepts include existential **presupposition** (e. g. Strawson 1964b), various senses of referentiality and **specificity** (e.g. Fodor and Sag 1982), assumed familiarity of Prince (1981b), the familiarity condition on definite descriptions (e.g. Heim 1982), the activation and identifiability statuses of Chafe (1994) and Lambrecht (1994), the hearer-old/new and discourse-old/new statuses of Prince (1992), and the (in **focus**, activated, familiar, uniquely identifiable, referential, type identifiable) cognitive statuses of Gundel *et al.* (1993).

Relational givenness/newness, by contrast, involves a relation between two complementary parts, X and Y, of the semantic/conceptual **representation** of a sentence. X (what the sentence is about) is given in relation to Y in the sense that it is independent, and outside the scope of, what is predicated in Y. Y is new in relation to X in the sense that it is new information asserted, questioned, etc. about X. This partition, which is encoded across languages by intonational prominence, syntactic structure, and/or special **topic** and focus morphemes, does not necessarily correspond to the syntactic division between grammatical subject and predicate in the sentence, though it may. It reflects how the informational content of a particular event or state of affairs expressed by a sentence is conceptualized and represented and how truth value is to be assessed. Some examples of relational givenness/newness pairs include presupposition-focus (e.g. Chomsky 1971; Jackendoff

1972), topic-comment (e.g. Gundel 1974), theme-rheme (e.g. Valldui 1992), and topic-predicate (Erteschik-Shir 1997).

It has often been observed that given information tends to precede new information in a sentence. However, this given–new order is not absolute even in a single language and in some (especially VSO and VOS) languages there is a tendency to prefer relationally new before relationally given order. The order of given and new can also be affected by the interaction of referential and relational givenness. Topics with a high degree of referential givenness (activated or in focus) are often postposed to sentence-final position, following the relationally new part of the sentence or utterance. For example, cleft sentences, where the (relationally given) topic follows relationally new information, are typically appropriate only when the topic also has a high degree of referential givenness. Thus, (1) would be an appropriate response to *What will we talk about today?*, since what we are going to talk about today is already activated, and possibly in focus of attention, by virtue of just having been mentioned in the question.

(1) It's information structure that we will talk about today.

However, (1) would not be appropriate as the first sentence in a lecture. Even though it can be assumed that something will be talked about, this fact is a new topic which is not necessarily already activated for the addressee. By contrast, the pseudo-cleft in (2), where relationally given precedes relationally new, is appropriate in either context (*see* Gundel 1988 and Gundel and Mulkern 2007 for further discussion).

(2) What we will talk about today is information structure.

Referential givenness/newness and relational givenness/newness are logically independent, as seen in (3) (from Gundel 1980):

(3) A. Who called?
    B. Pat said SHE called.

If *SHE* in (3) is used to refer to Pat, it is referentially given in virtually every possible sense. The

intended referent is presupposed, specific, referential, familiar, activated, in focus, uniquely identifiable, hearer old, and discourse old. But the subject of the embedded sentence is at the same time relationally new, and therefore receives a focal accent here. It instantiates the variable in the topic of the sentence, *x* called, thus yielding the relationally new information expressed in (3).

The two kinds of givenness/newness also differ in other respects. While relational givenness/newness is necessarily associated with linguistic representations, the meanings of sentences or utterances, referential givenness/newness is not specifically linguistic at all. Thus, one can just as easily characterize a visual or non-linguistic auditory stimulus, for example, a house or a tune, as familiar or not, in focus or not, and even specific or not. Corresponding to this essential difference is the fact that referential givenness statuses such as familiarity are uniquely determined by the **knowledge** and attention state of the addressee at a given point in the **discourse**. Relational givenness notions like topic, by contrast, may be constrained or influenced by the discourse **context** (as all aspects of meaning are in some sense), but they are not uniquely determined by it. As Sgall *et al.* (1973) point out, a sentence like *Yesterday was the last day of the Davis Cup match* could be followed by *The match was won by Australia* or by *Australia won the match*. While the latter two sentences could each have an interpretation where the topic (what is relationally given) is the Davis Cup match and the new information is that Australia was the winner, it is also possible in exactly the same discourse context to interpret the first of these sentences as new information about the match and the second as new information about Australia. Which of these possible interpretations is the intended one depends on the interests and perspective of the speaker, and would also be reflected in the **prosody**.

One place where the linguistic context often seems to determine the relational given–new (topic–comment/focus) structure is in question–answer pairs, which is why these provide one of the more reliable contextual tests for relational givenness/newness concepts. Thus, (4b) is judged to be an appropriate answer to the **question** in (4a) because the location of the prominent pitch accent is consistent with an interpretation where the topic is who the Twins played and the focus/new information is the Yankees. But (4c), where the location of the prominent pitch accent requires an interpretation where the topic is who played the Yankees, is not an appropriate response to (4a).

(4) a. Who did the Twins play?
      b. The Twins played the YANKEES.
      c. #The TWINS played the Yankees.

As questions restrict other aspects of the semantic appropriateness of a possible answer, the fact that they constrain the appropriateness of linguistic forms that encode different relational givenness/newness partitions is consistent with the idea that this distinction is part of the conceptual/semantic representation of natural language sentences.

JEANETTE GUNDEL

See also: Focus; information structure; presupposition; reference; topic

Suggestions for further reading

Gundel, J.K. (1988) 'Universals of topic-comment structure', in M. Hammond, E. Moravczik and J. Wirth (eds) *Studies in Syntactic Typology*, Amsterdam: John Benjamins.
Gundel, J.K. and Fretheim, T. (2003) 'Information structure', in J. Verschueren, J.O. Östman, J. Blommaert and C. Bulcaen (eds) *Handbook of Pragmatics*, Amsterdam: John Benjamins.
Prince, E. (1981) 'Toward a taxonomy of given and new information', in P. Cole (ed.) *Radical Pragmatics*, New York: Academic Press.

Grammaticalization

Grammaticalization is the subfield of historical linguistics that studies the sources of grammatical forms and the changes they typically undergo. The expression 'grammatical forms' covers a variety of phenomena, including case, number, and gender markers of nouns and person, tense, and aspect markers of verbs. The term grammaticalization is also applied to changes of lexical items (nouns, verbs, adverbs, and adjectives) into grammatical items (prepositions, conjunctions, auxiliary verbs, and definite and indefinite articles) and the emergence of grammatical constructions such as those for forming negation and the passive. Grammaticalization is part of (and inseparable from) the more general study of change in language. Consequently, any principles of change that are discovered apply equally to grammatical and to lexical change; there are no changes that are specific to changes in grammatical forms (Hopper 1991). Like all names of scientific fields, the expression 'grammaticalization' is both a label for the field of study and a term applied to the phenomena that are studied.

Grammaticalization involves structural changes and semantic changes, it being impossible to say which has historical precedence. Structural changes comprise reanalysis and phonological reduction. In reanalysis, adjacent forms are rebracketed: [I am going] [to sell my pig] "I'm on my way to sell my pig" becomes [I am going to] [sell my pig] and eventually [going to] assumes the meaning of future tense. [A cup] [full of nails] is reanalyzed as [a cupful] [of nails] and [a cupful] is understood as a quantifying phrase determining 'nails' (and no longer refers to 'a cup' as such). A typical concomitant of reanalysis is a reversal of the roles of head and satellite. The head of an expression stands duty for the entire expression, while satellites are subordinate parts. Hence, 'a cup full of nails' is singular, because the head is 'cup', whereas 'a cupful of nails' is plural, the head being 'nails'. The second but not the first can occur in contexts where a plural noun phrase is required (*cf.* 'they scattered a cupful of nails over the workbench' vs. *they scattered a cup full of nails over the workbench'). An especially common type of reanalysis is the collapsing of a phrase into a shorter form. The English adhortative 'let's' is an example: clearly derived from 'let us', it now serves to introduce an adhortative construction, as in 'let's stay home tonight'.

The example of 'let's' illustrates another frequent accompaniment of grammaticalization, phonological reduction. When [going] [to sell] was reanalyzed as [going to] [sell], 'going to' was free to be reduced to 'gonna' (whereas in [going] [to college], with no reanalysis, this reduction is not possible.) The French future tense as in (je) chanterai 'I will sing' came about when the Old French descendents of Latin cantare habeo 'I have to sing' were collapsed into a single word: [cantar][ayo]> [cantarayo]> [chanterai] (Benveniste 1968). Such changes typically bring about paradigms in which the verb has person and number affixes that were formerly pronouns, and tense, modality and aspect affixes that were once auxiliaries.

The semantic changes that accompany grammaticalization have been described as a weakening of **meaning**, and as a shift from concrete to abstract, for which the term 'bleaching' has been used (for the history of the study of grammaticalization, *see* Lehmann 1995). In recent years this negative characterization has fallen out of favour as linguists came to see forms undergoing grammaticalization as spreading into wider contexts and increasing their pragmatic usefulness (Traugott 1995; Traugott and Dasher 2002). For example, the ancestor of the modal auxiliary 'can' meant in Old English 'know how to'. It occurred exclusively with human subjects. In later stages of English the restriction to humans was modified to include a wider variety of forms, including inanimates: 'These trees can grow to a height of 100 meters'. But this widening distribution of the form presupposes a semantic change from knowledge to ability and then to the expression of possibility. The English 'going to/gonna' construction provides another example. There is a change from the sense of purpose, as in Shakespeare's ' … letters to my friends, And I am going to deliver them' (*Two Gentlemen of Verona*, III, 1), that is, 'I am on my way to deliver them', to a predictive future tense in which neither motion nor purpose is expressed, as in 'The ice carvings are going to melt'.

Such examples illustrate the place of **pragmatics** in semantic change. They highlight the fact that changes result not from purely language-internal factors but from verbal interactions among speakers, specifically the role of what Geis and Zwicky (1971) called invited **inferences**. Traugott and Dasher (2002) argue that invited inferences are central to an account of change. **Discourse** and pragmatics rather than local semantics are the driving force behind change. An utterance like 'I am going to deliver the letters' is understood to report an action and

at the same time an **intention** of the speaker. But the speaker allows the listener to infer that the delivery of the letters is an intention and a future event. This inference becomes generalized to all uses of 'be going to', which eventually assumes the present day meaning of 'future tense'. Traugott and Dasher (2002: 36–37) present as an example the case of 'as/so long as'. In Present Day English it has a conditional meaning, as in:

> Galligan told the jury that it is proper for police to question a juvenile without a parent present *as long as* they made a 'reasonable effort' to notify the parent.

In earlier forms of English, both spatial and temporal meanings were possible. An Old English medical text (Lacnunga) has the following example:

> wring þurh linenne clað on þæt eage *swa lange swa* him ðearf sy
> wring through linen cloth on that eye *as long as* him need be
> 'squeeze (the medication) through a linen cloth onto the eye as long as he needs'

Here, the temporal expression *swa lange swa* 'as long as' invites the inference that the procedure should be continued 'if' it is needed. In later stages of the language the conditional meaning becomes more salient. The history of 'so/as long as' is one of a gradual weakening of the temporal meaning and its replacement by the more purely grammatical meaning of a conditional.

Grammaticalization is gradual (Lichtenberk 1991) and unidirectional (Haspelmath 1999b; Hopper and Traugott 2003). Grammaticalization is gradual in that the term is not applied to discontinuous leaps such as borrowings and ad hoc transformations between lexical classes such as the use of a preposition like 'up' as a verb in 'They have upped their prices'. Unidirectionality refers to the hypothesis that grammaticalization is irreversible and tends strongly to evolve in the direction of increased pragmatic relevance and semantic diffuseness. This hypothesis is challenged by several of the authors in Love (2001) on the grounds that (1) there are exceptions, and (2) that grammaticalization does not involve changes distinct from linguistic change in general. Neither of these objections has, however, been denied by its proponents. Hopper and Traugott (2003) contains a detailed response to these and other criticisms.

Grammaticalization has significant implications for general linguistics. It points to the essential fluidity of grammar. It also suggests that the appearance of fixed forms and rules is illusory, that the grammar–lexicon distinction is less sharp than is commonly assumed, and that grammatical structure itself is emergent, that is, subject to constant revision by speakers. While the paths of grammaticalization are constrained by universal and cognitive factors (see the impressive catalogue of examples in Heine and Kuteva 2002), its proximate causes are in discourse, through frequency of use (Bybee and Hopper 2001), pragmatic inferencing (Traugott and Dasher 2002), and the routinization (Haiman 1994) of word combinations.

PAUL J. HOPPER

See also: Discourse; discourse analysis; discourse markers; discourse particles; historical pragmatics; implicature; indexicals; interactional linguistics; lexical pragmatics; meaning; metaphor; pragmatics; semantics-pragmatics interface; syntax-pragmatics interface

Suggestions for further reading

Aitchison, J. (2001) *Language Change: Progress or Decay?*, Cambridge: Cambridge University Press.
Heine, B., Claudi, U. and Hünnemeyer, F. (1991) *Grammaticalization: A Conceptual Framework*, Chicago, IL: University of Chicago Press.

Grice, H.P.

Herbert Paul Grice (known universally as Paul) was an English philosopher of language, who is widely recognized as the father of modern **pragmatics**. Whilst we may owe the term 'pragmatics' to Charles **Morris** (1938), Grice certainly ranks highly among a select few to whom credit is due for shaping the discipline as we know it today. Grice's theory of **conversation**

(*see* Neale 1992), which was presented in his William James Lectures at Harvard in 1967, formed the foundations upon which much of modern pragmatics has been built.

A large proportion of Grice's working life was spent at Oxford, where he was a fellow and tutor at St John's College. In 1967, he moved to the University of California, Berkeley, where he taught until 1986, despite having officially retired in 1980. During his time at Oxford, Grice was heavily influenced by what has become known as **ordinary language philosophy**, a movement championed by John **Austin**. Ordinary language philosophers believed in the study of actual language use as opposed to the study of formal languages. They opposed the central tenets of the highly influential 'idealized' language philosophy of, for example, Frege and Russell. For ordinary language philosophers there was such a vast difference between the **semantics** of idealized, formal languages and the semantics of natural language that they believed study of the former could never shed light on the latter. Grice's main aim in his theory of conversation was to suggest ways in which the essential differences between the two movements might be reconciled. In effect, he proposed a distinction between semantics, the theory of linguistic meaning, and pragmatics, the study of language use, a distinction which allowed idealized and ordinary language philosophy to coexist.

In the William James Lectures, Grice proposed that human verbal **communication** is a cooperative activity driven by the mutual expectation that, in general, participants will obey a **cooperative principle** and conversational **maxims** of quantity, quality, relation and manner. He drew a distinction between **what is said** in an utterance and the **implicatures** of that utterance. Together with the cooperative principle and maxims this distinction provided the first systematic way of drawing a line between the content of whatever direct **speech act** was performed (the literal meaning of the words being said, or the **proposition** expressed) and any wider **meaning** the speaker intended to convey (what the speaker might mean over and above the words uttered).

It is worth remembering, however, that despite the fact that Grice is probably best known for his theory of conversation, this formed only one small part of his work. Indeed, it could be argued that his theory of conversation was, actually, just one part of his 'theory of meaning' (first presented in Grice's 1957 paper 'Meaning'), which itself was a part of much a larger programme on reasons, **reasoning** and **rationality** (Grice 2001b).

Grice's 'Meaning' is one of the most influential philosophical papers of the past fifty years, and has had a profound influence on linguists and philosophers. The approach presented in the paper is neatly summed up by a quote from his 1989 *Retrospective Epilogue*: 'what words mean is a matter of what people mean by them' (Grice 1989: 340). Meaning was to be understood in terms of **propositional attitude** psychology: ultimately, the meaning of words was to be analyzed in terms of the beliefs, desires and **intentions** of communicators who uttered them. In this paper, Grice drew a distinction between **natural and non-natural meaning**, and attempted to characterize non-natural meaning (meaning$_{NN}$) in terms of the expression and recognition of intentions.

The connections between the different facets of Grice's work are not immediately obvious. In part, this is because Grice was notoriously reticent about being published. Indeed, Grice apparently did not even regard his seminal 1957 paper 'Meaning' as worthy of publication. Dale (1996: 14; fn. 31) notes that 'Grice originally wrote the paper for a seminar that he and [Peter] Strawson were to give in 1948, but was reluctant to publish it. Strawson had the article typed out and submitted it for publication without Grice's knowledge. Strawson only told Grice after the article was accepted for publication.'

The William James Lectures themselves were never published as a whole (at least not until his 1989 anthology, which contained revised versions). For various reasons, the first of the lectures to be published were Lectures VI and VII, parts of which appeared in revised form as Grice (1968b), and Lectures V and VI, parts of which were published, again in revised form, as Grice (1969). It was not until 1975 that Lecture II – the lecture in which Grice introduced his cooperative principle and maxims, and the notion of implicature – was published. Confusingly, the paper was entitled 'Logic and Conversation', which was the title Grice had given the entire lecture series.

There has been much less discussion of how Grice's theories of conversation and meaning fit into his larger programme on reasons, reasoning and rationality (though *see* Chapman 2005 and Allott 2007). This is largely because this dimension of Grice's work was only published quite recently as Grice (2001b). His later work, however, can be interpreted as a continuation of his exploration into the themes of his earlier works. Grice was committed to seeing humans as rational beings. We have reasons for our attitudes and actions and have evolved to interpret the behaviour of others in terms of the reasons behind it. Moreover, the way we interpret the actions and utterances of others constitutes in itself a form of reasoning. Thanks largely to Grice's influential work it is now increasingly recognized that verbal communication is more than a simple coding–decoding process. Any attempt to characterize language use should reflect the fact that it is an intelligent, inferential activity involving the expression and recognition of intentions. Grice died in California in 1989 but his legacy lives on not just in pragmatics and the **philosophy of language**, but also in psychology and the cognitive sciences.

TIM WHARTON

See also: Austin, J.; conventionality; conversation; cooperative principle; explicit/implicit distinction; generalized conversational implicature, theory of; history of pragmatics; implicature; meaning; metarepresentation; Morris, C.; natural and non-natural meaning; neo-Gricean pragmatics; ordinary language philosophy; philosophy of language; post-Gricean pragmatics; pragmatics; proposition; propositional attitudes; radical pragmatics; rationality; reasoning; relevance theory; scalar implicature; semantics-pragmatics interface; theory of mind; utterance interpretation; what is said

Suggestions for further reading

Chapman, S. (2005) *Paul Grice, Philosopher and Linguist*, Basingstoke: Palgrave Macmillan.
Grice, H.P. (1989) *Studies in the Way of Words*, Cambridge, MA: Harvard University Press.

Habermas, J.

Jürgen Habermas is one of the world's most influential philosophers. Over the past decades he has produced an extensive corpus of work that has impacted not only on philosophy but also on sociology, psychology, communication studies, political theory and legal theory. A core element of Habermas's philosophical approach is his program of **formal pragmatics**. The aim of this program is to identify and reconstruct the universal **presuppositions** that underlie the **communicative competence** of speakers and make mutual understanding possible. For this reason, Habermas used the term 'universal pragmatics' when he first delineated its main features in his programmatic article 'What is Universal Pragmatics?' (Habermas 1976). However, later on he preferred to use the term 'formal pragmatics' to distinguish it from Apel's program of transcendental pragmatics (Apel 1992, 1994) and to underscore its affinity with formal **semantics**. The core idea behind Habermas's project is that not only language but also speech, that is, the use of sentences in utterances, is susceptible to formal philosophical analysis and not merely to empirical analysis of particular situations of use as is done in **sociolinguistics**, for example. A comprehensive philosophical account of human **communication** thus requires complementing formal semantics with formal pragmatics. Whereas the former examines the propositional content of utterances in order to provide an account of **what is said** in a **speech act**, the latter examines the force of speech acts in order to explain the interpersonal relations that are established in communication. According to

Habermas, the latter type of analysis, unlike the former, has a philosophical significance that goes beyond its intrinsic value for understanding human communication. It has important implications for theories of action, rationality, society and morality. The key hypothesis behind Habermas's program of formal pragmatics is that human communication is governed by a genuine kind of **rationality** (he calls it 'communicative rationality') that is not reducible to instrumental rationality. Whereas the **linguistic competence** of speakers may be conceived as being limited to the capacity of understanding grammatically well-formed expressions of a language, the communicative competence of speakers involves at the very least the ability to use linguistic expressions in order to reach understanding with someone about something (or, in Habermas's own terminology, to engage in 'communicative action'). This communicative ability, however, is genuinely different from and irreducible to the capacity to act instrumentally or strategically in order to achieve extra-communicative goals. In order to prove this hypothesis, Habermas draws from **speech act theory** as it was originally developed by J. **Austin** (Austin 1975) and J. **Searle** (Searle 1969, 1979b, 1983). In contradistinction to these authors, however, Habermas's aim is not to provide a comprehensive descriptive account of each of the rules that govern the use of specific types of speech acts, important as that task may be. Instead, his analysis of speech acts aims to identify the unavoidable rational presuppositions that make communication possible.

These rational presuppositions can be identified by focusing on the difference between the mere production of a grammatically correct sentence by a speaker and its use in a situation of possible understanding. Habermas explains this difference by reference to the *relations to reality* in which every sentence is first embedded through the act of utterance. In being uttered, a sentence is placed in relation to (1) a certain state of affairs, (2) a certain speaker's **intention**, and (3) a certain interpersonal relationship. It is thereby placed under validity claims that it need not and cannot fulfill as a nonsituated sentence, as a purely grammatical formation. These three dimensions of validity (what Habermas calls 'the validity basis of speech') are the key **heuristic** cues that interlocutors have at their disposal in trying to understand each other's speech acts. The guiding idea is a generalization of the conception of **meaning** as truth conditions characteristic of formal semantics. According to the latter, we understand the propositional content of an **assertion** when we know its truth conditions, that is, when we know what would be the case if it were true. Generalizing this view to cover both the propositional content of an utterance and the force of the different speech acts that can be performed by it, Habermas claims that we understand a speech act when we know what makes it acceptable. Now, as we just saw, **knowledge** of the acceptability-conditions of speech acts involves at least three dimensions: a speaker, a hearer, and the world. Thus, in order to understand each other's speech acts, interlocutors must be able to share the knowledge implicit in the propositional content of the speech act and hence they must assess the *truth* claim of the utterance. They must share the normative presuppositions inherent in the interpersonal relation established through the illocutionary act (i.e. they must assess the *rightness* claim inherent in it) and they must also assess the *sincerity* with which the speech act is uttered. Truth, rightness, and sincerity are three universal validity claims that speakers (implicitly or explicitly) raise with their speech acts and which they must be prepared to justify by offering reasons if challenged by the hearer. Following Dummett's account of meaning in terms of assertibility conditions (Dummett 1975, 1976), Habermas claims that knowing the kinds of reasons with which a speaker could vindicate the validity claims raised with her speech act is an indispensable part of understanding its meaning. Here lies the key connection between formal pragmatics and theories of action, rationality, and social order. To the extent that interlocutors can check the acceptability of their reasons by participating in reflexive practices of argumentation (what Habermas calls 'rational discourses'), communication can generate binding and bonding effects that have a rational foundation and make consensual action coordination possible.

In order to fill in the details of this general program of formal pragmatics, Habermas has engaged in discussion and criticism of central aspects of speech act theory such as the classification of basic types of speech acts and the account of the relationship between the illocutionary and perlocutionary component of speech acts. He has also criticized the shortcomings of the major competitors to formal pragmatics: truth-conditional semantics (Dummett 1976) and intentionalist semantics (Bennett 1976; Grice 1989; Schiffer 1972). His analyses are spread over multiple writings, from the original statement of the program in 'What is Universal Pragmatics?' (Habermas 1976) to his major philosophical work *The Theory of Communicative Action* (Habermas 1981). They also extend to some more recent discussions in his book *Truth and Justification* (Habermas 1999). Over this long period of time he has proposed important modifications of classical speech act theory and has also refined and revised his own pragmatic theory of meaning in light of numerous suggestions and criticisms (Apel 1994; Lafont 1999; Schnädelbach 1992; Skjei 1985; Thompson 1982; Tugendhat 1985; Wellmer 1992; Wood 1985). Most of these writings are compiled in an English anthology entitled *On the Pragmatics of Communication* (Habermas 1998). For further analysis and discussion of Habermas's program, *see* Apel (1992, 1994), Cooke (1994), Heath (1995, 2001), Honneth and Joas (1991), Johnson (1993), Lafont (1999, 2002) and Wellmer (1992).

CRISTINA LAFONT

See also: Assertion; Austin, J.L.; communication; competence, communicative; competence, linguistic; explicit/implicit distinction; formal pragmatics; heuristic; intention; meaning;

pragmatics; presupposition; proposition; rationality; Searle, J.; semantics; sociolinguistics; speech act theory; speech act type; utterance interpretation; what is said

Suggestions for further reading

Cooke, M. (1994) *Language and Reason: A Study of Habermas's Pragmatics*, Cambridge, MA: MIT Press.

Habermas, J. (1998) *On the Pragmatics of Communication*, ed. M. Cooke, Cambridge, MA: MIT Press.

Lafont, C. (1999) *The Linguistic Turn in Hermeneutic Philosophy*, Cambridge, MA: MIT Press.

Hedges

Conducting one of the first explorations of the linguistic hedging phenomenon, Lakoff (1972: 195) defines hedges as 'words whose job is to make things fuzzier or less fuzzy'. In functional grammar, hedging or modalization refers to 'either yes or no' or 'both yes or no' (Halliday and Matthiessen 2004: 147). The functions of hedging, as depicted by Markkanen and Schröder (1987), include modifying the **definiteness** of an utterance or the weightiness of the information given in it; modifying or even hiding the attitude of the writer to the **propositions** put forward in the text; protecting the writer from the possible attacks of the audience; hiding who is responsible for the truth value of what is being said; appearing modest; and in scientific genres, fuzziness, in the form of imprecise numerical expressions, serves to background previous theories, especially those one believes are wrong.

Hedging takes different linguistic forms. Fraser's (1975) pragmatic Performative Model states that modal verbs or semi-modals can be used to modify the illocutionary force of performative verbs by stressing the inevitability and desirability of the locution. The most common forms of hedging have been identified as follows (e.g. Lakoff 1972; Prince *et al.* 1982; Brown and Levinson 1987; Simpson 1990; Crompton 1997; Fortanet *et al.* 1998; Hyland 1998b):

(1) Modal auxiliary verbs are the most straightforward and widely used means of expressing hedging in English academic writing. The most common verbs are *may, might, can, could, would* and *should*.

(2) Modal lexical verbs are **speech act** verbs that are used to perform acts such as doubting and evaluating rather than merely describing, for example, *to see, to appear, to believe, to assume, to suggest, to estimate, to tend, to think, to argue, to indicate, to propose*, and *to speculate*.

(3) Adjectives, nouns and adverbs. Probability adjectives include *possible, probable* and *un/likely*. Nouns include *assumption, claim, possibility, estimate* and *suggestion*. Examples of adverbs, or non-verbal modals, are *perhaps, possibly, probably, practically, presumably, virtually* and *apparently*.

(4) Approximators of degree, quantity, frequency and time, such as *approximately, roughly, about, often, occasionally, generally, usually, somewhat, somehow* and *a lot of*.

(5) Introductory phrases such as *I believe, to our knowledge, it is our view that, we feel that*, etc. which express the writer's personal doubt and indirect involvement.

(6) If-phrases, for example, *if true* and *if anything*.

(7) Compound hedges are phrases made up of several hedges. The most common forms are a modal auxiliary combined with a lexical verb with a hedging content (e.g. *it would appear*), and a lexical verb followed by a hedging adverb or adjective where the adverb or adjective reinforces the hedge already inherent in the lexical verb (e.g. *it seems reasonable/probable*). Such compound hedges can be double hedges (e.g. *it may suggest that; it seems likely that; it would indicate that; this probably indicates*), triple hedges (*it seems reasonable to assume that*), quadruple hedges (e.g. *it would seem somewhat unlikely that, it may appear somewhat speculative that*), and so on.

Studies of hedges have primarily been conducted in **academic discourse** such as biology research articles (Hyland 1994, 1996, 1998b; Myers 1989, 1997), economics (Bloor and Bloor 1993; Bloor 1996) and medicine (Salager-Meyer 1994, 1997). Hyland (1998b) discusses hedging functions and their linguistic realizations and confirms the importance of hedges as a rhetorical means of gaining communal adherence to knowledge claims. Varttala (2001) finds noticeable disciplinary differences in the use of hedges in scientific research articles. Examining different disciplines, Markkanen and Schröder (1997) argue that some disciplines such as linguistics and **philosophy** employ more hedging than others such as natural sciences and technology, due to discipline-specific bases of **argumentation**.

WINNIE CHENG and LEUNG CHI KONG

See also: Academic discourse; complaints; definiteness; disagreement; evidentials; meta-pragmatics; morphopragmatics; refusals; socio-linguistics; translation, pragmatics of; vagueness

Suggestions for further reading

Hyland, K. (2000) 'Hedges, boosters and lexical invisibility: noticing modifiers in academic texts', *Language Awareness*, 9: 179–97.
Kenesei, I. and Harnish, R. (eds) (2001) *Perspectives on Semantics, Pragmatics and Discourse: A festschrift for Ferenc Kiefer*, Amsterdam: John Benjamins.
Maat, H. P. (2007) 'How promotional language in press releases is dealt with by journalists', *Journal of Business Communication*, 44: 59–95.

Heuristic

A 'heuristic' is a strategy that helps make decisions, or discover solutions to problems. What is special about heuristics, though, is that they are a fast, informal – *intuitive* – way of doing so. In making decisions, we rarely have all the facts at our disposal, and even if we did, our minds would not have the capacity to weigh up potentially infinite possible options. Human **rationality** is not unbounded. It is 'bounded' (Simon 1956), and evolution has left us with economical 'rules-of-thumb' that enable us to make the most of our finite cognitive capacity.

Much current work in evolutionary psychology conceives of the mind as an 'adaptive toolbox', as a set of dedicated cognitive mechanisms – or 'modules' – likely to have evolved in small incremental steps (Barkow *et al.* 1995; Sperber 2001b). One way in which such mechanisms might improve overall cognitive efficiency is by

providing what Gigerenzer *et al.* (1999) call 'fast and frugal heuristics', which apply to a particular domain, and yield reliable conclusions when applied to input from this domain. As Gigerenzer and Selten (2002: 7) put it: 'heuristics are middle-ranged, that is, they work in a class of situations … What we call the adaptive toolbox contains a number of these "middle-range" tools, not a single hammer for all purposes.'

On the face of it, having to trust heuristics may seem disadvantageous, especially since they are not foolproof. Gigerenzer and Selten (2002) suggest not. They ask us to consider a thought experiment in which two teams are set the task of designing a robot that can catch a ball (no such robot exists). One team adopts the unbounded 'omniscientific' approach and programmes a robot with all the necessary **knowledge** of the projected parabolas a ball might follow, along with myriad other instruments to perform the calculations that will get the robot to the right place to wait and catch the ball. The other team study what cricketers or baseball players actually do (the first team dismisses this idea because, since sportsmen aren't conscious of the measurements and calculations they are using when they catch a ball, interviewing them or watching them would serve no purpose). On the basis of this approach, they programme the robot to follow what has been called the *gaze heuristic*. The robot does not move immediately the ball is airborne. Instead, it makes a rough estimate of whether the ball is going to land in front of it or behind it. The robot then starts running in the appropriate direction, whilst fixing its gaze on the ball and adjusting its running speed so that the angle between the eye and the ball remains the same. Using this method, the robot does not need to calculate where the ball will land. Provided it can move quickly enough, it will catch the ball whilst it is running.

Many such heuristics have been identified. They include the *recognition heuristic*, by which we tend to assign higher value to objects with which we are familiar and the *contagion heuristic*, by which we tend to avoid contact with objects that have come into contact with other objects we regard as contaminated. Emotions may be heuristics. Faced with a dangerous animal, for example, fear puts our body into the state it needs to be in to either fight or run away: we don't need to reason ourselves into feeling frightened (though we sometimes try to reason our way out of it).

There are clear implications for **pragmatics**. After all, the central question in pragmatics is how it is that hearers accurately and seemingly effortlessly infer speaker **meaning**. Heuristics would seem to be an appropriate choice. Levinson (2000) makes use of what he calls an 'I-heuristic', which yields default **inferences** in the form of conclusions that are automatically drawn but may be overruled by contextual information. **Relevance theory**'s cognitive approach (Sperber and Wilson 1995) sees cognition and **communication** as relying heavily on fast and frugal heuristics, which make it possible to pick out potentially relevant inputs to cognitive processes and process them in a way that enhances their relevance. Both these approaches diverge from more traditional, Gricean accounts of intentional communication (Grice 1989) – indeed, from philosophical characterizations of utterance comprehension generally – which rationally reconstruct the comprehension process in the form of conscious and reflective inferences about the mental states of others.

Having said that, it's worth noticing that in more recently published work, Grice (2001b: 17) describes a view of inference in which inferential processes did not always have to be conscious and explicit: 'we have … a "hard way" of making inferential moves; [a] laborious, step-by-step procedure [which] consumes time and energy … A substitute for the hard way, the quick way, … made possible by habituation and intention, is [also] available to us.' Perhaps a heuristic is what **Grice** had in mind.

TIM WHARTON

See also: Artificial intelligence; cognitive pragmatics; generalized conversational implicature, theory of; Grice, H.P.; modularity of mind thesis; modular pragmatics; neo-Gricean pragmatics; philosophy of language; philosophy of mind; post-Gricean pragmatics; rationality; reasoning; relevance theory; social cognition; utterance interpretation

Suggestions for further reading

Barkow, J., Cosmides, L. and Tooby, J. (1995) *The Adapted Mind: Evolutionary Psychology and the Generation of Culture*, Oxford: Oxford University Press.
Gigerenzer, G. and Selten, R. (eds) (2002) *Bounded Rationality: The Adaptive Toolbox*, Cambridge, MA: MIT Press.

Historical Pragmatics

A mere fifteen years ago, historical pragmatics would have been an unlikely candidate for an encyclopedia of **pragmatics**. This is not to say that scholars working in earlier times were not engaged, at least occasionally, in activities that could be labelled historical pragmatics. A good example is Salmon's ([1967] 1987) study of the colloquial language of Shakespeare's Falstaff plays, which has much to say about the pragmatic functions of linguistic items in a particular historical context. However, such early studies generally lack the underpinning of pragmatic theory, and the fact that they touch on issues that might be labelled pragmatic was often a by-product of the study rather than a central focus. Moreover, such studies were disconnected: they did not represent a coherent research programme. Things began to change with the publication of various programmatic statements (Schlieben-Lange 1983; Fries 1983; Stein 1985; Jucker 1994; Sell 1994; *see also* Sitta 1980 and Busse 1991), and an emerging critical mass of relevant publications. Perhaps the key moment was the publication of Andreas H. Jucker's edited collection, *Historical Pragmatics*, in 1995. This raised the profile of the field and lent it definition. It also contributed to stabilizing its name (previously, such terms as 'new philology' (Fleischman 1990) and 'diachronic textlinguistics' (Fries 1983) had been possible candidates), though, as we shall see, this issue of labels is far from settled. The last ten years have seen a prolific growth in relevant and substantial publications and also the founding of the *Journal of Historical Pragmatics*, whose first issue appeared in the year 2000.

To appreciate the differences between the various strands of work that constitute historical pragmatics, we must first consider the fields of pragmatics and historical language studies. Work falling within what has been dubbed the Anglo-American view of pragmatics is considered distinct from other areas of language in that it deals with **context**. It is nevertheless treated as another component in a theory of language, adding to the usual phonetics, phonology, morphology, grammar/**syntax** and **semantics**. Work falling within what has been dubbed the Continental European view of pragmatics does not exclude the kind of topic areas discussed in the Anglo-American view, but it encompasses much beyond them and has a rather different perspective. Thus, pragmatics is not simply about adding a contextual dimension to a theory of language – it is a 'general cognitive, social, and cultural perspective on linguistic phenomena in relation to their usage in forms of behaviour' (Verschueren 1999: 7). There is a 'micro' versus 'macro' difference of emphasis here, which can be seen in the different focus studies have (e.g. a specific linguistic feature and a fairly limited linguistic context versus a linguistic feature, its (wider) co-text and cognitive and social contexts). This difference is also reflected in historical language studies. Historical linguistics focuses on language change. Studies typically consider a linguistic feature – a word, inflection, grammatical construction – and account for the way it changes over time, focusing largely on 'internal' issues of language change. Philology, in contrast, focuses on historical language at a particular point in time. Studies typically consider linguistic features and account for their role in relation to the text in which they appear and/or context(s) of that text. Philology also includes palaeography and text-editing. If diachronic change is considered in this tradition, the focus is on 'external' issues.

Table 3 presents three schemes for classifying research trends in historical pragmatics.

Although the three schemes can be aligned, there can be no claim of an exact match, not

least of all because they were designed for somewhat different purposes. Of particular note is the fact that the status of 'historical pragmatics' as a superordinate label is not secure. An illustration of this concerns the historical entries in the *Handbook of Pragmatics* (Horn and Ward 2004) and the *Handbook of Discourse Analysis* (Schiffrin *et al.* 2001). Traugott's (2004) contribution to the former is labelled 'Historical Pragmatics', yet focuses solely on what falls into the 'micro' category. Brinton's (2001) contribution to the latter is labelled 'Historical Discourse Analysis', and discusses work in all categories represented in the middle column of the table. This division clearly suited the remit of these volumes: Horn and Ward (2004) take an Anglo-American view of pragmatics, and thus appropriated the term 'historical pragmatics' for what would be encompassed within this narrow view, leaving the broader vision to fall under the term **'discourse'** (*see also* Jucker *et al.* (1999) and the notion of 'historical dialogue analysis'). The debate here is not just about labels: a full pragmatic account needs to encompass more than the micro. As even Traugott (2004: 560) states:

> [h]istorical pragmatics requires going beyond decontextualised examples of semantic change, and paying attention to the discourse contexts in which the changes occur. To achieve a full picture, a macro-approach taking external factors such as cultural changes into consideration is, of course, also necessary.

Let us consider the earliest scheme presented in Table 3, that of Jacobs and Jucker (1995), in more detail. Pragmaphilology involves studying the pragmatics of historical texts at a particular point of time, focusing on 'the contextual aspects of historical texts, including the addressers and addressees, their social and personal relationship, the physical and social setting of text pro-

Table 3 Three schemes for classifying research trends in historical pragmatics

Arnovick (1999)	Brinton (2001)	Jacobs and Jucker (1995)
Micro	Discourse-oriented historical linguistics	Pragma-historical linguistics
	Diachronically oriented discourse analysis	Diachronic pragmatics
Macro	Historical discourse analysis proper	Pragmaphilology

duction and text reception, and the goal(s) of the text' (Jacobs and Jucker 1995: 11). Examples include the discussion of **advertising** (Gotti 2005), news discourse (Jucker 2005), letters (Fitzmaurice 2002), courtroom discourse (Kryk-Kastovsky 2006a), and work on specific literary texts (Magnusson 1999 on Shakespeare and Pakkala-Weckström 2005 on Chaucer). (Further examples are to be found in the collections by Skaffari *et al.* (2005) and Dossena and Taavitsainen (2006).) Diachronic pragmatics involves studying change in pragmatic phenomena over time, focusing on 'the linguistic inventory and its communicative use across different historical stages of the same language' (Jacobs and Jucker 1995: 11). Within this category Jacobs and Jucker (1995) make a further distinction, based on methodology. Some studies proceed on a 'form to function' basis, i.e. they consider how a particular form has undergone functional change. Studies might track, for example, lexical or grammatical material such as pragmatic/**discourse markers** (for example, *while, well, indeed, even*) (Brinton 1996; Jucker 1997; Traugott and Dasher 2002: chapter 4); **speech act** verbs (for example, of promising, cursing, complimenting) (Traugott 1991; *see also* Culpeper and Semino 2000; and Taavitsainen and Jucker 2007); or terms of address (some papers in Taavitsainen and Jucker 2003). Other studies proceed on a 'function to form' basis, i.e. they consider how a particular function has changed the forms it employs. Studies might track particular speech act functions (Arnovick 1999; some papers in Jucker and Taavitsainen 2008), social functions such as (im)**politeness** (some papers in Culpeper and Kádár, to appear), or genre functions (Biber and Finegan 1997). Pragmahistorical linguistics involves studying the role of pragmatics in language change. Pragmatics is understood here in a fairly restricted sense, usually relating to discourse or **information structure**/processing. Typical exemplars of this strand of work have considered the role of pragmatics in word-order change (Bech 1998; Bernardez and Tejada 1995).

Any attempt to classify academic work involves a certain amount of simplification. Many of the studies cited in the above paragraph cannot be considered 'pure' examples of a particular strand of research in historical pragmatics. Often, it is more a matter of emphasis and perspective. In particular, the boundary between pragmaphilology and diachronic pragmatics is fuzzy. Many studies focus on a particular linguistic aspect in a particular text and context. To some extent, these studies could be considered pragmaphilological. However, they are unlike the studies mentioned in the above paragraph in that they are less holistic, having a specific focus on a particular linguistic feature or set of features, much as one would find in diachronic pragmatic studies. In fact, these studies do make a contribution to diachronic pragmatic endeavours by filling in part of the diachronic picture. They often mention diachronic issues, typically by citing other studies of the same linguistic phenomena for other periods (rather than undertaking the research themselves). In a sense, then, we have an intermediary category, which we might label 'diachronic pragmaphilology'. Example studies include Hope (1994), Busse (2002) and Walker (2007) on the English second-person pronouns *you* and *thou* in specific genres (mostly witness depositions and drama) in specific periods; Archer (2005) on **questions** and answers in the English courtroom of 1640 to 1760; and Brown and Gilman (1989) and Kopytko (1995a) on linguistic politeness in Shakespeare's plays.

The conceptual and theoretical apparatus of historical pragmatic studies is various, but, broadly speaking, as we move from the more micro to the more macro, we move from the more cognitive and universal to the more social and local. Elizabeth C. Traugott's work has played a significant role in shaping the theoretical input to the more micro approaches. Traugott (1982) hypothesized that meanings of linguistic expressions tend to shift from propositional to interpersonal meanings, with quite often an intermediate stage of textual **meaning** (these categories of meaning, of course, echo those of Halliday, e.g. Halliday 1978). A good example is Jucker's (1997) discussion of how *well* developed into a pragmatic marker with the potential for expressing interpersonal meanings (compare 'I am never well', an assertion about health or well-being, and 'Well, I never!', an expression of surprise). Such processes of change are sometimes discussed under the label '**grammaticalization**', to which Traugott's work has contributed much (*see also* Traugott's later notion of 'subjectification' (Traugott 1989, 1995) and her notion of 'intersubjectification' (Traugott 2003)). Other authors (e.g. Erman and Kotsinas 1993) have preferred to talk of 'pragmaticalization', because items such as pragmatic markers can be seen as lying outside the grammar and not having grammatical functions. This, however, rather depends on what you consider 'the grammar' to be. Traugott and Dasher (2002: 158–59) argue that pragmatic markers belong to the grammar, just as one would consider, for example, sentence adverbials to be part of the grammar. Whatever the label, the processes of change discussed are in fact fairly similar, both involving the increasing importance of meanings considered typically pragmatic. The development of pragmatic meanings in relation to semantic change has been explained in terms of **Grice**'s conversational **implicature** (particularly as developed in **Neo-Gricean pragmatics**). Thus, one-off, context-sensitive, particularized implicatures are said to evolve into preferred, contextually-stable generalized implicatures, which may then become part of the semantic meaning of the item (*cf.* Levinson 2000). Of particular note here is Traugott's invited inferencing theory of semantic change, which aims at providing a full, step-by-step account of how pragmatic meanings develop (Traugott 1999; Traugott and Dasher 2002).

More macro historical pragmatic work (leaning towards pragmaphilology) is not in fact generally atheoretical, despite non-pragmatic historical language philology often being so. Theories or at least concepts, often cultural and/or social in orientation and drawn from diverse fields of study, are used to account for how pragmatic meanings are generated and interpreted in particular contexts, and for how those very contexts are to be analyzed and understood. To take just one example, the work of the cognitive-sociologist Ervin Goffman is deployed both indirectly via face-oriented politeness theories, and directly in studies such as Bax (2001), which uses Goffman's notion of frame analysis (Goffman 1974). Typically, the theories and concepts used were not devised for historical purposes, which leads to the crucial issue of the applicability or otherwise of a particular theory or concept.

In fact, pragmatic theories are not only based on and devised for relatively recent language, but are also largely based on and devised for spoken data. But there are no actual records of spoken data prior to the invention of the tape-recorder. All, however, is not lost. For one thing, as we go further back into the past the gap between the characteristics of writing and of speech narrows. As Fleischman puts it:

> I am convinced that many of the disconcerting properties of medieval vernacular texts [...] can find more satisfying explanations if we first of all acknowledge the extent to which our texts structure information the way a spoken language does, and then proceed to the linguistic literature that explores the pragmatic underpinning of parallel phenomena in naturally occurring discourse.
>
> (1990: 23)

Further, much can be inferred about spoken interaction from historical speech-related text-types (e.g. trial proceedings, play-texts, didactic works in dialogue form), as well as from more colloquial written genres such as personal letters (*see* Culpeper and Kytö 2000). It is worth noting that how colloquial a particular genre is at a particular point in time is partly culturally determined. Thus, personal letters in East Asia are traditionally considerably more formal than their European counterparts. There is also secondary data available in the form of conversation manuals, prescribing modes of approved conversational behaviour. A more radical approach, and one that is gaining ground, is to recognize that pragmatics need not be constrained by medium (*cf.* Stein 1992). Indeed, more recent research has pointed out the interactional qualities of written language (*cf.* G. Myers 1999). Jacobs and Jucker (1995: 10) rightly argue that 'written texts can be analyzed as communicative acts in their own right'. Any pragmatic discussion of a linguistic feature in a historical text must, therefore, take on board the fact that a, if not the, key contextual aspect of that feature will be the genre of which it is a part.

Methodologically, historical pragmatics encounters huge challenges (see the discussions in Jacobs and Jucker 1995; Jucker 2000; Fitzmaurice and

Taavitsainen 2007). One particular difficulty attends diachronic pragmatics. If one tracks a particular function and how it changes the forms it employs, one needs to assume that the particular function one is tracking is stable (if the enterprise is to be meaningful). But this assumption cannot be strongly held. For example, if tracking the speech act of **apology** over time, one may observe different forms being employed. Simultaneously, however, what actually counts as an apology may be changing as well, so that the forms one observes do not have a stable relationship with a function. As Jacobs and Jucker (1995: 19) point out, illocutionary force is not clearly the best *tertium comparationis*. A further methodological problem for historical pragmatics is that many of the methods of synchronic pragmatics (e.g. questionnaires, discourse completion tasks or role-plays) are unavailable because the interactants of that period are dead. Instead, methodological approaches include, on the one hand, detailed qualitative analyses, often drawing upon social historical research and/or contemporary social commentaries in order to help reconstruct contexts. While some have argued that it is impossible to reconstruct speaker meaning in the past (Stetter 1991: 74, 79, cited in Arnovick 1999: 12), approximate reconstructions are possible. In fact, even studies on present-day data rely on approximate reconstruction. On the other hand, the use of corpus-based methods by which researchers reveal and/or track patterns of usage, relationships with the co-text and aspects of context, are becoming increasingly popular (e.g. Jucker and Taavitsainen 2008).

JONATHAN CULPEPER

See also: Anglo-American and European Continental traditions; corpus linguistics; cross-cultural pragmatics; discourse; discourse markers; discourse particles; generalized conversational implicature, theory of; grammaticalization; implicature; inference; information structure; neo-Gricean pragmatics; parentheticals; politeness; semantics

Suggestions for further reading

Brinton, L.J. (2004) 'Historical discourse analysis', in D. Schiffrin, D. Tannen and H.E. Hamilton (eds) *The Handbook of Discourse Analysis*, Oxford: Blackwell.
Jacobs, A. and Jucker, A.H. (1995) 'The historical perspective in pragmatics', in A.H. Jucker (ed.) *Historical Pragmatics: Pragmatic Developments in the History of English*, Amsterdam: John Benjamins.

History of Pragmatics

Pragmatics, the study of language use in social situations, is a fairly recent addition to the language sciences. The term 'pragmatics' is generally said to date back to the 1930s work of the semiotician and behaviourist Charles **Morris** and his distinction between the three parts of **semiotics**: syntactics, **semantics** and pragmatics. The foundations for pragmatics as a linguistic discipline are rooted in the work of ordinary language philosophers and speech act theorists, such as Ludwig **Wittgenstein**, John L. **Austin**, John **Searle** and Herbert P. **Grice**. From the 1970s onwards pragmatics split into a more formal (Huang 2007) and more functional enterprise (Mey 2001). This discussion focuses on the history of pragmatics (from the Greek *prâgma* = act) as a study of linguistic action and interaction in society (Nerlich and Clarke 1996) and in particular on its origin in five approaches which one can distinguish in Europe and America: (1) the British approach which emerged from **ordinary language philosophy** with Wittgenstein, Austin and Searle, and which has dominated the field until the present; (2) the school of British contextualism and functionalism; (3) the French approach which is based on the theory of enunciation elaborated by Emile Benveniste; (4) the German approach, which is associated with the critical theory movement around Jürgen **Habermas** and Karl Otto Apel, and saw pragmatics as part of a general theory of (communicative) action. The Austinian conception of pragmatics was successfully amalgamated with those developed in France and in Germany. These traditions were affiliated in various ways with (5) the development of American **pragmatism** as a new philosophy which emerged in the United States in the latter part of the nineteenth century, and which made the three-way split between syntactics, semantics and pragmatics popular in linguistics, philosophy and semiotics.

A pragmatic perspective on language has its deeper roots in antiquity, that is in **rhetoric**, as one of the three 'liberal arts' or the 'trivium' (rhetoric, grammar, logic). This triple distinction is mirrored in Morris's semiotic triplet, and in the 'pragmatic perspective' adopted by medieval theologians reflecting on the efficacy or power of words and phrases in religious and other rituals (Rosier-Catach 1994, 2004). The pragmatic perspective is also based in Immanuel Kant's philosophy of the 'active (transcendental) subject' and John Locke's philosophy of the 'semiotic act' (Taylor 1992). However, unlike Givón (2005), I would not say that Kant's work was the opening to modern pragmatics.

The various strands of thought which built on these older foundations clustered around certain pragmatic keywords which are still central to pragmatic thinking today:

British (1)	speech act, **meaning**, use, **intention**
British (2)	**context**, situation, function
German	agenthood of (transcendental) subject, dialogue, pronouns, speech act
French	subjectivity, markers of subjectivity, **indexicals**, enunciation
American	meaning as action, the triadic sign relation.

Many of those generating pragmatic insights *avant la lettre* rejected an older philosophical theorem, namely, that language represents thoughts (or ideas), and that only language that represents thoughts or the world is worthy of philosophical inquiry. For pragmatic thinkers, by contrast, language is not only there to represent true or false states of affairs, but it is used to influence others in certain ways, to communicate with others, to act upon others, and to make them act in certain ways, even to change the world.

In Germany, the representational theory of language was undermined in the tradition of Kant. Kant's theory of the active organizing powers of the mind gave impetus to a **philosophy of language** based on the mental but intrinsically dialogical acts of the speaker and hearer, especially in the works of Johann Severin Vater, August Ferdinand Bernhardi, and Wilhelm von Humboldt, which were published during the first two decades of the nineteenth century.

In Britain, the representational theory of language was overthrown in the writings of the Scottish school of common sense philosophy, in particular the work of Thomas Reid. According to Reid, Aristotle had been wrong in relegating the study of speech acts other than the **proposition** to the rhetoric wastebasket. Reid wants to study what came to be known as speech acts, such as **questions**, **commands** and promises. He stressed that, unlike the statement, these other sentences are fundamentally 'social operations', because their success necessarily depends on the uptake by others. Reid's views on language spread widely, from Scotland to England, mainly Cambridge, to the United States and to France. One Cambridge philosopher, who knew Scottish common sense philosophy just as well as Kantianism, was John Grote. In the 1860s, he developed a theory of meaning as use and of thinking as a social activity based on **communication** (Gibbins 2007). His focus on 'living meaning' as opposed to 'fossilized' or historical meaning had parallels with the theory of meaning developed by Michel Bréal at the same time and can be regarded as a direct precursor of ordinary language philosophy.

Whereas Reid had mainly focused on speech acts as social acts and thus contributed to **speech act theory** *avant la lettre*, the English philosopher Benjamin Humphrey Smart developed around 1830 a contextualist theory of meaning or 'sematology' as his contribution to a general theory of signs. He took up Locke's threefold division of **knowledge** into (1) *physicology* or the study of nature, (2) *practology* or the study of human action, and (3) *sematology*, the study of the use of signs for our knowledge. For Smart, sematology (as later semiotics for Morris, and going back to the medieval trivium) had three parts: grammar, logic, and rhetoric. In all three parts Smart makes it clear that signs do not 'mean' ideas, they are *used* to mean something in *context*, something he had learned from the Scottish common sense philosophy.

Another follower of Reid's philosophy, the Frenchman Adolphe Garnier, formulated, around 1850, a theory of speech acts (orders and promises, for example) which sounds astonishingly modern and takes into account the **power** relations involved in giving and accepting orders. However, Garnier's speech act theory went almost unnoticed. It was only at the beginning of the twentieth century that the legal philosopher Adolf Reinach formulated a similar, but much more elaborate, theory of speech acts, or what Reinach called, with Reid, 'social acts', based, in part, on Edmund Husserl's phenomenology (Vonk 1992).

In Germany as elsewhere psychology gradually began to inspire pragmatic insights. Friedrich Herbart proposed that language could only be understood in the context of human action. This view was repeated (without direct reference to Herbart, but totally in his spirit) by William Dwight Whitney in the United States (who also stressed the social dimension of language as an institution and inspired Ferdinand de Saussure), by Johan Nicolai Madvig in Denmark (who stressed the role of context and developed, like Grote and later Wittgenstein, a theory of meaning as use; Hauger 1994), and by Philipp Wegener in Germany (who studied not only language in context, but also what he called the 'dialogic speech-act', and what Grice later called 'conversational **implicatures**').

Inspired by French and German psychology, the father of 'semantics', Michel Bréal, began to study how language is used to express emotions, beliefs, wishes, and demands, that is, to accomplish speech acts. He also analyzed the traces left in speech of the speaker using language, as for example the function of markers like *nevertheless*, *hopefully*, etc. Furthermore, like Reid and others, he criticized what Austin later called the 'descriptive fallacy' in linguistic thinking and proclaimed that language is not only there to say things like 'the cat is on the mat' but also to express desires, demands and volition. The topic of subjectivity in language formed the basis of a new theory of enunciation, as elaborated by Charles Bally, Gustave Guillaume and Emile Benveniste.

Bréal not only initiated a study of subjectivity and indexicality in language, he also promoted a functionalist approach to language. For Bréal, as for other 'functionalists' of that time (such as Wegener and later Gardiner), function was the primary force of language change. Forms do not change in sound or meaning all by themselves, but because they are used with a specific function by the language user in **discourse** and in a certain situation. Other French functionalists were the psychologists Frédéric Paulhan and Henri Delacroix. Paulhan, in particular, established an explicit theory of speech acts in the context of a theory of linguistic functions which is directly comparable to that developed by Karl Bühler in Germany. Using an example that has become commonplace in pragmatic writing, he pointed out that one can say that a statement such as 'It's raining' has been understood if the addressee takes an umbrella when he leaves the house. We don't have to look at mental **representation** but at human behaviour instead.

The German functionalists and speech act theorists *avant la lettre* at the turn of the nineteenth to the twentieth century, especially Anton Marty and Karl Bühler, were influenced by rationalist linguists such as Whitney, Madvig, Wegener, and Bréal. They were also influenced by new developments in psychology, such as the descriptive psychology or act psychology developed by Franz Brentano, the psychology of Gestalt, phenomenological psychology, as well as developments in social behaviourism.

As early as 1908, Marty developed a synchronic and functional semasiology which included pragmatic insights, and which was strongly influenced by Brentano's philosophy and Wegener's theory of language. Bühler (who was also a great admirer of Wegener) was working in the context of the Würzburg school of psychology, and he knew the work of Marty and Husserl well. He established the most elaborate theory of pragmatics in Germany, of which his organon model was the central part. In this model he places the linguistic sign in its context of use, bringing into the model the speaker and hearer (forgotten in the semiotic triangle popularized by Charles K. Ogden and Ivor A. Richards) and the reference to 'things'. The organon model, depicted by a triangle overlaid upon a circle, shows that every sign is at one and the same time a symptom (indicator, index) by virtue of its dependence on the sender (whose internal state it expresses), a signal by virtue of its appeal to the recipient (whose behaviour it controls), and a symbol by virtue of its assignment to the objects and states of affairs (to which it refers). And so, every sentence is at one at the same time *expression*, *appeal*, and *representation*. These are also the three main functions of language use.

This functional and semiotic theory of language was further elaborated by linguists, such as Erwin Koschmieder. In the 1930s he discussed speech acts, especially what came to be known as performatives, such as *Hiermit eröffne ich die Versammlung* ('I hereby open the meeting, i.e. declare the meeting to be opened'), and he also pointed out that *Hiermit schreibe ich einen Brief* ('I am hereby writing a letter') is impossible.

At the same time, the English school of contextualism (Sir Alan Henderson Gardiner, Bronislaw Malinowski, John Rupert Firth) also rediscovered the 'power of words' in context. Gardiner wanted to analyze 'acts of speech', Firth whole 'speech events', and Malinowski, the anthropologist, wanted to study meaning as action in the context of situation (Senft 2007).

Charles Morris is well known for having introduced the tripartition of semiotics into *semantics*, as the study of the relationship between words and the world, *syntactics*, as the study of the relationship between words and words, and *pragmatics*, as the study of the relationship between words and their users. Morris was inspired in part by some principles of American pragmatism (Charles Sanders **Peirce** and William James), but also by Charles Ogden and Ivor Armstrong Richards's theory of signs and symbols, as well as by developments in logical positivism and behaviourism.

The problem of 'meaning' became the focus of philosophical thinking worldwide, but especially in England, from the turn of the century until the mid-twentieth century, leading up to the 'linguistic' and then 'pragmatic' turns in the philosophy of language, inaugurated by ordinary language philosophy. Many psychologists, philosophers and linguists shared what the pragmatist philosopher John Dewey called a 'pragmatic *Weltanschauung*'. This was not unknown to Austin, who had read Gardiner, Morris, Peirce, Wittgenstein and others. However, it seems that Austin did not wish to be associated, either with the contextualist-functionalist pragmatics developed on his doorstep, nor with the pragmatist, behaviourist and semiotic pragmatics developed on the other side of the ocean by Morris, nor with the formal type of pragmatics developed by

ideal language philosophers, such as Rudolf Carnap. He rejected Morris's tripartition of semiotics which divided up what was to be regarded as a whole, namely, actual language use or 'the way we use words in situations' (Austin [1940] 1963). Surprisingly, Austin did not use the term 'pragmatics' (the last component in the triadic model of semiotics) in this article, as he implicitly argues for an integration of syntactics and semantics into pragmatics. And this is where modern pragmatics begins.

BRIGITTE NERLICH

See also: Anglo-American and European Continental traditions; Austin, J.L.; context; contextualism; Grice, H.P.; Habermas, J.; meaning; Morris, C.; ordinary language philosophy; Peirce, C.S.; philosophy of language; pragmatics; pragmatism; rhetoric; Searle, J.; semantics; semiotics; societal pragmatics; speech act theory; Wittgenstein, L.

Suggestions for further reading

Nerlich, B. (2005) 'History of pragmatics', in K. Brown (ed.) *Encyclopedia of Language and Linguistics*, Amsterdam: Elsevier.

Nerlich, B. and Clarke, D.D. (1996) *Language, Action, and Context: The Early History of Pragmatics in Europe and America, 1780–1930*, Amsterdam and Philadelphia, PA: John Benjamins.

——(1999) 'Protopragmatic theories of language, 1780–1930', in P. Schmitter (ed.) *Geschichte der Sprachtheorie, Volume 4: Sprachtheorien der Neuzeit II: Der Epistemologische Kontext Neuzeitlicher Sprach- und Grammatiktheorien*, Tübingen: Gunter Narr Verlag.

Honorific Language

All human languages contain expressions that are recognized by their speakers as pertaining to matters of respect or deference. Such repertoires are thereby associated with a socio-pragmatic model of conduct: acts of uttering certain expressions are understood as acts of deference, as ways of performing respect to others, while other expressions are contrastively associated with the absence of deference, or with disrespect and rudeness. Given their cross-linguistic ubiquity, such 'honorific' forms have been the subject of extensive comparative study (*see* Agha 1994 for a review of the literature). Indeed, the range of studies now available has transformed our understanding of how language serves to mark deference relations and, by extension, social relations of many other kinds (Agha 2007).

In the older literature on this topic, the term 'honorific' is used narrowly for *positively*-valued, *referent*-focal, *lexemic* signs of *deference* to interlocutory *others*. However, each of these italicized expressions represents a specific value of a distinct typological variable, all of which together define a larger space of cross-cultural and cross-linguistic variation: (1) The presence of *positively*-valued honorifics creates correlative partitions within a language of neutral or negatively-valued repertoires, yielding a punctuated cline of deference level and polarity (at the other end of which lie forms of abuse and profanation, Leach 1966). (2) The person to whom deference is indexed may be the utterance's *referent* or the incumbent of some other speech-act role, such as addressee, bystander, or overhearer; deference to more than one such indexical focus (Agha 1993) may be implemented concurrently in a single utterance, though languages differ in the subtlety and complexity of such effects. (3) Honorific repertoires often contain non-*lexemic* signs, including sentence-configurational, prosodic, gestural, and other signs, and thus differ in semiotic range (Agha 2007: 179–85). (4) Patterns of *deference* are often linked to cultural models of more specialized types of conduct, e.g. taboo, avoidance, **gender** roles, courtly ritual, class relations, the propitiation of kin, ancestors, or deities, and thereby differ in sociological valence relative to these models. (5) Differences in patterns of deference to *others* are readily linked to matters of self-presentation and demeanour, and thus to effects at distinct orders of indexicality (Silverstein 1996) from which individuals acquire ascribed statuses and identities. Locating the narrow concerns of the early literature within this larger typological frame is essential to the comparative study of honorific language.

The honorific forms of a language never comprise a distinct 'language' (in the sense of a separate and complete grammatical system). They belong to distinct socio-pragmatic registers of conduct in which linguistic and non-linguistic

signs are often deployed together. An honorific register is a reflexive model of pragmatic behaviour that treats selected behaviours, including the use of linguistic expressions, as stereotypically indexical of deference (Agha 1998). Although honorific repertoires occur in all languages, they differ cross-linguistically in repertoire size (number of expressions), grammatical range (number of form-classes in which they are found), prosodic qualities, and other features. All known languages possess honorific titles and terms of address (e.g. noun phrase categories such as names, kin terms, occupational or other social role designators, and corresponding nouns and noun classifiers that function as status-differentiating titles), though such expressions differ across languages in repertoire size, grammatical range, deference level, polarity, and the relative ranking of repertoires. Honorific pronouns are cross-linguistically common and, in many languages, pronominal repertoires are extremely large due to the pronoun-like use of person-denoting common nouns (Agha 2007: 278–300, 308–10). Many languages differentiate honorific forms for common nouns and verbs (e.g. Tibetan, Urdu, Japanese, Persian, Samoan) and dependent categories such as case markers (Korean) and other inflectional forms (Agha 2007: Chapter 7). Javanese has more than 800 such lexemes, from which many more complex locutions can be formed, while in Japanese honorifics are differentiated by productive morphological affixes so that the number of expressions is indefinitely large. In many languages, honorific utterances tend to have a characteristic pitch, speech rate, amplitude, or other prosodic quality (Irvine 1990, 1992). In many others, the use of linguistic honorifics is normatively accompanied by characteristic non-linguistic behaviours, such as distinctive patterns of bodily comportment, gesture, eye-gaze, and the like, which comprise more or less elaborate systems of etiquette (Errington 1988; Haviland 1979; Kummer 1992).

The fact that honorific registers are reflexive models of conduct has several implications for the study of honorific language. First, honorific expressions cannot be identified by linguists without appeal to metapragmatic judgements of register value by native speakers. Although some honorific expressions are marked by grammatical affixes in many languages, other expressions in any language carry no overt morphemic mark identifying them as such (*see* Agha 1998 for examples and discussion). Thus, the only general method of identification available to linguists relies on the ability of native speakers to differentiate honorific expressions (including criterial affixes) from the rest of the language and to typify their values-in-use. The range of metapragmatic activities relevant to the study of honorifics is much wider than traditional elicitation. It includes naturally occurring metapragmatic commentaries on types of speech, speakers, social settings and scenarios of use, as well as purely implicit evaluations (including non-descriptive cues in response behaviours) that discriminate the appropriateness or lack thereof of naturally occurring speech forms in **context** (Agha 2007).

Second, all speakers of a language do not acquire or adhere to perfectly identical models of its honorific registers, and such variation is itself socially consequential. For complex systems (e.g. Javanese, Japanese, Tibetan) not all speakers are able to identify all honorific forms. Some speakers routinely treat specific social categories of persons (e.g. upper-class or aristocratic speakers) as better able to describe the purest forms of positively valued honorific speech, treating other social categories of speakers as less proficient, less able to grasp the nuances of the system. Hence, stereotypes about the indexical values of expressions are internally linked to metasemiotic judgements about exemplary and non-exemplary speakers, to judgements about their mental, and characterological qualities, and dependent conceptions of their group-relative social entitlements. Such frameworks for evaluating social identity typically function **culture**-internally as multi-level and internally motivated semiotic diagrams for inferring the characteristics of co-present interlocutors in social interaction (Agha 1998).

Third, the continuous historical existence of a register depends upon mechanisms for the replication of its forms and values over changing populations (e.g. from generation to generation). The group of users of any register continuously renews itself through demographic changes of various kinds (births, deaths, migration, etc.). Hence, the differentiable existence of that register – an awareness of its forms, values, and

appropriate use – must be communicable to new members of the group in order for the register to persist in some relatively constant way over time. Socialization within the family plays a role in the early acquisition of many registers. However, processes of register socialization continue through adult life as well. Although explicit prescriptions play a role in one or more of the institutions through which registers are replicated across populations, more implicit metapragmatic activity, such as jocular accounts of defective speech (Agha 1998), the implicit modelling of speech for bystanders (Errington 1998), mass media representations of defective speech, metadiscursive practices of schooling, and many others, also play a role (Agha 2003).

Finally, register models are ideologically inflected frameworks for reckoning social conduct. To say that models of register value exist in a society is merely to say that socially regular patterns of metapragmatic evaluation can be observed and documented as data. However, several models often compete with each other society-internally and, insofar as they co-exist within a single society, appear to be mutually distorting ideological alternatives in one or more sense. For instance, speakers may differ in the elaborateness of the repertoires they command (Errington 1988: 168), often caused by differences of socialization, or in the values they assign to specific forms within larger repertoires. Some forms of any honorific register are subject to competing valorizations that serve the positional interests of specific social groups and institutions (Hill 1992; Agha 2003). Any given speaker's judgements about honorific usage invariably reflect a socially positioned perspective on the register. If the individual is socialized to its institutionally dominant form, the model evidenced in his or her judgements, while socially positioned, may also have a very wide social domain (i.e. may also be evidenced in the metapragmatic judgements of many individuals) and may reflect an institutionally legitimated or 'official position' on the register.

Honorific register systems are thus social indexical sign systems of considerable interest. They infuse grammatical organization with sociopragmatic values through the work of ideologies and institutions. Such value-frameworks differentiate and rank specific forms of conduct (and actors who engage in such conduct) in ways that semiotically motivate distinctive patterns of exemplary behaviour, social interaction, positional entitlement, classifications of persons into entitlement-bearing groups, and other features of social organization. The continuance of such value-mediated frameworks depends on the continued vitality of the ideologies and institutions that replicate register models in social life. Needless to say, any such register model is subject to dialectical tensions of the kinds discussed above, and is thus subject to periods of emergence, growth, or decline in the face of competing models (Agha 2007: 206–32, 268–77).

Our current understanding of these systems derives from, but moves considerably beyond, the results of early work on this topic (*see* Agha 1994: 278–86 for a review of the early literature). Brown and Gilman's (1960) study of polite pronouns gave the field its early impetus by suggesting that cultural ideologies of hierarchy and egalitarianism (or '**power**' and 'solidarity') can be linked directly to patterns of language use. Yet, many of their limiting assumptions – that polite expressions 'semantically' encode preexisting relationships, that pronouns are polite expressions of pre-eminent interest, that cultural norms and ideologies are uniformly shared within societies – have been superseded by later research. Attempts to reconstruct honorific norms as abstract rules in various neo-Gricean frameworks (Lakoff 1973; Leech 1983; Brown and Levinson 1987) fail to account for the cross-cultural diversity of norms attested in the comparative record (Gu 1990; Hymes 1986; Matsumoto 1988, 1989). A more poignant difficulty with such approaches is their inability to theorize society-internal variation. It is now well known that speakers differ in patterns of honorific usage within every known language community (Hill 1992; Irvine 1992; Errington 1988), and that such differences themselves constitute society-internal emblems of speaker distinction from which persons draw entitlement to deference by others (Agha 1998). Once we recognize that patterns of honorific usage within register systems link respectfulness (to others) to respectability (of self), the study of such systems requires a shift from rule-based explanations (of other-directed norms) to a reflexive account of the capacity of sign systems concurrently to index

several types of role and relationship under specifiable conditions (Agha 2007: Chapters 6 and 7).

Differences of indexical focus (i.e. of the contextual target of deference) are also linked to differences of repertoire type. Some honorific repertoires (e.g. Australian affinal vocabularies) mark deference to co-present others, such as addressees and bystanders. Others (e.g. Tibetan *sÈeÙsa*) mark deference to any referent that can be denoted by a linguistic expression, whether or not such referent is co-present, alive, as yet born, or directly perceivable (deities, etc.). In addressee and bystander systems, any semiotic display that is perceivable by a co-present person – linguistic expressions, **prosody**, gestures, modes of bodily comportment, clothing, etc. – can become culturally enregistered as indexical of deference to that person (Haviland 1979; Errington 1988; Kummer 1992). However, referent-focal repertoires tend to consist only of linguistic expressions since, in such cases, the default focus of deference is identified not through interlocutory co-presence but through linguistic denotation (Agha 2007: 317ff.). Many languages contain repertoires of several kinds, varying in degrees of elaboration.

Any honorific register mediates social relations of a range and variety larger than what is ideologically grasped in native stereotypes of indexicality. This is due to a simple fact: honorific expressions are rarely encountered in isolation from other co-occurring signs. Hence, the framing of honorific expressions by accompanying signs can co-textually yield various kinds of interactional tropes, such as tropes of secondary focus (deferring to one person in order to defer to another), transposed origo (deferring to someone from another's point of view), veiled aggression (using honorific forms in acts that are otherwise hostile or coercive), hyperpoliteness (as in cases of **irony** or sarcasm), and many others (for examples and discussion *see* Agha 2007: 322–32). The analytic distinction between *stereotypic indexical effects* (effects stereotypically associated with honorific forms; Agha 1998) and *text-level indexical effects* (emergent effects, mediated by text-configurations in which 'honorific' forms co-occur with other signs; Agha 2007: 24–27) thus enables the systematic study of a much wider range of social relations during acts of honorific use than is straightforwardly described by users in everyday accounts of what 'honorific language' is, and what its uses are.

ASIF AGHA

See also: Discourse; historical pragmatics; indexicals; metapragmatics; performativity; politeness; semiotics; sociolinguistics

Suggestions for further reading

Agha, A. (1994) 'Honorification', *Annual Review of Anthropology*, 23: 277–302.
——(1998) 'Stereotypes and registers of honorific language', *Language in Society*, 27: 151–93.
——(2007) *Language and Social Relations*, Cambridge: Cambridge University Press.

Humour

The term 'humour' is usually used as a technical expression that encompasses all further pre-theoretical notions in the field, such as 'comical', 'laughable', and 'ridiculous'. While the forms and genres of humour may differ widely, humour is assumed to be universal. There have been claims that some **cultures** do not have **irony** or humorous puns. However, these claims are difficult to assess, especially in light of recent studies that attest to the universal nature of punning phenomena across samples of language families (Guidi, to appear).

It is also generally assumed that humour derives from the perception of two opposed concepts (scripts/frames) that co-occur (overlap) in the text. The most common theories associated with this position are Raskin's (1985) Semantic Script Theory of Humour (SSTH) and Attardo and Raskin's General Theory of Verbal Humour (GTVH). Attardo (1997) claims that these theories fall under the cognitive and/or psychological incongruity-resolution family of humour theories (*see* Martin 2007). Other approaches utilizing the same incongruity mechanism but more or less different terminology have been proposed within different areas of linguistics.

Both the SSTH and the GTVH assume no boundary between **semantics** and **pragmatics**.

Furthermore, they claim that humorous texts violate the **cooperative principle**, for example, by withholding relevant information in order to produce a surprising punch line, as in the joke in which Holmes wakes Watson and asks what he can observe. Watson notes the position of the stars, the clouds in the night sky, and similar details. Holmes replies 'No, Watson, someone stole our tent.'

There has been some discussion of this claim by scholars seeking to deny the violation of the cooperative principle. The problem that these attempts run into is that humorous texts are often obviously untruthful, irrelevant, deliberately obscure, etc. Conversely, accounts that incorporate violations of the cooperative principle need to explain the affiliative and prosocial effects of some kinds of humour. For example, one can tell the above Watson/Holmes joke without incurring the kind of social sanctions one would incur for lying, or reporting an otherwise untruthful event. Discussion of some of these ideas can be found in Attardo (1994: Chapter 9), and Yus (2003) for relevance-theoretic accounts. It should be noted that humour may violate any pragmatic principle and in general any linguistic rule. However, the rule violation tends to be restricted to the smallest extent. Consider again the joke above. While the violation of the maxim of relevance and quantity in the failure of the speaker to inform the hearer that the tent has gone missing prior to the punch line is the source of the incongruity exploited for humour, other implicatures are drawn in a perfectly normal fashion: for example, Watson responds to Holmes completely relevantly, and presumably truthfully, etc.

The SSTH is based on and accounts for jokes, i.e. short, simple text, with usually only one source of humour. Furthermore, it is deliberately limited to the semantic/pragmatic factors described above. The GTVH broadens the scope of the theory, introducing such aspects as the target of the joke, the verbalization used, etc. The GTVH was further expanded to address long texts and texts in non-verbal modalities (while confusingly preserving the original name). Thus expanded, the GTVH interacts with **stylistics** and other approaches to literary texts. Discussion of these approaches can be found in Attardo (2001).

Most of the research in the pragmatics of humour, however, has taken place in the field of conversation/**discourse analysis**. There is no comprehensive bibliography of the field. A bibliography can be found in Attardo (2005, 2008), Norrick (1993) and Glenn (2003). A common distinction (Sacks *et al.* 1974) is between improvised contextual conversational humour and prepared, often rehearsed, acontextual humour (so-called canned jokes). However, studies have shown that the distinction is less clear cut than assumed, since canned jokes can be contextualized to varying degrees (Zajdman 1991). The placement and function of laughter was a central topic for conversation analysts. Other topics investigated include whether humour is disruptive of the conversational structure, for example in the placement of puns. The claim that this was the case, as humour tended to occur in second turns, has been challenged recently (Atonopoulou and Sifianou 2004). Other foundational studies included Tannen (1984a) and Davies (1984), which both anticipated and defined the field by studying in depth individual conversations.

Within this area of research the topic of the functions of humour in **conversation** has attracted most attention. Typically working on written **transcriptions** of conversation, these analyses focus on how speakers use humour within the interaction, for example, by creating in-group bonding among the participants. The list of functions that has emerged is clearly skewed towards the affiliative side (i.e. researchers tend to focus on solidarity rather than conflict) and much less on the aggressive side of humour (with some exceptions). Overall, the lists of functions of humour developed in sociology have not been improved upon and lately the claim that humour can have any function (within contextual admissibility) has been put forward (Priego-Valverde 2003). This would of course severely limit the interest of studies investigating functions of humour.

Other more recent approaches are based on quantitative studies and have made some startling contributions. For example, the widely held belief that women tend to produce less humour and are passive recipients of male humour (Crawford 2003; Kotthoff 2006) has been challenged by the results of Janet Holmes and her

associates (Holmes *et al.* 2001). They show that New Zealand women in a workplace setting produced more humour than men. Other studies have found no difference between the amount of humour produced by men and women (Günther 2003). Overall, it seems fair to say that studies using representative corpora of conversations have successfully challenged the previous paradigm. Other topics in variationist studies of humour with a more or less sociolinguistic slant exist. A survey can be found in Attardo (2005) and Attardo (2008).

Laughter is often confused with humour. Laughter is a specific phonatory phenomenon consisting of staccato syllables, which may occur as a reaction to a humorous exchange, but by no means always does so. In fact, research on laughter in conversation has shown that laughter can be used to signal that the upcoming turn will be humorous and that often speakers initiate laughter. Laughter may occur in situations that have no humorous aspect at all and can express embarrassment or other emotions (relief, anger). Conversely, humour may not be accompanied by laughter on delivery (the so-called 'deadpan delivery') or on reception (for instance, because the hearer may fail to comprehend a humorous turn, or may decline to participate in the humorous frame). See Chafe (2007) for further discussion of laughter.

A significant distinction, which has not received the attention it deserves, is that between humour **competence** and humour performance. Humour competence describes the set of **knowledge** needed by speakers to perform adequately in their speech community as humour producers and receivers. Humour performance captures the actual production and reception of humour in a given situation or **context** (Attardo 2003). Semantic and pragmatic theories such as the SSTH and the GTVH, and cognitive theories of humour, fall clearly under the competence side. The performance side of this distinction has been explored much less and often not in these terms. Studies on conversational data fall under the performance side. Work exists on the **prosody** of humour performance, especially the tone of voice and facial expressions associated with irony, but also on the delivery of jokes (Pickering *et al.*, to appear). Recent work in conversation/

discourse analysis is also beginning to address failure of humour, a performance topic which has been largely neglected (Hay 1994, 1996; Priego-Valverde 2003).

SALVATORE ATTARDO

See also: Cooperative principle; discourse; implicature; irony

Suggestions for further reading

Attardo, S. (1994) *Linguistic Theories of Humor*, Berlin: Mouton de Gruyter.

Chafe, W. (2007) *The Importance of Not Being Earnest: The Feeling behind Laughter and Humor*, Amsterdam and Philadelphia, PA: John Benjamins.

Martin, R. (2007) *The Psychology of Humor: An Integrative Approach*, Burlington, MA: Elsevier.

Hyperbole

Hyperbole is, according to classical rhetoric, 'a figure or trope of bold exaggeration' (Preminger 1974: 359). Overstatement more generally includes any extravagant statement of amplification used to express emotion and not to be taken literally. Overstatements can be semantically interpreted as claims higher (or lower) on some scale than warranted, as argued in Norrick (1982). At the far end of any scale of comparison we find Extreme Case Formulations (ECFs) built around extreme expressions such as *every, all, none, best, least, always, perfectly*, and *absolutely*, according to Pomerantz (1986). Thus, ECF is a sub-category of hyperbole. Pomerantz says ECFs are used mainly in complaint sequences to defend or counter challenges to accusations, justifications and so on, e.g. *You never write, She always wins, Nobody cares about me*. As Edwards (2000) demonstrates, ECFs do not adhere to any single logical formula or grammatical rule. They cut across grammatical categories, including statements containing extreme adjectives (*total, absolute*), all-quantifiers (*all, every, no, none*) and related nouns like *everybody, nothing*, adverbs (*always, never*), and phrases like *as good as it gets* and *brand new* as well as superlative constructions with optional expressions involving *ever*, e.g.

the greatest story ever told. ECF is a participants' category, describable through the empirical study of conversational interaction. Nevertheless, we can say that ECFs are generally recognizable even out of context as semantically extreme. Edwards (2000: 364) says ECFs 'do not have automatic rhetorical effects', but his findings in fact jibe rather nicely with the traditional rhetorical analysis of hyperbole as a figure of amplification by which the speaker signals emotional involvement through an exaggerated formulation (*see* Norrick (2004) for a comparison of hyperbole and ECF specifically, and McCarthy and Carter (2004) for a corpus investigation of hyperbole).

Overstatement occurs any time a speaker makes a claim higher (or lower) on some scale than warranted, while ECFs make claims involving the end points on such scales. Thus, we hear *about five thousand* in the following excerpt (from the London–Lund Corpus (LLC) 3.1) not as a literal numerical claim, but as an aggrandizement signalling emotion.

> A: I had about five thousand books to take back to Senate House yesterday.

The speaker says *five thousand books* when there are actually only ten or twenty. Overstatements and ECFs also often contain **hedges**, like *about* in the phrase *about five thousand books*, but they do not thereby necessarily lose their hyperbolic effect. Still, as Edwards (2000) points out, ECFs generally occur unhedged, because the force of ECFs is taken as doing nonliteral in any case.

Proverbs, known for their apodictic mode of expression, often employ hyperbole. Any proverb containing absolute modifiers and adverbs like *all, no, always* and *never* is likely to involve overstatement, as in *The grass is always greener on the other side*. Proverbs incorporating hyperbole, like proverbs more generally, are taken as 'doing nonliteral'. Participants in interaction treat hyperboles in proverbs as if they did not make literal statements. Instead, hyperboles signal the speaker's investment in a point, emphasizing or highlighting it, and they are taken as insisting or denying in an extreme way.

Overstatement interacts with the nonliteral in complicated ways. First, since ECFs are heard as nonliteral, counterexamples are not heard as contradictions. In saying *my brother never rings up* in the following passage (from LLC 1–12), B speaks hyperbolically rather than factually, as seen in her following statement where she goes on to confirm that he in fact does ring up (*when sh-he does ring up or when he used to*):

> A: she says none of us sort of go to see her or anything but and my brother never rings up
> B: [m]
> A: but when [sh-] he does ring up or when he used to he used to get this same tirade

Second, hyperbole may enter discourse in figurative form. In the passage below from the LLC (3–4), the speaker mixes the metaphoric hyperbole of *fry* with the ECF of *never hear a word*.

> A: they say the noise there is intolerable and that in the summer of course it's a question of fry and and be audible or um open your windows and never hear a word

Never hear a word overstates the difficulty of hearing and comprehending, while *fry* both overstates on the temperature scale and shifts metaphorically from overheated rooms to pans on cooking ranges.

Third, overstatement may be just one component of a **metaphor** in the traditional sense. In calling a teacher *an iceberg of a woman* in the following passage (from LLC 3–1), the speaker expresses herself both figuratively, in identifying a human with a mountain of ice, and hyperbolically, in choosing *iceberg* rather than some more appropriate vehicle in temperature and size.

> A: There was A and B and some other bitchy iceberg of a woman

Instead of a simple overstatement like *absolutely unfeeling*, the speaker deploys an image with extreme connotations.

Fourth, though somewhat less obviously, even an explicit comparison between a human and a snail, as in the example below from the LLC (3–1), creates a tension between incongruent domains.

> A: … and Arabella poor Arabella was lame and walked [s]
> B: [m]

> A: you know slower than a snail

Again *slower than a snail* is hyperbolic in overstating the slowness of the pace via comparison with a snail. Moreover, according to Ortony (1979a, 1979b), any time the vehicle for a comparison comes from a category without obvious relevance for the object, the incongruity will have a metaphoric feel to it and may draw attention to itself. Thus, even similes like that in the foregoing example are metaphoric to varying degrees. When the explicit comparison *as slow as a snail* becomes implicit in the phrase *snails's pace*, in the continuation of the foregoing excerpt, the metaphor and overstatement remain.

> A: walked the whole length of this vast dining hall at this snail's pace

The metaphoricity and overstatement of *snail's pace* can be seen in other more or less formulaic implicit comparisons such as *lightning fast*, etc.

Regarding the **humour** of hyperbole, ECF is not generally perceived as funny, although formulations with superlatives often are. *There is no bug larger than that* is oddly sterile, whereas the essentially equivalent *That's the biggest bug I've ever seen* could spark humour. Hyperbole regularly accompanies irony (Colston and Keller 1998; Colston and O'Brien 2000b) and this hooks it with humour as well. In the passage later, Brandon and Ned are discussing movies, when Ned invokes irony in the narrow sense of *mentioning* a proposition opposite to what he believes and hopes to convey, as in the analysis by Sperber and Wilson (1981) and Sperber (1984).

> Brandon: I watched The Fountainhead just a couple weeks ago.
> Ned: Boy I'll bet *that's* a great movie.
> Brandon: {laughing} It's a terrible movie.

Ned's straightforwardly ironic *I'll bet that's a great movie* elicits more laughter than it seems to deserve, but it has little effect on the conversation otherwise. Brandon reverts immediately to the literal *terrible*, rather than joining in the ironic approach. The perception of incongruity which forms the basis for humour and laughter according to Bateson (1953), Koestler (1964) and others derives from the discrepancy between what is said and what we perceive to be the case, for instance, between calling a movie great and believing it was terrible. This evokes the simultaneous perception of an object within two contrasting frames of reference or the compatibility with opposed semantic scripts, as in Attardo and Raskin (1991).

NEAL R. NORRICK

See also: Discourse analysis; figurative interpretation; humour; inference; irony; metaphor; proverbs; psycholinguistics; relevance theory; rhetoric; scalar implicature; semantics; stylistics; understatement

Suggestions for further reading

Gibbs, R.W., Jr (1994) *The Poetics of Mind*, Cambridge: Cambridge University Press.
Norrick, N.R. (1993) *Conversational Joking*, Bloomington, IN: Indiana University Press.
Tannen, D. (1989) *Talking Voices*, Cambridge: Cambridge University Press.

Idiom

Idioms are traditionally defined as strings of words whose overall meanings are not given as a function of the meanings of their individual parts. American English, for instance, has several thousand idioms, including classic expressions such as 'pop the question', 'blow your stack', 'kick the bucket', 'red herring', 'take advantage of' and 'let the cat out of the bag'. These formulaic expressions are often viewed as 'noncompositional' or 'fixed', such that their meanings must be directly stipulated in the mental lexicon in the same way that the meanings of individual words are listed in a dictionary. People presumably produce and understand idioms as wholes, rather than being generated and comprehended by generative rules of language. For this reason, the study of how people use and understand idioms has historically been considered uninformative in revealing insights into the underlying architecture of the 'language processor' that is designed to produce and parse novel expressions.

However, there are several reasons to dispute these common assumptions about idioms. Many idioms are not fixed or frozen, but are decomposable or analyzable with the meanings of their parts contributing independently to their overall figurative meanings (Gibbs 1994; Nunberg *et al.* 1994). For instance, in the idiomatic phrase 'pop the question', people can recognize that the noun 'question' refers to a 'marriage proposal' when the verb 'pop' is used to refer to the manner of uttering it. Similarly, the 'law' of 'lay down the law' refers to the rules of conduct in certain situations when the verb phrase 'laying down' is used to refer to the act of invoking the law. Idioms such as 'pop the question', 'spill the beans' and 'lay down the law' are 'decomposable' because each of their components obviously contributes to their overall figurative interpretations. Other idioms whose individual parts contribute less to its overall figurative **meaning** are more 'nondecomposable' or 'nonanalyzable' (e.g. 'kick the bucket', 'shoot the breeze'). Yet many nonanalyzable idioms, even ones thought to be most fixed or frozen such as 'kick the bucket', still retain some degree of compositionality. For example, people judge the phrase 'kick the bucket' to be more appropriate in a **context** where the person died quickly, as opposed to dying in a longer, protracted manner (Hamblin and Gibbs 1999). This intuition is motivated by the **semantics** of 'kick' which alludes to a fast, sudden action. In this way, people appear to be analyzing some aspects of the word meanings even when using or understanding nonanalyzable idioms.

The partial analyzability of most idioms also explains why these phrases exhibit tremendous lexical variation (Gibbs 1994; Glucksberg 2001; Langlotz 2006; Moon 1998b). For instance, the main verbs in many idioms can be changed without disrupting these phrases' figurative meanings, as seen in the following examples: 'set/start the ball rolling', 'fit/fill the bill', 'throw/toss in the towel', 'lower/let down one's guard', 'step into/fill someone's shoes' and 'play/keep one's cards close to the chest'. Nouns can also vary in many idioms without disrupting their figurative meanings, such as the changes that can be made in the following pairs of expressions: 'a piece/slice of the action', 'a skeleton in the closet/cupboard', 'the calm/lull before the storm' and 'a ballpark figure/estimate'. Not surprisingly, then, the analyzability of many idioms also explains why they are to varying degrees syntactically productive. Thus, 'John laid down the law' can be altered into a passive construction like 'The law was laid down by John' without disrupting its figurative meaning. The fact that idioms are analyzable to different degrees suggests that an analyzable–nonanalyzable continuum makes more theoretical sense than any rigid distinction between creative speech and conventional language, or between literal and nonliteral meaning.

Speakers create and continue to use idioms for a variety of pragmatic and cognitive reasons. Idioms, like **metaphors** and many other figurative expressions, are often used for reasons of **politeness**, to avoid responsibility for the import of what is communicated, to express ideas that are difficult to communicate using literal language, and to express thoughts in a compact and vivid manner. Conventional phrases like 'blow your stack' are important to social interaction for manipulating others, asserting separate identity and asserting group identity (Wray and Perkins 2000). Knowing the right idiomatic phrase to use in some situation is critical to marking a speaker as having the right status to be considered a valued member of some community. At the same time, as suggested earlier, idioms are not frozen or fixed, as speakers can re-form standard expressions for different pragmatic reasons (Carter 2004). For instance, one person spoke of his grandfather in a **conversation** with a friend in the following way: 'He's been on like you know doomed to die death's door for about three years now' (Carter 2004: 130). By alluding to the phrase 'to be at/ on death's door', the speaker is able to distance himself from an unpleasant **topic**, while doing so in a playful manner. Speakers' familiarity with idioms also makes both standard phrases, and creative instantiations of them, relatively easy to produce and understand in **discourse** (Gibbs 1994).

Yet the important empirical demonstrations on the analyzability of many idioms suggest that the internal semantics of these expressions might be correlated in systematic ways with the concepts to which they refer. In this way, many idioms are created, and continue to have pragmatic value in discourse precisely because

people think in conventional metaphorical and metonymic ways. Much research in **cognitive linguistics** and **psycholinguistics** supports this view (Gibbs 1994; Kovecses 2000). For example, the idiom 'John spilled the beans' maps our **knowledge** of someone tipping over a container of beans onto a person who is revealing some previously hidden secret. English speakers understand 'spill the beans' to mean 'reveal the secret' because there are underlying conceptual metaphors, such as THE MIND IS A CONTAINER and IDEAS ARE PHYSICAL ENTITIES, that structure their conceptions of minds, secrets, and disclosure. Although the existence of these conceptual metaphors does not predict that certain idioms must appear in the language, the presence of these independent conceptual metaphors by which we make sense of experience provides a partial motivation for why specific phrases (e.g. 'spill the beans') are used to refer to particular events (e.g. the revealing of secrets). Other idioms, such as 'send shivers down my spine', which refers to being fearful, is motivated by a conceptual metonymy of PHYSICAL AGITATION STANDS FOR FEAR. Most generally, many idioms have important pragmatic and social functions that are closely tied to entrenched patterns of both metaphorical and metonymic thought.

RAYMOND W. GIBBS, JR

See also: Cognitive linguistics; metaphor; psycholinguistics

Suggestions for further reading

Fernando, C. (1996) *Idioms and Idiomaticity*, Oxford: Oxford University Press.
Gibbs, R. (2007) 'Idiomaticity and formulaic language', in D. Gearearts and H. Cuykens (eds) *Handbook of Cognitive Linguistics*, New York: Oxford University Press.
Langlotz, A. (2006) *Idiomatic Creativity*, Amsterdam: Benjamins.

Implicature

The concept of implicature (both conversational and conventional) has its origins in the work of the Oxford philosopher H.P. **Grice**, though some proto-Gricean ideas can be traced back at least to the first-century BC rhetorician Dionysius (de Jonge 2001; Horn 2004, 2006) and the fourth-century rhetoricians Servius and Donatus. The ideas were later reiterated by the nineteenth-century English philosophers John Stuart Mill and Augustus De Morgan (Horn 2004).

Conversational implicature

A conversational implicature is 'a component of speaker meaning that constitutes an aspect of what is meant in a speaker's utterance without being part of what is said' (Horn 2004: 3; *see also* Huang 2007: 27). It is derived via Grice's (1989) **cooperative principle** and its attendant **maxims of conversation**. For example, when one utters the sentence in (1a), he or she (ceteris paribus) conversationally implicates (1b). (I use '+>' to signify 'conversationally implicate'.)

   (1) a. Some of John's friends like spending money on a sports car.
        b. +> Not many/most/all of John's friends like spending money on a sports car

Conversational implicatures are characterized by a number of distinctive properties (Grice 1989; Levinson 1983, 2000; Huang 1991a, 1994: 4–5, 2000a: 206–7, 2003, 2007: 32–35). The first property is defeasibility or cancellability – conversational implicatures can simply vanish in certain linguistic or non-linguistic **contexts**. How? They are cancelled if they are inconsistent with (i) semantic **entailments**, (ii) background or ontological assumptions, (iii) contexts, and/or (iv) priority conversational implicatures. As an illustration, contrast (2) with (3).

   (2) John and Mary bought a semi-detached house in London.
       +> John and Mary bought a semi-detached house in London together, not one each
   (3) The Americans and the Russians tested an atom bomb in 1962.
       ~ +> The Americans and the Russians tested an atom bomb in 1962 together, not one each

The utterance in (3) has the potential 'togetherness' conversational implicature, as indicated in

(2). However, this potential conversational implicature is not in keeping with background or ontological assumptions. Given our **knowledge** about history, it was impossible for the USA and the USSR to test an atom bomb together in 1962, because they were enemies at that time. Consequently, the potential 'togetherness' conversational implicature is defeated by inconsistent real-world knowledge. (The symbol '~+>' is used here to stand for 'do not conversationally implicate'.) Notice that defeasibility or cancellability is a necessary but not a sufficient condition for conversational implicature (Horn 2007b).

A second property exhibited by conversational implicatures is non-detachability – any linguistic expression with the same semantic content tends to carry the same conversational implicature. (A principled exception is those conversational implicatures that arise via the maxim of manner.) This is because conversational implicatures are attached to the semantic content, rather than the linguistic form, of **what is said**. Therefore, they cannot be detached from an utterance simply by replacing the relevant linguistic expressions with their synonyms. This is illustrated in (4), which indicates that the use of any linguistic expression that is synonymous with *almost* will give rise to the same conversational implicature.

   (4) The boy almost/nearly drowned /came close to drowning in an outdoor hot-tub.
       +> The boy did not (quite) drown in an outdoor hot-tub

A third property of conversational implicatures is calculability – conversational implicatures can transparently be derived via the cooperative principle and its component maxims. A fourth property is non-conventionality – conversational implicatures, though dependent on the saying of what is coded, are non-coded in nature (Grice 1989: 39). In other words, they rely on the saying of what is said but they are not part of what is said. A fifth property is reinforceability – conversational implicatures can be made explicit without producing too much of a sense of redundancy. This is because conversational implicatures are not part of the conventional import of an utterance. For example, the conversational implicature in (5) is made explicit in (6). But (6) is not judged to be semantically redundant.

(5) The coffee is warm.
    +> The coffee is not hot
(6) The coffee is warm, but not hot.

The sixth property of conversational implicatures is universality – conversational implicatures tend to be universal, because they are motivated rather than arbitrary. For instance, if a language has 'all' and 'some', the use of the semantically weaker 'some' will universally carry the conversational implicature 'not all'. In Huang (2007: 35), data are drawn from Modern Standard Arabic, Catalan, Chinese, Modern Greek, Kashmiri and Malagasy to illustrate this point. The final property is indeterminacy – conversational implicatures may sometimes be difficult to determine. Suppose one says (7). He or she may generate a range of indeterminate conversational implicatures.

(7) Mary's boss is a machine.
    +> Mary's boss is cold, or/and
    +> Mary's boss is efficient, or/and
    +> Mary's boss is a workaholic, or/and
    +> ...

A conversational implicature can be engendered in two distinct ways. On the one hand, it can arise from strictly observing the maxims of conversation. In Huang (2007: 27), I called conversational implicatures thus induced conversational implicatures$_O$. As an illustrating example, take (8).

(8) John went to a music shop and bought a CD.
    +>John first went to a music shop and then bought a CD

In this example, the conversational implicature is derived from following Grice's (1989) fourth sub-maxim of manner (Be orderly). By this sub-maxim, the speaker is expected to arrange the events in the order in which they took place, and the addressee is expected to draw **inferences** in such a way.

On the other hand, a conversational implicature can be generated by way of the speaker's ostentatiously flouting the maxims. In Huang (2007: 29), I dubbed conversational implicatures thus engendered conversational implicatures$_F$.

This is the case with the generation of the conversational implicature in Mary's response in (9), which deliberately exploits Grice's maxim of relation.

(9) John: Wasn't that a boring lecture?
    Mary: Did you remember to call Helen yesterday?
    +> e.g. The lecturer is standing behind you and he may hear what you said

There is thus the first Gricean dichotomy between conversational implicature$_O$ and conversational implicature$_F$, namely, the distinction between those conversational implicatures that are generated from a simple assumption that the speaker is observing both the maxims of conversation and the cooperative principle, and those that are engendered in more complex ways on the basis of the speaker flouting a maxim but nevertheless observing the cooperative principle. Grice's major achievement was to have provided a unified analysis of both types.

A second Gricean dichotomy, independent of the first, is between those conversational implicatures which arise without requiring any particular contextual conditions and those which do require such conditions. Grice (1989) and later Levinson (2000) called the first kind generalized conversational implicatures (GCIs) and the second kind particularized conversational implicatures (PCIs). By way of illustration, consider the two conversational implicatures in Mary's utterance in (10).

(10) John: How did yesterday's guest lecture go?
     Mary: Some of the faculty left before it ended.
     +> (a) Not many/most/all of the faculty left before it ended
     +> (b) The lecture didn't go well

The conversational implicature (a) in (10) has a very general currency. Any utterance of the form 'Some x are Y' will have the default interpretation 'Not many/most/all x are Y'. This interpretation will go through without needing any particular context, hence (a) is a GCI. By contrast, the conversational implicature (b) in (10) depends crucially on context of some kind. Mary's reply points to a possible connection, namely, if some of the faculty left a lecture before it ended, the lecture may not have gone well. Without such a specific connection, we will not have the relevant conversational implicature, thus (b) is a PCI. The theoretical importance of this Gricean dichotomy has recently been subject to heated debates. Hirschberg (1991: 42–44), Welker (1994: 21–23) and Carston (2002), for example, doubted whether such a distinction can be maintained. However, Levinson (2000) put forward a rigorous defense of it (*see also* Grice 1989: 37–38 for further discussion).

Since its inception, Grice's classical theory of conversational implicature has revolutionized pragmatic theorizing, generating a large number of neo- and post-Gricean reinterpretations, revisions and reconstructions. Horn (1989, 2004) put forward a bipartite model. On Horn's view, all of Grice's maxims (except the maxim of quality) can be replaced with two fundamental and antithetical neo-Gricean pragmatic principles: the Q [uantity]-principle ('Make your contribution sufficient; say as much as you can') and R[elation]-principle ('Make your contribution necessary; say no more than you must'), resulting in Q- and R-implicatures, respectively. Arguing for a clear separation between pragmatic principles governing an utterance's surface form and pragmatic principles governing its informational content, Levinson (2000) proposed that the original Gricean program (the maxim of quality apart) be reduced to three neo-Gricean pragmatic principles: what he dubbed the Q[uantity]-, I[nformativeness]-and M[anner]-principles. Each of the three principles has two sides: a speaker's maxim, which specifies what the principle enjoins the speaker to say and a recipient's corollary, which dictates what it allows the addressee to infer. A simplified version of these three principles is given:

(11) Levinson's Q-principle
Speaker: Do not say less than is required (bearing the I-principle in mind).
Addressee: What is not said is not the case.
(12) Levinson's I-principle
Speaker: Do not say more than is required (bearing the Q-principle in mind).
Addressee: What is generally said is stereotypically and specifically exemplified.

(13) Levinson's M-principle
Speaker: Do not use a marked expression without reason.
Addressee: What is said in a marked way conveys a marked message.

The operation of the Q-, I- and M-principles gives rise to Q-, I- and M-implicatures, respectively. Furthermore, Q-implicatures can be divided into three types: (i) $Q_{-scalar}$, (ii) $Q_{-clausal}$ and (iii) $Q_{-alternate}$ (Huang 2007: 42–44). On the other hand, in **relevance theory** (Sperber and Wilson 1995), the majority of classical and neo-Gricean GCIs is reanalyzed as an explicature – a **proposition** that is an inferential development of one of the linguistically given incomplete conceptual representations or **logical forms** of the sentence uttered. Conversational implicatures in the relevance-theoretic sense, called r-implicatures in Huang (2007: 195), are largely PCIs in the classical and neo-Gricean sense. In a similar way, Recanati (2004b) reduced some cases of conversational implicature to pragmatically enriched said. Also, Bach (2004b) argued that certain aspects of speaker meaning are neither part of what is said nor of what is conversationally implicated. Consequently, on Bach's view, these cases of conversational implicature are in fact conversational **implicitures**, that is, what is implicit in what is said (*see also* Bach 2006b). Finally, it is worth mentioning that there have also been various attempts to integrate the classical and neo-Gricean pragmatic theories of conversational implicature with other current linguistic theories. These linguistic theories include accommodation theory (Thomason 1990), decision theory (Merin 1999), game theory (Benz *et al.* 2006), bidirectional optimality theory (Blutner 2004) and **speech act theory** (Vanderveken 2002).

Conventional implicature

We turn next to the second category of implicature put forward by Grice, namely, conventional implicature. (In fact, Frege's 1892, 1918–19 analysis of the *Andeutung* relation is a direct precursor of Grice's concept of conventional implicature, *see* Bach 1999a; Feng 2006; Horn 2007b). An *Andeutungen* or conventional implicature is a non-truth-conditional meaning which is not derivable from general considerations of cooperation and **rationality**, but arises solely from the conventional features attached to particular lexical items and/or linguistic constructions involved. A few standard examples are given in (14)–(18). (I use '+>>' to stand for 'conventionally implicate'.)

(14) *p* therefore *q* +>> *q* follows from *p*
She is an Italian; she, therefore, knows how to cook pastas.

(15) *p* but *q* +>> *p* contrasts with *q*
John is poor but he is honest.

(16) Even *p* +>> contrary to expectation
Even his servant has the money to spend on a luxury cruise.

(17) *p* moreover *q* +>> *q* is in addition to *p*
David can read German. Moreover, he can write poems in the language.

(18) *p* so q +>> *p* provides an explanation for *q*
Sue is reading linguistics. So her father has bought her a dictionary of linguistics.

In (14), the conventional implicature triggered by the use of *therefore* is that being Italian provides some good reason for knowing how to cook pastas. In (15), there is a conventional implicature of contrast between the information contained in *p* and that contained in *q* (Grice 1989: 25, 88). In (16), *even*, being epistemic in nature, conventionally implicates some sort of unexpectedness, surprise or unlikeliness (Farncescotti 1995). In (17), the use of *moreover* brings in the conventional implicature that the statement made in *q* is additional to the statement made in *p* (Grice 1989: 121). Finally in (18), the conventional implicature contributed by *so* is that the fact that Sue is reading linguistics explains why her father has bought her a dictionary of linguistics. Other representative lexical items that are considered to engender conventional implicatures in English include *actually, also, anyway, barely, besides, however, manage to, on the other hand, only, still, though, too* and *yet*.

What, then, are the essential properties of conventional implicature? From a traditional point of view, conventional implicatures are considered to have the following properties (Grice 1989; Huang 2007: 55–57; Levinson 1983: 127–28). First, conventional implicatures are not derived from Grice's cooperative principle

and its component maxims, but are attached by convention to particular lexical items and/or linguistic constructions. They are therefore an arbitrary part of **meaning**, and must be learned ad hoc. Second, conventional implicatures are not calculable via any natural procedure, but are rather given by convention, thus they must be stipulated. Third, conventional implicatures are not cancellable, that is, they cannot be defeated. Fourth, conventional implicatures are detachable, because they depend on the particular lexical expressions and/or linguistic constructions used. Finally, conventional implicatures do not tend to be universal.

It should be pointed out that unlike the concept of conversational implicature, the notion of conventional implicature is not taken to be very coherent. Even Grice himself (1989: 46) warned that 'the nature of conventional implicature needs to be examined before any free use of it, for explanatory purposes, can be indulged in'. Horn (2004: 6), himself a neo-Gricean, has gone a step further by claiming that 'the role played by conventional implicature within the general theory of meaning is increasingly shaky'. Since its inception, conventional implicature has been subject to numerous attempts to reduce it to semantic entailment, conversational implicature, and **presupposition** (Levinson 1983: 128), and more recently, to part of what is said (Bach 1999a; but *see* Barker 2003 for a different view), part of tacit performatives (Rieber 1997), vehicles for performing second-order speech acts (Bach 1999a), and procedural meaning in relevance theory (Blakemore 2004).

But recently, Potts (2005) has made a brave attempt to resurrect the concept of conventional implicature. He 'retain[ed] Grice's brand name but alter[ed] the product' (Horn 2007b) by focusing on expressives like epithets, attributive adjectives and honorifics and supplements like non-restrictive relatives, **parentheticals** and appositives rather than lexical items such as *but, therefore* and *even*. He isolated four essential properties of conventional implicature. The first of these properties is conventionality – conventional implicatures are part of the conventional meaning of the expressions involved. The second property is commitment – conventional implicatures are commitments, and thus engender entailments. The third property is speaker orientation – the commitments are made by the speaker of the utterance. The final property is independence – conventional implicatures are logically and compositionally independent of what is said, or in Potts's parlance, of the 'at-issue' entailments (*see also* von Heusinger and Turner 2006). Taking the view that conventional implicature is semantic in nature, Potts developed a logic of the notion by modeling it with a type-driven, multi-dimensional semantic translation language (*see* Feng 2006: 138–45, Horn 2007b for criticisms). Feng (2006) presented another development of Grice's concept of conventional implicature. The properties extracted by him for conventional implicature are (i) non-truth-conditionality, (ii) speaker orientation, (iii) infallibility, (iv) occurrency, (v) dependency, and (vi) context-sensitivity. He further argued that properties (i)–(iv) are intimately associated with subjectivity. Finally, contrary to Potts's view, Feng maintained that conventional implicature has both a semantic and pragmatic character. This is why a conventional implicature is so named by Grice.

> [I]t is so named because it involves both linguistic and contextual information. It is conventional because it is associated with the conventional linguistic meaning of a certain expression. … It is implicated rather than said because its full content requires contextual information, and does not affect the truth conditions of the utterance.
>
> (Feng 2006: 184)

This view is also echoed in Horn (2007b: 50), who said that:

> [conventional implicature] is semantic insofar as it involves an aspect of the conventional meaning of a given expression rather than being computable from general principles of rational behavior or communicative competence, but it is pragmatic insofar as it involves considerations of appropriateness rather than truth of the sentence in which it appears.

Whether belonging to **semantics** or straddling the semantics-pragmatics boundary, Potts's and Feng's recent works have shown rather encouragingly that the Fregeo-Gricean concept of conventional implicature is, after all, not that incoherent.

YAN HUANG

See also: Context; cooperative principle; Grice, H.P.; impliciture; logical form; maxims of conversation; neo-Gricean pragmatics; pragmatics; relevance theory; scalar implicature; what is said

Suggestions for further reading

Grice, H.P. (1989) *Studies in the Way of Words*, Cambridge, MA: Harvard University Press.
Horn, L.R. (2004) 'Implicature', in L.R. Horn and G. Ward (eds) *The Handbook of Pragmatics*, Oxford: Blackwell.
Huang, Y. (2007) *Pragmatics*, Oxford: Oxford University Press.

Impliciture

The notion of conversational impliciture (impliciture for short) was put forward by the philosopher of language Kent Bach. What, then, is an impliciture? Consider first (1).

(1) a. John is ready.
   b. John is too young.
   c. This dictionary is expensive.
   d. John is late.
   e. John prefers blondes.
   f. John needs a boat.
   g. The mayor has just arrived.
   h. Even John's grandma can surf the internet.

On Bach's (1994a, 1994b, 1999b, 2001, 2004b, 2006b) view, each of the sentences in (1) expresses an incomplete **proposition**. In other words, it is sub-propositional. Consequently, it cannot be evaluated truth-conditionally. Bach dubbed propositional fragments of this kind 'propositional radicals', which need to be completed or filled in contextually to become fully propositional. The pragmatic process of completion will provide extra conceptual content or material to the propositional radicals in (1), resulting in the corresponding minimal but full propositions in (2). The full and determinate propositions in (2) can then be assigned a truth value.

(2) a. John is ready [to join the navy]
   b. John is too young [to vote]
   c. This dictionary is expensive [relative to other dictionaries]
   d. John is late [for the seminar]
   e. John prefers blondes [to brunettes]
   f. John needs a boat [to cross the river]
   g. The mayor has just arrived [at the town hall]
   h. Even John's grandma can surf the internet [in addition to John's grandpa]

Next, let us move to (3).

(3) a. I've eaten lunch.
   b. I've been to China.
   c. She has nothing to wear.
   d. Everyone likes classical music.
   e. France is hexagonal.
   f. John and Clare are married.
   g. The police moved in and the suspects were arrested.
   h. You are not going to die.
   i. There are nine thousand students in this university town.
   j. Yan has got two doctorates.
   k. John and Mary painted a portrait of Mandela.

According to Bach, unlike in (1), each of the sentences in (3) expresses a full, though minimal proposition. Put slightly differently, it does not contain a conceptual gap, and as such does not require the insertion of any additional conceptual elements. But a proposition of this kind, called a 'skeletal' proposition by Bach, falls short of what the speaker intends to mean. Consequently, it needs to be expanded. The pragmatic process of expansion will flesh out the proposition expressed by the sentence uttered and engender a richer proposition. The pragmatically enriched proposition will then be identical with what the speaker has intentionally meant, thus allowing the assignment of an appropriate truth value to it. The pragmatically expanded propositions of (3) are given in (4).

(4) a. I've eaten lunch [today]
   b. I've been to China [before]
   c. She has nothing [appropriate/suitable] to wear [for tonight's party]
   d. Everyone [in John's family] likes classical music
   e. France is [approximately/roughly] hexagonal
   f. John and Clare are married [to each other]
   g. The police moved in and [as a result] the suspects were arrested
   h. You are not going to die [from that cut]
   i. There are [approximately] nine thousand students in this university town
   j. Yan has got [exactly/precisely] two doctorates
   k. John and Mary painted a portrait of Mandela [together]

Clearly, in both (2) and (4), each of the bracketed elements of **meaning** contributes to what is communicated. The result of completion and expansion, that is, the vehicle of each of the pragmatically completed or enriched propositions, Bach called a 'conversational impliciture' or 'impliciture' for short, because it is what is implicit in **what is said**. More specifically, an impliciture is an implicit strengthening, weakening or specification of what is said. In other words, on Bach's view, there is no pragmatic intrusion into what is said, because certain aspects of communicative content do not need to be recognized as either part of what is said or part of what is implicated. Rather, they constitute a middle ground between what is said and what is implicated. Stated in this way, impliciture represents a third category of communicated content – a category that is intermediate between **Grice**'s what is said and what is implicated. As Bach pointed out, an impliciture goes beyond what is said, but unlike a conversational **implicature**, which is an additional proposition external to what is said, an impliciture is built out of what is said. Further, Horn (2004) told us that an impliciture cannot be constitutive of what is said, because it can be felicitously cancelled, as can be seen in (5). Neither can it be derived as a conversational implicature, because it is truth-conditionally relevant.

(5) a. John is ready, but not to join the navy.
   b. John prefers blondes, but to brunettes.
   c. I've eaten lunch, but not today.
   d. John and Clare are married, but not to each other.
   e. Police moved in and the suspects were arrested, but the latter is not necessarily the result of the former.

An impliciture will then provide input to the classical Gricean inferential mechanism (the **cooperative principle** and its component **maxims of conversation**) yielding conversational implicatures as output. Thus, in Bach's theory, the traditional Gricean dichotomy between what is said and what is implicated is replaced by a trichotomy between what is said, what is implicit and what is implicated, with what is implicit constituting the middle level of speaker-meaning (*see also* Huang 2007).

One of the main attractions of Bach's model is that, as pointed out by Horn (2004), the classical Gricean semantic conception of what is said, along with a post-semantic orthodox Gricean characterization of what is implicated, is retained in a neo-classical way. But there may be one or two objections to the postulation of Bach's notion of impliciture. The main objection is that it is not clear that impliciture can really be distinguished from conversational implicature. First, as Bach was aware, like a (certain type of) conversational implicature, an impliciture is cancellable, vague and indeterminate, and detachable. Second, contrary to what Horn pointed out above, like an impliciture, a conversational implicature can also intrude upon truth-conditional content. This is the case with the determination of **indexicals** and related phenomena in the working out of the classical Gricean notion of what is said. In addition, there is a type of 'intrusive' construction such as the conditional, comparative, disjunction and *because*-clause, where 'the truth conditions of the whole depend in part on the implicatures of the parts' (Levinson 2000: 235). Third, as I argued in Huang (2007: 227–31), given the Cohen-Recanati scope principle (Cohen 1971; Recanati 1993), impliciture (and explicature and the pragmatically enriched said) cannot be distinguished from conversational implicature. Fourth, to the best of my knowledge, at present there is no experimental work in **pragmatics** that can distinguish alleged different types of pragmatic meanings and **inferences** such as impliciture and conversational implicature (Huang 2007: 227). A second drawback of Bach's analysis (if it is a drawback) is that the retention of the classical Gricean notion of what is said and what is implicated is achieved only at the expense of postulating a further representational level between what is said and what is implicated (*see also* Carston 2002 and Vincente 2002 for a critique of Bach's notion of impliciture from a relevance-theoretical point of view).

YAN HUANG

See also: Grice, H.P.; implicature; indexicals; neo-Gricean pragmatics; pragmatics; proposition; relevance theory; what is said

Suggestions for further reading

Bach, K. (1994a) 'Conversational impliciture', *Mind and Language*, 9: 124–62.
——(1994b) 'Semantic slack: what is said and more', in S.L. Tsohatzidis (ed.) *Foundations of Speech Act Theory: Philosophical and Linguistic Perspectives*, London: Routledge.

Indefiniteness

Indefiniteness is a property of noun phrases (NPs; also sometimes called determiner phrases, or DPs) which is exemplified at least by indefinite descriptions (e.g. *a hat, an old man*) and some (other) quantified NPs (*several/some/many children*). Exactly where to draw the boundaries of this category depends on how the property is defined, and that has not been completely agreed on. The term 'indefinite' suggests that indefinites lack **definiteness**, and most attempts to define the category begin with that contrast.

Definiteness has long been associated with **reference**, the idea being that use of a definite NP allows the speaker to communicate to the addressee about some determinate entity. The next question is how that happens. Following the classic analysis of Russell (1905), one proposal is that uniqueness is the essence of definiteness. It is true that typically definite descriptions, pronouns, and proper names require a unique referent. Following this approach, then, the essence of indefiniteness would be the lack of such a requirement. This seems to be borne out by examples such as (1):

(1) Mary is talking about *a/the movie she saw last night*.

In this example, use of the indefinite article *a* seems to leave it open as to whether Mary saw more than one movie, whereas the definite *the* implies that she saw only one. This is quite consistent with Russell's analysis, according to which indefinites merely assert existence, while definites assert uniqueness in addition. Some other cases require a bit more explanation. For example, when the descriptive content of the NP is such as to exclude more than one referent, as with superlatives (e.g. *the world's fastest Indian*), *the* is usually required and *a* is not allowed. The explanation here may be pragmatic: use of the indefinite article carries an **implicature** (Grice 1975, 1989) of at least the possibility of additional instances meeting the descriptive content of the NP, which conflicts with that content in these cases.

The most common test for indefiniteness relies on the ability of indefinite NPs to occur naturally in locating existential sentences. These are *there be* sentences which include a specification of location. Examples are given in (2):

(2) a. There was a large green banana on top of the fridge.
    b. There were several/some/many children standing at the door.

Definite NPs cannot occur naturally in such sentences. This test suggests that the essence of indefiniteness may have something to do with the introduction of items into the universe of **discourse** – novelty, in some sense – while definite NPs are assumed to have familiar referents, already in the universe of discourse. This idea has been a popular one (*see* e.g. Heim 1982). However, pinning down the exact sense of 'novelty' has proved more difficult. Consider example (3):

(3) There is a pile of tyres over there. Hand me *one of them* please.

The NP *one of them* would be classified as indefinite. But its semantic value is located among a group of items which have already been introduced into the universe of discourse, although of course it is true that that NP does not single out any particular tyre. Added to this is the fact that some NPs which are intuitively indefinite, like *most children*, are also not natural in locating existentials.

Given that failure to occur in locating existentials does not line up exactly with intuitive indefiniteness, linguists have defined a slightly different pair of categories, labeled 'weak' (for those NPs which do occur in existentials, including most indefinites), and 'strong' (for those which do not – definites, plus a few intuitively indefinite types). According to the formal definition given by Barwise and Cooper (1981), weak NPs place no independent constraints on the truth conditions of sentences in which they occur; instead, the only thing that matters is their overlap with other categories mentioned. Strong NPs, in contrast, impose a **presupposition** of some type. To get a sense of what this means, contrast the examples containing weak NPs in (4) with those containing strong NPs in (5):

(4) a. A child is sleeping.
    b. Several children are sleeping.
    c. Many children are sleeping.
(5) a. The child is sleeping.
    b. Most of the children are sleeping.
    c. Those children are sleeping.

The truth conditions of the sentences in (4) require only that the right number of entities are both children and sleeping – at least one for (4a), several for (4b), and many for (4c). However, to know whether the sentences in (5) are true, one must know more than this: for (5a) there must be only one child in the discourse **context**, for (5b) the sleeping children must outnumber the awake ones, and for (5c) the sleepers must be the ones whom the speaker is indicating.

When indefinite NPs occur in a sentence with **negation** (frequently expressed in English with *not*) or a modal (e.g. *must, probably*), scope ambiguities arise which result in differences in **specificity**. An example is given in (6):

(6) Mary didn't find a serious error in her paper.

If negation takes scope over the indefinite *a serious error*, its interpretation is nonspecific and the sentence means that Mary didn't find any serious errors. However, the indefinite may alternatively take wide scope relative to the negation, in which case the sentence means that there was a serious error which Mary failed to find. This is the specific reading for the indefinite. The adjective *certain* can often be used to disambiguate a sentence in favour of the specific reading: *Mary didn't find a certain serious error* has only the wide scope reading for the indefinite.

It has been suggested that a similar kind of nonspecific-specific **ambiguity** may occur in a simple sentence without negation or a modal (Chastain 1975; Fodor and Sag 1982). For example, sentence (7):

(7) A student in the syntax class cheated on the final.

may be used to assert simply that there was a cheater (a nonspecific understanding), or predicate cheating of a particular individual (potentially a referential understanding). Ludlow and Neale (1991), following Kripke (1977), argued that the referential construal of an utterance like (7), although perhaps conveyed by means of the utterance, is nevertheless not semantically encoded in it. The distinction between what is semantically encoded in an utterance and what is only conveyed pragmatically continues to be a topic of investigation (see, for example, Szabó 2005).

BARBARA ABBOTT

See also: Definiteness; given/new distinction; presupposition; reference; specificity

Suggestions for further reading

Abbott, B. (2004) 'Definiteness and indefiniteness', in L.R. Horn and G. Ward (eds) *The Handbook of Pragmatics*, Malden, MA: Blackwell.
Haspelmath, M. (1997) *Indefinite Pronouns*, Oxford: Oxford University Press.

Indexicals

An indexical expression is an expression whose semantic value varies across **contexts** by virtue of its **meaning**. For instance, since it is part of the meaning of the indexical singular term 'I' that it refers to whoever plays the appropriate role in the context at hand (typically, the speaker), occurrences of 'I' in different contexts may refer to different individuals.

At least according to a common view of the identity conditions for expressions, an ambiguous expression such as 'bank' is associated with contrasting semantic profiles, and the choice of the appropriate sense of 'bank' within a given conversational exchange depends on contextual factors, such as the speaker's **intentions** or the **topic** of discussion. Yet, the contextual sensitivity of an ambiguous expression is not of a semantic nature, in the sense that it does not depend on that expression's meaning. The case of indexical expressions is importantly dissimilar: different occurrences of 'I' are occurrences of an English expression endowed with a stable, fixed meaning, albeit one able to yield a semantic value only with respect to this or that context. In this sense, it is the trademark of the form of context-dependence typical of indexical expressions that it is meaning-governed.

The meaning of an indexical may be presented in terms of a descriptive condition, which is able to select an appropriate referent with respect to a given context. For instance, the meaning of 'I' may be presented by means of the description 'the speaker', and the meaning of 'here' may be summarized in terms of the description 'the location of speaking'. Yet conditions of this sort are not synonymous with their associated indexicals, because a sentence such as, say, 'I am hungry' is not truth-conditionally equivalent to the sentence 'the speaker is hungry'. This observation has led some philosophers of language to the distinction between two kinds of 'meaning' for indexicals; in the classic terminology suggested by David Kaplan, a character and a content (Kaplan 1989a; *see also* Perry 1977, 1979; Lewis 1980; and Braun 1995a; *see* **Bar-Hillel** 1954 for pioneering observations in this respect). The character of 'I', for instance, is related to the aforementioned descriptive condition, but the content of 'I' with respect to a context is merely the individual who happens to play the required role. For this reason, simple indexical expressions such as 'I', though endowed with a descriptive content, behave as rigid designators, and, at least accord- ing to some, provide the paradigm for directly referential expressions (Kaplan 1989a).

The distinction between the character and the content of an indexical generates intriguing semantic results. For instance, if it is assumed that the speaker is always at the location of speaking at the time of speaking (in technical jargon, if it is assumed that all contexts are *proper* contexts), the sentence 'I am here now' turns out to be true with respect to all contexts, even though it does not express a necessary content (Kaplan 1989a). The notion that all contexts are proper contexts has however been challenged on pragmatic grounds: arguably, there are true uses of 'I am not here now', for instance recordings of that sentence in an answering machine (Vision 1985; Sidelle 1991; Corazza *et al.* 2002; Predelli 2005).

Expressions such as 'this' or 'that' occupy a special place among indexicals. Although the context-dependence they display is clearly meaning-governed, these **demonstrative** expres- sions, unlike so-called pure indexicals such as 'I', are associated with a referent only with respect to a *demonstration*. The relationship between demonstratives and demonstrations has been approached from different viewpoints in the semantic and pragmatic literature (Kaplan 1989a; Bach 1992; Braun 1996; Salmon 2002; Caplan 2003). According to widespread con- sensus, however, the referent of a use of a demonstrative may be determined only with respect to a variety of pragmatic assumptions that are of no relevance for pure indexicals: the referent of a particular use of 'this', for instance, may be established only on the basis of wider contextual parameters, having to do with the speaker's intentions and/or the relevant con- versational setting (according to Recanati 2004b, this fact has important repercussions with respect to the **semantics-pragmatics interface**).

It is uncontroversial that simple pure index- icals such as 'I' or 'now', and demonstratives such as 'this' or 'that', are indexical expressions in the sense indicated above. Less uncon- troversial is the decision pertaining to the index- ical status of a variety of other expressions. So- called comparative adjectives provide a case in point. The extension for 'tall', for instance, apparently depends on the contextually relevant comparison class, given that what is tall for a normal human being may fail to be tall with respect to the class of basketball players. It is, however, debatable whether this evidence suf- fices for including adjectives such as 'tall' within the class of indexical expressions, that is, within the class of expressions endowed with a non- constant character (for different views on this matter, *see* Stanley and Szabó 2000; Szabó 2001 and Cappelen and Lepore 2005a). Similar con- siderations apply to a variety of other expressions. For instance, the adjective 'green' may arguably truly be applied to a given object (say, a russet leaf painted in a green hue) with respect to some contexts, but not to others. According to the so- called contextualist viewpoint, however, this form of context-dependence is not assimilable to indexi- cality, and may be explained only on the basis of a novel approach to the semantics-pragmatics interface (Travis 1997; for objections see Cappelen and Lepore 2005a and Predelli 2005).

Also particularly controversial is the inclusion of proper names among indexical expressions. The main evidence in favour of an approach of this sort is provided by the obvious fact that many individuals share a common proper name, such as 'John Smith'. According to the indexical theory of names, contexts provide suitable inter- pretation parameters, and a referent for 'John Smith' may be obtained only in a context- dependent fashion, in the sense of context- dependence exemplified by expressions such as 'I' or 'here' (Recanati 1993; for criticism *see* Predelli 2001).

STEFANO PREDELLI

See also: Ambiguity;   Bar-Hillel,   Y.; communication; context; contextualism; deixis; demonstratives; disambiguation; meaning; philo- sophy of language; reference; semantic minimal- ism; semantics; semantics-pragmatics interface; utterance interpretation; what is said

Suggestions for further reading

Kaplan, D. (1989) 'Demonstratives', in J. Almog, J. Perry and H. Wettstein (eds) *Themes from Kaplan*, Oxford: Oxford University Press.
Nunberg, G. (1993) 'Indexicality and deixis', *Linguistics and Philosophy*, 16: 1–43.

Infant-Directed Talk and Pragmatics

Linguistic input to young language learners is typically saturated with clues to speakers' intended meanings as well as to the conventional linguistic structures that speakers use to articulate those meanings. Human infants are admirably prepared to take advantage of these pragmatic clues, and skill at mining the input for such clues gains power with development.

Even *in utero*, infants are already learning something about the language being spoken around them. For instance, they perceive and remember rhythms and pitches presented to them before birth. Merely two days after birth, infants can modify sucking patterns if this is rewarded by presentation of a rhyming passage read to them by their mothers during the third trimester of pregnancy (DeCasper and Spence 1986). Newborn infants also display a preference for their mothers' voice over that of a stranger (DeCasper and Fifer 1980), and they prefer to listen to their native language rather than a foreign language (Moon *et al.* 1993). These findings point to an impressively early-developing social attunement which is suggested to promote strong ties with one's social group (Kinzler *et al.* 2007; Stern 1985) and to guide infants to attend to meaning-relevant aspects of **communication** (Fernald 1993, 2001).

Caregivers in many **cultures** also make systematic modifications to their speech in ways that complement infants' preferences and contribute to communicatively meaningful exchanges. Infant-directed speech (or 'motherese') typically departs from adult-directed speech in a variety of ways, including increased pitch, exaggerated pitch contours corresponding to communicative goals (e.g. approval, prohibition, comfort, and attention-bid), and simplified sentence structure (e.g. *see* Kuhl 2004). Infants prefer infant-directed speech over adult-directed speech, a propensity that directs their attention to the rich input parents tailor for them (Cooper and Aslin 1990). Infants are skilled at extracting structure of all sorts from linguistic input (e.g. *see* Jusczyk 1997), and the salient and enriched nature of infant-directed speech facilitates such extraction (Saffran *et al.* 2006). Additionally, infants appear to be better able to learn certain types of information, such as the onsets and offsets of words, when speech is infant-directed as opposed to adult-directed (Thiessen *et al.* 2005).

Regarding comprehension of **pragmatics** specifically, a small amount of evidence suggests infants as young as five months can also discriminate at least some of the different communicative goals conveyed in infant-directed speech. For example, they smile more to presentations of infant-directed approval in comparison to prohibition (Fernald 1993). These and similar findings lead to the conclusion that, in Fernald's words, 'the melody carries the message' (1989: 1505). Based on sensitivity to **prosody**, then, infants seem able to extract **meaning** from speech adults direct to them even before they comprehend actual words and grammatical structures.

Infant-directed speech also facilitates language learning by promoting acquisition of phonological structure. Parents exaggerate vowels, an acoustic modification that is associated with infants' later language-relevant speech–sound discrimination (Liu *et al.* 2003). Speech provided in contingent interactions also facilitates phonological development. Infants learn phonological forms more easily when parents provide vocalization contingent on infants' own babbling (Goldstein and Schwade 2008). Infants are better able to detect subtle differences between speech sounds when a live speaker interacts contingently with them as opposed to the same sounds being conveyed in a videotaped presentation (Kuhl *et al.* 2003).

Infants make use of other sources of information beyond strictly verbal channels in the language-learning enterprise. Infants under the age of one year, for instance, more readily learn sound–object associations when objects are moved at the same time the sound is provided (Gogate and Bahrick 1998). In studies of naturalistic mother–infant dyads, mothers tended to move objects at the same time they offered labels. This demonstrates that in addition to modifications to speech, parents also provide information in other modalities in ways that are responsive to infants' sensitivities (Gogate *et al.* 2000). As infants develop, their reliance on synchrony for learning words decreases (e.g. Fernald *et al.* 1998), and they become better able to use other cues to determine word–object mappings, including socio-pragmatic information, especially **intention**-reading skills (e.g. Tomasello 2003). Interestingly, the synchrony engaged in by parents also decreases, suggesting that parents adapt modifications to mesh with infants' changing abilities.

Social understanding undergoes important developments across the first two years of life (e.g. Tomasello and Carpenter 2007). Increased sophistication in this arena allows infants and toddlers to actively and purposefully search the communicative environment for meaning-relevant social clues including emotional expressions, line of regard, gestures, actions, and other indicators of the speaker's thoughts and communicative intent (Carpenter *et al.* 1998; Tomasello 2003; Woodward 2000). For example, younger infants are prone to link labels with objects they are focused on when hearing those labels. In contrast, older infants actively take the speaker's focus of attention into account in establishing new word–object links (Baldwin 1991, 1993; Hollich *et al.* 2000; Pruden *et al.* 2006). This and similar abilities enable the developing child to more actively and successfully participate in the communicative venture.

In addition to the changes we see across normative development, there are also intriguing individual differences in parental production of, and child responsiveness to, pragmatic cues that appear to have consequences for language acquisition. Vocabulary acquisition in young Western infants is positively associated with the frequency of parental 'follow-in' labeling, in which parents provide labels for objects to which infants are already attending. Conversely, frequently redirecting infants' attention to an external referent before labeling, a style known as 'lead-in' labeling, is negatively related to infant vocabulary growth (Akhtar *et al.* 1991, but *see* Akhtar and Gernsbacher 2007 for a discussion of cultural differences). However, when such lead-ins are successful in recruiting infants' attention, this negative relationship disappears (Shimpi and Huttenlocher 2007). This finding suggests that infants' ability to flexibly reorient attention in response to a parent's direction matters for language. Indeed, among Western infants, vocabulary development in the first 18 months is positively associated with higher frequencies of responding to parents' attempts to engage their infants' attentional focus on an external referent (Morales *et al.* 2000).

Research on **autism** further underscores the significance of sociopragmatic factors in early language acquisition. Whereas typically-developing infants prefer to listen to infant-directed talk in comparison to a non-speech analog (Vouloumanos and Werker 2004), children with autism (a developmental disorder characterized by impairments in social functioning and language, especially pragmatic components) tend to show the reverse preference. Additionally, heightened preference for the non-speech analog among children with autism is associated with greater neurophysiological abnormality in response to speech sounds, another finding that highlights the importance of social factors in typical language development and function (Kuhl *et al.* 2005). Differences in word-learning behavior are also observed when examining autistic populations. In comparison to typically-developing, age-matched children, children with autism are more likely to map words onto objects to which they themselves are attending, even when the speaker intends to refer to something else (Baron-Cohen *et al.* 1997; Preissler and Carey 2005). This leaves them prone to word-learning errors, which may not only slow language learning but also contribute to pragmatic oddity in their speech.

In conclusion, infant-directed talk is a rich, multifaceted, multi-modal stimulus. Normally-developing human infants seem eminently prepared to capitalize on it for social purpose, be that purpose to commune meaningfully with caregivers, or to make sense of the details of the linguistic system. Of course, this in turn furthers social exchange. Put another way, infant-directed talk is the human infant's pragmatic playground.

MEREDITH MEYER and DARE BALDWIN

See also: Autism spectrum disorders; child language acquisition; development, pragmatic; pragmatics; prosody and pragmatics; social cognition; theory of mind; word learning, role of mindreading in

Suggestions for further reading

Baldwin, D.A. and Meyer, M. (2007) 'How inherently social is language?', in E. Hoff and

M. Shatz (eds) *Blackwell Handbook of Language Development*, Malden, MA: Blackwell.

Kuhl, P.K. (2004) 'Early language acquisition: cracking the speech code', *Nature Reviews Neuroscience*, 5: 831–43.

Saffran, J.R., Werker, J. and Werner, L. (2006) 'The infant's auditory world: hearing, speech, and the beginnings of language', in R. Siegler and D. Kuhns (eds) *Handbook of Child Development*, New York: Wiley.

Inference

One of the basic forms of **reasoning**, inference is closely tied to the relation of implication, or its converse, consequence. If one **proposition** implies another, then the latter proposition is a consequence of the former. In its most basic sense, inference is the drawing of consequences. It is useful therefore to distinguish between the consequences that a proposition *has*, and the consequences that it is necessary (or permissible, or reasonable) to *draw*. There is some disagreement among logicians as to whether the distinction is a tenable one. Some are of the view that an ideally rational individual will draw all consequences of any proposition he or she holds. Others hold that the rational thing to do is to draw only those consequences that are relevant to the agent's interests and circumstances there and then. On the first view, every rule of implication (or what is the same thing, rule of consequence) is a rule of inference. On the second, the rules of inference are disjoint from the rules of implication. Even so, it is nowhere in doubt that implication furnishes a constraint upon inference, as follows. An agent's inference of proposition *B* from proposition *A* requires that *A* implies *B*.

Also embedded in this second position is the claim that, whereas implication is strictly a propositional relation, inference is a linguistic and/or mental act performed on propositions by reasoning agents. (There was a time when every school child was told 'Propositions imply. People infer.') Accordingly, implication can be adequately characterized by its syntactic and semantic properties alone. But getting inference right requires that we also take account of pragmatic factors, that is to say, factors affecting an agent's use of the propositions involved. These factors include the agent's goals and the cognitive resources he or she possesses for their attainment – resources such as information, time and computational capacity. So seen, inference is a matter of belief or commitment change. The tension between these two positions on consequence-having and consequence-drawing is also reproduced within present-day belief revision theory. In what is regarded as the classical or Alchourrón, Gärdenfors and Makinson (AGM) approach to belief revision, belief is closed under consequence (Alchourrón *et al.* 1985). In other words, a perfectly rational agent will draw all consequences of anything he believes. Against this approach is the objection that requiring belief to be closed under consequence imposes on reasoning agents a task that is both computationally too complex for them and irrelevant to their interests (Harman 1986).

Given that implication is a condition on correct inference, inference will vary in kind with variations in implication type. Accordingly, it is customary to recognize a distinction between deductive and inductive inferences, governed by implications that are deductive in the first case, and probabilistic in the second case. If *A* deductively implies (or entails) *B*, then the inference of *B* from *A* is likewise deductive. Deductive inference is truth-preserving. This means that if *A* deductively implies *B* and *A* is true, then in drawing *B* as a consequence we may be wholly assured of *B*'s truth as well. However, if *A* probabilistically implies *B*, the inference from *A* to *B* is inductive. Though not truth-preserving, correct inductive inferences are likelihood-enhancing. What this means is that if *A* probabilistically implies *B*, then although *A* does not verify *B*, it does offer it some degree of positive confirmation. Another way of saying this is that if the probability of *B* given *A* is sufficiently high, then *A* is inductively evidential for *B*. The literature also reveals a growing tendency among theorists to acknowledge a third category of inference called **abduction**. Whereas deductive inference is truth-preserving and inductive inference is likelihood-enhancing, abduction is sometimes described as ignorance-preserving. Abductive inference is typified by (though not limited to) what is called 'inference to the best explanation'. This is a form of reasoning in which from the fact, if true, that a certain proposition H would explain a certain known state of affairs, it is concluded that it is reasonable to conjecture that H and (provisionally and defeasibly) to make it a 'working hypothesis'. The idea that abduction is ignorance-preserving derives from C.S. **Peirce**'s insistence that the fact that H has been successfully abduced is no reason to believe it to be true. In other words, Peirce thinks that abductive success is not inductively evidential for H.

It is well to emphasize that as implication varies as to type, so too does inference. Over the past forty years, studies in logic, computer science, linguistics and psychology have discussed types of implication not adequately elucidated by the deductive–inductive–abductive trichotomy, each associated with a corresponding type of inference. Prominently included here are inferences variously characterized as defeasible, nonmomotonic, default and plausibilistic. These inferences in turn form a kind of hierarchy, with defeasible inference at the top. An inference is defeasible when, although reasonably drawn, it embeds the possibility of error (Hart 1994; McCarthy and Hayes 1969). Nonmonotonic inference is a major species of defeasible inference. It is a presently reasonable inference whose reasonability may be lost upon admittance of new information (Makinson 1994). Default reasoning is a particular kind of nonmonotonic reasoning (Reiter 1980). It is typified by what computer scientists call '**negation** as failure'. For example, from the 'failure' of the airport's departures board to list a late-night flight to London, it may be inferred that there is no such flight.

Negation as failure is linked to a species of implication of particular interest to students of **pragmatics**. It was dubbed by H.P. **Grice** (1975) 'conversational **implicature**', which is an instance of presumptive reasoning like default inference. For example, the information that one speaker imparts to another during **conversation** implicates that it is relevant to the **topic** of the discussion. So, in **default** of information to the contrary, one may presume that what one's interlocutor tells one is relevant to the issue at hand. A further type of presumptive reasoning arises from the pragmatic notion of **presupposition** (Kempson 1975; Stalnaker 1973). If A presupposes B, we may state that in saying

that A, a speaker is implicitly also saying that B. A hearer may take B as a default. That is, he may presume it to be the case unless he learns otherwise. Plausibilistic reasoning is weaker than probabilistic reasoning (Rescher 1976). If you hold that something is probable, you signal (or conversationally implicate) that it is something that warrants a positive degree of belief. But if you say only that it is plausible, you signal that it is worthy of consideration. In some respects, abduction may also be classified as plausibilistic.

The present hierarchy of inference types does not fit smoothly into the deduction–induction–abduction trichotomy, and in some respects cuts across it. To take just two examples, inductive inference is typically both defeasible and nonmonotonic, and deductive inference is nonmonotonic with regard to soundness even if monotonic with regard to validity. The monotonicity of validity provides that new information can never change a deductively valid argument into a deductively invalid argument. But since that same information might falsify a prior premise, thus rendering the original inference unsound, deductive soundness is not monotonic.

Except for those who see no difference between consequences-had and consequences-to-be-drawn, the systematic study of reasoning has two main components. One is a theory of the implication relation that governs the inference process. Theories of implication also typically include accounts of conditionality (Lycan 2001). This is motivated by the fact that whenever A implies B, there is a sense of 'if … then' in which the corresponding conditional sentence 'If A then B' is true. The second component of the study of reasoning investigates the various additional factors that are involved in consequence-driven changes of mind – factors, again, such as an agent's goals, the cognitive standards required to attain them, the cognitive resources needed to meet the standard, and so on. Broadly speaking, logicians have concentrated on the first task, and linguists and psychologists have focused on the second. But the border is far from sealed. Psychologists who study implication include Daniel Kahneman and Amos Tversky (1974), Philip Johnson-Laird and his colleagues (Johnson-Laird and Byrne 1991), John MacNamara (1994), Lance Rips (1994) and Gerd

Gigerenzer (2004) and his colleagues. Likewise, among linguists who study implication relations one might mention George Lakoff (1970), Dan Sperber and Deirdre Wilson (1995), and Gregory Carlson and Francis Jeffry Pelletier (1995) and their colleagues. In contrast, logicians who study the non-implicational aspects of inference, such as the goals of the agent, the agent's resource limitations, the relevance of information to goals, and so on, include (in addition to Harman) Bernd van Linder and his colleagues (1995, 2002), Frank Veltman (2000), Raymond Reiter (2001), and Dov Gabbay and John Woods (2003, 2005).

JOHN WOODS

See also: Abduction; computational pragmatics; entailment; Grice, H.P.; implicature; negation; Peirce, C.S.; reasoning

Suggestions for further reading

Evans, J. St. B.T. (2007) *Hypothetical Thinking*, Hove and New York: Psychology Press.
Levinson, S.C. (2000) *Presumptive Meanings: The Theory of Generalised Conversational Implicature*, Cambridge, MA: MIT Press.
Stanovich, K. (1999) *Who is Rational? Studies of Individual Differences in Reasoning*, Mahwah, NJ: Erlbaum.

Inferential Comprehension

Whereas scientific disciplines, such as logic, have specific definitions for **inference**, the same term in **cognitive psychology** is a general purpose expression that also describes non-demonstrative mental processes involved in comprehension. This way of viewing inference covers a wide range of phenomena that include not only deduction, but also invalid inference-making, categorization, drawing on encyclopaedic memory, **metaphor** comprehension, **implicature**-making, reference resolution, and much more. For the purposes of the present entry, we will begin by showing what investigations into logical comprehension yield before expanding into other areas that have been studied in the cognitive literature more generally.

Inference-making and deductive logic

It is tempting to present the cognitive field of **reasoning** as a partner of logic since correct responses on reasoning tasks are based on logical norms and incorrect responses are indications of faulty reasoning. Nevertheless, the logical criterion goes only so far in describing human comprehension. Consider the case of conditional (*if-then*) arguments, the most investigated in the psychological literature. It is well established that *modus ponens* (to infer *q* from the premises *If p then q; p*) is carried out at rates that are at least 90 per cent while *modus tollens* (to infer *not-p* from *If p then q; not-q*) typically yields correct responses that are at rates of about 60 per cent (Evans *et al.* 1993). This difference results because *modus tollens* involves **negations** and a *reductio ad absurdum* argument. Obviously, not all logical inferences behave similarly.

The study of conditional arguments also reveals that participants in experiments often accept fallacies such as affirmation of the consequent (to accept *p* from the premises *If p then q; q*) and denial of the antecedent (to accept *not-q* from the premises *If p then q; not-p*). The rates of correct responses to the potential fallacies (i.e. to respond that the conclusion is not justified) range from 20 per cent to 70 per cent (Evans *et al.* 1993). Most researchers assume that these fallacies are accepted because the conditional is interpreted as a biconditional (*If p then q* implies *If q then p*). How this occurs, and under what conditions, is a topic of debate that has preoccupied pragmatists (see, for example, Horn 2000).

There are, of course, other features that distinguish human comprehension from classic formal logical systems. For example, non-monotonicity, which concerns the way general beliefs and rules are revised, can undermine even the most basic *modus ponens* argument (Byrne 1989). To appreciate this, consider two premises:

> If Mary meets her friend, then she will go to a play.
> Mary meets her friend.

Whereas nearly all participants endorse the conclusion *Mary will go to the play*, under these conditions, fewer than half do so when a third premise is added to the set:

If Mary has enough money, then she will go to a play.

Clearly, inference comprehension is affected by the surrounding **context**.

Beyond deductive inference

The study of inference-making is not confined to comparing formal deductive logical procedures to informal ones. It also concerns other classes of inference such as induction. To appreciate induction, consider a statement such as 'Goldfish thrive in sunlight' and then determine how likely it is that 'Tunas thrive in sunlight'. In order to make the judgement, one relies on the categorization implied. Much research has been devoted to this area and it shows how powerful categorization is (for a comprehensive review, *see* Heit 2000).

Consider a common categorization task where a child, who is shown a cat, is told that it can see in the dark. When shown another cat she is likely to answer that it too can see in the dark. The idea is that people assume that members of the same category share many properties and that such categorization licenses inferences. Children as young as two and a half years of age will project an enduring property from one object of the category to another, even when category membership conflicts with appearance (Gelman and Markman 1986). To return to the example above, consider the child who is shown the cat that can see in the dark. When shown a cat that looks quite different, she is still likely to answer that it too can see in the dark. However, when presented with a skunk, even one that looks like that first cat, she is less likely to think that it can see in the dark.

The study of inference comprehension is also not confined to deduction and induction. The text-comprehension literature, which is strongly influenced by studies on memory, investigates the way explicit phrases in a text combine with long-term **knowledge** to produce new pieces of information through inference. Theoretical discussion in that literature concerns lines of demarcation between those inferences that are considered automatic and those that are considered 'strategic'. According to one prominent account (McKoon and Ratcliff 1992), inferences

involving co-reference (where a pronoun picks out a previously mentioned noun) are likely to be automatic. However, 'instrument' inferences (Corbett and Dosher 1978), which involve inferring, for example, that a broom was used when reading that *a janitor sweeps the floor*, are likely to require strategic effort.

Another, broader way to view inferential comprehension is through a Gricean lens (Grice 1989). This involves distinguishing sentence meaning from speaker's meaning and attributing mental states to the speaker. The passage from sentence meaning to speaker meaning can then be explained by an inferential process that is guided by the expectation that the speaker has complied with the **cooperative principle**, which leads to a set of **maxims of conversation**. According to **Grice**, inference-making is prompted when a maxim is violated or exploited. For instance, consider an utterance containing a metaphoric reference (e.g. *You are the sun*). By virtue of violating the maxim of quality (speak truthfully), the utterance triggers an inferential process that ultimately leads the listener to the speaker's intended meaning.

Much like researchers in the reasoning literature, Grice was concerned with the way logical terms could have a logical meaning that differs from the one used in everyday exchanges. For instance, the order of conjuncts is immaterial in logical uses of *and* ($P \& Q = Q \& P$). However, in everyday **conversation** P *and* Q readily implies P *and then* Q or P *and thus* Q (making order of conjuncts relevant). These inferences can appear so common that Grice coined the term '**generalized conversational implicatures**' for them. They are pragmatic inferences linked to **propositions** that appear to be generally common, making them valid pragmatically, but not logically.

Experimental pragmatics

Much like in the traditional psycholinguistic literature, many theorists propose that there exists a class of quick, light pragmatic inferences (Levinson 2000). To test this notion, experimentalists have focused specifically on what are often called scalar inferences (or **scalar implicatures**) as a test case. These are inferences that refine the **meaning** of (what are typically) logical terms. For example, the term *some* in *I ran into some of your children today* can be narrowed to mean *some but not all*. This interpretation raises an inconsistency because the semantic meaning of *some* is, in fact, compatible with *all*. Opposing views concerning this inconsistency have led to experimental procedures in the post-Gricean era.

There are also those theorists (e.g. Levinson 2000) who propose that a scalar implicature is generated automatically every time a term that is weak on the scale of informativeness is used. That is, the use of *some*, by being less informative than *all*, automatically prompts the inference *not all* by virtue of the fact that the speaker would have used the more informative term if he or she could have. Likewise, a speaker's use of *or* prompts the rejection of *and*, the use of *might* the rejection of *must*, and *good* the rejection of the more informative *excellent*. In contrast, **relevance theory** (Sperber and Wilson 1995) argues that the semantic reading of a term such as *some* could be good enough, not needing narrowing at all and, when there is narrowing, it is determined by context every time. Generally, in line with relevance theory, current data show that semantic meanings of weak terms are readily accessible to children and adults while narrowed meanings are associated with extra effort. This leads to intriguing developmental trends and reaction-time slowdowns (Breheny *et al.* 2006; Pouscoulous *et al.* 2007).

Since it is semantically underdetermined and relies on the addressee identifying the speaker's **intention**, definite reference is another area of **utterance interpretation** that both fits into a Gricean framework and can be investigated experimentally. Consider how one has to derive the speaker's intention when he or she says 'I used to work for that paper' (while pointing to the latest edition of a newspaper). One constraint advanced to determine the speaker's meaning when using **reference** is common ground (also called mutual knowledge) which is roughly knowledge common to both interlocutors and known by both to be common (Clark *et al.* 1983). The experimental literature on definite reference, much like the case for scalar terms, investigates whether common ground is automatic or intervenes only when needed. To be brief, the cognitive literature shows that closing the gap between the spoken

utterance and the speaker's meaning is often effortful (as measured by reaction times and eye-tracking), indicating that there is some amount of inference-making in direct reference too (*see* Noveck and Reboul 2008).

Taken together, the two phenomena – scalar inference and definite reference – reveal what factors are in play when discussing utterance interpretation from a pragmatic perspective. These are code (the words used), the (non-demonstrative) inferences they engender in context, and a role for intentions (**theory of mind**). As the last two sets of experimental pragmatic investigation indicate, there is a school of thought that assumes that language resolves meaning practically automatically. This kind of claim has prompted others to defend an effortful inferential approach to determining speaker's meaning.

IRA NOVECK

See also: Experimental pragmatics; inference; reasoning; relevance theory; utterance interpretation

Suggestions for further reading

Noveck, I.A. and Sperber, D. (eds) (2004) *Experimental Pragmatics*, Basingstoke: Palgrave Macmillan.
Traxler, M. and Gernsbacher, M.A. (2006) *Handbook of Psycholinguistics*, 2nd edn, San Diego, CA: Academic Press.

Information Structure

The term 'information structure' has been used since Halliday (1967) to refer to the distribution and encoding of given and new information in a sentence. It includes two distinct senses of given versus new information that have not often been carefully distinguished in the literature (*see* Gundel 1999a; Gundel and Fretheim 2003). One sense, relational givenness/newness, concerns the partition of the semantic-conceptual **representation** of a sentence into two complementary parts, X and Y. X is given in relation to Y in the sense that it is independent and outside the scope of what is predicated in Y, and

Y is new in relation to X in the sense that it is new information asserted, questioned, etc. about X. Information structure in this sense includes such concepts as psychological subject and predicate (von der Gabelentz 1868; Paul 1880), presupposition-focus (Chomsky 1971; Jackendoff 1972), topic-comment (e.g. Gundel 1974, 1988), and theme-rheme (e.g. Vallduví 1992).

Information structure has also been construed more broadly to include referential givenness/ newness, the information status that an entity has, or is assumed to have, in the addressee's mind, the **discourse** (model), or some real or possible world. Representative examples include existential **presupposition** (Strawson 1964b), various senses of referentiality and specificity (e. g. Fodor and Sag 1982), the familiarity condition on definite descriptions (e.g. Heim 1982), activation and identifiability statuses of Chafe (1994) and Lambrecht (1994), hearer-old/new and discourse-old/new statuses of Prince (1992), levels of accessibility of Ariel (1988), and the cognitive, i.e. memory and attention, statuses of Gundel *et al.* (1993). Although the two senses of givenness/newness are distinct and logically independent, it is generally agreed that they are empirically connected in that topics, which are relationally given, must have at least minimal referential givenness, as there must be an individuated entity for the utterance, sentence or **proposition** to be about, and in order for a predication to be assessed in relation to that entity. Some authors (e.g. Gundel 1988) have proposed that topics must be familiar, citing association of topics with **definiteness**. Others (e.g. Reinhart 1981) propose that topics only have to be referential, since indefinites can sometimes appear in structural positions reserved for topics. An attempt to reconcile the different positions is presented in Gundel and Fretheim (2003).

Information structure in the referential givenness/newness sense is associated with the choice between different forms of referring expressions (e.g. definite descriptions, **demonstratives**, pronouns) across languages. The most common and consistent way of marking information structure in the relational givenness/newness sense is through placement of a prominent pitch accent within the comment/ **focus** (*see* Lee *et al.* 2007 and references cited

therein). In many languages, the (relationally new) focus/comment receives a different pitch accent than a contrastive or new **topic**. For example, *Fred ate the beans* as an answer to *What did Fred eat?* would have what Pierrehumbert (1980) calls an H* (high tone) accent on *beans*, and a complex L + H* (low tone followed by high tone) accent on *Fred* (Pierrehumbert 1980). But in response to the question *What about the beans, who ate them?*, *Fred* would have an H* accent and *beans* would have an L + H* accent. However, not all languages distinguish prosodically between focus/comment and a contrastive or newly introduced topic. Thus, according to Vallduví and Vilkuna (1998), focus/comment (their 'rheme') and contrast (their 'kontrast') are 'associated with a single high tone accent' in Finnish; and the distinction between the two is coded syntactically rather than prosodically (*see also* Fretheim 1992 for Norwegian).

Languages also encode information structure through word order and different syntactic structures. The structure most widely and consistently used for encoding information structure across languages is one where a constituent referring to the topic is adjoined to the left or right of a full sentence comment/focus (e.g. *The beans, Fred ate (them) yesterday*). Such constructions are relatively unmarked in 'topic-prominent' languages like Chinese (Li and Thompson 1976). In some languages, information may also be marked morphologically through topic or focus markers (*see* Kuno 1972; Gundel 1988; inter alia). Other syntactic structures that encode information structure include different types of cleft sentences (e.g. *It was Fred who ate the beans, What Fred ate was the beans*). While the possibility of syntactic expression of information structure appears to be universal, languages differ in both the manner and consistency with which information structure is directly mapped onto syntactic structure (Birner and Ward 1998; Hedberg 2000; Gundel 2002; inter alia). See Gundel (1988) and Gundel and Fretheim (2003, 2004) for more detailed discussion.

Information structure is typically characterized as a pragmatic phenomenon, since sentences which describe the same basic event or state of affairs may differ in information structure and sentences/utterances with different information structures are appropriate in different **contexts**.

For example, both *Fred ate the beans* and *What Fred ate was the beans* can be used to describe a situation in which Fred ate beans. However, only the former sentence, with focal stress on *Fred*, is an appropriate answer to *Who ate the beans?*. While context influences, and in some cases severely constrains, information structure, as it does all aspects of **meaning** and interpretation (Sperber and Wilson 1995), it uniquely determines a single information structure only in a few cases, such as answers to *wh*-**questions**. Moreover, information structural distinctions sometimes correlate with profound differences in meaning, with corresponding differences in truth-conditional effects. For example, *Dogs must be carried* has different interpretations, depending on the position of focal stress (Halliday 1967). Focal stress on the subject, *dogs*, makes available an information structure where the whole sentence is focus/comment ('sentence focus' of Lambrecht 1994) and a corresponding interpretation that it is necessary to carry a dog, i.e. no dogless people are allowed (for example, to enter a particular place). This interpretation is not available, however, with focal stress on *carried*, which can only mean that if you have a dog, you must carry it. The expression and interpretation of information structure can therefore not be completely reduced to general principles governing human interaction or to other cognitive/pragmatic factors that are not specifically linguistic.

JEANETTE GUNDEL

See also: Definiteness; focus; given/new distinction; presupposition; reference; topic

Suggestions for further reading

Gundel, J.K. (1988) 'Universals of topic-comment structure', in M. Hammond, E. Moravczik and J. Wirth (eds) *Studies in Syntactic Typology*, Amsterdam: John Benjamins.

Gundel, J.K. and Fretheim, T. (2003) 'Information structure', in J. Verschueren, J.O. Östman, J. Blommaert and C. Bulcaen (eds) *Handbook of Pragmatics*, Amsterdam: John Benjamins.

Lambrecht, K. (1994) *Information Structure and Sentence Form: Topic, Focus and the Mental Representation of Discourse Referents*, Cambridge: Cambridge University Press.

Institutional and Professional Discourse

The study of institutional and professional discourses sheds light on how organizations work, how 'lay' people and experts interact and how **knowledge** and **power** circulate within the routines, systems and common sense practices of work-related settings. The analysis of such discourses ranges from the most micro studies, typically drawing on **conversation analysis** and interactional **sociolinguistics**, to more wide-ranging definitions of **discourse**. The latter definitions draw on the critical perspective of Michel Foucault, which relates to the orders and relations that are part of what Dorothy Smith calls the 'ruling apparatus' (Smith 1987: 160).

Most studies of institutional and workplace life involve professionals, and the two terms 'institutional' and 'professional' are often used interchangeably. However, there are useful distinctions to be made between institutional and professional discourse (Sarangi and Roberts 1999). The latter is acquired by professionals as they become teachers, doctors, human resource personnel and so on. Institutional discourse is characterized by rational, legitimate accounting practices which are authoritatively backed up by a set of rules and regulations governing an institution. So, for example, in the medical setting, the diagnosis and agreed course of action or the clinicians' working up of narratives into a case are professional discourses, but the gatekeeping functions of selection, assessment and training rely on institutional discourse.

However, in most settings, professionals are using both types of discourses. For example, Cicourel (1981) shows that the recoding of patient information into abstract categories both relates to clinical treatment but also, institutionally, to the systematic organization of patient care. At this level, the more abstract categories feed into the accounting practices and rules which construct the institution. Record-keeping is an obvious site where professional knowledge is recontextualized into a form where it can be institutionally managed.

The relationship between professional and institutional discourse is also apparent in some of the 'frontstage' and 'backstage' work of professionals (Goffman 1959). Much of the frontstage work is between the expert and the lay client/applicant in service encounters in healthcare (Fisher and Todd 1983; West 1984; Heritage and Maynard 2006), educational settings (Sinclair and Coulthard 1975; Mehan 1979) or in legal settings (Atkinson and Drew 1979). In institutional settings, the backstage is where professional knowledge is produced and circulated, but also where staff and professional groups do the institutional work. The backstage work is where, for example, care plans and records are discussed and made accountable, where decisions are ratified and the initial professional frontstage work is reshaped and reframed to fit into institutional categories.

Within the tradition of conversation analysis and **pragmatics**, the defining characteristic of institutional encounters is that they are asymmetrical and goal-oriented. This, in turn, involves particular constraints on what is allowable, and special aspects of **reasoning** or **inference** (Drew and Heritage 1992: 21–24). These goals are highly **context**-specific. For example, emergency calls to the police require a very different response from home visits by health visitors which consist of several less well-defined goals.

Similarly, the constraints on contributions vary depending on the overall function of the event. Courtroom interaction (Atkinson and Drew 1979), police interrogations (Heydon 2005) and cautions (Rock 2007) and job interviews (Roberts and Campbell 2005) have clearly ritual and formal components which constrain turn-taking and what are allowable contributions. The particular institutional encounter also entails 'special inferences' (Levinson 1979) which are drawn from both background knowledge and from the structural properties of the activity. Levinson illustrates this with some particularly telling examples from courtroom testimony of a rape victim where the defence lawyer uses a line of questioning about what the victim was wearing to create a set of inferences that she was inappropriately and provocatively dressed.

Most institutional and professional encounters involve some kind of sorting and labelling in which gatekeepers (Erickson and Shultz 1982) make assessments of people in order to make decisions about scarce resources. But these are not objective processes, relying instead on evaluations of socio-pragmatic **competence**:

> [G]atekeeping encounters are not a neutral and 'objective' meritocratic sorting process. On the contrary, our analysis suggests that the game is rigged, albeit not deliberately, in favour of those individuals whose communication style and social background are most similar to those of the interviewer with whom they talk.
> (Erickson and Shultz 1982: 193)

For those who do not have 'a feel for the game' and are challenged by the institutional discourse of 'impartiality, symmetry, balance, propriety, decency and discretion' (Bourdieu 1991: 130), the institutional encounter can lead to less good advice, failure to secure a job or in even more high stakes encounters, as in asylum seeker interviews, deportation from a safe country to a dangerous one (Maryns 2006).

Institutions take on a special kind of asymmetry when interactants do not share socio-pragmatic conventions for managing the task, the social relations and **politeness** requirements of the encounter. There are both gendered (Mullany 2007) and ethno-linguistic aspects to this asymmetry. Pragmatic differences in **intercultural communication** in the business world can lead to **misunderstandings** and stereotypes. In ethnically stratified societies, there is a communicative dimension to discrimination when different linguistic practices and socio-cultural knowledge produce inequality (Erickson and Shultz 1982; Gumperz 1982a, 1982b; Roberts *et al.* 1992; Holmes and Stubbe 2003b; Campbell and Roberts 2007). So institutions and organizations are held together by talk and wider discourses, but they are also places of potential struggle, misunderstanding and exclusion which are at least, in part, the product of socio-pragmatic differences.

CELIA ROBERTS

See also: Assessment, pragmatic; context; conversation analysis; discourse; discourse analysis; inference; intercultural communication; misunderstanding

Suggestions for further reading

Drew, P. and Heritage, J. (1992) *Talk at Work*, Cambridge: Cambridge University Press.

Gumperz, J. (ed.) (1982b) *Language and Social Identity*, Cambridge: Cambridge University Press.

Sarangi, S. and Roberts, C. (eds) (1999) *Talk, Work and Institutional Order: Discourse in Medical, Mediation and Management Settings*, Berlin: Mouton de Gruyter.

Intention

The term 'intention' covers distinct aspects of the process which translates desires and goals into behaviour, including action planning and **representation,** goal-directedness and action control. Depending on which aspect is considered, the term 'intention' comes to designate different objects. At one extreme, intentions are acknowledged as separate mental states on a par with beliefs and desires. Understood as mental states, intentions certainly play an important role in the aetiology of action, but are not reducible to the causal antecedent of certain events, i.e. actions. As several philosophers have pointed out, intentions in this sense might indeed never result in actions. At the other extreme, intentions seem to lose their independence, becoming identified with the mental component of the action itself. The intention to flex a finger, for example, is nothing but the mental component controlling the action of flexing the finger – that component whereby we can distinguish between the intentional action of flexing a finger and the unintentional movement of flexing the finger as an automatic reflex.

A range of compound nouns may be used to capture different types of intention: future intention, immediate intention, prior intention, intention-in-action, motor intention, etc. This vertical articulation of the concept of intention has been followed in recent years by a horizontal articulation. Deriving from the exploration of intentions from an inter-subjective point of view, this further expansion comprises the concept of collective intention or we-intention, as opposed to I-intention.

Prior intention versus intention-in-action

Introduced by John **Searle** (1983), this distinction addresses some of the problems raised by earlier versions of the causal theory of action, i.e. the view that what sets actions apart from mere happenings is that they are caused by certain mental events. One problem with which this view is confronted is how to account for those actions that do not seem to be preceded by any intention to cause them. Searle's strategy is to distinguish between the intention formed prior to the action and causing the action as a whole (prior intention) and the mental component of the action, proximately causing the physiological chain leading to overt behaviour (intention-in-action). According to Searle (1983), all intentional actions have intentions-in-action but not all have prior intentions. Similar – though not strictly equivalent – distinctions have been introduced by Brand (1984), who differentiates immediate from prospective intentions, and Mele (1992), who discriminates between proximal and distal intentions.

Action-intention and aim-intention

Focusing on the fundamental ambiguity of the term intention, which is used to denote both plan-states and end-states (*see* Velleman 1989), Tuomela (2005) distinguishes between action-intention, concerning the direct execution of an action (e.g. when agents intend to open the window), and aim-intention, concerning a certain state or event to be brought about. In contrast to action-intention, aim-intention does not require the agent to believe that he or she, with some likelihood, can alone bring about or see to it that the action or its result event comes about. Rather, the agent is assumed, by his or her action, to contribute to the aimed result. An aim-intention can in typical cases be rendered as 'the agent intends, by his or her actions, to bring about a state or event E', where E can in principle be any kind of state. We-intention (see below) can be conceived as a particular form of aim-intention (Tuomela 2005).

Motor intention

Sometimes used as a synonym of intention-in-action, the concept of motor intention addresses the notion of how intention-in-action is represented at a neural level (Haggard 2005). Underlying the concept of motor intention is the idea – largely supported by empirical evidence – that brain areas activated during the representation of executed actions, simply imagined actions and other's observed actions partly overlap. The concept of motor intention can be taken to describe the intersection between these representations. In contrast to a semantic mode of representation, it has been proposed that motor intentions encode a 'pragmatic' representation of the action goal (Jeannerod 1994). Understood as pragmatic representations, motor intentions fall between a sensory function (extracting from the environment attributes relevant to the execution of an action) and a motor function (encoding certain aspects of the action itself).

Collective intentions: I-intention versus We-intention

The notion of collective intention derives from the idea that individual intentions alone cannot explain collective action. Activities such as going for a walk together (Gilbert 1996), jointly operating a water pump (Bratman 1999), preparing a hollandaise sauce by one pouring the oil and one stirring the sauce (Searle 1990b), and pushing a broken-down car together (Tuomela 1995) have served as illustrations of the phenomenon. These activities – it has been argued – are not analyzable in terms of individual intentions, but require a collective intention (sometimes called *shared* or *joint* or *we-intention* in the literature). Note that, within this framework, the term 'collective intentionality' is often understood to refer not only to the phenomenon of collective intentions in the context of collective actions, but also to all mental states and activities exhibiting a collective 'aboutness' or **intentionality**.

Communicative intention

Developed by **Grice** (1989) in the context of his pragmatic theory, the concept of communicative intention includes, as part of its content, that the audience recognize this very intention by taking into account the fact that they are intended to recognize it (Grice 1989). So conceived, communicative intentions (a) always occur in the context of a social interaction with a partner, (b) are overt, in the sense that they are intended to

be recognized by the partner, and (c) their satisfaction consists precisely in the fact that they are recognized by the partner. Based on conditions (b) and (c), communicative intention plays a critical role in distinguishing between **communication** and other non-communicative forms of social interaction (e.g. information extraction; Bara, to appear). Recent attempts have been made to apply these notions to the study of the neural correlates of **social cognition** (*see* Frith and Frith 2006).

CRISTINA BECCHIO and CESARE BERTONE

See also: Intentionality; social cognition

Suggestions for further reading

Jacob, P. and Jeannerod, M. (2005) 'The motor theory of social cognition: a critique', *Trends in Cognitive Sciences*, 9: 21–25.
Pacherie, E. (2006) 'Towards a dynamic theory of intentions', in S. Pockett, W.P. Banks and S. Gallagher (eds) *Does Consciousness Cause Behavior? An Investigation of the Nature of Volition*, Cambridge, MA: MIT Press.
Searle, J. (1998) *Mind, Language and Society: Philosophy in the Real World*, New York: Basic Books.

Intentionality

Mental acts such as beliefs, desires, wants, or expectations are directed at an object; they have content. In other words, they are *about* something. This 'aboutness' is referred to in the **philosophy of mind** and language as intentionality. The Latin term 'intendere' means 'to point' at something, 'to aim' in a particular direction – just as an arrow aims at a target, so a mental state aims at an object. Derived from Aristotle, through Avicenna and medieval doctrines of **knowledge** and experience, intentionality was brought to the forefront of philosophical discussions in the nineteenth century by Franz Brentano (1874). It was subsequently developed by Brentano's students, most notably Edmund Husserl (1900–901), the founder of German phenomenology, where phenomenology is the study of conscious experience, the ways things ('phenomena') are presented to consciousness. It has to be remembered that not all mental states are intentional: feeling dizzy, for example, is not intentional. Moreover, not all intentional mental states are conscious: there can be unconscious beliefs and desires.

Brentano proposed that objects of consciousness are all in the mind. When John sees a brown dog, intentionality amounts to a relation between John and the act of seeing, the properties of which are spelled out by adverbs 'brownly' and 'dogly'. Phenomenologists later replaced this theory by defining intentionality as a relation between an experiencer and a mental object, and subsequently a real object. For Husserl (1913), **meaning** is contained in a *noema*, the objective content of consciousness. These ideas were further developed in the twentieth century by Heidegger.

Intentionality is of primary importance for linguistic **pragmatics** in that intentional acts provide the meaning of expressions. Meaning expressed in language is a sub-type of such noematic, intentional meaning. Linguistic utterances are carriers of speaker's meaning (vehicles of thought) and inherit intentionality from corresponding mental acts/states. Just as my thought has content (is intentional), so my linguistic expression of this thought has content (is intentional). This can be exemplified by **indexical** expressions such as personal or demonstrative pronouns, which contain an act of demonstration as part of their meaning. For example, the meaning of the **demonstrative** 'that' is not entirely contained in the word: the word is an open symbol (indexical, deictic) that requires an external assignment of the exact referent. In contemporary linguistics, the standard distinction is made between linguistic meaning (character) and semantic content (Kaplan 1989a). Intentionality is a useful concept for researching pragmatic ambiguities and helps explain the **default** status of certain interpretations (*see* Jaszczolt 1999). In contemporary **philosophy of language**, intentionality has been regarded either as a feature of conscious states (Searle 1983, 1992) or as brain states with informational content (Fodor 1975, 1981). According to Fodor's realist stance, intentionality is present in the head in the form of computations in the brain: there are no mental states, there are only brain states. There are ample approaches to

intentionality in current research on language and mind (*see* Lyons 1995). In some circles intentionality is currently referred to as representationality (*cf.* Strawson 2005; Woodfield 1994).

KASIA M. JASZCZOLT

See also: Propositional attitudes; reference

Suggestions for further reading

Lyons, W. (1995) *Approaches to Intentionality*, Oxford: Clarendon Press.
Searle, J.R. (1983) *Intentionality: An Essay in the Philosophy of Mind*, Cambridge: Cambridge University Press.
Smith, D.W. and Thomasson, A.L. (eds) (2005) *Phenomenology and Philosophy of Mind*, Oxford: Clarendon Press.

Interactional Linguistics

This article gives an overview of the theoretical and methodological concepts and goals of the research programme called 'interactional linguistics'. This programme is grounded on the premise that language should be analyzed not in terms of context-free linguistic structures but in terms of the actions that are implemented in interaction. With this in mind, interactional linguistics takes an interdisciplinary approach to a linguistic analysis that aims at the understanding of how language is shaped by the actions it is used for.

Historical development

Interactional linguistics can be seen as an alternative to the traditional Saussurian and Chomskyan view of language as a system of signs that should be described without reference to the **context** in which it is used. On the contrary, interactional linguistics adopts the view of ethnomethodological **conversation analysis** (CA) that language use is fundamentally action-oriented. Even though CA's primary research interest lies in the investigation of participants' methods for the organization of social interaction, and not in the linguistic make-up of those methods, this interactional perspective on language has inspired many linguists. Thus, interactional linguistics maintains that linguistic analysis should acknowledge the fact that language is used in and for the purpose of interaction.

Already in the 1980s, British linguists combined phonetic analysis with CA methods and showed that phonetic structures are systematically shaped by interaction and should thus be described as a product of the speech exchanges in which they are produced (Local and Kelly 1986; Kelly and Local 1989). In the German research context, the methodological practices of CA have been further combined with the theoretical insights of contextualization theory, which claims that speakers use specific linguistic and paralinguistic features to evoke interpretative frames. These frames are used by participants to 'construct' a context of interpretation permitting **inferences** about 'what is going on' in the speech event (Gumperz 1982a). CA and contextualization theory constitute the methodological and theoretical basis of research in interactional linguistics.

Research methods and principles

Research in interactional linguistics is strictly empirical and is based on naturally occurring talk-in-interaction. Everyday **conversation** is understood to be the primary environment for language use, and it is recognized as the main object of investigation, but institutional talk also falls into the area of interest. Data are audiotaped and/or videotaped for the purpose of multiple listening/viewing and then transcribed according to a **transcription** system which captures not only the words but also relevant auditory details of the style of delivery such as, for example, pauses, hesitation phenomena and cut-offs. With the aid of the transcript, the data can be listened to or watched repeatedly in order to thoroughly analyze the linguistic resources that prove important for the construction and interpretation of language-related social actions.

The analytical categories developed from the data are understood as an integral part of the sequential context in which they occur. Grammatical analysis, for example, is not to be guided a priori by traditional concepts such as 'clause' or 'sentence'. Instead, linguistic units are viewed as the result of an ongoing, real-time process of coordination and interaction between participants.

Their description is not only form-related but also includes an account of their function in talk-in-interaction.

Methods of validation and verification in interactional linguistics draw mainly on principles of sequential analysis. With reference to Wootton (1989: 244ff.), Couper-Kuhlen and Selting (1996a) name the following five types of evidence for the relevance of a linguistic category: (i) the relationship to prior turns, (ii) co-occurring evidence within the turn, (iii) subsequent treatment in interaction, (iv) discriminability, and (v) deviant cases. It is advocated that all linguistic categories should be warranted by demonstrating participants' orientation to them.

Objects of research

The programme of interactional linguistics comprises all objects of research that are of interest to linguists. Research can be either language-specific or cross-linguistic. So far, most studies have focussed either on **syntax** (Auer 1996; Selting 1996, 2005, 2008) or phonetics/**prosody** (Couper-Kuhlen 1992, 1996a, 2004; Kern 2007) and the relations between them, but recently lexico-**semantics** has also been attended to (Couper-Kuhlen and Thompson 2005; Deppermann 2005). The following areas have been of particular interest: (i) turn-taking, (ii) **sequence organization**, and (iii) action formation. Within these areas, investigations have focused on the role of linguistic structures (iv) for the construction of turns and units smaller than turns, such as 'sentences', 'clauses' and 'phrases', in and for interaction, and (v) for the constitution of conversational activities, styles and genres. An additional area of interest is the ways linguistic structures and phenomena are used and modified in specific interactions, such as institutional settings, **communication** between children and adults, or between participants with communicative disorders. Linguistic analysis then is aimed at the deconstruction of sequentially interpreted turns and actions into their constitutive linguistic features.

Studies in interactional linguistics

In the past decade, many empirical studies demonstrating the interdependence of language and linguistic structure with interaction have been published (e.g. the collection in Couper-Kuhlen and Selting 1996a, Selting and Couper-Kuhlen 2001, Couper-Kuhlen and Ford 2004, and Hakulinen and Selting 2005). Researchers have shown convincingly that the constitution and interpretation of conversational actions and activities depend on their linguistic structure as much as they depend on their positioning within an action sequence.

FRIEDERIKE KERN

See also: Conversational turn-taking; conversation analysis; institutional and professional discourse; intercultural communication; prosody and pragmatics; sequence organization

Suggestions for further reading

Couper-Kuhlen, E. and Selting, M. (1996) 'Towards an interactional perspective on prosody and a prosodic perspective on inter-action', in M. Selting and E. Couper-Kuhlen (eds) *Prosody in Conversation: Interactional Studies*, Cambridge: Cambridge University Press.
——(2001) 'Introducing interactional linguistics', in M. Selting and E. Couper-Kuhlen (eds) *Studies in Interactional Linguistics*, Amsterdam and Philadelphia, PA: Benjamins.
Selting, M. and Couper-Kuhlen, E. (2001) 'Forschungsprogramm "interaktionale linguistik"', *Linguistische Berichte*, 187: 257–86.

Intercultural Communication

'Intercultural' refers to comparison of cultures in contact, while 'crosscultural' refers to comparisons of different cultures in situations of non-contact (and 'intracultural' describes behaviour within a **culture**) (Gudykunst 2002a). The 1960s mark the official birth of intercultural communication in the USA. By that time, North America had experienced waves of immigration which fed a multicultural workforce and stimulated the need to address practical issues of **communicative competence** and miscommunication (Goldstein 1997; Gudykunst and Mody 2002).

While intercultural communication analysis in Europe, Australia and Asia has tended to concentrate on the study of micro-categories of verbal behaviour (e.g. back-channelling, turn-taking, **discourse markers**, **silence**), the North American tradition of cross-cultural communication, with its emphasis on theory testing and development, has concentrated on macro-analytical dimensions (e.g. adaptation, accommodation, uncertainty management) (Gudykunst 2002b). For example, the Australian workplace, populated by successive waves of immigration, has been fertile ground for intercultural communication research from the perspective of cultural differences and preferences (Clyne 1994, 2003; Goldstein 1997).

In the 1990s, the North American perspective of intercultural communication as inherently problematic had been replaced by a more reflexive, data-driven approach to authentic interactions. So, for example, Poncini (2004) in her analysis of intercultural meetings convincingly argues that communicative misunderstandings are often too simplistically attributed to cultural differences, and that **linguistic competence** (in English) alone cannot account for **misunderstanding**. Evidence from further empirical research suggests that a reappraisal is necessary of the role of 'culture' in business interactions (Bargiela-Chiappini and Nickerson 2002).

Intercultural communication sits at the intersection of a range of disciplines from the humanities and social sciences, e.g. linguistics, **pragmatics**, social and cultural psychology, and anthropology. Traditionally, the study of language from an anthropological perspective has involved treating language as a component of culture. A discipline which is of particular interest to intercultural communication, because it is concerned with 'capturing the elusive connection between larger institutional structures and processes and the textual detail of everyday encounters' (Duranti 2003: 323), is linguistic anthropology. Unlike social psychology, linguistic anthropology considers culture not as a cognitive but as a social construct.

Through its 'pragmatic poetic turn' (Silverstein 2004: 623), linguistic anthropology has moved towards the formulation of an analytical approach that reveals the 'cultural' in everyday language. A manifestation of such epistemology is 'culturally contexted conversation analysis' (Moerman 1988: 6), where culture is revealed in talk and is accessed through ethnographically enriched **conversation analysis**. This development provides a rich conceptual grounding for intercultural communication analysis. In this sense, intercultural communication could be defined as culturally situated, and therefore **context**-dependent **discourse**, where 'discourse' is cultural **knowledge** that 'lives and dies in textual occasions' (Silverstein 2004: 634).

In turn, culture as socio-historically situated and emergent from, and transformed by, the 'doings and sayings' of people (Silverstein 2004: 622) is an attractive re-conceptualization for interculturalists seeking an alternative to essentialist positions. According to this perspective, cultures are 'values and meanings expressed through genred (patterned) interactions'. Yet, they are also 'ideational or conceptual in that language in use displays evidence of (creation and transformation of) knowledge, feeling and belief' (Silverstein 2004: 622).

Progress in the theoretical development of intercultural communication has been notoriously slow (Gudykunst 2002b). From within pragmatics, Blommaert (1991: 26) argues that a linguistic theory of intercultural communication should be an interactional theory and should contain macro-concepts that enable generalization of findings. The advantages of such a theory would include an understanding of 'culture' as manifested through discourse, thus leading to the collapse of the traditional (micro, meso, macro) levels of analysis.

Conceptual progress in intercultural communication also depends on a shift in social psychology from an exclusive socio-cognitive to a socio-cultural understanding of the self. It has been argued that the cultural shaping of the self derives from one's philosophical and religious heritage, as witness the analytical view of the world that we have in the West which has been inherited from the Greeks (Cross and Gore 2003). Compare the Judaeo-Christian promotion of the independent self with the holistic and interpersonal sense of being of members of many Asian peoples whose social identity is defined in relational terms. These paradigmatic developments partly explain differences between Western and Eastern motivational and affective systems (Cross and Gore 2003).

The European tradition of intercultural communication, with its preference for qualitative (e.g. pragmalinguistic and ethnographic) studies of, for example, business and corporate settings, is also responsible for the construct of 'interculturality'. Interculturality is defined as the process and the condition of cultures-in-contact. It seeks to capture both the dynamics and the inherent or generic properties of intercultural exchanges as manifested through discourse (Bargiela-Chiappini 2004).

Interculturality pivots on the performance of cultural alignment achieved through language-in-use. In so doing, it denotes the 'cultural' as essentially interactional. In this sense, interculturality is an attempt to overcome the disputes and conceptual divides created by conflictual understandings of 'discourse', 'culture' and 'context'. Moreover, interculturality is not predicated on limiting evaluative criteria of communicative efficiency or effectiveness. Its full potential as a theoretical construct emerges from the analysis of denotational text. For as Silverstein (2004: 631) writes, 'all cultural study is hermeneutic (and dialectic) in nature, seeking to interpret the interactionally significant (i.e. efficacious) "meaning" of denotational text'.

FRANCESCA BARGIELA-CHIAPPINI

See also: Competence, communicative; competence, linguistic; context; conversational turn-taking; conversation analysis; cross-cultural pragmatics; culture; discourse; discourse markers; interlanguage pragmatics; meaning; pragmatics; silence

Suggestions for further reading

Kotthoff, H. and Spencer-Oatey, H. (eds) (2007) *The Handbook of Intercultural Communication*, Berlin: Mouton de Gruyter.

Piller, I. (2009) *Intercultural Communication: A Critical Introduction*, Edinburgh: Edinburgh University Press.

Spencer-Oatey, H. and Franklin, P. (2009) *Intercultural Interaction: A Multidisciplinary Approach to Intercultural Communication*, Basingstoke: Palgrave.

Interlanguage Pragmatics

Interlanguage pragmatics (ILP) represents a research domain at the intersection of

pragmatics and **second language acquisition** (SLA). It examines how speakers understand and produce social action in a second language (L2), and how they develop the ability to do so. ILP's key themes intersect with major research topics in the wider field of SLA and were to some degree, but not exclusively or consistently, extended from interlanguage grammar to pragmatics (for recent comprehensive reviews of L2 pragmatic development, *see* Bardovi-Harlig 2001a, 2001b; Kasper and Roever 2005; Kasper and Rose 2002).

From the late 1970s to the early 1980s, researchers began to explore such topics as the comprehension of indirectness (Carrell 1979), pragmatic awareness (Rintell 1979; Walters 1979), the development of pragmatic and **discourse** competence in cross-sectional (Scarcella 1979) and longitudinal perspective (Schmidt 1983), pragmatic transfer (Olshtain 1983; Scarcella 1983), the influence of social-affective factors on the development of pragmatic ability (Schmidt 1983), and the effect of instruction on the classroom learning of L2 pragmatics (Wildner-Bassett 1984). These themes were partly infused by sources from outside of SLA, such as Hymes's theory of **communicative competence**, **Searle**'s **speech act theory**, **Grice**'s theory of conversational **implicature**, and cognitive-psychological models of utterance processing. Some studies were specifically concerned with the relationship between grammar and pragmatics (Walters 1980). However, it took an explicitly articulated research agenda, proposed towards the end of the millennium by Bardovi-Harlig (1999), and a seminal study by Bardovi-Harlig and Dörnyei (1998) to bring the connection between grammar and pragmatics to the forefront.

A continuing line of investigation took grammar-focused SLA research into pragmatics. The discovery that morphosyntax develops in ordered sequences inspired researchers to look for similar acquisitional regularities in pragmatics, although it was not before another decade that the first longitudinal study by Schmidt (1983) saw a successor (Ellis 1992). In the case of transfer, a topic going back to the behaviourist beginnings of SLA, conceptual apparatus and explanatory constructs were available for application and adaptation to pragmatics, but the literature on pragmatic

transfer – the effect that pragmatic **knowledge** of languages other than L2 has on the use and development of L2 pragmatic knowledge (Kasper 1992) – made little reference to SLA theory and research on cross-linguistic influence. The main impetus to examine pragmatic transfer came from **cross-cultural pragmatics**, the comparative study of speech acts or discourse phenomena in different languages. One of the few psycholinguistically informed studies on the topic is an investigation by Takahashi (1996) on pragmatic transferability, and unfortunately it remained a singular case. On the whole, the interest in transfer has somewhat waned in recent years. Social-psychological theories of inter-group relations made a promising early entrance to interlanguage pragmatics with Schmidt's (1983) study of Wes, a Japanese artist living in Hawaii, a test case of Schumann's (1978) acculturation model, but then receded to the background again (although it was only in pragmatics and discourse that the predictions of the acculturation model were borne out).

In the decade from 1990 to 2000, the research agenda on developmental interlanguage pragmatics was substantially broadened. Continuing already active cognitive and (psycho)linguistic perspectives, a few studies adopted verbal report methodology in order to examine speech act production in a process perspective (Robinson 1992; Cohen and Olshtain 1993). Takahashi and Roitblat (1994) were the first to adopt a reaction time design to investigate learners' comprehension of conventionally indirect **requests** in real time. A more extensive literature on an earlier topic addresses pragmalinguistic and sociopragmatic awareness, either as topics in their own right (Bardovi-Harlig and Dörnyei 1998; Takahashi 1996) or in conjunction with speech act production (Bergman and Kasper 1993; Maeshiba *et al.* 1996). An important innovation in this period was a research program on the testing of pragmatics. Operationalizing the pragmatic component in Bachman's (1990) model for the testing of communicative abilities, Hudson *et al.* (1992, 1995) launched a prototypical multiple method framework for testing speech acts. Subsequently, the prototype was applied to the testing of speech acts in Japanese (Yamashita 1996), followed by further validation studies on instrument effects (Hudson 2001) and test characteristics (Brown 2001).

Research on the instructed learning of pragmatics is perhaps the most prolific and theoretically diverse area in the wider domain. It was here that socially grounded theories of L2 pragmatic learning first evolved. Within the broader area of classroom research, a dual bifurcation can be observed. Until recently, the two traditional sub-areas, interventional and observational research, advanced under two different metatheoretical orientations. Since the 1990s, interventional classroom research, which aims to determine the effect of different instructional arrangements on the learning of L2 pragmatics, has almost exclusively been framed by cognitive processing constructs, especially the noticing hypothesis and concepts of explicit/implicit learning and teaching (Lyster 1994). By contrast, observational studies, which examine the processes of L2 pragmatic learning in instructional settings as they occur without experimental manipulation, engage a variety of socially grounded perspectives. In the first of these, Poole (1992) analyzed the emergence of interactional style in adult ESL classes under a language socialization framework. Other theoretical approaches to L2 **pragmatic development** in language classrooms followed soon, notably Vygotskyan theory and situated learning theory (Ohta 1995), and socioculturally informed approaches to the development of interactional practices (Hall 1993, 1999).

About the same time that classroom research on L2 pragmatic learning began to be enriched by views of L2 pragmatic learning as a socially grounded activity, researchers became interested in two social domains outside of classroom settings. A series of studies by Bardovi-Harlig and Hartford (1990, 1993, 1996) on the learning of speech acts in academic advising sessions inaugurated a productive line of research on interlanguage pragmatics in institutional environments (for a recent collection, *see* Bardovi-Harlig and Hartford 2005). Other settings that have increasingly come under scrutiny as contexts for L2 pragmatic learning are study abroad and home stay contexts (Barron 2003; DuFon and Churchill 2006; Marriott 1993; for recent update). Under the influence of poststructural theories, the relationship of identity and L2

pragmatic learning has been of increasing interest since Siegal's (1995, 1996) ethnographic study of Western women in Japan.

In this millennium, existing topics have been continued, revitalized and reshaped through new technologies, synergies of theories and research methodologies, and in response to societal changes in the wake of migration and globalization. More longitudinal studies are now seen on trajectories of L2 pragmatic development by children (Achiba 2003) and adults (Barron 2003). After a hiatus of almost two decades, with Takahashi's (2005) study on the effect of motivation on attention to pragmatic resources, the social-psychological study of individual differences in pragmatic development has come to the fore again, complementing cognitive theories of L2 learning. Taguchi laid the ground work for a promising new line of experimental research on speech act comprehension (Taguchi 2007a) and production (Taguchi 2007b) in real time, based on a framework that integrates SLA research on task difficulty and fluency with pragmatic theory on speech acts and **politeness**. The relationship between grammar and pragmatics, a continued focus of interest (Schauer 2006), has acquired a new dimension with Bardovi-Harlig's (2006) proposal to investigate the role of formulaic constructions in L2 pragmatic development. The first meta-analysis on the effect of instruction in pragmatics (Jeon and Kaya 2006) shows superior outcomes for explicit instruction, although the small sample of included studies suggests cautious interpretation. Interventional classroom research is now conducted under diverse research paradigms, including cognitive processing models as well as socially grounded theories of interaction and learning. Recent studies have shown how **conversation analysis** can be deployed for teaching culture-specific conversational openings (Liddicoat and Crozet 2001) and speech act sequences (Félix-Brasdefer 2006a; Huth and Taleghani-Nikazm 2006) and for evaluating its own effectiveness for the instructed learning of pragmatics.

Technological advancements have led researchers to investigate the affordances of computer-mediated **communication** for pragmatic development. Through telecollaboration, foreign language students interact with L1 speaking peers in an environment that significantly expands interactional opportunities beyond the classroom and demonstrably advances sociolinguistic and pragmatic L2 abilities (Belz and Kinginger 2002; Kinginger 2000; Kinginger and Belz 2005). Likewise, L2 pragmatics tests are now available through web-based platforms (Liu 2006; Röver 2005), a significant step in enabling test-takers' participation independent of their location.

Together with its themes and questions, ILP has incorporated theoretical perspectives from different domains in **applied linguistics** and other social sciences. The emergence and steady expansion of socially grounded perspectives on language, **meaning**, action, cognition, and learning in the social sciences at large and applied linguistics in particular have enriched and diversified the field of interlanguage pragmatics as well. (Neo)Vygotskyan sociocultural theory (Ohta 2005), language socialization (Li 2007), and conversation analysis (Ishida 2006; Kasper 2006; Taleghani-Nikazm 2002a) are some of the most prominent theoretical and analytical resources that now guide interlanguage pragmatics research. These resources pull into view new connections between language-mediated social action, interactional organization and the wider social **context**, and the shifting constructions of identities and social relations. This work has also called into question, if not retired, stable and essentializing notions of '**culture**' and 'language', and not least the increasingly problematic division between 'native' and 'nonnative' speakers. As multilingualism becomes the norm even in traditionally 'monolingual' societies (Hall *et al.* 2006), and uses of English, Spanish or Chinese as lingua francas increasingly rival their use for 'intralingual' communication (Canagarajah 2007; House 2003), pragmatics is prone to develop hybrid shapes and forms. This will in turn transform what it means to be 'pragmatically competent' in these varieties and raise new questions about the development of such competencies.

GABRIELE KASPER

See also: Applied linguistics; assessment, pragmatic; competence, communicative; competence, pragmatic; communication failure; conversation analysis; cross-cultural pragmatics; culture; discourse; experimental pragmatics; Grice, H.P.; implicature; intercultural communication; politeness; psycholinguistics; Searle, J.; second language acquisition; speech act theory

Suggestions for further reading

Alcón Soler, E. and Martínez-Flor, A. (eds) (2008) *Investigating Pragmatics in Foreign Language Learning, Teaching and Testing*, Clevedon: Multilingual Matters.
Bardovi-Harlig, K. and Hartford, B. (eds) (2005) *Interlanguage Pragmatics: Exploring Institutional Talk*, Mahwah, NJ: Lawrence Erlbaum.
Kasper, G. and Rose, K.R. (2002) *Pragmatic Development in a Second Language*, Oxford: Blackwell.

Internet Language

Pragmatics faces a challenge in relation to computer-mediated communication (CMC: *see* Herring 1996). 'Classical' pragmatics evolved primarily in a context of spoken language interaction (as suggested by such terms as '*speech* acts' and maxims such as 'Do not *say* what you believe to be false'). CMC maintains the emphasis on interaction, but the criteria which define the nature of face-to-face **conversation** do not apply, and the technology permits and motivates new kinds of interaction. As a result, several principles of pragmatics need revision if they are to take into account what actually happens when people communicate through computers.

In many modes of CMC – notably email, chat, bulletin boards, blogs, and most website correspondence – communication does not take place in real time, and so lacks the simultaneous feedback which is critical to the success of face-to-face interaction. Even in so-called 'instant' messaging, there is a lag before a reaction to a message is received. Only in audio CMC (such as Skype) or video CMC (such as iChat) do we get anything resembling a traditional conversation; and even here, audio lag and picture breakdown is routine. One does not, in everyday conversation, see the body of one's interlocutor fragment into a thousand pixels when it moves! The linguistic result of this new state of affairs is that senders have to make their messages more autonomous, looking out for ambiguity or unintentional tone, and avoiding conventions which are likely to be misunderstood (such as using CAPITALS, which will be perceived as 'shouting'). Receivers have to revise their expectations, understanding the constraints which have led messages to be typed in unconventional ways, often using nonstandard spelling, capitalization, and punctuation, heavy **ellipsis**, and novel expressions, such as emoticons (Baron 2000; Crystal 2004).

Face-to-face conversation is typically one-to-one; and where there are several listeners it is not possible to take in and respond separately to simultaneous multiple responses. By contrast, in CMC modes, interaction is often one-to-many, and multiple responses are the norm (Davis and Brewer 1997). In a chatroom, members simultaneously send their own messages and comment on messages sent by others. The messages arrive on screen in unpredictable ways, with semantic threads interweaving; and varying time-delays ('lag') from different computers can cause disruption to normal turn-taking expectations (Hutchby 2001). A message on Topic A from one member can appear on screen when most other members have moved on to Topic B or C. To manage all this, new strategies and states of mind need to be devised. Senders may have to explain which message they are reacting to. Receivers have to relax their expectations of relevance.

Even if only two people are involved and there is no lag, turn-taking notions (such as adjacency-pairing) have to be revised. A typical sequence in an instant messaging dialogue is:

> P makes point A
> P makes supplementary point B
> Q responds to point B (Q1)
> P makes supplementary point C
> Q responds to point A (Q2)
> Q responds to point C (Q3)
> P responds to Q1

and so on. It is a kind of interaction which has no precedent, and which requires both sides to work out appropriate reaction strategies. For example, a Q response to P might be being typed while seeing a new point from P coming

up on screen. Q has to decide whether to send the message being typed or to rewrite it because P's remark has made it redundant. If Q sends it without change, both parties need to tacitly recognize that it is no longer relevant.

Anonymity has a great deal to do with the distinctive pragmatics of CMC. This is not the first medium to allow anonymous interaction, but CMC is certainly unprecedented in the scale and range of situations in which people can hide their identity, especially in chatgroups and forums, where it is routine to use nicknames ('nicks') and hide personal characteristics such as age and **gender** (Wallace 1999). Operating behind a false persona seems to make people less inhibited: they may feel emboldened to talk more and in different ways from their real-world linguistic repertoire. They must also expect to receive messages from others who are likewise less inhibited, and be prepared for negative outcomes. There are obviously inherent risks in talking to someone we do not know, and instances of harassment, insulting or aggressive language ('flaming'), and subterfuge are common (Cherny 1999).

Multiple and often conflicting notions of truth therefore co-exist in Internet situations, ranging from outright lying through mutually aware pretence to playful trickery. It is of course possible to live out a lie or fantasy logically and consistently, and it is on this principle that the games in virtual worlds operate and the nick-named people in chatgroups interact. But it is by no means easy to maintain a consistent presence through language in a world where multiple interactions are taking place under pressure, where participants are often changing their names and identities, and where **cooperative principles** can be arbitrarily jettisoned. In Gricean terms, all basic principles are disturbed (Grice 1975).

The **maxim** of quality is disturbed by 'spoofing' – an unattributed utterance introduced into a chatroom conversation by one of the participants (in a game, sometimes by the software) in order to disrupt proceedings. The result can be a fresh element of fun injected into a chat which is palling, with everybody knowing what is going on and willingly participating. Equally, because spoofing can confuse other participants, many groups are critical of it.

Because there is no way of knowing whether the content of a spoof is going to be true (with reference to the rest of the conversation) or false, such utterances introduce an element of anarchy into the cooperative ethos of conversation. A similar problem arises with 'trolling', the sending of a message (a 'troll') specifically intended to cause irritation to others.

The maxim of quantity can be undermined. At one extreme there is 'lurking' – a refusal to communicate. 'Lurkers' are people who access a chatgroup and read its messages but do not contribute to the discussion. The motives include a new member's reluctance to be involved, academic curiosity (researching some aspect of Internet culture), and voyeurism. 'Spamming' typically refers to the sending of a single message to many recipients, producing electronic 'junk mail', or the sending of many messages to one user, as when a group of people electronically attack a company's policy. Either way, people find themselves having to deal with quantities of unwanted text (Stivale 1996).

The maxim of manner can be challenged. Contributions should be orderly and brief, avoiding obscurity and **ambiguity**. Brevity is certainly a recognized desideratum in most CMC interactions, in terms of sentence length, the number of sentences in a turn, or the amount of text on a screen. In chatgroups, however, there can be an extraordinary degree of disorder, chiefly because of the way participants are all 'talking at once', which can make interactions extremely difficult to follow. And although web page designers constantly affirm the importance of 'clear navigation' around a page, the amateurishness of many web pages means that the manner maxim is repeatedly broken.

The maxim of relevance – that contributions should clearly relate to the purpose of the exchange – is also undermined. What is the purpose of a CMC exchange? In some cases, it is possible to define this easily – a search for information on a specific topic on the Web, for example. In others, several purposes can be present simultaneously, such as an email which combines informational, social, and ludic functions. But in many cases it is not easy to work out what the purpose of the exchange is. People often seem to post messages not in a spirit of real communication but just to demonstrate their

electronic presence to other members of a group – to 'leave their mark' for the world to see (as with graffiti). From the amount of topic-shifting in some forums we might well conclude that no subject-matter could ever be irrelevant. The notion of relevance is usually related to an ideational or content-based function of language; but here we seem to have a situation where content is not privileged, and where factors of a social kind are given precedence. Incorporating new functional dimensions of this kind is one of the many challenges facing pragmatic theory.

DAVID CRYSTAL

See also: Conversational turn-taking; cooperative principle; electronic health discourse; Grice, H.P.; maxims of conversation

Suggestions for further reading

Crystal, D. (2006) *Language and the Internet*, 2nd edn, Cambridge: Cambridge University Press.
Maricis, I. (2005) *Face in Cyberspace: Facework, (Im)politeness and Conflict in English Discussion Groups*, Acta Wexionensia 57/2005, Vaxjo, Sweden: Vaxjo University Press.
Wallace, P. (1999) *The Psychology of the Internet*, Cambridge: Cambridge University Press.

Irony

How do we go about interpreting an ironic utterance such as *You're sharp, aren't you?* (Flash 2004). Given the speaker's ostensive ironic intent, does that guarantee that we activate the appropriate interpretation initially or even exclusively? Or could the process also involve the *literal* ('piercing') and *metaphoric* ('smart') interpretations of the utterance, regardless of their inappropriateness?

An unresolved issue within pragmatics and psycholinguistics is whether our cognitive machinery is adept at swiftly and accurately homing in on a single, contextually appropriate interpretation (Gibbs 1986, 1994; Sperber and Wilson 1995) or whether it is less efficient at sieving out interpretations based on salient (coded and prominent) word and phrase meanings which might be derived irrespective of contextual information and speakers' intent (Giora 1997, 2003). Within the field of nonliteral language, this translates into whether accessible but incompatible message-level interpretations are involved even when contextual information is highly supportive of an alternative interpretation. The debate within irony research thus revolves around the role of salience-based yet incompatible interpretations in shaping contextually compatible ironic but non-salient interpretations in contexts strongly benefiting such interpretations.

What kind of contexts may benefit ironic interpretations? On one view, titled 'the direct access model' (Gibbs 1986, 1994, 2002), a context displaying some contrast between what is expected (by the protagonist) and the reality that frustrates it, while further conveying negative emotions, will both predict and facilitate ironic interpretations (Colston 2002; Gibbs 1986, 2002: 462; Utsumi 2000). On another view, titled 'the constraints-based model', a context involving contextual factors inviting an ironic interpretation (such as speakers known for their nonliteralness) will raise an expectation for an ironic utterance which, in turn, will facilitate irony interpretation exclusively (Pexman et al. 2000). (For a detailed review of the existing models of irony, see Giora 2003: 61–102.)

However, experiments in which one varies characteristics deemed effective by the direct access or constraints-based models have not demonstrated an increase in irony predictability or observed facilitation of irony interpretation (Giora et al. 2009). Although findings in Gibbs (1986) can be viewed as demonstrating similar processing times for ironies and equivalent salience-based (literal) interpretations, they may also be viewed as demonstrating quite the opposite, namely, that irony is more difficult to derive than salience-based interpretations (Dews and Winner 1997; Giora 1995).

Another way to induce an expectation for an ironic utterance has been studied by Giora et al. (2007) who increased uses of ironies in contexts preceding ironic targets. Still, while these contexts gave rise to an expectation for another ironic utterance (as might be also envisaged by Kreuz and Glucksberg 1989), this expectation did not facilitate ironical interpretations of those utterances compared to their salience-based (e.g. literal) interpretations. In spite of their contextual

inappropriateness, only salience-based interpretations were facilitated initially, even when comprehenders were allowed lengthy (1,000 msec) processing time.

Another environment privileging ironic interpretation is that shared by intimates who rely on a rich common ground and who are willing to join in the fun (Clark 1996; Clift 1999; Eisterhold et al. 2006; Gibbs 2000; Kotthoff 2003; Pexman and Zvaigzne 2004). However, a check of the way friends respond to their mates' ironic turns shows that they mostly respond to the salience-based (e.g. literal 'what is said') interpretation of the irony, either by addressing it directly or by extending the ironic turn on the basis of the salience-based interpretation (Eisterhold et al. 2006; Giora and Gur 2003; Kotthoff 2003). For instance, the irony cited above (*You're sharp, aren't you?*) is followed by an utterance (*I like my men to have 'brains' and a 'bit of class'*) that elaborates on the salient (metaphoric) meaning of the irony. Such response patterns testify to the high accessibility of irony's salience-based interpretations which may therefore lend themselves to further elaborations.

Indeed, most of the behavioural evidence in irony research argues in favour of a salience-based rather than contextually compatible initial model of irony interpretation (Colston and Gibbs 2002; Dews and Winner 1999; Giora 1995; Giora and Fein 1999; Giora et al. 1998, 2007; Ivanko and Pexman 2003; Katz et al. 2004; Katz and Pexman 1997; Pexman et al. 2000; Schwoebel et al. 2000). Corpus-assisted studies too support the view that salience-based interpretations are highly functional in irony interpretation (Partington 2007). Among other things, it is, in fact, the initial activation of incompatible, salience-based interpretations that makes irony interpretation a complex and error-prone process (Anolli et al. 2001; Lagerwerf 2007), as also demonstrated by some notorious misunderstandings (e.g. taking Swift's 'A Modest Proposal' literally; see Booth 1974).

The view that irony interpretation is a complex process also gains support from neurological studies. For instance, irony has been shown to recruit the right hemisphere, which is adept at inferencing and remote associations. Salient meanings and salience-based interpretations (familiar literals and familiar metaphors), however, rely more heavily on the left hemisphere, which reduces the range of possible alternatives to the most salient ones (Eviatar and Just 2006; Giora *et al.* 2000; Kaplan *et al.* 1990; McDonald 1999; Peleg and Eviatar 2008; Shamay-Tsoory *et al.* 2005a; Wakusawa *et al.* 2007). Furthermore, neurologically impaired populations were also found to fare better on salience-based interpretations than on (non-salient) ironic interpretations. For instance, populations impaired on theory of mind (the ability to distinguish between our own mental states and those of others), such as autistic individuals (including individuals with Asperger syndrome, a high-functioning variant of autism), individuals with closed head injury, brain damage (especially right-hemisphere damage) and schizophrenia performed worse than normal controls on irony compared to familiar (metaphoric and literal) interpretations (Baron-Cohen *et al.* 1993, 1997; Channon *et al.* 2005; Giora *et al.* 2000; Kaland *et al.* 2005; Kasari and Rotheram-Fuller 2005; Leitman *et al.* 2006; Martin and McDonald 2004; McDonald 2000; Mitchley *et al.* 1998; Mo *et al.* 2008; Stratta *et al.* 2007; Thoma and Daum 2006; Tompkins and Mateer 1985; Wang *et al.* 2006; Winner *et al.* 1998).

Developmentally, findings which show that irony acquisition occurs rather late, between 6 and 9 years of age (Bernicot *et al.* 2007; Creusere 2000; Hancock and Purdy 2000; Winner 1988), and decays earlier than simpler tasks (Bara *et al.* 2000), also support the view that interpreting irony might be a complex process. And while adults mostly make do with contextual information (Bryant and Fox Tree 2005), children, in addition, often rely on prosodic cues when detecting irony (Ackerman 1981, 1983, 1986; Capelli *et al.* 1990; de Groot *et al.* 1995; Milosky and Ford 1997; Winner 1988; Winner *et al.* 1988; but see Attardo *et al.* 2003 and Bryant and Fox Tree 2005, who found that there is no specific tone of voice for irony).

This diverse array of findings, coupled with observed scarcity (7–10 per cent) of ironic turns among friends (Attardo *et al.* 2003; Eisterhold *et al.* 2006; Gibbs 2000; Partington 2007; Rockwell 2004; Tannen 1984a), elementary-school teachers (Lazar *et al.* 1989), and others (Haiman 1998; Hartung 1998) and the failures to detect them (Attardo 2002; Rockwell 2004) bring out irony's complex nature. Such complexity is pre-

dicted by theories which assume that salience-based albeit incompatible interpretations play a major role in irony interpretation (Clark and Gerrig 1984; Colston 1997b, 2002; Currie 2006; Dews and Winner 1999; Giora 1995; Kumon-Nakamura *et al.* 1995; Recanati 2004b; Sperber and Wilson 1995: 242), while further triggering inferential processes such as implicature derivation (Attardo 2000, 2001; Carston 2002: 160; Grice 1975) and theory of mind (Curcó 2000; Happé 1993, 1995; Sperber and Wilson 1995; Wilson 2006; Wilson and Sperber 1992). Although by the age of 6 years we can distinguish between our own and others' mental states, even as adults we often fail to recruit this ability initially (Keysar 1994, 2000; Keysar *et al.* 2003), although this may vary culturally (Wu and Keysar 2007).

However, theories assuming that context can effect immediate if not exclusive activation of nonsalient but contextually compatible interpretations (Gibbs 1994; Katz *et al.* 2004; Pexman *et al.* 2000; Utsumi 2000) cannot, at this stage, explain a wide range of findings accumulated during the last two decades of irony research. Still, testing the initial effect of a *cluster* of contextual factors, including their relative weight, might shed further light on the nature of irony interpretation.

RACHEL GIORA

See also: Autism spectrum disorders; clinical pragmatics; conventionality; development, pragmatic; experimental pragmatics; explicit/implicit distinction; humour; inference; inferential comprehension; neuropragmatics; pragmatic language impairment; right-hemisphere damage and pragmatics; schizophrenic language; theory of mind; traumatic brain injury and discourse

Suggestions for further reading

Barbe, K. (1995) *Irony in Context*, Amsterdam: John Benjamins.
Gibbs, R.W. Jr and Colston, H.L. (eds) (2007) *Irony in Language and Thought: A Cognitive Science Reader*, New York and London: Lawrence Erlbaum Associates.
Martin, A.R. (2007) *The Psychology of Humor: An Integrative Approach*, Burlington, MA: Elsevier.

K

Knowledge

Set at the centre of a network of related notions like reality, **meaning**, understanding, reason and truth, knowledge is probably the most debated concept in the history of Western thought. With the rise of scientific psychology in the second half of the nineteenth century and of **cognitive science** another hundred years later, the notion of knowledge has become crucial to our comprehension of ourselves, insofar as the mind has been conceived of as a knowledge engine. There is no way of encapsulating the concept of knowledge in a brief entry, so we will limit ourselves to outlining a few roles that it plays in **pragmatics** and **communication**. We recommend that the reader consult the entries on cognitive science and **representation and computation** for further discussion and references.

Pre-theoretically at least, the following domains of knowledge can be kept distinct in the study of communication: (1) knowledge that each agent has about herself; (2) knowledge that each agent has about the interlocutor(s); (3) knowledge that each agent has about the process of communication; (4) knowledge that each agent has about the specific communicative exchange in which she is currently engaged; and (5) knowledge that each agent has about the world within which the exchange takes place. There can be overlaps between two or more of these domains. How each such domain is viewed and described depends on how one conceives of knowledge. Furthermore, since the cybernetic turn at the middle of the twentieth century (Wiener 1948; Ashby 1956; Bateson 1972) the

mind has been viewed as a knowledge engine: a system that dynamically generates and employs knowledge. Therefore, the question concerning the nature of knowledge is closely related to the question concerning the nature and the 'structure' of the mind and of its activities. There are basically two large perspectives concerning these issues, which we will call descriptionist and constructivist perspectives.

Because we are accustomed to dealing with knowledge as it appears to be hosted in sentences, drawings and other external, publicly accessible reifications of human thought, it may appear commonsensical to think that knowledge has an objective nature and that it exists before the subject and independently of it. The subject then may or may not have access to knowledge. In this perspective, knowledge is conceived of as reified into a (potentially infinite) set of statements whose meaning and truth are independent not only of the individual subject, but of any subject at all. Large bodies of mind and brain sciences have straightforwardly adopted this view to describe knowledge as a mental phenomenon. To the traditional locus of 'accessible' knowledge – the external world of books and encyclopaedias – these research communities have added a second, substantially identical locus placed in the realm of mental events and activities. Such events and activities, like the knowledge that they employ, are mostly or completely outside the scope of subjectivity. In this tradition, the mind is made up of an array of subpersonal components and processes that collect, store, retrieve and manipulate representations as pieces of knowledge. The functioning of the representational mind, that is, of the knowledge engine, is independent of the subjective mind and impenetrable to it. The subjective mind may access some products of the functioning of the representational mind, possibly adding qualitative feels (qualia) to them, but its role is marginal, often to the point of theoretical or practical eliminativism. The unconscious in Freudian psychology, the computational machinery of cognitive science, or language processing in mainstream **psycholinguistics** are examples of mental functions and activities that are thought to be representational and knowledge-intensive, yet to fall outside the scope of subjectivity (Searle 1992 criticizes this view). Analogously, several conditions of neuropsychological interest are often explained in terms of the patient's defective access or lack of access to relevant portions of her own knowledge base. The standard interpretation of anomia (nominal aphasia), for example, is in terms of the inability to access (part of) one's own lexicon.

Many theorists, however, do not accept this view. An alternative is to regard mental knowledge (or all kinds of knowledge) as the subject's construction rather than as an objectively given, albeit internalized, description which she can or cannot access. Constructivism is a broad array of theories characterized by the idea that knowledge is inseparable from the subject. In this perspective, knowledge is a property of the meaningful ways in which an agent interacts with the world and with herself. By definition, a meaningful interaction exists only in the first person, and the first person exists only in the here and now. Therefore, knowledge is actively and continuously constructed by the interacting mind. The representational mind (that is, the knowledge engine) and the subjective or phenomenal mind (that is, consciousness and experience) become one and the same thing. A consequence of this view is the need to distinguish between the knowledge that an agent's mind actually represents at a certain moment – like her experience of walking and the relevant thoughts and bodily feelings – and the knowledge that is merely embedded in the way she acts, like the 'knowledge' about balancing that her body implements as she walks. While in the descriptionist approach outlined above the difference between the two is at most a question of 'levels of representation', here the difference is

qualitative. (Of course, the agent may theorize about bodily balancing. The knowledge employed for this purpose, however, is not directly the 'implicit' bodily knowledge, but a more or less detailed description thereof.) **Intentionality**, that is, the semantic (meaningful) relation between the mind and the world, is a crucial notion in this framework. The forms that intentionality takes in a certain agent depend on the agent's biological nature and endowment (Johnson 1987; Maturana and Varela 1987; Tirassa et al. 2000) as well as on her previous interactions and on the activities in which she is currently engaged. This typically leads to the adoption of a methodology that is close to or includes phenomenology (Merleau-Ponty 1945; Varela 1996).

Let us now turn our attention to knowledge as it is employed in communication. First, each agent has to possess knowledge about herself. First-person experience and the awareness thereof are the basis of human agency: the reasons why an agent communicates are grounded in her beliefs, emotions, goals (both global and local), values, and so on. The standard jargon of psychology and cognitive science, typically cast in terms of elementary, subpersonal systems and microprocesses, has a hard time capturing the nature and functioning of human planning, action, and understanding. **Relevance theory** (Sperber and Wilson 1995) is probably the most renowned theory of pragmatics grounded in the standard jargon and general perspective of cognitive science. It may be interesting to note that, however satisfactory as a theory of language comprehension, relevance theory has never been able to become a theory of language generation or of dialogue, nor has it ever even tried to.

Most other theories of communication since Grice (1957) are cast in terms of mental states or, more precisely, in some variation of the so-called Belief-Desire-Intention (BDI) framework (Rao and Georgeff 1992). Such a framework appears to be well suited to the description of human activity, whether private, generally social or specifically communicative (Tirassa 1999). Mental states can be studied in terms of their intrinsic nature, their functional role in the mind's internal dynamics and in its relations with the external world, their biological and evolutionary import, and so on. The use of a

BDI framework, however, is still neutral about the nature of the mind. In the descriptionist framework, mental states are abstract, objectively given states of a control system, and actions are behaviours or operators that are performed in an objectively given internal or external world (e.g. Fikes and Nilsson 1971; Newell and Simon 1972; Newell 1990; Cohen and Levesque 1990a, 1990b). In this view, it makes sense to say that a thermostat can perceive the external temperature, decide to turn on (or off) the heater and act upon such beliefs and **intentions**, issuing appropriate commands to the heater itself. This is viewed not as a metaphor, but as a simple, handy model of what goes on inside an animal's or a human being's mind. Instead, in the phenomenological or constructivist framework (Guidano 1987, 1991), beliefs, desires and intentions are phenomenal experiences that exist in the first person. The same view is then extended to the mental states involved in communication and generally in social cognition (Gallagher 2001; Gallagher and Hutto 2008; Tirassa and Bosco 2008).

Second, if communication is conceived of in terms of an agent affecting the mental states of another (Grice 1957), then knowledge of one's interlocutor(s) is also crucial. An agent must have an idea of what her partner's mental states are in order to affect them and to understand how (and even that) another agent is trying to affect hers. The ability to possess knowledge of others' minds is the faculty commonly known as mindreading, or **theory of mind** (Premack and Woodruff 1978). The descriptionist view will typically conceive of this kind of knowledge as a theory proper that is made up of a list of facts and a set of **reasoning** rules concerning the minds of others (Fodor 1992). In this case, there is no particular reason to distinguish it from the knowledge that the agent has about herself, which also consists in a similar set of **propositions** and rules. The constructivist view will more likely conceive of mindreading in terms of intersubjectivity, and will probably be careful to keep it distinct from self-knowledge. Indeed, there are complex ongoing debates concerning the nature of mindreading (Whiten 1991; Baron-Cohen et al. 1993; Lewis and Mitchell 1994; Carruthers and Smith 1996) and its relation with self-knowledge (Goldman 1993;

Gopnik 1993; Nichols and Stich 2002; Bosco et al. 2009). These debates often involve developmental aspects, which are particularly interesting in the area of communication, because many empirical studies appear to show that human infants have substantially no theory of mind during the first 9–12 months of life. If this were true, it would be impossible for infants to engage in intentional communication with their caregivers (Risjord 1996) and, at least under certain perspectives, to even acquire language during this period (Bloom 2000). These considerations have been influential in the development of alternative accounts of the nature and the ontogeny of mindreading and communication (Airenti 1998, 2004; Tirassa et al. 2006a, 2006b).

Third, agents must have knowledge about the process of communication itself. This is a complex area which includes knowledge of language, knowledge of **speech acts** (including their locutionary, illocutionary and perlocutionary aspects), knowledge of the nature and the structure of **conversation** (including the allocation of turns, the repair system, etc.), knowledge of **rhetoric** and of the structure of dialogue and **discourse**, and knowledge of social customs and habits (including the nature and the management of 'face', **politeness**, and so on). Here, the general logic of the difference between descriptionist and constructivist approaches can be captured as follows. The descriptionist approach will view dialogue and conversation as characterized by an intrinsic, grammar-like or script-like structure that prescribes to a greater or lesser extent what move is appropriate to the ongoing exchange or should be played by each interlocutor at each time, as well as how the various structural and linguistic components of such moves relate to each other and to the overall script (Schegloff and Sacks 1973; Rumelhart 1975; Schank and Abelson 1977; Airenti et al. 1993a). In the constructivist perspective, the descriptionist approach appears to unduly expel subjectivity from the study of the mind's activities and to commit the fallacy that Searle (1990a) calls 'explanatory inversion': the belief that regularities found in conversation (or generally in human activities) are caused or generated by the application of internal rules. Thus, constructivist approaches to communication (Winograd and Flores 1986; Tirassa and

Bosco 2008) will view the meaning and relevance of the communicative moves and of their components as founded in each interlocutor's dynamics of mental states and in how such dynamics relate to each agent's subjectively perceived situation.

Fourth, communicators must have knowledge of the dynamics, the current status and the contents of the specific communicative exchange in which they are engaged. This has to include at least some (however rough) knowledge of each participant's current status and situation, knowledge of what has gone on explicitly and implicitly up to the present time, knowledge of what has been mentioned or referenced in the previous utterances, knowledge of the **presuppositions** and the **implicatures** of such utterances, knowledge of the material setting of the conversation (for example, it may be a face-to-face interaction or an interaction that occurs on the telephone or on email), and so on. According to some theories (Clark 1992, 1996; Airenti *et al.* 1993a), a larger or smaller part of this knowledge has a peculiarly public status. The idea is that communicative actions take place in a joint (mental) space which includes part or all of the above phenomena: such space is jointly set up and modified by the interactants and becomes their common knowledge. Some mental states of the interactants also belong to this public space; of course, if communicative actions are thought of as mental events the two things become one. Here, the descriptionist view will conceive of the public space as something that exists before and independently of the mental dynamics (and, of course, the subjectivity) of the interactants. This is typical, for example, of the 'joint plan' theories of dialogue in **artificial intelligence** and classical cognitive science (Cohen *et al.* 1990; Grosz and Kraus 1996, 1999). The constructivist view will conceive of the public space as a one-sided mental state which is unilaterally built by each interactant. Successful interaction depends on each interlocutor constructing a public space which is identical to, or at least compatible with, those of the others (Tirassa and Bosco 2008). Sometimes the whole notion of public space is interpreted as

a form of collective intentionality (Bratman 1992; Searle 1995; Tuomela 1995).

Fifth, the last kind of knowledge integral to communication is the general world knowledge that is needed to deal with the current exchange. This may include, for example, knowledge of the entities to which **reference** has been made, background knowledge, 'encyclopaedic' knowledge, and so on. The descriptionist view will conceive of this kind of knowledge in terms of semantic networks (Collins and Quillian 1969; Quillian 1968; Woods 1975), frames (Minsky 1974) and other representational codes. The constructivist perspective will view it in terms of an agent's capacity to experience the current situation as related to past ones and to the overall situation in which she finds herself (Clancey 1997a, 1997b; Glenberg 1997). Further, researchers adopting the constructivist perspective will probably view lexical knowledge as part of this category. In this perspective, to know what salt is in understanding a sentence like 'Pass the salt, please' is not different from knowing what happened at Waterloo in understanding 'This is a Waterloo'. Actually, the very idea that words, phrases and sentences have intrinsic meanings that pre-exist interpretation may be viewed as a token of the descriptionist idea that knowledge is objective and pre-exists the subjective mind.

DAVIDE MATE and MAURIZIO TIRASSA

See also: Artificial intelligence; cognitive pragmatics; cognitive psychology; cognitive science; computational pragmatics; cooperative principle; experimental pragmatics; explicit/implicit distinction; intentionality; philosophy of mind; propositional attitude; representation and computation

Suggestions for further reading

Maturana, H.R. and Varela, F.J. (1987) *The Tree of Knowledge: The Biological Roots of Human Understanding*, Boston, MA: Shambhala Press.
Newell, A. (1990) *Unified Theories of Cognition*, Cambridge, MA: Harvard University Press.
Searle, J.R. (1992) *The Rediscovery of the Mind*, Cambridge, MA: MIT Press.

L

Language Evolution

In 1866, the Société de Linguistique de Paris banned the presentation of *any* theory purporting to explain the evolution of the human language faculty. During the years following the publication of Charles Darwin's *Origin of Species* there had been an explosion in the number of (increasingly) far-fetched accounts offered and the Société felt its reputation for scientific rigour was at stake.

The area is indeed fraught with problems. A major problem is that language faculties don't fossilize. A palaeontologist will never find a section of an early hominid's language module among the strata of a cliff, or a grammatical structure hidden in a piece of flint. There is no fossil record of any kind through which to sift, and as a consequence many theories are simply not testable. In addition to this problem, other traditional methods of evolutionary research, such as the analysis and comparison of analogous traits within related species, are unavailable. The combinatorial, recursive system that is language appears to be uniquely human. While there are many complex **animal communication** systems (*see* Hauser 1996), none have anything in common with the core features of human language. Even our closest relative, the chimpanzee, has neither the cognitive ability to acquire language nor the physical prerequisites for producing it if they could.

Reflecting the concerns of the Société de Linguistique de Paris, (retrospectively at least), Stephen Jay Gould (1989: 14) warned against *Kiplingesque* 'just-so stories' in accounts of language evolution: 'the universals of language are so different from anything else in nature … [that] origin as a side consequence of the brain's enhanced capacity, rather than a simple advance in continuity from ancestral grunts … seems indicated'. For someone who has said so much about language, Noam Chomsky was notoriously reticent (at one time at least) on the question of its evolution. Chomsky (1988: 167) stated that 'in the case of such systems as language or wings, it is not easy even to imagine a course of selection that might have given rise to them'. Indeed, he was largely thought to advocate a view that a language faculty could have emerged by way of a single genetic mutation (*see* Piatelli-Palmarini 1989).

Despite the numerous problems, over the past twenty years or so there has been a massive resurgence of interest in the evolution of not only language, but also **communication** and cognition. Modern theories of language evolution are constrained by advances in evolutionary psychology, and are helped by the increasing number of researchers – from disciplines as diverse as neuroscience, behavioural genetics and archaeology – becoming involved in the field (*see* Christiansen and Kirby 2003 for a review).

Various aspects of human language have been proposed as the core around which the human language faculty evolved. For Terrence Deacon (1997), it is the fact that language uses 'symbols' – humans are, to use the title of Deacon's book, the 'symbolic species'. For Jean Aitchison (1996), it is 'the naming insight' deployed by children in the early stages of the acquisition of language. For Andrew Carstairs-McCarthy (1999), it is subject-predicate structure which, he argues, has its origins in syllable structure. Michael

Corballis (2002) proposes that language evolved from manual gestures. Steve Mithen (2005) suggests it was the propensity early hominids possessed for making music that led eventually to the evolution of language. In 2002, Chomsky himself joined the discussion (Hauser *et al.* 2002). This paper sought to sever the link between the evolution of language and the evolution of communication and argued that language – in the sense of a 'narrow syntax' (2002: 2) which generates linguistic **representations** and maps them on to the language of thought – could have evolved as a by-product of other human computational abilities, such as number or navigation.

For those working in **pragmatics**, it is interesting to note that all these proposals are based on a view of ancestral hominid linguistic communication that is a simple coding-decoding affair (*see* Dessalles 2007 for an exception). Such a view of communication is also adopted in one of the seminal papers on the topic, Pinker and Bloom (1990). However, it is problematic. If linguistic communication began as a pure coding-decoding process, we need to explain why it changed in character so drastically at a certain stage, and became inferential (*see* Sperber 2000). Most accounts ignore the fact that it is not just language that is unique, but also the way we use it. An act of linguistic communication is a meeting of minds. Human communicators are simultaneously engaged in a massive amount of multilayered **intention** attribution and expression.

A further assumption in much work is that the evolution of the human linguistic ability preceded the development of the kind of mental capacity necessary to handle these multilayered **metarepresentations**. This view is also problematic, since without some capacity for inferential communication it is hard to see how a language faculty could have been adaptive. Natural selection is a process by which advantageous heritable characteristics or traits increase in prevalence within successive generations of a particular organism, and disadvantageous ones decrease. But any organism, who acquired through mutation some novel linguistic coding-decoding ability, would have had no advantage within his or her community. These abilities would have been entirely useless, as this organism

would have had no one to talk to and no one to listen to. In the development of other cognitive mechanisms, such as face recognition and colour categorization, there is a clear domain of information in the environment that is present *before* the mechanism evolves. What in the environment could have resulted in mutations toward a language faculty being selected for? As Sperber (1990: 757) puts it:

> Either we deny with Piatelli-Palmarini and others that the language faculty has been selected, or we deny that the domain of information relevant to the language faculty was empty before the emergence of the faculty itself.

Sperber considers the second possibility, and proposes that metarepresentational abilities developed before linguistic abilities (Origgi and Sperber 2000; Sperber 2000, 2001a; Sperber and Origgi 2005). Humans with an evolving metarepresentational capacity would have had a system of inferential **prelinguistic communication** before a language faculty evolved, and a more plausible evolutionary scenario presents itself. The biological evolution of the language faculty may have resulted from the emergence of ever more precise coded signals, which increased the efficiency of inferential communication by saving effort and making its effects more precise (*see* Wharton 2006).

One feature of much work on the evolution of the human metarepresentational capacity is that while there is disagreement about precisely how it developed, there is at least agreement that it could indeed have evolved, or at least begun to evolve, independently of communication. Cosmides and Tooby (2000) suggest that the ability to entertain a representation of a situation as something other than a true belief about the world would have improved human adeptness in reacting and responding to local aspects of the environment. Another view – the Machiavellian Intelligence Hypothesis (Whiten and Byrne 1988a) – proposes that the metarepresentational capacity might have developed in response to the particular challenge for humans of dealing with the complexity of social interaction (*see also* Dunbar 1998a). The ability to interpret behaviour in terms of underlying mental states would have given our ancestors strong predictive powers. It would therefore have been adaptive to become increasingly adept at working out the thoughts and feelings of others (Humphrey 1984). In the human case, it is argued, the challenge of social interaction led to a spiralling of cognitive abilities which enabled individuals to better compete with their conspecifics and perhaps outmanoeuvre them. Tomasello *et al.* (2005) point out that as well as evolving the ability to compete and deceive, humans also evolved the ability to collaborate and cooperate. This disposition to share intentions, which includes a metarepresentational ability, may form the foundation upon which human interaction (and possibly human **culture**) is built.

This account has a lot going for it. The proposal that humans were capable of entertaining thoughts complex enough for full-blown inferential communication, or **meaning**, is not inconsistent with aspects of all the approaches discussed above. But one of the strongest benefits of taking this approach is that the human metarepresentational ability is just the kind of existing computational system to make an excellent candidate for being recruited into use as a rudimentary **syntax** (in the way Hauser *et al.* 2002 suggest language in the narrow sense may be a 'by-product' of other abilities). The degree of metarepresentation required for overt inferential communication presupposes considerable recursive ability, and linguistic syntax could quite plausibly have been inherited from the syntax of the language of thought. Put simply, we should not ignore the possibility that, in evolutionary terms, the human pragmatic ability came before the linguistic one.

TIM WHARTON

See also: Animal communication, pragmatics of; cognitive anthropology; cognitive psychology; communication; competence, pragmatic; meaning; metarepresentation; pragmatics; social cognition; theory of mind; utterance interpretation

Suggestions for further reading

Desalles, J.-L. (2007) *Why We Talk: The Evolutionary Origins of Language*, New York: Oxford University Press.

Hauser, M. (1996) *The Evolution of Communication*, Cambridge, MA: MIT Press.
Origgi, G. and Sperber, D. (2000) 'Evolution, communication and the proper function of language', in P. Carruthers and A. Chamberlain (eds) *Evolution and the Human Mind: Modularity, Language and Meta-Cognition*, Cambridge: Cambridge University Press.

Legal Pragmatics

Legal pragmatics may be said to have begun as a research area at the same time that **pragmatics** itself emerged. John **Austin**, in his *How to Do Things With Words* (1962), illustrated his approach to the **philosophy of language** by using legal and quasi-legal utterances to illustrate performative utterances, in contrast to constatives. His examples include 'I give and bequeath my watch to my brother' which, he states, may occur in a will. A further example is 'I do' or 'I take this woman to be my lawful wedded wife' which may be considered quasi-legal, since it is the conventional utterance at a religious marriage ceremony, and is consequentially considered to have a legal effect. Austin set up felicity conditions for these performatives. Such conditions would be based on what the law requires for such utterances to be felicitous, or legally operative (Olivecrona 1971). For example, a preparatory condition of a will of the form 'I bequeath … ' would be the ownership by the speaker of what he or she plans to bequeath. One of the preparatory conditions of the ritual utterance at a marriage ceremony would be the unmarried status of the speaker at the time the performative is uttered; otherwise, the speaker would be committing bigamy.

Further research on **speech acts** in written legal texts has been carried out by Kurzon (1986), who studied legislative texts, in particular. He noted the almost exclusive use of *hereby* not only in terms of its occurrence in legal performatives, but also its function as an indication of a performative. Legislative texts, interestingly also called 'act' (*cf.* 'speech act') as well as 'statute' in English, consist primarily of directive speech acts, though declarations may occur, too. The statute itself is a declaration expressed in the form of the passive of *to enact*: 'Be it enacted … '.

Other types of written legal documents that have also been pragmatically analysed include contracts (Trosborg 1995a), and wills (Tiersma 1999).

Spoken legal discourse has also been analysed from a pragmatic perspective. Starting from Danet's (1980) seminal article on legal discourse, which included a discussion about **questions** and answers in legal proceedings (e.g. the Watergate hearings in the Senate in the early 1970s), considerable research has been carried out on **discourse** in the courtroom. This work has analysed the type of questioning of witnesses by counsel, especially to show the different types of speech acts used to elicit information advantageous to the particular lawyer, but detrimental to the position of the opposing side. This may be seen in terms of **power** – the asymmetrical relationship between the counsel and witness, and even the asymmetrical relationship between judge and counsel. The pragmatics of power may be especially seen in defence counsel's questioning of a rape victim (Ehrlich 2001), or a witness belonging to a socially disadvantaged or linguistically disadvantaged group, e.g. aborigines (Eades 2000). The form of question may be seen as highlighting the power of the lawyer vis-à-vis the witness. While *wh*-questions allow the addressee to tell his or her story, which is often the case with expert witnesses or witnesses brought by the lawyer's side, *yes/no* or polar questions are used to obtain only a 'yes' or a 'no' without any elaboration. Even a 'Yes, but … ' may be disallowed. A lawyer in court would use polar questions, and expect 'yes' or 'no' as answers, when questioning the opposing side's witnesses, and a witness that he or she has brought, but who turns out to be a hostile witness.

Another effect of the asymmetrical power relationships that exist in legal discourse could be the lack of **politeness**. What happened in the past, however, when judges insulted witnesses – e.g. Lord Justice Jeffreys in the trial of Lady Alice Lisle: 'But you Blockhead, I ask you whether you did see any body else?' (Kryk-Kastovsky 2006b: 220) – would not happen today. Not only do judges maintain a correct and polite stand in relation to all those present in the court proceedings, but they also keep the lawyers in check to ensure that the proceedings are fair. Another area in which politeness has been studied is in inter-judicial relations where

in their published opinions (judgements) judges sitting on the same bench refer to colleagues on the bench, to judges in lower courts (in appeal cases), or refer to counsel who appeared before them. Again, there seems to be an attempt to maintain polite discourse, although differences have been discerned in the judicial behaviour of American and English judges, where the latter appear to be more polite (Kurzon 2001).

Other pragmatic fields relevant to legal pragmatics, especially in spoken discourse in the courtroom, include **presuppositions**, turn-taking, and **silence**. The area of presupposition in questions may be illustrated with the well known utterance 'Have you stopped beating your wife?' which presupposes that the addressee beat his wife in the past. In this case, even an appropriate *wh*-question may have a similar effect, since 'When did you last beat your wife?' also presupposes previous domestic violence on the part of the addressee.

In courtroom discourse, the turn-taking rules (Sacks *et al.* 1974) are not altogether suspended, but they do not have the flexibility that one finds in natural **conversation**. Judges and lawyers usually select the next speaker – the judge may address the lawyer or the witness, and the lawyer may address the witness. Attempts by a witness to obtain a pause on the part of the counsel by selecting him- or herself may be considered contempt of court. This is linked to the power relationship discussed above, when a witness would like to answer a *yes/no* question with a 'yes, but … '. The witness's turn has been circumscribed as a short one-word answer, which by the rules of courtroom procedure would immediately give the turn back to counsel.

Where speech is expected, but none occurs, is a central issue in criminal investigations. This relates not only to the interpretation that may be given to a suspect's silence, but also to the rights of the suspect that have to be protected. The right of silence has been studied both in the British context (Gudjonsson 1991; Kurzon 1995, 1996), and in the American context – the well known Miranda warning (Leo and Thomas 1998). Courts cannot interpret a suspect's silence as admission, despite the fact that in natural conversation a refusal to answer a question is usually understood as a tactic of avoiding a compromising answer. The silent addressee may, for example, have something to hide. In legal proceedings, such an interpretation has to be rejected. However, in current English law, in a situation where a suspect is silent about a particular matter during police investigation which he or she then brings up at trial, this silence may be commented upon, and interpreted as it would be in normal conversation.

The analysis of pragmatic features in legal discourse does not suggest a different approach from the pragmatic analysis of other discourses, except for the conventional and traditional restrictions that are placed on the participants when engaging in legal discourse. It is this set of restrictions, for example, as felicity conditions to speech acts, that seems to identify legal discourse as a fruitful area of pragmatic research, as Austin discovered over a half a century ago.

DENNIS KURZON

See also: Austin, J.L.; police-suspect interviews; silence; speech act theory; question

Suggestions for further reading

Gibbons, J. (2003) *Forensic Linguistics: An Introduction to Language in the Justice System*, Malden, MA: Blackwell.

Kryk-Kastovsky, B. (2005) 'Legal pragmatics', in K. Brown (ed.) *Encyclopedia of Language and Linguistics*, Oxford: Elsevier Science.

Lexical Pragmatics

The basic idea of lexical pragmatics was launched by a now classic paper (McCawley 1978). Discussing several examples, McCawley argued that 'a lexical item and a syntactically complex equivalent of it may make different contributions to the interpretation of a sentence without making different contributions to its semantic structure' (McCawley 1978: 257). Alluding to **Grice**'s (1967) **maxims of conversation**, McCawley demonstrated that the difference between the linguistically encoded semantic structure and the suggested interpretation (presumptive meaning) is a consequence of general principles of cooperative behaviour and as such is systematic and predictable. As a consequence,

he claims, there is no need to formulate idiosyncratic restrictions that must be incorporated into the relevant lexical entries in order to restrict the system of interpretations. The suggested division of labour between **semantics** and **pragmatics** has important consequences for keeping semantics simple and for applying the semantic tool of decomposition.

Lexical pragmatics investigates the mechanisms by which linguistically specified word meanings are modified in use. Following Wilson (2003) and Carston (2002), we can distinguish three basic phenomena:

(i) 'Narrowing' refers to using a lexical item to convey a more restricted interpretation than the semantically encoded one. Examples are the use of the word *drink* to mean 'alcoholic drink' or the use of *smoke* to mean 'smoke your joint' (at least in Amsterdam, where everybody knows the **request** 'please smoke inside'). Further examples concern the interpretation of reciprocals (Dalrymple *et al.* 1998), adjectives (Lahav 1989), and polysemous nouns such as *opera*, *concert*, *school*, and *government* (Nunberg 1979).

(ii) 'Approximation' refers to a case of interpretive broadening where the interpretation of a word with a restricted core meaning is extended to a family of related interpretations. Cases in point are loose uses of numbers (e.g. *1,000 students* used to mean 'about 1,000 students'; *cf.* Krifka 2007a), geometric terms (e.g. *square* used to mean 'squarish'; *cf.* Wilson 2003), colour adjectives, where the precise colour value can deviate from the lexically addressed focal colour (e.g. *red* in *red nose*, *red bean*, and *red flag*). Recanati (2004b) introduced the term 'modulation' for describing the underlying mechanism of contextual modification. A precise model of this mechanism is one of the big challenges for lexical pragmatics.

(iii) 'Metaphorical extension' refers to a type of broadening that extends the space of possible interpretation much more radically than approximation. A good introductory example is the perception verbs in English (*cf.* Sweetser 1990). Following

John Locke and Ferdinand de Saussure, Sweetser (1990) claims that the feature of arbitrariness could be taken at least as a sufficient condition for the presence of semantic information. It is certainly an arbitrary fact of English that *see* (rather than, say, *buy* or *smell*) refers to visual perception when it is part of the utterance ('I *see* the tree'). Given this arbitrary association between a phonological word and its **meaning**, however, it is by no means arbitrary that *see* can also have an epistemic reading as in 'I *see* what you're getting at'. Moreover, it is not a coincidence that other sensory verbs such as *smell* or *taste* are not used to express an epistemic meaning. Sweetser (1990) sketches an explanation for such facts and insists that they have to do with conceptual organization. It is our **knowledge** about the inner world that accounts for vision and knowledge being highly related, in contrast to, say, smell and knowledge or taste and knowledge, which are only weakly related for normal human beings. If this claim is correct, then the information that *see* may have an epistemic meaning but *smell* and *taste* do not, no longer needs to be stipulated semantically. Instead, this information is pragmatic in nature, having to do with the utterance of words within a conceptual setting, and can be derived by means of some general mechanism of conceptual interpretation. Other cases of metaphoric extension are more radical extensions of the semantically specified interpretation, as illustrated by the following examples: 'The president has been *under fire* for his veto'; 'My memory is *a little foggy*'.

To give a categorization of different basic phenomena does not mean to assume different computational mechanisms for explaining these phenomena. Rather, it is theoretically much more satisfying to look for a unified theory of lexical pragmatics. Presently, we find two main attempts for realizing such a unified approach. The first one is based on **relevance theory** (RT; Sperber and Wilson 1995); the second one is based on **optimality-theory pragmatics**

(OTP; Blutner 1998; Blutner and Zeevat 2004a; Blutner *et al.* 2005). Both approaches agree on a number of important assumptions. For instance, both approaches take a naturalistic stance with regard to pragmatics and pursue the same main goal: developing a cognitive psychological model of lexical interpretation. This contrasts with the normative character that is normally attributed to the Gricean approach. Further, both approaches claim that the linguistic semantics encoded by a natural language expression underdetermines what is communicated by an utterance of that expression. Taking a lead from Atlas (e.g. Atlas 2005), both theories reject the doctrine of literal meaning (that **logical form** conforms to literal meaning), and assume **contextualism** instead, i.e. the claim that the mechanism of pragmatic interpretation is crucial both for determining what the speaker says and what he means.

There are also important differences between the two approaches. OTP follows the neo-Gricean idea of assuming that two countervailing principles determine the interpretation mechanism (Atlas and Levinson 1981; Horn 1984; Blutner 1998; e.g. Atlas 2005; Horn 2005): the Q-principle and the R-principle. The first principle is oriented to the interests of the hearer and looks for optimal interpretations; the second principle is oriented to the interests of the speaker and looks for expressive optimization. In optimality theory (OT), these principles correspond to different directions of optimization where the content of the optimization procedure is expressed by particular OT constraints. In contrast, RT sees the communicative principle of relevance as the only effective principle. According to this principle, utterances convey a presumption of their own optimal relevance. That means that any given utterance can be presumed (i) to be at least relevant enough to warrant the addressee's processing effort and (ii) to be the most relevant one compatible with the speaker's current state of knowledge and her personal preferences and goals.

Obviously, both RT and OTP account for the resolution of the conflict between communicative effect and (processing) effort. This observation, and the fact that both approaches have a number of 'free parameters' for fitting the empirical data, make a direct comparison relatively difficult. The notion of blocking, which is present in OTP but missing in RT, is presumably a substantial difference between the two approaches. Although it is not really clear if the mechanism of blocking is a real processing mechanism that takes place online in natural language interpretation, its role in directing language acquisition and language change is strongly supported. The general idea is that a specialized item can block a general/regular process that would lead to the formation of an otherwise expected interpretation equivalent to it. For example, in English the specialized mass terms *pork*, *beef*, and *wood* usually block the grinding mechanism in connection with the count nouns *pig*, *cow*, and *tree*. This explains the following contrasts: 'I ate *pork*/?*pig*'; 'I like *beef*/? *cow*'; 'The table is made of *wood*/?*tree*'. It is important to note that blocking is not absolute, but may be cancelled under special contextual conditions (*cf.* Blutner 1998). This suggests that the blocking phenomenon is pragmatic in nature and may be explicable on the basis of Gricean principles.

McCawley (1978) makes the interesting claim that verbs such as *cause* and *make* are neutral with regard to the directness of causation but are given an interpretation of indirect causation through conversational **implicature** (as is famously exemplified by the periphrastic phrase *cause to die* where the direct causation interpretation is blocked by the existence of the semantically equivalent verb *kill*). Interestingly, McCawley cites examples demonstrating that periphrastic causatives can be used for direct causation in cases where there is no lexical causative. This provides direct evidence for the idea of blocking: the interpretation of periphrastic causatives depends not only on their own linguistic meaning but on what alternatives the lexicon provides for expressing the interpretation in question.

The RT approach to lexical pragmatics has been developed in Carston (2002), Wilson (2003), and Wilson and Sperber (2002), inter alia. The main idea is that the linguistically encoded meaning of a word is no more than an indication to the actual interpretation or utterance meaning. Hence, the interpretation is not decoded but has to be inferred by a pragmatic mechanism. Furthermore, understanding any utterance, literal, loose or metaphorical, is a matter of seeing its intended relevance, as specified in the relevance-theoretic comprehension procedure. In other words, RT:

> suggests the following answers to the basic questions of lexical pragmatics: lexical-pragmatic processes are triggered by the search for relevance, they follow a path of least effort, they operate via mutual adjustment of explicit content, **context** and cognitive effects, and they stop when the expectations of relevance raised by the utterance are satisfied (or abandoned).
>
> (Wilson 2003: 282)

The idea to use OTP for formalizing lexical pragmatics was proposed by Blutner (2000) (*see also* Blutner 2004; Blutner and Zeevat 2004a; Blutner *et al.* 2005). There are several case studies demonstrating the power of the formalism. Jäger and Blutner (2000, 2003) suggested an OTP analysis of the different reading of German *wieder* (again). Henriëtte de Swart (2006) provided an OTP approach to the pragmatics of **negation** and negative indefinites. Referring to the stage level/individual level contrast, Maienborn (2004, 2005) argued against the popular view that the distinction between stage level predicates and individual level predicates rests on a fundamental cognitive division of the world that is reflected in the grammar. Instead, she proposed a pragmatic explanation of the distinction, and she gives, inter alia, a **discourse**-based account of Spanish *ser/estar*. Other applications include the pragmatics of dimensional adjectives (Blutner and Solstad 2000), the analysis of Dutch *om/rond* (Zwarts 2006), the pragmatics of negated antonyms (Blutner 2004; Krifka 2007b), the approximate interpretation of number words (Krifka 2007a), and several examples of semantic change (Eckardt 2002).

Recent developments concern the role of fossilization in lexical pragmatics as a mechanism for sanctioning certain interpretations (e.g. Blutner 2007; Blutner and Zeevat, to appear). The idea of fossilization was introduced in Geis and Zwicky's (1971) paper about 'invited **inferences**' as a mechanism for conventionalization of implicatures. A closely related approach is Morgan's (1978) theory of short-circuited implicatures where some fundamentally pragmatic mechanism has become partially grammaticalized. Using this idea, Horn and Bayer (1984) propose an elegant account of so-called neg-raising, i.e. the availability (with certain predicates) of lower clause understandings for higher clause negations. Here is an example:

(1) a. Surface form: Robert doesn't think Stefan left.
    b. Interpretation: Robert thinks Stefan didn't leave

There is a principal difficulty for pragmatic treatments of these neg-raising interpretations. The difficulty has to do with the existence of lexical exceptions to neg-raising, i.e. we find pairs of virtual synonyms of which one member allows the lower clause understanding and the other blocks it. One of Horn and Bayer's (1984) examples concerns opinion verbs. For instance, Hebrew *xogev* 'think' permits neg-raising readings while *maamin* 'believe' does not. Interestingly, the opposite pattern obtains in Malagasy. In French, *souhaiter* 'hope, wish' exhibits neg-raising, but its near-synonym *esperer* does not – although its Latin etymon *sperare* did. Horn and Bayer (1984) argue that conversational implicatures may become conventionalized ('pragmatic conventions') and this conventionalization sanctions neg-raising.

The short-circuiting of implicatures as a matter of convention has important empirical consequences for lexical pragmatics. Inter alia, these consequences were discussed in connection with the classical pattern of constructional iconicity (or Horn's (1984) division of pragmatic labour) stating that unmarked forms preferentially correspond to unmarked meanings and marked forms preferentially correspond to marked meanings. McCawley (1978) listed numerous cases of constructional iconicity in the lexicon; the most famous one was mentioned already in connection with *kill* (denoting direct causation) and *cause to die* (denoting indirect causation). Krifka (2007a) observed that the phenomenon is the decisive factor in determining the precise/vague interpretation of measure expressions. Interestingly, there are also examples of anti-iconicity. They are found in connection with semantic broadening. A good example can be found in Dutch, where besides the preposition *om* (= Engl. 'round'; German 'um') the

word *rond* is in use, which is a word borrowed from French. It refers to the ideal shape of a circle. Starting with its appearance the form *rond* comes in competition with the original (and unmarked) form *om*. The result is a division of labour as demonstrated in the following examples (*cf.* Zwarts 2003, 2006):

(2) a. Ze zaten rond (?om) de televisie
       ('They sat round the television')
    b. Een man stak zijn hoofd om (?rond) de deur
       ('A man put his head round the door')
    c. De auto reed om (?rond) het obstakel heen
       ('The car drove round the obstacle')

Interestingly, the marked form *rond* is semantically close to the ideal shape of a circle (unmarked meaning) whereas the unmarked form *om* is semantically close to the detour interpretation (marked interpretation).

A theoretical solution that accounts for iconicity and anti-iconicity is in terms of a mechanism of cultural evolution simulating the real process of conventionalization (e.g. Van Rooy 2004). Here, the actual frequencies of marked and unmarked interpretations play a significant role in determining the result of conventionalization. Hence, the actual parameters of use are often decisive for the result of conventionalization.

REINHARD BLUTNER

See also: Abduction; context; experimental pragmatics; explicit/implicit distinction; formal pragmatics; generalized conversational implicature, theory of; Grice, H.P.; implicature; maxims of conversation; neo-Gricean pragmatics; optimality-theory pragmatics; post-Gricean pragmatics; pragmatics; radical pragmatics; rationality; relevance theory; semantics-pragmatics interface

Suggestions for further reading

Blutner, R. (1998) 'Lexical pragmatics', *Journal of Semantics*, 15: 115–62.
——(2004) 'Pragmatics and the lexicon', in L. Horn and G. Ward (eds) *Handbook of Pragmatics*, Oxford: Blackwell.

Wilson, D. (2003) 'Relevance and lexical pragmatics', *Italian Journal of Linguistics/Rivista di Linguistica*, 15: 273–91.

Literary Pragmatics

According to Banfield (2003: 475), 'the term "literary pragmatics" does not have widespread use with a well-defined referent; it stands less for a unified theory than for an area of research.' As an 'area of research', concerned with what and how literary texts communicate, literary pragmatics has developed in response to insights provided by pragmatic theory over the past few decades. It does not have, as Banfield notes, 'a widespread use with a well-defined referent' because of the different approaches to **pragmatics** that have provided the insights and because of the different types of relationship between literary analysis and pragmatic theory (with, on the one hand, a literary pragmatics that is essentially literary analysis using ideas from pragmatics and, on the other hand, literary pragmatics that is properly grounded in, a proper part of, pragmatic theory). A further complication results from the different understandings, or definitions, of the term 'literary' and the contested special nature of literary **communication**.

One early attempt to give shape to this new field of research, the Åbo Symposium on Literary Pragmatics (1988) (*see* Sell 1991), illustrates the wide diversity of approaches currently being pursued. Based partly on the experience of this symposium, Sell (1998) argues that there is a crucial distinction to be drawn between 'formalist' and 'historical' literary pragmatics. Formalist literary pragmatics focuses on analyses based on 'systems' or 'sets of conventions', or pragmatic processes (depending on the preferred pragmatic theory) that help to characterize what is distinctive about literary communication. (Work by Pratt (1977) and others on **speech act theory** and literary communication and Banfield (1982) on 'unspeakable sentences'/free indirect **discourse** are placed in this category.) Just as 'Russian formalism' sought to characterize literariness in terms of the linguistic properties of literary texts, so 'formalist' literary pragmatics can be seen as an attempt to characterize literariness

in terms of pragmatic properties. This project is contrasted with the 'historical' literary pragmatics that Sell favours, which is 'interdisciplinary' in that it seeks connections between literary studies, pragmatics, history and sociocultural studies and uses ideas from pragmatics to the benefit of literary analysis. With such a range of disciplinary backgrounds, research in this kind of literary pragmatics is inevitably interpretive rather than explanatory. It draws ideas and insights from social pragmatic theory as found, for example, in Brown and Levinson (1987), in an attempt to build up an interpretation of the **context**, defined in broad terms, in which a literary text is written and read. **Politeness** theory, for example, is used to offer insights into and help articulate the nature of the assumed and actual relationships existing between writers and readers. Sell (1998: 534) argues that politeness is rarely treated in literary studies despite being 'the most basic aspect of the writer-reader relation'. One way in which Sell develops this idea is in his distinction between 'selectional' politeness, referring to the choice of what to talk about in the context of what is considered appropriate or (relatively) taboo, and 'presentational' politeness, referring to the (relative) degree of help given to the reader, the relative accessibility or obscurity of literary texts.

A different kind of literary pragmatics – one providing an account of literary communication grounded in an explanatory pragmatic theory dealing in mental **representations** and processes – is made available by the **relevance theory** account of poetic effects. This account (*see* Sperber and Wilson 1995, mainly chapter 4, sections 6 and 8) depends on the notion of weak **implicature**. This notion is briefly illustrated here with respect to poetic **metaphor**. Sperber and Wilson (1995) contrast the following two metaphors:

(1) This room is a pigsty.
(2) His ink is pale.

Examples of 'standardized metaphor' such as in (1), it is argued, 'give access to an encyclopaedic schema with one or two dominant and highly accessible assumptions' (Sperber and Wilson 1995: 236). The information that pigsties are filthy and untidy is taken from the encyclopaedic entry of the concept PIGSTY and used to implicate that a certain room is filthy and untidy. The context (assumptions stored under PIGSTY) is readily accessible and hence the implicatures are relatively determinate and strong. Even so, it is argued, the relative indirectness of the utterance encourages the hearer to process a little more deeply than would normally be the case for more cognitive effects (in accordance with the communicative principle of relevance), in order to recover 'an image, say of filthiness and untidiness beyond the norm, beyond what could have been satisfactorily conveyed by saying merely 'This room is filthy and untidy" (Sperber and Wilson 1995: 236).

The utterance in (2), said by Flaubert of the poet Leconte de Lisle, is an example of a more creative, or poetic, metaphor. Unlike the case in example (1), there is no readily accessible context that can be used to achieve a satisfactory range of contextual implications, an interpretation consistent with the communicative principle of relevance. The context is, therefore, extended to provide a wider range of weak implicatures. Sperber and Wilson (1995: 237) suggest that the only immediately recoverable relevant implicature is that Leconte de Lisle 'has the character of a man who would use pale ink'. They then suggest that 'some other implications – that Leconte de Lisle's writing lacks contrasts, that it may fade – have further relevant implications in a context to which has been added the premise that what is true of his handwriting is true of his style'. Different addressees would be expected to access different, or different ranges of, weak implicatures.

Poetic effects generally are characterized in terms of such weak implicatures, of the making marginally more manifest of a range of weakly manifest assumptions. The effect of this, it is claimed, is to create 'common impressions rather than common **knowledge**' (Sperber and Wilson 1995: 224). Utterances communicating poetic effects can 'create this sense of apparently affective rather than cognitive mutuality' (Sperber and Wilson 1995: 224). 'Apparently' non-propositional affective effects, in other words, can be described in purely propositional terms as a wide range of minute cognitive effects. This kind of analysis can be extended to the communication of poetic

effects in literary texts, at least at the local level of poetic metaphor or the poetic use of other kinds of language use. (*See*, for example, Blakemore 2008 on apposition, MacMahon 2007 on sound patterning and Sperber and Wilson 2008, which includes an analysis of poetic effects from literal description.) This account represents an attempt to provide a precise description and explanation of what Sperber and Wilson (1995: 57) refer to as 'the vaguer effects of verbal communication': it explains the impossibility of adequate paraphrase (it is impossible to spell out precisely which range of implicatures is communicated, to determine the boundary between implicatures and mere implications) and it explains variety of response (different sets of implicatures derived by different addressees may be instances of equally successful communication).

This relevance-based literary pragmatics has produced an extensive range of analyses of literary texts as well as theoretical debate about the way in which literary communication should be described and explained (*see* Yus 2008 for a complete list of work in this area). One of the currently important theoretical issues arises from developments in **lexical pragmatics**, in particular the emphasis on the need for a distinction between decoded and communicated concepts. In (1), for example, it is now argued that an ad hoc concept PIGSTY* is communicated, a concept denoting places that are really filthy and untidy (as well as real pigsties), rather than simply the decoded concept PIGSTY. In (2), the concept PALE* is communicated, rather than PALE, its denotation including characteristics of a writer's style as well as a colour shade. In moving from PALE to PALE* it is now accepted that the relevant properties are not simply taken from one encyclopaedic entry and transferred to another: the properties required emerge in the inferential process of constructing an ad hoc concept on the basis of a decoded concept. (The property indicated by 'fading' of ink on paper is not the same property of 'fading' as applied to reputation; 'weakness' and 'lacking contrasts' refer, likewise, to different properties in respect of ink and style.)

An important question arises: do concepts (or the construction of concepts) such as PALE* differ from concepts (or the construction of concepts) such as PIGSTY*? It could be argued that

PALE* is more indeterminate: it is likely to be the case that a wider range of concepts (PALE*, PALE**, PALE***, etc.) will be constructed by different addressees. The range of PIGSTY* concepts is likely to be much narrower with a smaller degree of indeterminacy. Although the emergent property issue is important here for the interpretation of poetic metaphor, the ad hoc concept issue is of more general significance for the analysis of poetic effects. The definition of poetic effects, therefore, has to be revised in the light of these changes: poetic effects need to be explained not only in terms of the communication of a wide range of implicatures but also in terms of the construction of a particular kind of ad hoc concept.

The characterization of poetic effects in Sperber and Wilson (1995), outlined above, claimed that non-propositional effects are merely apparent. The underlying idea was that a description and explanation had to be framed in propositional terms for it to fall squarely within the domain of pragmatic theory. It could be argued, however, that the implicature account fails to adequately represent the full force of what is communicated, that thoughts containing affective representations are essential to literary communication (Pilkington 2000). The suggestion occurs in recent work that non-conceptual information may play an important role in, for example, the interpretation of creative metaphor. Carston (2002: 321, 356) suggests that some encyclopaedic information 'may be represented in analogue (as opposed to digital) format, perhaps as mental images of some sort' and goes on to suggest that they may play a role in metaphor interpretation: 'could it be that we derive conceptual representations ... through scrutinising the internal image, rather as we might form thoughts through looking at an external picture?'

If literary pragmatics can be said to be beginning to establish itself, not as a loose area of research, but as a unified discipline, then it is as an explanatory account of literary communication grounded in relevance theory and based on the relevance theory account of poetic effects, where progress is being made. It is clear, however, that this account requires revision in the light of developments in lexical pragmatics and that there are many unresolved issues. They include, most importantly, the challenge posed

to literary pragmatics by the role of analogic format information/non-propositional effects in **utterance interpretation** generally and in literary interpretation more particularly.

ADRIAN PILKINGTON

See also: Dramatic discourse; implicature; metaphor; politeness; relevance theory; speech act theory

Suggestions for further reading

Pilkington, A. (2000) *Poetic Effects*, Amsterdam: John Benjamins.
Sell, R. (1991) *Literary Pragmatics*, London: Routledge.
Sperber and Wilson (2008) 'A deflationary account of metaphor', in R.W. Gibbs (ed.) *The Cambridge Handbook of Metaphor and Thought*, Cambridge: Cambridge University Press.

Logical Form

A logical form is the semantic **representation** of an interpreted sentence. It can depart quite radically from grammatical form. Consider (1):

(1) If he misses the plane, then he will be late.

Here there is a grammatically subordinate clause, followed by a main clause. This kind of sentence is usually represented, in logical form, as a material conditional:

(2) $P \rightarrow Q$

where 'P' represents the 'if' clause and 'Q' the 'then' clause and where the subordination has been replaced by coordination. Consider, further, (3):

(3) All men are mortal.

Here there is a traditional subject predicate form (*c.f.* Strawson 1974). This is usually represented, in logical form, as fundamentally a material conditional; first, informally:

(4) For any object, in the domain of **discourse**, which we shall arbitrarily call 'x',

if that object is a man, then that object is mortal.

then, formally:

(5) ∀x (Man(x) → Mortal(x))

where '∀' is the universal quantifier and 'x' the name of the arbitrarily chosen object. The curious consequence of this method of revealing the logical form of universally quantified statements is that in a domain of discourse where there are no objects that we would want to call 'men', (5) is still true. Universally quantified **propositions**, unlike natural universally quantified sentences, have no existential commitments.

This general view of logical form is able to claim at least two significant successes. The first relates to expressions referring to non-existing objects. For example, one of the most notorious sentences from the archives is:

(6) The present King of France is wise.

This sentence is, on the face of it, neither true nor false, but it is a declarative sentence and, on a classical view, ought to be one or the other. It can be made one or the other if it is recognized that the logical form bears little relationship to the grammatical form. The assumption is that (6) consists of three 'smaller' propositions:

(6a) There is a King of France.
(6b) There is only one King of France.
(6c) That one King of France is wise.

(6a) is the existential clause, (6b) is the uniqueness clause, and (6c) is the predicative clause. More formally:

(6i)   ∃x KoF(x)
(6ii) ∀y(KoF(y) → y = x)
(6iii) Wise(x)

or, when conjoined:

(7) ∃x(KoF(x) & ∀y(KoF(y) → y = x) & Wise(x)).

On this analysis, this proposition is false, and so consistent with classical demands on **semantics**, because the first conjunct is false and this falsity

is sufficient for the falsity of the conjunction. Russell, the original architect of this account (1905), was not modest about what he had achieved. Of the analysis he said: 'This clears up two millennia of muddle-headedness about "existence", beginning with Plato's *Theaetetus*' (Russell 1946: 785; *c.f.* Ostertag 1998; Reimer and Bezuidenhout 2004; Neale 2005b).

The second significant success relates to adverbial modification. For example, another notorious sentence from the archives is:

(8) John buttered the toast at midnight with a knife in the kitchen.

This sentence entails all of (9) to (12):

(9)   John buttered the toast with a knife in the kitchen.
(10) John buttered the toast at midnight in the kitchen.
(11) John buttered the toast at midnight with a knife.
(12) John buttered the toast.

and more. These **entailments** cannot be demonstrated without additional assumptions about logical form. One way to capture these entailments is to assume that (8) consists of 'smaller' propositions that make **reference** to events:

(8a) There is an event.
(8b) Such an event is a buttering.
(8c) The agent of the event is John.
(8d) The patient of the event is toast.
(8e) The time of the event is midnight.
(8f) … etc. …

In this way, the logical form of (8) can be revealed as along the lines of:

(13) ∃e ((buttering, e) & (Agent, e, John) & (patient, e, toast) & … etc. …))

On the assumption, therefore, that (8) can be decomposed into a set of propositions making reference to events and, optionally, semantic roles, all the entailments in (9) to (12) can be demonstrated and warranted by the rule of conjunction reduction. See Thomson (1977), Martin (1978), Davidson (1980), Lombard

(1986), Bennett (1988), Higginbotham *et al.* (2000), Lowe (2002: part IV, and Pietroski (2005) for more on the metaphysics of events and their articulation in logical form.

The term 'logical form' is also used in certain syntactic theories where it refers to the level of abstract syntactic structure where interpretations are assigned. The term is also used in certain pragmatic theories where it refers to (possibly indeterminate and pragmatically 'enrichable') lexical **meaning**. The precise meaning of the term is therefore sensitive and relative to whether the discourse in which it appears is concerned with **syntax**, semantics or **pragmatics**.

KEN TURNER

See also: Ambiguity; Bar-Hillel, Y.; disambiguation; entailment; Grice, H.P.; implicature; impliciture; maxims of conversation; philosophy of language; presupposition; radical pragmatics; relevance theory; what is said

Suggestions for further reading

Lycan, W. (1984) *Logical Form in Natural Language*, London: MIT Press.

Preyer, G. and Peter, G. (eds) (2002) *Logical Form and Language*, Oxford: Clarendon Press.

Sainsbury, M. (2001) *Logical Forms: An Introduction to Philosophical Logic*, Oxford: Blackwell.

M

Maxims of Conversation

In his William James Lectures delivered at Harvard in 1967, H.P. **Grice** provided a range of insights that would prove to be hugely influential in the development of modern **pragmatics**. During the course of the seven talks that made up the lecture series, Grice explored a number of issues relating to **meaning** and **conversation**. His famous **maxims of conversation** – presented in Lecture II, alongside his **cooperative principle** – are probably the most well known aspect of this work.

In this second lecture, Grice elaborated on earlier work (*see* Grice 1957) in which he argued that communication is a rational, purposive, inferential activity. As well as this (indeed, *because* of this) Grice proposed that communication was fundamentally cooperative, and that participants work towards a 'common aim' (1967: lecture II, 11; 1989: 29). Early in this lecture he formulated his cooperative principle: '"Make your conversational contribution such as is required, at the stage at which it occurs, by the accepted purpose or direction of the talk-exchange in which you are engaged"' (1967: lecture II, 6; 1987: 26).

But the cooperative principle (or CP, as it is often referred to) is quite vague. What makes a 'contribution' cooperative? Grice's answer to this question was that the CP can be broken down into a number of different maxims of conversation – *Quantity*, *Quality*, *Relation* and *Manner* – the idea being that speakers will, on the whole, make sure that their conversational contributions comply with these maxims, and hence the CP. Grice presented the four maxims as follows:

The category of *Quantity* relates to the quantity of information to be provided, and under it fall the following maxims:

(1) 'Make your contribution as informative as required (for the current purposes of the exchange)', and possibly
(2) 'Do not make your contribution more informative than is required' [...]

Under the category of *Quality* falls a super-maxim: 'Try to make your contribution one that is true', and two more specific maxims:

(1) 'Do not say what you believe to be false'
(2) 'Do not say that for which you lack adequate evidence'.

Under the category of *Relation* I place a single maxim, namely 'Be relevant' [...]
Finally, under the category of *Manner* [...] I include the super-maxim 'Be perspicuous' and various maxims such as:

(1) 'Avoid obscurity of expression'
(2) 'Avoid ambiguity'
(3) 'Be brief (avoid unnecessary prolixity)'
(4) 'Be orderly'
(1967: lecture II, 7–8; 1989: 26–27)

But how do the maxims work in practice? How does the hearer actually put the linguistic meaning of what has been said together with the assumption that the speaker is being cooperative (and therefore complying with the maxims), and any other necessary world knowledge, in order to finally arrive at the intended interpretation of the utterance in question? Let's see how Grice's ideas might work in relation to the example provided in the entry on the cooperative principle, repeated below as (1):

(1) Peter: Is John asleep yet?
     Mary: His light is on and I can hear music.

The first question Peter asks himself about Mary's utterance is whether all she wants to communicate to him is that the light in John's room is on, and that she can hear music coming from the room. He will justifiably conclude that this is not the case, on the grounds that if that was all she wanted to communicate, it would not satisfy the maxims (and hence would fail to satisfy the CP). For example, it would fail to satisfy the *Maxim of Quantity*, since Mary's contribution would not be as informative as is required for the current purposes of the exchange. Nor would it satisfy the *Maxim of Relation*, since her contribution would not be relevant in the context of the exchange.

Peter, however, can assume that Mary *is* obeying the CP and maxims, and hence will look for a way of interpreting her utterance such that these apparent violations can be disposed of. If Mary is being cooperative, then she must think that the fact that John's light is on, and that music is coming from his room, is informative and relevant in some way as a response to Peter's question. Peter knows that most people turn out their light before they go to sleep, and he knows that it is unlikely that John would be playing music in his room if he had already gone to sleep. Moreover, he knows (or at least presumes) that Mary is also aware of these facts. He infers, then, that what she intended to communicate is that because John's light is on, and music is coming from his room, John has not yet gone to sleep. This is the only way that her utterance can be interpreted on the assumption that she is observing the CP and maxims; only in this way is her response both informative and relevant.

We thus have a framework on which to flesh out the intuitive sketch of Peter's inferential processes provided in the entry on the cooperative principle. In cases such as the one above, when there is an *apparent* violation, a hearer is going to reason along roughly these lines: x has said y and by doing so has apparently violated a maxim; if, however, by saying y, x also meant z then x wouldn't have violated the maxim; x must therefore have meant z. This provides a clearer idea of how **implicatures** are derived: by saying y, x implicates z if retrieving z is necessary in order for x not to be a violation of the CP and maxims.

It is important not to confuse Grice's claims about the rational, cooperative nature of conversation with the much stronger claim (which Grice certainly did *not* endorse) that *all* conversations are cooperative, and that the maxims are *always* obeyed. Indeed, Grice listed four ways in which the maxims may fail to be fulfilled.

In the first way, a speaker might 'violate' a maxim covertly, in which case she would be lying or misleading another (and would not, therefore, be complying with the CP). In the second way, a speaker may 'opt out' (1967: lecture II, 12; 1989: 30) of the CP and maxims, and make it clear he/she is unwilling to participate in a conversation at all. A politician being harassed by journalists might simply utter 'No comment' on his way out of the courtroom.

The third and fourth ways in which the maxims may be violated have received a great deal of attention in the literature on pragmatics, for these violations enable Grice to provide an account of how a range of different types of implicature are generated. In the third way, Grice described how a speaker may be faced by a 'clash' of maxims. Sometimes, for example, it may be impossible for a speaker to fulfil one of the maxims without violating one of the others. Consider the example in (2) below, one of Grice's originals. Grice sets out the following context: 'A is planning with B an itinerary for a holiday in France. Both know that A wants to see his friend C; if to do so would not involve too great a prolongation of his journey' (1967: lecture II, 15; 1989: 32).

(2) A: Where does C live?
     B: Somewhere in the South of France.

B's reply to A's question clearly violates the first *Maxim of Quantity* ('Make your contribution as informative is as required'). However, if what B has said amounts to all that he knows about where it is that C lives, then he *cannot* make his contribution as informative as is required without violating the second *Maxim of Quality* ('Do not say that for which you lack adequate evidence'). B therefore implicates that he does not know where C lives.

The fourth and final way in which maxims might be violated is probably the most well-known, and provided Grice with an analysis of the process of, among other things, figurative interpretation. These examples included an *overt* violation of one of the maxims, and can be contrasted with the earlier example (see (1) above) in which the violation is only *apparent*. Consider example (3) (for Grice's example see 1967: lecture II, 17; 1989: 34). Peter is talking to Mary about their flatmate John, who is inconsiderate, unfriendly and has failed to pay his share of the rent for a third consecutive month:

(3) Peter: He's an absolute joy to live with.

It is perfectly obvious to Mary that Peter has said something he does not believe, and Peter is well aware of this (and Mary is aware that Peter is aware of it). However, he has done so overtly, and whilst he is clearly violating the first *Maxim of Quality* ('Do not say what you believe to be false') she will infer that he is at least still obeying the cooperative principle. (This is the principal difference between those implicatures generated by an apparent violation – in which a hearer presumes the speaker is violating neither the CP nor the maxims – and one generated by open, deliberate 'flouting' – in which the hearer presumes that while the speaker is still conforming with the CP, a maxim has indeed been violated.) Mary will therefore search for another related proposition to the one Peter is expressing. For Grice, the most obvious one in this case would be the opposite proposition to the one he has expressed: i.e. that John is absolute hell to live with. This example involves the figurative interpretation of a case of **irony**. Other figures of speech Grice characterized as relying on the flouting of maxims include **metaphor**, **hyperbole** and meiosis (or **understatement**).

The maxims of conversation are not unproblematic, and have been far from immune from

criticism. One criticism is that while they are designed to make the CP less general and less vague, they themselves are quite general and vague. Many theoretical terms are left unexplained. The *Maxim of Relation*, for example, expects speakers to 'Be relevant', but what exactly constitutes relevance? Grice himself was aware of the problems inherent in his use of this term:

> Though the formulation itself is terse, its formulation conceals a number of problems which exercise me a great deal; questions about what different kinds of foci of relevance there may be, how these shift in the course of a talk-exchange, how to allow for the fact that subjects of conversation are legitimately changed and so on. I find the treatment of such questions exceedingly difficult, and I hope to revert to them in a later lecture.
>
> (1967: lecture II, 8; 1989: 27)

Relevance theory (Sperber and Wilson 1995; Carston 2002) began as an attempt to deal with the issue of what precisely relevance is.

Another problem concerns the question of where the maxims come from. Are we born with them? Do they vary from culture to culture? (See Keenan 1976 for discussion.) Again, Grice is not unaware of the problem, though he finds his own answer unsatisfactory:

> A dull but, no doubt at a certain level, adequate answer is that it is just a well-recognized empirical fact that people do behave in these ways; they learned to do so and have not lost the habit of doing so [...] I am, however, enough of a rationalist to want to find a basis that underlies these facts [...]; I would like to be able to think of the standard type of conversational practice not as merely as something we all or most do *in fact* follow but as something that is it *reasonable* for us to follow ...
>
> (1967: lecture II, 10; 1989: 29)

Although Grice did not return to questions of **reasoning** and **rationality** in the William James Lectures (he focussed mainly on issues of meaning), an often overlooked fact is that he spent a great deal of time during the final few years of his life exploring the question of what precisely constituted rational behaviour, and what constituted reasoning. His work on rationality, inference and reasoning is published in Grice (2001b), and there are fascinating links with this, and his work on meaning and conversation.

Despite any problems there may have been with them, the maxims have been hugely influential. For many, the CP and maxims represent the dawn of modern pragmatics. Most people working within pragmatics accept that hearers are guided in the interpretive process by some sort of expectation that a speaker is meeting certain standards. From this it follows that speakers behave in predictable ways and hearers can therefore recognize the best hypothesis about the speaker's meaning by inferring the one that satisfies those expectations the speaker is aiming at, or standards he/she is trying to meet. Neo-Gricean pragmatists (Atlas 2005; Gazdar 1979a; Horn 1984, 1996, 2006; and Levinson 1983, 2000) view these standards in a way that remains quite faithful to Grice's (1967) framework. Whilst doing away with Gricean maxims, relevance theory (Sperber and Wilson 1995) remains true to Grice's original insights: that communication is a rational, inferential activity, and that central to the process of **utterance interpretation** is the fact that utterances raise certain expectations.

TIM WHARTON

See also: Conversation; explicit/implicit distinction; Grice, H.P.; implicature; meaning; natural and non-natural meaning; neo-Gricean pragmatics; philosophy of language; post-Gricean pragmatics; pragmatics; radical pragmatics; rationality; reasoning; semantics-pragmatics interface; utterance interpretation; what is said

Suggestions for further reading

Grice, H. P. (1987) *Studies in the Way of Words*. Cambridge, MA: Harvard University Press. Chapter 2.
Neale, S. (1992) 'Paul Grice and the philosophy of language', *Linguistics and Philosophy*, 15: 509–59.

Meaning

While **semantics** is often thought of as the study of meaning in language, **pragmatics** can be said to be the study of meaning in utterances. How we view the relation between semantics and pragmatics depends in some ways on how we think of meaning.

The question of the nature and source of meaning for linguistic expressions has long been debated within the analytical philosophical tradition. One apparently plausible view is that words are associated with an image or idea of their referent in our mind and the image or idea could serve as the meaning of the word (*see* Locke 1690). One often discussed problem with this view is the lack of objectivity of meaning that it entails: your idea of a cat may differ from mine and yet we both seem to use 'cat' with the same meaning. A related issue concerns the structure of these mental ideas. For instance, what is the structure of the idea that serves as the meaning of 'brown cow' and how does it relate to the ideas for 'brown' and 'cow'?

Gottlob Frege is widely credited with the founding of modern semantics (*see* Frege 1984). He argued that not only should meanings be objective but they should also be compositional: any account of linguistic meaning must show how the meaning of a complex expression is derived as a function of the meaning of the lexical items involved and the syntactic structure of the expression. This requirement cannot be avoided because of the productivity, systematicity and infinite nature of humans' abilities to understand sentences of their language.

Frege rejected simple referential theories of meaning (*see* Mill 1843) where meanings of expressions are just their referents, for on these accounts, co-referential expressions share meanings. But many expressions which differ in meaning share referents (e.g. 'the morning star' and 'the evening star' both refer to Venus) and many meaningful expressions lack **reference** (e.g. 'unicorn'). Thus, Frege conjectured that the meaning (sense) of an expression determines its referent but distinguished between sense and referent, the former being an abstract mode of presentation of the referent.

Frege's notion of an abstract sense is rejected in more behaviouristic alternatives, like Quine's account (*see* Quine 1960), according to which only the public practices of language users could determine what expressions mean. While making meaning less mysterious, this line brings with it the 'indeterminacy of translation': that for any set of behaviours one can provide any number of theories to explain it. Thus, meaning becomes unstable and we could say that there is no one meaning for any given expression.

Davidson attempted to restore the stability of meaning by arguing that meaning can be analyzed in terms of truth (*see* Davidson 2001). Like Frege and Quine, Davidson took a holistic approach to meaning where sentences are the primary carriers of meaning while the words which make up sentences derive their meanings from the contributions they make to the meaning of the sentences in which they figure.

Non-holistic alternatives look at the information content of sub-sentential expressions independently of that of sentences. These approaches analyze the meaning of linguistic expressions (sentences, phrases, words) in terms of abstract objects such as properties and **propositions** (Russell 1919). From this perspective, the analysis of 'meaning' looks at the ultimate source of content for expressions. For instance, 'cat' may express cathood in virtue of causal relations between the word and the kind. This causal relation could arise for a number of reasons, e.g. social practices (*see* Kripke 1972; Putnam 1975). An alternative to this externalist, causal view analyzes the contents of expressions in terms of relations among expressions. One version of the relational view looks at inferential relations among expressions (*see* Laurence and Margolis 1999 for a useful overview of the debate between so-called 'externalist' and 'internalist' views of the source of content).

The above accounts of meaning do not draw any distinction between meaning in language and meaning in utterances and, in fact, tend to assume that the latter is dependent on the former. An alternative view, exemplified notably in the work of **Grice** (*see* Grice 1989), holds that meaning in a language derives from what individual speakers who use the language mean. Grice aimed to analyze meaning generally in terms of the **intentions** of speakers. The first step in this project is to analyze what it is for a speaker to mean something by an utterance:

'U meant something by uttering x' is true iff, for some audience A, U uttered x intending:

   (i) A to produce a particular response r
  (ii) A to think (recognize) that U intends (i)
 (iii) A to fulfil (i) on the basis of his fulfilment of (ii)

                  (Grice 1969/1989: 92)

A primary feature of this analysis and of subsequent proposals that are Gricean in spirit is the idea that to communicate something or, more generally, to mean something, the speaker's actions have to be overt or public. Grice builds this aspect into the definition via the reflexive second clause: I mean some thing only if I intend that you recognize my intention that you respond in a particular way. A second feature is the idea that meaning emerges as the result of a rational transaction among individuals who must engage in a good deal of folk psychological **reasoning**. This is emphasized in Grice's clarification of clause (iii), which is to be understood such that the recognition of the intention gives the audience a reason to respond as the speaker intends, rather than being a mere cause.

As influential and popular as Grice's ideas about speaker meaning have been, the details of his various attempted analyses have come under sustained criticism (*see* Grice 1969; Schiffer 1972). In particular, the way Grice tries to capture the overtness of speaker meaning is widely thought to be insufficient. It is widely deemed to be necessary to replace clause (ii) above with a condition that requires it to be 'common **knowledge**' or 'mutually known' that the speaker has an intention to produce a particular response (*see* Schiffer 1972; Clark and Marshall 1981).

Grice's notion of speaker meaning connects with core ideas in pragmatics via the notions of conversational **implicature** and **what is said**. There is widespread agreement that the total signification of an utterance, what the speaker means, is the sum of what the speaker says, or explicitly communicates, and what the speaker implicates (*see* Carston 2002 for saying vs. explicating). In cases of figurative language, what is said can be considered to be null: the speaker only makes as if to say something (*see* Neale 1992 for discussion) and implicates all of the figurative meaning.

In a series of papers, Grice developed his programme of reducing meaning in language (the 'timeless meaning of an expression') to speakers' meaning (Grice 1957, 1968b, 1969, 1982). Broadly speaking, what the speaker says in uttering u is determined by the timeless meaning of the utterance type, S, of u. In turn, the constituents of S have the meaning they do in virtue of the fact that speakers have the practice of using those constituents in that way.

While in broad outline this programme makes sense, there is a question of how the account could be compositional. In practice, Grice has to rely on the idea that speakers use words to make reference to either their denotata (objects, properties and the like) or to express concepts which in turn carry the content inherited by the word. In addition, the Gricean theorist has to rely on some set of compositional semantic rules for either composing meanings or translating linguistic expressions into mental **representations**. Different versions of the latter, mentalist programme can be found in Sperber and Wilson (1995) and Kamp and Reyle (1993). Such mentalist accounts owe a debt to the work of Fodor (*see* Fodor 1987, 1990) who argues, inter alia, that if the content of linguistic expressions is inherited from the content of mental representations, linguistic meanings can nevertheless be both objective and external. Putnam (1975) makes basically the same point.

Lewis (1969) put forward another early attempt to analyze linguistic meaning as a product of rational interaction among language users. Lewis used the game theory of Schelling (1960) to show how conventions of meaning could be maintained without any prior agreement (i.e. without requiring some kind of linguistic system to be established). In the process, Lewis defined a notion of 'common knowledge' which is to be distinguished from the standard concept employed in game theory (involving an ideally rational individual) and which can be used to characterize how actual individuals might reasonably solve a coordination problem (*see* Cubitt and Sugden 2003). In fact, according to Lewis, adherents to a convention do not need to have anything other than first-order beliefs

about prior adherence (i.e. they do not need to have actual beliefs about the beliefs of other adherents). In a similar vein, Sperber and Wilson's (1995) notion of 'mutual manifestness' provides the basis of a psychologically plausible way of stating the 'overtness' condition in the analysis of what it is for a speaker to mean something.

The question of the psychological plausibility of various views of meaning has been given recent impetus from studies of children learning their first words and from pre-linguistic infants. From a psychological perspective, any account of meaning should be compatible with what we know about language learning. Traditionally, research into **child language acquisition** has focussed more on how children acquire language: whether solely by statistical techniques (association) or in virtue of additional initial constraints such as those posited in Universal Grammar by Generative Linguists (*see* Chomsky 1986). Such previous research took for granted what it is that children are learning, and, in the case of phonology and **syntax**, this was a reasonable assumption. However, in the case of the semantic properties of language, it is a question of genuine interest what it is that children are learning. That is, we can look at children producing their first words in a meaningful fashion (from around 14 months onward) and ask what is the nature of the symbolic element they have grasped. If, on the one hand, we treat words as simply being associated with meanings (properties, objects), then we could say that children are learning symbols of the type of formal language which is the model of many analyses of natural language semantics. If, on the other hand, we treat words as utterance types, i.e. as types of intentional action for making reference to objects and properties, then we could say that children are learning words as these types of intentional action.

Although the evidence is by no means conclusive, there is reason to think that children are learning words as Gricean utterance types rather than simply symbols associated with meanings. First, it has been demonstrated that, although children can and do associate word forms with extra-linguistic entities, when faced with a novel word, they do not simply associate that word with the most salient referent. Rather, they seek to infer the referential intention of the user of the novel word to learn its referent (*see* Baldwin 1993;

Baldwin *et al.* 1996). Second, children only begin to use words as symbols after the development of general abilities to understand actions as intentional or goal-directed (from around 12 months onward). Thus, although from about 8 months of age children are able to discriminate word forms from adult speech (Jusczyk 1999) and they do make associations between words and extra-linguistic objects from this age (Xu 2007), it seems they are not able to grasp what words are until they are able to recognize their use as constituents of intentional acts (*see* Bloom 2000 and Tomasello 2003 for more discussion of this point).

Another line of evidence comes from very young infants engaging in **non-verbal communication**. It seems that from around 14 months, infants both comprehend and produce non-verbal gestures as Gricean acts of **communication**. That is, they see these acts as the making overt of an intention to recognize an informative intention (*see* Tomasello *et al.* 2007 for a review of the evidence). For instance, given the very same pointing gesture on the part of an experimenter, children will treat it as communicative or not depending on whether there are cues that the experimenter is making some informative intention 'mutually known', for example, through eye contact (*see* Behne *et al.* 2005). So it seems likely that infants are already Gricean communicators when they come to learn words in their language.

RICHARD BREHENY

See also: Child language acquisition; conventionality; cooperative principle; explicit/implicit distinction; Grice, H.P.; intention; philosophy of language; prelinguistic communication; reference; relevance theory; semantic externalism/internalism; word learning, role of mindreading in

Suggestions for further reading

Bloom, P. (2000) *How Children Learn the Meanings of Words*, Cambridge, MA: MIT Press.
Grice, H.P. (1989) *Studies in the Way of Words*, Cambridge, MA: Harvard University Press.
Laurence, S. and Margolis, E. (1999) 'Concepts and cognitive science', in E. Margolis and S. Laurence (eds) *Concepts: Core Readings*, Cambridge, MA: MIT Press.

Media Discourse
'Media discourse' defined

The term '**discourse**' is a problematic term within the disciplines of linguistics and **discourse analysis**. Depending upon the individual analyst and analytical framework being utilized, its definition can range from the largely descriptive, such as 'an extended piece of text, which has some form of internal organisation, coherence or cohesion' (Sinclair and Coulthard 1975, cited in Mills 1997: 9), to the more sociolinguistic, such as 'language in use' (Brown and Yule 1983). However, a definition that further encompasses the notion that language and the social world are inextricably linked is one that sees 'discourse' as 'language as a form of social practice' (Fairclough 1989: 22). This encapsulates the notion that spoken and written texts both reflect the social world and the societies in which they are produced, as well as perform social functions. For the purposes of this discussion, it will be assumed that the study of 'discourse', as opposed to 'language', involves examining not only the textual features of a given text, but also the wider processes involved in the production and consumption of texts and, critically, how texts reflect and enact social practices.

Such social practices are, typically, the serving of ideological goals within texts. On a simplistic level, a text featuring the sentence 'Women should not be allowed to work', for example, can be said to be both a reflection of how the institution and society from which that text is born might be sexist, while at the same time it enacts that sexist ideology. That is principally achieved through the use of the negated modal auxiliary 'should not'.

Media discourse, then, can be narrowly defined as the language used in spoken and written mass media texts. Many analysts have utilized this definition in their work, such as O'Keeffe (2006), who performs conversation analyses of broadcast media texts, or Bell (1991, 1998), whose work centres upon explaining discursive structures by gaining a holistic understanding of the practices associated with the construction of media discourse. This work also focuses upon explaining the discursive features of media texts.

A more critical definition of media discourse would, however, be one which is used by Fairclough (1992, 1995a, 1995b) and van Dijk (1988, 1991, 1993) amongst others. These theorists see media discourse as a term that encapsulates not only the language used within media texts, but also as the processes involved in the construction of media texts. Analysis of media discourse using this type of definition therefore examines the ways in which the language used within mass media texts reflects and enacts ideologies and encodes point of view. Others whose work adopts this definition and approach include Fowler (1991), Fowler *et al.* (1979) and Machin and van Leeuwen (2007).

Media discourse and pragmatics

The study of media discourse and **pragmatics** overlaps in two key areas: in the types of critical approaches to the analysis of media discourse, and in more descriptive, stylistic, discursive approaches to media texts.

In critical approaches to media texts (see below), the application of pragmatic concepts and insights can highlight the ways in which the texts perform social functions, and therefore encode ideologies and points of view of speakers or authors.

Even in more descriptive approaches, such as O'Keeffe's (2006) work on broadcast **conversations**, the analysis of pragmatic markers, such as **hedges**, **discourse markers** and response tokens form a key part of understanding how media texts are structured, as well as identifying interpersonal meanings created by speakers or text producers. The existence of **deixis** in broadcast media texts has also been noted by O'Keeffe when exemplifying the structure and nature of broadcast interactions. However, the use of deictic expressions in this instance is similar to those in spoken discourse in general.

Critical approaches

The application of the concepts that underpin pragmatic study can be used in critical analyses of media discourse, especially in seeking to establish the embedded existence of opinion or point of view in written and spoken media texts.

Such inquiries show how the examination of **propositions**, implications and **presuppositions** in texts can highlight the existence of stance and point of view within texts, and therefore the dominant ideology of the text. As van Dijk (1998b) points out, the analysis of propositions present within media texts can lead to a greater understanding of the ideological stance adopted within texts. On a basic level, an analysis of propositions merely involves establishing the stances expressed by clauses and sentences, especially by examining the use of adjectives and verbs.

(1) In fact, this alleged exercise in dragging Labour into the modern age is a charade.
(Editorial 1988, *Daily Mail*)

In the editorial from the *Daily Mail* in (1), an implicit proposition is that the Labour Party's leader at the time, Neil Kinnock, is being dishonest in concealing the fact that Labour is not modernizing and reviewing its policies despite claims to the contrary. This is achieved through the use of the copula creating a categorical **assertion**, alongside the noun phrase 'a charade'. Readers, because of the categorical assertion, are presented with a strong commitment to this representation of reality being true. Similarly, the use of the adjective 'alleged' within the sentence also indicates that an anti-Labour stance is encoded.

More importantly, the concepts of presupposition and implication can also be applied to media texts. The way in which the concept of presupposition can be applied to media discourse analysis is seen in (2) below.

(2) Was Mr Foot's unfitness to lead his party really all a figment of journalistic imagination?
(Editorial 1983, *Daily Mail*)

The **rhetorical question** asked in the *Daily Mail* editorial encodes a presupposition, as the text producer presupposes that Foot is indeed viewed as an unfit leader, through use of the adjective phrase 'unfitness to lead'. The overall effect upon the reader of the text is of an identity having been constructed for Foot that sees him as a professional failure, but in such a way that presupposes that readers share in this conceptualization of Foot's leadership. Here, it is possible to see how the text producer has assumed from the outset that a particular proposition is true (that Foot is an unfit leader). At the same time, this strategy encodes the *Daily Mail*'s Conservative and anti-Socialist ideology through the use of the presupposition.

Media texts also frequently encode implications. These have a similar social function to the use of presuppositions, in that implications are further evidence of media discourse reflecting and enacting social practices, as well as encoding ideological stance.

(3) By any standard, the new Ministers look an impressive team. But is Mr Wilson playing them in the right positions?
(Editorial 1974, *Daily Mail*)

One such example can be found in (3), where the use of the lexical perception verb 'to look' encodes the implication that although the Cabinet appears impressive, it is not necessarily the case. Reinforced by the rhetorical question that follows, this has the function of encoding a negative stance towards 'Mr Wilson', the then prime minister, which serves to subtly suggest to readers that Wilson has made poor decisions.

(4) It is a relief that, as Foreign Secretary, the wily and pragmatic Jim Callaghan will take charge of Common Market negotiations.
(Editorial 1974, *Daily Mail*)

Similarly, in (4) from the same text, the main clause 'It is a relief', through the use of the noun 'relief', contains the implication that it was expected that Wilson would make a less sensible choice when selecting a Cabinet member. This again highlights one of the social functions of the text as being to reflect a negative orientation towards Wilson and therefore to enact an anti-Labour Party ideology.

(5) Can Mr Callaghan seriously present himself in the role of the man who is to stand up to the unions and operate the squeeze?
(Editorial 1978, *Daily Telegraph*)

The use of **questions**, rhetorical or otherwise, in media discourse can also often contain impli-

cations. In (5), the use of a question encodes the implication that the then prime minister Jim Callaghan would want to 'stand up to the unions and operate the squeeze'. This suggests to readers that 'standing up to unions' is a positive thing to do, and encodes a right-wing ideology, or at least an anti-union perspective. In identifying the implications in questions such as this, media discourse analysts can further highlight how texts contain ideological stances and serve to enact or reflect those ideologies.

In all the examples given, application of pragmatic concepts allows for a greater understanding of the social function of the media texts being analyzed. By uncovering encoded presuppositions and implications, the analyst can highlight further how media texts are examples of language as a form of social practice and how they enact or reflect ideological stances.

DEAN HARDMAN

See also: Discourse; discourse analysis; political discourse; power; presupposition; proposition; rhetorical questions

Suggestions for further reading

Fairclough, N. (1995) *Media Discourse*, London: Edward Arnold.
van Dijk, T. (1998) 'Opinions and ideologies in the press', in A. Bell and P. Garrett (eds) *Approaches to Media Discourse*, Oxford: Blackwell.

Metaphor

Metaphor appears to be a paradigmatically pragmatic phenomenon. It involves a gap between the conventional **meaning** of words and their occasion-specific use, of precisely the kind that motivates distinguishing **pragmatics** from **semantics**. This assumption is so widespread that it has received little explicit justification, but at least two obvious considerations can be offered in its support. First, metaphorical interpretation is importantly parasitic on literal meaning. If a hearer doesn't know the literal meanings of the relevant expressions, she will only accidentally succeed in interpreting an utterance metaphorically. In children, the general ability to comprehend and to knowingly produce metaphors (especially those based on abstract similarities) develops later than the capacity for literal speech (Vosniadou 1987). Moreover, various cognitive and brain disorders, such as **autism** (Happé 1995), schizophrenia (Langdon *et al.* 2002b), and lesions in the **right hemisphere** (Brownell *et al.* 1990) significantly impair metaphorical comprehension, while there are no converse cases of impairment in literal comprehension with preserved capacity to interpret metaphors. Second, metaphorical interpretation depends not just on **knowledge** of the conventional meanings of the words uttered and their mode of combination, but also on substantive and wide-ranging **presuppositions** (real or mutually pretended) about the referents of the relevant expressions. As a result, the same sentence can receive dramatically different metaphorical interpretations in distinct **contexts**. For instance, sentence (1):

(1) Juliet is the sun.

will be interpreted quite differently when spoken by Romeo (very crudely, as meaning *Juliet is beautiful*), by his friend Benvolio (*Juliet is dangerous*) and by his rival Paris (*Juliet is the most important socialite in Verona*).

Until recently, however, the basic premise that metaphor is pragmatic was closely associated with two more specific assumptions. First, metaphorical interpretation is 'indirect' in the sense that it is attempted only after the search for a cooperative and relevant literal interpetation fails. Second, metaphor is an instance of manner **implicature** (Grice 1975), akin to an utterance of (2):

(2) Miss X produced a series of notes that corresponded closely with the score of 'Home Sweet Home'.

which is intended to convey that Miss X sang in an unusual, probably unappealing, way. Both assumptions have been the focus of recent critical attention.

The indirectness of metaphorical interpretation was challenged by Gibbs (1990, 1994), who found no difference in processing time for literal and metaphorical speech. Indeed, Glucksberg *et al.* (1982) found that subjects actually took

longer to access the literal meaning of sentences that also had plausible metaphorical interpretations, even when they were explicitly told to focus only on literal meaning. These findings have been widely taken to support relevance theoretic and other contextualist accounts (Sperber and Wilson 1986, 1995; Bezuidenhout 2001; Recanati 2001a; Carston 2002). According to these accounts, metaphorical meaning is a form of direct and explicit meaning, and hence belongs to '**what is said**' rather than to what is implicated. However, more recent studies (Blasko and Connine 1993; Gentner and Wolff 1997; Brisard *et al.* 2001; Noveck *et al.* 2001; Giora 2002, 2003; Bowdle and Gentner 2005) suggest that unfamiliar and novel metaphors do take significantly longer to process than either literal utterances or familiar metaphors. This supports the contextualist view that metaphor forms a continuum with literal meaning. But it also threatens to undermine on-line processing as a criterion for theoretical classification, since this would divide metaphors into heterogeneous classes based on their familiarity and aptness. Instead, it seems plausible to take 'indirectness' as claiming that a good rational reconstruction of successful metaphorical **communication** will first rule out a literal interpretation as being contextually inappropriate, and also appeal to that literal meaning in determining the speaker's intended meaning. The claim that metaphor is indirect in this sense is supported by the patterns of justification and concession that speakers engage in when they are challenged on their intended metaphorical meanings (Camp 2006).

The assimilation of metaphor to implicature is rendered problematic by at least five major differences between the two. First, contents communicated metaphorically can be felicitously reported as 'what the speaker said', either by echoing the speaker's original words, or with a literal paraphrase (Bezuidenhout 2001). Second, metaphorically communicated contents are available for explicit response by others. For instance, if Benvolio responded to Romeo's utterance of (1) by saying 'No she isn't', this would most naturally be construed as a response to the claim that she is beautiful (Hills 1997; Bezuidenhout 2001). Third, metaphorical meanings appear not to be capable of cancellation by the speaker (Leezenberg 2001; this test is unreliable, however; *see* Camp 2006 for discussion). Fourth, metaphors can serve as a 'springboard' for implicatures (Tsohatzidis 1994; Stern 2000). By uttering (1), Romeo implicates that he admires and wants to be with Juliet. Fifth, complete sentences can be interpreted metaphorically when embedded within larger sentences which are otherwise literal. For instance, Benvolio could respond (rather flatfootedly) to Romeo's utterance of (1) by saying (3):

(3) If Juliet is the sun, then I guess you'll never be satisfied with any of the other girls in Verona.

Taken together, these differences constitute a strong case against treating metaphors as implicatures. It is much less clear, though, how metaphor should be analyzed. Contextualists advocate placing metaphor within 'what is said' as a form of loose talk. Semanticists claim that metaphor should be treated as a contextually variable form of semantic meaning, either by adding hidden structure to the postulated **logical form** of the sentence uttered (Stern 2000; Leezenberg 2001), or by allowing 'free enrichment' or modulation of that logical form (Hills 1997). However, these same differences from implicature are also exhibited by other uses of language, most notably sarcasm and malapropisms, which are intuitively very far from 'what is said', let alone semantic meaning. One alternative possibility is to recognize a third pragmatic category of word-based speaker's meaning (Camp 2006). 'What is said' could then be tied relatively closely to sentence meaning, as Grice (1975) originally suggested, and the class of implicatures could remain a comparatively homogeneous one.

In addition to theoretical considerations about metaphor's place in the linguistic taxonomy, a very different topic also deserves consideration: how is metaphorical interpretation achieved? First, can any general account be offered of how hearers recognize the appropriateness of a metaphorical interpretation (the 'detection problem')? Relevance theorists claim that a metaphorical interpretation is automatically preferred because it is most accessible in context. While this may be true of many conversational metaphors, it is less plausible as an account of novel and especially poetic metaphors, which often require significant

interpretive effort. Second, how do hearers determine the specific content that the speaker intends? There are two leading cognitive models here. Very roughly, on the category-transfer model (Glucksberg and Keysar 1993; Glucksberg *et al.* 1997), prominent properties associated with the metaphorical vehicle (e.g. with 'the sun' in (1)) are predicated of the subject (e.g. Juliet). By contrast, on the structure-mapping model (Gentner 1983; Gentner and Wolff 1997; Gentner *et al.* 2001), structural similarities between the concepts or schemas associated with the two terms are cultivated. Recently, the two models have begun to converge toward a hybrid view, on which more conventionalized, conversational metaphors are interpreted by transfer, and more novel metaphors are interpreted structurally (Glucksberg 2001; Bowdle and Gentner 2005). However, both views still require significant modification in order to cover the full range of cases in a psychologically plausible and computationally tractable way. This is especially true for metaphors that don't fit the standard '*a* is *F*' format, where *a* is literal and *F* is metaphorical (White 1996; Camp 2003).

ELISABETH CAMP

See also: Explicit/implicit distinction; Grice, H.P.; hyperbole; idiom; implicature; irony; literary pragmatics; neo-Gricean pragmatics; relevance theory; rhetoric; what is said

Suggestions for further reading

Camp, E. (2006) 'Metaphor in the mind: the cognition of metaphor', *Philosophy Compass*, 1: 154–70.
Moran, R. (1997) 'Metaphor', in C. Wright and R. Hale (eds) *A Companion to Philosophy of Language*, Oxford: Basil Blackwell.
Reimer, M. and Camp, E. (2006) 'Metaphor', in E. Lepore and B. Smith (eds) *The Oxford Handbook of Philosophy of Language*, Oxford: Oxford University Press.

Metapragmatics

The term 'metapragmatics' has been used in the description of a number of aspects of language in use (Caffi 1998; Verschueren 2004). The prefix *meta* ('above', 'beyond') marks a shift in perspective that is tied to reflexivity, or the ability not only to create utterances, but also to recognize and talk about features of those utterances. This usage originates in Tarski's ([1935] 1956) description of *Metasprache* ('metalanguage'). Metapragmatics is concerned with a particular type of reflexivity, one that is in evidence when speakers indicate in some way that they are aware of pragmatic features and potential pragmatic interpretations of utterances. Among the indicators of metapragmatic awareness that have been identified are linguistic action verbs, deictic expressions, contextualization cues, **hedges**, **discourse markers** and some formulaic constructions. These particular indicators represent highly salient examples of reflexivity at work, but less salient effects may remain unanalyzed. There is every reason to suspect that **knowledge** at the meta-level, such as metapragmatic awareness, is more pervasive in its effect than we have been able to document so far. It may turn out to be the case, as Verschueren (1999: 188) has proposed, that 'there is no language use without a constant calibration between pragmatic and metapragmatic functioning'.

Some of the most easily identified indicators of metapragmatic functioning are linguistic action verbs. Beginning with **Austin**'s (1962) explicit performatives (*I apologize*), a large number of expressions have been recognized as containing verbs that identify the type of **speech act** being performed. The clearest evidence of metapragmatic awareness comes when a speaker not only performs a speech act (*I will help you*), but another speaker can report it by identifying the pragmatic function thereby performed (*She promised that she would help me*). In using the verb *promise*, the speaker is labeling an utterance token as a specific type of linguistic action. As Lee (1997: 139) points out, 'the performative verbs are explicitly metalinguistic, but their functioning depends on their place in a whole system of grammatical categories that are structured around principles of indexicality and metaindexicality'.

It was in the study of indexicality that some of the original observations on metapragmatic awareness were made. Speakers are clearly aware of contextual effects when they use expressions, first described as 'shifters' (Jakobson 1971) and later known as **indexicals** or deictics. As Hanks

(1993: 129) has noted, 'deictics could be viewed as metapragmatic devices insofar as they regiment the relation between a referential object and a pragmatic context relative to which it is individuated'. Awareness of contextual effects is evident in the use of aspect, tense, modality, **evidentials** and a range of indexical expressions. As illustrated in the earlier example of a reported promise, the speaker demonstrates an awareness of the need to 'shift' pronouns (*I, you → she, me*), tense and modality (*will → would*) as the **context** changes. This type of metapragmatic awareness is analyzed in Lucy (1993).

Other features of language use involving awareness of contextual effects have been described as 'contextualization cues' (Gumperz 1982a), which include paralinguistic features and code-switching. Taking an example of code-switching (Gumperz 1982a: 76), we can see how one speaker ('reporting on what her father said about her children's inability to speak Spanish') creates an interactive context through the use of the different languages to illustrate her point.

> To this day he says that … uh … it's a shame that they don't speak … uh … Spanish. *Estan como burros. Les abla uno y* (they are like donkeys. someone talks to them and): 'What he say, what's he saying.'

Showing her awareness of the **pragmatics** of interaction, this speaker creates a performed version, with little explicit marking of turn-taking, of what her father thinks and says. The selection and juxtaposition of appropriate expressions in Spanish and English is a good illustration of the metapragmatics identified by Caffi (1998: 581) as 'that area of the speakers' competence which reflects the judgements of appropriateness on one's own and other people's communicative behavior'.

Within that same area we might also include hedges, particularly those that seem to be tied to aspects of **Grice**'s (1975) **cooperative principle** and the accompanying **maxims**. Speakers can indicate their awareness of, and desire not to be in violation of, maxims such as quality (*As far as I know*) and quantity (*I won't bore you with all the details*) as they work out what to include in their talk. As Brown and Levinson (1987: 189) also note, certain hedges seem to indicate awareness of the need for **politeness** strategies in the context of possible impositions (*I'm sorry to bother you, but ...*). We might think of hedges in general as a form of metapragmatic commentary on the status of the accompanying utterance relative to the current interaction. Sentence adverbs (*Obviously, Seriously*), connectors (*Actually, For example*), **parentheticals** (*I mean, You know*) and other discourse markers are also used by speakers to indicate how their utterances fit into the current interaction and how they should be interpreted.

Certain formulaic constructions also allow speakers to comment on potential pragmatic interpretations of their utterances. In an example of a formulaic disclaimer (Overstreet and Yule 2001: 46), the underlying formula of *not X (or anything), but Y* is instantiated in the disclaimer *I don't want to sound like your mother or anything, but I think you should wait.* By using a disclaimer, the speaker can project a potentially unwanted characterization (*sound like your mother*) and disavow it prior to stating something that might be problematic in the interaction (*I think you should wait*). This type of construction allows speakers to mention constraints on possible interpretations of their behaviour as part of what Goffman (1959: 208) described as 'impression management' during interaction. This is clearly a metapragmatic function.

Metapragmatics has become a wide-ranging area of study. It has prompted some scholars to review fundamental assumptions about **communication** in terms of metapragmatic principles (Mey 2001), others to investigate the development of metapragmatic awareness in children (Gombert 1992), and others to use pragmatic expectations in interaction to study metapragmatics in use (Bublitz and Hübler 2007).

MARYANN OVERSTREET

See also: Austin, J.L.; communication; context; cooperative principle; deixis; evidentials; Grice, H.P.; hedge; indexicals; maxims of conversation; parentheticals; politeness; speech act theory

Suggestions for further reading

Caffi, C. (1998) 'Metapragmatics', in J. Mey (ed.) *Concise Encyclopedia of Pragmatics*, Amsterdam: Elsevier.

Verschueren, J. (2004) 'Notes on the role of metapragmatic awareness in language use', in A. Jaworski, N. Coupland and D. Galasinski (eds) *Metalanguage: Social and Ideological Perspectives*, Berlin and New York: Mouton de Gruyter.

Metarepresentation

Two cognitive mechanisms which are probably uniquely human are language and thinking, and currently, both of them are considered to involve **representations**. Furthermore, an essential property of both linguistic representations (e.g. a sentence) and mental representations (thought) is recursion – a representation can be embedded within another higher-order representation. The term 'metarepresentation' is used to refer to such higher-order representations which contain further representations.

It is useful to distinguish types of lower-level representations, according to their cognitive functions, in order to illustrate a variety of human metarepresentational capacities. Sperber (2000) suggests the following three main categories: mental representations (e.g. thoughts), public representations (e.g. utterances) and abstract representations (e.g. sentences, **propositions**). Any one of them can be embedded in a higher-order representation, which is typically a thought or an utterance: for example, a mental representation of a mental representation ('Mary believes that John believes that the price of petrol will go up soon'), a public representation of a public representation ('Mary said that John said that the price of petrol will go up soon'), a mental representation of a public representation ('John believes that Mary said that price of petrol will go up soon'), or a public representation of a mental representation ('John said that Mary believes that the price of petrol will go up soon'). An abstract representation, such as '*boring* and *tedious* are synonymous', can also be embedded in a mental representation and/or a public representation, e.g. 'John said that Mary believes that *boring* and *tedious* are synonymous.' Unlike utterances and thoughts, which are attributed to a particular person(s), abstract representations are considered to be non-attributive.

Metarepresentational capability in the mental domain has been investigated most systematically in **theory of mind** research. Pretend play among toddlers, which is considered to be an important precursor to an understanding of mind, has been seen as a prime example of how metarepresentational ability can be manifested at an early stage of development (Leslie 1987). It has been argued that toddlers' deferred imitation and mirror self-recognition are also explained by their early metarepresentational capability (Gopnik and Meltzoff 1994; Perner 1991; Whiten 1996). During their preschool period, children's maturing metarepresentational ability is demonstrated by their understanding of mental states such as beliefs and **intentions**, as well as by their autobiographical memory. Metarepresentational capability is also considered to provide cognitive machinery for self-consciousness, or reflection on one's own mental states (Rosenthal 1997). Autistic patients, who are known to have difficulty in understanding other people's minds, also show deficits in self-awareness, and both are explained, at least in part, by their metarepresentational impairment (Frith and Happé 1999).

Metarpresentational capability is also essential in **communication** (Noh 2000; Wilson 2000). The most discussed topic in this area may be that of deception (Sperber 2000; Whiten and Byrne 1988b). In order to understand the speaker's intention to deceive, the hearer needs to be able to infer that the speaker intends her to believe what he says and that the speaker himself does not believe what he says. To avoid the possibility of being deceived, the hearer should be able to construct a fourth-order metarepresentation such as 'the speaker intends that I should believe that the speaker intend that I should believe P' (Sperber 2000: 125).

More generally, **propositional attitudes**, or the speaker's attitudes towards a proposition expressed in an utterance, are instances of metarepresentation. A metarepresentational ability to ascribe certain propositional attitudes to the speaker enables us to understand what the speaker meant by the utterance, which typically deviates from what is linguistically encoded by the utterance (Sperber and Wilson 1995). Propositional attitudes can be communicated overtly or tacitly. In the case of jokes or ironies, the attitude that the speaker does not believe the proposition expressed has to be tacit, for it to be

successful. Alternatively, the speaker's propositional attitudes can be overtly marked, i.e. it can be linguistically encoded. Attitudinal adverbials such as *certainly, definitely, probably*, and *maybe* or predicates such as *I know, I wonder* and *I suppose*, for instance, encode particular propositional attitudes. It has been shown that until about 4 years of age, children cannot adequately distinguish between the propositional attitudes expressed by the predicates *I know* and *I think* (Moore *et al.* 1989). Children come to understand the concept of false belief around the same time, between 4 and 5 years of age, which indicates that children's metarepresentational capability becomes robust enough to understand a variety of mental states by then (Matsui *et al.* 2006).

Understanding propositional attitudes is one of main difficulties autistic patients are known to have (Baron-Cohen 1995; Happé 1994a). It has been claimed that their difficulty can be explained by a general lack of metarepresentational ability (Leslie and Roth 1993). Unlike normally developing 2-year-olds, young autistic children typically do not engage in pretend play, an indication of early metarepresentational capacity. Verbally able autistic patients have particular difficulty in understanding a non-literal interpretation of an utterance, due to their inability to infer the speaker's propositional attitudes. It has been suggested that to ascribe certain propositional attitudes to a speaker requires the ability to select appropriate contextual information, and autistic patients may have deficits in this ability (Happé 1996; Jolliffe and Baron-Cohen 1999).

It has been argued that non-human primates, great apes in particular, have some capacity for metarepresentation (Boysen and Kuhlmeier 2002; Suddendorf and Whiten 2001; Whiten and Byrne 1991). For example, great apes have shown some capacity for mirror self-recognition, pretend play, and deliberate deception (Byrne and Whiten 1990; Gallup 1970; Russon *et al.* 2002). Given that there has been no convincing evidence to suggest that non-hominid primates share metarepresentational ability with humans, it may be plausible to assume that human-like representational capacity emerged as a result of an evolutionary arms race (Byrne and Whiten 1988). The sophisticated human metarepresentational ability and that of our closest evolutionary ancestors are by no means comparable, and it is the evolution of linguistic communication that is likely to have contributed to the emergence of the advanced metarepresentational ability in humans (Sperber 2000).

TOMOKO MATSUI

See also: Propositional attitude; representation and computation; theory of mind

Suggestions for further reading

Recanati, F. (2000) *Oratio Obliqua, Oratio Recta: An Essay on Metarepresentation*, Cambridge, MA: MIT Press.
Sperber, D. (ed.) (2000) *Metarepresentations: A Multidisciplinary Perspective*, New York: Oxford University Press.

Misunderstanding

Most modern pragmatic accounts of how utterances are understood have their roots in the pioneering work of H. Paul **Grice** (1957, 1989). Grice proposed that **utterance interpretation** is an intelligent, inferential activity, involving the expression and attribution of **intentions**. It is a two-stage process. In the first stage, a hearer decodes the linguistic meaning of the words they have heard, and in the second the hearer uses this **meaning** as a premise from which to work out, or 'infer', the meaning the speaker actually intended to convey – the speaker meaning. The distinction between linguistic meaning and speaker meaning corresponds roughly to the respective domains of **semantics** and **pragmatics** (*see* Atlas 2005; Carston 2002; Horn 2006; Levinson 2000; Recanati 2004b; Sperber and Wilson 1995). It follows from the fact that utterance interpretation takes place in two stages that there are two stages within which misunderstandings might occur. Let's consider each in turn.

A code is a system which reliably correlates signals with messages, allowing two information-processing systems to communicate along a 'channel' that exists between them (*see* Shannon and Weaver 1949). In Morse code, for example, the sender and receiver are Morse code operators,

each working with an encoding 'key' with which they tap out the signals that represent the message to be conveyed. The 'channel' along which the message travels is typically a telegraph wire. One of the strengths of Morse code, and one of the reasons it caught on so quickly, was that messages could be successfully transmitted despite the considerable amount of background noise and distortion that was often caused by interference along the telegraph wires. At a level of background noise above which the human voice can barely be discerned, let alone satisfactorily understood, the dots and dashes of Morse could be easily decoded by an operator. In states of emergency, or during times of war – anytime when it was vital not to be misunderstood – Morse became hugely important.

Human language, like **animal communication** systems, is a code. It is a system that pairs signals (words) with messages (the meanings those words convey). The 'channel' along which vocal signals are carried is the air through which sound waves travel from the speaker's vocal folds to the hearer's ears. Inherent in this 'channel' are a number of factors which might sometimes hinder decoding of the signal. In the same way that interference on the telegraph wire might occasionally render even Morse code unintelligible, I'm sure we have all experienced times during which background noise drowns out the voice we are listening to on a radio, or a train hurtling through a train station might make a part of someone's utterance entirely inaudible. In such instances, misunderstanding can easily occur.

But since, as Grice showed, utterance interpretation is much more than a process of coding and decoding, there is a huge potential for misunderstanding. Indeed, it could be argued that the way humans use language actually makes misunderstanding far *more* likely than misunderstanding is in other animal communication systems, which rely strictly on a process of coding and decoding. In this second stage of utterance interpretation, **context** is all important. Consider examples (1) to (4):

(1) She put it there!
(2) Mary gave John a file.
(3) The president's wife can't bear children.
(4) You simply must come to the party. Everyone else will be there!

All of these utterances contain examples of the phenomenon known as linguistic under-determinacy. What is linguistically encoded in each of these utterances falls well short of what the utterance is intended to convey. In (1), a hearer must infer to whom or what the **indexicals** 'she', 'it' and 'there' refer. Examples (2) and (3) are ambiguous – (3) multiply so – and the hearer must disambiguate certain words. In (4), the speaker's use of the phrase 'everyone else' is not, presumably, intended to mean literally everyone else in the world, and the hearer must infer which group of people 'everyone' is intended to apply to (everyone at work, every person within a certain group of friends, etc.).

The situation becomes even more complex when you consider the fact that speakers are often deliberately obtuse, and say one thing while meaning something else entirely. Consider the implied meaning (or **implicature**) in example (5) below, in which what the speaker intends to convey by this utterance is the precise opposite of what he or she has actually said:

(5) Another beautiful day! (Said whilst looking out of the window at the pouring rain.)

The more you think about the gap that needs to be bridged between linguistic meaning and speaker meaning, the broader that gap becomes. What's surprising in the human case is not that misunderstandings occur but, when you consider how many millions and millions of communicative acts are taking place each second, that on the whole we manage to avoid them so effortlessly, and so often.

Grice's own account of the inferential processes at work in utterance interpretation appealed to a **cooperative principle** and conversational **maxims** (Grice 1967). According to Grice, **conversation** is in the main a cooperative activity: 'Our talk exchanges do not normally consist of a succession of disconnected remarks, and would not be rational if they did' (Grice 1967: lecture II, 6; 1989: 26). It would not be rational for a speaker to formulate utterances in such a way that they are wide open to misunderstanding. On the whole, we do all we can to make it as easy as we can for our interlocutors to engage with us successfully.

While aspects of Grice's original framework are problematic, his central insight – that hearers are guided in the interpretive process by an expectation that speakers will be meeting certain standards – remains (Sperber and Wilson 1995; Levinson 2000). Likewise, his claim that utterance interpretation is indeed a two-stage process has led to a vast literature that explores the fact that the second, inferential stage exploits the human ability to interpret the actions of others in terms of the mental states behind these actions: the ability known as mind-reading or **theory of mind** (Baron-Cohen 1995).

There is a growing literature on the problems that arise in **communication** and general social interaction among individuals whose theory of mind ability is impaired in some way (Happé 1994b). The autobiographical works of Donna Williams (1992, 1994, 1999), who is autistic, document all too well the isolation and loneliness of an individual who simply did not have the ability to interpret the behaviour of others in terms of the mental states motivating that behaviour. Williams' linguistic ability was almost entirely intact, but she lived in a state of constant misunderstanding. She could understand words, but not what people meant by them. She could not bridge the gap between linguistic and speaker meaning.

Children whose linguistic ability is quite sophisticated, but whose theory of mind ability is still developing, often produce utterances that are difficult, or even impossible, to understand. Below is an example of the kind of thing I mean (adapted from something my own daughter uttered when she was three). There was no previous utterance, and she provided no context in which to process it. I recall it coming completely out of the blue:

(6) He was really mean to me today.

My daughter's utterance was well formed grammatically, but the problem was that while my daughter knew exactly who she was talking about, and presumed I did too, I did not. Before a certain age, young children simply presume that everything that they know is also known by the people they are talking with. They presume, if you like, that all background **knowledge** is *shared* background knowledge, and it takes a while for them to develop an appreciation that this is not always the case.

The intended context, the set of beliefs or assumptions used by the hearer in the interpretation of an utterance (Sperber and Wilson 1995), can be drawn from just about *any* piece of shared background knowledge (Gumperz 1992) that is available to *both* speaker and hearer. Philosophers have called this 'common knowledge' (Lewis 1969) or 'mutual knowledge' (Schiffer 1972), and it is often referred to in psychological circles as 'the common ground' (Clark 1996).

If two people are reminiscing about the scenery in a place they once visited, the name of which they cannot recall, there is liable to be a serious misunderstanding if, unbeknownst to each other, they are actually thinking about two different places. Examples are not hard to recall. Indeed, instances of glaring misunderstanding, caused by genuine cases in which shared background knowledge is presumed to be shared, but is not shared, are so atypical that we often dwell on them, and joke about them.

As well as sharing sufficient background knowledge to construct a context, communicators must also somehow assess and reassess the salience or relevance of background knowledge in interpreting behaviour. Otherwise, shared knowledge can itself be liable to cause misunderstandings. A few years ago, I attended a talk at the university at which I was working. As it happened, I genuinely had to leave before the end of the talk to catch a train. A piece of background knowledge that I and a colleague (uniquely) shared was that we had read some work of the person who was giving the talk and found it, well, a little dull to say the least. As luck would have it, however, I found the talk extremely thought-provoking and the speaker not only had some excellent ideas, but was also engaging and very entertaining. As a consequence, time flew by and I only realized that I had to leave when I happened to glance at my watch. A few days later, my colleague told me that she had found the talk as boring as she had expected and knew that I had too because she saw me looking at my watch! My colleague had mistaken my looking at my watch as behaviour intended for her. Moreover, she had interpreted it as relevant to her, in the sense that she thought I had intended it to interact with background knowledge we both possessed. As such, there was a complete misunderstanding.

As well as misunderstandings that occur on a 'micro' level (where the misunderstanding arises because of a lack, or presence, of shared knowledge between two people), there are other 'macro'-level factors involved in some misunderstandings. In England, for example, an utterance such as (5) might be considered an appropriate way of breaking the ice with someone: sarcasm and **irony** are quite prevalent in British culture and most people share that piece of background knowledge and pick up on it quite quickly. I once uttered that very utterance whilst looking out of a rainy schoolroom window in Brighton and turning to one of my new (non-British) students. The following exchange occurred:

(7) Tim: Another beautiful day!
    Student: Really? I don't like the rain at all.

People working within the 'ethnographic approach' to communication focus not only on **linguistic competence** (as is the case with most linguists), but also on the tacit social and cultural knowledge that governs appropriate use of language within a **culture**, otherwise known as **communicative competence** (Gumperz 1964; Hymes 1964a, 1972b). This resulted in the exploration of factors that might influence a speaker to choose to produce a certain utterance in preference to others: What is it that makes certain utterances more or less appropriate in a certain circumstance? What rules govern the appropriateness of certain behaviours? What are the cultural constraints that make some utterances feasible and others simply unfeasible? Individuals with native-like mastery of the language spoken in a country they are visiting for the first time, with well developed theory of mind abilities, yet who lack this cultural dimension of communicative competence, still leave themselves open to being misunderstood.

TIM WHARTON

See also: Animal communication, pragmatics of; conversation; disambiguation; explicit/ implicit distinction; Grice, H.P.; implicature; indexicals; inference; inferential comprehension; meaning; philosophy of language; post-Gricean pragmatics; pragmatics; proposition; radical pragmatics; rationality; reasoning; semantics-pragmatics interface; what is said

Suggestions for further reading

Clark, H. (1996) *Using Language*, Cambridge: Cambridge University Press. Part II, Foundations.
Sperber, D. and Wilson, D. (1995) *Relevance*: *Communication and Cognition*, Oxford: Blackwell. Chapter 1.

Mitigation

Mitigation has a growing importance within **pragmatics**. In fact, we have by now a blooming field, which identifies many rhetorical devices (e.g. **hedges**, bushes, shields, approximators) that express mitigation and that relates it to **politeness**, indirectness, fuzziness, **vagueness**, reduced commitment, and defenses. It is studied as a pragmatic phenomenon, particularly (but not only) in **contexts** such as medical and therapeutic discourse (e.g. Martinovski and Marsella 2003, 2005; Delbene 2004; Caffi 2006) and legal discourse (Danet and Kermish 1978; Danet 1980, 1985; Adelswärd *et al.* 1988; Drew 1990; Linell *et al.* 1993; Martinovski 2000, 2006; Kurzon 2001; Perez de Ayala 2001).

Mitigation (from Latin 'mitigare' meaning 'to make mild or gentle') is defined as a discursive process, the main function of which is minimization of vulnerability (Martinovski 2000). It is a product of the integration of discursive moves, argumentation lines, communicative acts, and rhetorical devices (Martinovski 2006). Mitigation involves strategic, emotional, linguistic, and **theory of mind** processes on different levels of consciousness (Martinovski *et al.* 2005). It can have two orientations: self-orientation, i.e. downplay of one's own vulnerability (see example 1) and other-orientation, i.e. downplay of others' vulnerability (see example 2) (Fraser 1980; Martinovski 2000).

In example (1), the examined is asked to admit that he hit a man with the door of a car.

(1) Examiner: So you moved towards Nilsson then
Examined: THE DOOR moved towards Nilsson I moved inside the car

The examined does not say 'yes' or 'no', but emphasizes through the use of topicalization that it was the door which hit the man, not him. The examined mitigates responsibility for action and damages by implicitly admitting action and denying **intention**.

In example (2), a daughter asks her father how his health check went. He knows that he has metastasized terminal stomach cancer. The father mitigates the bad news by his choice of modally weak verbs.

(2) Daughter: Dad, what did the doctors say about the tests you did?
Father: It seems that I might have some small polyps in my intestine.

Mitigations are realized on sequence and utterance levels in recognizable combinations of mitigation structures. These structures include directives performed by indirect means, distancing constructs such as disclaimers and 'or something/anything' (*see* Overstreet and Yule 2001), evasive answers, rhetorical devices such as tag questions, hedges (e.g. 'more or less', 'like', 'sort of') (Danet 1978), parenthetical verbs (e.g. guess, think, feel) (Fraser 1980), elliptic clauses, cut-off words, self-repetitions, overlap, pauses, lower voice, smiles, gestures, modal expressions, expressions of unclear quantity, impersonal constructions and narratives. These structures seem to be independent of language and **culture** (Martinovski 2000).

Vulnerability is interpreted differently according to culture and activity. Positive-politeness cultures (Brown and Levinson 1978) prefer to mitigate or downplay positive communicative acts such as praise and congratulations as opposed to negative communicative acts such as rejections and bad news. Negative-politeness cultures pay more attention to mitigation as avoidance of **disagreement** (Holmes 1984a: 345) or as softening of 'impact of some unpleasant aspect of an utterance on the speaker or the hearer' (Danet 1980: 525). In these contexts, communicative acts such as accusations, **refusals** and **irony** (Giora *et al.* 2005) are often mitigated. Holmes builds on Fraser (1980) and describes mitigation as a kind of attenuation, which is the opposite of boosting of **meaning**. Attenuation and boosting are described as strategies for modification of illocutionary force. For instance, mitigated denials become corrections (see example 1), while mitigated admissions become accounts (Martinovski 2000). Holmes claims that mitigation can be understood only in contrast to boosting. Mitigation is thus used to reduce the anticipated negative effect of a **speech act**. Finally, Holmes distinguishes between modification of attitude to a **proposition** (e.g. modal expressions) and modification of attitude to a hearer. This applies both to mitigation and boosting. Similarly, Flowerdew (1991) sees the function of mitigation as indicating an interpersonal exchange that goes beyond truth conditions and as a pragmatic strategy for modification of meaning.

Discourse mitigation is altered and coloured by specific activities. Caffi (1999) adopts a relation-oriented stance in describing doctor–patient dialogues. She defines mitigation as weakening or downgrading of interactional parameters, which affects allocation and shuffling of rights and obligations. In this sense, mitigation affects interactional efficiency, on the one hand, and the monitoring of relational, emotive distance between interlocutors, on the other hand. Mitigation is defined in terms of 'responsibility management in **discourse**, involving cognitive and emotive aspects' (Caffi 1999: 884).

In legal settings, mitigation is used to describe self-defense or defense related to responsibility for wrongdoing or evaluation of wrongdoing, often without denial of responsibility. It is expressed not only in the answers of witnesses but also in the **questions** and the utterances of examiners (Jacquemet 1994; Martinovski 2000). Mitigation of one's own guilt may cause aggravation of others' guilt (Martinovski 2000, 2006). Witnesses tend to use mitigation in reference to their own credibility more often than in relation to their moral positions or actions (Martinovski 2000, 2006). Examiners formulate utterances in a directed manner, which aims to soften the vulnerability of their clients or to aggravate or challenge the vulnerability of their opponent.

Mitigation and politeness are separate phenomena (Martinovski 2006). In non-legal discourse, mitigation is directed towards social face-work rather than defense behaviour, accusations, credibility, and guilt issues, i.e. in courts people can mitigate without being polite. Perez de Ayala (2001) discusses mitigation in terms of negative face and distinguishes between private and public face. Private negative face-work is described as 'the basic claims or territories, … freedom of action and freedom of imposition' (Brown and Levinson 1978: 61), whereas public negative face-work addresses the right not to suffer impositions in the public sphere (Perez de Ayala 2001). The assumed function of mitigation is to minimize threat to face and avoid conflict. However, Perez de Ayala finds that in the Question Time sessions in the British Parliament, politicians use politeness to engage in conflict, to attack and threaten each other rather than to avoid and diminish threat to others' face (as defined in Brown and Levinson 1978). The Parliamentary Question Time is described as a political fight. A trial is also a form of verbal fight governed by some restrictions on behaviour such as turn-giving order. However, in a trial some of the participants act with their public face and others, such as the witnesses, act with their private face. In that sense, the function of mitigation in courts is to monitor the co-existence of pubic and private negative face related to legal responsibility.

Future studies on mitigation are expected to cover a greater diversity of languages, cultures and multi-party activities using authentic data for analysis.

BILYANA MARTINOVSKI

See also: Argumentation theory; cognitive anthropology; cognitive pragmatics; compliments; cross-cultural pragmatics; cultural scripts; disagreement; discourse analysis; discourse markers; discourse particles; ellipsis; hedge; indefiniteness; institutional and professional discourse; intentionality; interactional linguistics; irony; legal pragmatics; meaning; narrative discourse; politeness; power; pragmatics; rhetoric; silence; speech act theory; speech act type; theory of mind; understatement; vagueness

Suggestions for further reading

Caffi, C. (ed.) (2006) *Mitigation*, Studies in Pragmatics 4, The Netherlands: Elsevier.
Fraser, B. (1980) 'Mitigation', *Journal of Pragmatics*, 31: 341–50.

Martinovski, B. (2006) 'Framework for analysis of mitigation in courts', *Journal of Pragmatics*, 38: 2065–86.

Modular pragmatics

A module is a cognitive system of a certain nature. To claim about any cognitive system, such as face recognition, the **syntax** of some natural language or a particular type of speech act, that it is modular is to ascribe to it a certain nature as a cognitive system. Unfortunately, there is no common understanding of the meaning of the notion of 'a module'. A variety of different theories about different cognitive systems have been made employing a notion of **modularity**.

A leading intuition that has enriched discussions in terms of or about 'modularity' is the possibility of a cognitive system being independent of other cognitive systems. The cognitive system of face recognition, for example, is independent of the cognitive systems of language, since babies who are unable to produce or understand a word, do recognize faces of some familiar persons.

Independence of a cognitive system with respect to other systems can take place on different levels. First, there is domain independence of a system, which means that the system processes only inputs of a certain type, produces only outputs of a certain type, or constitutes an input/output system of a certain type. Second, there is process independence of a system, which includes having restricted access to data (being 'informationally encapsulated') as well as not being accessible to consciousness. Third, there is neural independence of a system, which means it is associated with certain brain regions or processes. Fourth, there is developmental independence of a system, which means it developed in a child independently of the extent to which other cognitive systems have developed in it.

Theories that have used a notion of 'modularity' have included several additional, related ideas. In Chomsky's studies of language, innateness (what is genetically determined) plays a major role. In Fodor's theory of modularity, a module operates in a mandatory manner. Degrees of independence have also been suggested. Theoretical

frameworks that involve modules of some type have included a 'central' cognitive system that processes outputs of modules while having access to general belief and desire systems. Some frameworks include 'interface' systems as well.

Issues of modularity in **pragmatics** arise first with respect to the whole domain of pragmatics within an overarching theory of natural language, and second with respect to certain cognitive systems within pragmatics. A comprehensive system of language use is not modular, since common instances of language use involve access to the central, non-modular systems of belief and desire in creating or comprehending conversational **implicatures**. Hence, pragmatics is not a modular system. However, parts of pragmatics have been claimed to be modular (Kasher 1984a). The most interesting example is that of speech acts. Basic **speech act types** are those that appear in every natural language. **Assertion**, **question** and **command** are basic speech act types. Each of them is modular to the extent that the related cognitive systems manifest independence on the four levels mentioned above. For example, in work done by Kasher, Zaidel and associates it has been shown that deficits in assertion, command and question are related to damage of different brain regions (Soroker *et al.* 2005; Zaidel *et al.* 2000, 2002).

ASA KASHER

See also: Cognitive science; modularity of mind thesis

Suggestions for further reading

Chomsky, N. (1982) *On the Generative Enterprise: A Discussion with Riny Huybregts and Henk van Riemsdijk*, Dordrecht: Foris.
Fodor, J.A. (1983) *The Modularity of Mind*, Cambridge, MA: MIT Press.
Sperber, D. and Wilson, D. (2002) 'Pragmatics, modularity and mind reading', *Mind and Language*, 17: 3–23.

Modularity of Mind Thesis

Although the notion of modularity of mind has historical precursors, the term was introduced in

1983 by Jerry Fodor. In his influential book *The Modularity of Mind*, Fodor argued that perceptual systems are modular. A module is defined as an independent, innate, computational mechanism that is characterized by nine properties: (1) Domain specificity: modules are activated by a restricted class of inputs; (2) Informational encapsulation: modular processes can only access information in their dedicated database; they are impenetrable to information from the outside (Pylyshyn 2003); (3) Mandatoriness: modules are not under voluntary control and they are necessarily triggered by the relevant stimuli; (4) Inaccessibility: higher cognitive mechanisms only have limited access to the internal processes of modules; (5) Rapidity: computational processes are fast; (6) Shallow, i.e. non-conceptual outputs (for example, the visual module delivers a representation of the shape and the location of the object from the subject point of view; the subsequent, subject-independent recognition of the object is performed by a non-modular, central system); (7) Neural localization: modules are localized in a relatively small region of the brain; (8) Breakdown: modules display characteristic and specific patterns of breakdown; and (9) Development: modules follow a characteristic pace and sequence of growth.

Despite the title of his book, Fodor thinks that only a small portion of the mind is modular. In his view, only perceptual systems possess all the distinctive properties of modules. In particular, perceptual processes are characterized by informational encapsulation, which is regarded as the crucial property of modules (Fodor 1983, 2000). By contrast, thought processes (such as **reasoning**, decision-making, conceptualization) are holistic and unencapsulated, since they can take as input whatever information is in one's mind. As a consequence, Fodor is a strong opponent of the massive modularity thesis, i.e. the idea that the mind is largely, if not entirely, composed of modules.

In recent years, the massive modularity thesis has been defended by many authors belonging to different areas of **cognitive science**, such as **philosophy of mind**, **cognitive psychology**, **cognitive pragmatics**, neuropsychology and **cognitive anthropology**. Massive modularity can be conceived of in a strong or weak sense. According to the strong massive modularity

thesis, every central process is modular: the human mind does not contain any general-purpose mechanism. According to a weaker massive modularity thesis, central processes are largely modular, but there presumably are also non-modular, general-purpose processes.

As stated by many authors (e.g. Barrett and Kurzban 2006; Butterfill 2007), there is much disagreement and misunderstanding about what modules (in particular, conceptual modules) are. The crucial challenge facing the massive modularity thesis is to find a nontrivial notion of modularity, one that ensures that modules are real components of the cognitive architecture (see, for example, Carruthers 2006; Sperber 1996a, 2001b). Clearly, conceptual modules neither deliver shallow outputs nor are completely isolated from other conceptual processes. It is also possible to imagine a non-domain-specific module, such as Sperber's (1996a) formal logic module. Concerning encapsulation, two significant analyses were proposed by Carruthers and Sperber. According to Carruthers (2006), what is essential to massive modularity is that cognitive systems are frugal in both the amount of information required for processing and the complexity of the algorithms. Examples of frugal rules could be the heuristics rules proposed by Gigerenzer *et al.* (1999). For example, a cognitive mechanism using the Take the Best heuristics does not need to search for all the information possessed by the agent. When one has to decide which of two German cities is the larger, a frugal algorithm looks for information concerning the properties of those respective German cities that have correlated best with size in the past (having a top-division football team, having an underground, and so on). The property of frugality ensures computational fastness. Now, fast and frugal systems are not encapsulated in a narrow-scope sense, as there is not a large body of information such that that information cannot influence cognitive processes. Still, fast and frugal systems are characterized by wide-scope encapsulation, in the sense that they cannot be affected by most of the information held in the mind.

The solution proposed by Carruthers is a clear answer to the problem raised by Fodor's conceptual argument against the modularity of thought. The answer runs as follows: to be sure, a mind endowed with perfect **rationality** would be characterized by an unencapsulated reasoning process, which can take as an input any kind of information, depending on cognitive, linguistic, or objective **contexts**. However, the human mind is just partially rational, as it is constrained by attention and memory limitations. It follows that a wide-scope encapsulated module is compatible with it.

The analysis of the architectural aspects of the mind carried out by Dan Sperber (1996a, 2001b) also addresses the problem of the context sensitivity of reasoning and **communication**. However, contrary to Carruthers, Sperber (2005) believes that central modules are not necessarily activated by every input belonging to the right domain. In his view, mandatoriness at a conceptual level would lead to a computational explosion. To avoid this problem, a cognitive system for resource allocation has evolved. Every input to a perceptual or cognitive system is characterized by a degree of relevance, which is a positive function of the cognitive benefits that the system would gain from processing this input and a negative function of the computational effort required for processing. Correspondingly, every cognitive system strives for the maximization of relevance, i.e. selects the input that grants the highest probability of maximizing relevance (known as the cognitive principle of relevance; Sperber and Wilson 2002). In this framework, the mind is organized as a network of modular systems, which could be individually encapsulated but which together give rise to holistic effects (Sperber 1996a), as different contexts change the respective relevance of the various possible inputs.

Other authors who defend the massive modularity thesis adopt a weaker notion of modularity, in which domain specificity rather than encapsulation is the core property of central mechanisms (e.g. Baron-Cohen 1995). Sometimes the hypothesis of a cognitive *mechanism* is also discharged (Carey and Spelke 1994; Gopnik and Meltzoff 1997), and the emphasis is shifted to a specific corpus of innate **knowledge** that is generally inaccessible to consciousness (in analogy with Chomsky's syntactic knowledge). A different notion of modularity is defended in cognitive neuropsychology, which focuses on the property of neural localization (from which specific

patterns of breakdown follow; *see* Coltheart 2001; Shallice 1988). Cognitive neuropsychology rejects both cognitive impenetrability and innateness as necessary conditions for modularity. Even domain specificity is not a necessary condition. In fact, while some neuropsychological double dissociations concern specific domains (e.g. **theory of mind** versus theory of inanimate bodies), other dissociations (e.g. long-term memory versus working memory) concern nonspecific domains.

A further notion of modularity was proposed by Karmiloff-Smith (1992), who adopts a developmental perspective. For Karmiloff-Smith, the mind is not modular at birth, but modularization is a gradual process that takes place during development. The starting point is characterized by domain-specific predispositions that focus infants' attention to specific inputs. Complementary to this process of progressive modularization is a process of representational redescription, whereby the information contained in the cognitive system becomes increasingly explicit and accessible to consciousness. Particular attention to the developmental aspect was also given by Segal (1996), who proposes a distinction between synchronic and diachronic modularity. Synchronic modules reflect a static capacity, while diachronic modules follow a genetically and developmentally determined pattern of growth, such as occurs in the parameterization process of Chomskyan syntactic knowledge (Chomsky 1981).

The Darwinian approach to psychology is a theoretical perspective that has produced many concrete hypotheses about specialized, fitness-promoting cognitive mechanisms, such as the cheater detection system (Cosmides and Tooby 1989, 1992), the mating-selection system (Buss 1994) and the mindreading system (Baron-Cohen 1995). The massive modularity thesis is strictly tied to an evolutionary (or Darwinian) perspective on the mind (Cosmides and Tooby 1992; Pinker 1997), according to which mental mechanisms are the outcome of natural selection processes. In this approach, specialized cognitive systems are also called Darwinian modules (Samuels *et al.* 1999). Among the many arguments that have been proposed to defend massive modularity, it is worth mentioning the engineering argument, the error argument, the poverty of the stimulus argument, and the combinatorial explosion argument (Cosmides and Tooby 1989, 1992; *see also* Frankenhuis and Ploeger 2007). According to the engineering argument, natural selection favoured specialized cognitive mechanisms because they tend to provide rapid, reliable, and efficient solutions to specific adaptive problems. As in any hypothesis formulated in a Darwinian framework, this argument does not imply that a specialized system should be expected for any kind of problem.

The error argument highlights that a general-purpose learning device should possess some criteria for distinguishing between success and failure. However, what counts as success or failure depends on the particular domain, and thus an evolved system that is specific to a given domain has a high probability of being selected. The poverty of the stimulus argument generalizes the Chomskyan argument for syntactic knowledge. It states that organisms could not learn ex nihilo how to handle adaptive problems during their lifetime, because they have no time to run the necessary trial-and-error, statistical-based process. For that reason, cognitive systems endowed with domain-specific procedures have been favoured by natural selection. The combinatorial explosion argument points to the combinatorial explosion that a general-domain system would have to handle in order to imagine, compare, and select all the possible alternative actions. Instead, computational time and cost are drastically reduced in a domain-specific system, which is triggered by limited types of inputs and runs on domain-specific rules.

We have already pointed out that Fodor is at one and the same time a strong defender of the modularity of the 'perceptual' mind and a strong opponent of the modularity of central cognition (the latter for a priori, conceptual reasons). The background of his arguments for the holistic nature of cognition is a sceptical attitude towards evolutionary psychology (Fodor 2000) and, more recently, against Darwinism in general (Fodor 2008; but *see* Dennett 2008 for an efficacious reply). In Fodor's view, all the arguments for evolutionary psychology presuppose a Lamarckian-finalistic notion of evolution. Moreover, when efficacious, they are arguments for innateness, i.e. for the existence of innate knowledge, and not for the existence of innate domain-specific mechanisms. Other authors, who are not

opposed to the massive modularity thesis, still do not find the various conceptual and empirical arguments proposed in support of it compelling (Samuels 2006) and in turn criticize the fuzziness of the notions involved (but *see* Carruthers 2006). Even within the 'massive modularity community' there are worries about some empirical hypotheses that have been formulated in the evolutionary paradigm. Sperber and colleagues, for example, present a relevance-based account of the 'cheater-detection problem' as an alternative to Cosmides and Tooby's modular solution (Sperber *et al.* 1995).

Many authors have criticized the modularity hypothesis. Among the most radical criticisms is Prinz (2006) who presents much empirical evidence that in his view contradicts the modularity of both perceptual and cognitive processes (but *see* Samuels 2006 for replies). More generally, recent neurophysiological data on the activity of neurons which have both perceptual and motor properties (Rizzolatti *et al.* 2008) casts doubt on the traditional separation between perception and action which underlies even basic, Fodorian modularity.

CRISTINA MEINI

See also: Animal communication, pragmatics of; autism spectrum disorders; cognitive psychology; cognitive science; modular pragmatics

Suggestions for further reading

Kasher, A. (1984) 'Pragmatics and the modularity of mind', *Journal of Pragmatics*, 8: 539–57; revised version in S. Davis (ed.) (1991) *Pragmatics*, Oxford: Oxford University Press.
Seok, B. (2006) 'Diversity and unity of modularity', *Cognitive Science*, 30: 347–80.

Morphopragmatics

At the interface of morphology and **pragmatics**, morphopragmatics, as pioneered by Wolfgang U. Dressler and Lavinia Merlini Barbaresi (1987, 1994) and expanded in Dressler and Kiefer (1990), deals with regular pragmatic meanings obtained through the sole application of morphological rules, given certain sets of contextual conditions. These rules may be totally responsible for the added utterance meanings (e.g. endearment and playfulness via diminutive formation), with the wordbase being either neutral (English: *dogg-y*) or contributory (English: *dear-ie*; Italian: *piccol-ino* 'small-DIM') or even contrary (Italian: *gross-ino* 'big-DIM') to the effect pursued.

The authors assume the priority of pragmatics over **semantics** (Dressler and Merlini Barbaresi 2001, contrary to Kiefer 2004), i.e. they do not derive morphopragmatic meanings from semantic meanings, but assume that a morphopragmatically relevant rule possesses some non-semantic, autonomous pragmatic feature. In Italian diminutives, for example, the pragmatic effects cannot be derived from a semantic meaning [small], with its allosemes [unimportant] and [young]. These effects are based on an autonomous pragmatic feature [fictive], and on a derived, more specific feature [non-serious]. Evidence of that is the fact that many of these pragmatic effects can also be obtained by augmentatives, which share with diminutives the pragmatic feature [fictive], but certainly not their semantic meaning [big]. In Italian, saying to somebody:

(1) mangi come un maial-ino
    you eat like a pig-DIM
    'you eat like a little piggy'

would have the same pragmatic effect as:

(2) mangi come un maial-one
    you eat like a pig-AUGM
    'you eat like some huge pig'

In both cases, the evaluative suffix is capable of hedging the critical remark, i.e. of downgrading the illocutionary force of the evaluative **assertion**, by adding some playful character. A non-suffixed version like:

(3) mangi come un maiale
    'you eat like a pig'

would be insulting and likely to cause the addressee's angry retort.

The pragmatic meaning of the evaluative suffix, as in (1) and (2), is first of all intended to

apply to a whole **speech act**, but a specific landing site is necessary as a base for attaching an evaluative suffix. And, in this case, the only eligible landing site is *maiale*.

Fictiveness is conceptualized as a departure from conventionally accepted standards of **meaning**, which glide according to the speaker's evaluation. It creates fuzziness as, for example, in the Italian dialogue:

(4) Greengrocer: Quante mele? Customer: Faccia un chil-etto.
    'How many apples?' 'Make (it) a kilo-DIM' (= about a kilo)

Here the diminutive does not diminish the value of the measure term, of course, but it creates imprecision.

In many languages, evaluatives have the power to modify speech acts, but not to the point of moving them to a different class of speech acts. In addition, they are capable of modifying the speech situation by introducing a whole series of positive or negative pragmatic meanings, ranging from endearment, playfulness (in examples 1 and 2), pleasantness, cosiness, empathy or sympathy, to **irony**, sarcasm, meanness and derision. An example of self-irony is:

(5) Dutch: wij zijn een dom volk-je
    German: Wir sind ein dummes Völk-chen.
    we are a silly people-DIM
    'we're sort of silly people'

A speech situation that mostly favours the use of diminutives is one in which adults address small children or speak about them In these cases, even mass nouns, normally excluded from diminutive formation, can be diminutivized, as in Italian and Viennese German:

(6) No, non toccare l'acqu-etta
    Nein, rühr das Wass-erl nicht an!
    No, not touch the water-DIM (don't touch …)

Small children themselves also use diminutives when referring to items in their own world. The first meanings that we appreciate in their use of dimunitives are pragmatic rather than semantic (Dressler and Merlini Barbaresi 2001;

Savickiene and Dressler 2007). At early stages, that is, children do not connect diminutive suffixes to the semantic notion of smallness, which they express by the use of the adjective 'small'. This is evidence corroborating the authors' assumption of the priority of pragmatics over semantics.

Other patterns having morphopragmatic effects are excessives in Hungarian, German, Dutch, Danish and Ancient Greek. Excessives express the highest possible intensification, as in referring to God in Danish:

(7) Den aller-hellig-ste Fader
    'The very holi-est Father'

Here, the superlative meaning is radicalized to an absolute peak, allowing no further comparison. In **discourse**, excessives put an end to any further discussion, as in the German dialogue expressing an indirect invitation to urgently leave the place:

(8) A: Es ist höch-ste   B: Es ist aller-höch-ste
       Zeit.   Zeit.
       It is highest time   It is all-highest time
    A: It's high time   B: It is the very last
       (we left).   moment.

Morphopragmatic studies have been applied to the French ironic-intimate suffix–*o* (which may trigger a truncation of the base), as in *les social-os* (from the base *socialiste*) (Kilani-Schoch and Dressler 1999) and the Japanese honorific suffix–*masu*, which indexes social and psychological distance in **conversation**.

LAVINIA MERLINI BARBARESI and
WOLFGANG U. DRESSLER

See also: Hedge; honorific language; hyperbole; interlanguage pragmatics; irony; mitigation; request; semantics-pragmatics interface; speech act theory; understatement

Suggestions for further reading

Crocco Galéas, G. (1992) *Gli Etnici Italiani: Studio di Morfologia Naturale*, Padua: Unipress.
Dressler, W.U. (ed.) (1997) *Studies in Pre- and Proto-Morphology*, Vienna: Verlag der Oesterreichischen Akademie der Wissenschaften.
Merlini Barbaresi, L. (1999) 'The pragmatics of the "diminutive"–y/ie suffix in English', in C. Schaner-Wolles, J. Rennison and F. Neubarth (eds) *Naturally!*, Turin: Rosenberg & Sellier.

Morris, C.

Charles W. Morris was born on 23 May 1901 in Denver, Colorado. After studying engineering and psychology, he earned a bachelor of science degree at Northwestern University in 1922. Deciding that his primary interests were philosophical, Morris became a student of pragmatist George Herbert Mead at the University of Chicago. In his dissertation titled 'Symbolism and Reality: A Study in the Nature of Mind' (Morris 1925) and articles published during the 1930s, Morris assembled a synthesis of the **semiotics** of Charles **Peirce**, the social behaviourism of Dewey and Mead, and the logical positivism of Rudolf Carnap and Otto Neurath. Morris quickly rose to a prominent position in American **philosophy**. Morris organized the fifth and sixth International Congresses for the Unity of Science (1939 and 1941). His relationships with German philosophers were essential to bringing many of them to America during World War II. Morris held academic appointments as an instructor in philosophy at the Rice Institute in Texas (1925–31), an associate professor of philosophy at the University of Chicago (1931–47), a lecturer at the University of Chicago (1948–58) and a research professor at the University of Florida (1958–71). Morris was a Fellow of the American Academy of Arts and Sciences, and served as President of the Western Division of the American Philosophical Association in 1936–37. Morris died on 15 January 1979 in Gainesville, Florida.

The non-reductive and pluralistic naturalism of **pragmatism** is evident in Morris's efforts to construct a theory of language and signs. The scientific method, applied to all areas of inquiry, produces **knowledge** about humans and their environment which aids with philosophical questions. Neither philosophy alone, nor any single science's knowledge, can determine the reality of anything, including the nature of **meaning**, signs, and language. Morris inherited this perspective towards philosophical problems from earlier pragmatists. The psychological functionalism developed by Dewey, Mead, and James Angell at Chicago during the late 1890s synthesized the latest scientific knowledge into a theory of mind inspired by evolution: all aspects of mind are functions of purposive organic activity, explained by their survival value. Morris defended functionalism against its rivals in *Six Theories of Mind* (Morris 1932), and during the 1930s he labelled his own version as the 'neo-pragmatism' advancing the movement.

Also committed to the pragmatist view, emphasized particularly by Peirce, that intelligence essentially involves the creation and proper functioning of signs, Morris focused on their nature. Biology, psychology, sociology, anthropology, and linguistics together contribute to semiotics: the study of semiosis or the use of signs. To be a legitimate scientific field in its own right, semiotics must define its subject matter, the nature of signs, and delimit its methodological orientation to the objectively available evidence. Morris, following Mead, accordingly adopted the standpoint of pragmatic social behaviourism towards signs. The meaning of signs consists in their practical use; the practical use of signs is embedded in the behavioural habits of organisms; and complex signs and language arise in the social conduct of humans. Morris's large debt to Mead, as well as his selective appropriation of Mead's theories of mind and **communication**, is especially evident in his editorial work on Mead's lectures, brought together in *Mind, Self, and Society: From the Standpoint of a Social Behaviorist* (Morris 1934).

Morris's behaviourism offers an elimination of any subjectivity to signs. Signs exist in the natural world and do not essentially involve internal mental **representations**, but only the behavioural habits of response to stimuli. This behaviourism departs from Peirce's semiotic theory of signs as thought processes, and rejects Peirce's view of persons as signs themselves. Psychology may additionally formulate relationships between signs and mental experiences or conceptual processes, but such theorizing is not part of semiotics. Peirce's discrimination of sign, object, and interpretant within the semiotic process is transformed by Morris in *Foundations of the Theory of Signs* (Morris 1938) into the tripartite division of

sign, object, and person within the natural world. Morris then divides the field of semiotics into **syntax**, **semantics**, and **pragmatics**. This tripartite division of semiotics conveniently embraces logical positivism's treatment of analytic a priori **propositions** as merely syntactical truths, having no mental or metaphysical significance (following Carnap 1937). Morris's division of semiotics also found a fitting place for semantical propositions whose truths depend on nothing more than the correspondence between the meaning of the sign and the existence of the entity so designated. By adding pragmatics, Morris hoped to enfold the unity of science movement within the pragmatist camp, as *Logical Positivism, Pragmatism, and Scientific Empiricism* (Morris 1937) suggests. Carnap (1942) quickly adopted Morris's general approach to semiotics. However, advocates of logical positivism and scientism tended to isolate pragmatics as dealing only with features of communication largely irrelevant to knowledge, truth, and science.

Morris's *Signs, Language, and Behavior* (Morris 1946) more carefully defines syntax, semantics, and pragmatics as follows. Pragmatics 'deals with the origins, uses, and effects of signs within the total behavior of the interpreters of signs' (1946: 219), and thus has the widest scope of any semiotic study. Semantics concerns just the relations between signs and the objects they signify, narrowing semiotic study to the strict literal meaning of signs and propositions. Syntactics concerns the formal relations between signs themselves, further narrowing semiotic study to the logical and grammatical rules that govern sign use. Morris's wide definition of pragmatics, by covering all linguistic behaviours, does not limit that field's study to meanings conveyed by speakers beyond what is explicitly or literally communicated. Morris resisted the notion that any firm dichotomy could be found between explicit and implicit meaning, or that any simplistic division could be made between syntactical signs, semantical signs, and pragmatical signs. Further, the three factors of sign-behaviour, the designative, appraisive, and prescriptive factors, are found to varying degrees in all communication. Only the most refined and sophisticated languages facilitate sign-usage for just one or another factor, and such usage heavily depends on social **context** in any case.

Morris's impact on philosophy and linguistics faded during the 1940s and 1950s, as pragmatism was displaced by analytic and scientistic approaches more concerned with formal and factual truth. Hostility towards pragmatism from University of Chicago philosopher Mortimer Adler and president Robert Hutchins further ensured the marginalization of Morris and semiotics. Undeterred, Morris applied his semiotics to a variety of fields in *Paths of Life: Preface to a World Religion* (Morris 1942), *The Open Self* (Morris 1948), *Varieties of Human Value* (Morris 1956), and *Signification and Significance* (Morris 1964), pursuing his dream that scientific knowledge of humanity will inspire the wisdom necessary to keep pace with technological and cultural change. *The Pragmatic Movement in American Philosophy* (Morris 1970) is an outstanding insider's account of pragmatism's figures and phases. However, Morris himself had almost no influence on the next generation of pragmatists in philosophy, who were more interested in insights from Ludwig **Wittgenstein**, Thomas Kuhn, or W.V. Quine. Morris's greatest student, the semiotician Thomas Sebeok, pursued and improved upon several of Morris's ideas, including those collected in *Writings on the General Theory of Signs* (Morris 1971).

JOHN SHOOK

See also: History of pragmatics; Peirce, C.S.; pragmatism

Suggestions for further reading

Black, M. (1949) 'The semiotic of Charles Morris', in M. Black (ed.) *Language and Philosophy*, Ithaca, NY: Cornell University Press.

Fiordo, R.A. (1976) *Charles Morris and the Criticism of Discourse*, Bloomington, IN: Indiana University Press.

Rossi-Landi, F. (1975) 'Signs about a master of signs', *Semiotica*, 13: 155–97.

N

Narrative Discourse

From the mid-1980s onwards, narrative studies moved away from the abstract, formalist concerns of literary narratology towards a contextualist stance that went hand-in-hand with the interdisciplinary expansion of the 'narrative turn' across the humanities and social sciences. Narrative analysis thus broadened to include the study of 'natural' narratives alongside written literature, and the questions asked increasingly drew attention to the actual situation in which storytelling took place and the functions narratives might perform. In line with the emphasis on situated interaction, researchers concerned with the pragmatic aspects of narrative tend to focus on oral stories (although not exclusively so), especially narratives of personal experience. The context of the interaction varies considerably, including stories told at family meal times (Ochs *et al.* 1992; Blum Kulka 1993), in peer groups (Kyratzis 2000, Georgakopoulou 2003) and in interview situations, be they research generated (Wortham 2000; Jones 2002), in medical discourse (He 1996; Mishler 1997) or in a law court (Barry 1991; Harris 2001b). Given the diverse and interdisciplinary nature of studying narrative discourse, the application of pragmatic theory tends to be eclectic and overlap with other fields of interest, especially **sociolinguistics**, **stylistics**, **conversation analysis** and **psycholinguistics**.

From a contextualist perspective, narrative discourse is understood as one means by which speakers make sense of themselves, the world around them, and position themselves in relation to others. In order to differentiate this from other kinds of texts and talk, narrative is minimally defined as a series of temporally ordered events (Labov 1972). Other factors may be considered as optional prompts of narrativity (that is, the perception of a text as more or less like a narrative), including the climactic organization of events around a problematic situation with a recognizable beginning, middle and end (Ryan 2006). Over the last four decades, numerous models have been put forward to describe narrative form. Within linguistics, Labov's (1972) six-part outline has been highly influential, particularly of interest for the multifaceted concept of evaluation (Schiffrin 1997; Gwyn 2000). While pragmatics has not gone on to shape definitions of narrative per se (debated recently by Rudrum 2005), the need to account for social purpose has given rise to Martin and Plum's (1997) typology of story genres. This typology differentiates narratives of personal experience from Anecdotes, Exemplums and Recounts.

The linguistic resources of narrative discourse have come under scrutiny for their interrelated structural and pragmatic functions. Longacre (1983) and Labov (1972) identify devices used to indicate the narrative peak (the pivotal moment where climax moves into resolution), the use of which may also be interpersonally motivated by the demand for vividness and relevance. **Discourse markers** (Norrick 2001), repetition and cohesion (Bauman 1984) all serve to organize relations between narrative segments, but, crucially, play equal roles in managing interaction between narrator(s) and their audience. **Deixis** and **evidentials** (Mushin 2000) are important for their part in constructing narrative perspective, and also for their indexical nature.

Anaphora and **reference** operate within cognitive sequencing constraints as narrative processing takes place in real time (Emmott 1997; Herman 2000). More generally, mentions of time and place (Georgakopoulou 2003) contribute to plot structure and simultaneously reinforce the co-constructed nature of storytelling. This kind of linguistic analysis is not limited to English language narratives, but is also manifest in cross-linguistic comparisons. Examples include (but are not limited to) the analysis of storytelling in Japanese (Hinds 1984; Clancy 1992), Chinese (Norment 1994), and European languages such as German (Ahrenholz 2000).

It is the pervasive concern with **context** that dominates the broader study of narrative discourse. Both the localized interactional setting and its relationship to wider cultural issues are important. Likewise, the role of the audience in co-constructing narratives is considered vital, whether that collaboration takes place as a story of explicitly shared experience (for example, between friends) or less overtly through the interventions of the researcher. The shared knowledge between listener and speaker and the capacity to interpret **inferences** correctly (or lack thereof) are seen as vital components in successful storytelling. Sociolinguistic studies provide many examples of where variation according to ethnicity and **gender** result in different patterns of and uses for narrative discourse, giving rise to potential miscommunication. Notable examples that focus on gendered interaction include the analysis of storytelling within same sex groups (Coates 1996, 2001), mixed sex groups (Abney 1994) and in young boys and girls (Kyratzis 2000). Researchers have also considered the distinctive narrative discourse of ethnic groups, including work on Maori storytelling (Holmes 1998b), Jewish (Schiffrin 1996) and Greek communities (Georgakopoulou 1997). Storytelling within the family as a site for socialization is a site for further cross-cultural comparisons including Israeli (Blum Kulka *et al.* 1993), Scandinavian (Aukrust and Snow 1998), Central American (Melzi 2000) and Japanese (Minami 1994) contexts.

Children's acquisition of narrative skills brings another perspective to bear on the social and cognitive factors involved in storytelling. There is rich literature documenting children's progressive use of narrative structure (Peterson and McCabe 1983; Clarke 1985) especially the evolving use of reference (Clancy 1992) and evaluation (Page 2006). Sociolinguistic studies of narrative pragmatics also contribute to wider debates about literacy, where the potential disadvantages raised by inattention to cross-cultural variation in narrative participation take centre stage (Michaels 1981; Heath 1982). Children's storytelling also intersects with research in psycholinguistics (Bokus 1991; Harriet 1987) and work on language disorders.

Studies of literary narrative tend to be more text-immanent and treat the contextual interaction between author and reader in a more diffuse and mediated manner. Nonetheless, concepts from pragmatics have been usefully put to use in the analysis of narrative literature. This includes stylistic work which examines speech acts and implicature as they occur in the dialogue of fictional prose and drama (Carter and Simpson 1989). More contentiously, attempts to conceptualize literary narratives as speech acts in and of themselves raised considerable dispute (Genette 1990), especially regarding whether literary narratives should be given special status or not (Pratt 1977). Searle's work was also important for developing the idea that certain sentences were unspeakable in narrative (Banfield 1982). Recently, pragmatics has been useful in the developing narrative theories of fictionality (Walsh 2003) and cognitively oriented work on storyworlds (Herman 2002).

While there is not, as such, a narrowly defined concept as narrative pragmatics, the vast and varied range of narratives enumerating in different contexts and made possible through interaction in different media will no doubt provide a significant discourse form of interest to pragmatics for some time yet to come.

RUTH PAGE

See also: Context; culture; discourse; gender; literary pragmatics; psycholinguistics; sociolinguistics; stylistics

Suggestions for further reading

Chafe, W.L., Freedle, R. and John, W. (eds) (1980) *The Pear Stories: Cognitive, Cultural and*

Linguistic Aspects of Narrative Production, Norwood, NJ: Ablex.

Herman, D. (2002) *Story Logic: Problems and Possibilities of Narrative*, Lincoln, NE and London: University of Nebraska Press.

Thornborrow, J. and Coates, J. (eds) (2005) *The Sociolinguistics of Narrative*, Studies in Narrative, volume 6. Amsterdam: Benjamins.

Natural and Non-Natural Meaning

The notion of non-natural meaning (meaning$_{NN}$) is central to much of the work of the philosopher of language H.P. **Grice**. In the 1940s, Grice wrote a paper entitled 'Meaning' (published in 1957) in which he argued that the kind of **meaning** which typically involves a linguistic convention or code should, ultimately, be characterized in terms of the beliefs, desires and **intentions** of communicators. In Grice's words, 'what words mean is a matter of what people mean by them' (1989: 340).

However, before beginning the account of meaning$_{NN}$ offered in his 1957 paper, Grice noticed that 'mean' can be used in a different way. He therefore distinguished another sense of the word, which he called natural meaning (meaning$_N$). In contrast with meaning$_{NN}$, which relies on the presence of a certain set of nested intentions, meaning$_N$ exists as the result of a causal co-variation between two states of affairs: it is sometimes called indicator meaning. Compare the difference between examples of meaning$_N$ in (1) and (2) with the examples of meaning$_{NN}$ in (3) and (4):

(1) Those black clouds mean rain.
(2) That hissing sound means there's a snake under the table.
(3) That remark means 'it is raining'.
(4) *Il y a un serpent sous la table* means 'there is a snake under the table'.

Grice developed a series of tests to distinguish meaning$_N$ from meaning$_{NN}$. The first of these was based on the idea that cases of meaning$_N$ are factive, in the sense that *x* means$_N$ *p* or *x* meant$_N$ *p* entails *p*. By contrast, cases of meaning$_{NN}$ are non-factive. Consider the utterance in (2). If Sue's utterance of (2) is true, then it will

indeed always follow that there is a snake under the table. If, for example, there isn't a snake under the table, then Peter, on hearing Sue's utterance, could legitimately respond 'Well, it looks like that hissing sound *didn't mean* there was a snake under the table.' Compare this with a scenario in which Peter asks Sue what Pierre meant by the remark 'Il y a un serpent sous la table', to which Sue replies with the utterance in (4). Here, the utterance can be true whether or not there actually is a snake under the table, and her remark will still mean$_{NN}$ the same thing (and Pierre will still have meant$_{NN}$ the same thing by his utterance of it) regardless of the facts of the matter.

After setting meaning$_N$ to one side, Grice then moved through a series of carefully constructed examples in order to identify precisely what type of intentions are required in cases of meaning$_{NN}$. In the first of these examples, Grice considered whether performing an action with the intention of inducing a thought or belief in another person – or informing them of something – amounted to meaning$_{NN}$. It plainly does not. In order to incriminate someone I might drop their handkerchief near the scene of a murder in order to induce the police into believing they are the murderer. However, the fact that I have this intention is entirely incidental to the response of the police. The two are not linked in any way, since the 'audience' is entirely unaware of my intention: the handkerchief does not mean$_{NN}$ anything (though the police may think it means$_N$ something!). Grice then turns to a series of further examples, in which a communicator provides *overt* evidence of their intention to inform.

For Grice, such examples were still problematic. Even if someone openly shows something to someone (and, in doing so, provides overt evidence of an intention to inform), there is still a sense in which the presence of the communicator's intentions are at least partly incidental to the occurrence of the intended response. In such a situation, according to Grice, we still do not have a case of meaning$_{NN}$. Grice asks us to consider the case in which King Herod presents the head of St John the Baptist to Salome. Here, Salome can infer that St John the Baptist is dead solely on the strength of the evidence presented, and independently of any intentions Herod has in presenting her with his head. Grice wanted to distinguish between merely overtly showing someone a particular object, or a certain type of behaviour, and something being meant$_{NN}$ by the object or behaviour in question (or by the person responsible for using it in a certain meaningful$_{NN}$ manner). His solution was ingenious:

Compare the following two cases:

(1) I show Mr. *X* a photograph of Mr. *Y* displaying undue familiarity to Mrs. *X*.
(2) I draw a picture of Mr. *Y* behaving in this manner and show it to Mr. *X*.

I find that I want to deny that in (1) the photograph (or my showing it to Mr. *X*) meant$_{NN}$ anything at all, while I want to assert that in (2) the picture (or my drawing and showing it) meant$_{NN}$ something (that Mr. *Y* had been unduly familiar), or at least that I had meant$_{NN}$ by it that Mr. *Y* had been unduly familiar. What is the difference between the two cases? Surely that in case (1) Mr. *X*'s recognition of my intention to make him believe that there is something between Mr. *Y* and Mrs. *X* is (more or less) irrelevant to the production of this effect by the photograph. Mr. *X* would be led by the photograph at least to suspect Mrs. *X* even if, instead of showing it to him, I had left it in his room by accident; and I (the photograph shower) would not be unaware of this. But it will make a difference to the effect of my picture on Mr. *X* whether or not he takes me to be intending to inform him (make him believe something) about Mrs. *X*, and not to be just doodling or trying to produce a work of art.

(Grice 1989: 218)

In any act which provides evidence of an intention to inform, notice that there are two layers of information to be retrieved by the audience. The first is the information being pointed out – in Grice's example, the fact that Mr. *Y* is being unduly familiar with Mrs. *X*. The second is the information that this first layer is being pointed out intentionally. In the Herod example, whilst he does provide overt evidence of his intention to inform (the second layer), the audience –

Salome – can derive the basic layer of information (that St John the Baptist is dead) without reference to this intention. According to Grice, for a case to count as one of meaning$_{NN}$, this basic layer should *not* be entirely derivable without reference to the second layer. Grice concluded his formulation of meaning$_{NN}$ as follows:

'*A* meant something by *x*' is roughly equivalent to '*A* uttered *x* with the intention of inducing a belief by means of the recognition of this intention'.

(Grice 1989: 219)

Grice's account of meaning$_{NN}$ inspired a great deal of discussion. Philosophers such as Strawson (1964a), Searle (1965, 1969) and Schiffer (1972) constructed a range of increasingly complex counter-examples, many designed to show the need for ever higher levels of **intentionality**. Grice dealt with these counter-examples in his 1968b and 1969 papers and revised his formulation (*see* Avramides 1989 for discussion). Less remarked upon have been the problems that arise as a result of pragmatists focusing solely on meaning$_{NN}$. Intentional verbal **communication**, after all, involves a mixture of both meaning$_{NN}$ *and* meaning$_N$ (*see* Wharton 2009).

TIM WHARTON

See also: Conventionality; entailment; Grice, H.P.; meaning; metarepresentation; neo-Gricean pragmatics; philosophy of language; post-Gricean pragmatics; pragmatics; propositional attitudes; radical pragmatics; relevance theory; Searle, J.

Suggestions for further reading

Avramides, A. (1989) *Meaning and Mind: An Examination of a Gricean Account of Language*, Cambridge, MA: MIT Press.
Grice, H.P. (1989) *Studies in the Way of Words*, Cambridge, MA: Harvard University Press.

Negation, Pragmatics of

The ability to negate or deny is a ubiquitous property of being human. It is the sine qua non of such fundamental properties of linguistic

communication as truth/falsity assessment, contradiction, **presupposition**, **entailment**, **scalar implicature**, counterfactuality, **irony**, and lying. From ancient Greek and Indian philosophers to contemporary linguists, logicians, and psychologists, negation has played a central role in the investigation of natural and formal linguistic systems. This role has also been an intriguing one, given the conceptual clash between the simplicity of the formal negation operator (a one-place connective of propositional logic that toggles the truth of *p* to the falsity of not-*p* and vice versa) and the complexity displayed by the form and function of actual negative expressions in natural language.

Since Parmenides, Plato, and Aristotle, it has been recognized that the logical symmetry of negative and affirmative **propositions** in logic belies a fundamental asymmetry in natural language. It was Plato who first observed that negative sentences are less valuable than affirmative ones, in being less specific or less informative. The ontological, epistemological, psychological, and grammatical priority of affirmatives over negatives is further supported by Aristotle (*Metaphysics* 996b14–16) – 'The affirmative proposition is prior to and better known than the negative (since affirmation explains denial just as being is prior to not-being)' – and St Thomas Aquinas:

> The affirmative enunciation is prior to the negative for three reasons … With respect to vocal sound, affirmative enunciation is prior to negative because it is simpler, for the negative enunciation adds a negative particle to the affirmative. With respect to thought, the affirmative enunciation, which signifies composition by the intellect, is prior to the negative, which signifies division … With respect to the thing, the affirmative enunciation, which signifies *to be*, is prior to the negative, which signifies *not to be*, as the having of something is naturally prior to the privation of it.
>
> (St. Thomas, book I, lesson XIII; Oesterle 1962: 64)

Not only are negatives (e.g. 'Hartford is not the capital of Massachusetts') less informative than affirmatives (e.g. 'Hartford is the capital of Connecticut') (*cf.* Leech 1983: 100ff.), they are also more marked morphosyntactically (few languages have affirmative markers) and psychologically more complex and harder to process (*cf.* Just and Carpenter 1971: 248–49, and other work reviewed in Horn 1989: chapter 3). Many philosophers, linguists, and psychologists have situated this asymmetry in logic or **semantics**, often as the view that every negation presupposes a corresponding affirmative. For Bergson (1911: 289), negation is necessarily 'of a pedagogical and social nature', while for Wood (1933: 421) it is 'infected with error and ignorance'. According to Wittgenstein (1953a: §447), 'the feeling is as if the negation of a proposition had to make it true in a certain sense in order to negate it'. For Givón (1978: 70), ~*p* (e.g. 'My wife is not pregnant') logically presupposes *p*. Psycholinguistic studies have shown that negation is easier to process when the denied proposition, if not already in the discourse model, is at least a plausible addition to it (e.g. 'The whale is not a fish/#bird'; *cf.* Wason 1965; Horn 1989: chapter 3; Yamada 2003). Others have variously analyzed negation as a modality, a **propositional attitude**, and a **speech act**. But in such analyses the pragmatic cart is being placed before the semantic horse.

Not every negation is a speaker denial, nor is every speaker denial a linguistic negation. However, the prototypical use (or, following Volterra and Antinucci 1979: 203, the core) of negation is indeed as a denial of a proposition attributable to, or at least considered by, someone relevant to the discourse **context**. While affirmation standardly introduces a proposition into the **discourse** model, negation – in its 'chief use' (Jespersen 1917: 4), its 'most common use' (Ayer 1952: 39), its 'standard and primary use' (Strawson 1952: 7) – is directed at a proposition that is already in or that can be accommodated by the discourse model.

Further, there is a specialized metalinguistic or **echoic use** of negation in English and other languages (Horn 1989: chapter 6; Carston 1996). In examples like (1), a speaker objects metalinguistically to a previous utterance on any grounds whatever, including its phonetic or grammatical form, register, or associated presuppositions or **implicatures**:

(1) a. That wasn't a bad year – it was horrible.
   b. She didn't "buy her some INsurance" – she bought some inSURance.
   c. The king of France isn't bald – there is no king of France.
   d. I'm not his brother – he's my brother!

Horn (1989) draws on the behaviour of polarity licensing and lexical incorporation to argue that the distinction between metalinguistic and descriptive negation involves a pragmatic **ambiguity** or built-in duality of use.

The avoidance of 'negative face' (Goffman 1967a) prompts the universal tendency for logical (contradictory) negation to undergo pragmatic strengthening: the speaker euphemistically weakens her negative statement, counting on the hearer to strengthen its negative force (Horn 1989: chapter 5). The result is contrary negatives in contradictory clothing ranging over, as illustrated by, affixal negation, 'neg-raising', and simple litotes (Horn 1991; van der Wouden 1996):

(2) a. contrariety in affixal negation
     He is unhappy
     (> ~[He is happy])
     I disliked the movie
     (> ~[I liked the movie])
   b. 'neg-raising' effects
     I don't believe it'll snow
     (≈ I believe it won't snow)
     I don't want you to go
     (≈ I want you not to go)
   c. simple litotes (**understatement**)
     She's not pleased
     (may convey 'She's displeased')
     You don't like squid
     (may convey 'You dislike squid')

In each case a formally contradictory negation is strengthened to a specific, contrary understanding, given social and cultural constraints against the direct expression of the stronger contrary. I say you don't like squid to avoid acknowledging your antipathy directly, while counting on your willingness to fill in the intended strengthened (contrary) interpretation online. This same practice is responsible for the conventionalized 'neg-raising' effect seen in (2b), in which a higher negation is interpreted outside the scope of certain predicates of opinion, desire,

or likelihood as if it had lower-clause scope. Again, the contrary **meaning** ('x believes that not-p') is stronger than (unilaterally entails) the corresponding contradictory ('x does not believe that p').

Other aspects of the **pragmatics** of negation include the acquisition and development of metalinguistic negation (Drozd 1995) and negative polarity (van der Wal 1996), the scalar nature of polarity licensing (Krifka 1995a; van der Wouden 1997; Israel 2001, 2004, to appear), the role of pragmatics in the expression of sentential negation (Tottie 1991; Schwenter 2005), and the psychological persistence of negated information (as in Nixon's celebrated 'I am not a crook'; *cf.* Giora 2007).

LAURENCE HORN

See also: Echoic use; indefiniteness; lexical pragmatics; presupposition; semantics-pragmatics interface

Suggestions for further reading

Givon, T. (1978) 'Negation in language: pragmatics, function, ontology', in P. Cole (ed.) *Syntax and Semantics 9: Pragmatics*, New York: Academic Press.

Horn, L. (1989) *A Natural History of Negation*, Chicago, IL: University of Chicago Press; reissued 2001, Stanford, CA: CSLI.

Israel, M. (to appear) *The Least Bits of Grammar: Pragmatics, Polarity, and the Logic of Scales*, Cambridge: Cambridge University Press.

Neo-Gricean Pragmatics

In their joint seminar at the 1987 Stanford LSA Linguistic Institute, Steve Levinson and Larry Horn outlined a neo-Gricean model of **pragmatics**, differentiating it from the more radical post-Gricean model propounded within **relevance theory** (RT). The neo-Gricean umbrella has since extended to varied undertakings sharing essential premises and goals with Grice's framework while differing from the original on several particulars. Examples range from revised programs for **implicature** (Harnish 1976; Sadock 1978; Atlas and Levinson 1981; Horn

1984, 2007a; Levinson 1983, 2000) and formal models of implicature projection and cancellation (Gazdar 1979a; Hirschberg 1985) to theories of **anaphora** (Levinson 1991, 2000; Huang 1991a, 1994) and minimalist characterizations of **what is said** (Bach 1994a, 2001; Saul 2002a, 2002b; Borg 2004a; Horn, to appear a).

Over the years, the communal neo-Gricean umbrella has sprung some leaks. Most notably, Levinson (2000), addressing the issue of pragmatic 'intrusion' into propositional content, takes implicatures as input to truth conditions. This is a radical departure from Gricean analysis. The traditional analysis, with some modifications, has been defended by Horn (2004, 2006, to appear a), Russell (2006), and Geurts (2009), for whom the move to a 'truth-conditional pragmatics', subscribed to variously by Sperber, Wilson, Carston, Recanati, and Levinson, is neither a necessary nor desirable innovation.

One question is what the truth conditions under debate are truth conditions of. As Bach (2001) has stressed, a sentence may (directly or indirectly) express more than one **proposition**, thus violating the widely assumed but never explicitly defended 'one sentence, one proposition' dictum. By the same token, a given sentence – classic examples include the unbracketed versions of (1a) and (1b):

(1) a. I haven't had breakfast {today}.
    b. Chris is ready {for the exam}.

– may express no actual proposition, but rather a propositional radical: the speaker uttering the non-bracketed material in each case may well communicate the full sentences above, enriched by the bracketed addenda. For Bach, this communicated proposition is an **impliciture** (an implicit component of what is said), while for Carston (2002, 2004b) it is an explicature. Neo-Griceans have challenged the latter term, given that the enriched proposition is not explicitly communicated and is cancellable.

Another parameter of variation involves quantificational **domain restriction**, where the semantically minimalist neo-Gricean positions of Bach, Cappelen and Lepore, and Borg square off against the maximalist view of incompleteness endorsed by Stanley, Szabó, and others. Stanley and Szabó (2000), Bach (2000),

Neale (2000), Recanati (2004b), and King and Stanley (2005) provide lively skirmishes in this ongoing conflict.

While Levinson (2000) regards **generalized conversational implicatures** (GCIs) as default meanings, studies in empirical pragmatics (e.g. Noveck and Posada 2003; Bott and Noveck 2004; Breheny *et al.* 2006) suggest that children and adults do not first construct GCI-based enriched meanings and then, if the 'default' interpretation proves inconsistent with the local **context**, deconstruct such meanings and recover the minimal implicature-free **meaning**. To the extent that such empirical work on GCIs and processing time can be substantiated and extended, this is an interesting result, but the 'automatic' enrichment or default interpretation accounts threatened by such work are not those of the Gricean tradition. **Grice** himself distinguished particularized and generalized implicature as 'only if' and 'unless' conditions, respectively. This distinction depends on whether an implicature is 'carried by saying that p on a particular occasion in virtue of special features of the context' or whether 'the use of a certain form of words in an utterance would normally (in the absence of special circumstances) carry such-and-such an implicature' (Grice 1989: 37). An implicature may arise in a default context without constituting a default or automatic **inference**. In the Gricean tradition, GCIs cannot be 'default inferences' both because they are not defaults and because they are not inferences. By definition, an implicature is an aspect of speaker meaning, not hearer interpretation.

In the years since the appearance of Levinson (2000), the question of automaticity in pragmatics has taken another turn. Beginning with Chierchia (2004), several scholars (e.g. Fox 2006) have argued that generalized – in particular, scalar – implicatures must be algorithmically generated within the grammar; others (Sauerland 2004; Russell 2006) have challenged this conclusion. The move to grammaticize implicatures is one front in the attack on Gricean foundations. Another is Davis's (1998, 2003) reconstruction of conversational implicatures as part of conventional meaning (on which *see* Saul 2001). In both cases, implicatures are essentially stipulated rather than derived from general principles of rational interchange (*cf.* Horn 2006, to appear a, for a neo-Gricean response).

As for local versus global computation of **scalar implicatures**, recent work concurs that the original (neo-)Gricean program must be modified to cope with a restricted range of cases in which upper bounding can enter into the pragmatic (re)interpretation of what scalar predications communicate. Thus, given (2) or (3):

(2) Drinking warm coffee is better than drinking hot coffee.
(3) If you're convicted of a felony, you'll spend at least a year in jail, and if you're convicted of murder, you'll be executed.

the hearer must retroactively accommodate the meanings of *warm* and *felony* to express 'warm but not hot' and 'non-murder felony', respectively. Geurts (2009) offers a helpful survey of the domain. He distinguishes between marked L[evinson]-type cases and unmarked C[herchia]-type cases of putative locality effects and argues that only the former represent true (although not insoluble) problems for the classical neo-Gricean approach to enrichment.

On another issue, the prevailing (but not unanimous) neo-Gricean view is more neo than Gricean. On the standard view (Horn 1972 et seq.), my predicating a weak scalar value like *some, possible, or,* or *warm* will typically (although non-monotonically) induce an upper-bounding quantity-based implicature to the effect that (for all I know) no stronger value on the same scale (*all, certain, and, hot*) obtains. Indeed, it is this upper-bounding implicature that is the basis for the neo-Gricean account of the lexicalization asymmetry codified within the logical square of opposition (Horn 1989: §4.5; to appear b), i.e. the non-occurrence of lexical items corresponding to the values *not all, not and, not always,* etc. On this view, the systematic, cross-linguistically attested restriction on the lexicalization or direct expression of values mapping onto the O vertex of the square is attributable to the mutual quantity implicature relation typically obtaining between the I and O subcontraries (e.g. *some* and *not all* respectively) together with the marked status of **negation** dictating the preference for I over O forms.

But there is considerable evidence that the traditional pragmatic analysis is not actually tenable for number words as in *Chris has three children.* Such predications are semantically underspecified rather than assigned the weak, 'at least n' values by linguistic means; the propositional content is filled in from the context of utterance. Arguments for this position, first given by Carston (1988) and Koenig (1991), are supported in recent work by Horn (1992), Geurts (1998), Bultinck (2005), and others. But this finding for the cardinals does not carry over to scalar values more generally. (See Horn (2006: §4) for a defense of the neo-Gricean implicature-based account of the upper bound of *most*-statements (i.e. the move from *most F are G* to 'not all F are G') in response to Ariel's (2004) brief for treating the upper bound as semantically encoded.) Furthermore, a now considerable body of empirical work indicates that the acquisition and processing of cardinals differs along several parameters from that of other scalar values (*cf.* Papafragou and Musolino 2003 and Hurewitz *et al.* 2006). Given the asymmetry between the cardinals and their inexact scalar cousins, it is not obvious how the explicature-based program for scalar operators is equipped to draw the necessary distinctions here, any more than Levinson's approach (2000: 87–90), which retains the original (Horn 1972) neo-Gricean line for both cardinal and general scalar predications.

A bone of perennial contention in neo- and **post-Gricean pragmatics** is the proper treatment of 'what is said'. Relevance theorists (e.g. Carston 2002) have questioned the utility of this notion (to the extent that it cannot be identified with explicature). Recanati (2001c) distinguishes a Gricean notion of what-is-said$_{min}$ from what-is-said$_{max}$, with only the latter playing a significant role within his 'truth-conditional pragmatics'. Even the self-described semantic minimalists Cappelen and Lepore (2005a) endorse an inflationary view of what is said, incorporating pragmatically inferred expansions.

Grice's notion of what is said is flawed in that, as Bach (2001) and Saul (2002a) have stressed, we must give up Grice's edict that saying something entails meaning it, i.e. that we can't say what we don't mean. This constraint becomes implausible when we consider slips of the tongue, non-literality, and performances or rehearsals. (Recall in this connection Austin's

(1962) distinction between locutionary and illocutionary acts: saying ≠ stating.) Communicative **intention** does not determine what is said.

But as demonstrated by Bach, Saul, and Borg, the death-knell for a relatively orthodox or (in Saul's terms) austere conception of what is said may be premature. Bach (2001) proposes a 'syntactic correlation constraint' which is based on Grice's position (1989: 87) that what is said must correspond to 'the elements of [the sentence], their order, and their syntactic character'; aspects of enriched content not directly linked to the utterance cannot be part of what is said. Many have been sceptical of this view, from Cappelen and Lepore (2005a) to Recanati (2001c, 2004b) and the relevance theorists. In Carston's words (2005: 310), '[i]t is hard to see what this conception of "what is said" buys one'. Saul (2006) and Horn (to appear a) try to respond to Carston's doubts by invoking the intuitive distinction between misleading and lying.

Another departure from scripture by both neo- and post-Griceans lies in the inventory of conversational **maxims**. Grice's fourfold set of macroprinciples and nine actual maxims has been revised both upward (Leech 1983) and downward. The neo-Gricean program of Horn (1984, 1989, 2007a) begins by following Grice's lead (1989: 371) in ascribing a privileged status to Quality, on the grounds that without the observation of Quality, or Lewis's (1969) convention of truthfulness, it is hard to see how any of the other maxims can be satisfied (though *see* Sperber and Wilson 1995 for a dissenting view). The remaining maxims are subsumed under two countervailing functional principles whose role in **communication** and language change traces back to Paul (1889) and Zipf (1949). Within this Manichaean model, implicatures may be generated by either the Q Principle (essentially 'Say enough', generalizing Grice's first submaxim of Quantity and collecting the first two 'clarity' submaxims of Manner) or the R Principle ('Don't say too much', subsuming the second Quantity submaxim, Relation, and Brevity). The hearer-oriented Q Principle is a lower-bounding guarantee of the sufficiency of informative content, exploited to generate upper-bounding (typically scalar) implicata. By contrast, the R Principle is an upper-bounding

correlate of Zipf's principle of least effort dictating minimization of form. It is exploited to induce strengthening implicata and is widely involved in meaning change.

Horn's dualistic framework is subdivided by Levinson (2000) into an opposition of Q, I (= R), and M (= Manner) **heuristics**. The division of pragmatic labour (Horn 1984) predicts that given two co-extensive expressions, a relatively unmarked form – briefer and/or more lexicalized – will tend to become R-associated with a particular unmarked, stereotypical meaning/use/situation. The periphrastic or less lexicalized expression, typically more complex or prolix, will tend to be Q-restricted to those situations outside the stereotype, for which the unmarked expression could not have been used appropriately (e.g. *kill* versus *cause to die*). Levinson's (2000) version of the division of pragmatic labour involves not Q but his M[anner] heuristic, given that the species of minimalism involved in the step from *some* to *not all* is defined by information rather than complexity of production or processing. As Levinson concedes, however, the Q and M patterns are closely related, since each is negatively defined and linguistically motivated: H infers from S's failure to use a more informative and/or briefer form that S was not in a position to do so. R-based (for Levinson, I-based) inference is not negative in character and is socially rather than linguistically motivated.

While the more reductionist RT model appears simpler, the dialectical neo-Gricean approaches may offer a more explanatory account of maxim clash, synonymy and homonymy avoidance, and pragmatic factors in lexical choice and lexical change (on which *see* Traugott and Dasher 2002). In any case, the RT program is arguably not as monist as it appears, given that relevance itself is calibrated as a minimax of effort and effect. As Carston (1995: 231) puts it, '[h]uman cognitive activity is driven by the goal of maximizing relevance: that is ... to derive as great a range of contextual effects as possible for the least expenditure of effort'.

LAURENCE HORN

See also: Explicit/implicit distinction; Grice, H.P.; implicature; maxims of conversation;

meaning; post-Gricean pragmatics; relevance theory; scalar implicature; semantic minimalism; what is said

Suggestions for further reading

Horn, L. (2006) 'The border wars: a neo-Gricean perspective', in K. Turner and K. von Heusinger (eds) *Where Semantics Meets Pragmatics*, Oxford: Elsevier.
——(to appear) 'William James + 40: issues in the investigation of implicature', in K. Petrus (ed.) *Meaning and Analysis: Themes from H. Paul Grice*, Online. Available HTTP: www.yale.edu/linguist/faculty/doc/horn07_petrus.pdf (accessed 17 March 2008).
Levinson, S. (2000) *Presumptive Meanings: The Theory of Generalized Conversational Implicature*, Cambridge, MA: MIT Press.

Neuropragmatics

A growing number of investigators in **pragmatics** have been concerned to examine the neural basis of pragmatic phenomena. This has given rise to a branch of study in pragmatics called neuropragmatics. Stemmer and Schönle (2000: 233) state that '[n]europragmatics is concerned with how the brain and mind uses language, that is how it comprehends and produces verbal pragmatic behaviour in healthy as well as neurologically impaired individuals'. For these investigators, this is an interdisciplinary effort that draws upon fields as diverse as linguistics, neuropsychology, neuroscience, **cognitive science**, computer science, **philosophy**, sociology and anthropology. Although neuropragmatics has benefited from technological developments such as the expansion in brain imaging techniques (e.g. functional magnetic resonance imaging, fMRI), further progress may well be threatened by a lack of clear theoretical direction. While Stemmer and Schönle (2000: 234) may be somewhat overstating the point when they remark that 'there is currently no theoretical model of pragmatic processing', it is at least true to say that in the absence of theoretical frameworks, findings from increasingly sophisticated imaging and other techniques lack full significance. In this discussion, we examine some of the studies that have contributed to this vibrant area of enquiry.

Neuropragmatic studies have examined a diverse range of pragmatic phenomena including **speech acts**, **implicatures**, sarcasm, **metaphor**, **discourse** (e.g. **narrative discourse**) and **humour**. These studies have been conducted in subjects with intact cognitive and language skills as well as in subjects with identifiable clinical disorders and brain pathology (e.g. **right-hemisphere damage**). Uchiyama *et al.* (2006) examined the neural substrates of sarcasm in twenty normal adult volunteers using fMRI. A scenario-reading task was used in which a situation was described. This description was then followed by comments from a protagonist. The comments represented sarcastic, non-sarcastic or contextually unconnected remarks in relation to the situation. These investigators found that sarcasm detection activated the left temporal pole, the superior temporal sulcus, the medial prefrontal cortex and the inferior frontal gyrus. The left inferior frontal gyrus was activated more prominently by sarcasm detection than by the first sentence. Uchiyama *et al.* (2006: 100) concluded that sarcasm detection 'recruits the medial prefrontal cortex, which is part of the mentalizing system, as well as the neural substrates involved in reading sentences'.

The large majority of neuropragmatic investigations have examined aspects of pragmatics in adults with clinical disorders. Stemmer and Schönle (2000: 234) state that '[u]ntil today, most research in neuropragmatics has been limited to providing detailed descriptions of aspects of pragmatic abilities in brain-damaged populations'. These populations include subjects with left- and right-hemisphere damage, individuals who have sustained **traumatic brain injury** and subjects with neurodegenerative disorders such as Parkinson's disease and **dementia**. Studies have also examined the neural basis of pragmatic phenomena in schizophrenic subjects. In what follows, we review the findings of some of these studies.

Zaidel *et al.* (2002) examined the relationship between the performance of thirty-one subjects with left-brain damage on a Hebrew version of the Right Hemisphere Communication Battery (RHCB; Gardner and Brownell 1986) and the extent and location of lesions in different regions of the left hemisphere. The RHCB contains eleven subtests, many of which test aspects of language pragmatics. Zaidel *et al.* found a negative correlation between subtest scores on the Hebrew version of the RHCB and lesion extent in frontal and temporal perisylvian regions. In specific terms, verbal humour negatively correlated with the extent of lesion in the left inferior temporal gyrus; indirect **requests** negatively correlated with the extent of lesion in the middle and inferior frontal, superior temporal and supramarginal gyri; pictorial metaphors negatively correlated with the extent of lesion in the left superior temporal gyrus; verbal metaphors negatively correlated with the extent of lesion in the left middle temporal gyrus and in the junction of the superior temporal and supramarginal gyri; sarcasm negatively correlated with the extent of lesion in the left middle and inferior frontal gyri. On only one subtest was there any correlation with extent of lesion in subjects with right-brain damage – narrative comprehension negatively correlated with the extent of lesion in the junction area of the superior temporal and supramarginal gyri. These findings, Zaidel *et al.* conclude, fail to support the right prefrontal hypothesis of pragmatic deficit. Other studies of the neural basis of pragmatic deficits include an investigation by Kasher *et al.* (1999) of the processing of conversational implicatures by subjects with left- or right-brain damage. In this study, both groups of subjects displayed weak correlations between performance on an implicatures battery and the extents of lesions in the left perisylvian language area or its right-hemisphere homolog.

Shamay-Tsoory *et al.* (2005a) examined the neural substrates of sarcasm and its underlying social cognitive processes (i.e. **theory of mind** (ToM) and emotion recognition) in subjects with right prefrontal and posterior damage. Subjects with prefrontal damage displayed impaired performance on a sarcasm task, with those with right ventromedial lesions exhibiting the greatest deficits understanding sarcasm. Right prefrontal damage was associated with ToM deficits and right-hemisphere damage was associated with deficits in emotion recognition. These investigators concluded that 'the right frontal lobe mediates understanding of sarcasm by integrating affective processing with perspective taking' (2005a: 288). Soroker *et al.* (2005) examined the neural basis of the processing of basic speech acts

(i.e. **question**, **assertion**, request, **command**) by right-hemisphere-damaged and left-hemisphere-damaged subjects. These investigators found no correlation between the location and extent of lesion in the perisylvian cortex of the right-hemisphere-damaged subjects and performance on these speech acts.

While numerous studies have examined the neural substrates of cognitive impairments in traumatic brain injury (TBI), few studies have sought to investigate the neural basis of pragmatic impairments in this clinical population. Two notable exceptions are investigations by Shamay-Tsoory *et al.* (2005a, 2005b). As discussed above, Shamay-Tsoory *et al.* (2005a) found that subjects with prefrontal damage, and particularly those with right ventromedial lesions, exhibited deficits understanding sarcasm. Forty-one adults were included in this study, thirty of whom had brain contusions and haematomas following TBI. Shamay-Tsoory *et al.* (2005b) report that patients with ventromedial prefrontal lesions were significantly impaired in understanding ironic utterances and in identifying social faux pas compared to patients with posterior lesions and normal control subjects. These investigators relate the difficulties of these patients with **irony** and faux pas to underlying ToM deficits. The most severe ToM deficit was associated with lesions in the right ventromedial area.

The group of neurodegenerative disorders is wide ranging and includes individuals with Parkinson's disease, motor neurone disease, multiple sclerosis and dementia as a result of Alzheimer's disease, amongst other cerebral pathologies. The neural substrates of pragmatic impairment in these clinical populations are increasingly being investigated. Monetta and Pell (2007) examined the comprehension of metaphorical language in seventeen subjects with Parkinson's disease. Subjects with Parkinson's disease who had impaired working memory on a measure of verbal working memory span were also impaired in the processing of metaphorical language. Monetta and Pell conclude that metaphor comprehension is dependent on fronto-striatal systems for working memory which are often compromised in the early course of Parkinson's disease. Chapman *et al.* (2005) used single photon emission computed tomography (SPECT) imaging in a study of discourse in nineteen subjects with early-stage frontotemporal lobar degeneration (FLD is a frontal dementia). These investigators found that across FLD subtypes, discourse profiles were consistently associated with distinctive patterns of SPECT hypometabolism in the left frontal, right frontal or left temporal lobes.

Few studies have examined the neural substrates of pragmatic processing in schizophrenia. A notable exception is a study by Kircher *et al.* (2007) who examined processing of metaphoric sentences by twelve schizophrenic patients using fMRI. In the twelve control subjects in this study, reading metaphors as opposed to literal sentences produced signal changes in the left inferior frontal gyrus. In the schizophrenic subjects, an area 3 cm dorsal to the left inferior frontal gyrus was activated by the same metaphor activity. The severity of concretism was also found to negatively correlate with the response in the inferior frontal gyrus. Comparisons of the metaphor versus baseline conditions in control and patient groups revealed stronger signal changes in the right superior/middle temporal gyrus in the control subjects and in the left inferior frontal gyrus in the patients. Kircher *et al.* (2007: 287) conclude that '[t]he inferior frontal and superior temporal gyri are key regions in the neuropathology of schizophrenia. Their dysfunction seems to underlie the clinical symptom of concretism, reflected in the impaired understanding of non-literal, semantically complex language structures.'

As is clear from the studies examined above, neuropragmatic research is beginning to bring a much needed alternative perspective to the study of pragmatic phenomena. This research is highly varied and is constrained only by the rate of development in methods and technology on the one hand and our theoretical understanding of pragmatic phenomena on the other hand. As further progress is made on both these fronts, neuropragmatics will continue to reveal the neural substrates that make the use of language possible.

LOUISE CUMMINGS

See also: Autism spectrum disorders; clinical pragmatics; cognitive pragmatics; dementia and pragmatics; irony; psycholinguistics; psychotic discourse; right-hemisphere damage and pragmatics;

schizophrenic language; theory of mind; traumatic brain injury and discourse

Suggestions for further reading

Bara, B.G. and Tirassa, M. (2000) 'Neuropragmatics: brain and communication', *Brain and Language*, 71: 10–14.
Stemmer, B. and Schönle, P.W. (2000) 'Neuropragmatics in the 21st century', *Brain and Language*, 71: 233–36.

Non-Verbal Communication, Pragmatics of

When we speak our speech is augmented by a range of non-verbal behaviours. These behaviours indicate our internal state by conveying attitudes to the **propositions** we express or information about our emotions or feelings. As Abercrombie (1968: 55) puts it 'we speak with our vocal organs, but we converse with our whole body'. The approach favoured by many linguists is to sift these behaviours out, in order to focus better on the rule-based grammar that constitutes language. However, the pragmatist has to cast a broader net. The central aim of **pragmatics** is to describe and explain the process of **utterance interpretation** and utterances, after all, have non-linguistic as well as linguistic properties.

The two-thousand-or-so words that make up this entry could quite easily be devoted to a discussion of what precisely the term 'non-verbal communication' means. A notion which at first sight appears to be quite an intuitive one is not unproblematic. Does non-verbal mean non-*vocal*? Surely not: from the fact that a visual rather than a vocal channel is exploited in **sign language**, it does not follow that we should characterize the gestures of sign language as being the same as the spontaneous, manual gestures used during speech by the hearing population. Sign languages are verbal in every sense. Equally, there are communicative behaviours used by humans that *are* vocal, but which we would not want to class as verbal. I'm thinking here of elements of affective **prosody**, such as a sad or happy tone of voice. As a more extreme example, a deliberate cough can be used to communicate, but a cough is hardly a form of 'verbal communication' in any useful sense of the term.

One of the ways people have attempted to resolve this problem of definition is to adopt the term 'paralinguistic' as a kind of catch-all term. But there is disagreement here too. Some argue that the language/paralanguage distinction cannot be satisfactorily maintained at all (*see* McNeill and Duncan 1999). Others treat 'paralanguage' as including only those vocal aspects of language use that are not strictly speaking part of language: intonation, stress, affective tone of voice, rate of speech (Crystal 1969). This has the slightly unintuitive result that non-vocal behaviours such as facial expression and gesture are *non*-linguistic, even though rising pitch in the voice is so often associated with rising eyebrows. The position taken in this paper is that the domain of non-verbal communication (or paralinguistics, if you prefer) should include all of those aspects of **communication** that are not part of language per se, but are nonetheless somehow involved with the message or **meaning** a communicator conveys. Of course, much depends here on how we define 'language' and 'communication'. Unfortunately, lack of space prevents a more in-depth discussion (*see* Wharton 2009).

But just to define the term is not really to get very far. The real task is not merely to stipulate at what point verbal communication ends and non-verbal communication begins, but to describe and explain how the two dimensions interact. There have been attempts to explain this interaction. Linguists working within functionalist frameworks (e.g. Bolinger 1983) have addressed non-verbal communicative behaviours. The same is true of conversational analysts and discourse analysts (Goodwin 1981; Brown and Yule 1983; Schiffrin 1994) and those looking at human interaction and communication from a more sociological, ethnomethodological perspective (Goffman 1964; Garfinkel 1967; Gumperz 1972; Hymes 1972b). However, few have sought to offer a cognitive explanation of the phenomena they describe. Moreover, distinctions that are important from the point of view of modern pragmatics are sometimes left unexplored, and the question of how the non-verbal properties of utterances might interact with the linguistic ones is largely ignored. Also, these approaches miss what is perhaps the most crucial development in pragmatics over the past thirty years. This is the fact that, since the work of H.P. **Grice** (1957, 1989), it has been recognized that human communication is an intelligent, inferential activity based on the expression and attribution of **intentions**.

Similar problems exist in the numerous studies of non-verbal communication which have their roots in disciplines outside linguistics. In work on **gestural communication**, for example, pragmatics takes very much a second place to description of the gestures themselves. Consider the following from Adam Kendon (1992: 328):

> If I clear my throat in the midst of an utterance this is not treated as part of what I am 'saying'. If I uncross my legs, take a drag on my cigarette or sip my coffee while another is speaking, such actions are not attended to by other participants as if they are contributions to the conversation. Overt acts of attention to activities of this sort are generally not made at all. Whereas spoken utterances and bodily movements, if perceived as gestures, are regarded as vehicles of explicitly intended messages, directly relevant to the business of the conversation, other aspects of behaviour are not regarded in this light.

But whilst they do not contribute to what a speaker is 'saying', clearing the throat and uncrossing the legs can certainly contribute to the overtly intended speaker's meaning, just as bodily movement (and, indeed, aspects of the spoken utterance) might convey information accidentally, or even be intended by the 'speaker' to convey information covertly. While there has been a huge amount of valuable descriptive and classificatory work on gesture (and Kendon's contribution has been enormous), his comments reflect the fact that in accounts of human non-verbal communication generally, distinctions that are central to **semantics** and pragmatics play very much a secondary role. Even worse, on those occasions when pragmatic notions are introduced, an element of inconsistency sometimes creeps in. For instance, Kendon (2004: 15) writes that the term 'gesture' is 'a label for actions that have *manifest deliberate expressiveness*' (italics added). But the work of David McNeill is concerned almost entirely with 'gestures' that are largely not under a communicator's conscious control, and therefore, presumably, do not have manifest deliberate expressiveness.

Such problems are not confined to accounts of gestural communication. In his account of facial expression Alan Fridlund (1994: 146) abstracts away from pragmatic notions entirely: 'I have circumvented these "levels of intentionality" issues in the interests of space, and use intentionality in a purely functionalist sense'. In this he is adopting a similar position to Kendon (2004: 15): '[T]he judgement of an action's intentionality is a matter of how it appears to others and not a matter of some *mysterious process by which the intention or intentions themselves that may guide the action may be known*' (italics added). But the aim of a pragmatic framework is very much to engage with these 'mysterious' processes and examine the role they play. Indeed, one of the main achievements of Grice's pioneering work has been to allow the demystification of such processes to begin.

So where do we begin? My own work on the pragmatics of non-verbal communication (*see* Wharton 2003a, 2003b, 2009) takes as its starting point notions that lie at the heart of Gricean pragmatics and **relevance theory**: notions such as **inference, inferential comprehension, intentionality** and **natural and non-natural meaning**. Doing this allows us to focus on those specifically pragmatic questions that might take us a step closer to explaining how non-verbal behaviours work. These questions include: (1) What is the relation between non-verbal behaviours and intentional communication?; (2) How do non-verbal behaviours contribute to utterance interpretation, and are they all interpreted in the same way? (3) What is the relation between *natural* non-verbal behaviours and *non-natural* non-verbal behaviours?

Turning to question (1), a feature of Grice's (1957) account of intentional communication that is not without controversy is the line he draws between 'showing' and non-natural meaning (meaning$_{NN}$), where meaning$_{NN}$ typically involves a linguistic convention or code. This distinction has had a great effect on the development of pragmatics. Following Grice, pragmatists have tended to focus on the notion of meaning$_{NN}$ and have abstracted away from cases of showing, which include the intentional display of 'natural' phenomena such as facial expression, gesticulation or even affective tone of voice. But while there is room for disagreement on whether cases of 'showing' always amount to cases of meaning$_{NN}$, there is little doubt that cases of 'showing' do qualify as cases of intentional communication of the kind a pragmatic theory should be able to handle: *meaning* and *communicating* do not always line up. Intentional verbal communication, then, involves a mixture of natural and non-natural meaning, and an adequate pragmatic theory should take account of both.

Turning to question (2), it seems clear that all non-verbal behaviours do not work in the same way, and I have suggested they fall into two distinct subsets – natural *signs* and natural *signals* – only one of which fits straightforwardly with Grice's distinction between natural and non-natural meaning. This distinction between natural signs and natural signals is based on the one made in Marc Hauser's (1996) work on **animal communication**. Natural signs (e.g. tree rings, footprints in the snow) carry information which provides evidence for a certain conclusion (about the age of the tree or the presence of an animal). Indeed, Grice's notion of natural meaning was largely constructed by considering natural signs. However, Hauser's work enables us to distinguish such signs from natural signals (e.g. the alarm calls of vervet monkeys, the waggle dance of honey bees), which have the *function* of conveying information (Millikan 1984; Origgi and Sperber 2000; Sperber 2007). These signals are inherently communicative and owe their continued existence to the fact that they convey information. I argue that the existence of natural signals presents problems for Grice's distinction between natural and non-natural meaning.

The sign–signal distinction seems to apply not only to animal but also to human behaviour. Some natural human behaviours (e.g. shivers) are signs rather than signals: they carry information for observers, but do not have an indicating function. I suggest that they are interpreted purely inferentially, as providing evidence for a certain conclusion. Other human behaviours (e.g. smiles) are signals: they are inherently communicative, and do have an indicating function. I suggest that these have a coded element and are best analyzed using the notion of a *natural code* (or natural signal, in the ethological sense). If some natural behaviours are coded, we would predict that they are interpreted by specialized neural machinery. This prediction appears to be borne out. Both non-human primates and humans have neural mechanisms dedicated to recognizing faces and to processing facial expressions (Gazzaniga and Smiley 1991).

Turning finally to question (3), while we feel many non-verbal behaviours to be 'natural' in the Gricean sense, some are clearly *non*-natural. At the beginning of his 1992 book, David McNeill argues convincingly that gesture is best seen as ranging along a continuum between natural display and language proper. So at the one end are those gestures that McNeill calls 'gesticulation', the movements of the arms and hands that accompany speech, and at the other is sign language proper. In between gestures fit into a range of others classes including, for example, 'emblems', cultural-dependent symbolic gestures used to convey a wide range of both positive and negative meanings: the British 'thumbs up' signal and the two-fingered insult are two examples (*see* McNeill 1992: 57–59 for an overview). Prosodic inputs to the process of utterance interpretation are also often described as ranging along a continuum from the natural, e.g. an angry, friendly or agitated tone of voice (Gussenhoven 2002; Pell 2002), to the properly linguistic, e.g. lexical stress or lexical tone. Ladd (1980), Gussenhoven (2002, 2004) and Wichmann (2002) suggest that there is considerable cross-linguistic variation in the way 'universal paralinguistic meanings' are realized, to a point where they may become heavily stereotyped or even fully grammaticalized and part of language proper.

But adopting a pragmatic perspective suggests there is another possibility. The fact that prosodic patterns and their interpretations become stereotyped or vary from language to language does not provide conclusive evidence that they are *linguistically* coded. Whilst the notion of a cultural, as opposed to a linguistic, code has played little role in analyses of prosody, it is one

that is familiar in the study of gesture. Culture-specific 'emblems', whilst clearly *non-linguistic*, are equally clearly non-natural in Grice's sense. We have, then, a further notion which can be used in future exploration into the pragmatics of non-verbal behaviours: non-natural, non-linguistic, *cultural codes*.

TIM WHARTON

See also: Animal communication, pragmatics of; communication; conversation analysis; discourse analysis; ethnomethodology; gestural communication; Grice, H.P.; inference; inferential comprehension; intentionality; meaning; natural and non-natural meaning; pragmatics; proposition; propositional attitude; relevance theory; semantics; signed language, pragmatics of; utterance interpretation

Suggestions for further reading

Hinde, R. (ed.) (1972) *Non-Verbal Communication*, Cambridge: Cambridge University Press.
Wharton, T. (2009) *Pragmatics and Non-Verbal Communication*, Cambridge: Cambridge University Press.

Normative Pragmatics

Whereas **pragmatics** generally deals with the ways speakers use expressions, normative pragmatics stems from the assumption that it is *rules* of their usage that are crucial and hence concentrates on the study of the rules. The basic paradigm is that of language as a kind of game like chess or football. Just as it is the rules of the game that make pieces of wood into pawns or kings, or events of kicking a round thing through a square thing into scoring a goal, it is the rules of our 'language games' that make the types of sounds we make (or inscriptions we produce) into words and expressions meaning thus and so. This view of language is not alien to the later **Wittgenstein**, but it was propagated especially by the American philosopher Wilfrid Sellars and elaborated by Robert Brandom and his followers.

Sellars was an influential philosopher and one of the founding fathers of analytic philosophy in the USA. He was deeply influenced by the teaching of Rudolf Carnap and his fellow logical empiricists from the Vienna Circle, but he almost completely reassessed the doctrines of logical empiricism and developed his own distinctive philosophical system. His **philosophy of language** is mostly presented in his papers (*see* especially Sellars 1949, 1953, 1954, 1969).

Whereas Carnap (1942) saw the **semantics** of language as a matter of expressions representing certain entities and considered pragmatics as a matter philosophically not so interesting, Sellars' view of semantics is much more dynamic and his border between semantics and pragmatics much less clear-cut. But as Sellars stressed the role of *rules* for human linguistic conduct, his version of pragmatics became *normative*. However, he urges that our language games are rule-governed neither in the sense of merely displaying regularities, nor in the sense of being a matter of following explicit rules. He claims that they are rule-governed in a specific sense and speaks about 'pattern governed behaviour' (*see also* Peregrin 2008). Sellars (1954: 209) states that 'an organism may come to play a language game – that is to move from position to position in a system of moves and positions and to do it "because of the system" without having to *obey rules* and hence without having to be playing a *meta*language game'.

Sellars (1974: 423–24) claims that, in general, our linguistic activities fall into three basic kinds:

(1) Language entry transitions: The speaker responds to objects in perceptual situations, and in certain states in himself, with appropriate linguistic activity.
(2) Intra-linguistic moves: The speaker's linguistic conceptual episodes tend to occur in patterns of valid **inference** (theoretical and practical), and tend not to occur in patterns which violate logical principles.
(3) Language exit transitions: The speaker responds to such linguistic conceptual episodes as 'I will now raise my hand' with an upward motion of the hand, etc.

Inherent to all these activities, according to Sellars, are certain *proprieties* and in this sense the activities are governed by rules. However, the rules are of the kind that Sellars calls 'rules of criticizing' (as opposed to 'rules of doing'; *see*

Sellars 1992: 76). This means that, for example, the most important of the three kinds of transitions, the intra-linguistic moves, or inferences in the narrow sense of the word, should be seen not as telling us *what to do*, but rather what to *avoid* and, hence, are really more the rules of what *not* to do. They delimit a space of what is approvable. If you assert that Fido is a dog, then you should not deny that Fido is a mammal; and if you do deny it, you are a legitimate target of criticism.

As a result, any content a linguistic expression comes to have comes to it from the rules governing its usage within our linguistic practices (rules not necessarily explicit, but often implicit to the practices in the sense that we take some ways of the practices as proper while others are improper). This wholly eschews the Carnapian picture of pragmatics as a mere supplementum to semantics. On the contrary, semantics falls out as an appendix to pragmatics, though a distinctively normative one. And normativity becomes, for Sellars (1949: 297), the hallmark of **rationality**: 'To say that man is a rational animal, is to say that man is a creature not of *habits*, but of *rules*'.

This also breathes new life into the already mentioned parallel between language and chess (*see* Peregrin 2001 for details). Just as a piece of wood becomes a chess pawn solely in virtue of the fact that we let it be governed by certain rules of the chess game, an expression comes to mean thus and so in force of the fact that we let it be governed by rules of our language games. Hence, just as the rules of chess constitute a space in which we can enjoy chess games, the rules of our language games constitute the space of meaningfulness in which we can enjoy our distinctively human meaningful talk (the space of meaningfulness is also called the *space of reasons* by Sellars, in view of the fact that the most direct projection of the rules of inference onto our linguistic practices is giving reasons).

The phenomenon of rules within the context of our linguistic practices was also discussed thoroughly by Wittgenstein in his *Philosophical Investigations* (1963). Wittgenstein famously pointed out the diversity of our 'language games', but at the same time he paid a lot of attention to the problem of how we can learn, follow and maintain rules that are inherent to these games. He pointed out some crucial aspects of rules that are not immediately obvious, especially that not all rules may be explicit, for in order to be able to follow an explicit rule, we would need to interpret it, and to interpret it correctly, we would need some further rule, which would lead us into an infinite regress. Another thing he pointed out is that it is hard to see how the examples of application of the rules we are shown when we are taught the language could allow us to really grasp a unique rule (which made Kripke 1982b interpret Wittgenstein as a sceptic, an interpretation which has led to huge disputes).

For Brandom (1994, 2000, 2008), this view of language became part and parcel of his project of *inferentialism*. Like Wittgenstein, Brandom sees language as a way of carrying out an activity, the activity of playing certain language games. But unlike many postmodern followers of Wittgenstein, he is convinced that one of the games is 'principal', namely, the game of giving and asking for reasons. It is this game, according to Brandom, that is the hallmark of what we are – thinking, concept-possessing, rational beings abiding by the force of better reason.

Brandom points out that language games are governed by inferential rules. As he puts it, our language is *inferentially articulated*, because the inferential rules are what are needed to make language into a vehicle of the game of giving and asking for reasons. To be able to give reasons, we must be able to make claims that can serve as reasons for other claims. Hence, our language must provide for sentences that *entail* other sentences. To be able to ask for reasons, we must be able to make claims that count as a challenge to other claims. Hence, our language must provide for sentences that are *incompatible* with other sentences. Accordingly, our language must be structured by these **entailment** and incompatibility relations.

In fact, for Brandom the level of inference and incompatibility is merely a deconstructible superstructure, underlain by certain normative statuses, which communicating people acquire and maintain via using language. These statuses comprise various kinds of *commitments* and *entitlements*. Thus, for example, when I make an **assertion**, I commit myself to giving reasons for it when it is challenged (that is what makes it an assertion rather than just babble) and I *entitle*

everybody else to reassert my assertion reflecting any possible challenges to me. I may commit myself to a claim without being entitled to it, i.e. without being able to give any reasons for it. I can be committed to all kinds of claims, but there are certain claims commitment to which blocks my entitlement to certain other claims.

Brandom's idea is that living in a human society is steering within a rich network of normative social relationships and enjoying many kinds of normative statuses, which reach into many dimensions. Linguistic **communication** institutes an important stratum of such statuses (commitments and entitlements) and to understand language means to be able to keep track of the statuses of one's fellow speakers, to keep score of them, as Brandom puts it. And the social distribution is essential because it provides for the multiplicity of perspectives that makes the objectivity of linguistic content possible.

This interplay of commitments and entitlements is also the underlying source of the relation of incompatibility (i.e. commitment to one claim excluding the entitlement to others). Additionally, there is the relation of inheriting commitments and entitlements. By committing myself to *This is a dog* I commit myself also to *This is an animal*, and being entitled to *It is raining* I am entitled also to *The streets are wet*. The same applies to the relation of co-inheritance of incompatibilities (*A* is in this relation to *B* iff whatever is incompatible with *B* is incompatible with *A*). This provides for the inference relation (more precisely, it provides for its several layers).

Brandom's response to the Wittgensteinian challenge regarding the impossibility of explicitness of all rules of language is that, indeed, at least the most fundamental of them must be implicit. They exist through the speakers' *normative attitudes*, their treatings of the utterances of others (and indeed of their own) as correct or incorrect. But though the rules exist only as underpinned by the attitudes, which are manifested within the 'causal order', the rules themselves do not exist within the 'causal order'. In other words, though we may be able to describe, in a descriptive idiom, how a community can come to employ a normative idiom, the latter is not translatable into the former.

Inferentialism is a species of pragmatism and of the use-theory of **meaning** – our expressions are seen as tools which we employ to do various useful things (though they should not be seen as self-standing tools like a hammer, but rather as tools like, say, a toothed wheel that can do useful work only in cooperation with its fellow tools). Also, inferentialism gives pride of place to the practical over the theoretical. It leads to seeing language as a tool of social interaction rather than as an abstract system. Thus, any explication of concepts such as language or meaning must be rooted in an account of what one *does* when one communicates. Hence, semantics, as Brandom (1994: 83) puts it, 'must answer to pragmatics'.

A theory of **speech acts** within the normative setting is developed by Lance and Kukla (2009). Their idea is that every kind of speech act can be characterized by the normative input conditions that are supposed to be fulfilled when the act takes place, and the normative output conditions resulting from the act's taking place.

Thus, for example, the input condition for an imperative is that its utterer is entitled to give orders to the addressee, whereas the output condition is that the addressee is committed to doing what he or she is ordered to do.

JAROSLAV PEREGRIN

See also: Inference; pragmatism; Wittgenstein, L.

Suggestions for further reading

Brandom, R. (1994) *Making It Explicit*, Cambridge, MA: Harvard University Press.

DeVries, W.A. (2007) *Wilfrid Sellars*, Chesham: Acumen.

Lance, M.N. and Kukla, R. (2009) *'Yo!' and 'Lo!': The Pragmatic Topography of the Space of Reasons*, Cambridge, MA: Harvard University Press.

O

Optimality-Theory Pragmatics

Introduction

The area of **pragmatics** is characterized by **defaults** and preferences. This is exactly the reason to be interested in the application of optimality theory (OT) to pragmatics. Interpretation is clearly an optimization problem: what is the best interpretation of an utterance in a **context**? If pragmatics were formalizable using optimality theory, it would mean that a system of ranked constraints could deal with the optimization problem, capturing exactly the preferences and defaults that human language users use when interpreting utterances. It would also lead to an integrated pragmatics, in which the waste-basket structure of the field is overcome and in which a single account given by a small number of principles predicts conventional and conversational **implicature**, explicature, **presupposition**, **disambiguation**, pronoun resolution, rhetorical structure, **politeness** marking and other aspects of interpretation.

At the same time, there is a sense in which there is no place for semantics and pragmatics in a complete optimality theoretic account of language. Production OT is the original OT, developed for phonology as an account of what is the appropriate surface phonological structure for a given abstract phonological **representation**. And the focus of the optimization problem on what is the appropriate pronunciation for a given abstractly specified linguistic structure is no accident – that is where natural generalizations are achievable, not in the other direction. The same model has been followed in optimality theoretic syntax where the aim has

been to assign a surface structure to some characterization of the semantics (at various depths of abstraction), because this is where natural generalizations are possible. If production OT is the right account, the theory of interpretation can be read off from the relevant components of production: the **meaning** is given by the inverse of the relation between input and output characterized by the phonological and syntactical constraint systems.

The first point to be made here is that this is not a notion of meaning that can be ignored. It is necessary for any pragmatics to be able to account for unusual modes of expression such as 'How late is it?' for 'What time is it?' or 'cause to die' for 'kill', given that these can be blocked by other forms or receive an extra meaning in the context. OT production syntax excels at blocking of forms and at neutralization: giving the same pronunciation to different words or at assigning the same form to two different meanings.

Yet, it is not difficult to show that it is not enough. To see this, consider a central principle of OT pragmatics known as DOAP ('Do not overlook anaphoric possibilities') (Hendriks and de Hoop 2001; Williams 1997), or as *ACCOMMODATE (Blutner 2000) or as *NEW (Zeevat 2001). This principle militates against interpretationsthat do not identify enough material.

(1) a. John kissed Mary in the garden and Bill Susan.
    b. Jim committed suicide. He bought a rope at the grocer's.
    c. Alena broke her skis. She lost her only means of transport.

In (1a), it is natural to assume that Bill kissed Susan in the garden too and not somewhere else. In (1b), the rope is preferentially interpreted as the instrument of the suicide, and in (1c), the event of Alena breaking her skis is normally interpreted as the event that was the loss of her only means of transport. Now consider the case that these **inferences** are not made (the relevant identifications are omitted from the relevant semantic representation). By OT syntax there is no reason why (1) would not give the optimal forms anymore: it would neutralize the difference between the versions of the semantic representation with and without the *NEW-inference. Production OT therefore does not capture the fact that the inferences are obligatory.

The same points can be made with respect to PLAUSIBLE (possibly realized by a system of OT constraints along the lines of Boersma 2001) and the weakest one RELEVANCE. PLAUSIBLE would deal with lexical and other forms of disambiguation and with stereotypical interpretation, RELEVANCE with maximizing the relation of the interpretation to the goals and **questions** that are activated in the **conversation**. In (2a), the preferred interpretation is that Bill's pushing caused John to fall, the dispreferred interpretation that the pushing was the next thing that happened. The preference is clearly a question of plausibility given that in (2b) the preferences are reversed. It does not seem though that the sequence would be any less syntactically optimal in either case if the pushing followed the falling, or the smiling is the cause of the falling. Or, at least, the need in that case to insert *then* in (2a) or *because* in (2b) has no syntactic reason.

(2) a. John fell. Bill pushed him.
    b. John fell. Bill smiled at him.

In **Grice**'s example in (3), the garage is interpreted as a means to achieve the goal of A, i.e. a garage that is open and that sells petrol. If it were not, and B is just choosing to state some irrelevant fact, the syntactic form would be just the same.

(3) A: I am out of petrol.
    B: There is a garage just around the corner.

While there is some debate about the precise formulation of the constraints mentioned and not everyone has all three, there are few proposals for other constraints that cannot be reinterpreted as production constraints. There also seems to be little disagreement about the ordering: PLAUSIBLE > *NEW > RELEVANCE. Coherence (*NEW) cannot be bought at the price of PLAUSIBILITY. And one cannot make an utterance more relevant by sacrificing coherence or plausibility. But there is considerable disagreement about how to put the OT syntax and phonology together with pragmatics.

Architecture

Pragmatics can be studied as the optimization problem of assigning the correct interpretation to an utterance in a context. One thing that seems to be non-starter is the idea that OT pragmatics is completely independent of OT syntax and phonology, having its own constraints. Yet, this is not such an impossible idea because of learning. Consider the following proposal for word recognition from Boersma (2001).

Let the set of constraints be of the form: 'interpret surface form α as the word ω in context of type C'.

The learning data which lead to the ranking of the constraints in this set are utterances of words by adult speakers in contexts, which are by hypothesis given by the appropriate adult OT phonology and which necessarily occur in contexts. Apart from the contexts, they are in fact just the same as the learning data for learning production phonology. If the finite characterization of the contexts is good enough, the learned system will assign the word ω to surface form α in a context c only if α is an optimal pronunciation of ω. Conversely, α is only optimal for ω if there is a context in which α is interpreted as ω.

Boersma's proposal can be extended to morphemes and configurational patterns (syntactic functions, constructions or other potential syntactic bearers of meaning). It can be changed by taking instead of the word ω the concept associated with the word ω (or with the morpheme or with the configurational pattern). The constraint system now gives a sequence of partially related concepts. *NEW prefers maximally related concepts, among themselves and with the given context and RELEVANCE selects the more relevant possibilities from the ones that are still allowed.

This seems feasible and offers an explanation for production monitoring, the amply confirmed fact that speakers listen to their own productions and improve and correct them on the basis of their attempts to interpret what they are saying (the insertion of *then* and *because* for the dispreferred readings in (2) would be due to monitoring). Unfortunately, it also predicts a similar monitoring process in interpretation, for which there seems to be no evidence at all. One may also feel that this is a wasteful architecture: what is there for production should play a role in interpretation as well.

Though Boersma invented the approach given above, he in fact defends a different position in which the production and interpretation constraints are mixed and ranked with respect to each other. This system should exhibit symmetry: it characterizes the same relation when it is run in production mode (with semantic input and forms as candidates) and in interpretation mode (with forms as input and semantic candidates).

This is different from the original proposal of Smolensky (1996) of just letting the production constraints do the semantic job. Above, an argument was presented that this is not enough – there are cases where extra pragmatics is needed. But the real problem for a system of this kind is the Rat/Rad problem (actually, rather a large set of problems in phonology and syntax): the production system solving the interpretation problem predicts that the faithful interpretation Rat always wins. Other versions of connecting pragmatics with syntax and phonology are Blutner's strong bidirectionality, in which a production is only optimal if its input is its optimal interpretation and, conversely, an interpretation is only optimal for a form, if its form is its optimal production. The weak version of bidirectionality defines superoptimal pairs of productions and interpretations as those that cannot be improved by better superoptimal pairs. These versions can be seen as formalizations of the pragmatic proposals of Horn (1984) or Levinson (2000) in which the speaker and the hearer perspective are conditioned on each other.

Then there are asymmetric versions. One can hold that production is bidirectional, but

interpretation is not or, conversely, that interpretation is bidirectional, but production is not. The problems with these notions mirror the problems with Smolensky's version: care should be taken that pragmatic constraints are present and that something like Boersma's solution to the Rat/Rad problem should be incorporated.

The author of this article contends that the natural language interpretation process has recruited the generation system to define the set of possible interpretations: the full intentional state of a production is the object perceived in interpreting an utterance. Pragmatics is then the perceptual bias in this process of distal perception of generations: PLAUSIBILITY reflects the a priori probability of the perception, *NEW the bias to re-identify the already perceived in the new material and RELEVANCE the bias to perceive the utterance as something that makes sense given the activated goals and questions. In this view, the architecture of pragmatics is like that of **relevance theory**: pragmatics enriches an underspecified meaning.

While few would deny that some kind of bidirectionality is involved in the explanation of pragmatic phenomena, little agreement is emerging about how to meet the excellent critical work of Hale and Reiss (1998), Gärtner (2003) or Beaver and Lee (2003).

Analyses

Not much troubled by these foundational questions, OT pragmatics has been successfully applied to a wide range of semantic, pragmatic, lexical and syntactic phenomena such as pronouns (Bresnan 2001; Beaver 2004), reflexives (Mattausch 2007 building on Levinson 2000), differential case marking (Zeevat and Jäger 2002 building on Aissen 1999, de Swart 2007), word order freezing (Lee 2001; Zeevat 2006), stereotypical meaning (Blutner 2000), articles (de Swart *et al.* 2007), **discourse particles** (Zeevat 2003; Malchukov 2004) and connectors, **negation** (Swart 2006), rhetorical structure (Zeevat 2008), case marking (de Hoop and Lamers 2006), scope alternations (Hendriks and de Hoop 2001), intonation (Blutner 2000; de Hoop 2003a; Hendriks and de Hoop 2001; Schwarzschild 1999), and many others. A typical feature of the treatments is that they constrain both production and interpretation and get their mileage out of the interaction between the two directions: this may well be the defining characteristic of OT pragmatics.

To demonstrate, Lee (2001) describes the following effect in Hindi (similar effects are known from many languages): subjects and objects are not inherently ordered and topical objects may be fronted. But this effect disappears when there is no case marking: then the order is subject–object. Lee can explain these features by assuming ordering constraints for the production system that allow both the **topic** and the subject to occur first and by requiring that the input is recovered by running the competition in reverse. This, in effect, lets the pragmatics directly explain a syntactic fact.

Perhaps the most exciting aspect of OT pragmatics comes from the fact that OT comes with an account of learning. Moreover, if one has an account of learning, one can iterate the learning and obtain an account of language change. This has led to interesting accounts of asymmetries in language acquisition (Hendriks and Spenader 2006) and to first attempts at evolutionary explanation in linguistics using OT or OT inspired systems. Jäger (2003) is able to explain the full typological distribution of differential case marking by his model of **language evolution**. It seems possible in these and future systems to show that pragmatics and frequency are the key factors in explaining language change and language evolution.

HENK ZEEVAT

See also: Abduction; disambiguation; formal pragmatics; grammaticalization; language evolution; lexical pragmatics; neo-Gricean pragmatics; presupposition; radical pragmatics; relevance theory

Suggestions for further reading

Blutner, R. (2000) 'Some aspects of optimality in natural language interpretation', *Journal of Semantics*, 17: 189–216.
Hendriks, P. and de Hoop, H. (2001) 'Optimality theoretic semantics', *Linguistics and Philosophy*, 24: 1–32.
Zeevat, H. (2008) 'Discourse structure in optimality theoretic pragmatics', in C. Sidner, J. Harpur, A. Benz and P. Kühnlein (eds) *Proceedings of the 2nd Workshop on Constraints in Discourse*, Amsterdam and Philadelphia, PA: John Benjamins.

Ordinary Language Philosophy

Ordinary Language Philosophy (henceforth OLP) is a particular approach to philosophy that takes traditional philosophical difficulties and puzzlements to result from unclarity of one sort or another with respect to our concepts. It also takes the attainment of clarity to require, not a theory of this or that concept, or of language, but rather a careful and deliberate consideration of the sorts of everyday **contexts** in which the words of our philosophizing would normally and ordinarily be natural and in place. The ordinary language philosopher (henceforth OLPer) takes it that words are natural and in place when we do some work with them that is called for under the circumstances and for which their history has fitted them; and he further takes it that there is no better way of gaining clarity with respect to the concepts expressed by our words than to consider the (different sorts of) work that these words are fitted to do under various circumstances. Relevant here is Ludwig **Wittgenstein**'s (1963) likening of words to tools, or instruments, and John **Austin**'s ([1962] 1975) exploration of the different things we do with words and of the conditions of doing them 'felicitously', as he puts it.

In a way, Wittgenstein and Austin mark the two poles of a sort of magnetic field that defines OLP. Other philosophers whose work could reasonably be said to exemplify OLP – Gilbert Ryle, Peter Strawson, Norman Malcolm, Elizabeth Anscombe and D.Z. Phillips, among others – would be located somewhere in between Wittgenstein and Austin, in closer proximity to one or the other. Then there will be other philosophers – G.E. Moore, John Wisdom, Richard Hare, and more recently Bernard Williams, Stanley Cavell, John McDowell, and Charles Travis, among others – whose relation to the field, while defining of their work, is more complex. In this article, I shall of necessity present a grossly generic characterization of OLP, one that abstracts from some very important differences among its central practitioners, but that nonetheless captures, I hope, something like its essence.

Philosophical questions, the OLPer takes it, are essentially conceptual questions – as opposed, most importantly, to empirical questions (*cf.* Wittgenstein 1963: 109). (Note that the distinction between empirical question and conceptual question is itself a conceptual distinction.) This means that for the OLPer the general form of philosophical difficulty is that of 'not knowing one's way about' (Wittgenstein 1963: 123) – being unclear with respect to what one says, means, or thinks. This understanding of the nature of philosophical difficulty should be contrasted with the prevailing understanding, according to which the basic philosophical question is whether or not one should hold this or that view about this or that subject, where it is already taken to be clear what the view itself is, and what question(s) it is supposed to answer.

Consider any of the traditional philosophical questions, for example, 'Can we know the external world (the future, what other people think or feel)?', or 'What makes a human action morally right?', or 'Are we responsible for our actions?', or 'What (if anything) is the soul and how might it be related to the body?', or 'In what consists our understanding of our words?', or 'What is time (justice, beauty …)?'. The OLPer is suspicious of the prevailing conception of philosophy according to which one of us might give one answer to such a question and the other give an opposing answer to it, and one of the two answers would be just right and the other just wrong. It is much more likely that we are unclear about the question – about what *we* mean or wish to know in raising it – the OLPer would say. If we could only clarify the question to ourselves, the OLPer believes, we would most likely find nothing to disagree about. For unless our intended question turns out to have been empirical, it is a question about our concepts – about what our words do and can mean – and this, the OLPer contends, is something with respect to which we must already be in deep and pervasive, even if not perfect, agreement. Otherwise, we would not have been able to speak to and understand each other in the way that we do. (It *might* be the case that we 'disagree' in what our words mean. If so, this would

have to manifest itself in our finding it hard to speak to and understand each other, and not only when we do philosophy. This possibility could be set aside here, because at least most philosophical apparent disagreements arise among people who can and do smoothly and effectively speak to each other when they don't philosophize, and by means of the very words that tend to give them trouble when they philosophize.)

In taking its cue from suspected unclarities in what we or others say, think, or mean, OLP continues the work of the Socrates of the early Platonic dialogues. Famously, this Socrates did not charge his fellow Athenians with holding the wrong views, but rather with being unclear with respect to the views they professed to hold, an unclarity that his procedures were designed to bring out. A Socratic point that OLP takes to heart is that taking oneself to know perfectly well what one means, or says, is compatible with one's being found, or even later on finding oneself, to have meant or said nothing clear.

In taking it that at the root of at least very many philosophical difficulties lies misunderstanding with respect to the question one attempts to answer, OLP was even more clearly anticipated by Immanuel Kant (1998). Kant argues that when 'empiricists' and 'rationalists' give contrasting answers to questions like 'Does the world have a beginning in time?' or 'Is the world made of absolutely simple and non-divisible parts?', both sides are attempting to answer a question that rests on a misunderstanding. The competing answers are therefore neither correct nor incorrect, but 'lacking in sense', as Kant puts it. For both Kant and the OLPer, what philosophical difficulty calls for is diagnosis that would make the parties give up their original question as only seemingly making sense, as opposed to arbitration that would find at least one of the two parties incorrect in its answer. For such a diagnosis to be successful, it must be informed by thorough understanding of the processes and considerations that have brought the philosophical question or difficulty to its present form.

The difference between Kant and the OLPer is that the former thought he had, whereas the latter thinks that the organic open-endedness of language makes it impossible to have, a general theory that fully spells out, once and for all, the conditions for the legitimate or intelligible employment of each of our philosophically potentially troublesome words, or concepts. In attempting to show that, and how exactly, we fail to make sense, or fail to make the sense we have taken ourselves to make – in raising a philosophical question or in putting forth an answer to it – the OLPer relies on nothing more than what we all must rely on when, in the everyday, we try to figure out what sense, if any, someone has made with his or her words. The OLPer relies, namely, on his or her familiarity with the normal and ordinary uses of the words; on his or her sense of their potential, when special need arises – philosophical, poetical, or more mundane – to mean more than, or just differently from, what they normally and ordinarily mean; and on his or her appreciation of the speaker's or thinker's (personal, practical, moral, spiritual, intellectual …) situation. In other words, the OLPer has no more solid ground for his or her proposed diagnoses of philosophical difficulties than our more or less shared sense of what makes (what) sense, and under what conditions. But neither do we have more solid ground when, outside philosophy, we speak to (and sometimes for) others, and respond to what they say.

Only half a century ago, OLP was widely taken to hold the promise for a fresh start in philosophy. Nowadays, it is widely believed to have somehow been discredited. The most prevalent complaint against OLPers is that they fail to note the important distinction between the 'semantic' question of whether some 'assertoric' form of words makes sense – in the sense of being a suitable candidate for assessment in terms of truth and falsity – and the 'pragmatic' question of whether, and under what conditions, it would make sense for us actually to utter this form of words assertorically, as it were. This complaint, which was originally raised by Paul **Grice** and John **Searle**, seems to me to rest on a gross misunderstanding. OLPers such as Wittgenstein and Austin have not failed to notice the widely assumed distinction between 'semantics' and 'pragmatics'. They *question* it, or its philosophical usefulness. They take the widely shared assumption that it ought in principle to be possible for us to tell what our words 'refer' to, or mean, apart from a consideration of what use(s) we normally and ordinarily make of them, to lie at the root of many philosophical difficulties. It may be that for those already committed to the assumption, nothing would count as proving it wrong; but for those who have come to question its usefulness and to see it as responsible for many philosophical difficulties, its being noncompulsory might be all that need be shown. For the latter, OLP may still prove to constitute a viable alternative to traditional forms of philosophizing.

AVNER BAZ

See also: Assertion; Austin, J.L.; context; contextualism; Grice, H.P.; meaning; philosophy of language; pragmatics; Searle, J.; semantics; semantics-pragmatics interface; Wittgenstein, L.

Suggestions for further reading

Austin, J. (1979) *Philosophical Papers*, Oxford: Oxford University Press.
Cavell, S. (1979) *The Claim of Reason*, Oxford: Oxford University Press.
Wittgenstein, L. (1963) *Philosophical Investigations*, trans. G.E.M. Anscombe, Oxford: Basil Blackwell.

P

Parentheticals

Parentheticals are expressions of varying length, complexity, function and syntactic category, which are interpolated into the current string of the utterance. Expressions that have been argued to be parenthetical in nature include sentence adverbials and adverbial clauses, one-word expressions (e.g. English *like, say, what*), comment clauses (e.g. English *I think, I suppose, you know*, German *glaube ich*, French *je pense*), reporting verbs (e.g. English *he said, said she*), vocatives, nominal appositions, non-restrictive relative clauses (NRRC), question tags, and various types of full or elliptical clauses (*cf.* Dehé and Kavalova 2007 and Kaltenböck 2007 for overviews).

In **syntax**, a contradiction exists between far-reaching structural independence of the parenthetical from its host utterance on the one hand and linear order and certain existing hierarchical relations on the other hand. Accordingly, parentheticals have either been argued to be external to the syntactic structure of their host sentence (e.g. Haegeman 1988; Peterson 1999; Espinal 1991; Burton-Roberts 1999b), or loosely related to it, for example, in terms of adjunction (Ross 1973; Emonds 1973, 1976, 1979; McCawley 1982; Corver and Thiersch 2002; Potts 2002; D'Avis 2005; Vries 2005, 2007) or insertion (Ackema and Neeleman 2004). Those approaches that assume structural independence account for linearization and apparent surfacing relationships along the lines of semantic association (e.g. Peterson 1999), **utterance interpretation** (e.g. Haegeman 1988), or serialization in the phonetic component (e.g. Haider 2005).

In prosodic research, parentheticals have been argued to be in their own intonational domain and marked by a change in pitch level, loudness and tempo. Prosodic cues indicating phrase-level boundaries before and after the parenthetical include pauses (e.g. Altmann 1981; Astruc 2005; Bolinger 1989; Payà 2003a; Taglicht 1998), falling-rising pitch at the end of the immediately preceding domain (e.g. Local 1992) and the blocking of sandhi rules (e.g. Frota 2000). We also know that the intonational features of parentheticals depend on various factors, among them length, relative weight and syntactic make-up and position (e.g. Bolinger 1989). Certain types of relatively short parentheticals, such as comment clauses, reporting verbs, question tags and vocatives, may be prosodically integrated into an adjacent domain (e.g. Crystal 1969; Taglicht 1998; Wichmann 2001; Gussenhoven 2004; Peters 2006; Dehé 2007). While shorter parentheticals are more likely to be prosodically integrated than longer ones (e.g. Peters 2006), empirical research has shown that the placement of an intonational boundary before NRRCs or other types of sentential parentheticals is far from obligatory, and that it depends on position, prosodic make-up and discourse factors (Watson and Gibson 2004; Dehé, to appear).

In **pragmatics**, parentheticals have been approached from various perspectives. In an early study by Urmson (1952), certain types of parentheticals, comment clauses in particular, are seen as expressions which do not have any descriptive function and do not contribute to the truth-conditionality of the host utterance, but which attach an illocutionary commitment to it (*cf.* also Hand 1993). The hearer is guided towards a proper assessment of the statement. Similarly, comment clauses, interrogative parentheticals (e.g. English *do you think*, *do you know*) and tag questions have been analyzed as mitigators in more recent **speech act** theoretic approaches, i.e. as insertions used to modify, correct, reinforce or soften a speech act performed by the host utterance (e.g. Mittwoch 1979; Fraser 1980; Schneider 2007a, 2007b). They function as a **hedge** on the illocutionary force of the frame utterance (Hand 1993). Apart from this mitigating function, the insertion of a parenthetical may also lead to the addition of another speech act to the one performed by the host.

Looking at *as*-parentheticals, nominal appositives, NRRCs and certain types of adverbs in particular, Potts (2002, 2005) proposes that parentheticals should be analyzed as contributing conventional **implicatures** (Grice 1975). They are thus 'logically and compositionally independent of the at issue-entailments' (Potts 2005: 89). Cf. Blakemore (2007) for a critical discussion of this approach.

In terms of **relevance theory** (Sperber and Wilson 1995), parentheticals are generally inserted in pursuit of optimal relevance (Blakemore 2005a, 2006, 2007). On the one hand, their use leads to an increase of the costs of the utterance in at least two ways: the inserted additional material (word or phrase) increases the hearer's linguistic processing efforts, and its marked prosodic behaviour may increase the hearer's phonological processing efforts. On the other hand, the additional linguistic material may diminish the effort of memory and **inference** in that it helps the hearer to achieve early and correct **disambiguation** and **reference** assignment, and thus assists the hearer in deriving the intended cognitive effects. Similarly, the departure from normal **prosody** may guide the hearer towards the intended interpretation (Wilson and Wharton 2006). Overall, the insertion of a parenthetical increases the cognitive effects of an utterance and helps to achieve optimal relevance. As Blakemore (2006) argues, some parenthetical expressions may yield cognitive effects of their own, while others only contribute to the relevance and overall interpretation of the host. Specific types of parentheticals that have been analysed in the framework of relevance theory include *and*-parenthetical clauses (Blakemore

2005a; Kavalova 2007), sentential adverbs (Ifantidou-Trouki 1993) and parenthetical *what* (Dehé and Kavalova 2006).

In the framework of **conversation analysis** (Schegloff 2007), parentheticals have been seen as located at the interface of turn-taking and **sequence organization** (Mazeland 2007). Parentheticals, analyzed as separate turn constructional units (TCUs), may be inserted within an ongoing TCU or, in a multi-unit-turn, between TCUs. Their insertion initiates a subsidiary activity, that is, parentheticals are used to specify, exemplify, explicate, clarify, characterize, elaborate on or delimit a referent or reference introduced prior to the parenthetical in the TCU interrupted by it (Mazeland 2007). They are designed to get a response, i.e. as a sequence (Schegloff 2007). The characteristic prosodic features of parentheticals are seen as a key device to signal their status as separate TCUs.

In a theory of **information structure**, parentheticals have been argued to function as 'partitions' (Taglicht 1984; Ziv 2002). Specifically, comment clauses, vocatives and certain types of adverbs are used to set off the marked theme (or 'link' in Valld
ví's 1992 sense) from what follows in the main utterance, and to link it to information in the preceding utterance. Dehé and Kavalova (2006) argue that the one-word parenthetical *what* helps the hearer to recognize the **focus** of the sentence.

Certain parentheticals such as comment clauses have been argued to be subject to a process of **grammaticalization**, developing from pronoun–verb combinations to epistemic adverbs or **discourse markers** (Thompson and Mulac 1991; Aijmer 1997; Dehé and Wichmann, to appear).

Overall, parentheticals are a multifaceted phenomenon and further research needs to be done to fully account for it.

NICOLE DEHÉ

See also: Discourse markers

Suggestions for further reading

Blakemore, D. (2006) 'Divisions of labour: the analysis of parentheticals', *Lingua*, 116: 1670–87.
Dehé, N. and Kavalova, Y. (eds) (2007) *Parentheticals*, Amsterdam: John Benjamins.

Peirce, C.S.

Charles Sanders Peirce (1839–1914), pronounced 'purse', was an American philosopher and founder of philosophical **pragmatism**. Within his vast and wide-ranging work, Peirce developed what he called his semeiotic (also spelled 'semiotic'), a theory of signs meant to provide a naturalistic account of the mind (Short 2007). The semeiotic of Peirce is often confused with the **semiotics** of Charles W. **Morris**. This confusion stems, in part, from Peirce's definition of semiosis, which he provides in his manuscript 'Pragmatism' (*Essential Peirce*, 2: 411):

> [B]y 'semiosis' I mean ... an action, or influence, which is, or involves, a cooperation of three subjects, such as a sign, its object, and its interpretant, this tri-relative influence not being in any way resolvable into actions between pairs.
>
> (Peirce 1992b)

This 'cooperation of three subjects' seemingly resembles Morris's threefold division of semiosis into **syntax**, **semantics**, and **pragmatics**, at least at first blush. Peirce's theory of signs, however, is much more robust and ambitious than Morris's theory of language.

For Peirce, all objects are signs. By object, Peirce means anything that we can think. He defines signs as things that serve to convey **knowledge** of other things, which are said to stand for or represent (*Essential Peirce*, 2: 13). A sign is thus a representamen that creates in the mind another sign, which Peirce refers to as an interpretant. Elsewhere, Peirce refers to what the representamen conveys as the **meaning** of the sign (*Collected Papers*, 1.339) (Peirce 1931–58). Here, we recognize Peirce's three subjects in cooperation: the object the sign represents, the representamen, and the interpretant. It is important to note that all three are kinds of signs for Peirce, including the object represented.

Peirce initially divided signs into three kinds: icons, indices, and symbols. This division of signs fits into Peirce's three general categories of phenomena: Firstness (Quality or Feeling), Secondness (Reactivity), and Thirdness (Lawlikeness). Peirce defines an icon as that which 'stands for its object because as a thing perceived it excites an idea naturally allied to the idea that object would excite' (*Essential Peirce*, 2: 13). For Peirce, icons are not connected to their objects, but merely cause similar interpretants as their objects due to being likenesses of those objects. Peirce uses the example of a photograph as an icon. However, indices actually connect with their objects through pointing to or causing us to attend to the objects. The example of an index that Peirce provides is that of a weathercock, which points to the direction of the wind. Symbols are representamen of objects 'regardless of any *factual* connection therewith, but solely and simply because [they] will be interpreted to be ... representamen' (*Essential Peirce*, 2: 163). According to Peirce, symbols are interpreted as representamen of specific objects based upon habit, conventional or natural. Symbols are constituted as signs mainly by being used as signs for objects rather than by having natural likeness to objects, as icons do, or by indicating other objects, as indices do (*Collected Papers*, 2.307).

Perhaps the most contentious and misunderstood element of Peirce's semeiotic, especially as it relates to pragmatics, has been that of the *interpretant*, by which was not meant *interpretation*. Peirce defined the interpretant of a symbol as 'an outgrowth of the symbol' (*Essential Peirce*, 2: 322). Elsewhere, Peirce referred to an interpretant as the outcome of a sign (*Collected Papers*, 5.473). The interpretant is a representamen caused by another representamen 'in the Quasi-mind that is the Interpreter' (*Collected Papers*, 4.536). An interpretant is thus a sign of another sign that is a likeness, an indication, or a **representation** of another object. Any sign caused by another sign is an interpretant of that sign.

Regarding pragmatics, as developed by Charles S. Morris, the American pragmatist John Dewey was a harsh critic. Dewey claimed that Morris completely misinterpreted Peirce's concept of an interpretant. Morris had taken interpretant to mean the user of the language, rather than the system of signs within which a sign is used (*The Later Works*, 15.141–52) (Dewey 1925–53). In addition, Dewey believed it a mistake to attempt to divide the semiotic into three separate dimensions (syntax, semantics, and pragmatics) because each was inextricably embedded in the other two. In the first chapter of Dewey's co-authored book, *Knowing and the*

Known, Arthur F. Bentley claims that the separation of semantics and pragmatics from one another 'is to leap from Peirce back towards the medieval' (*The Later Works*, 16.33).

There is an interesting difference in categorization between Peirce's semeiotic and the typical inclusion of semiotics (including pragmatics) in the category of linguistics. Peirce claimed that logic was the science of the theory of signs, which was divided into three branches: Speculative Grammar (the theory of the nature and meaning of signs); Critic (the classification of arguments); and Methodeutic (the principles pertaining to guiding valuable research) (*Essential Peirce*, 2: 272). As a field of study, Peirce placed Linguistics within the category of Classificatory Psychics, which is a branch of what Peirce referred to as Psychical Sciences (*Essential Peirce*, 2: 259–61). If pragmatics is within the field of linguistics, this classification fits not only Peirce's placement of the field within Psychics, but is also closely aligned with Rudolf Carnap's (1942: 8–10) definition of pragmatics:

> If in an investigation explicit reference is made to the speaker, or, to put it in more general terms, to a user of a language, then we assign it to the field of *pragmatics* … If we abstract from the user of a language and analyze only the expressions and their designata, we are in the field of *semantics*.

This places pragmatics apart from what Peirce intended with his theory of signs as the science to which logic pertains. Carnap's framing of pragmatics also indicates the separation of Peirce's semeiotic from the semiotic developed by Morris, which shifted focus from the interpretant as a sign caused by another sign to the interpretation by the user of language. Although Peirce had insisted on the importance of use in the functioning of a symbol, for Peirce that habitual use was a fundamental part of his theory of signs that could not be placed into a separate category of analysis.

MARK DIETRICH TSCHAEPE

See also: Abduction; context; discourse; Habermas, J.; indexicals; knowledge; meaning; Morris, C.; philosophy of language; philosophy of mind; pragmatism; reasoning; semantics; semiotics; theory of mind

Suggestions for further reading

Deledalle, G. (2001) *Charles S. Peirce's Philosophy of Signs: Essays in Comparative Semiotics*, Bloomington, IN: Indiana University Press.

Fisch, M.H. (1986) *Peirce, Semeiotic, and Pragmatism*, ed. K.L. Ketner and C.J.W. Kloesel, Bloomington, IN: Indiana University Press.

Hausman, C.R. (1993) *Charles S. Peirce's Evolutionary Philosophy*, Cambridge: Cambridge University Press.

Performative Pragmatics

Drawing on Felman's remark that 'What is really at stake in the play – the real conflict – is, in fact, the opposition between two views of language, one that is cognitive, or constative, and another that is performative' ([1980] 2003: 13), Douglas Robinson has outlined a general performative linguistics (Robinson 2003) and a more restricted performative pragmatics (Robinson 2005).

A constative linguistics/pragmatics would be an approach to language that is oriented to *structural abstraction* (abstract systems of linguistic structures are more real and more significant than what people do with those structures), *objectivity* (those abstract structures do exist and can and should be described accurately, and it is the job of language to describe the world objectively as well), and *rule-governedness* (**communication** is made possible by the fact that human speakers of a language are governed more or less mechanically by a set of rules that transform abstract linguistic structures into understandable messages). By contrast, a performative linguistics/pragmatics would be an approach to language that is oriented to *people doing things with words* (it is the people that matter, the people and what they do, how they interact, how they create drama), *the performative power of words to transform human realities* (it is the act of people creating **meaning** with words that gives shape to our beliefs and values, social and cultural structures), *emergent collaboration* (it is the collaborative work of people in groups that gives words their power to shape reality, in both regulatory and transformative ways: both imposing order and overstepping the order already in place), and *the importance of the body* (we perform our lives in our bodies, and our bodies both shape and store how we perform and how we feel about how we and others perform) (*see* Robinson 2005: 8, 11). Put briefly, the constative linguist is interested in those aspects of language that are not susceptible to (pre)conscious *choice* – the areas in which language seems to work mechanically – while the performative linguist is interested in those aspects of language that are dramatic, dialogical, relational, (re)performed in ever new ways by groups of language users.

The constative phonologist, syntactician, or semantician, for example, studies general linguistic patterns that are taken to be more or less stable from **context** to context, while the performative phonologist, syntactician, or semantician would study the deliberate use of accent (for example), sentence structure, or word meanings for specific contextual dramatic purposes. By the same token, the constative pragmatician studies 'from above' (outside the interactive subjectivities of individual participants in specific language use contexts) the stable contextual, speech act, turn taking, and uptake structures of a language, and the structural markers that signal when a given pragmatic structure is being employed, while the performative pragmatician studies what people do with the dramatic aspects of verbal communication (context, implicit and explicit verbal actions, the sequence of turns taken by speakers, the possibility of **misunderstanding** and tension between conflicting interpretations). Briefly, both constative and performative pragmaticians study 'people doing things with words'. However, where the constative pragmatician attempts to idealize that subject matter *out* of the realm of people actually doing things with words, in order to study 'speaker types', 'listener types', 'context types', and '**speech act types**', the performative pragmatician seeks to develop strategies for analyzing actual 'performed' interactions in groups.

Other linguistic theorists have drawn distinctions similar to that between constative and performative linguistics/pragmatics: the linguistic study of sentences versus the metalinguistic study of utterances (Bakhtin [1929] 1984: 182–83),

scientistic versus dramatistic approaches to human action (Burke [1945] 1969), language as rule versus language as resource (Halliday 1978), segmentationalist versus integrationalist linguistics (Harris 1980, 1981, 1988, 1998), objectivist versus **cognitive linguistics** (Lakoff 1987), linguistics proper versus critical language study (Fairclough 1989, 1997), the product tradition versus the action tradition (Clark 1992), and Cartesian/rational versus non-Cartesian/relational pragmatics (Kopytko 1993, 1995b, 1998, 2001, 2003).

Performative pragmatics grows out of close rereadings of J.L. **Austin** (1961) and H. Paul **Grice** (1975), specifically the generative power of **performativity** and **implicature**. The radical rethinkings of Austin offered by Derrida (1988: iterability), Felman ([1980] 2003: the speaking body), and Butler (1990: performative identities) open up many new avenues for performative pragmatics. Grice has received considerably less performative attention, but Altieri's (1981) Gricean concept of *expressive implicature* draws analytical attention to the ways in which conversational **intentions** are staged as style. Robinson's (2003, 2005) concept of *conversational invocature* explores the dramatic use of allusion, paraphrase, and anticipatory completion to implicate unstated intentions.

In addition, sociolinguists like Garfinkel (1967) and sociologists like Goffman (1974) have drawn our attention to the performative aspects of pragmatic interactions as well. Garfinkel does this through what he calls '**ethnomethodology**', while for Goffman it is achieved through his 'dramaturgical' discussions of language use contexts in terms of 'stages', 'scenes', and 'framings'.

Garfinkel theorizes social interaction as *always* managed locally, through emergent collaboration, which is always what he calls 'another first time'. Unlike his younger colleague at UCLA in the 1960s, Harvey Sacks, whose **conversation analysis** is a constative study of the structure of **conversations**, Garfinkel was interested in how people structure conversations – what people do to each other with words in groups. Garfinkel's theory was that we tend to structure conversations by trusting each other to know what we know and obey the rules we unconsciously try to obey, and then to put pressure on them to live up to that trust.

Goffman, on the other hand, looks at how we frame our social actions, including speech – how we work individually and collectively to impose a contextualized order on speech. What happens when someone unexpectedly changes or 'rekeys' a frame? How does the rest of the group adjust? What sorts of metapragmatic strategies (Bateson 1955; Silverstein 1976; Shiffrin 1980) do they use to explain and participate in the rekeying? Goffman's performative principles include an insistence that (a) people do the keying (create contexts); (b) people keying events (creating contexts) tend to forget that that's what they're doing, tend to ignore the constructedness of contexts, and to react to them as 'givens'; (c) people can rekey an event at any time, which also means that no one actor can perfectly control how a frame is keyed; (d) even though people 'mimic' existing frameworks for conversation, in keying those frameworks they reperform them in novel ways, so that no keyed event can ever be taken as a mere 'example' of a framework (1974: 79), and (e) every time a frame is rekeyed, it is weakened a little, so that eventually a frame could be exhausted and become no longer usable (1974: 182).

Although constative and performative approaches to the study of language are diametrically opposed to each other, for the most part there is no reason to assume that we must decide which approach is the 'correct' or 'appropriate' path for linguistics to take, and banish the other. There are aspects of language that are so stable that it is virtually impossible to vary them contextually and still be understood. We will, therefore, continue to need constative phonology, morphology, **syntax**, and **semantics**. It is, however, difficult to imagine a principled justification for the abstract idealization of people doing things with words out of the realm of people and doing. Indeed, constative pragmatics would seem to be more a carryover of Saussurean methodologies than a necessary pragmatic orientation. It is one that notoriously generates methodological double binds that are nearly impossible to escape, such as how one might identify an implicit performative based solely on imagined formal markers, so as not to have to invoke actual people doing things with words to make the classification stick. **Pragmatics** is the study of language in contextualized social interactions, and as such would appear to require a performative – or action-oriented, or cognitive, or relational – approach.

DOUGLAS ROBINSON

See also: Austin, J.L.; cognitive anthropology; cognitive linguistics; cognitive pragmatics; cognitive psychology; cognitive science; context; conversational turn-taking; conversation analysis; cooperative principle; ethnomethodology; Grice, H.P.; implicature; maxims of conversation; metapragmatics; misunderstanding; performativity; speech act theory

Suggestions for further reading

Robinson, D. (2003) *Performative Linguistics: Speaking and Translating as Doing Things With Words*, London and New York: Routledge.
——(2005) *Introducing Performative Pragmatics*, London and New York: Routledge.

Performativity
Performativity defined

The concept of performativity, often accorded the status of a theoretical framework, is a productive one in the disciplines of linguistics, linguistic anthropology, social theory and **philosophy**. Its application in the 1990s and first decade of the twenty-first century has been principally in **gender** and 'queer' studies and has introduced new controversy into these two arenas. The notion of performativity, it is claimed, allows theorists to examine how 'identities are constructed iteratively through complex citational processes' (Parker and Sedgwick 1995: 2).

Performativity, as it has been understood since the first publication of Judith Butler's seminal work *Gender Trouble* in 1990, must be distinguished from performance. The latter presupposes the existence of a prior subject, who then performs of his/her own volition. In her elaboration of performativity, Butler argues that there is no pre-existing subject. The subject only emerges through **discourse**: there is no 'doer behind the deed' (Butler 1990: 25).

Butlerian performativity takes forward an idea introduced by **Austin** (1962) in *How to Do Things* *with Words*, which is recognized as the canonical work on the performative. One of Austin's assertions is that a **speech act** *does* something. One type of speech act is called a 'performative' precisely because Austin recognizes a class of verbs which bring about a new state of affairs; in the stating, there is also the doing of an action. Obvious examples would be verbs like 'I bet' or 'I promise' or 'I arrest you' in which the uttering initiates the enactment denoted by the verb.

Austin first distinguishes performatives from another class of utterances – constatives. He defines a constative as a statement which can be judged to be true or false (Austin 1962: 3), e.g. 'the sun rises every morning'. On the other hand, a performative cannot immediately be judged to be true or false since the validity of the act can only be sustained by what are termed felicity conditions. As Austin puts it, a performative has to be 'happy'. The felicity conditions that Austin sets out require that the utterance is spoken by an appropriate person, that there is correct and complete execution of the utterance, and that it must be carried out with correct, appropriate **intentions**. If any of these felicity conditions are violated, the performative is invalidated.

Austin also recognizes that constatives may behave as performatives. In the act of stating, we are also performing an act, and the statement itself is also subject to tests of 'felicitousness' (1962: 133–38). Butler recognizes that discursive performativity is constructed more frequently through constative verbs than by performative verbs. She illustrates this claim with her example of the way a child is 'gendered' at birth, with the constative proclamation 'It's a girl!' (1993: 232). Moreover, in Althusserian theory (Althusser 1971), the child is interpellated by this speech act into a subjectivity that can have no existence outside this call to being. Althusser's work argues that ideology interpellates subjects, or more literally hails them, so that in responding to the discourse they are forced to acknowledge that it refers to them. In this way, his theory suggests, the individual is constituted as a subject.

Performativity can be both discursive and embodied. Gendered subjects signal their identity by bodily acts which are socially sanctioned, meaningful in a social **context** and rigidly

policed. A key assumption of performativity theory is that once subjectivity has been discursively furnished, the child must also surrender to embodied performativity. This embodying is enacted by a forcible 'citation' of the regulatory norms of femininity/masculinity (Butler 1993: 232). Although Austin's theory emphasized speaker/actor intention, according to performativity theory, a subject's volitionality is strictly attenuated. Gender is compulsory and Butler offers just two choices: citation of the norm, or deliberate, and punishable transgression of it.

In this theory, performing gender instantiates merely the effect of gender. Butler describes the process of citation as 'the repeated stylization of the body, a set of repeated acts within a highly rigid regulatory frame that congeal over time to produce the appearance of substance, of a natural sort of being' (1999: 43–44). The 'rigid, regulatory frame' refers to the kind of policing of gendered behaviour that forms the means of its social construction within a **culture**. Gender, writes Butler, 'is a *compulsory* performance in the sense that acting out of line with heterosexual norms brings with it ostracism, punishment and violence' (1991: 24). Despite our attachment to the gender binary, gender categories are by their nature permeable, rather than rigid; this is a corollary of the fact that there is no original to copy (1993: 9, 14, 21). The citation of acts, within a compulsory frame, then, forms a border between male and female which must be rigorously maintained. Butler further undermines the notion of any naturalness underlying the categories of male and female with her example of the phenomenon of drag (male bodied actors dressed and performing as women on stage). Clearly, if such an individual can convincingly cite the norms of the 'opposite' gender, then this exposes the non-naturalness of gender, and the fragility of these categories. In a sense, the acts have been 'resignified' in a way that might allow for the proliferation of genders, and in so doing 'undermine the naturalness of binary gender and heterosexuality' (1999: 180). That sense of naturalness can only be restored by ensuring that the appropriate acts are always cited by the 'right' gendered bodies. Gender, she explains, is a convenient fiction, naturalized only by repetition of the approved norms.

Performativity in linguistics

Work in the 1970s and 1980s in **socio-linguistics** (e.g. Labov 1972; Trudgill 1974) had proposed that language variation exhibited by speakers revealed pre-existing identities such as social class, ethnicity or regional affiliation. This work assumed a determining relationship between social identity and speech variety, as manifest by 'markers' – variables which could reliably be judged to index the implicated identity. More recent work in the sociolinguistics of language and gender or language and sexual identity has argued for a reversal of this relationship. Instead, it is presupposed that identity materializes through discourse and that speakers exert some agency in making choices from a 'symbolic marketplace' (Eckert 1996) of linguistic variables.

One of the first and most influential investigations of the explanatory power of performativity theory is a collection edited by Livia and Hall (1997a) entitled *Queerly Phrased*, whose introduction announced '[i]t is time to bring performativity back to its disciplinary origins' (Livia and Hall 1997b: 13). This book explores a number of discursive performances of non-normative sexualities in different social contexts and different historical periods. Examples include queer performance by gay deaf signers, Jewish gay men, lesbian discourse and the discursive indexing of transsexual identity. Importantly, in queer linguistics, no one-to-one correspondence is assumed between language and identity. Instead, identity emerges discursively, and signifiers must be decoded by local negotiation. Identity signals, then, vary by social and cultural context and by purpose.

A demonstration of the workings of such a negotiation is an analysis of the discursive enactment of male heterosexuality by Cameron (1997), using an explicitly performativist framework. In it she details the work of performing heterosexual masculinity: the linguistic repudiation of stigmatized identities such as homosexual men and a discursive differentiation from women, together with the policing and display of hegemonically masculine behaviours and ideologies. Paradoxically, the young male subjects of the study use the conventionally feminine genre of 'gossip' to enact this. Gossip, in this case, has been resignified for the purpose of doing masculinity.

It is evident that in performing gender, normative speakers learn to manipulate a large repertoire of signifiers which are understood in local contexts as an appropriate performance of gender (Eckert 1996). Non-normative speakers have access to the same signifiers, but will use these to resist and disrupt performative norms, or to stretch the tolerances of femininity and masculinity (Bucholtz 1999). Linguistic performances of gender dissonance are detailed in Morrish and Sauntson (2007). The primary focus of this work is lesbian **conversation** and language used by lesbians to index lesbian identity. The performance of coming out, for example, is often not in the form of a (constative) performative 'I am a lesbian', but may be covertly revealed in acts of **silence** and non-compliance with gender norms. Taking issue with Butler's presentation of performativity as a choice between compliance and transgression, Morrish and Sauntson argue that volitionality is more of a continuum. The sexually transgressive subject experiences limits to agency, and identity revelation may be balanced with strategic concealments. Coincidentally, these concealments may be read by other lesbians and gay men as linguistic performances of homosexuality.

Performativity has emerged as a key idea from queer theory and gender theory. It has given rise to a postmodern turn in sociolinguistics that continues to influence new work in language and gender/sexual identity. If Judith Butler has questioned the validity of the gender binary, it remains a useful analytical concept in sociolinguistic work where performativity theory has enhanced our understanding of femininity, masculinity, and of how gender and heterosexual norms may be resisted.

LIZ MORRISH

See also: Austin, J.L.; gender; intentionality; performative pragmatics; speech act theory; speech act type

Suggestions for further reading

Butler, J. ([1990] 1999) *Gender Trouble: Feminism and the Subversion of Identity*, New York: Routledge.

Salih, S. (2002) *Judith Butler*, London: Routledge.
Wilchins, R. (2004) *Queer Theory, Gender Theory: An Instant Primer*, Los Angeles, CA: Alyson Books

Perspective-Taking/Point of View

Four areas of investigation associated with the idea of perspectivalism or alternative points-of-view (POVs) will be briefly discussed, with the first being of least direct relevance to **pragmatics** and the last of most relevance: (i) linguistic relativism, (ii) information structuring, (iii) lexical selection, and (iv) deictic centring. This is by no means an exhaustive list of doctrines or domains of inquiry that have perspectivalist implications.

When they think of the notion of perspective, many people will think of the doctrine of linguistic relativity, i.e. the Whorfian hypothesis that language determines thought. After all, Whorfianism seems to imply that one's language forces one to see the world from a particular perspective. Those who find this doctrine questionable are likely to find the idea of perspective-taking equally suspect. However, the doctrine of linguistic relativity does not embody a notion of POV that is of central interest to pragmatics, even though some ideas proposed by contemporary linguistic relativists such as Levinson (2003) are tangentially related to the deictic notion of POV discussed later.

Another domain in which the notion of alternative perspectives plays a role is the domain of discourse- or **information structure**. The way a speaker structures the information content of her message determines a particular POV on the situation being described. Simple examples involve active versus passive constructions. An employee unhappy about his situation would be wise to ask his boss 'Why was I not given a pay raise?' rather than 'Why didn't you give me a pay raise?', since the former backgrounds the boss's agency in the matter of the pay raise, whereas the latter comes across as directly confrontational.

Confining our attention to a single language or a single dialect of a language so as to make it clear that nothing Whorfian is afoot, it is possible to see *all* uses of expressions within a language as implicitly harbouring a POV. Thus, McConnell-Ginet (2008) suggests that a speaker's lexical choices can present matters from a POV. Moreover, she suggests that this POV may be

pernicious, because speakers may not recognize the implicit bias in their lexical choices. For example, when a speaker uses the pronominal form 'he' as an allegedly neutral way to refer to people in general, this may act to exclude women. If a job advertisement reads 'Anyone interested in applying should submit his resume to the following address', women may be less inclined to apply for the job, even though the 'his' here is ostensibly a 'gender neutral' use.

Once one looks for such biases hidden in people's lexical choices, they can be found all over the place. McConnell-Ginet (2008) gives an example of an airline employee saying to a quadriplegic passenger 'We'll have to get the people off the plane first before you can disembark', suggesting that the airline employee thinks of quadriplegics as non-persons. However, although McConnell-Ginet may be right to note that lexical choices can reveal hidden biases, we should also note that using an underspecified form like 'people' to refer to a more restricted class, such as 'people able to help themselves off the aircraft', is a pervasive linguistic strategy, and one that is perfectly legitimate. Relevance theorists, neo-Griceans, and other pragmatists have long noted that **utterance interpretation** requires a hearer to enrich underspecified forms on the basis of contextually available background information. It would be cognitively inefficient to have lexical forms to encode all the contextually specific sub-groups of people that one might want to refer to. Moreover, even though a speaker can always use an underspecified form together with explicit additional descriptive material to indicate a restricted **reference**, this would be an inefficient use of cognitive resources if the hearer can be relied on to access this extra descriptive content from the conversational common ground. Thus, the airline employee could have said 'We'll have to get the people able to help themselves off the aircraft off the plane first before you can disembark'. But this is unnecessary if the hearer can supply this enrichment himself from **context**.

A perspectivalist notion that is clearly central to pragmatics is the idea that many words encode a deictic centre or POV. Addressees must rely on common ground information to figure out the POV that the speaker is adopting to portray the situation being talked about.

Some of the clearest examples involve the verbs 'come' and 'go' in English, which are discussed by Fillmore (1997). Contrast utterances of 'Are you coming?' and 'I'll come to your office later'. In the former utterance, the deictic centre is the speaker's location and the addressee's motion must be towards the speaker. In the latter utterance, the deictic centre is the addressee's location and the direction of motion is reversed. It is not possible to do justice to the complexities of verbs of motion here. For one thing, there are many ways to shift the deictic centre by manipulating **discourse** context. Moreover, the centre need not be the location of either the speaker or hearer, but could be that of some third party or even some neutral landmark.

A similar sort of flexibility of deictic centre is built into many indexical and demonstrative expressions, such as 'here' and 'there', 'now' and 'then', 'these' and 'those', as well as into terms of spatial reference, such as 'front' and 'back'. (See Levelt (1996) and Levinson (2003) for discussion of the spatial reference cases.) The traditional picture of such indexical and demonstrative expressions is that the deictic centre is tied to the speaker and to the time and place of the speaker's utterance. However, Smith (1989), Predelli (1998), Schlenker (2004), Bezuidenhout (2005) and others have noted many interesting ways in which the deictic centre can shift away from the speaker's here and now.

One of the most interesting types of shift in POV involves a literary style known as the 'free indirect style' or as 'represented speech and thought', discussed for example by Kuroda (1973) and Banfield (1982). In this style, the narrator switches to the POV of the person whose thought and speech is being reported, and temporal **indexicals** and adverbials must be interpreted from the reportee's POV rather than the reporter's POV. A made-up example in this style is as follows: 'Mary sat down at her desk. She would need to think about how to deal with Sam. Today's meeting had been a disaster!' The tenses indicate that the events being described happened in the past. However, the interpretation of 'today' is not tied to the time of the report but to the 'internal' time, the time of Mary's own ruminations on her day.

ANNE BEZUIDENHOUT

See also: Context; deixis; demonstratives; indexicals; information structure; stylistics

Suggestions for further reading

Chafe, W. (1994) *Discourse, Consciousness, and Time: The Flow and Displacement of Conscious Experience in Speaking and Writing*, Chicago, IL: University of Chicago Press.
Keysar, B., Barr, D.J., Balin, J.A. and Brauner, J.S. (2000) 'Taking perspective in conversation: the role of mutual knowledge in comprehension', *Psychological Science*, 11: 32–38.

Phatic Communication

The term 'phatic' (from Greek *phátos*: spoken) was originally used in the phrase 'phatic communion' which was coined by the anthropologist Bronisław Malinowski (1923). Malinowski observed that in some types of communicative interaction (e.g. greeting, gossiping) the situation in which the conversational exchange takes place consists in, and is largely created by, 'what happens linguistically'. In this type of **communication** – in which the **meanings** of the words used are almost irrelevant – linguistic expressions fulfil a social function. They establish an atmosphere of sociability and personal communion between people (a sense of being in positive rapport with each other) through overcoming silence, which is inherently unpleasant and somewhat threatening. While the phrase 'phatic communion' is closely associated with ritualized aspects of social interaction, the more recent expressions 'phatic communication' and 'phatic speech' place greater emphasis on the function of conversational exchanges described as phatic.

Jakobson (1960) characterizes the 'phatic function' of language as its use to focus on the channel of communication itself, rather than on the information conveyed by the language code. He points out that prolonged phatic **conversations** sometimes occur precisely when the communication process is threatened (for instance, by the insecurity of the interlocutors). From this perspective, various more or less conventionalized ways of opening and ending conversations, as well as maintaining them (e.g. back-channelling devices, such as 'uh-huh') are described as phatic. Laver (1974) takes up Malinowski's views and examines in some detail the connection between the relative social status of the interlocutors and the appropriate choice of linguistic expression in a phatic exchange. Coupland (2000) is a collection of articles which looks at small talk as a form of phatic communication from the sociolinguistic perspective.

Despite the growing number of publications on phatic communication, this type of social interaction calls for much further research on a number of issues, including the three which are briefly outlined here. First, analyses of phatic communication are often couched in terms of the distinction between cognitive (propositional) and social information. To give but one example, Schneider (1988: 11) observes that phatic speech 'does not convey much cognitive information […] but it is always loaded with social information'. Clearly, this claim and similar claims can be explanatory only if the terms 'cognitive' (i.e. 'propositional') information and 'social information' are given reasonably explicit theoretical contents. However, while the propositional mode of mental **representation** has been explored extensively within **cognitive psychology** and **pragmatics**, the theoretical content of the term 'social information' remains something of a mystery. For this reason, the description of phatic communication as the communication of social information has little explanatory value. Second, the production and the comprehension of phatic communicative acts are generally seen as regulated by social conventions about the way particular **topics** (which might be called 'phatic topics') are brought up in particular types of social situation. On the one hand, this makes it difficult to explain communicative acts which have a phatic function, although they are not conventionally phatic, as illustrated by (1):

(1) Several people (who have never met before) have been waiting at a bus stop in North London for about twenty minutes. One of them walks some distance up the road to see if there is a bus coming. He then rejoins the others and says (facing another person who is also waiting impatiently): 'No sign of a bus. I suppose they'll all come together.' She replies: 'Oh yes. They travel in convoys.'

This conversational exchange has the key features of phatic exchanges. The main point of the two utterances does not lie with their propositional contents; rather, the main purpose of the exchange is to establish a sense of solidarity between the interlocutors. But it is not clear how this conversation, and many similar conversations, can be analyzed in terms of social conventions or why they might need to be explained in this way. On the other hand, many phatic conversations in which social conventions about topic choice and language use do play a role cannot be fully explained in terms of conventionalization or standardization (for a discussion of these terms *see* Bach and Harnish 1982). As Lyons (1968: 417) points out, utterances are not simply phatic or non-phatic, but may be more or less phatic:

We must therefore distinguish between that aspect of the 'use' of utterances which may be referred to their function in 'phatic communion' and that part of their 'use' which is to be distinguished as their meaning (if they have meaning in terms of our definition). In saying this, we recognize that, even when both these aspects are present, either one or the other may be the dominant part of the 'use' of the utterance.

There is ample evidence to support this view. The following is a clear example of a conventional phatic exchange, in which the words used are informative to some appreciable degree:

(2) Conversation between two colleagues who have met by chance in a corridor at their place of work.
 [1] A: Hi. How are you?
 [2] B: Fine. Thanks. And you?
 [3] A: Busier than I'd like to be, but generally okay.

A's **question** in [1] is standardly used as a greeting, but it is also an expression of some interest in the hearer's well-being. B's reply in [2] expresses a similar interest and, despite being a conventional phatic string, leaves A the option to give a more or less informative answer. In fact, by providing more information than a formulaic phatic reply would do, A conveys a more positive social attitude towards B (than he would have done by using a formulaic phatic utterance). Examples like these suggest that the degrees of phaticness of a given utterance, or conversational exchange as a whole, can be explained only in the context of a general theory of human communication. Third, as is well known, phatic communication varies across **cultures** in a number of respects. They include the types of situation in which phatic conversation is appropriate, the length of phatic talk at a particular stage of a conversation (say, the beginning or end) and the topics which are appropriate for use in phatic communication.

Attempts to address these issues within the framework of a general pragmatic theory have been few (e.g. Žegarac 1998; Žegarac and Clark 1999a, 1999b) and remain controversial (*see* Ward and Horn 1999). Working within the framework of **relevance theory** (Sperber and Wilson 1995), Žegarac and Clark (1999a) start from the observation that the 'phaticness' of a communicative act largely depends on **context**. For example, the utterance 'It's sunny, but there's a rather cold wind' may be very phatic in one situation (e.g. as part of a chat over coffee between two people who do not expect they will be going out), while not being phatic in a different setting (e.g. if the interlocutors are getting ready to go sailing). These authors argue that the main difference between phatic and non-phatic communicative acts concerns what the most relevant communicated information (which they assume is always propositional) is about and how this information is communicated. In phatic communication, the most relevant information is about the positive rapport between the interlocutors, whereas in non-phatic communicative interaction, the main relevance lies with information which builds to a greater extent on the meanings of the words used. On this approach, the **knowledge** of conventions about conducting phatic exchanges merely facilitates (but does not explain the possibility of) phatic communication. Topics and communicative acts which are frequently used in phatic communication are very cognitively salient. Therefore, they are readily available for use in situations where phatic communication seems appropriate. Žegarac and Clark's relevance-theoretic analysis also identifies

two universal properties of good conventional phatic topics. A topic is suitable for use in phatic communication if (a) the interlocutors can reliably presume (even if they are complete strangers) that the topic is potentially relevant to them in readily conceivable circumstances, and (b) the topic is not very relevant in the immediate situation of communication (or the conversational exchange will be commensurably less phatic or not phatic at all).

VLADIMIR ŽEGARAC

See also: Cognitive psychology; cognitive science; communication; context; conventionality; conversation; culture; intercultural communication; knowledge; proposition; relevance theory; representation and computation

Suggestions for further reading

Coupland, J., Coupland, N. and Robinson, J.D. (1992) '"How are you?": negotiating phatic communion', *Language in Society*, 21: 207–30.
Malinowski, B. (1923) 'The problem of meaning in primitive languages', in C. Ogden and I.A. Richards (eds) *The Meaning of Meaning*, London: Routledge and Kegan Paul.
Žegarac, V. (1998) 'What is phatic communication?', in V. Rouchota and A. Jucker (eds) *Current Issues in Relevance Theory*, Amsterdam: John Benjamins.

Philosophy of Language
Introduction: preliminaries and game plan

Philosophy of language is an extraordinarily rich field. It has a history stretching back, in the Western tradition, to the pre-Socratics. And, in the last century or so, it has been of central concern in both the Anglo-American and Continental traditions. Obviously, a brief survey cannot hope to cover such intellectual abundance. What's more, as this encyclopedia itself attests to, **pragmatics** is an equally rich academic endeavour. Any mere overview of their intersection must, then, narrow its focus. As a result, my specific topic will be: What has Anglo-American philosophy of language contributed to the study of utterance meaning in **context**?

The game plan is as follows. I present two traditional perspectives in philosophy of language, and describe some illustrative contributions of each to pragmatics. I end by explaining how these two philosophical perspectives have recently been combined, thereby affording a still richer and deeper contribution to pragmatics.

Two traditional perspectives in philosophy of language

It is a simplification, not to say artificial, to summarize twentieth-century Anglo-American philosophy of language in terms of only two dominant perspectives. Nevertheless, given the expository purposes of this article, that's mostly what I will do.

One tradition, call it the System Perspective, thinks of a language as a collection of formal rules: rules which are so simple as to require no insight to apply them. A language, on this view, is like an algebra, with its axioms and rules of proof. System Theorists have mainly focused on two kinds of rules: those of **syntax** (which describe how minimal linguistic elements are put together into complex wholes) and those of **semantics** (which describe what each minimal linguistic element means in the language, and how the meaning of complexes depends upon such part-meanings, together with the contributions of syntax). It is no accident that these two, syntax and semantics, also constitute the core of artificial logical languages: System Theorists self-avowedly take such languages as their models, not least because one of their aims is to capture logical relations among natural language sentences.

This may sound very much like the project of Chomskyan generative grammar. And, indeed, Chomsky's earliest work finds its roots in the System Perspective. But there remains a fundamental difference. For the philosopher of language who inclines towards the System Perspective, and in sharp contrast to the approach of generative grammarians, the rules presented are not designed to capture how we humans mentally process language, any more than formal logic seeks to characterize the psychological processes involved in human **reasoning**. To offer a standard comparison: for the System Theorist, to describe a language is akin to laying out the

rules of chess itself, as opposed to offering a description of the thinking processes within a given chess player. (For discussion, *see* George 1989; Iten *et al.* 2007; Katz 1981, 1985; Lewis 1975b; Soames 1984, 1985).

The parallel between a language as construed by the System Theorist and an algebra leads to the next key feature of the System Perspective: its understanding of what a 'linguistic item' is. A linguistic item, on this view, whether a word, phrase or sentence, is something that exists in abstraction from use and users. Linguistic items are types, as opposed to tokens/instances/utterances of those types. (For those unfamiliar with the type/token contrast, think of the difference between the novel *War and Peace* itself and the tens of thousands of copies of this novel. Each copy has a certain weight and extension, a certain location, etc. This is like the *tokens* of linguistic symbols: they are spatiotemporally located specific instances, with all the associated physical features of physical objects. But the novel itself is not located in any one place, has no specific weight, etc. This is like a linguistic type.) Linguistic items, on this view, are thus outside us. Indeed, they are outside the physical world as a whole: like numbers, sentences, phrases and words – the types, that is – are not spatiotemporal entities. And, crucially, it is these types that are the proper object of study according to the System Perspective.

To each perspective there corresponds a theory of what meanings are. Speaking roughly, what I am calling the System Perspective takes meanings to be extra-mental things. And, consonant with its view of linguistic items, meanings are also abstract for the System Theorist: they include sets of possible worlds, sets of properties, and functions (in the mathematical sense of a mapping) from two truth values to one truth value. (Notice, since it will be important in what follows, that all of these meaning-entities have something to do with truth.)

The second traditional perspective could not be more different. According to the Use Perspective, as I will call it, a language is a sociocultural practice. It emphasizes what we *do* with language. Describing a language, on the Use Perspective, is more like describing a folk dance than it is recounting the abstract rules of a formal game. What's more, it is crucial for Use

Theorists that humans do not merely use languages to *describe* the world (which, insofar as usage comes into it at all, is the implicit focus of the System Perspective). As they stress, we also use it to get married, issue verdicts, name ships, make promises, etc. Related to this, a 'linguistic item' according to the Use Perspective is a **speech act** – a linguistic token, rather than a type. Thus, linguistic items are not so much abstract posits as concrete performances.

Just as the System Perspective has an associated view of what meanings are, the Use Perspective does as well. Words on this second view are tools. And their meanings, rather than being abstract objects such as mathematical functions and sets of possible worlds, are actions that we humans perform linguistically. For instance, the meaning of 'Hello' is not some truth-relevant quasi-mathematical *entity*. Instead, to give the meaning of 'Hello' it is enough to say: 'One uses this word to greet people.'

Since it will prove important in the final section of this article, it is worth stressing here again that the aim of the Use Theorist is to capture linguistic action, rather than inner mental 'goings on'. Even though various psychological activities take place when we speak and understand, they are not supposed, even by the Use Theorist, to be relevant to the philosophy of language proper. (Recalling the comparison with a folk dance, there seems no need for a cultural ethnographer to speculate about the psychological mechanisms that permit people to perform a dance. He or she need merely describe its motions, its cultural significance, and so forth.)

To sum up so far, the System Perspective, as I have labeled it, treats a language as an algebra-like collection of syntactic and semantic rules. The items of a language are abstract (types, rather than tokens) and their meanings are abstract too (e.g. functions and sets of worlds). It is essential to stress that inclining towards this perspective does not entail adopting every tenet noted above. For instance, some of those that are best classed as System Theorists nonetheless eschew possible worlds in favour of structurally rich **propositions**, and some recognize contents that go beyond truth conditions. Taking that into account, central figures who lean towards the System Perspective include Frege (1892, 1918), **Wittgenstein** (1922) in his early

writings, Tarski (1944), Davidson (1967) and Montague (1968). The Use Perspective, in contrast, treats a language as a socio-cultural activity. The items of a language are spatio-temporally located speech acts, and linguistic meanings are the actions one can perform using language. Noting again that I am simplifying for the purposes of exposition, key figures in this tradition include **Austin** (1961, 1962), the later Wittgenstein (1953b, 1958), and Strawson (1956).

Illustrative contributions of each perspective to pragmatics

I turn now to the respective contributions of the two philosophical perspectives to the study of utterance meaning in context. Two contributions from the System Perspective come immediately to mind. First, the System Perspective tells us about the standing meaning of words, phrases and sentences, that is, what they mean *in the common language*. This is vital for pragmatics because utterances in context receive part of their meaning from the meaning of the types of which they are tokens. In particular, the System Perspective addresses, at least in part, the question of how utterances of words and sentences manage to be about our world: they manage this because they are tokens of types which, as the System Perspective highlights, are themselves about our world.

One might reasonably complain: 'We don't need all the formal complexity and abstractness of the System Perspective to tell us about the standing meaning of linguistic items. We merely need to describe the use to which the various linguistic tools are put.' But, I would insist, this overlooks a more specific contribution of the System Perspective. Only given the resources of the System Perspective can we explain the unbounded *productivity* of human speech: the System Perspective's rules are recursive (i.e. the output of a rule can serve, once again, as an input) and the meaning of each sentence is determined compositionally (i.e. the meaning of the type is exhausted by what its minimal linguistic elements mean, and how those parts are put together by the syntactic rules). These two features yield a potential infinity of meaningful expression types, including ones that have never before been tokened. The need for this kind of complex machinery can be illustrated with a relatively simple example. The study of utterances in context needs to say how a particular use of, for example, 'Last night I dreamed that I spoke with a tiny pink elephant in the University of Western Ontario student centre' manages to mean what it does. This requires saying what this sentence type means, which in turn requires the kind of complex and abstract rules afforded by the System Perspective.

Second, the System Perspective has afforded invaluable insights into an important way in which utterance meaning, in a specific context, typically outstrips the standing meaning of the linguistic expression used. Specifically, it has provided insights into certain features of utterance meaning that, though they do not *derive* entirely from standing meaning alone, are nevertheless highly *constrained* by it. Examples of this kind of linguistically constrained contribution by context include **demonstratives** ('this', 'that'), pure **indexicals** ('here', 'now', 'I'), and tense markers.

The details are not especially important for present purposes. Nonetheless, here is a brief example to spell out the idea. To account for how (certain) context-sensitive words help to fix utterance content, philosophers such as Kaplan (1989a) and Stalnaker (1970, 1978) introduced the notion of a *character*. This is a function (again, in the mathematical sense of 'function') from certain aspects of a context to a truth-relevant entity. For instance, the standing meaning of 'I once lived here' would be such a character: specifically, a function from triples of <person, time, location> to a proposition about the person who is the speaker in the context, to the effect that he or she lived at the location of the context at some point prior to the time of the context. Hence, should this sentence be spoken by, say, Noam Chomsky, in Boston, on January 1st, 2009, the character of the sentence would, by means of a language-internal rule, deliver as output the content NOAM CHOMSKY ONCE LIVED IN BOSTON AT SOME POINT PRIOR TO JANUARY 1st, 2009. The key point is that the System Perspective not only helps us understand utterance meaning as deriving directly from context-insensitive type meaning, it also helps us understand how utterance meaning is fixed by variable context.

Let's turn now to some illustrative contributions from the Use Perspective. These come in two flavours: literal and non-literal utterance content. Use Theorists pointed out early on that there at least two kinds of content that are literal – indeed, contents which derive wholly from the meaning of the type itself – but which the System Perspective tended to ignore. These are contents that seemingly do not alter the truth conditions of the utterance, but nevertheless contribute to its literal meaning. One sub-variety, which **Grice** labeled 'conventional **implicatures**', shows something about the speaker's attitude towards the truth conditions of the utterance, e.g. that he or she finds them surprising, or in tension with each other. Instances include 'surprisingly', 'but', and 'therefore'. Thus, putting things roughly, to say 'Surprisingly, John won' is truth conditionally equivalent to 'John won.' However, using the former sentence is a way of linguistically indicating surprise.

Syntactic mood affords another example of non-truth-conditional content that attaches to the expression type. Mood is an indicator of illocutionary force potential. Thus, the sentences 'Chomsky left' and 'Did Chomsky leave?' pertain to the exact same topic, that is, their truth-conditional contents are identical. But they are by no means synonymous sentences. Instead, the declarative mood of the former sentence encodes, as part of its content in the language, that the illocutionary force is assertoric, whereas the interrogative mood of the latter sentence encodes that the illocutionary force is interrogatival. Crudely, the import of these illocutionary forces is that the first sentence has a 'use-theoretic' content USED TO STATE, while the second sentence has a 'use-theoretic' content USED TO ASK. Other force indicators are more specific and, rather than attaching to syntactic mood, they are carried by an explicitly performative verb, such as 'promise', 'swear' and 'pronounce'. Thus, the expressions 'I promise to – ' and 'I swear to – ' wear their use-theoretic contents on their sleeves: the first has as part of its content USED TO PROMISE while the second has as part of its content USED TO SWEAR.

In addition to linguistically constrained contributions to literal content that involve pragmatics, the Use Perspective has contributed enormously to our understanding of non-literal usages. Such features of utterance content, that are shaped more by speaker's **intentions** than by standing meaning, include conversational implicatures, speaker's **reference**, metaphorical speech, and indirect speech acts. Each of these is described elsewhere in this volume. It suffices, then, to provide a quick example of each. Saying 'I am French' to convey that one is a good cook illustrates conversational implicature: the speaker says one thing but implies another. An example of speaker's reference would be using 'Jake's mother' to speak of Jake's much older sister. This phrase does not itself designate the sister. Yet, in the right circumstances, a speaker may manage nonetheless to refer to Jake's sister with these words. Metaphorical speech is familiar to all. For instance, Dylan Thomas famously wrote about his father, 'Do not go gentle into that good night', meaning that the latter should fight to remain alive. Finally, indirect speech acts include using an interrogative, the assigned use of which is asking a **question**, to make a **request**. 'Do you have any cold beer in the fridge?' may be used, in context, not to enquire but to request politely. Use Theorists who made such contributions in this regard include Donnellan (1966), Grice (1975) and **Searle** (1975b, 1979a).

To recapitulate, I have summarized recent Anglo-American philosophy of language by presenting two (idealized) traditions: the System Perspective and the Use Perspective. I have also illustrated some of the contributions of each tradition to pragmatics, here understood as the study of utterance meaning in context. Many more examples could be presented, but the above provide sufficient background to move forward. The final section will describe a revolutionary means of combining the two perspectives.

Combining the two perspectives

Our problem amounts to this. Given that the two perspectives are complementary in numerous ways, we ought to combine them. Yet, they appear to be in deep conflict about many fundamental matters. So, unifying them seems difficult if not impossible.

Let's first revisit the obstacles to unification. The two perspectives disagree about what a language is (a collection of formal rules versus a socio-cultural practice), what a linguistic item is (an abstract type versus a concrete performance) and about what meanings are (abstract truth-relevant entities versus actions). In short, one tradition focuses on users and usage, while the other abstracts away from them. Another problem for combining the two perspectives is what I will call the 'ontological gap'. Linguistic types are abstract entities. Existing outside space and time, they cannot themselves cause utterances. And, in turn, no collection of utterances, no matter how large, in and of itself constitutes a type. On a related note, Use Theorists are wont to insist on the many diverse actions we perform with language, and on the contextually bound, creative jumble that is actual talk, whereas System Theorists highlight the pristine elegance and compositional-recursive power of languages themselves. Even setting aside their disagreements about what languages, linguistic items and meanings are, then, how can the two perspectives be combined, if there is such an enormous metaphysical gulf between their respective objects of study?

Yet, as noted, there are many reasons to hope for a unification of the two perspectives. In particular, each covers the other's omissions. In terms of content, both truth-theoretic meaning and use-theoretic meaning (e.g. conventional implicatures and illocutionary force) are necessary for a complete account of natural language. Similarly, non-literal content is important, but so is literal content: it's essential to keep in mind the enormous part that standing meaning, i.e. the meaning of the type, plays in fixing utterance content. And in terms of philosophical orientation, it seems that language is productive and rich in both senses canvassed in the last paragraph: context-invariant generative capacity *and* creative usage in context.

In short, while it seems hard to unify the two perspectives, there are strong reasons for doing so. The solution I would like to draw attention to is inspired by the work of the linguist-philosophers Chomsky (1986), Fodor (1983), and especially Sperber and Wilson (1995). They reject a common commitment of both traditional perspectives, namely, that psychology is irrelevant to the philosophy of language. Yes, language is a system of symbols but, crucially, it is a system which we humans *know*. And it is precisely because knowledge of linguistic rules is stored in the mind/brain that it can give rise to use.

The first advantage of this approach is that it bridges the ontological gap. Abstract entities may not cause utterances, but mental states can. And, while no collection of utterances can give rise to types, mental processes can extract type meaning from a collection of tokens. So, knowledge of the system bridges the gulf between linguistic types and tokens. In a similar vein, we can admit both kinds of creativity (i.e. within the language itself and in usage) by distinguishing, as Chomsky does, between **competence** and performance. The former consists in the rules known. Importantly, however, linguistic competence is only one of the causes of performance: our performance (i.e. actual speech) is an interaction effect of such knowledge with much else besides. That's why we get gloriously near-anarchic speech from such highly structured linguistic rules.

Recognizing that we know the system also makes it easy to accommodate all the varieties of content discussed above. With respect to literal content of utterances, our knowledge of language includes (a), (b) and (c):

(a) Knowledge of the truth-relevant content of context insensitive minimal elements;
(b) Knowledge of the character of context sensitive minimal elements;
(c) Knowledge of the non-truth-conditional content of minimal elements.

(In addition, to account for the productivity of speech, note that we also know the recursive syntactic rules for putting the minimal elements together, and the semantic rules for computing the meaning of a complex expression on the basis of its syntax and the truth-theoretic and use-theoretic content of its parts.) With respect to non-literal content, we also know many non-linguistic facts which allow us to interpret speech in ways that knowledge of language alone would not permit. We know general facts about the world and about people, and we know specific facts about the speech situation. Finally, we are able to combine such knowledge with the information that language proper affords. It is this diversity of mental capacities that allows us to go from the literal content of the utterance in context, as afforded by highly constrained linguistic rules, to non-literal contents.

I would summarize the proposed unification with a slogan: 'Language is by equal measures a system of symbols which we know and use'. That is, it is fundamentally and essentially all three. This merges the two traditional philosophical perspectives. It thereby allows their independent contributions to come together, yielding a still deeper and richer contribution of recent Anglo-American philosophy of language to the study of utterance content in context.

ROBERT J. STAINTON

See also: Assertion; Austin, J.L.; Bar-Hillel, Y.; competence, linguistic; competence, pragmatic; context; cooperative principle; demonstratives; explicit/implicit distinction; formal pragmatics; Grice, H.P.; implicature; indexicals; intention; logical form; maxims of conversation; metaphor; modular pragmatics; modularity of mind thesis; neo-Gricean pragmatics; ordinary language philosophy; philosophy of mind; primary pragmatic processes; proposition; propositional attitudes; question; radical pragmatics; reasoning; reference; relevance theory; scalar implicature; Searle, J.; semantic minimalism; semantics-pragmatics interface; speech act theory; utterance interpretation; Wittgenstein, L.

Suggestions for further reading

Carston, R. (2002) *Thoughts and Utterances: The Pragmatics of Explicit Communication*, Oxford: Blackwell.

Lycan, W.G. (2000) *Philosophy of Language: A Contemporary Introduction*, London: Routledge.

Stainton, R.J. (1996) *Philosophical Perspectives on Language*, Peterborough, ON: Broadview.

Philosophy of Mind

Debates within philosophy of mind often begin by examining the relationship between minds and bodies. Since minds and bodies seem so different, it is natural to see them as different sorts of substances. This view, called mind–body dualism, has been so associated with René

Descartes (1641, 1649) that it is often called 'Cartesian dualism'. These Cartesian dualists cannot see how a merely physical thing could, inter alia, think, talk, exhibit consciousness, exhibit **rationality**, or see itself and others as having minds. Hence, something distinct must serve as the seat of these mental features – a mental substance. Although initially appealing, this view has two major drawbacks. First, it fails to explain how mental substances are any more capable of having these features than physical substances – it simply asserts that the former substance has them. Second, dualists portray mental features as being so distinct from physical features that an obvious fact – that the mind and body interact – becomes deeply mysterious. Dualists must either deny mind–body interaction or generate some suitable explanation as to how such radically distinct things can interact with one another. Each of these options has sustained critiques so severe that many have been led to adopt some form of monism – either everything is mental (idealism) or the more widely held view that everything is physical or material (physicalism or materialism).

In the wake of Chomsky's (1959) attack on behaviourism, two major materialist theories about the nature of mental states have emerged: the (psychophysical) identity theory and functionalism. The identity theory identifies mental states with states of the human central nervous system (Place 1956; Smart 1959). Just as scientists have established such identities as 'water = H$_2$O' and 'lightning = electrical discharge', it is hoped that scientists could generate identities between a mental category and a neurological category, as in the oft-used example of 'pain = c-fibre firing'. Functionalists, however, criticized this theory for being too restrictive and chauvinistic (Putnam 1967). Inspired by the idea that thought is quite like computation, and noting that computing devices can be constructed out of a number of different physical materials, yet still execute the same function, program, or algorithm, philosophers thought that thinking and feeling could also take place in a number of different materials. Putnam argued that whether some entity counts as a mental state is not determined by what it is made out of, but rather by what it does, i.e. its functional role in the mind. For example, anything that performs the

same function as pain – being caused by tissue damage, causing further mental states, leading to overt behaviour, etc. – counts as being a pain. Since creatures like the octopus, with nervous systems very different from that of a human, have parts that play functionally isomorphic roles to pain in humans (not to mention robots or Martians!), pain cannot be identified as c-fibre firing. Since pain and other mental states are, in Putnam's words, 'multiply realizable' in different sorts of things, mental states should be identified by their functional role and not by what they are made out of.

Despite being the most widely held theory about the nature of mental states (for varieties *see* Block 1980a, 1980b), functionalism has been criticized for being too liberal in its articulation of mentality. Block (1978) argues that there is no way for a functionalist to identify the functional roles of mental states in such a way that avoids having complex systems that lack a mind (e.g. groups of organisms, economic systems) count as functionally isomorphic to minds – and hence, counting as genuine minds – without adding the sort of chauvinistic constraints functionalism sought to avoid. Trying to require a certain sort of sensory input or behavioural output in order to be a mind – the sort of thing that an economic system would lack – will end up excluding bizarre creatures that functionalists might want to count as having a mind. Block insists that what these complex systems lack, and what functionalism fails to capture, is the qualitative nature of consciousness.

Philosophy of mind struggles with identifying mentality with any of these physical or functional states because it seems as though these states fail to capture 'qualia' – the elusive phenomenological 'what it's like' to be in pain or see red. Dualists argue that even if we achieved a complete account of the neural correlates of conscious experience in humans, we are still left with a set of mysteries, namely what Chalmers (1996) calls 'the hard problem' of consciousness: Why does this neurological activity go on with *any* qualitative character? And why is there not some *different* phenomenological feeling to brain activity like this? Hence, despite its drawbacks, dualism still lives as a live alternative to materialist accounts of cognition, and the debate over consciousness continues (*see* Block *et al.* 1995).

Another area of focus in philosophy of mind concerns the **propositional attitudes**. Despite the intuitive claim that these are real entities that are the causes of other mental states and behaviour (Fodor 1987), and despite the fact that many accounts of **theory of mind** invoke these states to explain, predict, and understand the behaviour of ourselves and others, the very existence and explanatory utility of these attitudes has been called into question. Some believe that we do not need to assume that they are real entities in order to exploit their utility (as mere explanatory fictions) in understanding and predicting behaviour (Dennett 1987). Others criticize these states as ancient relics of an untenable theory about how the mind works (Churchland 1981) which should be eliminated altogether from our discourse about the mind. If the field of **pragmatics** essentially involves these attitudes, it may be vulnerable to these concerns.

Many debates within philosophy of mind are intertwined with debates in **philosophy of language**. Both fields are interested in **intentionality**, **meaning**, and **reference** – how it is that certain things can represent, refer to, or be about other things – and explore the complex relationships between the meaningfulness of thought and the meaningfulness of language. In addition to worries about how material things can give rise to consciousness or meaningfulness, philosophy of mind also explores the extent to which material things can give rise to **rationality** and **reasoning**, and the structure of minds and concepts, including claims about the **modularity of mind thesis**.

J. ROBERT THOMPSON

See also: Artificial intelligence; cognitive science; intentionality; meaning; modularity of mind thesis; philosophy of language; pragmatics; propositional attitudes; rationality; reasoning; reference; semantic externalism/internalism; semantics-pragmatics interface; theory of mind

Suggestions for further reading

Block, N., Flannagan, O. and Guzeldre, G. (eds) (1995) *Consciousness*, Cambridge, MA: MIT Press.
Chalmers, D. (2005) *Philosophy of Mind: Contemporary Readings*, Oxford: Oxford University Press.
Ravenscroft, I. (2005) *Philosophy of Mind: A Beginner's Guide*, Oxford: Oxford University Press.

Police–Suspect Interviews

Police interviews with suspects are a unique form of **institutional discourse** with a highly significant social function. Yet, they have been the subject of surprisingly little attention from a specifically pragmatic perspective. Nevertheless, several pragmatic concepts are of relevance and interest in this context.

The **power** dynamics of the police-suspect interview have been an area of particular research interest (Harris 1984, 1989, 1995; Haworth 2006; Heydon 2003, 2005; Newbury and Johnson 2006; Thornborrow 2002; *see also* Shuy 1998: 174–85). This has largely focused on the asymmetric power dynamic created by the discursive roles of questioner and responder allocated to participants. Yet, it has also revealed that, despite the inherent institutional power of the police interviewer, the discursive dynamics are not completely one-sided, especially since the institutional purpose of the interview is to obtain information (and indeed evidence) from the mouth of the interviewee. Special attention has been paid to the **question** types utilized by interviewers and their pragmatic function (Harris 1984; Haworth 2006; Newbury and Johnson 2006; *see also* Johnson (2002) on the pragmatic implications of 'so'-prefaced questions), and to discursive strategies of resistance utilized by interviewees (Harris 1989; Haworth 2006; Newbury and Johnson 2006). However, given the institutional purpose of the interview such resistance may be discursively successful but ultimately damaging to the interviewee's legal position (Haworth 2006), and overall the literature demonstrates that power and control ultimately always remain with the interviewer.

In a study of a different manifestation of power relations in the police–suspect interview, Ainsworth (1993) analyzes the invocation of suspects' rights during US police interrogations as performative speech acts. Focusing on the right to consult a lawyer, Ainsworth (1993: 262)

highlights that legal doctrine requires 'direct and unqualified assertions' of these rights in order for them to have legal effect. As a result of strict principles of interpretation applied by the courts, which run entirely counter to pragmatic models of **communication**, Ainsworth demonstrates that the use of ambiguous language, **implicature**, or even **hedges** can be sufficient to deprive interviewees of basic legal rights, despite the clear intended (if not literal) **meaning** of their utterance.

Shuy (1998) also uses pragmatic concepts to reveal injustices in US police interrogations. He considers in some depth the **speech act** of confession. Shuy (1998: 9) observes that 'most confessions are not made up of relatively clear and unambiguous performatives … Instead, confessions are often pieced together by means of an interrogation by law enforcement officers' and are thus 'dialogically constructed'. He provides a number of case studies in which he was involved as a linguistic expert, and where this process of dialogic construction led to flawed confession statements.

In the UK, police–suspect interviews have a significant dual function, being both investigative and evidential. In addition to their original interview-room setting as part of the initial police investigation, interview data are subsequently transcribed and presented as evidence to judge and jury in court. This future evidential function of the interaction and its consequent recontextualization in the courtroom have several important interactional consequences.

First, this means that interviewers' turns often have the function of eliciting, indeed creating, specific pieces of evidence in the form of interviewees' responses. This is especially important in establishing the *mens rea*, or 'mental' element of an offence, such as **intention** or **knowledge**. This needs to be established explicitly and unambiguously in order to be legally robust. The result is communicatively superfluous **requests** for explicit accounts of an interviewee's state of mind even when this is already apparent by implication (referred to by Stokoe and Edwards (2008) as 'silly questions').

Second, the evidential requirement for explicitness leads to difficulties with context-dependent language such as **deixis**, which is used in the interview room but is then recontextualized into

the courtroom, whereby its intended point of **reference** becomes lost (Haworth, to appear). The use by interviewees of context-dependent and under-determined language often leads to repairs from interviewers, who are more oriented to the future **context** and function of the utterances. But it is also still used by interviewers, indicating the difficulty of maintaining the needs of multiple contexts and audiences for utterances simultaneously (Haworth, to appear).

A further important concept in the UK police-suspect interview context is the inferential meaning of **silence**. Despite the so-called 'right of silence', section 34 of the Criminal Justice and Public Order Act 1994 states that if, on being questioned, a suspect fails to mention a 'fact', and this fact is later relied upon as part of their defence, the court is entitled to 'draw inferences' as to why they did not mention this sooner. The nature of these **inferences** is not specified, but the clear implication is that silence, or rather the absence of a (legally) effective response to a police question, can be taken as a sign of guilt. This arguably gives legal effect to the usual inferential meaning accorded to the absence of an explanation or denial in the face of an accusation. Yet, prior to the introduction of this provision, such inferences were not legally permitted to be drawn.

However, despite legal references to the 'right of silence', in interviews where that right is asserted, there is generally very little actual silence. Most interviewees still conform to the expected interview format by supplying some form of verbal answer, often in the form of the formulaic 'no comment'. This can be seen as the interviewee still being cooperative to some extent, in that it provides at least some response to the question and functions as a formal invocation of the interviewee's rights.

As a final general point, it should be borne in mind that the institutional function of police-suspect interviews and the procedures involved can vary considerably between different legal jurisdictions. The goal orientation of the interview will therefore be slightly different (e.g. the preparation of a written monologic summary in Holland (Komter 2002) compared to the direct creation of verbal evidence in the UK). This will have inevitable interactional consequences. Further, police-suspect interviews have a different institutional goal to the police-witness interview. This is an important functional distinction which is often overlooked.

KATE HOWARTH

See also: Ambiguity; context; deixis; explicit/ implicit distinction; implicature; inference; institutional and professional discourse; legal pragmatics; performative pragmatics; performativity; power; question; silence; speech act theory; speech act type

Suggestions for further reading

Cotterill, J. (ed.) (2002) *Language in the Legal Process*, Basingstoke: Palgrave.

Heydon, G. (2005) *The Language of Police Interviewing: A Critical Analysis*, Basingstoke: Palgrave.

Politeness

For many linguists it is Robin Lakoff's article on the logic of politeness, written over three decades ago in 1973, which marks the beginning of what is now a burgeoning research field into linguistic politeness. During the decades since the publication of Lakoff's article, politeness research has developed as a multidisciplinary, multifaceted and challenging area of study both theoretically and methodologically, with much of its most fruitful work emerging within the fields of **pragmatics** and **sociolinguistics**. This is evident in Christie's introductory editorial in the first issue of the *Journal of Politeness Research*, in which she states: 'the journal offers a focused outlet for work on politeness that cuts across disciplines, languages, cultures and contexts, and our aim is to bring together key theoretical debates as well as the findings of empirical studies' (2005: 6). Politeness is also a topic of wide interest and appeal, not only to academic researchers and teachers but also to ordinary people. To see this is the case, one has only to note the number of entries under 'politeness' on the internet, along with the variety of definitions, approaches, concerns (and misconceptions) displayed there, in addition to the numerous references to 'politeness' (or, more often, the lack of it) in the media as well as the occasional political campaign encouraging 'respect' and 'courtesy'.

While there is no canonical definition of politeness, most research-based definitions include an element of appropriate social and interactive behaviour, consideration and concern for the feelings of other people and some reference to 'face'. Relatively few researchers give precise definitions of politeness. Holmes and Stubbe (2003b: 5) define it, very generally but succinctly, as showing 'mutual respect and concern for the feelings or face needs of others'. Those who do attempt more precise definitions usually present politeness as a multifaceted and complex phenomenon. Locher (2004: 91), for example, provides two definitions, one which relates to speaker politeness and one which relates to the hearer, both calling for 'a qualitative approach to data that takes the dynamics of interaction into account'. But undoubtedly the most often cited definition of politeness is still Brown and Levinson's, whose work on 'some universals in language usage' has been immensely influential for more than two decades and is only fairly recently being seriously challenged both theoretically and methodologically. Drawing on the work of both Goffman (1967b, 1971) and **Grice** (1975), Brown and Levinson (1987) construct their theory of 'universal politeness' around the concept of 'face', which they define as 'that public self-image that every member wants to claim for himself' (1987: 61). Brown and Levinson consider face to be universal, as well as the consequent face threatening acts (FTAs) which occur in many, if not most, interactions despite linguistic and cultural differences. Their assumption is that 'in the context of the mutual vulnerability of face', rational agents will seek to avoid face-threatening acts by employing 'certain strategies to minimize the threat' (1987: 68). It is the detailed elucidation of these strategies which is the primary concern of Brown and Levinson's work. These strategies are oriented mainly either towards positive politeness (the positive 'face' of the hearer, i.e. 'the positive self-image he claims for himself' (*sic*)) or negative politeness (partially satisfying or redressing the hearer's negative face, i.e. 'his [*sic*] basic want to maintain claims of territory and self-determination') (1987: 70).

Brown and Levinson's face-oriented model of politeness has generated a huge amount of research, much of it critical. While it is arguable that Brown and Levinson have for too long dominated the field of politeness research, the strength of their model, and probably one of the reasons for its dominance for such a lengthy period, is 'its coherence, level of detail and testability, supported by cross-cultural empirical evidence' (Harris 2007: 128). In fact, the vast amount of criticism directed at Brown and Levinson, and the application of their model to a variety of languages, cultures and situations, has proved extremely insightful and productive in creating a large literature on a wide range of issues (negative versus positive politeness, individualism versus collectivism, deference versus volition, universalism versus cultural relativity) as well as in raising some searching questions which recent theories have begun to address. Of particular interest has been criticism from speakers of Asian languages, who have queried the 'universality' of Brown and Levinson's model (Matsumoto 1988, 1989; Ide 1989; Gu 1990; Mao 1994 and others). Chinese, Japanese and Korean scholars in particular have mainly questioned whether Brown and Levinson's model is applicable to 'collective' societies, and such criticisms have centred on deference, especially as evidenced in the use of **honorifics**. Ide (1989) and Matsumoto (1988, 1989) have challenged the capacity of Brown and Levinson's model to explain discernment in more hierarchic societies where the group appears to predominate over the individual. However, as Byon (2006) maintains, recently there are also more positive responses from scholars of Asian languages to Brown and Levinson's work. For example, Fukada and Asato (2004) and Pizziconi (2003) claim that the use of honorifics in Japanese is more subject to individual volition and the dynamics of particular interactions than was previously thought. Thus, Brown and Levinson's model has perhaps been most fruitful in eliciting further research and controversy from those who have challenged its validity and applicability. Negative and positive politeness strategies, and particularly the issue of their mutual exclusiveness, have also come in for some sharp but productive criticism (*see* Harris 2001a, 2003).

However, more recently there have been important developments which go beyond the critical application of Brown and Levinson's model and present a challenge to the basic premises of the paradigm itself. Beginning perhaps with Eelen (2001), a number of researchers have taken a more radical approach to politeness which Watts (2005: xix) has defined as:

a shift in emphasis away from the attempt to construct a model of politeness which can be used to predict when polite behaviour can be expected or to explain postfactum why it has been produced and towards the need to pay closer attention to how participants in social interaction perceive politeness.

Such a shift, most often characterized as the postmodern approach (Terkourafi 2005) or the discursive approach (Haugh 2007b), has had a number of consequences. As Watts suggests above, one of these is the contention that politeness is most fruitfully analyzed not as a normative system of prescripts which are predictive but rather as a social practice which is both dynamic and interactive. According to the latter view, politeness is enacted through a **discourse** where neither **power** nor politeness is a 'given' but must be contested through a discourse which often becomes a site of 'struggle' or 'dispute'.

A further consequence of this shift of emphasis is that postmodern approaches to politeness theory tend to favour a hearer-oriented model of politeness rather than the speaker-oriented model of Brown and Levinson and many of the researchers who have been significantly influenced by their work. For a postmodernist, the **intentions** of the speaker count for less (and are also less accessible) than the evaluation of what has been said by the hearer. This has several further consequences in that recent politeness theorists (Eelen 2001; Mills 2003; Watts 2003; Locher 2004) tend also to emphasize both the crucial importance of the situated evaluation of what is considered polite and, methodologically, the desirability of research which makes use of natural language data, primarily in the form of longer stretches of recorded discourse in situated contexts.

Equally significant is the recent contention that seeing politeness as a contested concept established through situated discourse rather than as a set of strategic choices which serve to mitigate possible face threats to individuals has resulted in the increasing attention paid to the question of impoliteness by current (im)politeness theorists (Culpeper 1996, 2005; Culpeper *et al.* 2003; Harris 2001a; Cashman 2006). Studied much less frequently in the past than politeness, impoliteness cannot now be regarded merely as the polar opposite (or the absence) of politeness. For Brown and Levinson, who wrote relatively little on the topic, impoliteness constituted mainly an attack on face and was often associated with particular syntactic and/or lexical forms. However, in a hearer-oriented model Mills (2003: 122), writing insightfully about politeness and **gender**, argues rather that 'impoliteness has to be seen as an assessment of someone's behaviour rather than a quality intrinsic to an utterance'. Moreover, what is polite or impolite can be significantly dependent on differences in such contextual features as culture, class, gender and age. The social and cultural expectations of the participants in any interactive situation play a crucial role, and even such forms which are conventionally associated with politeness, such as 'please' and 'thank you', may be interpreted differently in different contexts and can be manifestly impolite when used in certain circumstances with a particular intonation.

Terkourafi (2005: 242) presents a perceptive and interesting critique of recent politeness theories, and especially of the dangers of placing politeness research firmly within social theory, where 'accounting for aspects of politeness as a social phenomenon takes priority over accounting for its pragmatic aspects'. She raises some particularly pertinent questions with regard to the postmodernists' argument for the ultimate abandonment of norms and their consequent declaration of the impossibility of a predictive theory of (im)politeness (Watts 2003: 25; Eelen 2001: 249). Going further, Terkourafi (2005: 245–46) also suggests that methodologically, the postmodernists have offered relatively little that is new and that:

the descriptive tools used are those of the traditional theories, namely, conversation-

analytic terms (Mills 2003, Watts 2003), and face-related terms (Watts 2003). ... Thus, although advancing a very interesting and challenging critique, postmodern theories would, at least in the way they deal with the data, seem unable to bring the paradigm change within politeness studies to which they aspire.

A recent approach which Terkourafi (2005) doesn't consider is that taken by Spencer-Oatey (2000, 2002, 2005), which focuses on the relationship between (im)politeness and rapport, drawing primarily on social pragmatics, politeness theory and face. Spencer-Oatey's work is more clearly within pragmatics, and although she too has been influenced by the work of Brown and Levinson, she widens their concept of face to the management of social relations more generally and uses the term 'rapport' instead of politeness. Spencer-Oatey has a long-standing interest in **intercultural communication,** and her experience underpins the model she puts forward. This model elaborates 'the bases of rapport' as involving three separate components: interactional goals; face sensitivities; and sociality rights and obligations. Taking both a social pragmatic and a cognitive pragmatic perspective, her work attempts to provide what might be considered a possible (and promising) alternative way forward to postmodernism by focusing on the interrelationship between politeness, **communication** and culture. Spencer-Oatey (2005: 117) says that further case studies are now necessary in order to:

determine the extent to which the rapport management issues that occur in authentic interactions can be explained with reference to these elements [those previously quoted], and whether they are adequate for analysing the similarities and differences that occur across cultures, contexts and individuals.

A further alternative to postmodernism is Christie's (2007) interesting attempt to devise a model of politeness which provides a link between the social and the pragmatic by means of **relevance theory**.

A final welcome development in the inter-relationship between politeness and pragmatics is the fairly recent extension of politeness research beyond the scope of interactive encounters between individuals to a consideration of the different discourse types associated with certain professional and institutional contexts. Such an extension was initially proposed by Robin Lakoff in her 1989 article. As Lakoff suggests, examining such contexts may well force us to see (im)politeness from different perspectives, which tend to foreground different features. Such examination will enable us to revisit in new ways the notion of the existence of (im)-politeness 'norms' from institutional and/or professional points of view. Work within a number of such contexts has begun, including medical contexts (Arronsson and Rundstrom 1989; Speirs 1998; Mullany, 2009), political contexts (Harris 2001a; Perez de Ayala 2001; Blas-Arroyo 2003), legal contexts (Penman 1990; Trinch 2001) and business and work contexts (Bargiela-Chiappini and Harris 2006). In terms of the latter context, the pioneering research of Janet Holmes *et al.* (Holmes and Stubbe 2003b; Holmes and Schnurr 2005), in conjunction with the *Wellington Language in the Workplace Project*, has proved especially relevant. It has widened the scope of (and interest in) (im)politeness studies in a particular direction, as well as providing substantial amounts of data on the nature of politeness in a variety of work contexts. As Harris (2003) argues, work and professional contexts differ significantly in the ways that interactant relationships are manifested and negotiated. (Im)politeness theory provides us with one means of both elucidating and explaining such differences.

SANDRA HARRIS

See also: Business discourse; cognitive pragmatics; communication; complaints; compliments; context; conversation analysis; cross-cultural pragmatics; disagreement; discourse; gender; Grice, H.P.; honorific language; humour; institutional and professional discourse; intention; intercultural communication; mitigation; political discourse; power; pragmatics; relevance theory; societal pragmatics; sociolinguistics; speech act type

Suggestions for further reading

Arundale, R.B. (2006) 'Face as relational and interactional: a communication framework for research on face, facework, and politeness', *Journal of Politeness Research*, 2: 193–216.
Lakoff, R. and Ide, S. (2005) *Broadening the Horizon of Linguistic Politeness*, Amsterdam: John Benjamins.

Political Discourse

The philosophical approaches of Aristotle and Machiavelli can be regarded as the two main roots for the meanings of *politics* used in the field of 'language and politics' (*see* Holly 1990; Chilton 2004; Wodak and de Cillia 2006; Reisigl 2008). These approaches emphasize ethics and morals, on the one hand, and violence and hegemony, on the other. The Aristotelian goal to discover the best form of government is thus linked to definitions of ethics and morals, i.e. values for a given society, what is believed to be 'good' or 'bad'. The definition of values always depends on the historical context and the political system: what might have been 'good' for a totalitarian state like Nazi Germany was certainly experienced as 'bad' for democratic systems. The second ideological position endorses 'the dark view of political power'. All politics is necessarily driven by a quest for power, but power is inherently unpredictable, irresponsible, irrational, and pervasive. This view has been articulated most prominently by Michel Foucault (Foucault 1972a; Wodak 2005), but traces and roots can be detected in many authors from Niccolò Machiavelli (Zorn 1972) to Antonio Gramsci (1977).

Research in the field of language and politics has expanded enormously in recent years. The field is huge and covers research on the language and **discourse** of specific politicians, the many ways politics is discussed and reported in the media, and patterns of **communication** in political organizations (see later). Moreover, macro-topics such as language politics and language change related to political change are also part of this field (Blommaert and Verschueren 1999; de Cillia *et al.* 2001, 2003; Gruber and Menz 2004; Panagl and Wodak 2004; Spolsky 2004; Wright 2004; Blommaert 2005; Shohamy 2006).

Rhetoric is one of the oldest academic disciplines and was already concerned with aspects of political communication in ancient times (*see* Holly 1990: 6ff.). After World War II, Harold Lasswell and Nathan Leites (1965) published one of the most important studies on quantitative **semantics** in the field of language and politics, developing approaches from communication and mass media research. The famous economist Friedrich von Hayek (1967) discussed the impact of language on politics during his stay at the London School of Economics. Simultaneously, research started in Central Europe, mainly in Germany, in the late 1940s. Moreover, the novel *1984* by George Orwell was a significant point of departure for the development of the entire field (*see* Chilton 2006). Of course, all this research was influenced by the massive use of propaganda in World War II and in the emerging Cold War in the 1950s.

'Political linguistics' (*Politolinguistik*) was the first attempt to create a new academic discipline for the research of political discourse (*see* Wodak and de Cillia 2006, for an extensive overview). Klein (1997) argued that the 'linguistic study of political communication' should be defined as a sub-discipline of linguistics. He cited the critical linguistic research that started in the wake of National Socialism and was conducted primarily by Victor Klemperer (1975; 2005) and Rolf Sternberger *et al.* (1957) as paving the way for the new discipline (Schmitz-Berning 2000). Both Klemperer and Sternberger sampled, categorized and described the words used during the Nazi regime. Many words had acquired new meanings, other words were forbidden (loanwords from other languages, like *cigarette*), and neologisms (new words) were created. Similar language policies were adopted by communist totalitarian regimes (Wodak and Kirsch 1995). Controlling language in this way implies the attempt to control the (minds and thoughts of) people. Because these first studies provoked criticism for being inadequate from the perspective of linguistic theory, a new methodological approach, *Politolinguistik*, emerged in the late 1960s. It drew on various linguistic sub-disciplines (**pragmatics**, text linguistics, media research).

Burkhardt (1996: 5) proposed the use of 'political language' as the generic term comprising 'all types of public, institutional and private talks on political issues, all types of texts typical of politics as well as the use of lexical and stylistic linguistic instruments characterizing talks about political contexts'. From 1990 onwards, research on political discourse expanded while drawing on sociological approaches (Goffman 1959; Edelman 1977) and sociolinguistic research, for example, on the functions of pronouns like 'we', 'us', 'them', and so forth (Wilson 1990). Research into communication in political organizations (European Union: Muntigl *et al.* 2000; Mokre *et al.* 2003; Wodak and Weiss 2007), on parliamentary debates (Holly 1990; Ilie 2006; Bayley 2004; Wodak and van Dijk 2000), on the unique (charismatic) style of politicians (Fairclough 2000), on political speeches (commemorative speeches: Ensink and Sauer 2003; Martin and Wodak 2003; Wodak and de Cillia 2007; Reisigl 2008), on right-wing political rhetoric (Wodak and Pelinka 2002; Rydgren 2005), on strategies of manipulation and persuasion (van Dijk 2006; Chouliaraki 2007), and on interviews of politicians in the media (Clayman and Heritage 2002; Machin and Niblock 2006; Talbot 2007) have become mainstream in discourse studies. Nowadays, many refereed journals publish research from this area (e.g. *Discourse and Society*; *Journal of Language and Politics*; *Critical Discourse Studies*; *Discourse and Communication*; *TEXT and TALK*).

Chilton (2004: 201–5) lists twelve propositions which could serve as a possible framework for the field of language and politics (I only list the most important ones in the following). (1) *Political discourse operates indexically.* This implies that one's choice of language (a politician's choice or a layperson's choice) will always signal, explicitly or implicitly, some political distinction (the choice of a specific accent or lexical items, or the choice of address forms, etc.). (2) *Political discourse operates as interaction.* For example, features such as interruptions or overlaps might indicate hierarchy or rank. Moreover, interactions of any kind (dialogues, negotiations or debates) serve to find common representations of the world, to mark agreements or **disagreements**. (3) *Modal properties of language subserve political interaction.* Many claims put forward by politicians stay vague. Others are claims for truth, confidence, trust, credibility or even legitimization (of actions or positions). Hence, in English, the use of 'can', 'must', 'should', 'could', etc. implies such agenda. (4) *Binary conceptualizations are frequent in political discourse.* Most politicians attempt to present themselves in positive ways and their political opponents in negative ways (van Dijk 1984; Reisigl and Wodak 2001). The discursive construction of 'us' and 'them' in all politically used textual genres necessarily lies at the core of persuasive rhetoric. Binary concepts are also used in attributing a range of characteristics to 'us' and 'them' which emphasize positive or negative connotations. (5) *Political discourse involves metaphorical reasoning.* **Metaphors** serve as arguments (*Topoi*), for example, in legitimizing restrictions on migrants who are often depicted as 'floods' or 'waves', and so forth (Kienpointner 1992). Other spatial metaphors (the 'path schema') are regularly used in indicating actions or positions which a political group endorses ('being at crossroads', 'boarding the train', 'choosing directions', etc.) (Musloff 2004).

Chilton's framework is related to Burkhardt's (1996) dimensions of concrete textual analysis (from word to text and image; *see also* Wodak and de Cillia 2006; Wodak 2008, 2009). For example, modality can be analyzed through lexical or visual analysis. Binarity involves lexical choices, rhetorical structures, the analysis of pronouns, arguments, and address forms; and so forth. A further important premise inherent in political communication relates to the dimension of persuasion. Political language and discourse inherently serve to convince hearers/viewers/listeners of a specific ideological position, of actions to be implemented or of a programme which needs to be endorsed. Hence, all genres in the field of politics necessarily involve persuasive elements which enhance the position and opinion of the text producer in a televised interview, in a parliamentary debate or in a speech at a specific occasion.

RUTH WODAK

See also: Ambiguity; anaphora, pragmatics of; argumentation theory; Austin, J.L.; communication; competence, communicative; context; corpus linguistics; deixis; discourse; discourse analysis; discourse coherence; discourse cohesion; discourse markers; discourse particles; ellipsis; Habermas, J.; implicature; intentionality; meaning; media discourse; metaphor; politeness; power; presupposition; question; quotation; rhetoric; rhetorical questions; vagueness

Suggestions for further reading

Chilton, P. (2004) *Analysing Political Discourse: Theory and Practice*, London: Routledge.
Martin, J.R. and Wodak, R. (eds) (2003) *Re-Reading the Past: Critical and Functional Perspectives on Time and Value*, Amsterdam: John Benjamins.
Reisigl, M. and Wodak, R. (2001) *Discourse and Discrimination*, London: Routledge.

Post-Gricean Pragmatics

Paul **Grice** is generally regarded as the founding figure of the tradition in which utterance meaning is analyzed in terms of speaker's **intentions**. As Grice (1957: 219) put it in his seminal paper 'Meaning', "'A meant$_{NN}$ something by x' is roughly equivalent to "A uttered x with the intention of inducing a belief by means of the recognition of this intention"', where meaning$_{NN}$ stands for non-natural meaning, or what is communicated (**what is said** plus **implicatures**), as distinguished from **natural meaning** where meaning that p entails that it is the fact that p. In other words, the speaker means something by uttering x when he or she intends the addressee to produce a response, recognizing that this production of a response is what the speaker intends (*see also* Grice 1969). The view is further supported by Grice's account of rational communicative behaviour. This is spelled out in Grice's **cooperative principle** and **maxims of conversation** (Grice 1975) which capture the predictability of speaker's meaning, some aspects of which are context-free and some context-bound.

Post-Gricean research develops these two aspects of the theory of linguistic communication. It revises Grice's set of maxims in order to reduce redundancy and overlap and aims at a more cognitively adequate generalization. These revisions adopt various degrees of reductionism. **Neo-Gricean pragmatics** remains close to the spirit of Grice's original maxims which were reanalyzed as (i) Horn's (1984, 1988, 2007a) maximization of information content (Q principle) and minimization of form (R principle) and (ii) its less reductionist variant in Levinson's (1987a, 1995, 2000) three heuristics: the Q principle (as above), aided by the minimization of content ('Say as little as necessary', I principle) and minimization of form ('Do not use a prolix, obscure or marked expression without reason', M principle). At the other end of the spectrum, **relevance theory** replaces the maxims with one principle defined separately for **communication** ('Every act of ostensive communication communicates a presumption of its optimal relevance') and for cognition ('Human cognition tends to be geared to the maximisation of relevance'; Sperber and Wilson 1995: 260). In spite of the differences in the number of principles, these post-Gricean endeavours are surprisingly similar in adhering to the overarching idea of the trade-off between informativeness and economy (expending the least effort). The principle of relevance is also spelled out in terms of a balance between two such driving forces: the processing effort and the cognitive effect in **conversation**, understood as minimizing the cost and at the same maximizing the information content.

Subsuming the generalizations under one principle is useful for discussing cognition and the psychology of utterance processing. On the other hand, detailed spelling out of interlocutors' rational behaviour in neo-Gricean pragmatics benefits attempts at formalization such as **optimality-theory pragmatics** (*see* Blutner and Zeevat 2004b). It also aids applications to the study of semantic change, as for example in Traugott's principles of **historical pragmatics**, which are founded on neo-Gricean heuristics (Traugott and Dasher 2002; Traugott 2004). The main difference between neo-Griceans and relevance theory lies perhaps in 'whose meaning' they model: while the neo-Griceans follow the original perspective and consider utterance meaning, including implicature, to be speaker's intended meaning, relevance theorists discuss intentional communication from the perspective of the addressee's reconstruction of speaker's assumptions (*see also* Saul 2002b).

One of the main research topics in post-Gricean pragmatics concerns the influence of pragmatic meanings, be they inferred or automatically bestowed, on truth-conditional content. Following Grice's (1978) principle of Modified Occam's Razor which says that senses are not to be multiplied beyond necessity, and since the so-called Atlas-Kempson thesis of semantic underdetermination in the 1970s (*see* Jaszczolt, to appear a), many post-Griceans have subscribed to the view that **syntax** renders a semantically underdetermined **representation** of **meaning** which is further enriched, embellished, modulated, etc. by the output of pragmatic processing. What is said (Recanati 1989, 2004b) and the relevance-theoretic notion of explicature (Carston 1988, 1998a, 2001, 2002) exemplify such a pragmatics-rich unit that corresponds to the development of the **logical form** of the uttered sentence, even though their proponents offer different principles for its delimitation (availability principle and functional independence, respectively) and uphold different hypotheses concerning the psychology of utterance processing that allows addressees to arrive at such a unit (*see* Jaszczolt 2006; Carston 2007; Recanati 2007). The most radical form of this semantics-pragmatics mix is called **Contextualism**. It considers such enrichment (or, more generally, modulation of the output of syntax) to be always present. In Recanati's (2005: 179–80) words, '[c]ontextualism ascribes to modulation a form of necessity which makes it ineliminable. Without contextual modulation, no proposition could be expressed.'

In a recent strand of post-Gricean research called Default Semantics, the question of the delimitation of what is said is revised more fundamentally. What is said is assumed to be the main, primary, or most salient meaning but its relation to the logical form of the sentence is less restrictive than on the previous accounts. We know from experimental evidence that in the majority of cases speakers communicate their main message (primary meaning) through implicit content (Nicolle and Clark 1999; Pitts 2005; Sysoeva and Jaszczolt 2007). A fortiori, the unit of meaning which relies on the development of the logical form (what is said, explicature) should not be of main interest to a true post-Gricean interested in intentional communication. Instead, what is needed is a unit of primary intentional meaning in which this reliance on syntactic representation can be relaxed. Primary meanings of Default Semantics, represented formally as so-called merger representations, offer such a unit. The syntactic constraint which stipulates that what is said or is explicit must be a development of the logical form of the sentence is abandoned. The truth-conditional content pertains to the main meaning intended by the model speaker and recovered by the model addressee, irrespective of its relation to the logical form of the sentence. In other words, the logical form can not only be enriched but in some cases can be overridden when the primary meaning corresponds to what is traditionally dubbed an implicature (*see* Jaszczolt 2005, 2006, to appear b).

Other new aspects of post-Gricean contextualism include debates about the unit on which pragmatic processes operate, where views range from Grice's original proposition-based (thought-based), 'global' **inference** (Jaszczolt 2005) to very 'local', sometimes even word- or morpheme-based inference (Levinson 2000). In the past few years, theoretical debates have begun to be supported with evidence from experimental research. Cancellability of implicatures and aspects of what is said are also newly reopened topics in this paradigm (Weiner 2006; Blome-Tillmann 2008).

Not all post-Gricean pragmaticists subscribe to the contextualist semantics/pragmatics mix. Bach (2004a, 2006a) and Horn (2006) advocate an alternative construal in the form of radical minimalism in which the **proposition**, and thereby also truth conditions, are rejected. According to Bach, the semantic properties of a sentence are analogous to syntactic and phonological properties. The object of study of **semantics** is grammatical form rather than a proposition. Contextualists are accused of making a mistake in upholding propositionalism, the view that the grammatical form of a sentence, as in (1a), has to be completed to become fully propositional, as in (1b), evaluable by means of a truth-conditional analysis:

(1a) Tom isn't old enough.
(1b) Tom isn't old enough to stay alone in the house.

In general, questions which are currently at the forefront of post-Gricean research fall into the following categories:

(i) What principles govern **utterance interpretation**?
(ii) How does pragmatic content interact with semantic content?

and, for those who do not shun psychologism in **pragmatics**,

(iii) What are the properties of the interpretation process?

Question (i) concerns the **heuristics** for rational and intentional communicative behaviour. Question (ii) pertains to the boundary dispute between semantics and pragmatics in the contextualism–**semantic minimalism** debate (*see* Recanati 2002b on truth-conditional pragmatics Jaszczolt 2005; Recanati 2005, on contextualism, and Borg 2004a and Cappelen and Lepore 2005a on minimalism). Question (iii) is spelled out as the debate over pragmatic inference vis-à-vis automatic interpretation. Cross-cutting questions (i) to (iii) is the controversy between the proponents (e.g. Stanley 2002; Stanley and Szabó 2000) of the grammatical basis of pragmatic enrichment ('bottom-up' process) and those (e.g. Recanati 2002b, 2004b) advocating the theory of free, not linguistically triggered, 'top-down' enrichment. This controversy is discussed predominantly with respect to quantifier **domain restriction** as in (2b):

(2a) Everybody submitted an article.
(2b) *Every pragmaticist invited to contribute to this Encyclopedia* submitted an article.

As Stanley (2002: 152) puts it, '[m]uch syntactic structure is unpronounced, but no less real for being unpronounced'. However, according to Recanati (2002b: 302), enrichment is free, 'not linguistically triggered' but 'pragmatic through and through'.

Constructions and phenomena that are most frequently studied in post-Gricean pragmatics include those expressions which were traditionally regarded as giving rise to semantic **ambiguity**. They include **negation**, sentential connectives, definite and indefinite descriptions, various quantifying expressions, and **propositional attitude** reports.

KASIA M. JASZCZOLT

See also: Ambiguity; defaults in utterance interpretation; experimental pragmatics; explicit/implicit distinction; implicature; impliciture; meaning; neo-Gricean pragmatics; scalar implicature; semantics-pragmatics interface

Suggestions for further reading

Horn, L.R. (2007) 'Neo-Gricean pragmatics: a Manichaean manifesto', in N. Burton-Roberts (ed.) *Pragmatics*, Basingstoke: Palgrave.

Huang, Y. (2007) *Pragmatics*, Oxford: Oxford University Press. Chapters 2, 6 and 7.

Jaszczolt, K.M. (2002) *Semantics and Pragmatics*, London: Longman. Chapters 10 and 11.

Power

As both **pragmatics** and power have proved to be complex and problematic concepts, defining the relationship between them is not likely to be straightforward or simple. Indeed, in his influential book *Understanding Pragmatics*, Verschueren (1999: 91) refers to 'power' only very briefly, with a single index reference to 'institutionally defined power' in a section entitled 'The Social World'. Jacob Mey (2001), in contrast, has quite a lot to say about power in his equally well-known book *Pragmatics: An Introduction*. Mey's definition of general pragmatics, i.e. '[p]ragmatics studies the use of language in human **communication** as determined by the conditions of society' (2001: 6), relates directly to power, though still implicitly. He concludes that:

> Pragmatics, especially in its social-critical variety, aims at increasing [...] freedom and independence by making the users of language conscious of, unveil and (if necessary) oppose, the institutional and linguistic conditions of power that they are living under.
>
> (2001: 320)

Mey goes on to advance the term 'critical pragmatics', which he takes to focus on 'those areas where language use was critically determined by relations of power in society, placing the language users in a "critical" position' (2001: 316).

Mey's book on pragmatics points the way towards defining how a number of studies within

linguistics, if not specifically pragmatics, have focussed on the relationship between language and power. Both Thornborrow (2002) and Locher (2004) are perhaps most helpful in discussing in an accessible way how definitions of power have gone from an emphasis on individual agency (*see* Dahl 1961) through versions which define power in a more abstract hegemonic and ideological sense (*see* Lukes 1974). The latter approach has proved most clearly relevant to **discourse**, i.e. power is seen as 'a contextually sensitive phenomenon, as a set of resources and actions which are available to speakers and which can be used more or less successfully depending on who the speakers are and what kind of speech situation they are in' (Thornborrow 2002: 8). Thornborrow goes on to say that from this perspective 'power can be accomplished in discourse both on a structural level, through the turn and type of space speakers are given and can get access to, and, on an interactional level, through what they can effectively accomplish in that space' (2002: 8). Locher (2004: 39–40) adds what is implicit in Thornborrow, i.e. that 'power is relational, dynamic and contestable', and that 'the exercise of power involves a latent conflict and clash of interests, which can be obscured because of a society's ideologies'. Though neither of these studies makes explicit reference to pragmatics as such, both provide some thoughtful and perceptive insights into how pragmatics and power intersect in a variety of **contexts**, which are predominantly institutional and hence role-related. They also involve the close analysis of a considerable amount of natural language data by means of a methodology which owes as much to pragmatics as to the **conversation analysis** which both explicitly acknowledge (*see* Haworth 2006 for a further recent example).

Mey (2001) clearly regards 'critical pragmatics' as subsuming what is more commonly referred to as 'critical discourse analysis' (CDA) and considers at some length the 'Lancaster School', which centres around the work of Norman Fairclough and his co-researchers (2001: 316). In *Language and Power*, Fairclough (2001) does not, apparently, consider CDA (or critical language studies) to be a sub-discipline of pragmatics. He does devote a very brief section to pragmatics (2001: 7–8), but makes evident in this section the weaknesses of pragmatics in addressing the kinds of questions, most of them significantly concerned with power, which are central to CDA. One of the most recent publications emanating from CDA (Wodak and Chilton 2005) likewise makes no explicit reference to pragmatics. Its aim is very similar to that of Fairclough, i.e. 'to bring the study of language into engagement with the powers of social action in the real world in which we live' (Scollon 2005: 101). This is not to say that CDA does not make use of pragmatics as a methodology, given that an account of 'the study of language use' (Verschueren's 1999 definition of pragmatics) is unarguably an essential part of engaging with the powers of social action in the real world.

Perhaps the most significant writer identified explicitly with the relationship between pragmatics and power is Jürgen **Habermas** (1979, 1984, 1990). A social theorist rather than a linguist, Habermas has attempted on a grand scale, i.e. through the study of 'universal pragmatics', to embed the study of language within a more general theory of social action. The concept of power is a crucial one for Habermas, though his work has had relatively little influence on linguistic pragmatics. One of the most important distinctions is between what Habermas calls 'communicative discourse', which is oriented towards reaching an understanding, and 'strategic discourse', which is oriented to power. The latter is essentially goal-directed, bringing power to bear through the systems of linguistic constraints which operate most obviously in institutional contexts. For Habermas, communicative discourse is distorted by power and inequality, which is primarily made manifest in diverse discourse contexts through speakers' differing rights to particular **speech acts**. However, like Grice (1975), Habermas does not attempt to bring his theories to bear on natural language data. In fact, he states that:

> formal (universal) pragmatics – which in its reconstructive intention […] is directed to the universal presuppositions of communicative action – seems to be hopelessly removed from actual language use.
>
> (Habermas 1984: 328)

Unlike the work of **Grice**, whose work has been hugely influential on both linguistics and pragmatics, there has as yet been very little attempt on the part of linguists to apply Habermas's theories to 'actual language use' (but *see* Harris 1995).

In addition, it is worth taking into account that Brown and Levinson (1987), who also wish to establish pragmatic 'universals' of language usage (of **politeness**), initially base their work on Grice, but add a distinct and important 'power' component in their formula for computing the 'weightiness' of a Face Threatening Act (FTA). Brown and Levinson tend to see power primarily as a 'given', which is largely inherent in particular situations, roles or individuals. Following on from Brown and Levinson (1987), some recent work on power and politeness is also of relevance to those readers who are interested more generally in pragmatics and power (*see* Harris 2003; Holmes and Stubbe 2003b; Locher 2004; Harris *et al.* 2006; Harris 2007). It is particularly interesting to note in this context the recent work of several linguists who are writing about (im)politeness in the postmodern tradition (*see* Mills 2003 and Watts 2003). These theorists have largely rejected the 'strategy'-based paradigm of Brown and Levinson and its emphasis on predictability and individual volition, with power seen largely as a 'given' in a particular situation. Though such writers have both foregrounded the concept of power and challenged its status as a 'given' (regarding power rather as something negotiable which must in many contexts be established through discourse struggle and dispute), they appear at the same time to have retained an analytical methodology which owes considerably more to pragmatics than to social theory.

SANDRA HARRIS

See also: Anglo-American and European Continental traditions; communication; context; conversation analysis; cooperative principle; discourse; discourse analysis; formal pragmatics; Grice, H.P.; Habermas, J.; institutional and professional discourse; maxims of conversation; police-suspect interviews; politeness; political discourse; pragmatics; speech act type

Suggestions for further reading

Cotterill, J. (2003) *Language and Power in Court: A Linguistic Analysis of the O J Simpson Trial*, Basingstoke: Palgrave Macmillan.

Hutchby, I. (1996) 'Power in discourse: the case of arguments on a British talk radio show', *Discourse and Society*, 7: 481–97.

Wilson, J. (1990) *Politically Speaking*, Oxford: Blackwell.

Pragma-Dialectics

For almost thirty years, argumentation has been studied within the pragma-dialectical framework of Frans van Eemeren and Rob Grootendorst (1984, 1995, 2004). This framework is of interest to the reader of **pragmatics** because the central concept of a critical discussion that is aimed at resolving differences of opinion draws on a speech act analysis of language: 'The theory of speech acts is ideally suited to provide the theoretical tools for dealing with verbal **communication** that is aimed at resolving a difference of opinion in accordance with the pragma-dialectical principles' (van Eemeren and Grootendorst 2004: 62). A difference of opinion can only be resolved in a reasonable way in this framework if it is subjected to each of the following discussion stages: the confrontation stage, the opening stage, the argumentation stage and the concluding stage. At each of these stages, the protagonist and antagonist may perform only certain types of **speech acts**. For example, assertives may be used to express a standpoint in the confrontation stage, to advance argumentation in the argumentation stage and to uphold or retract a standpoint in the concluding stage. In ordinary language use, much less in argumentative **discourse**, speech acts do not exist in isolation or have little or nothing to do with other speech acts or the wider context. To capture the relevance of speech acts to each other, and so facilitate the move from argument interpretation to evaluation, van Eemeren and Grootendorst propose an integration of the theory of speech acts of **Austin** (1962) and **Searle** (1969, 1979b) with Grice's theory of rational verbal exchanges (1975, 1989): 'an integration of Searlean communicative insight and Gricean interactional insight offers, in our view, the best starting-point

for approaching argumentative discourse and texts' (van Eemeren and Grootendorst 2004: 76).

To achieve this integration, Grice's **Cooperative Principle** is redefined as a 'broader' Communication Principle that covers 'the general principles that language users in principle observe and expect others to observe in verbal communication and interaction' (2004: 76). These principles include clarity, honesty, efficiency and relevance, each of which is realized by rules of language use that function as speech act alternatives to Grice's **maxims**. In this way, the principle of clarity is implemented by the following rule of language use: You must not perform any speech acts that are incomprehensible (2004: 77). This rule corresponds to two of Searle's felicity conditions – the propositional content condition and the essential condition – which combine to give identity conditions on the performance of speech acts (*see* van Eemeren and Grootendorst 1992 for discussion of identity conditions). The second, third and fourth rules of language use – You must not perform any speech acts that are insincere, redundant or meaningless, respectively – implement the principles of honesty and efficiency and correspond to Searle's sincerity condition (second rule) and preparatory conditions (third and fourth rules). The fifth rule of language use – You must not perform any speech acts that are not in an appropriate way connected with previous speech acts or the communicative situation (van Eemeren and Grootendorst 2004: 77) – implements the principle of relevance. This rule does not correspond to a speech act condition. Nor does it refer to the performance of an individual speech act. Rather, it stipulates that a speech act must be a relevant addition to the speech acts that have gone before and to the communicative situation. A speech act that expresses rejection of a preceding speech act may be as relevant a contribution as one that expresses acceptance. The model of a critical discussion, van Eemeren and Grootendorst argue, provides a framework for determining what constitutes an appropriate or relevant sequel in a particular case.

Speech acts in pragma-dialectics are systematically connected with the rules for a critical discussion. Specifically, a rational participant in argumentative discussion 'performs only speech acts which accord with a system of rules acceptable to all discussants which furthers the creation of a dialectic which can lead to a resolution of the dispute at the centre of the discussion' (van Eemeren and Grootendorst 1984: 18). Speech acts that violate one of the rules for a critical discussion and undermine attempts to resolve a difference of opinion are characterized as fallacies:

> Any infringement of one or more of the rules, whichever party commits it and at whatever stage in the discussion, is a possible threat to the resolution of a difference of opinion and must therefore be regarded as an incorrect discussion move. In the pragma-dialectic approach, fallacies are analyzed as such incorrect discussion moves in which a discussion rule has been violated.
>
> (van Eemeren and Grootendorst 1995: 136)

The fallacy of *petitio principii* (begging the question) occurs when the protagonist attempts to make use of a **proposition** to defend his standpoint that is not part of the 'shared premises' (rule 3) between discussants. This proposition cannot be amongst these shared premises as it is the very proposition that divides the discussants. The fallacy of *argumentum ad hominem* (argument against the man) has three different variants (abusive, circumstantial and *tu quoque* variants), each of which involves the violation of different rules of critical discussion. In the *tu quoque* variant, a discussant attempts to show that there is a contradiction in that an opponent is currently attacking (or defending) a standpoint that he previously defended (or attacked). In this form of *ad hominem*, the discussant is violating rule 14 in asking the opponent to retract his opposition to the standpoint on the ground of an inconsistency with a prior standpoint rather than on the ground of the discussant's own conclusive defence of it. The discussant is also violating rule 1 of a critical discussion, in that he is denying his opponent the unconditional right to advance a standpoint, even a standpoint that he previously opposed. The extent to which pragma-dialectics offers a more satisfactory analysis of the fallacies than an approach identified by Charles Hamblin

as the 'standard treatment' is a topic of some debate (*see* Woods 1991).

LOUISE CUMMINGS

See also: Argumentation theory; fallacy theory; inference; reasoning; rhetoric

Suggestions for further reading

Houtlosser, P. and van Rees, A. (eds) (2006) *Considering Pragma-Dialectics*, Mahwah, NJ: Lawrence Erlbaum.
van Eemeren, F.H. (ed.) (2002) *Advances in Pragma-Dialectics*, Newport News, VA: Vale Press and Amsterdam: Sic-Sat.
van Eemeren, F.H. and Grootendorst, R. (2004) *A Systematic Theory of Argumentation: The Pragma-Dialectical Approach*, Cambridge: Cambridge University Press.

Pragmatic Language Impairment

Pragmatic language impairment (PLI) refers to difficulties with the pragmatic use of language, particularly the use of relevant **context** in interpretation. PLI is used clinically to describe difficulties in understanding language in context, in understanding non-literal **meaning**, in using pragmatic cues in **conversation** and in communicating with others. Both production and comprehension are affected in PLI while structural language is relatively spared. PLI occurs in populations of children with specific language impairment (SLI) (children who have specific difficulties with language in the absence of explanatory factors), where pragmatic language impairment is a central component of their language difficulty (McTear and Conti-Ramsden 1992; Bishop 2000; Adams and Lloyd 2005). Pragmatic language impairment is also found in association with disorders such as **autistic spectrum disorder** (ASD), **right-hemisphere** brain lesions or **traumatic brain injury**.

Pragmatic language development is characterized by an increasing ability to use context to construct meaning which is relevant to the interpretation intended by the speaker (Gernsbacher 1990; Milosky 1992; Airenti *et al.* 1993a; Sperber and Wilson 1995; Wilson 2000). In the 1980s children identified as having a **communication** disorder in the presence of fluent speech and articulation were referred to as having 'semantic-pragmatic deficit syndrome' (Rapin and Allen 1983, 1998), 'conversational disability' (Conti-Ramsden and Gunn 1986), 'semantic-pragmatic disorder' (Bishop and Rosenbloom 1987) 'pragmatic disability' (McTear and Conti-Ramsden 1992), and 'semantic-pragmatic difficulties' (Vance and Wells 1994). Common characteristics of these children were identified. Communication generally broke down due to complex comprehension difficulties which resulted in poor communicative interaction due to a reliance on learned scripts, atypical choice of words and word-finding difficulties. The semantic deficits in 'semantic-pragmatic disorder' were found to be common in language impaired children (Bishop 2000), particularly word-finding problems (Dockrell *et al.* 1998; McGregor 1997). The pragmatic difficulties, described as a lack of coherence, a lack of understanding of speaker-listener roles and a lack of understanding of the relevance of language in conversation, are also seen in children with autistic spectrum disorder, leading to the suggestion that PLI is on the autistic spectrum (Brook and Bowler 1992; Gagnon *et al.* 1997; Boucher 1998). However, more recent studies found cases where children with PLI had little evidence of autistic features (Bishop *et al.* 1998; Botting and Conti-Ramsden 1999) or pervasive developmental disorder not otherwise specified (Bishop and Norbury 2002). Bishop therefore suggested that PLI refers to children without autistic spectrum disorder whose primary deficit is pragmatic impairment (difficulty using language in a given context).

It is generally agreed that children with PLI show a delay in pragmatic language **development** compared to typically developing children. Studies focussing on conversational abilities of children with PLI found that these children interpreted language literally and failed to understand the **intention** of the speaker in asking a **question** or the relevance of the previous utterance or context (Adams and Bishop 1989; Bishop *et al.* 1998; Perkins 2005). The delay in the ability to understand contextual meaning and in constructing **inferences** is also evident on verbal and pictorial story tasks (Smith and Leinonen 1992; Vance and Wells 1994; Norbury and Bishop 2002) especially when

inferential load is increased. However, when inferring referents (pronoun resolution), children with PLI perform similarly to their peers. Though somewhat delayed in inferring semantic meaning from context (enrichment), this ability is in line with their language level (Botting and Adams 2005). Disproportionate difficulties are evident when the pragmatic language complexity is increased, for example integrating inferences and generating relevant inferences in verbal contexts. Some researchers suggest that a cognitive or memory processing load is implicated (Bara *et al.* 2001) or increased processing costs (Sperber and Wilson 1995). Studies using **relevance theory** (Sperber and Wilson 1995) to investigate pragmatic language comprehension used questions requiring pragmatic abilities and targeting the generation of **implicatures**. Typically developing English and Finnish children (aged three to seven years) were found to gradually develop the ability to use the given context and their own knowledge to successfully interpret questions requiring the processing of implicatures (Ryder and Leinonen 2003; Loukusa *et al.* 2008). Children with PLI (aged seven to eleven years) perform significantly below their peers and children with SLI without pragmatic impairment, when answering questions targeting implicature(s) based on verbal scenarios and stories (Ryder *et al.* 2008). Difficulties in utilizing and integrating relevant contextual information (given in the scenario, or read-aloud story text) are significantly reduced when answers are strongly supported by pictures (this decreases memory load). Children with PLI perform similarly to their peers if answers are available in pictures.

In the clinical setting, identification of children with PLI has proved difficult. These children may have resolved structural deficits, pass standard structural language tests and fail to meet the criteria for ASD, but pragmatic deficits are still evident. There has been difficulty in achieving an **assessment** with reliable outcome measures which is compounded by a lack of normative data (Botting and Conti-Ramsden 1999; Adams and Lloyd 2005). Identifying children with PLI is generally made on the basis of the elimination of other explanations. Clinicians use pragmatic assessment tools (e.g. language and social behaviour profiles or checklists) which identify many of the characteristics of the communicative behaviours of children with pragmatic difficulties. These tools assist diagnosis and eliminate autistic symptomology (Shulman 1985; Prutting and Kirchner 1987; Bray and Wiig 1987; Prinz and Werner 1987; Phelps-Terasaki and Phelps-Gunn 1992; Bishop 2003a). Other language impairments (difficulties in the production and comprehension of grammar, of vocabulary and verbal memory) are eliminated using standard language tests. Perkins (1998) suggests that the usefulness of addressing structural language deficits in the clinical setting has resulted in **pragmatics** being characterized as a higher-level, cognitively-based process/ component which is dissociated from structural language components. As such, it has been viewed as a secondary consequence of SLI (Bishop 2000). However, research increasingly suggests that the development of language is dependent on interaction, and pragmatic abilities such as understanding others' intentions or using context appropriately are an integral part of language development (Tomasello 2003). Neurolinguistic evidence (Locke 1997) suggests that for children with PLI, this development is atypical as they experience language differently (their irrelevant or unusual utterances receive different reaction and feedback from interlocutors).

Pragmatic language impairment can occur as a result of brain injury. In adults, right-hemisphere lesions are linked to the irrelevant use of context, a failure to understand figurative language, sarcasm, **humour**, indirect questions and, more generally, to derive meaning from social context. In some adults with right-hemisphere lesions or with traumatic brain injury, pragmatic language difficulties are comparable to the language difficulties found in individuals with high-functioning autism and Asperger syndrome. For these populations, pragmatic language impairment exists alongside difficulties in drawing together diverse information to construct higher-level meaning in context, as seen in local and global processing tasks, planning tasks, perceptual processing tasks, and frontal lobe deficits such as impulsiveness (Martin and McDonald 2003).

The difficulties in pragmatic language impairment are socially realized. The suggestion that PLI lies on an autistic continuum is attributed to the similarity in many of the communicative difficulties, e.g. literal interpretation and lack of understanding of speaker/listener roles and intentions. Others argue that the development of pragmatic language understanding depends on interaction and the different communicative experiences of PLI children leads to atypical language development. On this view, pragmatic impairment is seen as an integral part of the development of language use and comprehension and not as a separate component. This suggests that communicative interaction, including reaction and feedback, is responsible for the variation in the language development of children with PLI. It is clear that early intervention would be important on this view. However, there is still debate about the nature of pragmatic language development, including the role of memory and cognitive load. More research is needed with a view to providing clinicians with appropriate tools for assessment and therapy to meet the needs of these children.

NUALA RYDER

See also: Assessment, pragmatic; autism spectrum disorders; clinical pragmatics; communication; competence, pragmatic; context; conversation; development, pragmatic; implicature; inference; intention; meaning; metarepresentation; question; relevance theory; right-hemisphere damage and pragmatics; semantics; traumatic brain injury and discourse; utterance interpretation

Suggestions for further reading

Norbury, C.F. and Bishop, D.V.M. (2002) 'Inferential processing and story recall in children with communication problems: a comparison of specific language impairment, pragmatic language impairment and high-functioning autism', *International Journal of Language and Communication Disorders*, 37: 227–51.

Perkins, M.R. (2007) *Pragmatic Impairment*, Cambridge: Cambridge University Press.

Ryder, N., Leinonen, E. and Schulz, J. (2008) 'Cognitive approach to assessing pragmatic language comprehension in children with specific language impairment', *International Journal of Language and Communication Disorders*, 43: 427–47.

Pragmatics

Pragmatics is a rapidly growing field in contemporary linguistics. But what is pragmatics? It can generally be defined as the study of language in use. However, such a definition may be too general to be of much use.

Since at least Levinson (1983), the study of pragmatics has been acknowledged to be split between two schools of thought: the **Anglo-American and (European) Continental traditions**. Within the Anglo-American conception of linguistics and the **philosophy of language**, pragmatics may be defined as the systematic study of **meaning** by virtue of, or dependent on, the use of language. The central topics of inquiry include **implicature**, **presupposition**, **speech acts, deixis**, and **reference**, all of which originate in twentieth-century analytical philosophy (see, for example, Huang 2007: 2, Levinson 2000, but also Levinson 1983, who added **conversation analysis** to the above list). This is known as the component view of pragmatics. On this view, a linguistic theory consists of a number of core components: phonetics, phonology, morphology, **syntax**, and **semantics**. Each of these core components has a relatively properly demarcated domain of inquiry. Pragmatics, then, is just another core component placed in the same contrast set within a linguistic theory. By contrast, other 'hyphenated' branches of linguistics such as anthropological linguistics, educational linguistics, and **sociolinguistics** lie outside this contrast set of core components. The component view of pragmatics is to some extent a reflection of the modular conception of the human mind, namely, the claim that the mental architecture of *Homo sapiens* is divided roughly into a basic dichotomy between a central processor and a number of distinctive, specialized mental systems known as modules (Fodor 1983; *see also* Cummings 2005: 140–60; Huang 2007: 198–201).

The notion of implicature (both conversational and conventional) was put forward by the British philosopher H.P. **Grice** (Grice 1989). Conversational implicature is any utterance meaning implied by a speaker and inferred by an addressee which goes beyond **what is said** in the strict sense. It is derived from the speaker's saying of what is said via the **cooperative principle** and its attendant **maxims of conversation**. Since its inception, the classical Gricean theory of conversational implicature has remained one of the two foundation stones of current pragmatic theorizing. Further, it has been the impetus to a staggering amount of research, giving rise to **neo-Gricean pragmatics** (Levinson 2000; Huang 2004b; Horn 2007a), **relevance theory** (a reductionist revision of the classical Gricean programme; Sperber and Wilson 1995), novel concepts like **impliciture** (Bach 1994a) and pragmatically enriched what is said (Recanati 2004b), and interesting work in **experimental pragmatics** (Noveck and Sperber 2004). In addition, classical and neo-Gricean pragmatics has integrated with other current linguistic theories to bring about bidirectional **optimality-theoretic pragmatics** (Blutner and Zeevat 2004a, 2004b), game-theoretic pragmatics (Benz *et al.* 2006) and decision-based pragmatics. By contrast, conventional implicature is a non-truth-conditional meaning which is not derived in any general, natural way from the saying of what is said, but arises solely from the conventional features attached to particular lexical items and/or linguistic constructions.

Presupposition is a **proposition** whose truth is taken for granted in the utterance of a sentence. The main function of presupposition is to act as a precondition of some sort for the appropriate use of the sentence. This background assumption will remain in force when the sentence that contains it is negated. Presupposition has long been considered to be a linguistic phenomenon that is balanced on the edge between semantics and pragmatics, but how much is semantics and how much is pragmatics is debatable (see, for example, Huang 2007).

A notion introduced by the British philosopher J.L. **Austin**, speech acts refer to the uttering of a linguistic expression, the function of which is not just to say things but actively to do things or to perform acts as well. Since **speech act theory** was established in the 1960s (Austin 1962; Searle 1969), it has remained to date another cornerstone of pragmatics. On the one hand, cultural and interlanguage variations in speech acts have been a major pursuit of **cross-cultural pragmatics** and **interlanguage pragmatics** (*see*, for example, Huang 2006a). On the other hand, the integration of speech acts with intentional logic has given rise to what is called illocutionary logic in **formal pragmatics**. Various aspects of speech act theory have also been formalized in **artificial intelligence** and **computational pragmatics**.

Deixis is the phenomenon whereby features of **context** of utterance or speech event are encoded by lexical and/or grammatical means in a language. There are three major categories of deixis: person, space, and time deixis. Person deixis is concerned with the identification of the interlocutors or participant roles in a speech event. Space deixis is the specification of location in space relative to that of the participants at utterance time in a speech event. Finally, time deixis is concerned with the encoding of temporal points and spans relative to the time at which an utterance is produced in a speech event. In addition, two minor categories of deixis can be identified: social and discourse deixis. Social deixis is the codification of the social status of the speaker, the addressee, or a third person or entity referred to, as well as the social relationships holding between them. Discourse, text or textual deixis is concerned with the use of a linguistic expression within some utterance to point to the current, preceding or following utterances in the same spoken or written discourse (*see*, for example, Huang 2007).

Finally, reference is the relationship between a linguistic expression and an entity, activity, property, relationship, etc. or a set of entities, activities, properties, relationships, etc. in the external world, to which it refers. In other words, referring is an act of a speaker picking out a particular entity or a particular set of entities, denoted by a linguistic expression, in the external world. It is performed through the speaker's utterance of that linguistic expression on some occasion. Defined thus, reference is essentially a context-dependent aspect of utterance meaning and it therefore falls within the domain of pragmatics (*see*, for example, Lyons 1977; Carlson 2004).

By contrast, within the European Continental conception of linguistics, pragmatics is taken to present a functional perspective on all core components and 'hyphenated' areas of linguistics and beyond. Verschueren (1999: 7, 11), for example, claimed that pragmatics constitutes 'a general functional (i.e. cognitive, social and cultural) perspective on linguistic phenomena in relation to their usage in forms of behaviour'. Elsewhere, he elaborated by saying that '[p]ragmatics should be seen … as a specific perspective … on whatever phonologists, morphologists, syntacticians, semanticists, psycholinguists, sociolinguists, etc. deal with' (Verschueren 1995: 12). This represents the perspective view of pragmatics. Consequently, within the wider Continental tradition, the empirical orbit of pragmatics has been considerably widened, encompassing not only much that goes under the rubric of those non-core branches of linguistics such as sociolinguistics, **psycholinguistics**, and **discourse analysis**, but also some that falls in the province of certain neighbouring social sciences.

However, there has recently been some convergence between the two traditions. On the one hand, important work has been done on micropragmatic topics such as implicature, speech acts, and presupposition from a Continental, perspective point of view. On the other hand, research in the Anglo-American conception has been extended not only to some core topics in formal syntax such as **anaphora** (*see*, for example, Levinson 2000; Huang 1994, 2000, 2004a, 2006b) and the lexicon in **lexical pragmatics** (Blutner 2004; Horn 2007) but also certain 'hyphenated' domains of linguistics such as computational linguistics, historical linguistics, and clinical linguistics, giving rise to computational pragmatics, **historical pragmatics** (Traugott 2004), and **clinical pragmatics** (Cummings 2005, 2008, 2009). This is also true in relation to **cognitive science**. One case in point is relevance theory, which has taken many insights from **cognitive psychology**. Another case is the recent emergence of experimental pragmatics. Further, each side of the divide complements, and has much to learn from, the other side. Whereas the strength of the Anglo-American branch lies mainly in theory, and philosophical, cognitive, and formal pragmatics, the Continental camp has much to offer in empirical work, and socio- (or societal), cross- (or inter-) cultural, and interlanguage pragmatics.

Computational, experimental, and socio- (or **societal**) **pragmatics**, for example, can be taken to be branches of what may be called macro-pragmatics – the study of the use of language in all aspects. Current topics of inquiry in macro-pragmatics can roughly be divided into two groups: cognitive-oriented and social or cultural-oriented. The former includes **cognitive pragmatics**, psycho-pragmatics (including both developmental and experimental pragmatics), computational pragmatics, and clinical pragmatics. The latter includes socio- (or societal) pragmatics, cross- (or inter-) cultural pragmatics, and interlanguage pragmatics.

Cognitive pragmatics has its roots in the emergence of modern cognitive science in the 1970s. A typical example of cognitive pragmatics is relevance theory. Grounded in a general view of human cognition, the central tenet of relevance theory is that the human cognitive system works in such a way as to tend to maximize relevance with respect to **communication**. Thus, the communicative principle of relevance is responsible for the recovery of both the explicit and implicit content of an utterance. Furthermore, it is hypothesized that pragmatics, which incorporates the relevance-theoretic comprehension procedure, is a sub-module of '**theory of mind**', that is, a variety of mind-reading (Sperber and Wilson 1995; Huang 2007). Another significant cognitive approach to pragmatics is cognitive pragmatics theory (Airenti *et al.* 1993a, 1993b). This offers an explanation of the cognitive processes that are involved in intentional verbal and nonverbal communication. These theorists contend that a 'partner' (addressee) in communication establishes the communicative intention of an 'actor' (speaker) by identifying the behaviour game that the actor intends him or her to play. Pragmatic phenomena are accounted for in terms of the complexity of the inferential steps (the 'inferential load') that are needed to refer an utterance to a particular behaviour game and the complexity of the underlying mental representations. Cognitive pragmatics theory has been applied to studies of developmental pragmatics in children (Bucciarelli *et al.* 2003), the comprehension of pragmatic phenomena in head-injured subjects (Bara *et al.* 1997, 2001) and pragmatic decay in subjects with Alzheimer's disease (Bara *et al.* 2000). In these cases, cognitive pragmatics theory overlaps with clinical and **neuropragmatics**.

Psycho-pragmatics is the psycholinguistic study of aspects of language in use and mind. It is primarily concerned with the issue of how human beings acquire, store, produce, and understand the use of language from the vantage point of psychology. Within psycho-pragmatics, developmental pragmatics studies the empirical development of **pragmatic competence** in children, utilizing both observations and experiments. Topics that have been discussed in developmental pragmatics include the acquisition of **scalar implicature**, **metaphor**, and **irony**. Using both psycholinguistic and neurolinguistic methods, experimental pragmatics investigates, through carefully controlled experiments, such important pragmatic issues and theories as scalar implicatures, felicity conditions on speech acts, reference, metaphor, neo-Gricean pragmatic theory, and relevance theory (Noveck and Sperber 2004; Huang 2004b). One point to note here is that the majority of work in experimental pragmatics has been carried out from the perspective of relevance theory. The importance of psycho-pragmatics, as pointed out by Cummings (2005), is that it has a crucial role to play not only in the formulation and development of pragmatic theories but also in the testing and revision of these theories.

Computational pragmatics is the systematic study of the relation between utterances and context from an explicit computational point of view. This includes the relation between utterances and action, the relation between utterances and **discourse**, and the relation between utterances and their uttering time, place, and environment. Two sides to the question of how to compute the relation between linguistic aspects and context aspects can be identified. On the one side, given a linguistic expression, one needs to work out how to compute the relevant properties of the context. On the other side, in the case of language generation, the task is to construct a linguistic expression that encodes the contextual information a speaker intends to convey. Given the relevant properties of the context, one needs to work out how to compute the relevant properties of the linguistic expression. This study of the relation between linguistic aspects and context aspects requires the building-up of explicit computational **representations** at either side of the relation. A particularly important topic of inquiry in computational pragmatics is **inference**. **Abduction**, the resolution of reference, the generation and interpretation of speech acts, and the generation and interpretation of discourse structure and coherence relations, have figured prominently in computational pragmatics (Bunt and Black 2000; Jurafsky 2004).

Finally, clinical pragmatics involves the application of pragmatic concepts, theories, and findings to the assessment, diagnosis, and treatment of pragmatic aspects of language disorders. It studies such pragmatic concepts and phenomena as Grice's cooperative principle and its attendant maxims, conversational implicature, speech acts, inferences, context, non-literal meaning, deixis, and **conversation** and discourse from a clinical perspective. Pragmatic deficits have been examined in a variety of clinical groups including children and/or adults with developmental language disorder, **autism spectrum disorder**, learning disability, left- or **right-hemisphere damage** of the brain, closed head injury, Alzheimer's disease, and schizophrenia (Cummings 2005, 2008, 2009). Insofar as most of these clinical groups are defined by an underlying neurological condition, and a large amount of research involves children, clinical pragmatics overlaps to some degree with developmental pragmatics, and neuropragmatics, the study of the neuroanatomical basis of language in use.

We move next to the second group of branches of macro-pragmatics. Socio- (or societal) pragmatics sits at the interface between sociolinguistics and pragmatics and studies the use of language in relation to society. One topic that has long been the focus of socio-pragmatic research is **politeness**. Politeness, broadly defined to encompass both polite friendliness and polite formality, is concerned with the actions people take to maintain their face and that of the people they are interacting with. Defined in this way, politeness functions as a precondition of human communication. Since its publication in 1978, Brown and Levinson's (1987) now classic 'face-saving' theory has generated an enormous amount of cross-cultural/linguistic research on politeness. Other topics that have attracted attention in socio-pragmatics include social deixis, social conventions on the performance of speech acts, and social factors which constrain language in use such as the overriding of conversational implicature by the Malagasy taboo on exact identification (Huang

2007). From a macro point of view, the hand of societal pragmatics can be detected in any area that pertains in any way to society, dealing with topics as diverse as language in education, pragmatics and social struggle, and what is called 'critical pragmatics' (Mey 2001).

Cross- (or inter-)cultural pragmatics is the systematic study of the use of language across different **cultures** and languages. Since the 1980s, a principal concern of cross-cultural pragmatics has been the issue of how particular kinds of speech acts, especially such face-threatening acts (FTAs) as **requests**, **apologies** and **complaints**, are realized across different cultures and languages. One of the most influential investigations is the large-scale Cross-Cultural Speech Act Realization Patterns Project (CCSARP) carried out in the 1980s. In this project, the realization patterns of requesting and apologizing in German, Hebrew, Danish, Canadian French, Argentinian Spanish, and British, American, and Australian English were compared and contrasted (Blum-Kulka *et al.* 1989). Since then, strategies for the performance of certain types of FTAs in a much wider range of languages have been examined. These languages include Catalan, Chinese, Danish, Dutch, German, Greek, Hebrew, Japanese, Javanese, Polish, Russian, Thai, Turkish, four varieties of English (British, American, Australian and New Zealand), two varieties of French (Canadian and French), and eight varieties of Spanish (Argentinian, Ecuadorian, Mexican, Peninsular, Peruvian, Puerto Rican, Uruguayan, and Venezuelan). As a result of these studies, it has now been established that there is indeed extensive cross-cultural/linguistic variation in directness/indirectness in the expression of speech acts, especially in FTAs, and that these differences are generally associated with the different means that different languages utilize to realize speech acts. These findings have undoubtedly contributed to our greater understanding of cross-cultural/linguistic similarities and differences in face-redressive strategies for FTAs (*see*, for example, Huang 2007).

More recently, the exploration of speech acts has been extended to interlanguage, giving rise to interlanguage pragmatics (Kasper and Blum-Kulke 1993; Achiba 2003; Barron 2003). What, then, is an interlanguage? Simply put, an interlanguage is a stage on a continuum within a rule-governed language system that is developed by second or foreign language learners on their path to acquiring the target language. This language system is intermediate between the learner's native language and his or her target language. It gives rise to the phenomenon of what Slobin (1996: 89) called 'first language thinking in second language speaking'. Of these studies, some have investigated how a particular type of speech act is performed by non-native speakers in a given interlanguage; others have compared and contrasted the similarities and differences in the realization patterns of given speech acts between native and non-native speakers in a particular (inter)language. The best studied interlanguage is that developed by speakers of English as a second language. Other interlanguages that have been investigated include Chinese, German, Hebrew, Japanese, and Spanish (see, for example, Huang 2007).

Finally, mention should be made of conversation analysis. Since Levinson (1983), conversation analysis has become a branch of macro-pragmatics. Originating with a breakaway group of sociologists known as ethnomethodologists (Garfinkel 1972), conversation analysis is concerned with the discovery and description of the methods and procedures that participants employ systematically to display their understanding of the structure of naturally occurring, spontaneous conversations in face-to-face interaction. In conversation, there are rules governing sequential organization such as the turn-taking system, the formulation of adjacency pairs, and the mechanism for opening or closing a telephone call. There are also norms regulating participation in a conversation such as those for how to hold the 'floor', for how to interrupt, and for how to remain silent. Other interesting structural devices of conversation include preference organization, the pre-sequence system, and the repair mechanism (Levinson 1983; Sacks 1992; Hutchby and Wooffitt 2008). Given that conversation is the most important spoken manifestation of language, conversation analysis or conversation(al) pragmatics has to be closely linked to prosodic pragmatics – a study of how **prosody** like intonation can affect the interpretation of a variety of linguistic phenomena in relation to context (see, for example, Hirschberg 2004). Furthermore,

since rules, norms, and regulations for conversational interaction may vary from culture to culture, society to society, and language to language, conversation(al) pragmatics may overlap with the ethnography of speaking and cross-cultural pragmatics.

As a subdiscipline of linguistics, pragmatics is developing rapidly, and will continue to develop rapidly. One thing is certain: the future of pragmatics is bright!

YAN HUANG

See also: Anaphora, pragmatics of; Anglo-American and European Continental traditions; clinical pragmatics; cognitive pragmatics; computational pragmatics; conversation analysis; cross-cultural pragmatics; deixis; experimental pragmatics; implicature; interlanguage pragmatics; neo-Gricean pragmatics; neuropragmatics; presupposition; reference; relevance theory; societal pragmatics; speech act theory; what is said

Suggestions for further reading

Cummings, L. (2005) *Pragmatics: A Multidisciplinary Perspective*, Edinburgh: Edinburgh University Press.
Huang, Y. (2007) *Pragmatics*, Oxford: Oxford University Press.
Mey, J.L. (2001) *Pragmatics: An Introduction*, 2nd edn, Oxford: Blackwell.

Pragmatism

Derived from πραγμα (deed or act), pragmatism is an American philosophical movement inspired by C.S. **Peirce**. Peirce used the term after reflecting upon Kant's *Critique of Pure Reason*, where Kant had used *pragmatisch*, meaning 'relation to some definite human purpose' (Morris 1970: 9). The term generally refers to a philosophical position in which one holds that **meaning** lies in the consequences of one's actions or beliefs. Pragmatism is 'often identified as a theory of meaning first stated by Charles Peirce in the 1870s; revived primarily as a theory of truth in 1898 by William James; and further developed, expanded, and disseminated by John

Dewey and F.C.S. Schiller' (Thayer 1968: 5). All four of these pragmatists advocated the use of techniques derived from the natural sciences in understanding human engagement with the world. This turn towards the natural sciences, especially biology and evolutionary theory, was especially influential to the later development of **pragmatics** by Charles S. **Morris**.

Peirce's theories of pragmatism are considered closest to pragmatics and the **philosophy of language**, especially because of his semeiotic. Peirce had initially defined his pragmatic maxim as: 'Consider what effects, that might conceivably have practical bearings, we conceive the object of our conception to have. Then, our conception of these effects is the whole of our conception of the object' (*Collected Papers*, 5.402) (Peirce 1931–58). Peirce, however, quickly rejected the term because he felt that it had been incorrectly defined when popularized by William James. In his lecture 'What Pragmatism Means', James (1910: 53) had stated:

> Theories thus become instruments, not answers to enigmas, in which we can rest. We don't lie back upon them, we move forward, and, on occasion, make nature over again by their aid. Pragmatism unstiffens all our theories, limbers them up and sets each one at work. Being nothing essentially new, it harmonizes with many ancient philosophic tendencies. It agrees with nominalism for instance, in always appealing to particulars; with utilitarianism in emphasizing practical aspects; with positivism in its disdain for verbal solutions, useless questions and metaphysical abstractions.

In harsh reaction to what he believed was James's misuse of his term, especially regarding nominalism and practical aspects, Peirce adopted the term 'pragmaticism', the maxim of which he claimed was: 'The entire intellectual purport of any symbol consists in the total of all general modes of rational conduct which, conditionally upon all the possible different circumstances and desires, would ensue upon the acceptance of the symbol' (*Collected Papers*, 5.438) (Peirce 1931–58). This later maxim of pragmaticism is probably closest to the term 'pragmatics', as conceived by

Charles Morris, as being the semiotic method by which to understand the relations between signs and persons who use and understand those signs.

Morris claimed that pragmatics had been derived from the pragmatism of Peirce, James, Dewey, and George Herbert Mead. According to Morris, all four had provided points of view in which signs were linked with the habitual behaviour of organisms. Morris (1938: 109) claimed:

> If from pragmatism is abstracted the features of particular interest to pragmatics, the result may be formulated somewhat as follows: The interpreter of a sign is an organism; the interpretant is the habit of the organism to respond, because of the sign vehicle, to absent objects which are relevant to a present problematic situation as if they were present.

The pragmatists did not find much sympathy with Morris's claims concerning the connection between pragmatism and pragmatics. In fact, Morris's definition of pragmatics may signify a break between philosophy of language as it was to develop in the mid-to-late twentieth century and philosophical pragmatism which, following World War II, would come to be eclipsed by the philosophy of language in the United States. However, some philosophers of language, such as W.V.O. Quine and Donald Davidson, utilized aspects of pragmatism in their work. For instance, Quine used the methods of natural science in order to address questions of meaning. This technique is especially close to that of John Dewey, as put forth in his 1938 book *Logic: The Theory of Inquiry* (*Later Works*, 12) (Dewey 1925–53). The theorists working in **ordinary language philosophy**, inspired by Ludwig **Wittgenstein**, Gilbert Ryle, J.L. **Austin** and John **Searle**, are also considered to hold positions closely akin to pragmatism, especially because of their insistence on meaning being constituted by use. The contemporary exemplar of the combination of these two traditions is the later work of Richard Rorty, who combined a version of Dewey's instrumentalism with the later Wittgenstein's understanding of meaning (*cf.* Rorty 1979).

Works pertaining to the philosophy of language by 'neo-pragmatists', such as Rorty,

Hilary Putnam, and Ian Hacking, have caused a resurgent interest in pragmatism and the pragmatic approach to language. There is also a continual interest in Peirce's theory of signs, which is perhaps best represented by the work of philosophers in Finland, especially that of Ahti-Veikko Pietarinen and Sami Pihlstrom.

MARK DIETRICH TSCHAEPE

See also: Abduction; context; discourse; Habermas, J.; history of pragmatism; indexicals; knowledge; meaning; Morris, C.; Peirce, C.S.; philosophy of language; philosophy of mind; reasoning; semantics; semiotics; theory of mind

Suggestions for further reading

Kuklick, B. (1977) *The Rise of American Philosophy – Cambridge, Massachusetts, 1860–1930*, New Haven, CT: Yale University Press.
Pietarinen, A.-V. (2006) *Signs of Logic: Peircean Themes on the Philosophy of Language, Games, and Communication*, Dordrecht: Springer.
Wiener, P.P. (1949) *Evolution and the Founders of Pragmatism*, Cambridge, MA: Harvard University Press.

Prelinguistic Communication

Before we can speak of **pragmatics** in prelinguistic communication, we need to know when infants start communicating intentionally. Although the early face-to-face interactions that young babies participate in with their caregivers have been called 'proto-conversations' because of their turn-taking structure and mutual responsiveness (Bateson 1975), the general consensus is that it is only later, around age 9–12 months, that infants' communication is clearly intentional (see, for example, Bates *et al.* 1975 on infants' early showing, giving, pointing and reaching gestures, and Harding and Golinkoff 1979 on the **intentionality** of infants' prelinguistic vocalizations). It is also important to know whether, once infants are communicating intentionally, they do so with some understanding of how **communication** works, that is, by influencing the psychological states of the recipients, and not just their physical behaviour

(Shatz 1983; Moore and Corkum 1994; Phillips *et al.* 1995). As we will see later, evidence suggests that infants do have some such understanding around their first birthdays.

The study of pragmatics in infants' prelinguistic communication began in earnest in the 1970s (e.g. Bates *et al.* 1975; Bruner 1975). Much of the early work focused on the variety of **speech acts** prelinguistic infants are able to perform with gestures. These range from the classic proto-imperatives and proto-declaratives (used to **request** and to share attention to objects, respectively; Bates *et al.* 1975) to refusing, protesting, commenting (Carpenter *et al.* 1983), representing (Acredolo and Goodwyn 1990), questioning (Chouinard 2007), and many others (*see* Ninio and Snow 1996 for a review, and Tomasello *et al.* 2007 for some examples of the infinite variety of meanings infants can express with gestures).

Much of the research on pragmatics in prelinguistic communication has focused on one particular gesture: pointing. Pointing is a particularly interesting gesture in this context because, compared with symbolic gestures and words, it provides very little information in itself regarding the precise message the pointer is intending to communicate: both pointer and recipient must take into account the common ground they share in order for the point to be understood (Tomasello *et al.* 2007). Beginning around 12 months, preverbal infants are able to interpret adults' points – even points that are deliberately ambiguous for experimental purposes – and they do so according to pragmatic principles such as what is given/new in their shared experience with the adult. For example, if an adult points ambiguously toward a group of three objects, 12- and 14-month-olds can identify which object she is referring to based on which of those objects they have and have not shared with her previously (Tomasello and Haberl 2003; Moll and Tomasello 2007). If the adult points ambiguously to another group of objects, all of which are familiar to the infant and the adult, 14-month-olds correctly assume she is pointing to the one they have previously shared together in a special way (Moll *et al.* 2008). And when the adult points to a single object, 14-month-olds know what she wants them to do with it, based, again, on their shared experience with that particular adult (Liebal *et al.* 2009).

In infants' production of pointing, too, there is strong evidence for a rich view of prelinguistic communication. Twelve-month-olds point with the prosocial motives of sharing attention and interest with others (Liszkowski *et al.* 2004) and informing others helpfully (Liszkowski *et al.* 2006). When they point, they take into account not just the current attentional state of the recipient (Liszkowski *et al.* 2008a) but also what the recipient knows or does not know from previous experience (Liszkowski *et al.* 2008b). Twelve-month-olds can even point to request and refer to absent referents (Liszkowski *et al.* 2007a; Liszkowski *et al.*, to appear). Together, these findings suggest that 12-month-old infants see communication as taking place on a mental level, as a transfer of information or alignment of attitudes between partners that should be tailored to the needs of the recipient.

Another productive line of research in this area concerns infants' ability to repair failed communications. Infants as young as 12–14 months are able to repair different types of **misunderstandings** (e.g. Golinkoff 1986; Liszkowski *et al.* 2007b; Marcos and Kornhaber-le Chanu 1992). Given their limited communicative means, at this age they typically do so by simply repeating or augmenting their signal. Over the next few months, with more words at their disposal, infants become increasingly able to reformulate their requests and attune them to the type of misunderstanding experienced (e.g. Golinkoff 1986; Marcos 1991; Marcos and Kornhaber-le Chanu 1992).

When infants begin learning their first words they continue to use their pragmatic skills, interpreting novel language based on the common ground or joint attentional focus they share with their partner, and on an understanding of the partner's **intentions** (*see* Tomasello 2001 for a review). Indeed, there is evidence of continuity between early pragmatic skills and later language development. Smith (1998) found that various pragmatic skills at 10 months predicted children's scores on tests of language development at 2 years, for example. Even during the prelinguistic period there are relations between some types of pointing and infants' understanding of others' intentions

(Camaioni *et al.* 2004). Along with the pragmatic skills we see in infants' earliest **gestural communication**, these kinds of developmental continuities and relations with early **theory of mind** skills support social-pragmatic theories of language development (e.g. Bruner 1983; Tomasello 2003).

Thus, although prelinguistic infants still have a long way to go toward adult **communicative competence**, it seems clear that some basic pragmatic skills are present before children have learned any language. This suggests that pragmatics is a basic feature of human communication in general, not just language alone. This claim receives further support from another nonverbal population of children: young deaf children who have not been exposed to any conventional language. These children are able to convey a wide range of complex messages with the gestures and signs they invent themselves (e.g. Butcher *et al.* 1991). This complexity – in production or comprehension – is simply not seen in our nearest primate relatives, the great apes. Although they have a large repertoire of communicative gestures (and are even able to tailor their gestures to the recipient's attentional state), apes do not show anything like the flexibility, creativity, range of speech acts, and use of shared information seen in human 1-year-old infants (*see* Tomasello 2008 for a review).

MALINDA CARPENTER

See also: Animal communication, pragmatics of; child language acquisition; communication failure; context; cooperative principle; deixis; development, pragmatic; gestural communication; given/new distinction; infant-directed talk and pragmatics; intention; intentionality; knowledge; language evolution; misunderstanding; perspective taking/point of view; reference; request; sharedness; speech act theory; theory of mind; word learning, the role of mindreading in

Suggestions for further reading

Ninio, A. and Snow, C.E. (1996) *Pragmatic Development*, Boulder, CO: Westview Press.
Tomasello, M. (2008) *Origins of Human Communication*, Cambridge, MA: MIT Press.

Tomasello, M., Carpenter, M. and Liszkowski, U. (2007) 'A new look at infant pointing', *Child Development*, 78: 705–22.

Presupposition

The term 'presupposition' has been used to cover a very broad category of semantic and pragmatic phenomena that have an essential bearing on the understanding of utterances (*see* Levinson 1983). It refers to **propositions** whose truth is taken for granted in an utterance and without which the utterance cannot be assigned a truth-value. Presuppositions remain in force when the utterance is negated (Green 1989: 71). For example, both the utterance 'It's great that Mary passed the Pragmatics exam' and its negation 'It's not great that Mary passed the Pragmatics exam' presuppose the proposition *Mary passed the Pragmatics exam*, whereas 'I think that Mary passed the Pragmatics exam' does not. Presuppositions are typically generated by lexical items or linguistic constructions, such as *it's great that* above. These items and constructions are called presupposition triggers. Some presupposition triggers include definite descriptions (e.g. The King of France is/isn't wise>> There is a King of France), factive verbs (e.g. John knows/doesn't know that Mary passed the Pragmatics exam>> Mary passed the Pragmatics exam), change-of-state verbs (e.g. Mary has/hasn't stopped smoking>> Mary has been smoking), iteratives (e.g. Mary cried/didn't cry again>> Mary cried before), implicative verbs (e.g. Mary managed/didn't manage to pass the Pragmatics exam>> Mary tried to pass the Pragmatics exam), temporal clauses (e.g. After she passed the Pragmatics exam, Mary got/didn't get drunk>> Mary passed the Pragmatics exam), cleft sentences (e.g. It was/wasn't Mary who got drunk>> Someone got drunk), comparatives (e.g. Pat is a better linguist than Lou>> Pat is a linguist and Lou is a linguist), and counterfactual conditionals (e.g. If I were a vascular surgeon, I would/wouldn't have made a lot of money>> I am not a vascular surgeon).

So far, presupposition seems to be defined in semantic terms relating, on the one hand, to the **meaning** of the proposition expressed and its **negation** and, on the other hand, to the meaning of particular linguistic expressions. However, presuppositions are also sensitive to contextual factors such as our **knowledge** about the world. For example, whereas 'Mary married/didn't marry before she got a promotion' presupposes *Mary got a promotion*, the utterance 'Mary resigned before she got a promotion' does not, because our background knowledge tells us that people do not get promotions after they have left their jobs. In other words, the presupposition is related to the **pragmatics** of the sentence.

Presuppositions exhibit a number of distinctive properties, such as (a) constancy under negation and (b) defeasibility or cancellability, which is often related to what is known as the projection problem. The constancy-under-negation test isolates the presuppositions of an utterance among all possible **inferences** that can be drawn from it. An utterance of a sentence S presupposes a proposition p if and only if (a) if S is true, then p is true, and (b) if S is false, then p is still true. In these terms, while 'Mary managed to pass the Pragmatics exam' is associated with the inferences *Mary tried to pass the Pragmatics exam* and *Mary passed the Pragmatics exam*, only the former is a presupposition, since it also an inference of the negation of the initial utterance, i.e. 'Mary didn't manage to pass the Pragmatics exam'. Given that the latter inference follows the truth-value of the utterance (i.e. it is true when the utterance is true and false when the utterance is false/negated), it constitutes one of its **entailments**.

Unlike entailments, presuppositions seem to disappear (a) when background knowledge blocks their generation (b) when they are inconsistent with conversational **implicatures** and (c) in some linguistic **contexts**. An example of (a) is the utterance 'Mary resigned before she got a promotion', where the presupposition *Mary got a promotion*, which is normally generated by the temporal clause, is cancelled because it is inconsistent with our background knowledge. As an example of (b), the utterance 'If Mary has lied, John will be angry that she has done so' implicates that perhaps Mary has not lied. In this context, the factive adjective *angry* fails to trigger the putative presupposition that Mary has lied. As an example of (c), even though 'Mary knows/doesn't know that John passed his driving test' presupposes *John passed his driving test*, in the linguistic context of first person subject, as in

'I don't know that John passed his driving test' the presupposition is cancelled. As Gazdar (1979a) has observed, first person subject sentences deny the speaker's knowledge and hence what they would otherwise presuppose. Thus, two contradictory presuppositions arise, i.e. the one which is triggered by *know* and the other which is triggered by *not*. In such cases, denials override contradictory presuppositions. Importantly, this peculiarity in the use of *know* as a trigger cannot be accounted for in truth-conditional semantic terms, since it does not relate to the truth conditions of the containing sentence. Rather, it relates to the commonly held general assumption that, when speakers do not know something, they cannot be taken to verify its truth. A further example of (c) concerns presuppositions that are blocked in certain intrasentential contexts. For example, a presupposition may be triggered by the first part of a sentence, but then overtly denied in the second part, as in 'Mary doesn't regret marrying young, because in fact she never did marry young'. In this case, the putative presupposition triggered by the factive *regret* is cancelled in the second clause.

At this point the issue of defeasibility of presuppositions merges with the projection problem, which concerns the behaviour of presuppositions in complex sentences. The projection problem originates in the compositional account of meaning that is commonly attributed to Frege. This account specifies that the meaning of a compound expression is a function of the meaning of its parts (*see* Janssen 1997). In these terms, the truth of a complex sentence depends on the truth of its parts. It follows that the conjunction of a part of a sentence and its negation leads to contradiction. However, the presupposition of the first part of 'Mary doesn't regret marrying young, because in fact she never did marry young', namely *Mary married young*, is explicitly negated in the second part, namely *she never did marry young*, without creating a contradiction. In other words, the presupposition of a part of a sentence does not become a presupposition of the whole sentence and the truth of the parts does not become the truth of the whole, *contra* Frege. Stating the problem in this way suggests an implicit comparison of presuppositions with entailments. The projection problem and its solution have worried linguists of various theoretical

backgrounds (see, for example, Karttunen 1973; Fillmore 1985; and Kempson 1988). It manifests itself systematically in the presence of certain conjunctions, modal operators, belief-contexts, and negation. Apparently, presuppositional phenomena can neither be accounted for truth-conditionally, nor are they a set of irregularly occurring inferences.

As already noted in relation to the constancy-under-negation test, presuppositions survive the negation of a sentence, while entailments fail such negation. Similarly, presuppositions survive and entailments fail when sentences are embedded in modal operators such as *it's possible that*, *it's probable that*, etc. For example, the utterance 'My sister ate five apples yesterday' generates the inferences *My sister ate four apples yesterday* (if she ate five, she also ate any number of apples smaller than five) and *I have a sister*. The former inference is an entailment and the latter inference a presupposition. If the sentence is embedded in a modal operator, to become 'It's possible that my sister ate five apples yesterday', the entailment fails whereas the presupposition survives: if my sister did not eat five apples, it does not necessarily mean that she ate four, whereas it is still true that I have a sister. Moreover, presuppositions may be suspended in conditional constructions such as 'Mary doesn't regret eating apples – if in fact she actually did do so'. Thus, it is possible for the speaker to suspend her commitment to the presupposition she has expressed, without any apparent anomaly or contradiction in **communication**. However, it is also possible for presuppositions to disappear in the context of if-clauses or disjunctions, as in 'If Mary had five apples yesterday, she will regret eating them' or 'Either Mary had five apples yesterday, or she will regret eating them'. Even though *Mary ate apples* is a presupposition triggered by the factive verb *regret* in the second clause taken in isolation in each of these examples, it is defeated in the context of such connectives as *if ... then* and *either ... or*. Similarly, presuppositions are defeated in the context of verbs expressing propositional attitudes as in 'Mary believes that she is pregnant', which does not presuppose *Mary is pregnant*. However, there are cases in which a belief context does not block presuppositions, as in 'Mary believes that she is pregnant again', which presupposes *Mary was pregnant before*.

In view of these aspects of the projection problem, Karttunen (1973) claimed that presuppositions are not cancellable. Rather, they are simply satisfied in the local context, which is dynamic and developing on line and filters out unwanted presuppositions during the derivation of the utterance. He further classified presuppositional contexts into three types: (a) plugs, which block all the presuppositions of lower clauses of a sentence (as in metalinguistic negation); (b) holes, which allow the presupposition of a clause of a sentence to become a presupposition of the whole sentence (as in propositional negation); and (c) filters, which prevent some, but not all, presuppositions of a clause from becoming presuppositions of the whole sentence (as in belief contexts, for example). Karttunen's filtering satisfaction analysis seems descriptively adequate, but does not provide a conceptual motivation for the proposed three-way classification. Moreover, it does not treat negation as a unitary phenomenon, since it adopts the position that sentence meaning is affected in different ways by propositional (within-sentence) negation and metalinguistic negation (the former being a hole and the latter a plug).

Fillmore's (1977) theory of a scenes-and-frames **semantics** seems to propose a solution to the double-negation problem created by the analysis of presuppositions. In Fillmore's terms, a lexical frame is associated with prototypical instances of scenes. Scenes and frames are said to activate each other and to be mutually retrievable. A single situation, then, may be framed in different ways, so that in the end it is understood as different facts. For example, both *stingy* and *thrifty* have to do with spending little money. But in using the former, the speaker describes one's behaviour implicitly contrasting it with *generous*. In using the latter, the speaker contrasts this behaviour with being *wasteful* (Fillmore 1982: 125). This analysis creates the possibility of distinguishing between contrasts within frames and contrasts across frames. For example, in uttering 'Mary's not stingy – she's really generous', the speaker accepts the scale of measurement, namely, the stingy–generous one, and informs the addressee that there is an error in its application with respect to Mary's character. In 'Mary's not stingy – she's thrifty', the speaker is stating that Mary's character is not to be evaluated on the stingy–generous scale, but rather on the thrifty–wasteful scale. In these terms, negation is a unitary phenomenon. But while the negation test (within sentence negation) holds in the normal or within-frame cases of negation, metalinguistic negation is a case of cross-frame negation. It has also been pointed out that this across-frames metalinguistic negation strongly and crucially presupposes the previous speaker's utterance with which the current speaker disagrees (Marmaridou 2000: 146). Therefore, in 'Mary doesn't regret marrying young, because in fact she never did do so', the negation operator does not reject Mary's feeling of regret (within sentence negation), but rather rejects the applicability of the term used (the verb *regret*) to the situation in which it is used (Mary's presumed early marriage) by the previous speaker.

Gazdar (1979a) has argued that presuppositions are cancellable and has claimed that what a presupposition trigger does is merely generate a potential presupposition, which will become real if not defeated. So, with respect to the projection problem, the presupposition of the clause of a complex sentence will become a presupposition of the whole sentence if it is not cancelled by certain linguistic or non-linguistic factors. Gazdar further proposes a cancellation mechanism involving a set of procedures that are meant to apply in the following hierarchical order: (a) background assumptions, (b) contextual factors, (c) semantic entailments, (d) conversational implicatures, and (e) presuppositions. Thus, potential presuppositions are actualized only if they do not clash with propositions incrementally arising in the previous steps of the procedure. Conceptually motivated as this proposal seems to be, it does not always make correct predictions about an utterance, as Soames (1982) has pointed out. In the utterance 'If someone in the linguistics department won the research grant, it was John who won it', the cleft construction of the second clause of this utterance generates the potential presupposition *Someone won the research grant*. According to Gazdar's theory, this presupposition is cancelled because it clashes with the conversational implicature generated by the if-clause, namely, that the speaker is uncertain as to whether anyone in the linguistics department won the research grant. However, the speaker is talking about the linguistics department and does not implicate that she is uncertain as to whether anyone at all, possibly from other departments, won the grant, i.e. she is not doubtful about the possibility that the grant was won by someone outside the linguistics department. Therefore, on the basis of the speaker-generated conversational implicature, the presupposition *Someone won the research grant* should be actualized, which seems to be an incorrect prediction.

Dynamic approaches to the projection problem include what has been termed accommodation analysis, of which there are two versions (of a formal semantic and a pragmatic hue, respectively). In the framework of discourse representation theory, Van der Sandt (1992) argues that presuppositions are anaphors, in that they can be analyzed in the same way that pronominal or other anaphors are analyzed. If their antecedent cannot be found in the preceding text, they can be contextually accommodated. Hence, accommodation is a process of repair in **conversation** with the help of context, a commonsensical mechanism in fact (Jaszczolt 2002a: 181; Jaszczolt 2002b). For example, in 'If John has grandchildren, his children will be happy' the expression *his children* presupposes that *John has children*. But this presupposition is not bound to or generated by the conditional clause, since the existence of grandchildren is conditional and hence does not guarantee the existence of parents (i.e. John's children). Rather, the presupposition is generated by global accommodation in context (what we know about John) and thus becomes a presupposition of the whole sentence. Supporting evidence for this analysis comes from 'If John has grandchildren, his children will be happy; they wanted to have offspring long ago', in which *they* is anaphoric on *his children* and not on *grandchildren*.

In an alternative, but related, theory, that of accommodation, an account is provided of how deviant usages are brought back into line with the expectations of a cooperative interlocutor (Heim 1992; Huang 2000a, 2007). In this dynamic process of 'repair', if a speaker said 'I'm sorry I'm late, my car broke down' upon entering a board meeting room, the presupposition *The speaker has a car* would be generated by accommodation, i.e. it would simply be added to the discourse context, by the speaker's

cooperative addressees, as if it had been there all along. In these terms, accommodation is a mechanism that is used to achieve increments in the discourse context with new, non-controversial assumptions. Thus, it can be regarded as a special case of exploitation of **Grice**'s **maxims of conversation** to generate pragmatic inferences (*see* Lee 2005). The tension between an essentially semantic and a pragmatic account of presupposition, evident since its inception, seems to have been resolved in a neo-Gricean programme by the recognition that this phenomenon cannot be accounted for at a single level of analysis. Therefore, attempts have been made to reduce the presuppositions of a positive sentence to its entailments and those of a negative sentence to conversational implicature (*see* Atlas 2004 for a development of these ideas).

Finally, within the tradition of **cognitive linguistics**, Fauconnier (1985) has analyzed presuppositions as propositions arising within mental spaces, thereby establishing this phenomenon as, primarily, a conceptual one. In his analysis, utterances consist of two parts: a space-builder (SB_M), which creates a mental space, and a proposition (Prop) establishing relations between elements within that space. For example, in 'Mary dreamt that she had stopped smoking', *Mary dreamt* builds the space of Mary's dream, while *she had stopped smoking* establishes the relation between Mary and smoking within Mary's dream-world. Similarly, the Prop may be divided into the asserted part A (*Mary doesn't smoke now*) and a presupposed part P (*Mary smoked before*). Moreover, the notion of parent space (e.g. that established by a complex sentence) is introduced as a space containing another space. In this analysis, the projection problem is accounted for in terms of a set of rules (R) and strategic principles (SP) that specify whether a presupposition satisfied in space M (a part of a complex sentence) can or must be satisfied in parent space R (the whole of the complex sentence). For example, given the utterance 'Mary dreamt that she had stopped smoking', this account does not only specify why *she had stopped smoking* is blocked, but also under what pragmatic conditions *she smoked before* is or is not inherited by the whole utterance, thereby also providing a conceptual motivation for Karttunen's filters.

Fauconnier's analysis is promising in formally associating conceptual processes with pragmatic knowledge. It is also compatible with the idea that presupposition-creating utterances instantiate a conceptual relationship between figure and ground. The figure is what is specifically asserted, negated, etc., whereas presuppositions constitute the ground against which the figure is perceived. In communication terms, the figure receives immediate attention and is informationally focal, whereas the ground remains in the shade and is hence not open to questioning or subject to debate (Burton-Roberts 1989: 452). Such conceptual approaches to presupposition have been used in highlighting the communicative value of presuppositions (Marmaridou 2000: 153–60), which are shown to confer on the speaker the power to create realities and directly involve the addressee in them. This is effected while language is being used and cognitive mechanisms, such as space building, are necessarily activated.

SOPHIA MARMARIDOU

See also: Anaphora, pragmatics of; assertion; cognitive linguistics; entailment; generalized conversational implicature, theory of; implicature; inference; negation; neo-Gricean pragmatics; proposition; propositional attitude; semantics-pragmatics interface

Suggestions for further reading

Huang, Y. (2007) *Pragmatics*, Oxford: Oxford University Press.
Jaszczolt, K.M. (2002) *Semantics and Pragmatics: Meaning in Language and Discourse*, London: Longman.
Marmaridou, S.S.A. (2000) *Pragmatic Meaning and Cognition*, Amsterdam and Philadelphia: John Benjamins.

Primary Pragmatic Processes

Philosophers of language and linguists have long accepted the idea that speakers can, by their uses of words, imply things that go beyond the meanings encoded in the words themselves. By this means, speakers can indirectly communicate

more than they actually say. In his 1956 paper 'Logic and Conversation', H.P. **Grice** was interested in characterizing such implicit **communication**. He called the sorts of implicit messages that he had in mind 'conversational implicatures' and contrasted such **implicatures** both with what is strictly and literally said and with what is conventionally implicated. Moreover, he was clear that the sort of implication he had in mind was not a logical or analytic **entailment** of **what is said**. Rather, it is *by saying* that *p* (i.e. performing the act of saying that *p*) in a certain conversational **context** that a speaker implicates a further **proposition** *q*. What proposition is implicated is something that the hearer must work out on the basis of his **knowledge** of a set of conversational **maxims** together with certain contextual assumptions, including an assumption that the speaker is being cooperative. Within the class of conversational implicatures, Grice made a further distinction between generalized and particularized conversational implicatures. Grice's distinctions can be summarized in the following tree diagram (Figure 3).

Grice proposed various tests that could be used to determine whether an assumption was a conversational or conventional implicature, as opposed to an entailment or part of what is said. He argued that conversational implicatures are cancellable (either explicitly or implicitly), non-detachable, and calculable.

Grice's initial proposals led to an explosion of work on the notion of an implicature. His distinctions have been challenged, refined, and modified. For example, neo-Griceans such as Laurence Horn and Stephen Levinson have refined Grice's notion of a **generalized conversational implicature** (GCI). Others, such as Bach (1999a), have challenged the notion of conventional implicature, arguing that there is no such category and that cases that Grice analyzed as conventional implicatures can be reanalyzed either as constituents of what is said or as conversational implicatures. There have also been challenges to Grice's category of GCI. Relevance theorists such as Carston (1988, 2002) have argued that many cases that have been categorized as Gricean GCIs should in fact be classified as constituents of what is said by an utterance, i.e. of the utterance's 'explicature', to

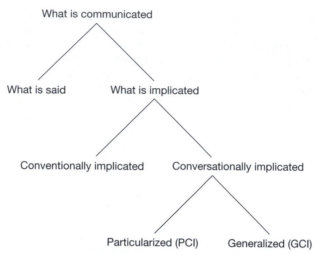

What is communicated

What is said   What is implicated

Conventionally implicated   Conversationally implicated

Particularized (PCI)   Generalized (GCI)

Figure 3 Grice's distinctions.

use the technical term that relevance theorists use for the informal notion of what is said. Finally, there have been challenges even to Grice's root distinction between what is said versus what is implicated. Bach (1994a) has argued that we should replace Grice's two-way distinction with a three-way distinction between what is said, what is implicit in what is said, and what is implicated. Bach dubs contents belonging in the middle category '**implicitures**'.

While all the argumentative threads alluded to in the previous paragraph involve reactions to Grice's ideas, they are also bound up with each other, in the sense that there is disagreement amongst theorists on how to handle particular cases. Consider, for example, a particular utterance *u* of the sentence 'Mary got pregnant and got married'. Unless the speaker of *u* does something to block this, *u* will be understood to convey that Mary's pregnancy occurred before her marriage. Carston treats this temporal sequencing information as part of the explicature of *u*. However, Levinson treats it as a GCI derived by default by means of his Informativeness Principle, and Bach treats it as an ordinary conversational implicature. Or consider an utterance *u** of the sentence 'Mary has finished', uttered in a context in which what is at issue is whether or not Mary has completed work on her Ph.D. dissertation. Carston would regard the proposition that Mary has finished

working on the dissertation as an explicature of *u**, whereas Bach would treat it as an impliciture.

Even though there may be disagreement amongst these theorists as to how to classify particular cases and as to the usefulness or otherwise of Grice's original categories of communicated content, there is consensus about one thing, namely, that pragmatic **reasoning** is not confined to the derivation of conversational implicatures, but is also involved in the derivation of utterance content that is (logically and possibly temporally) *prior* to implicated content. For example, consider *u** again. Suppose this is uttered in response to a query as to whether Mary is eligible for a university lectureship. Then *u** will conversationally imply that Mary is eligible for the job, and pragmatic reasoning will be required to derive that implicature. But this implicature follows only if the hearer antecedently recovers the content that Mary has finished her Ph.D. dissertation (i.e. the explicature/ impliciture of *u**), and that content too requires pragmatic reasoning for its recovery.

It is useful to follow Recanati (1993) and call the sorts of pragmatic processes needed to derive explicatures/implicitures *primary* pragmatic processes (PPPs) and the processes needed to derive classical Gricean implicatures *secondary* pragmatic processes (SPPs). PPPs themselves are a heterogeneous group and, again following

Recanati, we can distinguish at least the following sorts of primary processes:

(1) *Saturation*: This is a process in which there is something like a 'slot' or 'hidden variable' in the underlying semantic **representation** which indicates that some contextual value must be sought to fill that slot to arrive at a complete interpretation.

(2) *Free enrichment*: This is a process in which the hearer must supply content that goes beyond what is semantically encoded, but which is guided purely by the hearer's contextual knowledge rather than by some hidden **indexical**.

(3) *Transfer*: This is a process in which a hearer must seek an interpretation that requires a shift from what is semantically encoded to another referential domain or another property domain.

It is somewhat contentious to provide illustrations of these processes, since different theorists treat examples differently. One theorist may treat something as a case of free enrichment that another theorist treats as a case of saturation. And even Recanati himself has changed his mind about particular cases. A case in point is the utterance of so-called 'meteorological sentences', such as 'It's raining'. Typically, when someone utters such a sentence, he or she will be taken to have expressed a proposition that includes information about the location of the rain (which could be the speaker's location but could also be indefinitely many other places, depending on which place is contextually salient in the conversational context). Some have argued that the verb 'rain' contains a hidden location variable in its semantic interpretation, so that recovery of the location intended by the speaker will be a case of slot-filling or saturation. Others have insisted that the intended location is recovered by means of free enrichment (*see* Recanati 2002a for an overview of this debate).

The category of pragmatic transfer comes from the work of Nunberg (1993), who appeals to the idea of transfer to account both for cases of *deferred reference* and for cases of *metonymy*. An example of the former is a case in which a speaker points to a spot on a map and utters the sentence 'The treasure is here' intending to refer to the place represented by the spot on the map. An example of the latter is a case in which a speaker uses the sentence 'The ham sandwich wants his cheque' to refer to the customer who ordered the ham sandwich. In subsequent work, Nunberg (2004) differentiates between two sorts of transfer, which he calls **reference** and property transfer, respectively. Cases of metonymy are now analyzed as cases of property transfer rather than reference transfer. That is, 'The ham sandwich wants his cheque' does not refer in a deferred way to the ham sandwich orderer, but rather refers directly to the ham sandwich orderer and predicates a transferred property of the orderer, one he acquires in virtue of being the orderer of the sandwich.

Two of Recanati's three categories of PPPs (saturation and free enrichment) are similar in certain respects to the two sorts of pragmatic processes that Bach (1994a) claims are involved in the derivation of implicitures:

(4) *Completion*: This is a process in which semantically encoded content that is conceptually incomplete (i.e. content that amounts merely to a propositional schema or 'gappy' proposition rather than to a full proposition) is completed by information available in the pragmatic context.

(5) *Expansion*: This is a process in which a complete propositional content is elaborated on because it is pragmatically insufficient in some way (e.g. under-informative).

Bach argues that completion is involved in examples such as utterance *u** above – the utterance of the sentence 'Mary has finished'. He argues that this is a syntactically complete sentence, since 'finish' does not sub-categorize for an obligatory following event nominal (as does the verb 'complete', which is shown by the unacceptability of *'Mary has completed'). However, it is conceptually incomplete, because we know that finishings require events that are finished. The hearer must supply the unarticulated event on the basis of contextual knowledge.

Bach's process of expansion is illustrated by so-called quantifier **domain restriction**. Suppose someone plans an elaborate roast beef dinner for his boss, her husband, and his new girlfriend. If, when asked the next day how his

dinner went, he replies 'Everyone was a vegetarian', he will be taken to have said that all his
dinner guests were vegetarians (and to have
conversationally implicated that the dinner was
a disaster). But, according to Bach, what the
speaker has strictly said is that everyone in the
universe is a vegetarian, something that is pragmatically inappropriate in the context. Thus, the
hearer will search the context for some more
appropriate restriction on the domain of quantification. Inasmuch as expansion is guided
purely by assumptions that are part of the
common ground between speaker and hearer, it
would seem to be similar to Recanati's process of
free enrichment. Again though, using the case of
domain restriction to illustrate expansion is controversial, since some people have argued that
contextual quantifier domain restriction is guided
by hidden variables, making such restriction
more akin to Bach's process of completion or
Recanati's process of saturation (*see* Stanley 2000
and Lepore 2004 for more discussion).

While many theorists are in agreement that
utterance interpretation involves the sorts of
PPPs identified by Recanati and Bach, there is
disagreement as to the nature of these processes.
Recanati has argued that PPPs are non-inferential
in character, whereas relevance theorists such as
Carston (2002) argue that they are inferential in
nature, as are the processes involved in secondary
pragmatic processing. The problem is that if both
PPPs and SPPs are inferential, it becomes harder
to distinguish between explicatures/implicitures
on the one hand and implicatures on the other
hand, which are the outputs of PPPs and SPPs,
respectively. Relevance theorists have presented
two sorts of considerations to distinguish these
processes and their respective outputs.

First, relevance theorists argue that PPPs are
distinguishable from SPPs by their *inputs*. The
input to PPPs are representations of semantically
underspecified **logical forms** (LFs) that must
be developed into fully propositional forms by
some sort of contextual modulation of the input
forms. However, the input to SPPs are sets of
fully propositional forms (the implicated premises), including the propositional form that is
the output of whatever PPP was used. Second,
Sperber (1997) has argued that we need to distinguish between spontaneous, fast, effortless and
unconscious **inference** on the one hand and

explicit, slow, effortful and conscious inference
on the other hand. As an example of a spontaneous inference he gives the case of someone's
hearing the doorbell ringing and spontaneously
forming the belief that a person is at the door.
One suggestion then would be that PPPs are
spontaneous inferences and SPPs are effortful
and conscious inferences.

Recanati (2002b) criticizes the idea that SPPs
are necessarily effortful, slow and under voluntary control. He argues instead that SPPs have
the property of what he calls 'availability', by
which he means that the interpreter can become
aware of the input to the process (namely, what
the speaker said), of the output of the process
(namely, what was implicated), and of the inferential relation that holds between input and
output. That is, SPPs are available to introspective awareness; they are *reflective* processes,
even though they are often spontaneous and
more or less automatic. Because such inferences
are 'available', because they are inferences *for*
the interpreter, we can say that these processes
belong to the 'personal' level, rather than a
sub-personal level.

PPPs have just the opposite characteristics.
These processes belong to a sub-personal,
unconscious level and are not available to introspective awareness. An interpreter may be aware
of the output of such processes (what the speaker
has said), but he or she will be unable to recover
the input by means of introspection. After all,
the input will, according to relevance theorists,
be an underspecified LF-representation – something that is the output of the hearer's mental
grammar at interface between the language
system proper and what Chomsky (1995b) calls
the conceptual-intentional system. To call such
sub-personal, non-reflective, processes inferential
is to use the word 'inferential' in a very broad
(and not very helpful) sense. In this sense, any
mapping between one system of representations
and another would count as an inference.

One other reason Recanati gives for doubting
that PPPs are inferential is to point out they are
local processes rather than processes that operate
at the level of complete, truth-evaluable propositions. Hence, they do not seem to be even
potentially truth-preserving (a property generally
taken to be constitutive of a valid inference).
Taking the three primary processes in turn, first,

saturation is simply the assignment of a contextual value to a hidden variable. There is no propositional content available as a premise in reasoning until such a value is assigned, unless we assume that the inference in question is a meta-representational one. However, conclusions about representations (i.e. about the *vehicles* of **meaning** as opposed to the meanings themselves) would seem to be an unnecessary detour and secondary at best.

Second, free enrichment takes an underspecified concept as input (e.g. 'finish') and yields a more elaborated concept as output (e.g. 'finish writing a dissertation'). This elaborated concept is what enters into the compositional process which results in the propositional content that is assigned to the speaker's utterance. To say that a proposition with the underspecified concept as constituent plays a role as a premise in an inference whose conclusion is the proposition with the elaborated concept, is to assign a cognitive role to literal sentence meaning, something that relevance theorists have argued against. Third, in property transfer, the property of being X (e.g. a ham sandwich) gives access to the property of being Y (e.g. a ham sandwich orderer) because of some contextual association between these things. For example, it could be that these things are associated because they are both elements of some mental script or schema for a restaurant visit. Such associations can be non-inferential.

For further arguments in the debate between inferentialism and non-inferentialism about PPPs, *see* Carston (2002) and Recanati (2002b). This debate has ramifications also for discussions about **metaphor**. Wilson and Carston (2006) argue in favour of a view about concept modulation in metaphor that stresses the inferential nature of such modulation.

ANNE BEZUIDENHOUT

See also: Generalized conversational implicature, theory of; Grice, H.P.; implicature; impliciture; neo-Gricean pragmatics; relevance theory; semantics-pragmatics interface

Suggestion for further reading

Recanati, F. (2004) *Literal Meaning*, Cambridge: Cambridge University Press.

Proposition

A proposition is that part of a sentence or **utterance interpretation** that displays and preserves truth or falsity and that enters into logical relations with other propositions. Propositions are distinct from utterances and sentences. In this way, utterances are evaluated relative to certain felicity conditions and **contexts**. 'John is next to Jane' and 'John is next to Jane', *as utterances*, that is, spoken at different times and possibly in different contexts and with different purposes, are two different utterances. Sentences are evaluated relative to a certain grammar. 'John is next to Jane' and 'John is next to Jane', *as sentences*, that is, as sequences of words in a certain order, and presumably with a specifiable constituency, are the same sentence. The sentences 'John is next to Jane' and 'Jane is next to John' are different sentences (because different word orders are in play). Propositions are evaluated relative to certain truth conditions. The sentences 'John is next to Jane' and 'Jane is next to John', although different sentences, express the *same* proposition, because the first cannot be true without the second also being true. The sentence 'Jane and John are next to each other' also expresses the same proposition. And any of these sentences, when translated into any other natural language, will also express exactly the same proposition.

Following the above reasoning, propositions are clearly not linguistic objects. So the question arises: What kind of objects are they? There is a degree of very interesting controversy in the answer to this question. One answer is to say that propositions are (Platonistic) abstract objects which are independent of minds and languages (*cf.* Hale 1987; Jubien 1997). This is a somewhat mysterious answer for it fails to specify what, and indeed where, this abstract realm, populated by abstract objects, is and it fails to explain how abstract independent objects (causally) interact with concrete, dependent objects like minds and users of languages. A second answer states that propositions are that which can act as the linguistic **meaning** of a sentence (*cf.* Loux 2002; Lycan 1984). The trouble with this answer is that the linguistic meaning of a sentence is not a more lucid notion than that of proposition and so this answer is merely a case of *obscurum per*

obscurius. A third answer is to say that propositions are the content of **what is said**, where
'the content of what is said' may have a pragmatic character. Something close to this answer
can be found in the recent debates of
'**contextualism**' (e.g. Preyer and Peter 2005,
2007). A fourth answer is to say that propositions are the contents of psychological states
such as hopes, desires and beliefs. Further discussion of this answer can be found in the
voluminous literature on **propositional attitudes** (e.g. Schiffer 1987, 2003; Richard 1990;
Crimmins 1992).

Another response to 'What kind of objects
are they?' is to deny that the question is felicitous. This answer is preferred by anyone
who gets severe ontological indigestion at the
slightest mention of abstract objects. Strawson
(1952), who does not have an entry for 'proposition' in his index, is one early candidate.
(Note that the linguistic phenomenologies of,
for example, Austin (1962) and Searle (1969)
both depend upon some conception of the
proposition and so, despite the evident pragmatic character of their philosophies, do not
fundamentally challenge the question's felicity
conditions.)

Propositions are, therefore, for some – the
ontologically profligate – the ultimate foundations for all theories of language. For others –
the ontologically cautious – they provide no
foundation at all. This dichotomy has determined thinking about language for all of the last
century. There is no evidence that its influence
will wane any time soon.

KEN TURNER

See also: Assertion; Austin, J.L.; Bar-Hillel, Y.;
contextualism; demonstratives; generalized conversational implicature, theory of; Grice, H.P.;
neo-Gricean pragmatics; philosophy of language;
philosophy of mind; propositional attitudes;
Searle, J.; speech act theory

Suggestions for further reading

Gibson, M.I. (2004) *From Naming to Saying: The
Unity of the Proposition*, Oxford: Blackwell.
King, J. (2007) *The Nature and Structure of Content*,
Oxford: Oxford University Press.

Nuchelmans, G. (1973) *Theories of the Proposition:
Ancient and Medieval Conceptions of the Bearers of
Truth and Falsity*, Amsterdam: North-Holland
Publishing Company.

Propositional Attitudes

When speakers report on people's mental states,
they often use expressions which identify the
type of this mental state (e.g. belief, doubt, fear)
and its content, referred to in the form of a *that*-
clause, as in (1).

(1) Ben believes that Alaska is an island.

Such mental states were called propositional
attitudes by Bertrand Russell. However, it is now
often disputed whether the object of such attitudes should be construed as a **proposition** or
perhaps as a sentence, thought, or a structure of
some kind.

Linguists are predominantly interested in the
semantics and **pragmatics** of propositional
attitude reports. Attitude reports belong to the
class of so-called intensional contexts in which
substitution of coreferential expressions is not
truth-preserving (*salva veritate*). For example,
although 'Alaska' has the same referent as the
definite description 'the U.S. state purchased
from the Russian tsar Alexander II in 1867 for
$7.2 million', substituting this phrase for the
proper name 'Alaska' as in (1') may affect the
truth value: Ben may not know that the proper
name and the description are coreferential.

(1') Ben believes that the U.S. state purchased
from the Russian tsar Alexander II in
1867 for $7.2 million is an island.

This lack of substitutivity poses theoretical problems for the theory of **meaning**, as well as
practical problems for human **communication**.
These two problems are interconnected: satisfactory solutions to both take into account the
guise, the way of thinking about the referent,
that can be ascribed to the speaker and assumed
as shared by interlocutors – the so-called mode
of presentation, modelled to a greater or lesser
extent on Frege's notion of sense (Frege 1892; *cf.*
Schiffer 1992, 1996; Crimmins and Perry 1989;

Crimmins 1992; Forbes 1990, 1997; Jaszczolt 1999, 2000). At the other end of the spectrum are approaches that deny modes of presentation any role in the **logical form** of propositional attitude constructions (Salmon 1986; Soames 1987, 1995). It has also been suggested that the verb *believe* is context-sensitive (Richard 1990, 1995; Pelczar 2004, 2007). The general problem with these categories of solutions is this: when the semantic significance of the mode of presentation is denied, the truth conditions cease to be intuitive. When the modes of presentation or some other form of context-dependence are admitted to the logical form, semantics ceases to be compositional. From the pragmatic, contextualist perspective, however, it seems that modes of presentation, the guises under which speakers talk about beliefs, are necessary for representing intentional meaning and should figure in the contextualist semantic **representation**, arguably by making use of a more relaxed, pragmatic version of compositionality of meaning.

Propositional attitude constructions are standardly regarded as ambiguous between a transparent reading and an opaque reading. For example, (2) has two logical forms in (2a) and (2b), corresponding to the wide and narrow scope of the existential quantifier. '$\exists x$' stands for existential quantification ('there is an x ... '), 'KoP' for 'king of Poland', '$\wedge$' for logical conjunction ('and'), '$\forall y$' for universal quantification ('for all ys ... '), '$\rightarrow$' for logical implication ('if ... then'), and 'Bel$_B$' for 'Ben believes that' (*see* Russell 1905, 1919; Quine 1956; Neale 1990).

(2) Ben believes that the king of Poland is a polyglot.

(2a) $\exists x (KoP(x) \wedge \forall y (KoP(y) \rightarrow y = x) \wedge Bel_B$ Polyglot (x))

(2b) $Bel_B \exists x (KoP(x) \wedge \forall y (KoP(y) \rightarrow y = x) \wedge$ Polyglot (x))

(2a) reflects the reading that is transparent to substitutions. When a speaker uses (2a), he/she ascribes to Ben a belief about a particular, identifiable individual (*de re*). A report with the form as in (2b) ascribes to Ben a belief that there is someone whom he calls the king of Poland and that that individual has a certain property (*de dicto*). The philosophical literature on the subject

focuses on the semantics of the attitude sentences. In pragmatics we are interested in the utterance, the **speech act** of reporting on someone's beliefs, and hence must also recognize the situation in which the holder of the belief is referentially mistaken. Imagine that while using the definite description 'the king of Poland' Ben intentionally refers to 'the king of Sweden'. The logical form corresponding to this utterance is that in (2c), where 'KoS' stands for 'king of Sweden'. If the objective is to represent the speaker's intended meaning, we are faced with many different possible semantic representations instead of a clear **ambiguity** *de re/de dicto*.

(2c) $\exists x (KoS(x) \wedge \forall y (KoS(y) \rightarrow y = x) \wedge Bel_B$ Polyglot (x))

Such a contextualist, pragmatics-rich approach to meaning is currently dominant and propositional attitude research also reflects this orientation.

The *de re/de dicto* distinction must not be confused with the distinction between factive and nonfactive attitudes and factive and nonfactive verbs. Factive verbs engender a proposition whose truth entails that the proposition expressed in the embedded *that*-clause is itself true. For example, (3) entails (4).

(3) Anna knows that whales are mammals.

(4) Whales are mammals.

Nonfactive verbs, such as *believe* or *think*, do not have this property.

KASIA M. JASZCZOLT

See also: Definiteness; intentionality; reference

Suggestions for further reading

Jaszczolt, K.M. (2000) 'The default-based context-dependence of belief reports', in K.M. Jaszczolt (ed.) *The Pragmatics of Propositional Attitude Reports*, Oxford: Elsevier Science.

Richard, M. (1990) *Propositional Attitudes: An Essay on Thoughts and How We Ascribe Them*, Cambridge: Cambridge University Press.

Schiffer, S. (1992) 'Belief ascription', *Journal of Philosophy*, 89: 499–521.

Prosody and Pragmatics

In his textbook on pragmatics, Levinson (1983) acknowledged that the absence of prosody, particularly intonation, was a serious omission, but he justified the omission on two grounds: first, that there was as yet no agreement on how to analyze intonation, and second, that the area was understudied. Twenty-five years on, the American autosegmental model has clearly become the international standard in intonational phonology (e.g. Ladd 1996; Gussenhoven 2004) and for typological comparison (Jun 2005). This model decomposes the pitch contour into underlying pitch targets, or 'tones', (H – high or L – low). Other models, however, continue to have currency, including variations of the British system of holistic contours (fall, rise, fall-rise, etc). None is sufficient to explore the pragmatic function of prosody, since many effects are generated not by 'local' categorical phonological choices, but by 'global' gradient features, such as the overall pitch range of an utterance. Further, prosody has a number of components, of which intonation is just one. It also includes tempo and duration, loudness and voice quality. All these features combine to create 'tone of voice'.

Levinson's second caveat, that the area was understudied, is easier to counter. Interest in the contribution of prosody to pragmatic meaning has grown markedly in the intervening decades, albeit in a fragmented way, and from a wide variety of theoretical perspectives. These developments have been dominated by the Anglo-American view of **pragmatics**, which focuses on the role of prosody in relation to other linguistic systems, for example in resolving syntactic ambiguities, signalling **information structure**, discourse structure, and identifying **speech acts** (for an overview *see* Hirschberg 2004). The European view of pragmatics is broader, including the above phenomena but also adopting a wider cognitive, social and cultural perspective on **meaning** in **context**, with corresponding foci in the study of prosody. In broad terms, the function of speech prosody has been studied in relation to referential meaning, discourse meaning, utterance meaning (speech acts) and interpersonal meaning or attitude. Not surprisingly, these topics are approached from within very

different theoretical frameworks, and are also differently motivated.

Approaches and methods

Early descriptions of the relationship between intonation and meaning (e.g. O'Connor and Arnold 1961) were pedagogically motivated, a tradition continued more recently by Wells (2006). In the last two decades, in contrast, work has been largely driven by the needs of speech technology: speech synthesis, automatic speech recognition, and latterly interactive dialogue systems. Much of this work has been carried out either experimentally, using laboratory speech, or based on automatic analysis of speech corpora. Any contribution to linguistic theory has usually been secondary to the intended application. A separate development has taken place which combines insights from **conversation analysis** (CA) and contextualization theory within interactional **sociolinguistics**. CA has always been aware of prosody, captured impressionistically in early **transcription** systems (e.g. Jefferson 1985), but it was rarely the focus of analysis. The easy availability of speech analysis software has since allowed researchers to focus explicitly on phonetic features. This work is best represented by two seminal collections of papers on prosody in **conversation**, Couper-Kuhlen and Selting (1996b) and Couper-Kuhlen and Ford (2004). Finally, researchers working in **relevance theory**, a cognitive approach to **communication**, have turned their attention to the role of prosody in the inferential process (Vandepitte 1989; House 1990; Fretheim 2002; Wilson and Wharton 2006).

Referential meaning

The mapping of **syntax** to prosody has a long tradition (e.g. Selkirk 1984), in relation to both phrasing and prominence location. The mapping of syntactic boundaries onto intonation phrase boundaries is important for signalling referential meaning, for example in the realization of structurally ambiguous utterances (e.g. *He spoke to the woman in the garden* where the **ambiguity** lies in the scope of the prepositional phrase). Boundary placement is also important for the identification of **parentheticals** (Bolinger 1989;

House 2006b; Dehé 2007). Prosody also plays a part in the signalling of information structure, especially in languages such as English with less flexible constituent ordering, by means of the location and shape of prosodic prominences (accents). In the utterance *Don't buy him a book; he's got hundreds of books*, the second occurrence of *book(s)* is deaccented in Standard British English because it is 'given' information. Much of the discussion in this area revolves around notions of givenness or accessibility, and tends to assume an almost iconic (inverse) relationship between prosodic prominence and psychological salience. Information status is seen variously as gradient (Hajikova 1993) or categorical. Chafe proposed three degrees, given, accessible and new (Chafe 1994: 73 in Baumann and Grice 2006: 1639), while Gundel *et al.* (1993) have six degrees of givenness. Recent papers on **focus** by Baumann and Grice (2006) and Baltazani (2006) found no one-to-one relationship between prominence type, including tone choice, and degree of accessibility. Accent location is also important in spoken **idioms** where a shift of accent can destroy the idiomatic quality of the utterance (Ashby 2006), while both phrasing and prominence characterize grammaticalized items such as **discourse markers** (Wichmann *et al.*, to appear).

Discourse meaning

Studies of prosody in **discourse** include work on topic structure, speech acts, and interaction management. Intonational topic structuring has a long tradition, going back to notions of 'paragraph intonation' and 'paratones' (Brown 1977; Brown and Yule 1983) which examined pitch trends across spoken texts. Studies of scripted monologue observe co-occurrences of phonetic features signalling a new **topic**: a long pause, followed by a high (and sometimes delayed) pitch peak and increased amplitude (Lehiste 1975; Wichmann *et al.* 2000). However, pauses are an unreliable indicator of topic boundaries (Yang 2004) especially in spontaneous conversation, when speakers often want to close, or abandon, old topics and introduce new ones without ceding their turn. This results in the so-called 'rush through' (e.g. Schegloff 1998; Walker 2003) where, instead of slowing down

and pausing, the speaker accelerates into the new topic which is then marked only by an upwards shift of pitch and volume (Couper-Kuhlen 2004). The height of an initial accent can also indicate close cohesive relations between consecutive spoken sentences (Douglas-Cowie and Cowie 1998; Wichmann 2000). The processing of discourse is guided partly by the use of pragmatic markers or discourse markers, such as *still, anyway, well, so,* and *now,* and their prosodic patterning is of interest to speech technologists and discourse analysts alike. For example, utterance-initial *now* tends to be unstressed if it is a discourse marker but stressed if it is a time adverbial. The wide range of functions of discourse markers in English, and their prosodic patterns, have been described in a corpus study by Aijmer (2002). Studies of individual discourse markers cover a number of languages including English *you know* (Holmes 1986b), *well* (Bolinger 1989), *now* and *well* (Hirschberg and Litman 1993), *anyway* (Ferrara 1997) and Swedish *men* 'but' (Horne *et al.* 2001).

Prosody, particularly intonation, is also known to contribute to the pragmatic force of an utterance. Many prosodic studies of speech acts have focused particularly on question intonation in different languages (e.g. Bartels 1999; Grønnum and Tøndering 2007; Vella 2007). Typically, yes/no questions, for example, are thought to display final rising contours (Hedberg *et al.* 2004), but Haan *et al.* (1997) have also shown that **questions** tend to be overall higher in pitch range. There is as yet little published typological research that would shed light on the universality of such observations. Some regional varieties of British English, for example, have very different patterns associated with question and statement (e.g. Wells and Peppe 1996). The intonation of **requests** (with *please*) has been shown to vary with the **power** relations between speaker and hearer. A request with a final rising tone, similar to question intonation, suggests that compliance is optional, while a final falling tone renders the request closer to a **command** (Wichmann 2004). Computational studies have expanded the notion of speech act to include a wider variety of functions ('dialog acts') including backchannel responses, 'agreement', and 'evaluation' (Jurafsky 2004: 588), with the aim of establishing the cues that will enable automatic identification, e.g. Shriberg *et al.* (1998), Jurafsky *et al.* (1998).

A dialog act that is crucial to maintaining conversation is the use of backchannels or 'continuers' (Schegloff 1982: 81) such as *mm, uh huh, right, yes* and *Ok.* These typically display a rising contour and overall higher pitch than other 'affirmative words', and tend to be cued by final rising contours of the interlocutor (Benus *et al.* 2007). Timing has also been found to be an important parameter (e.g. Noguchi and Den 1998). However, while backchannels are generally assumed to be supportive (hence, 'continuer'), they can also subtly indicate the opposite. Müller (1996) notes that the absence of melodic and rhythmic integration is a sign of 'disaffiliation', i.e. backchannels that are not fully supportive. An important cross-cultural concern is the fact that the contours that invite or cue backchannel responses have been found to vary across languages (Ward and Tsukahara 2000; Caspers and Wichmann 2001), showing that this is a potential source of cross-cultural **misunderstanding**.

Studies of conversational interaction include extensive focus on the prosodic correlates of turn-taking, including turn completion, turn continuation, and cues to imminent turn completion. A rising tone, for example, typically suggests continuation while a falling tone suggests completion (Yngve 1970; Cutler and Pearson 1986; Couper-Kuhlen and Selting 1996b; Couper-Kuhlen and Ford 2004; Szczepek Reed 2004). Methods range from CA-type case studies to quantitative analyses, and a number of varieties of UK English have been studied including Tyneside (Local *et al.* 1986) and London Jamaican (Local *et al.* 1985). The prosody of interruptions, competitive and non-competitive, and turn sequencing has been described by, for example, French and Local (1983), Auer (1996) and Wells and Corrin (2004).

Affect, attitude and interpersonal meaning

The interpersonal meanings expressed by prosody remain the most elusive of functions to be accounted for. There is now renewed interest in how it works, because of the development of human–machine dialogue systems. This has prompted the desire to generate machine voices

that sound 'friendly' or 'polite', along with the aim to recognize when human customers are irate, frustrated or just plain exasperated (Ang *et al.* 2002). But the nurturing of participant relationships, or 'rapport management' (Spencer-Oatey 2000), is also of interest for pragmatics in general. One element in the expression of 'rapport' is the vocal expression of emotion. This is of interest to many, including psychologists, neuroscientists, sociolinguists, clinical linguists, and speech engineers. Yet, it remains very difficult to establish clear phonetic correlates between recognizable emotions and speech (see Scherer 1986; Murray and Arnott 1993; Abelin 2004) even though the recognition of some emotions appears to be universal (Scherer 2000).

A prime area of methodological difficulty is that there is little agreement on the taxonomy of emotions, only a multiplicity of terms or 'labels'. Research into prosodic correlates has focused mainly on 'primary' emotions such as happiness, anger, sadness and fear, and these appear to be typically characterized in terms of pitch (height, range, contour). So-called 'secondary' emotions, such as affection and surprise, are characterized by variation in voice quality (Murray and Arnott 1993). Methodological problems also include the difficulty of acquiring emotional data ethically, leading to the use of actors, but material in the public domain (e.g. talk shows) has recently been used to create a corpus of emotional speech (Cowie 2000).

The role of emotion in the interpretation of utterances is controversial. In semiotic terms, an expression of emotion would normally be seen as a 'natural' sign. While such a sign may have communicative effects, these are not its function and it is thus not inherently communicative. Wharton (2003b), and Wilson and Wharton (2006), however, suggest that there is a distinction between an unintentional display of emotion and an intentional 'showing' of emotion with communicative intent. This deliberately-shown, natural behaviour is, in terms of relevance theory, a form of encoding procedural meaning. The function of procedural meaning is 'to facilitate the identification of the speaker's meaning by narrowing the search space for inferential comprehension.' (Wilson and Wharton 2006: 1571).

Many of the labels used in relation to affective prosody are more suitably categorized as 'attitudinal', i.e. indicating a stance or behaviour towards an interlocutor rather than the mental state of the speaker, and thus fall more clearly within the field of pragmatics. Attitude or '(dis) affiliation' has been shown within CA studies to be signalled rhythmically (e.g. Müller 1996) and by melodic mimicry (Couper-Kuhlen 1996b). It has also been described in terms of (im)politeness theory (e.g. Culpeper *et al.* 2003). Ito (2003) claims that a breathy voice quality is an indicator of **politeness** in Japanese, while other studies suggest that some 'attitudinal' effects are caused by a mismatch between **proposition** and prosody, or between prosody and context. Work on the effect of context on perceived attitude was carried out by Ladd *et al.* (1986) and more recently by Payà (2003b). A mismatch between tone of voice and proposition can, for example, indicate **irony** (*see* Tepperman *et al.* 2006 on 'Yeah right').

In general, while much is known about the prosodic correlates of information structure, speech acts, discourse structures and emotions, less is known about how these features are systematically exploited to generate implied meanings. There remains much to be learnt about the role of prosody in managing 'rapport', including politeness, and also its role in conflict talk. It is equally important to continue to extend prosodic research to languages other than English, not only in order to extend linguistic typology but also to explore the role that prosody can potentially play in cross-cultural (mis)understanding.

ANNE WICHMANN

See also: Computational pragmatics; conversational turn-taking; cross-cultural pragmatics; disambiguation; discourse cohesion; discourse markers; given/new distinction; idiom; inference; information structure; interactional linguistics; irony; natural and non-natural meaning; politeness; speech act theory

Suggestions for further reading

Arndt, H. and Janney, R.W. (1987) *Intergrammar: Toward an Integrative Model of Verbal, Prosodic and Kinesic Choices in Speech*, Berlin: De Gruyter.

Hirschberg, J. (2004) 'Pragmatics and intonation', in L.R. Horn and G. Ward (eds) *The Handbook of Pragmatics*, Oxford: Blackwell.
Wichmann, A. and Blakemore, D. (eds) (2006) 'Prosody and pragmatics', *Journal of Pragmatics*, 38: 1537–792.

Proverbs

The linguistic units called proverbs in a **culture** constitute a diverse, organically developed and developing collection. Lexica and anthologies can mislead us into thinking there is some fixed, monolithic group of items called proverbs – as opposed to an ad hoc assortment of certain recurrent sayings from the discourses of a language community, indeed, really, from a particular *community of practice* (Eckert and McConnell-Ginet 1992; Wenger 1998). We should not expect to discover a single characteristic *proverbiality* or a single inclusive definition of the proverb, and we should not be surprised when isolated proverbs contradict each other. Hence Taylor's (1962) famous remark that the definition of the proverb is too difficult to reward the effort.

What we generally call proverbs are recurrent, pithy, often formulaic and/or figurative, fairly stable and generally recognizable units. Proverbs are generally used to form a complete utterance or make a complete conversational contribution. This differentiates them from non-sentential items like proverbial phrases, **idioms**, binomials, etc. Proverbs make apodictic statements like *Money talks* or they evoke a scenario applicable to a range of analogous situations, as in *Little strokes fell great oaks*. In supplying ready-made responses to recurrent types of situations, proverbs seem to suggest particular evaluations or courses of action.

Despite Taylor's warning about defining the proverb, paremiologists have proposed various sorts of definitions through the years. Barley (1974: 880) argues that in defining items of folklore we should 'forget the genres and concentrate on the features', and he develops a feature-matrix definition for the proverb and related items (compare Norrick (1985) and Harnish (1993)). Ultimately, perceptions of proverbs are built around prototypes. Most prototypical are proverbs which sketch a scenario generalizable to comment on a range of analogous situations like *The early bird catches the worm*. Next come formulaic examples, which tend to make a literal statement like *Easy come, easy go*, and so on. The notion of *proverbiality* is itself even more clearly a matter of prototypicality (compare Arora (1984)). Honeck and Welge (1997) develop a scale of proverbiality based on prototypical proverbs, but by their criteria, there can be no clear line between proverbs, clichés, literary allusions and popular sayings like *When you're hot, you're hot*. This fact presents a problem for any effort to define the proverb in purely structural terms. Two noteworthy attempts in this direction are Milner (1969a, 1969b) and Dundes (1975). Milner (1969a: 200) argues that the most characteristic form of the traditional saying 'consists of a statement in four parts', while Dundes (1975) says, first, that only underlying formulas provide the basis for definition and, second, that the basic unit of classification is a descriptive element consisting of a topic and a comment – an analysis parallel to that which Georges and Dundes (1963) had proposed for riddles.

Proverbs often represent structures which are ungrammatical in normal sentence grammar. Like other idiomatic structures, proverbs represent an anomaly in any generative paradigm (Chafe 1968). Proverbs often contain archaic and dialect words and structures, e.g. *Them as has gits*. They may even come from other languages entirely, as in *Che sarà, sarà*. Proverbs are also often constructed around formulas which fail to conform to normal sentence grammar, e.g. *Like father, like son*. Since proverbs are typically conversational, it makes more sense to think of them as potentially complete contributions to conversation. Nevertheless, the syntactic structures of proverbs are interesting in themselves, e.g. those without verbs like *No rose without a thorn* or lacking nouns like *Slow and steady wins the race*. When proverbs are elliptical, hearers must mobilize rhetorical principles to work out discourse inferences, as Nordahl (1999) argues. Along with truly formulaic structures, proverbs exhibit various patterns of repetition, e.g. *An eye for an eye*, *You gotta do what you gotta do*, as discussed in Norrick (1989).

So-called transformational defects of proverbs have been described by Fraser (1970), Newmeyer (1972) and Dobrovolskij (1997, 1999), but

proverbs freely occur in variant-related forms and remain highly recognizable even when manipulated – hence the use of recognizable chunks like *early bird* in contexts like *the early bird satellite* and *early bird air fares*, and the creation of *anti-proverbs* (Mieder 1982; Mieder and Litovkina 1999). Moon (1998a: 88–89) demonstrates that transformability has now become a statistical corpus fact rather than an intuitive game. Her corpus investigations show that certain set phrases, including proverbs, tend, to appear in specific variant forms, while others simply do not.

Moon stresses the correlations between frequency, form, type of idiomaticity and discourse function. Colourful, stylistically marked and metaphorical expressions like proverbs are rare and often manipulated in contexts where they appear. As little recurrent texts in themselves, proverbs represent 'strongly coded' (Meleuc 1972) structures through, for example, **prosody**, hyperbole, personification, special syntax and lexis. Moreover, proverbs are sometimes conventionally tied to particular recurrent speech events or exchanges. As Norrick (1994) shows, for instance, proverbial formulas can be used for greetings such as *Fancy meeting you here*. Utterances of proverbs count as indirect speech acts in the sense of Searle (1975b). In using *Praise a fair day at evening*, I can mean what I say about praise and times of day, but also convey a general warning to my hearer. Figurative proverbs allow us to be doubly indirect, since they require listeners to apply the proverbial scenario to the present context and draw appropriate conclusions of their own (compare Taylor (1962: 169), Arewa and Dundes (1964: 70) and Barley (1972: 740)).

Proverbs often have striking images. Cognitive linguists argue that metaphors organize our perceptions, but the picture is far from clear (compare Burger (1996, 1998)). Proverbs contain specialized images from pre-industrial life, not basic-level metaphors or images familiar to speakers today. Thus, *The apple doesn't fall far from the tree* is confusing and ambiguous by comparison with *Like father, like son*. Proverbs frequently mix metaphors, combining images from separate source domains into complex collages. *Every cloud has a silver lining* draws first on the metaphoric domain of weather phenomena, then switches to a domain where silver represents something precious. The lining is mysterious, fitting, as it does, neither with clouds nor with silver. The result is a jumble of incongruous metaphors from unrelated domains, which cannot really resolve themselves. Seitel (1969) shows how fully metaphoric proverbs express a scenario applicable to a range of parallel social contexts.

Lakoff and Turner (1989) propose the Great Chain Metaphor (GCM) as a theory of how we understand proverbs. The Great Chain Metaphor is not really a metaphor. Rather, it is an 'ensemble' of principles by which we interpret proverbs, including The Great Chain, which reflects our folk theory about the attributes and behaviour of humans, animals, plants, complex physical objects, and natural physical things. Krikmann (1994) argues that the GCM does not really get at the difficult issues like how to figure out just how the proverb applies in any specific case, how good the interpretation is, how well it fits the context and what sort of force it has with the recipient. Honeck and Temple (1994) argue that the GCM is too complicated compared to other approaches. Much of the GCM simply recapitulates creative problem solving of the sort we must do in understanding all kinds of language. Norrick (2007) shows that the GCM fails to take into account intertextual relations between proverbs and all sorts of other texts, and their significance for contextual proverb interpretation.

The assumption that standard proverb meanings are generally accessible provides the foundation for the use of proverbs in tests of language understanding by psycholinguists. These tests examine (1) Polysemy: *A rolling stone gathers no moss* has two standard interpretations 'a person on the move remains young' and 'a person on the move remains poor'; (2) Pun: *No news is good news* means literally 'news is never positive' or on the punning interpretation 'the absence of new information leaves hope that nothing bad has happened'; (3) **Hyperbole**: *A watched pot never boils* (*see* Norrick (1982) on overstatement and extreme case formulations in proverbs); (4) **Irony**: *All geese are swans*; (5) **Tautology**: *Boys will be boys* (*see* Wierzbicka (1987) and Fraser (1988)); and (6) Paradox: preposterous claims like *The pen is mightier than the sword* and vicious circles like *Never say never* (*see* Golopentia-Eretescu (1970, 1971) and Norrick (1989)). Finally, we can note semantic relations between proverbs, because these relations often come up in the literature – even Sacks (1992) mentions them. These relations include (1) Synonymy: *Strike while the iron is hot* – *Make hay while the sun shines*; (2) Implicational Series: *It's not over till it's over* – *Never say die*; and (3) Antonymy: *He who hesitates is lost* – *Fools rush in* (Norrick 1984).

NEAL R. NORRICK

See also: Ambiguity; cognitive linguistics; ellipsis; humour; hyperbole; idiom; inference; irony; metaphor; psycholinguistics; quotation; rhetoric; semantics; stylistics; tautology

Suggestions for further reading

Abrahams, R.D. (1968) 'Introductory remarks to a rhetorical theory of folklore', *Journal of American Folklore*, 81: 143–58.
Firth, R. (1926) 'Proverbs in native life, with special reference to those of the Maori', *Folklore*, 37: 134–53.
Kirshenblatt-Gimblett, B. (1973) 'Toward a theory of proverb meaning', *Proverbium*, 22: 821–27.

Psycholinguistics

Psycholinguistics is the study of how the mind acquires, stores and handles language. The most important areas it covers are language processing, language acquisition, language disorders and language in the brain. Psycholinguistic perspectives also shape research into **animal communication**, **language evolution** and bilingualism. A recurrent question in many of these contexts is whether language is part of general cognition or independent of it.

The field is essentially a multidisciplinary one. It relies most heavily upon **cognitive psychology** and linguistics for its principles, but there are important connections with neurolinguistics, speech sciences, phonetics and phonology, education and computer modelling. Studies of language processing rely quite extensively upon pragmatic theory. The extent of the debt is not always acknowledged, but with the emergence of **experimental pragmatics** (Noveck and Sperber 2004), the links between the two fields seem set to become stronger.

The dominant approach in psycholinguistics is evidence-driven. It is informed by established cognitive theory and can draw upon detailed models, developed over fifty years, of how the mind and brain handle language. This tradition is heavily reliant upon an experimental methodology with its own set of task types, but observational data and **discourse analysis** are also used, as are the insights provided by brain imaging. A second approach is theory-driven, using the principles laid down by linguists (Chomskyan accounts are much favoured) as a framework for interpreting evidence relating to the nature of **linguistic competence**.

Some of the major areas of psycholinguistics are covered elsewhere in this volume: language acquisition in the entries for **child language acquisition**, **pragmatic development** and **theory of mind**, and language disorders under **autism spectrum disorders**, **clinical pragmatics**, **dementia**, **pragmatic language impairment** and **right-hemisphere damage**. This entry focuses upon models of language processing. The term 'processing' is sometimes restricted to the receptive skills (speech processing and visual processing), but here it is taken to include the productive skills as well.

Memory features prominently in cognitive accounts of language use (Gathercole and Baddeley 1993). Linguistic and world **knowledge** are held to be stored in long term memory (LTM). Processing entails retrieving information from LTM and holding it briefly in a short-term store, known as working memory (WM), while an utterance is being assembled or analyzed. The most important feature of WM is its limited capacity. If a task is too demanding or if there are multiple demands upon the language user's attention, processing may be compromised. It is therefore beneficial for certain processes such as word recognition to become highly automatic: in an expert user, they make minimal demands upon attention.

Psycholinguistic accounts of how language is produced and understood tend to favour a two-stage approach, which separates perceptual processes relating to linguistic form from conceptual ones relating to text **meaning** and external knowledge.

Language production

In models of language production, a distinction is generally observed between a pre-linguistic phase, involving planning and syntactic assembly, and a linguistic phase where the speaker or writer assembles and delivers a form of words. A process of encoding turns abstract concepts into words and phrases. The part played by pragmatic information is explicitly acknowledged in most accounts. Thus, Levelt's (1989) influential model of speech assembly recognizes that planning is informed by the speaker's understanding of turn-taking, Gricean **cooperative principles**, **deixis** and speaker **intentions**. Similarly, the widely discussed Hayes and Flower model of writing (Hayes 1996) has a rhetorical component which incorporates the speaker's goals, predisposition and beliefs and his or her estimate of the costs and benefits of producing the utterance. Hayes and Flower also specify the environment in which the writing task takes place, with account taken of the audience, the text so far and the composing medium.

An important issue in speech production is the tension between the complex syntactic decisions that a speaker needs to make and the time-constrained nature of most speech events. One solution is to propose that much language is stored in the mind in the form of chunks which can be produced fully formed in response to particular semantic and pragmatic imperatives (Wray 2002a). Formulaic language is said to consist not simply of multi-word lexical items but of many other kinds of recurrent sequence, including fillers that buy planning time (*what I'm trying to say is* …), **idioms**, frozen **metaphors** and syntactic patterns (e.g. *should have done* or *wish I'd known* associated with contexts of regret). This may seem to place a heavy burden upon lexical storage, but recent evidence confirms that the human mind possesses an enormous capacity for storing information.

Studies of writing processes have explored the differences between skilled and unskilled writers. Often quoted is the distinction made by Scardamalia and Bereiter (1987) between knowledge telling, a linear citing of information characteristic of the work of novice writers, and knowledge transforming, which takes full account of the target reader, the argument structure and the writer's goals. Bereiter and Scardamalia (1987: 110–30) also provide insights into the experience of writing acquisition, notably the adjustment that a child has to make from transmitting information in an interactive speech mode to transmitting it in a non-interactive writing mode and tracking the reader's state of knowledge. There has been interest in the cognitive demands imposed by writing (Kellogg 1994; Levy and Ransdell 1996). Keystroke logging (Sullivan and Lindgren 2006) provides detailed evidence of errors of execution made by writers using PCs. It also provides insights into the editing decisions that are made when a text does not fulfil a writer's original plan. Many such decisions relate to overall goals, to pragmatic intentions, to the foregrounding of important information, to clarity of expression or to inadequate identification with the reader's point of view. Skilled writing is generally agreed to be characterized by more detailed planning and more extensive and methodical revision.

Decoding

In accounts of receptive skills (Perfetti 1985; Pisoni and Remez 2005), a distinction is usually made between an initial perceptual phase, in which the input is analyzed into linguistic units, and a conceptual phase, when a meaning-based **representation** is constructed. The former, often referred to as decoding, requires the detection of lexical and syntactic forms in the input.

In lexical terms, the language user seeks a match between sounds reaching the ear or characters on the page and entries in his or her mental lexicon (Dahan and Magnuson 2006; McQueen 2007; Rastle 2007). A particularly intractable issue in studies of auditory decoding concerns the way in which word forms vary in connected speech. Exemplar models propose that language users do not store a single idealized word type against which the input can be matched, but multiple examples based upon actual tokens (Bybee and Hopper 2001; Tomasello 2003).

In identifying a word, cues provided by the input are evaluated at various levels of representation (how well do the sounds or letters match a given word at phoneme/grapheme, syllable or word level?). Likely candidates are identified and are activated (weighted) according to their closeness to the input and to factors such as frequency. Information about each candidate is accessed, including its meaning, word class

and combinatorial possibilities. Finally, as evidence accrues, one word becomes so activated that it emerges as indisputably the best match and recognition occurs.

A question raised by activation accounts of word recognition concerns the role of **context** (Morris 2006). Is recognition initially determined solely by perceptual information, with non-linguistic cues brought to bear very shortly afterwards? Or are all sources of evidence available to the processor at the outset? Research has produced conflicting findings, but opinion tends to favour the view that priority is briefly given to input. Much quoted in this regard is a finding by Swinney (1979) suggesting that where a word is ambiguous, all its potential senses are retrieved by the listener or reader, even where the context strongly favours one of them.

Theories of syntactic analysis have to conform to a presumption in psycholinguistics that decoding takes place on-line (Marslen-Wilson and Tyler 1980). Listeners attempt to make sense of what they hear at a very brief delay behind the speaker; readers analyze the text as their eyes move across the page. Syntactic parsing is thus not postponed until a clause is complete. Instead, listeners and readers rely upon probability, upon distributional cues and upon factors such as animacy in order to anticipate the structure of the input they are processing (van Gompel and Pickering 2007). There may be 'garden path' effects that are created by sentences which initially appear to favour one interpretation on semantic, pragmatic or syntactic grounds but then endorse another (*The rescuers found … they had lost their way*). Sentences of this type place heavy demands upon the processor. There are three alternative views of how listeners or readers respond (Mitchell 1994). They might adopt a single interpretation and revisit the form of words if the interpretation proves to be inappropriate. They might foreground a favoured interpretation but carry others in reserve in case of need. Or they might accept an indeterminate representation until such time as the **ambiguity** is resolved.

Syntactic parsing is assisted by punctuation and by patterns of intonation, which often correspond to syntactic boundaries. Once such a boundary is reached, the unit that has been processed is turned into an abstract representation, a unit of meaning, and it may become difficult for the listener to report the actual words that were used.

The output of decoding

Most psycholinguistic models embrace the semantic-pragmatic notion of 'sentence meaning' and represent the outcome of decoding as a context-independent **proposition**. This is a simplification for reasons that are not always made clear. One concerns word meaning. Many psycholinguistic accounts of lexical access (retrieving information about a word) assume that a single sense becomes available when a word is identified. However, the mental lexicon clearly has to supply a range of possible senses, which can only be narrowed down once account is taken of context (compare TURN in *turn a corner*, *turn a page* and *turn a handle*). A similar reservation attaches to syntactic parsing. A piece of English speech can be parsed into a structure that corresponds to the present progressive, but that form can refer to a temporary state, an ongoing event or a future plan. Until context is invoked, these alternatives have to be held in reserve by the processor. In short, the product of decoding cannot be as precise as the term 'proposition' might suggest to a semanticist, and the boundary between the perceptual and conceptual phases is not as sharply defined as psycholinguists sometimes imply.

From sentence meaning to speaker meaning

Nevertheless, many psycholinguistic accounts of meaning construction adhere closely to the traditional pragmatic distinction between sentence meaning and speaker meaning. The early models of van Dijk and Kintsch (1983) feature a text-based level where propositional information is established on a sentence-by-sentence basis and a situational level where external information is added. Their more recent construction-integration model (Kintsch 1988) consists of two stages: a construction stage where meanings are activated in the form of a loose network of connections, and an integration stage where a boost is given to context-relevant information. Another influential account represents comprehension as entailing the construction of a mental model of a text, in which propositional meaning is enhanced by world knowledge, interpretation and selection (Johnson-Laird 1983). The model is continuously updated as more information is added. A model may be indeterminate, with language users accepting a version that is incomplete but adequate for their purposes. This occurs especially when complex information has to be processed or when a text only requires processing at a relatively shallow level.

Concepts from **pragmatics** make an important contribution to cognitive accounts of meaning construction. A developing mental model is enriched by means of **inferences** (Singer 1994), which compensate for facts that a speaker has taken for granted or for links between points of information that have not been explicitly signalled. Psycholinguistic research into how meaning representations are retrieved indicates that, after a short delay, many individuals cannot distinguish between information that was provided by the text and information they supplied themselves through bridging inferences (Bransford *et al.* 1972). By contrast, elaborative inferences appear not to reshape the mental model, and decay quite quickly if not sustained by evidence. Psycholinguistics recognizes a further type of inference known as instantiation (Anderson and Ortony 1975), whereby a single aspect of a schematic concept becomes foregrounded by reference to co-text (the redness of TOMATO is salient in the phrase *a face like a tomato*, but its softness is salient in *squashed like a tomato*).

Much attention has been given to the question of **reference**, usually referred to as anaphor resolution (Garrod and Sanford 1994). It appears to be an automatic, on-line process but slows reading when there is ambiguity or when processing is inefficient. There is a marked difference between skilled and unskilled readers in the ability to match pronouns to antecedents that are at some distance (Yuill and Oakhill 1992: 86–94). Experimental tasks using ambiguous anaphors (*John phoned Bill. He said he was ill.*) provide insights into how an antecedent is chosen. Factors include parallel position, current **topic** and proximity, though sometimes these criteria may be in conflict. There has been much discussion of the type of representation that supports anaphor resolution. A reader, and in particular a listener, has to sustain an awareness of what the current topic is in addition to a **discourse** representation of everything that has been said so far. Sanford and Garrod's (1981) memory focus model distinguishes between an explicit focus on elements of a text that are currently foregrounded and an implicit focus on other information being carried forward.

In addition, ambiguity has to be resolved. The most obvious examples are lexical in nature (Simpson 1994). As already noted, a lexical item may indicate a range of possible senses until account is taken of its context. The conflicting indications provided by homophones and homographs must also be dealt with. A special instance of ambiguity is offered by figurative language. While frozen metaphors can be stored in the mind as pre-assembled formulae, much interest attaches to how novel ones are understood (Cacciari and Glucksberg 1994). A traditional view assumes a three-stage operation in which the receiver forms a literal interpretation of the utterance, relates it to the immediate context and to world knowledge and then seeks a non-literal interpretation. Against this hypothesis, there is evidence that individuals take longer to reject as 'false' a statement that is potentially metaphorical (*Some desks are junkyards*) than one which is not (*Some desks are roads*). Some researchers report that metaphors take no longer to process than comparable literal statements, provided they are clearly contextualized. This might suggest a parallel processing model like those proposed for 'garden path' situations, where the language user carries forward alternative interpretations (metaphorical and literal) until such time as the producer's intentions become clear.

The discourse representation

An aspect that merits separate consideration is the integration of sentence-level information into an evolving discourse representation. Here, the reader or listener has to judge the relevance of incoming information (allowing it to decay if it appears redundant), to trace logical connections with what has gone before, which may not be explicitly represented in the text, and to check whether the new information is consistent with what has already been understood. The last

process (termed self-monitoring) may result in **misunderstandings** being corrected or pragmatic inferences adjusted. A characteristic of children acquiring reading is their failure to self-monitor and identify conflicting information (Oakhill and Garnham 1988: 115–18).

In constructing a discourse representation, macro-information has to be distinguished from micro-information and a hierarchical model has to be built of the overall line of argument. Skilled comprehenders build more complex representations than weak comprehenders. According to Gernsbacher's (1990) structure building framework, skilled comprehenders are more able to determine when to initiate a new conceptual structure. Weak comprehenders operate linearly, repeatedly starting new structures instead of elaborating existing ones.

An 'effort after meaning' is said to drive the receptive language skills. It accounts for the way in which a representation is constantly updated and revised as earlier assumptions are challenged (Sanford and Garrod 1981). It is also seen in the extent to which listeners and readers foreground parts of a text that are associated with their own goals (Anderson and Pichert 1978). There are obvious parallels here with **relevance theory**, which affords a more principled account. Here, and in many other instances mentioned previously, psycholinguistics and pragmatics pursue similar agendas, but do so independently and sometimes using different terminology and terms of reference. A closer alignment between the two fields would clearly be advantageous to both.

JOHN FIELD

See also: Ambiguity; anaphora, pragmatics of; artificial intelligence; child language acquisition; cognitive psychology; context; experimental pragmatics; inference; inferential comprehension; information structure; lexical pragmatics; metaphor; modularity of mind thesis; neuropragmatics; proposition; reference; relevance theory; theory of mind

Suggestions for further reading

Field, J. (2004) *Psycholinguistics: The Key Concepts*, London: Routledge.

Gaskell, M.G. (ed.) (2007) *The Oxford Handbook of Psycholinguistics*, Oxford: Oxford University Press.

Gleason, J.B. and Ratner, N.B. (1998) *Psycholinguistics*, Fort Worth, TX: Harcourt Brace.

Psychotic Discourse

To understand psychotic talk, one needs first and foremost to establish 'what talk is', that is, what is the meaning of **discourse** and how will **communication** be defined? Recent studies in psychotic discourse are grounded in the interactional approach to communication. As noted by Schiffrin (1994), this approach privileges situated meaning, **context**, the co-construction of talk and the recipient's interpretations. The notion of situated meaning derives from Goffman (1974: 8): 'a concern for what one individual can be alive to at a particular moment', notwithstanding that in most situations 'many different things are happening simultaneously' (1974: 9). It takes into account the participants' constant verbal and nonverbal signals to each other, conveyed either intentionally or non-intentionally. In Goffman's terms, participants engaged in interaction would be constantly signalling information given (intentional) and information given-off (non-intentional). What is crucial in interpreting **meaning** in communication is how the listener (the recipient) actually understands what talk (and interaction) is about, that is, how communicative primacy may be attributed to information either given or given off. Also, interactional meaning is constantly being negotiated among the participants. The dynamic notion of frames (Bateson 1972; Goffman 1974; Tannen 1993) captures this ongoing linguistic and social work, where participants jointly construct talk. Frames may be a way of understanding particular and local interactional contexts. They address the interpreter's question of 'what is the meaning of what's going on here?' or 'how does the speaker mean what he or she says and does?' (taking into account information both given and given-off). Frames are signalled indirectly through conveyed messages (what Tannen calls 'metamessages'). To assess the meaning of a given message (for example, how a greeting was intended and to whom it was addressed), participants make use of situated **inferences** derived from contextualization cues (Gumperz 1982a, 1992). These signals may be prosodic (pitch, tone, voice quality, etc.), paralinguistic (pace of talk, pauses, overlaps, etc.) or nonverbal (postural configurations, distancing, eye gaze, etc.). Contextualization cues are typically understood as information given off: 'they are almost never consciously noted or assigned conventional meanings' (Schiffrin 1994: 402). Contextualization cues signal how social and linguistic messages are framed – what is the context of talk. These cues not only signal changes in contexts but also constitute these very contexts (Schiffrin 1989). In understanding psychotic discourse, these verbal and nonverbal devices make up the building blocks to understand 'what's going on here?'.

The study of doctor–patient interaction – within the above theoretical framework – aims at contributing to a better understanding of the processes involved in the use of language and communication, that is, to the very essence of psychiatry. According to Foucault (1994), the doctor is responsible for transforming the patient's symptoms into signs that are meaningful within a semiological system. Therefore, the doctor's description is in fact a linguistic and discursive operation that results in inserting the patient's symptoms in a predetermined schema for a certain disease.

Atypical framing practices may be at stake in psychotic discourse (Goffman 1974). Thus, the notion of coherence seems particularly interesting to understand such practices. Recent studies in this field (Ribeiro 1994; Pinto 2000; Ribeiro and Pinto 2005) discuss how psychotic patients may display unexpected verbal and nonverbal behavior. Consequently, coherence breaks down at various points. It breaks down within the exchange system. The patient does not follow **conversational turn-taking** rules, that is, he or she does not alternate speaker and hearer roles. It also breaks down in the action structure. The patient does not provide the expected sequencing of actions that characterizes doctor–patient interviews (within the domain of **speech acts**); for instance, the doctor's questions often remain unanswered as well as his or her summons unattended. Finally, coherence breaks down in the propositional content (utterance meaning). The patient fails to refer to what is being talked about, ignoring the **topics** introduced by the doctor and often presenting unclear referents (Ribeiro 1994). Some of these processes are captured in the descriptive definitions for the manifestation of disordered speech and communication (Andreasen 1979a, 1979b).

Language, thought and communication disorders

In the past, thought disorder was regarded as key to identify certain types of psychosis (Kraepelin 1925; Bleuler 1950). Kraepelin and Bleuler, for instance, regarded *flight of ideas* (when the patient shifts from one topic to an unrelated one, providing many details in the context of pressured speech) as one of the main symptoms of a manic state. *Looseness of association* (Bleuler 1950) was believed to be a pathognomic symptom (a symptom closely associated with a certain disorder or illness) of schizophrenia. However, the term 'thought disorder' has been under criticism for decades (Andreasen 1979a, 1979b; Chaika 1982; Taylor *et al.* 1994; Berembaum and Barch 1995; P. Thomas 1995). First, it relies on a correlation between thought and speech that is unattainable, as the interface between the two remains unclear (Chaika 1990). Second, the concept of thought disorder 'is not a unitary construct' (Berembaum and Barch 1995: 350), but rather encompasses several heterogeneous cognitive components, ranging from memory and attention problems to linguistic and discursive ones. Third, most common definitions of thought in handbooks of psychiatry are tautological, obscure and vague. As a consequence, the category 'thought disorder' remains an indefinite entity.

Based on the criticisms of the circular correlation between thought and speech, Andreasen (1979a, 1979b) coined the term 'disorganized speech', as it translates what can indeed be observed, that is, the patient's speech. Relying on empirical studies, Andreasen has reorganized the disorders by providing descriptive definitions. These definitions are closely related to some of the principles that underlie the notions of topic, topic shift, and conversational turn, thus assuming implicitly the notion of discourse as co-constructed by the participants while engaged in talk-in-interaction.

Psychosis, schizophrenia, mania

In the 1970s, there were many efforts to understand the use psychotics make of language (Rochester and Martin 1979). In acute psychosis, studies indicated that manics have similar performances to schizophrenics, so that what is usually attributed to schizophrenic behavior (a cluster of speech disorders) also occurs in manics (Andreasen and Powers 1974; Harrow and Quinlan 1977; Simpson and Davis 1985; Chaika 1990). A few studies have discussed the possibility of a general psychosis factor that may cut across psychotic diagnosis. Although thought pathology has been regarded as one of the primary symptoms of schizophrenia (Bleuler 1950; Chapman and Chapman 1973; Arieti 1974, among others), disturbances in thinking and perception are now known to occur also in manic patients (Akiskal and Puzantian 1979; Harrow *et al.* 1982, among others). Recent studies have found linguistic differences between manic and schizophrenic patients, pointing to the latter's low syntactic complexity (King *et al.* 1990; Taylor *et al.* 1994; Annand *et al.* 1994). However, from an interactional point of view these studies present some methodological problems. The results derive from experimental research, which is grounded in a model of communication focused only on the speaker's meanings and intentions, disregarding the listener's contributions. Also, the data collection is based uniquely on audiotapes, which in turn have only a verbatim transcription. If we believe that communication is a two-way process, to which all participants are expected to contribute, one would have to consider not only the linguistic code but also other contextualization cues (prosodic, nonverbal) in the co-construction of meaning in talk and interaction.

Communication in psychotic discourse: frame and topic

Frames and topics are interesting ways of understanding coherence in psychotic discourse (Ribeiro 1994; Pinto 2000). Framing captures the dynamic and fleeting nature of situational contexts (as some frames are brought to the foreground, while others are inhibited and become background). Ribeiro (1993, 1994) discusses how a patient in an acute psychotic crisis (a manic episode) may attend and respond (albeit in a bizarre way) to the institutional frames proposed by the doctor in a doctor–patient interview: the patient identifies who she is, where she is, who brought her to the hospital. Turns alternate and both participants, doctor and patient, contribute to the development of the interview. Each response (from either the doctor or the patient) ratifies a previous contribution, and talk goes on. In the institutional frames, the doctor controls the turn structure (gets the floor and introduces questions), while the patient provides information, requests help, and asks to leave. However, in the frames of the psychotic crisis – what Goffman (1974) has labeled psychotic fabrications – the patient establishes what talk is about. Within such framings, the patient mostly speaks as a young child addressing his or her mother. This is a common regressive behavior in psychosis (Cameron 1964; Kasanin 1964; Sullivan 1964). There is a transformation from ordinary behavior, where the doctor is treated literally (and not metaphorically) as the patient's mother. Goffman states that 'one of the upsetting things "psychotics" do is to treat literally what ordinarily is treated as **metaphor**, or at least to seem to do so' (1974: 115). Dialogic and reflexive frames emerge: first, the patient speaks as a very small child and summons her mother ('mama! mama!'); then reflexively, the patient as the mother provides a response ('what is it, my child?'). Such paired turns (composed of adjacency pairs of question/answer, greeting/greeting, command/response) attest to the dialogic nature of cognitive processes (Ribeiro 1994). In psychotic discourse, consistent frames emerge portraying a multitude of speakers addressing distinct listeners. Contextualization cues (prosodic and kinesic features, speech play, role switching and persona/audience cues, speech action and discourse markers) signal changes in frames.

Topic (what talk is about) provides a natural criterion for distinguishing instances of a speaker's deviant discourse from a discourse that matches our expectations about coherence. Also, research on patients' **conversations** in a psychiatric ward indicates that topic is the main criterion used to ground the perception of the other as mentally ill (Pinto 1995). The complex step-by-step process of topic introduction and topic development reveals the amount of effort that participants must undertake in interaction to assure topic continuity. When doctors face inconsistencies in the patient's discourse, they may use a number of strategies to keep the communicative channel open: they constantly summon the patient to the interview, they acknowledge the patient's statements, and they address some of his or her questions (Ribeiro 1994; Pinto 2000). In doing so, doctors are constantly reassessing their assumptions about the patient's topic of talk.

Psychotic talk often presents a 'loss of goal directedness' (Bleuler 1950) or derailment (Andreasen 1979a). The speaker ceases to contribute to the sequential (or cyclic) development of topics, thus thwarting topic continuity (Pinto 2000). Referents may be introduced with no meaningful relationship to each other. Often, the speaker gets farther and farther off the track. Word associations tend to be governed by rhythmic relationships (sound play) rather than by semantic and pragmatic ties (Ribeiro 1994). To complicate matters further, both doctor and patient fail to identify each other's topics. As a result, the process of topic negotiation often breaks down, few topics are expanded, and others are recycled with no pre-established agenda.

Narrative and coherence in psychotic discourse

In narrating, we make sense of experience, of what is happening with and around us (Labov 1972; Bruner 1990). It is how past experience and events are contextualized. In medical discourse, the analysis of patients' talk as **narrative** has proved to be helpful in understanding the experience of illness (Mishler 1986; Clark and Mishler 1992; Good 1994).

Can stories emerge within a psychiatric interview with a patient in an acute psychotic crisis? To what extent are they relevant to the purpose of the interview? In spite of speech and communication disorders (such as tangentiality, incoherence, derailment, among others), Ribeiro states that 'bits of a story can be pieced together, thus providing the doctor with crucial clues to the patient's past and present illness, family and social history, and chief complaint' (2000: 284). In interviews with a patient in a psychotic episode, narrative works to describe the patient's personal topic agenda and its complex layering of **references** (or multiple contextual embeddings).

Different frameworks for analyzing narratives are used in discourse studies in psychiatry. Labov's structural/functional framework – a narrative is 'a method of recapitulating a past experience by matching a verbal sequence of clauses to the sequence of events which, we infer, actually occurred' (1972: 359–60) – has been used by researchers to analyze discourse cohesion and coherence. Labov's framework presents a schematic structure: stories would often have an abstract, orientation(s), complicating actions, evaluation(s), a coda, and a resolution. The evaluation component is considered most relevant as it is used by the narrator to indicate the point of the story: why it is being narrated. Also, temporal order constitutes the main thread of coherence. In psychiatric interviews, however, patients' stories are often presented in a quite fragmented form and do not adhere to the temporal order principle. Also the orientation section (who, where, when, what) often lacks sequential ties. Ribeiro (2000) describes a story ('the Bozo narrative') told by a patient in a fragmented but yet still coherent discourse. The story seems to accomplish at least three functions: (1) it creates textual cohesion in a discourse often filled with unrelated topics; (2) it provides a referent – Bozo, the clown – which seems to clarify contradictory utterances and interactional moves, providing the listener with important clues as to the patient's performance and identity; and (3) it integrates different interactive contexts which would otherwise conflict, thus creating some conversational coherence.

Ribeiro and Cabral Bastos (2005) discuss a narrative that is constructed in a noncanonical form by a patient in a manic episode (in a psychiatric interview situation). There are bits of information that often lack development. The orientation sections point to emotions and cultural values; however, they lack specific time and place references and most referents are left inconclusive. Chaika (1990) discusses an experimental task with twenty-two patients (fourteen had diagnoses of schizophrenia and eight of mania), who were interviewed individually and

asked to produce a narrative after each patient had seen a short movie (*The Ice Cream Stories*). They all seemed to understand the requirements and indicated cooperation. Chaika states that all patients completed the experiment and produced a 'decodable' narrative, 'albeit not necessarily by the usual strategies for comprehension' (1990: 136). Compared to 'normals', they displayed competence in the use of cohesive ties (contradicting Rochester and Martin 1979), but there was digression and lack of adherence to a 'macrostructure' in the narrative: 'personal memories and other extraneous factors interfered' (Chaika 1990: 145). In some extreme cases (five out of the twenty-two psychotic narrations), there were problems in establishing a required referent as well as structuring the story (for example, providing an introduction). All the above studies merit further investigation in studies of discourse and language use in mental health contexts.

Talk and interaction in a psychiatric interview

Psychiatry relies on clinical practice where the patient's **communicative competence** is one of the aspects being assessed (Ribeiro and Pinto 2005). A successful assessment of the patient's mental state requires that the patient addresses the institutional topics of the psychiatric interview. While some interactional processes may facilitate communication, others may inhibit it. Open-ended questions, for example, allow for the production of more spontaneous and lengthy responses, where stories may then emerge. And probing questions about details of a narrative, for instance, might reveal specific information that would otherwise not be evaluated.

The interactional approach to studies in communication (Schiffrin 1994) brought to light aspects of communication which have deep implications for psychiatry. It calls for a balance between the institutional agenda introduced and maintained by the doctor on one hand, and the personal topics brought up by the patient on another, allowing for a more conversational encounter, where the patient may introduce narratives and the doctor may align him- or herself as a listener of stories (Mishler 1986).

Psychotic discourse is a term that encompasses a gamut of multiple undetermined and unconventional discursive behaviors. In order to be communicatively competent, that is, to use language in context, one needs to activate not only the linguistic system but also other more complex mental functions such as memory, attention and consciousness (Andreasen 2001). Research on various fields has not been able to identify yet whether and how the multiple mental functions that constitute 'normal' human activity come into play when using discourse. Psychotic discourse is then a generic label that has been used to refer to a set of unexpected or abnormal verbal and/or non-verbal manifestations. From an interactional approach, it ranges from atypical phonological and lexical choices to a series of disconnected discursive sequences, in which both circular topic discontinuity and atypical framing dynamics position the listener away from the interactional process of the joint construction of meaning.

BRANCA TELLES RIBEIRO and DIANA DE SOUZA PINTO

See also: Autism spectrum disorders; clinical pragmatics; communication failure; competence, communicative; competence, pragmatic; context; conversation; conversational turn-taking; conversation analysis; cultural scripts; deixis; discourse; discourse analysis; discourse coherence; discourse cohesion; implicature; inference; intention; intentionality; interactional linguistics; meaning; narrative discourse; reference; relevance theory; schizophrenic language; sociolinguistics; topic; utterance interpretation

Suggestions for further reading

Andreasen, N. (2001) *The Brave New Brain*, New York: Oxford University Press.
Chaika, E.O. (1990) *Understanding Psychotic Speech: Beyond Freud and Chomsky*, Springfield, IL: Charles C. Thomas.
Ribeiro, B.T. (1994) *Coherence in Psychotic Discourse*, New York: Oxford University Press.

Q

Question

Speech acts are rule governed. There are rules that we have to follow when we intend to perform a speech act of a particular type in a certain natural language. If we intend to pose a question to a person in order to elicit an answer, we are required by the rules that govern the **speech act type** of posing a question to be able to recognize an answer as such and to distinguish between an answer to our question and a reaction to it that is not an answer, such as 'I don't know' or a few seconds of **silence**. This is a general requirement, independent of any particular natural language. If we intend to pose a question in a certain natural language, then we are required by the rules that govern the speech act type of posing a question in that language to use certain features of the language, such as the interrogative grammatical form of the language, if it has one, or its interrogative intonation, if it has one.

Wittgenstein, a most influential twentieth-century philosopher, used the term 'language game' to mark practices, such as asking. A language game can be described as being governed by some rules. A specification of a language game is a full and accurate presentation of the rules that govern the practice. A specification of a speech act type is such a presentation of the rules that govern each performance of a speech act of that type.

It has been commonly assumed that question is a single speech act type. Instances of posing a question have usually been taken to constitute attempts on the part of the speaker to get information of a certain kind from the addressee of the speech act. Typical instances of a sincere usage of the sentence 'what is your address?', under typical circumstances of addressing the speech act to a certain addressee, are intended as attempts to know the addressee's address on grounds of the addressee's specification of it.

Such typical instances of sincerely using an English sentence in the interrogative, in a speech act addressed to a certain addressee, manifest two of the rules that govern speech acts of asking: (a) a speech act is performed by the speaker, as intended to be addressed to a certain addressee, and (b) the speech act counts as an attempt on the part of the speaker to get information from the addressee. Assuming that speakers are rational agents, two additional rules become manifest: a precondition of sincerely posing a question is that (c) the speaker does not know the answer and is interested in knowing it, and (d) the speaker has a reason to assume the addressee of one's speech act knows the answer. All of these rules seem to be followed when a typical speech act of posing a question is under consideration.

However, a consideration of additional instances of sincerely using interrogative sentences shows that there are some circumstances in which one or more of these rules do not have to be followed. We sincerely ask ourselves all kinds of questions when we are not our own addressees. We pose questions we know the answers to in order to examine the **knowledge** of some addressee. We pose questions we and our addressees know the answer to in order to create a rhetorical effect. Sometimes we pose a question we are sure our addressee cannot answer in order to teach the addressee some lesson. Thus, posing a question is a family of different speech act types, each of which is governed by a separate system of rules, both generally and in every natural language.

Questions have been extensively studied as speech acts that play a role under special circumstances of interaction, such as interviews, interrogations and academic discussions (Crawford Camiciottoli 2008; Emmertsen 2007; Gnisci and Pontecorvo 2004). However, such studies shed light on the nature of these interactions more than on question as a speech act type. A study of brain localization of speech act types has revealed an intricate relationship between questions and **requests** (Soroker *et al.* 2005).

ASA KASHER

See also: Rhetorical question; speech act theory; speech act type

Suggestions for further reading

Chisholm, W.S. (ed.) (1984) *Interrogativity: A Colloquium on the Grammar, Typology, and Pragmatics of Questions in Seven Diverse Languages*, Amsterdam: John Benjamins.

Searle, J.R. (1969) *Speech Acts*, Cambridge: Cambridge University Press.

Somerville, J. (2002) *The Epistemological Significance of the Interrogative*, Aldershot: Ashgate.

Quotation

In its typical form a quotation is an iconic sign for a linguistic **representation**. Its main varieties are (1) metalinguistic citation, (2) direct quotation/speech, (3) mixed quotation and (4) scare quoting:

(1) 'Brussels' rhymes with 'muscles'.
(2) Then she said, 'Will you write a letter?' and I said, 'Sure'. (Hash 1999)
(3) Quine says that quotation ' … has a certain anomalous feature'. (Davidson 1979b: 28)
(4) A boy tells Grossman of 'his' house in Jaffa. He has never seen it, but his grandfather did. (Grant 2000)

Quotations are often classified in reference to W. V.O. Quine's distinction between 'use' and 'mention' (Quine 1940). In (1), the words *Brussels* and *muscles* are not used but mentioned (more precisely, the quotations *'Brussels'* and *'muscles'* are used to mention the names *Brussels* and *muscles* as types). In (2), we have a similar situation, with the difference that the strings *'Will you write a letter?'* and *'Sure'* are presented as standing for uttered tokens. In (3), which appears to combine direct with indirect speech – the quotation is under the scope of *says that – has a certain anomalous feature* fulfils its ordinary, quotation-independent function in the quoting sentence but is mentioned at the same time. A similar description applies to *his* in (4) with the difference that the quotation does not occur within the scope of a verb of saying. Note that, if quotation is defined as involving mention of a linguistic representation, then so-called 'indirect quotation/speech' is not a variety of quotation in the strict sense because it does not appear to function as an iconic sign in C.S. **Peirce**'s sense.

Syntactic and semantic inertness

It has been repeatedly observed that just about anything can be quoted. This is certainly true with metalinguistic citation and direct quotation:

(5) 'No me gusta la carne!' is my favourite Spanish sentence.
(6) And then she said 'I won't blah blah this and blah blah that'.

In both (5) and (6), it is clear that the quoted strings do not make an ordinary syntactic and semantic contribution to the quoting sentence. This is true of all quotations that involve only mention, not use, regardless of whether they have a bona fide English **syntax** and **semantics**, or include foreign words as in (5), non-words as in (6) or even representations of noises (see (10) and (11)). Accordingly, many scholars propose that quoted strings are syntactically and semantically 'inert' with respect to the phrase or clause in which they are embedded (Davidson 1979b: 37; García-Carpintero 1994: 261; Recanati 2001b: 651). Such inertness, however, cannot extend to quotations that involve use together with mention, as in (3) and (4), precisely because the quoted strings *are* used in those examples. Still, there remain difficulties with the account in terms of simultaneous use and mention: even in mixed and scare quoting, strings different from English words can be tokened:

(7) If you were a French academic, you might say that the parrot was *un symbole du Logos*. (Barnes 1985: 18)

Though the French string *un symbole du Logos* is made to fulfil the same syntactic and semantic role that its translated equivalent *a symbol of the Logos* would, it cannot be said to be *used* in (7) in any simple sense: an explanation of what it means for a non-English string to be used in an English sentence is required.

The mechanism(s) of quotation

Though nearly everyone agrees that quotation possesses an iconic (pictorial) dimension, there is no general consensus that this is the essential mechanism on which quotation works. Thus, writers from Tarski (1983: 156) to Gómez-Torrente (2005) claim that, in cases like (1) and (2), enclosing a string between quotation marks creates a term made up of the inverted commas and a so-called interior. A quotation, then, is a composite name that refers to its interior. However, contrary, to appearances, the name has no internal structure: it is monomorphemic. Other writers hold that inverted commas function essentially as indexical signs. Thus, the popular 'demonstrative theory', championed notably by Sørensen (1961) and Davidson (1979b), has it that a pair of inverted commas is a sort of **demonstrative** pronoun that points at its interior. These theories have the advantage of offering a direct explanation for the inertness of quotations: on the monomorphemic theory, the interior is a meaningless part of a morpheme, not any more meaningful than *let* in *letter* (*cf.* Quine 1940: 26); on the demonstrative account, the interior is the demonstratum, and like any demonstratum it is part not of the sentence but of the extra-sentential **context**. However, these theories meet with serious difficulties when faced with quotations involving use as well as mention. There is no way a name or a demonstrative pronoun can be substituted for the quotes in (3) and (4) (*cf.* Recanati 2001b: 654).

Another popular account of the way quotation works is the so-called 'identity theory', which holds that the quotation and what it mentions are one and the same thing. Thus, in (1), the nouns *Brussels* and *muscles* are used – albeit anomalously – to mention themselves (see, e.g. Searle 1969: 74–76; Washington 1992: 582). The attractive simplicity of this account may conceal some serious difficulties. For example, *Brussels* and *muscles* in (1) are tokens, but they refer to types or lexemes. No 'simple identity' is at play here.

A further major line of thinking is represented by the 'demonstration theories' of Clark and Gerrig (1990) and Recanati (2001b). These theorists view quotations essentially as depictive or iconic acts whose purpose is to illustrate certain features exemplified by the uttered token, e. g. a linguistic form, a meaning, the speaker's pronunciation, age, emotional state, etc. (Clark and Gerrig 1990: 769; Clark 1996: 175). Recanati (2001b: 649) suggests that these acts are sometimes 'linguistically recruited' to fill a slot in a phrase or clause. He then talks of 'closed quotation' (as in (1), (2), (5), (6), (8)), and uses the term 'open quotation' for those cases in which a linguistic demonstration is not recruited (examples (3), (4), (7)). Typically, closed quotations are metalinguistic referring expressions, but open quotations are not. In this respect, Recanati's version of the demonstration theory is at odds with all other major theories, which hold that *all* quotations are referential expressions.

Marks

There is a debate as to whether quotation is marked in a linguistically conventional way. The debate suffers from the almost exclusive focus on written language in discussions of quotation. Thus, the only serious contenders for the title of conventional linguistic markers of quotation have been single or double inverted commas, with some allowances made for italics. To 'conventionalists', quotation is essentially a semantic phenomenon. The **meaning** of quotation marks affects **logical form**, hence, this meaning is truth-conditionally relevant (*cf.* Cappelen and Lepore 2005b). This is so even when those marks are not overtly realized in the quoting sentence, either because the writer failed to use inverted commas, or because the quotation occurs in speech. Thus, conventionalists have to assume that spoken quotations exhibit some counterpart of quotation marks. However, very little research has been done into this issue, and the question remains open whether there are conventional linguistic markers of spoken quotation. Defenders of semantic accounts, usually the monomorphemic or the demonstrative theory, also have to deal with the fact that quotation marks were nonexistent in written European languages until the Middle Ages and that their use did not generalize until the Modern period. On the other side of the theoretical divide, one finds scholars who endorse pragmatic accounts of quotation, usually some form of the identity or demonstration theories. For these scholars, whatever signals there are, these are optional 'pragmatic indicators' (Clark and Gerrig; Recanati) or disambiguating marks (Saka 1998). These theorists do not have to face the issues just raised, but they have to explain the (sometimes) truth-conditional impact of quotations with more than an appeal to the conventional meaning of quotation marks.

Metalinguistic predicates

Metalinguistic predicates often signal the presence of a quotation, though not systematically. They can combine with two types of mention: 'autonymous', in which a token of an expression is produced in order to refer to another token of that expression or to a type which it instantiates, as in (8); and 'heteronymous', i.e. mention by means of a NP that is not iconically related to the expression mentioned, as in (9) (*see* Recanati 2000: 137):

(8) 'Collateral damage' is a despicable expression.
(9) *That* is a despicable expression.

The predicate *be a despicable expression* requires a metalinguistic argument, but that argument need not be a quotation. It can be a mentioning expression that works non-iconically. Likewise for these heteronymous variants of the quotations in (1) and (2):

(1') *The name of the Belgian capital* rhymes with *a name for fibrous tissue.*
(2') Then she said *something I pretended not to hear.*

Notice that heteronymous mentions are usually purely metalinguistic referential expressions, and that explains why they cannot substitute for the quotations in (3) or (4), where some form of use accompanies mention.

Extension to non-linguistic representations

Some scholars stress the similarities between quoting and some forms of iconic gesturing (Clark and Gerrig 1990; Recanati 2001b; De Brabanter, to appear). It appears difficult to find a cut-off point between prototypical cases of quotation – where the interior of the quotation consists of linguistic material only – and less typical cases – where the interior of (what may still be) a quotation comprises non-linguistic sounds or even non-sonic gesturing:

(10) Then the camel went [SPEAKER IMITATES A CAMEL BELCH].
(11) Piano student plays passage in manner μ
Teacher: It's not [PLAYS PASSAGE IN MANNER μ] – it's [PLAYS PASSAGE IN MANNER μ']. (Horn 1989: 564; quoted in Recanati 2001b: 648–49)
(12) Then Joe went [SPEAKER IMITATES SOMEONE KEEPING A LOW PROFILE].

If one accepts that (10) contains a quotation of non-linguistic sounds – a tempting conclusion, given the presence of quotative *went* – then there seems to be no principled reason to deny that (11) contains quotations. But if it is possible to quote musical passages, i.e. sounds not produced by vocal organs, then there is little reason to deny that (12) contains a (sort of) quotation too. Clearly, it is the iconic nature of the communicative behaviour that unites these various cases. One possible line of objection against such an extension of the notion of quotation may consist in requiring quotations to be metarepresentations. Whereas all examples of quotations until (8) were metarepresentational, (10) and (11) may not be (depending on whether the camel 'meant' something by belching and on whether music is representational), and (12) clearly is not, since the gestures there refer to non-signalling behaviours.

Quotation and metarepresentation

Those scholars like Wilson (2000), who approach quotation from the metarepresentational angle, tend to regard quotations as just one type of **metarepresentation**. Quotations are higher-order linguistic representations of lower-order linguistic representations. But the mechanism on which quotation is said to work – representation by resemblance – is also that on which the other types of metarepresentations work (2000: 425). In metarepresentations of thought, resemblance is usually 'interpretive': the higher-order representation shares a number of logical and contextual implications with the represented thought (2000: 426). In quotation, resemblance can be mainly formal (metalinguistic citation or direct quotation) or interpretive (indirect quotation) or both (mixed and scare quoting) (*see* Noh 2000).

As opposed to the line adopted in the preceding sections, relevance theorists emphasize the commonalities between representations that formally resemble their object (roughly, quotations that meet the iconicity criterion) and those that resemble it interpretively (roughly, indirect quotations and representations of thought). They also underline the commonalities between quotations and a series of linguistic devices (e.g. hearsay adverbs like *allegedly* or parentheticals like *as X says*) which, though not strictly quotational, signal that certain utterances or thoughts are to be attributed to other cognitive agents. Like quotation, these devices are interesting in that they appeal to a metacommunicative ability that is 'a sub-part of a more general metapsychological ability, or "theory of mind"' (Wilson 2000: 440).

PHILIPPE DE BRABANTER

See also: Conventionality; demonstratives; echoic use; evidentials; indexicals; metarepresentation; Peirce, C.S.; philosophy of language

Suggestions for further reading

Cappelen, H. and Lepore, E. (2007) *Language Turned on Itself: The Semantics and Pragmatics of Metalinguistic Discourse*, Oxford: Oxford University Press.

De Brabanter, P. (ed.) (2005) *Hybrid Quotations*, Belgian Journal of Linguistics, 17, Amsterdam: Benjamins.

Rey-Debove, J. (1997) *Le Métalangage: Etude Linguistique du Discours sur le Langage*, Paris: Armand Colin.

R

Radical Pragmatics

Theories of grammar and **semantics** posit sets of rules (or principles) which allow for the construction of natural language sentences and for their compositional interpretation. These theories are broadly taken to be empirical theories and hence are subject to (dis-)confirmation given data from language users. In particular, it is incumbent on a theory of grammar to explain our judgements of acceptability of sentence forms. For example, the theory should explain why informants regularly attest to the ill-formedness of (1) and to the well-formedness of (2):

(1) John thinks Mary likes himself.
(2) John thinks Mary likes him.

Similarly, semantic theories ought to explain judgements concerning truth and falsity and concerning **entailment** relations. For example, a semantic theory should explain the judgement that (3) could not be true if John did not see Bill but (4) could be true, while (5), the **negation** of (4), could not be true if John saw Bill:

(3) John saw Mary and Bill.
(4) John saw Mary or Bill.
(5) John didn't see Mary or Bill.

While linguists in the modern era (from the middle of the last century) would largely recognize the above empirical desiderata as being central for theories of grammar and interpretation, there is a question about the scope of each of these theories. Should all judgements of acceptability be captured by grammatical theories? Should all the implications attested to by informants follow from the compositional interpretation assigned by semantic theories? In the context of early modern linguistics, the default presumption seems to have been that the answer is affirmative in both cases. That is, putting aside performance limitations, the only competencies relevant to linguistic judgements are *ipso facto* grammatical (including semantic) competencies.

What became known as the radical pragmatics movement (*see* Cole 1981) diverged from this orthodoxy. Radical pragmatics recognized that there are competencies surrounding the use of linguistic expressions, competencies that directly affect informants' judgements, which are distinct from those involved in determining the structure of an expression and assigning it an interpretation. Probably the best known articulation of this idea is in **Grice**'s pragmatic theory (*see* Grice 1989), which shows how semantic theories can be greatly simplified where judgements about **meaning** can be accounted for via the mechanism of conversational **implicature** rather than derived by entailment from conventional meaning. For example, while informants might be inclined to say that (4) implies that John did not see both Mary and Bill, the implication does not need to be encoded in the conventional meaning of 'or' but follows as an **inference** about what the speaker means in addition to what the speaker's words mean. The simplification this account affords semantic theory can be demonstrated by considering the fact that if 'A or B' conventionally entailed not both A and B, then the 'or' in (5) would have to be a homonymous lexeme encoding a different, 'inclusive', meaning. Grice's theory of implicature allows us to say there is just one 'or' which has an inclusive meaning. Other interpretations are derived inferentially.

Grice's pragmatic principles are not the only principles of use that may figure in informants' judgements. For example, Reinhart (1983b) proposed that a principle of efficiency of **reference** lies behind judgements that (6) is ill-formed if the pronoun is meant to refer to John:

(6) John likes him.

The principle says, roughly, that the speaker should use the most efficient means of reference, unless there is good reason not to do so. In the case of (6), although 'him' could refer to John, it is highly ambiguous, potentially referring to any male individual. By contrast, there is a more efficient alternative, 'himself', which unambiguously gives rise to the same overall interpretation. Given that there is an obviously more efficient alternative, (6) is judged infelicitous.

Reinhart's account greatly simplified the rules of grammar embodied in the so-called binding principles to cover just those cases where there was semantic binding. Other theories attempt to reduce more of the binding principles to **pragmatics** (*see* Huang 1994; Levinson 2000), and other areas of grammar – such as quantifier scope assignment – have been analyzed in terms of pragmatics (*see* Kempson and Cormack 1981). In each case, the relative merits of a pragmatic analysis compared to a grammatical account boils down to how well it explains the data. But where empirical coverage is the same, then methodological considerations tend to apply: which account makes appeal to the smallest number of otherwise unmotivated assumptions overall? The most well-known methodological principle is referred to by Grice as Modified Occam's Razor: Do not multiply senses beyond necessity. However, while this principle is often invoked, it rarely stands as the only methodological consideration that makes pragmatic accounts persuasive. Returning to (4), for instance, it is not simply that the Gricean account of the 'not both A and B' implication obviates the need to say that 'or' is ambiguous. Other methodological considerations (scope of the account, universality) carry far more weight. In this example, disjunction is just one case among very many

(including quantifiers, modals, scalar adjectives) that conforms to a pattern predicted by Grice's theory. Moreover, such implications arise universally across languages.

Another important domain of inquiry for pragmatics is **presupposition**. A presupposition is unlike an entailment in that it can *project* out of non-veridical embedding operators. So, while the entailments of a sentence do not survive when the sentence is negated (7a, b), they apparently do survive where presupposition triggers like 'know' are involved (8a, b):

(7) a. Mary killed John $\implies$ John died
   b. Mary didn't kill John $\not\implies$ John died
(8) a. John knows that it is raining $\implies$ It is raining
   b. John doesn't know that it is raining $\implies$ It is raining

As a phenomenon studied by linguists and philosophers of language, presupposition has been viewed as a property of lexical triggers (like 'know') or constructions (like 'to stop V-ing'). Hence, it is a linguistic property (*see* Karttunen 1974). However, presuppositions, as in (8b), behave suspiciously like pragmatic conversational implicatures in that they are cancellable and non-detachable (*see* Levinson 1983 for discussion of these properties and their application to presupposition). An alternative approach inspired by Stalnaker (1974, 1998) argues that to explain the phenomenon of presupposition, we need an account of what speakers presuppose in uttering a sentence rather than what sentences themselves presuppose. The Stalnakerian approach represents the most radical approach to presupposition but it has few takers. A large impediment to the widespread acceptance of the radical pragmatic analysis of presuppositions has to do with the fact that sometimes presuppositions do not project, as the presupposition does in (8b) above, but are somehow absorbed by other parts of the sentence. For instance, consider that (9) has no presupposition because the presupposition of the sentence in the consequent of the conditional is 'satisfied' by the sentence in the antecedent:

(9) If it's raining, then John knows that it's raining.

It would appear that to explain this type of projection fact using only pragmatics one would need a theory of the pragmatics of sub-utterances. So far, no such theory has been forthcoming. Instead, alternative theories of linguistic meaning proposed by Heim (1983b) and Kamp (1981) have adapted some of Stalnaker's ideas to make it possible to describe the effect of early parts of a sentence on the interpretation of later parts. Although similar in terms of the way they account for projection facts, these so-called *dynamic semantic theories* come in two varieties. The theory developed by Heim is closer in spirit to the work of Karttunen and Strawson in that presupposition phenomena are treated as fundamentally linguistic, semantic phenomena. By contrast, the dynamic accounts of presupposition that follow Kamp (found in van der Sandt 1992 and Geurts 1999) assume that the truth-conditional properties of utterances are not necessarily read off the sentence alone but are subject to the operation of a constrained set of contextual rules. This is a kind of moderately radical pragmatic approach in that it treats the phenomenon in question as the product of some pragmatic rules but it does not attempt to explain the phenomena as deriving from inferences we make about the speaker in **context** using only general principles of **conversation** (as in the radical pragmatics of Grice and Stalnaker).

In linguistics as in other disciplines, what appears to pose a radical challenge to orthodoxy in one period of history can become orthodoxy in another period. For early modern linguistics, the application of Grice's ideas to explain semantic phenomena was a great departure from standard methods. Today, almost all linguists accept that if you can use general pragmatic principles to explain some phenomena, then that route is to be preferred. More recently, another fundamental working assumption has been challenged, namely, the idea that the truth conditions of an utterance can be derived from the structure of the sentence (once certain linguistic elements are assigned an interpretation in context). Today's radicals propose that, although truth conditions sometimes do not go beyond the content determined by the sentence's meaning, they can on occasion be enriched by post-linguistic pragmatic inference.

Pragmatic enrichment can best be illustrated by considering (10), which implies that John's ostracization was preceded by, and a result of, his inebriation. It is widely agreed that these temporal and causal implications of conjunction should be treated as conversational implicatures (*see* Gamut 1991 for a good textbook discussion):

(10) At the party, John got drunk and no one talked to him.

(11) illustrates how such an implicature can somehow become embedded within the scope of an operator and hence have an effect on the truth conditions of the utterance:

(11) It's always the same at parties, either John gets drunk and no one talks to him or no one talks to him and he gets drunk.

According to standard assumptions about conversational implicatures, they are implications that arise independently of the truth conditions of the utterance and so they should not affect truth conditions in the way that they appear to in this example and many others. If the implicature of each conjunct of (11) does not affect the truth conditions, then each conjunct should say the same thing as the other and so (11) should strike us as an abuse of disjunction, saying effectively, 'Always, A or A'. It seems clear in this case that the temporal and causal implications of each conjunct fall within the scope of the disjunction. So it would appear that purely pragmatic implications can affect truth conditions. That is, truth conditions can be affected by content that is not represented anywhere in the structure of the sentence but is derived by the application of rules or principles for the employment of the sentence in context.

Following on from Kamp's theory, the moderately radical treatment of this enrichment phenomenon (found in Lascarides and Asher 1993) holds that the product of a circumscribed set of defeasible pragmatic rules can be allowed to affect the representations of the truth conditions of the **discourse**. There is reason, however, to be sceptical that a circumscribed set of pragmatic rules can account for all enrichment phenomena given that any pragmatic effect (including all figurative effects) can become embedded in this way (*see* Carston 2002 for an overview of the phenomena and Breheny 2002 for a discussion of the shortcomings of the moderate view). Other moderately radical accounts, such as that found in Bach (1994a) and Levinson (2000), are subject to similar concerns. Recanati (2004b) extends the moderately radical view by arguing that any pragmatic effect can intrude into truth conditions via a **primary pragmatic process** which applies to the product of grammatical rules. For Recanati, general pragmatic principles (such as that proposed by Grice and Stalnaker) only apply to the output of these primary processes. A more thoroughly radical pragmatic approach to enrichment is taken by relevance theorists (*see* Sperber and Wilson 1995; Carston 2002). They argue that all pragmatic effects, whether implicature or enrichment, can be accounted for by the one set of general pragmatic principles concerning the conduct of the speaker.

Whether moderately radical or not, all of these accounts of enrichment accept that truth conditions can be affected by factors other than the sentence's meaning in context. They are all referred to as contextualist accounts. **Contextualism** is rejected by semantic conservatives who would argue that all apparent cases of enrichment can be explained away. For example, Stanley (2000) holds that many apparent enrichments are the product of interpreting covert linguistic elements in sentences. Other accounts, such as Cappelen and Lepore (2005a), hold that radicals' assumptions about enrichment are based on poor methodology, since they conflate intuitions about the main point of an utterance with intuitions about the truth conditions of the sentence uttered.

RICHARD BREHENY

See also: Anaphora, pragmatics of; contextualism; explicit/implicit distinction; generalized conversational implicature, theory of; Grice, H.P.; implicature; impliciture; meaning; presupposition; primary pragmatic processes; relevance theory; semantics-pragmatics interface

Suggestions for further reading

Carston, R. (2002) *Thoughts and Utterances*, Oxford: Blackwell.

Levinson, S.C. (1983) *Pragmatics*, Cambridge: Cambridge University Press.
Stalnaker, R. (1998) *Context and Content*, Oxford: Oxford University Press.

Rationality

In the present practical sense of the term, rationality is, generally speaking, the capacity of identifying particular actions as justified under certain circumstances of belief and desire. Principles of practical rationality are principles that direct activity. When they are actively followed, under given circumstances, the actions performed are considered justified. A simple example of such a principle would be the following. If you believe a yes-no **question** has just been addressed to you, and you are interested in responding in a linguistically appropriate way, say 'Yes' if you believe that you understand the question and that this is the right answer.

Theoretically interesting principles of practical rationality are much more general in nature. Assume a person is interested in purchasing a publication that consists of two volumes. In one bookstore one finds the set of the two volumes. In another, close bookstore only one of the volumes is available for the same price. Under such circumstances, it would be justified to buy the volumes from the first bookstore rather than from the second one. Generally speaking, one of the principles that regulate rational decision making tells us to opt for the most effective among the possible actions, when they are equal in all other respects.

Now, assume a person who is interested in purchasing a two-volume publication knows that it is available in two bookstores, both of which are close to his residence. In one of them the price is much lower than in the other one. Under such circumstances, it would be justified to buy the volumes from the bookstore that sells them for a cheaper price. Generally speaking, another principle that is involved in regulating rational decision making tells us to opt for the least costly among the possible actions, when they are equal in all other respects. Combining the two rationality principles we have just mentioned, we get the following principle:

(R) Given a desired end and a variety of means, one is to choose that action which most effectively and at least cost attains that end, ceteris paribus.

(see Richards 1971)

Speech acts are actions. Hence, principles that regulate rational activity in general, such as (R), apply to speech acts as well. The desired end of a speech act is the state to be attained by performing it in the given **context** of utterance. By answering a question, for example, the state to be attained is, in many contexts of utterance, one in which the hearer, who posed the question, is now aware of what the speaker believes is the answer to it. The given means are the speech acts that can be performed in the context of utterance. Applying principle (R) to such circumstances, one has to answer the posed question as fully as possible, according to one's beliefs, and not be more informative than is required under the circumstances.

These practical consequences of (R) constitute parts of **Grice**'s system of conversational **maxims**, which are involved in creating conversational **implicatures** (Grice 1967). It was shown in Kasher (1976) that all those maxims follow from (R) and some additional assumptions. Other rationality principles have also been introduced and used for explanation in **pragmatics**. Horn introduced a pair of principles:

(H-Q) Make your contribution sufficient, say as much as you can (given Principle H-R).
(H-R) Make your contribution necessary, say no more than you must (given Principle H-Q).
    (see Horn 2004 which rests on his work during the preceding three decades).

Notice that (H-Q) represents the 'most effective' and (H-R) the 'at least cost' parts of (R). Levinson introduced variants of these maximization and minimization principles and added a third one:

(L-M) Use marked expressions, which indicate that the situation is not an ordinary one, only for a reason.

(see Levinson 2000)

ASA KASHER

See also: Grice, H.P.; implicature; relevance theory; speech act theory

Suggestion for further reading

Mele, A.R. and Rawling, P. (eds) (2004) *The Oxford Handbook of Rationality*, New York: Oxford University Press.

Reasoning

Reasoning is a systematic mental process that generates or evaluates implications among **propositions**. These implications fall into two principal categories: deductions and inductions. In logic, implications or **entailments** occur between sentences expressed in a formalized language. They are proved using rules of **inference** that are sensitive only to the **logical form** of the sentences. However, in everyday life, inferences occur, not between sentences, but between the propositions that sentences in a natural language express in a particular situation, or that derive from perception, memory, or imagination. The recovery of the particular proposition that an everyday sentence expresses depends on the **meaning** of the sentence, on the **reference** of its constituents, on **knowledge,** and on a process of **inferential comprehension.** This article is accordingly about how **pragmatics** can affect all stages of reasoning from propositions.

A valid deduction has a conclusion that must be true given that its premises are true: the conclusion does not go beyond the information in the premises. If a deduction is to be useful, it makes explicit a proposition that was not explicit in the premises. Consider the following example:

If the battery is dead then the light hasn't come on.
The light *has* come on.
Therefore, the battery isn't dead.

The two premises are consistent with just a single possibility in which the light has come on and the battery is not dead. So the conclusion adds no new information, but it does make explicit a proposition that wasn't expressed as such in the premises.

Any set of premises validly implies infinitely many different conclusions. The premises above, for instance, yield the following sequence of conclusions:

> The battery isn't dead.
> The battery isn't dead or Hitler is dead, or both.
> The battery isn't dead or Hitler is dead or Mussolini is dead, or all three.
> and so on … ad infinitum.

Unless you are a logician, you are unlikely to draw any of these conclusions other than the first one. Yet, they are all valid: they must be true if the premises are true. What, then, determines the conclusions that you do draw in daily life? The answer depends on three pragmatic constraints which are akin to **Grice**'s (1978) conversational conventions (*see* Johnson-Laird and Byrne 1991: chapter 2). First, you tend to draw conclusions that are parsimonious, e.g. you don't just form a conjunction of the premises. Second, you do not draw conclusions that throw information away by adding disjunctive alternatives to those consistent with the premises, as in the series above. Third, you draw conclusions that make explicit propositions that were not explicit in the premises.

One other factor is crucial to the conclusions that you draw. As **relevance theory** predicts, much depends on your goals (*see* Sperber and Wilson 1995). Given the problem:

> Ann is taller than Beth.
> Ann is taller than Cate.
> What follows?

you will probably respond 'nothing', because the premises fail to yield a definite order in the heights of the three individuals. But, if you want to know who is tallest, then there is a relevant answer: Ann is the tallest (van der Henst *et al.* 2002a).

Pragmatics influences the interpretation of sentential connectives, such as 'if', 'and', and 'or'. Unlike their analogues in logic, they do not have constant interpretations. In the paradigm case, the chameleon-like shifts in the meaning of conditionals affect your reasoning. For example, you are likely to make this valid deduction:

> If she bought a book then she didn't buy a magazine.
> In fact, she did buy a magazine.
> Therefore, she didn't buy a book.

But, you are unlikely to make this inference from a similar conditional:

> If she bought a book then she didn't buy a novel.
> In fact, she did buy a novel.
> Therefore, she didn't buy a book.

The reason is that you know that a novel *is* a book.

Grice (1975) took the view that conditionals have the same meaning as the truth-functional connective of material implication in logic, but that this meaning is modified by pragmatic factors. Others have rejected this analysis (e.g. Gazdar 1979a: 83–85). In psychology, the model theory of reasoning proposes a compromise (Johnson-Laird and Byrne 2002). The core meaning of a conditional is specified, not in terms of truth values, but in terms of possibilities. Hence, *If she bought a book then she didn't buy a magazine* is consistent with these three possibilities, as corroborated experimentally by Barrouillet *et al.* (2000):

She bought a book.	She didn't buy a magazine.
She didn't buy a book.	She didn't buy a magazine.
She didn't buy a book.	She bought a magazine.

These possibilities correspond to the cases in which a material implication in logic is true.

The meaning of the clauses, co-reference between them, and knowledge can modulate the core meaning of conditionals in two different ways. On the one hand, it can block one or more of these possibilities, as occurs in the case of *If she bought a book then she didn't buy a novel*. Your knowledge that a novel is a book blocks the possibility in which she didn't buy a book but did buy a novel. On the other hand, modulation can introduce temporal, spatial, or other relations between the clauses of a conditional. In one possibility consistent with the conditional:

> If she fell off her bike then she grazed her knee.

there is a spatio-temporal sequence of events: first, she was on her bike, then she fell off it, and finally she grazed her knee. The conditional supports inferences that these events are possible. A corollary is that the mere truth of the two clauses does not suffice for the conditional to be true: if she grazed her knee and then fell off her bike, the conditional is false. In general, no sentential connectives in natural language can be interpreted in a truth functional way, because modulation can always introduce spatial, temporal, and other relations between their clauses.

The model theory postulates that logical form plays no role in reasoning, and that instead the process is semantic: a conclusion is valid if it holds in all the possibilities consistent with the premises. The key step in induction is an extension of modulation. Knowledge and beliefs go beyond the information in the starting point of an inference, and eliminate without a secure warrant one or more possibilities consistent with its premises (Johnson-Laird 2006). The process of inference itself, given that it depends on envisaging possibilities, is also affected by beliefs. Individuals are more likely to reject an invalid conclusion if it is unbelievable than if it is believable. Presumably, they search harder for a counterexample to an unbelievable conclusion.

The model theory is based on a principle of truth: mental models do not represent the possibilities consistent with **assertions** in a fully explicit way, but instead represent clauses, whether affirmative or negative, only when they are true in a possibility (Johnson-Laird 2006). The result is a much more parsimonious **representation** than the representation of meanings in logic (using truth tables). But, the principle has a devastating effect on some inferences. Consider this inference about the cards in a hand:

If there is a king then there is an ace, or else if there isn't a king then there is an ace. There is a king. What follows?

As the mental models predict, nearly everyone infers that there is an ace, but the inference is invalid. One of the conditionals could be false, and the first conditional could be false because there is a king but no ace. Such invalid inferences occur with other sentential connectives,

and they are endemic, occurring in all domains of reasoning. And they are a direct consequence of the pragmatic principle of representing what is true rather than false, what is possible rather than impossible, what is permissible rather than impermissible (except in the case of explicit prohibitions), and what is an instance of a concept rather than a non-instance.

Finally, pragmatics plays a major role in a reasoning problem that has been studied in **cognitive psychology** more often than any other. In Wason's (1966) selection task, you have to select evidence to find out whether a general claim about four cards is true or false, for example:

If a card has an 'A' on one side then it has a '2' on its other side.

The four cards are laid out in front of you: A, B, 2, and 3, and you know that each of them has a letter on one side and a number on the other side. Most individuals select the A card and sometimes the 2 card too. They fail to select the 3 card. Yet, if this card has an A on its other side, the general claim is false. To anyone who has studied logic, the error of omission in the selection task is puzzling. On one account, the failure is a result of the principle of truth: individuals fail to represent the case in which the conditional is false, A and *not 2*, and so they fail to base their selections on this counterexample. The remedy is any procedure that makes the counterexample salient. Sperber *et al.* (1995) have a similar view, and argue that the counterexample has to be relevant. With appropriate manipulations of the effort or the effect of thinking about the counterexample, their participants were likely to make the correct selections. Their most successful case was to frame the general claim as one that an engineer had made after repairs to a machine printing cards according to its specification. Hence, the claim could be interpreted as ruling out the possibility of an 'A' and a '3' (*see also* Girotto *et al.* 2001).

Whether the selection task reflects reasoning is a moot point. Some theorists have argued that it does, but that the probability calculus rather than logic provides the appropriate norm (Oaksford and Chater 1998). In contrast, Sperber *et al.* (1995) argued that individuals are guided, not by reasoning of any sort, but by their intuitions about what is relevant, and that these intuitions arise from the pragmatic system underlying all sorts of comprehension. This view and the modulation hypothesis concur that the interpretation of premises – that is, the process leading to the representation of the particular propositions that they express – is decisive in reasoning.

PJ.L.

See also: Abduction; argumentation theory; cognitive pragmatics; cognitive psychology; cognitive science; entailment; fallacy theory; generalized conversational implicature, theory of; Grice, H.P.; implicature; inference; inferential comprehension; knowledge; logical form; meaning; post-Gricean pragmatics; proposition; psycholinguistics; rationality; relevance theory; representation and computation; scalar implicature

Suggestions for further reading

Byrne, R.M.J. (2005) *The Rational Imagination*, Cambridge, MA: MIT Press.
Noveck, I.A. and Sperber, D. (ed.) (2004) *Experimental Pragmatics*, New York: Palgrave Macmillan.
Politzer, G. and Macchi, L. (2000) 'Reasoning and pragmatics', *Mind and Society*, 1: 73–93.

Reference

Reference has something to do with the way language relates to the world. When we go beyond that vague and general statement, however, we quickly get into areas of dispute. One point of issue is whether reference is solely a pragmatic relation. It is clear that the ordinary sense of the word 'refer' allows us to say that speakers use linguistic expressions to refer to entities (or to refer their addressees to entities). We are speaking here of what is sometimes termed 'singular reference'. As this sense of 'refer' has to do with the use of language, it reflects a pragmatic conception of reference. According to this conception, the essence of reference is getting one's addressee to attend to a particular entity, in order to predicate some

property of that entity. To speak of expressions themselves as referring is a derivative way of speaking, like speaking of knives cutting. Just as we do not really think that knives can cut on their own, we should not think that expressions can refer on their own. (See, for example, Strawson 1950a and Bach 2006c for pragmatic views, arrived at for reasons which we will not discuss here.)

However, there is also a tradition of using the term 'reference' for a semantic relation – that which holds between linguistic expressions and what they stand for or apply to in the world, abstracting away from occasions of use. This tradition goes back at least to Frege's classic 1892 paper 'Über Sinn und Bedeutung', whose title is often translated 'On Sense and Reference'. On this view, reference contrasts with sense, or **meaning**, in one sense of 'meaning'. As Frege explained it, sense is the mode of presentation of a referent: expressions with different senses, such as *the Corsican who ruled France* and *the emperor who lost at Waterloo*, may present the same referent by expressing different properties which that referent has. Two other pairs of terms marking a similar kind of distinction are 'denotation' and 'connotation' from the work of Mill (1843), which predated Frege's by fifty years; and 'extension' and 'intension', although frequently the term 'extension' is reserved for general terms, e.g. ordinary nouns, verbs, and adjectives.

Another issue is what kinds of linguistic expressions can be properly said to refer (on the semantic view) or to be used to refer (on the pragmatic view). Most scholars would agree that at least a subset of noun phrases (NPs; sometimes also called 'determiner phrases', or DPs) are referring expressions. The category of NPs itself includes pronouns (*she, these*), proper names (*Socrates, Benazir Bhutto*), definite, indefinite, and **demonstrative** descriptions (*the/a/that large box of chocolates*), and quantificational NPs (*all/most/ several classically trained pianists*). Within the category of NPs, which subtypes are associated with the referring function is a source of differences of opinion.

For some philosophers, to speak of a NP as referring or referential requires the NP, or a use of the NP, to guarantee an actual referent as a part of the **proposition** being expressed. The most restrictive view of this type was probably that of Russell, who suggested ultimately that only the demonstrative determiner *this* could be so used (Russell 1918: 177). Thus, on Russell's view (oversimplifying somewhat) to say *This is red* while standing in front of a red barn and pointing at it would be to express a proposition consisting of the barn itself and the property of being red. Bach holds a similar view, but allows that only some pure **indexicals**, such as *I* and *today*, are correctly regarded as referring (*cf.* Bach 2006c: 542). (Indexicals are expressions like *now*, *you* and *that barn* whose semantic value depends solely (pure indexicals) or in part on features of the **context** in which they are used.) Others, who agree with Russell and Bach that referring expressions contribute a referent to propositions, feel nonetheless that more kinds of NPs are up to the task: proper names, and a broader class of pronouns and other indexicals would be included (Kaplan 1989a, 1989b; Salmon 1986).

Probably a majority of philosophers of language accept Russell's (1905) analysis of definite descriptions – NPs that begin with *the*, like *the Corsican who ruled France*. According to this analysis, definite descriptions are quantificational NPs. *The Corsican who ruled France was short* means 'There was one and only one entity from Corsica who ruled France, and that entity was short', which is a general statement, not a referential one. However, Donnellan (1966) argued that in addition to what he called the 'attributive' use, which reflects Russell's analysis, definite descriptions also have a referential use, on which they serve simply to pick out an entity. When the president of the Teetotallers' Union asks *Who is the man drinking a martini?*, the cocktail is an essential part of the **question** and this is an attributive use. But a questioner in a bar context may just want to ask about a particular individual, and any other description (e.g. *the guy in the blue shirt*) might have done as well. It has even been argued that indefinite descriptions may be referential, most notably when they initiate a chain of reference, as in *A cat strolled into the room. It sat down and meowed* (Chastain 1975; *see also* Fodor and Sag 1982).

Donnellan was unclear on whether his attributive-referential distinction reflects a semantic **ambiguity** or whether instead it can be accounted for in purely pragmatic terms. Kripke (1977), citing the theory of **implicature** of

Grice (1975), favoured the latter view, arguing that Donnellan's referential use concerns speaker's reference rather than semantic reference, and Ludlow and Neale (1991) used many of Kripke's arguments to dispute the claims of referentiality for indefinite NPs. Following Kripke, scholars have been at pains to distinguish the semantic content actually encoded in an utterance from propositions which the speaker wishes to convey, and which the addressee grasps as the result of an utterance, but which are not actually encoded in it. However, there continues to be a lack of agreement on exactly where to draw the line between **what is said** in an utterance and what is conveyed by **inference** (see, for example, Reimer and Bezuidenhout 2004: section II, on Donnellan's referential-attributive distinction; on the issue of the semantics-pragmatics divide, *see* Szabó 2005).

On the semantic view of reference, the concept extends naturally to general terms, and in fact expressions of almost any type (*cf.* MacBride 2006). Thus, *water* refers to the totality of water, *green* refers to the totality of green things, *extrapolate* refers to the totality of instances of extrapolation, and so forth. Frege himself argued that whole sentences refer to their truth value. He also held that the reference of complex expressions is determined by the referents of their parts (plus the way those parts are combined syntactically). This is the principle of compositionality, which is believed to account for our ability to produce and understand novel sentences without limit. It is natural, given this picture, to suppose that all of the contentful expressions in a sentence – starting with the words, and continuing with the phrases composed of those words up to the level of the sentence – are referential and help to compose the reference of the whole sentence. (The grammar of Montague 1973 is very much in this spirit.)

BARBARA ABBOTT

See also: Definiteness; deixis; demonstratives; indefiniteness; indexicals; specificity

Suggestions for further reading

Bach, K. (1987) *Thought and Reference*, Oxford: Clarendon Press.

Evans, G. (1982) *The Varieties of Reference*, ed. J. McDowell, Oxford: Clarendon Press.

Sainsbury, R.M. (1999) 'The essence of reference', in E. Lepore and B.C. Smith (eds) *The Oxford Handbook of Philosophy of Language*, Oxford: Clarendon Press.

Refusals

Pragmatics is concerned with analyzing the **meaning** of utterances in interaction. More specifically, many pragmatics researchers have focussed on developing criteria for identifying different **speech acts** such as **compliments**, **apologies**, **complaints** and refusals and on describing the ways in which they are expressed in different languages (Olshtain and Weinbach 1987; Blum-Kulka *et al.* 1989; Ylanne-McEwen 1993; Bardovi-Harlig *et al.* 2006; Félix-Brasdefer, to appear). Refusals provide interesting contrasts in preferred pragmatic choices of strategy across different **cultures**, as well as in preferred structures for expressing a refusal.

Definition

The core component of a refusal is an utterance expressing unwillingness to comply with a proposal, e.g. a **request**, invitation or offer (Kline and Floyd 1990; Chen *et al.* 1995; Houck and Gass 1996; Daly *et al.* 2004). Refusals are highly face-threatening speech acts because they involve the rejection of a request which the communicator felt it was legitimate to make. They are complex speech acts, often characterized by extended sequences of turn taking and negotiation (Félix-Brasdefer, to appear: 2). In this context, **politeness** theory predicts that direct refusals will be a less preferred option (Folkes 1982), and that when they occur they will be mitigated to redress the face threat to the requester (Houck and Gass 1996: 49; Besson *et al.* 1998). However, analyses of authentic refusal sequences indicate that this is not always what occurs, as will become apparent.

Methodology

Most research on refusals has used some variant of the discourse completion task (DCT), which has been popularized by the influential Cross-Cultural Speech Act Research Project (Blum-Kulka *et al.* 1989), to elicit (usually written) data from student subjects (e.g. Takahashi and Beebe 1987; Besson *et al.* 1998; Beebe *et al.* 1990; Bresnahan *et al.* 1999; Itoi 1997). Some researchers have devised oral versions of DCTs using taped stimuli (e.g. Kinjo 1987; Walkinshaw 2007), or interviews where the DCT was read aloud and the response recorded on audio tape (e.g. Nelson *et al.* 2002). Others have added concurrent verbal reports to the DCT exercise which are then replayed to the participants during a retrospective interview (Robinson 1992). (See entry on complaints for a discussion of the strengths and weaknesses of this methodology.)

Role plays have also been extensively used in eliciting refusals (e.g. Folkes 1982; Widjaja 1997; Sasaki 1998; Gass and Houck 1999; Turnbull 2001; Da Silva 2003; Felix-Brasdefer 2006b; Taguchi 2007b). In a study involving ESL Japanese students living in American host families, for example, Houck and Gass (1996) used videorecorded open-ended role plays of familiar situations in which the students were encouraged to refuse a request. Other studies have involved role plays followed by verbal reports or interviews to investigate the speakers' perceptions of refusals (Félix-Brasdefer 2006b, 2008), and many use a combination of DCTs and role plays. However, as Sasaki (1998) points out, these methods often elicit rather different data, so the results are not always comparable.

There is also research describing refusals collected in naturally occurring interaction. Using data from the Wellington Language in the Workplace project, for example, Daly *et al.* (2004) describe the very direct refusals found in exchanges between members of a close-knit factory team. Others have shown considerable ingenuity in eliciting authentic or near-authentic refusals from participants (e.g. Beebe and Cummings 1996; Al-Khatib 2006). Turnbull (2001: 39) elicited telephone refusals from students who were asked to sign up for an experiment involving tests of logical and mathematical skills at an unattractively early hour on a Saturday morning. Morrison (2005) invited students to a social event and then (1) offered food and drink until it was refused and (2) issued genuine invitations to events that they were likely to refuse (e.g.

kick-boxing classes). Overall, such research suggests that authentic refusals tend to be longer, more complex, and more emotional in tone than written DCT responses (Beebe 1985b; Bardovi-Harlig and Hartford 1992), and that role play provides data that is generally closer on these dimensions to authentic responses (Gass and Houck 1999; Turnbull 2001; Morrison and Holmes 2003).

Results

Research on refusals has tended to focus on identifying *strategies* for refusing and on pragmatic and linguistic features of the *structure* of refusals (e.g. Ueda 1972; Rubin 1983; Beebe and Cummings 1996). Refusal strategies have been categorized as *direct* (with or without **hedges** or intensifiers), *indirect* (e.g. challenging some feature of the request, asking for more information, offering an alternative, blaming someone else), or *avoidance* (e.g. saying nothing, postponing a response, changing the **topic**) (*cf.* Rubin 1983; Blum-Kulka and Olshtain 1984; Beebe *et al.* 1990; Félix-Brasdefer 2008). Responses often include more than one strategy. Many studies report differences in preferred refusal strategies and their frequencies by groups from different linguistic and cultural backgrounds (Stevens 1993; Nelson *et al.* 2002; Al-Issa 2003).

In terms of structure, refusals often include the following three components: (1) respond positively (e.g. 'I would like to ... '), (2) expression of regret, and (3) provide an excuse (Takahashi and Beebe 1987; Beebe *et al.* 1990). However, the precise way these components are expressed varies in different socio-cultural **contexts** (Wootton 1981; Chen *et al.* 1995; Liao and Bresnahan 1996), and the order of **discourse** components is very contextually variable (e.g. Kinjo 1987).

Results also tend to reflect the methodology used in a study. DCT research using native speakers often elicits linguistically complex refusals, using a number of politeness strategies to address the face needs of the requester (Besson *et al.* 1998; Gass and Houck 1999). Authentic refusals in contrast, are often very direct (Saeki and O'Keefe 1994; Daly *et al.* 2004). In sociolinguistic terms, direct refusals are often interpreted as indicators of closeness and solidarity (Daly *et al.* 2004; Al-Khatib 2006; Félix-Brasdefer 2006b), while indirect refusals generally express respect to those of higher status (Takahashi and Beebe 1987; Stevens 1993; Kwon 2004; Oktoprimasakti 2006).

Reported differences in the production of refusals between native and non-native speakers can be attributed not only to lack of control of subtle pragmalinguistic components (Tanck 2002), but also to the transfer of cultural values from L1 to L2 (Chen 1996; Gass and Houck 1999; Al-Issa 2003). Takahashi and Beebe (1987) also noted that negative pragmatic transfer occurred more with advanced ESL students. Ironically, it seemed that a greater ability in English allowed the learners to express English refusals in a more Japanese-like way. Finally, there is much research demonstrating that classroom instruction in second language pragmatics benefits subjects in acquiring socio-pragmatic skills (Bardovi-Harlig 2001c; Takahashi 2001; Tateyama 2001; Kasper and Rose 2002; Da Silva 2003; Alcón 2005; Koike and Pearson 2005; Riddiford 2007).

Conclusion

Research on refusals identifies considerable differences in the structure of refusals elicited by different methods, with obvious implications both for researchers and practitioners. Refusing appropriately also requires attention to a range of potentially relevant social variables which may be weighted very differently in different socio-cultural contexts. The overriding message from many studies of the acquisition of pragmatic proficiency is that while there is always a certain amount of individual variation, mastery improves over time, and especially time spent in the target language setting (Schauer 2006). Reassuringly for teachers, explicit instruction generally speeds up the process.

JANET HOLMES and NICKY RIDDIFORD

See also: Apologies; applied linguistics; competence, communicative; competence, pragmatic; complaints; compliments; context; conversation; conversational turn-taking; conversation analysis; cross-cultural pragmatics; disagreement; discourse; discourse analysis; discourse markers;

discourse particles; ethnomethodology; hedge; intercultural communication; misunderstanding; politeness; power; request; sociolinguistics; speech act theory

Suggestions for further reading

Bardovi-Harlig, K., Félix-Brasdefer, J.C. and Omar, A.S. (eds) (2006) *Pragmatics and Language Learning, Volume 11*, Honolulu, HI: University of Hawaii Press.

Gass, S.M. and Houck, N. (1999) *Interlanguage Refusals: A Cross-Cultural Study of Japanese English*, New York: Mouton de Gruyter.

Kasper, G. and Rose, K.R. (2002) *Pragmatic Development in a Second Language*, Oxford: Blackwell.

Rehabilitation, Communication

Recovery from **communication** disorders is a prolific area of research. Examples of rehabilitation interventions reported in the literature include practicing different language and communication skills through a wide range of activities including drama, role playing, poetry reading, writing workshops, music therapy and discussion groups. The goal of a rehabilitation intervention is to provide opportunities for patients to use communicative skills effectively in order to obtain a successful outcome. This is achieved by increasing patients' ability to communicate and by helping them recognize their residual abilities and learn compensatory strategies. A rehabilitation intervention should be planned on the basis of careful communicative **assessment** in which patients' deficits and residual abilities are highlighted.

People express their communicative ability via different expressive means, for instance, using linguistic, gestural and paralinguistic modalities. However, the majority of studies in the literature have focused primarily on remediation of the linguistic modality. Moreover, although communicative deficits characterize different neuropsychological and psychiatric disorders (due to congenital or acquired cerebral pathologies), such as, for example, aphasia, **right-hemisphere damage**, **traumatic brain injury** (TBI) and schizophrenia, the majority of studies have focused on the treatment of aphasic patients.

Traditional therapies for aphasia start by identifying the impaired element in the patients' language system and then involve specific treatment of the impaired component. The main acquired language deficits consist of difficulty producing words at a motor planning level (apraxia of speech) and at the stages of conceptual and lexical-semantic processing. Rehabilitative treatments for apraxia of speech focus on improving patients' ability, through repeated practice, to articulate target sounds (*see* Ballard 2001). Rehabilitative treatments of conceptual and lexical-semantic processing provide diverse interventions according to the damaged cognitive component that is dedicated to a specific aspect of word processing (*see* Basso 2003).

The major limitation of interventions that focus exclusively on language is that, after therapy, patients often have difficulty solving communicative problems in everyday life situations. The pragmatic approach has been developed to overcome this limitation. The pragmatic view has shifted the focus of therapeutic practice from the patient's linguistic ability to the effective use of language in a given **context**. Functional pragmatic therapies also focus on a patient's residual communicative abilities, such as gestural and prosodic skills, and look for alternative and compensatory communicative strategies with respect to the defective ones (Carlomagno *et al.* 2000). Aten *et al.* (1982) was first to develop a successful formal pragmatic therapy program, the *Functional Communication Treatment*, in which aphasic patients are confronted with simulated everyday life situations and trained in the use of non-verbal communicative strategies. Holland (1991) further expanded this treatment by introducing *Conversational Coaching* therapy. The aim of this method, based on the use of short monologues, is to train patients to control the quality of the monologue depending on the degree of familiarity with the listener – from relatives to unknown persons – and the informativeness of the script – from known information to improbable events. A further example of the functional pragmatic approach to intervention, backed by experimental evidence, is *Promoting Aphasics' Communicative Effectiveness* (Davis and Wilcox 1985). The treatment requires that therapist and patient sit facing one another across a table on which are a set of printed stimulus cards. In turn, each participant takes a card and, without showing it, he tries to describe it to the other person. The therapeutic basis of this treatment is that it involves a progressive exercise within the setting of natural **conversation,** supported by a therapist eliciting compensatory strategies and providing useful feedback, which improves the patient's linguistic and communicative performance.

An important setting for practicing pragmatic therapies is role-playing (Schlanger and Schlanger 1970), in which the patient has the opportunity to enact everyday life situations. Further, within the pragmatic approach, Marshall (1999) highlighted the usefulness of group therapy. Group communication treatments focus on initiating conversation and conveying a message, understanding the communication disorder, being aware of personal goals and progress and having confidence in being able to communicate in personally relevant situations (Elman and Bernstein-Ellis 1999). The aim of socially oriented conversational aphasia groups is to promote interpersonal exchanges similar to natural peer communication. **Discourse** management features include establishing the feel of discourse equality, focusing on everyday events and genres, employing multiple communication modes, mediating communication, calibrating corrections, aiding turn allocation and employing teachable moments (Simmons-Mackie *et al.* 2007). Within the small group setting, Avent (1997, 2004) demonstrated the importance of cooperation with the *Aphasia Treatment Program*, which is based on the principle that in a small group, members share information, work cooperatively on tasks and are encouraged to maximize individual and group learning.

Ehrlich and Sipes (1985) described a model of group intervention for TBI patients based on the functional pragmatic approach. Treatment consisted of four modules that were focused on improving non-verbal communication, appropriate communication in context, message repair and message cohesiveness. The therapist role-played and videotaped both appropriate and inappropriate examples of target behavior. The videos were examined and reviewed by the group under the supervision of the therapist, who pointed out the inappropriate behavior and suggested possible appropriate alternatives. After

treatment patients showed improvements in the reformulation of inappropriate messages, sentence cohesion and in the introduction and development of conversational **topics**. In particular, TBI patients have been found to have social communication problems (*see* Dahlberg *et al.* 2006). Social communication interventions include treatments such as group discussion, forming communication goals, modeling, role playing, feedback, self-monitoring, behavioral rehearsal and social reinforcement (*see* McGann *et al.* 1997; Struchen 2005). For example, Bellon and Rees (2006) examined the role of social context on language and communication skills among TBI patients, demonstrating the notable benefits of carefully structured supportive social networks. The key component of their rehabilitation intervention was the presence of a mentor, who prompted the patients and gave them cues and models of positive behavior; this kind of social support stimulated patients' positive self-image, positive self-talk and inter-personal language. Ylvisaker (2006) presented an intervention for TBI patients based on self-coaching which was aimed at improving planned, goal-oriented and successful behavior. In particular, the patients' improved metacognitive skills (see **theory of mind**) increased their ability to self-monitor and self-evaluate during a communicative interaction (Ylvisaker and Szekeres 1989).

Another group of diverse rehabilitative treatments focus on training the partners who communicate with patients with acquired brain injury. The common goal of such interventions, conducted both with aphasic (Kagan *et al.* 2001; Lyon *et al.* 1997; Worrall and Yiu 2000) and TBI patients (Togher *et al.* 2004), is to improve conversational interaction by training the communication partner rather than the person with the communication deficit.

Few studies are available in the literature concerning interventions that address the communicative problems of patients with right-hemisphere damage (*see* Halper and Cherney 1998). The principal forms of treatment and strategies have been derived from treatment of other populations, such as aphasic and brain injury patients (for a discussion, *see* Tompkins 1995).

Controlled studies and systematic reviews of the literature have demonstrated the advantages of cognitive linguistic therapies for aphasic patients (Cicerone *et al.* 2005), especially when associated with an increased intensity of treatment (Denes *et al.* 1996). Empirical data also support the effectiveness of functional pragmatic therapy after TBI, even though the limited number of studies on small samples needs further confirmation (Cicerone *et al.* 2005; *see also* Cappa *et al.* 2005). Furthermore, a systematic review of the empirical evidence for social communication interventions for TBI subjects appears to support the effectiveness of this type of therapy, although further studies are still necessary (Struchen 2005).

FRANCESCA M. BOSCO

See also: Assessment, pragmatic; clinical pragmatics; cognitive pragmatics; competence, communicative; pragmatics; schizophrenic language

Suggestions for further reading

Basso, A. (2003) *Aphasia and Its Therapy*, New York: Oxford University Press.
Carlomagno, S., Blasi, V., Labruna, L. and Santoro, A. (2000) 'The role of communication models in assessment and therapy of language disorders in aphasic adults', *Neuropsychological Rehabilitation*, 10: 337–63.
Elman, R. (ed.) (2007) *Group Treatment of Neurogenic Communication Disorders: The Expert Clinician's Approach*, San Diego, CA: Plural Publishing.

Relevance Theory

Relevance theory treats as foundational three of **Grice**'s assumptions about verbal communication (Grice 1989: Chapters 1–7, 14, 18). The first is that sentence **meaning** is a vehicle for conveying a speaker's meaning, where a speaker's meaning is an overtly expressed **intention** that is fulfilled by being recognized. The second is that a speaker's meaning cannot be simply perceived or decoded, but has to be inferred from his or her behaviour, together with background information. The third is that in inferring a speaker's meaning, the hearer is guided by the expectation that utterances should meet certain standards (in Grice's framework, the **cooperative principle** and **maxims of**

conversation, and in relevance theory, a presumption of optimal relevance automatically conveyed by every utterance).

However, relevance theory differs significantly from Grice as to the goals and methods of **pragmatics**. Grice's goals were philosophical or semantic. His analysis of speaker's meaning was intended to shed light on traditional semantic notions such as sentence meaning and word meaning, and his accounts of the derivation of **implicatures** were rational reconstructions of how a speaker's meaning *might* be inferred, rather than empirical hypotheses about what actually goes on in hearers' minds. The goal of relevance theory is to produce a psychologically plausible theory of **communication**. The methods proposed are those of **cognitive psychology**, including modelling of cognitive processes, experimental tests, studies of communication pathologies (e.g. **autism spectrum disorders**), and evolutionary insights.

In the last twenty-five years, relevance theorists have contributed to debate on a variety of central theoretical pragmatic topics, including the **explicit/implicit distinction** (Wilson and Sperber 1981; Sperber and Wilson 1995: chapter 4; Carston 2002: Chapter 2), pragmatic enrichment and the linguistic underdeterminacy thesis (Carston 1988, 2002: Chapters 2–5; Sperber and Wilson 1995: Chapter 4; Matsui 2000; Ifantidou 2001; Noh 2000; Wilson and Sperber 2002), **lexical pragmatics** (Carston 1997, 2002: Chapter 5; Sperber and Wilson 1998a; Wilson and Sperber 2002; Wilson and Carston 2007a), **rhetoric** and figurative interpretation (including **metaphor**, **irony**, **hyperbole** and **understatement**) (Sperber and Wilson 1981, 1990a, 1995: Chapter 4; 1998b; Wilson and Sperber 1992; Carston 2002: Chapter 5; Wilson 2006; Vega Moreno 2007; Wilson and Carston 2007b; Sperber and Wilson 2008), the communication of **speech act** and **propositional attitude** information (Wilson and Sperber 1988; Sperber and Wilson 1995: Chapter 4; Ifantidou 2001; Noh 2000) and the derivation of stylistic and poetic effects (Sperber and Wilson 1995: Chapter 4; 2008; Pilkington 2000).

Relevance theorists have also contributed to applied research on **experimental pragmatics**, **pragmatic development** and impairment (e.g. in autism spectrum disorders), and the psychology of **reasoning** (Jorgensen *et al.* 1984; Happé 1993; Sperber *et al.* 1995; Happé and Loth 2002; van der Henst *et al.* 2002a; Noveck and Sperber 2004, 2007; van der Henst and Sperber 2004; Breheny *et al.* 2006; Southgate *et al.*, to appear), to theoretical research on lexical semantics, the **semantics-pragmatics interface**, non-truth-conditional semantics, **discourse markers**, **discourse particles**, interjections and non-verbal communication (Blakemore 1987, 2002; Wilson and Sperber 1988, 1993; Blass 1990; Carston 1999; Papafragou 2000; Iten 2005; Wharton 2009), and to theories of **translation**, **literary pragmatics**, **narrative discourse**, **discourse coherence** and genre (Blass 1990; Gutt 1991; Pilkington 2000; Unger 2006). A broader concern has been with the place of pragmatics in mental architecture. Here, I will outline the main assumptions of the theory (while attempting to clear up a few common objections or misconceptions), and end by sketching some of the broader implications of this approach.

Relevance and cognition

Relevance theory is based on a definition of relevance and two principles of relevance: a Cognitive Principle and a Communicative Principle. (The aim of the definition is not to capture any of the ordinary-language senses of the word 'relevance', but to provide a useful theoretical concept which has enough in common with these ordinary-language senses to justify the name.) The theory starts from the assumption that relevance plays a fundamental role not only in communication but in cognition. Relevance is therefore defined not only for utterances or other communicative acts, but for all external stimuli or internal mental **representations** capable of providing an input to cognitive processes. Thus, sights, smells, utterances, thoughts, memories or conclusions of **inferences** all provide potentially relevant inputs (for an individual, at a time).

Intuitively, an input is relevant to an individual when it interacts with a **context** of mentally represented assumptions (derived from perception, memory or inference) to achieve a worthwhile effect: for instance, by answering a **question**, settling a doubt, correcting a mistake,

suggesting a hypothesis or a plan of action, and so on. These worthwhile effects are described as positive cognitive effects. A positive cognitive effect may be a true contextual implication (derived from interaction between input and context, but from neither input nor context alone), a warranted strengthening of an existing assumption, or a warranted revision of an existing assumption. A single input may achieve several cognitive effects. For instance, the sight of an empty taxi rank when I am rushing to an appointment may make me revise my assumption that I left home early enough, contextually imply that I need an alternative means of transport, and strengthen my suspicion that today is not my lucky day. According to relevance theory, other things being equal, the greater the positive cognitive effects achieved, and the smaller the processing effort required (in order to represent the input, access contextual information and derive any cognitive effects), the greater the relevance of the input (to the individual who processes it, at the time) (Sperber and Wilson 1995: 260–66).

A fundamental problem for human cognition is that at any point in our waking lives, a huge variety of potential inputs are competing for our attention. It may be that there is no general answer to the question of how attention and processing resources are allocated among these competing inputs, but relevance theory claims there is one. The central claim of relevance theory is that, as a result of constant selection pressures, the human cognitive system has developed a variety of dedicated (innate or acquired) mental mechanisms or biases which tend to allocate attention to inputs with the greatest expected relevance, and process them in the most relevance-enhancing way. This claim is expressed in the First, or Cognitive, Principle of Relevance (Sperber and Wilson 1995: 260–66):

Cognitive Principle of Relevance
Human cognition tends to be geared to the maximization of relevance.

It follows from the Cognitive Principle that the human cognitive system is capable (at least to some extent) of monitoring expected cognitive effects and processing effort and allocating resources in such a way that a competing potential input is helped by a comparatively high level of expected effect and hindered by a comparatively high level of expected effort. As a result, the spontaneous working of our perceptual mechanisms tends to pick out the most relevant potential inputs, the spontaneous working of our memory retrieval mechanisms tends to activate the most relevant potential contextual assumptions, and the spontaneous working of our inferential mechanisms tends to yield the most relevant conclusions (for suggestions about how a relevance-oriented cognitive system might be implemented, *see* Sperber and Wilson 1996; Barrett 2005; Sperber 2005).

A common objection to the Cognitive Principle is that it is too vague and general to be falsifiable. (For early discussion, *see* the multiple review of Sperber and Wilson 1987a in Adler *et al.* 1987, and continuing commentary in Sperber and Wilson 1987b; Garnham and Perner 1990; Politzer 1990; Chiappe and Kukla 1996; and Sperber and Wilson 1990b, 1996; for more recent discussion, *see* the papers in Burton-Roberts 2007 and Romero and Soria, to appear.) However, it would be straightforwardly falsified by evidence that human attention and processing resources are systematically allocated on some other basis: for instance, to inputs which are informative without being relevant, which yield many associations but few inferential effects, which are cheap to process regardless of any expected effects, or which have many expected effects regardless of the processing costs incurred. The Cognitive Principle also makes a number of testable predictions about human perceptual, memory retrieval and inferential mechanisms. Here, I will consider just one.

The claim that human inferential mechanisms tend spontaneously to derive the most potentially relevant conclusions, ignoring others which are logically valid but have few expected effects, was experimentally tested by van der Henst *et al.* (2002a). Participants were presented with pairs of premises such as (1a) and (1b) (a so-called 'determinate relational problem') or (2a) and (2b) (a so-called 'indeterminate relational problem') and simply asked 'What follows?':

Determinate relational problem
(1) a. A is taller than B
      b. B is taller than C

Indeterminate relational problem
(2) a. A is taller than B
      b. C is taller than B

In principle, psychologists should be reluctant to use open-ended questions of this type in experiments on reasoning, for fear that (since every set of premises yields an infinity of logically valid conclusions) the result would be a computational explosion. In practice, such questions are often asked, and participants typically give a single answer or none at all, because they interpret the question as 'What *of relevance* follows?'. This is something that psychologists of reasoning seem to take for granted and don't discuss, let alone explain. The goal of van der Henst *et al.*'s experiment was to investigate the role of relevance in the actual derivation of conclusions. The results showed that 45 per cent of participants presented with indeterminate relational problems responded that nothing follows (as compared with only 8 per cent for determinate relational problems, which yield a highly salient and potentially relevant conclusion). These results confirm the prediction that human inferential mechanisms do not simply derive logically valid conclusions regardless of their potential relevance.

Moreover, participants who did draw conclusions from the indeterminate relational problems tended to produce 'single-subject' conclusions (e.g. 'B is shorter than A and C') rather than 'double-subject conclusions' (e.g. 'A and C are taller than B'), even when, as in (2a) and (2b), this involved the additional effort of substituting one lexical item for another and altering the **syntax** of the premises. Van der Henst *et al.* argue that the additional effort is justified by the fact that single-subject conclusions have greater expected relevance than double-subject conclusions, since they are more likely to combine with available contextual assumptions to lead on to further conclusions. This surprising result is predictable on the assumption that human inferential mechanisms are relevance oriented, and hard to explain in other terms (*see also* van der Henst and Sperber 2004).

Relevance and communication

The Cognitive Principle of Relevance has important consequences for pragmatics. In order to communicate, a speaker needs the addressee's attention. If attention tends automatically to go to what is most relevant at the time, then the success of communication depends on the addressee taking the utterance to be relevant enough to be worthy of his or her attention. Thus, a speaker, by the very act of communicating, indicates that the addressee is intended to see the utterance as relevant enough to be worth processing, and this is what the Communicative Principle of Relevance states (Sperber and Wilson 1995: 266–78):

> *Communicative Principle of Relevance*
> Every utterance conveys a presumption of its own optimal relevance.

The Communicative Principle of Relevance is a law-like generalization about what happens when an utterance is addressed to someone. It is not a rule or maxim that speakers are expected to follow, but which they may occasionally violate (e.g. because of a clash with other maxims, or in order to trigger an implicature, as in Grice's account of figurative utterances). Relevance theorists have consistently argued that the very act of communicating creates precise and predictable expectations of relevance, which are enough on their own to guide the hearer towards the speaker's meaning. In this framework, there is no essential connection between (real or apparent) maxim violation and the derivation of implicatures, and many of Grice's examples must be reanalyzed (on clashes, *see* Sperber and Wilson 1995: 272–76; on blatant maxim violation, *see* Wilson and Sperber 2002; *see also* Sperber and Wilson 1995: 158–63).

The presumption of optimal relevance mentioned in the Communicative Principle has a precise content. The addressee is entitled to presume that the utterance is at least relevant enough to be worth processing. This follows directly from the Cognitive Principle. If attention and processing resources are automatically allocated to inputs with the greatest expected relevance, then the speaker manifestly intends the addressee to presume that the utterance is more relevant than other inputs competing for his or her attention at the time. In many circumstances, the hearer can also presume that the speaker has aimed higher than this. The

speaker wants to be understood. An utterance is most likely to be understood when it simplifies the hearer's task by demanding as little effort from him or her as possible, and encourages the hearer to pay it due attention by offering him or her as much effect as possible. It is therefore manifestly in the speaker's interest for the addressee to expect not merely relevance enough, but as much relevance as is compatible with the speaker's abilities and preferences, and this is what the presumption of optimal relevance states (Sperber and Wilson 1995: 266–78):

> *Presumption of optimal relevance*
> a. The utterance is at least relevant enough to be worth processing.
> b. It is the most relevant one compatible with the speaker's abilities and preferences.

The Communicative Principle and the definition of optimal relevance ground the following practical **heuristic** for inferring the speaker's meaning (Sperber and Wilson 2002; Wilson and Sperber 2002):

> *Relevance-guided comprehension heuristic*
> a. Follow a path of least effort in constructing an interpretation of the utterance (and in particular in resolving **ambiguities** and referential indeterminacies, adjusting lexical meaning, supplying contextual assumptions, deriving implicatures, etc.).
> b. Stop when your expectations of relevance are satisfied.

A hearer using this heuristic should proceed in the following way. The aim is to find an interpretation that satisfies the presumption of optimal relevance. To achieve this, the decoded sentence meaning must be enriched at the explicit level, and complemented at the implicit level by supplying contextual assumptions which will combine with it to yield enough cognitive effects to make the utterance relevant in the expected way. What route should a hearer follow in disambiguating, assigning **reference**, adjusting lexical meaning, constructing a context, deriving contextual implications, etc.? According to the relevance-guided comprehension heuristic, the hearer should follow a path of least effort, and stop at the first overall interpretation that satisfies the expectations of relevance that the utterance itself has raised.

What makes it reasonable for the hearer to follow a path of least effort is that the speaker is expected (within the limits of his or her abilities and preferences) to have made the utterance as easy as possible for the hearer to understand. Since relevance varies inversely with effort, the very fact that an interpretive hypothesis is easily accessible gives it an initial degree of plausibility (an epistemic advantage specific to communicated information).

What makes it reasonable for the hearer to stop at the first interpretation which satisfies the expectations of relevance raised by the utterance is that a speaker who knowingly produced an utterance with two or more significantly different interpretations, each yielding the expected level of cognitive effect, would put the hearer to the gratuitous extra effort of choosing among them, and the resulting interpretation (if any) would not satisfy clause (b) of the presumption of optimal relevance. Thus, when a hearer following the path of least effort finds an interpretation that is relevant in the expected way, in the absence of contrary evidence, this is the best possible interpretive hypothesis. Since comprehension is a non-demonstrative inference process, this hypothesis may well be false. This can happen when the speaker formulates the utterance in a way that is inconsistent with the expectations raised, so that the normal inferential routines of comprehension fail. Failures in communication are common enough. What is remarkable and calls for explanation is that communication works at all.

A common objection to the Communicative Principle and the presumption of optimal relevance is that they are too vague to be falsifiable. However, this claim is often based on a misconception. It has been suggested, for instance, that a hearer looking for the most relevant interpretation of an utterance can never be sure of having found it, since by spending a little more effort, it may be possible to achieve substantially greater effects, and hence more relevance. But according to relevance theory, the hearer's goal is not to find the *most relevant interpretation*: it is to construct an overall interpretation on which the utterance satisfies the presumption of *optimal relevance* (or, in more complex cases, on

which the speaker might have thought it would satisfy – or at least seem to satisfy – the presumption of optimal relevance) (Sperber 1994; Wilson 2000). Moreover, as shown earlier, the relevance-guided heuristic has a clear stopping point.

The Communicative Principle of Relevance would be straightforwardly falsified by evidence that communicators systematically orient to some other property of utterances than optimal relevance. This could happen, for instance, if speakers systematically aim at literal truthfulness rather than optimal relevance, or produce utterances which are informative without being relevant, or prefer to save their own effort even if the result is not relevant enough to be worth processing. Here, relevance theory comes into direct conflict with Grice's framework. For Grice, the first Quality maxim ('Do not say what you believe to be false') was the most important of all the maxims (Grice 1989: 27, 371), and from this it should follow that considerations of literal truthfulness systematically outweigh those of informativeness, relevance or perspicuity. The theoretical consequences of this difference between the Gricean and relevance theory frameworks were discussed in Wilson and Sperber (2002) and experimentally tested by van der Henst *et al.* (2002b).

In an initial experiment, van der Henst *et al.* simply approached strangers in the street and asked 'Do you have the time, please?', giving no indication of why the question was being asked. The prediction was that, if the speaker's watch showed (say) 11.13, in the absence of any indication that some crucial implications would be lost, an answer rounded to the nearest five minutes would be easier for the hearer to process, and hence more likely to be produced by a speaker aiming at optimal relevance. And indeed, 97 per cent of participants with analogue watches gave a rounded answer, while 57 per cent of participants with digital watches went to the extra effort of producing a rounded answer rather than simply reading off a strictly accurate (and literally truthful) answer, thus confirming the prediction that speakers systematically aim at optimal relevance rather than literal truthfulness.

In a second experiment, the experimenters asked 'Do you have the time, please? My watch has stopped', giving an explicit indication that a strictly accurate answer would be more relevant. Here, the percentage of rounders fell from 97 per cent to 49 per cent (only results for participants with analogue watches were reported in this experiment), suggesting that speakers tend to provide strictly accurate (i.e. literally truthful) answers when they expect them to be relevant. In a third experiment, the experimenters asked 'Do you have the time, please? I have an appointment at 4.00', at different intervals in the half hour leading up to the imaginary appointment. The results showed that speakers tended to give more strictly accurate answers as the time of the imaginary appointment approached (when some crucial implications might be lost by rounding). These results are straightforwardly predictable on the assumptions of relevance theory, and hard to explain in frameworks where a maxim of literal truthfulness is seen as the most important of all the maxims (for further tests of the Cognitive and Communicative Principles, *see* van der Henst and Sperber 2004).

Broader implications

When pragmatics emerged as a distinct discipline at the end of the 1960s, analytic philosophy was dominated by **philosophy of language** and the **cognitive sciences** were in their infancy. As the cognitive sciences have expanded, the focus in philosophy has shifted from philosophy of language to **philosophy of mind**. The development of pragmatics reflects this shift, with increasing emphasis on psychological plausibility and experimental testing. However, there is some tension between more linguistically oriented and more cognitively oriented approaches.

One of Grice's most original contributions was to treat meaning as a primarily psychological phenomenon and only derivatively a linguistic one. Rather than claiming that linguistic meaning is the only type of meaning amenable to scientific treatment, he suggested, on the contrary, that speaker's meaning is a proper subject for investigation in its own right. More linguistically oriented approaches tend to idealize away from properties of the context that are hard to formalize, and focus on aspects of interpretation (e.g. **presuppositions**, default inferences or **generalized implicatures**) which exhibit a kind of code-like regularity. In this way, they hope to extend the methods of formal semantics to a sub-part of the pragmatic domain. However, the resulting analyses are unlikely to generalize to the whole domain of pragmatics. Relevance theory and other cognitively oriented approaches treat verbal comprehension as a psychological process. The challenge is precisely to explain how the closed formal system of language provides effective pieces of evidence which, combined with contextual information, enable hearers to infer speakers' meanings.

Conceived in this way, pragmatics is relevant to linguistics because of the light it sheds on the semantics-pragmatics interface. However, its main relevance is to cognitive psychology, and in particular to the study of mindreading and inference mechanisms. According to relevance theory, **utterance interpretation** is carried out neither by general-purpose reasoning abilities (as Grice and Fodor suggest), nor by a general **theory of mind** mechanism (as many cognitive psychologists assume), but by a domain-specific inferential mechanism (the relevance-guided comprehension heuristic) which applies only to overt communicative acts (Sperber 2000, 2001b, 2005; Sperber and Wilson 2002; Wilson 2005). Thus, pragmatics provides a valuable case study for the investigation of central cognitive processes, which, precisely because of their context-dependence, are seen by Fodor (1983, 2000) as a major mystery for cognitive psychology and philosophy of mind.

DEIRDRE WILSON

See also: Autism spectrum disorders; clinical pragmatics; cognitive psychology; communication; context; cooperative principle; development, pragmatic; disambiguation; echoic use; evidentials; experimental pragmatics; explicit/implicit distinction; formal pragmatics; Grice, H. P.; heuristic; hyperbole; implicature; inference; inferential comprehension; intention; irony; lexical pragmatics; literary pragmatics; maxims of conversation; meaning; metaphor; metarepresentation; modularity of mind thesis; natural and non-natural meaning; philosophy of language; philosophy of mind; post-Gricean pragmatics; prelinguistic communication; rationality; reasoning; reference; rhetoric; speech act theory;

stylistics; theory of mind; utterance interpretation; word learning, the role of mindreading in

Suggestions for further reading

Carston, R. (2002) *Thoughts and Utterances: The Pragmatics of Explicit Communication*, Oxford: Blackwell.

Sperber, D. and Wilson, D. (1995) *Relevance: Communication and Cognition*, 2nd edn, Oxford: Blackwell.

Wilson, D. and Sperber, D. (2004) 'Relevance theory', in L. Horn and G. Ward (eds) *The Handbook of Pragmatics*, Oxford: Blackwell.

Representation and Computation

The notion of representation is one of the most important and controversial in psychology. Leaving aside the acceptations that were given of it in the first decades of scientific psychology – which include the works of Frederick Bartlett (1932) and even of behaviourists like Edward C. Tolman (1948), as well as the main body of Gestalt psychology – its contemporary history traces back to the cybernetic turn that took place around the middle of the twentieth century. Kenneth Craik (1943) was among the first in modern psychology to argue that the mind operates not directly on external reality, but on internally created models thereof, which it manipulates and uses to understand, simulate and predict world events and dynamics.

Positions of this sort fitted well into the burgeoning **cognitive psychology**. This discipline viewed the mind/brain as a computer and, via its close relation to **artificial intelligence**, was to give rise in the 1970s to **cognitive science**. A Turing machine (Church 1936; Turing 1936) is an abstract characterization of digital computers. It is comprised of a set of data, which is written on a tape as tokens of a finite symbolic alphabet (e.g. made of zeros and ones), and a set of procedures that operate on them. It was all too natural in the heyday of cognitive science to equate – or straightforwardly identify – Craik's mental models with the data of a Turing machine, their constitutive elementary items with the symbols in its formal alphabet, and their manipulation on the part of the mind with the operation of its programs (e.g. Thagard 1996).

Over the decades that followed, the attempt to identify the code, or the codes, in which **knowledge** is supposedly represented in the mind gave rise to a major research area. The debate was far from merely philosophical or metaphorical. In an oft-quoted passage, Zenon Pylyshyn (1991: 219) stated that, differently from what happens in other sciences:

> in cognitive science our choice of notation is critical precisely because the theories claim that representations are written in the mind in the postulated notation: that at least some of the knowledge is explicitly represented and encoded in the notation proposed by the theory … What is sometimes not appreciated is that computational models are models of what literally goes on in the mind.

Each representational code is well suited for a corresponding set of **reasoning** rules, and vice versa: the form of the data and the form of the procedures mirror each other, so that to identify the one practically means to identify the other. However, it was generally maintained that the mind's program(s), once identified, would turn out to be comparatively simple: 'An ant, viewed as a behaving system, is quite simple. The apparent complexity of its behaviour over time is largely a reflection of the complexity of the environment in which it finds itself' (Simon 1981: 64). In Herbert Simon's famous metaphor, the mind, like the ant, is a simple set of programs, and the complex environment in which it finds itself – and which makes it appear more complex than it actually is – is the set of representations over which it operates. Therefore, the real issue was held to be the identification of the code in which the representations are 'written in the mind'. Once this code was identified, the mind and its functioning would be substantially understood.

In the 1960s and 1970s many such codes were proposed to capture the nature of human representations: the most notable among them, apart from classical and nonclassical logic, were semantic networks (Quillian 1968; Collins and Quillian 1969; Woods 1975), production rules (Newell and Simon 1972), frames (Minsky 1974), schemata (Bobrow and Norman 1975), scripts (Schank and Abelson 1977; Schank 1980), and mental models (Johnson-Laird 1983; the phrase 'mental models' has a specific, more technical meaning in Johnson-Laird's work than in Craik's account).

Each proposed notation had its own theoretical specifications and often its own computational and empirical or experimental correlates. What all of them appeared to have in common is the idea that mental representations are coded symbolically and are structured and computable. That representations are coded symbolically means that they are, to quote Pylyshyn again, 'written in the mind in the postulated notation'; that they are computable means that they can be the input and – once transformed by the program – the output of the mind's functioning. Taken together these properties mean that the mind/brain is a digital computer. That representations are structured means that the elementary items of which they are composed are linked to each other in complex ways and grouped into meaningful aggregates. Knowledge of restaurants, for example, has to include or be linked to knowledge about rooms, tables, menus, waiters, dishes, money, and so on; knowledge of money has to include or be linked to knowledge about value, trade, banknotes, coins, cheques, jobs, wages, robberies and so on; knowledge of robberies has to include or be linked to knowledge about property, law, banks, guns, police, handcuffs, jails and so on. Each such node may also point to specific examples or instances of the concept which the system has encountered. Thus, an intelligent agent's overall knowledge system consists in a huge network or graph with different types of nodes and links to connect them. This is in practice a hypertext. Computational theories of representation differ with regard to what structure the hypertext is supposed to have, what types of nodes and links it may contain, what types of **inference** may be drawn by the processor while it traverses the hypertext, and so on.

Other researchers, while subscribing to the computational paradigm, maintained instead that representations have an analogical nature (most notably Shepard 1980 and Kosslyn 1983) or that they can have both a symbolic and an analogical nature (Paivio 1986). These views gained popularity, albeit in a different form, when parallel distributed models of representation (later known under labels like connectionism or neural networks) were developed (McClelland *et al.* 1986; Rumelhart *et al.* 1986).

With a partial exception for the controversy about symbolic versus connectionist approaches (Fodor and Pylyshyn 1988; Smolensky 1988), the whole debate about representational codes lost much of its momentum during the 1980s and the 1990s. This was caused by several reasons. It became generally understood that if the mind/brain is a digital computer, then all properly constructed representational systems are equivalent, because ultimately they all are materially reduced to the finite alphabet used by the machine that is supposed to be the mind/brain. This thought was encapsulated in the so-called physical symbol system hypothesis which stated that '[a] physical symbol system has the necessary and sufficient means for general intelligent action' (Newell and Simon 1976: 41; it may be interesting to note that this is actually a postulate, not a hypothesis). It also led to the idea that successful computational intelligence – whether natural (e.g. Barkow *et al.* 1992; Pinker 1997) or artificial (e.g. Minsky 1988, 1991) – should probably employ different representational and reasoning subsystems according to the features of the **context** and of the task at hand (but *see* Fodor 2000).

The field of knowledge representation thus became largely a matter of sheer engineering (e.g. Davis *et al.* 1993; Brachman and Levesque 2004). With a major emphasis on formal and computational issues and little or no interest in psychological plausibility, knowledge representation is currently considered a province of artificial intelligence more often than of psychology or cognitive science. Simultaneously, many cognitive scientists lost interest in a research topic which was no longer meant to capture the real nature of the (human) mind.

Another reason for the decline of interest in knowledge representation outside artificial intelligence was the growing understanding of the many limits of the classical view. Let us reconsider the assumption that the mind does not operate on the world, but only on the representations of the world that it entertains. This position, which constitutes one of the foundations of computational functionalism, is known as methodological solipsism (Fodor 1980). It requires that the mind/brain be connected to the world via noncognitive subsystems known as modules (Fodor 1983). Thus, the representational and reasoning system only needs to satisfy constraints of completeness, correctness, consistency and, possibly, efficiency, while truth, or, at least, appropriateness to reality, is maintained via nonrepresentational connections to the external world.

A problem with this view is that it only functions on a closed-world assumption. This is the assumption that all that exists to the system has to be either explicitly coded in its knowledge base or formally deducible from what is coded. However, the closed-world assumption gives rise to computationally intractable problems known as the frame problem (McCarthy and Hayes 1969) and the qualification problem (McCarthy 1980). These problems follow from the requirement that each and every effect that a certain action may have or, respectively, each and every precondition that must hold for such action to be executable, must be explicitly stated in the knowledge base or formally deducible from it. Some researchers think that these two problems imply the impossibility of a computational system operating intelligently in the real open world (Searle 1980; Dreyfus 1992). Others proposed instead that they can be overcome by coding the entire body of knowledge that a computational system would need, which is in practice a description of the whole relevant universe. This was attempted, for example, with the CYC project (Lenat and Feigenbaum 1991; the name of the project comes from the 'psych' syllable in 'encyclopaedia') (see Smith 1991 for a criticism of CYC and of its underlying assumptions). It may be interesting to remark that this position also corresponds to the standard position of computational psychology and artificial intelligence that everything in the mind has to be innate: learning from experience is viewed as impossible both in natural and in artificial agents, although the solutions to this impasse seem to differ in the two cases.

A seemingly different attempt to overcome the difficulties of methodological solipsism is to work with agents so simple as to not need a knowledge base at all. Mainstream autonomous robotics rejected the whole idea of representation and claimed that cognition can and should be understood without recurring to it: internal models of the world are useless because 'the world is its own best model' (Brooks 1990: 6). This allowed investigators to 'build complete creatures rather than isolated cognitive simulators', as proposed by Rodney Brooks (1991a) in the title of a paper. On the one hand, however, these creatures hardly reach the intelligence level of a simple arthropod (or of any other computer), and scaling up to the human species appears impossible for principled reasons (Kirsh 1991; Tirassa et al. 2000). On the other hand, because their control systems ultimately function on zeros and ones, autonomous robots have been interpreted as an integral part of the symbolic paradigm and therefore of the research programme of classical artificial intelligence (Vera and Simon 1993).

Thus, the most radical criticism of the classical view is the claim that the mind/brain is indeed a representational organ, but that the nature of representations is not that of a formal code. John **Searle** (1992) argued that the representational and computational structures that have typically been theorized in cognitive science lack any acceptable ontology. Not being observable or understandable either in the third person (because all that we can objectively see is neurons or circuitries and not frames or other representational structures) or in the first person (because frames and other representational structures are 'cognitively impenetrable', that is, inaccessible to subjectivity or introspection), these structures just cannot exist. Searle (1983) rejected the assumption – undisputed from Craik to Simon – that the representational mind/brain operates on formal internal models detached from the world and argued instead that its main feature is **intentionality** (see also Brentano 1874), a term which has been variously viewed as synonymous with connectedness, aboutness, meaningfulness, **semantics** or straightforwardly consciousness.

The idea that representations are constructed (or simply happen) at the interaction of the conscious mind/brain and the external world is also a major tenet of the area known as situated or embodied cognition (e.g. Gibson 1979; Johnson 1987; Varela et al. 1991; Hutchins 1995; Clark 1997; Clancey 1997b; Glenberg 1997; Tirassa et al. 2000). Representations here are viewed as neither structured symbolic codes nor as the objects of formal manipulation, but as (at least partially culturally constructed) artefacts that are interposed between the internal and the external worlds and that generate a continuous dynamical reconceptualization of **meaning**. Thus, many researchers in situated cognitive science are constructivist with regard to the nature of knowledge, which they view as a continuously renewed product of consciousness and as tightly bound to action and experience, and practitioners of phenomenology with regard to their methodology, which follows from the idea that the mind only exists in the first person immersed in time (Heidegger 1927; Merleau-Ponty 1945; Varela *et al.* 1991; Varela 1996).

MAURIZIO TIRASSA and MARIANNA VALLANA

See also: Artificial intelligence; cognitive anthropology; cognitive psychology; cognitive science; computational pragmatics; inference; information structure; intentionality; knowledge; modularity of mind thesis; philosophy of mind; rationality; reasoning; Searle, J.

Suggestions for further reading

Clancey, W.J. (1997) *Situated Cognition: On Human Knowledge and Computer Representations*, Cambridge: Cambridge University Press.
Lindsay, P.H. and Norman, D.A. (1977) *Human Information Processing*, 2nd edn, New York: Academic Press.
Varela, F.J., Thompson, E. and Rosch, E. (1991) *The Embodied Mind: Cognitive Science and Human Experience*, Cambridge, MA: MIT Press.

Request

Making a request is a seemingly simple act that is performed by an utterance of an appropriate sentence under appropriate circumstances. To be sure, speech acts of request share with speech acts of other types a number of major features, but their own type is of much additional interest.

Being speech acts of a certain type, requests are rule governed. The rules that govern them determine the nature of requests, by specifying the ends of these speech acts as well as by governing the means through which they are achieved.

The nature of the ends can be grasped by considering an ordinary request, such as the one performed by an utterance of the sentence 'I request that you include recommendations for additional readings in your chapter', made by an editor of a book, addressed to an author of a chapter, to appear in the book. The request may seem to be an expression of the editor's wish that chapters of the book include recommendations for additional readings. On the background of that speech act of request it is reasonable to assume that the editor entertains such a wish. However, this is not the wish expressed by making the speech act. Strictly speaking, the expressed wish is confined to the addressed author's chapter, in which one is requested to include recommendations for additional readings. Satisfaction of the latter wish is, indeed, a necessary condition for satisfaction of the former wish, but an expression of the latter is not tantamount to an expression of the former.

The special nature of the means can also be grasped by considering a common request, such as the one performed by an utterance of the sentence 'Could you please repeat the question?', as made by a person, addressed to another one, who has just posed a **question**, under ordinary circumstances. As much as this is a seemingly simple speech act of request, it involves two special features that have to be noticed and explained. The first feature which indicates that this is a speech act of request is the use of the word 'please'. This is an interesting marker of request. On the one hand, it does not have, to appear for the performed speech act to be one of request. To see this, consider another speech act that is different from the previous one only by not including 'please' in the sentence. The resulting speech act will naturally be understood as one of request. On the other hand, when 'please' appears as a marker, it emphasizes the **speech act type**. It is always used for a reason and understanding that reason is part of understanding the speech act (*see* White 1993 for a discussion of an inter-language usage of 'please').

A second feature of that speech act of request is that the sentence used in its performance is in the interrogative. Moreover, the speech act performed can be taken to be a question. One can easily imagine circumstances under which such a sentence can be used for asking a question about the addressee's ability without making any request. This special feature of speech acts of request reveals a distinction between direct and indirect requests. Theories have attempted to explain our natural understanding of a speech act of question as a speech act of request (*see* Searle 1975b). The reasons underlying usage of indirect speech acts have also been investigated. See House (2006a) and Pinker *et al.* (2008) for different frameworks of explanation. Interestingly, some brain-damaged persons who suffer a **right-hemisphere** injury lose the ability to understand indirect requests (*see* Gibbs 2003 for a broad discussion).

Speech acts of request have been thoroughly studied in the context of **politeness** research. Studies such as seminal work by Brown and Levinson (1987) have deepened our understanding of politeness, but not that of requests as a speech act type. The same holds for studies of the acquisition of requests and its usage in different types of social contexts. An exception is the case of brain localization studies of request that found an intricate relationship between requests, questions and **commands** (*see* Soroker *et al.* 2005).

ASA KASHER

See also: Neuropragmatics; speech act theory; speech act type

Suggestions for further reading

Searle, J.R. (1969) *Speech Acts*, Cambridge: Cambridge University Press.
Vanderveken, D. (1990) *Meaning and Speech Acts*, vol. 1, New York: Cambridge University Press.

Rhetoric

As the discipline of **pragmatics** has emerged and developed, it has found a natural relationship with several older disciplines interested in the use and functions of language and the roles language plays in a variety of activities. Perhaps chief among these is rhetoric, conceived generally as the art of persuasion (Kennedy 1963). Many of rhetoric's traditional methods for achieving

purposes through language use have been modified in ways that are instructive for contemporary work in pragmatics.

In the Western tradition, rhetoric finds its roots in the works of the Greeks (Enos 1993). Even before Plato introduces the term in the *Gorgias* (Schiappa 1999; Cole 1991), we see references to the organized use of persuasive techniques as employed by such figures as Corax and Tisias. More systematic developments appear in the form of textbooks, like that of Aristotle's *Rhetoric*, with its stress on argument and style. What makes Aristotle's treatment distinctly rhetorical is the primary consideration he gives to audiences in the discussion of his central triad of *logos, ethos*, and *pathos*. People are moved to accept claims through the way they are invited to complete the argument, the weight granted to the arguer's character, and the way they are moved by the appeal. Aristotle also laid stress on three types of rhetorical speech: the deliberative, which concerns debate, primarily in the political realm; the epidictic, or the ceremonial use of language, such as that used in funeral orations; and the judicial, or forensic, involving the detailed examinations of the courts. Aristotle's foundations received constructive emendations during the later Hellenistic period and from the great Roman rhetoricians. Cicero (106–43 BCE), both a skilled theorist and practitioner, placed rhetoric above philosophy and law, with it encompassing the skills of both. Among his contributions of significance were the rhetorical canons that came to influence teaching into the eighteenth century.

The parts of rhetoric captured in these canons involve invention (*inventio*), arrangement (*dispositio*), style (*elocutio*), memory (*memoria*), and delivery (*pronuntiatio*). Invention concerns the creation of the content of a speech and deciding which strategy to use in conveying it. Such strategies are one way of understanding Aristotle's topics. Arrangement concerned the laying out of the argument or speech through its component parts, from introduction, through the proof, to the conclusion. The style referred to the best figures to use in presenting the case to the audience. Then came memory, or use of mnemonics to remember a speech. And finally, there is the actual delivery of the speech. In terms of the interest of rhetoric for pragmatics, it is the first three of these that retain the greatest importance.

Succeeding Cicero, Quintilian (35–96 CE) also made important contributions to the development of rhetoric. In many ways his influence was on the attention given to the orator, now conceived of as a good man. Rhetoric becomes the discourse of a good man, and attention is shifted away from its elements.

These core elements of rhetoric retained their influence for many centuries, added to and subtracted from in less significant ways, and served as the focus of the curriculum, along with logic and grammar. But that influence diminished until it disappeared altogether, not to be resurrected in any serious way until the work of Chaïm Perelman (1912–84) in the twentieth century. Together with Lucie Olbrechts-Tyteca, Perelman returned to the rhetoric of Aristotle to produce a theory of argumentation modern enough to combat what they took to be the negative influence of demonstrative proof (Perelman and Olbrechts-Tyteca 1969). They called their theory of argumentation a 'New Rhetoric' because it was thoroughly grounded in rhetorical features, chief among which were a focus on context and audience. While logical proofs have an internal relation of parts and exhibit a self-evidence that puts them beyond the bounds of argumentation, arguments themselves are always *for* an audience and aim for the adherence of that audience to the claims advanced. To understand the relationship between arguers and audiences, Perelman and Olbrechts-Tyteca draw freely on the content of the rhetorical tradition, adopting topics (or *loci*) and rhetorical figures to their own end. For example, the emphasis they give to figures is on their effects. Hence, the argumentative nature cannot be decided in advance. This leads them to focus on three types of effect: choice, presence, and communion. The effect of an oratorical definition can reveal it to be a figure of choice in a case where the structure of a definition is used not to give the meaning of a word but to bring forward aspects of a case or situation that would otherwise be overlooked (1969: 172–73). In a similar way, 'presence' concerns the display of certain elements in a speech on which the speaker wishes to place emphasis so as to bring them to the attention of the audience in a particularly vivid way.

Perelman and Olbrechts-Tyteca also introduce important features of their own, including the still controversial concept of a universal audience rooted in each particular audience and providing in some way the standard of reasonableness that will govern the argumentative situation.

These innovations from the tradition of rhetoric coincided with the emergence of interests in language use characterized by the work of people like the philosopher H.P. **Grice** (1913–88). Although rhetoric often seems disconnected from the interests of pragmatics, since it is taken to be primarily prescriptive while pragmatics is descriptive, Perelman's work has been instrumental in challenging such a division (Perelman 1982). Further, it can be important when interpreting the utterances or written texts of people to recognize the ways in which speakers or writers have intentionally drawn on principles of rhetoric in organizing a case (Bitzer 1968).

Scholars have drawn attention to the differences between rhetoric and pragmatics (Dascal and Gross 1999) and the problems that need to be addressed for a more fruitful interchange to emerge. The propositional mental states operative in **post-Gricean pragmatics**, for example, are not easily assimilated with the 'proofs' associated with character and emotion. But efforts to develop more cognitive theories of rhetoric (Tsur 1992; Fahnestock 2005), some by stressing the rationality of the emotions (Nussbaum 2001), hold promise for addressing such concerns.

CHRISTOPHER W. TINDALE

See also: Argumentation theory; context; Grice, H.P.; logical form; post-Gricean pragmatics; proposition; topic; utterance interpretation

Suggestions for further reading

Dascal, M. and Gross, A. (1999) 'The marriage of pragmatics and rhetoric', *Philosophy and Rhetoric*, 32: 107–30.

Perelman, Ch. and Olbrechts-Tyteca, L. (1969) *The New Rhetoric: A Treatise on Argumentation*, trans. J. Wilkinson and P. Weaver, Notre Dame, IN: University of Notre Dame Press.

Tindale, C.W. (2004) *Rhetorical Argumentation: Principles of Theory and Practice*, Thousand Oaks, CA: Sage Publications.

Rhetorical Questions

Rhetorical questions still hold a fascination for scholars of various scientific disciplines. Since Antiquity, when it first emerged among rhetorical figures, the rhetorical question has captured the interest of rhetoricians and linguists alike on account of its complexity and elusiveness. Historically, the analysis of rhetorical questions has been approached from several scholarly perspectives. A number of studies have addressed their rhetorical use, particularly in fiction, political speeches and courtroom examinations (Ilie 1995a), while others have concentrated on their linguistic structure and pragmatic functions. Of more recent date are the cross-cultural and **translation** studies of rhetorical questions (Ilie 1995b).

Cicero and Quintilian classified rhetorical questions as figures of thought, pointing to the fact that their interrogative form deviates from ordinary interrogative functions. In *Institutio Oratoria*, Quintilian makes the distinction between two fundamental interrogative strategies: *to ask*, i.e. to require information by means of a straightforward **question**, and *to enquire*, i.e. to emphasize a point in order to prove something by means of a rhetorical figure, such as the rhetorical question.

In the field of linguistics, several theoretical schools have grappled with the description of the features and uses of rhetorical questions. Focusing exclusively on **syntax**, structuralist grammarians pointed to relevant aspects of rhetorical questions, such as their emphatic and dual nature (Poutsma 1928; Scheurweghs 1959) and their polarity shift (Curme 1931). (The polarity shift consists in the fact that a rhetorical question usually displays an affirmative or negative form which is opposite to that of its implied answer.) Significant contributions to the study of rhetorical questions within the framework of transformational-generative approaches have been made by Borkin (1971), Sadock (1971, 1974) and Pope (1976). Sadock studied sentences with the surface form of questions but with the semantic value and some of the syntactic properties of declaratives. He called these sentences 'queclaratives'. According to Sadock, queclaratives display the same polarity shift as rhetorical questions and share certain semantic properties with tag questions. The questions that Pope chooses to investigate are

yes-no questions and wh-questions. Unlike previous approaches, which took for granted that rhetorical questions have no answers, Pope's approach starts from the assumption that rhetorical questions involve specific answers (belonging to rhetorical question-answer pairs). However, the impossibility of accounting for the shift in focus between rhetorical and non-rhetorical questions at deep structure level is one of the major difficulties encountered by structuralists and transformational-generativists.

As earlier studies show, the complex nature and multifunctionality of rhetorical questions cannot be captured and defined exclusively by syntactic, semantic or syntactico-semantic analysis. A major inadequacy of those descriptions is that they focus almost exclusively on syntactic and/or semantic aspects, while ignoring the pragmatic factors involved in specific **contexts** and situations of use.

An integrative pragmatic approach to the study of questions and responses has been used by Ilie (1994) to account for context-based varieties and functions of rhetorical questions, and to distinguish them from genuine questions and other special types of questions (such as echo questions, leading questions and examination questions). Several systematic examinations of the linguistic and rhetorical behaviour of rhetorical questions in several **discourse** genres indicate that rhetorical questions have an interrogative form like any other question, but they do not function as standard questions, viz. they do not convey or expect a genuine elicitation of information. Actually, rather than request information from the hearer, rhetorical questions normally provide information about the speaker's state of mind, opinion and/or emotions, as illustrated in the following two examples:

(1) A: Are you and him together again?
    B: Have you seen any pigs flying?
                        (excerpt from the British TV
                         series *Firm Friends*)

The question uttered by B in (1) has the syntactic form of a yes-no interrogative and, if it were a genuine question, it would basically elicit a choice between an affirmative and a negative answer. However, B's obvious purpose is to use this question as an indirect answer to A's question.

The ironic undertone of B's rhetorically used question is meant to reinforce a strong denial that is conveyed by an idiomatic expression which refers to a prototypically unlikely situation. So the answer to be inferred by questioner A is a most categorical 'no'.

A particular feature of rhetorical questions is the polarity shift between the rhetorical question and the implied answer in the sense that a question with an affirmative interrogative form normally implies a negative answer, as in (1), whereas a question with a negative interrogative form normally implies an affirmative answer, as illustrated in (2):

(2) M: Am I allowed to tell you that you are very beautiful?
    A: Isn't this the country of free speech? [Change of scene]
                        (excerpt from the British TV series *The House of Eliott*)

The sarcastic undertone of A's rhetorical question is meant to reinforce her reluctantly implied affirmative answer to M's question. However, although the rhetorical answer is affirmative, A's attitude to M's utterance is anything but positive. In both examples the interrogative form of the utterance conveys an implicit challenge directed at the interlocutor, while the underlying message is a forceful statement. In other words, rhetorical questions constitute a special use, not a special category of questions. Consequently, rhetorical questions have to be interpreted as pragmatic, rather than grammatical categories. Since a rhetorical question functions as a crossbreed between a question and a statement, it shares certain features with each of these two utterance types: on the one hand, it can be followed by a verbalized answer like any other question, and, on the other, it indirectly conveys an **assertion** or a denial like any statement.

It has occasionally been suggested that conducive or leading questions share a basic feature with rhetorical questions, namely, that they indirectly convey a particular answer that is easily inferred by the addressee. However, on closer inspection, there are significant differences between these questions in terms of addresser goals and expectations, on the one hand, and addressee goals and expectations, on the other hand. While leading questions actually elicit a particular verbalized answer, rhetorical questions do not elicit a verbalized answer, but only imply a particular answer, which is inferrable by the addressee and to which the addresser is strongly committed. Thus, rhetorical questions serve to synchronize addresser and addressee beliefs with the purpose of confirming their shared beliefs about the world. This is, according to Rohde (2006: 134), a major condition for the felicitous use of rhetorical questions: 'the addresser and the addressee must share prior commitments to similar and obvious answers'.

On reconsidering the definition of rhetorical questions, five distinctive features are particularly relevant and need to be taken into account:

(i) the discrepancy between the interrogative form of the rhetorical question and its communicative function as a statement: because of this double nature, rhetorical questions must comply with constraints on both questions and statements;

(ii) the polarity shift between the interrogative form of the rhetorical question and its implied answer;

(iii) the implicitness and the exclusiveness of the answer to a rhetorical question, which is assumed to be shared by the addresser and the addressee;

(iv) the addresser's firm commitment to the implied answer;

(v) the multifunctionality of the rhetorical question which may function simultaneously as an ironic or sarcastic remark, a reminder, a criticism or a warning, to name but a few.

The pragmatic definition of rhetorical questions advanced by Ilie (1994: 128) offers a synthetic explanation of their nature and functioning: 'A rhetorical question is a question used as a challenging statement to convey the addresser's commitment to its implicit answer in order to induce the addressee's mental recognition of its obviousness and the acceptance, verbalised or non-verbalised, of its validity'. Therefore, in pragmatic terms, a rhetorical question can be described as having the literal illocutionary force of a question and the perlocutionary effect of a statement.

A systematic examination of responses to rhetorical questions can contribute not only to providing a better understanding of the addresser's **intentions** and of the effects of these intentions on the addressee(s), but also to throwing light on the specific functions of rhetorical questions and on the interaction between addresser and addressee. As has already been mentioned, rhetorical questions are usually not meant to elicit answers, but to express feedback, a standpoint, an attitude or an ironic or sarcastic stance, as illustrated in example (3):

(3) Winfrey: Not only that, you grew up with Bonanza and Pa and –
Landon: That's right.
Winfrey: Yeah, I mean, what could be better than that?
Landon: That's right.
(*The Oprah Winfrey Show*, 10 December 1986)

The dynamics of the dialogue indicate that Winfrey uses the interrogative 'what could be better than that?' as a rhetorical question to convey a strong appreciative attitude. Landon's response to her rhetorical question is obviously not an answer, since no answer has been elicited, but a reply to Winfrey's unstated admiration: 'nothing (could be better than that)'. Landon does not answer the question, but acknowledges shared commitment with the implied answer by overtly expressing agreement with the rhetorical question's underlying statement. For further discussion of the functions of rhetorical questions in talk shows, the reader is referred to Ilie (1998, 1999).

Situations of confrontation and **disagreement** occur whenever there is a mismatch between the addresser's assessment of the addressee's degree of shared **knowledge** and the latter's actual knowledge, or whenever the addressee misinterprets the illocutionary force of the rhetorical question. An illustration of the former case can be found in example (4):

(4) Harry: Yes, I was missing [during the General Strike], I'm sure.
Sarah: Well, sure you were missing?
Harry: Where was I missing?
Sarah: How should I know where you were missing?
(Wesker 1964: 19)

The knowledge gap conveyed by Harry's genuine question 'Where was I missing?' is real, but the elicited answer cannot be provided by the addressee, who shares the same knowledge gap. Sarah uses instead a rhetorical question to indirectly provide a negative answer to Harry's question: 'There is no way I should know … '. While admitting her lack of knowledge in a disclaimer, she implicitly reproaches Harry for having made an incorrect assessment of their shared knowledge and for addressing the question unjustifiably to someone lacking the necessary information. This example shows clearly that, due to their multifunctionality, rhetorical questions can be used as multi-purpose responses to genuine questions. Sarah's commitment to the implied rhetorical answer makes it possible for the rhetorical question to function as a response to a regular question. While a plain denial would have simply conveyed Sarah's confessed inability to provide an informative answer, the rhetorical question can express at the same time her reaction of disculpation, reproach and protest at being confronted with Harry's inadequate question.

The occurrence of rhetorical questions in several discourse genres (political, legal, journalese, literary, etc.) and their multiple communicative functions (as challenges, responses, disagreements, accusations, ironical remarks, etc.) provide evidence for the fact that rhetorical questions are meant to be heard as questions and understood as statements.

CORNELIA ILIE

See also: Assertion; context; disagreement; discourse analysis; inference; inferential comprehension; intention; knowledge; negation, pragmatics of; question; speech act theory; utterance interpretation

Suggestions for further reading

Ilie, C. (1994) *What Else Can I Tell You? A Pragmatic Study of English Rhetorical Questions as Discursive and Argumentative Acts*, Stockholm: Almqvist & Wiksell International.
——(1995) 'The validity of rhetorical questions as arguments in the courtroom', in F.H. van Eemeren, R. Grootendorst, J.A. Blair and

C.A. Willard (eds) *Special Fields and Cases. Proceedings of the Third International Conference on Argumentation*, Amsterdam: SICSAT.
——(1999) 'Question-response argumentation in talk shows', *Journal of Pragmatics*, 31: 975–99.

Right-Hemisphere Damage and Pragmatics

Deficits in pragmatic language ability are common to a number of clinical populations. This discussion reviews the current state of knowledge of pragmatic disorders following right-hemisphere damage (RHD). Brain damage in the right hemisphere may occur due to a wide range of conditions such as stroke (haemorrhagic or ischaemic), brain tumours, epilepsy, and neural infections. In the mid-twentieth century, researchers conducted the first systematic investigations of language comprehension following RHD and concluded that RHD patients had verbal communication disorders, which were different from the communication disorders found in left-hemisphere damaged individuals (Eisenson 1962; Weinstein 1964).

Since then, several studies have investigated the verbal communication abilities of RHD individuals. Most of those studies have focused their attention on the pragmatic aspects of language (for reviews *see* Joanette *et al.* 1990; Tompkins 1995; P.S. Myers 1999; Cummings 2007a). **Pragmatics** refers to the use of language in **context** including both physical context and aspects such as speaker **intention**, mood and the emotional state of the speaker.

Since **Austin** (1962), **Grice** (1969), and **Searle** (1969), we know that verbal messages can convey a speaker's intention. Thus, the comprehension of non-literal speech acts requires the ability to grasp both the literal and non-literal meanings of a message, and disentangle what the speaker says from what he or she intends to say. Following Searle's framework, research was developed that distinguished sentence meaning from speaker meaning and literal language from non-literal language. Since then, a number of studies that have specifically tested the comprehension of indirect **requests** (Foldi 1987; Weylman *et al.* 1989) by RHD individuals have proposed that these individuals have a tendency

to understand language 'literally', in other words they process only the literal meaning of utterances. For example, RHD individuals would answer the question 'Could you pass the salt?' with 'yes' or 'no' instead of with the appropriate action (e.g. passing the salt). However, other studies have shown that RHD individuals do not present with such deficits in comprehension or production when speech is used within a natural context (Stemmer *et al.* 1994; Brownell and Stringfellow 1999; Vanhalle *et al.* 2000; Champagne *et al.* 2003).

Following these results, researchers assessed non-literal language in the context of Grice's framework. RHD individuals were shown to exhibit deficits in comprehension of Grice's conversational **implicatures**, specifically indirect request (e.g. *The door is open*, meaning *Close the door*) (Kasher *et al.* 1999), indirect **refusal** (Hatta *et al.* 2004), and the maxims of relation and quantity (Kasher *et al.* 1999; Champagne *et al.* 2003).

RHD individuals demonstrate difficulty in grasping the non-literal meaning of other pragmatic aspects of language such as **metaphor** (Winner and Gardner 1977; Brownell *et al.* 1984; Giora *et al.* 2000; Rinaldi *et al.* 2004) and **idioms** (Myers and Linebaugh 1981; Van Lancker and Kempler 1987).

Some studies have shown that RHD individuals exhibit **discourse** deficits, such as deficits in **conversation** (Marini *et al.* 2005; Lehman Blake 2006), difficulty in generating **inferences** (Brownell *et al.* 1986; Schneiderman *et al.* 1992; Tompkins *et al.* 2004; Saldert and Ahlsen 2007), understanding and producing central themes (Hough 1990; Schneiderman *et al.* 1992) and managing contextual information.

Modern pragmatic theories have influenced the study of language comprehension and production in RHD. For example, the ability to understand metaphors (Giora *et al.* 2000) has been evaluated taking into account different subtypes of metaphors (e.g. conventional vs. non-conventional). Since Kaplan *et al.* (1990) and Sabbagh (1999), the role played by perception and comprehension of the speaker's intention has become the focus of studies assessing non-literal language styles such as **irony**, sarcasm or non-conventional indirect requests in RHD individuals. Researchers have examined if

RHD patients are able to use **theory of mind** and **prosody** to establish speakers' intentions (Lalande *et al.* 1992; Baum and Dwivedi 2003; Pell 2006, 2007; Harciarek *et al.* 2006). Research on prosody has suggested that patients with RHD have difficulty using information provided about the mood of an individual (e.g. angry versus happy; Joanette *et al.* 1990; Pell 2006) and understanding the attitude of a speaker (Pell 2007). Similar results have been found in research on discourse and inferences generation, suggesting that RHD individuals have a diminished capacity to understand conversational speech.

The study of theory of mind in RHD individuals has added to our understanding of their problems in non-literal language comprehension. Indeed, the interpretation processes involved in understanding non-literal language such as irony or indirect requests have been defined as an exercise in mind-reading, as such interpretation necessitates the inference of the speaker's intention, beliefs and desires (Grice 1969). To understand how a listener can interpret an ironic utterance or an indirect request, one must understand what the listener knows and what the speaker thinks the listener knows. Many studies have found that RHD individuals seem to have a reduced capacity to understand the speaker's motivation. This limited capacity impairs their ability to understand irony (Kaplan *et al.* 1990; Winner *et al.* 1998), indirect requests (Siegal *et al.* 1996; Surian and Siegal 2001) and **humour** (Cheang and Pell 2006). Studies that have specifically tested the attribution of mental states by RHD individuals have systematically reported that RHD individuals are unable to assess the speaker's mental state, beliefs, prior **knowledge**, or intention (Siegal *et al.* 1996; Winner *et al.* 1998; Happé *et al.* 1999; Surian and Siegal 2001; Griffin *et al.* 2006; Champagne-Lavau and Joanette 2007). The problems that individuals with RHD have in distinguishing a joke from a lie, or an ironic statement from a lie were thus attributed to a problem in understanding the intentions of the story's protagonist (Kaplan *et al.* 1990; Winner *et al.* 1998). Accordingly, a speaker can facilitate **communication** with the individual with RHD by explicitly providing the communicative intention behind non-literal statements (Cheang and Pell 2006).

It is important to note that pragmatic deficits are not present in all RHD individuals and that patterns of performance may vary from one RHD individual to another (Joanette *et al.* 1991; Martin and McDonald 2003; Champagne *et al.* 2004). To account for such heterogeneity in the RHD population, researchers have investigated the role of general cognitive deficits, central coherence abilities, executive functions and lesion site in pragmatic deficits (Martin and McDonald 2003; Monetta and Champagne 2004). The performance of individuals with RHD in pragmatic tasks has been shown to be affected by a number of factors including working memory (Tompkins *et al.* 1994; Saldert and Ahlsen 2007), executive dysfunction in terms of lack of inhibition (Tompkins 1995; McDonald and Pearce 1996; Champagne *et al.* 2004; Champagne-Lavau *et al.* 2007), reduced flexibility (Brownell *et al.* 1986), and reduced attention resources (Monetta and Joanette 2003; Monetta *et al.* 2006).

In conclusion, research since the mid-twentieth century has shown that individuals with RHD are impaired in the use of language in context, although not all of them seem to have this problem. Our understanding of pragmatic deficits in RHD individuals has been increased by understanding theory of mind, emotion, and other non-specific cognitive abilities. Further research must address the development of adapted rehabilitation according to the different patterns of pragmatic deficits existing in the RHD population.

LAURA MONETTA and MAUD CHAMPAGNE-LAVAU

See also: Clinical pragmatics; communication; context; conventionality; conversation; cooperative principle; discourse; discourse coherence; generalized conversational implicature, theory of; Grice, H.P.; humour; idiom; implicature; inference; intention; irony; metaphor; neuropragmatics; rehabilitation, communication; request; schizophrenic language; Searle, J.; speech act theory; theory of mind

Suggestions for further reading

Brownell, H.H., Griffin, R., Winner, H., Friedman, O. and Happé, F. (2000) 'Cerebral lateralization and theory of mind', in S. Baron, H. Tager-Flusberg and D. Cohen (eds) *Understanding Other Minds: Perspectives from Autism and Cognitive Neuroscience*, Oxford: Oxford University Press.

Joanette, Y., Champagne-Lavau, M., Kahlaoui, K. and Ska, B. (2007) 'The future of our knowledge about communication impairments following a right-hemisphere lesion', in

M.J. Ball and J.S. Damico (eds) *Clinical Aphasiology. Future Directions. A Festschrift for Chris Code*, Hove and New York: Psychology Press.

Martin, I. and McDonald, S. (2003) 'Weak coherence, no theory of mind, or executive dysfunction? Solving the puzzle of pragmatic language disorders', *Brain and Language*, 85: 451–66.

S

Scalar Implicature

A scalar **implicature** is a conversational implicature that is derived from a set of salient contrastive alternates ordered in informational strength. The derivation of a scalar implicature is the result of **Grice**'s (1989) first sub-maxim of Quantity or Horn's (1984) and Levinson's (2000) Q[uantity]-principle, hence a scalar implicature is also called a Q-scalar implicature or a scalar Q-implicature.

In its narrow sense, a scalar implicature is engendered from a Q- or Horn-scale. There are two types of Horn: (i) positive Horn scales, and (ii) negative Horn scales. A prototype positive Horn scale is defined in (1) (Levinson 2000: 82; *see also* Horn 1972; Ducrot 1972; Gazdar 1979a; Matsumoto 1995).

(1) A positive Horn scale
  A set of linguistic alternates $<x_1, x_2, \dots, x_n>$ such that $S(x_i)$ unilaterally entails $S(x_j)$, where S is an arbitrary simplex sentence-frame, and $x_i > x_j$ and where $x_1, x_2, \dots, x_n$ are:
  a. equally lexicalized items, of the same word class, from the same register; and
  b. 'about' the same semantic relations, or from the same semantic field.

Some examples of positive Horn scales are given in (2).

(2) a. Quantifiers
      <all, most, many, some>
    b. Connectives
      <and, or>
    c. Adjectives
      <ancient, old>
    d. Adverbs
      <always, often, sometimes>
    e. Number words
      <n, … 6, 5, 4, 3, 2, 1>
    f. Modals
      <must, should, may>
    g. Verbs
      <adore, love, like>

As an illustrating example, consider (2d). In this contrast set, *always* is semantically stronger than *often*, which in turn is semantically stronger than *sometimes*. This is because *always* entails *often*, which in turn entails *sometimes*, but not vice versa. The three adverbs are relatively equally lexicalized. All of them are adverbs of frequency, that is, they are from the same semantic field. More or less the same can be said of (2a) to (2c), and (2e) to (2g). In contrast, the sets in (3) are ruled out as genuine Horn scales.

(3) a. *<iff, if>
    b. *<regret, know>
    c. *<(p because q), (p and q)>

(3a) violates the equal lexicalization condition specified in (1a); there is no unitary lexeme in English, which standardly means the same as 'if and only if'. Put in a slightly different way, *iff* (which is in a special register) and *if* are not lexicalized to the same degree. Next, the reason why both (3b) and (3c) are excluded is that the two lexical expressions in each set are not about the same semantic relation, thus contradicting the same semantic relation condition in (1b).

We move next to a negative Horn scale, which is defined in (4) and exemplified in (5) (Levinson 2000: 82).

(4) A negative Horn scale
For each well-formed positive Horn scale of the form $<x_1, x_2, \ldots , x_n>$, there will be a corresponding negative scale of the form $<\sim x_n, \ldots ,\sim x_2,\sim x_1>$, regardless of the relative lexicalization of the **negation**.

(5) <not some, not all> i.e.<none, not all>

Given a Horn scale, if a speaker asserts a lower-ranked or semantically weaker alternate (i.e. a rightwards expression in the ordered set), then he or she conversationally Q-implicates that he or she is not in a position to assert any of the higher-ranked or semantically stronger ones (i.e. leftwards in the ordered set) in the same set. Thus, the use of positive (6a) gives rise to the Q-scalar implicature in (6b), and the **assertion** of negative (7a) generates the Q-scalar implicature in (7b). ('Conversationally imply' is symbolized by +>.)

(6) a. Some of John's friends can speak Chinese.
b. +> Not many/most/all of John's friends can speak Chinese
(7) a. Not all of John's friends can speak Chinese.
b. +> Not none of John's friends can speak Chinese; some of them can

One interesting point to note is that sometimes scalar predicates in the same semantic field form two Horn scales linked by a (sub)contrary relationship rather than a single unified Horn scale, systematically engendering two opposite sorts of pragmatic **inference** (Horn 1989: 239–40; Levinson 2000: 86–87; Israel 2004; Huang 2007). This is illustrated by the paired Horn scales in (8). For example, in the 'evaluation' scalar domain, there are two opposite scales: a positive 'excellent' scale and a negative 'terrible/awful' scale.

(8) a. Quantity
<all, most, many, some>
<none, hardly any, few>
b. Epistemic modality

<necessary, likely, possible>
<impossible, unlikely, uncertain>
c. Temperature
<boiling, hot, warm>
<freezing, cold, cool, lukewarm>
d. Preference
<adore, love, like>
<loathe, hate, dislike>
e. Evaluation
<excellent, good, alright/OK>
<terrible/awful, bad, mediocre>

Finally, mention should also be made of the fact that under certain circumstances, a Horn scale can be inverted. For example, the order of the number words in the Horn scale in (9a) is reversed. Consequently, (9b) gives rise to the Q-scalar implicature in (9c).

(9) a. < ... 6, 7, 8, 9, 10, ... >
b. John has cut down his smoking to ten cigarettes a day.
c. +> John hasn't cut down his smoking to less than ten cigarettes a day

However, as pointed out by Sadock (1984), this kind of scale-reversal seems to be restricted to number words. Now contrast (9) with (10). In the latter, the order of the scalar items in the Horn scale is not reversed. The assertion of (10b) then generates the Q-scalar implicature in (10c).

(10) a. < ... 12, 11, 10, ... >
b. John hasn't cut down his smoking to ten cigarettes a day.
c. +> John has cut down his smoking to more than ten cigarettes a day

Of particular interest here is that the direction of Q-scalar implicatures engendered in an affirmative sentence like (9b) and in its negative counterpart like (10b) is exactly the opposite. The same is also true of the direction of scalar or pragmatic **entailments** here (*see also* Israel 2004).

Having discussed scalar implicature in its narrow sense, I now turn to scalar implicature in its broad sense. A scalar implicature in its broad sense can be generated from a Horn-like scale, where while the lexical expressions are informationally ranked, the stronger items do not entail the weaker ones.

(11) <succeed, try>
   a. John tried to recover the lost files on his computer.
   b. +> John didn't succeed in recovering the lost files on his computer
   c. John succeeded in recovering the lost files on his computer without even trying.

(12) <divorce, separate>
   a. John: Have they divorced?
      Mary: They have separated.
   b. +> They haven't divorced yet
   c. They have divorced without separating.

(13) <David Beckham's autograph, Michael Owen's autograph>
   a. I have got Owen's autograph.
   b. +> The speaker hasn't got Beckham's autograph
   c. I have got Beckham's autograph without getting Owen's autograph.

As the (c) sentences in (11) to (13) show, the stronger expressions do not entail the weaker ones in these scales. But the uttering of the (relevant) (a) sentences does give rise to scalar-like implicatures, as in the (b) sentences. This type of scalar implicature I called Q-ordered alternate implicatures in Huang (2007).

Notice next that the Horn-like scales in (11) to (13) are of two types: those like Horn scales, which are given by the lexicon without requiring any specific **context**, as in (11), and those which are given by general assumptions about the world, context and/or other pragmatic factors, as in (12) and (13). The former can be based on different structures of the lexicon such as taxonomies, metonymies, and helices. The latter is essentially a nonce scale, that is, a contextually given ad hoc scale. Such a scale can be based on any partially ordered contrastive sets in a contextually salient way. Levinson (2000) called this kind of pragmatically defined set a Hirschberg scale (Hirschberg 1991; *see also* Fauconnier 1975; Harnish 1976; Coulson 2001). Furthermore, he categorized scalar implicatures derivable from a Horn or Horn-like scale as **generalized conversational implicatures** and those acting on a Hirschberg scale as particularized conversational implicatures.

Needless to say, both Horn-like scales and Hirschberg scales can also be based on alternates that contrast semantically but not on an informational asymmetry. This is the case of (14) and (15). But in these examples, although their generation follows exactly the same Q-inferential **reasoning**, the weak Q-implicatures engendered are not Q-scalar ones. In Huang (2007), I called such an implicature Q-unordered alternate implicature.

(14) A Horn-like scale
   a. < ... white, red, blue, green, yellow ... >
   b. The flag is white.
   c. +> The flag is not, for example, red, blue or green, or
      +> The flag is not white and red, or
      +> The flag is only/all white.

(15) A Hirschberg scale
   a. < ... French, German, Italian, Russian, Spanish ... >
   b. John: Do they teach any modern languages in that school?
      They teach French, German and Russian there.
   c. +> They don't teach, for example, Italian and Spanish in that school

Finally, two related issues should be mentioned *en passant*. First, the analysis of number words as scalar expressions is highly controversial (see, for example, Scharten 1997; König 1991; Levinson 2000; Carston 2002; Bultinck 2005). Second, scalar implicature has recently been subject to interesting studies in **experimental pragmatics** (see, for example, Papafragou and Musolino 2003; Noveck and Sperber 2004).

YAN HUANG

See also: Context; experimental pragmatics; Grice, H.P.; implicature; impliciture; maxims of conversation; neo-Gricean pragmatics; pragmatics

Suggestions for further reading

Hirschberg, J. (1991) *A Theory of Scalar Implicature*, New York: Garland.
Horn, L.R. (1989) *A Natural History of Negation*, Chicago, IL: University of Chicago Press.
Levinson, S.C. (2000) *Presumptive Meanings: The Theory of Generalized Conversational Implicature*, Cambridge, MA: MIT Press.

Schizophrenic Language

The characteristic symptoms of schizophrenia have often been conceptualized as falling into two broad categories – *positive* and *negative* symptoms (Green and Walker 1985; Frith 1993; Andreasen *et al.* 1995). Positive symptoms reflect an excess or distortion of normal functions, whereas negative symptoms reflect a reduction or loss of normal functions. The positive symptoms criteria include distortion or exaggeration of inferential thinking (delusions), perception (hallucinations), language and **communication** (disorganized speech), and behavioural monitoring (grossly disorganized or catatonic behaviour). Negative symptoms include restrictions in the range and intensity of emotional expression (affective flattening), in the fluency and productivity of thought and speech (alogia) and in the initiation of goal-directed behaviour. A third category – *disorganized symptoms* – includes disorganized speech (thought disorder), disorganized behaviour and poor attention.

Language disorder has long been considered a diagnostic indicator of schizophrenia (American Psychiatric Association 1994; Bleuler 1950; Kraepelin 1971). The fourth edition of the *Diagnostic and Statistical Manual of Mental Disorders* (DSM-IV; American Psychiatric Association 1994) is a descriptive approach to the diagnosis of schizophrenia, based on descriptions of the clinical features of the disorder. This manual presents diagnostic criteria for schizophrenia reflecting the opinion of the raters regarding what is appropriate or inappropriate language behaviour during the diagnostic interview. An intrinsic relationship exists between diagnosis and classification of schizophrenia, and the use of language in the context of the psychiatric clinical interview.

Clinicians have developed a tradition of measuring thought disorder through verbal behaviour, possibly confusing linguistic failures and disturbances in thought content, thought structure and cognitive processes (Andreasen and Grove 1986). The term 'formal thought disorder' has been used to identify structural failures in speech unique to schizophrenia and to distinguish schizophrenia from mania and other phenomena of disturbed thought content. Tracy (1998) recommends instead the use of the term 'psychotic speech disorder'. Research using lexical priming

has built considerable evidence suggesting that in schizophrenia thought intrusions and derailments in **discourse** arise from the hyperactive functioning of semantic networks. McGrath (1991) reviewed studies in the area of language and thought disorder, and attributed failure to structure discourse at higher levels to lack of executive planning and editing of information. Rodriguez-Ferrera *et al.* (2001) studied the relationship between language and thought disorder in schizophrenia and found that general intellectual impairment is an important determinant of poor language test performance in schizophrenia, to which presence of formal thought disorder may also contribute.

The topic of language and schizophrenia has been studied from different methodological points of view. Studies have been structured around the various levels of linguistic analysis from phonology to discourse, dependent on the tools and theoretical bases available in each discipline (cognition, psychopathology, physiopathology, linguistics and social sciences). In addition, researchers have applied tools borrowed from the current theory of language at the time the investigation was being performed.

Most of the schizophrenic language studies conducted during the 1950s and 1960s were verbal behaviour studies that required verbal responses from speakers (Lorenz and Cobb 1954; Gottschalk and Gleser 1964; Tucker and Rosenberg 1975; Andreasen 1979a, 1979b; Allen and Frith 1983). It was found that participants with schizophrenia did not show deviant word association. Word production measurements contribute little to the understanding of the use of language in **context** and its effect on the thought processes, communicative and social interactions of speakers with schizophrenia.

Syntactic deviance studies have shown that participants with schizophrenia appear to produce language that is syntactically less complex than that of the average adult (Morice and Ingram 1983; Thomas *et al.* 1990, 1996). Morice and Ingram (1983) and Thomas *et al.* (1990, 1996) conclude that this impoverished use of syntax reflects a premorbid deficit in syntactic production, probably a sign of abnormal neurodevelopment. A number of studies have reported that as syntactic complexity increases, so does semantic deviance (Morice and Ingram 1983;

Morice and McNicol 1986). The application of the semantic priming method to the study of word association of speakers with schizophrenia has shown an increased semantic priming effect (Manschreck *et al.* 1988; Kwapil *et al.* 1990; Spitzer *et al.* 1993; Weisbrod *et al.* 1998; Minzenberg *et al.* 2002).

Deviant cohesion between discourse elements and unclear **reference** for pronouns, phrases and clauses has been reported as highly characteristic of speakers with schizophrenia. Because of these failures, the language of these speakers becomes increasingly incomprehensible to the listener as it deviates from initial referents and context (Tracy 1998). Rochester and Martin (1979), using a functional linguistic approach to the description of the language of speakers with schizophrenia, reported that these speakers use fewer cohesive devices than normal speakers and rely significantly more on the use of situational reference.

A review of the literature shows clearly that the study of language in schizophrenia underwent a paradigmatic shift similar to the study of normal language, from the level of word units (e.g. Pavy 1968; Maher 1972), through sentence cohesion (Rochester and Martin 1979; Harvey 1983; Ragin and Oltmanns 1986), to a level related to the **pragmatics** of language (**speech acts** in particular) and to the discourse unit (Wodak and Van de Craen 1987; Wrobel 1990; Ribeiro 1994; Tényi *et al.* 2002; Meilijson *et al.* 2004).

Early studies have shown that the primary language impairment in schizophrenia is in the area of pragmatic performance. Bleuler's (1950) first description of patients with schizophrenia is illuminating in this respect, stating that although they may generate a great deal of speech, it is not intended to convey anything or to communicate with the environment. Pavy (1968) argued that the prominence of discourse failures in the language of patients with schizophrenia makes formal analysis of discourse necessary. Frith (1993), defining 'pragmatics' as the processes by which we use language to communicate our ideas and wishes to others, stated that the disturbances of language in schizophrenia lie at the level of language use rather than language **competence**. Griffin *et al.* (1994) have assessed the pragmatic abilities of participants with

chronic schizophrenia through a test of pragmatic language, **discourse analysis** and narrative analysis. Results showed poor pragmatic abilities in all areas assessed, with relevancy of content being the most problematic area. Done *et al.* (1998) argued that the language disturbances in schizophrenia do not result from a deficiency in generation of syntax *per se*. Rather, they reflect the way in which individuals with schizophrenia use language.

Meilijson *et al.* (2004) applied the Pragmatic Protocol (Prutting and Kirchner 1987) in order to attain a general profile of pragmatic abilities of participants with schizophrenia. This protocol represents a wide range of pragmatic behaviours that enables the extraction of patterns or clusters of dimensions on which the subject performs well or poorly. In addition, the protocol enables comparisons with other adult populations, specifically with hemispheric brain-damaged subjects. The participants with schizophrenia exhibited a high degree of inappropriate pragmatic abilities compared to participants with Mixed Anxiety Depression disorder and participants with Hemispheric Brain Damage, as previously assessed by Prutting and Kirchner (1987). Clustering analysis yielded five distinct parameter clusters (**Topic**, Speech Acts, Turntaking, Lexical and Nonverbal). Topic was found to be the most inappropriate cluster in the general profile of participants with schizophrenia: topic management represents an essential level of organization in discourse, necessary for the establishment of **discourse coherence** (Mentis and Prutting 1991). The highly inappropriate performance in the Topic cluster is consistent with earlier clinical observation (Bellack *et al.* 1989; Bleuler 1950; Brown 1973; De Decker and Van de Craen 1987; Rutter 1985; Wrobel 1990). Speech Acts correlate with all other clusters and the three clusters of Turntaking, Lexical and Nonverbal are relatively independent of each other. Clustering of the participants with schizophrenia focused on the latter clusters and produced three groups with distinct profiles: Minimal Impairment, Lexical Impairment and Interactional (Turntaking and Nonverbal) Impairment.

Within the modular framework of pragmatics, a Neuropragmatic Battery of tests was developed to assess basic speech acts (BSA) and conversational

implicatures (see pages 572–74 in Kasher *et al.* 1999 for a description of the battery). This study examined the processing of BSA of participants with chronic schizophrenia, based on the theoretical framework of **modular pragmatics** of language (Kasher 1982, 1991a, 1994, 1998). The BSA test (Soroker *et al.* 2005) was used to assess the comprehension and production of BSA (**Questions**, **Assertions**, **Requests** and **Commands** in verbal and nonverbal modes) by individuals diagnosed with chronic schizophrenia, compared to a psychiatric control group (Mixed Anxiety Depression disorder) and to a group of individuals with hemispheric brain damage. Individuals with schizophrenia produced significant deficits in BSA processing and performance relative to the comparison groups. As a general trend, the performance of participants with schizophrenia was similar to that of subjects with left-brain damage in the verbal variables and subjects with right-brain damage in the nonverbal variables (Meilijson 1999).

Gricean implicatures are **inferences** that attribute to a speaker an implicit **meaning** that goes beyond the explicit linguistic meaning of an utterance. Tényi *et al.* (2002) found that participants with schizophrenia made significantly more mistakes during the decoding of the violated **maxim** of relevance compared to a normal control group. Meilijson (1999) found that participants with schizophrenia failed to decode verbal and nonverbal implicatures compared to psychiatric and normal control groups.

Language disorders in schizophrenia have been related to theories of the evolution of language (DeLisi 2001). Crow (1997) developed a theory of the human evolution of hemispheric speciation and language and proposed how it may relate to schizophrenia. According to this theory, the origins of psychosis are to be sought in the genetic mechanisms associated with the evolution of language and the descent of Homo sapiens from a pongid ancestor. Crow (1998: 289) further stated that schizophrenia is 'the price Homo sapiens pays for language'. That is, the part of our genetic endowment that makes language possible is failure-prone but so valuable that even when it fails as manifested in schizophrenia, it is preserved in the gene pool.

SARA MEILIJSON

See also: Assertion; assessment, pragmatic; clinical pragmatics; command; communication failure; competence, pragmatic; conversation; conversational turn-taking; cooperative principle; discourse cohesion; generalized conversational implicature, theory of; Grice, H.P.; implicature; language evolution; lexical pragmatics; maxims of conversation; modular pragmatics; neuropragmatics; pragmatic language impairment; pragmatics; psychotic discourse; question; request; right-hemisphere damage and pragmatics; speech act theory; speech act type; stylistics; topic

Suggestions for further reading

Fine, J. (2006) 'Language in Psychiatry: A Handbook of Clinical Practice', London: Equinox.
Ribeiro, B.T. (1994) *Coherence in Psychotic Discourse*, Oxford: Oxford University Press.

Searle, J.

John Searle (Denver, 1932–) has been one of the most influential contributors to **speech act theory** and **pragmatics** in the last forty years. Searle studied philosophy, politics and economics at Christ Church College, Oxford, from 1952–55, on a Rhodes Scholarship from the University of Wisconsin (1949–52). Sir Peter Strawson, who was one of his two tutors in philosophy (the other was J.O. Urmson), had the most influence on his philosophical outlook, and it is useful to think of Searle's philosophy in the light of Strawson's advocacy of descriptive as opposed to speculative metaphysics. Searle received a B.A. with First Class Honours in 1955. He was awarded a senior scholarship from St Anthony's College, Oxford, and was appointed as a research lecturer at Christ Church from 1956–59. Searle worked with Peter Strawson, Peter Geach and J.L. **Austin** at Oxford on a D.Phil. which was conferred in 1959. The title of his thesis was 'Problems Arising in the Theory of Meaning out of the Notions of Sense and Reference'. In the fall of 1959, he took up a position in the philosophy department at the University of California at Berkeley. In 1964, Searle was the first tenured professor at Berkeley to join the free speech movement, though he came to think that later student protests got out of hand. His book *The Campus War* (1971) provides an incisive analysis of the structure of student protest movements. Searle is now the Slusser Professor of Philosophy at Berkeley. He has been a member of the American Academy of Arts and Sciences since 1977 and received the National Humanities Medal, USA, in 2004.

Searle's work, which ranges widely over philosophy in more than 220 articles and books, can be divided roughly into four stages. The first stage, which includes his primary contributions to speech act theory and pragmatics, is represented in *Speech Acts* (1969), *Expression and Meaning* (1979b) and *The Foundations of Illocutionary Logic* (1985), the latter with Daniel Vanderveken. A spin-off from this early work is Searle's well known argument that, contrary to Hume's famous contention, it is possible to derive an 'ought' from an 'is', that is, a moral statement from a descriptive statement. The argument rests on Searle's identification of the factual conditions that determine when someone has performed an act of promising, and the observation that from that and the constitutive rules for promising, it follows that the speaker has an obligation. The second stage is constituted by his work on issues in the **philosophy of mind**, which aimed to provide a foundation for his theory of speech acts. Searle's famous Chinese room thought experiment is the basis for his critique of strong **artificial intelligence** in 'Minds, Brains and Programs' (1980). In this paper, Searle argues that manipulation of **syntax** (symbols characterized independently of content) is never by itself sufficient for **semantics** (or content). In *Intentionality* (1983), Searle gives a theory of the directedness or aboutness of thought and relates it to issues in the theory of **meaning** and speech acts. He is well known also for his argument against indeterminacy of meaning and **translation** in 'Indeterminacy, Empiricism and the First Person' (1987), and for his defense of the connection principle. This is the principle that every mental state is either conscious or potentially conscious, which he argues much work in **cognitive science** ignores (Searle 1990a). Searle gives his non-reductive account of the nature and place of consciousness in the natural world in *The Rediscovery of the Mind*

(1992). The third stage is constituted by his work on the nature of social reality and the role of collective **intentionality** in our understanding of constitutive rules and institutions. It is represented primarily by *The Construction of Social Reality* (1995). The final stage is represented by a development of Searle's earlier work in *Intentionality* on the nature of free action in *Rationality in Action* (2001).

Searle's main contributions to speech act theory and pragmatics develop against the background of J.L. Austin's pioneering work on performative utterances and Paul **Grice**'s work on conversational **implicature**. Searle's contributions include his framework for analyzing the structure of speech acts (Searle 1969, 1979b: chapter 1, 1985), his account of indirect speech acts (Searle 1979b: chapter 2), his theory of **metaphor** (Searle 1979b: chapter 4), and his argument for **radical pragmatics** (Searle 1979b: chapter 5), the view that token sentence meaning underdetermines the satisfaction conditions of literal utterances of them.

Speech act theory

Searle's framework for analyzing speech acts is illustrated using promising, for which he gives a set of necessary and sufficient conditions and a corresponding set of rules (Searle 1969: 57–64). For brevity, we consider only the rules, where '*Pr*' is an illocutionary force indicating device for promising (e.g. 'I promise to … ').

> *Propositional content rule:*
> Rule 1. *Pr* is to be uttered only in the **context** of a sentence (or larger stretch of **discourse**) T, the utterance of which predicates some future act A of the speaker S.
> *Preparatory rules:*
> Rule 2. *Pr* is to be uttered only if the hearer H would prefer S's doing A to his not doing A, and S believes H would prefer S's doing A to his not doing A.
> Rule 3. *Pr* is to be uttered only if it is not obvious to both S and H that S will do A in the normal course of events.
> *Sincerity rule:*
> Rule 4. *Pr* is to be uttered only if S intends to do A.

Essential rule:

Rule 5. The utterance of *Pr counts as* the undertaking of an obligation to do A.

These categories govern every **speech act type** (Searle 1969: 66–67). The essential rule gives the illocutionary point of a speech act, around which its other features are organized. Illocutionary act type is determined by illocutionary point (e.g. directing versus representing), the relative positions of S and H (e.g. general versus private), the degree of commitment undertaken (e.g. insisting versus suggesting), propositional content (e.g. S will do A versus H will do A), how that relates to S's and H's interests (e.g. boasting versus lamenting), expressed psychological state (e.g. **intention**, desire, belief), and how it relates to the **conversation** (e.g. as **question**, reply, or objection).

Searle's taxonomy of illocutionary acts employs three main differentia: (1) illocutionary point, (2) direction of fit, and (3) expressed psychological state. An utterance's direction of fit is determined by whether it aims to match the world (*word*-to-world ↓) or to have the world match it (*world*-to-word ↑). Description is word-to-world; **command** is world-to-word. The taxonomy includes five main categories: *assertives* (↓), which aim to represent something as being the case (e.g. reporting); *commissives* (↑), which commit the speaker to doing something (e.g. promising); *directives* (↑), which aim to get the audience to do something (e.g. ordering); *expressives* (no direction of fit), which aim to express a psychological state (e.g. congratulations); and *declaratives* (↕), which aim to make something the case (e.g. adjourning a meeting). Declaratives rely on extra-linguistic conventions for their performance. They have a dual direction of fit because they both bring something about and represent what they bring about.

Indirect speech acts

Searle shows how implicit **knowledge** of the structure of speech acts is exploited in *indirect* speech acts, that is, speech acts performed by way of another (Searle 1979b: chapter 2). In illustration, consider examples exploiting the first three types of conditions for directives (1979: 44).

(1) Preparatory conditions
    H can do A.

(2) Sincerity conditions
    S wants H to do A.
(3) Propositional content conditions
    S predicates a future act A of H.

For example, S can utter 'Can you pass the salt?' at the dinner table to **request** that H pass the salt by exploiting their shared knowledge of the *preparatory conditions* for such a request. H recognizes that the question about his ability cannot be serious and also that it is about a preparatory condition for requesting him to pass the salt. H knows that S knows this as well and so reasons that S intends him so to reason and so to take S to be requesting that H pass the salt. Similarly, S can utter 'I want you to go now' to request that H leave by exploiting their shared knowledge that that is the *sincerity condition* for a request that H leave. Finally, S can ask 'Will you take the trash out?' to request that H take the trash out by exploiting their shared knowledge that the **topic** of the question is the *propositional content* of a request that H take out the trash.

Metaphor

On Searle's account (Searle 1979b: chapter 4), in metaphor, as in indirect speech acts and in **irony**, speaker meaning comes apart from literal meaning. This implies that in principle the 'metaphorical speaker's meaning' can be expressed in a paraphrase. For example, Disraeli's 'I have climbed to the top of the greasy pole' might be paraphrased as 'I have become prime minister after great difficulty'. Metaphors work by a number of background principles of interpretation, according to Searle. For example, S uses 'Sam is a pig' to say that Sam is gluttonous. H knows it is literally false, assumes S aims to communicate something, looks for a feature Sam shares in common with pigs, and fixes gluttony as the best fit. Not all metaphors exploit similarity, however, as in 'Time flies', for example. So other principles are needed as well. Searle identifies six basic principles (Searle 1979b: 103–9), without suggesting they are exhaustive. There are three general stages in **reasoning** from a metaphor 'S is P' to its interpretation 'S is R'.

Stage 1: Figure out that the speaker doesn't mean what he literally says.

Stage 2: Employ shared principles to figure out what range of properties are candidates for R.

Stage 3: Narrow down the properties in the relevant range to the right one or ones.

According to Searle, metaphors are often used to fill semantic gaps, that is, to express things we can think but don't have words for. That is why we are often dissatisfied with paraphrases. For example, we do not have a verb that expresses what is conveyed metaphorically by 'The ship ploughed the sea'. Nonetheless, on Searle's view, a **proposition** is conveyed by this utterance. When a live metaphor that fills a semantic gap becomes a dead metaphor, the dead metaphor's literal meaning fills the semantic gap.

Radical pragmatics

Searle was an early proponent of radical pragmatics, according to which conventional meaning and rules for context-sensitive terms do not fix truth conditions for literally intended utterances even relative to contextual features taken as input to the rules (Searle 1979b: chapter 5). The flavour of the argument can be conveyed by reflecting on how 'The cat is on the mat' is to be understood in nonstandard contexts, such as one in which the cat and mat are suspended by wires so that, though the cat is above and in contact with the mat, it exerts no pressure on it, or in which the cat and the mat are in outer space. That we do not know what to say in such cases, Searle argues, shows that 'in general the literal meaning of a sentence only determines a set of truth conditions relative to a set of background assumptions which are not part of the semantic content of the sentence; and ... the notion of similarity plays an essential role in any account of literal predication' (1979: 81).

KIRK LUDWIG

See also: Communication; competence, linguistic; competence, pragmatic; context; contextualism; conversation; cooperative principle; generalized conversational implicature, theory of; Grice, H. P.; implicature; indexicals; intentionality; literary pragmatics; maxims of conversation; ordinary language philosophy; performative pragmatics; philosophy of language; post-Gricean pragmatics; proposition; propositional attitude; radical pragmatics; reasoning; relevance theory; semantics-pragmatics interface; speech act theory; utterance interpretation; what is said

Suggestions for further reading

Lepore, E. and Van Gulick, R. (1991) *John Searle and His Critics*, Cambridge: Blackwell.
Smith, B. (ed.) (2003) *John Searle*, Cambridge: Cambridge University Press.
Tsohatzidis, S.L. (ed.) (2007) *John Searle's Philosophy of Language: Force, Meaning and Mind*, Cambridge: Cambridge University Press.

Second Language Acquisition

The term 'second language acquisition' refers to the acquisition of a new language by children and adults who already have full **knowledge** of their first language. It is thus distinct from childhood bilingualism, or simultaneous language acquisition, which refers to the **child language acquisition** of two languages simultaneously, with exposure to both languages beginning in infancy or soon after (Genesee 2000; Meisel 2001, 2004). Child second language acquisition, also known as sequential bilingualism, refers to the acquisition of a second language after age three or four, when much of the first language is already in place (Gass and Selinker 2001; Lakshmanan 1994; McLaughlin 1978). There is disagreement on exactly when child second language acquisition ends and adult second language acquisition begins (Gass and Selinker 2001), but age eight or nine is often taken as the upper boundary for true child second language acquisition (Bialystok and Miller 1999; Schwartz 2003).

The input that child and adult learners receive in their second language takes many different forms. Like child language acquisition, second language acquisition involves naturalistic exposure to the target language. However, the amount and type of input are different for second language learners immersed in the language on the one hand, and foreign language learners with classroom-only exposure to a foreign language on the other hand (Ellis 1989; Pica 1983). Further, second language learners often receive negative evidence about the target language in the form of explicit and/or implicit instruction (Bley-Vroman 1989, 1990; Doughty and Williams 1998; *see* White 1991 on positive versus negative evidence in the classroom). There is a debate in the field of **applied linguistics** concerning the degree to which linguistic knowledge learned through explicit instruction can become internalized, implicit linguistic knowledge (Ellis 2005; Ellis 2002; Krashen 1981; Norris and Ortega 2000; *see* Ellis 2006 for an overview of the issues in grammar teaching). On the relationship between second language theory and second language instruction, see the papers in Eckman *et al.* (1995).

In addition to the target language input, a potential source of knowledge for second language learners is their native language. Early morpheme-order studies (Bailey *et al.* 1974; Dulay and Burt 1974; Larsen-Freeman 1975) focused on developmental sequences across second language learners from different native language backgrounds, and found little effect of the native language (but *see* Larsen-Freeman and Long 1991). However, there is much evidence from other studies that second language learners are influenced by their native language in the acquisition of the target language, a process known as transfer (Dechert and Raupach 1989; Gass and Selinker 1992; Odlin 1989, among many others). Transfer has traditionally been divided into positive transfer or facilitation, which helps learners acquire properties of the target (second) language, and negative transfer or interference, which hinders learners in their course of acquisition (Odlin 1989). Generative approaches to second language acquisition look at transfer at the level of grammatical categories and features (Schwartz and Sprouse 1994, 1996; Schwartz 1998; Vainikka and Young-Scholten 1994, 1996; *see* White 2003 for an overview).

The role that age plays in second language acquisition has received much attention in the literature. Early studies focused on how age affects ultimate attainment of the target language, and found that younger age of exposure to the target language is related to better performance on the target language phonology and syntax (Johnson and Newport 1989, 1991; Oyama 1978; Patkowski 1980; for critiques and replications of the Johnson and Newport 1989

study, *see* Bialystok and Miller 1999; Birdsong and Molis 2001; DeKeyser 2000, among others). Following the proposal of Lenneberg (1967) that first language acquisition is subject to critical period effects, many researchers have argued that age effects in second language acquisition are a result of biological maturation (Hyltenstam and Abrahamsson 2003; Long 1990; Patkowski 1980; Pulvermüller and Schumann 1994). At the same time, it has been argued that non-biological factors, such as the type and amount of target language input, and learners' motivation and attitude, may account for, or at least contribute to, differences between child and adult second language learners (Flege *et al.* 1997; Klein 1995; for a variety of approaches to age effects, see the papers in Singleton and Lengyel 1995 and Birdsong 1999; *see* Birdsong 2004, 2006 for an overview). As pointed out by Long (1990) and Birdsong (2004), a biologically determined critical period should prevent native-like attainment in all learners past a certain age. While Coppieters (1987) found that even highly advanced adult second language learners in fact did not exhibit native-like attainment, much literature since then has pointed out the existence of adult second language learners who do perform near-natively on phonology (Bongaerts 1999) and syntax (Birdsong 1992; White and Genesee 1996). For a review of the recent literature on near-nativeness, *see* Bongaerts (2005) and Sorace (2003).

Within the field of generative approaches to second language acquisition, the critical period issue takes the form of a debate concerning whether innate mechanisms underlying language acquisition, in the form of universal grammar, are available to adult learners. In a highly influential proposal, Bley-Vroman (1989, 1990) argued that first language acquisition by children and second language acquisition by adults are fundamentally different processes. Bley-Vroman argued that while child language acquisition is guided by innate linguistic mechanisms, adult second language acquisition relies on problem-solving, instruction, and explicit strategies. Much work in the field of generative second language acquisition over the past twenty years has debated this view. Proponents of the deficit view argue that adult learners are impaired with regard to all or some aspects of language acquisition and/or constrained to those aspects of universal grammar instantiated in their native language (Hawkins and Chan 1997; Hawkins and Hattori 2006; Meisel 1997; Schachter 1990; Tsimpli and Dimitrakopoulou 2007). On the other side of the debate, proponents of the full access to universal grammar view argue that innate linguistic mechanisms remain active throughout adulthood, and that differences between children and adults stem from other sources (Epstein *et al.* 1996, 1998; Schwartz and Sprouse 1994, 1996; *see* White 2003 for an overview). On the influential full transfer/full access model of second language acquisition (Schwartz and Sprouse 1994, 1996), second language learners transfer the grammatical characteristics of their native language to the second language, but are then able to acquire new aspects of the target language through direct access to universal grammar.

Evidence for full access views of second language acquisition comes from two different sources. The first source of evidence comes from developmental comparisons between child and adult second language learners, under a research program put forth by Schwartz (1992, 2003). On the assumption that innate linguistic knowledge is available to child second language learners, evidence of similar developmental sequences among children and adults (with the native language held constant) is used to argue that such knowledge is available to adult learners as well (Gilkerson 2006; Schwartz 2003; Unsworth 2005). The second source of evidence comes from studies of poverty-of-the-stimulus phenomena with adult second language learners. When adult learners are able to master aspects of the second language which are not instantiated in the native language, not obvious from the input, and not explicitly taught in the classroom, this provides evidence that innate linguistic knowledge is at work (Dekydtspotter *et al.* 1997; Dekydtspotter *et al.* 2001; Montrul and Slabakova 2003; Kanno 1998, among others). Much of this work has been done with phenomena at the syntax-semantics interface (*see* Slabakova 2006 for an overview). The **syntax-pragmatics interface** has also been examined in recent literature, both in second language acquisition (Sorace 2003, 2005) and childhood bilingualism (Serratrice *et al.* 2004).

Second language acquisition is a growing field. It encompasses a variety of perspectives on how languages are learned (Doughty and Long 2003), including **interlanguage pragmatics** and approaches in applied linguistics, as well as generative approaches (White 2003) and, more recently, psycholinguistic perspectives and techniques (*see* Marinis 2003 for an overview). The study of second language acquisition is also closely related to the study of attrition and incomplete acquisition of the first language under the influence of a dominant second language (Montrul 2008; Polinsky 1997). Many of the same issues, including the role of transfer and the effects of age, are studied with regard to both second language acquisition and first language attrition.

TANIA IONIN

See also: Applied linguistics; child language acquisition; competence, communicative; competence, linguistic; competence, pragmatic; communication failure; cross-cultural pragmatics; development, pragmatic; intercultural communication; interlanguage pragmatics; psycholinguistics; semantics; semantics-pragmatics interface; sociolinguistics; specificity; syntax-pragmatics interface

Suggestions for further reading

Doughty, C. and Long, M. (eds) (2003) *The Handbook of Second Language Acquisition*, Oxford: Blackwell.
Gass, S. and Selinker, L. (2001) *Second Language Acquisition: An Introductory Course*, Mahwah, NJ: Lawrence Erlbaum.
White, L. (2003) *Second Language Acquisition and Universal Grammar*, Cambridge: Cambridge University Press.

Semantic Externalism/Internalism

Semantic content is the aspect of a mental state or linguistic expression that is responsible for its semantic features: its truth- and **reference**-conditions. Semantic internalism in the **philosophy of language** and the **philosophy of mind** is the view that the semantic content of a subject's thoughts or utterances is determined by his or her internal states. Internalists allow that **what is said** may depend on outside factors, for example, on the conventions of the linguistic community; but they insist that *what is meant* is internally individuated. Further, internalists would agree that as actual history goes, we acquire contents (or concepts that constitute those contents) through interacting with the external world. However, they would see this as an account of how contents are caused, and not how they are constituted. They would insist that no outside factor makes a difference to the content of our thoughts and utterances, unless it makes a difference to some of our internal features. Hence, two subjects who agree in all their internal features (both physically and in terms of how things seem to them) share their semantic contents. Externalists deny this.

There are several distinct motivations and arguments for externalism. One is a conviction that any naturalistic account of reference (or **representation**, or **intentionality**) should explain reference in terms of causal or nomological relations between the subject and her environment. Causal or nomological (Fodor 1987), informational (Dretske 1986) and teleosemantic (Millikan 1984; Papineau 1987) accounts of content all agree that features of a subject's environment and his or her history are constitutive of the content of mental states.

A second, different motivation arises from a general criticism of a certain Cartesian view of the mind. On this view, one of Descartes' central mistakes was the belief that one could be a thinking being even if one existed alone in the whole world. Descartes offers a view of a subject that is hopelessly cut off from the world. In contrast, these critics claim that the very possibility of our thoughts referring to the external world depends on the world partly constituting our mental acts (McDowell 1986; McCulloch 1995; Campbell 2002).

A third group of arguments (often combined with either of the previous two) is based on observations about the semantics of expressions that belong to some specific types, especially proper names, natural kind terms and certain **indexical** expressions. The arguments often rely on thought experiments where parallel utterances of internally identical subjects in indistinguishable situations have different truth- and reference-conditions.

For example, adopting an idea of Hilary Putnam (Putnam 1975, 1993), suppose that there is a planet somewhere in the universe we may call 'Twin Earth' which, through some cosmic coincidence, is just like Earth down to the last detail of its composition and its history. Imagine Oscar, an inhabitant of Earth, and his atom-by-atom replica Twin Oscar, living on Twin Earth. When Oscar says 'Aristotle enjoyed walking', he refers to Aristotle; and so his utterance is true if, and only if, the famous philosopher who lived on Earth enjoyed walking. But Twin Oscar's parallel utterance is about a different person, and it will be true if this other man, who spent his life on Twin Earth (and was also called 'Aristotle'), enjoyed walking. The truth-conditions of their utterances are different and therefore, assuming that content is responsible for truth-conditions, the contents of their utterances are also different. This means that internal sameness does not imply sameness of content: the content of (some of) our sentences depends on factors outside the individual. 'Meanings ain't in the head', as Hilary Putnam famously stated on the basis of similar arguments about natural kind terms (Putnam 1975, 1993). The view gets support from the 'causal' theory of proper names and natural kind terms suggested, for example, by Saul Kripke (Kripke 1972). On this theory, the reference of a proper name used on a given occasion depends on a causal chain leading from an event of naming an object to the present use of the name.

Similar considerations apply to many indexical expressions: if Oscar says to his friend Lucinda 'you are late', his utterance is true if Lucinda was late; but Twin Oscar's parallel utterance is true if *his* friend, Twin Lucinda, was late. Again, according to defenders of externalism, the truth-conditions, and hence the content of these utterances are different, despite the internal sameness of the users of the utterances. Thought-experiments involving internally identical subjects in two different linguistic communities were used by Tyler Burge (Burge 1979) to argue that the use of words in a linguistic community can also be an external determinant of the contents of thoughts and utterances. This view is known as 'social externalism'.

An internalist could agree that, for example, 'Aristotle' refers to different individuals when used by Oscar and Twin Oscar, but claim that this is due simply to the fact that Oscar and

Twin Oscar themselves are different individuals, and not due to some factors external to them (Searle 1983). According to an alternative internalist view, difference in reference does not in itself imply a difference in content. Peter Lasersohn suggested a semantic theory of predicates expressing personal tastes which relativizes the truth-value of relevant sentences without relativizing semantic content (Lasersohn 2005). A similar view could be adopted for the Twin Earth cases allegedly supporting the externalist conclusion: it could be argued that the semantic value (i.e. truth-value or denotation) of expressions is determined by a content which remains constant in different utterances, together with the varying contextual elements which are external to the semantic content (Farkas 2008). The positive arguments for internalism are based on some features traditionally associated with semantic content: first, that what we mean by an expression is usually available to introspection; second, that the content of our thoughts is explanatory in our actions. It has been argued that externalism is incompatible with both of these features (Fodor 1987: chapter 2; Ludlow and Martin 1998).

KATALIN FARKAS

See also: Context; indexicals; intentionality; reference; semantic minimalism; what is said

Suggestions for further reading

Putnam, H. (1993) 'Meaning and reference', in A.W. Moore (ed.) *Meaning and Reference*, New York: Oxford University Press.
Searle, J.R. (1983) *Intentionality*, Cambridge: Cambridge University Press.

Semantic Minimalism

Semantic minimalism is an attempt to answer two questions: 'What counts as semantic content?' and 'What work does semantic content do?' The answer the theory gives to both these questions is minimal (hence the name). First, semantic content is exhausted by the contributions made by the syntactic constituents of a sentence together with their mode of composition. Second, the role played by this kind of content is much more constrained than is often supposed. With respect to the first question, semantic minimalism holds that content is entirely determined by syntax – there is nothing to be had 'for free', as it were, at the semantic level. Specifically, minimalism holds that it is not possible for features of the **context** of utterance to permeate semantic content unless their presence is demanded by something at the syntactic level. Furthermore, the syntactic elements which can trigger pragmatic intrusion are themselves limited to unarguably context-sensitive elements, such as words like 'here' and 'now'. (Thus, minimalism is not the thesis that semantic content is context-invariant, but that contextual infiltration of **semantics** is very limited.) So take utterances of the following sentences:

(1) She took out her key and opened the door.
(2) Jack is tall.
(3) The bridge will hold.

The semantic minimalist allows that context does contribute an element to the semantic content in each of these cases: context is needed to determine a value for the tense markers in the sentences, to provide a referent for 'she' in (1) and (possibly) to provide the salient Jack in (2). However, there are also a number of other ways in which we might think context contributes in these cases. For instance, the message conveyed by (1) will contain the so-called 'bridging inference' that the door was opened *with the key*. The utterance of (2) will convey that Jack is tall for some salient comparison class, say tall for a four-year-old or tall for a Frenchman, and (3) will convey a richer message concerning the conditions the speaker takes to be relevant, perhaps that the bridge will hold while the troops cross it. Yet, the minimalist argues that all of these additional pragmatic effects, which are not triggered by anything obvious in the syntax of the sentence, lie outside the semantic realm and are instead part of a pragmatic speaker-meaning (see **Grice, H.P.**). This demonstrates one aspect of the minimalist's conservative answer to our second question above concerning the work semantic content can do. For as (1)–(3) show, it is not the job of semantic content, according to the minimalist, to capture our intuitive judgements of what speakers say when they utter sentences.

Opponents of minimalism, commonly known as 'contextualists' (see work by Recanati 2002b, 2004b, Travis 1997, Atlas 2005 and the relevance theorists Sperber and Wilson 1995 and Carston 2002), advance two main claims. The first of these claims is that minimal meanings are not possible: some/many/all sentences in natural language are not truth-evaluable prior to pragmatic enrichment (of the non-syntactically triggered sort). Thus, if semantics concerns truth-evaluable entities, then semantic content must be open to rich pragmatic effects. (See Carston 2002, Recanati 2004b and Bach 1994b, 2006a. Bach is an interesting figure here for, although he argues that sentences may express only incomplete propositional radicals, he also rejects **contextualism**. Instead, Bach allows that semantics may deal with non-truth-evaluable entities, with truth-evaluation (often) possible only at the level of the speech act. However, we might think that careful work is needed to maintain a clear distinction between this stance and that of at least some contextualists.) The second of the contextualists' claims is that minimal meanings are redundant. Even where sentences are truth-evaluable without rich pragmatic effects, the resulting minimal meanings are (often) theoretically inert – they are not consciously accessible nor do they play a role in explaining communicative success – thus they cannot be the correct subject matter for semantics (*see* Carston 2002; Recanati 2004b).

In response minimalists have tried to argue that minimal meanings are possible. Thus, they seek to defuse the myriad examples raised by contextualists which purport to show pragmatic influence on semantics, usually by insisting on a rigid distinction between semantic content and pragmatic speech act content. They also argue that there is a role for minimal meanings to play – Soames (2002) and Cappelen and Lepore (2005a) argue for their role in communication, while Borg (2004a) tries to locate their use elsewhere. Minimalists dispute the assumption that semantic content need be immediately accessible to speakers in communicative exchanges. Indeed, some minimalists have argued that a major ground of support for minimalism comes from the thesis of the **modularity of mind**, in which case the idea that semantic content does not feed directly to consciousness would not be

exceptional (Borg 2004a, 2004b. A discussion of the different versions of minimalism can be found in Borg 2007). However, the success of these moves is open to question and the debate remains a lively one in the contemporary literature.

Finally, it is worth noting the existence of an intermediary position here. Such a position seeks to retain the minimalist assumption that syntax provides the sole route to semantic content but also to embrace the contextualist contention that there is a wealth of semantically relevant context-sensitivity in natural language. There are various ways in which this position might be realized. For instance, we might seek to complicate the syntax of natural language sentences by positing a range of 'hidden indexicals' which provide the syntactic triggers for the additional context-sensitivity demanded by contextualists (Stanley and Szabo 2000; Stanley 2000, 2005; note that Cappelen and Lepore argue that this position is a form of contextualism). Alternatively, we might seek to introduce additional complexity into the way in which sentences map to truth-conditions, holding that the context-sensitivity demanded by contextualists lies within the circumstances of evaluation, not in a truly indexical content for sentences. This sort of position has been labelled 'non-indexical contextualism' by some (*see* McFarlane 2007; Predelli 2005). Or we might perhaps claim with Rothschild and Segal (to appear) that what the contextualist data show is that most terms in natural language are themselves indexical and that their semantic axioms are exactly on a par with those for commonly recognized indexicals like 'this' and 'that'.

The debate between minimalism and contextualism is part of a long tradition of disputes about where the boundary between semantics and **pragmatics** is situated (with minimalism following the path of so-called 'formal approaches to meaning', as found in Frege, early **Wittgenstein**, and Carnap, and contextualists pursuing the 'speech act' school of thought, found in the later Wittgenstein, **Austin** and **Searle**). This boundary dispute is one which doesn't show any signs of being decisively settled in the near future. Furthermore, at times the debate can seem like a purely terminological squabble. However, it is important to note that choices between theories like minimalism and contextualism do have consequences, particularly given the ambition, shared by many of the current participants to the debate, of providing a theory with cognitive reality. For this reason it seems likely that the future of the debate lies at least in part with advances in experimental techniques which may help reveal the course of language processing in the individual and the structures of the mind (see **experimental pragmatics**).

EMMA BORG

See also: Context; contextualism; demonstratives; experimental pragmatics; explicit/implicit distinction; Grice, H.P.; indexicals; meaning; modularity of mind thesis; neo-Gricean pragmatics; post-Gricean pragmatics; primary pragmatic processes; radical pragmatics; relevance theory; Searle, J.; semantics-pragmatics interface; speech act theory; what is said

Suggestions for further reading

Borg, E. (2004) *Minimal Semantics*, Oxford: Oxford University Press.
Cappelen, H. and Lepore, E. (2005) *Insensitive Semantics: A Defense of Semantic Minimalism and Speech Act Pluralism*, Oxford: Blackwell.
Preyer, G. and Peter, G. (eds) (2007) *Context Sensitivity and Semantic Minimalism: New Essays on Semantics and Pragmatics*, Oxford: Oxford University Press.

Semantics

Though the term 'semantics', like the related term 'semasiology', goes back to the nineteenth century, one of its most influential definitions comes from Charles **Morris**'s division of **semiotics**:

syntax: the formal relation of signs to each other;
semantics: the relation of signs to the objects to which the signs are applicable;
pragmatics: the relation of signs to interpreters.
            (adapted from Morris 1938, 1955)

In this characterization, which has proved so important in the development of theoretical linguistics, we see semantics suspended between grammar, on the one hand, and language use, on the other hand. In it we can see the idea of abstracting regularities from the complex flux of people's linguistic interaction, explicitly stated by Rudolf Carnap (1942: 9; cited in Morris 1955: 218):

> If in an investigation explicit reference is made to the speaker, or, to put it in more general terms, to the user of a language, then we assign it to the field of pragmatics. (Whether in this case reference to designata is made or not makes no difference for this classification.) If we abstract from the user of the language and analyze only the expressions and their designata, we are in the field of semantics. And if, finally, we abstract from the designata also and analyze only the relations between the expressions, we are in (logical) syntax. The whole science of language, consisting of the three parts mentioned, is called semiotic.

This view of the relationship between **syntax** and semantics can be seen continued in Generative Grammar (Chomsky 1957, 1965, 1988) with its autonomous syntactic and semantic modules. In other theories, for example, Functional Grammar (Dik 1997), Cognitive Grammar (Langacker 1987, 1991a), and more recently Construction Grammar (Goldberg 2006), this assumption is rejected. These theories in their various ways deny that generalizations about grammar can be made without reference to **meaning**.

Rudolf Carnap, quoted above, represents along with other scholars like Charles **Peirce** (1992b, 1998), Gottlob Frege (1980), and Alfred Tarski (1944, 1956), the tradition of philosophers and logicians who in the nineteenth and twentieth centuries applied to the **philosophy of language** and semiotics the methods so successful in the analysis of logical systems and mathematics. This tradition's impact on linguistics accelerated with the work of the logician Richard Montague (Montague 1974), who famously proposed that the methods of a formal language like logic could be used to analyze the semantics of natural languages:

> [I]ndeed, I consider it possible to comprehend the syntax and semantics of both

kinds of language within a single, natural and mathematically precise theory.

(Montague 1974: 222)

In formal approaches like Montague Grammar, meaning is equated, in what is usually described as Tarski's theory of truth, with a set of truth conditions. Thus, truth and falsity can be assigned to the declarative sentences of natural languages depending on two parameters: the meaning of a sentence and the facts of the world.

In this view, semantic analysis consists of three stages: first, a translation from a natural language like English into a formal language whose syntax and semantics are explicitly defined; second, the establishment of a mathematical model of the situations that the language describes; third, a set of procedures for checking the mapping between the expressions in the logical language and the modeled situations. Essentially, these algorithms check whether the expressions are true or false of the modeled situations.

This approach captures the view that sentences of languages are about something, typically the world and the things that are in it, and that speakers may quantify these things. However, this basic semantics captures only a little of the semantic potential of a natural language. Early extensions include the incorporation of modality by theories like possible worlds (Kripke 1980; Lewis 1973, 1986), which reflect our ability to talk about the many possible ways the world might have been. Similarly, moving beyond eternal sentences entails recognizing the dependence of truth on time: a sentence might be true today but might not have been true yesterday. Early attempts to model this simply stipulated temporal integers, so that a sentence is assigned a truth value relative to a world and a time (Lewis 1970; Montague 1968).

This step presages the long debate in this literature on the role of **context** in the interpretation of meaning, or in this view, the assignment of truth values. In a sense, this revisits Morris's proposed distinction between semantics and **pragmatics**; and this debate can be characterized loosely as attempting the task of deciding where semantics ends and pragmatics begins. More and more context-dependent elements have been identified in the literature, the determination of which affects the truth value of the sentence. A clear case is **deixis**, such as the italicized deictic expressions (or **indexicals**) in (1):

(1) *I*'m *here now.*

Early attempts to model this feature of language included stipulating further indices for spatial coordinates and participants. However, this approach faltered in the face of criticism, for example Cresswell (1973), that context dependence is not limited to obvious indexicals and consequently that such information is in principle limitless. Other elements identified as context-dependent include quantifiers (Stanley and Szabó 2000) such as *all* in (2), gradable adjectives (Kennedy 2007) like *tall* in (3), and the related 'adjectives of personal taste' (Lasersohn 2005) like *fun* in (4):

(2) She broke all the bottles.
(3) Fred is tall.
(4) This game is fun.

Each of these expressions seems to need access to aspects of the context to be interpreted: the relevant domain for *all*; *tall* against the relevant scale, for example, young boys or adult basketball players; *fun* needs to be related to a particular judge or judges.

One interpretation of this debate is that the linguistic or semantic content of expressions independent of interpreters, to paraphrase Morris, seems to be shrinking under examination; or, to put it the other way around, the recognition of the underspecification of meaning seems to be growing, towards a position often termed **contextualism**. A defense against this process is mounted by advocates of **semantic minimalism** (Borg 2004a; Cappelen and Lepore 2005a).

Other scholars have pointed out that the context is not static but evolves in natural **communication** such as **conversations**. Studies of **anaphora**, **definiteness** and **presupposition** have revealed speakers' efforts to package their messages against the changing context, in particular to take account of their hearers' **knowledge** and interpretive task. There have been a number of proposals to model formally the influence of discourse context on meaning, including File Change Semantics (Heim 1983b, 1989) which uses the metaphor of files for information states in **discourse**; Dynamic Semantics (Groenendijk and Stokhof 1991; Groenendijk *et al.* 1996), where meaning is viewed as the potential to change information states; and Discourse Representation Theory (Kamp and Reyle 1993) which, like the related theory of Segmented Discourse Representation Theory (Asher and Lascarides 2003), formalizes a level of discourse structure.

A quite distinct view of semantics is portrayed in cognitive semantics, which is part of a wider approach that calls itself **cognitive linguistics**. Cognitive linguists (e.g. Johnson 1987; Lakoff 1987; Langacker 1987) disagree fundamentally with formal approaches by rejecting what they term objectivism: the idea that language directly models or maps reality (Lakoff 1988: 123–24). In its place they assert that meaning relies on conceptualization, which underlines how a speaker construes a situation. It follows from this that semantic structures are based on, indeed are themselves conceptual structures. This approach seeks to reflect research on concepts and conceptual categories in the **cognitive psychology** literature and, in particular, incorporates embodiment theory (Gibbs 2005; Johnson 1987). This is the view that many of the conceptual structures and processes that we find in language derive from bodily experience, including vision; kinesthesia, the bodily experience of muscular effort or motion; and somesthesia, the bodily experience of sensations such as pressure. Conceptual structures, like image schemas (Johnson 1987), have been used to build topographical models of semantic structure, for example, in analyzing the traditional problem of polysemy in prepositions (Brugman and Lakoff 1988; Tyler and Evans 2003).

Possibly the most influential work in cognitive semantics has been in reassessing **metaphor**, metonymy and other linguistic strategies that have been traditionally viewed as figurative language. Dispensing with the traditional distinction between literal and figurative language, where the latter is seen to represent rhetorical or decorative additions, cognitive semanticists see metaphor as a basic and universal part of human understanding. In this view it is basic to our attempts to categorize the world, especially in our attempts to integrate novel concepts into our existing knowledge system. Conceptual metaphor theory (Lakoff and Turner 1989) views metaphor as an analogical mapping from a source domain to a target domain. The mapping is seen as structured and as having key features such as systematicity, asymmetry and abstraction. Systematicity, for example, arises from the fact that some metaphors seem to consist of more than an extension to a single sense of a word. Instead, they are used to structure a whole conceptual domain in terms of another. Thus, a conceptual metaphor like LOVE IS A JOURNEY (Lakoff and Johnson 1980) licenses a series of metaphorical sentences like *Look how far we've come*, *We're at a crossroads in our relationship*, *Our marriage is on the rocks*, etc. More recently, the theory of conceptual integration or blending (Fauconnier and Turner 2002) has focused on the on-line processing of novel complex analogies, such as (5):

(5) In France, Bill Clinton wouldn't have been harmed by his relationship with Monica Lewinski.

(Taylor 2002: 530)

A traditional subfield of semantics is lexical semantics, which is concerned with characterizing word meaning and relations between semantic words. Attempts to completely specify word meaning by means of semantic components or features (see, for example, Katz and Fodor 1963) have tended recently to have the more conservative aim of using semantic features to characterize grammatical processes, i.e. identifying certain units of meaning that are shared by different lexical items and which predict the grammatical rules they undergo. Authors such as Pinker (1989) and Levin and Rappaport Hovav (1992, 2005), for example, have postulated components of verb-internal semantic structure which may allow us to correctly characterize variations in verbal argument structure, such as locative alternation in (6) and dative shift in (7):

(6) a. He loaded newspapers onto the van.
    b. He loaded the van with newspapers.
(7) a. He sent the money to his parents.
    b. He sent his parents the money.

Semantic components, it is argued, allow us to give a motivated explanation of the links between individual verbs, their argument structures, and the alternations they undergo. This line of enquiry, in what may be termed grammatical semantics (Mohanan and Wee 1999), has also investigated the semantics/grammar interface in areas such as causatives and event structure (Pustejovsky 1992; Tenny and Pustejovsky 2000). Two influential decompositional semantic theories are Jackendoff's (1990) Conceptual Semantics and Pustejovsky's (1995) Generative Lexicon.

An important application of lexical semantic theories is computational lexicon building where models of lexical content and relations have been in used in a wide range of computational applications, for example, information extraction and machine translation. Three major digital lexicon projects are WordNet (Fellbaum 1998b), FrameNet (Fillmore *et al.* 2003) and SIMPLE (Lenci *et al.* 2000). Each of these builds into their applications specific theories of conceptual **representation** and semantic networks.

JOHN SAEED

See also: Anaphora, pragmatics of; cognitive linguistics; context; contextualism; definiteness; deixis; discourse; domain restriction; indexicals; metaphor; philosophy of language; pragmatics; presupposition; semantic minimalism

Suggestions for further reading

Chierchia, G. and McConnell-Ginet, S. (2000) *Meaning and Grammar: An Introduction to Semantics*, 2nd edn, Cambridge, MA: MIT Press.

Saeed, J.I. (2009) *Semantics*, 3rd edn, Oxford: Wiley-Blackwell.

Ungerer, F. and Schmid, H.-J. (2006) *An Introduction to Cognitive Linguistics*, 2nd edn, London: Longman.

Semantics-Pragmatics Interface

Semantics and **pragmatics** have both developed sophisticated methods of analysis of **meaning**. The question to address is whether their objects of study can be teased apart or whether each sub-discipline accounts for different contributions (in the sense of qualitatively different outputs or different types of processes) that produce one unique object called 'meaning'. Traditionally, semantics was responsible for compositionally construed sentence meaning, in which the meanings of lexical items and the structure in which they occur were combined. The best developed approach to sentence meaning is undoubtedly truth-conditional semantics. Its formal methods permit the translation of vague and ambiguous sentences of natural language into a precise metalanguage of predicate logic and provide a model-theoretic interpretation to so construed **logical forms**. Pragmatics was regarded as a study of utterance meaning, and hence meaning in **context**, and was therefore an enterprise with a different object of study. However, the boundary between them began to be blurred, giving rise to the so-called semantic underdetermination view. Semantic underdetermination was a revolutionary idea for the theory of linguistic meaning. It was a reaction to generative semantics of the 1960s and 1970s which attempted to give syntactic explanations to inherently pragmatic phenomena. We have to note the importance of the Oxford ordinary language philosophers (John L. **Austin**, H. Paul **Grice**, Peter F. Strawson) and Ludwig **Wittgenstein** in Cambridge in the late phase of his work, and subsequently the work of Gerald Gazdar, Bruce Fraser, Jerry Morgan, Jay Atlas, Ruth Kempson, Deirdre Wilson, Stephen Levinson, Larry Horn, and many others, in opening up the way for the study of pragmatic **inference** and its contribution to truth-conditional **representation**, now understood as Gricean, intended meaning with intuitive truth-conditions. I list below some important landmarks.

Grice (1978) remarked that pragmatic processes of **disambiguation** and **reference** assignment to **indexical** expressions sometimes have to be taken into consideration before the sentence's truth conditions can be assessed. At the same time, Kempson (1975, 1979, 1986) and Atlas (1977, 1979, 1989) suggested that **negation** in English should not be regarded as ambiguous between narrow-scope and wide-scope as Bertrand Russell had proposed, but was instead semantically underdetermined. In other words, the celebrated example (1) is not

semantically ambiguous between (1') and (1")
but instead the scope of negation is pragmatically determined in each particular utterance
on the basis of the recovery of the speaker's
intentions.

(1) The king of France is not bald.
(1') $\exists x \ (KoF(x) \ \land \ \forall y \ (KoF(y) \ \rightarrow \ y \ = \ x) \ \land$
$\neg Bald \ (x))$
(1") $\neg \exists x \ (KoF(x) \ \land \ \forall y \ (KoF(y) \ \rightarrow \ y \ = \ x) \ \land$
$Bald \ (x))$

(1') is a presupposing reading: there is a person
who fulfils the property of being the king of
France, there is only one such person, and whoever fulfils this property is not bald. The reading
in (1") is non-presupposing: the king of France is
not bald because there is no such person. Since
(1') entails (1"), the semantic underdetermination
(sense-generality) view has both formal and cognitive support: the logical forms in (1') and (1")
are not disjoint and (1') and (1") do not correspond
to separate, independent thoughts. A battery of
tests was proposed in order to tell **ambiguity**
and underdetermination apart (Zwicky and
Sadock 1975; *see also* Jaszczolt 1999). The
boundary became more and more blurred. Linguists began to adopt the underdetermination
stance to an increasing set of expression types
and we can talk about the beginning of an
orientation called **radical pragmatics** (Cole
1981), sense-generality (Atlas 1989), or **contextualism** (Recanati 2004b, 2005). According
to this view, semantic analysis takes us only part
of the way towards the recovery of utterance
meaning and pragmatic enrichment completes
this process. In other words, the logical form
becomes enriched (or, to use a more general
term, modulated; *see* Recanati 2004b, 2005) as a
result of pragmatic inference and the entire
semantic-pragmatic product becomes subjected
to the truth-conditional analysis (see, for example, Carston 1988, 1998a, 2002; Atlas 1989,
2005; Wilson 1975; Recanati 1989, 2004b,
2005; Sperber and Wilson 1995). For example,
sentence (2) is normally enriched with the consequence sense of *and* before being subjected to
the truth-conditional analysis as in (2').

(2) Tom dropped the vase and it broke.
(2') Tom dropped the vase *and as a result* it broke.

This widening of the content of semantic representation resulted in the reallocation of some of
the meanings which Grice classified as implicit to
the truth-conditional content of the utterance.
One of the main research questions now became
to delimit the scope of such an enriched, truth-
conditional representation, called **what is said**
(Recanati 1989) or explicature (Carston 1988;
Sperber and Wilson 1995) vis-à-vis **implicatures**. Carston (1988) argued that enrichment
stops as soon as optimal relevance (in the sense
of **relevance theory** of Sperber and Wilson) is
reached. She proposed that a criterion for classification is provided by the functional independence principle, according to which implicatures
have their own, independent logical forms and
they function as separate premises in **reasoning**. Identifying some problems with the formal
definition of functional independence, Recanati
(1989) offered the availability principle. According to this principle, an aspect of meaning is part
of what is said when it conforms to our pre-
theoretic intuitions (but *see* Carston's 1998a
response).

Another aspect of the post-Gricean boundary
dispute concerns the so-called 'middle level' of
meaning. For Kent Bach (1994b, 2001; also
Horn 2006), there is what is said and what is
implicated. However, there is also part of an
utterance's content that he believes is implicit in
what is said. People often speak loosely, non-
literally, and it is more efficient to do so because
inference is fast, while speech production is
relatively slow. For example, (3) may be uttered
by a mother comforting a child who cut his
finger (from Bach 1994b: 267). But what the
mother meant was not the content of the sentence alone (the minimal **proposition** in (3'))
but instead an expansion in (3").

(3) You are not going to die, Peter.
(3') There is no future time at which you will
die, Peter.
(3") You are not going to die from this cut,
Peter.

Similarly, utterances of sentences which are
semantically incomplete, although they correspond to complete syntactic forms, such as (4),
are further completed to reflect the speaker's
meaning, as for example in (4').

(4) Bill is not good enough.

(4') Bill is not a good enough singer to be a chorister in King's College Choir.

Such expansions and completions are neither what is said nor implicatures: they are **implicitures** in that they are implicit in what is said. They constitute the middle level of meaning, while the label 'what is said' is reserved for what is explicitly uttered. Next, Levinson (1995, 2000) also proposes a middle level of meaning, but he founds it on very different principles, taking into consideration the **modularity** issue. Levinson discusses utterance-type meanings, so-called presumptive (**default**) interpretations, which are arrived at without the help of context. For example, (2') is for him such a presumptive meaning, the result of the process of the generalized (context-free) conversational implicature. Such utterance-type meanings don't belong either to semantics or to pragmatics, where both are understood as separate modules producing one, single representation of meaning. Presumptive meanings belong to the middle level of conventions of language use.

An opposite tendency in this respect is represented by Default Semantics (Jaszczolt 2005), according to which a representation of utterance meaning is created as a merger of the output of a variety of linguistic and non-linguistic sources. These sources include word meaning and sentence structure, cognitive defaults (pertaining to the way our mental operations normally proceed), social-cultural defaults (interpretations that are standard for the given **culture** and society), and conscious pragmatic inference. Merger representation is the only level of meaning and its construction does not give preference to any of the sources listed above, to the extent that the logical form of the uttered sentence may occasionally be replaced by an implicit form if that implicit proposition is the primary intended meaning. In other words, there is no syntactic constraint on the semantic representation and (3) above may on occasion give rise to, say, (3''').

(3''') There is nothing to worry about, Peter.

The composition of meaning proceeds according to the principles of pragmatic compositionality (Recanati 2004b).

It can be safely said that the union of truth-conditional semantics with Gricean, intention-based pragmatics continued and developed without major paradigm shifts until the early years of the twenty-first century. The 'intrusion' of the output of pragmatic processes was largely taken for granted, even as the **explicit/implicit distinction** engendered many theoretical disputes and much experimental research (concerning, for example, the nature of pragmatic processes that produce what is said versus those that produce implicatures, and the automatic or inferential status of these processes). The field was mainly divided into those who accepted the default, automatic nature of the pragmatic enrichments of sentence meaning (e.g. Levinson 2000; Horn 2004; Recanati 2004b, 2007; Jaszczolt 2005), albeit differentiated by associating different properties to default interpretations, and those for whom pragmatic additions are always inferential (Sperber and Wilson 1995; Carston 2002, 2007), albeit on a very liberal definition of the term 'inferential'. Until this time, the characteristic that united post-Griceans was adherence to a stronger or weaker form of contextualism: the view that pragmatic processes influence the truth conditions of the utterance. This view was subsequently dubbed by Recanati 'truth-conditional pragmatics':

> [V]arious contextual processes come into play in the determination of an utterance's truth conditions; not merely saturation – the contextual assignment of values to indexicals and free variables in the logical form of the sentence – but also free enrichment and other processes which are not linguistically triggered but are pragmatic through and through. That view I will henceforth refer to as 'Truth-conditional pragmatics' (TCP).
>
> (Recanati 2002b: 302)

Opponents of this view include those who postulate slots in the syntactic representation of the sentence for each instance of pragmatic enrichment. For linguists of this orientation, pragmatic enrichment can be explained in terms of filling in slots in the logical form: '[m]uch syntactic structure is unpronounced, but no less real for being unpronounced' (Stanley 2002: 152; *see also*

Stanley and Szabó 2000; King and Stanley 2005). But it seems that the onus of proof lies on those who postulate such syntactic slots. With no compelling syntactic evidence or argumentation, it is a more supportable methodological move to assume that pragmatic enrichment can be free from syntactic constraints.

Recanati advocates a strong version of contextualism. On this view, contextual modulation is always present: there is no level of meaning which is truth-evaluable and unaffected by top-down enrichment. The most radical of such contextualist stances is so-called meaning eliminativism. According to this position, meaning construction does not proceed through the stage of abstraction from past uses and formulation of a core, context-independent meaning, but instead is permeated by context-dependent modulation from the start – in the spirit of the late Wittgensteinian view of meaning as use.

This family of post-Gricean contextualist stances was challenged in the early years of the twenty-first century by so-called **semantic minimalism**, a view according to which the object of study of semantic theory should be strictly separated from post-Gricean intrusion of pragmatic processes. There are currently three versions of semantic minimalism: Emma Borg's (2004a) minimal semantics, Herman Cappelen and Ernie Lepore's (2005a) insensitive semantics, and Kent Bach's (2004a, 2006a) radical semantic minimalism. Borg advocates modular semantics, governed by the rules of deduction, and distinguishes so-called 'liberal' truth conditions from verification conditions. The sentence 'The melon is red' is true if and only if the melon is red in some way or another, that is, either its skin or its flesh is red. The exact meaning, and the exact correspondence to the situation in the world that would make this sentence true, are the domain of verification conditions and fall outside the domain of semantic theory. Cappelen and Lepore offer a semantics of sentences according to which only those context-dependent expressions which are necessary for obtaining a complete semantic, truth-conditional representation are further specified. They propose a (short) list of such expressions, including personal pronouns, **demonstratives**, adverbs such as 'here', 'now', 'yesterday', adjectives like 'actual' and 'present', and tense indicators. A natural

consequence of this minimalist construal of meaning is the discrepancy between the object of study of semantic theory and the meaning of the speaker's utterance. This discrepancy is alleviated by supplementing minimal semantics with so-called speech act pluralism: each minimal representation may correspond to a wide variety of **speech acts** which it is capable of conveying. Finally, Bach offers the most radical form of semantic minimalism, according to which the semantic properties of the sentence should be regarded as analogous to its syntactic and phonological properties:

> The semantics-pragmatics distinction is not fit to be blurred. What lies on either side of the distinction, the semantic and the pragmatic, may each be messy in various ways, but that doesn't blur the distinction itself. Taken as properties of sentences, semantic properties are on a par with syntactic and phonological properties: they are linguistic properties. Pragmatic properties, on the other hand, belong to acts of uttering sentences in the course of communicating. Sentences have the properties they have independently of anybody's act of uttering them. Speakers' intentions do not endow them with new semantic properties.
>
> (Bach 2004a: 27)

On this construal, truth conditions are redundant as a tool because the object of study is not the proposition, not even in its minimal version, but the grammatical form itself. In other words, the completion of incomplete propositions such as (4) – so-called propositional radicals – does not fall within the domain of semantics: this would mean adopting propositionalism, which he strongly opposes and which he regards as a weakness of both Borg's and Cappelen and Lepore's accounts.

Several pertinent questions arise at this juncture of the semantics-pragmatics boundary dispute. The most important among them are perhaps (i) whether minimalism can be regarded as compatible with contextualism, each of them arguably having a distinct set of objectives and a distinct object of study; (ii) whether the powerful tool of truth conditions should be regarded as dispensable in semantics, as Bach suggests, but be applicable to freely enriched what is said, as contextualists have it; (iii) whether the pragmatic contribution to what is said is conscious and inferential or automatic; and (iv) at what phase exactly does this pragmatic elaboration take place in utterance processing. We have to wait for future developments in the dispute to bring answers to these questions. Recent research also testifies to the shift from the narrowly construed semantics-pragmatics interface to more broadly conceived interfaces that involve **syntax**, sociology (in the sense of standard social practices governed by laws of economy and efficiency), anthropology, and **cognitive science**.

KASIA M. JASZCZOLT

See also: Ambiguity; generalized conversational implicature, theory of; neo-Gricean pragmatics; ordinary language philosophy; philosophy of language; post-Gricean pragmatics; radical pragmatics; semantic minimalism

Suggestions for further reading

Atlas, J.D. (1989) *Philosophy without Ambiguity: A Logico-Linguistic Essay*, Oxford: Clarendon Press.
Jaszczolt, K.M. (to appear) 'Semantics and pragmatics: the boundary issue', in K. von Heusinger, P. Portner and C. Maienborn (eds) *Semantics: An International Handbook of Natural Language Meaning*, Berlin: Mouton de Gruyter.
Recanati, F. (2005) 'Literalism and contextualism: some varieties', in G. Preyer and G. Peter (eds) *Contextualism in Philosophy: Knowledge, Meaning, and Truth*, Oxford: Clarendon Press.

Semiotics

Semiotics is the discipline that aims to study, classify, and explain signs as they are used in intellectual and artistic forms, from gestures and words to paintings and mathematical theorems. A sign is anything that is perceived to stand for something other than itself. So, a word such as *cat* is not perceived by English speakers simply as a random sequence of sounds, but rather as a unitary sound structure that stands for a specific kind of mammal. Similarly, most people would not perceive a cross figure as just two lines crossing at right angles, but rather as a symbol standing for various concepts, including 'addition' in arithmetic and 'Christianity' in religion. Since the mid-twentieth century, semiotics has grown into a truly broad field of inquiry, which is applied to the study of any **meaning**-making activity and enterprise, from body language to **advertising** and clothing fashion (Nöth 1990).

The term 'semeiotics' (spelled now as 'semiotics') – from Greek *sêmeiotikos* ('observant of signs') – was coined by Hippocrates (c.460–c.370 BCE), the founder of Western medicine, to designate the diagnosis of the symptoms produced by the human body. The particular physical form that a symptom (called a *semeion* 'mark') takes constitutes a vital clue for finding its aetiological source. It was St Augustine (354–430 CE), the early Christian church father and philosopher, who first elaborated a theory of non-medical semiotics in his *De Doctrina Christiana* (Deely 2001). St Augustine distinguished between two main types of signs: natural signs (*signa naturalia*) and conventional signs (*signa data*). Natural signs lack human **intentionality** and include symptoms, the rustling of leaves, the colours of plants, animal signals, and so on. Conventional signs are the direct products of human intentionality. They include not only words, but also witting gestures and symbols of all kinds. Sign theory was extended in the medieval period, when the Scholastics proposed that signs are structures composed of two parts – a *signans* ('that which does the signifying') and a *signatum* ('that which is signified'). At about the same time, the scientist Roger Bacon (c.1214–94) developed one of the first typologies of signs. But it was John Locke (1632–1704) several centuries later who put forward the specific proposal of using sign theory as an investigative framework for studying philosophical issues (Deely 2001). The idea of semiotics as an autonomous discipline did not surface until the late nineteenth century, when the Swiss linguist Ferdinand de Saussure (1857–1913) put this notion forward in his *Cours de Linguistique Générale* (Saussure 1916). Saussure used the term *sémiologie* (English *semiology*) to designate what he thought was a 'new' discipline. Today, 'semiotics' is the preferred designator, due primarily to the influence of the American philosopher Charles S. **Peirce** (1839–1914), who elaborated the first truly comprehensive analysis of sign structure and function (Peirce 1931: 58).

Following on the coat-tails of Saussure and Peirce, a number of twentieth-century scholars developed semiotics into the sophisticated discipline that it has become today. Among them are Ludwig **Wittgenstein** (1889–1951) who suggested that signs were pictures of reality; Charles **Morris** (1901–79) who saw signs as shapers of behaviour; Roman Jakobson (1896–1982) who drafted a widely used model of **communication** based on the subjectivity of sign exchange; Roland Barthes (1915–80) who illustrated the power of using semiotics for decoding the hidden mythic meanings in pop culture; Algirdas J. Greimas (1917–92) who made the study of **narrative** a central target of semiotics; Thomas A. Sebeok (1920–2001) who projected semiotic inquiry into the larger study of cross-species communication (Sebeok 2002); and finally Umberto Eco (b. 1932) who contributed significantly to our understanding of how we interpret texts.

Today, a blend of Saussurean and Peircean semiotics is used to carry out all kinds of analyses. Essentially, Saussurean semiotics sees signs as arbitrary 'descriptors of reality'. Saussure (1916) named the physical form of the sign, the 'signifier', and the concept that it elicits, the 'signified'. The two parts are inseparable cognitively. When we utter the word *cat* the image of a specific mammal inevitably comes to mind and, in fact, such an image cannot be blocked; vice versa, when we see such a mammal before us the word *cat* also comes automatically to mind. In effect, both components exist in tandem, not separately. Peirce saw the sign instead as a construct resulting from an informed hunch. Signs were thus 'evaluators of reality', or interpretants of reality, as he termed them. What does *cat* mean? It depends on who uses that word sign and where it is used, varying from 'a domestic companion' to a 'sacred animal' (akin to a sacred cow in some societies). Thus, while the sign refers to virtually the same mammal in different **cultures** (no matter what signifier is used), its interpretant varies considerably (Merrell 1997). Peirce also developed a comprehensive typology of signs, of which icon, index, and symbol are fundamental constituents. A sign forged as a simulation of something is an icon.

For example, when the V-sign formed by raising the index and middle fingers of the hand in the shape of a 'V' is used to stand for the letter V, it is an icon. When it is used instead to point to two things at once (in a vertical orientation of the hand) it is an index – a sign that relates objects in relation to the sign user. Lastly, when it is used to stand for 'victory' or 'peace', it is a symbol. Such meanings can only be inferred within specific historical and social contexts.

The meanings associated with sign use are of two kinds – denotative and connotative (Barthes 1968). Denotative meaning allows people to determine if a sign refers to something concretely. For example, when we see a feline creature and use the word *cat* to refer to it, we are using that word denotatively. All other uses of the word are connotative. For instance, when we say something like 'He let the *cat* out of the bag', we are referring to qualities perceived in cats, not to a specific real cat. Connotation covers a broad range of meaning-making, including **metaphor**, metonymy, and other figurative modes of **reference**. The cognitive or social functions of signs also determine whether or not we will interpret them denotatively or connotatively. The signs in the alphabet code, for instance, have denotative meaning when we use them to compose words. However, when we use them symbolically, they can only be interpreted connotatively. The letter X, for instance, has connotative meanings when used in such expressions as 'X-Rated' or 'X-Files'. The notion of code is used extensively in semiotics. It is defined simply as a system of signs with specific functions. Codes underlie the construction of texts. They are amalgams of signs that cohere into meaningful wholes. A novel, for instance, is a verbal text constructed with words (which are, more accurately, the signifiers of the text) in order to communicate some overarching message.

Today, semiotic theory is used extensively as a critical and investigative tool in various domains of inquiry, from culture studies to media analysis. It was Barthes (1957) who drew attention to the interpretive power of semiotics. As he showed in *Mythologies*, semiotics makes it possible to flesh out recurring elements of connotative meaning in television programmes, sports spectacles, brands, and other modern texts in a systematic fashion. Since these elements lie generally below the threshold of awareness, it is useful indeed to have at our disposal a discipline that allows us to bring them out into the open for examination and evaluation.

MARCEL DANESI

See also: Cognitive linguistics; culture; deixis; indexicals; meaning; metaphor; Morris, C.; Peirce, C.S.; reference; semantics

Suggestions for further reading

Cobley, P. (ed.) (2001) *The Routledge Companion to Semiotics and Linguistics*, London: Routledge.
Danesi, M. (2002) *Understanding Media Semiotics*, New York: Oxford University Press.
——(2007) *The Quest for Meaning: A Guide to Semiotic Theory and Practice*, Toronto: University of Toronto Press.

Sequence Organization

Conversation analysis (CA) has a basic interest in the systematic ways in which utterances are constructed to demonstrate why they are produced at that particular moment in the interaction. One aspect of this sequence organization is how utterances relate to immediately preceding ones. An early observation of Harvey Sacks was that actions performed in **conversation** tend to come in pairs, like greeting-greeting, question-answer or invitation-acceptance/declination, with each action being performed by a different speaker (Sacks 1992: vol. I). Later, such pairings were conceptualized as adjacency pairs (Sacks 1992: vol. II: 521–69; Schegloff 1968; Schegloff and Sacks 1973: 295–96; Schegloff 2007: 13–21). Such pairs consist of two adjacently placed utterances produced by different speakers in which the first pair part (FPP) served to initiate an exchange, while the second pair part (SPP) offers a response to it. Furthermore, these utterances are 'pair-type related': a FPP gets a SPP of the same 'type', as in a greeting gets a greeting in return, a **question** receives an answer, and so on. The basic rule of operation of adjacency pairs (APs) is that on the recognizable production of a FPP, its speaker should stop and a next speaker should start to produce a SPP of the

same pair type (Schegloff 2007: 14). This 'rule' can be used quite flexibly in various circumstances, while its basic features are still oriented to by the participants. The central thesis of Schegloff's book *Sequence Organization* is that the AP-format is the basic building block of most, if not all, recognizable sequences in conversation. The AP relationship has two aspects: the FPP projects a particular relevance for the 'filler' of the 'slot' following after it, while the SPP demonstrates a particular understanding of the turn just preceding.

While many FPPs project the relevance of a particular kind of action, there are others for which there are alternative kinds of response. One of these responses is 'positive' and another 'negative', for instance, an acceptance or a declination of an invitation, an agreement versus a **disagreement** with an assessment. Such alternatives tend to be formatted differently: the positive, 'preferred' SPPs mostly come fast and are formulated in a straightforward manner, while the negative, 'dispreferred' responses are often delayed, uttered hesitantly and accompanied by accounts (Pomerantz 1984). Here the notion of preference should be understood in a structural way, not as a reference to personal preferences. The underlying issue is one of 'alignment' and 'progressivity'. Positive SPPs are 'in line' with the preceding FPP and add to a smooth progression of the interaction, while negative SPPs require some sort of reorientation (*cf.* Lerner 1996a).

Taking the AP-format as the basic type of a minimal sequence, such basic sequences can be expanded in various ways. Schegloff (2007) distinguishes three general types of sequence expansion: pre-expansion, insert expansion, and post-expansion. In pre-expansion, a basic AP is preceded by a pre-sequence in which the possibilities for the success of that base-sequence are explored (2007: 28–57). Before uttering an invitation, for instance, one may ask 'Are you doing anything tonight?'. This may lead to some exchanges before the actual invitation is launched, at least to the extent that the conditions for it have been established as being positive. Other types can involve pre-offers, pre-announcements (Terasaki 2004) and other pre-tellings. A separate case has been characterized as 'preliminaries to preliminaries', as in 'Can I ask you a question?'

(Schegloff 1980). The general function of these various kinds of preliminaries can be taken to be the avoidance of 'dispreferred' alternatives, like having a suggestion rejected or an opinion disagreed with.

In the second type of expansion, insert expansion (Schegloff 1972, 2007: 97–114), a second sequence is inserted between the FPP and the SPP. This is done at the initiative of the projected SPP speaker, that is, the production of the projected SPP is deferred 'in order to address matters which need to be dealt with in order to enable the doing of the base SPP' (2007: 99). These 'matters' can be concerned with the FPP just produced ('post-first insert expansion'), or with contingencies of what is to be done next ('pre-second insert expansion'). Here is an example of a post-first insertion by a next-turn-repair-initiation (from Schegloff 2007: 102):

A: Have you ever tried a clinic?
B: What?
A: Have you ever tried a clinic?
B: ((sigh)) No, I don't want to go to a clinic

Post-first insertion sequences are a specific type of a very general phenomenon in conversation called repair sequences. The organization of repair can be quite complicated and a substantial part of CA research has been devoted to clarifying the varieties of its organization (Schegloff *et al.* 1977; Schegloff 1992, 2007: 100–60). Repair sequences are addressed to solving problems of hearing and understanding the preceding talk, which can, therefore, be initiated at any time in a conversation. Such sequences can be initiated by the speaker of the 'trouble source' (self-initiated repair) or by another speaker (other-initiated repair). The repair itself, the 'solution' to the problem, can be executed by the original speaker (self-repair) or by another speaker (other-repair). In the case of 'post-first insert expansion', it may be other-initiated, self-repair which does the job, taking possibly just one insertion sequence before the projected SPP can be produced (as in the example above). 'Pre-second insert expansions' may be initiated in order to collect additional information before a **request** can be sensibly honoured, for instance, 'Where are you now?' after a request for directions (Psathas 1991).

As an AP is opened by a FPP, it can be closed by a SPP, a two-part sequence. Quite often, people have more to say which is still part of that particular sequence; that is what Schegloff (2007: 115–68) calls post-expansion. A minimal form of this is the addition of a 'sequence closing third', like 'Oh', 'Okay' or an assessment (or combination of these) that is clearly designed to close off the sequence. More extended forms are also possible, for instance, by uttering a repair initiation, by a 'news mark' like 'oh really?', which can lead to elaboration of the **topic**, or by some indication of disagreement of the SPP, which can result in a more or less extended argument.

As CA has increasingly used video data, it has become clear that in face-to-face encounters, the sequential arrangements mentioned above are co-organized in various ways by the use of visual cues. These cues include most prominently gaze direction, as well as observable actions in the environment and the manipulation of material artefacts. These aspects are especially prominent in the work of Charles Goodwin and Christian Heath (*cf.*, for instance, Goodwin 1984, 2000a, 2002; Heath 1984, 1986; Heath and Luff 2000; also Egbert 1997b; Fox *et al.* 1996).

There are two structural locations in conversations where one often sees a series of adjacency pairs, at the opening and closing of a conversational encounter. Conversational openings have been studied mostly in telephone calls, where the telephone ring can be considered a FPP, for which answering the phone is the SPP (Schegloff 1968). This is, of course, a presequence, most often followed by a series of APs dealing with identifications, greetings and inquiries, before a specific topic is launched (Schegloff 1979b, 1986). Conversational closings also tend to engender a series of APs, dealing with summaries, arrangements, closing implicative exchanges such as 'well', 'okay' and 'good' and leave-takings (Schegloff and Sacks 1973).

PAUL TEN HAVE

See also: Communication failure; conversation; conversation analysis; conversational turn-taking; ethnomethodology; telephone conversation; transcription

Suggestions for further reading

Sacks, H. (1992) *Lectures on Conversation*, I and II, ed. G. Jefferson, Oxford: Blackwell.

Schegloff, E.A. (2007) *Sequence Organization in Interaction: A Primer in Conversation Analysis*, vol. 1, Cambridge: Cambridge University Press.

Schegloff, E.A., Jefferson, G. and Sacks, H. (1977) 'The preference for self-correction in the organization of repair in conversation', *Language*, 53: 361–82.

Sharedness

Human beings share different things: food, living and sleeping places, experiences, and states of the mind such as emotions and beliefs. The pervasive desire to share with others is typically human, and it sustains our normally cooperative approach to social and cultural matters. How did the capacity to share phylogenetically evolve, how does it ontogenetically develop, what is the cognitive architecture that implements it, and why is it fundamental for intentional **communication**?

Phylogenetically, Tomasello *et al.* (2005) point out that primates are intensely competitive creatures. In addition to competing with others (and coordinating with others like all social animals), human beings have also evolved the capacity and the motivation for collaborating with one another. Collaborative interactions require interactants to have the capacity to read the intentional states of others. But collaboration also requires the motivation to share feelings, experiences and activities with other persons under the auspices of mutual assistance.

In terms of ontogeny, Tomasello and Carpenter (2007) hypothesize that there is a uniquely human line of development for sharing psychological states with others, which is present in nascent form as infants indulge in affective exchanges with caregivers. Trevarthen (1998) calls the face-to-face communication between infants and caregivers in the first months of life 'primary intersubjectivity'. This communication consists of eye gaze, vocalization, and rhythmic turn-taking patterns. The cooperative dimension of human cognition emerges most clearly around the first year of life, when children begin to show joint attention and joint **intentions** (Tomasello *et al.* 2005).

Remarkably, infants' early **representations** do not seem to distinguish between self and other, and are essentially symmetric, i.e. both actors share the same state with no role complementarity (imitation is a good example; Meltzoff and Moore 1997). Such dyadic sharing probably depends on the mirror neural circuit, involving the prefrontal medial cortex, the temporo-parietal junctions and the temporal lobes (Kohler *et al.* 2002). Only after the so-called '9-months revolution' (Tomasello *et al.* 2005) do infants acquire the ability to discriminate the mental states of oneself and others. This transition is probably marked by the maturation of the 'Who-system', the neural circuit underlying the distinction between one's own actions and those of others (Georgieff and Jeannerod 1998). With the 9-months revolution, infants shift from dyadic sharing (the basis for imitative and symmetric behaviours) to triadic sharing (where an object is shared between the self and the other). From now on, infants are able to conceive of themselves as separate from others: true shared experiences require not only commonality but also differentiation, i.e. the recognition of others as separate individuals (Bara, to appear).

This process allows children to acquire subjective sharedness, to be distinguished from the absolute sharedness of infants (for whom the caregiver has access to all their states: from the infant's point of view, the mother *knows* what he feels like). The maturation of the ability to subjectively share is based upon the new possibility for the child of understanding the differences between his or her own mental states and the mental states of other agents. Subjectively, this corresponds both to the final maturation of sharedness and to the birth of privateness (Tirassa *et al.* 2006b). In the state of subjective sharedness, children are able to assume a point of view, grasping the fact that they can know something the other does not know, and that only through communication can they assume that something becomes shared with the other.

Let us now explore the necessity of the notion of sharedness for explaining intentional communication (Bara, to appear). In order to introduce the concept of shared beliefs – a concept which is indispensable when we are dealing with mental states in communication – I must first differentiate between three types of beliefs: individual, common (also called mutual) and shared beliefs. I will do so in an intuitive fashion, allowing myself a certain definitional leeway. In the case of individual belief, agents believe a certain thing, or believe that other agents believe a certain thing, but they do so in a totally autonomous fashion, with no connection existing between the agents themselves. Often in a given context, all the agents have the same individual beliefs: all agents generally share **knowledge** of their surrounding environment, or a certain amount of knowledge which is culturally transmitted. For instance, A may share with B the fact that both love opera, and with all pacifists the opinion that atomic weapons should be banned, and with all humans the fact that we are born of a mother and a father. Much human interaction is based on this type of belief, which is spread over a more or less wide group of people, and which we will call common belief or mutual belief.

Clark (1996) speaks of common ground, meaning the sum of knowledge, beliefs and suppositions that two people share. Common ground enables us to identify a series of cultural communities, which may be classified according to the type of beliefs a community shares. A cultural community is a group of people who possess profound knowledge which other cultural communities do not possess. Hepatologists do not all live together in a large hepatological village: what makes a community of these people is the set of shared beliefs, practices, terminology, conventions, values, habits, and knowledge concerning the liver and its diseases. Egyptians are experts on Egypt, Catholics on Catholicism, mechanics on cars, philatelists on postage stamps, socialists on socialism, cocaine addicts on cocaine, teenagers on adolescence and so on. Each type of expert knowledge consists of facts, procedures, norms and assumptions that the members of the community assume they can take for granted in other members. Knowledge is ranked: some information is of central importance, and must necessarily form part of each member's repertoire, while other information is only peripheral.

However, having common beliefs is not a sufficient condition for communication to take place. Suppose that a person is in a foreign country whose language she does not know and she wishes to convey her mental state to other interlocutors. She will not employ a gesture whose **meaning** she is familiar with, unless she thinks the other participants are also cognizant of its meaning. Everyone present might happen to know the gesture at an individual level, and yet never use it, because they are not aware that all the others are also aware of the meaning it conveys. The conclusion, therefore, is that in order to communicate, in addition to possessing common beliefs, each participant must also be aware of the fact that all the other participants possess those very same common beliefs.

I define a shared belief as that belief which is not only common to all the participants engaged in a communicative event, but which each participant is aware is possessed by all the other participants. From a psychological standpoint, shared belief has a crucial feature: it is subjective (one-sided), and not objective as is common belief. In actual fact, no-one can ever be certain that another person has knowledge of a certain type: she may at most assume that he has it, and she may be convinced that they share it. To be certain, she should in some way be able to observe the mental states of others in a direct manner, and not simply infer them from circumstances. In theory, a counter-Galileo might pretend to share with others the belief that the earth is round, but be privately convinced that it is flat, without anyone ever suspecting what was really going on in his mind. Taking up a subjective position where shared belief is concerned means assuming that each agent has a space of shared beliefs which contains all the beliefs which the agent herself is convinced she shares with a given partner, or with a group of people, or with humanity in its entirety.

The formal connection between individual belief and shared belief has been clarified by Airenti *et al.* (1993a):

$$\mathrm{SH}_{AB}\, p \equiv \mathrm{BEL}_A\, (p \wedge \mathrm{SH}_{BA}\, p)$$

where SH_{AB} means that both the agents A and B reciprocally hold the belief that p. What the formula expresses is that when actress A takes p as shared by B and herself, this means that on the one hand she herself takes p as being true, and that on the other hand she believes that *B* also takes *p* as being shared by both of them. Circularity derives from the fact that sharedness is present on both sides of the formula, both in the *definiens* and in the *definiendum*.

One important difference between mutual belief and shared belief is that the former is objectively common to both interlocutors. This means that both *A* and *B* really do believe that *p*, and both should therefore possess the same mental state corresponding to that *p*. Shared belief, on the contrary, assumes a subjective viewpoint, since no agent can ever be sure that all the other participants possess the same beliefs she holds. Hence, shared belief always expresses the standpoint of one of the interlocutors. *A* may take a certain fact as shared by both *B* and herself, but this assumption is subjective, one which does not necessarily correspond to the real mental states possessed by *B*. No one can open another person's brain and look inside in order to check what beliefs the other person actually does hold. And subjective assumptions regarding sharedness play an important part in non-standard communication, especially in cases of failure and deceit (Airenti *et al.* 1993b).

Even as Tomasello and colleagues (2005, 2007) empirically demonstrate the genetic structure of shared intention, I argue that it is logically necessary for shared belief to be primitive, that is, irreducible to private beliefs. The crucial role that sharedness plays within communication is best exemplified by the notion of communicative intention. Grice (1975) defines communicative intention as the intention to communicate something, plus the intention that that intention to communicate something be recognized as such. In more formal notation, *A* has the communicative intention that *p* towards *B*, when *A* intends that the following two facts be shared by *B* and herself: that *p*, and that she intended to communicate to *B* that *p*.

Unique to the human species, intentional communication depends upon the capacity to share mental states with one another and on the motivation to share these states. Through the development of an understanding of the differences between what is privately believed and what is openly shared, children learn to recognize and recover communicative failures and to

plan and uncover deceit. Finally, through the exploitation of shared beliefs children learn to master one of the most sophisticated forms of communication, **irony** (Bara, to appear).

BRUNO G. BARA

See also: Cognitive pragmatics; communication; communication failure; competence, communicative; competence, pragmatic; cooperative principle; development, pragmatic; intention; intentionality; irony; knowledge; language evolution; misunderstanding; perspective taking/point of view; prelinguistic communication; representation and computation; theory of mind

Suggestions for further reading

Bara, B.G. (to appear) *Cognitive Pragmatics*, Cambridge, MA: MIT Press.
Tirassa, M., Bosco, F.M. and Colle, L. (2006) 'Sharedness and privateness in human early social life', *Cognitive Systems Research*, 7: 128–39.
Tomasello, M., Carpenter, M., Call, J., Behne, T. and Moll, H. (2005) 'Understanding and sharing intentions: the origins of cultural cognition', *Behavioral and Brain Sciences*, 28: 675–91.

Signed Language, Pragmatics of

Signed languages are the primary languages of deaf communities worldwide. These languages exhibit grammatical complexity on a par with spoken languages. Lexicalization and diachronic patterns of grammatical change are also similar, as are stages of first language acquisition. The single important difference between signed and spoken languages is in their articulatory structure: they are produced by configurations of the hands, face and body that are perceived visually instead of by structures of the vocal tract perceived auditorily. *Ethnologue* (Gordon 2005) lists 121 signed languages known to exist (several of them are extinct), but it is thought that this list is far from complete. Even though it is often assumed that signed language is 'universal', signed languages for the most part are not mutually intelligible.

Pragmatics of spatial association

Signed languages are articulated with the hands and body within a three-dimensional space. Because linguistic expression reflects the language producer's conceptualization of referents and events that also exist in some space, it is not surprising that signers take advantage of the space that their hands move around in to reflect relational features of conceptualized real-world spaces. Signers convey relationships between referents, ideas and abstract entities by iconic positioning in space. For example, proximity in space is equivalent to proximity in conceptualized relationship, which is described for Danish Sign Language by Engberg-Pedersen (1993, 1995) and for American Sign Language (ASL; Winston 1995), among others.

Engberg-Pedersen (1993) outlines a number of ways in which signers work such deictic and anaphoric spatial referencing into their **discourse**. If two items share some semantic affinity, the signer is likely to cluster her articulation around a single point in space. If an entity typically occupies a space relative to the signer during some regular event, the signer will use a deictic **reference** to this canonical location even if the referent is not physically there at the time. An iconic convention occurs when the signer maps a conceptualized spatial relation between two entities onto spatial positioning in linguistic expression. Note that this is aided by the signer's physiology of having two hands, which can be positioned relationally in space. Thus, if two entities are understood as existing far away from each other, the two hands may be positioned in two locations far apart to iconically represent this conceptualized distance. In the abstract, if two ideas are widely disparate, they may be represented in space similarly. Finally, the convention of comparison obtains when two items are being compared, with one positioned in a leftward location and the other rightward. Again, this convention holds whether the items are physical or abstract. Referring to spatial locations where entities have been positioned previously pragmatically evokes that entity for both signer and addressee. This is achieved through mechanisms such as pointing to the space (considered pronominal (Liddell 2003) in many signed languages), eye gaze toward

the space, beginning or ending the path movement of a dynamic verb at that location (e.g. beginning the path movement for GIVE at a location conveys that the referent positioned at that space is the giver), leaning the body towards that space and positioning another item at or near the space (as semantic affinity) (Winston 1995).

Information ordering

In ASL, as in many other signed languages, the utterance-final position is a position of focus or stress (Wilbur 1997). Thus, signed languages tend to have flexible word and constituent ordering, largely influenced by the **pragmatics** of the situation and intent. Topic-comment structure is prevalent, with numerous categories able to take topic marking, such as noun phrases, locative phrases, temporal elements, and full clauses (Janzen *et al.* 1999). **Topics** are chosen as grounding information for the focused or stressed information to follow, and are marked by raised eyebrows and a slight backward head tilt that continue throughout the articulation of the topic phrase. The topic and comment may be separated by a slight pause with no additional overt linker. Thus, the relationship between topic and comment constituents is largely inferential. Topic marking in ASL signals topic shift; if a topic is maintained, it loses topic marking, and is highly reduced in form. The higher the topicality of an element, the more likely it is to be 'null', that is, to receive no overt mention in the clause at all (Janzen 2007). A common progression through a stretch of discourse begins with a referent introduced as new information. Once it is introduced, it may next appear as a topic-marked constituent. If it is then maintained as a topic, it may further appear as a non-topic-marked pronoun. If it is continued, it is taken as highly accessible and becomes null.

Utterance-final position can also indicate scope relations (Shaffer 2004). Modal verbs in ASL may appear verb-initially or clause-finally. Clause-final modals (SHOULD, MUST, etc.) have scope over the entire **proposition**. As well, modals with epistemic reading appear clause-finally but not verb-initially in ASL. Shaffer (2004: 190) gives as one example the clause-final modal SHOULD in the sentence

LIBRARY HAVE DEAF LIFE, SHOULD 'I'm sure the library has *Deaf Life* [magazine]' to indicate the signer's degree of commitment to the proposition that the library has the magazine in its holdings.

Referencing and pragmatics

Pragmatic inferencing takes place inter-subjectively when a speaker or signer intends a **meaning** that is not directly coded in a lexical item or construction (Traugott and Dasher 2002). An example of this in ASL is the use of first person referencing mechanisms when the signer shifts her perspective in a **narrative** passage to that of a third person referent. When the signer assumes the perspective of the third person referent, she may use a first person pronoun (or other referencing mechanism) to convey reference to that third person entity. This is not unlike the use of *I* in English for reported speech in a construction like 'She's like "I don't think so!"', although such usage in signed languages appears to go well beyond instances of reported speech. Similarly, if the signer has been a participant in the event or interaction being reported, while now taking a third person's perspective on that interaction, she can conceptualize herself as occupying a location in conceptual space from the third person's viewpoint. For example, in a sequence of perspective shifts in an ASL narrative (Janzen 2004), the signer describes an interaction between a group of people she is part of and a police officer. When she shifts to the perspective of the officer, she and the others in the group are conceptualized as facing the officer from a short distance away. This conceptual space corresponds to a more distal location in her articulation space, and she may use a third person pronoun to refer to that location, thus conveying a reference to herself. Essentially, she herself is being viewed in a relational space from the third person's view on that space. Critical is that the first person pronoun does not actually encode third person meaning and the third person pronoun does not encode first person meaning, but in the right interaction **context**, this meaning can be an invited **inference**, as Traugott and Dasher call it, available to the addressee.

Simultaneous constructions

In articulation, the hands may represent two different elements simultaneously. Because movements in articulation space frequently represent the movement paths of these elements, the two hands may be used to articulate two simultaneous but distinct actions (Leeson and Saeed 2004; *see also* Vermeerbergen *et al.* 2007). In these cases, the relationship between the hands in space represents iconically a spatial relationship between the two elements, therefore indicating inferentially the interaction of these elements in both time and space.

Even though signed languages are produced by different articulators than those for spoken languages and are perceived visually, linguistic expressions in both language types function in similar ways. Signed languages, however, incorporate aspects of iconic spatial organization and referencing that are not as readily available in spoken language systems. Pragmatic inferencing in signed language, as in spoken language, depends crucially on the choice of linguistic expression within the intersubjective context of use.

TERRY JANZEN

See also: Cognitive pragmatics; context; deixis; ellipsis; focus; indexicals; inference; information structure; meaning; narrative discourse; perspective taking/point of view; proposition; reference; semantics-pragmatics interface; topic; utterance interpretation

Suggestions for further reading

Pizzuto, E. (2007) 'Deixis, anaphora and person reference in signed languages', in E. Pizzuto, P. Pietrandrea and R. Simone (eds) *Verbal and Signed Languages: Comparing Structures, Constructs and Methodologies*, Berlin and New York: Mouton de Gruyter.

Slobin, D.I. (2006) 'Issues of linguistic typology in the study of sign language development of Deaf children', in B. Schick, M. Marschark and P.E. Spencer (eds) *Advances in the Sign Language Development of Deaf Children*, Oxford and New York: Oxford University Press.

Wilcox, S. and Wilcox, P. (1995) 'The gestural expression of modality in ASL', in J. Bybee and S. Fleischman (eds) *Modality in Grammar and Discourse*, Amsterdam and Philadelphia, PA: John Benjamins.

Silence

Silence has been treated in the past as a phenomenon in psychoanalysis (Schön 1987), and as a metaphysical issue (Picard 1952; Dauenhauer 1980), countered by **Wittgenstein**'s famous aphorism at the end of *Tractatus*: 'what we cannot speak about we must pass over in silence' (Wittgenstein 1974: 74), recommending silence to metaphysical discourse. We also find discussions of silence as a phenomenon in theatrical performances, e.g. the silences of Chekhov, Beckett, Pinter (*see*, e.g. Kane 1984; Benston 1993), in art and **culture** in general (Steiner 1967), and in holocaust studies (Wajnryb 2001). There have been other individual articles appearing occasionally, each author presenting his own general interpretation of silence as a communication device, relating to different aspects of silence. Bruneau (1973) speaks of three forms of silence: psychological, interactive and sociocultural silence, while Jensen (1973) relates to five functions of silence: linking, affecting, revelational, judgemental and activating. Johannesen (1974) presents four contexts in which silence functions: in cognitive processes, in normal interpersonal communication, in political and civil life, and in counselling and psychotherapy; and offers twenty meanings of silence.

Silence has also been a topic among feminists concerning the silence of women in that they have not been given a voice in society. Lakoff (1975) gave a general survey of women's language and the silencing of women, which was followed by many works on related topics such as women writers and their silencing (Olsen 1978), and a woman's silence following sexual harassment (Clair 1998).

Silence became an integral part of **pragmatics**, and of linguistics in general, with the publication of a collection of articles edited by Tannen and Saville-Troike (1985). Saville-Troike (1985), in her introductory chapter, deals with a model of silence in **communication**, in which she distinguishes between institutionally determined silence, group-determined silence and

individually determined silence, or negotiated silence. The other articles in the book look at silence from different pragmatic and linguistic aspects in various contexts, e.g. witness hesitancy in the courtroom (Graffam Walker 1985), silence and noise in church services (Maltz 1985), silence among the Finns (Lehtonen and Sajavaara 1985).

The first book-length study of silence from a pragmatic (and sociolinguistic) perspective was Jaworski (1993), who made use of the concept of prototypicality as well as **relevance theory** in his analysis. Several years later, Jaworski also edited a further collection of articles (Jaworski 1997a), including the linguistics and pragmatics of silence (Sobkowiak 1997; Sifianou 1997), as well as silence in artistic performance (Jaworski 1997b; Withers 1997), silence in religious ritual (Szuchewicz 1997), silence among women (Dendrinos and Pedro 1997), and again the silent Finn (Sajavaara and Lehtonen 1997).

Other work on silence in this period includes the pragmatic analysis of the right of silence in criminal proceedings (Kurzon 1995, 1998), and Bilmes's (1994) distinction between absolute silence and notable silence. The former type of silence relates to the absence of all sound, which probably, according to the American avant-garde composer John Cage, among others, is non-existent (Cage 1967), for absolute silence may be found only in outer space where there is no air to carry sound waves. In pragmatics, however, we are not concerned with absolute silence, or with the lack of noise in nature. The pragmatic feature is the lack of speech, Bilmes's 'notable silence', defined as 'the absence of some particular sound', which would be silence in social interaction. More precisely, a pragmatic approach to silence would examine the lack of speech in situations in which dialogue – at least two-way social verbal interaction – is taking place.

In studies of silence in social interaction, focus has been placed on the silence of one of the interlocutors in a **conversation**. A participant may either not participate – he or she is present physically but does not join in the conversation, or may not answer **questions** or comments directed at him or her. Pragmatic research investigates not only the various circumstances in which such a silence may take place, but also how such a silence may be interpreted. This has been suggested in previous research discussed above. A number of models have been suggested in this regard. Saville-Troike (1985), as mentioned above, has suggested a comprehensive framework in which silence in social interaction may be investigated. Kurzon (1998) has focused in his model on the second type of silence in which the participant does not respond to talk directed at him or her. We may draw an initial distinction between intentional and unintentional silence. In the former, the addressee refuses to respond as a deliberate act on his or her part. This may be seen, too, as a non-verbal instance of a violation of **Grice**'s **cooperative principle**. This type of silence is often discussed in research on police and lawyer interrogation. In such a context, the addressee may refuse to cooperate with the police, because he or she either does not want to incriminate him- or herself, or does not want to divulge information that may incriminate others. At times social pressure may have had its effect on the addressee in his or her refusal to respond. Unintentional silence, in contrast, is usually psychological in essence. The addressee may feel shy in the situation in which he or she finds him- or herself (*see also* Berger 2004). Another example of a silent response to questions is the student in a classroom who keeps silent – either intentionally or unintentionally – because he or she either does not know the answer to the question, or is not sure of the answer, or does know the answer, but does not want to be in the limelight.

As well as silence in conversation, there are other circumstances in which silence may be examined from a pragmatic perspective or, more precisely, from a sociopragmatic perspective. We may, therefore, distinguish between textual silence, e.g. the silence of readers in a library, and situational silence, e.g. the silence in cemeteries, places of worship and at remembrance ceremonies (Kurzon 2007a). A more specific study of situational silence is Kurzon (2007b), which deals with the intertextuality of silence and copyright law in the case of musical performances.

However, the term 'silence' has also been used to relate to the linguistic zero and other omissions in syntactic structure, e.g. agent deletion after a passive verb. This cannot be considered

silence in its **meaning** of 'lack of talk', but reflects the expansion of the meaning of the term 'silence'; it is frequently used metaphorically to relate to a **topic** a speaker, usually intentionally, does not mention.

DENNIS KURZON

See also: Gender; intentionality; legal pragmatics; police-suspect interviews; societal pragmatics

Suggestions for further reading

Sifianou, M. (1995) 'Do we need to be silent to be extremely polite? Silence and FTAs', *International Journal of Applied Linguistics*, 5: 95–110.
Vainiomäki, T. (2004) 'Silence as a cultural sign', *Semiotica*, 150: 347–61.

Social Cognition

Broadly speaking, social cognition is concerned with the cognitive processes that shape and define our interactions with the social world (for comprehensive introductions, *see* Fiske and Taylor 1991, 2008; Moskowitz 2005). Precisely because it is concerned with the interaction between multiple cognitive agents rather than individuals in isolation, social cognition is often taken to be more complex and multifaceted than cognition in general. It is explicitly and unashamedly mentalistic in nature, as the term 'cognitive' suggests. Indeed, its roots can be traced to the rise of **cognitive psychology**, which articulates a conception of the human mind as an information-processing system. Social cognition adopts this mentalistic approach and asks how it can be used to make sense of those around us. As such, it attempts to provide an account of how information is received, encoded, organized and otherwise used to mediate our social behaviour. It is, then, neither an empirical domain nor a particular theory. It is instead a conceptual approach to social psychology, in much the same way that **cognitive science** is (or, at least, can be seen as) a conceptual approach to psychology in general. Having said that, it is also often used in a looser sense (just as the term 'cognitive science' is) to refer to the psychology of social behaviour in general.

The scope of social cognition is thus extremely broad. It includes, for example, the study of prejudice, stereotypes, the judgment of others, the formation of impressions, and the mental representation of others and the self. This is, of course, just a small subset of possible topics, chosen to reflect the diversity of phenomena that can be studied under a social cognitive approach. Ultimately, any aspect of cognition that is not entirely egocentric is open to social cognitive research, as is the interaction of social traits with various aspects of individual cognition, for example, perception, personality, motivation, memory, and attention.

Pragmatics is therefore just one of many topics that might be approached from a social cognitive perspective. Nevertheless, the real-time interactivity that is inherent in most human **communication** makes it arguably the most social act we can engage in. It is thus no surprise that among the psychological phenomena that are most studied by social cognitive scientists are the very same ones that regularly appear in discussions of **pragmatic competence**. The most obvious example is **theory of mind**, but there are many others such as **intentionality**, **reference**, imitation, joint attention and gaze recognition. In fact, it is hard to think of social cognitive phenomena that are not relevant to pragmatics and communication in some way or other.

One historically popular avenue of social cognitive research is into the process of social categorization and how this can give rise to schemas – abstract, higher-order knowledge structures that specify the typical qualities of a particular stimulus type, and the relationships between those qualities. For example, when we think of a librarian a number of associated traits may come to mind, some by definition (works in a library), others more arbitrarily and perhaps less reliably (e.g. wears glasses). Once placed into these categories, individuals are often perceived to possess all the qualities associated with that group, even though many of those qualities will not have been used to diagnose their membership of the category. When shared across a social group, schemas can give rise to stereotypes, another popular and active area of study.

An example of how this approach can inform matters of linguistic interest is in the investigation of the Whorfian hypothesis (Whorf 1956b). This hypothesis can be read as a statement that the process of categorization and the creation of schemas are dependent in some important way on one's linguistic system. Another example is to consider linguistic development not only a matter of learning the names for certain classes of things, but also learning what those classes are in the first place. A third example, which is of most relevance to pragmatics, is to observe that the **cooperative principle** (Grice 1975) can be understood as just such a schema, as a generalization about the nature of intentional communication. It is then by making use of this **knowledge**, and an assumption that this schema is being adhered to, that listeners are able to converge upon the correct (that is, the intended) speaker **meaning**, and in doing so overcome the problem of linguistic underdeterminacy.

The later elaboration of **Grice**'s observations, by himself and others, took place, at least initially, largely within the domains of formal logic and the **philosophy of language**. This had the consequence that, at least in the eyes of those observers of a cognitive bent, it began to move 'away from common sense, away from psychological plausibility' (Sperber and Wilson 1995: 24). It was with this in mind that **relevance theory**, an explicitly cognitive theory of communication and pragmatics, was developed by Sperber and Wilson (1995). Other approaches have since followed (e.g. Bara, to appear; Pickering and Garrod 2004; Tomasello *et al.* 2005). These are sometimes contrasted with relevance theory, but that need not be the case. The enterprise of **cognitive pragmatics** (Bara, to appear), for example, couches itself as an alternative to relevance theory on the grounds that it emphasizes the interactive, social aspect of communication. However, the two approaches may be consonant with each other. Whether or not they are will turn on whether the individual cognitive traits posited by relevance theory can be shown to give rise to the social phenomena that are the focus of cognitive pragmatics theory. The term 'social cognition' is seldom mentioned in these discussions, and indeed in pragmatics more generally, but the research that all of these frameworks have stimulated could, for the most part, be classified and studied under such a banner. Conversely, most research that goes by the name of social cognition may not necessarily deal directly with communication, language and other matters of import to pragmatists, but much of it will nevertheless inform and appeal to those who consider such matters to be fundamentally social phenomena.

THOMAS C. SCOTT-PHILLIPS

See also: Autism spectrum disorders; cognitive pragmatics; cognitive psychology; cognitive science; communication; competence, pragmatic; inference; intention; intentionality; pragmatics; prelinguistic communication; reference; relevance theory; theory of mind; Wittgenstein, L.; word learning, the role of mindreading in

Suggestions for further reading

Fiske, S.T. and Taylor, S.E. (1991) *Social Cognition*, 2nd edn, New York: McGraw-Hill.
Moskowitz, G.B. (2005) *Social Cognition: Understanding Self and Others*, New York: Guilford Press.

Societal Pragmatics

Societal pragmatics is a **pragmatics** that explicitly relates to the societal conditions of the user (the user being the focal point of all pragmatic thinking; *see* Haberland and Mey 1977, 2002). The way we envision society will naturally have a strong influence on how we see a societal pragmatics; and hence the various definitions and also the interrelationships with other parts of pragmatics dealing with social issues will be subject to variation.

In this contribution, I will base myself on the notion that society is not just a conglomerate of individuals contracting some bonds of interaction which they then dub 'social' (in a 'Thatcherite' vein of thinking, one could even envision society as simply a superfluous superstructure on the individual relationships of family, work, personal interaction and so on). Compare Baroness Thatcher's famous quote: 'And, you know, there is no such thing as society. There are individual men and women, and there are families' (excerpt from an interview with Margaret Thatcher on 'Aids, Education and the Year 2000', *Woman's Own*, 3 October 1987, pp. 8–10).

Consequently, I will take my point of departure in society as an organized whole of users, whose placements are based on the relationships of production and consumption. I will mitigate the strict Marxist conception of class, as determined by these relations, by allowing for an extended view of the individual as determined not just by economic conditions but also by how he or she is placed in the societal discourse (a term borrowed from Michel Foucault 1966, 1972b). This placement, in a more contemporary view of class, is not only dependent on the material products that the worker brings forth; **knowledge**, in particular specialized knowledge and technological know-how, and in general educational credentials, can compensate for the lacking marketable assets that the worker would have to rely on in a strictly classical view of labour. A consideration of language as 'symbolic capital', as offered by Bourdieu (1982, 1986) or an extension of the notion of 'property' and 'product' in the sense of Max Weber (1978) is therefore appropriate to account for the shifting values of manual versus mental labour in our contemporary society (Macy 1998).

Individuals act dialectically upon society as a whole and upon other individuals, and they do this in virtue of their placement in the total web of social relations. These include, in addition to economic conditions, such personal attributes and affordances as education, consciousness, psychological make-up, personal interests; in other words, the entire life world of an individual, including not least the language he or she has at his or her disposal.

It is this latter aspect which is paramount in all reflection on societal pragmatics. In the spirit of Kant, an examination of the conditions that make language use, and in particular, a certain language use, possible is appropriate here. As an example, consider the well established theory of **speech acts**. The conditions for speech acting, as embodied in **Grice**'s **cooperative principle** (Grice 1975, 1978, 1981), have principally to do with the utterer of the words that embody the act in question. Mostly, the addressee is not mentioned at all, neither are the conditions that would determine proper reception, rather than correct production, of a particular act. In other words, the speech acts that we are considering are mainly 'speaker-centred'.

In contrast, a pragmatic view of speech acting would place the indexical centre, the 'origo' of these acts (Bühler 1934; Koyama 2009) in the common domain of addresser and addressee, the societal discourse. ('Origo' was first defined in the 1930s by the German psychologist Karl Bühler as the referential-indexical centre for **deixis**, understood as the way one refers linguistically to the personal, temporal, and other dimensions of a text, and symbolized in deictic expressions such as *he, she, now, then, there, yesterday*, etc.; Mey 2000).

A speech act such as ordering or promising can only be executed if the conditions for uttering and reacting to the utterance are in harmony with this **discourse**. A congratulation should not be uttered, and cannot be received, when the utterer's conditions are inappropriate (he or she not having the proper 'stance' for displaying this kind of empathy; *see* Heritage 2007), or if the receiver is unable to identify with the underlying **intention** because of what he or she perceives as a 'non-congratulatory' condition on his or her own part. The 'felicity conditions' for a well functioning speech act (Searle 1975b; but compare Goffman 1983: 53) are, so to speak, built into the societal discourse, rather than being found in the individual utterer.

In a more general way, these conditions can be called 'affordances', in the sense first defined by the visual psychologist James J. Gibson (1979; *see* Mey 2001: 220). By this I mean that for any activity to be successful, it has to be 'expected', not just in the sense that somebody is waiting for the act to be performed, but rather in a general sense: this particular kind of act is apposite in this particular discursive interaction. Conversely, once the societal conditions are appropriate, the shape of the particular act may vary widely. Thus, when we perform a speech act of offering condolences, what we actually say is of less importance as regards content (in the sense that it is more or less predictable), than is the framing of the act by which society has provided us with a 'template' for dealing with precisely these occasions.

The so-called 'indirect' speech acts are a prime example of this societal 'affordability'. It does not always matter *what* I say, or in which linguistic garb I clothe my speech act. When the discursive preparation (understood as the ensemble of societal affordances) is right, almost any utterance will have the potential of being accepted as adequate. I can think of dozens of ways to thank a person, or of asking him or her to open a window or allow passage on the bike path, on the street, or in the subway. While many of these ways are codified (linguistically and/or otherwise), they all crucially depend on the *situation* being there to 'carry' them, as Bourdieu has called it (1986: 79). The 'carrying wave' is represented by the societal affordances upon which and by which the individual utterances are 'modulated', are 'being carried', as Bourdieu expresses it.

This 'wave' is not to be interpreted deterministically, as if it were commandingly penetrating our language capacity in all its nooks and crannies. Rather, it is to be understood as the sum of all affordances that a particular situation, understood as the 'anchoring' of the interlocutors in societal reality (to use Koyama's (2009) felicitous metaphor) has to offer. But neither is the language user allowed to disregard the parameters of use that Bourdieu has termed the 'objective structures defining the social conditions' (1986: 78). Speech acting is a free choice: the user picks a suitable act in accordance with what he or she perceives as the relevant context. But the fact itself of speech acting, including the rights afforded and the limits set, is a matter of societal discern. When I choose to express my condolences by way of a 'written speech act' in the form of a greeting card, I am free to pick whatever I find suitable among the display at the local drug store (and usually I find very little, so I may prefer to make up my own). But the institution of 'offering condolences', either by voice or by some kind of other medium, is prescribed by the societal affordances; and the same goes for all kinds of speech acting, and in fact for all use of language.

Let me illustrate what I have said so far by appealing to the aforementioned notion of 'indirect speech act'. Here, I want to reiterate that properly speaking, and *pace* the philosophers, there are no isolated, 'naked' speech acts, but only speech acts 'dressed for the occasion', that is, as spoken in a particular situation. Such *situated* speech acts are dependent, for their interpretation, on the 'history' of the act, that is to say, not only on that which comes before, but also, and most importantly, on what comes after (in a 'retrospective' account). But without a conversational participant, without a situation, there is neither a 'before' nor an 'after'. This is why indirect speech acts are crucially dependent, not only on the *utterer's* intention, but on the interpretation that the *hearer* gives it *in the situation*, possibly involving a renewed exchange with the original utterer, as in the following Japanese example (adapted from Haugh 2007a):

A visitor to the Edo-Tokyo Museum is sitting down on a bench, and starts to unwrap a package of food. A museum attendant, upon seeing this, approaches the visitor and says:

> (Attendant) *Mooshiwake gozaimasen ... mooshiwake gozaimasen ...*
> ('I'm very sorry ... I'm very sorry ... ')
> (Visitor)   *A, ikenai?*
> ('Oh, it's not allowed?'; literally 'it doesn't go')
> (Attendant) *Mooshiwake gozaimasen ...*
> ('I'm very sorry')
>
> (Haugh 2007a: 86)

whereupon the visitor (having made the correct **inference** that eating and drinking is not allowed in the museum) quietly packs up and leaves the room.

Notice here that the expression *mooshiwake gozaimasen* ('I'm very sorry') has nothing to do with the actual situation as such; it is a very general, super-polite way of proffering an excuse or an **apology**. Uttering *mooshiwake gozaimasen*, the museum attendant makes no mention of any regulations or prohibitions with regard to the consumption of food and drink in a public place like a museum; no appeal is made to authority, sanctions, proper visitor behaviour, and the like. Yet, this 'indirect speech act' of warning/reminding/admonishing/prohibiting and so on is immediately (and correctly) taken up by the visitor, who interprets the actual utterance of 'apologizing' (Searle's 'primary illocution') as an indirect speech act of 'not allowing' (the 'secondary illocution' in Searle's terminology; Searle 1975b: 62; *cf.* Mey 2001:113).

In conclusion, I would like to underscore that societal pragmatics neither aspires to be a comprehensive theory of human social behaviour, nor asserts that its explanations should cover everything that linguists and pragmaticists over

the years have occupied themselves with in theory and practice. Rather, societal pragmatics offers a *perspective* on human linguistic behaviour (Haberland and Mey 1977, 2002; Verschueren 1987, 1999) which should be present in all our thinking about language and in our deliberations about its use. The prime and main concern of societal pragmatics should be the question that I raised more than twenty years ago: Whose language are we speaking, and whose voices are we listening to, when we engage in linguistic interaction? (Mey 1985).

JACOB L. MEY

See also: Austin, J.L.; cognitive pragmatics; conversation analysis; cooperative principle; deixis; discourse; Grice, H.P.; inference; inferential comprehension; intention; legal pragmatics; metapragmatics; pragma-dialectics; pragmatics; reference; refusals; Searle, J.; sociolinguistics; speech act theory; understatement; utterance interpretation

Suggestions for further reading

Gorayska, B. and Mey, J.L. (2004) *Cognition and Technology: Co-existence, Convergence, and Co-evolution*, Amsterdam and Philadelphia: John Benjamins.

Sohn-Rethel, A. (1978) *Intellectual and Manual Labour: A Critique of Epistemology*, London: Macmillan.

Thomas, J. (1996) *Meaning in Interaction: An Introduction to Pragmatics*, London: Longman.

Sociolinguistics

Sociolinguists aim to explain the relationship between language and society. This is a broad brief, covering all aspects of the relationship between linguistic variation and social variation (including attitudes to language), between language and social **context**, and between language and social meaning. The last of these is where the interests of sociolinguistics and **pragmatics** most obviously overlap, and it is this area that has burgeoned in the last two decades (Eckert 2002).

Early sociolinguistic studies focused on linguistic variation in multilingual communities (e.g. Gumperz 1958; Gumperz and Hymesymes 1964; Bright 1966) and explored the ways in which social categories and social contexts influence language choice. Gumperz's influential analyses of the socio-pragmatic significance of code-switching (Blom and Gumperz 1972; Gumperz 1978) provide an early example of the close links between sociolinguistics and pragmatics. The closely related area of the sociology of language, pioneered by Fishman (1968, 1972b), examined patterns of language maintenance and shift. Initially, this was among minority groups in the USA (Fishman 1966), but later extended to other societies (e.g. Fishman 1978; Clyne 1985; Janse and Tol 2003; Choi 2005), and to issues of societal multilingualism, language policy, and planning (e.g. Fishman 1978, 1983, 2000; Williams and Morris 2000; Ricento 2000; Wright 2003). The intersection of language and **culture** also attracted the attention of early sociolinguists, especially those with anthropological training (e.g. Hymes 1964b). Reflecting interest in non-Western cultures, ethnographic frameworks for language analysis took account not only of factors such as setting, channel, participants and **topic**, but also genre, message form, key (emotional tone), and act sequence (Hymes 1974; Saville-Troike 2003). These components could be regarded as enclosing the seeds of a socially-oriented pragmatics. Attention to the different functions of speech in different communities by these early sociolinguists also laid groundwork which later proved fruitful in pragmatics (Levinson 1979, 1983).

Social dialectology is another important strand of sociolinguistics. It initially engaged in extensive surveys describing the speech of urban centres in the USA (Labov 1966; Wolfram and Shuy 1974) and Britain (Trudgill 1974; Macauley and Trevelyan 1977; Milroy 1980), though soon extended worldwide. Although these continue to be central research areas in current sociolinguistics – they now also encompass the analysis and quantification of pragmatic or **discourse particles** such as *like* and *you know* (e.g. Holmes 1986b; Irwin 2000; Watt 2002), **discourse markers** (e.g. Cheshire 2007) and quotatives (e.g. Macaulay 2001; Tagliamonte and D'Arcy 2004) – they will not be discussed further in this article, which focuses on the more obvious area of the intersection of sociolinguistics and pragmatics.

A distinction can be made between the analysis of the **meaning** of utterances in interaction (pragmatics), and the examination of the distribution of particular patterns identified in such analyses by sociolinguists. Pragmatics is concerned with developing criteria for identifying what counts as a **compliment**, a **refusal**, a **complaint** or a **hedge** and a booster, while sociolinguists are more interested in the distribution of such **speech acts** and forms among different social groups, for example, by **gender**, social class, ethnic group, and so on (e.g. Johnson and Roen 1992; Holmes 1995; Ruhi 2002; Lauwereyns 2002). But while some research can usefully be classified in this way, boundaries are never so neat. This has been especially apparent in the areas of **politeness** research and **cross-cultural pragmatics**.

The development within pragmatics of theories of politeness has offered many insights into the differing ways in which people use **discourse** in context, and into the reasons why discourse is not consistently brief, truthful, relevant, and clear (Brown and Levinson 1987). Early work in pragmatics was undertaken largely by philosophers (Searle 1969; Grice 1975) using artificially constructed, de-contextualised utterances. While these served well to explore the logical constraints on inferring meaning, sociolinguists quickly pointed to the importance of social context, as well as the contribution of the larger discourse context in interpreting the social meaning of an utterance. The analysis of **classroom discourse**, for example, illustrated the relevance of the institutional context, of **power** relations, and of the type of talk in which participants were engaged to understanding the pragmatic meaning of an utterance (Sinclair and Coulthard 1975; Stubbs 1983a). More recently, analyses of **institutional discourse** which engage with issues of power and politeness in workplace interaction further demonstrate the crucial importance of integrating social dimensions into pragmatic analyses in more sophisticated ways (Candlin 2002; Holmes and Stubbe 2003b; Harris 2003; Locher 2004). This predominantly qualitative research conceptualizes power as social practice, dynamic and contestable, and negotiated in social interaction. The illustrative analytical material ranges from law courts, through radio interviews to workplace meetings and business transaction.

These studies take the position that linguistic politeness is culturally determined, hence, rules for polite behaviour differ from one speech community to another. Different speech communities express particular speech functions or speech acts differently: greetings, gratitude, compliments, insults, refusals, **requests**, complaints, terms of address, and so on. Norms for social interaction also differ. Cross-cultural research has thus benefited from the insights of pragmatic and sociolinguistic analysis. While some researchers describe the communicative norms of particular (usually non-Western) groups (e.g. Tanaka 2000; Yi 2002; Okada 2006; Cao 2007), others explicitly identify areas of potential miscommunication between people from different socio-cultural backgrounds. With this goal, Gumperz (1982a, 1982b, 1996) developed 'interactional sociolinguistics', a framework which pays particular attention to the linguistic and non-linguistic clues which account for how people use conversational inferencing to interpret conversational interaction within its ethnographic context. He and his colleagues have explored in depth the problems facing minority group members in the process of attempting to obtain employment, or trying to access the social benefits to which they are entitled (Gumperz *et al.* 1979; Gumperz and Roberts 1991; Roberts *et al.* 1992; Campbell and Roberts 2007).

Critical Discourse Analysis (CDA) is another approach which provides analyses of interest to sociolinguists since it is concerned with investigating how language is used to construct and maintain power relationships in society. It is also concerned to uncover the hidden relationships between language and ideology (van Dijk 1998a; Thornborrow 2002; Fairclough 2003), that is, how discourse may prop up a particular view of 'reality'. So, for example, a CDA approach focuses on the ways in which lexical choices such as *riot* versus *protest* versus *demonstration*, or *hooligans* versus *protestors* versus *demonstrators* subtly convey different ideological positions and different political sympathies (Lee 1992). **Discourse analysis** is thus another area which clearly overlaps with pragmatics, since analysing discourse is precisely how researchers in pragmatics identify the social meanings encoded in language in interaction.

The intersection of sociolinguistic and pragmatic research is a paradigmatic case of the fruitful integration or intertwining of quantitative and qualitative research. Sociolinguists traditionally use a range of methods to collect large quantities of data, for example, surveys, questionnaires, interviews, etc. However, an examination of the contents of recent issues of the core journals in sociolinguistics, *Language in Society* and the *Journal of Sociolinguistics*, indicates that sociolinguists' interests and methods have broadened considerably over the last twenty years. Work such as Cheshire's (2007) analysis of the social class distribution, as well as the pragmatic functions, of general extenders such as *and stuff, or something* in the speech of British teenagers, illustrates clearly that the two types of analysis are increasingly intertwined.

The extensive impact of social constructionist approaches has similarly resulted in further integration of pragmatic and sociolinguistic analyses. In 1995, Thomas characterised sociolinguists as interested in the way language '*reflects* social relations', while pragmaticists, she suggested, were concerned with 'the way people use language in order to change or maintain social relationships' (J. Thomas 1995: 132). Sociolinguists describe the individual's sociolinguistic repertoire and resources, and the systematic contextual constraints which operate on language use; pragmaticists describe how those resources are used in interaction (J. Thomas 1995: 185–89). The distinction that Thomas makes is, however, steadily eroding. Since 1995, research undertaken by people who identify as sociolinguists, and who publish in sociolinguistics journals, examines the way people use language dynamically to signal and negotiate different facets of their social identity in relation to others in particular contexts (e.g. Eckert and McConnell-Ginet 1995; Holmes 1997; Schilling-Estes 2004; Kiesling 2005; Holmes and Schnurr 2006; O'Hanlon 2006; Burkette 2007). Rather than defining people by assigned group membership, a more dynamic approach describes how certain socio-pragmatic, discursive and linguistic choices 'index' (Ochs 1992, 1996) or culturally encode social categories such as gender through their association with particular roles, activities, traits, and stances (Cameron and Kulick 2003, 2006). These sociolinguistic indices are then available to emphasise particular aspects of social identity in different contexts (e.g. McElhinney 1995, 2003; Meyerhoff 1999; Hall 2003). So a female manager may express herself drawing on normatively feminine linguistic features while discussing office furnishings, but make use of features indexing an authoritative, normatively masculine, or a mature stance, when dealing with a confrontational challenge in a meeting (Holmes 2006; Holmes and Schnurr 2006).

The most recent field to emerge from the cross-fertilisation of sociolinguistics and pragmatics is variational pragmatics. This sub-discipline is committed to challenging the assumption that language communities of native speakers constitute homogeneous entities, and to exploring the impact of factors such as region, social class, gender, age, and ethnicity on communicative language use in context (Schneider and Barron 2005a; Wolfram and Schilling-Estes 2006: 93–101). Variational pragmatics identifies five levels of pragmatic analysis, ranging through forms (e.g. discourse markers, hedges), speech acts, discourse sequences (e.g. openings), topic, and turn-taking patterns (Schneider 2001; Barron 2005; Schneider and Barron 2005a). Research to date includes both qualitative and quantitative studies (Schneider and Barron 2005b), analyzing material of direct interest to both sociolinguists and pragmaticists.

Sociolinguistics is concerned with 'unraveling the theoretical significance of language variation' (Coupland 2001: 3), and in the process sociolinguists have provided valuable theories of language change, social variation in speech communities, social networks, ways of speaking, social context, interpersonal relations, the role of inferencing in **intercultural communication**, and much more. These theoretical concepts have increasingly impinged on concepts in pragmatic theory, as this entry has illustrated. An adequate sociolinguistic theory provides a motivated account of the way language is used in a community, and of the choices people make when they use language. This inevitably involves consideration of pragmatic as well as linguistic features, and pragmatic as well as social factors or dimensions, as discussions of sociolinguistic theory indicate (Figueroa 1994; Coupland 2001). Thus, we can expect sociolinguists to continue to explore the implications of pragmatic theories

and concepts within a range of socio-cultural contexts, with benefits for both disciplines.

JANET HOLMES

See also: Apologies; applied linguistics; competence, communicative; competence, pragmatic; compliments; complaints; context; conversation; conversational turn-taking; conversation analysis; cooperative principle; cross-cultural pragmatics; disagreement; discourse; discourse analysis; discourse markers; discourse particles; ethnomethodology; gender; Grice, H.P.; hedge; honorific language; humour; inference; intercultural communication; maxims of conversation; misunderstanding; phatic communication; politeness; political discourse; power; refusals; relevance theory; request; Searle, J; speech act theory; stylistics; topic

Suggestions for further reading

Clyne, M. (2006) 'Some thoughts on pragmatics, sociolinguistic variation, and intercultural communication', *Intercultural Pragmatics*, 3: 95–105.
Coupland, N. (2001) 'Introduction: sociolinguistic theory and social theory', in N. Coupland, S. Sarangi and C.N. Candlin (eds) *Sociolinguistics and Social Theory*, Harlow: Pearson.
Gumperz, J.J. (ed.) (1982) *Language and Social Identity*, Cambridge: Cambridge University Press.

Specificity

The term 'specificity' is commonly used in the literature on the **semantics** and **pragmatics** of indefinite noun phrases. Noun phrases are categorized with respect to **definiteness** versus **indefiniteness** and indefinite noun phrases are further categorized with respect to specificity. Specificity with indefinites encompasses at least three separate phenomena: scopal specificity, epistemic specificity, and partitivity (Farkas 1994, 2002a).

Scopal specificity is defined in terms of the indefinite's interpretation outside the scope of an operator, such as an intensional verb, a modal, or **negation** (Dahl 1970; Ioup 1977; Karttunen

1976). Thus, the indefinite in (1) and (2) is ambiguous between scopally specific and non-specific readings, with the continuations in (a) and (b) disambiguating in favour of one of the readings. Specificity on this view is equated with wide scope (1a, 2a).

(1) Sarah would like to read a book about butterflies …
   a. … but she can't find it.
   [scopally specific]
   b. … but she can't find one.
   [scopally non-specific]
(2) Amanda did not buy a yellow shirt …
   a. … because she didn't like it.
   [scopally specific]
   b. … because the store sold only green ones. [scopally non-specific]

Further, indefinites exhibit exceptional scope-taking behaviour. Unlike quantificational phrases, indefinites are able to escape scope islands such as *if*-clauses and *that*-clauses (Fodor and Sag 1982), as in (3a), while also allowing intermediate scope, above the island but below a higher quantifier (Abusch 1994; Farkas 1981; Ruys 1992), as in (3b). Indefinites are not restricted to readings inside the scope island (3c). Many analyses have treated such long-distance indefinites as (3a) and (3b) in terms of choice functions: the determiner is translated into a variable that ranges over choice functions, which map any non-empty set in their domain to a member of this set (Chierchia 2001; Kratzer 1998; Matthewson 1999; Reinhart 1997; Schwarz 2001; Winter 1997). On this view, scopal specificity becomes equivalent to a choice function interpretation. On an alternative approach, Schwarzschild (2002) analyzes long-distance indefinites as indefinites with an implicit **domain restriction**.

(3) Every student read every book that a professor had recommended.
   a. paraphrase of the widest-scope reading of the indefinite:
   There is a particular professor, such that every student read every book recommended by that professor.
   b. paraphrase of the intermediate scope reading of the indefinite:

For every student X, there is a particular professor Y, such that X read every book that Y had recommended [professors co-vary with students]
   c. paraphrase of the narrow scope reading of the indefinite:
   Every student read every book that was recommended by some professor or other [professors co-vary with books]

A phenomenon closely related to, but distinct from, scopal specificity is epistemic specificity, also known as identifiability, speaker **knowledge**, and referentiality (Farkas 1994, 2002a; Fodor and Sag 1982; Groenendijk and Stokhof 1980; Ioup 1977; Jayez and Tovena 2006). An epistemically specific (referential) indefinite makes **reference** to an entity that is known by the speaker and/or inherently identifiable (Farkas 2002b), as in (4a) versus (4b). Formal accounts of epistemic specificity in different frameworks include Groenendijk and Stokhof (1980), Farkas (2002b), and von Heusinger (2002). Epistemic specificity is closely linked to scopal specificity in that some semantic analyses of long-distance indefinites make reference to epistemic specificity (Fodor and Sag 1982; Kratzer 1998). However, other analyses of scopal specificity do not involve epistemic specificity (Reinhart 1997; Winter 1997).

(4) a. A student cheated on the exam. It was the guy who sits in the very back.
   [epistemically specific, identifiable]
   b. A student cheated on the exam. I wonder which student it was.
   [epistemically non-specific, unidentifiable]

Many accounts of both scopal and epistemic specificity discuss *a/an*-indefinites in English, arguing for **ambiguity** between specific and non-specific readings (Fodor and Sag 1982; Kratzer 1998; Reinhart 1997), as in (1) through (4). There is also much literature on indefinites cross-linguistically which are unambiguously specific or non-specific. In English, much attention has been given to both scopal and epistemic specificity of *a certain*-indefinites (Farkas 2002b; Hintikka 1986; Schwarz 2001; Jayez and Tovena 2006 on *un certain* in French) as in (5).

Additionally, *some*-indefinites as in (6) are treated as epistemically non-specific (Becker 1999; Farkas 1994, 2002b), and *this*-indefinites as in (7) as epistemically specific (Ionin 2006).

(5) Sarah would like to read a certain book about butterflies, but she can't find it/#one.
(6) Susan rented some movie for us to watch yesterday. #It was *The Maltese Falcon.*

(Farkas 2002b)

(7) Mary wants to see this new movie. #I wonder which movie it is.

(Ionin 2006)

Cross-linguistically, scopal (non-)specificity been shown to play a role in the nominal systems of Lillouet Salish (Matthewson 1999), West Greenlandic (van Geenhoven 1996), and Hungarian (Farkas 1997), as in (8), among other languages. On the basis of cross-linguistic data, Farkas (2002a) proposes a scale for scopal specificity, from widest-scope to incorporated nominals (Farkas and de Swart 2003). Epistemic (non-) specificity has been shown to be relevant for the nominal systems of a number of languages, including Hebrew (Givón 1981; Borer 2005; see discussion in Ionin 2006), Russian (Haspelmath 1997; Kagan 2007), as in (9), and Sissala (Blass 1990). For an overview of relevant cross-linguistic data, *see* Haspelmath (1997) and Lyons (1999).

(8) Hungarian, from Farkas (2002b)
  a. Minden gyerek látott   egy-egy filmet.
     every   child   see.Past a-a   movie.Acc
     'Every child saw a movie.' [obligatory narrow scope of the indefinite]
  b. Minden gyerek látott   egy filmet.
     every   child   see.Past a   movie.Acc
     'Every child saw a movie.' [either wide or narrow scope reading of the indefinite]
(9) Russian, from Kagan (2007)
  #Ja xochu vyjti zamuzh za   kakogo-to
  I   want marry-Inf to   some
  shveda.
  Swede.
  '#I want to marry some Swede.' [epistemic non-specificity]

Most of the discussion of scopal and epistemic specificity concerns indefinites. While epistemic specificity (referentiality) has also been discussed with regard to definites (Donnellan 1966; Kaplan 1978; Stalnaker 1970), the case for the existence of specific versus non-specific definites is less persuasive than that for specific versus non-specific indefinites (Heim 1991). Lyons (1999) reports that while many languages use determiners to mark (scopal and/or epistemic) specificity on indefinites, as shown in (5) through (9), no language is known to do so for definites.

A rather different view of specificity is one that treats it as partitivity or presuppositionality (Enç 1991; Diesing 1992). Unlike definiteness, which (on some analyses) is associated with **presuppositions** of uniqueness and existence (Heim 1991), partitivity is associated with a presupposition of existence only, as shown in (10). Presuppositional/partitive indefinites include overt partitives in English (de Hoop 2003b) as in (10b) and accusative-case-marked indefinites in Turkish (Enç 1991; but Kelepir 2001 argues for an alternative analysis in terms of choice functions). A closely related phenomenon is D-linking with wh-phrases (Pesetsky 1987, 2000). D-linked wh-phrases such as *which student* presuppose the existence of a relevant set, as shown in (11).

(10) a. The professor came to the party. #The other professors did not.
        [presupposes the existence of a unique, salient professor]
     b. One of the professors came to the party. The other professors did not.
        [presupposes the existence of a salient set of professors]
(11) a. Who did you meet? [non-D-linked wh-phrase does not presuppose the existence of a particular set of people]
     b. Which student did you meet? [D-linked wh-phrase presupposes the existence of a relevant set of students]

Diesing (1992), following observations in Milsark (1974, 1977), argues that *a*-indefinites and *some*-indefinites in English are ambiguous between presuppositional (strong, quantificational, specific) and non-presuppositional (weak, cardinal, non-specific) readings, as shown in (12). The status of an indefinite NP as presuppositional or not has consequences for such syntactic phenomena as occurrence in *there*-constructions and scrambling (Diesing 1992) (for instance, the indefinite in (12a) is obligatorily non-presuppositional). An alternative view treats indefinites as unambiguously non-presuppositional, and attributes the existence presupposition to sentence-level phenomena like topic-focus configurations (Reinhart 1995) (for instance in (12b), *some ghosts* is a contrastive topic). A number of other accounts also link specificity (epistemic or partitive) to presuppositionality (Geurts 2002) or topicality (Prince 1981a; Endriss 2006). The question is still open as to whether the different types of specificity with indefinites can be subsumed under a single approach to specificity, or constitute entirely separate phenomena (Farkas 2002a).

(12) From Diesing (1992)
   a. There are some ghosts in my house. [non-presuppositional, asserts the existence of ghosts]
   b. SOME ghosts are in the pantry; the others are in the attic. [presuppositional, presupposes the existence of ghosts]

Specificity of all three types has been examined in language acquisition studies. Following Bickerton (1981), specificity was argued to play a role in the acquisition of English articles by both first language learners (Cziko 1986) and second language learners (Huebner 1983; Master 1987; Thomas 1989). While early acquisition work did not distinguish between scopal and epistemic specificity, more recent work has examined the effects of scopal specificity in **child language acquisition** (Schaeffer and Matthewson 2005) and scopal versus epistemic specificity in **second language acquisition** (Ionin *et al.* 2004). Specificity as partitivity has also been examined with regard to article use both by children (Schafer and de Villiers 2000; Wexler, to appear) and adults (Ko *et al.* 2006). The relationship between presuppositionality and scrambling has been examined in both child language acquisition (Krämer 2000; Ketrez 2005; Schaeffer 2000) and second language acquisition (Unsworth 2005). An issue that has received much attention is whether young children's errors with articles and nominal scrambling (such as overuse of *the* in a partitive indefinite context, as in (13))

stem from pragmatic difficulties, such as an incompletely developed **theory of mind** (Maratsos 1976; Karmiloff-Smith 1979; Krämer 2000; Schaeffer 2000; Schaeffer and Matthewson 2005), or whether they stem from the semantic effects of specificity (Matthewson *et al.* 2001; Wexler, to appear). Much progress has been made, but much work remains to be done on how specificity in its different forms influences the course of language development across different ages and types of populations.

(13) From Maratsos (1976) (shortened):

Story: Once there was a lady. She had lots of girls and boys, about *four girls and three boys*. One of them started laughing and giggling. Let's see. Who was laughing and giggling like that? – Children's response: *The boy* (or: *The girl*)

TANIA IONIN

See also: Ambiguity; assertion; child language acquisition; context; definiteness; deixis; demonstratives; development, pragmatic; discourse; domain restriction; given/new distinction; implicature; indefiniteness; maxims of conversation; pragmatics; presupposition; reference; second language acquisition; semantics; semantics-pragmatics interface; theory of mind; topic

Suggestions for further reading

Farkas, D. (2002) 'Specificity distinctions', *Journal of Semantics*, 19: 213–43.
Ionin, T. (2006) '*This* is definitely specific: specificity and definiteness in article systems', *Natural Language Semantics*, 14: 175–234.
Lyons, C. (1999) *Definiteness*, Cambridge: Cambridge University Press.

Speech Act Theory

Over the past fifty years, work within speech act theory (Austin 1962; Bach and Harnish 1979; Searle 1969, 1979b) has been some of the most influential in the development of modern **pragmatics**. Insights from this framework continue to shape the discipline today. Before looking at the central tenets of the theory, it is worth briefly considering the philosophical backdrop against which it came into being.

In the early and mid-twentieth century, the most common approach to analytic **philosophy of language** was 'ideal' language philosophy. This was a highly formal approach, which explored natural language using logical and mathematical languages such as propositional logic and predicate calculus. The main protagonists of this approach included Bertrand Russell, Gottlob Frege, Alfred Tarski and later the 'logical positivists' led by Rudolf Carnap. Central to ideal language philosophy were the notions of truth, falsity and truth conditions. A truth-conditional theory of **meaning** takes it that the meaning of a sentence amounts to a specification of the conditions under which that sentence is true. The idea sounds unintuitive, but can be clearly illustrated. Consider the statement in (1):

(1) Dogs can fly.

If you know the meaning of this sentence, you know that the (albeit unlikely) conditions which have to obtain for it to be true is that dogs have to be able to fly. Truth-conditional semanticists argue that knowing the meaning of that sentence *just is* knowing the truth conditions, and that by specifying the truth conditions of a sentence, you therefore capture the essence of its meaning. Consider sentence (2). What are the truth conditions of this sentence?

(2) Os cães podem voar.

If you don't speak Portuguese, you won't know the truth conditions. You might argue, well of course I don't, because I don't know what it means. But truth-conditional semanticists argue in the other direction. You don't know what it means, they claim, because you don't know the truth conditions.

Carnap's logical positivists took the ideal language approach to surprising extremes (see, for example, Ayer 1936). In effect, they suggested that if there was no way of working out whether a particular sentence was true or not (or, in their terms, 'verifying' it), that sentence was meaningless. Thereafter, the logical positivists set about the task of purifying philosophy by sifting out a number of claims that, on their principle of

verifiability, came out as meaningless. Many ethical statements – statements such as 'X is good' or 'Y is bad' – came out either as having no meaning at all or as having a very different sort of meaning from what had previously been thought. The meaning of 'x is good', as uttered by a particular speaker, might, for instance, reduce to the statement 'I like X' or 'I approve of X', either of which could then be tested for truth or falsity.

In the 1940s and 1950s, a group of philosophers at Oxford began to question this method. They felt that rather than shedding light on the crucial features of language, this method obscured them. Instead of studying 'ideal' languages, they wanted to study 'ordinary' language, and they became known as the ordinary language philosophers. Among this group, we might single out John **Austin**, Peter Strawson, J. Urmson and H. Paul **Grice**. Although he was at Cambridge, and it is unlikely that the Oxonians knew much about his work, Ludwig **Wittgenstein** had come to similar conclusions in his *Philosophical Investigations* (1958).

The basic idea behind speech act theory is that while the formal approach to the philosophy of language can tell you all sorts of things about sentence meaning, it misses one major fact about language. It misses the fact that to use language is *to do* something – that when we speak, we are performing actions. Austin's response to the logical positivists was this. You can't reduce meaning to truth because many sentences both in the language of philosophy and in everyday language aren't *intended* to be true or false. Approaching them from the perspective of truth is therefore to misunderstand what they are doing.

There are some varieties of sentence that are obvious candidates for the kind of thing Austin had in mind. Consider (3) and (4) below:

(3) Would you like another cup of coffee?
(4) Leave me alone.

How could we say, for instance, whether a **question** (such as the one in (3)), or an order (such as the one in (4)), are true or false? But Austin pointed out that as well as these kinds of sentences, there was trouble amongst the declarative sentences on which all truth-conditional theories thrive. He claimed that there were a number of declarative sentences that, just as with questions and orders, don't lend themselves to being analyzed in terms of truth and falsity. Examples (5) to (8) are examples from Austin's posthumously published book *How to Do Things with Words* (1962: 5):

(5) 'I do (take this woman to be my lawful wedded wife)' – as uttered in the course of the marriage ceremony.

(6) 'I name this ship the *Queen Elizabeth*' – as uttered when smashing the bottle against the stern.

(7) 'I give and bequeath my watch to my brother' – as occurring in a will.

(8) 'I bet you sixpence it will rain tomorrow.'

And here is what Austin (1962: 6) had to say about them:

In these examples it seems clear that to utter the sentence (in, of course, the appropriate circumstances) is not to *describe* my doing of what I should be said in so uttering to be doing or to state that I am doing it: it is to do it. None of the utterances cited is either true or false: I assert this as obvious and do not argue it … To name the ship *is* to say 'I name etc.'. When I say, before the registrar or altar, etc. 'I do', I am not reporting on a marriage: I am indulging in it.

Austin called sentences/utterances such as those in (5) to (8) *performative* utterances, and contrasted them with sentences/utterances that *do* describe states of affairs in the world, which he called *constatives*. Consider (9) and (10) and note how they compare with Austin's previous examples (6) and (7):

(9) Yesterday evening, in a moving ceremony, the Queen named the ship *Queen Elizabeth*.

(10) I gave my brother a lovely watch for Christmas.

An utterance of (9) *describes* (to use Austin's term) or reports a particular state of affairs (the state of affairs that on a particular evening, in a moving ceremony, the Queen named a particular ship).

This can be contrasted directly with (6), which doesn't describe the naming: it *is* the act of naming. An utterance of (10) describes the state of affairs in which 'I' gave 'my brother' a watch as a Christmas gift. This can be contrasted with (7), which doesn't describe an act of giving, it *is* an act of giving (or bequeathing). The acts in question Austin called *speech acts*, hence the expressions 'speech act theory' and '**speech act types**'.

Whilst denying that sentences such as those in (5)–(8) could be analyzed in term of truth conditions, Austin did recognize that there were certain conditions that had to hold if the act that is being performed is to be performed successfully. If, whilst strolling along the harbour front in the early hours of the morning, I utter (6) and swing an empty champagne bottle against the stern of a boat moored nearby, I have hardly succeeded in naming that boat. In order to carry out the act of naming a boat or ship, it is required that I have a certain authority invested in me.

In order for a performative utterance to 'work', then, there are conditions that have to be met. Austin called these *felicity conditions* – the set of conditions that must be in place for the act in question to come off successfully (Austin (1962: 12) called successful performatives 'happy performatives'). He distinguished three main categories. In the first category, felicity conditions might include the presence of a conventional procedure which, in appropriate circumstances, and in the presence of appropriate people, has some kind of conventional effect. In the second category of felicity conditions, the procedure must be carried out correctly and completely. The third and final category noted that felicity conditions often rely on the people involved in the speech act having the thoughts, **intentions** and feelings required by the procedure. If the correct felicity conditions were not present, or were present but failed to be observed in some way, it might result in a *misfire* or an *abuse*. In the case of a misfire, the whole act fails to come off – if the man uttering (5) is already married, for example. In the case of an abuse, the act comes off but only in some way insincerely – if the man uttering (5) intends to run off with the maid-of-honour immediately after the ceremony, for example (*see* Levinson 1983).

The first two thirds or so of Austin's book examines ways in which the constative/performative distinction might be maintained. Are there, for example, grammatical or syntactic criteria by means of which performatives can be identified? Can they be distinguished from constatives on purely linguistic grounds? Austin concludes that there are no grammatical or syntactic properties by means of which performatives can be identified, and looks for an explanation as to why this is the case. He divides performatives into two classes: *explicit performatives* (in sentences such as (6) and (8), which contain explicitly performative verbs such as 'name' and 'bet') and *implicit performatives* (such as those in sentences (11)–(13)):

(11) I'll come to your party. (Uttered as a promise)
(12) There's a bull in that field. (Uttered as a warning)
(13) A fiver says it'll lose! (Uttered extending the hand offering to make a bet)

Austin proceeds with a two-stage argument. In the first stage of the argument, he suggests it should be possible to distinguish between performative and non-performative verbs: all you need to look for is a particular kind of asymmetry between the first person singular of the present tense and all other persons and tenses. Using this criterion, it should be possible to go through a dictionary listing all verbs with this particular characteristic. Then, in the second stage of the argument, Austin suggests that all implicit performative utterances (such as those in (11) to (13) above) might be capable of being paraphrased as utterances containing explicit performative verbs. This would provide an explanation of how it is that performatives come in such a variety of linguistic shapes.

So far so good. But anyone who has read *How to Do Things with Words* knows that the story contains a twist. Beneath the painstaking argument taking place on the surface there is considerable guile, even cunning. At this point in the book, Austin plays his trump card, and the argument takes a seismic shift. Having introduced the distinction between constative and performative sentences/utterances, and having used the latter as an argument against ideal language philosophy, Austin decides that actually there is *no* systematic way to work out which utterances are performative and which are constative. Moreover, he suggests that the distinction should be dropped! Once the distinction is dropped, however, it becomes clear that Austin's real claim is that *all* utterances, not just the ones that he has called performatives, are used to perform speech acts. All sentences/utterances are performatives in some way.

Austin goes on to distinguish three main types of speech act that are performed when someone says something. The first of these is the *locutionary act*. This is the act of saying something. Saying 'there is a bull in that field' is to perform a locutionary act (the notion is parallel to the semantic notion of the **proposition** expressed, or Grice's **what is said** (Grice 1989)). The second type of act is the *illocutionary act*. This is the act performed *in* saying something. So in saying 'there is a bull in that field', I might be warning you. Other illocutionary acts include asserting, complaining, apologizing, commanding, requesting, threatening, suggesting, etc. The third type of speech act is the *perlocutionary act*. The perlocutionary act is the act performed *by* saying something. So, by saying 'there is a bull in that field', I may frighten you. The perlocutionary act is one that results in an actual effect on the hearer: misleading him, embarrassing him, amusing him, convincing him of something, persuading him to do something.

Post Austin, the main concern of speech act theorists has been with illocutionary acts. John **Searle**, who was a student of Austin at Oxford, picked up the baton on Austin's premature death in 1960. His 1969 book *Speech Acts* is an attempt to integrate the speech act framework within a modern linguistic theory. Without Searle, speech act theory would arguably still be a subject only taught on philosophy courses, as opposed to courses on linguistics and pragmatics. In his later work *Expression and Meaning*, Searle suggested a range of problems with the original taxonomy of illocutionary acts that Austin presented and provided his own classificatory system. Searle proposed five classes of speech act – representatives (speech acts such as asserting), commissives (promising and swearing), expressives (thanking and congratulating), directives (requesting or suggesting) and declarations (appointing) – and developed three main principles by which these classes could be differentiated. Searle also developed considerably

Austin's notion of felicity conditions. His work is hugely important.

Speech act theory does not provide all the answers, but as with other important contributions to linguistic theory, it enables us to ask new questions. According to one, radical interpretation of **ordinary language philosophy**, the study of meaning cannot be divorced from the study of language use. Construed in this way, speech act theory is an *alternative* to the kind of formal approach advocated by ideal language philosophers. Notice in the extended Austin quote above that he appears to use the terms 'sentence' and 'utterance' interchangeably. This was because at the time he wrote those words the modern distinction between sentences and utterances, or **semantics** and pragmatics, did not exist. A more moderate interpretation would be that speech act theory might be able to *supplement* formal semantics. Put differently, while Austin's intention was to say that the study of semantics is, in effect, better construed as the study of pragmatics, the real contribution of speech act theory was to confirm that when it comes to the study of meaning, there are different levels to consider. In the late 1960s, the work of H.P. Grice, himself one kind of ordinary language philosopher (albeit an atypical one), suggested ways in which the work of the formalists and the speech act theorists might finally be reconciled.

TIM WHARTON

See also: Apologies; assertion; Austin, J.L.; command; complaints; conversation; evidentials; explicit/implicit distinction; Grice, H.P.; meaning; ordinary language philosophy; philosophy of language; pragmatics; proposition; request; Searle, J.; semantics-pragmatics interface; speech act type; truth-conditional/non-truth-conditional meaning; what is said; Wittgenstein, L.

Suggestions for further reading

Austin, J. (1962) *How to Do Things with Words*, Oxford: Clarendon Press; 2nd edn 1980, Oxford: Oxford University Press.
Levinson, S. (1983) *Pragmatics*, Cambridge: Cambridge University Press.

Searle, J. (1965) 'What is a speech act?', in M. Black (ed.) *Philosophy in America*, London: Allen and Unwin.

Speech Act Type

At a preliminary stage of a scientific study of some family of phenomena, it seems natural to devise a taxonomy of these phenomena, a division of all of them into classes that are collectively exhaustive and mutually exclusive. A simple example is the classification of animals into species. Animals are obviously different from each other. Every animal belongs to some species and no animal belongs to two species.

Speech acts are no exception. At an early stage of their systematic study during the twentieth century, philosophers, who studied them more than scholars of other disciplines, introduced taxonomies of speech acts. The first taxonomy was introduced by J.L. **Austin** in his seminal book *How to Do Things with Words* (1962), which includes lectures delivered at Harvard University in 1955, on the basis of views formed in 1939. Austin (1962: 150–51) described the following classes of speech act: *Verdictives*, 'typified by the giving of a verdict'; *Exercitives*, such as 'appointing, voting … advising, warning'; *Commissives*, 'typified by … undertaking; they commit you to doing something'; *Behabitives*, which are 'a very miscellaneous group, and have to do with attitudes and social behaviour. Examples are apologizing, congratulating … '; and *Expositives*, which 'are difficult to define. They make plain how our utterances fit into the course of an argument or conversation … Examples are: "I reply", "I argue", "I concede" … '. Austin himself found the last two classes 'most troublesome'.

Searle discussed the weaknesses in Austin's taxonomy and presented an alternative one: *Assertives, Directives, Commissives, Expressives* and *Declarations* (Searle 1975a). Searle's taxonomy is an improvement on Austin's taxonomy, not because the classes are more sharply delineated and none are 'most troublesome'. Searle's taxonomy is a significant advancement in the study of speech acts, because it rests on a rich and quite clear conceptual framework rather than on a broad variety of intuitions. Searle's taxonomy rests on a list of significant dimensions of difference between speech acts. Major examples are:

(1) Differences in the point of speech acts of a type. Every speech act is intentional, done for a purpose. A speech act type determines the type of purposes served by using speech acts of that type. The purpose of a promise is to create and undertake an obligation on the part of the speaker. The point of an **assertion** is to represent a fact.

(2) Differences in the direction of fit between words and the world. In assertion, the words used should, roughly speaking, fit the given world, while in **commands** the world should be changed in order to fit the words.

(3) Differences in the expressed psychological states. For example, a **request** expresses a desire, while an **apology** expresses regret.

(4) Differences in the strength with which the point of the speech act is presented. For example, 'I suggest that so and so' is weaker than 'I insist that so and so'.

The importance of Searle's list of differences is that it enables us to make a significant step beyond his taxonomy. It is a step towards a systematic answer to the major theoretical question: What is a speech act type? To take the differences (1)–(4) as examples, the emerging theory of speech acts says a speech act is an intentional act, done with words, that has a certain point (1), a certain direction of fit (2), is an expression of a certain psychological state (3), and has a certain strength (4). Searle and Vanderveken (1985) and Vanderveken (1990) have systematically presented answers to that major theoretical question, along similar lines. An additional theoretical insight gained in these studies is that 'there are a rather limited number of basic things we do with language' (Searle 1975a: 29).

Kasher (1977) claimed that a specification of a speech act type should consist of all conceptual components of an intentional act, namely ends and means, roles and products.

Ends: A speech act of assertion manifests the speaker's purpose at the **context** of utterance to represent a fact. Sentences, as used in performance of speech acts in given contexts of utterance, are means that can be used by speakers in pursuit of their purposes.

Means: There are many sentences that can be used in posing a **question** as to the way from where the speaker is to where the speaker wants to be, such as *How do I get to Jerusalem Street?*, *What is the way to Jerusalem Street?* or *Where is Jerusalem Street?*. They are all means that can be used for attaining the same end. How we opt for some means rather than others depends on different considerations, such as those of **rationality** in speech activity.

Roles: Not every person is in a position of properly using certain verbal means in order to serve one's purpose. In order to be in a position to properly use a command, *Do not park your car here!*, for example, a speaker has to play a certain role in a certain hierarchy, such as that of a police officer or the proprietor of a parking lot.

Products: A performance of a speech act, in an appropriate context of utterance, often changes the situation beyond one's having spoken rather than kept silent. On many occasions, a performed speech act has a product that is present in circumstances beyond those of the utterance and its memory. Thus, for example, a proper usage of *I promise to answer your question* creates an undertaken obligation to answer the question referred to in the promise.

Such an analysis of components of speech act types eliminates from common descriptions of speech act types part of an air of arbitrariness from which they suffer. Mere lists of conditions become more reasonable portrayals of components of speech act types as intentional act types.

An open question of much theoretical importance is which of the components of speech acts suggested by these studies are innate in the human mind and which are acquired during linguistic development on the basis of common experience. The distinction between the innate and the acquired is of supreme theoretical interest. The innate is taken to reflect an essential aspect of our human mind, which in turn is an essential aspect of our being human (i.e. being Homo sapiens).

Theories of various parts of human cognition, including natural language, have used the concept of 'modularity' (*see* Fodor 1983 for a most influential presentation of this element of Chomsky's approach to natural language). A module, in a broad sense of the term, is a cognitive system that is independent of other systems in several respects. Using the computer analogy for describing the main features of a module, cognitive independence is manifest in the nature of the input the system is able to process, in the nature of the program and its data, in the background process of the program development and in the nature of the underlying hardware. It is assumed that the modularity of a system is an innate feature of it.

Using the conceptual framework of theories of the **modularity of mind**, one can formulate interesting hypotheses about speech act types. Kasher (1984b) argued that there is a pragmatic module that consists of the **knowledge** of certain speech act types, such as assertion, question and command. In Kasher (1991b) a distinction between 'core pragmatics' and 'amplified core pragmatics' was introduced, designating a difference between speech act types that are modular (and innate) and speech act types in the broad sense of 'things done with words', to use Austin's apt expression. Each of the latter involves a basic speech act type, which is modular, as well as additional elements, related to some human institution, such as promise, which is informal, or acquittal, which is formal.

If speech act types such as assertion, question and command are modular and innate, the theoretical problem arises of why there are innate systems of rules that govern speech acts of these types rather than many others as well. An answer would consist of two parts. First, the whole variety of speech act types has been shown to be reducible to a small number of speech act types (see the above mentioned works by Searle and Vanderveken). It would be reasonable to assume that a speech act type is not innate if it is reducible to another speech act type that is innate. Second, a speech act type that is not

reducible to other speech act types has to be explained as a natural element of the innate ingredients of the human mind. Assertion, for example, seems to be such a natural element, because the point of it is **representation** of facts, which is a natural element of the mind. It cannot be mastered by the human mind on grounds of human experience that is independent of any representation system. Our hypothesis is that question is similarly related to the idea of problem processing, and command to norm following. Putting such hypotheses to empirical tests and theoretical consideration remains a subject matter of cognitive research programmes in **pragmatics**.

Studies of speech acts in different natural languages and contexts of utterance abound. Many of them are of some theoretical or empirical interest, some of them of much interest. However, what they illuminate is usually a certain natural language or a certain sphere of human activity rather than a certain speech act type or speech act types in general. For example, a study of what is shared by occurrences of wh-words in English, in which they appear as interrogative pronouns (as in *Who read the book?*) and in relative clauses (as in *I met the man who wrote the book*), can illuminate parts of English **syntax** and **semantics**, but hardly the nature of the speech act type of question. Similarly, a study of speech acts in e-mails can reveal fascinating facts about e-mail correspondence, but is not expected to change our views of the nature of speech acts in general or any speech act in particular, unless it uncovers a speech act type that occurs just in e-mails. Any study of a speech act type or speech act types in general within the framework of a certain system illuminates the system itself. If the system is that of a certain natural language, then we usually learn about it, not about what extends beyond its confines. If the system is that of a certain activity, such as e-mail correspondence, we usually learn about that activity, not about other activities. If the system is natural language as part of the human mind, we learn about natural language in general.

ASA KASHER

See also: Assertion; command; question; request; speech act theory

Suggestions for further reading

Burkhardt, A. (ed.) (1990) *Speech Acts, Meaning and Intentions: Critical Approaches to the Philosophy of John R. Searle*, Berlin and New York: Walter de Gruyter.
Tsohatzidis, S.L. (ed.) (1994) *Foundations of Speech Act Theory: Philosophical and Linguistic Perspectives*, London: Routledge.

Stylistics

Stylistics is concerned with the formal characteristics and interpretative significance of linguistic choices and patterns in texts. Its earliest developments in continental Europe were the results of the work of scholars such as Bally (1909) and Spitzer (1948) in the first half of the twentieth century. An Anglo-American tradition began to develop in the mid-twentieth century, initially under the influence of Russian and Prague formalism on the one hand, and Practical Criticism on the other hand. This tradition has continued to flourish as a result of an ongoing interaction with developments in linguistics and literary criticism.

The term 'stylistics' can be used in relation to two distinct but overlapping lines of research, which may be labelled, respectively, 'general stylistics' and 'literary stylistics'. General stylistics primarily aims to investigate the 'styles' that are perceived as characteristic of particular genres, registers, or language varieties more generally. As such, it is closely related to **sociolinguistics** and **discourse analysis**. Literary stylistics is concerned with the study of the relationship between the language of literary texts on the one hand and readers' responses and interpretations on the other. It therefore has a close relationship with poetics, narratology, and literary criticism (*see also* Verdonk 2002 and Wales 2001). The term 'linguistic stylistics' can also be used, either as an alternative to 'general stylistics', or to refer specifically to studies that aim to test and develop particular linguistic theories by applying them to (literary) texts (*see* Wales 2001).

General stylistics was established in the 1960s and 1970s by a series of studies on how language varies depending on **context** and purpose (Crystal and Davy 1969; Enkvist 1973). These studies were concerned with identifying the linguistic features (or, in Enkvist's terms, 'style markers') that characterize different registers or genres, and provided linguistic descriptions of the styles of, for example, newspaper reporting and legal documents. Leech (1966) provided an early account of the language of **advertising**. Work in general stylistics gained new impetus in the 1980s and 1990s when more sophisticated approaches to context were developed in **pragmatics** and discourse analysis. This made it possible to explain more systematically how linguistic choices are connected to factors such as the relationship between speaker/writer and hearer/reader, and the maintenance of dominant ideologies (e.g. Carter and Nash 1990; Hickey 1989; Simpson 1993; Toolan 1992). In recent years, the comparative study of registers and genres has also benefited from the application of methods developed in **corpus linguistics** (Biber 1988; Stubbs 1996).

By contrast, literary stylistics is concerned with the styles of particular literary texts, authors, periods or genres and, more specifically, with the way in which linguistic choices in literary texts relate to readers' responses and interpretations. Since the mid-twentieth century, much work in this area was inspired by Roman Jakobson's well known claim that 'a linguist deaf to the poetic function of language and a literary scholar indifferent to linguistic problems and unconversant with linguistic methods are equally flagrant anachronisms' (Jakobson 1960: 377). In the 1960s, literary stylisticians were particularly concerned with poetry. The influence of the Formalist tradition (Jakobson 1960; Mukařovský 1964) led to the investigation of how poets use linguistic deviation and parallelism to achieve foregrounding effects, namely, to make some parts or aspects of texts highly salient and interpretable (e.g. Leech 1969). The dominance of Chomsky's generative grammar in linguistics is evident in a number of studies from the 1960s that attempt to characterize the styles of individual texts or authors in terms of the application of particular rules or transformations (Ohmann 1964; Thorne 1965). Since the 1970s, M.A.K. Halliday's systemic functional approach to language has inspired a wide range of studies on how systematic linguistic choices at different levels of language can result in the perception of distinctive styles and in the projection of particular world views, especially in novels and short stories (e.g. Fowler 1986, 1996; Halliday 1971; Leech and Short 1981, 2007). The study of the language of prose fiction has also led to the development of systematic accounts of the linguistic projection of characters' viewpoints and of the representation of characters' speech and thought (Fowler 1986; Leech and Short 1981, 2007; Short 1996). Advances in pragmatics, **conversation analysis** and discourse analysis since the 1970s have made it possible to analyze systematically fictional dialogue, both in prose fiction and drama, in order to explain how characters' conversational behaviour affects the way in which they are perceived by readers or audiences (Carter and Simpson 1989; Culpeper *et al.* 1998; Herman 1995; Short 1989a).

Since the 1980s, some work in literary stylistics has been influenced by the rise of critical linguistic and critical discourse analysis, and has been concerned with how literary texts participate in the maintenance and negotiation of **power** relationships and ideologies (Burton 1982; Fowler 1986, 1996; Mills 1995; Toolan 2001; Weber 1992). Developments in **cognitive linguistics**, and **cognitive science** more generally, have drawn the attention of stylisticians to the possibility of combining linguistic analysis with relevant models of cognition, in order to attempt to explain readers' interpretation of texts. This line of research has come to be known as 'cognitive stylistics' or 'cognitive poetics' (Gavins and Steen 2003; Semino and Culpeper 2002; Stockwell 2002), and includes work on how readers imagine text worlds and plots (Emmott 1997; Gavins 2007; Werth 1999), how they perceive characters (Culpeper 2001), and how they may experience 'schema refreshment', or, in other words, have their existing assumptions challenged (Cook 1994; Semino 1997). Cognitive **metaphor** theory has been exploited in order to study the role of distinctive metaphorical patterns in the language of particular texts (Freeman 1993), characters (Semino 2002) or authors (Freeman 1995). Fauconnier and Turner's (2002) blending theory has also been applied to the analysis of how the language of particular literary works results in particular effects and interpretations (Semino 2006; Sweetser 2006). **Relevance theory** has similarly been applied to the analysis of how **meaning** is constructed in the reading of literary texts (Pilkington 2000).

Stylisticians are also increasingly taking advantage of the availability of a variety of electronic language corpora, and of techniques for automatic text analysis. Corpus-based methods have been applied, for example, to the study of individual texts (Hoover 1999; Louw 1993), of the styles of particular authors (Mahlberg 2007), and of particular textual phenomena, such as speech, writing and thought presentation in fictional and non-fictional narratives (Semino and Short 2004). The pedagogical potential of stylistic analysis has been explored in a number of studies (Brumfitt and Carter 1986; Clark and Zyngier 2003; Short 1989b; Widdowson 1992), and some important informant-based work has been carried out at the interface between stylistics, **cognitive psychology** and the empirical study of literature (Emmott *et al.* 2006; Short and van Peer 1989; Steen 1994; van Peer 1986).

The borderline status of literary stylistics between linguistics and literary criticism regularly sparks controversy, especially in relation to the validity of the claims that can be made about meanings and effects on the basis of linguistic analysis (Fish 1980; Fowler 1971; Mackay 1996; Short *et al.* 1998; Toolan 1996). Arguably, however, these controversies are not a symptom of disease but rather evidence of the continuing vitality of the field.

ELENA SEMINO

See also: Cognitive linguistics; cognitive psychology; cognitive science; context; conversation analysis; corpus linguistics; discourse analysis; literary pragmatics; metaphor; narrative discourse; perspective taking/point of view; pragmatics; relevance theory; sociolinguistics

Suggestions for further reading

Leech, G.N. and Short, M.H. (2007) *Style in Fiction*, London: Longman.
Simpson, P. (2004) *Stylistics: A Resource Book for Students*, London: Routledge.
Weber, J.-J. (ed.) (1996) *The Stylistics Reader: From Roman Jakobson to the Present*, London: Arnold.

Syntax-Pragmatics Interface

It has been recognized since the 1960s (Lees and Klima 1963) that the acceptability of sentences depends on the referential and predicative intents imputed to the speaker, although this fact was not always represented in such baldly pragmatic terms. In fact, many or most of the constraints discussed in the syntax literature either must be stated ultimately in pragmatic terms or describe constructions whose use conveys pragmatic information about the beliefs of the speaker – beliefs about the world (**presuppositions**), about the **propositional attitudes** of the addressee, or about the structure of the ongoing **discourse**. An extensive catalogue may be found in Green (2001).

What kind of information is pragmatic?

In a sense, all pragmatic information is ultimately indexical information (Bar-Hillel 1954; Nunberg 1993; Levinson 2004). However, it is not linguistic forms (words, morphemes, expressions) that carry pragmatic information, but the facts of their utterance: pragmatic information is information about the relation between the user of the form and the act of using the form. More precisely, pragmatic information is information about the speaker's model of the addressee, and the hearer's model of the speaker (potentially recursively). (The choice of 'addressee' and 'hearer' in this sentence is not accidental. Speakers plan speech with a particular audience in mind, but everyone who hears it has access to the same rules for interpreting it.) Since acts are interpreted at multiple levels of granularity, this built-in indeterminacy or margin of error is present for acts involved in choosing words and construction types, as well as for acts of uttering sentences containing or instantiating them.

Some illustrative phenomena

In English and probably all other natural languages, there are truth-conditionally equivalent alternatives to practically every describable construction. To the extent that this is true, the alternatives turn out to have different pragmatic values. Horn (1984, 1993) offers a detailed and convincing explanation of why this is inevitable.

The factors which might enter into the choice between or among truth-conditionally equivalent constructions are numerous. To take one of the most familiar examples, one might choose a passive construction over its active counterpart in order to represent the patient as the **topic**. Or one might use a passive to defer information about the agent to the end of the sentence, where it will be more perceptually prominent, naturally receiving sentence stress. On the other hand, using the passive allows expression of the agent to be entirely suppressed. This enables a speaker to accommodate the fact that it is unknown or irrelevant who the agent is, or just avoid saying who the agent is, even if he does know, for whatever reason.

Using a passive also commonly implies a belief that the event described caused a certain effect in some contextually salient sentient individual (Lakoff 1971; Davison 1980; Fukada 1986). Often the affected individual is the subject, as in (1a) and (1b). However, it can be any contextually salient legal person including, but not limited to, the speaker or addressee, as in (1c) and (1d):

(1) a. He was interrogated for three hours.
    b. He was awarded a Pulitzer Prize for that photograph.
    c. The evidence was destroyed in the fire.
    d. This idea has been attacked as simplistic and naive.

The effect can be negative, as in (1a), or positive, as in (1b). Only the details of the **context** in which the sentence is uttered could tell us which it is in (1c). The jarring effect of (2a) is attributable to the fact that the referent of the term 'dog' is clearly affected, but the construction does not consistently represent that term as a subject (*cf.* 2b):

(2) a. #A car hit your dog, but he's OK now.
    b. Your dog was hit by a car this afternoon, but he's OK now.

Truth-conditionally equivalent sentences may also differ from each other in rhetorical function (i.e. in what gets asserted and what is presupposed), or in how they reflect the speaker's assumptions about the structure of the discourse.

In addition, syntactic choices like Extraposition and Relative Clause Extraposition that position multi-word constituents towards the end of the sentence may enable a speaker to compensate for (perceived) difficulties in producing or parsing a complex utterance.

Belief/attitude/value cases

One set of cases where 'stylistic variants' exhibit a difference in rhetorical value involves constructions with sentential complements as in (3) and (4), or adjuncts as in (5). The (a) sentences in these sets differ from the (b) sentences in that the italicized subordinate clause represents a presupposed or otherwise subordinate **proposition** in the (a) sentences, but has independent declarative illocutionary force in the (b) sentences:

(3) a. I bet *it'll float if you throw it in the lake.*
 b. It'll float if you throw it in the lake, I bet. [S-LIFTING]
(4) a. That *Sandy thought it was Tuesday* is obvious/clear.
 b. It's obvious/clear that Sandy thought it was Tuesday. [EXTRAPOSITION]
(5) a. Someone *who said the girls were supposed to bring two quarts of potato salad* called.
 b. Someone called who said the girls were supposed to bring two quarts of potato salad. [RELATIVE CLAUSE EXTRAPOSITION]

Thus, depending on the sense intended for *bet* in (3a), (3a) is either a wager or a speculation. But (3b) can only be a speculation – *bet* does not have a performative interpretation in that construction (Ross 1975; Horn 1986). And while both (4a) and (4b) could be used to assert something about the claim that Sandy had some belief about the identity of a day, only (4b) could be used to actually make the claim that Sandy had that belief (Morgan 1975; Horn 1986). In the case of (5), the (a) sentence reports who called, while the (b) sentence reports what someone said the girls were supposed to bring (Ziv 1976).

Other constructions reflect particular kinds of beliefs speakers have about the objects of their discourse. For example, use of the INTERNAL DATIVE construction (Green 1974) in (6b) implies that the speaker believes that the referents of the subject and beneficiary noun phrases were alive at the same time:

(6) a. Win this one for the Gipper/me.
 b. Win me/#the Gipper this one.

Wierzbicka (1986b) has argued that use of the internal dative construction reflects more generally the speaker's greater interest in the referent of the indirect object noun phrase.

Although the examples cited here have been from English, it would be surprising to find a language where custom didn't link beliefs or attitudes to the use of particular words or constructions. Sakakibara (1995) gives detailed examples of the speaker beliefs associated with the use of Japanese long distance reflexives (*cf.* Huang 2004a for additional discussion of the pragmatics of **anaphora**).

Reflections of discourse structure

Language scholars have long recognized that there are correlations between the order of syntactic constituents in a sentence and the discourse function of the information which a particular constituent references (Mathesius 1928; Firbas 1964; Halliday 1967; Kuno 1972; Gundel and Fretheim 2004; Ward and Birner 2004; also Prince 1981b; Zaenen 1982; Horn 1986). In general, and all other things being equal, the first phrase in a sentence tends to be intended to denote familiar (or TOPICAL, or GIVEN, or OLD, or presupposed, or predictable, or THEMATIC) material, while phrases toward the end of the sentence tend to denote NEW (or FOCUSSED, or asserted, or RHEMATIC) material. Other things are not always equal, however. Sentence stress or intonational accent (higher pitch which falls off rapidly and is perceived as louder) also correlates with information being treated as new (Schmerling 1976), and new information may be expressed in phrases that occur toward or at the beginning of a sentence if they bear the main sentence stress (Olsen 1986).

Further, as Prince (1981b) demonstrated, 'familiar', 'predictable', 'given', 'old', 'theme', and 'sentence topic' do not denote interchangeable notions, and different writers have used the same term to refer to rather different categories. Still, the various writers seem to have been addressing the same point, summarized by Horn's (1986) observation that the initial slot in a sentence tends to be reserved for material taken to refer to the discourse theme or sentence topic (i.e. what the sentence is about). Typically, this is material that the speaker (reflexively) assumes to be familiar to the addressee, and preferentially, it is material which is either salient (assumed by the speaker to be in the addressee's consciousness) or presupposed (taken as noncontroversial) (Horn 1986: 171). It is not surprising, then, that syntactic rules of languages provide for numerous alternative constructions which differ in the order of phrases while preserving truth-conditional **semantics** and illocutionary force. This is true even in a 'fixed word order' language like English, where passive constructions, the *there*-construction, topicalization, clefting, and predicate preposings, as well as the *tough*-construction and extraposition all offer alternative orders for sentence components. Ward's (1988) analysis of preposings is illustrative (*see* Aissen 1975; Milsark 1977; Napoli and Rando 1978; Prince 1978, 1981c, 1984 for discussions of clefts, preposings, and existential and presentational *there*-constructions).

Reflections of perceived difficulty

Speakers may take advantage of constructions like EXTRAPOSITION and HEAVY NP SHIFT which allow a constituent, to appear at the end of the sentence to put the longest or most conversationally significant constituent last. It is not clear whether this option serves to make the sentence easier to articulate (*cf.* Olsen 1986) or easier to keep track of, or whether the motivation is altruistic – accommodating the addressee's likely strategies or difficulties in parsing – or some combination of these. Length and discourse significance seem to be at least partially independent factors. Longer postposed noun phrases tend to sound better, even if they have no more semantic content, but of two noun phrases of equal length, the more significant-sounding sounds better, as illustrated in (7) (*see* Arnold *et al.* 2000 for related discussion.)

(7) a. #Harry gave to Hermione the butter beer.
    b. Harry gave to Hermione the entire sheaf.

Representing the pragmatic value of syntactic constructions

In the early years of generative grammar, the distribution of linguistic expressions in sentences was taken to be an exclusively formal matter, and the relevant notion of identity among expressions was assumed to be identity of form. However, as early as 1965, attempts were made to incorporate various kinds of pragmatic conditions into the framework then available for syntactic description (Lakoff 1965). At the same time, addressing other issues, Chomsky (1965) proposed indexing nodes in constituent structure trees for coreference so that the kind of identity required for personal and relative pronouns could be represented as syntactic information. Morgan (1968, 1970) provided early demonstrations that the kind of identity required varies from syntactic construction to construction. Later proposals to encode contingent assumptions about real-world relations among situations as syntactic information were equally doomed, as they led to theory-internal logical contradictions (Morgan 1973a).

As linguists began to appreciate **Grice**'s paper 'Logic and Conversation' (Grice 1989: chapter 2), they began to describe relations between grammaticality and usage. Although Morgan (1975) had demonstrated that making a strict separation in grammatical descriptions between constraints on form and constraints on usage was not as simple as it looked, given the fact that certain forms induced **implicatures** which are not induced by semantically equivalent forms, this warning went largely unheeded. Gordon and Lakoff's (1971) conversational postulates incorporated **speech act** participants' beliefs and **intentions** into syntactic derivations in the guise of constraints on derivations that referred to other possible derivations (a sort of precursor of optimality syntax (e.g. Grimshaw 1997) and pragmatics (Blutner 2004)). However, it obscured the fact that the relation between the use of a form and its interpretation in context depends on the speaker's and addressee's beliefs and intentions about each other's beliefs and intentions (Cohen and Perrault 1979; Cohen and Levesque 1990b, 1991; Green 1996a) and not on any other kinds of contingent facts.

A better approach (one that is more consistent with these facts and with the better understanding of implicature now available) will minimize the number of grammatical constraints on the syntactic combination of grammatical categories and integrate them with construction-specific pragmatic constraints of the sorts discussed here and with independently necessary constraints on their semantics. Such an approach would be, in effect, a complex function on a theory of **communication** which entailed the integration of such more or less universal principles as Grice's **cooperative principle** and the strategies of relevance and quantity (cf. Horn 1984) that derive from it (strategies for referring, predicating, focussing, etc.) with **culture**-specific interpretations (or implementations) of **politeness** principles (cf. Brown and Levinson 1987; Green 1996a). All of these aspects of **pragmatics** refer directly to language users' intentions and beliefs, linking them to the conventions of usage (Morgan 1978) that the construction-specific constraints encode. Such a treatment, in contrast to known predecessors, would remove many sentences judged unacceptable from the realm of the ungrammatical and would predict instead (a) that the use of such sentences will cause hearers to make certain **inferences** about their speaker, (b) that some of these inferences may result in the sentence being considered inappropriate, given what else the hearer knows about the speaker and the subject matter, or contradictory, or ineffective for the purpose the hearer imputes to the speaker, and (c) that the speaker is aware at some level of (a) and (b).

Pollard and Sag (1994) take a first step toward such an approach, treating speaker's presuppositions and other categories of propositional attitudes as part of the **representation** for lexical and phrasal expressions. As discussed in Green (1994, 2000), such representations might be very detailed, incorporating much of the same sort of information as might be expressed in a representation in Discourse Representation Theory (Kamp 1981; Kamp and Reyle 1993). One concern of Pollard and Sag (1994: 332–35), however, is that while background presuppositions have to be projected from lexical items to phrases containing them, it has been known since the early 1970s that the

projection is not a function of tree geometry (Morgan 1973b; Karttunen and Peters 1979), or even of the semantic class of predicates and operators in the structural projection path. Morgan showed that neither the problem nor the solution is strictly linguistic, but depends instead on beliefs attributed by the interpreter to the speaker and agents and experiencers of propositional attitude verbs in the sentence. Morgan's account, and Gazdar's (1979a) formalization of it, show that conversational implicatures of the utterance of a sentence limit the presuppositions of that sentence uttered in context to the subset of presuppositions associated with the lexical items in it that are consistent with the speaker's assumptions and intended implicatures.

Conversational implicature, of course, is a function of a theory of human behaviour generally, not something specifically linguistic (Grice 1989; Green 1993), because it is based on inference of intentions for actions generally, not on properties of the artefacts (sentence and utterance tokens) that are the result of linguistic actions. Conversational implicatures arise from the assumption that it is reasonable (under the particular circumstances of the speech event in question) to expect the addressee to infer that the speaker intended the addressee to recognize the speaker's intention from the fact that the speaker uttered whatever the speaker uttered. Thus, it would be naive to anticipate that the filtering in the projection of presuppositions or other associated propositional attitudes could be represented as any kind of formal function on constituent structure (like the constraints on the projection of agreement or subcategorization or unbound dependency information), precisely because conversational implicature is inherently indeterminate (Morgan 1973b; Gazdar 1979a; Grice 1989).

This does not necessarily mean that a projection principle for pragmatic information is logically impossible. Background propositions of a phrase can be computed as a conjunction of the background propositions of its parts, along the lines suggested by Pollard and Sag (1994: 333) and Wilcock (1999). This sort of context inheritance principle would be completely consistent with the inherently indeterminate character of Gricean conversational implicature. If that

conjunction should happen to contain predications that are inconsistent with each other, or
predications that are inconsistent with what is
predicated by the sentence as a whole, that does
not pose a formal or logical problem, or even a
linguistic problem, but only a practical sort of
problem for an agent constrained to construe the
speaker's behaviour in uttering the sentence as
rational. Doing that requires using **knowledge**
of principles of sense and/or **reference** transfer
(Nunberg 1995, 2004) and lexical rules, as well
as beliefs about what is sensible and what is silly.
A common way of resolving a conflict involving
lexical presuppositions is to interpret one or
more of the presupposition-bound phrases involved
as intended figuratively in a way that allows
propositions intended to be conveyed to be
regarded as all true. In any case, the resolution
of such contradictions is precisely what the
cooperative principle was invented for (Grice
1989; Green 1996b) and what the computation
of implicatures is about, as Morgan and Gazdar
demonstrated.

GEORGIA M. GREEN

See also: Anaphora, pragmatics of; Bar-Hillel,
Y.; given/new distinction; Grice, H.P.; indexicals;
intention; neo-Gricean pragmatics; pragmatics;
presupposition

Suggestion for further reading

Horn, L.R. and Ward, G. (2004) *Handbook of
   Pragmatics*, Oxford: Blackwell.

T

Tautology

The notion of tautology enters the **philosophy of language** with **Wittgenstein**'s *Tractatus Logico-Philosophicus* (Wittgenstein 1922). There tautology is defined as a truth-functional **proposition** that is 'true for all the truth-possibilities of the elementary propositions' (4.46, 34). In the contemporary literature, the applicability of the term has been expanded beyond sentential logic to include any proposition that is true as a matter of form, especially those that are true as a result of syntactic repetition, e.g. sentences of the forms 'A is A', 'All As are As', 'A or not A' or 'If A, then A'. Following the Wittgensteinian line, all tautologies are considered to be semantically vacuous, that is, true but devoid of content.

The use of utterances of tautological form in non-vacuous **speech acts** was noted by **Grice** (1975), who contends that statements like 'Women are women' or 'War is war' are 'totally noninformative and so, at that level, cannot but infringe the first **maxim** of Quantity in any conversational context' (33). The speaker's choice to utter a particular tautology in the **context** of a given **conversation** then forms the basis of an **implicature** which leads the listener to infer non-vacuous content when confronted with such an utterance. Some theorists have worked on the details of the Gricean pragmaticist approach to tautological utterances based on the maxim of quantity (Levinson 1983; Fraser 1988; Autenreith 1997). Tautologies say nothing and, since a cooperative speaker would always strive to make his conversational contributions meaningful, the **meaning** requires an **inference** on the part of the listener. Levinson (1983) argues that since one can assume the speaker is making as informative a contribution as required, the speaker's utterance takes on a 'dismissive or topic-closing quality' (111). Nothing was said because there is nothing to say. Autenreith (1997) argues that the meaning results from an implicature that the proposition is not actually a tautology, that only the first use of the noun phrase in utterances of the form 'A is A' is predicative. Hence, when we hear 'After 1905, Bertrand Russell was Bertrand Russell', the first use of the name points to Russell the man. The second use is non-referential as it refers only to a description which is assumed by the listener to contain the common sense properties attached to the noun phrase 'Bertrand Russell', thereby breaking the symmetry and giving the proposition the implied meaning.

Opposition to this pragmaticist approach centres on the claim that the listener's inference is not based on conversational context, but rather on conventional semantic aspects of the language in which the tautology is uttered (Wierzbicka 1987, 1988; Davis 1998). It is argued that meaningful tautologies are the exception rather than the rule, something that should not be the case if pragmatic considerations of quantity or relevance were all that were in play. Further, considering English language tautologies of the form 'A is A', it is argued that the type of noun phrase employed in the tautology radically alters the interpretation. When the tautology is formed using an abstract noun phrase, such as in the case of 'Business is business', the utterance is interpreted as expressing 'a sober attitude towards complex human activities'. In contrast, when the noun phrase employed is plural and refers to a group of humans, e.g. 'Boys will be boys', the interpretation inferred is one of 'tolerance for human nature'. And if an article is a part of the noun phrase, as in 'A deal is a deal', then the tautological utterance is to be understood as an attempt to enforce an obligation. It is therefore more than a universal conversational implicature, the argument goes, that would lead someone to understand the difference between 'War is war' and 'A war is a war'. The implicature turns in crucial ways upon semantic aspects of the particular language.

A central piece of linguistic evidence cited by the 'radical semanticist' camp in opposition to the 'radical pragmaticist' view is the non-translatability of non-trivial utterances of tautological form. Wierzbicka (1987) argues that the standard meaning attached to the sentence 'Boys will be boys' is not conveyed to a native speaker when the sentence is translated into French, German, Polish, or Russian in a fashion that preserves the tautological form. She also points to non-trivial tautological utterances in Korean and Japanese that have well defined meanings for members of the respective linguistic communities, but which are not the meanings ordinary speakers would naturally attribute to such statements translated into English. This question of the translatability of tautologies has become the basis for anthropological linguistic investigations into tautological utterances in different languages, e.g. Farghal (1992) examines tautological **speech acts** in Jordanian colloquial Arabic, Okamoto (1993) in Japanese, Molnár (2004) in Hungarian, and Zeldovich (2005) in Russian and Polish.

Ward and Hirschberg (1991) take issue with the question of translatability, arguing that there are word for word translatable tautological utterances between English and French, and Spanish and Turkish. As such, the mechanism for interpreting tautological utterances is not purely a matter of **semantics** as radical semanticists such as Wierzbicka and Davis claim. At the same time, they seek to augment the Gricean pragmatic account in line with the semanticist challenge by distinguishing between the mechanisms employed for different classes of tautological utterances. But where the partitioning for the semanticists is based on the type of noun phrase,

for Ward and Hirschberg the distinctions are based upon syntactic elements, e.g. whether the utterance is equative, 'A is A', disjunctive, 'A or not A', or conditional, 'If A, then A'.

Bulhof and Gimbel (2001, 2004) follow Ward and Hirschberg in pointing to tautologies that are translatable without loss of meaning, from Dutch political slogans to the passage 3:14 in Exodus, 'I am who I am'. While on the one hand, such examples are problematic for the semanticist position of Wierzbicka and Davis, the proposed explanation of their translatability is entirely consistent with Wierzbicka's taxonomy of tautologies. The group of translatable tautologies, it is argued, are those in which the operative noun phrase has both a sharply delimited sense in which degrees or quantity is irrelevant and a vague sense in which the noun phrase may be more or less appropriate. For example, one might say of a friend in her third trimester that 'She is looking *very* pregnant', but one could also use the term 'pregnant' in such a way that there is pregnant and not pregnant and questions of degree make no sense. The use of a tautology with such a term, for example, 'You are pregnant or you are not', implies that when the speaker uses the operative term, in this case 'pregnant', it should be interpreted in the sharply delimited sense as that is the only case in which the tautology holds true. In this way, the tautologies are not code for a non-tautological proposition that must be inferred by the listener. Rather, they are intended to be the tautologies they are, that is, true statements in line with Grice's maxim of quality. Thereby, 'deep tautologies' are a category of tautological utterance consistent with the semanticist view, because their meaning requires categorization by type of noun phrase, but is entirely unpacked by Gricean maxims accounting for their translatability.

STEVEN GIMBEL

See also: Implicature; maxims of conversation; translation, pragmatics of

Suggestions for further reading

Ward, G. and Hirschberg, J. (1991) 'A pragmatic analysis of tautological utterances', *Journal of Pragmatics*, 15: 507–20.

Wierzbicka, A. (1987) 'Boys will be boys: radical pragmatics vs. radical semantics', *Language*, 63: 95–114.

Telephone Conversation

Fifteen years ago, Hopper (1992: 3) wrote that 'we are the people of the phone', enjoying its services (e.g. quick access) and grumbling about its disservices (e.g. telemarketing, obscene calls). Since its invention, the telephone has undoubtedly been the most important medium of electronic communication. Even though at some point other means of electronically mediated communication, such as e-mails, have threatened to undermine its primacy, the advent of mobile telephones has rapidly redressed the balance by establishing their omnipresence in the lives of most people worldwide (see, e.g. Laurier 2001; Arminen 2007). In its early years, telephone communication tended to be brief and direct, but as it became more accessible and cheaper, interaction through the telephone came closer to face-to-face interaction (McArthur 1992: 1029); in fact, nowadays it constitutes an interactional genre of its own (Schegloff 1993: 4547).

The initiation and expansion of research into telephone **conversation** is to be credited to **conversation analysis**, whose practitioners set out to explore the orderliness and overall sequential organization of interaction. To this end, telephone calls offered an advantageous site mainly for various methodological reasons, e.g. both analyst and interlocutors lack visual resources (*see* Schegloff 1979a: 24–27). Moreover, telephone calls are analytically advantageous sites since they constitute well bounded events with clear beginnings and endings. Despite their seeming unworthiness for sustained investigation, they constitute interactional achievements and 'the primordial site of sociality' (Schegloff 1986: 112). Besides the seemingly mundane and more-or-less automatically produced turns of openings and closings, they perform a multiplicity of tasks, such as the 'the constitution or reconstitution of the relationship of the parties for the present occasion' (Schegloff 1986: 113).

Research to date concerns mainly openings, but also, on a smaller scale, closings (see, e.g. Schegloff and Sacks 1973; Placencia 1997;

Pavlidou 1997, 2002) and topic management (Luke 2002), an imbalance that has been attributed to the great complexity of the latter phenomena. Research on opening telephone interactions pioneered by Sacks ([1963] 1995) was expanded and elaborated by Schegloff (1968, 1979a, 1986) in the direction of identifying a set of four core sequences typical of such openings in North America. These are: (1) a summons/answer sequence, which establishes the openness of the channel and the availability of two parties to talk; (2) an identification and/or recognition sequence, which establishes the identities of the parties; (3) a greeting sequence; and (4) an exchange of 'howareyou' sequences. Among closely related people, the identification sequence may be absent since identification is normally achieved through voice recognition of the call answerer's initial response and greetings. Closing sections, on the other hand, involve two core sequences: (1) a pre-closing sequence (e.g. an exchange of OKs) which offers a warrant for undertaking the closing; and (2) a terminal exchange (e.g. farewells), which achieves a cooperative termination of a conversation (Schegloff and Sacks 1973).

This early work by Sacks and Schegloff has served as the springboard, after the 1980s in particular, for a plethora of studies. These studies include Hopper's (1992) book on telephone call openings and numerous articles relevant to different languages, most of which compare their findings to those in American English. The interested reader should refer to Godard (1977) on French, Bakakou-Orfanou (1988–89) and Sifianou (1989, 2002) on Greek, Houtkoop-Steenstra (1991) on Dutch, Placencia (1992) on Ecuadorian Spanish, Halmari (1993) on Finnish, Lindström (1994) on Swedish, Pavlidou (1994, 1997) on Greek and German, Taleghani-Nikazm (2002b) on Persian, Park (2002) on Japanese and Korean, Sun (2004) on Chinese, and Lee (2006) on Korean. A more recent mature body of theoretical appraisal and empirical research on diverse communities is to be found in the volume edited by Luke and Pavlidou (2002).

One of the issues extensively debated in the literature is the extent of universality or culture-specificity of the canonical pattern of telephone call openings (established by Schegloff), with many scholars providing evidence for culturally specific features. For instance, the Dutch call answerers have been shown to prefer self-identification by name (Houtkoop-Steenstra 1991), which is also the case for Swedes unless they are family members (Lindström 1994). This preference is in contrast to practices elsewhere – America (Schegloff 1979a), Greece (Pavlidou 1994; Sifianou 2002) and Korea (Lee 2006) – where other recognition is preferred. Variation has also been detected in other components of an opening. For example, greetings are more dispensable in Greek (Sifianou 2002), Chinese (Sun 2004) and Korean (Lee 2006) than initial enquiries, which are the dispensable sequences in Swedish (Lindström 1994) and German (Pavlidou 1994). To such claims of cultural variation, Hopper (1992: 90) responds that the core sequences constitute a kind of template for participants and any divergences indicate adaptation to local contexts. Schegloff (2002) claims that his initial account of telephone call openings was meant neither as a claim to universality nor as a basis for cross-cultural comparisons. Such openings should be seen as parts of the specific interactions to which they belong rather than as independent constructs to be compared with similar constructs from other societies.

Research on telephone interaction has largely concentrated on landline telephone talk. However, recent technological advances and the expansion of mobile telephony have widened the research horizons to include burgeoning research on interaction via mobile phones. In this respect, Hutchby and Barnett (2005) argue that, despite modifications (such as locational enquiries and the absence of identification) in the organization of talk between landline and mobile telephone interactions, the norms remain largely the same. Such modifications are claimed to be related to the facilities afforded by mobile telephony (e.g. display of callers' name or number and/or distinct ringing tone). These claims have been challenged by other researchers (see Arminen 2005), who contend that landline and mobile phone interaction and their respective openings differ systematically. The opening sequences on a mobile telephone are a systematically reduced version of the landline norm, reflecting technological advances and subsequent social change (Arminen and Leinonen 2006; Arminen 2007). Thus, it appears that the research area is expanding and will continue to do so with the prospect of technological advances such as the increasing use of videophones and mobile multimedia (see Hutchby 2001).

MARIA SIFIANOU

See also: Conversation; conversation analysis

Suggestions for further reading

Hopper, R. (1992) *Telephone Conversation*, Bloomington, IN: Indiana University Press.
Luke, K.K. and Pavlidou, Th.-S. (eds) (2002) *Telephone Calls: Unity and Diversity in Conversational Structure across Languages and Cultures*, Amsterdam and Philadelphia, PA: John Benjamins.

Theory of Mind

The term 'theory of mind' was originally used by Premack and Woodruff (1978) to refer to a cognitive ability to attribute certain mental states, such as belief, **knowledge**, **intention** and desire, to oneself and to others. Although it has been argued that such an ability can be found in non-human animals, most experimental evidence currently available suggests that animals' social behaviours require little understanding of mental states, and occur only in a narrow range of **contexts**, such as competing for food. The only known exception is found in our closest evolutionary relatives, the great apes, who are reported to be capable of intentionally manipulating others' perceptual states by concealing information. However, even their ability is limited to functioning only in competitive contexts, and not in cooperative contexts (Hare and Tomasello 2004).

As adults, we take it for granted that we can make inferences effortlessly about one another's mind, although we are aware that sometimes **misunderstanding** occurs. Adult-like understanding of another's mind, however, takes time to become fully functional. Meta-analysis of 178 studies on children's developing theory of mind reports that sometime between 4 and 5 years of age, normally developing children of any country, **culture** and **gender** become capable of understanding the concept of belief (Wellman *et al.* 2001). Standard false belief tasks, which typical 3-year-olds fail, have been widely recognized as a litmus test for developing theory of mind. Three types of false belief tasks have been used in investigations of children's belief understanding: 'location false belief' task after Wimmer and Perner (1983), 'content false belief' task after Perner *et al.* (1987), and 'appearance-reality' task after Flavell *et al.* (1983).

Although the focus of the majority of existing studies has been preschool children, acquisition of theory of mind in a child is a continuous process like any other aspect of cognitive development. Prior to passing false belief tasks, important precursors, such as understanding of pretence and implicit understanding of false belief, are observed in younger children (Clements and Perner 1994; Leslie 1987). During early school years, children come to understand second-order false belief, as well as individual differences in the interpretation of the same event (Carpendale and Chandler 1996; Perner and Wimmer 1985). Understanding a speaker's intentions and attitudes in verbal **communication** crucially involves theory of mind (Sperber and Wilson 2002; Matsui, to appear). An ability to engage in non-literal interpretation of utterances such as white lies and ironies also develops between 6 and 9 years of age (Winner and Leekam 1991). Further sophistication in understanding mind continues into adulthood, with some signs of decline in later adulthood (Happé *et al.* 1998). Clinical impairment in theory of mind is found in **autistic spectrum disorder** (Baron-Cohen 1995). Autistic patients generally have difficulty in understanding mental states, and even those patients who are verbal have deficits in the non-literal interpretation of utterances (Happé 1994a).

The relation between theory of mind and language has been one of the central topics in research in cognitive development. Children's acquisition of non-linguistic concepts of belief coincides with the time when they start comprehending mental state verbs such as *believe*, *think* and *know*. This occurs sometime between 4 and 5 years of age, when children start passing standard false belief tasks (Matsui *et al.* 2006; Moore *et al.* 1989). Several possibilities exist concerning the relation between **linguistic competence** in mental state discourse and non-linguistic

reasoning about mental states in children between 4 and 5 years. For example, some pre-linguistic understanding of beliefs may be a prerequisite for competence in **discourse** about beliefs (Bartsch and Wellman 1995). Alternatively, the development of general representational abilities may be essential for both an understanding of beliefs and mental state discourse (Perner 1991). Another possibility is that some understanding of linguistic **representation**, or more specifically, understanding syntactic structures associated with mental state verbs, is a prerequisite for understanding non-linguistic representation of belief (de Villiers and de Villiers 2000). This issue is still controversial (e.g. Astington and Baird 2005), but there is general agreement that by the time children pass standard false belief tasks, they are capable of understanding representation of belief both linguistically and non-linguistically.

There are two main accounts of how attribution of mental states can be achieved. The first is the 'theory-theory' approach, which claims that we are capable of constructing a folk theory of psychology. This theory enables us to predict and explain the actions of self and others (Gopnik and Wellman 1994). The content of folk psychological theories changes step by step in accord with the gradual increase in sophistication of a child's grasp of mental concepts. For example, according to this approach, 3-year-olds are viewed as having a theory based on the concept of desire, but not of belief, whereas 5-year-olds are seen to have acquired a theory which also crucially involves the concept of belief (Wellman and Bartsch 1988). The second is the 'simulation theory' approach, in which attribution of belief states is seen as an extended form of empathy (Goldman 2006). It claims that attribution of mental states to others is achieved through replication of one's own relevant mental states. Thus, in this account, recognition of one's own mental states is the primary process, which then provides the foundation for understanding mental states of others. Discovery of the mirror system (a neuro-cognitive mechanism that involves 'mirror' neurons which fire not only when an animal executes a certain action, but also when the animal observes the same action performed by other animals) has often been taken as neuropsychological evidence for the simulation account of theory of mind (Gallese and Goldman 1998).

Two main hypotheses about the cognitive architecture of theory of mind exist. The first, the **modularity** hypothesis, claims that theory of mind is an innate and domain-specific representational mechanism (Baron-Cohen 1995; Leslie 1994). The second, the conceptual-change hypothesis, claims that at some point between 4 and 5 years of age, children develop a fully functional representational mind, and that prior to that point, their conceptual system is unable to understand the mental state of belief (Perner 1991; Wellman *et al.* 2001). Recent findings that even 1- and 2-year-olds seem to understand the consequence of having a false belief favour the innateness hypothesis (Onishi and Baillargeon 2005; Southgate *et al.* 2007). However, the clear difference in conceptual ability in the mental domain between 3- and 5-year-olds, tapped by verbal false belief tasks, is still taken to indicate that there is a qualitative difference between infants' implicit social understanding and 5-year-olds' explicit grasp of the belief concept (Perner and Ruffman 2005).

TOMOKO MATSUI

See also: Autism spectrum disorders; development, pragmatic; experimental pragmatics; infant-directed talk and pragmatics; metarepresentation; pragmatic language impairment; prelinguistic communication; word learning, the role of mindreading in

Suggestions for further reading

Baron-Cohen, S., Tager-Flusberg, H. and Cohen, D.J. (2000) *Understanding Other Minds: Perspectives from Developmental Cognitive Neuroscience*, Oxford: Oxford University Press.

Topic

'Topic' (also called 'theme', 'psychological/logical subject') has been defined as both a pragmatic/ semantic and structural/syntactic category. Gundel (1988: 210) distinguishes syntactic topic, defined on syntactic structure, from pragmatic topic, defined as follows: 'An entity, E, is the topic of a sentence, S, iff in using S the speaker intends to increase the addressee's **knowledge** about, request information about, or otherwise get the addressee to act with respect to E.' This definition is intended to capture the intuitive characterization of topic as what the sentence is about, the domain within which the main predication is to be assessed (*see also* Reinhart 1981). It is central in explaining the association of topic with **definiteness**, including generics, across languages (Kuno 1972; Gundel 1974, 1985; Li and Thompson 1976; Lee 1999), since assessing a predicate in relation to the topic assumes the ability to uniquely identify it.

The association between topic, definiteness, and **presupposition** goes back at least to Strawson (1964b), who argues that definite descriptions are associated with presuppositions only if they are topics. According to Strawson, a sentence like *The king of France is bald* lacks a truth value if France has no king. However, *I dined with the king of France* (e.g. in response to *What did you do yesterday?*) is false, as the existence of a French king is part of what is asserted. It is not presupposed because the statement is about what the speaker did yesterday, not about the king. However, Reinhart (1981) and others maintain, based on indefinite topics, as in (1), that topics only have to be referential:

(1) A friend of mine, he just lost his job.

This position is challenged in Gundel (1985), who proposes that since the identifiability and familiarity restrictions on topics are pragmatic, they can sometimes be suspended.

Syntactic definitions typically associate topic with a constituent at the left periphery of the sentence, though they differ in the level of **representation** and hierarchical structure on which topic is defined (*cf.* Hockett 1961; Chomsky 1965; Halliday 1967; Gundel 1974; Kiss 1998, inter alia). Languages differ in the type of topic-marking structures they allow (e.g. some have topic-marking morphemes) as well as the consistency with which pragmatic topics are marked structurally (Li and Thompson 1976; Gundel 1988). However, all languages appear to mark topics syntactically by adjunction of a phrase to the left (or right) of a full sentence comment containing a co-indexed pronoun, as in (2), or a gap, as in (3):

(2) a. My job, I like it.
b. I like it, my job.
(3) My job I like.

Topics may also be adjoined to a sentence that lacks a co-indexed constituent, as in (4):

(4) My job, I'm going crazy.

However, there is no simple one-to-one mapping between pragmatic topic and structurally marked topic, even within a single language. Pragmatic topics do not have to be realized as syntactic topics; in fact, they need not be directly realized in a sentence at all. For example, the pragmatic topic of (5B) is the weather in Boston on a particular date:

(5) A. How's the weather in Boston today?
B. It's raining.

Moreover, while the initial phrase in (3) may represent the pragmatic topic (e.g. in response to *How's your job?*), it may also be the information **focus**, the complement of topic (e.g. in response to *Is there anything you like?*), and some languages distinguish the two interpretations prosodically (Gundel 1974, 1999a; Gundel and Fretheim 2004). Formal marking of topics may also be restricted to specific **discourse** functions, especially in languages where topic-marking structures are not basic. Some authors restrict the term to such formally marked topics. For example, Büring (1999) uses the term only for prosodically marked new and/or contrastive topics. Finally, syntactic topics may contain material that is arguably not part of the pragmatic topic, as in (6):

(6) Most Americans, they're going to be better off.

Since the referent of the phrase 'most Americans' is not a uniquely identifiable, or even specific, group, Prince (1998) argues that topic-marking is not the primary function of sentences like (6), (2), and (3) (*see also* Birner and Ward 1998). However, this conclusion is unwarranted if syntactic topic is distinguished from pragmatic/semantic topic. As argued in Gundel (1999b), the pragmatic topic in (6) is the N-set, Americans, not the whole quantified phrase, a position supported by paraphrases like (7):

(7) Americans, most (of them) are going to be better off.

JEANETTE GUNDEL

See also: Focus; given/new distinction; information structure; presupposition; reference

Suggestions for further reading

Gundel, J.K. (1988) 'Universals of topic-comment structure', in M. Hammond, E. Moravczik and J. Wirth (eds) *Studies in Syntactic Typology*, Amsterdam: John Benjamins.
Gundel, J.K. and Fretheim, T. (2004) 'Topic and focus', in L.R. Horn and G. Ward (eds) *The Handbook of Pragmatics*, Oxford: Blackwell.
Lambrecht, K. (1994) *Information Structure and Sentence Form: Topic, Focus and the Mental Representation of Discourse Referents*, Cambridge: Cambridge University Press.

Transcription

All approaches within pragmatics that are based on recordings of actual verbal interactions are faced with problems of 'catching' the phenomena of interest for careful study and for sharing the data with others. Just playing the recording, even repeatedly, does not seem to fully do the job, and in any case recordings are hard to distribute for many types of sharing. Therefore, researchers of this type of work have developed techniques to render spoken language in a textual format, an 'entextualization', mostly called transcription. Such a cross-modal rendering can never be a 'complete' representation of the original event. Both the recording process and the process of transcription itself necessarily involve a reduction of information.

An obvious first step in producing a transcription is to understand the words spoken, which can then be rendered in the format of the written version of the language used. For most types of pragmatic study, this is not sufficient.

Depending on one's analytic interests, the transcriber will add various types of production details, like timing and intonation. This means that any transcription is unavoidably selective and theory-laden (Bucholtz 2007; Duranti 2006; Ochs 1979). This has resulted in a wide variety of transcription styles, as well as efforts to establish transcription conventions corresponding to particular analytical traditions (an early overview is provided in Edwards and Lampert 1993). A rather successful style has been developed by Gail Jefferson (2004b) which is now quasi-obligatory for **conversation analysis** (CA), but also used in related disciplines.

In any style, and in any concrete application of it, the transcriber has to compromise between rendering the speech-as-spoken as faithfully as one can, and preserving an acceptable level of readability. The general solution is not to use purely phonetic symbols, but to start with standard orthography and to 'bend' it so as to suggest the way words were actually pronounced. As with any compromise, the result tends always to be problematic (Duranti 1997a: 138–44). Special problems arise when speakers produce sounds that cannot be caught in words, like laughing or crying. In those cases one can add a description, but this obscures the timing and coordination with speech, so it pays to try to render these actions in letters (Hepburn 2004; Jefferson 1985).

Jeffersonian transcription conventions were developed in response to the analytic needs that emerged in conversation analytic work. An early and still important theme in CA is the organization of **conversational turn-taking**. Therefore, it makes sense to note those details that are specifically relevant for turn-taking and to design the format to highlight that organization. Separate turns are made visibly distinct on the page by putting utterances by different speakers on separate lines, one below the other. It is also useful for analyzing turn-taking to mark various aspects of timing, of one turn in relation to another as well as within turns. Overlap onsets and endings are carefully marked, as well as various aspects of turn design that are involved in the projectability of the possible completion of a turn. These aspects include intra-turn pauses, audible inhalations and final or non-final intonation (cf. Jefferson 2004b; Psathas and Anderson 1990).

When video recording became more prominent, it also became necessary to note visual aspects of interaction. Researchers in this area have made various efforts to include visual phenomena, like gaze direction and gestures, within Jefferson-styled transcripts of speaking. This requires adding descriptions, schemata, or images like screen shots, and indications of timing in relation to the time line suggested by the transcription of the vocal part (cf. Goodwin 2000b; Heath 2004; Mondada 2007a).

With the advent of computer technology, certain conventions had to be adapted, but more importantly, it became possible to develop special software programs to facilitate transcribing. In Transana, for instance, one can play a digitized video recording in one window, while a sound wave is displayed in another window, and a transcript can be typed in a third window, and they are all coordinated in time. As Mondada (2007a) argues, these possibilities not only change the transcription process, but they also greatly facilitate a fine-grained analysis.

A different set of problems became urgent when CA researchers started to work on data in one language, say Japanese, while reporting their research in another language, say English. The usual solution is to present the transcript in three lines: first the original transcript, second a word-for-word translation, often with markers of linguistic function added, and third a gloss in colloquial English (Duranti 1997a: 154–60; Traverso 2002).

PAUL TEN HAVE

See also: Communication failure; conversation; conversational turn-taking; conversation analysis; ethnomethodology; sequence organization

Suggestions for further reading

Duranti, A. (1997) 'Transcription: from writing to digitized images', in A. Duranti, *Linguistic Anthropology*, Cambridge: Cambridge University Press.

Jefferson, G. (2004) 'Glossary of transcript symbols with an introduction', in G.H. Lerner (ed.) *Conversation Analysis: Studies from the First Generation*, Amsterdam and Philadelphia, PA: John Benjamins.

ten Have, P. (2007) 'Transcribing talk-in-
interaction', in P. ten Have, *Doing Conversation Analysis: A Practical Guide*, 2nd edn,
London: Sage.

Translation, Pragmatics of

There are multiple theories, even philosophies,
of translation (including interpreting) (*see* Venuti
1992; Gentzler 1993) but, in practice, translations (apart from academic exercises) are usually
commissioned by clients in order to achieve
some objective. The objective may be analogous
to that envisaged in the original source text (ST)
(e.g. a tourist brochure translated to attract foreign tourists), or it may be different (e.g. a letter
from judicial authorities used solely in translation, as a target text (TT), requesting help from
another jurisdiction). Some TTs simply report
on what a ST means (e.g. a letter in a foreign
language translated for its addressee).

Commissioned translations, therefore, are
intended to have a specific illocutionary force
and to bring about a certain perlocutionary
effect on a different readership and in a different
context from their STs. Yet many clients (and
perhaps some translators) assume that an 'accurate' translation will automatically produce the
desired effect, and thus a translation must simply
'say' what the original 'says'. But which, if any,
of the (usually) various ways of 'saying the same
thing' will incorporate the intended illocution and
potentially bring about the desired perlocution?
Or should translators adopt 'adaptive strategies'
(Wilss 1996: 90) to achieve such effects?

Impartial mediators (e.g. translating public
documents) will conscientiously seek semantic,
stylistic and pragmatic equivalence. Translators
working solely for the 'owner' of a text, though
freer, may lack expertise in drafting certain
genres (e.g. publicity leaflets or novels). Some
translation agencies go beyond translation,
offering help and advice in drafting texts for
specific purposes (*see* Gutt 2000: 66–67). In discussing the *skopos*, or purpose, of translations,
Nord (1997: 30–31) gives the extreme example
of someone commissioned to translate an
instruction manual who, instead of translating,
learns how the machine works and writes his
own instructions in the target language. Indeed,

some theorists perceive translators as full participants in any interaction, personally 'responsible for the texts and utterances they produce'
and able to 'inject the discourse with their own
voice' (Baker 2006: 105, 110).

A pragmatics of translation, then, attempts to
explain translation – procedure, process and
product – relating what TTs and their STs say
(locution), do (illocution) and potentially bring
about (perlocution) both on the textual level and
in their details. It focuses primarily on how TTs
may replicate the **speech acts** in, and of, the
corresponding STs. A translation of 'You're one
or Mr. Nizar's private patients, are you?' (Lodge
1995: 7) will attempt to convey the nurse's
request for information, her criticism of the
patient and the potential/desired perlocutionary
effect of humiliating him for 'buying' special
treatment within a free health service. An army
captain says to a young woman who has just shot
a deer 'I don't suppose you'd like to join my
regiment?' (Follett 1995: 56). The translation of
this utterance will aim to transfer the illocutionary force of a **compliment** on the lady's
shooting ability with the perlocutionary force of
making her feel flattered and attracted to the
speaker.

The transference of locutionary, illocutionary
and perlocutionary force may depend in complex ways on the relationships between ST and
TT contexts and **cultures**. In 'I give to Mary *for
her own use and benefit* all my shares in ICI', the
italicised phrase functions to rebut any possible
presumption of a trust, since under English law
Mary may become the legal owner but be
obliged to use the shares entirely for someone
else's benefit. A translator, therefore, will convey
this rebuttal even for a culture having no such
presuppositions, because they are crucial to
the purpose of the ST.

Within an overall focus on speech act transference, re-production or re-performance, a
pragmatics of translation will also address other
pragmatic categories. These may be preserved
by various strategies, as appropriate to each TT
context (*see* Hickey 1998: 220–23). Presupposition may be explicated. The compliment
embedded in 'You should go on Mastermind'
(Lodge 1989: 333) may be maintained for readers unfamiliar with *Mastermind* as 'Mastermind,
that intelligent people's contest'. A brief exegesis

may recreate the functioning of the **cooperative principle**. The indirect **request** in '"My car won't start", said James' may be followed by 'hoping for Jane's help'. ST **politeness** may be adapted to the TT culture's politeness system. 'Déjame cien euros' (literally 'Lend me 100 euros'), a perfectly (positive-)polite Spanish request, might become the equivalently (negative-)polite English request 'Could you possibly lend me 100 euros?' (*see* Hickey 2005: 317–30). **Discourse markers** may be analyzed. If 'actually' is an announcement of, and **apology** for, contradicting the hearer's assumption (*see* Hickey 1991), 'Actually, I'm not George' might be translated as 'I'm sorry to say I'm not George'.

Hedges can usually be conveyed by expansion. 'I rather think it's hopeless' (Brown and Levinson 1987: 145) might become 'I think it may be hopeless', though losing the English **understatement**. Marking, without further explanation, may signal **given/new** information as specific to a ST culture. Translating 'The coroner recorded an open verdict' as 'The official delivered what the English call an open verdict' will alert a readership without coroners or open verdicts to its implications. If the translator considers that the TT readers might miss the relevance of Mary's utterance to Peter's utterance in the exchange 'Peter: "I'm tired", Mary: "I'll make the meal"' (Sperber and Wilson 1995: 133), a translator might add 'Since you're tired'. Context-bound or language-specific STs, like jokes or puns, may be recontextualised in the TT context. 'Cleanliness is next to what, Jimmy? – Impossible, Miss' may recontextualise into the Spanish **proverb** 'En boca cerrada no entran moscas' (No flies get into closed mouths) as 'En boca cerrada no entran caramelos' (No sweets get into closed mouths). Usually translators attempt to preserve pragmatic **ambiguity**. In 'Why don't you send me the accounts?' a translator will not disambiguate between a request for information, a demand for the accounts to be sent or an accusation that the accounts have not been sent.

While translation is as ancient as the Tower of Babel, the radical insights offered by **pragmatics** will need more time to have their full impact on the priorities of its practitioners.

LEO HICKEY

See also: Ambiguity; apologies; compliments; context; cooperative principle; disambiguation; discourse markers; given/new distinction; hedge; performativity; politeness; pragmatics; presupposition; relevance theory; request; semantics; speech act theory; stylistics

Suggestions for further reading
Baker, M. (1992) *In Other Words: Coursebook on Translation*, London: Routledge.
Hatim, B. (1998) 'Pragmatics and translation', in M. Baker and K. Malmkjaer (eds) *Encyclopedia of Translation Studies*, London: Routledge.
Hickey, L. (2004) 'Perlocutionary pursuits: persuading of/that/to', in M.P. Navarro Errasti, R. Lores Sanz and S. Murillo Ornat (eds) *Pragmatics at Work: The Translation of Tourist Literature*, Bern: Peter Lang.

Traumatic Brain Injury and Discourse

Traumatic brain injury (TBI) commonly results in diffuse damage and multifocal lesions which are often concentrated in the temporal and medial-orbital zones of the frontal lobe (Gentry *et al.* 1988). Communication disturbances are seen frequently in TBI and vary in scope and severity. **Discourse** of individuals with TBI has been described as repetitive or overly talkative (Body and Parker 2005), confused and confabulatory (Hartley and Jensen 1992), or characterized by impoverished language content (Chapman *et al.* 1992; Hartley and Jensen 1992; McDonald 1998).

In examining communicative impairments following TBI, discourse has emerged as an important diagnostic consideration. Conventional language batteries assess language at the single word and sentence levels, at which most individuals with TBI have little difficulty. Examination of language function at the discourse level is better suited for delineating the subtle cognitive-communicative deficits seen in this population (Coelho *et al.* 1991a; McDonald 1992; Ewing-Cobbs *et al.* 1998). Discourse deficits have far-reaching consequences, affecting community re-integration, social adjustment, and overall quality of life (Galski *et al.* 1998;

Dijkers 2004). The subsequent sections focus primarily on assessment of cognitive-communicative impairments associated with TBI via discourse analyses. This is followed by a brief discussion of treatment issues.

Monologic discourse

Monologic discourse is non-interactive, as opposed to the other principal form of discourse – conversational discourse. Various tasks are employed to elicit monologic discourse, for example, procedural explanations (giving directions to a certain location), descriptions (describing a childhood memory), and story **narratives** (producing a new story or recounting one presented previously). Analyses of monologic discourse may take place at the microlinguistic, microstructural, macrostructural, or superstructural level, depending on the type of discourse elicited and the aim of assessment.

Microlinguistic analyses are within-sentence measures that typically examine basic lexical and grammatical processes. Information gained from these procedures usually relates to productivity, grammatical complexity and correctness, or number of **propositions** and content units. Findings from within-sentence analyses for individuals with TBI have been inconsistent. Normal (Mentis and Prutting 1987; Chapman et al. 1992; Coelho 2002) and deficient (Peach and Schaude 1986; Glosser and Deser 1990; McDonald 1993; Coelho et al. 2005a) performance has been observed for syntactic processing and tallies of propositions. By contrast, decreased productivity and efficiency, and a reduction in content units have been consistently noted in the discourse of individuals with TBI (Hartley and Jensen 1991; Coelho 1995; Tucker and Hanlon 1998; Stout et al. 2000; Coelho et al. 2005b). This finding suggests these analyses may be more sensitive to disruptions in discourse following TBI.

Microstructural analyses involve across-sentence measures such as cohesion. Within a text, cohesive ties establish meaningful relationships between consecutive sentences. Measures of cohesion may include frequency counts of cohesive devices or adequacy ratings of their use (i.e. complete or incomplete). Studies of cohesion in the TBI literature are equivocal, with normal performance reported in some investigations

(Ewing-Cobbs et al. 1998; Van Leer and Turkstra 1999; Hough and Barrow 2003) and impairments cited in others (Coelho et al. 1991b; Mentis and Prutting 1991; Davis and Coelho 2004).

Macrostructural analyses consider a text's local and global coherence. Coherence is an index of thematic unity between sentences (local) or between a sentence and the whole of the text (global). Coherence is typically assessed by means of rating scales (Glosser and Deser 1990; Van Leer and Turkstra 1999). Impairments in coherence following TBI have been consistently reported (Glosser and Deser 1990; McDonald 1993; Davis and Coelho 2004).

Superstructural analyses examine the structural framework that organizes semantic content within story narratives. The organization of story components is governed by rules that specify how the different components may be linked and in what order. This is referred to as story grammar. Story grammar analysis identifies episodes as the main structural unit. Episodes may be scored based on completeness (presence of essential story components) or efficiency (proportion of story within episodic structure). Impaired story grammar is characteristic of narrative discourse following TBI (Tucker and Hanlon 1998; Brookshire et al. 2000; Coelho 2002; Body and Perkins 2004).

Conversational discourse

Conversation is the most natural form of discourse (Coelho 2007). There are numerous analyses of conversational discourse including rating scales and checklists, measures of response adequacy and appropriateness, as well as turn taking and **topic** management. These analyses are discussed briefly later.

A variety of rating scales have commonly been used in the analysis of conversation. Examples include Clinical Discourse Analysis (Damico 1985), the Pragmatic Protocol (Prutting and Kirchner 1987), and the La Trobe Communication Questionnaire (Douglas et al. 2007). Scales vary widely in scope and dimension. Some rate non-verbal behaviours and verbal **communication** (Halper et al. 1996) while others rate aspects of the verbal message such as intelligibility and sentence formation (Ehrlich and Barry 1989). These scales are useful tools for rating communicative behaviours but require training to achieve acceptable inter-judge reliability (Coelho *et al.* 2005b). Checklists and rating scales have demonstrated that individuals with severe TBI have poor topic maintenance (Snow *et al.* 1987; Ehrlich and Barry 1989), poor initiation and fail to sufficiently engage their conversational partner (Coelho 1998; Ehrlich and Barry 1989).

Inappropriate turn taking may be a significant detriment to communication. Although turn taking is often considered in rating scales (e.g. Halper *et al.* 1996), additional information should be coded including the **context** of the error, patterns of errors, and number and length of turns (Coelho 1998) to aid in remediation. It has been shown that individuals with TBI generate a greater number of turns and that these turns tend to be shorter and less complex than the turns of non-TBI subjects (Campbell and Dollaghan 1990; Coelho *et al.* 1991c).

Response adequacy and appropriateness are also important considerations in the analysis of conversation. These dimensions are evaluated by classifying speaker initiations as obliges or comments and the speaker's responses in terms of adequacy (Coelho 1998). Various reports on conversational skills of individuals following TBI confirm that the non-injured partner generally needs to assume a greater proportion of the communicative burden to ensure a successful exchange of information in conversations (Coelho 1998; Coelho *et al.* 2002).

How topics are initiated and maintained in conversation, or topic management, is a critical skill for effective communication (Mentis 1994). The number of novel introductions and topic shifts may be counted (Coelho *et al.* 2002). They may be further classified into the place, type, reason for shift, and context in which they occurred (Garcia and Joanette 1994). Individuals with TBI tend to initiate less and have a decreased ability to manage ongoing topics in conversation (Coelho *et al.* 2002).

Although numerous measures may be applied to a conversational sample in order to quantify communicative effectiveness, the specific measures and level of analysis depend on the goals of the clinician (Coelho 1998). Measures of content and topic management have been shown to be most useful in identifying conversational impairments following TBI (Coelho *et al.* 2005b).

Management of discourse impairment following TBI

The limited research on treatment of discourse deficits following TBI has yet to specify a best clinical approach. Few discourse treatment programmes focus solely on discourse. Most address discourse in conjunction with social skills or cognitive functions. Suggested avenues for intervention of discourse impairments include: (1) discourse components, (2) higher order language, (3) social skills, and (4) cognitive abilities. The discourse components approach breaks down the impaired aspects of discourse and targets the underlying skills thought to contribute to that discourse ability (Cannizzaro and Coelho 2002). The higher order language approach integrates specific discourse skills with cognitive skills in a structured therapeutic framework (Biggs and Collis 1982; Penn *et al.* 1997). The social skills approach implements direct teaching and is specific to situations in which the individual encounters communicative difficulty (Ylvisaker *et al.* 2001). This type of intervention treats discourse as part of a more general communicative behaviour management programme. Finally, the cognitive abilities approach focuses on remediation of cognitive processes, such as attention, memory, and executive functions, which are thought to support discourse ability. On this approach, discourse performance becomes the outcome measure as opposed to the treatment target (Hartley and Jensen 1991; Coelho 2002; Youse 2005).

KAREN LE, JENNIFER MOZEIKO and CARL COELHO

See also: Assessment, pragmatic; clinical pragmatics; cognitive pragmatics; cognitive psychology; communication; competence, communicative; competence, pragmatic; conversation; conversational failure; conversational turn-taking; dementia and conversation; discourse analysis; discourse cohesion; narrative discourse; pragmatic language impairment; rehabilitation, communication; right-hemisphere damage and pragmatics; schizophrenic language

Suggestions for further reading

Bara, B.G. (to appear) *Cognitive Pragmatics*, Cambridge, MA: MIT Press.

Coelho, C.A., Youse, K.M., Le, K.N. and Feinn, R. (2003) 'Narrative and conversational discourse of adults with closed head injuries and non-brain-injured adults: a discriminant analysis', *Aphasiology*, 17: 499–510.

Martin, I. and McDonald, S. (2006) 'Weak coherence, no theory of mind, or executive dysfunction? Solving the puzzle of pragmatic language disorders', *Brain and Language*, 85: 451–66.

Truth-Conditional and Non-Truth-Conditional Meaning

Let's begin by making a few assumptions about the study of **meaning**. First, there is a distinction to be drawn between the study of linguistic meaning – what words and sentences mean – and the study of what the speaker intends to mean by their use of these words and sentences. This assumption lies at the heart of the distinction between **semantics** and **pragmatics**. Second, this distinction between semantics and pragmatics is reflected (in some way at least) in the fact that the process of **utterance interpretation** is a two-stage one which involves both semantic decoding and pragmatic **inference**. In the first stage, a hearer decodes the words they have heard, and in the second the hearer uses the linguistic meaning to work out (i.e. infer) the intended speaker meaning. The third and final assumption is that linguistically encoded meaning is not all cut from the same cloth. Most people working within semantics assume, broadly speaking, that there are two types of linguistic meaning: 'truth-conditional' and 'non-truth-conditional' meaning.

Truth-conditional semantics developed out of work in the **philosophy of language** in the early part of the twentieth century by, for example, Bertrand Russell, Alfred Tarski and Rudolf Carnap. Donald Davidson's (1967) seminal paper 'Truth and Meaning' built on the ideas of – in particular – Tarski and Carnap and suggested that providing the linguistic meaning of a sentence was equivalent to providing a characterization of the conditions under which that sentence is true – or the 'truth conditions' of that sentence.

The idea sounds a little unintuitive at first (and having taught truth-conditional semantics to undergraduate classes, I can vouch for this!). But it can be clearly illustrated, and the more you think about it, the more sense it makes. Consider the statement in (1):

(1) Grass is blue.

If you know the meaning of this sentence, you know – despite the fact that it is false – that the condition which is required for it to be true is that grass has to be blue. Truth-conditional semanticists argue that knowing the meaning of that sentence *just is* knowing the truth conditions and that by providing a specification of the truth conditions of a sentence you therefore capture the essence of its meaning. We'll consider just how such a specification might be achieved in a moment, but before that consider sentence (2). What are the truth conditions of this sentence?

(2) A grama é azul.

If I tell you that (2) is a sentence in Portuguese, you might well object by saying 'well I don't know the truth conditions of this sentence, because I don't know what it means' (provided you don't speak Portuguese, of course). However, with this objection you play right into the truth-conditional semanticists' hands. You don't know what the sentence means, they would claim, *because* you don't know the truth conditions.

Developing an earlier idea of Tarski's (1944), Davidson (1967) proposed that a specification of truth conditions could be provided by adopting a *truth theory*, or *T-theory*. This is a special kind of formal system which makes use of set theory, as well as various mathematical and logical languages, in order to describe properties of natural language. The T-theory works by pairing sentences from the natural language with 'sentences' from a 'metalanguage' (called *T-sentences*) which do the descriptive work. In order to make clear the distinction between object language and metalanguage, in the following example the former is Portuguese and the latter is English:

(3) [A grama é azul] is true if and only if (*iff*) grass is blue.

Now that I have specified the truth conditions of (2), you know what that Portuguese sentence means. Notice, though, that in most T-sentences the difference between object language and metalanguage is not signalled by using different natural languages. A T-sentence for (1), for example, would be as follows in (4):

(4) [Grass is blue] is true *iff* grass is blue.

Reasons of space prevent a more in-depth presentation. The interested reader looking for a thorough grounding in truth-conditional semantics is referred to Dowty *et al.* (1981), Larson and Segal (1995) and Lycan (1999).

Let's turn now to three more sentences:

(5) Some politicians are uninspiring.
(6) Some important politicians are uninspiring.
(7) Some politicians are inspiring.

We would, I think, all agree on the following truth conditions: for (5) to be true there have to be at least some uninspiring politicians, for (6) to be true there have to be some uninspiring politicians who are important and for (7) to be true there have to be some inspiring politicians. We would probably also agree that each of the words in each of the sentences contribute to the truth conditions of the sentences containing them. If, for example, we remove the word 'important' from sentence (6), the truth conditions change (in fact, they become the same as the truth conditions of (5)); if we change the word 'uninspiring' in (5) to 'inspiring', the truth conditions of (5) change (they become identical to the truth conditions of (7)). Every word in (5), (6) and (7) contributes to the truth-conditional content (or the **proposition** expressed, or **what is said**) in each example. We can therefore claim that the linguistic meaning each word encodes is truth-conditional meaning.

However, most semanticists agree that there are some linguistic constructions which do not contribute to truth conditions. Consider now the sentences in (8), (9) and (10):

(8) Obama is President.
(9) Is Obama President?
(10) Obama, be President!

While the sentence in (8) has truth conditions, (9) and (10) do not, since neither of them are capable of being true or false. Truth and falsity, after all, are properties that can only be associated with *declarative* sentences: interrogatives and imperatives cannot be true and cannot be false. How, then, does a theory of semantics deal with this kind of meaning? One way, proposed the philosopher of language John **Searle** (1979b) within the framework of **speech act theory**, is to exploit the clear linguistic similarities between (8), (9) and (10) and assume that the proposition expressed in each sentence (in speech act terms, the *descriptive* content) is actually the same in all three. What differs in the linguistic meaning is the illocutionary force that is being *indicated* by the alternative forms of word order: sentence (8) has the force of an **assertion**, sentence (9) has the force of a **question** and sentence (10) has the force of a **request** or order. According to speech act analysis, it is proposed that every sentence has two, different dimensions to its linguistic meaning: as well as a truth-conditional element, there is also a non-truth-condition, speech act element encoded by what are known as 'mood indicators' (word order, intonation) and which indicates the type of illocutionary force (or speech act being performed). (See Wilson and Sperber (1988) for a discussion of some of the problems with the speech act analysis of mood indicators.)

The distinction between describing and indicating – and, of course, the notion of illocutionary force – was central to speech act theory and many people working within the framework became particularly interested in other linguistic expressions which, they argued, conveyed non-truth-conditional meaning. Consider the use of the adverbial 'frankly' in (11):

(11) Frankly, some politicians are uninspiring.

Intuitions about adverbials such as these do vary, but most people agree that the illocutionary adverbial in example (11) does *not* contribute to truth conditions. The sentence in (11), they would claim, is true *iff* some politicians are uninspiring. The fact that the speaker is speaking frankly about this state of affairs does not affect the truth conditions of the state of affairs itself. One way to test these intuitions is to ask yourself under what conditions (11) is true. Would it still be true if some politicians are uninspiring but the speaker is not speaking frankly?

Speech act theorist J.L. Urmson (1952) claimed that not only were 'illocutionary' adverbials, such as the one in (11), non-truth-conditional, but also that 'attitudinal' adverbials, such as those in (12) and (13), were non-truth-conditional too. Illocutionary adverbials are those expressions that indicate the manner in which you are speaking; attitudinal adverbials indicate the attitude you have to the proposition you are expressing (so they are less to do with the way you are saying something, and more to do with how you feel about what you're saying).

(12) Fortunately, Obama is President.
(13) Happily, some Presidents are inspiring.

Indeed, Urmson also proposed that expressions known as **parentheticals**, as illustrated in italics in (14) and (15), are non-truth-conditional:

(14) Some politicians, *I believe*, are inspiring.
(15) Some famous politicians, *I think*, are uninspiring.

Intuitions here are less clear. Whilst Urmson's speech act account proposes that the adverbials in (12) and (13) merely indicate an attitude to what is being described, and that the parentheticals in (14) and (15) indicate the degree of support the speaker feels for the proposition being expressed, all these examples can be paraphrased in such a way that the adverbials and parentheticals *do* contribute to the truth conditions. Consider (16) to (19):

(16) It's fortunate that Obama is President.
(17) I'm happy that Obama is President.
(18) I believe some politicians are inspiring.
(19) I think some famous politicians are uninspiring.

Whichever way your intuitions go, the distinction between describing and indicating does indeed appear to capture aspects of the distinction between truth-conditional and non-truth-conditional meaning.

The philosopher H.P. **Grice**, famous for his **cooperative principle** and **maxims of conversation**, also provided an account of certain non-truth-conditional expressions (1967: lecture II, 6; 1989). Indeed, he even devised a category into which they fit: the category of conventional **implicature**. Consider (20) and (21), which are adapted from Grice's own examples (Grice 1961):

(20) It's Christmas Day and the shops are open.
(21) It's Christmas Day but the shops are open.

Grice's argument was that the truth conditions of two sentences, which only differ in the interchange of 'and' and 'but', are the same. So both (20) and (21) are true when (a) it is Christmas Day and (b) the shops are open. The difference in meaning between 'and' and 'but' – the fact that the second part somehow contrasts with the first part – could not be dealt with truth-conditionally. What is said in (21) is the same as what is said in (20), and the word 'but' conventionally implicates that there is some kind of contrast between the two parts of the sentence. There are a whole range of discourse connectives such as 'and' and 'but' that theorists have argued are best dealt with in non-truth-conditional terms, such as 'so', 'however', 'after all', etc. Indeed, **discourse markers** are the most widely researched non-truth-conditional expressions, and have been studied from a range of different perspectives: from the point of view of **discourse cohesion** (Halliday and Hasan 1976), **discourse coherence** (Mann and Thompson 1986), **sociolinguistics** (Schiffrin 1994) and **relevance theory** (Sperber and Wilson 1995; Blakemore 2002).

The truth-conditional/non-truth-conditional distinction is an important one for pragmatics. However, the assumptions listed at the beginning of this entry are very much that, i.e. assumptions. As such, they are not shared by everyone. Some linguists take the view that the study of semantics should coincide with the study of truth-conditional meaning. If semantics is construed in this way, then this has a range of implications for the **semantics-pragmatics interface** and the **explicit/implicit distinction**. In Gazdar's formal pragmatic approach, he adopts the formula that 'pragmatics = meaning *minus* truth conditions' (Gazdar 1979a). But surely non-truth-conditional expressions encode something? With regard to this latter question, Blakemore's work on 'procedural' meaning represents a major step forward (Blakemore 1987, 2002).

TIM WHARTON

See also: Assertion; cooperative principle; discourse analysis; discourse coherence; discourse cohesion; explicit/implicit distinction; formal pragmatics; Grice, H.P.; implicature; impliciture; indexicals; inference; maxims of conversation; meaning; philosophy of language; pragmatics; proposition; question; relevance theory; request; Searle, J.; semantics; semantics-pragmatics interface; sociolinguistics; speech act theory; utterance interpretation; what is said

Suggestions for further reading

Blakemore, D. (2002) *Relevance and Linguistic Meaning: The Semantics and Pragmatics of Discourse Markers*, Cambridge: Cambridge University Press. Chapter 2.

Fraser, B. (1998) 'Contrastive discourse markers in English', in A. Jucker and Y. Ziv (eds) *Discourse Markers: Descriptions and Theory*, Amsterdam: John Benjamins.

Wilson, D. and Sperber, D. (1988) 'Mood and the analysis of non-declarative sentences', in J. Dancy, J. Moravcsik and C. Taylor (eds) *Human Agency: Language, Duty, Value*, Stanford, CA: Stanford University Press.

U

Understatement

A number of definitions of understatement have been offered by linguists, philosophers, cognitive scientists, psychologists, literary theorists and other scholars. Among these definitions are the following:

(1) 'To state or represent less strongly or strikingly than the facts would indicate; set forth in restrained terms' (Random House 1999: 1422).
(2) 'Understatements are traditionally analyzed as saying, not the opposite of what is meant, but merely less than what is meant' (Wilson and Sperber 2007: 36).
(3) ' ... presenting something as less significant than it is' (Roberts and Kreuz 1994: 159).
(4) 'Deliberate underemphasis' (Kreuz et al. 1998: 92).
(5) ' ... where speakers conveyed their ironic messages by stating far less than was obviously the case' (Gibbs 2000: 13).

These definitions also neatly demonstrate the range of contemporary scholarship on understatement, which may be distilled into three essential goals. The first goal is the attempt in literary criticism and language and **culture** studies to identify and characterize the presence of different guises of understatement in varieties of languages, fiction and other texts and artifacts (definition (1) – Antoine 2000; Berntsen and Kennedy 1996; Briggs 1978; Carney 1993; Hübler 1983; Johnson 1959; Liggens 1981; Kreuz and Roberts 1993; Mao 1989; Singh 1973;

Spitzbardt 1963). The second goal is a definitional and categorical enterprise which attempts to explain the scope of understatement and how it fits into taxonomies of figurative forms (definition (2) – Colston and O'Brien 2000a; Cummings 2005; Gibbs and Colston 2007; Kitcher 1978; Lowrey 2002; Wilson and Sperber 2007). The third goal is the desire to delineate the comprehension and pragmatic effects of the use of understatement by speakers and writers, including how the form might accomplish these pragmatic effects (definitions (3) to (5) – Berntsen and Kennedy 1996; Colston 1997a; Colston and O'Brien 2000a; Demorest et al. 1983; Gibbs 2000; Gibbs and Colston 2006, 2007; Gibbs et al. 2000; Kreuz et al. 1998; Leggitt and Gibbs 2000; Roberts and Kreuz 1994; Winner et al. 1987). This brief treatment here will focus on the latter two of these goals.

Understatement has been included under the umbrella of verbal **irony** by most accounts (Gibbs 2000; Gibbs and Colston 2006) in that, like verbal irony, understatement typically involves an asserted expression that contradicts or contrasts with a referent **topic**. For instance, a speaker might assert that there is moderate rainfall (e.g. 'It seems to be raining') in reference to something reasonably different in magnitude (e.g. an extreme downpour). Although the contrast offered by verbal irony is stronger, or arguably of a different form than that for understatement, both tropes still work with this contrast (Colston and O'Brien 2000a). This relationship between understatement and verbal irony has indeed been useful in refining relatively loose traditional definitions of verbal irony that were initially based on notions of opposition (Wilson and

Sperber 2007). Other accounts, while recognizing the overlap between verbal irony and understatement, have focused more on how the figures nevertheless differ, particularly in how the different kinds of contrasts they portray between asserted and referent domains can achieve similar as well as subtly different pragmatic effects (Colston 1997a; Colston and O'Brien 2000a; Gibbs 2000; Gibbs and Colston 2007; Roberts and Kreuz 1994).

Perhaps the largest contemporary literature focuses on how understatement is comprehended, including the different pragmatic effects that understatement typically triggers when comprehended. This work has branched into several sub-goals, including how comprehension and pragmatic effect computation develop in children or might differ by personality (Colston 2007; Colston and Gibbs 2007; Demorest *et al.* 1983; Gibbs and Colston 2007; Winner *et al.* 1987), the emotional aspects of understatement understanding (Colston 1997a; Colston and O'Brien 2000a; Gibbs 2000; Gibbs and Colston 2006; Gibbs *et al.* 2000; Kreuz *et al.* 1998; Leggitt and Gibbs 2000; Roberts and Kreuz 1994), and the specific pragmatic effects of understatement, including emotional expression and others, and how they are brought about by the figure's form (Colston 1997a; Colston and Gibbs 2007; Colston and O'Brien 2000a; Gibbs 2000; Gibbs and Colston 2006; Gibbs *et al.* 2000; Kreuz *et al.* 1998; Leggitt and Gibbs 2000; Roberts and Kreuz 1994). Among the other pragmatic effects empirically demonstrated by understatement are surprise expression, **humour,** criticism, a meta-semantic indication that actual events are not as expected, and protection of the user of the understatement (Colston 1997a; Colston and O'Brien 2000a).

Among the challenges facing future scholars of understatement and similar forms is the determination of whether all the generally considered 'ironic' forms of expression can be subsumed under one theory of use, comprehension, definition and scope. It remains unclear whether such an attempt will work, or whether different theories will be necessary for the different functions of ironic forms, or indeed for the different tropes subsumed under the category verbal irony (Gibbs and Colston 2007). Further work is also required to establish which pragmatic effects are

brought about by the figurative form of understatement by itself versus the broader category of figurative or indirect language in general.

HERBERT L. COLSTON

See also: Humour; hyperbole; irony

Suggestions for further reading

Colston, H. and O'Brien, J. (2000) 'Contrast and pragmatics in figurative language: anything understatement can do, irony can do better', *Journal of Pragmatics*, 32: 1557–83.
Gibbs, R. (2000) 'Irony in talk among friends', *Metaphor and Symbol*, 15: 5–27.
Roberts, R. and Kreuz, R. (1994) 'Why do people use figurative language?', *Psychological Science*, 5: 159–63.

Utterance Interpretation

Consider the (attested) example in (1) below. Tim is in a music shop and has just tried out a beautiful vintage guitar, which is staggeringly expensive. Smiling broadly, and handing the lovely guitar back to his friend David, who owns the shop, Tim begins the following exchange:

(1) Tim: Well, I didn't like that at all.
    David: I didn't think you would. Awful, isn't it?

Given the **context** provided above, it's clear that both Tim and David mean the exact *opposite* of what they are saying, and are communicating to each other that they regard the guitar as a thing of rare beauty. The central question a theory of utterance interpretation needs to answer is how it is that hearers bridge the gap between what people say and what people mean by what they say.

While it's true that cases in which speakers say one thing and mean something entirely different are the clearest cases of the kind of gap that needs to be bridged, there are more complex factors at play. There's more to the gap between sentence **meaning** (the domain of **semantics**) and utterance meaning (the domain of **pragmatics**) than is evident in (1). As a result, there are a number of further challenges to which theories of utterance interpretation must rise. Consider the sign in (2), written on the door of a charity shop near where I live:

(2) Sorry! Guide dogs only.

Taken literally, the sign prohibits all creatures except guide dogs from entering the shop (including humans, presumably). However, it is unlikely that anyone – other than someone writing an entry in a pragmatics encyclopaedia – would read it this way. Instead, we recognize it is intended to convey something like 'If you own a dog, you can only bring that dog into this shop with you if it is a guide dog'. It communicates much more than the words themselves say. There's nothing implied, but in order for someone reading the sign to understand what the sign actually communicates, they need to do much more than simply understand the words.

Linguists call this kind of phenomenon linguistic underdeterminacy (sometimes semantic underdeterminacy), and distinguish it from the implied meaning in (1). The idea is that, irrespective of any **irony** or sarcasm that a speaker may intend, what is linguistically encoded in an utterance *still* more often than not falls well short of what it is intended to communicate in crucial ways. A couple of obvious examples are those in (3) and (4). Before the speaker of these utterances can be understood, **indexicals** must have **reference** assigned to them and an ambiguous word must be disambiguated:

(3) He lost it over there.
(4) The students are revolting!

Some less obvious examples are included below:

(5) I've literally got nothing to wear!
(6) Jack drinks too much.
(7) Have you seen Laura's painting?

If (5) is uttered in exasperation whilst preparing to go to a party, it is unlikely the speaker is intending to convey that they spend their entire life in the nude. What the speaker means by 'nothing' is something more akin to 'nothing suitable for the party'. The **proposition** expressed by an utterance of (6) will (probably)

include the fact that it is alcohol that Jack drinks too much of, and also information concerning what it is that Jack drinks too much to do: to operate machinery, for example, or to be entrusted with driving everyone home from a party. In (7), the precise nature of the relationship between Laura and the painting – whether it is one that she owns, one that she has painted, or one that she loves above any other – is information that is not included in the words themselves.

Various proposals have been made as to how the gap might be bridged and most modern accounts can be traced back to the work of H. Paul **Grice** (1957, 1989). Grice proposed that utterance interpretation is not just a matter of coding and decoding. Rather, it is a rational, inferential activity involving the expression and recognition of **intentions**. It is a two-stage process: in the first stage, a hearer decodes the words they have heard; in the second, the hearer uses the linguistic meaning to work out (or infer) the intended speaker meaning. Since **conversation** is a rational activity, hearers are guided in the interpretive process by the expectation that a speaker will be meeting certain standards. From this it follows that they will behave in certain predictable ways. A hearer can therefore recognize the best hypothesis about the speaker's meaning by arriving at an interpretation that satisfies those expectations the speaker is aiming at, or standards he or she is trying to meet.

Grice's own account of utterance interpretation appealed to a **cooperative principle** and conversational **maxims** (Grice 1967). In the exchange in (1) Tim and David are both overtly violating what Grice called the first *Maxim of Quality* ('Do not say what you believe to be false'). However, they are still being cooperative, and in interpreting the utterances they will both search for another proposition related to the one the speaker is expressing. For Grice, the most obvious candidate would be the opposite propositions to the ones actually expressed. David would therefore infer that Tim likes the guitar a great deal, and Tim will infer that David knew this would be the case, and that he likes it also.

But as far as the process of utterance interpretation is concerned, Grice's maxims only come into play once the hearer has successfully derived the proposition the speaker has expressed (or in Grice's terms, **what is said** by the speaker). Researchers, who have built on Grice's work, have noticed that the extra layers of meaning present in (5) to (7) are actually *part* of Grice's 'what is said'. As a result, different proposals have been made as to exactly how his framework, which only dealt with implied meaning (or **implicatures**), might be adapted to assimilate this. These proposals impact in various ways on how we might conceive of the distinction between semantics and pragmatics, between these notions and Grice's notion of what is said, and also the relationship between decoding and **inference**.

Relevance theory (Sperber and Wilson 1995), for example, does away with the notion of 'what is said' entirely, and pragmatically derived elements of the proposition expressed by the speaker are called *explicatures*. Bach (1994a) retains a minimal, semantic notion of what is said and calls pragmatically derived elements of the proposition expressed the level of **impli-citure** (note the second 'i'). Recanati (2004b) calls the kind of phenomena in (5) to (7) instances of *saturation*, and regards saturation as one of a group of processes that takes place in the derivation of pragmatic aspects of an enriched version of what is said. The debate continues (*see* Atlas 2005; Carston 2002; Horn 2006; Recanati 2004b). However, most people now agree that linguistic **communication** is indeed an inferential activity, and that hearers are guided in the interpretive process by an expectation that a speaker will meet certain standards (Levinson 2000; Sperber and Wilson 1995).

While Grice was a philosopher, a consequence of his pioneering work has been the recognition that a full-fledged theory of utterance interpretation will need to encompass ideas from disciplines beyond **philosophy**. Utterance interpretation, for example, involves inferential computations, which need to be explained. It also exploits the human ability to interpret the actions of others in terms of the mental states behind these actions, known as **theory of mind**. After Grice, the study of pragmatics has had to become truly cross-disciplinary with links to **cognitive science**, psychology and beyond.

Turning first to the question of what inferential computations might be involved in utterance interpretation, introductory logic books generally introduce the notion of inference by means of examples such as those below:

(8) Premise 1: If it's snowing, it's cold.
Premise 2: It's snowing.
Conclusion: It's cold.

This is a straightforward example of the process logicians call deduction. It is a foolproof argument, insofar as in any case where the two premises are true, the conclusion will also be true. But is it correct that the inferences made during the process of utterance interpretation are always true? This is probably not the case. The fact that **misunderstandings** occur is clear evidence that **inferential comprehension** is not foolproof and, hence, that the kind of inferential processes at work are not *all* deductive. Even in cases where a hearer interprets an utterance correctly, the inference is at best only an inference-to-the-best-explanation. Since misunderstandings do happen, hearers can *never* be sure that the interpretation they arrive at is the one intended by the speaker.

Some researchers (e.g. Levinson 1983) have suggested that interpretive inferences are inductive or probabilistic, such as the one in (9) (*see also* Brown and Yule 1983):

(9) Premise 1: When it rains, he usually carries an umbrella.
Premise 2: It's raining.
Conclusion: He's carrying an umbrella.

In contrast with the inference in (8), notice that even if the two premises in the example are true, the conclusion can still be false. Does this better explain the kind of inference at work in linguistic communication? This is not necessarily the case. There is no principled reason to deny that just because the inferences made in the process of utterance interpretation are *non-demonstrative* (or not foolproof), they cannot be at least partly deductive.

Moreover, the challenge of explaining what kind of inference takes place in utterance interpretation is complicated by a range of other factors. First, the kind of beliefs and assumptions that act as premises are not simply true or false, as they are in classical logic, but are held with a varying degree of strength or weakness. Second, while logic books introduce inference using the staged, step-by-step arguments in (8) and (9), the kind of inference involved in utterance interpretation appears to be spontaneous and fast. Implicatures are not arrived at laboriously; they are derived in an instant. Third and finally, appealing to one particular form of inference – whether it be deduction, induction or **abduction** – is to say nothing about the much more complex question of how the premises themselves are chosen from the potentially infinite number of beliefs or assumptions available. An account of utterance interpretation must constrain very tightly the number of plausible candidates.

Turning to the issue of theory of mind, there has been a huge amount of recent psychological research on the capacity for mental-state attribution among humans and non-human animals. It seems clear that the kind of metarepresentational abilities at work in utterance interpretation are related to this wider meta-psychological ability (Allen and Bekoff 1997; Baron-Cohen 1995; Happé 1994b). However, there are a variety of reasons to believe that there is much more to the processes at work in an act of utterance interpretation than general mind-reading abilities.

The principal reason is that it is often the case that what makes it possible for an individual to attribute an intention to another is observing not only their behaviour but also the consequences of their behaviour. Observing someone climbing a tree and rescuing a cat, we may infer that their intention in climbing that tree was to rescue the cat; observing someone jumping over a fence and picking some flowers, we may infer that their intention in jumping over the fence was to pick some flowers. In contrast to this, the only clue an audience has to the content of the complex intention which constitutes a speaker's meaning is the fact that the speaker has produced a certain utterance which falls far short of determining what he or she intends to convey. Until the hearer has understood the speaker's meaning, the speaker's behaviour will have no observable consequences from which his or her intentions can be inferred: the hearer can't *first* observe the effect of an utterance and *then* infer what it meant.

These and other problems suggest that utterance interpretation might be carried out by a specialized, domain-specific comprehension mechanism or module, which may form a sub-part of theory of mind (Sperber 2000; Sperber and Wilson 2002; Wilson 2005; Wilson and Sperber 2002). Seen this way, the process of utterance interpretation is characterized in terms of the automatic operation of an evolved, sub-conscious procedure or **heuristic** (Gigerenzer *et al.* 1999). This can be contrasted with the traditional view of the process of utterance interpretation Grice envisaged (though *see* Grice 2001b), in which it is characterized in terms of conscious, reflective inferences.

TIM WHARTON

See also: Animal communication, pragmatics of; conversation; disambiguation; explicit/implicit distinction; Grice, H.P.; implicature; impliciture; indexicals; inference; inferential comprehension; meaning; modular pragmatics; modularity of mind thesis; neo-Gricean pragmatics; philosophy of language; post-Gricean pragmatics; pragmatics; proposition; radical pragmatics; rationality; reasoning; semantics-pragmatics interface; what is said

Suggestions for further reading

Blakemore, D. (1992) *Understanding Utterances*, Oxford: Blackwell.
Sperber, D. and Wilson, D. ([1986] 1995) *Relevance: Communication and Cognition*, Oxford: Blackwell. Chapter 2.

V

Vagueness

'Vagueness' (Kempson 1977) consists of 'a closed set of identifiable items that can be interpreted based on the particular **context** in which they occur' (Cheng 2007: 162). These items signal 'to the hearer that the utterance, or part of it, is not to be interpreted precisely' (Cheng 2007: 162). Vagueness is defined variously as 'fuzziness, vague language, generality, **ambiguity** and even ambivalence' (He 2000: 7), vague language (Channell 1994), vague expressions (Carter and McCarthy 1997), imprecision (Crystal and Davy 1975), and loose talk (Sperber and Wilson 1995). Vague expressions are more pervasive in spoken **discourse**, particularly **conversations**, than written discourse, occur in a variety of contexts, and serve a variety of functions (Carter and McCarthy 1997; Biber *et al*. 1999; Jucker *et al*. 2003), although the use of vagueness varies across spoken genres (Cheng 2007). Cheng and Warren (2001, 2003) find Hong Kong Chinese and native speakers of English use vagueness to perform similar functions in social interaction, such as to achieve solidarity, cover up linguistic and knowledge deficiencies, show that they know the rules of information quantity in different speech situations, and protect one's face and that of others. Warren (2007) suggests that discourse intonation (Brazil 1997) can disambiguate vagueness or add extra layers of **meaning** to vague items based on the speaker's perceptions of the context.

Regarding linguistic realizations of vagueness, Crystal and Davy (1975: 112–14) identify types of lexical vagueness on a spectrum, from items which express 'total vagueness' like *thing, whatsit*

and so on, to examples such as *I've got some tomatoes, beans and things*, and the use of the suffix-*ish* in colloquial English. Brown and Yule (1983: 8–9) also note that spoken language contains a lot of 'general, non-specific' vocabulary. Dubois (1987: 531) describes the use of **hedges** such as *close to, about, around, on the order of*, and *something like* with numbers as 'imprecise' numerical expressions. Wierzbicka (1986a: 597) calls *just, at least, only, merely* and *at the most* 'approximatives'. Channell (1994) describes three categories of vagueness:

(a) vague additives to numbers: a word or phrase is added to a precise figure to signal a vague reading ('about', 'around', 'round', 'approximately');
(b) vagueness by choice of vague words or phrases ('and things', 'or something', 'and such', 'or anything', 'thing', 'thingy', 'whatsisname', 'whatnot');
(c) vagueness by **scalar implicature** ('most', 'many', 'some', 'few', 'often', 'sometimes', 'occasionally', 'seldom').

Research on vagueness has examined various discourse types, such as English plays (Graves and Hodge 1947), advertising (Leech 1966; Myers 1994), biomedical slide talks (Dubois 1987), academic writing on economics (Channell 1990), a group task that requires co-ordinated actions among the members (Erev *et al*. 1991), occupational standards (Drave 1995), ESL writing by Chinese students (Allison 1995), patents (Myers 1995), academic writing (Myers 1996), **telephone conversations** (Urbanová 1999), and both speech and writing across a number of genres (Channell 1985, 1994; Kennedy 1987). Examining Hong Kong English textbooks, Cheng (2007) notes that the examples of vague expressions are far too limited for the students to master effectively the important pragmatic use of language to meet their **communication** needs.

WINNIE CHENG

See also: Ambiguity; communication; context; conversation; discourse; hedge; knowledge; meaning; scalar implicature; telephone conversation; utterance interpretation

Suggestions for further reading

Cutting, J. (ed.) (2007) *Vague Language Explored*, London: Palgrave Macmillan.
Keefe, R. and Smith, P. (ed.) (1999) *Vagueness: A Reader*, Cambridge, MA: MIT Press.
Shapiro, S. (2006) *Vagueness in Context*, Oxford and New York: Oxford University Press.

What Is Said

Within the classical Gricean paradigm, a distinction is made between what is said and what is implicated (e.g. Grice 1989: 25). However, as pointed out by Levinson (2000: 170), **Grice**'s characterization of what is said is quite complex, though it may roughly be presented as follows:

(1) Grice's concept of what is said
   U said that p by uttering x if and only if:
   a. x conventionally means p
   b. U speaker-meant p
   c. p is the conventional meaning of x minus any conventional implicature

where U stands for the speaker/utterer, p for a **proposition**, and x for a linguistic expression.

Given the definition in (1), what is said is generally taken to be (i) the conventional **meaning** of a sentence uttered with the exclusion of any conventional **implicature**, and (ii) the truth-conditional propositional content of the sentence uttered (e.g. Grice 1989: 25; Levinson 1983: 97; Levinson 2000: 170; Neale 1992: 520–21; Clark 1996: 141).

According to Bach (2004b), the Gricean notion of what is said is needed in order to account for three kinds of cases. In the first, the speaker means what he or she says and something else as well, as in conversational implicatures and indirect **speech acts**. The second of these cases is where the speaker says one thing and means something else instead, as in non-literal utterances such as **metaphor, irony** and **hyperbole**. Third and finally, there is the case where the speaker says something and does not

mean anything at all by it. Cases in point may include translating, reciting or rehearsing in which the speaker says something with full understanding but does not use it to communicate (Bach 1994a; *see also* Huang 2007).

On Grice's (1989: 25) view, before one works out what is said, one has (i) **reference** to identify, as in (2); (ii) **deixis** to fix, as in (3); and (iii) **ambiguity** and ambivalences to resolve, as in (4).

(2) Advice given by the government during an outbreak of salmonella in the UK
   Fried eggs should be cooked properly and if there are frail or elderly people in the house, they should be hard-boiled.
(3) Accompanied by selecting gestures
   You and you, but not you, stand up!
(4) The plane taxied to the terminal.

To these, Levinson (2000: 172–86) added (iv) unpacking ellipsis, as in (5); and (v) narrowing generality, as in (6).

(5) If I can, you can.
(6) John had a glass of milk for breakfast this morning.

It turns out, however, that the interpretation of (2) to (6) involves pragmatic **inference** of some kind. In (2), the preferred antecedent of the pronoun *they* is *eggs* rather than *frail or elderly people*. This reading is dependent on what the speaker is most likely to intend to mean, and our real-world knowledge about who or what is or is not likely to be hard-boiled. The three uses of the deictic expression *you* in (3) can be properly determined only by a direct, moment by moment monitoring of the physical aspects of the speech event in which the sentence is uttered. The **disambiguation** of the lexical items *plane, taxi* and *terminal* in (4), due to Hirst (1987), may depend on whether or not the sentence is uttered at an airport. Next, the interpretation of the elided constituent in (5) requires also the physical aspects of **context**. Finally, *milk* in (6) has to be pragmatically narrowed down to 'cow's milk'. All this indicates that in examples like (2) to (6), there is pragmatic intrusion of some sort involved in the working out of what Grice called what is said (e.g. Levinson 2000; Huang 2004b).

What is said in the classical Gricean sense is, then, largely semantically based. It constitutes the semantic **representation** or linguistic meaning of the sentence uttered, together with a set of preconditions on the determination of the proposition expressed: (i) identifying reference, (ii) completing deixis, and (iii) disambiguating expressions. What is said is itself minimally but fully propositional. But as shown above, the working out of the preconditions involves pragmatic intrusion. Given all this, the question that arises next is whether the classical Gricean characterization of what is said needs to be redefined.

Relevance theorists

The relevance theorists (e.g. Sperber and Wilson 1995; Carston 2004b) argued for a broader, more pragmatic notion of what is said, though they do not use the term 'what is said'. What is said in the relevance-theoretic sense can roughly be divided into two parts: semantic representations and explicatures. Explicatures are responsible for the pragmatically enriched level of what Sperber and Wilson called explicit content. They cover both pragmatic resolution of **indexicals** and ambiguities, and minimal and enriched propositions.

Recanati

Like the relevance theorists, Recanati (2004b) also endorsed a wider, more pragmatic conception of what is said. Both the relevance theorists' and Recanati's notion of what is said (in what Levinson (2000) called the 'everyday sense of

what is stated') constitute what Berg (2002) termed 'contextually enriched content'. According to Recanati (2004b: 6), what is said has a semantic part (i.e. a semantic representation or sentence meaning), and a pragmatic part (i.e. the pragmatically enriched said). Elsewhere, Recanati dubbed the semantic part i-content (intuitive truth-conditional content of the utterance) (Recanati 2000) or 'what is said$_{min}$' (Recanati 2001c), as opposed to c-content (compositionally articulated content of the utterance) or 'what is said$_{max}$' for the pragmatic part. Notice that in Recanati's account, reference assignment, deixis identification, and disambiguation, and minimal and expanded propositions all belong to pragmatically enriched what is said.

Bach

In contrast to the relevance theorists and Recanati, Bach (1994a, 2001, 2004b) opted for a notion of what is said that is narrower than the original minimal Gricean concept. Following Grice (1989), Bach was of the view that what is said should be 'closely related to the conventional meaning of the ... sentence ... uttered' and must correspond to 'the elements of [the sentence], their order and their syntactic character' (Grice 1989: 87). In other words, according to Bach (1994a), the content of the original Gricean notion of what is said is a *structured* proposition, that is, a proposition which is associated with its syntactic form. Bach called this narrower criterion for what is said the 'syntactic correlation constraint'. What is said, thus understood, is closely linked with both the conventional, semantic content and the syntactic structure of the sentence uttered. This locutionary sense of what is said is roughly equivalent to Berg's (2002) characterization of what is said as being general content, as opposed to contextually enriched content. In addition, on Bach's account, reference resolution, deixis fixing, and disambiguation are also part of what is said. The semantic representation of what is said may be sub-propositional. In other words, it can be in the form of what Bach called propositional radicals. Propositional radicals and minimal propositions undergo a process of completion and expansion respectively to be transformed into what is implicit or what Bach called (conversational) **implicitures**. Implicitures then provide input to the classical Gricean inferential mechanism (the **cooperative principle** and its component **maxims of conversation**), yielding conversational implicatures as output. Thus, in Bach's theory, the traditional Gricean dichotomy between what is said and what is implicated is replaced by a trichotomy between what is said, what is implicit and what is implicated.

Levinson

Levinson (2000) retained the classical Gricean characterization of what is said. As mentioned previously, the Gricean semantic notion of what is said consists of semantic representations and a set of preconditions to determining the propositions expressed. But unlike Grice, Levinson allowed conversational implicatures to intrude onto the assignment of truth-conditional content. Put differently, on Levinson's view, conversational implicatures are not only needed to explain additional propositions classically 'post'-semantically. They are also required pre-semantically to account for reference determination, deictic resolution, disambiguation, ellipsis unpacking and generality-narrowing, as well as to affect truth conditions in complex constructions such as comparatives, conditionals and *because*-clauses.

By way of summary, what the relevance theorists, Recanati, Bach and Levinson have in common is the point of view that at least part of the original Gricean notion of what is said has to be understood as involving much more of a pragmatic contribution than Grice had acknowledged. But there are two points they cannot agree on. First, while the relevance theorists, Recanati and Levinson believed that there is substantial pragmatic intrusion into the original Gricean concept of what is said, Bach denied that there is such an intrusion, and posited a level intermediate between what is said and what is implicated. Second, the disagreement concerns the nature of the pragmatic inference under consideration. For the relevance theorists, Recanati and Bach, the pragmatic inference under discussion is of a special kind, which differs from conversational implicature; for Levinson, it is the same beast as conversational implicature. This difference certainly has implications for the

domain of **semantics** and that of **pragmatics**, the interface between semantics and pragmatics, and indeed for the theory of meaning as a whole (*see also* Huang 2007).

YAN HUANG

See also: Context; explicit/implicit distinction; Grice, H.P.; implicature; impliciture; neo-Gricean pragmatics; pragmatics; relevance theory; scalar implicature; semantics

Suggestions for further reading

Grice, H.P. (1989) *Studies in the Way of Words*, Cambridge, MA: Harvard University Press.
Huang, Y. (2007) *Pragmatics*, Oxford: Oxford University Press.
Levinson, S.C. (2000) *Presumptive Meanings: The Theory of Generalized Conversational Implicature*, Cambridge, MA: MIT Press.

Wittgenstein, L.

Ludwig Wittgenstein (1889–1951) is second only to Gottlob Frege (1848–1925) as the chief architect of the conceptual edifice in terms of which the twentieth century thought and spoke about language. His work is sometimes said to fall into two periods, often referred to with the labels the Early Wittgenstein and the Later Wittgenstein. The principal text of the early period is the *Tractatus Logico-Philosophicus*, published in German in 1921 and in an English translation, by C.K. Ogden, the following year. The principal text of the later period is *Philosophische Untersuchungen*, which appeared also as the *Philosophical Investigations* in an English translation, by G.E.M. Anscombe, in 1953. The exact relationship between the work of the Early and the Later Wittgenstein is a matter of not infrequent controversy (*cf.* Kenny 1973; Pears 1987, 1988). The present author favours a perspective that profiles a continuity, with certain occasional differences in emphases, temperament and style, over a complete sea change (*cf.* Bogen 1972; Coffa 1991; Soames 2003a: chapters 9–11; Soames 2003b: chapters 1–2; Beaney 2006; Losonsky 2006: chapter 7). Rather unusually, Stroll (2002) argues that there are three periods.

On the basis of the enormous legacy of unpublished writings, found after Wittgenstein's death, he claims that a new and original phase of philosophical development is discernible. The principal text of this third period is *On Certainty*, which appeared in 1969, edited by G.E.M. Anscombe and G.H. von Wright and translated by Denis Paul and G.E.M. Anscombe. This last period will not be discussed here.

The 'headline' arguments of the *Tractatus* revolve around the Picture Theory of Meaning. One argument gives an account of the nature and structure of language; another argument gives an account of the nature and structure of the world. A final argument attempts to establish that the nature and structure of (all meaningful) language is the way it is because the nature and structure of the world is the way *it* is: language, when analyzed in the appropriate way and with the appropriate logical tools, provides a *picture* of the world. The following quotation reveals what is perhaps the key move (and illustrates the uncompromising austerity of Wittgenstein's early style):

2.1 We make to ourselves pictures of facts.
2.11 The picture presents the facts in logical space, the existence and non-existence of atomic facts.
2.12 The picture is a model of reality.
2.13 To the objects correspond in the picture the elements of the picture.
2.131 The elements of the picture stand, in the picture, for the objects.
2.14 The picture consists in the fact that its elements are combined with one another in a definite way.
2.141 The picture is a fact.
2.15 That the elements of the picture are combined with one another in a definite way, represents that the things are so combined with one another.

With the benefit afforded by nearly a century of hindsight, these, and accompanying, arguments may be read as constituting the first systematic attempt to develop a truth-conditional **semantics** for natural language (*cf.* Soames 2003a). Useful commentary on the *Tractatus* can be found in Anscombe (1963), Mounce (1981), McDonough (1986) and Brockhaus (1991).

The 'headline' arguments of the *Investigations* revolve around Wittgenstein's remarks on the possibility of a private language and on the character of rule-following. These remarks are, in turn, embedded in further, often rhetorical and polemical, remarks on the determinacy of sense, the pursuit of essence, the nature of philosophy, language games, family resemblances, and what might now be called the natural ecology and evolution of **communication**. The taut reasoning of the *Tractatus* is replaced, in the *Investigations*, by what Wittgenstein himself called 'a number of sketches of landscapes which were made in the course of ... long and involved journeyings' (*Philosophical Investigations*, Preface) and there has, inevitably, ensued a huge exegetical literature on these, sometimes very evocative, sketches (e.g. Pitcher 1966; Kripke 1982b; Hunter 1985, 1990; Hilmy 1987; Hanfling 1989; Werhane 1992; Garver 1994; McGinn 1997; Wilson 1998; Baker and Hacker 2005a, 2005b). If, therefore, one of the core theses in the *Tractatus* is that there is only one meaningful use of language – the one that science employs and which is determined by the Picture Theory – then in the *Investigations* a multiplicity of meaningful uses is now recognized:

But how many kinds of sentence are there? Say assertion, question, and command? – There are *countless* kinds: countless different kinds of use of what we call "symbols", "words", "sentences". And this multiplicity is not something fixed, given once and for all; but new types of language, new language-games, as we may say, come into existence, and others become obsolete and get forgotten.
(§23; emphasis in original)

Commanding, questioning, recounting, chatting, are as much a part of *our natural history* as walking, eating, drinking, playing.
(§25; emphasis added)

This plurality of language-games allows Wittgenstein to attempt an account of the origin of philosophical problems: 'philosophical problems arise when language *goes on holiday*' (§38; emphasis in original). He elaborates on this aphorism as follows:

When philosophers use a word – 'knowledge', 'being', 'object', 'I', 'proposition', 'name' – and try to grasp the *essence* of the thing, one must always ask oneself: is the word ever actually used in this way in the language game which is its original home?

What *we* do is to bring words back from their metaphysical to their everyday use.

(§116; emphasis in original)

And when all of language is safely back where it should be and properly re-housed, philosophical problems, and indeed philosophy itself, completely disappear:

The real discovery is the one that makes me capable of stopping doing philosophy when I want to. – The one that gives philosophy peace, so that it is no longer tormented by questions which bring *itself* in question.

(§133; emphasis in original)

There are a number of puzzles in the *Investigations*. Most of these relate to Wittgenstein's views on the purposes of his inquiries. He gives some particularly stark statements about method: (i) 'There must not be anything hypothetical in our considerations. We must do away with all *explanation*, and description alone must take its place' (§109; emphasis in original). Again: (ii) 'Philosophy may in no way interfere with the actual use of language; it can in the end only describe it' (§124). Again: (iii) 'Say what you choose, so long as it does not prevent you from seeing the facts' (§79). And finally, and very tersely: (iv) 'To repeat: don't think, but look!' (§66). These, and other, remarks can easily be marshalled to neutralize any suggestion that the Later Wittgenstein is criticizing, and dismissing as mistaken, the Early Wittgenstein. Philosophy doesn't criticize. Philosophy doesn't refute:

Philosophy simply puts everything before us, and neither explains nor deduces anything. – Since everything lies open to view there is nothing to explain.

(§126)

The Early Wittgenstein, then, on this view, is merely engaging in a particular language-game

which the Later Wittgenstein, by his own remarks, is only attempting to describe and 'in no way interfere with'. The 'continuity hypothesis' of Wittgenstein's thought is, therefore, to be preferred over the 'sea-change hypothesis'.

The risks in the interpretation of the *Investigations*, and other of Wittgenstein's posthumously published work, are very great and should not be underestimated (*cf.* Kahane *et al.* 2007). Apart from its obvious fragmentary nature, and its occasional, almost whimsical asides (e.g. 'What is your aim in philosophy? – To shew the fly the way out of the fly-bottle' (§309)), none of this work is independent of translator or editorial intervention. Determining what Wittgenstein 'really meant' is, many would say, and the present author would agree, probably an impossible task. Perhaps the most heuristically sensible strategy is to take seriously two of the last sentences from the Preface of the *Investigations*: 'I should not like my writing to spare other people the trouble of thinking. But, if possible, to stimulate someone to thoughts of his own.'

KEN TURNER

See also: Anglo-American and European continental traditions; Grice, H.P.; normative pragmatics; ordinary language philosophy; Peirce, C.S.; philosophy of language

Suggestions for further reading

McGuinness, B. (1988) *Wittgenstein: A Life. Young Ludwig (1889–1921)*, London: Duckworth.
——(ed.) (2008) *Wittgenstein in Cambridge: Letters and Documents 1911–1951*, Oxford: Blackwell.
Monk, R. (1991) *Ludwig Wittgenstein: The Duty of Genius*, London: Vintage.

Word Learning, Role of Mindreading in

All over the world, independently of language spoken or IQ, children are impressively good at learning the **meaning** of words. They begin to utter their first words by their first birthday, and by the second half of their second year they learn over ten words per day. They learn in **conversation** without any explicit training.

According to an empiricist tradition concerning **child language acquisition**, lexical items are learnt by association. On this view, as words are typically uttered when the child is looking at the object to which the word refers (the referent), the sound and the referent are associated by a statistically reliable process. Despite being extremely simple from a cognitive-architectural perspective, this associative hypothesis has been challenged by a number of empirical arguments which suggest that more specific learning processes are involved, such as syntactic and pragmatic processes. In particular, considerable data suggest that children assume the speaker's perceptual and psychological perspective during word learning. Rather than being an associationist learner, the child seems to be an intentional interpreter who is skilled in understanding the role of joint attentional situations (Tomasello 1999). In the following discussion, the main arguments in support of this view will be summarized including the results of experimental studies (for an excellent analysis, *see* Bloom 2000 and Tomasello 1999).

A number of factors suggest that an associationist approach to word learning is problematic. First, the practice of ostensively referring to objects and people is not universal. Even in Western **culture**, it does not account for important aspects of the learning process. For example, verb meaning is typically learned by interpreting and planning actions ('*Give* me the cup, please') rather than by ostensive practice. Second, despite the fact that words are often uttered when the child is not looking at the object, the referential link is nonetheless correctly established. For example, even if the child is looking at a chair in front of him when the adult says 'truck', the child knows that the word 'truck' is never intended to refer to chairs. Finally, learning is extraordinarily fast, whereas a statistical-associative process would be much slower.

In a series of important experiments, Baldwin (1991) observed children's understanding of basic communicative **intentions** during lexical learning. In a well-known study, children were given one unknown object to play with, while another unknown object was put in a bucket close to the experimenter. When the children were not paying attention to their toy, the experimenter looked at the object in the bucket and uttered a new word. Eighteen-month-old children did not associate the new label with the object they were looking at, concentrating instead on the experimenter's gaze, presumably understanding that the adult *intended* to name that object. Although children follow the gaze of adults, this is not a blind instinct. Even 3-year-olds tend to override it when it is not relevant to understanding the speaker's intention, e.g. when the adult does not know the location of the object they are naming (Nurmsoo and Bloom 2008; *see also* Moll and Tomasello 2006).

Another interesting study revealed that in naming familiar artefacts, children increasingly tend to consider their history (Gutheil *et al.* 2004). Children ranging from 4 to 9 years of age were presented with a familiar artefact. The perceptual cues of the object were then radically altered so that the current function was presumably changed (e.g. a straw was crushed). When asked if the altered object was still a member of the artefact category, children tended to behave like adults, i.e. they tended to obliterate the perceptual cues and take into account the history of the artefact and presumably the creator's intentions (see German and Defeyter's (2000) hypothesis that younger children also assume an intentional attitude and consider the experimenter's intentions).

The precocious attitude to using folk psychological **reasoning** in naming objects has been demonstrated in a number of other studies. For example, Birch and Bloom (2002) showed that when hearing a proper name, even 2-year-olds tend to consider the experimenter's epistemic state, because they attribute the lexical label to the individual with whom the experimenter is familiar. As in adults, the effect disappears with common names. To conclude with a more recent experiment, Birch *et al.* (2008) showed that from 3 years of age, children spontaneously keep track of the speaker's reliability, favouring a previously veridical person when learning a new word (*see also* Koenig *et al.* 2004 for similar data concerning non-spontaneous learning, and Jaswal and Neely 2007).

An intense debate concerns the specificity of learning mechanisms. To restrict the analysis to researchers who are committed to the **modularity of mind thesis**, the processes of **inferential comprehension** involved in word learning fall within the domain of the alleged **theory of mind** mechanism (ToMM) underlying folk-psychological **competence** (Bloom 2000). A different perspective is defended by the neo-Gricean pragmatists Sperber and Wilson (2002). In their view, lexical learning involves a sub-module of ToMM, which specifically applies a relevance-based procedure to linguistic inputs. This suggestion originates from empirical arguments. For example, Sperber and Wilson observe that the set of possible interpretations of an action is typically much more restricted than the possible linguistic interpretations of an utterance, and that 2-year-olds, who fail standard theory of mind tasks, understand the multiple levels of **metarepresentation** involved in inferential comprehension in the linguistic domain. This empirical question concerning the architecture of the mind is still open, and an important role will presumably be played by clinical data on alleged dissociations between psychological and linguistic competences in individuals with **autism spectrum disorders**, Williams syndrome and other specific mental conditions (Rinaldi 2000).

CRISTINA MEINI

See also: Autism spectrum disorders; child language acquisition; Grice, H.P.; infant-directed talk and pragmatics; inferential comprehension; metarepresentation; relevance theory; theory of mind

Suggestion for further reading

Bloom, P. (2001) 'Précis of *How Children Learn the Meanings of Words*', *Behavioral and Brain Sciences*, 24: 1095–103.

Bibliography

Abdesslem, H. (2001) 'Politeness strategies in the discourse of drama: a case study', *Journal of Literary Semantics*, 30: 111–38.

Abelin, Å. (2004) 'Cross-cultural multimodal interpretation of emotional expressions – an experimental study of Spanish and Swedish', paper presented at *Speech Prosody 2004*, Nara, Japan, March 2004. Online. Available: www.isca-speech.org/archive/sp2004/sp04_647.pdf (accessed 26 August 2008).

Abercrombie, D. (1968) 'Paralanguage', *British Journal of Disorders of Communication*, 3: 55–59.

Abney, L. (1994) 'Gender differences in oral folklore narratives', *The SECOL Review: South-eastern Conference on Linguistics*, 18: 62–79.

Abu-Akel, A. (1999) 'Phoricity as a measure of clozaril's efficacy in treating disorganized schizophrenia', *Clinical Linguistics and Phonetics*, 13: 381–93.

Abusch, D. (1994) 'The scope of indefinites', *Natural Language Semantics*, 2: 83–135.

Achiba, M. (2003) *Learning to Request in a Second Language: Child Interlanguage Pragmatics*, Clevedon, UK: Multilingual Matters.

Ackema, P. and Neeleman, A. (2004) *Beyond Morphology: Interface Conditions on Word Order*, Oxford: Oxford University Press.

Ackerman, B.P. (1979) 'Children's understanding of definite descriptions: pragmatic inferences to the speaker's intent', *Journal of Experimental Child Psychology*, 28: 1–15.

——(1981) 'Young children's understanding of a speaker's intentional use of a false utterance', *Developmental Psychology*, 17: 472–80.

——(1983) 'Form and function in children's understanding of ironic utterances', *Journal of Experimental Child Psychology*, 35: 487–508.

——(1986) 'Children's sensitivity to comprehension failure in interpreting a nonliteral use of an utterance', *Child Development*, 57: 485–97.

Acredolo, L.P. and Goodwyn, S.W. (1990) 'Sign language in babies: the significance of symbolic gesturing for understanding language development', in R. Vasta (ed.) *Annals of Child Development: A Research Annual*, vol. 7, London: Jessica Kingsley.

Adams, C. (2002) 'Practitioner review: the assessment of language pragmatics', *Journal of Child Psychology and Psychiatry*, 43: 973–87.

Adams, C. and Bishop, D.V.M. (1989) 'Conversational characteristics of children with semantic-pragmatic disorder. I: exchange structure, turntaking, repairs and cohesion', *British Journal of Disorders of Communication*, 24: 211–39.

Adams, C. and Lloyd, J.T. (2005) 'Elicited and spontaneous communicative functions and stability of conversational measures with children who have pragmatic language impairments', *International Journal of Language and Communication Disorders*, 40: 41–65.

Adelswärd, V., Aronsson, K. and Linell, P. (1988) 'Discourse of blame: courtroom constructions of social identity from the perspective of the defendant', *Semiotica*, 71: 261–84.

Adler, J.E. *et al.* (1987) 'Open peer commentary on "Précis of *Relevance: Communication and Cognition*"', *Behavioral and Brain Sciences*, 10: 710–36.

Agha, A. (1993) 'Grammatical and indexical convention in honorific discourse', *Journal of Linguistic Anthropology*, 3: 131–63.

——(1994) 'Honorification', *Annual Review of Anthropology*, 23: 277–302.

——(1998) 'Stereotypes and registers of honorific language', *Language in Society*, 27: 151–93.

——(2003) 'The social life of cultural value', *Language and Communication* 23: 231–73.

——(2007) *Language and Social Relations*, Cambridge: Cambridge University Press.

Agre, P.E. (1995) 'Computational research on interaction and agency', *Artificial Intelligence*, 72: 1–52.

——(1997) *Computation and Human Experience*, Cambridge: Cambridge University Press.

Ahrenholz, B. (2000) 'Modality and referential movement in instructional discourse: comparing the production of Italian learners of German with native German and native Italian production', *Studies in Second Language Acquisition*, 22: 337–68.

Aijmer, K. (1997) '*I think* – an English modal particle', in T. Swan and O. Jansen Westvik (eds) *Modality in Germanic Languages: Historical and Comparative Perspectives*, Berlin: Mouton de Gruyter.

——(2002) *English Discourse Particles: Evidence from a Corpus*, Amsterdam and Philadelphia, PA: John Benjamins.

Ainsworth, J.E. (1993) 'In a different register: the pragmatics of powerlessness in police interrogation', *Yale Law Journal*, 103: 259–322.

Airenti, G. (1998) 'Dialogue in a developmental perspective', in S. Cmejrková, J. Hoffmannová, O. Müllerová and J. Svetlá (eds) *Proceedings of the 6th Conference of the International Association for Dialogue Analysis, Prague 1996*, Tübingen: Niemeyer.

Airenti, G. (2004) 'The development of the speaker's meaning', in C. Florén Serrano, C. Inchaurralde Besga and M.A. Ruiz Moneva (eds) *Applied Linguistics Perspectives: Language Learning and Specialized Discourse*, Zaragoza: Anubar.

Airenti, G., Bara, B.G. and Colombetti, M. (1993a) 'Conversation and behaviour games in the pragmatics of dialogue', *Cognitive Science*, 17: 197–256.

——(1993b) 'Failures, exploitations and deceits in communication', *Journal of Pragmatics*, 20: 303–26.

Aissen, J. (1975) 'Presentational *there*-insertion: a cyclic root transformation', in R. Grossman, J. San and T.J. Vance (eds) *Papers from the 11th Regional Meeting of the Chicago Linguistic Society*, Chicago, IL: Chicago Linguistic Society.

——(1999) 'Markedness and subject choice in optimality theory', *Natural Language and Linguistic Theory*, 17: 673–711.

Aitchison, J. (1996) *The Seeds of Speech*, Cambridge: Cambridge University Press.

——(1999) *Cutting Edge Advertising*, Singapore: Prentice Hall.

Akhtar, N. and Gernsbacher, M.A. (2007) 'Joint attention and vocabulary development: a critical look', *Language and Linguistic Compass*, 1: 195–207.

Akhtar, N., Dunham, F. and Dunham, P.J. (1991) 'Directive interactions and early vocabulary development: the role of joint attentional focus', *Journal of Child Language*, 18: 41–49.

Akiskal, H.S. and Puzantian, V.R. (1979) 'Psychotic forms of depression and mania', *Psychiatric Clinics of North America*, 2: 419–39.

Aksu-Koç, A. (1988) *The Acquisition of Aspect and Modality: The Case of Past Reference in Turkish*, Cambridge: Cambridge University Press.

——(2000) 'Some aspects of the acquisition of evidentials in Turkish', in L. Johanson and B. Utas (eds) *Evidentials: Turkic, Iranian and Neighbouring Languages*, Berlin: de Gruyter.

Aksu-Koç, A. and Slobin, D. (1986) 'A psychological account of the development and use of evidentials in Turkish', in W. Chafe and J. Nichols (eds) *Evidentiality: The Linguistic Coding of Epistemology*, Norwood, NJ: Ablex.

Albert, E. (1964) '"Rhetoric", "logic" and "poetics" in Burundi: cultural patterning of speech behavior', *American Anthropologist*, 66: 35–54.

Alchourrón, C.A., Gärdenfors, P. and Makinson, D. (1985) 'On the logic of theory change: partial meet, contraction and revision functions', *The Journal of Symbolic Logic*, 50: 510–30.

Alcón, E. (2005) 'Does instruction work for learning pragmatics in the EFL context?', *System*, 33: 417–35.

Alexander, D., Wetherby, A. and Prizant, B. (1997) 'The emergence of repair strategies in infants and toddlers', *Seminars in Speech and Language*, 18: 197–212.

Alibali, M.W., Flevares, L. and Goldin-Meadow, S. (1997) 'Assessing knowledge conveyed in gesture: do teachers have the upper hand?', *Journal of Educational Psychology*, 89: 183–93.

Alibali, M.W., Heath, D.C. and Myers, H.J. (2001) 'Effects of visibility between speaker and listener on gesture production: some gestures are meant to be seen', *Journal of Memory and Language*, 44: 169–88.

Alicke, M.D., Braun, J.C., Glor, J.E., Klotz, M.L., Magee, J., Sederholm, H. and Siegel, R. (1992) 'Complaining behaviour in social interaction', *Personality and Social Psychology Bulletin*, 18: 286–95.

Aliseda, A. (2006) *Abductive Reasoning: Logical Investigation into the Processes of Discovery and Evaluation*, Dordrecht: Springer.

Al-Issa, A. (2003) 'Socio-cultural transfer in L2 speech behaviours: evidence and motivating factors', *International Journal of Intercultural Relations*, 27: 581–601.

Al-Khatib, M.A. (2006) 'The pragmatics of invitation making and acceptance in

Jordanian society', *Journal of Language and Linguistics*, 5: 272–94.

Allan, K. and Burridge, K. (2006) *Forbidden Words: Taboo and the Censoring of Language*, Cambridge: Cambridge University Press.

Allen, C. and Bekoff, M. (1997) *Species of Mind*, Cambridge, MA: MIT Press.

Allen, H.A. and Frith, C.D. (1983) 'Selective retrieval and free emission of category exemplars in schizophrenia', *British Journal of Psychology*, 74: 481–90.

Allen, J.F. (1995) *Natural Language Understanding*, Redwood City, CA: Addison-Wesley Publishing Co.

Allen, J.F. and Core, M. (1997) *Draft of DAMSL: Dialog Act Markup in Several Layers*. Online. Available: www.cs.rochester.edu/research/cisd/resources/damsl/RevisedManual/Revised Manual.html (accessed 22 February 2008).

Allen, J.F. and Perrault, C.M. (1980) 'Analysing intentions in utterances', *Artificial Intelligence*, 15: 143–78.

Allen, J.F., Byron, D.K., Dzikovska, M., Ferguson, G., Galescu, L. and Stent, A. (2001) 'Towards conversational human-computer interaction', *AI Magazine*, 22: 27–38.

Allison, D. (1995) 'Why "often" isn't "always"', in D. Nunan, R. Berry and V. Berry (eds) *Language Awareness in Language Education*, Hong Kong: University of Hong Kong, Department of Curriculum Studies.

Allott, N. (2007) 'Relevance and rationality', unpublished thesis, University College London.

Allwood, J. (1976) 'Communication in action and cooperation', unpublished thesis, Göteborg University.

Alm, N. and Newell, A.F. (1996) 'Being an interesting conversation partner', in S. von Tetzchner and M. Jensen (eds) *Augmentative and Alternative Communication: European Perspectives*, London: Whurr Publishers.

Alm, N., Arnott, J.L. and Newell, A.F. (1989) 'Discourse analysis and pragmatics in the design of a conversation prosthesis', *Journal of Medical Engineering and Technology*, 13: 10–12.

Althusser, L. (1971) *Lenin and Philosophy and Other Essays*, London: New Left Books.

Altieri, C. (1981) *Act and Quality: A Theory of Literary Meaning and Humanistic Understanding*, Amherst, MA: University of Massachusetts Press.

Altmann, G.T.M. and Kamide, Y. (1999) 'Incremental interpretation at verbs: restricting the domain of subsequent reference', *Cognition*, 73: 247–64.

Altmann, G.T.M. and Steedman, M.J. (1988) 'Interaction with context during human sentence processing', *Cognition*, 30: 191–238.

Altmann, H. (1981) *Formen der 'Herausstellung' im Deutschen: Rechtsversetzung, Linksversetzung, Freies Thema und Verwandte Konstruktionen*, Tübingen: Niemeyer.

Alzheimer's Association (2007) *Newest Estimate of Worldwide Prevalence of Alzheimer's Disease = 26.6 Million*, Chicago: Alzheimer's Association. Online. Available: www.alz.org/prevention conference/pc2007/releases/61007_12am_worldprev.asp (accessed 7 April 2008).

American Psychiatric Association (1994) *Diagnostic and Statistical Manual of Mental Disorders*, 4th edn, Washington, DC: American Psychiatric Publishing.

——(2000) *Diagnostic and Statistical Manual of Mental Disorders (DSM-IV-TR)*, 4th edn, text revision, Washington, DC: American Psychiatric Association.

Anderson, B. (1991) *Imagined Communities: Reflections on the Origin and Spread of Nationalism*, London: Verso.

Anderson, L.B. (1986) 'Evidentials, paths of change, and mental maps: typologically regular assymetries', in W. Chafe and J. Nichols (eds) *Evidentiality: The Linguistic Coding of Epistemology*, Norwood, NJ: Ablex.

Anderson, R.C. and Ortony, A. (1975) 'On putting apples into bottles: a problem of polysemy', *Cognitive Psychology*, 7: 168–80.

Anderson, R.C. and Pichert, J.W. (1978) 'Recall of previously unrecallable information following a shift in perspective', *Journal of Verbal Learning and Verbal Behavior*, 12: 1–12.

Andreasen, N.C. (1979a) 'Thought, language and communication disorders. I. Clinical assessment, definition of terms, and evaluation of their reliability', *Archives of General Psychiatry*, 36: 1315–21.

——(1979b) 'Thought, language and communication disorders. II. Diagnostic significance', *Archives of General Psychiatry*, 36: 1325–30.

——(2001) *The Brave New Brain*, New York: Oxford University Press.

Andreasen, N.C. and Grove, W.M. (1986) 'Thought, language and communication in schizophrenia: diagnosis and prognosis', *Schizophrenia Bulletin*, 12: 348–59.

Andreasen, N.C. and Powers, P.S. (1974) 'Overinclusive thinking in mania and schizophrenia', *British Journal of Psychiatry*, 125: 452–56.

Andreasen, N.C., Arndt, S., Alliger, R., Miller, D. and Flaum, M. (1995) 'Symptoms and schizophrenia: methods, meanings and mechanisms', *Archives of General Psychiatry*, 52: 341–51.

Ang, J., Dhillon, R., Krupski, A., Shriberg, E. and Stolcke, A. (2002) 'Prosody-based automatic detection of annoyance and frustration in human-computer dialog', paper presented at The International Conference on Spoken Language Processing, Denver, CO, 2002. Online. Available: .www.speech.sri.com/cgi-bin/run-distill?papers/icslp2002-emotion.ps.gz (accessed 26 August 2008).

Annand, A., Wales, R.J., Jackson, H.J. and Copolov, D.L. (1994) 'Linguistic impairment in early psychosis', *The Journal of Nervous and Mental Disease*, 182: 488–93.

Anolli, L., Infantino, M.G. and Ciceri, R. (2001) '"You're a real genius!": irony as a miscommunication design', in L. Anolli, R. Ciceri and G. Riva (eds) *Say Not to Say: New Perspectives on Miscommunication*, Amsterdam: IOS Press.

Anscombe, G.E.M. (1963) *An Introduction to Wittgenstein's Tractatus*, 2nd edn, London: Hutchinson University Library.

Anselmi, D., Tomasello, M. and Acunzo, M. (1986) 'Young children's responses to neutral and specific contingent queries', *Journal of Child Language*, 14: 135–44.

Antoine, F. (2000) 'From understatement to overstatement in French', *French Studies Bulletin: A Quarterly Supplement*, 75: 13–17.

Antonopoulou, E. and Nikiforidou, K. (2002) 'Deictic motion and the adoption of perspective in Greek', *Pragmatics*, 12: 273–95.

Antonopoulou, E. and Sifianou, M. (2004) 'Conversational dynamics of humour: the telephone game in Greek', *Journal of Pragmatics*, 35: 741–69.

Aone, C. and Bennett, W.S. (1995) 'Evaluating automated and manual acquisition of anaphora resolution strategies', *Proceedings of the 33rd Annual Meeting of the Association for Computational Linguistics (ACL-95)*, Morristown, NJ: Association for Computational Linguistics.

Apel, K.-O. (1992) 'Is intentionality more basic than linguistic meaning?' in E. Lepore and R. van Gulick (eds) *John Searle and his Critics*, Oxford: Blackwell.

——(1994) *Selected Essays: Towards a Transcendental Semiotics*, edited by E. Mendieta, New Jersey: Humanities Press.

Archer, D. (2005) *Questions and Answers in the English Courtroom (1640–1760)*, Amsterdam and Philadelphia, PA: John Benjamins.

Arent, R. (1996) 'Sociopragmatic decisions regarding complaints by Chinese learners

and NSs of American English', *Hong Kong Journal of Applied Linguistics*, 1: 125–47.

Arewa, E.O. and Dundes, A. (1964) 'Proverbs and the ethnography of speaking folklore', *American Anthropologist*, 66: 70–85.

Argyle, M. (1975) *Bodily Communication*, London: Methuen.

Ariel, M. (1988) 'Referring and accessibility', *Journal of Linguistics*, 24: 65–87.

——(1990) *Accessing Noun-Phrase Antecedents*, London: Routledge.

——(2004) '*Most*', *Language*, 80: 658–706.

Arieti, S. (1974) *Interpretation of Schizophrenia*, New York: Basic Books.

Aristotle (1966) *Metaphysics*, edited by H. Apostle, Bloomington, IN: Indiana University Press.

——(1985) *The Complete Works of Aristotle*, edited by J. Barnes, Princeton, NJ: Princeton University Press.

——(2007) *On Rhetoric: A Theory of Civic Discourse*, trans. G. Kennedy, Oxford: Oxford University Press.

Arminen, I. (2005) 'Sequential order and sequence structure – the case of incommensurable studies on mobile phone calls', *Discourse Studies*, 7: 649–62.

——(2007) 'Mobile time-space – arena for new kinds of social actions', *Mobile Communication Research Annual*, volume 1. Online. Available: www.uta.fi/%7Eilkka.arminen/doc/Arminen mcra16.3.2007.pdf (accessed 26 April 2008).

Arminen, I. and Leinonen, M. (2006) 'Mobile phone call openings: tailoring answers to personalized summonses', *Discourse Studies*, 8: 339–68.

Arnauld, A. and Nicole, P. ([1662] 1996) *Logic or the Art of Thinking*, edited by J.V. Buroker, Cambridge: Cambridge University Press.

Arnold, J., Wasow, T., Losongco, A. and Ginstrom, R. (2000) 'Heaviness vs. newness: the effects of complexity and information structure on constituent ordering', *Language*, 76: 28–55.

Arnold, J.E., Tanenhaus, M.K., Altmann, R.J. and Fagnano, M. (2004) 'The old and thee, uh, new: disfluency and reference resolution', *Psychological Science*, 15: 578–82.

Arnovick, L.K. (1999) *Diachronic Pragmatics: Seven Case Studies in English Illocutionary Development*, Amsterdam and Philadelphia, PA: John Benjamins.

Arora, S.L. (1984) 'The perception of proverbiality', *Proverbium*, 1: 1–38.

Arronsson, K. and Rundstrom, B. (1989) 'Cats, dogs and sweets in the clinical negotiation of reality: on politeness and coherence in pediatric discourse', *Language in Society*, 18: 483–504.

Ashby, M. (2006) 'Prosody and idioms in English', *Journal of Pragmatics*, 38: 1580–97.

Ashby, W.R. (1956) *Introduction to Cybernetics*, London: Methuen.

Asher, N. (1993) *Reference to Abstract Objects in Discourse*, Dordrecht: Kluwer.

Asher, N. and Lascarides, A. (1998) 'The semantics and pragmatics of presupposition', *Journal of Semantics*, 15: 239–300.

——(2003) *Logics of Conversation*, Cambridge: Cambridge University Press.

Asperger, H. (1944) 'Autistic psychopathology in childhood', in U. Frith (ed.) *Autism and Asperger Syndrome*, Cambridge: Cambridge University Press.

Astington, J.W. and Baird, J.A. (2005) *Why Language Matters for Theory of Mind*, New York: Oxford University Press.

Aston, G. (1995) 'Say "thank you": some pragmatic constraints in conversational closings', *Applied Linguistics*, 16: 57–86.

Astruc, L. (2005) 'The intonation of extra-sentential elements in Catalan and English', unpublished dissertation, University of Cambridge.

Aten, J.L., Cagliuri, M.P. and Holland, A.L. (1982) 'The efficacy of functional communication therapy for chronic aphasic patients', *Journal of Speech and Hearing Disorders*, 47: 93–96.

Atkinson, J.M. and Heritage, J. (eds) (1984) *Structures of Social Action: Studies in Conversation Analysis*, Cambridge: Cambridge University Press.

Atkinson, M. and Drew, P. (1979) *Order in Court: The Organization of Verbal Interaction in Judicial Settings*, Cambridge: Cambridge University Press.

Atkinson, R.C. and Shiffrin, R.M. (1968) 'Human memory: a proposed system and its control processes', in K.W. Spence and J.T. Spence (eds) *The Psychology of Learning and Motivation, Vol. 2*, London: Academic Press.

Atlas, J.D. (1977) 'Negation, ambiguity, and presupposition', *Linguistics and Philosophy*, 1: 321–36.

——(1979) 'How linguistics matters to philosophy: presupposition, truth, and meaning', in D. Dinneen and C.-K. Oh (eds) *Syntax and Semantics 11: Presupposition*, New York: Academic Press.

——(1989) *Philosophy without Ambiguity: A Logico-Linguistic Essay*, Oxford: Clarendon Press.

——(2004) 'Presupposition', in L.R. Horn and G. Ward (eds) *The Handbook of Pragmatics*, Oxford: Blackwell.

——(2005) *Logic, Meaning, and Conversation: Semantical Underdeterminacy, Implicature, and Their Interface*, Oxford: Oxford University Press.

Atlas, J.D. and Levinson, S.C. (1981) 'It-clefts, informativeness and logical form', in P. Cole (ed.) *Radical Pragmatics*, New York: Academic Press.

Attardo, S. ([1996] 2005) 'Humor', in J. Verschueren, J.-O. Östman, J. Blommaert and C. Bulcaen (eds) *Handbook of Pragmatics*, Amsterdam: John Benjamins.

——(1994) *Linguistic Theories of Humor*, Berlin: Mouton de Gruyter.

——(1997) 'The semantic foundations of cognitive theories of humor', *HUMOR: International Journal of Humor Research*, 10: 395–420.

——(2000) 'Irony as relevant inappropriateness', *Journal of Pragmatics*, 32: 793–826.

——(2001) *Humorous texts: a semantics and pragmatics analysis*, Berlin: Mouton De Gruyter.

——(2002) 'Humor, irony and their communication: from mode adoption to failure of detection', in L. Anolli, R. Ciceri and G. Riva (eds) *Say Not to Say: New Perspectives on Miscommunication*, Amsterdam: IOS Press.

——(2003) 'Introduction: the pragmatics of humor', *Journal of Pragmatics*, 35: 1287–94.

——(2008) 'A primer for the linguistics of humor', in V. Raskin (ed.) *The Primer of Humor Research*, Berlin: Walter de Gruyter.

Attardo, S. and Raskin, V. (1991) 'Script theory revis(it)ed: joke similarity and joke representation model', *Humor*, 4: 293–347.

Attardo, S., Eisterhold, J., Poggi, I. and Hay, J. (2003) 'Multimodal markers of irony and sarcasm', *HUMOR: International Journal of Humor Research*, 16: 243–60.

Auer, P. (1996) 'On the prosody and syntax of turn-continuations', in E. Couper-Kuhlen and M. Selting (eds) *Prosody in Conversation: Interactional Studies*, Cambridge: Cambridge University Press.

Aukrust, V.G. and Snow, C.E. (1998) 'Narratives and explanations during mealtime conversations in Norway and the U.S.', *Language in Society*, 27: 221–46.

Austin, J.L. (1946) 'Other minds', *Proceedings of the Aristotelian Society*, Supplement 20: 148–87; reprinted in *Philosophical Papers* (1979), Oxford: Oxford University Press.

——(1950) 'Truth', *Proceedings of the Aristotelian Society*, Supplement 24: 111–28; reprinted in *Philosophical Papers* (1979), Oxford: Oxford University Press.

——(1956a) 'Ifs and cans', *Proceedings of the British Academy*, 42: 123–24; reprinted in *Philosophical*

Papers (1979), Oxford: Oxford University Press.

——(1956b) 'A plea for excuses', *Proceedings of the Aristotelian Society*, 57: 1–30; reprinted in *Philosophical Papers* (1979), Oxford: Oxford University Press.

——(1961) *Philosophical Papers*, ed. J.O. Urmson and G.J. Warnock, Oxford: Clarendon Press.

——(1962) *How to Do Things with Words*, Oxford: Clarendon Press.

——([1940] 1963) 'The meaning of a word', in C.E. Caton (ed.) *Philosophy and Ordinary Language*, Urbana, IL: University of Illinois Press.

——(1975) *How to Do Things with Words*, Oxford: Oxford University Press.

——(1979) *Philosophical Papers*, ed. J.O. Urmson and G.J. Warnock, 2nd edn, Oxford: Clarendon Press.

——(1980) *How to Do Things with Words*, 2nd edn, Oxford: Oxford University Press.

Autenreith, T. (1997) 'Tautologien sind tautologien', in E. Rolf (ed.) *Pragmatik, Implikaturen und Sprechakt: Linguistische Berichte*, Opladen, Germany: Westdeutscher Verlag.

Avent, J.R. (1997) *Manual of Cooperative Group Treatment for Aphasia*, Boston, MA: Butterworth and Heinemann.

——(2004) 'Group treatment for aphasia using cooperative learning principles', *Topics in Language Disorders*, 24: 118–24.

Avramides, A. (1989) *Meaning and Mind: An Examination of a Gricean Account of Language*, Cambridge, MA: MIT Press.

Ayer, A.J. (1936) *Language, Truth and Logic*, London: Victor Gollancz.

——(1940) *The Foundations of Empirical Knowledge*, London: Macmillan.

——(1952) 'Negation', *Journal of Philosophy*, 49: 797–815; reprinted in *Philosophical Essays* (1963), London: Macmillan.

Bach, K. (1984) 'Default reasoning: jumping to conclusions and knowing when to think twice', *Pacific Philosophical Quarterly*, 65: 37–58.

——(1992) 'Intentions and demonstrations', *Analysis*, 52: 140–46.

——(1994a) 'Conversational impliciture', *Mind and Language*, 9: 124–62.

——(1994b) 'Semantic slack: what is said and more', in S.L. Tsohatzidis (ed.) *Foundations of Speech Act Theory: Philosophical and Linguistic Perspectives*, London: Routledge.

——(1995) 'Standardization vs. conventionalization', *Linguistics and Philosophy*, 18: 677–86.

——(1997) 'The semantics-pragmatics distinction: what it is and why it matters', *Linguistische Berichte*, 8: 33–50; reprinted in K. Turner

(ed.) (1999) *The Semantics/Pragmatics Interface from Different Points of View*, Oxford: Elsevier Science.

——(1998) 'Standardisation revisited', in A. Kasher (ed.) *Pragmatics: Critical Concepts, Volume 4: Presupposition, Implicature, and Indirect Speech Acts*, London: Routledge.

——(1999a) 'The myth of conventional implicature', *Linguistics and Philosophy*, 22: 327–66.

——(1999b) 'The semantics-pragmatics distinction: what it is and why it matters', in K. Turner (ed.) *The Semantics-Pragmatics Interface from Different Points of View*, New York: Elsevier Science.

——(2000) 'Quantification, qualification and context', *Mind and Language*, 15: 262–83.

——(2001) 'You don't say?', *Synthese*, 127: 11–31.

——(2004a) 'Minding the gap', in C. Bianchi (ed.) *The Semantics/Pragmatics Foundations of Speech Act Theory: Philosophical and Linguistic Perspectives*, London: Routledge.

——(2004b) 'Pragmatics and the philosophy of language', in L.R. Horn and G. Ward (eds) *The Handbook of Pragmatics*, Oxford: Blackwell.

——(2006a) 'The excluded middle: semantic minimalism without minimal propositions', *Philosophy and Phenomenological Research*, 73: 435–42.

——(2006b) 'The top ten misconceptions about implicature', in B.J. Birner and G. Ward (eds) *Drawing the Boundaries of Meaning*, Amsterdam: John Benjamins.

——(2006c) 'What does it take to refer?', in E. Lepore and B.C. Smith (eds) *The Oxford Handbook of Philosophy of Language*, Oxford: Clarendon Press.

Bach, K. and Harnish, R. (1979) *Linguistic Communication and Speech Acts*, Cambridge, MA: MIT Press.

——(1982) *Linguistic Communication and Speech Acts*, Cambridge, MA: MIT Press.

Bachman, L. (1990) *Fundamental Considerations in Language Testing*, Oxford: Oxford University Press.

Baddeley, A.D. (1986) *Working Memory*, Oxford: Oxford University Press.

Bailey, N., Madden, C. and Krashen, S. (1974) 'Is there a "natural sequence" in adult second language learning?', *Language Learning*, 24: 235–43.

Bakakou-Orfanou, A. (1988–89) 'Telephone interaction: variation in switchboard requests', *Glossologia*, 7–8: 35–50.

Baker Graham, M. and Thralls, C. (1998) 'Connections and fissures: discipline formation in business communication', *Journal of Business Communication*, 35: 7–13.

Baker, G.P. and Hacker, P.M.S. (2005a) *Wittgenstein: Understanding and Meaning. Part I: Essays*, Oxford: Blackwell Publishing.

——(2005b) *Wittgenstein: Understanding and Meaning. Part II: Exegesis §§1–184*, Oxford: Blackwell Publishing.

Baker, M. (2006) *Translation and Conflict*, London: Routledge.

Bakhtin, M. ([1929] 1984) *Problems of Dostoevsky's Poetics*, ed. and trans. C. Emerson, Theory and History of Literature, vol. 8, Minneapolis, MN: University of Minnesota Press.

Baldwin, D.A. (1991) 'Infants' contribution to the achievement of joint reference', *Child Development*, 62: 875–90.

——(1993) 'Early referential understanding: infants' ability to recognize referential acts for what they are', *Developmental Psychology*, 29: 832–43.

——(2000) 'Interpersonal understanding fuels knowledge acquisition', *Current Directions in Psychological Science*, 9: 40–45.

Baldwin, D.A., Markman, E.M., Bill, B., Desjardins, R.N., Irwin, J.M. and Tidball, G. (1996) 'Infants' reliance on a social criterion for establishing word-object relations', *Child Development*, 67: 3135–53.

Ballard, K.J. (2001) 'Response generalization in apraxia of speech treatments: taking another look', *Journal of Communication Disorders*, 34: 3–20.

Bally, C. (1909) *Traité de Stylistique Française*, Heidelberg, Germany: Carl Winters.

Baltaxe, C. (1977) 'Pragmatic deficits in the language of autistic adolescents', *Journal of Pediatric Psychology*, 2: 176–80.

Baltazani, M. (2006) 'Intonation and pragmatic interpretation of negation in Greek', *Journal of Pragmatics*, 38: 1658–76.

Bamford, J. (2004) 'Gestural and symbolic uses of the deictic "here" in academic lectures', in K. Aijmer and A.-B. Stenström (eds) *Discourse Patterns in Spoken and Written Corpora*, Amsterdam: John Benjamins.

Banfield, A. (1982) *Unspeakable Sentences: Narrative and Representation in the Language of Fiction*, London: Routledge and Kegan Paul.

——(2003) 'Literary pragmatics', in W.J. Frawley (ed.) *International Encyclopaedia of Linguistics*, 2nd edn, Oxford: Oxford University Press.

Bara, B.G. (1995) *Cognitive Science: A Developmental Approach to the Simulation of the Mind*, Hove: Psychology Press.

——(to appear) *Cognitive Pragmatics*, Cambridge, MA: MIT Press.

Bara, B.G. and Tirassa, M. (1999) 'Communicative meaning in linguistic and extralinguistic communication', in S. Bagnara (ed.) *Proceedings of the 3rd European Conference on Cognitive Science*, Rome: Instituto di Psicologia Consiglio Nazionale delle Ricerche.

——(2000) 'Neuropragmatics: brain and communication', *Brain and Language*, 71: 10–14.

Bara, B.G., Bucciarelli, M. and Geminiani, G.C. (2000) 'Development and decay of extralinguistic communication', *Brain and Cognition*, 43: 21–27.

Bara, B.G., Cutica, L. and Tirassa, M. (2001) 'Neuropragmatics: extralinguistic communication after closed head injury', *Brain and Language*, 77: 72–94.

Bara, B.G., Tirassa, M. and Zettin, M. (1997) 'Neuropragmatics: neuropsychological constraints on formal theories of dialogue', *Brain and Language*, 59: 7–49.

Barak, A. (2007) 'Emotional support and suicide prevention through the internet: a field project report', *Computers in Human Behaviour*, 23: 971–84.

Barak, A. and Bloch, M. (2006) 'Factors related to perceived helpfulness in supporting highly distressed individuals through an online support chat', *CyberPsychology and Behavior*, 9: 60–68.

Barak, A. and Miron, O. (2005) 'Writing characteristics of suicidal people on the internet: a psychological investigation of emerging social environments', *Suicide and Life-Threatening Behavior*, 35: 507–24.

Barber, R., Snowden, J. and Craufurd, D. (1995) 'Frontotemporal dementia and Alzheimer's disease: retrospective differentiation using information from informants', *Journal of Neurology, Neurosurgery, and Psychiatry*, 59: 61–70.

Barch, D.M. and Berenbaum, H. (1997) 'The effect of language production manipulations on negative thought disorder and discourse coherence disturbances in schizophrenia', *Psychiatry Research*, 71: 115–27.

Bardovi-Harlig, K. (1999) 'Exploring the interlanguage of interlanguage pragmatics: a research agenda for acquisitional pragmatics', *Language Learning*, 49: 677–713.

——(2001a) 'Empirical evidence of the need for instruction in pragmatics', in K.R. Rose and G. Kasper (eds) *Pragmatics in Language Teaching*, New York: Cambridge University Press.

——(2001b) 'Pragmatics and second language acquisition', in R. Kaplan (ed.) *Handbook of Applied Linguistics*, Oxford: Oxford University Press.

——(2001c) 'Evaluating the empirical evidence: grounds for instruction in pragmatics?', in K. Rose and G. Kasper (eds) *Pragmatics in Language Teaching*, Cambridge: Cambridge University Press.

——(2006) 'On the role of formulas in the acquisition of L2 pragmatics', in K. Bardovi-Harlig, C. Félix-Brasdefer and A. Omar (eds) *Pragmatics and Language Learning, Volume 11*, Honolulu, HI: National Foreign Language Resource Center, University of Hawai'i at Manoa.

Bardovi-Harlig, K. and Dörnyei, Z. (1998) 'Do language learners recognize pragmatic violations? Pragmatic vs. grammatical awareness in instructed L2 learning', *TESOL Quarterly*, 32: 233–59.

Bardovi-Harlig, K. and Hartford, B.S. (1990) 'Congruence in native and nonnative conversations: status balance in the academic advising session', *Language Learning*, 40: 467–501.

——(1992) 'Experimental and observational data in the study of interlanguage pragmatics', *Pragmatics and Language Learning*, 3: 33–52.

——(1993) 'Learning the rules of academic talk: a longitudinal study of pragmatic development', *Studies in Second Language Acquisition*, 15: 279–304.

——(1996) 'Input in an institutional setting', *Studies in Second Language Acquisition*, 18: 171–88.

Bardovi-Harlig, K. and Hartford, B. (eds) (2005) *Interlanguage Pragmatics: Exploring Institutional Talk*, Mahwah, NJ: Lawrence Erlbaum.

Bardovi-Harlig, K., Félix-Brasdefer, J.C. and Omar, A.S. (eds) (2006) *Pragmatics and Language Learning, Volume 11*, Honolulu, HI: University of Hawaii Press.

Bargiela-Chiappini, F. (2004) 'Intercultural business discourse', in C.N. Candlin and M. Gotti (eds) *Intercultural Aspects of Specialized Communication*, Bern, Switzerland: Peter Lang.

——(ed.) (2005/2006) 'Special double issue on Asian business discourse(s)', *Journal of Asian Pacific Communication*, 15 (2): 207–320; 16 (1): 1–158.

——(ed.) (2009a) *The Handbook of Business Discourse*, Edinburgh: Edinburgh University Press.

——(2009b) 'Introduction: business discourse', in F. Bargiela-Chiappini (ed.) *The Handbook of Business Discourse*, Edinburgh: Edinburgh University Press.

Bargiela-Chiappini, F. and Gotti, M. (eds) (2005) *Asian Business Discourse(s)*, Bern, Switzerland: Peter Lang.

Bargiela-Chiappini, F. and Harris, S. (2006) 'Politeness at work: issues and challenges', *Journal of Politeness Research*, 2: 7–34.

Bargiela-Chiappini, F. and Nickerson, C. (1999) 'Business writing as social action', in F. Bargiela-Chiappini and C. Nickerson (eds) *Writing Business: Genres, Media and Discourses*, London and New York: Longman.

——(2002) 'Business discourse: old concepts, new horizons', *International Review of Applied Linguistics*, 40: 273–86.

——(2003) 'Intercultural business communication: a rich field of studies', *Journal of Intercultural Studies*, 24: 3–15.

Bar-Hillel, Y. (1954) 'Indexical expressions', *Mind*, 63: 359–79.

——(1970) *Aspects of Language*, Jerusalem: Magnes.

——(ed.) (1971) *Pragmatics of Natural Languages*, Dordrecht: Reidel.

Barker, C. (2002) 'The dynamics of vagueness', *Linguistics and Philosophy*, 25: 1–36.

Barker, S. (2003) 'Truth and conventional implicature', *Mind*, 112: 1–34.

Barkow, J.H., Cosmides, L. and Tooby, J. (1995) *The Adapted Mind: Evolutionary Psychology and the Generation of Culture*, Oxford: Oxford University Press.

——(eds) (1992) *The Adapted Mind: Evolutionary Psychology and the Generation of Culture*, New York and Oxford: Oxford University Press.

Barley, N. (1972) 'A structural approach to the proverb and maxim with special reference to the Anglo-Saxon corpus', *Proverbium*, 20: 737–50.

——(1974) '"The proverb" and related problems of genre-definition', *Proverbium*, 23: 880–84.

Barlow, M. (2000) *MonoConc Pro (MP2.2)*, Athelstan Publications. Online. Available www.athel.com/mono.html#monopro (accessed 14 May 2008).

Barnes, D. (1976) *From Communication to Curriculum*, Harmondsworth: Penguin.

Barnes, D. and Todd, F. (1977) *Communication and Learning in Small Groups*, London: Routledge and Kegan Paul.

Barnes, D., Britton, J. and Rosen, H. (1969) *Language, the Learner and the School*, Harmondsworth: Penguin.

Barnes, G. (1984) 'Evidentials in the Tucuya verb', *International Journal of American Linguistics*, 50: 255–71.

Barnes, J. (1985) *Flaubert's Parrot*, London: Picador.

Baron, N. (2000) *Alphabet to E-mail*, London and New York: Routledge.

Baron-Cohen, S. (1988) 'Social and pragmatic deficits in autism: cognitive or affective?', *Journal of Autism and Developmental Disorders*, 18: 379–402.

——(1989) 'Perceptual role-taking and proto-declarative pointing in autism', *British Journal of Child Psychology and Psychiatry*, 30: 285–98.

——(1995) *Mindblindness: An Essay on Autism and Theory of Mind*, Cambridge, MA: MIT Press.

——(2004) 'The extreme male brain theory of autism', *Trends in Cognitive Sciences*, 6: 248–54.

Baron-Cohen, S., Baldwin, D.A. and Crowson, M. (1997) 'Do children with autism use the speaker's direction of gaze strategy to crack the code of language?', *Child Development*, 68: 48–57.

Baron-Cohen, S., Jolliffe, T., Mortimore, C. and Robertson, M. (1997) 'Another advanced test of theory of mind: evidence from very high functioning adults with autism or Asperger Syndrome', *Journal of Child Psychology and Psychiatry*, 38: 813–22.

Baron-Cohen, S., Leslie, A. and Frith, U. (1985) 'Does the autistic child have a "theory of mind?"', *Cognition*, 21: 37–46.

Baron-Cohen, S., O'Riordan, M., Stone, V., Jones, R. and Plaisted, K. (1999) 'Recognition of faux pas by normally developing children and children with Asperger syndrome or high-functioning autism', *Journal of Autism and Developmental Disorders*, 29: 407–18.

Baron-Cohen, S., Ring, H.A., Bullmore, E.T., Wheelwright, S., Ashwin, C. and Williams, S. C.R. (2000) 'The amygdala theory of autism', *Neuroscience and Biobehavioural Reviews*, 24: 355–64.

Baron-Cohen, S., Tager-Flusberg, H. and Cohen, D.J. (eds) (1993) *Understanding other Minds: Perspectives from Autism*, Oxford: Oxford University Press.

Barrett, A. (2005) 'Model compilation for real-time planning and diagnosis with feedback', in L.P. Kaelbling and A. Saffiotti (eds) *Proceedings of the Nineteenth International Joint Conference on Artificial Intelligence*, Edinburgh: Professional Book Centre.

Barrett, H.C. (2005) 'Enzymatic computation and cognitive modularity', *Mind and Language*, 20: 259–87.

Barrett, H.C. and Kurzban, R. (2006) 'Modularity in cognition: framing the debate', *Psychological Review*, 113: 628–47.

Barron, A. (2003) *Acquisition in Interlanguage Pragmatics: Learning how to do Things with Words in a Study Abroad Context*, Amsterdam: Benjamins.

——(2005) 'Offering in Ireland and England', in A. Barron and K.P. Schneider (eds) *The Pragmatics of Irish English*, Berlin and New York: Mouton de Gruyter.

Barrouillet, P., Grosset, N. and Leças, J.-F. (2000) 'Conditional reasoning by mental models: chronometric and developmental evidence', *Cognition*, 75: 237–66.

Barry, A.K. (1991) 'Narrative style and witness testimony', *Journal of Narrative and Life History*, 1: 281–93.

Barsalou, L. (1983) 'Ad hoc categories', *Memory and Cognition*, 11: 211–27.

——(1987) 'The instability of graded structure in concepts', in U. Neisser (ed.) *Concepts and Conceptual Development*, New York: Cambridge University Press.

——(1993) 'Flexibility, structure, and linguistic vagary in concepts: manifestations of a compositional system of perceptual symbols', in A. Collins, S. Gathercole, A. Conway and P. Morris (eds) *Theory of Memory*, Hove: Lawrence Erlbaum.

Bartels, C. (1999) *The Intonation of English Statements and Questions: A Compositional Interpretation*, New York: Garland.

Barth, E.M. and Krabbe, E.C.W. (1982) *From Axiom to Dialogue: A Philosophical Study of Logic and Argumentation*, Berlin and New York: de Gruyter.

Barthes, R. (1957) *Mythologies*, Paris: Seuil.

——(1968) *Elements of Semiology*, London: Cape.

Bartlett, F.C. (1932) *Remembering: A Study in Experimental and Social Psychology*, Cambridge: Cambridge University Press.

Barton, D. (2007) *Literacy: An Introduction to the Ecology of Written Language*, Oxford: Basil Blackwell.

Bartsch, K. and Wellman, H.M. (1995) *Children Talk about the Mind*, Oxford: Oxford University Press.

Barwise, J. and Cooper, R. (1981) 'Generalized quantifiers and natural language', *Linguistics and Philosophy*, 4: 159–219.

Barwise, J. and Perry, J. (1983) *Situations and Attitudes*, Cambridge, MA: MIT Press.

Basso, A. (2003) *Aphasia and Its Therapy*, New York: Oxford University Press.

Basso, K. (1972) '"To give up on words": silence in Western Apache culture', in P. Giglioli (ed.) *Language and Social Context*, Harmondsworth: Penguin.

Bates, E., Benigni, L., Bretherton, I., Camaioni, L. and Volterra, V. (1979) *The Emergence of Symbols: Cognition and Communication in Infants*, New York: Academic Press.

Bates, E., Camaioni, L. and Volterra, V. (1975) 'The acquisition of performatives prior to speech', *Merrill-Palmer Quarterly*, 21: 205–24.

Bateson, G. (1953) 'The position of humor in human communication', in H. von Foerster (ed.) *Cybernetics – Circular, Causal and Feedback*

Mechanisms in Biological and Social Systems, New York: Josiah Macy, Jr. Foundation.

——(1955) 'The message "This is Play"', in B. Schaffner (ed.) *Group Processes: Transactions of the Second Conference*, New York: Josiah Macy, Jr. Foundation.

——(1972) *Steps to an Ecology of Mind*, New York: Ballentine.

Bateson, M.C. (1975) 'Mother-infant exchanges: the epigenesis of conversational interaction', in D. Aaronson and R.W. Rieber (eds) *Developmental Psycholinguistics and Communication Disorders*, New York: New York Academy of Sciences.

Baum, S.R. and Dwivedi, V.D. (2003) 'Sensitivity to prosodic structure in left- and right-hemisphere-damaged individuals', *Brain and Language*, 87: 278–89.

Bauman, G. (1996) *Contesting Culture*, Cambridge: Cambridge University Press.

Bauman, R. (1984) 'The making and breaking of context in West Texas oral anecdotes', in D. Schiffrin (ed.) *Meaning, Form and Use in Context: Linguistic Applications*, Georgetown University Round Table on Languages and Linguistics 1984. Washington, DC: Georgetown University Press.

Baumann, S. and Grice, M. (2006) 'The intonation of accessibility', *Journal of Pragmatics*, 38: 1636–57.

Bavelas, J.B., Chovil, N., Coates, L. and Roe, L. (1995) 'Gestures specialized for dialogue', *Personality and Social Psychology Bulletin*, 21: 394–405.

Bax, M. (2001) 'Historical frame analysis: hoaxing and make-believe in a seventeenth-century Dutch play', *Journal of Historical Pragmatics*, 2: 33–67.

Baxter, J. (2002a) 'Competing discourses in the classroom: a poststructuralist analysis of pupils' speech in public contexts', *Discourse and Society*, 19: 827–42.

——(2002b) 'A juggling act: a feminist poststructuralist analysis of girls' and boys' talk in the secondary classroom', *Gender and Education*, 14: 5–19.

——(2003) *Positioning Gender in Discourse: A Feminist Methodology*, Basingstoke: Palgrave.

Bayles, K.A. (1990) 'Language and Parkinson's disease', *Alzheimer Disease and Associated Disorders*, 4: 171–80.

Bayles, K.A. and Tomoeda, C. (1993) *Arizona Battery of Communication Disorders for Dementia*, Tucson, AZ: Canyonlands Publishing.

——(1994) *Functional Linguistic Communication Inventory*, Tucson, AZ: Canyonlands Publishing.

Bayley, P. (ed.) (2004) *Cross-Cultural Perspectives on Parliamentary Discourse*, Amsterdam: John Benjamins.

Beamer, L. (2003) 'Directness in Chinese business correspondence of the nineteenth century', *Journal of Business and Technical Communication*, 17: 201–37.

Beaney, M. (2006) 'Wittgenstein on language: from simples to samples', in E. Lepore and B. C. Smith (eds) *The Oxford Handbook of Philosophy of Language*, Oxford: Clarendon Press.

Beaver, D.I. (2001) *Presupposition and Assertion in Dynamic Semantics*, Stanford, CA: CSLI.

——(2004) 'The optimization of discourse anaphora', *Linguistics and Philosophy*, 27: 3–56.

Beaver, D.I. and Lee, H. (2003) 'Input-output mismatches in OT', in R. Blutner and H. Zeevat (eds) *Optimality Theory and Pragmatics*, New York: Palgrave Macmillan.

Bech, K. (1998) 'Pragmatic factors in language change: XVS and XSV clauses in Old and Middle English', *Folia Linguistica Historica*, 19: 79–102.

Becker, M. (1999) 'The "some" indefinites', in G. Storto (ed.) *UCLA Working Papers in Linguistics 3: Syntax at Sunset 2*, Los Angeles, CA: UCLA Department of Linguistics.

Beebe, L.M. (1985a) 'Speech act performance: a function of the data collection procedure?', paper presented at the Sixth Annual Colloquium on TESOL and Sociolinguistics at the 19th Annual TESOL Convention, New York, 1985.

——(1985b) 'Cross-cultural differences in the sociolinguistic rules of a speech act: the case of refusals', paper presented at the Sixth Annual Colloquium on TESOL and Sociolinguistics at the 19th Annual TESOL Convention, New York, 1985.

Beebe, L.M. and Cummings, M.C. (1985) 'Speech act performance: a function of the data collection procedures?' Paper presented at the TESOL Convention, New York.

——(1996) 'Natural speech act data versus written questionnaire data: how data collection method affects speech act performance', in S.M. Gass and J. Neu (eds) *Speech Acts Across Cultures: Challenges to Communication in a Second Language*, Berlin: Mouton de Gruyter.

Beebe, L.M. and Takahashi, T. (1989) 'Sociolinguistic variation in face-threatening speech acts: chastisement and disagreement', in M. Eisenstein (ed.) *The Dynamic Interlanguage*, New York: Plenum.

Beebe, L.M., Takahashi, T. and Uliss-Weltz, R. (1990) 'Pragmatic transfer in ESL refusals', in

R.C. Scarcella, E.S. Anderson and S.D. Krashen (eds) *Developing Communicative Competence in a Second Language*, New York: Newbury House.

Beeke, S. (2003) '"I suppose" as a resource for the construction of turns at talk in agrammatic aphasia', *Clinical Linguistics and Phonetics*, 17: 291–98.

Beeke, S., Maxim, J. and Wilkinson, R. (2007) 'Using conversation analysis to assess and treat people with aphasia', *Seminars in Speech and Language*, 28: 138–49.

Beeke, S., Wilkinson, R. and Maxim, J. (2003) 'Exploring aphasic grammar. 1: a single case analysis of conversation', *Clinical Linguistics and Phonetics*, 17: 81–107.

Befi-Lopes, D.M., Rodrigues, A. and Rocha, L.C. (2004) 'Pragmatic abilities in the discourse of children with and without specific language impairment', *Pro Fono: Revista de Atualizacao Cientifica*, 16: 57–66.

Behne, T., Carpenter, M. and Tomasello, M. (2005) 'One-year olds comprehend the communicative intentions behind gestures in a hiding game', *Developmental Science*, 8: 492–99.

Bell, A. (1991) *The Language of News Media*, Oxford: Blackwell.

——(1998) 'The discourse structure of news stories', in A. Bell and P. Garrett (eds) *Approaches to Media Discourse*, Oxford: Blackwell.

Bellack, A.S., Morrison, R.L. and Mueser, K.T. (1989) 'Social problem solving in schizophrenia', *Schizophrenia Bulletin*, 15: 101–16.

Bellman, R.E. (1957) *Dynamic Programming*, Princeton, NJ: Princeton University Press.

Bellon, M. and Rees, R. (2006) 'The effect of context on communication: a study of the language and communication skills of adults with acquired brain injury', *Brain Injury*, 20: 1069–78.

Belz, J.A. and Kinginger, C. (2002) 'The cross-linguistic development of address form use in telecollaborative language learning: two case studies', *Canadian Modern Language Review / Revue Canadienne des Langues Vivantes*, 59: 189–214.

Bennett, J. (1976) *Linguistic Behaviour*, Cambridge: Cambridge University Press.

——(1988) *Events and Their Names*, Oxford: Clarendon Press.

Bennison, N. (1998) 'Assessing character through conversation in *Professional Foul*', in J. Culpeper, M. Short and P. Verdonk (eds) *Exploring the Language of Drama: From Text to Context*, London: Routledge.

Benston, A. (1993) 'Chekhov, Beckett, Pinter: the strain upon the silence', in K. Burkman

and J. Kundert-Gibbs (eds) *Pinter at Sixty*, Bloomington, IN: Indiana University Press.

Benus, S., Gravano, A. and Hirschberg, J. (2007) 'The prosody of backchannels in American English', paper presented at the *16th International Congress of Phonetic Sciences*, Saarbrücken, Germany, August 2007. Online. Available: www1.cs.columbia.edu/~agus/files/benus_et_al_2007b.pdf (accessed 26 August 2008).

Benveniste, E. (1968) 'Mutations of linguistic categories', in W.P. Lehmann and Y. Malkiel (eds) *Directions for Historical Linguistics: A Symposium*, Austin, TX: University of Texas Press.

Benz, A., Jäger, G. and van Rooij, R. (2005) 'An introduction to game theory for linguists', in A. Benz, G. Jäger and R. van Rooij (eds) *Game Theory and Pragmatics*, Houndmills: Palgrave Macmillan.

——(2006) *Game Theory and Pragmatics*, London: Palgrave Macmillan.

Bereiter, C. and Scardamalia, M. (1987) *The Psychology of Written Composition*, Hillsdale, NJ: Erlbaum.

Berembaum, H. and Barch, D. (1995) 'The categorization of thought disorder', *Journal of Psycholinguistic Research*, 24: 349–76.

Berg, E., Björnram, C., Hartelius, L., Laakso, K. and Johnels, B. (2003) 'High-level language difficulties in Parkinson's disease', *Clinical Linguistics and Phonetics*, 17: 63–80.

Berg, J. (2002) 'Is semantics still possible?', *Journal of Pragmatics*, 34: 349–59.

Berger, C.R. (2004) 'Speechlessness: causal attributions, emotional features and social consequences', *Journal of Language and Social Psychology*, 23: 147–79.

Berger, K.W. and Popelka, G.R. (1971) 'Extra-facial gestures in relation to speech reading', *Journal of Communication Disorders*, 3: 302–8.

Bergman, M.L. and Kasper, G. (1993) 'Perception and performance in native and nonnative apology', in G. Kasper and S. Blum-Kulka (eds) *Interlanguage Pragmatics*, New York: Oxford University Press.

Bergson, H. (1911) *Creative Evolution*, trans. A. Mitchell, New York: Modern Library.

Berlin, B. (1992) *Ethnobiological Classification*, Princeton, NJ: Princeton University Press.

Berlin, B. and Kay, P. (1969) *Basic Color Terms: Their Universality and Evolution*, Berkeley, CA: University of California Press.

Berlin, B., Breedlove, D. and Raven, P. (1974) *Principles of Tzeltal Plant Classification*, New York: Academic Press.

Berman, S. (1987) 'Situation-based semantics for adverbs of quantification', in J. Blevins and A. Vainika (eds) *University of Massachusetts Occasional Papers 12*, Amherst, MA: University of Massachusetts.

Bernardez, E. and Tejada, P. (1995) 'Pragmatic constraints to word order, and word-order change in English', in A.H. Jucker (ed.) *Historical Pragmatics: Pragmatic Developments in the History of English*, Amsterdam: Benjamins.

Bernicot, J., Laval, V. and Chaminaud, S. (2007) 'Nonliteral language forms in children: in what order are they acquired in pragmatics and metapragmatics?', *Journal of Pragmatics*, 39: 2115–32.

Berntsen, D. and Kennedy, J. (1996) 'Unresolved contradictions specifying attitudes – in metaphor, irony, understatement and tautology', *Poetics: Journal of Empirical Research on Culture, the Media and the Arts*, 24: 13–29.

Besson, A., Rollof, M.E. and Paulson, G.D. (1998) 'Preserving face in refusal situations', *Communication Research*, 25: 183–99.

Beukelman, D. and Mirenda, P. (2005) *Augmentative and Alternative Communication: Supporting Children and Adults With Complex Communication Needs*, Baltimore, MD: Paul H. Brooks Pub. Co.

Bezuidenhout, A. (1997) 'Pragmatics, semantic underdetermination and the referential/ attributive distinction', *Mind*, 106: 375–409.

——(2001) 'Metaphor and what is said: a defense of a direct expression view of metaphor', *Midwest Studies in Philosophy*, 25: 156–86.

——(2002) 'Truth-conditional pragmatics', *Philosophical Perspectives*, 16: 105–34.

——(2005) 'Indexicals and perspectivals', *Facta Philosophica*, 7: 3–18.

Bezuidenhout, A. and Cutting, J.C. (2002) 'Literal meaning, minimal propositions and pragmatic processing', *Journal of Pragmatics*, 34: 433–56.

Bezuidenhout, A.L. and Morris, R.K. (2004) 'Implicature, relevance and default pragmatic inference', in I.A. Noveck and D. Sperber (eds) *Experimental Pragmatics*, London: Palgrave Macmillan.

Bhatia, V.K. (1993a) *Analysing Genres*, London: Pearson Education.

——(1993b) *Analysing Genre: Language Use in Professional Settings*, London: Longman.

——(2004) *Worlds of Written Discourse*, London: Continuum.

Bialystok, E. and Miller, B. (1999) 'The problem of age in second language acquisition: influences from age, structure and task', *Bilingualism: Language and Cognition*, 2: 127–45.

Biber, D. (1988) *Variation across Speech and Writing*, Cambridge: Cambridge University Press.

——(2006) *University Language: A Corpus-based Study of Spoken and Written Registers*, Amsterdam: John Benjamins.

Biber, D. and Finegan, E. (1997) 'Diachronic relations among speech-based and written registers in English', in T. Nevalainen and L. Kahlas-Tarkka (eds) *To Explain the Present: Studies in the Changing English Language in Honour of Matti Rissanen*, Helsinki: Société Néophilologique.

Biber, D., Conrad, S. and Cortes, V. (2004) '*If you look at …* : lexical bundles in university teaching and textbooks', *Applied Linguistics*, 25: 371–405.

Biber, D., Conrad, S. and Reppen, R. (1998) *Corpus Linguistics: Investigating Language Structure and Use*, Cambridge: Cambridge University Press.

Biber, D., Johansson, S., Leech, G., Conrad, S. and Finegan, E. (1999) *Longman Grammar of Spoken and Written English*, London: Longman.

Bickerton, D. (1981) *Roots of Language*, Ann Arbor, MI: Karoma.

Biggs, J.B. and Collis, K.F. (1982) *Evaluating the Quality of Learning: The SOLO Taxonomy*, New York: Academic Press.

Bilmes, J. (1994) 'Constituting silence: life in the world of total meaning', *Semiotica*, 98: 73–87.

Birch, D. (1991) *The Language of Drama*, London: Macmillan.

Birch, S. and Bloom, P. (2002) 'Preschoolers are sensitive to the speaker's knowledge when learning proper names', *Child Development*, 73: 434–44.

Birch, S., Vauthier, S. and Bloom, P. (2008) 'Three- and four-year-olds spontaneously use others' past performance to guide their learning', *Cognition*, 107: 1018–34.

Birdsong, D. (1992) 'Ultimate attainment in second language acquisition', *Language*, 68: 706–55.

——(ed.) (1999) *Second Language Acquisition and the Critical Period Hypothesis*, Mahwah, NJ: Lawrence Erlbaum.

——(2004) 'Second language acquisition and ultimate attainment', in A. Davis and C. Elder (eds) *The Handbook of Applied Linguistics*, Oxford: Blackwell.

——(2006) 'Age and second language acquisition and processing: a selective overview', *Language Learning*, 56: 9–49.

Birdsong, D. and Molis, M. (2001) 'On the evidence for maturational constraints in second language acquisition', *Journal of Memory and Language*, 44: 235–49.

Birner, B. and Ward, G. (1998) *Informational Status and Noncanonical Word Order*, Philadelphia, PA: John Benjamins.

Biro, J. and Siegel, H. (1997) 'Epistemic normativity: argument and fallacies', *Argumentation*, 11: 277–92.

Bishop, D.V.M. (2000) 'Pragmatic language impairment: a correlate of SLI, a distinct subgroup, or part of the autistic continuum?', in D.V.M. Bishop and L.B. Leonard (eds) *Speech and Language Impairments in Children: Causes, Characteristics, Intervention and Outcome*, Hove: Psychology Press.

——(2003a) *The Children's Communication Checklist*, London: Psychological Corporation.

——(2003b) 'Autism and specific language impairment: categorical distinction or continuum?', *Novartis Foundation Symposium*, 251: 213–26.

Bishop, D.V.M. and Adams, C. (1989) 'Conversational characteristics of children with semantic-pragmatic disorder: II. What features lead to a judgement of inappropriacy?', *British Journal of Disorders of Communication*, 24: 241–63.

Bishop, D.V.M. and Norbury, C.F. (2002) 'Exploring the borderlands of autistic disorder and specific language impairment: a study using standardised diagnostic instruments', *Journal of Child Psychology and Psychiatry*, 43: 917–29.

——(2005) 'Executive functions in children with communication impairments in relation to autistic symptomatology. 1: Generativity', *Autism*, 9: 7–27.

Bishop, D.V.M. and Rosenbloom, L. (1987) 'Classification of childhood language disorders', in W. Yule and M. Rutter (eds) *Language Development and Disorders*, London: Mac Keith Press.

Bishop, D.V.M., Chan, J., Adams, C., Hartley, J. and Weir, F. (1998) 'Conversational responsiveness in specific language impairment: evidence of disproportionate pragmatic difficulties in a subset of children', *Development and Psychopathology*, 12: 177–99.

Bitzer, L. (1968) 'The rhetorical situation', *Philosophy and Rhetoric*, 1: 1–14.

Black, A.W. (2003) 'Unit selection and emotional speech', paper presented at the *8th European Conference on Speech Communication and Technology*, Geneva, Switzerland, September 2003. Online. Available: www.cs.cmu.edu/~awb/papers/eurospeech2003/emph.pdf (accessed 27 August 2007).

Black, M. (1969) 'Austin on performatives', in K.T. Fann (ed.) *Symposium on Austin*, London: Routledge.

Blackmore, J. (2004) 'Quality assurance rather than quality improvement in higher education?', *British Journal of Sociology of Education*, 25: 383–94.

Blakemore, D. (1987) *Semantic Constraints on Relevance*, Oxford: Blackwell.

——(2000) 'Indicators and procedures: *nevertheless* and *but*', *Journal of Linguistics*, 36: 463–86.

——(2002) *Meaning and Relevance: The Semantics and Pragmatics of Discourse Connectives*, Cambridge: Cambridge University Press.

——(2002) *Relevance and Linguistic Meaning: The Semantics and Pragmatics of Discourse Markers*, Cambridge: Cambridge University Press.

——(2004) 'Discourse markers', in L.R. Horn and G. Ward (eds) *The Handbook of Pragmatics*, Oxford: Blackwell.

——(2005a) '"and"-parentheticals', *Journal of Pragmatics*, 37: 1165–81.

——(2005b) 'Discourse markers', in L.R. Horn and G. Ward (eds) *The Handbook of Pragmatics*, Oxford: Blackwell.

——(2006) 'Divisions of labour: the analysis of parentheticals', *Lingua*, 166: 1670–87.

——(2007) '"Or"-parentheticals, "that is"-parentheticals and the pragmatics of reformulation', *Journal of Linguistics*, 43: 311–39.

——(2008) 'Apposition and affective communication', *Language and Literature*, 17: 37–57.

Blas-Arroyo, J.L. (2003) '"Perdóneme que se lo diga, pero vuelve usted a faltar a la verdad, señor González": form and function of politic verbal behaviour in face-to-face Spanish political debates', *Discourse and Society*, 14: 395–423.

Blasko, D. and Connine, C. (1993) 'Effects of familiarity and aptness on metaphor processing', *Journal of Experimental Psychology: Learning, Memory and Cognition*, 19: 295–308.

Blass, R. (1990) *Relevance Relations in Discourse: A Study with Special Reference to Sissala*, Cambridge: Cambridge University Press.

Bleuler, E. ([1911] 1950) *Dementia Praecox or the Group of Schizophrenias*, New York: International University Press.

Bley-Vroman, R. (1989) 'What is the logical problem of foreign language learning?', in S. Gass and J. Schachter (eds) *Linguistic Perspectives on Second Language Acquisition*, Cambridge: Cambridge University Press.

——(1990) 'The logical problem of foreign language learning', *Linguistic Analysis*, 20: 3–49.

Bloch, M. (1998) *How We Think They Think: Anthropological Approaches to Cognition, Memory, and Literacy*, Boulder, CO: Westview Press.

Block, N. (1978) 'Troubles with functionalism', in N. Block (ed.) (1980) *Readings in Philosophy of Psychology, Volume 1*, Cambridge, MA: Harvard University Press.

——(ed.) (1980a) *Readings in Philosophy of Psychology, Volume 1*, Cambridge, MA: Harvard University Press.

——(1980b) 'Introduction: what is functionalism?', in N. Block (ed.) (1980a) *Readings in Philosophy of Psychology, Volume 1*, Cambridge, MA: Harvard University Press.

Block, N., Flannagan, O. and Guzeldre, G. (eds) (1995) *Consciousness*, Cambridge, MA: MIT Press.

Blom, J.-P. and Gumperz, J.J. (1972) 'Social meaning in linguistic structure: code-switching in Norway', in J.J. Gumperz and D. Hymes (eds) *Directions in Sociolinguistics*, New York: Holt, Rinehart, and Winston.

Blome-Tillmann, M. (2008) 'Conversational implicature and the cancellability test', *Analysis*, 68: 156–60.

Blommaert, J. (1991) 'How much culture is there in intercultural communication?', in J. Blommaert and J. Verschueren (eds) *The Pragmatics of Intercultural and International Communication*, Amsterdam: Benjamins.

——(2005) *Discourse*, Cambridge: Cambridge University Press.

Blommaert, J. and Verschueren, J. (1999) *The Diversity Debate*, London: Routledge.

Bloom, P. (2000) *How Children Learn the Meanings of Words*, Cambridge, MA: MIT Press.

——(2002) 'Mindreading, communication, and the learning of the names for things', *Mind and Language*, 17: 37–54.

Bloomfield, L. (1933) *Language*, New York: Henry Holt.

Bloor, M. and Bloor, T. (1993) 'How economists modify propositions', in W. Henderson, T. Dudley-Evans and R. Backhouse (eds) *Economics and Language*, London and New York: Routledge.

Bloor, T. (1996) 'Three hypothetical strategies in philosophical writing', in E. Ventola and A. Mauranen (eds) *Academic Writing: Intercultural and Textual Issues*, Amsterdam and Philadelphia, PA: John Benjamins.

Blum-Kulka, S. (1993) '"You gotta know how to tell a story": Telling, tales and tellers in American and Israeli narrative events at dinner', *Language in Society*, 22: 361–402.

Blum-Kulka, S. and Kasper, G. (1993) *Interlanguage Pragmatics*, Oxford: Oxford University Press.

Blum-Kulka, S. and Olshtain, E. (1984) 'Requests and apologies: a cross-cultural study of realisation patterns (CCSARP)', *Applied Linguistics*, 5: 196–213.

Blum-Kulka, S., House, J. and Kasper, G. (eds) (1989) *Cross-Cultural Pragmatics: Requests and Apologies*, Norwood, NJ: Ablex.

Blutner, R. (1998) 'Lexical pragmatics', *Journal of Semantics*, 15: 115–62.

——(2000) 'Some aspects of optimality in natural language interpretation', *Journal of Semantics*, 17: 189–216.

——(2004) 'Pragmatics and the lexicon', in L.R. Horn and G. Ward (eds) *Handbook of Pragmatics*, Oxford: Blackwell.

——(2007) 'Some experimental aspects of optimality-theoretic pragmatics', unpublished manuscript, University of Amsterdam.

Blutner, R. and Solstad, T. (2000) 'Dimensional designation: a case study in lexical pragmatics', in R. Blutner and G. Jäger (eds) *Studies in Optimality Theory*, Potsdam, Germany: University of Potsdam.

Blutner, R. and Zeevat, H. (2004a) 'Editors' introduction: pragmatics in optimality theory', in R. Blutner and H. Zeevat (eds) *Optimality Theory and Pragmatics*, Basingstoke: Palgrave Macmillan.

——(eds) (2004b) *Optimality Theory and Pragmatics*, Basingstoke: Palgrave Macmillan.

——(to appear) 'Optimality-theoretic pragmatics', in C. Maienborn, K. v. Heusinger and P. Portner (eds) *Semantics: An International Handbook of Natural Language Meaning*, Berlin: Mouton de Gruyter.

Blutner, R., de Hoop, H. and Hendriks, P. (2005) *Optimal Communication*, Stanford, CA: CSLI Publications.

Bobrow, D.G. and Collins, A. (1975) *Representation and Understanding*, New York: Academic Press.

Bobrow, D.G. and Norman, D.A. (1975) 'Some principles of memory schemata', in D.G. Bobrow and A. Collins (eds) *Representation and Understanding*, New York: Academic Press.

Boden, D. (1994) *The Business of Talk: Organizations in Action*, Cambridge: Polity Press.

Boden, D. and Zimmerman, D.H. (eds) (1991) *Talk and Social Structure: Studies in Ethnomethodology and Conversation Analysis*, Cambridge: Polity Press.

Body, R. and Parker, M. (2005) 'Topic repetitiveness after traumatic brain injury: an emergent, jointly managed behaviour', *Clinical Linguistics and Phonetics*, 19: 379–92.

Body, R. and Perkins, M.R. (2004) 'Validation of linguistic analyses in narrative discourse after traumatic brain injury', *Brain Injury*, 18: 707–24.

Boersma, P. (2001) 'Phonology-semantics inter-action in OT and its acquisition', in R. Kirchner, W. Wikeley and J. Pater (eds) *Papers in Experimental and Theoretical Linguistics*, volume 6, Edmonton, Canada: University of Alberta.

Bogen, J. (1972) *Wittgenstein's Philosophy of Language: Some Aspects of its Development*, London: Routledge and Kegan Paul.

Bokus, B. (1991) 'Children's pragmatic knowledge of narrative tasks', in J. Verschueren (ed.) *Pragmatics at Issue: Selected Papers of the International Pragmatics Conference, Antwerp, August 17–22, 1987*, Amsterdam, Netherlands: Benjamins.

Bolinger, D.L. (1977) 'There', in D. Bolinger, *Meaning and Form*, London: Longman.

——(1983) 'The inherent iconism of intonation', in J. Haiman (ed.) *Iconicity in Syntax*, Typological Studies in Language, volume 6, Amsterdam, Netherlands and Philadelphia, PA: John Benjamins.

——(1989) *Intonation and Its Uses: Melody in Grammar and Discourse*, London: Arnold.

——(1961) 'Contrastive accent and contrastive stress', *Language*, 37: 87–96.

Bongaerts, T. (1999) 'Ultimate attainment in L2 pronunciation: the case of very advanced late L2 learners', in D. Birdsong (ed.) *Second Language Acquisition and the Critical Period Hypothesis*, Mahwah, NJ: Lawrence Erlbaum.

——(2005) 'Introduction: ultimate attainment and the critical period hypothesis for second language acquisition', *International Review of Applied Linguistics in Language Teaching*, 43: 259–67.

Booth, W. (1974) *A Rhetoric of Irony*, Chicago: University of Chicago Press.

Borer, H. (2005) 'Things that count: null D', in H. Borer (ed.) *Structuring Sense: An Exo-Skeletal Trilogy. Book I: Determining Structures*, Oxford: Oxford University Press.

Borg, E. (2004a) *Minimal Semantics*, Oxford: Oxford University Press.

——(2004b) 'Formal semantics and intentional states', *Analysis*, 64: 215–23.

——(2007) 'Minimalism versus contextualism in semantics', in G. Preyer and G. Peter (eds) *Context-Sensitivity and Semantic Minimalism: New Essays on Semantics and Pragmatics*, Oxford: Oxford University Press.

Borkin, A. (1971) 'Polarity items in questions', *Proceedings from the 7th Regional Meeting of the Chicago Linguistic Society*, Chicago: Chicago Linguistic Society.

Borod, J., Rorie, K., Pick, L., Bloom, R., Andelman, F., Campbell, A., Obler, L., Tweedy, J., Welkowitz, J. and Sliwinski, M. (2000) 'Verbal pragmatics following unilateral stroke: emotional content and valence', *Neuropsychology*, 14: 112–24.

Bosch, P. (1988) 'Representing and accessing focused referents', *Language and Cognitive Processes*, 2: 207–31.

Bosco, F.M. and Bucciarelli, M. (2008) 'Simple and complex deceits and ironies', *Journal of Pragmatics*, 40: 583–607.

Bosco, F.M., Bucciarelli, M. and Bara, B.G. (2004) 'Context categories in understanding communicative intentions', *Journal of Pragmatics*, 36: 467–88.

——(2006) 'Recognition and recovery of communicative failures: a developmental perspective', *Journal of Pragmatics*, 38: 1398–429.

Bosco, F.M., Colle, L., De Fazio, A., Bono, S., Ruberti, S. and Tirassa, M. (2009) 'Th.o.m.a.s.: an exploratory assessment of theory of mind in schizophrenic subjects', *Consciousness and Cognition* 18: 306–19.

Bott, L. and Noveck, I. (2004) 'Some utterances are underinformative: the onset and time course of scalar inferences', *Journal of Memory and Language*, 51: 437–57.

Botting, N. and Adams, C. (2005) 'Semantic and inferencing abilities in children with communication disorders', *International Journal of Language and Communication Disorders*, 40: 49–66.

Botting, N. and Conti-Ramsden, G. (1999) 'Pragmatic language impairment without autism: the child in question', *Autism*, 3: 371–96.

Boucher, J. (1998) 'SPD as a distinct diagnostic entity: logical considerations and directions for future research', *International Journal of Language and Communication Disorders*, 33: 71–108.

Boulima, J. (1999) *Negotiated Interaction in Target Language Classroom Discourse*, Amsterdam: John Benjamins.

Bourdieu, P. (1977) *Outline of a Theory of Practice*, trans. R. Nice, Cambridge: Cambridge University Press.

——(1982) *Ce que parler veut dire: L'économie des échanges linguistiques*; trans. J. Thompson (1991) *Language and Symbolic Power*, Cambridge: Polity Press.

——(1984) *Questions de Sociologie*, Paris: Les Editions de Minuit.

——(1986) *Outline of a Theory of Practice*, Cambridge: Cambridge University Press.

——(1991) *Language and Symbolic Power*, ed. J. Thompson, trans. G. Raymond and M. Adamson, Cambridge, MA: Harvard University Press.

Bourgeois, M., Schulz, R., Burgio, L. and Beach, S. (2002) 'Skills training for spouses of patients with Alzheimer's disease: outcomes of an intervention study', *Journal of Clinical Geropsychology*, 8: 53–73.

Bowdle, B. and Gentner, D. (2005) 'The career of metaphor', *Psychological Review*, 112: 193–216.

Bowerman, M. and Levinson, S.C. (2001) 'Introduction', in M. Bowerman and S.C. Levinson (eds) *Language Acquisition and Conceptual Development*, Cambridge: Cambridge University Press.

Boxer, D. (1993a) 'Social distance and speech behavior: the case of indirect complaints', *Journal of Pragmatics*, 19: 103–25.

——(1993b) *Complaining and Commiserating: A Speech Act View of Solidarity in Spoken American English*, New York: Peter Lang.

——(1996) 'Ethnographic interviewing as a research tool in speech act analysis: the case of complaints', in S. Gass and J. Neu (eds) *Speech Acts Across Cultures: Challenges to Communication in a Second Language*, Berlin: Mouton de Gruyter.

——(2002) 'Discourse issues in cross-cultural pragmatics', *Annual Review of Applied Linguistics*, 22: 150–70.

Boysen, S.T. and Kuhlmeier, V.A. (2002) 'Representational capacities for pretense with scale models and photographs in chimpanzees', in R.W. Mitchell (ed.) *Pretending and Imagination in Animals and Children*, Cambridge: Cambridge University Press.

Brachman, R. and Levesque, H. (2004) *Knowledge Representation and Reasoning*, San Francisco, CA: Morgan Kaufmann.

Brand, M. (1984) *Intending and Acting*, Cambridge, MA: MIT Press.

Brandom, R. (1994) *Making It Explicit*, Cambridge, MA: Harvard University Press.

——(2000) *Articulating Reasons*, Cambridge, MA: Harvard University Press.

——(2008) *Between Saying and Doing*, Cambridge, MA: Harvard University Press.

Bransford, J.D., Barclay, J.R. and Franks, J.J. (1972) 'Sentence memory: a constructive versus interpretive approach', *Cognitive Psychology*, 3: 193–209.

Bratman, M. (1992) 'Shared cooperative activity', *The Philosophical Review*, 101: 327–41.

——(1999) *Faces of Intention*, Cambridge, MA: Cambridge University Press.

Braun, D. (1995a) 'What is Character?', *Journal of Philosophical Logic*, 24: 227–40.

——(1995b) 'Structured characters and complex demonstratives', *Journal of Philosophical Logic*, 24: 227–40.

——(1996) 'Demonstratives and their linguistic meaning', *Noûs*, 30: 145–73.

Bray, C.M. and Wiig, E.H. (1987) *Let's Talk Inventory for Children*, London: The Psychological Corporation.

Brazil, D. (1997) *The Communicative Value of Intonation in English*, Cambridge: Cambridge University Press.

Breheny, R. (2002) 'The current state of (radical) pragmatics in the cognitive sciences', *Mind and Language*, 17: 169–87.

Breheny, R., Katsos, N. and Williams, J. (2006) 'Are generalized scalar implicatures generated by default? An on-line investigation into the role of context in generating pragmatic inferences', *Cognition*, 100: 434–63.

Brentano, F. ([1874] 1973) *Psychology from an Empirical Standpoint*, trans. A.C. Rancurello, D.B. Terrell and L.L. McAlister, London: Routledge and Kegan Paul.

Bresnahan, M.J., Ohashi, R., Liu, W.Y., Nebashi, R. and Liao, C. (1999) 'A comparison of response styles in Singapore and Taiwan', *Journal of Cross-Cultural Psychology*, 30: 342–58.

Bresnan, J. (2001) 'The emergence of the unmarked pronoun', in G. Legendre, J. Grimshaw and S. Vikner (eds) *Optimality-Theoretic Syntax*, Cambridge, MA: MIT Press.

Briggs, A. (1978) 'Hadji Murat: the power of understatement', in M. Jones and R.F. Christian (eds) *New Essays on Tolstoy*, Cambridge: Cambridge University Press.

Briggs, C. (1996) *Disorderly Discourse: Narrative, Conflict and Inequality*, Oxford: Oxford University Press.

Bright, W.A. (ed.) ([1966] 1971) *Sociolinguistics. Proceedings of UCLA Sociolinguistics Conference, Los Angeles and Lake Arrowhead, California, 1964*, The Hague: Mouton.

Brinton, B. and Fujiki, M. (1984) 'Development of topic manipulation skills in discourse', *Journal of Speech and Hearing Research*, 27: 350–58.

Brinton, L.J. (1996) *Pragmatic Markers in English: Grammaticalization and Discourse Functions*, Berlin: Mouton de Gruyter.

——(2001) 'Historical discourse analysis', in D. Schiffrin, D. Tannen and H.E. Hamilton (eds) *The Handbook of Discourse Analysis*, Oxford: Blackwell.

Brisard, F., Frisson, S. and Sandra, D. (2001) 'Processing unfamiliar metaphors in a self-paced reading task', *Metaphor and Symbol*, 16: 87–108.

Britt, M.A. (1994) 'The interaction of referential ambiguity and argument structure in the parsing of prepositional phrases', *Journal of Memory and Language*, 33: 251–83.

Broadbent, D.E. (1958) *Perception and Communication*, Oxford: Pergamon.

Brockhaus, R.R. (1991) *Pulling Up the Ladder: The Metaphysical Roots of Wittgenstein's Tractatus Logico-Philosophicus*, La Salle, IL: Open Court.

Brogaard, B. (2008) 'Moral contextualism and moral relativism', *Philosophical Quarterly*, 58: 385–409.

Brook, S.L. and Bowler, D. (1992) 'Autism by another name? Semantic and pragmatic impairments in children', *Journal of Autism and Developmental Disorders*, 22: 61–81.

Brooks, R.A. (1990) 'Elephants don't play chess', *Robotics and Autonomous Systems*, 6: 3–15.

——(1991a) 'How to build complete creatures rather than isolated cognitive simulators', in K. VanLehn (ed.) *Architectures for Intelligence*, Hillsdale, NJ: Erlbaum.

——(1991b) 'Intelligence without representation', *Artificial Intelligence*, 47: 139–59.

Brookshire, B.L., Chapman, S.B., Song, J. and Levin, H.S. (2000) 'Cognitive and linguistic correlates of children's discourse after closed head injury: a three-year follow-up', *Journal of the International Neuropsychological Society*, 6: 741–51.

Brown, G. (1977) *Listening to Spoken English*, London: Longman.

Brown, G. and Yule, G. (1983) *Discourse Analysis*, Cambridge: Cambridge University Press.

Brown, J. (2001) 'Pragmatics tests: different purposes, different tests', in K. Rose and G. Kasper (eds) *Pragmatics in Language Teaching*, Cambridge: Cambridge University Press.

Brown, P. (1980) 'How and why women are more polite: a new perspective on language and society', *Reviews in Anthropology*, 3: 240–49.

——(1990) 'Gender, politeness, and confrontation in Tenejapa', *Discourse Processes*, 13: 123–41.

——(2002) 'Language as a model for culture: lessons from the cognitive sciences', in B. King and R. Fox (eds) *Anthropology Beyond Culture*, Oxford: Berg.

Brown, P. and Levinson, S.C. (1978) 'Universals in language usage: politeness phenomena', in E. Goody (ed.) *Questions and Politeness: Strategies in Social Interaction*, Cambridge: Cambridge University Press.

——(1987) *Politeness: Some Universals in Language Usage*, Cambridge: Cambridge University Press.

——(2008) 'Language as mind tools: learning how to think through speaking', in J. Guo, E. Lieven, N. Budwig, S. Ervin-Tripp, K. Nakamura and S. Ozcaliskan (eds) *Cross-linguistic Approaches to the Psychology of Language: Research in the Tradition of Dan Issac Slobin*, Mahwah, NJ: Erlbaum.

Brown, R. (1973) 'Schizophrenia, language and reality', *American Psychologist*, 28: 395–403.

Brown, R. and Gilman, A. (1960) 'The pronouns of power and solidarity', in T.A. Sebeok (ed.) *Style in Language*, Cambridge, MA: MIT Press.

——(1989) 'Politeness theory and Shakespeare's four major tragedies', *Language in Society*, 18: 159–212.

Brownell, H.H. and Stringfellow, A. (1999) 'Making requests: illustrations of how right-hemisphere brain damage can affect discourse production', *Brain and Language*, 68: 442–65.

Brownell, H.H., Potter, H.H., Bihrle, A.M. and Gardner, H. (1986) 'Inference deficits in right brain-damaged patients', *Brain and Language*, 27: 310–21.

Brownell, H.H., Potter, H.H., Michelow, D. and Gardner, H. (1984) 'Sensitivity to lexical denotation and connotation in brain-damaged patients: a double dissociation?', *Brain and Language*, 22: 253–65.

Brownell, H.H., Simpson, T., Bihrle, A., Potter, H. and Gardner, H. (1990) 'Appreciation of metaphoric alternative word meanings by left and right brain-damaged patients', *Neuropsychologia*, 28: 375–83.

Brown-Schmidt, S., Gunlogson, C. and Tanenhaus, M.K. (2008) 'Addressees distinguish shared from private information when interpreting questions during interactive conversation', *Cognition*, 107: 1122–34.

Brugman, C. and Lakoff, G. (1988) 'Cognitive topology and lexical networks', in S. Small, G. Cottrell and M. Tanenhaus (eds) *Lexical Ambiguity Resolution: Perspectives from Psycholinguistics, Neuropsychology and Artificial Intelligence*, San Mateo, CA: Morgan Kaufmann.

Brumark, A. (2006) 'Non-observance of Gricean maxims in family dinner table conversation', *Journal of Pragmatics*, 38: 1206–38.

Brumfitt, C.J. (2001) *Individual Freedom in Language Teaching: Helping Learners to Develop a Dialect of their Own*, Oxford: Oxford University Press.

Brumfitt, C.J. and Carter, R. (eds) (1986) *Literature and Language Teaching*, Oxford: Oxford University Press.

Bruneau, T.J. (1973) 'Communicative silences: forms and functions', *Journal of Communication*, 23: 17–46.

Bruner, J.S. (1975) 'The ontogenesis of speech acts', *Journal of Child Language*, 2: 1–19.

——(1983) *Child's Talk*, New York: Norton.

——(1990) *Acts of Meaning*, Cambridge, MA: Harvard University Press.

Brunner, J. and You, W. (1988) 'Chinese negotiation and the concept of face', *Journal of International Consumer Marketing*, 1: 27–43.

Bryant, G.A. and Fox Tree, J.E. (2005) 'Is there an ironic tone of voice?', *Language and Speech*, 48: 257–77.

Bublitz, W. and Hübler, A. (2007) *Metapragmatics in Use*, Amsterdam: John Benjamins.

Bucciarelli, M., Colle, L. and Bara, B.G. (2003) 'How children comprehend speech acts and communicative gestures', *Journal of Pragmatics*, 35: 207–41.

Bucholtz, M. (1999) '"Why be normal?": Language and identity practices in a community of nerd girls', *Language in Society*, 28: 203–23.

——(2007) 'Variation in transcription', *Discourse Studies*, 9: 784–808.

Bühler, K.L. (1934) *Sprachtheorie: die Darstellungsfunktion der Sprache*, trans. D.F. Goodwin (1990), *Theory of Language: The Representative Function of Language*, Amsterdam, Netherlands and Philadelphia, PA: John Benjamins.

——([1934]1982) 'The deictic field of language and deictic words', in R.J. Jarvella and W. Klein (eds) *Speech, Place and Action: Studies in Deixis and Related Topics*, Chichester: John Wiley and Sons Ltd.

Bulhof, J. and Gimbel, S. (2001) 'Deep tautologies', *Pragmatics and Cognition*, 9: 279–91.

——(2004) 'A tautology is a tautology, or is it?', *Journal of Pragmatics*, 36: 1003–5.

Bultinck, B. (2005) *Numerous Meaning: The Meaning of English Cardinals and the Legacy of Paul Grice*, Oxford: Elsevier.

Bunt, H.C. (1979) 'Conversational principles in question-answer dialogues', in D. Krallmann (ed.) *Zur Theorie der Frage*, Essen, Germany: Narr Verlag.

——(2000a) 'Dialogue pragmatics and context specification', in H.C. Bunt and W.J. Black (eds) *Computational Pragmatics, Abduction, Belief and Context: Studies in Computational Pragmatics*, Amsterdam: John Benjamins.

——(2000b) 'Dynamic interpretation and dialogue theory', in M.M. Taylor, F. Neel and D.G. Bouwhuis (eds) *The Structure of Multimodal Dialogue*, volume 2, Amsterdam and Philadelphia, PA: John Benjamins.

——(2006) 'Dimensions in dialogue annotation', *Proceedings of the 5th International Conference on Language Resources and Evaluation (LREC 2006)*, Paris: ELRA.

Bunt, H.C. and Black, W.J. (2000) 'The ABC of computational pragmatics', in H.C. Bunt and W.J. Black (eds) *Abduction, Belief and Context in Dialogue: Studies in Computational Pragmatics*, Amsterdam: John Benjamins.

Bunt, H.C., Morante, R. and Keizer, S. (2007) 'An empirically based computational model of grounding in dialogue', in S. Keizer, H. Bunt and T. Paek (eds) *Proceedings of the 8th SIGdial Workshop on Discourse and Dialogue*, Antwerp, Belgium.

Bunton, D. (1999) 'The use of higher level metatext in Ph.D theses', *English for Specific Purposes*, 18 (Supplement 1): S41-S56.

Burge, T. (1979) 'Individualism and the mental', reprinted in D.M. Rosenthal (ed.) (1991) *The Nature of Mind*, New York: Oxford University Press.

Burger, H. (1996) 'Phraseologie und Metaphorik', in E. Weigand and F. Hundsnurscher (eds) *Lexical Structures and Language Use*. Beiträge zur Dialogforschung 10. Tübingen: Niemeyer.

——(1998) 'Idiom and metaphor: their relation in theory and text', in P. Durco (ed.) *Phraseology and Paremiology*. Europhras 1997. Bratislava.

Büring, D. (1999) 'Topic', in P. Bosch and R. van der Sandt (eds) *Focus: Linguistic, Cognitive and Computational Perspectives*, Cambridge: Cambridge University Press.

Burke, K. ([1945] 1969) *A Grammar of Motives*, Berkeley, CA: University of California Press.

Burkette, A. (2007) 'Constructing identity: grammatical variables and the creation of a community voice', *Journal of Sociolinguistics*, 11: 286–96.

Burkhardt, A. (1996) 'Politolinguistik. Versuch einer Ortsbestimmung', in J. Klein and H. Diekmannshenke (eds) *Sprachstrategien und Sialogblockaden: Linguistische und Politikwissenschaftliche Studien zur Politischen Kommunikation*, Berlin and New York: de Gruyter Verlag.

Burkhardt, P. (2005) 'Online comprehension of definite NPs: inferential knowledge facilitates integration of bridging relations at an early point', poster presented at *CUNY Conference on Human Sentence Processing*, Tucson, AZ, April 2005.

——(2006) 'The given-new distinction: how context and definiteness impact referential interpretation', poster presented at *CUNY Conference on Human Sentence Processing*, New York City, NY, March 2006.

Burnard, L. and McEnery, A.M. (2000) *Rethinking Language Pedagogy from a Corpus Perspective*, Hamburg: Peter Lang.

Burton, D. (1980) *Dialogue and Discourse: A Sociolinguistic Approach to Modern Drama Dialogue and Naturally Occurring Conversation*, London: Routledge and Kegan Paul.

——(1982) 'Through glass darkly: through dark glasses', in R. Carter (ed.) *Language and Literature*, London: Allen and Unwin.

Burton-Roberts, N. (1989) *The Limits to Debate: A Revised Theory of Semantic Presupposition*, Cambridge: Cambridge University Press.

——(1999a) 'Apposition', in K. Brown and J. Miller (eds) *The Concise Encyclopaedia of Grammatical Categories*, Amsterdam: Elsevier.

——(1999b) 'Language, linear precedence and parentheticals', in P. Collins and D. Lee (eds) *The Clause in English*, Amsterdam: John Benjamins.

——(2007) *Pragmatics*, Basingstoke: Palgrave Macmillan.

Buss, D. (1994) *The Evolution of Desire*, New York: Basic Books.

Busse, D. (ed.) (1991) *Diachrone Semantik und Pragmatik: Untersuchungen zur Erklärung und Beschreibung des Sprachwandels*, Tübingen: Max Niemeyer Verlag.

Busse, U. (2002) *Linguistic Variation in the Shakespeare Corpus: Morpho-Syntactic Variability of Second Person Pronouns*, Amsterdam and Philadelphia, PA: John Benjamins.

Butcher, C., Mylander, C. and Goldin-Meadow, S. (1991) 'Displaced communication in a self-styled gesture system: pointing at the nonpresent', *Cognitive Development*, 6: 315–42.

Butler, J. (1991) 'Imitation and gender subordination', in D. Fuss (ed.) *Inside/Out: Lesbian theories, Gay Theories*, London: Routledge.

——(1993) *Bodies That Matter: On the Discursive Limits of "Sex"*, New York: Routledge.

——([1990] 1999) *Gender Trouble: Feminism and the Subversion of Identity*, New York: Routledge.

Butterfill, S. (2007) 'What are modules and what is their role in development?', *Mind and Language*, 22: 450–73.

Bybee, J.L. and Hopper, P. (eds) (2001) *Frequency and the Emergence of Language Structure*, Amsterdam: John Benjamins.

Byon, A.S. (2006) 'The role of linguistic indirectness and honorifics in achieving linguistic politeness in Korean requests', *Journal of Politeness Research*, 2: 247–75.

Byrne, R.W. (1989) 'Can valid inferences be suppressed?', *Cognition*, 39: 71–78.

——(1998) 'So much easier to attack straw men', *Behavioral and Brain Sciences*, 21: 116–17.

Byrne, R.W. and Whiten, A. (1988) *Machiavellian Intelligence: Social Expertise and the Evolution of Intellect in Monkeys, Apes and Humans*, Oxford: Clarendon Press.

——(1990) 'Tactical deception in primates: the 1990 database', *Primate Report*, 27: 1–101.

Cacciari, C. and Glucksberg, S. (1994) 'Understanding figurative language', in M.A. Gernsbacher (ed.) *Handbook of Psycholinguistics*, San Diego, CA: Academic Press.

Caffi, C. (1998) 'Metapragmatics', in J. Mey (ed.) *Concise Encyclopedia of Pragmatics*, Amsterdam: Elsevier.

——(1999) 'On mitigation', *Journal of Pragmatics*, 31: 881–909.

——(ed.) (2006) *Mitigation*, Studies in Pragmatics 4, Netherlands: Elsevier.

Cage, J. (1967) *A Year from Monday*, Middletown, CT: Wesleyan University Press.

Cahn, J.E. and Brennan, S.E. (1999) 'A psychological model of grounding and repair in dialog', in S.E. Brennan, A. Giboin and D.R. Traum (eds) *Proceedings of AAAI Fall Symposium on Psychological Models of Communication in Collaborative Systems*, North Falmouth, MA: American Association for Artificial Intelligence.

Calculator, S.N. (1988) 'Evaluating the effectiveness of AAC programmes for persons with severe handicaps', *Augmentative and Alternative Communication*, 4: 177–79.

Call, J., Carpenter, M. and Tomasello, M. (2004) '"Unwilling" versus "unable": chimpanzees' understanding of human intentional action', *Developmental Science*, 7: 488–98.

Camaioni, L. (1993) 'The development of intentional communication: a re-analysis', in J. Nadel and L. Camaioni (eds) *New Perspectives in Early Communication Development*, New York: Routledge.

Camaioni, L., Perucchini, P., Bellagamba, F. and Colonnesi, C. (2004) 'The role of declarative pointing in developing a theory of mind', *Infancy*, 5: 291–308.

Cameron, D. (1997) 'Performing gender identity: young men's talk and the construction of heterosexual masculinity', in S. Johnson and U. Meinhof (eds) *Language and Masculinity*, Oxford: Blackwell.

——(1998) '"Is there any ketchup, Vera?" Gender, power and pragmatics', *Discourse and Society*, 9: 437–55.

——(2000) *Good to Talk: Living and Working in a Communication Culture*, London: Sage.

Cameron, D. and Kulick, D. (2003) *Language and Sexuality*, Cambridge: Cambridge University Press.

——(2006) *The Language and Sexuality Reader*, London: Routledge.

Cameron, N.A. (1964) 'Experimental analysis of schizophrenic thinking', in J. S. Kasanin (ed.) *Language and Thought in Schizophrenia*, Berkeley, CA: University of California Press.

Camp, E. (2003) 'Saying and seeing-as: the linguistic uses and cognitive effects of metaphor', unpublished dissertation, University of California, Berkeley.

——(2006) 'Contextualism, metaphor, and what is said', *Mind and Language*, 21: 280–309.

Campbell, D. and Dillon, M. (1993) *The Political Subjects of Violence*, Manchester: Manchester University Press.

Campbell, J. (2002) *Reference and Consciousness*, Oxford: Oxford University Press.

Campbell, S. and Roberts, C. (2007) 'Migration, ethnicity and competing discourses in the job interview: synthesising the institutional and the personal', *Discourse and Society*, 18: 243–71.

Campbell, T.F. and Dollaghan, C.A. (1990) 'Expressive language recovery in severely brain injured children and adolescents', *Journal of Speech and Hearing Disorders*, 55: 567–81.

Canagarajah, S. (2007) 'Lingua franca English, multilingual communities, and language acquisition', *The Modern Language Journal*, 91: 923–39.

Candlin, C.N. (ed.) (2002) *Research and Practice in Professional Discourse*, Hong Kong: City University of Hong Kong Press.

Candlin, S. (2003) 'Issues arising when the professional workplace is the site of applied linguistic research', *Applied Linguistics*, 24: 386–94.

Cannizzaro, M.S. and Coelho, C.A. (2002) 'Treatment of story grammar following traumatic brain injury: a pilot study', *Brain Injury*, 16: 1065–73.

Canny, J.F. (1988) *The Complexity of Robot Motion Planning*, Cambridge, MA: MIT Press.

Cao, X. (2007) 'The effect of age and gender on the choice of address forms in Chinese personal letters', *Journal of Sociolinguistics*, 11: 392–407.

Capelli, C.A., Nakagawa, N. and Madden, C.M. (1990) 'How children understand sarcasm: the role of context and intonation', *Child Development*, 61: 1824–41.

Caplan, B. (2003) 'Putting things in contexts', *The Philosophical Review*, 112: 191–214.

Caplan, R., Guthrie, D. and Foy, J.G. (1992) 'Communication deficits and formal thought disorder in schizophrenic children', *Journal of the American Academy of Child and Adolescent Psychiatry*, 31: 151–59.

Caplan, R., Guthrie, D. and Komo, S. (1996) 'Conversational repair in schizophrenic and normal children', *Journal of the American Academy of Child and Adolescent Psychiatry*, 35: 950–58.

Cappa, S.F., Benke, T., Clarke, S., Rossi, B., Stemmer, B. and van Heugten, M. (2005) 'EFNS guidelines on cognitive rehabilitation: report of an EFNS task force', *European Journal of Neurology*, 12: 665–80.

Cappelen, H. and Lepore, E. (2005a) *Insensitive Semantics: A Defense of Semantic Minimalism and Speech Act Pluralism*, Oxford: Blackwell.

——(2005b) 'Varieties of quotation revisited', *Belgian Journal of Linguistics*, 17: 51–75.

Carey, S. and Spelke, E. (1994) 'Domain-specific knowledge and conceptual change', in L. Hirschfeld and S. Gelman (eds) *Mapping the Mind: Domain Specificity in Culture and Cognition*, Cambridge: Cambridge University Press.

Carletta, J., Isard, A., Isard, S., Kowtko, J., Doherty-Sneddon, G. and Anderson, A. (1997) 'The reliability of a dialogue structure coding scheme', *Computational Linguistics*, 23: 13–31.

Carlomagno, S., Blasi, V., Labruna, L. and Santoro, A. (2000) 'The role of communication models in assessment and therapy of language disorders in aphasic adults', *Neuropsychological Rehabilitation*, 10: 337–63.

Carlson, G.N. (1991) 'Cases of really direct reference: perception and ostention?', paper presented at *Semantics and Linguistic Theory (SALT) 1*, Cornell University, Ithaca, New York, April 1991.

——(2004) 'Reference', in L.R. Horn and G. Ward (eds.) *The Handbook of Pragmatics*, Oxford: Blackwell.

Carlson, G.N. and Pelletier, F.J. (eds) (1995) *The Generic Book*, Chicago, IL: University of Chicago Press.

Carnap, R. (1937) *The Logical Syntax of Language*, London: Routledge and Kegan Paul.

——(1942) *Introduction to Semantics*, Cambridge, MA: Harvard University Press.

Carney, L.S. (1993) 'Not telling us what to think: the Vietnam veterans memorial', *Metaphor and Symbolic Activity*, 8: 211–19.

Carpendale, J.I. and Chandler, M.J. (1996) 'On the distinction between false belief understanding and subscribing to an interpretive theory of mind', *Child Development*, 67: 1686–1706.

Carpenter, M., Nagell, K. and Tomasello, M. (1998) 'Social cognition, joint attention, and communicative competence from 9 to 15 months of age', *Monographs of the Society for Research in Child Development*, 63: 1–143.

Carpenter, R.L., Mastergeorge, A.M. and Coggins, T.E. (1983) 'The acquisition of communicative intentions in infants eight to fifteen months of age', *Language and Speech*, 26: 101–16.

Carrell, P. (1979) 'Indirect speech acts in ESL: indirect answers', in C. Yorio, K. Perkins and J. Schachter (eds) *On TESOL '79: The Learner in Focus*, Washington, DC: Teachers of English to Speakers of Other Languages.

Carruthers, P. (2006) *The Architecture of the Mind*, Oxford: Oxford University Press.

Carruthers, P. and Smith, P.K. (eds) (1996) *Theories of Theories of Mind*, Cambridge: Cambridge University Press.

Carstairs-McCarthy, A. (1999) *Origins of Complex Language*, Oxford: Oxford University Press.

Carston, R. (1988) 'Implicature, explicature and truth-theoretic semantics', in R. Kempson (ed.) *Mental Representation: The Interface between Language and Reality*, Cambridge: Cambridge University Press; reprinted in S. Davis (ed.) (1990) *Pragmatics: A Reader*, Oxford: Oxford University Press; and also in A. Kasher (ed.) (1998) *Pragmatics: Critical Concepts*, vol. IV, London: Routledge.

——(1995) 'Quantity maxims and generalized implicatures', *Lingua*, 96: 213–44.

——(1996) 'Metalinguistic negation and echoic use', *Journal of Linguistics*, 25: 309–30.

——(1997) 'Enrichment and loosening: complementary processes in deriving the proposition expressed?', *Linguistische Berichte*, 8: 103–27.

——(1998a) 'Postscript (1995) to Carston 1988', in A. Kasher (ed.) *Pragmatics: Critical Concepts*, vol. 4, London: Routledge.

——(1998b) 'Informativeness, relevance, and scalar implicature', in R. Carston and S. Uchida (eds) *Relevance Theory: Applications and Implications*, Amsterdam: John Benjamins.

——(1999) 'The semantics/pragmatics distinction: a view from relevance theory', in K. Turner (ed.) *The Semantics/Pragmatics Interface from Different Points of View*, Oxford: Elsevier Science.

——(2001) 'Relevance theory and the saying/implicating distinction', *UCL Working Papers in Linguistics*, 13: 1–34.

——(2002) *Thoughts and Utterances: The Pragmatics of Explicit Communication*, Oxford: Blackwell.

——(2004a) 'Explicature and semantics', in S. Davis and B. Gillon (eds) *Semantics: A Reader*, Oxford: Oxford University Press.

——(2004b) 'Relevance theory and the saying/implicating distinction', in L.R. Horn and G. Ward (eds) *The Handbook of Pragmatics*, Oxford: Blackwell.

——(2005) 'Relevance theory, Grice, and the neo-Griceans: a response to Laurence Horn's "Current issues in neo-Gricean pragmatics"', *Intercultural Pragmatics*, 2: 303–20.

——(2007) 'How many pragmatic systems are there?', in M.J. Frápolli (ed.) *Saying, Meaning and Referring: Essays on François Recanati's Philosophy of Language*, Basingstoke: Palgrave Macmillan.

——(2008) 'Linguistic communication and the semantics/pragmatics distinction', *Synthese*, 165: 321–45.

Carter, R. (2004) *Language and Creativity: The Art of Common Talk*, London: Routledge.

Carter, R. and McCarthy, M. (1995) 'Grammar and the spoken language', *Applied Linguistics*, 16: 141–57.

——(1997) *Exploring Spoken Discourse*, Cambridge: Cambridge University Press.

——(2006) *Cambridge Grammar of English*, Cambridge: Cambridge University Press.

Carter, R. and Nash, W. (1990) *Seeing through Language*, Oxford: Blackwell.

Carter, R. and Simpson, P. (eds) (1989) *Language, Discourse and Literature*, London: Unwin Hyman.

Casas, A.M., Fernandez, A.Y. and Remirez, J.R. (2004) 'Grammatical complexity and cohesion mechanisms in the communicative pragmatics of children with attention deficit hyperactivity disorder', *Revista de Neurología*, 38: S111–16.

Cashman, H.R. (2006) 'Impoliteness in children's interactions in a Spanish/English bilingual community of practice', *Journal of Politeness Research*, 2: 217–46.

Caspers, J. and Wichmann, A. (2001) 'Melodic cues to turn-taking in English: evidence from perception', *Proceedings of the Second SIGdial Workshop on Discourse and Dialogue*, Morristown, NJ: Association for Computational Linguistics.

Cassell, J. (1998) 'A framework for gesture generation and interpretation', in R. Cipolla and A. Pentland (eds) *Computer Vision in Human-Machine Interaction*, Cambridge: Cambridge University Press.

Casson, R.W. (1983) 'Schemata in cognitive anthropology', *Annual Review of Anthropology*, 12: 429–62.

——(ed.) (1981) *Language, Culture and Cognition*, New York: Macmillan.

Cavell, S. ([1969] 2002) *Must We Mean What We Say?* Cambridge: Cambridge University Press.

——(1995) 'What did Derrida want of Austin?', in S. Cavell, *Philosophical Passages: Wittgenstein, Emerson, Austin, Derrida*, Oxford: Blackwell.

Cazden, C. (1988) *Classroom Discourse: The Language of Teaching and Learning*, Portsmouth, NH: Heinemann.

Chafe, W. (1968) 'Idiomaticity as an anomaly in the Chomskyan paradigm', *Foundations of Language*, 4: 109–27.

——(1986) 'Evidentiality in English conversation and academic writing', in W. Chafe and J. Nichols (eds) *Evidentiality: The Linguistic Coding of Epistemology*, Norwood, NJ: Ablex.

——(1994) *Discourse, Consciousness and Time*, Chicago, IL: University of Chicago Press.

——(2007) *The Importance of Not Being Earnest: The Feeling behind Laughter and Humor*, Amsterdam and Philadelphia, PA: John Benjamins.

Chafe, W. and Nichols, J. (eds) (1986) *Evidentiality: The Linguistic Coding of Epistemology*, New Jersey: Ablex.

Chaika, E.O. (1982) 'Thought disorder or speech disorder in schizophrenia', *Schizophrenia Bulletin*, 8: 587–91.

——(1990) *Understanding Psychotic Speech: Beyond Freud and Chomsky*, Springfield, IL: Charles C. Thomas.

Chalmers, D.J. (1996) *The Conscious Mind: In Search of a Fundamental Theory*, Oxford: Oxford University Press.

Chambers, C.G., Tanenhaus, M.K., Eberhard, K.M., Filip, H. and Carlson, G.N. (2002) 'Circumscribing referential domains during real-time language comprehension', *Journal of Memory and Language*, 47: 30–49.

Chambers, C.G., Tanenhaus, M.K. and Magnuson, J.S. (2004) 'Action-based affordances and syntactic ambiguity resolution', *Journal of Experimental Psychology: Learning, Memory and Cognition*, 30: 687–96.

Champagne, M., Desautels, M.-C. and Joanette, Y. (2004) 'Lack of inhibition could contribute to non-literal language impairments in right-hemisphere-damaged individuals', *Brain and Language*, 91: 172–74.

Champagne, M., Virbel, J., Nespoulous, J.L. and Joanette, Y. (2003) 'Impact of right hemispheric damage on a hierarchy of complexity evidenced in young normal subjects', *Brain and Cognition*, 53: 152–57.

Champagne-Lavau, M. and Joanette, Y. (2007) 'Why RHD individuals have more difficulties with direct requests than indirect requests. A theory of mind hypothesis', *Brain and Language*, 103: 45–46.

Champagne-Lavau, M., Stip, E. and Joanette, Y. (2007) 'Language functions in right-hemisphere damage and schizophrenia: apparently similar pragmatic deficits may hide profound differences', *Brain*, 130: 67.

Chang, Y.-Y. and Hsu, Y.-P. (1998) 'Requests on e-mail: a cross-cultural comparison', *RELC Journal*, 29: 121–51.

Channell, J. (1985) 'Vagueness as a conversational strategy', *Nottingham Linguistic Circular*, 14: 3–24.

——(1990) 'Precise and vague quantities in academic writing', in W. Nash (ed.) *The Writing Scholar: Studies in the Language and Conventions of Academic Discourse*, Newbury Park, CA: Sage Publications.

——(1994) *Vague Language*, Oxford: Oxford University Press.

Channon, S., Pellijeff, A. and Rule, A. (2005) 'Social cognition after head injury: sarcasm and theory of mind', *Brain and Language*, 93: 123–34.

Chapman, L.J. and Chapman, J.P. (1973) *Disordered Thought in Schizophrenia*, Englewood Cliffs, NJ: Prentice Hall.

Chapman, S. (2005) *Paul Grice: Philosopher and Linguist*, Houndmills: Palgrave Macmillan.

Chapman, S., Ulatowska, H., Franklin, L., Shobe, A., Thompson, J. and McIntire, D. (1997) 'Proverb interpretation in fluent aphasia and Alzheimer's disease: implications beyond abstract thinking', *Aphasiology*, 11: 337–50.

Chapman, S.B., Bonte, F.J., Wong, S.B.C., Zientz, J.N., Hynan, L.S., Harris, T.S., Gorman, A.R., Roney, C.A. and Lipton, A. M. (2005) 'Convergence of connected language and SPECT in variants of fronto-temporal lobar degeneration', *Alzheimer Disease and Associated Disorders*, 19: 202–13.

Chapman, S.B., Culhane, K.A., Levin, H.S., Harward, H.H., Mendelsohn, D., Ewing-Cobbs, L., Fletcher, J.M. and Bruce, D. (1992) 'Narrative discourse after closed head injury in children and adolescents', *Brain and Language*, 43: 42–65.

Charles, M. (2009) 'Future horizons: Europe', in F. Bargiela-Chiappini (ed.) *The Handbook of Business Discourse*, Edinburgh: Edinburgh University Press.

Chastain, C. (1975) 'Reference and context', in K. Gunderson (ed.) *Minnesota Studies in the Philosophy of Science, Volume 7: Language Mind and Knowledge*, Minneapolis, MN: University of Minnesota Press.

Chaudron, C. and Richards, J.C. (1986) 'The effect of discourse markers on the comprehension of lectures', *Applied Linguistics*, 7: 113–27.

Cheang, H.S. and Pell, M.D. (2006) 'A study of humour and communicative intention following right hemisphere stroke', *Clinical Linguistics and Phonetics*, 20: 447–62.

Chen, H.J. (1996) 'Cross-cultural comparison of English and Chinese metapragmatics in refusal', unpublished Ph.D. Thesis, Indiana University.

Chen, R. (1993) 'Responding to compliments: a contrastive study of politeness strategies between American English and Chinese speakers', *Journal of Pragmatics*, 20: 49–75.

Chen, X., Ye, L. and Zhang, Y. (1995) 'Refusing in Chinese', in G. Kasper (ed.) *Pragmatics of*

Chinese as Native and Target Language, Second Language Teaching and Curriculum Center, Honolulu: University of Hawai'i Press.

Cheng, W. (2003) *Intercultural Conversation*, Amsterdam and Philadelphia, PA: John Benjamins.

——(2007) 'The use of vague language across spoken genres in an intercultural corpus', in J. Cutting (ed.) *Vague Language Explored*, London: Palgrave Macmillan.

——(2008) 'Concgramming: a corpus-driven approach to learning the phraseology of discipline-specific texts', *CORELL: Computer Resources for Language Learning*, 1: 22–35.

——(2009) 'Future horizons: Asia', in F. Bargiela-Chiappini (ed.) *The Handbook of Business Discourse*, Edinburgh: Edinburgh University Press.

Cheng, W. and Warren, M. (1999) 'Inexplicitness: what is it and should we be teaching it?', *Applied Linguistics*, 20: 293–315.

——(2001) 'The use of vague language in intercultural conversations in Hong Kong', *English World-Wide*, 22: 81–104.

——(2003) 'Indirectness, inexplicitness and vagueness made clearer', *Pragmatics*, 13: 381–400.

——(2005) '// → well I have a *DIF*ferent // ↘ *THIN*king you know //: a corpus-driven study of disagreement in Hong Kong business discourse', in F. Bargiela-Chiappini and M. Gotti (eds) *Asian Business Discourse(s)*, Frankfurt am Main: Peter Lang.

——(2006) 'I would say be very careful of: opine markers in an intercultural business corpus of spoken English', in J. Bamford and M. Bondi (eds) *Managing Interaction in Professional Discourse: Intercultural and Interdiscoursal Perspectives*, Rome: Officina Edizioni.

——(2007) 'Checking understandings: comparing textbooks and a corpus of spoken English in Hong Kong', *Language Awareness*, 16: 190–207.

Cheng, W., Greaves, C. and Warren, M. (2005) 'The creation of a prosodically transcribed intercultural corpus: The Hong Kong Corpus of Spoken English (prosodic)', *International Computer Archive of Modern English (ICAME) Journal*, 29: 47–68.

——(2006) 'From n-gram to skipgram to concgram', *International Journal of Corpus Linguistics*, 11: 411–33.

Cherny, L. (1999) *Conversation and Community: Chat in a Virtual World*, Stanford, CA: Center for the Study of Language and Information.

Cheshire, J. (2007) 'Discourse variation, grammaticalisation and stuff like that', *Journal of Sociolinguistics*, 11: 155–92.

Chew, C.L.G. (2009) 'Vietnam', in F. Bargiela-Chiappini (ed.) *The Handbook of Business Discourse*, Edinburgh: Edinburgh University Press.

Chiappe, D. and Kukla, A. (1996) 'Context-selection and the frame problem', *Behavioral and Brain Sciences*, 19: 527–28.

Chien, Y.-C. and Wexler, K. (1990) 'Children's knowledge of locality conditions in binding as evidence for the modularity of syntax and pragmatics', *Language Acquisition*, 1: 225–95.

Chierchia, G. (1995) *Dynamics of Meaning: Anaphora, Presupposition, and the Theory of Grammar*, Chicago, IL: University of Chicago Press.

——(2001) 'A puzzle about indefinites', in C. Cecchetto, G. Chierchia and M.T. Guasti (eds) *Semantic Interfaces: Reference, Anaphora, and Aspect*, Stanford, CA: CSLI Publications.

——(2004) 'Scalar implicatures, polarity phenomena, and the syntax/pragmatics interface', in A. Belletti (ed.) *Structures and Beyond: The Cartography of Syntactic Structures*, volume 3, New York: Oxford University Press.

Chierchia, G., Crain, S., Guasti, T., Gualmini, A. and Meroni, L. (2001) 'The acquisition of disjunction: evidence for a grammatical view of scalar implicatures', *Proceedings of the Boston University Conference on Language Development*, 25: 157–68.

Chierchia, G., Frazier, L. and Clifton, C. (2006) 'When basic meanings are not enough: processing scalar implicatures in adult language comprehension', unpublished manuscript, University of Massachusetts.

Chilton, P. (2004) *Analysing Political Discourse: Theory and Practice*, London: Routledge.

——(2006) 'Political terminology', in K. Brown (ed.) *Encyclopedia of Language and Linguistics*, Oxford: Elsevier.

Choi, J.K. (2005) 'Bilingualism in Paraguay: forty years after Rubin's study', *Journal of Multilingual and Multicultural Development*, 26: 233–48.

Choi, S. (1995) 'The development of epistemic sentence-ending modal forms and functions in Korean children', in J. Bybee and S. Fleischman (eds) *Modality in Grammar and Discourse*, Amsterdam: John Benjamins.

Chomsky, N. (1957) *Syntactic Structures*, The Hague: Mouton.

——(1959) 'A review of B.F. Skinner's *Verbal Behavior*', *Language*, 35: 26–58.

——(1965) *Aspects of the Theory of Syntax*, Cambridge, MA: MIT Press.

——(1971) 'Deep structure, surface structure and semantic interpretation', in D. Steinberg and L. Jacobovits (eds) *Semantics: An Interdisciplinary Reader in Philosophy, Linguistics and*

Psychology, Cambridge: Cambridge University Press.

——(1980) *Rules and Representations*, New York: Columbia University Press.

——(1981) *Lectures on Government and Binding*, Dordrecht: Foris.

——(1986) *Knowledge of Language: Its Nature, Origin and Use*, New York: Praeger.

——(1988) *Language and Problems of Knowledge. The Managua Lectures*, Cambridge, MA: MIT Press.

——(1995a) *The Minimalist Program*, Cambridge, MA: MIT Press.

——(1995b) 'Language and nature', *Mind*, 104: 1–61.

Chouinard, M.M. (2007) 'Children's questions: a mechanism for cognitive development', *Monographs of the Society for Research in Child Development*, 72: vii–ix, 1–112.

Chouliaraki, L. (ed.) (2007) *The Soft Power of War*, Amsterdam and Philadelphia, PA: John Benjamins.

Christiansen, M. and Kirby, S. (2003) 'Language evolution: consensus and controversies', *Trends in Cognitive Science*, 7: 300–307.

Christianson, K., Hollingworth, A., Halliwell, J. and Ferreira, F. (2001) 'Thematic roles assigned along the garden path linger', *Cognitive Psychology*, 42: 368–407.

Christie, C. (2002) 'Politeness and the linguistic construction of gender in parliamentary debate: an analysis of transgressions and apology behaviour', *Working Papers on the Web, Special Issue on Politeness and Context*, 3. Online. Available: www.shu.ac.uk/wpw/politeness/christie.htm (accessed 11 September 2008).

——(2005) 'Editorial', *Journal of Politeness Research*, 1: 1–7.

——(2007) 'Relevance theory and politeness', *Journal of Politeness Research*, 3: 269–94.

Christophersen, P. (1939) *The Articles: A Study of their Theory and Use in English*, Copenhagen: Munksgaard.

Church, A. (1936) 'An unsolvable problem of elementary number theory', *American Journal of Mathematics*, 58: 345–63.

Churchland, P.M. (1981) 'Eliminative materialism and the propositional attitudes', *Journal of Philosophy*, 78: 67–90.

Ciaramidaro, A., Adenzato, M., Enrici, I., Erk, S., Pia, L., Bara, B.G. and Walter, H. (2007) 'The intentional network: how the brain reads varieties of intentions', *Neuropsychologia*, 45: 3105–13.

Cicerone, K.D., Dahlberg, C., Malec, J.F., Langenbahn, D.M., Felicetti, T., Kneipp, S., Ellmo, W., Kalmar, K., Giacino, J.T., Harley, J.P., Laatsch, L., Morse, P.A. and Catanese, J. (2005) 'Evidence-based cognitive rehabilitation: updated review of the literature from 1998 to 2002', *Archives of Physical Medicine and Rehabilitation*, 86: 1681–92.

Cicourel, A. (1981) 'Notes on the integration of micro- and macro-levels of analysis', in K. Knorr-Cetina and A. Cicourel (eds) *Advances in Social Theory and Methodology*, London: Routledge.

Clair, R.P. (1998) *Organizing Silence: A World of Possibilities*, New York: State University of New York Press.

Clancey, W.J. (1997a) 'The conceptual nature of knowledge, situations and activity', in P.J. Feltovich, K.M. Ford and R.R. Hoffmann (eds) *Expertise in Context*, Cambridge, MA: AAAI Press/MIT Press.

Clancey, W.J. (1997b) *Situated Cognition: On Human Knowledge and Computer Representations*, Cambridge: Cambridge University Press.

Clancy, P.M. (1992) 'Referential strategies in the narratives of Japanese children', *Discourse Processes*, 15: 441–67.

Clark, A. (1997) *Being There*, Cambridge, MA: MIT Press.

Clark, E. (2007) 'Conventionality and contrast in language and language acquisition', *New Directions for Child and Adolescent Development*, 115: 11–23.

Clark, H. and Havilland, S. (1977) 'Comprehension and the given-new contract', in R. Freedle (ed.) *Discourse Production and Comprehension*, Norwood, NJ: Ablex.

Clark, H.H. (1977) 'Bridging', in P.N. Johnson-Laird and P.C. Wason (eds) *Thinking: Readings in Cognitive Science*, Cambridge: Cambridge University Press.

——(1979) 'Responding to indirect speech acts', *Cognitive Psychology*, 11: 430–77.

——(1992) *Arenas of Language Use*, Chicago, IL: University of Chicago Press.

——(1996) *Using Language*, Cambridge: Cambridge University Press.

Clark, H.H. and Marshall, C. (1981) 'Definite reference and mutual knowledge', in A.K. Joshi, B.L. Webber and I.A. Sag (eds) *Elements of Discourse Understanding*, Cambridge: Cambridge University Press.

Clark, H.H. and Fox Tree, J.E. (2002) 'Using uh and um in spontaneous speaking', *Cognition*, 84: 73–111.

Clark, H.H. and Gerrig, R. (1984) 'On the pretense theory of irony', *Journal of Experimental Psychology: General*, 113: 121–26.

——(1990) 'Quotations as demonstrations', *Language*, 66: 764–805.

Clark, H.H. and Schaefer, E.F. (1989) 'Contributing to discourse', *Cognitive Science*, 13: 259–94.

Clark, H.H. and Wilkes-Gibbs, D. (1986) 'Referring as a collaborative process', *Cognition*, 22: 1–39.

Clark, H.H., Schreuder, R. and Buttrick, S. (1983) 'Common ground and the understanding of demonstrative reference', *Journal of Verbal Learning and Verbal Behavior*, 22: 245–58.

Clark, J.A. and Mishler, E. (1992) 'Attending to patients' stories: reframing the clinical task', *Sociology of Health and Illness*, 14: 344–72.

Clark, U. and Zyngier, S. (2003) 'Towards a pedagogical stylistics', *Language and Literature*, 12: 339–51.

Clarke, M.A. (1985) 'Conversational narratives as altered states of consciousness', in D. Tannen and J.E. Alatis (eds) *The Interdependence of Theory, Data and Application*, Georgetown University Round Table on Languages and Linguistics 1985, Washington, DC: Georgetown University Press.

Clayman, S.E. (2002) 'Disagreements and third parties: dilemmas of neutralism in panel news interviews', *Journal of Pragmatics*, 34: 1385–401.

Clayman, S.E. and Heritage, J. (2002) *The News Interview*, Cambridge: Cambridge University Press.

Clear, J. (1993) 'From Firth principles: computational tools for the study of collocation', in M. Baker, G. Francis and E. Tognini-Bonelli (eds) *Text and Technology: In Honour of John Sinclair*, Amsterdam: John Benjamins.

Clements, G.N. (1975) 'The logophoric pronoun in Ewe: its role in discourse', *Journal of West African Languages*, 2: 141–77.

Clements, W.A. and Perner, J. (1994) 'Implicit understanding of belief', *Cognitive Development*, 9: 377–95.

Clibbens, J. (1997) 'Theory of relevance', in E. Björck-Åkesson and P. Lindsay (eds) *Communication ... Naturally: Theoretical and Methodological Issues in Augmentative and Alternative Communication. Proceedings of the Fourth ISAAC Research Symposium*, Vancouver, Canada: Mälardalen University Press.

Clift, R. (1999) 'Irony in conversation', *Language in Society*, 28: 523–53.

Clyne, M. (1985) 'Language maintenance and language shift: some data from Australia', in N. Wolfson and J. Manes (eds) *Language of Inequality: A Reader in Sociolinguistics*, The Hague: Mouton.

——(1994) *Intercultural Communication at Work: Cultural Values in Discourse*, Cambridge: Cambridge University Press.

——(2003) *Dynamics of Language Contact: English and Immigrant Languages*, Cambridge: Cambridge University Press.

Clyne, M., Ball, M. and Neil, D. (1991) 'Intercultural communication at work in Australia: complaints and apologies in turns', *Multilingua*, 10: 251–73.

Coates, J. (1996) *Women Talk*, Oxford: Blackwell.

——(2001) '"My mind is with you": story sequences in the talk of male friends', *Narrative Inquiry*, 11: 81–101.

Coelho, C.A. (1995) 'Discourse production deficits following traumatic brain injury: a critical review of the recent literature', *Aphasiology*, 9: 409–29.

——(1998) 'Analysis of conversation', in L.R. Cherney, B.B. Shadden and C.A. Coelho (eds) *Analyzing Discourse in Communicatively Impaired Adults*, Gaithersburg, MD: Aspen Publishers.

——(2002) 'Story narratives of adults with closed head injury and non-brain-injured adults: influence of socioeconomic status, elicitation task, and executive functioning', *Journal of Speech, Language, and Hearing Research*, 45: 1232–48.

——(2007) 'Management of Discourse Deficits following Traumatic Brain Injury: Progress, Caveats, and Needs', *Seminars in Speech and Language*, 28: 124–37.

Coelho, C.A. and Flewellyn, L. (2003) 'Longitudinal assessment of coherence in an adult with fluent aphasia', *Aphasiology*, 17: 173–82.

Coelho, C.A., Grela, B., Corso, M., Gamble, A. and Feinn, R. (2005a) 'Microlinguistic deficits in the narrative discourse of adults with traumatic brain injury', *Brain Injury*, 19: 1139–45.

Coelho, C.A., Liles, B. and Duffy, R. (1991a) 'The use of discourse analyses for the evaluation of higher level traumatically brain-injured adults', *Brain Injury*, 5: 381–92.

Coelho, C.A., Liles, B.Z. and Duffy, R.J. (1991b) 'Discourse analyses with closed head injured adults: evidence for differing patterns of deficits', *Archives of Physical Medicine and Rehabilitation*, 72: 465–68.

Coelho, C.A., Liles, B.Z. and Duffy, R.J. (1991c) 'Analysis of conversational discourse in head injured adults', *Journal of Head Trauma Rehabilitation*, 6: 92–99.

Coelho, C.A., Ylvisaker, M. and Turkstra, L.S. (2005b) 'Nonstandardized assessment approaches for individuals with traumatic brain injuries', *Seminars in Speech and Language*, 26: 223–41.

Coelho, C.A., Youse, K. and Le, K.N. (2002) 'Conversational discourse in closed-head-injured and non-brain-injured adults', *Aphasiology*, 16: 659–72.

Coffa, J.A. (1991) *The Semantic Tradition from Kant to Carnap: To the Vienna Station*, ed. L. Wessels, Cambridge: Cambridge University Press.

Cohen, A. and Olshtain, E. (1981) 'Developing a measure of sociocultural competence: the case of apology', *Language Learning*, 31: 113–34.

——(1993) 'The production of speech acts by EFL learners', *TESOL Quarterly*, 27: 33–56.

Cohen, L.J. (1971) 'Some remarks on Grice's views about the logical particles of natural language', in Y. Bar-Hillel (ed.) *Pragmatics of Natural Languages*, Dordrecht: Reidel.

Cohen, P.R. and Levesque, H.J. (1990a) 'Intention is choice with commitment', *Artificial Intelligence*, 42: 213–61.

——(1990b) 'Rational interaction as the basis for communication', in P.R. Cohen, J. Morgan and M.E. Pollack (eds) *Intentions in Communication*, Cambridge, MA: MIT Press.

——(1991) 'Teamwork', *Noûs*, 25: 487–512.

Cohen, P.R. and Perrault, C.R. (1979) 'Elements of a plan-based theory of speech acts', *Cognitive Science*, 3: 177–212.

Cohen, P.R., Morgan, J. and Pollack, M. (eds) (1990) *Intentions in Communication*, Cambridge, MA: MIT Press.

Cohen, S. (1999) 'Contextualism, skepticism, and the structure of reasons', *Philosophical Perspectives*, 13: 57–89.

Cole, A.T. (1991) *The Origins of Rhetoric in Ancient Greece*, Baltimore, MD: Johns Hopkins University Press.

Cole, M. (1996) *Cultural Psychology: A Once and Future Discipline*, Cambridge, MA: Harvard University Press.

Cole, P. (ed.) (1981) *Radical Pragmatics*, New York: Academic Press.

Coleman, L. (1990) 'The language of advertising', *Journal of Pragmatics*, 14: 137–45.

Collins, A.M. and Quillian, M.R. (1969) 'Retrieval time for semantic memories', *-Journal of Verbal Learning and Verbal Behaviour*, 8: 240–48.

Collins, J. and Blot, R. (2003) *Literacy and Literacies: Texts, Power, and Identity*, Cambridge: Cambridge University Press.

Collins, J., Slembrouck, S. and Baynham, M. (to appear) 'Scale, migration and communicative practice', in J. Collins, S. Slembrouck and M. Baynham (eds) *Globalization and Language Contact*, London: Continuum.

Colston, H.L. (1997a) '"I've never seen anything like it": overstatement, understatement, and irony', *Metaphor and Symbol*, 12: 43–58.

——(1997b) 'Salting a wound or sugaring a pill: the pragmatic functions of ironic criticism', *Discourse Processes*, 23: 25–45.

——(2002) 'Contrast and assimilation in verbal irony', *Journal of Pragmatics*, 34: 111–42.

——(2007) 'What figurative language development reveals about the mind', in A.C. Schalley and D. Khlentzos (eds) *Mental States: Volume 2: Language and Cognitive Structure*, Amsterdam: John Benjamins.

Colston, H.L. and Gibbs, R.W. Jr. (2002) 'Are irony and metaphor understood differently?', *Metaphor and Symbol*, 17: 57–80.

——(2007) 'A brief history of irony', in R. Gibbs and H. Colston (eds) *Irony in Language and Thought: A Cognitive Science Reader*, New York: Lawrence Erlbaum Associates.

Colston, H.L. and Keller, S. (1998) 'You'll never believe this: irony and hyperbole in expressing surprise', *Journal of Psycholinguistic Research*, 27: 419–513.

Colston, H.L. and O'Brien, J. (2000a) 'Contrast and pragmatics in figurative language: anything understatement can do, irony can do better', *Journal of Pragmatics*, 32: 1557–83.

——(2000b) 'Contrast of kind versus contrast of magnitude: the pragmatic accomplishment of irony and hyperbole', *Discourse Processes*, 30: 179–99.

Coltheart, M. (2001) 'Assumption and methods in cognitive neuropsychology', in B. Rapp (ed.) *The Handbook of Cognitive Neuropsychology*, Hove: Psychology Press.

Conti-Ramsden, G. and Gunn, M. (1986) 'The development of conversational disability: a case study', *British Journal of Disorders of Communication*, 21: 339–51.

Cook, G. (1989) *Discourse*, Oxford: Oxford University Press.

——(1994) *Discourse and Literature: The Interplay of Form and Mind*, Oxford: Oxford University Press.

——(2001) *The Discourse of Advertising*, 2nd edn, London and New York: Routledge.

Cook, G., Robbins, P. and Pieri, E. (2006) '"Words of mass destruction": British newspaper coverage of the genetically modified food debate, expert and non-expert reactions', *Public Understanding of Science*, 15: 5–29.

Cooke, M. (1994) *Language and Reason: A Study of Habermas's Pragmatics*, Cambridge, MA: MIT Press.

Cooper, R. (1996) 'The role of situations in generalized quantifiers', in S. Lappin (ed.)

The Handbook of Contemporary Semantic Theory, Oxford: Blackwell.

Cooper, R., Larsson, S., Matheson, C., Poesio, M. and Traum, D.R. (1999) *Coding Instructional Dialogue for Information States. Trindi Project Deliverable D1.1*. Online. Available: www.ling. gu.se/projekt/trindi/private/deliverables/D1.1/ D1.1.pdf (accessed 22 February 2008).

Cooper, R.P. and Aslin, R.N. (1990) 'Preference for infant-directed speech in the first month after birth', *Child Development*, 61: 1584–95.

Coppieters, R. (1987) 'Competence differences between native and near-native speakers', *Language*, 63: 544–73.

Corazza, E., Fish, W. and Gorvett, J. (2002) 'Who is I?', *Philosophical Studies*, 107: 1–21.

Corballis, M. (2002) *From Hand to Mouth: The Origins of Language*, Oxford: Oxford University Press.

Corbett, A.T. and Dosher, B.A. (1978) 'Instrument inferences in sentence encoding', *Journal of Verbal Learning and Verbal Behavior*, 17: 479–91.

Corver, N. and Thiersch, C. (2002) 'Remarks on parentheticals', in M. van Oostendorp and E. Anagnostopoulou (eds) *Progress in Grammar. Articles at the 20th Anniversary of the Comparison of Grammatical Models Group in Tilburg*. Online. Available: www.meertens.knaw.nl/books/pro gressingrammar (accessed 3 December 2007).

Cosmides, L. and Tooby, J. (1989) 'The logic of social exchange: has natural selection shaped how humans reason? Studies with the Wason selection task', *Cognition*, 31: 187–276.

——(1992) 'Cognitive adaptations for social exchange', in J. Barkow, L. Cosmides and J. Tooby (eds) *The Adapted Mind*, Oxford: Oxford University Press.

——(1994a) 'Beyond intuition and instinct blindness: toward an evolutionarily rigorous cognitive science', *Cognition*, 50: 41–77.

——(1994b) 'Origins of domain specificity: the evolution of functional organization', in L.A. Hirschfeld and S.A. Gelman (eds) *Mapping the Mind: Domain Specificity in Cognition and Culture*, Cambridge: Cambridge University Press.

——(2000) 'Consider the source: the evolution of adaptations for decoupling and meta-representation', in D. Sperber (ed.) *Meta-representations: A Multidisciplinary Perspective*, New York: Oxford University Press.

Cotton, S. and Gupta, S. (2004) 'Characteristics of online and offline health information seekers and factors that discriminate between them', *Social Science and Medicine*, 59: 1795–806.

Coulson, S. (2001) *Semantic Leaps*, Cambridge: Cambridge University Press.

Coulter, J. (1990) 'Elementary properties of argument sequences', in G. Psathas (ed.) *Interaction Competence*, Lanham, MD: University Press of America.

Coulthard, M. (1985) *An Introduction to Discourse Analysis*, London: Longman.

——(ed.) (1992) *Advances in Spoken Discourse Analysis*, London: Routledge.

——(1993) 'On beginning the study of forensic texts: corpus, concordance, collocation', in M. Hoey (ed.) *Data, Description and Discourse*, London: HarperCollins.

——(1994) 'On the use of corpora in the analysis of forensic texts', *Forensic Linguistics*, 1: 25–43.

——(2004) 'Author identification, idiolect, and linguistic uniqueness', *Applied Linguistics*, 25: 431–47.

Coulthard, M. and Brazil, D. (1992) 'Exchange structure', in M. Coulthard (ed.) *Advances in Spoken Discourse Analysis*, London: Routledge.

Coulthard, M. and Johnson, A. (2007) *An Introduction to Forensic Linguistics*, London: Routledge.

Coulthard, M. and Montgomery, M. (1981a) 'Developing a description of spoken discourse', in M. Coulthard and M. Montgomery (eds) *Studies in Discourse Analysis*, London: Routledge and Kegan Paul.

——(1981b) *Studies in Discourse Analysis*, London: Routledge and Kegan Paul.

Couper-Kuhlen, E. (1992) 'Contextualizing discourse: the prosody of interactive repair', in P. Auer and A. di Luzio (eds) *The Contextualization of Language*, Amsterdam: Benjamins.

——(1996a) 'Intonation and clause-combining in discourse: the case of *because*', *Pragmatics*, 6: 389–426.

——(1996b) 'The prosody of repetition: on quoting and mimicry', in E. Couper-Kuhlen and M. Selting (eds) *Prosody in Interaction*, Cambridge: Cambridge University Press.

——(2004) 'Prosody and sequence organization: the case of new beginnings', in E. Couper-Kuhlen and C.E. Ford (eds) *Sound Patterns in Interaction*, Amsterdam: Benjamins.

Couper-Kuhlen, E. and Ford, C.E. (eds) (2004) *Sound Patterns in Interaction*, Amsterdam: John Benjamins.

Couper-Kuhlen, E. and Selting, M. (1996a) 'Towards an interactional perspective on prosody and a prosodic perspective on interaction', in M. Selting and E. Couper-Kuhlen (eds) *Prosody in Conversation: Interactional Studies*, Cambridge: Cambridge University Press.

——(eds) (1996b) *Prosody in Interaction*, Cambridge: Cambridge University Press.

Couper-Kuhlen, E. and Thompson, S. (2005) 'A linguistic practice for retracting overstatements:

"concessive repair"', in A. Hakulinen and M. Selting (eds) *Syntax and Lexis in Conversation*, Amsterdam: Benjamins.

Coupland, J. (ed.) (2000) *Small Talk*, Harlow: Pearson.

Coupland, J. (2006) 'Dating advertisements: discourses of the commodified self', in D. Tannen and D. Kulick (eds) *Language and Sexuality Reader*, London: Routledge.

——(2007) 'Gendered discourses on the "problem" of ageing: consumerized solutions', *Discourse and Communication*, 1: 37–61.

Coupland, N. (2001) 'Introduction: sociolinguistic theory and social theory', in N. Coupland, S. Sarangi and C.N. Candlin (eds) *Sociolinguistics and Social Theory*, Harlow: Pearson.

Cover, T.M. and Thomas, J.A. (1991) *Elements of Information Theory*, New York: Wiley.

Cowan, J.L. (1964) 'The uses of argument – an apology for logic', *Mind*, 73: 27–45.

Cowie, A.P. (1998) *Phraseology: Theory, Analysis, and Applications*, Oxford: Clarendon Press.

Cowie, R. (2000) 'Describing the emotional states expressed in speech', paper presented at the ISCA Tutorial and Research Workshop on Speech and Emotion, Newcastle, Northern Ireland, September 2000. Online. Available: http://www1.cs.columbia.edu/~julia/papers/cowie00.pdf (accessed 26 August 2008).

Craik, F.I.M. and Lockhart, R.S. (1972) 'Levels of processing: a framework for memory research', *Journal of Verbal Learning and Verbal Behaviour*, 11: 671–84.

Craik, K.J.W. (1943) *The Nature of Explanation*, Cambridge: Cambridge University Press.

Crain, S. and Pietroski, P. (2002) 'Why language acquisition is a snap', *Linguistic Review*, 19: 163–83.

Crandall, E. and Basturkmen, H. (2004) 'Evaluating pragmatics-focused materials', *ELT Journal*, 58: 38–49.

Crawford Camiciottoli, B. (2004) 'Interactive discourse structuring in L2 guest lectures: some insights from a comparative corpus-based study', *Journal of English for Academic Purposes*, 3: 39–54.

——(2008) 'Interaction in academic lectures versus written text materials: the case of questions', *Journal of Pragmatics*, 40: 1216–31.

Crawford, M. (2003) 'Gender and humor in social context', *Journal of Pragmatics*, 35: 1413–30.

Creese, A. (1991) 'Speech act variation in British and American English', *PENN Working Papers*, 7: 37–58.

——(2005) *Teacher Collaboration and Talk in Multilingual Classrooms*, Clevedon: Multilingual Matters.

Cresswell, M.J. (1973) *Logics and Languages*, London: Methuen.

Creusere, M.A. (2000) 'A developmental test of theoretical perspectives on the understanding of verbal irony: children's recognition of allusion and pragmatic insincerity', *Metaphor and Symbol*, 15: 29–45.

Crimmins, M. (1992) *Talk about Beliefs*, Cambridge, MA: MIT Press.

Crimmins, M. and Perry, J. (1989) 'The prince and the phone booth: reporting puzzling beliefs', *Journal of Philosophy*, 86: 685–711.

Crismore, A. and Farnsworth, R. (1990) 'Metadiscourse in popular and professional science discourse', in W. Nash (ed.) *The Writing Scholar: Studies in Academic Discourse*, Newbury Park, CA: Sage Publications.

Crismore, A., Markkanen, R. and Steffensen, M. (1993) 'Metadiscourse in persuasive writing: a study of texts written by American and Finnish university students', *Written Communication*, 10: 39–71.

Croft, W. (2002) *Radical Construction Grammar: Syntactic Theory in Typological Perspective*, Oxford: Oxford University Press.

Croft, W. and Cruse, D.A. (2004) *Cognitive Linguistics*, Cambridge: Cambridge University Press.

Crompton, A. (1987) *The Craft of Copywriting*, London: Hutchison.

Crompton, P. (1997) 'Hedging in academic writing: some theoretical problems', *English for Specific Purposes*, 16: 271–87.

Cross, S.E. and Gore, J.S. (2003) 'Cultural models of the self', in M.R. Leary and T. Price (eds) *Handbook of Self and Identity*, New York: The Guilford Press.

Crow, T.G. (1997) 'Is schizophrenia the price that Homo sapiens pays for language?', *Schizophrenia Research*, 28: 127–41.

Crow, T.J. (1998) 'Precursors of psychosis as pointers to the Homo sapiens-specific mate recognition system of language', *British Journal of Psychiatry*, 172: 289–90.

Crystal, D. (1969) *Prosodic Systems and Intonation in English*, Cambridge: Cambridge University Press.

——(2001) *Language and the Internet*, Cambridge: Cambridge University Press.

——(2004) *A Glossary of Netspeak and Textspeak*, Edinburgh: Edinburgh University Press.

Crystal, D. and Davy, D. (1969) *Investigating English Style*, London: Longman.

——(1975) *Advanced Conversational English*, London: Longman.

Csomay, E. (2002) 'Variation in academic lectures: interactivity and level of instruction', in R. Reppen, S. Fitzmaurice and D. Biber (eds) *Using Corpora to Explore Linguistic Variation*, New York: John Benjamins.

Cubitt, R. and Sugden, R. (2003) 'Common knowledge, salience and convention: a reconstruction of David Lewis' game theory', *Economics and Philosophy*, 19: 175–210.

Culpeper, J. (1996) 'Towards an anatomy of impoliteness', *Journal of Pragmatics*, 25: 349–67.

——(1998) '(Im)politeness in dramatic dialogue', in J. Culpeper, M. Short and P. Verdonk (eds) *Exploring the Language of Drama: From Text to Context*, London: Routledge.

——(2001) *Language and Characterisation: People in Plays and Other Texts*, London: Longman.

——(2005) 'Impoliteness and entertainment in the television quiz show *The Weakest Link*', *Journal of Politeness Research*, 1: 35–72.

Culpeper, J. and Kádár, D. (to appear) *Historical (Im)Politeness*, Bern, Switzerland: Peter Lang.

Culpeper, J. and Kytö, M. (2000) 'Data in historical pragmatics: spoken discourse(re)cast as writing', *Journal of Historical Pragmatics*, 1: 175–99.

Culpeper, J. and Semino, E. (2000) 'Constructing witches and spells: speech acts and activity types in Early Modern England', *Journal of Historical Pragmatics*, 1: 97–116.

Culpeper, J., Bousfield, D. and Wichmann, A. (2003) 'Impoliteness re-visited: with special reference to dynamic and prosodic aspects', *Journal of Pragmatics*, 35: 1545–79.

Culpeper, J., Short, M. and Verdonk, P. (eds) (1998) *Exploring the Language of Drama: From Text to Context*, London: Routledge.

Cummings, L. (2000) 'Petitio principii: the case for non-fallaciousness', *Informal Logic*, 20: 1–18.

——(2002) 'Reasoning under uncertainty: the role of two informal fallacies in an emerging scientific inquiry', *Informal Logic*, 22: 113–36.

——(2004) 'Analogical reasoning as a tool of epidemiological investigation', *Argumentation*, 18: 427–44.

——(2005) *Pragmatics: A Multidisciplinary Perspective*, Edinburgh: Edinburgh University Press.

——(2007a) 'Pragmatics and adult language disorders: past achievements and future directions', *Seminars in Speech and Language*, 28: 98–112.

——(2007b) 'Clinical Pragmatics: A Field in Search of Phenomena?', *Language and Communication*, 27: 396–432.

——(2008) *Clinical Linguistics*, Edinburgh: Edinburgh University Press.

——(2009) *Clinical Pragmatics*, Cambridge: Cambridge University Press.

Curcó, C. (2000) 'Irony: negation, echo and metarepresentation', *Lingua*, 110: 257–80.

Curme, G.O. (1931) *Syntax*, Boston, MA: D.C. Heath and Company.

Currie, G. (2006) 'Why irony is pretence', in S. Nichols (ed.) *The Architecture of the Imagination*, Oxford: Oxford University Press.

Cutica, I., Bucciarelli, M. and Bara, B.G. (2006) 'Neuropragmatics: extralinguistic pragmatic ability is better preserved in left-hemisphere-damaged patients than in right-hemisphere-damaged patients', *Brain and Language*, 98: 12–25.

Cutler, A. and Fodor, J.A. (1979) 'Semantic focus and sentence comprehension', *Cognition*, 7: 35–41.

Cutler, A. and Pearson, M. (1986) 'On the analysis of turntaking cues', in C. Johns-Lewis (ed.) *Intonation in Discourse*, London: Croom Helm.

Cutting, J. (2001) 'The speech acts of the in-group', *Journal of Pragmatics*, 33: 1207–33.

Cutting, J. and Bock, K. (1997) 'That's the way the cookie bounces: syntactic and semantic components of experientially elicited idiom blends', *Memory and Cognition*, 25: 57–71.

Cuyckens, H., Sandra, D. and Rice, S. (1997) 'Towards an empirical lexical semantics', in B. Smieja and M. Tasch (eds) *Human Contact Through Language and Linguistics*, Frankfurt: Peter Lang.

Cziko, G. (1986) 'Testing the language biogram hypothesis: a review of children's acquisition of articles', *Language*, 62: 878–98.

D'Andrade, R. (1995) *The Development of Cognitive Anthropology*, Cambridge: Cambridge University Press.

D'Andrade, R. and Strauss, C. (eds) (1992) *Human Motives and Cultural Models*, Cambridge: Cambridge University Press.

D'Avis, F.J. (2005) 'Über Parenthesen', in F.J. D'Avis (ed.) *Deutsche Syntax: Empirie und Theorie*, Göteborg, Sweden: Acta Universitatis Gothoburgensis.

Da Silva, A.J.B. (2003) 'The effects of instruction on pragmatic development: teaching polite refusals in English', *Second Language Studies*, 23: 55–106.

Dagge, M. and Hartje, W. (1985) 'Influence of contextual complexity on the processing of cartoons by patients with unilateral lesions', *Cortex*, 21: 607–16.

Dahan, D. and Magnuson, J.S. (2006) 'Spoken word recognition', in M.J. Traxler and M.A.

Gernsbacher (eds) *Handbook of Psycholinguistics*, 2nd edn, London: Elsevier.

Dahan, D., Tanenhaus, M.K. and Chambers, C.G. (2002) 'Accent and reference resolution in spoken-language comprehension', *Journal of Memory and Language*, 47: 292–314.

Dahl, O. (1970) 'Some notes on indefinites', *Language*, 46: 33–41.

Dahl, R. (1961) *Who Governs? Democracy and Power in an American City*, New Haven, CT: Yale University Press.

Dahlberg, C., Hawley, L., Morey, H., Newman, J., Cusick, C.P. and Harrison-Felix, C. (2006) 'Social communication skills in persons with post-acute traumatic brain injury: three perspectives', *Brain Injury*, 20: 425–35.

Dale, R. (1996) 'Theory of meaning', unpublished thesis, City University of New York.

Dalrymple, M., Kanazawa, M., Kim, Y., Mchombo, S. and Peters, S. (1998) 'Reciprocal expressions and the concept of reciprocity', *Linguistics and Philosophy*, 21: 159–210.

Daly, N., Holmes, J., Newton, J. and Stubbe, M. (2004) 'Expletives as solidarity signals in FTAs on the factory floor', *Journal of Pragmatics*, 36: 945–64.

Damasio, A. (1999) *The Feeling of What Happens: Body and Emotion in the Making of Consciousness*, New York: Harcourt Brace.

Damico, J. (1985) 'Clinical discourse analysis: a functional language assessment technique', in C.S. Simon (ed.) *Communication Skills and Classroom Success: Assessment of Language-Learning Disabled Students*, San Diego, CA: College-Hill.

Danet, B. ([1978] 1980) 'Language in the legal process', *Law and Society Review*, 14: 445–564; presented at the Ninth World Congress of Sociology, Uppsala, Sweden, August 1978.

——(1985) 'Legal discourse', in T. Van Dijk (ed.) *Handbook of Discourse Analysis*, Amsterdam: North Holland.

Danet, B. and Kermish, N. (1978) 'Courtroom questioning: a sociolinguistic perspective', in L. Massery (ed.) *Psychology and Persuasion in Advocacy*, Washington, DC: Association of Trial Lawyers of America, National College of Advocacy.

Dascal, M. (1985) 'The relevance of misunderstanding', in M. Dascal (ed.) *Dialogue: An Interdisciplinary Approach*, Amsterdam and Philadelphia, PA: John Benjamins.

Dascal, M. and Gross, A. (1999) 'The marriage of pragmatics and rhetoric', *Philosophy and Rhetoric*, 32: 107–30.

Dauenhauer, B.P. (1980) *Silence: The Phenomenon and its Ontological Significance*, Bloomington, IN: Indiana University Press.

Davidson, D. (1967) 'Truth and meaning', *Synthese*, 17: 304–23; reprinted in *Inquiries into Truth and Interpretation* (1984), Oxford: Oxford University Press.

——(1979a) *Inquiries into Truth and Interpretation*, Oxford: Oxford University Press.

——(1979b) 'Quotation', *Theory and Decision*, 11: 27–40.

——(1980) *Essays on Actions and Events*, Oxford: Clarendon Press.

——(2001) *Inquiries into Truth and Interpretation*, 2nd edn, Oxford: Clarendon Press.

——(2007) 'East spaces in West times: deictic reference and political self-positioning in a post-socialist East German chronotrope', *Language and Communication*, 27: 212–26.

Davies, A. (1999) *An Introduction to Applied Linguistics: From Practice to Theory*, Edinburgh: Edinburgh University Press.

Davies, B. (1997) 'The construction of gendered identity through play', in B. Davies and D. Corson (eds) *Encyclopedia of Language and Education, Volume 3: Oral Discourse and Education*, London: Kluwer.

Davies, C.E. (1984) 'Joint joking: improvisational humorous episodes in conversation', in C. Brugman and M. Macaulay (eds) *Proceedings of the Tenth Annual Meeting of the Berkeley Linguistics Society*, Berkeley, CA: University of California Press.

Davis, B.H. and Brewer, J.P. (1997) *Electronic Discourse: Linguistic Individuals in Virtual Space*, Albany, NY: State University of New York Press.

Davis, G.A. and Coelho, C.A. (2004) 'Referential cohesion and logical coherence of narration after closed head injury', *Brain and Language*, 89: 508–23.

Davis, G.A. and Wilcox, M. (1985) *Adult Aphasia Rehabilitation: Applied Pragmatics*, Windsor: NFER-Nelson.

Davis, R., Shrobe, H. and Szolovits, P. (1993) 'What is a knowledge representation?', *AI Magazine*, 14: 17–33.

Davis, W. (1998) *Implicature, Intention, Convention, and Principle in the Failure of Gricean Theory*, Cambridge: Cambridge University Press.

——(2003) *Meaning, Expression, and Thought*, Cambridge: Cambridge University Press.

Davison, A. (1980) 'Peculiar passives', *Language*, 56: 42–66.

De Beaugrande, R.-A. and Dressler, W. (1981) *Introduction to Text Linguistics*, London and New York: Longman.

De Brabanter, P. (to appear) 'Uttering sentences made up of words and gestures', in E. Romero and B. Soria (eds) *Explicit Communication: Robyn*

Carston's Pragmatics, Basingstoke: Palgrave Macmillan.

De Cat, C. (2008) 'Experimental evidence for preschoolers' mastery of "topic"', in A. Gavaro and M. Freitas (eds) *Proceedings of GALA 2007*, Newcastle: Cambridge Scholars Publishing.

de Cillia, R., Krumm, H.-J. and Wodak, R. (2001) *Loss of Communication in the Information Age. Kommunikationsverlust im Informationszeitalter*, Vienna: Austrian Academy of Sciences.

de Cillia, R., Krumm, H.-J. and Wodak, R. (eds) (2003) *The Costs of Multilingualism: Globalisation and Linguistic Diversity*, Vienna: Austrian Academy of Sciences.

De Decker, B. and Van de Craen, P. (1987) 'Towards an interpersonal theory of schizophrenia', in R. Wodak and P. Van de Craen (eds), *Neurotic and Psychotic Language Behaviour*, Philadelphia, PA: Elevedon.

de Groot, A., Kaplan, J., Rosenblatt, E., Dews, S. and Winner, E. (1995) 'Understanding versus discriminating nonliteral utterances: evidence for a dissociation', *Metaphor and Symbol*, 10: 255–73.

de Hoop, H. (2003a) 'On the interpretation of stressed pronouns', in R. Blutner and H. Zeevat (eds) *Optimality Theory and Pragmatics*, New York: Palgrave Macmillan.

——(2003b) 'Partitivity', in L. Cheng and R. Sybesma (eds) *The Second Glot International State-Of-The-Article-Book*, Berlin: Mouton de Gruyter.

de Hoop, H. and Lamers, M. (2006) 'Incremental distinguishability of subject and object', in L. Kulikov, A. Malchukov and P. de Swart (eds) *Transitivity*, Amsterdam and Philadelphia, PA: John Benjamins.

de Jonge, C.C. (2001) '*Natura artis magistra*: ancient rhetoricians, grammarians, and philosophers on natural word order', in T. van der Wouden and H. Broekhuis (eds) *Linguistics in the Netherlands 2001*, Amsterdam: John Benjamins.

de Swart, H., Winter, Y. and Zwarts, J. (2007) 'Bare nominals and reference to capacities', *Natural Language and Linguistic Theory*, 25: 195–222.

de Swart, P. (2007) *Cross-linguistic variation in object marking*, Ph.D. dissertation, University of Nijmegen.

de Villiers, J.G. (2006) 'Syntactic and semantic patterns of pedantic speech in Asperger's Syndrome', in S. Hwang, B. Sullivan and A. Lommel (eds) *LACUS Forum XXXII: Networks*, Houston, TX: LACUS.

de Villiers, J.G. and de Villiers, P.A. (2000) 'Linguistic determinism and the understanding

of false beliefs', in P. Mitchell and K. Riggs (eds) *Children's Reasoning about the Mind*, Hove: Psychology Press.

——(2003) 'Language for thought: coming to understand false beliefs', in D. Gentner and S. Goldin-Meadow (eds) *Language in Mind: Advances in the Study of Language and Thought*, Cambridge, MA: MIT Press.

de Villiers, J.G., Fine, J., Ginsberg, G., Vaccarella, L. and Szatmari, P. (2007) 'Brief report: a scale for rating conversational impairment in autism spectrum disorder', *Journal of Autism and Developmental Disorders*, 37: 1375–80.

de Villiers, J.G., Stainton, R. and Szatmari, P. (2007) 'Pragmatic abilities in autism spectrum disorder: a case study in philosophy and the empirical', *Midwest Studies in Philosophy*, 31: 292–317.

Deacon, T. (1997) *The Symbolic Species*, London: Penguin.

Deborah, C. (2001) *Working with Spoken Discourse*, London: Sage.

DeCarrico, J. and Nattinger, J.R. (1988) 'Lexical phrases for the comprehension of academic lectures', *English for Specific Purposes*, 7: 91–102.

DeCasper, A.J. and Fifer, W.P. (1980) 'Of human bonding: newborns prefer their mother's voices', *Science*, 208: 1174–76.

DeCasper, A.J. and Spence, M.J. (1986) 'Prenatal maternal speech influences newborns' perception of speech sounds', *Infant Behavior and Development*, 9: 133–50.

Dechert, H. and Raupach, M. (eds) (1989) *Transfer in Language Production*, Norwood, NJ: Ablex.

Deely, J. (2001) *Four Ages of Understanding: The First Postmodern Survey of Philosophy from Ancient Times to the Turn of the Twentieth Century*, Toronto: University of Toronto Press.

Deetz, S. and McClellan, J. (2009) 'Critical studies', in F. Bargiela-Chiappini (ed.) *The Handbook of Business Discourse*, Edinburgh: Edinburgh University Press.

Dehé, N. (2007) 'The relation between syntactic and prosodic parenthesis', in N. Dehé and Y. Kavalova (eds.) *Parentheticals*, Amsterdam: John Benjamins.

Dehé, N. (to appear) 'Clausal parentheticals, intonational phrasing, and prosodic theory', *Journal of Linguistics*.

Dehé, N. and Kavalova, Y. (2006) 'The syntax, pragmatics, and prosody of parenthetical *what*', *English Language and Linguistics*, 10: 289–320.

——(2007) 'Parentheticals: an introduction', in N. Dehé and Y. Kavalova (eds) *Parentheticals*, Amsterdam: John Benjamins.

Dehé, N. and Wichmann, A. (to appear) 'The multifunctionality of epistemic parentheticals in discourse: prosodic cues to the semantic-pragmatic boundary', *Functions of Language*.

DeKeyser, R. (2000) 'The robustness of critical period effects in second language acquisition', *Studies in Second Language Acquisition*, 22: 499–533.

Dekydtspotter, L., Sprouse, R.A. and Anderson, B. (1997) 'The interpretive interface in L2 acquisition: the process-result distinction in English-French interlanguage grammars', *Language Acquisition*, 6: 297–332.

Dekydtspotter, L., Sprouse, R.A. and Swanson, K. (2001) 'Reflexes of mental architecture in second-language acquisition: the interpretation of "combien" extractions in English-French interlanguage', *Language Acquisition*, 9: 175–227.

Delbene, R. (2004) 'The function of mitigation in the context of a socially stigmatized disease: a case study in a public hospital in Montevideo, Uruguay', *Context*, 1: 241–66.

DeLisi, L.E. (2001) 'Speech disorders in schizophrenia: review of the literature and exploration of its relation to the uniquely human capacity for language', *Schizophrenia Bulletin*, 27: 481–96.

del-Teso-Craviotto, M. (2006) 'Words that matter: lexical choice and gender ideologies in women's magazines', *Journal of Pragmatics*, 38: 2003–21.

Demberg, V. and Moore, J.D. (2006) 'Information presentation in spoken dialogue systems', *Proceedings of the 11th Conference of the European Chapter of the Association for Computational Linguistics (EACL)*, Trento, Italy, April 2006.

Demorest, A., Silberstein, L., Gardner, H. and Winner, E. (1983) 'Telling it as it isn't: children's understanding of figurative language', *British Journal of Developmental Psychology*, 1: 121–34.

Dendrinos, B. and Pedro, E.R. (1997) 'Giving street directions: the silent role of women', in A. Jaworski (ed.) *Silence: Interdisciplinary Perspectives*, Berlin: Mouton de Gruyter.

Denes, G., Perazzolo, C. and Piani, F. (1996) 'Intensive vs. regular speech therapy in global aphasia: a controlled study', *Aphasiology*, 10: 385–94.

Dennett, D.C. (1987) *The Intentional Stance*, Cambridge, MA: MIT Press.

——(2008) 'Fun and games in Fantasyland', *Mind and Language*, 23: 25–31.

Dennis, M. and Barnes, M.A. (2001) 'Comparison of literal, inferential, and intentional text comprehension in children with mild or severe closed head injury', *Journal of Head Trauma Rehabilitation*, 16: 456–68.

Dennis, M., Lazenby, A.L. and Lockyer, L. (2001a) 'Inferential language in high-function children with autism', *Journal of Autism and Developmental Disorders*, 31: 47–54.

Dennis, M., Purvis, K., Barnes, M.A., Wilkinson, M. and Winner, E. (2001b) 'Understanding of literal truth, ironic criticism, and deceptive praise following childhood head injury', *Brain and Language*, 78: 1–16.

Deppermann, A. (2005) 'Conversational interpreting of lexical items and conversational contrasting', in A. Hakulinen and M. Selting (eds) *Syntax and Lexis in Conversation*, Amsterdam: Benjamins.

Derrida, J. (1977a) 'Signature event context', *Glyph*, 1: 172–97.

——(1977b) 'Limited Inc. abc', *Glyph*, 2: 162–254.

——(1988) *Limited Inc*, ed. Gerald Graff, Chicago, IL: University of Chicago Press.

Dersley, I. and Wootton, A. (2000) 'Complaint sequences within antagonistic argument', *Research on Language and Social Interaction*, 33: 375–406.

Descartes, R. [1641] 'Meditations on first philosophy', in J. Cottingham, R. Stoothoff and D. Murdoch (eds) (1988) *Descartes: Selected Philosophical Writings*, Cambridge: Cambridge University Press.

——[1649] 'The passions of the soul', in J. Cottingham, R. Stoothoff and D. Murdoch (eds) (1988) *Descartes: Selected Philosophical Writings*, Cambridge: Cambridge University Press.

Dessalles, J.-L. (2007) *Why We Talk: The Evolutionary Origins of Language*, New York: Oxford University Press.

Deutsch, J.A. and Deutsch, D. (1963) 'Attention: some theoretical considerations', *Psychological Review*, 70: 80–90.

Dewart, H. and Summers, S. (1995) *Pragmatics Profile of Everyday Communication Skills in Children*, Windsor: NFER Nelson.

Dewey, J. (1925–53) *The Later Works of John Dewey, Vol. 12, Logic: The Theory of Inquiry*, in J. A. Boydston (ed.) *The Collected Works of John Dewey*, Carbondale, IL: Southern Illinois University Press.

Dewey, J. and Bentley, A.F. (1949) *Knowing and the Known*, Boston, MA: Beacon Press.

Dews, S. and Winner, E. (1997) 'Attributing meaning to deliberately false utterances: the case of irony', in C. Mandell and A. McCabe (eds) *The Problem of Meaning: Behavioral and Cognitive Perspectives*, Amsterdam: Elsevier.

——(1999) 'Obligatory processing of the literal and nonliteral meanings of ironic utterances', *Journal of Pragmatics*, 31: 1579–99.

Diesing, M. (1992) *Indefinites*, Cambridge, MA: MIT Press.

Diessel, H. (1999) *Demonstratives: Form, Function and Grammaticization*, Amsterdam: John Benjamins.

——(2006) 'Demonstratives, joint attention, and the emergence of grammar', *Cognitive Linguistics*, 17: 463–89.

Dijkers, M. (2004) 'Quality of life after traumatic brain injury: a review of research approaches and findings', *Archives of Physical and Medical Rehabilitation*, 85: S21–S35.

Dik, S.C. (1997) *The Theory of Functional Grammar*, 2 vols, Berlin: Mouton de Gruyter.

Dipper, L., Bryan, K. and Tyson, J. (1997) 'Bridging inference and relevance theory: an account of right hemisphere damage', *Clinical Linguistics and Phonetics*, 11: 213–28.

Dobrovolskij, D. (1997) *Idiome im Mentalen Lexikon: Ziele und Methoden der Kognitiv Basierten Phraseologieforschung*, Trier, Germany: WVT Wissenschaftlicher Verlag Trier.

——(1999) 'Haben transformationelle defekte der idiomstruktur semantische ursachen?', in N. Fernandez Bravo, I. Behr and C. Rozier (eds) *Phraseme und Typisierte Rede*, Tübingen, Germany: Niemeyer.

Docherty, N.M. (2005) 'Cognitive impairments and disordered speech in schizophrenia: thought disorder, disorganization and communicative failure perspectives', *Journal of Abnormal Psychology*, 114: 269–78.

Docherty, N.M., DeRosa, M. and Andreasen, N.C. (1996) 'Communication disturbances in schizophrenia and mania', *Archives of General Psychiatry*, 53: 358–64.

Dockrell, J., Messer, D., George, I. and Wilson, G. (1998) 'Children with word finding difficulties: prevalence, presentation and naming problems', *International Journal of Language and Communication Disorders*, 33: 445–54.

Done, D.J., Leinonen, E., Crow, T.J. and Sacker, A. (1998) 'Linguistic performance in children who develop schizophrenia in adult life: evidence for normal syntactic ability', *British Journal of Psychiatry*, 172: 130–35.

Donnellan, K.S. (1966) 'Reference and definite descriptions', *Philosophical Review*, 77: 281–304.

Dore, J. and McDermott, R.P. (1982) 'Linguistic indeterminacy and social context in utterance interpretation', *Language*, 58: 374–98.

Dossena, M. and Taavitsainen, I. (eds) (2006) *Diachronic Perspectives on Domain-Specific English*, Bern, Switzerland: Peter Lang.

Doty, R. (1996) *Imperial Encounters: The Politics of Representation in North-South Relations*, Minneapolis: University of Minnesota Press.

Doughty, C. and Long, M. (eds) (2003) *The Handbook of Second Language Acquisition*, Oxford: Blackwell.

Doughty, C. and Williams, J. (eds) (1998) *Focus on Form in Classroom Second Language Acquisition*, Cambridge: Cambridge University Press.

Douglas, J.M., Bracy, C.A. and Snow, P.C. (2007) 'Exploring the factor structure of the La Trobe Communication Questionnaire: insights into the nature of communication deficits following traumatic brain injury', *Aphasiology*, 21: 1181–94.

Douglas-Cowie, E. and Cowie, R. (1998) 'Intonational settings as markers of discourse units in telephone conversations', *Language and Speech*, 41: 351–74.

Dowty, D.R., Wall, R.E. and Peters, S. (1981) *Introduction to Montague Semantics*, London: Springer.

Drave, N. (1995) 'The pragmatics of vague language: a corpus-based study of vagueness in National Vocational Qualifications', unpublished thesis, University of Birmingham, UK.

Dressler, W.U. and Kiefer, F. (1990) 'Austro-Hungarian morphopragmatics', in W.U. Dressler, H.C. Luschützky, O.E. Pfeiffer and J.R. Rennison (eds) *Contemporary Morphology*, Berlin: Mouton de Gruyter.

Dressler, W.U. and Merlini Barbaresi, L. (1987) *Elements of Morphopragmatics*, Duisburg: LAUD A194; reprinted in J. Verschueren (ed.) (1991) *Levels of Linguistic Adaptation*, Amsterdam: Benjamins.

——(1994) *Morphopragmatics: Diminutives and Intensifiers in Italian, German, and Other Languages*, Berlin: Mouton de Gruyter.

——(2001) 'Morphopragmatics of diminutives and augmentatives: on the priority of pragmatics over semantics', in I. Kenesei and R.M. Harnish (eds) *Perspectives on Semantics, Pragmatics, and Discourse*, Amsterdam: Benjamins.

Dretske, F. (1986) 'Misrepresentation', in R. Bogdan (ed.) *Belief: Form, Content and Function*, Oxford: Oxford University Press.

Drew, P. (1990) 'Strategies in the contest between lawyer and witness in cross-examinations', in J. Levi and A.G. Walker (eds) *Language in the Judicial Process*, New York: Plenum Press.

——(1998) 'Complaints about transgressions and misconduct', *Research on Language and Social Interaction*, 31: 295–325.

Drew, P. and Heritage, J. (eds) (1992) *Talk at Work: Interaction in Institutional Settings*, Cambridge: Cambridge University Press.

Dreyfus, H.L. (1992) *What Computers Still Can't Do: A Critique of Artificial Reason*, Cambridge, MA: MIT Press.

Drozd, K. (1995) 'Child English pre-sentential negation as metalinguistic exclamatory sentence negation', *Journal of Child Language*, 22: 583–610.

Du, J.S. (1995) 'Performance of face-threatening acts in Chinese: complaining, giving bad news, and disagreeing', in G. Kasper (ed.) *Pragmatics of Chinese as a Native and Target Language*, Manoa, Hawaii, HI: University of Hawaii Press.

Dubois, B.L. (1987) '"Something in the order of around forty to forty-four": imprecise numerical expressions in biomedical slide talks', *Language in Society*, 16: 527–41.

Ducrot, O. (1972) *Dire et Ne Pas Dire*, Paris: Hermann.

Dudley-Evans, T. and St John, M.J. (1998) *Developments in English for Specific Purposes*, Cambridge: Cambridge University Press.

DuFon, M.A. and Churchill, E. (eds) (2006) *Language Learners in Study Abroad Contexts*, Clevedon: Multilingual Matters.

Dulay, H. and Burt, M. (1974) 'Natural sequences in child second language acquisition', *Language Learning*, 24: 37–53.

Dulek, R. and Graham, M. (2009) 'Future horizons: North America', in F. Bargiela-Chiappini (ed.) *The Handbook of Business Discourse*, Edinburgh: Edinburgh University Press.

Dummett, M. (1975) 'What is a theory of meaning?', in S. Guttenplan (ed.) *Mind and Language*, Oxford: Oxford University Press.

——(1976) 'What is a theory of meaning? (II)', in G. Evans and J. McDowell (eds) *Truth and Meaning*, Oxford: Oxford University Press.

Dumolyn, J. (2008) 'Privileges and novelties: the political discourse of the Flemish cities and rural districts in their negotiations with the Dukes of Burgundy (1384–1506)', *Urban History*, 35: 5–23.

Dunbar, R.I.M. (1998a) 'Theory of mind and the evolution of language', in J. Hurford, M. Studdert-Kennedy and C. Knight (eds) *Approaches to the Evolution of Language: Social and Cognitive Bases*, Cambridge: Cambridge University Press.

——(1998b) 'The social brain hypothesis', *Evolutionary Anthropology*, 6: 178–90.

Duncan, S. (1972) 'Some signals and rules for taking speaking turns in conversations',

Journal of Personality and Social Psychology, 23: 283–92.

Dundes, A. (1975) 'On the structure of the proverb', *Proverbium*, 25: 961–73.

Dunkel, P.A. and Davis, J.N. (1994) 'The effects of signalling cues on the recall of English lecture information by speakers of English as a native or second language', in J. Flowerdew (ed.) *Academic Listening: Research Perspectives*, Cambridge: Cambridge University Press.

Dunn, A. (1990) 'The pragmatics of selected discourse markers in Swahili', Ph.D. dissertation, University of Illinois.

Duranti, A. (1997a) 'Transcription: from writing to digitized images', in A. Duranti, *Linguistic Anthropology*, Cambridge: Cambridge University Press.

——(1997b) *Linguistic Anthropology*, Cambridge: Cambridge University Press.

——(2003) 'Language as culture in U.S. anthropology: three paradigms', *Current Anthropology*, 44: 323–48.

——(2006) 'Transcripts, like shadows on a wall', *Mind, Culture, and Activity*, 13: 301–10.

Duranti, A. and Goodwin, C. (eds) (1992) *Rethinking Context: Language as an Interactive Phenomenon*, Cambridge: Cambridge University Press.

Eades, D. (2000) '*I don't think it's an answer to the question*: silencing aboriginal witnesses in court', *Language in Society*, 29: 161–95.

Eckardt, R. (2002) 'Semantic change in grammaticalization', in G. Katz, S. Reinhard and P. Reuter (eds) *Proceedings of the Sixth Annual Meeting of the Gesellschaft für Semantik, Sinn und Bedeutung VI*, Osnabrück: University of Osnabrück.

Eckert, P. (1996) 'Vowels and nail polish: the emergence of style in the preadolescent heterosexual marketplace', in N. Warner, J. Ahlers, L. Bilmes, M. Oliver, S. Wertheim and M. Chen (eds) *Gender and Belief Systems*, Berkeley, CA: Berkeley Women and Language Group.

——(1999) *The Linguistic Construction of Identity in Belten High*, Oxford: Blackwell.

——(2002) 'Constructing meaning in sociolinguistic variation', paper presented at the Annual Meeting of the American Anthropological Association, New Orleans, November 2002.

Eckert, P. and McConnell-Ginet, S. (1992) 'Think practically and look locally: language and gender as community-based practice', *Annual Review of Anthropology*, 21: 461–90.

——(1995) 'Constructing meaning, constructing selves: snapshots of language, gender and class from Belten High', in K. Hall and M. Bucholtz (eds) *Gender Articulated: Language and the Socially Constructed Self*, New York and London: Routledge.

——(2003) *Language and Gender*, Cambridge: Cambridge University Press.

Eckman, F., Highland, D., Lee, P., Milcham, J. and Rutkowski, R. (eds) (1995) *Second Language Acquisition Theory and Pedagogy*, Mahwah, NJ: Lawrence Erlbaum.

Edelman, G.M. (1992) *Bright Air, Brilliant Fire: On the Matter of the Mind*, New York: Basic Books.

Edelman, M. (1977) *Political Language*, New York: Academic Press.

Editorial (1974) 'Mr Wilson's Labour coalition', *Daily Mail*, 6 March 1974, 6.

Editorial (1978) 'Callaghan at bay', *Daily Telegraph*, 4 October 1978, 18.

Editorial (1983) 'Farewell of a bad loser', *Daily Mail*, 5 October 1983, 6.

Editorial (1988) 'Forward into the past', *Daily Mail*, 5 October 1988, 6.

Editorial (2005) 'Sorry, but do they really know what the word means?', *The Times*, 10 February 2005, 24.

Edstrom, A. (2004) 'Expressions of disagreement by Venezuelans in conversation: reconsidering the influence of culture', *Journal of Pragmatics*, 36: 1499–518.

Edwards, A.D. and Westgate, D. (1994) *Investigating Classroom Talk*, London: Falmer Press.

Edwards, D. (2000) 'Extreme case formulations: softeners, investment, and doing nonliteral', *Research on Language and Social Interaction*, 33: 347–73.

——(2005) 'Moaning, whinging and laughing: the subjective side of complaints', *Discourse Studies*, 7: 5–29.

Edwards, D. and Mercer, N. (1987) *Common Knowledge: The Development of Understanding in the Classroom*, London: Methuen.

Edwards, D. and Potter, J. (1992) *Discursive Psychology*, London: Sage.

Edwards, J.A. and Lampert, M.D. (eds) (1993) *Talking Data: Transcription and Coding in Discourse Research*, Hillsdale, NJ: Lawrence Erlbaum.

Eelen, G. (2001) *A Critique of Politeness Theories*, Manchester: St Jerome Press.

Efron, D. (1941) *Gesture and Environment*, New York: King's Krown.

Egan, A. (2007) 'Epistemic modals, relativism, and assertion', *Philosophical Studies*, 133: 1–22.

Egan, A., Hawthorne, J. and Weatherson, B. (2005) 'Epistemic modals in context', in G. Preyer and G. Peter (eds) *Contextualism in Philosophy: Knowledge, Meaning and Truth*, Oxford: Oxford University Press.

Egbert, M.M. (1997a) 'Schisming: the collaborative transformation from a single conversation to multiple conversations', *Research on Language and Social Interaction*, 30: 1–51.

——(1997b) 'Some interactional achievements of other-initiated repair in multi-person conversation', *Journal of Pragmatics*, 27: 611–34.

Ehlich, K. and Wagner, J. (eds) (1995) *The Discourse of International Negotiations*, Berlin: Mouton de Gruyter.

Ehrlich, J. and Barry, P. (1989) 'Rating communication behaviors in the head-injured adult', *Brain Injury*, 3: 193–98.

Ehrlich, J. and Sipes, A. (1985) 'Group treatment of communication skills for head trauma patients', *Cognitive Rehabilitation*, 3: 32–37.

Ehrlich, S. (2001) *Representing Rape: Language and Sexual Consent*, London: Routledge.

Eisenson, J. (1962) 'Language and intellectual modifications associated with right hemisphere damage', *Language and Speech*, 5: 49–53.

Eisterhold, J., Attardo, S. and Boxer, D. (2006) 'Reactions to irony in discourse: evidence for the least disruption principle', *Journal of Pragmatics*, 38: 1239–56.

Ekman, P. and Friesen, W. (1969) 'The repertoire of nonverbal behavior: categories, origins, usage, and coding', *Semiotica*, 1: 49–98.

Ellis, A.W. and Young, A.W. (1988) *Human Cognitive Neuropsychology*, London: Erlbaum.

Ellis, N. (2005) 'At the interface: how explicit knowledge affects implicit language learning', *Studies in Second Language Acquisition*, 27: 305–52.

Ellis, R. (1989) 'Are classroom and naturalistic acquisition the same?', *Studies in Second Language Acquisition*, 11: 305–26.

——(1992) 'Learning to communicate in the classroom: a study of two learners' requests', *Studies in Second Language Acquisition*, 14: 1–23.

——(2002) 'Does form-focused instruction affect the acquisition of implicit knowledge? A review of the research', *Studies in Second Language Acquisition*, 24: 223–36.

——(2006) 'Current issues in the teaching of grammar: an SLA perspective', *TESOL Quarterly*, 40: 85–107.

Elman, J.L., Bates, E.A., Johnson, M.H., Karmiloff-Smith, A., Parisi, D. and Plunkett, D. (1996) *Rethinking Innateness: A Connectionist Perspective on Development*, Cambridge, MA: MIT Press.

Elman, R.J. and Bernstein-Ellis, E. (1999) 'The efficacy of group communication treatment in adults with chronic aphasia', *Journal of Speech, Language and Hearing Research*, 42: 411–19.

Elugardo, R. and Stainton, R. (2004) 'Short-hand, syntactic ellipsis, and the pragmatic determinants of what is said', *Mind and Language*, 19: 442–71.

Emmertsen, S. (2007) 'Interviewers' challenging questions in British debate interviews', *Journal of Pragmatics*, 39: 570–91.

Emmott, C. (1997) *Narrative Comprehension: A Discourse Perspective*, Oxford: Oxford University Press.

Emmott, C., Sanford, A.J. and Morrow, L.I. (2006) 'Capturing the attention of readers? Stylistic and psychological perspectives on the use and effect of text fragmentation in narratives', *Journal of Literary Semantics*, 35:1–30.

Emonds, J. (1973) 'Parenthetical clauses', in C. Corum, T.C. Smith-Stark and A. Weiser (eds.) *You Take the High Node and I'll Take the Low Node*, Chicago, IL: Chicago Linguistic Society.

——(1976) *A Transformational Approach to English Syntax: Root, Structure-Preserving, and Local Transformations*, New York: Academic Press.

——(1979) 'Appositive clauses have no properties', *Linguistic Inquiry*, 10: 211–43.

Emslie, C., Ridge, D., Ziebland, S. and Hunt, K. (2007) 'Exploring men's and women's experiences of depression and engagement with health professionals: more similarities than differences? A qualitative interview study', *BMC Family Practice*, 8: 1–10.

Enç, M. (1991) 'The semantics of specificity', *Linguistic Inquiry*, 22: 1–25.

Endriss, C. (2006) *Quantificational topics: a scopal treatment of exceptional wide scope Phenomena*, Ph.D. dissertation, University of Potsdam, Germany.

Enfield, N. and Levinson, S.C. (eds) (2007) *Roots of Human Sociality*, London: Berg.

Enfield, N. and Stivers, T. (2006) *Person Reference in Interaction*, Cambridge: Cambridge University Press.

Enfield, N.J. (2003a) 'Speakers and implications for semantic analysis', *Language*, 79: 82–117.

——(2003b) 'The definition of what-d'you-call-it: semantics and pragmatics of recognition deixis', *Journal of Pragmatics*, 35: 101–17.

Engberg-Pedersen, E. (1993) *Space in Danish Sign Language: The Semantics and Morphosyntax of the Use of Space in a Visual Language*, Hamburg: Signum-Verlag.

——(1995) 'Point of view expressed through shifters', in K. Emmorey and J. Reilly (eds) *Language, Gesture, and Space*, Hillsdale, NJ: Lawrence Erlbaum.

Enkvist, N.E. (1973) *Linguistic Stylistics*, The Hague: Mouton.

Enos, R. (1993) *Greek Rhetoric before Aristotle*, Long Grove, IL: Waveland Press.

Ensink, T. and Sauer, C. (eds) (2003) *The Art of Commemoration*, Amsterdam: John Benjamins.

Epstein, S., Flynn, S. and Martohardjono, G. (1996) 'Second language acquisition: theoretical and experimental issues in contemporary research', *Behavioral and Brain Sciences*, 19: 677–758.

Epstein, S., Flynn, S. and Martohardjono, G. (1998) 'The strong continuity hypothesis in adult L2 acquisition of functional categories', in S. Flynn, G. Martohardjono and W. O'Neil (eds) *The Generative Study of Second Language Acquisition*, Hillsdale, NJ: Lawrence Erlbaum.

Erev, I., Wallsten, T.S. and Neal, M.M. (1991) 'Vagueness, ambiguity, and the cost of mutual understanding', *Psychological Science*, 2: 321–24.

Erickson, F. and Shultz, J. (1982) *The Counsellor as Gatekeeper: Social Interaction in Interviews*, New York: Academic Press.

Erkü, F. and Gundel, J.K. (1987) 'The pragmatics of indirect anaphors', in J. Verschueren and M. Bertocelli-Papi (eds) *The Pragmatic Perspective: Selected Papers from the 1985 International Pragmatics Conference*, Amsterdam: John Benjamins.

Erman, B. and Kotsinas, U.-B. (1993) 'Pragmaticalization: the case of *ba*' and *you know*', in J. Falk, K. Jonasson, G. Melchers and B. Nilsson (eds) *Stockholm Studies in Modern Philology*, volume 10, Stockholm: Almqvist and Wiksell International.

Errington, J.J. (1988) *Structure and Style in Javanese: A Semiotic View of Linguistic Etiquette*, Philadelphia, PA: University of Pennsylvania Press.

——(1998) *Shifting Languages: Interaction and Identity in Javanese Indonesia*, Cambridge: Cambridge University Press.

Erteschik-Shir, N. (1997) *The Dynamics of Focus Structure*, Cambridge: Cambridge University Press.

Eslami-Rasekh, Z. (2004) 'Face-keeping strategies in reaction to complaints: English and Persian', *Journal of Asian Pacific Communication*, 14: 181–97.

Espinal, M.T. (1991) 'The representation of disjunct constituents', *Language*, 67: 726–62.

Evans, J. St. B.T., Newstead, S.E. and Byrne, R. (1993) *Human Reasoning: The Psychology of Deduction*, Hillsdale, NJ: Erlbaum.

Evans, V. (2006) 'Lexical concepts, cognitive models and meaning-construction', *Cognitive Linguistics*, 17: 491–534.

——(2004) *The Structure of Time: Language, Meaning and Temporal Cognition*, Amsterdam: John Benjamins.

——(to appear) *How Words Mean: Lexical Concepts, Cognitive Models and Meaning Construction*, Oxford: Oxford University Press.

Eviatar, Z. and Just, M. (2006) 'Brain correlates of discourse processing: an fMRI investigation of irony and metaphor comprehension', *Neuropsychologia*, 44: 2348–59.

Ewing-Cobbs, L., Brookshire, B., Scott, M.A. and Fletcher, J.M. (1998) 'Children's narratives following traumatic brain injury: linguistic structure, cohesion, and thematic recall', *Brain and Language*, 61: 395–419.

Eysenck, M.W. and Keane, M.T. (1990) *Cognitive Psychology: A Student's Handbook*, Hove: Erlbaum.

Eysenck, M.W. and Keane, M.T. (1993) *Cognitive Psychology*, London: Lawrence Erlbaum.

Fahnestock, J. (2005) 'Rhetoric in the age of cognitive science', in R. Graff, A.E. Walzer, and J. Atwill (eds) *The Viability of the Rhetorical Tradition*, New York: State University of New York Press.

Fairclough, N. (1989) *Language and Power*, London and New York: Longman.

——(1992) *Discourse and Social Change*, Cambridge: Polity Press.

——(1995a) *Media Discourse*, London: Edward Arnold.

——(1995b) *Critical Discourse Analysis*, London: Longman.

——(1996) 'A reply to Henry Widdowson's "Discourse Analysis: A Critical View"', *Language and Literature*, 5: 49–56.

——(1997) *Critical Discourse Analysis: The Critical Study of Language*, Glenview, IL: Addison-Wesley.

——(2000) 'The discourse of social exclusion', in M. Reisigl and R. Wodak (eds) *The Semiotics of Racism: Approaches in Critical Discourse Analysis*, Vienna: Passagen Verlag.

——(2001) *Language and Power*, 2nd edn, London: Longman.

——(2003) *Analysing Discourse: Textual Analysis for Social Research*, London and New York: Routledge.

Farghal, M. (1992) 'Colloquial Jordanian Arabic tautologies', *Journal of Pragmatics*, 17: 223–40.

Farghal, M. and Al-Khatib, M.A. (2001) 'Jordanian college students' responses to compliments: a pilot study', *Journal of Pragmatics*, 33: 1485–502.

Farkas, D. (1981) 'Quantifier scope and syntactic islands', in R. Hendrik, C.S. Masek and M.F. Miller (eds) *Papers from the 7th Regional Meeting of the Chicago Linguistic Society*, Ithaca, NY: CLC Publications.

——(1994) 'Specificity and scope', in L. Nash and G. Tsoulas (eds) *Langues et Grammaires*, 1: 119–37. Paris: University of Paris 8.

——(1997) 'Dependent indefinites', in F. Corblin, D. Godard and J.M. Marandin (eds) *Empirical Issues in Formal Syntax and Semantics*, Bern, Switzerland: Peter Lang.

——(2002a) 'Specificity distinctions', *Journal of Semantics*, 19: 213–43.

——(2002b) 'Varieties of indefinites', in B. Jackson (ed.) *Proceedings of SALT 12*, Ithaca, NY: CLC Publications.

Farkas, D. and de Swart, H. (2003) *The Semantics of Incorporation*, Stanford, CA: CSLI Publications.

Farkas, D. and Sugioka, Y. (1983) 'Restrictive if/when clauses', *Linguistics and Philosophy*, 6: 225–58.

Farkas, K. (2008) 'Phenomenal intentionality without compromise', *The Monist*, 91: 278–98.

Farncescotti, R.M. (1995) '*Even*: the conventional implicature approach reconsidered', *Linguistics and Philosophy*, 18: 153–73.

Fauconnier, G. (1975) 'Pragmatic scales and logical structure', *Linguistic Inquiry*, 6: 353–75.

——(1985) *Mental Spaces: Aspects of Meaning Construction in Natural Language*, Cambridge, MA: MIT Press.

——(1994) *Mental Spaces*, Cambridge: Cambridge University Press.

——(1997) *Mappings in Thought and Language*, Cambridge: Cambridge University Press.

Fauconnier, G. and Turner, M. (2002) *The Way We Think: Conceptual Blending and the Mind's Hidden Complexities*, New York: Basic Books.

Feeney, A., Scrafton, S., Duckworth, A. and Handley, S. (2004) 'The story of *some*: everyday pragmatic inference by children and adults', *Canadian Journal of Experimental Psychology*, 58: 121–32.

Feinberg, J. (1964) 'Action and responsibility', in M. Black (ed.) *Philosophy in America*, London: Allen and Unwin.

Feldman, C.F. and Kalmar, D. (1996) 'You can't step in the same river twice: repair and repetition in dialogue', in C. Bazzanella (ed.) *Repetition in Dialogue*, Tübingen, Germany: Niemeyer.

Félix-Brasdefer, J.C. (2006a) 'Teaching the negotiation of multi-turn speech acts: using conversation-analytic tools to teach pragmatics in the FL classroom', in K. Bardovi-Harlig, J.C. Félix-Brasdefer and A. Omar (eds) *Pragmatics and Language Learning, Volume 11*, Honolulu, HI: National Foreign Language Resource Center, University of Hawaii at Manoa.

——(2006b) 'Linguistic politeness in Mexico: refusal strategies among male speakers of Mexican Spanish', *Journal of Pragmatics*, 38: 2158–87.

——(2008) 'Speech act perception in interlanguage pragmatics: exploring the minds of foreign language learners', *Language Awareness*, 17: 195–211.

Fellbaum, C. (1998a) 'A semantic network of English verbs', in C. Fellbaum (ed.) *WordNet: An Electronic Lexical Database*, Cambridge, MA: MIT Press.

——(1998b) *WordNet: An Electronic Lexical Database*, Cambridge, MA: MIT Press.

Felman, S. ([1980] 2003) *The Scandal of the Speaking Body: Don Juan with J.L. Austin, or Seduction in Two Languages*, Stanford, CA: Stanford University Press.

Feng, G.W. (2006) *A theory of conventional implicature and pragmatic markers in Chinese*, unpublished thesis, University of Reading.

Fernald, A. (1989) 'Intonation and communicative intent in mother's speech to infants: is the melody the message?', *Child Development*, 60: 1497–510.

——(1993) 'Approval and disapproval: infant responsiveness to vocal affect in familiar and unfamiliar languages', *Child Development*, 64: 657–74.

——(2001) 'Auditory development in infancy', in G. Bremner and A. Fogel (eds) *Blackwell Handbook of Infant Development*, Oxford: Blackwell Publishers.

Fernald, A., Pinto, J.P., Swingley, D., Weinberg, A. and McRoberts, G.W. (1998) 'Rapid gains in speed of verbal processing by infants in the second year', *Psychological Science*, 9: 228–31.

Ferrara, K.W. (1997) 'Form and function of the discourse marker "anyway": implications for discourse analysis', *Linguistics*, 35: 343–78.

Figueroa, E. (1994) *Sociolinguistics Metatheory*, Oxford: Pergamon.

Fikes, R.E. and Nilsson, N.J. (1971) 'STRIPS: a new approach to the application of theorem proving', *Artificial Intelligence*, 2: 189–208.

File, P. and Todman, J. (2002) 'An evaluation of the coherence of computer-aided conversations', *Augmentative and Alternative Communication*, 18: 228–41.

Fillmore, C.J. (1971a) *The Santa Cruz Lectures on Deixis*, Bloomington, IN: Indiana University Linguistics Club.

——(1971b) 'How to know whether you are coming or going', in K. Hyldgard-Jensen (ed.) *Liguistik 1971*, Frankfurt: Athenäum Verlag.

——(1975) 'An alternative to checklist theories of meaning' in C. Cogen, H. Thompson, G. Thurgood and K. Whistler (eds) *Proceedings of the First Annual Meeting of the Berkeley Linguistics Society*, Berkeley, CA: Berkeley Linguistics Society.

——(1977) 'Scenes-and-frames semantics', in A. Zampolli (ed.) *Linguistic Structures Processing*, Amsterdam: North Holland Publishing Company.

——(1982). 'Frame semantics' in The Linguistic Society of Korea (ed.) *Linguistics in the Morning Calm*, Seoul, South Korea: Hanshin Publishing Co.

——(1985) 'Frames and the semantics of understanding', *Quaderni di Semantica*, 6: 222–53.

——(1997) *Lectures on Deixis*, Stanford, CA: CSLI Publications.

Fillmore, C.J. and Atkins, B.T. (1992) 'Toward a frame-based lexicon: the semantics of RISK and its neighbors', in A. Lehrer and E.F. Kittay (eds) *Frames, Fields and Contrasts*, Hillsdale, NJ: Lawrence Erlbaum.

Fillmore, C.J., Johnson, C. and Petruck, M. (2003) 'Background to FrameNet', in T. Fontenelle (ed.) *FrameNet and Frame Semantics*, Special Issue of *International Journal of Lexicography*, 16: 235–50.

Fillmore, C.J., Kay, P. and O'Connor, M.K. (1988) 'Regularity and idiomaticity: the case of let alone', *Language*, 64: 501–38.

Fine, J., Bartolucci, G., Szatmari, P. and Ginsberg, G. (1994) 'Cohesive discourse in pervasive developmental disorders', *Journal of Autism and Developmental Disorders*, 24: 315–29.

Finocchiaro, M. (2005) *Arguing about Argument: Systematic, Critical and Historical Essays in Logical Theory*, Cambridge: Cambridge University Press.

Firbas, J. (1964) 'On defining the theme in functional sentence perspective', *Travaux Linguistiques de Prague*, 1: 267–80.

Firth, A. (ed.) (1995) *The Discourse of Negotiation: Studies of Language in the Workplace*, Oxford: Pergamon.

Fish, S. (1980) *Is there a Text in this Class?*, Cambridge, MA: Harvard University Press.

Fisher, S. and Todd, A. (eds) (1983) *The Social Organisation of Doctor-Patient Communication*, Washington, DC: Centre for Applied Linguistics.

Fishman, J.A. (1966) *Language Loyalty in the United States: The Maintenance and Perpetuation of Non-English Mother Tongues by American Ethnic and Religious Groups*, The Hague: Mouton.

——(1968) *Readings in the Sociology of Language*, The Hague and Paris: Mouton.

——(1972a) 'Domains and the relationship between micro and macrosociolinguistics', in J. Gumperz and D. Hymes (eds) *Directions in Sociolinguistics*, Oxford: Blackwell.

——(ed.) (1972b) *The Sociology of Language: An Interdisciplinary Social Science Approach to Language in Society*, Rowley, MA: Newbury House.

——(ed.) (1978) *Advances in the Study of Societal Multilingualism*, The Hague: Mouton.

——(1983) *Progress in Language Planning: International Perspectives*, Berlin and New York: Mouton.

——(2000) *Can Threatened Languages Be Saved?*, Clevedon: Multilingual Matters.

——(1991) *Social Cognition*, 2nd edn, New York, NY: McGraw-Hill.

Fiske, S.T. and Taylor, S.E. (2008) *Social Cognition: From Brains to Culture*, New York: McGraw-Hill.

Fitzmaurice, S.M. (2002) *The Familiar Letter in Early Modern English: A Pragmatic Approach*, Amsterdam and Philadelphia, PA: John Benjamins.

Fitzmaurice, S.M. and Taavitsainen, I. (eds) (2007) *Methods in Historical Pragmatics*, Berlin: Mouton de Gruyter.

Flash (2004) *Big Dopes with High Hopes*, Online. Available: www.abctales.com/node/506844 (accessed 13 September 2004).

Flavell, J.H., Flavell, E.R. and Green, F.L. (1983) 'Development of the appearance-reality distinction', *Cognitive Psychology*, 15: 95–120.

Flavell, J.H., Flavell, E.R., Green, F.L. and Moses, L.J. (1990) 'Young children's understanding of fact beliefs vs. value beliefs', *Child Development*, 61: 915–28.

Flege, J., Frieda, A. and Nozawa, T. (1997) 'Amount of native-language (L1) use affects the pronunciation of an L2', *Journal of Phonetics*, 25: 169–86.

Fleischman, S. (1990) 'Philology, linguistics, and the discourse of the medieval text', *Speculum*, 65: 19–37.

Flowerdew, J.F. (1991) 'Pragmatic modifications on the "representative" speech act of defining', *Journal of Pragmatics*, 15: 253–64.

——(1994) 'Research of relevance to second language lecture comprehension: an overview', in J. Flowerdew (ed.) *Academic Listening: Research Perspectives*, Cambridge: Cambridge University Press.

Flowerdew, J.F. and Tauroza, S. (1995) 'The effect of discourse markers on second language lecture comprehension', *Studies in Second Language Acquisition*, 17: 453–58.

Flowerdew, L. (1998) 'Application of learner corpus based findings and methods to pedagogy', in S. Granger and J. Hung (eds) *Proceedings of First International Symposium on Computer Learner Corpora, Second Language Acquisition and Foreign Language Teaching*, Hong Kong: The Chinese University of Hong Kong.

Fodor, J.A. (1975) *The Language of Thought*, New York: Thomas Y. Crowell.

——(1980) 'Methodological solipsism considered as a research strategy in cognitive psychology', *Behavioral and Brain Sciences*, 3: 63–109; reprinted in J. Haugeland (ed.) (1981) *Mind Design*, Cambridge, MA: MIT Press.

——(1981) *Representations: Philosophical Essays on the Foundations of Cognitive Science*, Brighton: Harvester Press.

——(1983) *The Modularity of Mind: An Essay on Faculty Psychology*, Cambridge, MA: MIT Press.

——(1987) *Psychosemantics*, Cambridge, MA: MIT Press.

——(1990) *A Theory of Content and Other Essays*, Cambridge, MA: MIT Press.

——(1992) 'A theory of the child's theory of mind', *Cognition*, 44: 283–96.

——(2000) *The Mind Doesn't Work That Way*, Cambridge, MA: MIT Press.

——(2008) 'Against Darwinism', *Mind and Language*, 23: 1–24.

Fodor, J.A. and Pylyshyn, Z.W. (1988) 'Connectionism and cognitive architecture: a critical analysis', *Cognition*, 28: 3–71.

Fodor, J.D. and Sag, I.A. (1982) 'Referential and quantificational indefinites', *Linguistics and Philosophy*, 5: 355–98.

Foldi, N.S. (1987) 'Appreciation of pragmatic interpretations of indirect commands: comparison of right and left hemisphere brain-damaged patients', *Brain and Language*, 31: 88–108.

Foley, W. and Van Valin, R. (1984) *Functional Syntax and Universal Grammar*, Cambridge: Cambridge University Press.

Folkes, V.S. (1982) 'Communicating the reasons for social rejection', *Journal of Experimental Social Psychology*, 18: 618–28.

Follett, K. (1995) *A Place Called Freedom*, London: Macmillan.

Fombonne, E., Zakarian, R., Bennett, A., Meng, L. and McLean-Heywood, D. (2006) 'Pervasive developmental disorders in Montreal, Quebec, Canada: prevalence and links with immunizations', *Pediatrics*, 118: 139–50.

Forbes, G. (1990) 'The indispensability of Sinn', *Philosophical Review*, 99: 535–63.

——(1997) 'How much substitutivity?', *Analysis*, 57: 109–13.

Ford, C.E. (2004) 'Contingency and units in interaction', *Discourse Studies*, 6: 27–52.

Ford, C.E. and Thompson, S.A. (1996) 'Interactional units in conversation: syntactic, intonational, and pragmatic resources for the management of turn', in E. Ochs, E.A. Schegloff and S.A. Thompson (eds) *Interaction and Grammar*, Cambridge: Cambridge University Press.

Ford, C.E., Fox, B.A. and Thompson, S.A. (1996) 'Practices in the construction of turns: the "TCU" revisited', *Pragmatics*, 6: 427–54.

——(2002) 'Constituency and the grammar of turn increments', in C.E. Ford, B.A. Fox and S.A. Thompson (eds) *The Language of Turn and Sequence*, New York: Oxford University Press.

Forsyth, D.A. and Ponce, J. (2003) *Computer Vision: A Modern Approach*, Harlow: Pearson Education.

Fortanet, I., Posteguillo, S., Palmer, J.C. and Coll, J.F. (1998) 'Disciplinary variations in the writing of research articles in English', in I. Fortanet, S. Posteguillo, J.C. Palmer and J. F. Coll (eds) *Genre Studies in English for Academic Purposes*, Castello, Italy: Publicacions de la Universitat Jaume I.

Foster-Cohen, S. (1994) 'Exploring the boundary between syntax and pragmatics: relevance and the binding of pronouns', *Journal of Child Language*, 21: 237–55.

Foucault, M. (1966) *Les Mots et les Choses*, Paris: Gallimard.

——(1971) *L'Ordre du Discours*, Paris: Gallimard.

——(1972a) *L'Ordre du Discours*, Paris: Gallimard.

——(1972b) *The Archaeology of Knowledge*, London: Tavistock.

——(1994) *O Nascimento da Clínica*, Rio de Janeiro: Forense Universitária.

Fowler, R. (1971) *The Languages of Literature*, London: Routledge.

——(1986) *Linguistic Criticism*, Oxford: Oxford University Press.

——(1991) *Language in the News: Discourse and Ideology in the Press*, London: Routledge.

——(1996) *Linguistic Criticism*, 2nd edn, Oxford: Oxford University Press.

Fowler, R., Hodge, R., Kress, G. and Trew, T. (1979) *Language and Control*, London: Routledge and Kegan Paul.

Fox, B.A., Hayashi, M. and Jasperson, R. (1996) 'Resources and repair: a cross-linguistic study of the syntactic organization of repair', in E. Ochs, E.A. Schegloff and S.A. Thompson (eds) *Interaction and Grammar*, Cambridge: Cambridge University Press.

Fox, D. (2006) 'Free choice and the theory of scalar implicatures', unpublished manuscript, Massachusetts Institute of Technology.

Fox, H. and Jasperson, R. (1995) 'A syntactic exploration of repair in English conversation', in P.W. Davis (ed.) *Alternative Linguistics: Descriptive and Theoretical Modes*, Amsterdam: John Benjamins.

Fox, J. R. (1967) *The Keresan Bridge: a problem in Pueblo Ethology*, Oxford: Berg Publishers.

Fox, R. and King, B. (eds) (2002) *Anthropology Beyond Culture*, Oxford: Berg.

Fraenkel, A.A. and Bar-Hillel, Y. (1958) *Foundations of Set Theory*, Amsterdam: North Holland Publishing Company.

Fraenkel, A.A., Bar-Hillel, Y. and Levy, A. (1973) *Foundations of Set Theory*, Amsterdam: Elsevier.

Fragman, C., Goodluck, H. and Heggie, L. (2007) 'Child and adult construal of restrictive relative clauses: knowledge of grammar and differential effects of syntactic context', *Journal of Child Language*, 34: 345–80.

Francis, G. and Hunston, S. (1992) 'Analysing everyday conversation', in M. Coulthard (ed.) *Advances in Spoken Discourse Analysis*, London: Routledge.

Frankenhuis, W.E. and Ploeger, A. (2007) 'Evolutionary psychology versus Fodor: arguments for and against the massive modularity hypothesis', *Philosophical Psychology*, 20: 687–710.

Fraser, B. (1970) 'Idioms within a transformational grammar', *Foundations of Language*, 6: 22–42.

——(1975) 'Hedged performatives', in P. Cole and J.L. Morgan (eds) *Syntax and Semantics 3: Speech Acts*, New York: Academic Press.

——(1980) 'Conversational mitigation', *Journal of Pragmatics*, 4: 341–50.

——(1988) 'Motor oil *is* motor oil', *Journal of Pragmatics*, 12: 215–20.

——(1990) 'Perspectives on politeness', *Journal of Pragmatics*, 14: 219–36.

——(1996) 'Pragmatic markers', *Pragmatics*, 6: 167–90.

——(2006) 'Towards a theory of discourse markers', in K. Fischer (ed.) *Approaches to Discourse Particles*, Amsterdam: Elsevier.

Frazier, L. (2006) 'Big fish in a small pond: accommodation and the processing of novel definites', paper presented at the *OSU Presupposition Accommodation Workshop*, Columbus, OH, October 2006.

Frazier, L. and Clifton, C. (2006) 'Ellipsis and discourse coherence', *Linguistics and Philosophy*, 29: 315–46.

Frazier, L., Clifton, C. and Carlson, K. (2007) 'Focus and VP ellipsis', *Language and Speech*, 50: 1–21.

Freedman, N. and Hoffman, S.P. (1967) 'Kinetic behavior in altered clinical states: an approach to the objective analysis of motor behavior during clinical interviews', *Perceptual and Motor Skills*, 24: 525–39.

Freeman, D.C. (1993) '"According to my bond": King Lear and recognition', *Language and Literature*, 2: 1–18.

Freeman, J.B. (2005) *Acceptable Premises: An Epistemic Approach to an Informal Logic Problem*, Cambridge: Cambridge University Press.

Freeman, M.H. (1995) 'Metaphor making meaning: Emily Dickinson's conceptual universe', *Journal of Pragmatics*, 24: 643–66.

Frege, G. (1892) 'Über Sinn und Bedeutung', *Zeitschrift für Philosophie und Philosophisch Kritik*, 100: 25–50; trans. 'On sense and reference', in P. Geach and M. Black (eds) (1952) *Translations from the Philosophical Writings of Gottlob Frege*, Oxford: Blackwell; and as 'On sense and meaning', in B. McGuinness (ed.) (1984) *Gottlob Frege: Collected Papers on Mathematics, Logic, and Philosophy*, Oxford: Blackwell.

——(1918) 'Thoughts', in B. McGuinness (ed.) (1984) *Gottlob Frege: Collected Papers on Mathematics, Logic, and Philosophy*, Oxford: Blackwell.

——(1918–19) *The Thought: A Logical Inquiry*, trans. A.M. Quinton and M. Quinton (1956) *Mind*, 55: 289–311.

——(1980) *Translations from the Philosophical Writings of Gottlob Frege*, edited by P. Geach and M. Black, Oxford: Blackwell.

——(1984) *Collected Papers*, Oxford: Oxford University Press.

French, P. and Local, J. (1983) 'Turn-competitive incomings', *Journal of Pragmatics*, 7: 701–15.

Frescura, M. (1995) 'Face orientations in reacting to accusatory complaints: Italian L1, English L1, and Italian as a community language', in L.F. Bouton (ed.) *Pragmatics and Language Learning: Monograph Series Volume 6*, Urbana-Champaign, IL: DEIL, University of Illinois.

Fretheim, T. (1992) 'Themehood, rhemehood and Norwegian focus structure', *Folia Linguistica*, 26: 111–50.

——(2002) 'Intonation as a constraint on inferential processing', paper presented at Speech Prosody 2002, Aix-en-Provence, France, April 2002. Online. Available: http://aune.lpl.univ-aix.fr/sp2002/pdf/fretheim.pdf (accessed 26 August 2008).

Fridlund, A. (1994) *Human Facial Expression: An Evolutionary View*, San Diego, CA: Academic Press.

Friedland, D. and Miller, N. (1998) 'Conversation analysis of communication breakdown after closed head injury', *Brain Injury*, 1: 1–14.

Fries, U. (1983) 'Diachronic textlinguistics', in S. Hattori and K. Inoue (eds) *Proceedings of the XIIIth International Congress of Linguistics*, 29 August–4 September 1982. Tokyo: Tokyo Press, 1013–15.

Frisson, S. and Pickering, M. (1999) 'The processing of metonymy: evidence from eye movements', *Journal of Experimental Psychology: Learning, Memory and Cognition*, 25: 1366–383.

Frith, C.D. (1992) *The Cognitive Neuropsychology of Schizophrenia*, Hove and Hillsdale, NJ: Lawrence Erlbaum Associates.

——(1993) *The Cognitive Neuropsychology of Schizophrenia*, Hove: Lawrence Erlbaum.

Frith, C.D. and Frith, U. (2006) 'The neural basis of mentalizing', *Neuron*, 50: 531–34.

Frith, U. and Happé, F. (1999) 'Theory of mind and self consciousness: what is it like to be autistic?', *Mind and Language*, 14: 1–22.

Frota, S. (2000) *Prosody and Focus in European Portuguese: Phonological Phrasing and Intonation*, New York and London: Garland.

Fukada, A. (1986) *Pragmatics and grammatical description*, Ph.D. dissertation, University of Illinois.

Fukada, A. and Asato, N. (2004) 'Universal politeness theory: application to the use of Japanese honorifics', *Journal of Pragmatics*, 36: 1991–2002.

Fuller, J.M. (2003) 'The influence of speaker roles on discourse marker use', *Journal of Pragmatics*, 35: 23–45.

Fung, L. and Carter, R.A. (2007) 'Discourse markers and spoken English: native and learner use in pedagogic settings', *Applied Linguistics*, 28: 410–39.

Gabbay, D.M. and Woods, J. (2003) *Agenda Relevance: A Study in Formal Pragmatics*, Amsterdam: North Holland.

——(2005) *The Reach of Abduction: Insight and Trial*, Amsterdam: North Holland.

Gabelentz, G. von der (1868) 'Ideen zu einer Vergleichenden Syntax: Wort- und Satzstellung', *Zeitschrift für Völkerpsychologie und Sprachwissenschaft*, 6: 376–84.

Gagnon, L., Mottron, L. and Joanette, Y. (1997) 'Questioning the validity of the semantic-pragmatic syndrome diagnosis', *Autism*, 1: 37–55.

Gallagher, S. (2001) 'The practice of mind: theory, simulation, or primary interaction?', *Journal of Consciousness Studies*, 8: 83–108.

Gallagher, S. and Hutto, D. (2008) 'Understanding others through primary interaction and narrative', in T. Racine, C. Sinha, J. Zlatev and E. Itkonen (eds) *The Shared Mind: Perspectives on Intersubjectivity*, Amsterdam: Benjamins.

Gallagher, T.M. and Darnton, B.A. (1978) 'Conversational aspects of the speech of language-disordered children: revision behaviors', *Journal of Speech and Hearing Research*, 21: 118–35.

Gallese, V. and Goldman, A. (1998) 'Mirror neurons and the simulation theory of Mind-reading', *Trends in Cognitive Sciences*, 2: 493–501.

Gallese, V. and Lakoff, G. (2005) 'The brain's concepts: the role of the sensory-motor system in reason and language', *Cognitive Neuropsychology*, 22: 455–79.

Gallup, G.G. Jr (1970) 'Chimpanzees: self-recognition', *Science*, 167: 86–87.

Galski, T., Tompkins, C. and Johnston, M.V. (1998) 'Competence in discourse as a measure of social integration and quality of life in persons with traumatic brain injury', *Brain Injury*, 12: 769–82.

Galton, A.P. (2008) *Temporal Logic*. Online. Available: http://plato.stanford.edu/entries/logic-temporal/ (accessed 19 February 2008).

Galvan, N. (2005) 'Family members' perspectives on pragmatic difficulties in frontotemporal dementia', unpublished dissertation, University of Western Ontario.

Gamut, L.T.F. (1991) *Logic, Language, and Meaning, vol. 1, Intensional Logic and Logical Grammar*, Chicago: University of Chicago Press.

Garcia, A. (1991) 'Dispute resolution without disputing: how the interactional organization of mediation hearings minimizes argument', *American Sociological Review*, 56: 818–35.

Garcia, L.J. and Joanette, Y. (1994) 'Conversational topic-shifting analysis in dementia', in R.L. Bloom, L.K. Obler, S. De Santi and J.S. Ehrlich (eds) *Discourse Analysis and Applications: Studies in Adult Populations*, Hillsdale, NJ: Lawrence Erlbaum.

——(1997) 'Analysis of conversational topic shifts: a multiple case study', *Brain and Language*, 58: 92–114.

García-Carpintero, M. (1994) 'Ostensive signs: against the identity theory of quotation', *The Journal of Philosophy*, 91: 253–64.

Gardner, H. (1985) *The Mind's New Science: A History of the Cognitive Revolution*, New York: Basic Books.

Gardner, H. and Brownell, H.H. (1986) *Right Hemisphere Communication Battery*, Boston, MA: Psychology Service, Veterans Administration Medical Center.

Gardner, R. (2000) 'Resources for delicate manoeuvres: learning to disagree', *Australian Review of Applied Linguistics*, supplement, 16: 31–47.

Garfinkel, H. (1967) *Studies in Ethnomethodology*, Englewood Cliffs, NJ: Prentice-Hall.

——(1972) 'Remarks on ethnomethodology', in J.J. Gumperz and D. Hymes (eds) *Directions in Sociolinguistics*, New York: Holt, Rinehart and Winston.

——(2002) *Ethnomethodology's Program: Working Out Durkheim's Aphorism*, edited and introduced by A.W. Rawls, Lanham, MD: Rowman and Littlefield.

Garnham, A. and Perner, J. (1990) 'Does manifestness solve problems of mutuality?', *Behavioral and Brain Sciences*, 13: 178–79.

Garnham, A., Oakhill, J. and Johnson-Laird, P. N. (1982) 'Referential continuity and the coherence of discourse', *Cognition*, 11: 29–46.

Garnham, W.A. and Perner, J. (2001) 'Actions really do speak louder than words – but only implicitly: young children's understanding of false belief in action', *British Journal of Developmental Psychology*, 19: 413–32.

Garrett, M. and Harnish, R. (2007) 'Experimental pragmatics: testing for implicitures', *Pragmatics and Cognition*, 15: 65–90.

Garrod, S.C. and Sanford, A.J. (1982) 'The mental representation of discourse in a focused memory system: implications for the interpretations of anaphoric noun phrases', *Journal of Semantics*, 1: 21–41.

——(1994) 'Resolving sentences in a discourse context: how discourse representation affects language understanding', in M.A. Gernsbacher (ed.) *Handbook of Psycholinguistics*, San Diego, CA: Academic Press.

Gärtner, H.-M. (2003) 'On the optimality-theoretic status of "unambiguous encoding"', in R. Blutner and H. Zeevat (eds) *Optimality Theory and Pragmatics*, New York: Palgrave Macmillan.

——(2004) 'On the optimality theoretic status of "unambiguous encoding"', in R. Blutner and H. Zeevat (eds) *Optimality Theory and Pragmatics*, London: Palgrave Macmillan.

Garver, N. (1994) *This Complicated Form of Life: Essays on Wittgenstein*, Chicago: Open Court.

Garvey, C. (1984) *Children's Talk*, New York: Fontana.

Gass, S.M. and Houck, N. (1999) *Interlanguage Refusals: A Cross-Cultural Study of Japanese-English*, New York: Mouton de Gruyter.

Gass, S.M. and Selinker, L. (eds) (1992) *Language Transfer in Language Learning*, Amsterdam: John Benjamins.

——(2001) *Second Language Acquisition: An Introductory Course*, Mahwah, NJ: Lawrence Erlbaum.

Gathercole, S.E. and Baddeley, A. (1993) *Working Memory and Language*, Hove: Erlbaum.

Gavins, J. (2007) *Text World Theory: An Introduction*, Edinburgh: Edinburgh University Press.

Gavins, J. and Steen, G. (eds) (2003) *Cognitive Poetics in Practice*, London: Routledge.

Gazdar, G. (1979a) *Pragmatics: Implicature, Presupposition and Logical Form*, New York: Academic Press.

——(1979b) 'A solution to the projection problem', in C.K. Oh and D.A. Dinneen (eds) *Syntax and Semantics, volume 11: Presupposition*, New York: Academic Press.

Gazzaniga, M.S. (1999) *The New Cognitive Neurosciences*, Cambridge, MA: MIT Press.

Gazzaniga, M.S. and Smiley, C. (1991) 'Hemispheric mechanisms controlling voluntary and spontaneous facial expressions', *Journal of Cognitive Neuroscience*, 2: 239–45.

Geertz, C. (1979) *Meaning and Order in Moroccan Society: Three Essays in Cultural Analysis*, Cambridge: Cambridge University Press.

Geis, M. (1982) *The Language of Television Advertising*, New York: Academic Press.

Geis, M. and Zwicky, A. (1971) 'On invited inference', *Linguistic Inquiry*, 2: 561–79.

Gellner, E. (1959) *Words and Things*, London: Gollancz.

Gelman, S.A. and Markman, E.M. (1986) 'Categories and induction in young children', *Cognition*, 23: 183–209.

Geluykens, R. (2007) 'On methodology in cross-cultural pragmatics', in B. Kraft and R. Geluykens (eds) *Cross-Cultural Pragmatics and Interlanguage English*, Munich: Lincom Europa.

Geluykens, R. and Kraft, B. (2007) 'Gender variation in native and interlanguage complaints', in B. Kraft and R. Geluykens (eds) *Cross-Cultural Pragmatics and Interlanguage English*, Munich: Lincom Europa.

Genesee, F. (2000) 'Introduction: syntactic aspects of bilingual acquisition', *Bilingualism: Language and Cognition*, 3: 167–72.

Genette, G. (1990) 'The pragmatic status of narrative fiction', *Style*, 24: 59–72.

Gentner, D. (1983) 'Structure-mapping: a theoretical framework for analogy', *Cognitive Science*, 7: 155–70.

Gentner, D. and Goldin-Meadow, S. (2003) *Language in Mind*, Cambridge, MA: MIT Press.

Gentner, D. and Wolff, P. (1997) 'Alignment in the processing of metaphor', *Journal of Memory and Language*, 37: 331–55.

Gentner, D., Bowdle, B.F., Wolff, P. and Boronat, C. (2001) 'Metaphor is like analogy', in D. Gentner, K. Holyoak and B. Kokinov (eds) *The Analogical Mind: Perspectives from Cognitive Science*, Cambridge, MA: MIT Press.

Gentry, L.R., Godersky, J.C. and Thompson, B. (1988) 'MR imaging of head trauma: review of the distribution and radiopathologic features of traumatic lesions', *American Journal of Radiology*, 150: 663–72.

Gentzler, E. (1993) *Contemporary Translation Theories*, London: Routledge.

Georgakopoulou, A. (1997) *Narrative Performances: A Study of Modern Greek Storytelling*, Amsterdam: Benjamins.

——(2001) 'Arguing about the future: on indirect disagreements in conversations', *Journal of Pragmatics*, 33: 1881–900.

——(2003) 'Plotting the "right place" and the "right time": place and time as interactional resources in narrative', *Narrative Inquiry*, 13: 413–32.

George, A. (1989) 'How not to become confused about linguistics', in A. George (ed.) *Reflections on Chomsky*, Oxford: Blackwell.

Georges, R.A. and Dundes, A. (1963) 'Toward a structural definition of the riddle', *Journal of American Folklore*, 76: 111–18.

Georgieff, N. and Jeannerod, M. (1998) 'Beyond consciousness of external reality: a "Who" system for consciousness of action and self-consciousness', *Consciousness and Cognition*, 7: 465–77.

Gerber, S. and Kraat, A. (1992) 'Use of a developmental model of language acquisition: applications to children using AAC systems', *Augmentative and Alternative Communication*, 8: 19–32.

German, T. and Defeyter, M. (2000) 'Immunity to functional fixedness in young children', *Psychonomic Bulletin and Review*, 7: 707–12.

Gernsbacher, M.A. (1990) *Language Comprehension as Structure Building*, Hillsdale, NJ: Erlbaum.

Gerrig, R. (1989) 'The time course of sense creation', *Memory and Cognition*, 17: 194–207.

Gershenson, O. (2003) 'Misunderstanding between Israelis and Soviet immigrants: linguistic and cultural factors', *Multilingua*, 22: 275–90.

Geurts, B. (1998) 'Scalars', in P. Ludewig and B. Geurts (eds) *Lexikalische Semantik aus kognitiver Sicht*, Tübingen: Gunter Narr Verlag.

——(1999) *Presuppositions and Pronouns*, Oxford: Elsevier.

——(2002) 'Specifics', in K. von Heusinger and K. Schwabe (eds) *Sentence Type and Specificity*, ZAS Papers in Linguistics, 24, Berlin: Zentrum für Allgemeine Sprachwissenschaft.

——(2009) 'Scalar implicatures and local pragmatics', *Mind and Language*, 24: 51–79.

Ghadessy, M., Henry, A. and Roseberry, R. (eds) (2001) *Small Corpus Studies and ELT: Theory and Practice*, Amsterdam and Philadelphia, PA: John Benjamins.

Ghaziuddin, M. and Gerstein, L. (1996) 'Pedantic speaking style differentiates Asperger syndrome from high-functioning autism', *Journal of Autism and Developmental Disorders*, 26: 585–96.

Gibbins, J.R. (2007) *John Grote, Cambridge University and the Development of Victorian Thought*, Exeter: Imprint Academic.

Gibbs, R.W. Jr (1986) 'On the psycholinguistics of sarcasm', *Journal of Experimental Psychology: General*, 115: 3–15.

——(1990) 'Comprehending figurative referential descriptions', *Journal of Experimental Psychology: Learning, Memory and Cognition*, 16: 56–66.

——(1994) *The Poetics of Mind*, Cambridge: Cambridge University Press.

——(2000) 'Irony in talk among friends', *Metaphor and Symbol*, 15: 5–27.

——(2002) 'A new look at literal meaning in understanding what is said and implicated', *Journal of Pragmatics*, 34: 457–86.

——(2003) 'Nonliteral speech acts in text and discourse', in A.C. Graesser, M.A. Gernsbacher and S.R. Goldman (eds) *Handbook of Discourse Processes*, Mahwah, NJ: Lawrence Erlbaum Associates.

——(2005) *Embodiment and Cognitive Science*, Cambridge: Cambridge University Press.

Gibbs, R.W. Jr and Colston, H.L. (2006) 'Figurative language', in M. Traxler and M.A. Gernsbacher (eds) *Handbook of Psycholinguistics*, Amsterdam: Elsevier.

——(2007) 'The future of irony studies', in R. Gibbs and H. Colston (eds) *Irony in Language and Thought: A Cognitive Science Reader*, New York: Lawrence Erlbaum Associates.

Gibbs, R.W. Jr and Moise, J. (1997) 'Pragmatics in understanding what is said', *Cognition*, 62: 51–74.

Gibbs, R.W. Jr, Leggitt, J.S. and Turner, E.A. (2000) 'What's special about figurative language in emotional communication', in S. Fussell (ed.) *The Verbal Communication of Emotions: Interdisciplinary Perspectives*, Mahwah, NJ: Lawrence Erlbaum.

Gibson, J.J. (1979) *The Ecological Approach to Visual Perception*, Boston, MA: Houghton Mifflin.

Giddens, A. (1991) *Modernity and Self-Identity: Self and Society in the Late Modern Age*, Cambridge: Polity Press.

Gigerenzer, G. (2004) 'Fast and frugal heuristics: the tools of bounded rationality', in D. Koehler and D. Harvey (eds) *The Blackwell Handbook of Judgement and Decision-Making*, Oxford: Blackwell.

Gigerenzer, G. and Selten, R. (eds) (2002) *Bounded Rationality: The Adaptive Toolbox*, Cambridge, MA: MIT Press.

Gigerenzer, G., Todd, P.M. and the ABC Research Group (1999) *Simple Heuristics That Make Us Smart*, Oxford: Oxford University Press.

Gilbert, M. (1996) *Living Together*, Lanham, MD: Rowman and Littlefield.

Gilbert, M.A. (1997) *Coalescent Argumentation*, Mahwah, NJ: Lawrence Erlbaum Associates.

Gilkerson, J. (2006) *Acquiring English particle verbs: age and transfer effects in second language acquisition*, Ph.D. dissertation, University of California at Los Angeles.

Gilmour, J., Hill, B., Place, M. and Skuse, D.H. (2004) 'Social communication deficits in conduct disorder: a clinical and community survey', *Journal of Child Psychology and Psychiatry*, 45: 967–78.

Gimenez, J. (2009) 'Mediated communication', in F. Bargiela-Chiappini (ed.) *The Handbook of Business Discourse*, Edinburgh: Edinburgh University Press.

Giora, R. (1995) 'On irony and negation', *Discourse Processes*, 19: 239–64.

——(1997) 'Understanding figurative and literal language: the graded salience hypothesis', *Cognitive Linguistics*, 7: 183–206.

——(2002) 'Literal vs. figurative language: different or equal?', *Journal of Pragmatics*, 34: 487–506.

——(2003) *On Our Mind: Salience, Context, and Figurative Language*, New York: Oxford University Press.

——(2007) '"A good Arab is *not* a dead Arab – a racist incitement": on the accessibility of negated concepts', in I. Kecskes and L.R. Horn (eds) *Explorations in Pragmatics*, Berlin: Mouton de Gruyter.

Giora, R. and Fein, O. (1999) 'Irony: context and salience', *Metaphor and Symbol*, 14: 241–57.

Giora, R. and Gur, I. (2003) 'Irony in conversation: salience and context effects', in B. Nerlich,

Z. Todd, V. Herman and D.D. Clarke (eds) *Polysemy: Flexible Patterns of Meanings in Language and Mind*, Berlin: Walter de Gruyter.

Giora, R., Fein, F., Kaufman, R., Eisenberg, D. and Erez, S. (2009) 'Does an "ironic situation" favor an ironic interpretation?', in G. Brône and G. Vandaele (eds) *Cognitive Poetics: Goals, Gains and Gaps*, Berlin: Mouton de Gruyter.

Giora, R., Fein, O. and Schwartz, T. (1998) 'Irony: graded salience and indirect negation', *Metaphor and Symbol*, 13: 83–101.

Giora, R., Fein, O., Ganzi, J., Levi, N.A. and Hadas, S. (2005) 'On negation as mitigation: the case of negative irony', *Discourse Processes*, 39: 81–100.

Giora, R., Fein, O., Laadan, D., Wolfson, J., Zeituny, M., Kidron, R., Kaufman, R. and Shaham, R. (2007) 'Expecting irony: context vs. salience-based effects', *Metaphor and Symbol*, 22: 119–46.

Giora, R., Meiran, N. and Oref, P. (1996) 'Identification of written discourse topics by structure coherence and analogy strategies: general aspects and individual differences', *Journal of Pragmatics*, 26: 455–74.

Giora, R., Zaidel, E., Soroker, N., Batori, G. and Kasher, A. (2000) 'Differential effects of right and left hemisphere damage on understanding sarcasm and metaphor', *Metaphor and Symbol*, 15: 63–83.

Girotto, V., Kemmelmeir, M., Sperber, D. and van der Henst, J.-B. (2001) 'Inept reasoners or pragmatic virtuosos? Relevance and the deontic selection task', *Cognition*, 81: 69–76.

Givón, T. (1978) 'Negation in language: pragmatics, function, ontology', in P. Cole (ed.) *Syntax and Semantics 9: Pragmatics*, New York: Academic Press.

——(1981) 'On the development of the numeral "one" as an indefinite marker', *Folia Linguistica Historica* 2: 35–53.

——(2005) *Context as Other Minds*, Amsterdam: John Benjamins.

Glenberg, A.M. (1997) 'What memory is for', *Behavioral and Brain Sciences*, 20: 1–55.

Glenn, P. (2003) *Laughter in Interaction*, Cambridge: Cambridge University Press.

Glosser, G. and Deser, T. (1990) 'Patterns of discourse production among neurological patients with fluent language disorders', *Brain and Language*, 40: 67–88.

Glucksberg, S. (2001) *Understanding Figurative Language: From Metaphors to Idioms*, Oxford: Oxford University Press.

Glucksberg, S. and Keysar, B. (1993) 'How metaphors work', in A. Ortony (ed.) *Metaphor*

and Thought, Cambridge: Cambridge University Press.

Glucksberg, S., Gildea, P. and Bookin, H. (1982) 'On understanding nonliteral speech: can people ignore metaphors?', *Journal of Verbal Learning and Verbal Behavior*, 21: 85–98.

Glucksberg, S., McGlone, M. and Manfredi, D. (1997) 'Property attribution in metaphor comprehension', *Journal of Memory and Language*, 36: 50–67.

Gnisci, A. and Pontecorvo, C. (2004) 'The organization of questions and answers in the thematic phases of hostile examination: turn-by-turn manipulation of meaning', *Journal of Pragmatics*, 36: 965–95.

Godard, D. (1977) 'Same setting, different norms: phone call beginnings in France and the United States', *Language in Society*, 6: 209–19.

Goddard, A. (2002) *The Language of Advertising: Written Texts*, 2nd edn, London: Routledge.

Goddard, C. (1997) 'Cultural values and "cultural scripts" of Malay (Bahasa Melayu)', *Journal of Pragmatics*, 27: 183–201.

——(2000) 'Communicative style and cultural values – cultural scripts of Malay(Bahasa Melayu)', *Anthropological Linguistics*, 42: 81–106.

——(2002) 'Ethnosyntax, ethnopragmatics, sign-functions, and culture', in N.J. Enfield (ed.) *Ethnosyntax: Explorations in Grammar and Culture*, Oxford: Oxford University Press.

——(2005) 'The lexical semantics of "culture"', *Language Sciences*, 27: 57–73.

——(2006) 'Ethnopragmatics: a new paradigm', in C. Goddard (ed.) *Ethnopragmatics: Understanding Discourse in Cultural Context*, Berlin: Mouton de Gruyter.

Goddard, C. and Wierzbicka, A. (eds) (2002) *Meaning and Universal Grammar: Theory and Empirical Findings*, 2 vols, Amsterdam: John Benjamins.

——(eds) (2004) 'Cultural scripts', *Intercultural Pragmatics*, 1: 153–274.

Goffman, E. (1959) *The Presentation of Self in Everyday Life*, London: Allen Lane, the Penguin Press.

——(1964) 'The neglected situation', *American Anthropologist*, 66: 133–36.

——(1967a) 'On facework: an analysis of ritual elements in social interaction', in A. Jaworski and N. Coupland (eds) *The Discourse Reader*, London: Routledge.

——(1967b) *Interaction Ritual: Essays on Face to Face Behavior*, New York: Anchor Books.

——(1971) *Relations in Public: Microstudies of the Public Order*, New York: Basic Books.

——(1974) *Frame Analysis: An Essay on the Organisation of Experience*, New York: Harper and Row.

——(1983) 'Felicity's condition', *American Journal of Sociology*, 1: 1–53.

Gogate, L.J. and Bahrick, L.E. (1998) 'Intersensory redundancy facilitates learning of arbitrary relations between vowel sounds and objects in seven-month-old infants', *Journal of Experimental Child Psychology*, 69: 133–49.

Gogate, L.J., Bahrick, L.E. and Watson, J.D. (2000) 'A study of multimodal motherese: the role of temporal synchrony between verbal labels and gestures', *Child Development*, 71: 876–92.

Golato, A. (2003) 'Studying compliment responses: a comparison of DCTs and recordings of naturally occurring talk', *Applied Linguistics*, 24: 90–121.

Goldberg, A. (1995) *Constructions: A Construction Grammar Approach to Argument Structure*, Chicago: University of Chicago Press.

——(2006) *Constructions at Work: The Nature of Generalization in Language*, Oxford: Oxford University Press.

Goldin-Meadow, S. and Butcher, C. (2000) 'Pointing toward two-word speech in young children', in J.S. Kita (ed.) *Pointing: Where Language, Culture and Cognition Meet*, New Jersey: Lawrence Erlbaum Associates.

Goldin-Meadow, S. and Sandhofer, C.M. (1999) 'Gesture conveys substantive information to ordinary listeners', *Developmental Science*, 2: 67–74.

Goldman, A.I. (1993) 'The psychology of folk psychology', *Behavioral and Brain Sciences*, 16: 15–28.

——(2006) *Simulating Minds: The Philosophy, Psychology and Neuroscience of Mind Reading*, New York: Oxford University Press.

Goldstein, M.H. and Schwade, J.A. (2008) 'Social feedback to infants' babbling facilitates rapid phonological learning', *Psychological Science*, 19: 515–22.

Goldstein, T. (1997) *Two Languages at Work: Bilingual Life on the Production Floor*, Berlin: Mouton de Gruyter.

Golinkoff, K., Hirsh-Pasek, L., Bloom, G., Hollich, L., Smith, A.L., Woodward, L., Akhtar, N., Tomasello, M. and Hollich, G. (eds) *Becoming a Word Learner: A Debate on Lexical Acquisition*, Oxford: Oxford University Press.

Golinkoff, R.M. (1986) '"I beg your pardon?": the preverbal negotiation of failed messages', *Journal of Child Language*, 13: 455–76.

——(1993) 'When is communication a "meeting of minds"?', *Journal of Child Language*, 20: 199–207.

Golopentia-Eretescu, S. (1970) 'Infinite proverbs', *Proverbium*, 15: 38–39.

——(1971) 'Paradoxical proverbs, paradoxical words', *Proverbium*, 17: 626–29.

Gombert, J.E. (1992) *Metalinguistic Development*, Chicago: University of Chicago Press; translation of Gombert, J.E. (1990) *Le Développement Métalinguistique*, Paris: Presses Universitaires de France.

Gómez-Torrente, M. (2005) 'Remarks on impure quotation', *Belgian Journal of Linguistics*, 17: 129–51.

Good, B. (1994) *Medicine, Rationality, and Experience: An Anthropological Perspective*, London: Cambridge University Press.

Goode, D. (2007) *Playing with My Dog Katie: An Ethnomethodological Study of Canine-Human Interaction*, Ashland, OH: Purdue University Press.

Goodenough, W. ([1964] 1957) 'Cultural anthropology and linguistics', in D. Hymes (ed.) *Language in Culture and Society*, New York: Harper and Row.

——(1981) *Culture, Language, and Society*, Menlo Park, CA: Benjamin/Cummings.

Goodglass, H., Kaplan, E. and Barresi, B. ([1972] 2001) *Boston Diagnostic Aphasia Examination*, 3rd edn, Baltimore, MD: Lippincott Williams and Wilkins.

Goodluck, H. (2007) 'Formal and computational constraints on language development', in E. Hoff and M. Schatz (eds) *Blackwell Handbook of Language Development*, Malden, MA: Blackwell Publishing.

Goodwin, C. (1979) 'The interactive construction of a sentence in natural conversation', in G. Psathas (ed.) *Everyday Language: Studies in Ethnomethodology*, New York: Irvington.

——(1980) 'Restarts, pauses and the achievement of a state of mutual gaze at turn beginning', *Sociological Inquiry*, 50: 272–302.

——(1981) *Conversational Organisation: Interaction between Speakers and Hearers*, New York: Academic Press.

——(1984) 'Notes on story structure and the organization of participation', in J.M. Atkinson and J. Heritage (eds) *Structures of Social Action: Studies in Conversation Analysis*, Cambridge: Cambridge University Press.

——(1986) 'Gestures as a resource for the organization of mutual orientation', *Semiotica*, 62: 29–49.

——(2000a) 'Action and embodiment within situated human interaction', *Journal of Pragmatics*, 32: 1489–522.

——(2000b) 'Practices of seeing: visual analysis – an ethnomethodological approach', in

T. van Leeuwen and C. Jewitt (eds) *Handbook of Visual Analysis*, London: Sage.

——(2002) 'Time in action', *Current Anthropology*, 43: 19–35.

——(ed.) (2003) *Conversation and Brain Damage*, New York: Oxford University Press.

Goody, E. (1995) *Social Intelligence and Interaction*, Cambridge: Cambridge University Press.

Gopnik, A. (1993) 'How we know our own minds: the illusion of first-person knowledge of intentionality', *Behavioral and Brain Sciences*, 16: 1–14.

Gopnik, A. and Graf, P. (1988) 'Knowing how you know: young children's ability to identify and remember the sources of their beliefs', *Child Development*, 59: 1366–71.

Gopnik, A. and Meltzoff, A. (1997) *Words, Thoughts, and Theories*, Cambridge, MA: MIT Press.

——(1994) 'Minds, bodies, and persons: young children's understanding of the self and others as reflected in imitation and theory of mind research', in S.T. Parker, R.W. Mitchell and M.L. Boccia (eds) *Self-Awareness in Animals and Humans: Developmental Perspectives*, Cambridge: Cambridge University Press.

Gopnik, A. and Wellman, H. (1994) 'The theory theory', in S. Gelman and L. Hirschfeld (eds) *Mapping the Mind*, Cambridge: Cambridge University Press.

Gordon, D. and Lakoff, G. (1971) 'Conversational postulates', *Papers from the 7th Regional Meeting of the Chicago Linguistic Society*, Chicago, IL: Department of Linguistics, University of Chicago; reprinted in P. Cole and J.L. Morgan (eds) (1975) *Syntax and Semantics 3: Speech Acts*, New York: Academic Press.

——(1975) 'Conversational postulates', in P. Cole and J.L. Morgan (eds) *Syntax and Semantics, Volume 3: Speech Acts*, New York: Academic Press.

Gordon, R.G. Jr (ed.) (2005) *Ethnologue: Languages of the World*, 15th edn, Dallas, TX: SIL International. Online. Available: www.ethnologue.com (accessed 1 March 2008).

Gotti, M. (2005) 'Advertising discourse in eighteenth-century newspapers', in J. Skaffari, M. Peikola, R. Carroll, R. Hiltunen and B. Wårvik (eds) *Opening Windows on Texts and Discourses of the Past*, Amsterdam and Philadelphia: John Benjamins.

Gotti, M. and Salager-Meyer, F. (2006) *Advances in Medical Discourse Analysis: Oral and Written Contexts*, Bern, Switzerland: Peter Lang.

Gottschalk, L.A. and Gleser, G.C. (1964) 'Distinguishing characteristics of the verbal communications of schizophrenic patients', in D. McRioch and E.A. Weinstein (eds), *Disorders of Communication*, Baltimore, MD: Williams and Wilkins.

Gould, S.J. (1989) 'Tires to sandals', *Natural History*, 98: 8–15.

Graffam Walker, A. (1985) 'The two faces of silence: the effect of witness hesitancy on lawyers' impressions', in D. Tannen and M. Saville-Troike (eds) *Perspectives of Silence*, Norwood, NJ: Ablex.

Graham, J.A. and Heywood, S. (1976) 'The effects of elimination of hand gesture and of verbal codability on speech performance', *European Journal of Social Psychology*, 5: 189–95.

Graham, K. (1977) *J.L. Austin: A Critique of Ordinary Language Philosophy*, Hassocks, UK: Harvester.

Graham, K. and Hodges, J. (1997) 'Differentiating the roles of the hippocampal complex and the neocortex in long-term memory storage: evidence from the study of semantic dementia and Alzheimer's disease', *Neuropsychology*, 11: 77–88.

Grainger, K. and Harris, S. (2007) 'Introduction to special issue on apologies', *Journal of Politeness Research*, 3: 1–9.

Gramsci, A. (1977) *Selections from Political Writings*, London: Lawrence and Wishart.

Granger, S. (1998) 'Prefabricated patterns in advanced EFL writing: collocations and formulae', in A. Cowie (ed.) *Phraseology: Theory, Analysis and Applications*, Oxford: Oxford University Press.

Granger, S. and Rayson, P. (1998) 'Automatic profiling of learner texts', in S. Granger (ed.) *Learner English on Computer*, London: Longman.

Grant, L. (2000) 'What lies beneath', *Guardian*, 24 October 2000. Online. Available: www.guardian.co.uk/Archive/Article/0,4273,4080686,00.html (accessed 4 July 2008).

Graves, H. and Hodge, A. (1947) *The Reader over Your Shoulder: A Handbook for Writers of English Prose*, London: Jonathan Cape.

Greatbatch, D. (1988) 'A turn-taking system for British news interviews', *Language in Society*, 17: 401–30.

Greaves, C. (2000) *ConcApp Version 4*, Edict Virtual Learning Centre. Online. Available: www.edict.com.hk/pub/concapp/ (accessed 14 May 2008).

Green, G.M. (1974) *Semantics and Syntactic Regularity*, Bloomington, IN: Indiana University Press.

——(1989) *Pragmatics and Natural Language Understanding*, Hillsdale, NJ: Lawrence Erlbaum Associates.

——(1993) *Rationality and Gricean Inference*, Cognitive Science Technical Report UIUC-BI-CS-93-09 (Language Series), Urbana, IL: Beckman Institute, University of Illinois.

——(1994) 'The structure of CONTEXT: the representation of pragmatic restrictions in HPSG', in J.H. Yoon (ed.) *Studies in the Linguistic Sciences: Proceedings of the Fifth Annual Conference of the Formal Linguistics Society of the Midwest*, Urbana, IL: Department of Linguistics, University of Illinois.

——(1995) 'The right tool for the job: techniques for analysis of natural language use', in L.F. Bouton (ed.) *Pragmatics and Language Learning*, Monograph Series, volume 6, Urbana: Division of English as an International Language, University of Illinois.

——(1996a) *Pragmatics and Natural Language Understanding*, 2nd edn, Hillsdale, NJ: Lawrence Erlbaum Associates.

——(1996b) 'Ambiguity resolution and discourse interpretation', in K. van Deemter and S. Peters (eds) *Semantic Ambiguity and Underspecification*, Stanford, CA: CSLI Publications.

——(2000) 'The nature of pragmatic information', in R. Cann, C. Grover and P. Miller (eds) *Grammatical Interfaces in HPSG*, Stanford, CA: CSLI Publications.

——(2001) *Pragmatic Motivation and Exploitation of Syntactic Rules*, Technical Report, University of Illinois. Online. Available www.linguistics.uiuc.edu/g-green/441/prmoex/index.html (accessed 30 March 2008).

Green, M. and Walker, E. (1985) 'Neuropsychological performance and positive and negative symptoms in schizophrenia', *Journal of Abnormal Psychology*, 94: 460–69.

Grenoble, L. and Riley, M. (1996) 'The role of deictics in discourse coherence: French *voici/voilà* and Russian *vot/von*', *Journal of Pragmatics*, 25: 819–38.

Grice, H.P. (1957) 'Meaning', *The Philosophical Review*, 66: 377–88; reprinted in *Studies in the Way of Words* (1989), Cambridge, MA: Harvard University Press.

——(1961) 'The causal theory of perception', *Proceedings of the Aristotelian Society*, Supplementary Volume, 35: 121–52.

——(1967) 'Logic and conversation', William James Lectures, Harvard University typescript; reprinted in H.P. Grice (1989) *Studies in the Way of Words*, Cambridge, MA: Harvard University Press.

——(1968a) 'The logic of conversation', unpublished manuscript, Department of Philosophy, University of California, Berkeley.

——(1968b) 'Utterer's meaning, sentence meaning and word meaning', *Foundations of Language*, 4: 225–42.

——(1969) 'Utterer's meaning and intentions', *Philosophical Review*, 78: 147–77.

——(1971) 'Meaning', in D. Steinburg and L. Jakobovits (eds) *Semantics: An Interdisciplinary Reader*, Cambridge: Cambridge University Press.

——(1975) 'Logic and conversation' in P. Cole and J. Morgan (eds) *Syntax and Semantics 3: Speech Acts*, New York: Academic Press, pp. 41–58.

——(1978) 'Further notes on logic and conversation', in P. Cole (ed.) *Syntax and Semantics*, volume 9, New York: Academic Press; reprinted in H.P. Grice (1989) *Studies in the Way of Words*, Cambridge, MA: Harvard University Press.

——(1981) 'Presupposition and conversational implicature', in P. Cole (ed.) *Radical Pragmatics*, New York: Academic Press.

——(1982) 'Meaning revisited', in N.V. Smith (ed.) *Mutual Knowledge*, New York: Academic Press; reprinted in *Studies in the Way of Words* (1989), Cambridge, MA: Harvard University Press.

——(1989) *Studies in the Way of Words*, Cambridge, MA: Harvard University Press.

——(2001a) *The Conception of Value*, Oxford: Oxford University Press.

——(2001b) *Aspects of Reason*, ed. R. Warner, Oxford: Clarendon Press.

Gries, S.Th. (2005) 'The many senses of *run*', in S.Th. Gries and A. Stefanowitsch (eds) *Corpora in Cognitive Linguistics: Corpus-Based Approaches to Syntax and Lexis*, Berlin: Mouton de Gruyter.

Griffin, P.S., Crowe, T.A., Byrne, M.E. and Penzien, S. (1994) 'Pragmatic language abilities in adult patients diagnosed with chronic schizophrenia', paper presented at American Speech, Language and Hearing Association Convention, New Orleans, November 1994.

Griffin, R., Friedman, O., Ween, J., Winner, E., Happe, F. and Brownell, H. (2006) 'Theory of mind and the right cerebral hemisphere: refining the scope of impairment', *Laterality*, 11: 195–225.

Griffiths, L. (2004) 'Electronic text-based communication: assumptions and illusions created by the transference phenomena', in G. Bolton, S. Howlett, C. Lago and J. Wright (eds) *Writing Cures: An Introductory Handbook of Writing in Counselling and Therapy*, London: Routledge.

Grimshaw, J. (1997) 'Projection heads and optimality', *Linguistic Inquiry*, 28: 373–422.

Grodner, D. and Sedivy, J.C. (to appear) 'The effect of speaker-specific information on pragmatic inferences', in N. Pearlmutter and E. Gibson (eds) *The Processing and Acquisition of Reference*, Cambridge, MA: MIT Press.

Grodner, D., Klein, N., Carbary, K. and Tanenhaus, M. (2007) 'Experimental evidence for rapid interpretation of pragmatic *some*', paper presented at *XPRAG*, Berlin, December 2007.

Groenendijk, J. and Stokhof, M. (1980) 'A pragmatic analysis of specificity', in F. Heny (ed.) *Ambiguity in Intensional Contexts*, Dordrecht: Reidel Publishing Company.

——(1991) 'Dynamic predicate logic', *Linguistics and Philosophy*, 14: 39–100.

Groenendijk, J., Stokhof, M. and Veltman, F. (1996) 'Coreference and modality', in S. Lappin (ed.) *The Handbook of Contemporary Semantic Theory*, Oxford: Blackwell.

Grønnum, N. and Tøndering, J. (2007) 'Question intonation in non-scripted Danish dialogues', paper presented at the 16th International Congress of Phonetic Sciences, Saarbrücken, Germany, August 2007. Online. Available: www.cphling.dk/johtnd/pub/gron_tond_icphs 2007.pdf (accessed 26 August 2008).

Grosz, B.J. and Kraus, S. (1996) 'Collaborative plans for complex group action', *Artificial Intelligence*, 86: 269–357.

——(1999) 'The evolution of shared plans', in M. Wooldridge and A. Rao (eds) *Foundations of Rational Agency*, Dordrecht: Kluwer.

Grosz, B.J. and Sidner, C.L. (1986) 'Attention, intentions, and the structure of discourse', *Computational Linguistics*, 12: 175–204.

Grosz, B.J., Joshi, A.K. and Weinstein, S. (1995) 'Centering: a framework for modelling the local coherence of discourse', *Computational Linguistics*, 21: 203–25.

Grosz, B.J., Sparck Jones, K. and Webber, B.L. (eds) (1986) *Readings in Natural Language*, San Mateo, CA: Morgan Kaufmann.

Gruber, H. and Menz, F. (2004) 'Introduction: language and political change: micro- and macro-aspects of a contested relationship?', *Journal of Language and Politics*, 3: 175–88.

Gu, Y. (1990) 'Politeness phenomena in modern Chineses', *Journal of Pragmatics*, 14: 237–57.

——(2006) 'Multimodal text analysis: a corpus linguistic approach to situated discourse', *Text and Talk*, 26: 127–67.

Guasti, M.T., Chierchia, G., Crain, S., Foppolo, F., Gualmini, A. and Meroni, L. (2005) 'Why children and adults sometimes (but not always) compute implicatures', *Language and Cognitive Processes*, 20: 667–96.

Gudjonsson, G. (1991) 'The "Notice to Detained Persons", PACE codes, and reading ease', *Applied Cognitive Psychology*, 5: 89–95.

Gudykunst, W.B. (2002a) 'Cross-cultural communication', in W.B. Gudykunst and B. Mody (eds) *The Handbook of International and Intercultural Communication*, 2nd edn, Thousand Oaks, CA: Sage.

——(2002b) 'Issues in cross-cultural communication research', in W.B. Gudykunst and B. Mody (eds) *The Handbook of International and Intercultural Communication*, 2nd edn, Thousand Oaks, CA: Sage.

Gudykunst, W.B. and Mody, B. (eds) (2002) *The Handbook of International and Intercultural Communication*, 2nd edn, Thousand Oaks, CA: Sage.

Guendouzi, J. and Müller, N. (2006) *Approaches to Discourse in Dementia*, Mahwah, NJ: Lawrence Erlbaum Associates.

Guidano, V.F. (1987) *Complexity of the Self: A Developmental Approach to Psychopathology and Therapy*, New York: Guilford.

——(1991) *The Self in Process: Toward a Post-Rationalist Cognitive Therapy*, New York: Guilford.

Guidi, A. (to appear) 'Are pun mechanisms universal? A comparative analysis across language families', *HUMOR: International Journal of Humor Research*.

Guilford, A.M. and O'Connor, J.K. (1982) 'Pragmatic functions in aphasia', *Journal of Communication Disorders*, 15: 337–46.

Gulli, A. and Signorini, A. (2005) 'The indexable web is more than 11.5 billion pages', poster presented at the International World Wide Web Conference, Chiba, Japan, May 2005.

Gumperz, J.J. (1958) 'Dialect differences and social stratification in a North Indian village', *American Anthropologist*, 60: 668–81.

——(1964) 'Linguistic and social interaction in two communities', *American Anthropologist*, 66: 137–54.

——(1972) *Discourse Strategies*, Cambridge: Cambridge University Press.

——(1978) 'The sociolinguistic significance of conversational code-switching', *RELC Journal*, 8: 1–34.

——(1982a) *Discourse Strategies*, Cambridge: Cambridge University Press.

——(1982b) (ed.) *Language and Social Identity*, Cambridge: Cambridge University Press.

——(1992) 'Contextualization and understanding', in A. Duranti and C. Goodwin (eds) *Rethinking Context*, Cambridge: Cambridge University Press.

——(2003) 'Response essay', in S. Eerdmans, C. Prevignano and P. Thibault (eds) *Language and Interaction: Discussions with John J. Gumperz*, Amsterdam: John Benjamins.

Gumperz, J.J. and Hymes, D. (eds) (1964) Special Issue: The Ethnography of Communication, *American Anthropologist*, 66: 1257–517.

——(eds) (1972) *Directions in Sociolinguistics: The Ethnography of Communication*, New York: Holt, Rinehart and Winston.

Gumperz, J.J. and Levinson, S.C. (eds) (1996) *Rethinking Linguistic Relativity*, Cambridge: Cambridge University Press.

Gumperz, J.J. and Roberts, C. (1991) 'Understanding in intercultural encounters', in J. Blommaert and J. Verschueren (eds) *The Pragmatics of Intercultural and International Communication*, Amsterdam: John Benjamins.

Gumperz, J.J., Jupp, T.C. and Roberts, C. (1979) *Crosstalk: A Study of Cross-Cultural Communication*, London: National Centre for Industrial Language Training.

Gundel, J.K. (1974) 'The role of topic and comment in linguistic theory', Ph.D. thesis, University of Texas at Austin; published in G. Hankamer (ed.) (1988) *Outstanding Dissertations in Linguistics*, New York: Garland.

——(1980) 'Zero NP-anaphora in Russian: a case of topic-prominence', in J. Kreiman and A. Ojeda (eds) *Proceedings from the 16th Meeting of the Chicago Linguistic Society: Parasession on Anaphora*, Chicago, IL: Chicago Linguistic Society.

——(1985) 'Shared knowledge and topicality', *Journal of Pragmatics*, 9: 33–107.

——(1988) 'Universals of topic-comment structure', in M. Hammond, E. Moravczik and J. Wirth (eds) *Studies in Syntactic Typology*, Amsterdam: John Benjamins.

——(1999a) 'On different kinds of focus', in P. Bosch and R. van der Sandt (eds) *Focus: Linguistic, Cognitive and Computational Perspectives*, Cambridge: Cambridge University Press.

——(1999b) 'Topic, focus, and the grammar-pragmatics interface', *Penn Working Papers in Linguistics*, 6: 185–200.

——(2002) 'Clefts in English and Norwegian: implications for the grammar-pragmatics interface', in V. Molnar and S. Winkler (eds) *The Architecture of Focus*, Berlin: Mouton de Gruyter.

Gundel, J.K. and Fretheim, T. (2003) 'Information structure', in J. Verschueren, J.O. Östman, J. Blommaert and C. Bulcaen (eds) *Handbook of Pragmatics*, Amsterdam: John Benjamins.

——(2004) 'Topic and focus', in L.R. Horn and G. Ward (eds) *The Handbook of Pragmatics*, Oxford: Blackwell.

Gundel, J.K. and Mulkern, A. (2007) 'Frequency differences in use of cleft sentences: a comparative study of English, Irish and Norwegian', in R.A. Nilsen, N.A. Appiah Amfo and K. Borthen (eds) *Interpreting Utterances: Pragmatics and its Interfaces. Essays in Honour of Thorstein Fretheim*, Oslo: Novus Press.

Gundel, J.K., Hedberg, N. and Zacharski, R. (1993) 'Cognitive status and the form of referring expressions in discourse', *Language*, 69: 274–307.

——(2001) 'Definite descriptions and cognitive status in English: why accommodation is unnecessary', *English Language and Linguistics*, 5: 273–95.

Gundel, J.K., Hegarty, M. and Borthen, K. (2003) 'Cognitive status, information structure, and pronominal reference to clausally introduced entities', *Journal of Logic, Language and Information*, 12: 281–99.

Gunnarsson, B.-L., Linell, P. and Bordberg, B. (eds) (1997) *The Construction of Professional Discourse*, London and New York: Longman.

Günther, U. (2003) 'What's in a laugh: humour, jokes and laughter in the conversational corpus of the BNC', unpublished thesis, University of Freiburg.

Günthner, S. (1997) 'Complaint stories: constructing emotional reciprocity among women', in H. Kotthoff and R. Wodak (eds) *Communicating Gender in Context*, Amsterdam: John Benjamins.

Gussenhoven, C. (2002) 'Intonation and interpretation: phonetics and phonology', in B. Bel and I. Marlien (eds) *Proceedings of the First International Conference on Speech Prosody*. Online. Available: www.mpi.nl/Members/AojuChen/Gussenhoven.2002 (accessed 21 January 2009).

——(2004) *The Phonology of Tone and Intonation*, Cambridge: Cambridge University Press.

Gustafson, L. (1993) 'Clinical picture of frontal lobe degeneration of the non-Alzheimer type', *Dementia*, 4: 143–48.

Gutheil, G., Bloom, P., Valderraman, N. and Freedman, R. (2004) 'The role of historical intuitions in children's and adults' naming of artefacts', *Cognition*, 91: 23–42.

Gutt, E.-A. (1991) *Translation and Relevance: Cognition and Context*, Oxford: Blackwell.

——(2000) *Translation and Relevance*, Manchester: St Jerome Publishing.

Gwyn, R. (2000) '"Really unreal": narrative evaluation and the objectification of experience', *Narrative Inquiry*, 10: 313–40.

Haan, J., van Heuven, V.J., Pacilly, J. and van Bezooijen, R. (1997) 'An anatomy of Dutch question intonation', in J.A. Coerts and H. de Hoop (eds) *Linguistics in the Netherlands*, Amsterdam and Philadelphia, PA: John Benjamins.

Haberland, H. and Mey, J.L. (1977) 'Pragmatics and linguistics', *Journal of Pragmatics*, 1: 1–16.

——(2002) 'Linguistics and pragmatics, 25 years after', *Journal of Pragmatics*, 34: 1671–82.

Habermas, J. ([1976] 1998) 'What is universal pragmatics?', in M. Cooke (ed.) *On the Pragmatics of Communication*, Cambridge, MA: MIT Press.

——(1979) *Communication and the Evolution of Society*, London: Heinemann.

——([1981] 1984/1987) *The Theory of Communicative Action*, trans. T. McCarthy, vols 1 and 2, Boston, MA: Beacon Press.

——(1990) *Moral Consciousness and Communicative Action*, Cambridge: Polity Press.

——(1998) *On the Pragmatics of Communication*, ed. M. Cooke, Cambridge, MA: MIT Press.

——([1999] 2003) *Truth and Justification*, trans. B. Fultner, Cambridge, MA: MIT Press.

Hadar, U. and Butterworth, B. (1997) 'Iconic gesture, imagery and word retrieval in speech', *Semiotica*, 15: 147–72.

Haegeman, L. (1988) 'Parenthetical adverbials: the radical orphanage approach', in S. Chiba (ed.) *Aspects of Modern Linguistics*, Tokyo: Kaitakushi.

Hagège, C. (1974) 'Les pronoms logophoriques', *Bulletin de la Société de Linguistique de Paris*, 69: 287–310.

Hagen, S. (ed.) (1999) *Business Communication Across Borders: A Study of Language Use and Practice in European Companies*, London: CILT Publications.

Haggard, P. (2005) 'Conscious intention and motor cognition', *Trends in Cognitive Science*, 9: 290–95.

Haider, H. (2005) 'Parenthesen: evidenz aus Bindungsverhältnissen', in F.J. D'Avis (ed.) *Deutsche Syntax: Empirie und Theorie*, Göteborg: Acta Universitatis Gothoburgensis.

Haiman, J. (1994) 'Ritualization and the development of language', in W. Pagliuca (ed.) *Perspectives on Grammaticalization*, Amsterdam: John Benjamins.

——(1998) *Talk is Cheap: Sarcasm, Alienation, and the Evolution of Language*, New York: Oxford University Press.

Hajičová, E. (1987) 'Focussing: a meeting point of linguistics and artificial intelligence', in P. Jocrand and V. Sgurev (eds) *Artificial Intelligence II: Methodology, Systems, Applications*, Amsterdam: North Holland.

Hajikova, E. (1993) *Issues of Sentence Structure and Discourse Patterns. Theoretical and Computational Linguistics*, vol. 2, Prague: Charles University.

Hakulinen, A. and Selting, M. (eds) (2005) *Syntax and Lexis in Conversation*, Amsterdam: John Benjamins.

Hale, B. (1987) *Abstract Objects*, Oxford: Blackwell.

Hale, M. and Reiss, C. (1998) 'Formal and empirical arguments concerning phonological acquisition', *Linguistic Inquiry*, 29: 656–83.

Hall, A. (2007) 'Do discourse connectives encode procedures or concepts?', *Lingua*, 117: 149–74.

——(2008a) 'Free enrichment or hidden indexicals?', *Mind and Language*, 23: 426–56.

——(2008b) 'Free pragmatic processes and explicit utterance content', unpublished thesis, University of London.

Hall, C., Slembrouck, S. and Sarangi, S. (2007) *Language Practices in Social Work: Categorization and Accountability in Child Welfare*, London: Routledge.

Hall, J.K. (1993) 'The role of oral practices in the accomplishment of our everyday lives: the sociocultural dimension of interaction with implications for the learning of another language', *Applied Linguistics*, 14: 145–66.

——(1999) 'A prosaics of interaction: the development of interactional competence in another language', in E. Hinkel (ed.) *Culture in Second Language Teaching and Learning*, Cambridge: Cambridge University Press.

Hall, J.K., Cheng, A. and Carlson, M. (2006) 'Reconceptualizing multicompetence as a theory of language knowledge', *Applied Linguistics*, 27: 220–40.

Hall, K. (2003) 'Exceptional speakers: contested and problematized gender identities', in M. Meyerhoff and J. Holmes (eds) *Handbook of Language and Gender*, Malden, MA: Blackwell.

Halliday, M.A.K. (1967) 'Notes on transitivity and theme in English. Part II', *Journal of Linguistics*, 3: 199–244.

——(1970) 'Functional diversity in language as seen from a consideration of modality and mood in English', *Foundations of Language*, 6: 322–61.

——(1971) 'Linguistic function and literary style: and inquiry into the language of William Golding's *The Inheritors*', in S. Chatman (ed.) *Literary Style: A Symposium*, Oxford: Oxford University Press.

——(1978) *Language as Social Semiotic: The Social Interpretation of Language and Meaning*, London: Edward Arnold.

——(1985) *An Introduction to Functional Grammar*, London: Edward Arnold.

——(1993) 'Quantitative studies and probabilities in grammar', in M. Hoey (ed.) *Data, Description, Discourse*, London: HarperCollins.

——(1994) *An Introduction to Functional Grammar*, London: Edward Arnold.

Halliday, M.A.K. and Hasan, R. (1976) *Cohesion in English*, London: Longman.

Halliday, M.A.K. and Matthiessen, M.I.M. (2004) *An Introduction to Functional Grammar*, 3rd edn, London: Arnold.

Halliday, M.A.K., Teubert, W. and Yallop, C. (2002) *Lexicology and Corpus Linguistics: An Introduction*, London: Continuum.

Halmari, H. (1993) 'Inter-cultural business telephone conversations: a case of Finns vs. Anglo-Americans', *Applied Linguistics*, 14: 408–30.

Halper, A.S. and Cherney, L. (1998) 'Cognitive-communication problems after right hemisphere stroke: a review of intervention studies', *Topic in Stroke Rehabilitation*, 5: 1–10.

Halper, A.S., Cherney, L.R., Burns, M.S. and Mogil, S.I. (1996) *Clinical Management of Right Hemisphere Dysfunction*, 2nd edn, Gaithersburg, MD: Aspen.

Hamblin, C.L. (1970) *Fallacies*, London: Methuen.

Hamblin, J. and Gibbs, R. (1999) 'Why you can't kick the bucket as you slowly die: verbs in idiom comprehension', *Journal of Psycholinguistic Research*, 28: 25–39.

Hamilton, H.E. (1994) *Conversations with an Alzheimer's Patient: An International Sociolinguistic Study*, Cambridge: Cambridge University Press.

Hamlin, J., Wynn, K. and Bloom, P. (2007) 'Social evaluation by preverbal infants', *Nature*, 450: 557–59.

Han, C.-H. (1992) 'A comparative study of compliment responses: Korean females in Korean interactions and in English interactions', *Working Papers in Educational Linguistics*, 8: 17–31.

Hancock, J.T. and Purdy, K. (2000) 'Children's comprehension of critical and complimentary forms of verbal irony', *Journal of Cognition and Development*, 12: 227–40.

Hand, M. (1993) 'Parataxis and parentheticals', *Linguistics and Philosophy*, 16: 495–507.

Hanes, K., Andrews, D. and Pantelis, C. (1995) 'Cognitive flexibility and complex integration in Parkinson's disease, Huntington's disease, and schizophrenia', *Journal of the International Neuropsychological Society*, 1: 545–53.

Hanfling, O. (1989) *Wittgenstein's Later Philosophy*, London: Macmillan Press.

——(2001) *Philosophy and Ordinary Language: The Bent and Genius of Our Tongue*, London: Routledge.

Hanks, W. (1993) 'Metalanguage and pragmatics of deixis', in J. Lucy (ed.) *Reflexive Language: Reported Speech and Metapragmatics*, Cambridge: Cambridge University Press.

——(1995) *Language and Communicative Practice*, Boulder, CO: Westview Press.

——(1996) *Language and Communicative Practices*, Boulder, CO: Westview Press.

——(2005) 'Explorations in the deictic field', *Current Anthropology*, 46: 190–220.

Hansen, H.V. (2002) 'The straw thing of fallacy', *Argumentation*, 16: 133–55.

Happé, F. (1993) 'Communicative competence and theory of mind in autism: a test of relevance theory', *Cognition*, 48: 101–19.

——(1994a) 'An advanced test of theory of mind: understanding of story characters' thoughts and feelings by able autistic, mentally handicapped, and normal children and adults', *Journal of Autism and Developmental Disorders*, 24: 129–54.

——(1994b) *Autism: An Introduction to Psychological Theory*, Cambridge, MA: Harvard University Press.

——(1995) 'Understanding minds and metaphors: insights from the study of figurative language in autism', *Metaphor and Symbolic Activity*, 10: 275–95.

——(1996) 'Studying weak central coherence at low levels: children with autism do not succumb to visual illusions: a research note', *Journal of Child Psychology and Psychiatry*, 37: 873–77.

——(1997) 'Central coherence and theory of mind in autism: reading homographs in context', *British Journal of Developmental Psychology*, 15: 1–12.

Happé, F. and Frith, U. (2006) 'The weak coherence account: detail-focused cognitive style in autism spectrum disorders', *Journal of Autism and Developmental Disorders*, 36: 5–25.

Happé, F. and Loth, E. (2002) '"Theory of mind" and tracking speakers' intentions', *Mind and Language*, 17: 24–36.

Happé, F., Brownell, H. and Winner, E. (1999) 'Acquired "theory of mind" impairments following stroke', *Cognition*, 70: 211–40.

Happé, F., Winner, E. and Brownell, H. (1998) 'The getting of wisdom: theory of mind in old age', *Developmental Psychology*, 34: 358–62.

Harciarek, M., Heilman, K.M. and Jodzio, K. (2006) 'Defective comprehension of emotional faces and prosody as a result of right hemisphere stroke: modality versus emotion-type-specificity', *Journal of the International Neuropsychological Society*, 12: 774–81.

Harding, C.G. and Golinkoff, R.M. (1979) 'The origins of intentional vocalizations in prelinguistic infants', *Child Development*, 50: 33–40.

Hare, B. and Tomasello, M. (2004) 'Chimpanzees are more skilful at competitive than cooperative cognitive tasks', *Animal Behavior*, 68: 571–81.

Harman, G. (1986) *Change in View: Principles of Reasoning*, Cambridge, MA: MIT Press.

Harnish, R.M. (1976) 'Logical form and implicature', in T. Beaver, J. Katz and D.T. Langendoen (eds) *An Integrated Theory of Linguistic Ability*, New York: Crowell.

——(1993) 'Communicating with proverbs', *Communication and Cognition*, 16: 256–90.

Harriet, J. (1987) 'Sentence connectors in French children's monologue performance', *Journal of Pragmatics*, 11: 607–21.

Harris, R. (1980) *The Language-Makers*, London: Duckworth.

——(1981) *The Language Myth*, London: Duckworth.

——(1988) *Language, Saussure, and Wittgenstein: How to Play Games with Words*, London and New York: Routledge.

——(1998) *Introduction to Integrational Linguistics*, Kidlington and Oxford: Pergamon.

Harris, S. (1984) 'Questions as a mode of control in magistrates' courts', *International Journal of the Sociology of Language*, 49: 5–27.

——(1989) 'Defendant resistance to power and control in court', in H. Coleman (ed.) *Working with Language: A Multidisciplinary Consideration of Language Use in Work Contexts*, Berlin: Mouton de Gruyter.

——(1995) 'Pragmatics and power', *Journal of Pragmatics*, 23: 117–35.

——(2001a) 'Being politically impolite: extending politeness theory to adversarial political discourse', *Discourse and Society*, 12: 451–72.

——(2001b) 'Fragmented narratives and multiple tellers: witness and defendant accounts in trials', *Discourse Studies*, 3: 53–74.

——(2003) 'Politeness and power: making and responding to "requests" in institutional settings', *Text*, 23: 27–52.

——(2007) 'Politeness and power', in C. Llamas, L. Mullany and P. Stockwell (eds) *Routledge Companion to Sociolinguistics*, London: Routledge.

Harris, S., Grainger, K. and Mullany, L. (2006) 'The pragmatics of political apologies', *Discourse and Society*, 17: 715–37.

Harrow, M. and Quinlan, D. (1977) 'Is disordered thinking unique to schizophrenia?', *Archives of General Psychiatry*, 34: 15–21.

Harrow, M., Grossman, L.S., Silverstein, M.L. and Meltzer, H.Y. (1982) 'Thought pathology in manic and schizophrenic patients', *Archives of General Psychiatry*, 39: 665–71.

Hart, L.A. ([1961] 1994) *The Concept of Law*, Oxford: Clarendon Press.

Hartley, L.L. and Jensen, P. (1991) 'Narrative and procedural discourse after closed head injury', *Brain Injury*, 5: 267–85.

——(1992) 'Three discourse profiles of closed-head-injured speakers: theoretical and clinical implications', *Brain Injury*, 6: 271–382.

Hartung, M. (1998) *Ironie in der Alltagssprache*, Opladen and Wiesbaden, Germany: Westdeutscher Verlag.

Harvey, D. (1996) *Justice, Nature, and the Geography of Difference*, Oxford: Blackwell.

Harvey, K., Brown, B., Crawford, P., Macfarlane, A. and McPherson, A. (2007) 'Am I normal? Teenagers, sexual health and the internet', *Social Science and Medicine*, 65: 771–81.

Harvey, P.D. (1983) 'Speech competence in manic and schizophrenic psychosis: the association between clinically rated thought disorder and cohesion and reference performance', *Journal of Abnormal Psychology*, 92: 368–77.

Harweg, R. (1968) *Pronomina und Textkonstitution*, Munich: Fink.

Hasan, R. (1984) 'Coherence and cohesive harmony', in J. Flood (ed.) *Understanding Reading Comprehension*, Delaware: International Reading Association.

Hash, G. (1999) *Oral History*, Umatilla, OR. Online. Available: www.ccrh.org/comm/umatilla/oralhis/grghash.htm (accessed 4 July 2008).

Haspelmath, M. (1997) *Indefinite Pronouns*, Oxford: Oxford University Press.

——(1999a) 'Explaining article-possessor complementarity: economic motivation in noun phrase syntax', *Language*, 75: 227–43.

——(1999b) 'Why is grammaticalization irreversible?', *Linguistics*, 37: 1043–68.

Hassall, T. (2001) 'Do learners thank too much in Indonesian?', *Australian Review of Applied Linguistics*, 24: 97–112.

Hatim, B. and Mason, I. (1990) *Discourse and the Translator*, London: Longman.

Hatta, T., Hasegawa, J. and Wanner, P.J. (2004) 'Differential processing of implicature in individuals with left and right brain damage', *Journal of Clinical and Experimental Neuropsychology*, 26: 667–76.

Hauger, B. (1994) *Johan Nicolai Madvig: The Language Theory of a Classical Philologist*, Münster, Germany: Nodus.

Haugh, M. (2007a) 'The co-constitution of politeness implicature in conversation', *Journal of Pragmatics*, 39: 84–110.

——(2007b) 'The discursive challenge to politeness research: an interactional alternative', *Journal of Politeness Research*, 3: 295–318.

Hauser, M. (1996) *The Evolution of Communication*, Cambridge, MA: MIT Press.

Hauser, M., Chomsky, N. and Fitch, T. (2002) 'The faculty of language: who has it, what is it and how did it evolve?', *Science*, 298: 1569–79.

Haverkate, H. (1992) 'Deictic categories as mitigating devices', *Pragmatics*, 2: 505–22.

Haviland, J. (1979) 'Guugu-Yimidhirr brother-in-law language', *Language in Society*, 8: 365–93.

Haviland, S. and Clark, H. (1974) 'What's new? Acquiring new information as a process in comprehension', *Journal of Verbal Learning and Verbal Behavior*, 13: 512–21.

Hawkins, J.A. (1978) *Definiteness and Indefiniteness*, Atlantic Highlands, NJ: Humanities Press.

——(1991) 'On (in)definite articles: implicatures and (un)grammaticality prediction', *Journal of Linguistics*, 27: 405–42.

Hawkins, R. and Chan, C. (1997) 'The partial availability of Universal Grammar in second language acquisition: the "failed functional features hypothesis"', *Second Language Research*, 13: 187–226.

Hawkins, R. and Hattori, H. (2006) 'Interpretation of English multiple wh-questions by Japanese speakers: a missing uninterpretable feature account', *Second Language Research*, 22: 269–301.

Haworth, K. (2006) 'The dynamics of power and resistance in police interview discourse', *Discourse and Society*, 17: 739–60.

——(to appear) 'Police interview discourse and its role as evidence', in M. Coulthard and A. Johnson (eds) *Routledge Handbook of Forensic Linguistics*, London: Routledge.

Hay, J. (1994) 'Jocular abuse patterns in mixed-group interaction', *Wellington Working Papers in Linguistics*, 6: 26–55.

——(1996) 'No laughing matter: gender and humour support strategies', *Wellington Working Papers in Linguistics*, 8: 1–24.

Hayek, F.A. von (1967) *Studies in Philosophy, Politics and Economics*, Chicago, IL: University of Chicago Press.

Hayes, J.R. (1996) 'A new framework for understanding cognition and affect in writing', in C.M. Levy and S. Ransdell (eds) *The Science of Writing*, Mahwah, NJ: Erlbaum.

He, A.W. (1996) 'Narrative processes and institutional activities: recipient guided storytelling in academic counselling encounters', *Pragmatics*, 6: 205–16.

He, Z.R. (2000) 'A further study of pragmatic vagueness', *Journal of Foreign Languages*, 125: 7–13.

Heath, C. (1984) 'Talk and recipiency: sequential organization in speech and body movement', in J.M. Atkinson and J. Heritage (eds) *Structures of Social Action: Studies in Conversation Analysis*, Cambridge: Cambridge University Press.

——(1986) *Body Movement and Speech in Medical Interaction*, Cambridge: Cambridge University Press.

——(2004) 'Analysing face to face interaction: video, the visual and material', in D. Silverman (ed.) *Qualitative Research: Theory, Method and Practice*, 2nd edn, London: Sage.

Heath, C. and Luff, P. (2000) *Technology in Action*, Cambridge: Cambridge University Press.

Heath, J. (1995) 'Threats, promises, and communicative action', *European Journal of Philosophy*, 3: 225–41.

——(2001) *Communicative Action and Rational Choice*, Cambridge, MA: MIT Press.

Heath, S.B. (1982) 'What no bedtime story means: narrative skills at home and school', *Language in Society*, 11: 49–76.

Hedberg, N. (2000) 'The referential status of clefts', *Language*, 76: 891–920.

Hedberg, N., Sosa, J.M. and Fadden, L. (2004) 'Meanings and configurations of questions in English', paper presented at Speech Prosody 2004, Nara, Japan, March 2004. Online. Available: www.isca-speech.org/archive/sp2004/sp04_309.pdf (accessed 26 August 2008).

Heidegger, M. (1927) *Sein und Zeit*, Tübingen, Germany: Mohr; trans. J. Macquarrie and E. Robinson (1962) *Being and Time*, London: SCM.

Heim, I. (1982) 'The semantics of definite and indefinite noun phrases', unpublished thesis, University of Massachusetts.

——(1983a) 'File change semantics and the familiarity theory of definiteness', in R. Bauerle, C. Schwarze and A. von Stechow (eds) *Meaning, Use and the Interpretation of Language*, Berlin: Walter de Gruyter.

——(1983b) 'On the projection problem for presupposition', in M. Barlow, D.P. Flickinger and M.T. Westcoat (eds) *Proceedings of the West Coast Conference on Formal Linguistics*, vol. 2., Stanford, CA: Stanford Linguistics Association.

——(1989) *The Semantics of Definite and Indefinite Noun Phrases*, New York: Garland Press.

——(1990) 'E-type pronouns and donkey anaphora', *Linguistics and Philosophy*, 13: 133–77.

——(1991) 'Articles and definiteness', in A.V. Stechow and D. Wunderlich (eds) *Semantics: An International Handbook Of Contemporary Research*, Berlin: De Gruyter.

——(1992) 'Presupposition projection and the semantics of attitude verbs', *Journal of Semantics*, 9: 183–221.

Heine, B. and Kuteva, T. (2002) *World Lexicon of Grammaticalization*, Cambridge: Cambridge University Press.

Heit, E. (2000) 'Properties of inductive reasoning', *Psychonomic Bulletin and Review*, 7: 569–92.

Held, G. (2005) 'Politeness in Italy', in L. Hickey and M. Stewart (eds) *Politeness in Europe*, Clevedon: Multilingual Matters.

Heller, D. and Wolter, L. (2008) '"That is Rosa": identificational sentences as intensional predication', in A. Grønn (ed.) *Proceedings of Sinn und Bedeutung 12*, Oslo: Department of Literature, Area Studies, and European Languages, University of Oslo.

Heller, D., Grodner, D. and Tanenhaus, M.K. (to appear) 'Taking perspective: evidence for real-time integration of information about common ground', in U. Sauerland and K. Yatsushiro (eds) *Palgrave Studies in Pragmatics: Language and Cognition*, Basingstoke: Palgrave Macmillan

Hendriks, P. and de Hoop, H. (2001) 'Optimality theoretic semantics', *Linguistics and Philosophy*, 24: 1–32.

Hendriks, P. and Spenader, J. (2006). 'When production precedes comprehension: An optimization approach to the acquisition of pronouns', *Language Acquisition: A Journal of Developmental Linguistics*, 13: 319–48.

Hepburn, A. (2004) 'Crying: notes on description, transcription, and interaction', *Research on Language and Social Interaction*, 37: 251–91.

Herbert, R.K. (1986) 'Say "Thank You" – or something', *American Speech*, 61: 76–88.

——(1989) 'The ethnography of English compliments and compliment responses: a contrastive sketch', in W. Oleksy (ed.) *Contrastive Pragmatics*, Amsterdam and Philadelphia, PA: John Benjamins.

——(1990) 'Sex-based differences in compliment behavior', *Language in Society*, 19: 201–24.

——(1991) 'The sociology of compliment work: an ethnocontrastive study of Polish and English compliments', *Multilingua*, 10: 381–402.

Heritage, J. (2007) 'Territories of knowledge, territories of experience: (not so) empathic moments in interaction', keynote speech delivered at the *XVth Symposium About Language and Society, Austin (SALSA)*, Austin, Texas, April 2007.

Heritage, J. and Maynard, D. (eds) (2006) *Communication in Medical Care: Interaction between Primary Medical Care and Patients*, Cambridge: Cambridge University Press.

Herman, D. (2000) 'Pragmatic constraints on narrative processing: actants and anaphora resolution in a corpus of North Carolina ghost stories', *Journal of Pragmatics*, 32: 959–1001.

——(2002) *Story Logic: Problems and Possibilities of Narrative*, Lincoln, NE and London: University of Nebraska Press.

Herman, V. (1995) *Dramatic Discourse*, London: Routledge.

Herring, S. (1996) *Computer-Mediated Communication: Linguistic, Social and Cross-Cultural Perspectives*, Amsterdam: John Benjamins.

Herrmann, E., Call, J., Hernández-Lloreda, M.-H., Hare, B. and Tomasello, M. (2007) 'Humans have evolved specialized skills of social cognition: the cultural intelligence hypothesis', *Science*, 317: 1360–66.

Hester, S. and Eglin, P. (eds) (1997) *Culture in Action: Studies in Membership Categorization Analysis*, Washington, DC: University Press of America.

Heydon, G. (2003) '"Now I didn't mean to break his teeth": applying topic management to problems of power asymmetry and voluntary confessions', in S. Sarangi and T. van Leuven (eds) *Applied Linguistics and Communities of Practice*, London: Continuum.

——(2005) *The Language of Police Interviewing*, Basingstoke: Palgrave Macmillan.

Heyes, C.M. (1998) 'Theory of mind in non-human primates', *Behavioral and Brain Sciences*, 21: 101–34.

Hickey, L. (ed.) (1989) *The Pragmatics of Style*, London: Routledge.

——(1991) 'Surprise, surprise, but do so politely', *Journal of Pragmatics*, 15: 367–72.

——(1998) 'Perlocutionary equivalence: marking, exegesis and recontextualisation', in L. Hickey (ed.) *The Pragmatics of Translation*, Clevedon: Multilingual Matters.

——(2005) 'Politeness in Spain: thanks but no "Thanks"', in L. Hickey and M. Stewart (eds) *Politeness in Europe*, Clevedon: Multilingual Matters.

Higginbotham, D.J. and Wilkins, D.P. (2006) 'The short story of Frametalker: an interactive AAC device', *Perspectives on Augmentative and Alternative Communication*, 15: 18–22.

Higginbotham, J., Pianesi, F. and Varzi, A. (eds) (2000) *Speaking of Events*, Oxford: Oxford University Press.

Higgins, R. (1973) 'The pseudocleft construction in English', Ph.D. dissertation, Massachusetts Institute of Technology.

Hill, J. (1992) 'Today there is no respect: nostalgia, "respect", and oppositional discourse in Mexicano (Nahuatl) language ideology', *Pragmatics*, 2: 263–80.

Hills, D. (1997) 'Aptness and truth in verbal metaphor', *Philosophical Topics*, 25: 117–53.

Hilmy, S.S. (1987) *The Later Wittgenstein: The Emergence of a New Philosophical Method*, Oxford: Basil Blackwell.

Hinde, R.A. (ed.) (1972) *Nonverbal Communication*, Cambridge: Cambridge University Press.

Hindermarsh, J. and Heath, C. (2000) 'Embodied reference: a study of deixis in workplace interaction', *Journal of Pragmatics*, 32: 1855–78.

Hinds, J. (1984) 'Topic maintenance in Japanese narratives and Japanese conversational interaction', *Discourse Processes*, 7: 465–82.

Hinkel, E. (1997) 'Indirectness in L1 and L2 academic writing', *Journal of Pragmatics*, 27: 361–86.

Hintikka, J. (1962) *Knowledge and Belief*, Ithaca, NY: Cornell University Press.

——(1986) 'The semantics of *a certain*', *Linguistic Inquiry*, 17: 331–36.

Hirschberg, J. (1985) 'A theory of scalar implicature', published thesis, University of Pennsylvania; published 1991 in the series *Outstanding Dissertations in Linguistics*, New York: Garland.

——(1991) *A Theory of Scalar Implicature*, New York: Garland.

——(2004) 'Pragmatics and intonation', in L.R. Horn and G. Ward (eds) *The Handbook of Pragmatics*, Oxford: Blackwell.

Hirschberg, J. and Litman, D. (1993) 'Empirical studies on the disambiguation of cue phrases', *Computational Linguistics*, 19: 501–30.

Hirst, G. (1987) *Semantic Interpretation and the Resolution of Ambiguity*, Cambridge: Cambridge University Press.

Hobbs, J.R. (1978) 'Resolving pronoun references', *Lingua*, 44: 311–38.

——(1979) 'Coherence and coreference', *Cognitive Science*, 3: 67–90.

Hobbs, J.R., Stickel, M.E., Appelt, D. and Martin, P. (1993) 'Interpretation as abduction', *Artificial Intelligence*, 63: 69–142.

Hockett, C.F. (1961) 'The problem of universals in language', in J.H. Greenberg (ed.) *Universals of Language*, Cambridge, MA: Cambridge University Press.

Hoey, M. (1991) *Patterns of Lexis in Text*, Oxford: Oxford University Press.

——(ed.) (1993) *Data, Description, Discourse: Papers on the English Language in Honour of John McH Sinclair*, London: HarperCollins.

——(2005) *Lexical Priming: A New Theory of Words and Language*, London and New York: Routledge.

Holland, A.L. (1991) 'Pragmatics aspects of intervention in aphasia', *Journal of Neurolinguistics*, 6: 197–211.

Holland, D. and Quinn, N. (1987) *Cultural Models in Language and Thought*, Cambridge: Cambridge University Press.

Hollich, G.J., Hirsh-Pasek, K., Golinkoff, R.M., Brand, R.J., Brown, E., Chung, H.L., Hennon, E. and Rocroi, C. (2000) 'Breaking the language barrier: an emergentist coalition model for the origins of word learning', *Monographs of the Society for Research in Child Development*, 65: 1–123.

Holliday, A. (1999) 'Small cultures', *Applied Linguistics*, 20: 237–64.

Holly, W. (1990) *Politikersprache: Inszenierungen und Rollenkonflikte im Informellen Sprachhandeln eines Bundestagsabgeordneten*, Berlin: De Gruyter.

Holmes, J. (2006) *Gendered Talk at Work: Constructing Gender Identity through Workplace Discourse*, New York and Oxford: Blackwell.

——(1984a) 'Modifying illocutionary force', *Journal of Pragmatics*, 8: 345–65.

——(1984b) 'Women's language: a functional-approach', *General Linguistics*, 24: 149–78.

——(1986a) 'Compliments and compliment responses in New Zealand English', *Anthropological Linguistics*, 28: 485–508.

——(1986b) 'Functions of "you know" in women's and men's speech', *Language in Society*, 15: 1–22.

——(1988) 'Paying compliments: a sex-preference politeness strategy', *Journal of Pragmatics*, 12: 445–65.

——(1995) *Women, Men and Politeness*, London: Longman.

——(1997) 'Women, language and identity', *Journal of Sociolinguistics*, 2: 195–223.

——(1998a) 'Apologies in New Zealand English', in J. Cheshire and P. Trudgill (eds) *The Sociolinguistics Reader: Gender and Discourse*, volume 2, London: Arnold.

——(1998b) 'Narrative structure: some contrasts between Maori and Pakeha story-telling', *Multilingua*, 17: 25–57.

——(2000) 'Politeness, power and provocation: how humour functions in the workplace', *Discourse Studies*, 2: 159–85.

——(2006) 'Sharing a laugh: pragmatic aspects of humor and gender in the workplace', *Journal of Pragmatics*, 38: 26–50.

Holmes, J. and Major, G. (2003) 'Talking to patients: the complexity of communication on the ward', *Vision: A Journal of Nursing*, 11: 4–9.

Holmes, J. and Schnurr, S. (2005) 'Politeness, humor and gender in the workplace: negotiating norms and identifying contestation', *Journal of Politeness Research*, 1: 121–49.

——(2006) 'Doing "femininity" at work: more than just relational practice', *Journal of Sociolinguistics*, 10: 31–51.

Holmes, J. and Stubbe, M. (2003a) 'Doing disagreement at work: a sociolinguistic approach', *Australian Journal of Communication*, 30: 53–77.

——(2003b) *Power and Politeness in the Workplace: A Sociolinguistic Analysis of Talk at Work*, London: Longman.

Holmes, J., Marra, M. and Burns, L. (2001) 'Women's humour in the workplace: a quantitative analysis', *Australian Journal of Communication*, 28: 83–108.

Honeck, R.P. and Temple, J.G. (1994) 'Proverbs: the extended conceptual base and great chain metaphor theories', *Metaphor and Symbolic Activity*, 9: 85–112.

Honeck, R.P. and Welge, J. (1997) 'Creation of proverbial wisdom in the laboratory', *Journal of Psycholinguistic Research*, 26: 605–29.

Hong, B. (1985) 'Politeness in Chinese: impersonal pronouns and personal greetings', *Anthropological Linguistics*, 27: 204–13.

Honneth, A. and Joas, H. (1991) *Communicative Action: Essays on Jürgen Habermas's 'The Theory of Communicative Action'*, Cambridge: Polity Press.

Hoover, D.L. (1999) *Language and Style in The Inheritors*, Lanham, MD: University Press of America.

Hope, J. (1994) 'The use of "thou" and "you" in Early Modern spoken English: evidence from depositions in the Durham ecclesiastical court records', in D. Kastovsky (ed.) *Studies in Early Modern English*, Berlin: Mouton de Gruyter.

Hopper, P.J. (1991) 'On some principles of grammaticalization', in E.C. Traugott and B. Heine (eds) *Approaches to Grammaticalization, Volume I: Theoretical and Methodological Issues*, Amsterdam: John Benjamins.

Hopper, P.J. and Traugott, E.C. (2003) *Grammaticalization*, 2nd edn, Cambridge: Cambridge University Press.

Hopper, R. (1992) *Telephone Conversation*, Bloomington and Indianapolis, IN: Indiana University Press.

Horn, L.R. (1972) 'On the semantic properties of logical operators in English', unpublished thesis, University of California–Los Angeles.

——(1984) 'Toward a new taxonomy for pragmatic inference: Q-based and R-based Implicature', in D. Schiffrin (ed.) *Meaning, Form, and Use in Context (GURT '84)*, Washington, DC: Georgetown University Press.

——(1985) 'Metalinguistic negation and pragmatic ambiguity', *Language*, 61: 121–74.

——(1986) 'Presupposition, theme and variations', in A.M. Farley, P. Farley and K.-E. McCullough (eds) *The 22nd Regional Meeting of the Chicago Linguistic Society: Parasession on Pragmatics and Grammatical Theory*, Chicago, IL: Chicago Linguistic Society.

——(1988) 'Pragmatic theory', in F.J. Newmeyer (ed.) *Linguistics: The Cambridge Survey*, volume 1, Cambridge: Cambridge University Press.

——(1989) *A Natural History of Negation*, Chicago: University of Chicago Press; reissued 2001, Stanford, CA: CSLI.

——(1991) 'Duplex negatio affirmat … : the economy of double negation', in L. Dobrin, L. Nichols and R. Rodriguez (eds) *Proceedings of the 27th Meeting of the Chicago Linguistic Society, Part Two: Parasession on Negation*, Chicago, IL: Chicago Linguistic Society.

——(1992) 'The said and the unsaid', in C. Barker and D. Dowty (eds) *SALT 2: Proceedings of the Second Conference on Semantics and Linguistic Theory*, Columbus, OH: Ohio State University.

——(1993) 'Economy and redundancy in a dualistic model of natural language', in S. Shores and M. Vikuna (eds) *SKY 1993: The 1993 Yearbook of the Linguistic Association of Finland*, Helsinki: Linguistic Association of Finland.

——(1996) 'Presupposition and implicature', in S. Lappin (ed.) *The Handbook of Contemporary Semantic Theory*, Oxford: Blackwell; 299–320.

——(2000) 'From *If* to *Iff*: conditional perfection as pragmatic strengthening', *Journal of Pragmatics*, 32: 289–326.

——(2004) 'Implicature', in L. Horn and G. Ward (eds) *The Handbook of Pragmatics*, Oxford: Blackwell.

——(2005) 'Current issues in neo-Gricean pragmatics', *Intercultural Pragmatics*, 2: 191–204.

——(2006) 'The border wars: a neo-Gricean perspective', in K. Turner and K. von Heusinger (eds) *Where Semantics Meets Pragmatics*, Oxford: Elsevier.

——(2007a) 'Neo-Gricean pragmatics: a Manichaean manifesto', in N. Burton-Roberts (ed.) *Advances in Pragmatics*, Basingstoke: Palgrave.

——(2007b) 'Toward a Fregean pragmatics: Voraussetzung, Nebengedanke, Andeutung', in I. Kecskes and L.R. Horn (eds) *Explorations in Pragmatics: Linguistic, Cognitive and Intercultural Aspects*, Berlin: Mouton de Gruyter.

——(to appear a) 'William James + 40: issues in the investigation of implicature', in K. Petrus (ed.) *Meaning and Analysis: Themes from H. Paul Grice*, Online. Available: www.yale.edu/linguist/faculty/doc/horn07_petrus.pdf (accessed 17 March 2008).

——(to appear b) 'Lexical pragmatics and the geometry of opposition: the mystery of **nall* and **nand* revisited', in J.-Y. Béziau (ed.) *Papers from the World Congress on the Square of Opposition*, Montreux, Switzerland; Online. Available: www.yale.edu/linguist/faculty/doc/horn07_SQUOP.pdf (accessed 17 March 2008).

Horn, L.R. and Bayer, S. (1984) 'Short-circuited implicature: a negative contribution', *Linguistics and Philosophy*, 7: 397–414.

Horn, L.R. and Ward, G. (2006) 'On the other hand: a response to some reflections on a recent handbook', *Intercultural Pragmatics*, 3: 107–10.

——(eds) (2004) *The Handbook of Pragmatics*, Oxford: Blackwell.

Hornby, M. (2005) *Oxford Advanced Learner's Dictionary of Current English*, 7th edn, Oxford: Oxford University Press.

Horne, M., Hansson, P., Bruce, G., Frid, J. and Filipsson, M. (2001) 'Cue words and the topic structure of spoken discourse: the case of Swedish *men* "but"', *Journal of Pragmatics*, 33: 1061–81.

Hornsby, J. and Longworth, G. (2006) 'Commentary on Austin', in J. Hornsby and G. Longworth (eds) *Reading Philosophy of Language: Selected Texts with Interactive Commentary*, Oxford: Blackwell.

Houck, N. and Gass, S.M. (1996) 'Non-native refusals: a methodological perspective', in S. M. Gass and J. Neu (eds) *Speech Acts Across Cultures: Challenges to Communication in a Second Language*, New York: Mouton de Gruyter.

Hough, M.S. (1990) 'Narrative comprehension in adults with right and left hemisphere brain-damage: theme organization', *Brain and Language*, 38: 253–77.

Hough, M.S. and Barrow, I. (2003) 'Descriptive discourse abilities of traumatic brain-injured adults', *Aphasiology*, 17: 183–91.

House, J. (1990) 'Intonation structures and pragmatic interpretation', in S. Ramsaran (ed.) *Studies in the Pronunciation of English*, London: Routledge.

——(2000) 'Understanding misunderstanding: a pragmatic-discourse approach to analyzing mismanaged rapport in talk across cultures', in H. Spencer-Oatey (ed.) *Culturally Speaking: Managing Rapport through Talk across Cultures*, London: Continuum.

——(2003) 'English as a lingua franca: a threat to multilingualism?', *Journal of Sociolinguistics*, 7: 556–78.

——(2006a) 'Communicative styles in English and German', *European Journal of English*, 10: 249–67.

——(2006b) 'Constructing a context with intonation', *Journal of Pragmatics*, 38: 1542–58.

House, J. and Kasper, G. (1981) 'Politeness markers in English and German', in F. Coulmas (ed.) *Conversational Routine*, The Hague: Mouton.

Houtkoop, H. and Mazeland, H. (1985) 'Turns and discourse units in everyday conversation', *Journal of Pragmatics*, 9: 595–619.

Houtkoop-Steenstra, H. (1991) 'Opening sequences in Dutch telephone conversations', in D. Boden and D. Zimmerman (eds) *Talk and Social Structure*, Berkeley: University of California Press.

Howarth, D. (2000) *Discourse*, Buckingham: Open University Press.

Huang, Y. (1991a) 'A neo-Gricean pragmatic theory of anaphora', *Journal of Linguistics*, 27: 301–35.

Huang, Y. (1991b) 'A pragmatic analysis of control in Chinese', in J. Verschueren (ed.) *Levels of Linguistic Adaptation*, Amsterdam: John Benjamins.

——(1992) 'Against Chomsky's typology of empty categories', *Journal of Pragmatics*, 17: 1–29.

——(1994) *The Syntax and Pragmatics of Anaphora*, Cambridge: Cambridge University Press.

——(1995) 'On null subjects and null objects in generative grammar', *Linguistics*, 33: 1081–123.

——(1996) 'A note on the head-movement analysis of long-distance reflexives', *Linguistics*, 34: 833–40.

——(2000a) *Anaphora: A Cross-linguistic Study*, Oxford: Oxford University Press.

——(2000b) 'Discourse anaphora: four theoretical models', *Journal of Pragmatics*, 32: 151–76.

——(2001) 'Reflections on theoretical pragmatics', *Waiguoyu*, 131: 2–14.

——(2002) 'Logophoric marking in East Asian languages', in T. Güldemann and M. von Roncador (eds) *Reported Discourse: A Meeting Ground for Different Linguistic Domains*, Amsterdam: John Benjamins.

——(2003) 'On neo-Gricean pragmatics', *International Journal of Pragmatics*, 13: 87–110.

——(2004a) 'Anaphora and the pragmatics-syntax interface', in L.R. Horn and G. Ward (eds) *The Handbook of Pragmatics*, Oxford: Blackwell.

——(2004b) 'Neo-Gricean pragmatic theory: looking back on the past; looking ahead to the future', *Waiguoyu*, 149: 2–25.

——(2006a) 'Speech acts', in K. Brown (ed.) *The Encyclopedia of Languages and Linguistics*, 2nd edn, vol. 11, New York: Elsevier Science.

——(2006b) 'Anaphora, cataphora, exophora, logophoricity', in K. Brown (ed.) *The Encyclopedia of Languages and Linguistics*, 2nd edn, vol. 1, New York: Elsevier Science.

——(2007) *Pragmatics*, Oxford: Oxford University Press.

Hübler, A. (1983) *Understatements and Hedges in English*, Amsterdam: Benjamins.

Huckin, T. (1997) 'Cultural aspects of genre knowledge', *AILA Review*, 12: 68–77.

Huddleston, R. and Pullum, G.K. (2001) *The Cambridge Grammar of the English Language*, Cambridge: Cambridge University Press.

Hudson, T. (2001) 'Indicators for pragmatic instruction: some quantitative measures', in K. Rose and G. Kasper (eds) *Pragmatics in Language Teaching*, Cambridge: Cambridge University Press.

Hudson, T., Detmer, E. and Brown, J.D. (1992) *A Framework for Testing Cross-Cultural Pragmatics*, Honolulu, HI: Second Language Teaching and Curriculum Center, University of Hawaii at Manoa.

——(1995) *Developing Prototypic Measures of Cross-Cultural Pragmatics*, Honolulu, HI: Second Language Teaching and Curriculum Center, University of Hawaii at Manoa.

Huebner, T. (1983) *A Longitudinal Analysis of the Acquisition of English*, Ann Arbor, MI: Karoma.

Hugill, D. (2004) 'Commercial negotiation: reaching for disagreement within an overall project of reaching for agreement', *Culture and Organization*, 10: 163–87.

Humphrey, N. (1976) 'The social function of the intellect', in P. Bateson and R. Hinde (eds) *Growing Points in Ecology*, Cambridge: Cambridge University Press.

——(1984) *Consciousness Regained*, Oxford: Oxford University Press.

Hüning, M. (2007) *TextSTAT – Simple Text Analysis Tool 2.7*, Department of Dutch Linguistics, Free University of Berlin. Online. Available: www.niederlandistik.fu-berlin.de/textstat/software-en.html (accessed 14 May 2008).

Hunston, S. (1995) 'A corpus study of some English verbs of attribution', *Functions of Language*, 2: 133–58.

——(2002) *Corpora in Applied Linguistics*, Cambridge: Cambridge University Press.

Hunston, S. and Francis, G. (2000) *Pattern Grammar: A Corpus-Driven Approach to the Lexical Grammar of English*, Amsterdam: John Benjamins.

Hunter, J.M.F. (1985) *Understanding Wittgenstein: Studies of Philosophical Investigations*, Edinburgh: Edinburgh University Press.

——(1990) *Wittgenstein on Words as Instruments: Lessons in Philosophical Psychology*, Edinburgh: Edinburgh University Press.

Hurewitz, F., Papafragou, A., Gleitman, L. and Gelman, R. (2006) 'Asymmetries in the acquisition of numbers and quantifiers', *Language Learning and Development*, 2: 77–96.

Hurford, J.R., Studdert-Kennedy, M. and Knight, C. (1998) *Approaches to the Evolution of Language: Social and Cognitive Bases*, Edinburgh: Edinburgh University Press.

Husserl, E. (1900–1) *Logical Investigations*, trans. J.N. Findlay, 1970, London: Routledge and Kegan Paul.

——(1913) *Ideas: General Introduction to Pure Phenomenology*, trans. W.R. Boyce Gibson (1931) London: George Allen and Unwin.

Hutchby, I. (2001) *Conversation and Technology: From the Telephone to the Internet*, Cambridge: Polity Press.

Hutchby, I. and Barnett, S. (2005) 'Aspects of the sequential organization of mobile phone conversation', *Discourse Studies*, 7: 147–72.

Hutchby, I. and Wooffitt, R. (2008) *Conversation Analysis: Principles, Practices and Applications*, 2nd edn, Cambridge: Polity.

Hutchins, E. (1980) *Culture and Inference*, Cambridge, MA: Harvard University Press.

——(1995) *Cognition in the Wild*, Cambridge, MA: MIT Press.

Huth, T. and Taleghani-Nikazm, C. (2006) 'How can insights from conversation analysis be directly applied to teaching pragmatics?', *Language Teaching Research*, 10: 53–79.

Hyland, K. (1994) 'Hedging in academic writing and EAP textbooks', *English for Specific Purposes*, 13: 239–56.

——(1996) 'Writing without conviction? Hedging in science research articles', *Applied Linguistics*, 17: 433–54.

——(1998a) 'Persuasion and context: the pragmatics of academic metadiscourse', *Journal of Pragmatics*, 30: 437–55.

——(1998b) *Hedging in Scientific Research Articles*, Amsterdam and Philadelphia, PA: John Benjamins.

——(1999) 'Talking to students: metadiscourse in introductory coursebooks', *English for Specific Purposes*, 18: 3–26.

——(2004) *Disciplinary Discourses: Social Interactions in Academic Writing*, Ann Arbor, MI: University of Michigan Press.

——(2005) *Metadiscourse: Exploring Interaction in Writing*, London: Continuum.

——(2006) *English for Academic Purposes: An Advanced Resource Book*, London: Routledge.

Hyland, K. and Milton, J. (1997) 'Qualification and certainty in L1 and L2 students' writing', *Journal of Second Language Writing*, 6: 183–206.

Hyland, K. and Tse, P. (2004) 'Metadiscourse in academic writing: a reappraisal', *Applied Linguistics*, 25: 156–77.

Hyltenstam, K. and Abrahamsson, N. (2003) 'Maturational constraints in SLA', in C. Doughty and M. Long (eds) *The Handbook of Second Language Acquisition*, Oxford: Blackwell.

Hymes, D. (1964a) 'Towards ethnographies of communication: the analysis of communicative events', *American Anthropologist*, 66: 12–25.

——(ed.) (1964b) *Language in Culture and Society: A Reader in Linguistics and Anthropology*, New York: Harper and Row.

——(1972a) 'Models of the interaction of language and social life', in J. Gumperz and D. Hymes (eds) *Directions in Sociolinguistics: The Ethnography of Communication*, New York: Holt, Rinehart and Winston.

——(1972b) 'On communicative competence', in J. Pride and J. Holmes (eds) *Sociolinguistics*, Harmondsworth: Penguin.

——(1974) *Foundations of Sociolinguistics*, Philadelphia: University of Pennsylvania Press.

——(1986) 'Discourse: scope without depth', *International Journal of the Sociology of Language*, 57: 49–89.

Iacono, T.A. (2003) 'Pragmatic development in individuals with developmental disabilities who use AAC', in J.C. Light, D.R. Beukelman and J. Reichle (eds) *Communicative Competence for Individuals who Use AAC: From Research to Effective Practice*, Baltimore, MD: Paul H. Brookes Publishing Co.

Ian, H. (2007) *The Discourse of Child Counseling*, Amsterdam: John Benjamins.

Ide, S. (1989) 'Formal forms and discernment: two neglected aspects of universals of linguistic politeness', *Multilingua*, 8: 223–48.

Iedema, R. and Sheeres, H. (2009) 'Organisational discourse' in F. Bargiela-Chiappini (ed.) *The Handbook of Business Discourse*, Edinburgh: Edinburgh University Press.

Ifantidou, E. (2001) *Evidentials and Relevance*, Amsterdam: John Benjamins.

——(2005) 'The semantics and pragmatics of metadiscourse', *Journal of Pragmatics*, 37: 1325–53.

Ifantidou-Trouki, E. (1993) 'Sentential adverbs and relevance', *Lingua*, 90: 69–90.

Ilie, C. (1994) *What Else Can I Tell You? A Pragmatic Study of English Rhetorical Questions as Discursive and Argumentative Acts*, Stockholm: Almqvist and Wiksell International.

——(1995a) 'The validity of rhetorical questions as arguments in the courtroom', in F.H. van Eemeren, R. Grootendorst, J.A. Blair and C.A. Willard (eds) *Special Fields and Cases. Proceedings of the Third International Conference on Argumentation*, Amsterdam: SICSAT.

——(1995b) 'On the translatability of rhetorical questions', in Y. Gambier and J. Tommola (eds) *Translation and Knowledge*, Finland: Åbo University.

——(1998) 'Questioning is not asking: the discursive functions of rhetorical questions in American talk shows', *Texas Linguistic Forum*, 39: 122–35.

——(1999) 'Question-response argumentation in talk shows', *Journal of Pragmatics*, 31: 975–99.

——(2006) 'Parliamentary discourse', in K. Brown (ed.) *Encyclopedia of Language and Linguistics*, Oxford: Elsevier.

Intachakra, S. (2004) 'Contrastive pragmatics and language teaching: apologies and thanks in English and Thai', *RELC Journal*, 35: 37–62.

Ionin, T. (2006) '*This* is definitely specific: specificity and definiteness in article systems', *Natural Language Semantics*, 14: 175–234.

Ionin, T., Ko, H. and Wexler, K. (2004) 'Article semantics in L2-acquisition: the role of specificity', *Language Acquisition*, 12: 3–69.

Ioup, G. (1977) 'Specificity and the interpretation of quantifiers', *Linguistics and Philosophy*, 1: 233–45.

Iran-Nejad, A., Ortony, A. and Rittenhouse, R.K. (1981) 'The comprehension of metaphorical uses of English by deaf children', *Journal of Speech and Hearing Research*, 24: 551–56.

Irvine, J. (1990) 'Registering affect: heteroglossia in the linguistic expression of emotion', in C. Lutz and L. Abu-Lughod (eds) *Language and the Politics of Emotion*, Cambridge: Cambridge University Press.

——(1992) 'Ideologies of honorific language', *Pragmatics* 2: 251–62.

Irwin, A. (2000) 'The explicit (re)production of power/knowledge as a means of (re)producing dominant discourses and power relations:

"you know" and "I know" in two contrasting London peer groups', *University of Surrey, Roehampton Working Papers in Linguistics*, 2: 44–92.

Ishida, H. (2006) 'Learners' perception and interpretation of contextualization cues in spontaneous Japanese conversation: backchannel cue Uun', *Journal of Pragmatics*, 38: 1943–81.

Ishida, M. (2006) 'Interactional competence and the use of modal expressions in decision-making activities: CA for understanding microgenesis of pragmatic competence', in K. Bardovi-Harlig, J.C. Félix-Brasdefer and A. Omar (eds) *Pragmatics and Language Learning, Volume 11*, Honolulu, HI: National Foreign Language Resource Center, University of Hawaii at Manoa.

Israel, M. (2001) 'Minimizers, maximizers, and the rhetoric of scalar reasoning', *Journal of Semantics*, 18: 297–331.

——(2004) 'The pragmatics of polarity', in L.R. Horn and G. Ward (eds) *The Handbook of Pragmatics*, Oxford: Blackwell.

Iten, C. (2005) *Linguistic Meaning, Truth Conditions and Relevance: The Case of Concessives*, Basingstoke, UK: Palgrave Macmillan.

Iten, C., Stainton, R. and Wearing, C. (2007) 'On restricting the evidence base for linguistics', in P. Thagard (ed.) *Philosophy of Psychology and Cognitive Science*, Oxford: Elsevier.

Ito, K. and Speer, S.R. (2008) 'Anticipatory effects of intonation: eye movements during instructed visual search', *Journal of Memory and Language*, 58: 541–73.

Ito, M. (2003) 'The contribution of voice quality to politeness in Japanese', paper presented at *Conference on Voice Quality: Functions, Analysis and Synthesis*, Geneva, Switzerland, August 2003.

Itoi, E. (1997) 'How to say "no": a comparative study of refusals between Japanese and New Zealand students', *The Society of English Studies*, 27: 149–72.

Ivanko, L.S. and Pexman, M.P. (2003) 'Context incongruity and irony processing', *Discourse Processes*, 35: 241–79.

Iverson, J.M. and Goldin-Meadow, S. (1997) 'What's communication got to do with it: gesture in blind children', *Developmental Psychology*, 33: 453–67.

——(2001) 'The resilience of gesture in talk: gesture in blind speakers and listeners', *Developmental Science*, 4: 416–22.

Jackendoff, R. (1972) *Semantic Interpretation in Generative Grammar*, Cambridge, MA: MIT Press.

——(1990) *Semantic Structures*, Cambridge, MA: MIT Press.

Jacobs, A. and Jucker, A.H. (1995) 'The historical perspective in pragmatics', in A.H. Jucker (ed.) *Historical Pragmatics: Pragmatic Developments in the History of English*, Amsterdam: John Benjamins.

Jacobs, J. (1991) 'Focus ambiguities', *Journal of Semantics*, 8: 1–36.

Jacquemet, M. (1994) 'T-offenses and meta-pragmatic attacks: strategies of interactional dominance', *Discourse and Society*, 5: 297–319.

Jaffe, A. (2000) 'Introduction: nonstandard orthography and nonstandard speech', *Journal of Sociolinguistics*, 17: 497–513.

Jäger, G. (2003) 'Learning constraint sub-hierarchies: the bidirectional gradual learning algorithm', in R. Blutner and H. Zeevat (eds) *Optimality Theory and Pragmatics*, New York: Palgrave Macmillan.

Jäger, G. and Blutner, R. (2000) 'Against lexical decomposition in syntax', in A.Z. Wyner (ed.) *Proceedings of the Fifteenth Annual Conference, IATL 7*, Haifa, Israel: University of Haifa.

——(2003) 'Competition and interpretation: the German adverb wieder ("again")', in C. Fabricius-Hansen, E. Lang and C. Maienborn (eds) *Handbook of Adjuncts*, Berlin: Mouton de Gruyter.

Jakobson, R. ([1957] 1971) *Selected Writings, Volume II: Word and Language*, ed. S. Rudy, Berlin and New York: Mouton de Gruyter.

——(1960) 'Closing statement: linguistics and poetics', in T.A. Sebeok (ed.) *Style in Language*, Cambridge, MA: MIT Press.

James, S.H. (1978) 'Effect of listener age and situation on the politeness of children's directives', *Journal of Psycholinguistic Research*, 7: 307–17.

James, S.L. and Seebach, M.A. (1982) 'The pragmatic function of children's questions', *Journal of Speech and Language Research*, 25: 2–11.

James, W. (1910) *Pragmatism: A New Name for Some Old Ways of Thinking*, New York: Longmans, Green, and Co.

Janse, M. and Tol, S. (eds) (2003) *Language Death and Language Maintenance: Theoretical, Practical, and Descriptive Approaches*, Amsterdam: John Benjamins.

Janssen, T. (1997) 'Compositionality', in J. van Benthem and A. ter Meulen (eds) *Handbook of Logic and Language*, Amsterdam: North-Holland Publishing Company.

Janzen, T. (2004) 'Space rotation, perspective shift, and verb morphology in ASL', *Cognitive Linguistics*, 15: 149–74.

——(2007) 'The expression of grammatical categories in signed languages', in E. Pizzuto, P. Pietrandrea and R. Simone (eds) *Verbal and Signed Languages: Comparing Structures, Constructs and Methodologies*, Berlin and New York: Mouton de Gruyter.

Janzen, T., Shaffer, B. and Wilcox, S. (1999) 'Signed language pragmatics', in J. Verschueren, J.-O. Östman, J. Blommaert and C. Bulcaen (eds) *Handbook of Pragmatics, Installment 1999*, Amsterdam and Philadelphia, PA: John Benjamins.

Jaswal, V. and Neely, L. (2007) 'Adults don't always know best: preschoolers use past reliability over age when learning new words', *Psychological Science*, 17: 757–58.

Jaszczolt, K.M. (1999) *Discourse, Beliefs, and Intentions: Semantic Defaults and Propositional Attitude Ascription*, Oxford: Elsevier Science.

——(2000) 'The default-based context-dependence of belief reports', in K.M. Jaszczolt (ed.) (2000) *The Pragmatics of Propositional Attitude Reports*, Oxford: Elsevier Science.

——(2002a) *Semantics and Pragmatics: Meaning in Language and Discourse*, London: Longman.

——(2002b) 'Against ambiguity and under-specification: evidence from presupposition as anaphora', *Journal of Pragmatics*, 34: 829–49.

——(2005) *Default Semantics: Foundations of a Compositional Theory of Acts of Communication*, Oxford: Oxford University Press.

——(2006) 'Default semantics', in K. Brown (ed.) *Encyclopedia of Language and Linguistics*, 2nd edn, Oxford: Elsevier.

——(to appear a) 'Semantics and pragmatics: the boundary issue', in K. von Heusinger, P. Portner and C. Maienborn (eds) *Semantics: An International Handbook of Natural Language Meaning*, Berlin: Mouton de Gruyter.

——(to appear b) 'Default semantics', in B. Heine and H. Narrog (eds) *The Oxford Handbook of Linguistic Analysis*, Oxford: Oxford University Press.

Jaworski, A. (1993) *The Power of Silence: Social and Pragmatic Perspectives*, Newbury Park, CA: Sage.

——(1994) 'Apologies and non-apologies: negotiation in speech act realisation', *Text*, 14: 185–206.

——(ed.) (1997a) *Silence: Interdisciplinary Perspectives*, Berlin: Mouton de Gruyter.

——(1997b) 'Aesthetic, communicative and political silences in Laurie Anderson's performance art', in A. Jaworski (ed.) *Silence: Interdisciplinary Perspectives*, Berlin: Mouton de Gruyter.

Jayez, J. and Tovena, L. (2006) 'Epistemic determiners', *Journal of Semantics*, 23: 217–50.

Jeannerod, M. (1994) 'The representing brain: neural correlates of motor intention and imagery', *Behavioral and Brain Sciences*, 17: 187–245.

Jefferson, G. (1973) 'A case of precision timing in ordinary conversation: overlapped tag-positioned address terms in closing sequences', *Semiotica*, 9: 47–96.

——(1985) 'An exercise in the transcription and analysis of laughter', in T.A. van Dijk (ed.) *Handbook of Discourse Analysis*, vol. 3, London: Academic Press.

——(1986) 'Notes on "latency" in overlap onset', *Human Studies*, 9: 153–83.

——(2004a) 'A sketch of some orderly aspects of overlap in natural conversation', in G.H. Lerner (ed.) *Conversation Analysis: Studies from the First Generation*, Amsterdam and Philadelphia, PA: John Benjamins.

——(2004b) 'Glossary of transcript symbols with an introduction', in G.H. Lerner (ed.) *Conversation Analysis: Studies from the First Generation*, Amsterdam and Philadelphia, PA: John Benjamins.

Jeffries, L. (2007) 'Journalistic constructions of Blair's apology for the intelligence leading to the Iraq War', in S. Johnson and A. Ensslin (eds) *Language in the Media: Representations, Identities, Ideologies*, London: Continuum.

Jensen, J.V. (1973) 'Communicative functions of silence', *A Review of General Semantics*, 30: 249–57.

Jeon, E.H. and Kaya, T. (2006) 'Effects of L2 instruction on interlanguage pragmatic development: a meta-analysis', in J.M. Norris and L. Ortega (eds) *Synthesizing Research on Language Learning and Teaching*, Amsterdam: Benjamins.

Jespersen, O. (1917) *Negation in English and Other Languages*, Copenhagen: Høst.

——(1922) *Language: Its Nature, Development and Origin*, London: Allen and Unwin.

Jian, G., Schmisseur, A. and Fairhurst, G. (2009) 'Organisational communication', in F. Bargiela-Chiappini (ed.) *The Handbook of Business Discourse*, Edinburgh: Edinburgh University Press.

Jiang, X.-Y. (2006) 'Cross-cultural pragmatic differences in US and Chinese press conferences: the case of the North Korea nuclear crisis', *Discourse and Society*, 17: 237–57.

Joanette, Y., Goulet, P. and Daoust, H. (1991) 'Incidence et profils des troubles de la communication verbale chez les cérébrolésés roits', *Revue de Neuropsychologie*, 1: 3–27.

Joanette, Y., Goulet, P. and Hannequin, D. (eds) (1990) *Right Hemisphere and Verbal Communication*, New York: Springer Verlag.

Johannesen, R.L. (1974) 'The functions of silence: a plea for communication research', *Western Speech*, 38: 25–35.

Johanson, L. and Utas, B. (eds) (2000) *Evidentials: Turkic, Iranian and Neighbouring Languages*, Berlin: de Gruyter.

Johns, A.M. (1986) 'The language of business', *Annual Review of Applied Linguistics*, 7: 3–17.

Johns, T. (1991) 'Should you be persuaded: two samples of data-driven learning materials', in T. Johns and P. King (eds) *Classroom Concordancing (English Language Research Journal 4)*, Birmingham: University of Birmingham.

——(2002) 'Data-driven learning: the perpetual challenge', in B. Kettemann and G. Marko (eds) *Teaching and Learning by Doing Corpus Analysis. Proceedings of the Fourth International Conference on Teaching and Learning Corpora*, Amsterdam: Rodopi.

Johnson, A. (2002) '*So … ?* pragmatic implications of *so*-prefaced questions in formal police interviews', in J. Cotterill (ed.) *Language in the Legal Process*, Basingstoke: Palgrave.

Johnson, C. and Maratsos, M. (1977) 'Early comprehension of mental verbs: think and know', *Child Development*, 48: 1743–47.

Johnson, D.M. (1992) 'Compliments and politeness in peer-review texts', *Applied Linguistics*, 13: 51–71.

Johnson, D.M. and Roen, D.H. (1992) 'Complimenting and involvement in peer reviews: gender variation', *Language in Society*, 21: 27–57.

Johnson, J. (1993) 'Is talk really cheap? Prompting conversation between critical theory and rational choice', *American Political Science Review*, 87: 74–93.

Johnson, J. and Newport, E. (1989) 'Critical period effects in second language learning: the influence of maturational state on the acquisition of English as a second language', *Cognitive Psychology*, 21: 60–99.

——(1991) 'Critical period effects on universal properties of languages: the status of subjacency in the acquisition of a second language', *Cognition*, 39: 215–58.

Johnson, J.M., Inglebret, E., Jones, C. and Ray, J. (2006) 'Perspectives of speech language pathologists regarding success versus abandonment of AAC', *Augmentative and Alternative Communication*, 22: 85–99.

Johnson, M. (1987) *The Body in the Mind: The Bodily Basis of Imagination, Reason and Meaning*, Chicago, IL: University of Chicago Press.

Johnson, M.H. and Morton, J. (1991) *Biology and Cognitive Development: The Case of Face Recognition*, Oxford: Blackwell.

Johnson, P.H. (1959) 'Modern fiction and the English understatement', *Times Literary Supplement*, 7 August, 3.

Johnson, R.H. (2000) *Manifest Rationality: A Pragmatic Theory of Argument*, Mahwah, NJ: Erlbaum.

Johnson-Laird, P.N. (1983) *Mental Models*, Cambridge, MA: Cambridge University Press.

——(2006) *How We Reason*, Oxford: Oxford University Press.

Johnson-Laird, P.N. and Byrne, R.M.J. (1991) *Deduction*, Hillsdale, NJ: Erlbaum.

——(2002) 'Conditionals: a theory of meaning, pragmatics, and inference', *Psychological Review*, 109: 646–78.

Jolliffe, T. and Baron-Cohen, S. (1999) 'A test of central coherence theory: linguistic processing in high-functioning adults with autism or Asperger syndrome: is local coherence impaired?', *Cognition*, 71: 149–85.

Jones, J.F. (1995) 'A cross-cultural perspective on the pragmatics of small-group discussion', *RELC Journal*, 26: 44–61.

Jones, R.L. (2002) '"That's very rude, I shouldn't be telling you that": older women talking about sex', *Narrative Inquiry*, 12: 121–43.

Jorgensen, J., Miller, G. and Sperber, D. (1984) 'Test of the mention theory of irony', *Journal of Experimental Psychology: General*, 113: 112–20.

Josephson, J.R. and Josephson, S.G. (eds.) (1994) *Abductive Inference: Computation, Philosophy and Technology*, Cambridge: Cambridge University Press.

Jubien, M. (1997) *Contemporary Metaphysics*, Oxford: Blackwell Publishers.

Jucker, A.H. (1994) 'The feasibility of historical pragmatics', *Journal of Pragmatics*, 22: 533–36.

——(1995) *Historical Pragmatics: Pragmatic Developments in the History of English*, Amsterdam and Philadelphia: Benjamins.

——(1997) 'The discourse marker "well" in the history of English', *English Language and Linguistics*, 1: 91–110.

——(2000) 'English historical pragmatics: problems of data and methodology', in G. di Martino and M. Lima (eds) *English Diachronic Pragmatics*, Naples, Italy: CUEN.

——(2005) 'News discourse: mass media communication from the seventeenth to the twenty-first century', in J. Skaffari, M. Peikola, R. Carroll, R. Hiltunen and B. Wårvik (eds) *Opening Windows on Texts and Discourses of the Past*, Amsterdam and Philadelphia, PA: John Benjamins.

Jucker, A.H. and Taavistainen, I. (2008) *Speech Acts in the History of English*, Amsterdam and Philadelphia, PA: John Benjamins.

Jucker, A.H., Gerd, F. and Franz, L. (eds) (1999) *Historical Dialogue Analysis*, Amsterdam: John Benjamins.

Jucker, A.H., Smith, S.W. and Lüdge, T. (2003) 'Interactive aspects of vagueness in conversation', *Journal of Pragmatics*, 35: 1737–69.

Jun, Sun-Ah (ed.) (2005) *Prosodic Typology: The Phonology of Intonation and Phrasing*, Oxford: Oxford University Press.

Jung, Y. (2009) 'Korea', in F. Bargiela-Chiappini (ed.) *The Handbook of Business Discourse*, Edinburgh: Edinburgh University Press.

Jurafsky, D. (2004) 'Pragmatics and computational linguistics', in L.R. Horn and G.L. Ward (eds) *The Handbook of Pragmatics*, Oxford: Blackwell.

Jurafsky, D. and Martin, J.H. (2000) *Speech and Language Processing: An Introduction to Natural Language Processing, Computational Linguistics and Speech Recognition*, Harlow: Pearson Education.

Jurafsky, D., Shriberg, E., Fox, B. and Curl, T. (1998) 'Lexical, prosodic, and syntactic cues for dialog acts', paper presented at ACL/COLING-98 Workshop on Discourse Relations and Discourse Markers, Montreal, Canada, August 1998.

Jusczyk, P. (1997) *The Discovery of Spoken Language*, Cambridge, MA: MIT Press.

——(1999) 'How infants begin to extract words from speech', *Trends in Cognitive Sciences*, 3: 323–28.

Just, M.A. and Carpenter, P.A. (1971) 'Comprehension of negation with quantification', *Journal of Verbal Learning and Verbal Behavior*, 12: 21–31.

Just, M.A., Cherkassky, V.L., Keller, T.A. and Minshew, N.J. (2004) 'Cortical activation and synchronization during sentence comprehension in high-functioning autism: evidence of underconnectivity', *Brain*, 127: 1811–21.

Just, M.A., Cherkassky, V.L., Keller, T.A., Kana, R.K. and Minshew, N.J. (2007) 'Functional and anatomical cortical underconnectivity in autism: evidence from an fMRI study of an executive function task and corpus callosum morphometry', *Cerebral Cortex*, 17: 951–61.

Kadmon, N. (2001) *Formal Pragmatics*, Oxford: Blackwell.

Kadmon, N. and Landman, F. (1993) 'Any', *Linguistics and Philosophy*, 16: 353–422.

Kagan, A., Black, S., Duchan, J.F., Simmons-Mackie, N. and Square, P. (2001) 'Training volunteers as partners using "supported conversation for adults with aphasia" (SCA): a controlled trial', *Journal of Speech, Language and Hearing Research*, 44: 624–38.

Kagan, O. (2007) 'Specificity and the speaker's worldview', paper presented at the Funny Indefinites Workshop, Berlin, July 2007.

Kahane, G., Kanterian, E. and Kuusela, O. (eds) (2007) *Wittgenstein and His Interpreters: Essays in Memory of Gordon Baker*, Oxford: Blackwell Publishing.

Kahneman, D. and Tversky, A. (1974) 'Judgement under uncertainty: heuristics and biases', *Science*, 185: 1124–31.

Kaland, N., Møller-Nielsen, A., Smith, L., Mortensen, E.L., Callesen, K. and Gottlieb, D. (2005) 'The Strange Stories test: a replication study of children and adolescents with Asperger syndrome', *European Child and Adolescent Psychiatry*, 14: 73–82.

Kaltenböck, G. (2007) 'Spoken parenthetical clauses in English: a taxonomy', in N. Dehé and Y. Kavalova (eds.) *Parentheticals*, Amsterdam: John Benjamins.

Kamp, H. (1981) 'A theory of truth and discourse representation', in J. Groenendijk, T. M.V. Janssen and M. Stockhof (eds) *Formal Methods in the Study of Language*, Amsterdam: Mathematical Centre.

Kamp, H. and Reyle, U. (1993) *From Discourse to Logic: Introduction to Modeltheoretic Semantics of Natural Language, Formal Logic and Discourse Representation Theory*, Dordrecht: Kluwer.

Kane, L. (1984) *The Language of Silence: On the Unspoken and the Unspeakable in Modern Drama*, Cranbury, NJ: Associated University Presses.

Kangasharju, H. (2002) 'Alignment in disagreement: forming oppositional alliances in committee meetings', *Journal of Pragmatics*, 34: 1447–71.

Kanner, L. (1943) 'Autistic disturbances of affective contact', *Nervous Child*, 2: 217–50.

——(1946) 'Irrelevant and metaphorical language in early infantile autism', *American Journal of Psychiatry*, 103: 242–46.

Kanno, K. (1998) 'The stability of UG principles in second-language acquisition: evidence from Japanese', *Linguistics*, 36: 1125–46.

Kant, I. (1996) *Critique of Pure Reason: Unified Edition with All Variants from the 1781 and 1787 Editions*, trans. W.S. Pluhar, ed. P. Kitcher, Indianapolis, IN: Hackett Publishing.

——(1998) *Critique of Pure Reason*, trans. P. Guyer and A.W. Wood, Cambridge: Cambridge University Press.

Kaplan, D. (1977) 'Demonstratives', in J. Almog, J. Perry and H. Wettstein (eds) (1989) *Themes from Kaplan*, New York: Oxford University Press.

——(1978) 'Dthat', in P. Cole (ed.) *Syntax and Semantics 9: Pragmatics*, New York: Academic Press.

——(1989a) 'Demonstratives: an essay on the semantics, logic, metaphysics, and epistemology of demonstratives and other indexicals', in J. Almog, J. Perry and H. Wettstein (eds) *Themes from Kaplan*, New York: Oxford University Press.

——(1989b) 'Afterthoughts', in J. Almog, J. Perry and H. Wettstein (eds) *Themes from Kaplan*, Oxford: Oxford University Press.

Kaplan, J.A., Brownell, H.H., Jacobs, J.R. and Gardner, H. (1990) 'The effects of right hemisphere damage on the pragmatic interpretation of conversational remarks', *Brain and Language*, 38: 315–33.

Kaplan, M. (2000) 'To what must an epistemology be true?', *Philosophy and Phenomenological Research*, 61: 279–304.

Karmiloff-Smith, A. (1979) *A Functional Approach to Child Language*, Cambridge: Cambridge University Press.

——(1992) *Beyond Modularity: A Developmental Perspective on Cognitive Science*, Cambridge, MA: MIT Press.

Karttunen, L. (1973) 'Presuppositions of compound sentences', *Linguistic Inquiry*, 4: 169–93.

——(1974) 'Presupposition and linguistic context', *Theoretical Linguistics*, 1: 181–94; reprinted in S. Davis (ed.) (1991) *Pragmatics: A Reader*, New York: Oxford University Press.

——(1976) 'Discourse referents', in J.D. McCawley (ed.) *Syntax and Semantics, volume 7: Notes from the Linguistic Underground*, New York: Academic Press.

Karttunen, L. and Peters, S. (1979) 'Conventional implicature', in C.K. Oh and D.A. Dinneen (eds) *Syntax and Semantics 11: Presupposition*, New York: Academic Press.

Kasanin, J.S. (1964) *Language and Thought in Schizophrenia*, New York: Norton.

Kasari, C. and Rotheram-Fuller, E. (2005) 'Current trends in psychological research on children with high-functioning autism and Asperger disorder', *Current Opinion in Psychiatry*, 18: 497–501.

Kasher, A. (1976) 'Conversational maxims and rationality', in A. Kasher (ed.) *Language in Focus: Foundations, Methods and Systems*, Dordrecht: Reidel; reprinted in A. Kasher (ed.) (1998) *Pragmatics: Critical Concepts*, vol. IV, New York: Routledge.

——(1977) 'What is a theory of use?', *Journal of Pragmatics*, 1: 105–20; reprinted in A. Margalit (ed.) (1979) *Meaning and Use*, Dordrecht: Reidel.

——(1982) 'Gricean inference revisited', *Philosophica*, 29: 25–44.

——(1984a) 'On the psychological reality of pragmatics', *Journal of Pragmatics*, 8: 539–57; revised and reprinted in A. Kasher (ed.) (1998) *Pragmatics: Critical Concepts*, vol. III, London: Routledge.

——(1984b) 'Pragmatics and the modularity of mind', *Journal of Pragmatics*, 8: 539–57; reprinted in S. Davis (ed.) (1991) *Pragmatics: A Reader*, New York and Oxford: Oxford University Press.

——(1991a) 'On the pragmatic modules: a lecture', *Journal of Pragmatics*, 16: 381–97.

——(1991b) 'Pragmatics and Chomsky's research program', in A. Kasher (ed.) *The Chomskyan Turn*, Oxford: Blackwell.

——(1994) 'Modular speech act theory: programme and results', in S.L. Tsohatzidis (ed.) *Foundations of Speech Act Theory*, London: Routledge.

——(1998) 'Pragmatics and the modularity of mind', in A. Kasher (ed.) *Pragmatics: Critical Concepts. Volume 6: Pragmatics: Grammar, Psychology, and Sociology*, London: Routledge.

Kasher, A., Batori, G., Soroker, N., Graves, D. and Zaidel, E. (1999) 'Effects of right- and left-hemisphere damage on understanding conversational implicatures', *Brain and Language*, 68: 566–90.

Kasper, G. (1986) 'Repair in foreign language teaching', in G. Kasper (ed.) *Language, Teaching and Communication in the Language Classroom*, Aarhus, Denmark: Aarhus University Press.

——(1992) 'Pragmatic transfer', *Second Language Research*, 8: 203–31.

——(2006) 'When once is not enough: politeness in multiple requests', *Multilingua*, 25: 323–49.

Kasper, G. and Blum-Kulka, S. (eds) (1993) *Interlanguage Pragmatics*, Oxford: Oxford University Press.

Kasper, G. and Roever, C. (2005) 'Pragmatics in second language learning', in E. Hinkel (ed.) *Handbook of Research in Second Language Learning and Teaching*, Mahwah, NJ: Erlbaum.

Kasper, G. and Rose, K. (2001) *Research Methods in Interlanguage Pragmatics*, Mahwab, NJ: Erlbaum.

——(2002) *Pragmatic Development in a Second Language*, Oxford: Blackwell.

Katsos, N. (2007) 'Pragmatic me, pragmatic you: the development of informativeness from a speaker's and a comprehender's perspective', paper presented at *XPRAG*, Berlin, December 2007.

Katsos, N., Breheny, R. and Williams, J. (2006) 'Structural and contextual effects on the interpretation of scalar terms', paper presented at *COST A33: Lisbon Meeting*, Lisbon, July 2006.

Katz, A.N. (1996) 'Experimental psycholinguistics and figurative language: circa 1995', *Metaphor and Symbolic Activity*, 11: 17–37.

Katz, A.N. and Pexman, P. (1997) 'Interpreting figurative statements: speaker occupation can change metaphor into irony', *Metaphor and Symbolic Activity*, 12: 19–41.

Katz, J.J. (1981) 'An outline of Platonist grammar', in J. Katz (ed.) *The Philosophy of Linguistics*, Oxford: Oxford University Press.

——(1985) *Language and Other Abstract Objects*, Totowa, NJ: Rowman and Littlefield.

Katz, J.J. and Fodor, J.A. (1963) 'The structure of a semantic theory', *Language*, 39: 170–210.

Katz, N.A., Blasko, G.D. and Kazmerski, A.V. (2004) 'Saying what you don't mean: social influences on sarcastic language processing', *Current Directions in Psychological Science*, 13: 186–89.

Kavalova, Y. (2007) '*And*-parenthetical clauses', in N. Dehé and Y. Kavalova (eds.) *Parentheticals*, Amsterdam: John Benjamins.

Kay, P. and McDaniel, C. (1978) 'The linguistic significance of the meanings of basic color terms', *Language*, 54: 610–46.

Keen, D. (2003) 'Communicative repair strategies and problem behaviours of children with autism', *International Journal of Disabilities, Development and Education*, 50: 53–63.

Keenan, E.L. (1987) 'A semantic definition of "indefinite NP"', in E.J. Reuland and A.G.B. ter Meulen (eds) *The Representation of (In)definiteness*, Cambridge, MA: MIT Press.

Keenan, E.L. and Westerståhl, D. (1997) 'Generalized quantifiers in linguistics and logic', in J. van Bentham and A. ter Meulen (eds) *Handbook of Language and Logic*, Amsterdam: Elsevier.

Keenan, E.O. (1976) 'On the universality of conversational implicatures', *Language in Society*, 5: 67–80.

Keesing, R. (1987) 'Models, "folk" and "cultural": paradigms regained?', in D. Holland and N. Quinn (eds) *Cultural Models in Language and Thought*, Cambridge: Cambridge University Press.

——(1972) 'Paradigms lost: the new anthropology and the new linguistics', *Southwestern Journal of Anthropology*, 28: 299–332.

Kelepir, M. (2001) *Topics in Turkish syntax: clausal structure and scope*, Ph.D. dissertation, Massachusetts Institute of Technology.

Kellogg, R.T. (1994) *The Psychology of Writing*, New York: Oxford University Press.

Kelly, J. and Local, J. (1989) *Doing Phonology: Observing, Recording, Interpreting*, Manchester: Manchester University Press.

Kelly, S. and Church, R.B. (1998) 'A comparison between children's and adults' ability to detect conceptual information conveyed through representational gestures', *Child Development*, 69: 85–93.

Kemmerer, D. (2006) 'The semantics of space: integrating linguistic typology and cognitive neuroscience', *Neuropsychologia*, 44: 1607–21.

Kempson, R.M. (1975) *Presupposition and the Delimitation of Semantics*, Cambridge: Cambridge University Press.

——(1977) *Semantic Theory*, Cambridge: Cambridge University Press.

——(1979) 'Presupposition, opacity, and ambiguity', in C.-K. Oh and D.A. Dinneen (eds) *Syntax and Semantics 11: Presupposition*, New York: Academic Press.

——(1986) 'Ambiguity and the semantics-pragmatics distinction', in C. Travis (ed.) *Meaning and Interpretation*, Oxford: Blackwell.

——(1988) 'Grammar and conversational principles', in F. Newmeyer (ed.) *Linguistics: The Cambridge Survey. Vol. II. Linguistic Theory: Extensions and Implications*, Cambridge: Cambridge University Press.

Kempson, R.M. and Cormack, A. (1981) 'Ambiguity and quantification', *Linguistics and Philosophy*, 4: 259–310.

Kendon, A. (1992) 'The negotiation of context in face-to-face interaction', in A. Duranti and C. Goodwin (eds) *Rethinking Context: Language as an Interactive Phenomenon*, Cambridge: Cambridge University Press.

——(1994) 'Do gestures communicate? A review', *Research on Language and Social Interaction*, 27: 175–200.

——(2004) *Gesture: Visible Actions as Utterance*, Cambridge: Cambridge University Press.

Kennedy, C. (2007) 'Vagueness and grammar: the semantics of relative and absolute gradable adjectives', *Linguistics and Philosophy*, 30: 1–45.

Kennedy, G. (1963) *The Art of Persuasion in Ancient Greece*, Princeton, NJ: Princeton University Press.

——(1987) 'Quantification and the use of English: a case study of one aspect of the learner's task', *Applied Linguistics*, 8: 264–86.

Kenny, A. (1973) *Wittgenstein*, Harmondsworth: Pelican Press.

Kern, F. (2007) 'Prosody as a resource in children's game explanations: some aspects of turn construction and recipiency', *Journal of Pragmatics*, 39: 111–33.

Kertesz, A. ([1982] 2006) *Western Aphasia Battery – Revised*, San Antonio, TX: Harcourt Assessment.

Kertesz, A., Davidson, W. and McCabe, P. (1998) 'Primary progressive semantic aphasia: a case study', *Journal of the International Neuropsychological Society*, 4: 388–98.

Ketrez, N. (2005) 'Children's scope of indefinite objects', Ph.D. dissertation, University of Southern California.

Keysar, B. (1994) 'The illusory transparency of intention: linguistic perspective taking in text', *Cognitive Psychology*, 26: 165–208.

——(2000) 'The illusory transparency of intention: does June understand what Mark means because he means it?', *Discourse Processes*, 29: 161–72.

Keysar, B. and Barr, D. (2005) 'Coordination of action belief in conversation', in J.C. Trueswell and M.K. Tanenhaus (eds) *Approaches to Studying World-Situated Language Use: Bridging the Language-as-Product and Language-as-Action Traditions*, Cambridge, MA: MIT Press.

Keysar, B., Barr, D.J., Balin, J.A. and Brauner, J.S. (2000) 'Taking perspective in conversation: the role of mutual knowledge in comprehension', *Psychological Science*, 11: 32–38.

Keysar, B., Lin, S. and Barr, D.J. (2003) 'Limits on theory of mind use in adults', *Cognition*, 89: 25–41.

Keysers, S.J., Miller, G.A. and Walker, E. (1978) 'Cognitive science in 1978', unpublished report submitted to the Alfred P. Sloan Foundation, New York.

Kiefer, F. (2004) 'Morphopragmatic phenomena in Hungarian', *Acta Linguistica Hungarica*, 51: 325–49.

Kienpointner, M. (1992) *Alltagslogik: Struktur und Funktion von Argumentationsmustern*, Stuttgart: Fromman-Holzboog.

Kiesling, S.F. (2005) 'Homosocial desire in men's talk: balancing and re-creating cultural discourses of masculinity', *Language in Society*, 34: 695–726.

Kilani-Schoch, M. and Dressler, W.U. (1999) 'Morphopragmatique interactionelle: les formations en–o du français branché', in I. Mel'čuk (ed.) *Dictionnaire Explicatif et Combinatoire du Français Contemporain. Recherches Lexico-Sémantiques IV*, Montreal: Les Presses de l'Université de Montréal.

Kim, M.S. (1994) 'Cross-cultural comparisons of the perceived importance of conversational constraints', *Human Communication Research*, 21: 128–51.

Kim, M.-S., Sharkey, W.F. and Singelis, T.M. (1994) 'The relationship between individuals' self construals and perceived importance of interactive constraints', *International Journal of Intercultural Relations*, 18: 117–40.

Kindler, H.S. (1988) *Managing Disagreement Constructively*, London: Kogan Page.

——(1996) *Managing Disagreement Constructively: Conflict Management in Organizations*, Menlo Park, CA: Crisp Publications.

——(2006) *Conflict Management: Resolving Disagreements in the Workplace*, Boston, MA: Thomson/Course Technology.

King, J.C. (2001) *Complex Demonstratives*, Cambridge, MA: MIT Press.

King, J.C. and Stanley, J. (2005) 'Semantics, pragmatics, and the role of semantic Content', in Z.G. Szabó (ed.) *Semantics versus Pragmatics*, Oxford: Oxford University Press.

King, K., Fraser, W.F. and Thomas, P. (1990) 'Re-examination of the language of psychotic subjects', *British Journal of Psychiatry*, 156: 211–15.

Kinginger, C. (2000) 'Learning the pragmatics of solidarity in the networked foreign language classroom', in J.K. Hall and L.S. Verplaetse (eds) *Second and Foreign Language Learning through Classroom Interaction*, Mahwah, NJ: Erlbaum.

Kinginger, C. and Belz, J.A. (2005) 'Socio-cultural perspectives on pragmatic development in foreign language learning: microgenetic case studies from telecollaboration and residence abroad', *Intercultural Pragmatics*, 2: 369–421.

Kinjo, H. (1987) 'Oral refusals of invitations and requests in English and Japanese', *Journal of Asian Culture*, 1: 83–106.

Kintsch, W. (1988) 'The use of knowledge in discourse processing: a constructive-integration model', *Psychological Review*, 95: 163–82.

Kinzler, K.D., Dupoux, E. and Spelke, E.S. (2007) 'The native language of social cognition', *The Proceedings of the National Academy of Sciences of the United States of America*, 104: 12577–580.

Kircher, T.T.J., Leube, D.T., Erb, M., Grodd, W. and Rapp, A.M. (2007) 'Neural correlates of metaphor processing in schizophrenia', *NeuroImage*, 34: 281–89.

Kirsh, D. (1991) 'Today the earwig, tomorrow man?', *Artificial Intelligence*, 47: 161–84; reprinted in D. Kirsh (ed.) (1992) *Foundations of Artificial Intelligence*, Cambridge, MA: MIT Press.

Kiss, K.E. (1998) 'Identificational focus vs information focus', *Language*, 74: 245–73.

Kitcher, P. (1978) 'Positive understatement: the logic of attributive adjectives', *Journal of Philosophical Logic*, 7: 1–17.

Klein, J. (1997) 'Kategorien der Unterhaltsamkeit: Grundlagen einer Theorie der Unterhaltung mit Rückgriff auf Grice', *Linguistische Berichte*, 176–88.

Klein, W. (1995) 'Language acquisition at different ages', in D. Magnusson (ed.) *The Lifespan Development of Individuals; Behavioral, Neurobiological, and Psychosocial Perspectives: A Synthesis*, Cambridge: Cambridge University Press.

Klemperer, V. ([1947] 1975) *LTI (Lingua Tertii Imperii): Die Sprache des Dritten Reiches*, Leipzig: Reclam.

——(2005) *LTI (Lingua Tertii Imperii). Notizbuch eines Philologen*, Leipzig: Reclam.

Klima, E.S. and Bellugi, U. (1979) *The Signs of Language*, Cambridge, MA: Harvard University Press.

Kline, S.L. and Floyd, C.H. (1990)'On the art of saying no: the influence of social cognitive development on messages of refusal', *Western Journal of Speech Communication*, 54: 454–72.

Knapp, M.L., Hopper, R. and Bell, R.A. (1984) 'Compliments: a descriptive taxonomy', *Journal of Communication*, 34: 12–31.

Knibb, J.A. and Hodges, J.R. (2005) 'Semantic dementia and primary progressive aphasia: a problem of categorization?', *Alzheimer Disease and Associated Disorders*, 19, Supplement 1: S7–S14.

Ko, H., Ionin, T. and Wexler, K. (2006) 'Adult L2-learners lack the maximality presupposition, too!', in K.U. Deen, J. Nomura, B. Schulz and B.D. Schwartz (eds) *The Proceedings of the Inaugural Conference on Generative Approaches to Language Acquisition–North America*, Honolulu, Storrs: University of Connecticut Occasional Papers in Linguistics, 4.

Koenig, J.-P. (1991) 'Scalar predicates and negation: punctual semantics and interval interpretations', in L. Dobrin, L. Nichols and R. Rodriguez (eds) *Proceedings of the 27th Meeting of the Chicago Linguistic Society, Part Two: Parasession on Negation*, Chicago, IL: Chicago Linguistic Society.

Koenig, M., Clement, F. and Harris, P. (2004) 'Trust in testimony: children's use of true and false statements', *Psychological Science*, 15: 694–98.

Koestler, A. (1964) *The Act of Creation*, New York: Macmillan.

Kohler, E., Keysers, C., Umiltà, M.A., Fogassi, L., Gallese, V. and Rizzolatti, G. (2002) 'Hearing sounds, understanding actions: action representation in mirror neurons', *Science*, 297: 846–48.

Koike, D.A. and Pearson, L. (2005) 'The effect of instruction and feedback in the development of pragmatic competence', *System*, 33: 481–501.

Komter, M.L. (2002) 'The suspect's own words: the treatment of written statements in Dutch courtrooms', *Forensic Linguistics*, 9: 168–92.

König, E. (1991) *The Meaning of Focus Particles: A Comparative Perspective*, London: Croom Helm.

Kopecka, A. and Narasimhan, B. (eds) (to appear) *Events of 'Putting' and 'Taking': A Crosslinguistic Perspective*, Amsterdam and Philadelphia, PA: John Benjamins.

Kopytko, R. (1993) 'Linguistic pragmatics and the concept of face', *VIEWS*, 2: 91–103.

——(1995a) 'Linguistic politeness strategies in Shakespeare's plays', in A.H. Jucker (ed.) *Historical Pragmatics: Pragmatic Developments in the History of English*, Amsterdam and Philadelphia, PA: John Benjamins.

——(1995b) 'Against rationalistic pragmatics', *Journal of Pragmatics*, 23: 475–91.

——(1998) 'Relational pragmatics: towards a holistic view of pragmatic phenomena', *Studia Anglica Posnaniensia*, 33: 195–211.

——(2001) 'From Cartesian towards non-Cartesian pragmatics', *Journal of Pragmatics*, 33: 783–804.

——(2003) 'What is wrong with modern accounts of context in linguistics?', *VIEWS*, 12: 45–60.

Kose, Y.S. (1997) *The pragmatics of Japanese sentence-final particles*, Ph.D. dissertation, University of Illinois.

Koshino, H., Carpenter, P.A., Minshew, N.J., Cherkassky, V.L., Keller, T.A. and Just, M. A. (2005) 'Functional connectivity in an fMRI working memory task in high-functioning autism', *NeuroImage*, 24: 810–21.

Kosslyn, S.M. (1980) *Image and Mind*, Cambridge, MA: Harvard University Press.

——(1983) *Ghosts in the Mind's Machine*, New York: Norton.

Kotthoff, H. (2003) 'Responding to irony in different contexts: cognition and conversation', *Journal of Pragmatics*, 35: 1387–411.

——(2006) 'Gender and humor: the state of the art', *Journal of Pragmatics*, 38: 4–25.

Kovecses, Z. (2000) *Metaphor: A Practical Introduction*, New York: Oxford University Press.

Koyama, W. (2009) 'Indexically anchored onto the deictic center of discourse: grammar, sociocultural interaction, and "emancipatory pragmatics"', *Journal of Pragmatics*, 41: 79–92.

Kraat, A. (1985) *Communication Interaction Between Aided and Natural Speakers: A State of the Art Report*, Toronto: Canadian Rehabilitation Council for the Disabled.

Kraepelin, E. ([1919] 1925) *Dementia Praecox and Paraphrenia*, Edinburgh: E. and S. Livingstone.

——(1971) *Dementia Praecox and Paraphrenia*, edited by G.M. Robertson, Huntington, NY: Robert E. Krieger.

Kraft, B. and Geluykens, R. (2002) 'Complaining in French L1 and L2: a cross-linguistic investigation', *EUROSLA Yearbook*, 2: 227–42.

——(2007) 'Defining cross-cultural and interlanguage pragmatics', in B. Kraft and R. Geluykens (eds) *Cross-Cultural Pragmatics and Interlanguage English*, Munich: Lincom Europa.

Krämer, I. (2000) *Interpreting indefinites: an experimental study of children's language comprehension*, Ph.D. dissertation, Utrecht University.

——(2003) 'Reference of pronominal and definite noun phrases in a story context: English children's comprehension', in B. Beachley, A. Brown and F. Conlin (eds) *Proceedings of the 27th Annual Boston University Conference on Language Development*, vol. 2, Somerville, MA: Cascadilla Press.

——(ed.) (2007) 'Language acquisition between sentence and discourse', *Lingua*, 117: 1833–988.

Krashen, S. (1981) *Second Language Acquisition and Second Language Learning*, Oxford: Pergamon.

Kratzer, A. (1977) 'What *must* and *can* must and can mean', *Linguistics and Philosophy*, 1: 337–55.

——(1989) 'An investigation of the lumps of thought', *Linguistics and Philosophy*, 12: 607–53.

——(1998) 'Scope or pseudo-scope? Are there wide-scope indefinites?', in S. Rothstein (ed.) *Events in Grammar*, Dordrecht: Kluwer.

Krauss, R.M., Chen, Y. and Chawla, P. (1996) 'Nonverbal behavior and nonverbal communication: what do conversational hand gestures tell us?', in M. Zanna (ed.) *Advances in Experimental Social Psychology*, Tampa, FL: Academic Press.

Krauss, R.M., Morrel-Samuels, P. and Colasante, G. (1991) 'Do conversational hand gestures communicate?', *Journal of Personality and Social Psychology*, 61: 743–54.

Kress, G. and Van Leeuwen, T. (2001) *Multimodal Discourse: The Modes and Media of Contemporary Communication*, London: Hodder.

Kreuz, R.J. and Glucksberg, S. (1989) 'How to be sarcastic: the echoic reminder theory of verbal irony', *Journal of Experimental Psychology: General*, 118: 374–86.

Kreuz, R.J. and Roberts, R.M. (1993) 'The empirical study of figurative language in Literature', *Poetics*, 22: 151–69.

Kreuz, R.J., Kassler, M.A. and Coppenrath, L. (1998) 'The use of exaggeration in discourse: cognitive and social facets', in S. Fussell and R. Kreuz (eds) *Social and Cognitive Approaches to Interpersonal Communication*, Mahwah, NJ: Lawrence Erlbaum Associates.

Krifka, M. (1992) 'A framework for focus-sensitive quantification', in C. Barker and D. Dowty (eds) *Proceedings of Semantics and Linguistic Theory (SALT) 2*, Working Papers in Linguistics no. 40, Columbus, OH: Ohio State University.

——(1993) 'Focus and presupposition in dynamic interpretation', *Journal of Semantics*, 10: 269–300.

——(1995a) 'The semantics and pragmatics of polarity items', *Linguistic Analysis*, 25: 146–80.

——(1995b) 'Focus and the interpretation of generic sentences', in G.N. Carlson and F.J. Pelletier (eds) *The Generic Book*, Chicago, IL: University of Chicago Press.

——(2007a) 'Approximate interpretation of number words: a case for strategic communication', in G. Bouma, I. Krämer and J. Zwarts (eds) *Cognitive Foundations of Interpretation*, Amsterdam: Koninklijke Nederlandse Akademie van Wetenschapen.

——(2007b) 'Negated antonyms: creating and filling the gap', in U. Sauerland and P. Stateva (eds) *Presupposition and Implicature in Compositional Semantics*, Houndmills: Palgrave Macmillan.

Krifka, M., Pelletier, F.J., Carlson, G.N., ter Meulen, A., Link, G. and Chierchia, G. (1995) 'Genericity: an introduction', in G.N. Carlson and F.J. Pelletier (eds) *The Generic Book*, Chicago, IL: University of Chicago Press.

Krikmann, A. (1994) 'The great chain metaphor: an open sesame for proverb semantics?', *Proverbium*, 11: 117–24.

Kripke, S. (1959) 'A completeness theorem in modal logic', *Journal of Symbolic Logic*, 24: 1–14.

——(1972) 'Naming and necessity', in D. Davidson and G. Harman (eds) *Semantics of Natural Language*, Dordrecht: Reidel.

——(1977) 'Speaker's reference and semantic reference', in P.A. French, T.E. Uehling Jr and H. Wettstein (eds) *Midwest Studies in Philosophy, Volume II: Studies in the Philosophy of Language*, Morris, MN: University of Minnesota.

——(1980) *Naming and Necessity*, Oxford: Blackwell.

——(1982a) *Naming and Necessity*, Cambridge, MA: Harvard University Press.

——(1982b) *Wittgenstein on Rules and Private Language: An Elementary Exposition*, Oxford: Basil Blackwell.

Kryk-Kastovsky, B. (2006a) 'Historical courtroom discourse: introduction', *Journal of Historical Pragmatics*, 7: 163–79.

——(2006b) 'Impoliteness in Early Modern English courtroom discourse', *Journal of Historical Pragmatics*, 7: 213–43.

Kuhl, P.K. (2004) 'Early language acquisition: cracking the speech code', *Nature Reviews Neuroscience*, 5: 831–43.

Kuhl, P.K., Coffey-Corina, S., Padden, D. and Dawson, G. (2005) 'Links between social and linguistic processing of speech in preschool children with autism: behavioral and electrophysiological evidence', *Developmental Science*, 8: F1–F12.

Kuhl, P.K., Tsao, F.-M. and Liu, H.-M. (2003) 'Foreign-language experience in infancy: effects of short-term exposure and social interaction on phonetic learning', *Proceedings of the National Academy of Sciences*, 100: 9096–101.

Kummer, M. (1992) 'Politeness in Thai', in R.J. Watts, S. Edie and K. Ehlich (eds) *Politeness in Language: Studies in its History, Theory and Practice*, Berlin: Mouton de Gruyter.

Kumon-Nakamura, S., Glucksberg, S. and Brown, M. (1995) 'How about another piece of the pie: the allusional pretense theory of discourse irony', *Journal of Experimental Psychology: General*, 124: 3–21.

Kuno, S. (1972) 'Functional sentence perspective: a case study from Japanese and English', *Linguistic Inquiry*, 3: 269–320.

Kuntz, K. and Orange, J.B. (2003) 'Pretesting the Perception of Conversation Index – dementia of the Alzheimer's type', *Journal of Speech-Language Pathology and Audiology*, 27: 63.

Kuroda, S.-Y. (1973) 'Where epistemology, style and grammar meet', in S. Anderson and P. Kiparsky (eds) *Festschrift for Morris Halle*, New York: Holt Rienhart and Winston.

Kurzon, D. (1986) *It is Hereby Performed … : Explorations in Legal Speech Acts*, Amsterdam: John Benjamins.

——(1995) 'The right of silence: a socio-pragmatic model of interpretation', *Journal of Pragmatics*, 23: 55–69.

——(1996) 'To speak or not to speak: the comprehensibility of the revised police caution (PACE)', *International Journal for the Semiotics of Law*, 9: 3–16.

——(1998) *Discourse of Silence*, Amsterdam: John Benjamins.

——(2001) 'The politeness of judges: American and English judicial behaviour', *Journal of Pragmatics*, 33: 61–85.

——(2007a) 'Towards a typology of silence', *Journal of Pragmatics*, 39: 1673–688.

——(2007b) 'Peters edition v. Batt: the intertextuality of silence', *International Journal for the Semiotics of Law*, 20: 285–303.

Kwapil, T.R., Hegley, D.C. and Chapman, L.J. (1990) 'Facilitation of word recognition by semantic priming in schizophrenia', *Journal of Abnormal Psychology*, 99: 215–21.

Kwon, J. (2004) 'Expressing refusals in Korean and in American English', *Multilingua*, 23: 339–64.

Kyburg, A. and Morreau, M. (2000) 'Fitting words: vague language in context', *Linguistics and Philosophy*, 23: 577–97.

Kyratzis, A. (2000) 'Tactical uses of narratives in nursery school same-sex groups', *Discourse Processes*, 29: 269–99.

Labov, W. (1966) *The Social Stratification of English in New York City*, Washington, DC: Center for Applied Linguistics.

——(1972) *Language in the Inner City*, Philadelphia, PA: University of Pennsylvania Press.

Labov, W. and Fanschel, D. (1977) *Therapeutic Discourse: Psychotherapy as Conversation*, New York: Academic Press.

Laclau, E. and Mouffe, C. (1985) *Hegemony and Socialist Strategy: Towards a Radical Democratic Politics*, London: Verso.

Ladd, D.R. (1996) *Intonational Phonology*, Cambridge: Cambridge University Press.

Ladd, D.R., Scherer, K. and Silverman, K. (1986) 'An integrated approach to studying intonation and attitude', in C. Johns Lewis (ed.) *Intonation in Discourse*, London: Croom Helm.

Ladd, R. (1980) *The Structure of Intonational Meaning*, Bloomington, IN: Indiana University Press.

Ladusaw, W.A. (1979) 'Polarity sensitivity as inherent scope relations', unpublished thesis, University of Texas at Austin.

Lafont, C. (1999) *The Linguistic Turn in Hermeneutic Philosophy*, Cambridge, MA: MIT Press.

——(2002) 'Continental philosophy of language', in N.J. Smelser and P.B. Baltes (eds) *International Encyclopedia of Social and Behavioral Sciences. Volume 3: Philosophy*, Oxford: Elsevier Science.

Lagerwerf, L. (2007) 'Irony and sarcasm in advertisements: effects of relevant inappropriateness', *Journal of Pragmatics*, 39: 1702–21.

Lahav, R. (1989) 'Against compositionality: the case of adjectives', *Philosophical Studies*, 55: 111–29.

Lakoff, G. (1965) 'On the nature of syntactic irregularity', Ph.D. dissertation, Indiana University; published as *Irregularity in Syntax* (1970), New York: Holt, Rinehart and Winston.

——(1970) 'Linguistics and natural logic', *Synthese*, 22: 151–271.

——(1972) 'Hedges: a study in meaning criteria and the logic of fuzzy concepts', *Chicago Linguistic Society Papers*, 8: 183–228.

——(1987) *Women, Fire and Dangerous Things: What Categories Reveal About the Mind*, Chicago, IL: University of Chicago Press.

——(1988) 'Cognitive semantics', in U. Eco, M. Santambrogio and P. Violi (eds) *Meaning and Mental Representations*, Bloomington, IN: Indiana University Press.

——(1990) 'The invariance hypothesis: is abstract reason based on image schemas?', *Cognitive Linguistics*, 1: 39–74.

Lakoff, G. and Johnson, M. (1980) *Metaphors We Live By*, Chicago, IL: University of Chicago Press.

——(1999) *Philosophy in the Flesh: The Embodied Mind and its Challenge for Western Thought*, New York: Basic Books.

Lakoff, G. and Thompson, H. (1975) 'Introduction to cognitive grammar', in C. Cogen, H. Thompson, G. Thurgood and K. Whistler (eds) *Proceedings of the First Annual Meeting of the Berkeley Linguistics Society*, Berkeley, CA: Berkeley Linguistics Society.

Lakoff, G. and Turner, M. (1989) *More Than Cool Reason: A Field Guide to Poetic Metaphor*, Chicago, IL: University of Chicago Press.

Lakoff, R. (1971) 'Passive resistance', in *Papers from the 7th Regional Meeting of the Chicago Linguistic Society*, Chicago, IL: Chicago Linguistic Society.

——(1973) 'The logic of politeness: or, minding your p's and q's', in C. Corum, T. Smith-Stark and A. Weiser (eds) *Papers from the Ninth Regional Meeting of the Chicago Linguistic Society*, Chicago, IL: Chicago Linguistic Society.

——(1974) 'Remarks on *this* and *that*', *Chicago Linguistic Society*, 10: 345–56.

——(1975) *Language and Woman's Place*, New York: Harper and Row.

——(1989) 'The limits of politeness: therapeutic and courtroom discourse', *Multilingua*, 8: 101–29.

——(2000) *The Language War*, Berkeley, CA: University of California Press.

——(2003) 'Nine ways of looking at apologies', in D. Schiffrin and D. Tannen (eds) *The Handbook of Discourse Analysis*, Oxford: Blackwell.

Lakshmanan, U. (1994) 'Child second language acquisition of syntax', *Studies in Second Language Acquisition*, 17: 301–29.

Lalande, S., Braun, C.M., Charlebois, N. and Whitaker, H.A. (1992) 'Effects of right and left hemisphere cerebrovascular lesions on discrimination of prosodic and semantic aspects of affect in sentences', *Brain and Language*, 42: 165–86.

Lambrecht, K. (1994) *Information Structure and Sentence Form: Topic, Focus and the Mental Representation of Discourse Referents*, Cambridge: Cambridge University Press.

Lance, M.N. and Kukla, R. (2009) *'Yo!' and 'Lo!': The Pragmatic Topography of the Space of Reasons*, Cambridge, MA: Harvard University Press.

Langacker, R. (1987) *Foundations of Cognitive Grammar, Volume I*, Stanford, CA: Stanford University Press.

——(1991a) *Foundations of Cognitive Grammar, Volume II*, Stanford, CA: Stanford University Press.

——(1991b) *Concept, Image, Symbol: The Cognitive Basis of Grammar*, Berlin: Mouton de Gruyter.

Langdon, R., Coltheart, M., Ward, P.B. and Catts, S.V. (2002a) 'Disturbed communication in schizophrenia: the role of poor pragmatics and poor mind-reading', *Psychological Medicine*, 32: 1273–84.

Langdon, R., Davies, M. and Coltheart, M. (2002b) 'Understanding minds and understanding communicated meanings in schizophrenia', *Mind and Language*, 17: 127–48.

Langley, D. (2006) 'Apologies across cultures: an analysis of intercultural communication raised in the Ehime Maru incident', *Asian EFL Journal*, 8: 97–122.

Langlotz, A. (2006) *Idiomatic Creativity*, Amsterdam: Benjamins.

Lappin, S. and Leass, H. (1994) 'An algorithm for pronominal anaphora resolution', *Computational Linguistics*, 20: 535–61.

Larousse Editorial (2003) *Le Petit Larousse Illustré*, Paris: Larousse.

Larsen-Freeman, D. (1975) 'The acquisition of grammatical morphemes by adult ESL students', *TESOL Quarterly*, 9: 409–30.

——(1980) *Discourse Analysis in Second-Language Research*, Rowley, MA: Newbury House.

Larsen-Freeman, D. and Long, M. (1991) *An Introduction to Second Language Acquisition Research*, London: Longman.

Larson, R. and Segal, G. (1995) *Knowledge of Meaning: An Introduction to Semantic Theory*, Cambridge, MA: MIT Press.

Larsson, S., Cooper, R. and Ericsson, S. (2001) 'GoDiS: flexible dialogue in multiple domains', in P. Kühnlein, H. Rieser and H. Zeevat (eds) *Proceedings of the 5th Workshop on Formal Semantics and Pragmatics of Dialogue (BI-DIALOG 2001)*, Bielefeld, Germany.

Lascarides, A. and Asher, N. (1993) 'Temporal interpretation, discourse relations, and common sense entailment', *Linguistics and Philosophy*, 16: 437–93.

Lasersohn, P. (1999) 'Pragmatic halos', *Language*, 75: 522–51.

——(2005) 'Context dependence, disagreement, and predicates of personal taste', *Linguistics and Philosophy*, 28: 643–86.

Lasswell, H.D. and Leites, N.C. (1965) *Language of Politics*, Cambridge, MA: MIT Press.

Laurence, S. and Margolis, E. (1999) 'Concepts and cognitive science', in E. Margolis and S. Laurence (eds) *Concepts: Core Readings*, Cambridge, MA: MIT Press.

Laurier, E. (2001) 'Why people say where they are during mobile phone calls', *Environment and Planning D: Society and Space*, 19: 485–504.

Lauwereyns, S. (2002) 'Hedges in Japanese conversation: the influence of age, sex and formality', *Language Variation and Change*, 14: 239–59.

Lave, J. (1988) *Cognition in Practice*, Cambridge: Cambridge University Press.

Lave, J. and Wenger, E. (1991) *Situated Learning: Legitimate Peripheral Participation*, Cambridge: Cambridge University Press.

Laver, J. (1974) *Semiotic Aspects of Spoken Communication*, London: Edward Arnold.

Laws, G. and Bishop, D. (2004) 'Pragmatic language impairment and social deficits in Williams syndrome: a comparison with Down's syndrome and specific language impairment', *International Journal of Language and Communication Disorders*, 39: 45–64.

Lazar, R.T., Warr-Leeper, G.A., Nicholson, C.B. and Johnson, S. (1989) 'Elementary school teachers' use of multiple meaning expressions', *Language, Speech, and Hearing Services in Schools*, 20: 420–30.

Leach, E. (1966) 'Anthropological aspects of language: animal categories and verbal abuse', in E. Lenneberg (ed.) *New Directions in the Study of Language*, Cambridge, MA: MIT Press.

Lee, B. (1997) *Talking Heads: Language, Metalanguage, and the Semiotics of Subjectivity*, Durham, NC and London: Duke University Press.

Lee, C. (1999) 'Contrasive topic: a locus of the interface. Evidence from Korean and English', in K. Turner (ed.) *The Semantics/Pragmatics Interface from Different Points of View*, Oxford: Elsevier Science.

Lee, C., Gordon, M. and Buring, D. (eds) (2007) *Topic and Focus: Cross-Linguistic Perspectives on Meaning and Intonation*, Dordrecht: Springer.

Lee, D. (1992) *Competing Discourses: Language and Ideology*, New York: Longman.

Lee, H. (2001) 'Markedness and word order freezing', in P. Sells (ed.) *Formal and Empirical Issues in Optimality-Theoretic Syntax*, Stanford, CA: CSLI Publications.

Lee, H.-K. (2005) 'Presupposition and implicature under negation', *Journal of Pragmatics*, 37: 595–609.

Lee, H.S. (2006) 'Second summonings in Korean telephone conversation openings', *Language in Society*, 35: 261–83.

Lee, I. (1998) 'Enhancing ESL students' awareness of coherence-creating mechanisms in writing', *TESL Canada Journal*, 15: 36–49.

Leech, G.N. (1966) *English in Advertising: A Linguistic Study of Advertising in Great Britain*, London: Longman.

——(1969) *A Linguistic Guide to English Poetry*, London: Longman.

——(1983) *Principles of Pragmatics*, London, New York: Longman.

——(1997) 'Introducing corpus annotation', in R. Garside, G. Leech and T. McEnery (eds) *Corpus Annotation*, London: Longman.

Leech, G.N. and Short, M.H. ([1981] 2007) *Style in Fiction*, London: Longman.

Lees, R.B. and Klima, E. (1963) 'Rules for English pronominalization', *Language*, 39: 17–28.

Leeson, L. and Saeed, J.I. (2004) 'Windowing of attention in simultaneous constructions in Irish Sign Language (ISL)', in T. Cameron, C. Shank and K. Holley (eds) *Proceedings of the Fifth Annual High Desert Linguistics Society Conference*, Albuquerque, NM: High Desert Linguistics Society.

Leezenberg, M. (2001) *Contexts of Metaphor*, Oxford: Elsevier Science.

Leggitt, J. and Gibbs, R. (2000) 'Emotional reactions to verbal irony', *Discourse Processes*, 29: 1–24.

Lehiste, I. (1975) 'The phonetic structure of paragraphs', in A. Cohen and S.G. Nooteboom (eds) *Structure and Process in Speech Perception*, New York: Springer Verlag.

Lehman Blake, M. (2006) 'Clinical relevance of discourse characteristics after right hemisphere brain damage', *American Journal of Speech and Language Pathology*, 15: 255–67.

Lehmann, C. (1995) *Thoughts on Grammaticalization*, Munich: Lincom Europa.

Lehtonen, J. and Sajavaara, K. (1985) 'The silent Finn', in D. Tannen and M. Saville-Troike (eds) *Perspectives of Silence*, Norwood, NJ: Ablex.

Leinonen, E. and Kerbel, D. (1999) 'Relevance theory and pragmatic impairment', *International Journal of Language and Communication Disorders*, 34: 367–90.

Leitman, D.I., Ziwich, R., Pasternak, R. and Javitt, D.C. (2006) 'Theory of mind (ToM) and counterfactuality deficits in schizophrenia: misperception or misinterpretation?', *Psychological Medicine*, 36: 1075–83.

Lemke, J. (1990) *Talking Science: Language Learning and Values*, Norwood, NJ: Ablex.

——(2000) 'Across the scales of time', *Mind, Culture and Activity*, 7: 273–90.

Lenat, D.B. and Feigenbaum, E.A. (1991) 'On the thresholds of knowledge', *Artificial Intelligence*, 47: 185–250; reprinted in D. Kirsh (ed.) (1992) *Foundations of Artificial Intelligence*, Cambridge, MA: MIT Press.

Lenci, A., Bel, N., Busa, F., Calzolari, N., Gola, E., Monachini, M., Ogonowski, A., Peter, I., Peters, W., Ruimy, N., Villegas, M. and Zampolli, A. (2000) 'SIMPLE: a general framework for the development of multilingual lexicons', *Journal of Lexicography*, 13: 249–63.

Lenk, U. (1998) 'Discourse markers and global coherence in conversation', *Journal of Pragmatics*, 30: 245–57.

Lenneberg, E. (1967) *Biological Foundations of Language*, New York: John Wiley and Sons.

Leo, R.A. and Thomas, G.C. (eds) (1998) *The Miranda Debate: Law, Justice and Policing*, Boston, MA: Northeastern University Press.

Leonard, L.B., Wilcox, M.J., Fulmer, K.C. and Davis, G.A. (1978) 'Understanding indirect requests: an investigation of children's comprehension of pragmatic meanings', *Journal of Speech and Hearing Research*, 21: 528–37.

Lepore, E. (2004) 'An abuse of context in semantics: the case of incomplete definite descriptions', in M. Reimer and A. Bezuidenhout (eds) *Descriptions and Beyond*, Oxford: Oxford University Press.

Lerner, G.H. (1989) 'Notes on overlap management in conversation: the case of delayed completion', *Western Journal of Speech Communication*, 53: 167–77.

——(1996a) '"Finding face" in the preference structures of talk-in-interaction', *Social Psychology Quarterly*, 59: 303–21.

——(1996b) 'On the "semi-permeable" character of grammatical units in conversation: conditional entry into the turn space of another speaker', in E. Ochs, E.A. Schegloff and S.A. Thompson (eds) *Interaction and Grammar*, Cambridge: Cambridge University Press.

——(2002) 'Turn-sharing: the choral co-production of talk-in-interaction', in C.E. Ford, B.A. Fox and S.A. Thompson (eds) *The Language of Turn and Sequence*, New York: Oxford University Press.

——(2004) 'Collaborative turn sequences', in G. H. Lerner (ed.) *Conversation Analysis: Studies from the First Generation*, Amsterdam and Philadelphia: John Benjamins.

Leslie, A.M. (1987) 'Pretense and representation: the origins of "theory of mind"', *Psychological Review*, 94: 412–26.

——(1994) 'ToMM, ToBy, and agency: core architecture and domain Specificity', in L. Hirschfeld and S. Gelman (eds) *Mapping the Mind: Domain Specificity in Cognition and Culture*, New York: Cambridge University Press.

——(2000) 'How to acquire a "representational theory of mind"', in D. Sperber (ed.) *Metarepresentations: A Multidisciplinary Perspective*, Oxford: Oxford University Press.

Leslie, A.M. and Roth, D. (1993) 'What autism teaches us about metarepresentation', in S. Baron-Cohen, H. Tager-Flusberg and D. Cohen (eds) *Understanding Other Minds: Perspectives from Autism*, Oxford: Oxford University Press.

Letts, C. and Leinonen, E. (2001) 'Comprehension of inferential meaning in language-impaired and language normal children', *International Journal of Language and Communication Disorders*, 36: 307–28.

Leudar, I., Thomas, P. and Johnston, M. (1992) 'Self repair in dialogues of schizophrenics: effects of hallucinations and negative symptoms', *Brain and Language*, 43: 487–511.

Levelt, W.J.M. (1989) *Speaking*, Cambridge, MA: MIT Press.

——(1996) 'Perspective taking and ellipsis in spatial descriptions', in P. Bloom, M. Peterson, L. Nadel and M. Garrett (eds) *Language and Space*, Cambridge, MA: MIT Press.

Levin, B. and Rappaport Hovav, M. (1992) 'Wiping the slate clean: a lexical semantic exploration', in B. Levin and S. Pinker (eds) *Lexical and Conceptual Semantics*, Oxford: Blackwell.

——(2005) *Argument Realization*, Cambridge: Cambridge University Press.

Levinson, S.C. (1979) 'Activity types and language', *Linguistics*, 17: 365–69.

——(1983) *Pragmatics*, Cambridge: Cambridge University Press.

——(1987a) 'Minimization and conversational inference', in J. Verschueren and M. Bertuccelli-Papi (eds.) *The Pragmatic Perspective*, Amsterdam: John Benjamins.

——(1987b) 'Pragmatics and the grammar of anaphora', *Journal of Linguistics*, 23: 379–434.

——(1991) 'Pragmatic reduction of the binding conditions revisited', *Journal of Linguistics*, 27: 107–61.

——(1995) 'Three levels of meaning', in F.R. Palmer (ed.) *Grammar and Meaning. Essays in Honour of Sir John Lyons*, Cambridge: Cambridge University Press.

——(1996) 'Frames of reference and Molyneux's question: crosslinguistic evidence', in P. Bloom, M.A. Peterson, L. Nadell and M.F. Garrett (eds) *Language and Space*, Cambridge, MA: MIT Press.

——(1997) 'From outer to inner space: linguistic categories and non-linguistic thinking', in J. Nuyts and E. Pederson (eds) *Language and Conceptual Representation*, Cambridge: Cambridge University Press.

——(1998) 'Studying spatial conceptualization across cultures: anthropology and cognitive science', *Ethos*, 26: 7–24.

——(2000) *Presumptive Meanings: The Theory of Generalized Conversational Implicature*, Cambridge, MA: MIT Press.

——(2003) *Space in Language and Cognition: Explorations in Cognitive Diversity*, Cambridge: Cambridge University Press.

——(2004) 'Deixis' in L.R. Horn and G. Ward (eds) *The Handbook of Pragmatics*, Oxford: Blackwell.

Levinson, S.C. and Burenhult, N. (2009) 'Semplates: a new concept in lexical semantics?', *Language* 85: 150–72.

Levinson, S.C. and Wilkins, D. (eds) (2006) *Grammars of Space*, Cambridge: Cambridge University Press.

Levy, C.M. and Ransdell, S. (1996) *The Science of Writing*, Mahwah, NJ: Erlbaum.

Lewis, C. and Mitchell, P. (eds) (1994) *Children's Early Understanding of the Mind: Origins and Development*, Hillsdale, NJ: Erlbaum.

Lewis, D. (1969) *Convention: A Philosophical Study*, Cambridge, MA: Harvard University Press.

——(1970) 'General semantics', *Synthese*, 22: 18–67.

——(1973) *Counterfactuals*, Oxford: Blackwell.

——(1975a) 'Adverbs of quantification', in E. Keenan (ed.) *Formal Semantics of Natural Language*, Cambridge: Cambridge University Press.

——(1975b) 'Languages and language', in K. Gunderstone (ed.) *Language, Mind and Knowledge: Minnesota Studies in the Philosophy of Science*, vol. II, Minneapolis, MN: University of Minnesota Press; reprinted in A.P. Martinich (ed.) (1990) *The Philosophy of Language*, 2nd edn, New York: Oxford University Press.

——(1976) 'General semantics', in B.H. Partee (ed.) *Montague Grammar*, New York: Academic Press.

——(1980) 'Index, context, and content', in S. Kanger and S. Öhman (eds) *Philosophy and Grammar*, Dordrecht: Reidel.

——(1986) *The Plurality of Worlds*, Oxford: Blackwell.

——(1996) 'Elusive knowledge', *Australasian Journal of Philosophy*, 74: 549–67.

Li, C.N. and Thompson, S.A. (1976) 'Subject and topic: a new typology of language', in C. N. Li (ed.) *Subject and Topic*, New York: Academic Press.

Li, D. (2007) 'Pragmatic socialization', in P. Duff and N. Hornberger (eds) *Encyclopedia of Language and Education, Volume 8: Language Socialization*, Berlin: Springer.

Li, P. (2006) 'Factors affecting the degrees of severity in the realization of the speech act of complaint', *Foreign Language Teaching and Research*, 38: 56–60.

Liao, C. and Bresnahan, M.I. (1996) 'A contrastive pragmatic study on American English and Mandarin refusal strategies', *Language Sciences*, 18: 703–27.

Liberman, K. (2004) *Dialectical Practice in Tibetan Philosophical Culture: An Ethnomethodological Inquiry into Formal Reasoning*, Lanham, MD: Rowman and Littlefield.

Lichtenberk, F. (1991) 'On the gradualness of grammaticalization', in E.C. Traugott and B. Heine (eds) *Approaches to Grammaticalization, Volume I: Theoretical and Methodological Issues*, Amsterdam: John Benjamins.

Liddell, S.K. (2003) *Grammar, Gesture, and Meaning in American Sign Language*, Cambridge: Cambridge University Press.

Liddicoat, A.J. and Crozet, C. (2001) 'Acquiring French interactional norms through Instruction', in K.R. Rose and G. Kasper (eds) *Pragmatics in Language Teaching*, Cambridge: Cambridge University Press.

Liebal, K., Behne, T., Carpenter, M. and Tomasello, M. (2009) 'Infants use shared experience to interpret pointing gestures', *Developmental Science*, 12: 264–71.

Liebal, K., Carpenter, M. and Tomasello, M. (submitted) 'Infants' use of shared experience in declarative pointing', *Child Development*.

Liggens, E. (1981) 'Irony and understatement in Beowulf', *Parergon: Bulletin of the Australian and New Zealand Association for Medieval and Renaissance Studies*, 29: 3–7.

Lin, Y.-H. (2000) 'Agreement and disagreement of vowel features: mid vowel assimilation in Yanggu', *Language and Linguistics*, 1: 139–59.

Lindsay, P.H. and Norman, D.A. (1977) *Human Information Processing*, New York: Academic Press.

Lindström, A. (1994) 'Identification and recognition in Swedish telephone conversation openings', *Language in Society*, 23: 231–52.

Linell, P., Alemyr, L. and Jönsson, L. (1993) 'Admission guilt as a communicative project in judicial settings', *Journal of Pragmatics*, 19: 153–76.

Liszkowski, U., Albrecht, K., Carpenter, M. and Tomasello, M. (2008a) 'Infants' visual and auditory communication when a partner is or is not visually attending', *Infant Behavior and Development*, 31: 157–67.

Liszkowski, U., Carpenter, M. and Tomasello, M. (2008b) 'Twelve-month-olds communicate helpfully and appropriately for knowledgeable and ignorant partners', *Cognition*, 108: 732–39.

——(2007a) 'Pointing out new news, old news, and absent referents at 12 months of age', *Developmental Science*, 10: F1–F7.

——(2007b) 'Reference and attitude in infant pointing', *Journal of Child Language*, 34: 1–20.

Liszkowski, U., Carpenter, M., Henning, A., Striano, T. and Tomasello, M. (2004) 'Twelve-month-olds point to share attention and interest', *Developmental Science*, 7: 297–307.

Liszkowski, U., Carpenter, M., Striano, T. and Tomasello, M. (2006) 'Twelve- and 18-month-olds point to provide information for others', *Journal of Cognition and Development*, 7: 173–87.

Liszkowski, U., Schäfer, M., Carpenter, M. and Tomasello, M. (to appear) 'Prelinguistic infants, but not chimpanzees, communicate about absent entities', *Psychological Science*.

Liu, H.-M., Kuhl, P.K. and Tsao, F.-M. (2003) 'An association between mothers' speech clarity and infants' speech discrimination skills', *Developmental Science*, 6: F1–F10.

Liu, J. (2006) *Measuring Interlanguage Pragmatic Knowledge of EFL Learners*, Frankfurt am Main: Lang.

Livia, A. and Hall, K. (eds) (1997a) *Queerly Phrased: Language, Gender, and Sexuality*, Oxford: Oxford University Press.

——(1997b) '"It's a girl!": bringing performativity back to linguistics', in A. Livia and K. Hall (eds) *Queerly Phrased: Language, Gender, and Sexuality*, Oxford: Oxford University Press.

Lloyd, L.L., Koul, R. and Arvidson, H. (1993) 'ISAAC governance and related activities: AAC master's and doctoral theses', *Augmentative and Alternative Communication*, 9: 196–225.

Local, J.K. (1992) 'Continuing and restarting', in P. Auer and A. di Luzio (eds) *The Contextualization of Language*, Amsterdam: John Benjamins.

Local, J.K. and Kelly, J. (1986) 'Projection and "silences": notes on phonetic and conversational structure', *Human Studies*, 9: 185–204.

Local, J.K., Kelly, J. and Wells, W.H.G. (1986) 'Towards a phonology of conversation: turn-taking in Tyneside English', *Linguistics*, 22: 411–37.

Local, J.K., Wells, W. and Sebba, M. (1985) 'Turn delimitation in London Jamaican', *Journal of Pragmatics*, 9: 309–30.

LoCastro, V. (1997) 'Politeness and pragmatic competence in foreign language education', *Language Teaching Research*, 1: 239–67.

Locher, M. (2004) *Power and Politeness in Action: Disagreements in Oral Communication*, Berlin: Mouton de Gruyter.

——(2006) *Advice Online: Advice-Giving in an American Internet Health Column*, Philadelphia, PA: John Benjamins.

Lock, S., Wilkinson, R. and Bryan, K. (2001) *Supporting Partners of People With Aphasia in Relationships and Conversation (SPPARC): A Resource Pack*, Bicester: Speechmark.

Locke, J. (1690) *An Essay Concerning Human Understanding*, London: Thomas Tigg.

Locke, J.L. (1997) 'A theory of neurolinguistic development', *Brain and Language*, 58: 265–326.

Locke, T. (2004) *Critical Discourse Analysis*, London: Continuum.

Lodge, D. (1989) *Nice Work*, London: Penguin.

——(1995) *Therapy*, London: Secker and Warburg.

Lodge, D.N. and Leach, E.A. (1975) 'Children's acquisition of idioms in the English language', *Journal of Speech and Hearing Research*, 18: 521–29.

Loh, T. (1993) *Responses to Compliments Across Languages and Cultures: A Comparative Study of British and Hong Kong Chinese*, Hong Kong: Department of English, City Polytechnic of Hong Kong.

Lombard, L.B. (1986) *Events: A Metaphysical Study*, London: Routledge and Kegan Paul.

Long, M. (1990) 'Maturational constraints on language development', *Studies in Second Language Acquisition*, 12: 251–85.

Longacre, R.E. (1983) *The Grammar of Discourse*, New York and London: Plenum.

Lord, C. and Paul, R. (1997) 'Language and communication in autism', in D.J. Cohen and F.R. Volkmar (eds) *Handbook of Autism and Pervasive Developmental Disorders*, New York: John Wiley and Sons.

Lorenz, M. and Cobb, S. (1954) 'Language patterns in psychotic and psychoneurotic subjects', *Archives of Neurology and Psychiatry*, 72: 665–73.

Lorenzo-Dus, N. (2001) 'Compliment responses among British and Spanish university students: a contrastive study', *Journal of Pragmatics*, 33: 107–27.

Losonsky, M. (2006) *Linguistic Turns in Modern Philosophy*, Cambridge: Cambridge University Press.

Louhiala-Salminen, L. (2009) 'Business communication', in F. Bargiela-Chiappini (ed.) *The Handbook of Business Discourse*, Edinburgh: Edinburgh University Press.

Loukusa, S., Leinonen, E., Jussila, K., Mattila, M.-L., Ryder, N., Ebeling, H. and Moilanen, I. (2007a) 'Answering contextually demanding questions: pragmatic errors produced by children with Asperger syndrome or high-functioning autism', *Journal of Communication Disorders*, 40: 357–81.

Loukusa, S., Leinonen, E., Kuusikko, S., Jussila, K., Mattila, M.L., Ryder, N., Ebeling, H. and Moilanen, I. (2007b) 'Use of context in pragmatic language comprehension by children with Asperger syndrome or high-functioining autism', *Journal of Autism and Developmental Disorders*, 37: 1049–59.

Loukusa, S., Ryder, N. and Leinonen, E. (2008) 'Answering questions and explaining answers: a study of Finnish-speaking children', *Journal of Psycholinguistic Research*, 37: 219–41.

Louw, W. (1993) 'Irony in the text or insincerity in the writer? The diagnostic potential of semantic prosodies', in M. Baker, G. Francis and E. Tognini-Bonelli (eds) *Text and Technology: In Honour of John Sinclair*, Amsterdam: John Benjamins.

Loux, M.J. (2002) *Metaphysics: An Introduction*, 2nd edn, London: Routledge.

Love, N. (ed.) (2001) Special Issue: Grammaticalization, *Language Sciences*, 23: 93–340.

Lowe, E.J. (2002) *A Survey of Metaphysics*, Oxford: Oxford University Press.

Lowe, V. (1994) 'Unsafe convictions: "unhappy" confessions in *The Crucible*', *Language and Literature*, 3: 175–95.

Lowrey, B. (2002) 'Notes on meiosis', *Verbatim: The Language Quarterly*, 27: 9–11.

Lubinski, R. and Orange, J.B. (2000) 'A framework for the assessment and treatment of functional communication in dementia', in L. Worrall and C. Frattali (eds) *Neurogenic Communication Disorders: A Functional Approach*, New York: Thieme.

Lucy, J.A. (1985) 'Whorf's view of the linguistic mediation of thought', in B. Blount (ed.) *Language, Culture, and Society*, 2nd edn, Prospect Heights, IL: Waveland Press.

——(1992a) *Grammatical Categories and Cognition: A Case Study of the Linguistic Relativity Hypothesis*, Cambridge: Cambridge University Press.

——(1992b) *Language Diversity and Thought*, Cambridge: Cambridge University Press.

——(ed.) (1993) *Reflexive Language: Reported Speech and Metapragmatics*, Cambridge: Cambridge University Press.

——(1997) 'Linguistic relativity', *Annual Review of Anthropology*, 26: 291–312.

Lucy, J.A. and Gaskins, S. (2001) 'It's later than you think: the role of language-specific categories in the development of classification behavior', in M. Bowerman and S.C. Levinson (eds) *Language Acquisition and Conceptual Development*, Cambridge: Cambridge University Press.

Lucy, J.A. and Gaskins, S. (2003) 'Interaction of language type and referent type in the development of nonverbal classification preferences', in D. Gentner and S. Goldin-Meadow (eds) *Language in Mind*, Cambridge, MA: MIT Press.

Ludlow, P. and Martin, N. (eds) (1998) *Externalism and Self-Knowledge*, Stanford, CA: CSLI Publications.

Ludlow, P. and Neale, S. (1991) 'Indefinite descriptions: in defense of Russell', *Linguistics and Philosophy*, 14: 171–202.

Luke, A. (1997) 'The material effects of the word: "stolen children" and public discourse', *Discourse: Studies in the Cultural Politics of Education*, 18: 343–68.

Luke, K.K. (2002) 'The initiation and introduction of first topics in Hong Kong telephone calls', in K.K. Luke and Th.-S. Pavlidou (eds) *Telephone Calls: Unity and Diversity in Conversational Structure across Languages and Cultures*, Amsterdam and Philadelphia, PA: John Benjamins.

Luke, K.K. and Pavlidou, Th.-S. (eds) (2002) *Telephone Calls: Unity and Diversity in Conversational Structure across Languages and Cultures*, Amsterdam and Philadelphia, PA: John Benjamins.

Lukes, S. (1974) *Power: A Radical View*, London: Macmillan.

Lycan, W.G. (1984) *Logical Form in Natural Language*, London: MIT Press.

——(1999) *Philosophy of Language: A Contemporary Introduction*, New York: Routledge.

——(2001) *Real Conditionals*, Oxford: Oxford University Press.

Lynch, M. (1985) *Art and Artifact in Laboratory Science: A Study of Shop Work and Shop Talk*, London: Routledge and Kegan Paul.

Lyon, J.G., Cariski, D., Keisler, L., Rosenbek, J., Levine, R., Kumpula, J., Ryff, C., Coyne, S.

and Blanc, M. (1997) 'Communication partners: enhancing participation in life and communication for adults with aphasia in natural settings', *Aphasiology*, 11: 693–708.

Lyons, C. (1999) *Definiteness*, Cambridge: Cambridge University Press.

Lyons, J. (1968) *Introduction to Theoretical Linguistics*, Cambridge: Cambridge University Press.

——(1977) *Semantics*, vols 1 and 2, Cambridge: Cambridge University Press.

Lyons, W. (1995) *Approaches to Intentionality*, Oxford: Clarendon Press.

Lyster, R. (1994) 'The effect of functional-analytic teaching on aspects of French immersion students' sociolinguistic competence', *Applied Linguistics*, 15: 263–87.

Maat, H.P. (1998) 'Classifying negative coherence relations on the basis of linguistic evidence', *Journal of Pragmatics*, 30: 177–204.

Macaulay, R. (2001) '"You're like *why not?*" The quotative expressions of Glasgow adolescents', *Journal of Sociolinguistics*, 5: 3–21.

Macauley, R.K.S. and Trevelyan, G.D. (1977) *Language, Education and Employment in Glasgow*, Edinburgh: Edinburgh University Press.

MacBride, F. (2006) 'Predicate reference', in E. Lepore and B.C. Smith (eds) *The Oxford Handbook of Philosophy of Language*, Oxford: Clarendon Press.

MacFarlane, J. (2005) 'The assessment sensitivity of knowledge attributions', in T. Gendler and J. Hawthorne (eds) *Oxford Studies in Epistemology*, Oxford: Oxford University Press.

Machin, D. and Niblock, S. (2006) *News Production: Theory and Practice*, London: Routledge.

Machin, D. and van Leeuwen, T. (2007) *Global Media Discourse*, London: Routledge.

Mackay, R. (1996) 'Mything the point: a critique of objective stylistics', *Language and Communication*, 16: 81–93.

Maclaran, R. (1982) *The semantics and pragmatics of the English demonstratives*, Ph.D. dissertation, Cornell University.

MacMahon, B. (2007) 'The effects of sound patterning in poetry: a cognitive pragmatics approach', *Journal of Literary Semantics*, 36: 103–20.

MacNamara, J. (1994) *The Logical Foundations of Cognition*, New York: Oxford University Press.

Macnamara, J., Baker, E. and Olson, C. (1976) 'Four-year-olds' understanding of "pretend", "forget" and "know": evidence for propositional operations', *Child Development*, 47: 62–70.

Macy, M.W. (1998) 'Social class', in J.L. Mey (ed.) *Concise Encyclopedia of Pragmatics*, Amsterdam and Oxford: Elsevier.

Maes, P. (ed.) (1991) *Designing Autonomous Agents: Theory and Practice from Biology to Engineering and Back*, Cambridge, MA: MIT Press.

Maeshiba, N., Yoshinaga, N., Kasper, G. and Ross, S. (1996) 'Transfer and proficiency in interlanguage apologizing', in S. Gass and J. Neu (eds) *Speech Acts Across Cultures*, Berlin: Mouton de Gruyter.

Magnani, L. (2001) *Abduction, Reasoning and Science: Processes of Discovery and Explanation*, Dordrecht: Kluwer; New York: Plenum.

Magnusson, L. (1999) *Shakespeare and Social Dialogue: Dramatic Language and Elizabethan Letters*, Cambridge: Cambridge University Press.

Maher, B.A. (1972) 'The language of schizophrenia: a review', *British Journal of Psychiatry*, 120: 3–17.

Mahlberg, M. (2007) 'Clusters, key clusters and local textual functions in Dickens', *Corpora*, 2: 1–31.

Maienborn, C. (2004) 'A pragmatic explanation of the stage level/individual level contrast in combination with locatives', in B. Agbayani, V. Samiian and B. Tucker (eds) *Proceedings of the Western Conference on Linguistics (WECOL)*, volume 15, Fresno, CA: CSU.

——(2005) 'A discourse-based account of Spanish ser/estar', *Linguistics*, 43: 155–80.

Majid, A. and Bowerman, M. (eds) (2007) 'Cutting and breaking' events: a cross-linguistic perspective', *Cognitive Linguistics*, 18: 319–30.

Makinson, D. (1994) 'General patterns in non-monotonic reasoning', in D.M. Gabbay, C. Hagger, J.A. Robinson and D. Nute (eds) *Handbook in Artificial Intelligence and Logic Programming, Volume 3, Nonmotonic and Uncertain Reasoning*, Oxford: Oxford University Press.

Malchukov, A.L. (2004) 'Towards a semantic typology of adversative and contrast marking', *Journal of Semantics*, 21: 177–98.

Malinowski, B. (1923) 'The problem of meaning in primitive languages', in C. Ogden and I.A. Richards (eds) *The Meaning of Meaning*, London: Routledge and Kegan Paul.

Maltz, D.N. (1985) 'Joyful noise and reverent silence: the significance of noise in Pentecostal worship', in D. Tannen and M. Saville-Troike (eds) *Perspectives of Silence*, Norwood, NJ: Ablex.

Manes, J. and Wolfson, N. (1981) 'The compliment formula', in F. Coulmas (ed.) *Conversational Routine: Explorations in Standardized Communication Situations and Prepatterned Speech*, The Hague and New York: Mouton.

Mann, W. and Thompson, S. (1986) 'Relational propositions in discourse', *Discourse Processes*, 9: 57–90.

——(1988) 'Rhetorical structure theory: toward a functional theory of text organisation', *Text*, 8: 243–81.

Manning, C.D. and Schütze, H. (1999) *Foundations of Statistical Natural Language Processing*, Cambridge, MA: MIT Press.

Manschreck, T.C., Maher, B.A. and Milavetz, J. J. (1988) 'Semantic priming in thought disordered schizophrenic patients', *Schizophrenia Research*, 1: 61–66.

Mao, L. (1994) 'Beyond politeness theory: "face" revisited and renewed', *Journal of Pragmatics*, 21: 451–86.

Mao, R. (1989) 'On three issues of understatement', *Wai guo yu / Journal of Foreign Languages*, 6: 57–60.

Maratsos, M. (1976) *The Use of Definite and Indefinite Reference in Young Children*, Cambridge: Cambridge University Press.

March, E.G., Wales, R. and Pattison, P. (2006) 'The uses of nouns and deixis in discourse production in Alzheimer's disease', *Journal of Neurolinguistics*, 19: 311–40.

Marcos, H. (1991) 'Reformulating requests at 18 months: gestures, vocalizations and words', *First Language*, 11: 361–75.

Marcos, H. and Kornhaber-le Chanu, M. (1992) 'Learning how to insist and how to clarify in the second year', *International Journal of Behavioral Development*, 3: 359–77.

Marini, A., Carlomagno, S., Caltagirone, C. and Nocentini, U. (2005) 'The role played by the right hemisphere in the organization of complex textual structures', *Brain and Language*, 93: 46–54.

Marinis, T. (2003) 'Psycholinguistic techniques in second language acquisition research', *Second Language Research*, 19: 144–61.

Markkanen, R. and Schröder, H. (1987) 'Hedging and linguistic realizations in German, English, and Finnish philosophical text: a case study', *Erikoiskielet ja käännösteoria, Vakki-seminaari*, VII: 47–57.

——(1997) *Hedging and Discourse: Approaches to the Analysis of a Pragmatic Phenomenon in Academic Texts*, Berlin and New York: Walter de Gruyter.

Marmaridou, S.S.A. (2000) *Pragmatic Meaning and Cognition*, Amsterdam and Philadelphia, PA: John Benjamins.

Marquez Reiter, R. (2000) *Linguistic Politeness in Britain and Uruguay*, Amsterdam: John Benjamins.

——(2005) 'Complaint calls to a caregiver service company: the case of Desahogo', *Intercultural Pragmatics*, 2: 481–514.

Marr, D. (1982) *Vision: A Computational Investigation into the Human Representation and Processing of Visual Information*, San Francisco, CA: Freeman.

Marriott, H. (1993) 'Acquiring sociolinguistic competence: Australian secondary students in Japan', *Journal of Asian Pacific Communication*, 4: 167–92.

Marshall, R. (1999) *Introduction to Group Treatment for Aphasia: Design and Management*, Woburn, MA: Butterworth-Heinemann.

Marslen-Wilson, W. and Tyler, L.K. (1980) 'The temporal structure of spoken language understanding', *Cognition*, 88: 1–71.

Marti, L. (2006) 'Unarticulated constituents revisited', *Linguistics and Philosophy*, 29: 135–66.

Martin, I. and McDonald, S. (2003) 'Weak coherence, no theory of mind, or executive dysfunction? Solving the puzzle of pragmatic language disorders', *Brain and Language*, 85: 451–66.

——(2004) 'An exploration of causes of non-literal language problems in individuals with Asperger syndrome', *Journal of Autism and Developmental Disorders*, 34: 311–28.

Martin, J.R. and Plum, G.A. (1997) 'Construing experience: some story genres', *Journal of Narrative and Life History*, 7: 299–308.

Martin, J.R. and Wodak, R. (eds) (2003) *Re-Reading the Past: Critical and Functional Perspectives on Time and Value*, Amsterdam: John Benjamins.

Martin, R.A. (2007) *The Psychology of Humor: An Integrative Approach*, Burlington, MA: Elsevier.

Martin, R.M. (1978) *Events, Reference, and Logical Form*, Washington, DC: The Catholic University of America Press.

Martinovski, B. (2000) *The Role of Repetitions and Reformulations in Court Proceedings: A Comparison Between Sweden and Bulgaria*, Gothenburg Monographs in Linguistics 18, Göteborg University, Sweden.

——(2006) 'Framework for analysis of mitigation in courts', *Journal of Pragmatics*, 38: 2065–86.

Martinovski, B. and Marsella, S. (2003) 'Dynamic reconstruction of selfhood: coping processes in discourse', Proceedings of Joint International Conference on Cognitive Science, Sydney, Australia.

——(2005) 'Theory of mind and coping strategies', Proceedings of Artificial Intelligence and Social Behavior, Hatfield, UK.

Martinovski, B., Mao, W., Gratch, J. and Marsella, S. (2005) 'Mitigation theory: an integrated approach', Proceedings of Conference on Cognitive Science, Stresa, Italy.

Maryns, K. (2006) *The Asylum Speaker: Language in the Belgian Asylum Procedure*, Manchester: St Jerome.

Master, P. (1987) *A cross-linguistic interlanguage analysis of the acquisition of the English article system*, Ph.D. dissertation, University of California at Los Angeles.

Mathesius, V. ([1928] 1967) 'On linguistic characterology with illustrations from modern English', in J. Vachek (ed.) *A Prague School Reader in Linguistics*, Bloomington, IN: Indiana University Press.

Matheson, C., Poesio, M. and Traum, D.R. (2000) 'Modelling grounding and discourse obligations using update rules', *Proceedings of the 1st Annual Meeting of the North American Chapter of the Association for Computational Linguistics (NAACL)*, Morristown, NJ: Association for Computational Linguistics.

Mathy-Laikko, P. and Yoder, D. (1986) 'Future needs and directions in augmentative communication', in S. Blackstone (ed.) *Augmentative Communication: An Introduction*, Rockville, MD: American Speech Language Hearing Association.

Matsui, T. (2000) *Bridging and Relevance*, Amsterdam: John Benjamins.

——(ed.) (to appear) *Pragmatics and Theory of Mind*, Amsterdam: John Benjamins.

Matsui, T., Yamamoto, T. and McCagg, P. (2006) 'On the role of language in children's early understanding of others as epistemic beings', *Cognitive Development*, 21: 158–73.

Matsumoto, Y. (1988) 'Re-examination of the universality of face', *Journal of Pragmatics*, 12: 403–26.

——(1989) 'Politeness and conversational universals: observations from Japanese', *Multilingua*, 8: 207–21.

——(1995) 'The conversational condition on Horn scales', *Linguistics and Philosophy*, 18: 21–60.

Mattausch, J. (2007) 'Optimality, bidirectionality and the evolution of binding phenomena', *Research on Language and Computation*, 5: 103–31.

Matthewson, L. (1999) 'On the interpretation of wide-scope indefinites', *Natural Language Semantics*, 7: 79–134.

Matthewson, L., Bryant, T. and Roeper, T. (2001) 'A Salish stage in the acquisition of English determiners: unfamiliar "definites"', in *The Proceedings of SULA: The Semantics of Under-Represented Languages in the Americas*, Amherst, MA: University of Massachusetts Occasional Papers in Linguistics, 25.

Maturana, H.R. and Varela, F.J. (1980) *Autopoiesis and Cognition: The Realization of the Living*, Dordrecht: Reidel.

——(1987) *The Tree of Knowledge: The Biological Roots of Human Understanding*, Boston, MA: Shambhala Press.

Mauner, G., Tanenhaus, M. and Carlson, G. (1995) 'Implicit arguments in sentence processing', *Journal of Memory and Language*, 34: 357–82.

Mauranen, A. (1993) 'Contrastive ESP rhetoric: metatext in Finnish-English economics texts', *English for Specific Purposes*, 12: 3–22.

——(2001) 'Reflexive academic talk: observations from MICASE', in R.C. Simpson and J.M. Swales (eds) *Corpus Linguistics in North America: Selections from the 1999 Symposium*, Ann Arbor: University of Michigan Press.

Maybin, J. (1991) 'Children's informal talk and the construction of meaning', *English in Education*, 25: 34–49.

——(1994) 'Children's voices: talk, knowledge and identity', in D. Graddol, J. Maybin and B. Stierer (eds) *Researching Language and Literacy in Social Context*, Clevedon: Multilingual Matters Ltd.

Maynard Smith, J. and Harper, D.G.C. (2003) *Animal Signals*, Oxford: Oxford University Press.

Mazeland, H. (2004) 'Responding to the double implication of telemarketers' opinion queries', *Discourse Studies*, 6: 95–115.

——(2007) 'Parenthetical sequences', *Journal of Pragmatics*, 39: 1816–69.

McArthur, T. (1992) 'Telephone', in T. McArthur (ed.) *The Oxford Companion to the English Language*, Oxford: Oxford University Press.

McCarthy, J. (1968) 'Programs with common sense', in M. Minsky (ed.) *Semantic Information Processing*, Cambridge, MA: MIT Press.

——(1980) 'Circumscription: a form of nonmonotonic reasoning', *Artificial Intelligence*, 13: 27–39.

——(2007) *What is Artificial Intelligence?*. Online. Available: http://www-formal.stanford.edu/jmc/whatisai/whatisai.html (accessed 14 February 2008).

McCarthy, J. and Hayes, P.J. (1969) 'Some philosophical problems from the standpoint of artificial intelligence', in B. Meltzer and D. Michie (eds) *Machine Intelligence 4*, Edinburgh: Edinburgh University Press.

McCarthy, M. (2002) *Discourse Analysis for Language Teachers*, Cambridge: Cambridge University Press.

McCarthy, M. and Carter, R. (2004) '"There's millions of them": hyperbole in everyday conversation', *Journal of Pragmatics*, 36: 149–84.

McCarthy, R.A. and Warrington, E.K. (1990) *Cognitive Neuropsychology: A Clinical Introduction*, Orlando, FL: Academic Press.

McCawley, J.D. (1978) 'Conversational implicature and the lexicon', in P. Cole (ed.) *Syntax and Semantics 9: Pragmatics*, New York: Academic Press.

——(1981) *Everything that Linguists Have Always Wanted to Know about Logic (But Were Ashamed to Ask)*, Chicago, IL: University of Chicago Press.

——(1982) 'Parentheticals and discontinuous constituent structure', *Linguistic Inquiry*, 13: 91–106.

McClelland, J.L., Rumelhart, D.E. and the PDP Research Group (1986) *Parallel Distributed Processing: Explorations in the Microstructure of Cognition, Vol. 2: Psychological and Biological Models*, Cambridge, MA: MIT Press.

McConnell-Ginet, S. (2008) 'Words in the world: how and why meanings can matter', *Language*, 84: 497–527.

McCoy, K.F., Bedrosian, J. and Hoag, L.A. (2003) 'Pragmatic theory and utterance-based systems: application of the cooperative principle', in S. von Tetzchner and M.H. Jensen (eds) *Perspectives on Theory and Practice in Augmentative and Alternative Communication: Proceedings of the Seventh Biennial Research Symposium of the International Society for Augmentative and Alternative Communication*, Toronto, Canada: ISAAC.

McCoy, K.F., Bedrosian, J.L., Hoag, L.A. and Johnson, D.E. (2007) 'Brevity and speed of message delivery trade-offs in augmentative and alternative communication', *Augmentative and Alternative Communication*, 23: 76–88.

McCulloch, G. (1995) *The Mind and its World*, London and New York: Routledge.

McCulloch, W.S. and Pitts, W. (1943) 'A logical calculus of the ideas immanent in nervous activity', *Bulletin of Mathematical Biophysics*, 5: 115–37.

McDermott, J. (1982) 'RI: a rule-based configurer of computer systems', *Artificial Intelligence*, 19: 39–88.

McDonald, S. (1992) 'Communication disorders following closed head injury: new approaches to assessment and rehabilitation', *Brain Injury*, 6: 283–92.

——(1993) 'Pragmatic language skills after closed head injury: ability to meet the informational needs of the listener', *Brain and Language*, 44: 28–46.

——(1998) 'Communication and language disturbances following traumatic brain Injury', in B. Stemmer and H.A. Whitaker (eds) *Handbook of Neurolinguistics*, San Diego, CA: Academic Press.

——(1999) 'Exploring the process of inference generation in sarcasm: a review of normal and clinical studies', *Brain and Language*, 68: 486–506.

——(2000) 'Neuropsychological studies of sarcasm', *Metaphor and Symbol*, 15: 85–98.

McDonald, S. and Pearce, S. (1996) 'Clinical insights into pragmatic theory: frontal lobe deficits and sarcasm', *Brain and Language*, 53: 81–104.

McDonough, R.M. (1986) *The Argument of the 'Tractatus': Its Relevance to Contemporary Theories of Logic, Language, Mind, and Philosophical Truth*, Albany: State University of New York Press.

McDowell, J. (1986) 'Singular thought and the extent of inner space', in P. Pettit and J. McDowell (eds) *Subject, Thought and Context*, Oxford: Clarendon Press.

McElhinney, B. (1995) 'Challenging hegemonic masculinities: female and male police officers handling domestic violence', in K. Hall and M. Bucholtz (eds) *Gender Articulated: Language and the Socially Constructed Self*, London: Routledge.

——(2003) 'Fearful, forceful agents of the law: ideologies about language and gender in police officers' narratives about the use of physical force', *Pragmatics*, 13: 253–84.

McEnery, T. and Wilson, A. (1996) *Corpus Linguistics*, Edinburgh: Edinburgh University Press.

McFarlane, J. (2007) 'Semantic minimalism and nonindexical contextualism', in G. Preyer and G. Peter (eds) *Context-Sensitivity and Semantic Minimalism: New Essays on Semantics and Pragmatics*, Oxford: Oxford University Press.

McGann, W., Werven, G. and Douglas, M. (1997) 'Social competence and head injury: a practical approach', *Brain Injury*, 11: 621–28.

McGinn, M. (1997) *Wittgenstein and the Philosophical Investigations*, London: Routledge.

McGrath, J. (1991) 'Ordering thoughts on thought disorder', *British Journal of Psychiatry*, 158: 307–16.

McGregor, K. (1997) 'The nature of word-finding errors of preschoolers with and without word-finding deficits', *Journal of Speech, Language and Hearing Research*, 40: 1232–44.

McIntyre, D. (2004) 'Point of view in drama: a socio-pragmatic analysis of Dennis Potter's *Brimstone and Treacle*', *Language and Literature*, 13: 139–60.

——(2006) *Point of View in Plays: A Cognitive Stylistic Approach to Viewpoint in Drama and Other Text-types*, Amsterdam: John Benjamins.

McKenna, K. and Bargh, J. (2000) 'Plan 9 from cyberspace: the implications of the internet for personality and social psychological research', *Journal of Personality and Social Psychology*, 75: 681–94.

McKoon, G. and Ratcliff, R. (1992) 'Inference during reading', *Psychological Review*, 99: 440–66.

McLaughlin, B. (1978) *Second Language Acquisition in Childhood*, Hillsdale, NJ: Lawrence Erlbaum Associates.

McNamara, P. and Durso, R. (2003) 'Pragmatic communication skills in patients with Parkinson's disease', *Brain and Language*, 84: 414–23.

McNeil, N.M., Alibali, M.V. and Evans, J.L. (2000) 'The role of gesture in children's comprehension of spoken language: now they need them, now they don't', *Journal of Nonverbal Behavior*, 24: 131–50.

McNeill, D. (1985) 'So you think gestures are nonverbal?', *Psychological Review*, 92: 350–71.

——(1992) *Hand and Mind*, Chicago, IL: University of Chicago Press.

McNeill, D. and Duncan, S. (1999) 'Growth points in thinking for speaking', in D. McNeill (ed.) *Language and Gesture: Window into Thought and Action*, Cambridge: Cambridge University Press.

McNeill, D. and Levy, E. (1982) 'Conceptual representations in language activity and gesture', in R. Jarvella and W. Klein (eds) *Speech, Place, and Action*, Chichester: John Wiley and Sons.

McQueen, J.M. (2007) 'Eight questions about spoken word recognition', in M.G. Gaskell (ed.) *The Oxford Handbook of Psycholinguistics*, Oxford: Oxford University Press.

McTear, M. (2004) *Spoken Dialogue Technology: Toward the Conversational User Interface*, New York: Springer Verlag.

McTear, M. and Conti-Ramsden, G. (1992) *Pragmatic Disability in Children*, London: Whurr.

Medin, D., Coley, J., Storms, G. and Hayes, B. (2003) 'A relevance theory of induction', *Psychonomic Bulletin and Review*, 10: 517–32.

Mehan, H. (1979) *Learning Lessons: Social Organization in the Classroom*, Cambridge, MA: Harvard University Press.

Meier, A.J. (1998) 'Apologies: what do we know?', *International Journal of Applied Linguistics*, 8: 215–31.

——(2004) *Conflict and the Power of Apologies*. Online. Available: http://web.fu-berlin.de/phin/phin30/p30t1.htm (accessed 29 February 2008).

Meilijson, S.R. (1999) *The language of patients with chronic schizophrenia: aspects of the theory of core and central pragmatics*, unpublished thesis, Tel Aviv University.

Meilijson, S.R., Kasher, A. and Elizur, A. (2004) 'Language performance in chronic schizophrenia: a pragmatic approach', *Journal of Speech, Language and Hearing Research*, 47: 695–713.

Meisel, J. (1997) 'The acquisition of the syntax of negation in French and German, contrasting first and second language development', *Second Language Research*, 13: 227–63.

——(2001) 'The simultaneous acquisition of two first languages: early differentiation and subsequent development of grammars', in J. Cenoz and F. Genesee (eds) *Trends in Bilingual Acquisition*, Amsterdam: John Benjamins.

——(2004) 'The bilingual child', in T. Bhatia and W. Ritchie (eds) *The Handbook of Bilingualism*, Oxford: Blackwell.

Mele, A.R. (1992) *Springs of Action*, Oxford: Oxford University Press.

Meleuc, S. (1972) 'Struktur der maxime', in J. Ihwe (ed.) *Literaturwissenschaft und Linguistik. Bd. 2.3: Zur Linguistischen Basis der Literaturwissenschaft 2*, Frankfurt am Main: Athenäum.

Meltzoff, A.N. and Moore, M.K. (1997) 'Explaining facial imitation: a theoretical model', *Early Development and Parenting*, 6: 179–92.

Melzi, G. (2000) 'Cultural variations in the construction of personal narratives: Central American and European American mothers' elicitation styles', *Discourse Processes*, 30: 153–77.

Mentis, M. (1994) 'Topic management in discourse: assessment and intervention', *Topics in Language Disorders*, 14: 29–54.

Mentis, M. and Briggs-Whittaker, J. (1995) 'Discourse topic management in senile dementia of the Alzheimer's type', *Journal of Speech and Hearing Research*, 28: 1054–66.

Mentis, M. and Prutting, C.A. (1987) 'Cohesion in the discourse of normal and head-injured adults', *Journal of Speech and Hearing Research*, 30: 583–95.

——(1991) 'Analysis of topic as illustrated in a head injured and a normal adult', *Journal of Speech and Hearing Research*, 34: 583–95.

Mercer, N. (1995) *The Guided Construction of Knowledge: Talk amongst Teachers and Learners*, Clevedon: Multilingual Matters.

Mercer, N., Dawes, L., Wegerif, R. and Sams, C. (2004) 'Reasoning as a scientist: ways of helping children to use language to learn science', *British Educational Research Journal*, 30: 359–77.

Merin, A. (1997) 'If all our arguments had to be conclusive, there would be few of them',

Arbeitspapiere SFB 340 101, Stuttgart: University of Stuttgart.

——(1999) 'Information, relevance, and social decision making: some principles and results of decision-theoretic semantics', in L.S. Moss, J. Ginzburg and M. de Rijke (eds) *Logic, Language, and Computation*, volume 2, Stanford, CA: CSLI.

Merleau-Ponty, M. (1945) *Phénoménologie de la Perception*, Paris: Gallimard; trans. Colin Smith (1981) *Phenomenology of Perception*, London: Routledge.

Merrell, F. (1997) *Peirce, Signs, and Meaning*, Toronto: University of Toronto Press.

Mey, J.L. (1985) *Whose Language? A Study in Linguistic Pragmatics*, Amsterdam and Philadelphia, PA: John Benjamins.

——(1993) *Pragmatics: An Introduction*, Oxford: Blackwell.

——(2000) *When Voices Clash: A Study in Literary Pragmatics*, Berlin: Mouton de Gruyter.

——(2001) *Pragmatics: An Introduction*, 2nd edn, Oxford: Blackwell.

——(2005) 'What is in a (hand)book? Reflection on a recent compilation: review of Horn, L. R. and Ward, G. (eds) (2004) *The Handbook of Pragmatics*', *Intercultural Pragmatics*, 2: 347–53.

Meyer, R. (1993) *Compound Comprehension in Isolation and in Context*, Tübingen, Germany: Max Niemeyer Verlag.

Meyerhoff, M. (1999) 'Sorry in the Pacific: defining communities, defining practices', *Language in Society*, 28: 225–39.

Michaels, S. (1981) '"Sharing time": children's narrative styles and differential access to literacy', *Language in Society*, 10: 423–42.

Mieder, W. (1982) *Anti-Sprichwörter*, Wiesbaden, Germany: Verlag für Deutsche Sprache.

Mieder, W. and Litovkina, A.T. (1999) *Twisted Wisdom: Modern Anti-proverbs*, Burlington, VT: University of Vermont.

Mikkelsen, L. (2004) *Specifying who: on the structure, meaning and use of specificational copular clauses*, Ph.D. dissertation, University of California, Santa Cruz.

Mill, J.S. (1843) *A System of Logic, Ratiocinative and Inductive*, London: John W. Parker.

Miller, G.A. (1956) 'The magical number seven, plus or minus two: some limits on our capacity for processing information', *Psychological Review*, 63: 81–97.

——(2003) 'The cognitive revolution: a historical perspective', *TRENDS in Cognitive Sciences*, 7: 141–44.

Miller, G.A., Galanter, E. and Pribram, K.H. (1960) *Plans and the Structure of Behavior*, New York: Holt, Rinehart and Winston.

Millikan, R.G. (1984) *Language, Thought and Other Biological Categories*, Cambridge, MA: MIT Press.

——(1998) 'Language conventions made simple', *The Journal of Philosophy*, 95: 161–80.

Mills, S. (1995) *Feminist Stylistics*, London: Routledge.

——(1997) *Discourse*, London: Routledge.

——(2003) *Gender and Politeness*, Cambridge: Cambridge University Press.

Milner, G.B. (1969a) 'What is a proverb?', *New Society*, 332: 199–202.

——(1969b) 'Quadripartite structures', *Proverbium*, 14: 379–83.

Milosky, L.M. (1992) 'Children listening: the role of world knowledge in comprehension', in R. Chapman (ed.) *Processes in Language Acquisition and Disorders*, St Louis, MO: Mosby.

Milosky, L.M. and Ford, J.A. (1997) 'The role of prosody in children's inferences of ironic intent', *Discourse Processes*, 23: 47–61.

Milroy, L. (1980) *Language and Social Networks*, Oxford: Blackwell.

Milroy, L. and Perkins, L. (1992) 'Repair strategies in aphasic discourse: towards a collaborative model', *Clinical Linguistics and Phonetics*, 6: 27–40.

Milsark, G. (1974) *Existential sentences in English*, Ph.D. dissertation, Massachusetts Institute of Technology.

——(1977) 'Toward an explanation of certain peculiarities of the existential construction in English', *Linguistic Analysis*, 3: 1–29.

Minami, M. (1994) 'English and Japanese: a cross-cultural comparison of parental styles of elicitation', *Issues in Applied Linguistics*, 5: 383–407.

Minsky, M. (1974) *A Framework for Representing Knowledge*, MIT AI Laboratory Memo 306, Cambridge, MA; reprinted in P.H. Winston (ed.) (1975) *The Psychology of Computer Vision*, New York: McGraw-Hill; and also in J. Haugeland (ed.) (1981) *Mind Design*, Cambridge, MA: MIT Press.

——(1975) 'A framework for representing knowledge', in P. Winston (ed.) *The Psychology of Computer Vision*, New York: McGraw-Hill.

——(1988) *The Society of Mind*, New York: Simon and Schuster.

——(1991) 'Logical versus analogical or symbolic versus connectionist or neat versus scruffy', *AI Magazine*, 12: 34–51.

Minzenberg, M.J., Ober, B. and Vinogradov, S. (2002) 'Semantic priming in schizophrenia: a review and synthesis', *Journal of the International Neuropsychological Society*, 8: 699–720.

Mishler, E.G. (1986) *Research Interviewing: Context and Narrative*, Cambridge, MA: Harvard University Press.

——(1997) 'The interactional construction of narratives in medical and life-history interviews', in B-L. Gunnarsson, P. Linell, B. Nordberg and C.N. Candlin (eds) *The Construction of Professional Discourse*, London: Longman.

Mitchell, D.C. (1994) 'Sentence parsing', in M.A. Gernsbacher (ed.) *Handbook of Psycholinguistics*, San Diego, CA: Academic Press.

Mitchell, P., Robinson, E.J., Nye, R.M. and Isaacs, J.E. (1997) 'When speech conflicts with seeing: young children's understanding of informational priority', *Journal of Experimental Child Psychology*, 64: 276–94.

Mitchell, T. (1997) *Machine Learning*, New York: McGraw Hill.

Mitchley, N.J., Barber, J., Gray, J.M., Brook, D.N. and Martin, G.L. (1998) 'Comprehension of irony in schizophrenia', *Cognitive Neuropsychiatry*, 3: 127–38.

Mithen, S. (2005) *The Singing Neanderthals: The Origins of Music, Language, Mind and Body*, London: Weidenfeld and Nicolson.

Mithun, M. (1999) *The Languages of Native North America*, Cambridge: Cambridge University Press.

Mittwoch, A. (1979) 'Final parentheticals with English questions: their illocutionary function and grammar', *Journal of Pragmatics*, 3: 401–12.

Miyuki, S. (1998) 'Investigating EFL students' production of speech acts: a comparison of production questionnaires and role plays', *Journal of Pragmatics*, 30: 457–84.

Mo, S., Su, Y., Chan, R.C.K. and Liu, J. (2008) 'Comprehension of metaphor and irony in schizophrenia during remission: the role of theory of mind and IQ', *Psychiatry Research*, 157: 21–29.

Moerman, M. (1988) *Talking Culture: Ethnography and Conversation Analysis*, Philadelphia, PA: Pennsylvania University Press.

Mohanan, T. and Wee, L. (eds) (1999) *Grammatical Semantics: Evidence for Structure in Meaning*, Stanford and National University of Singapore: Centre for the Study of Language and Information.

Mokre, M., Weiss, G. and Bauböck, R. (eds) (2003) *Europas Identitäten, Mythen, Konstruktionen, Konflikte*, Frankfurt am Main: Campus.

Moll, H. and Tomasello, M. (2006) 'Level I perspective-taking at 24 months of age', *British Journal of Developmental Psychology*, 24: 603–13.

——(2007) 'How 14- and 18-month-olds know what others have experienced', *Developmental Psychology*, 43: 309–17.

Moll, H., Richter, N., Carpenter, M. and Tomasello, M. (2008) 'Fourteen-month-olds know what "we" have shared in a special way', *Infancy*, 13: 90–101.

Molnár, G. (2004) 'Translatability and tautological structures', *Hungarian Studies*, 18: 73–98.

Mondada, L. (2007a) 'Commentary: transcript variations and the indexicality of transcribing practices', *Discourse Studies*, 9: 809–21.

——(2007b) 'Multimodal resources for turn-taking: pointing and the emergence of possible next speakers', *Discourse Studies*, 9: 194–225.

Monetta, L. and Champagne, M. (2004) 'Processus cognitifs sous-jacents déterminants les troubles de la communication verbale chez les cérébrolésés droits', *Rééducation Orthophonique*, 219: 27–41.

Monetta, L. and Joanette, Y. (2003) 'The specificity of the contribution of the right hemisphere to verbal communication: the cognitive resources hypothesis', *Journal of Speech-Language Pathology*, 11: 203–11.

Monetta, L. and Pell, M.D. (2007) 'Effects of verbal working memory on metaphor comprehension in patients with Parkinson's disease', *Brain and Language*, 101: 80–89.

Monetta, L., Ouellet-Plamondon, C. and Joanette, Y. (2006) 'Simulating the pattern of right-hemisphere-damaged patients for the processing of the alternative metaphorical meanings of words: evidence in favor of a cognitive resources hypothesis', *Brain and Language*, 96: 171–77.

Montague, R. (1968) 'Pragmatics', in R. Klibansky (ed.) *Contemporary Philosophy–La Philosophie Contemporaine*, vol. 1, Florence: La Nuova Italia Editrice; reprinted in R. Thomason (ed.) (1974) *Formal Philosophy: Selected Papers of Richard Montague*, New Haven, CT: Yale University Press.

——(1973) 'The proper treatment of quantification in ordinary English', in J. Hintikka, J. Moravcsik and P. Suppes (eds) *Approaches to Natural Language: Proceedings of the 1970 Stanford Workshop on Grammar and Semantics*, Dordrecht: Reidel; reprinted in R. Thomason (ed.) (1974) *Formal Philosophy: Selected Papers of Richard Montague*, New Haven, CT: Yale University Press.

——(1974) *Formal Philosophy: Selected Papers of Richard Montague*, New Haven, CT: Yale University Press.

Montrul, S. (2008) *Incomplete Acquisition in Bilingualism: Re-Examining the Age Factor*, Amsterdam: John Benjamins.

Montrul, S. and Slabakova, R. (2003) 'Competence similarities between native and near-native speakers: an investigation of the preterite/imperfect contrast in Spanish', *Studies in Second Language Acquisition*, 25: 351–98.

Monzoni, C.M. (2008) 'Introducing direct complaints through questions', *Discourse Studies*, 10: 73–87.

Moon, C., Cooper, R.P. and Fifer, W.P. (1993) 'Two-day-olds prefer their native language', *Infant Behavior and Development*, 16: 495–500.

Moon, R. (1998a) 'Frequencies and forms of phrasal lexemes in English', in A.P. Cowie (ed.) *Phraseology: Theory, Analysis, and Applications*, Oxford: Oxford University Press.

——(1998b) *Fixed Expressions and Idioms in English*, Oxford: Clarendon Press.

Moore, C. and Corkum, V. (1994) 'Social understanding at the end of the first year of life', *Developmental Review*, 14: 349–72.

Moore, C., Bryant, D. and Furrow, D. (1989) 'Mental terms and the development of certainty', *Child Development*, 60: 167–71.

Moore, R.C. (1986) 'Problems in logical form', in B. Grosz, K. Jones and B. Webber (eds) *Readings in Natural Language Processing*, Los Altos, CA: Morgan Kaufman.

Morales, M., Mundy, P., Delgado, C.E.F., Yale, M., Messinger, D.S., Neal, R. and Schwartz, H. (2000) 'Responding to joint attention across the 6- to 24-month age period and early language acquisition', *Journal of Applied Developmental Psychology*, 21: 283–98.

Morante, R., Keizer, S. and Bunt, H.C. (2007) 'A dialogue act based model for context updating', in R. Artstein and L. Vieu (eds) *Proceedings of the Eleventh Workshop on the Semantics and Pragmatics of Dialogue (DECALOG 2007)*, Trento, Italy.

Morell, T. (2004) 'Interactive lecture discourse for university EFL students', *English for Specific Purposes*, 23: 325–38.

Morgan, D.L. and Krueger, R.A. (1993) 'When to use focus groups and why', in D.L. Morgan (ed.) *Successful Focus Groups*, Newbury Park, CA: Sage.

Morgan, G. (2000) 'Discourse cohesion in sign and speech', *International Journal of Bilingualism*, 4: 279–300.

Morgan, J.L. (1968) 'Some strange aspects of *if*', in C.-J.N. Bailey, B.J. Darden and A. Davison (eds) *Papers from the 4th Regional Meeting of the Chicago Linguistic Society*, Chicago, IL: Chicago Linguistic Society.

——(1970) 'On the criterion of identity for noun phrase deletion', *Papers from the 6th Regional Meeting of the Chicago Linguistic Society*, Chicago: Chicago Linguistic Society.

——(1973a) 'How can you be in two places at once when you're not anywhere at all?', in C. Corum, J.C. Smith-Stark and A. Weiser (eds) *Papers from the 9th Regional Meeting of the Chicago Linguistic Society*, Chicago, IL: Chicago Linguistic Society.

——(1973b) *Presupposition and the representation of meaning: prolegomena*, Ph.D. dissertation, University of Chicago.

——(1975) 'Some interactions of syntax and pragmatics', in P. Cole and J. Morgan (eds) *Syntax and Semantics 3: Speech Acts*, New York: Academic Press.

——(1978) 'Two types of convention in indirect speech acts', in P. Cole (ed.) *Syntax and Semantics 9: Pragmatics*, New York: Academic Press.

Mori, J. (1999) *Negotiating Agreement and Disagreement in Japanese: Connective Expressions and Turn Construction*, Amsterdam: John Benjamins.

Morice, R.D. and Ingram, J.C.L. (1983) 'Language complexity and age of onset of schizophrenia', *Psychiatry Research*, 9: 233–42.

Morice, R.D. and McNicol, D. (1986) 'Language changes in schizophrenia: a limited replication', *Schizophrenia Bulletin*, 12: 239–51.

Morris, C.W. (1925) 'Symbolism and reality: a study in the nature of mind', dissertation, University of Chicago; reprinted in A. Eschbach (ed.) (1993) *Foundations of Semiotics*, Amsterdam and Philadelphia, PA: John Benjamins.

——(1932) *Six Theories of Mind*, Chicago, IL: University of Chicago Press.

——(1934) 'Introduction', in C.W. Morris (ed.) *Mind, Self, and Society: From the Standpoint of a Social Behaviorist*, by George H. Mead, Chicago, IL: University of Chicago Press.

——(1937) *Logical Positivism, Pragmatism, and Scientific Empiricism*, Paris: Hermann et Cie.

——(1938) *Foundations of the Theory of Signs*, in O. Neurath (ed.) *International Encyclopedia of Unified Science*, vol. 1, no. 2, Chicago, IL: University of Chicago Press.

——(1942) *Paths of Life: Preface to a World Religion*, New York: Harper.

——(1946) *Signs, Language, and Behavior*, New York: Prentice-Hall.

——(1948) *The Open Self*, New York: Prentice-Hall.

——(1955) *Signs, Language and Behavior*, New York: George Braziller.

——(1956) *Varieties of Human Value*, Chicago, IL: University of Chicago Press.

——(1964) *Signification and Significance: A Study of the Relations of Signs and Values*, Cambridge, MA: Harvard University Press.

——(1970) *The Pragmatic Movement in American Philosophy*, New York: George Braziller.

——(1971) *Writings on the General Theory of Signs*, The Hague: Mouton.

Morris, R.K. (2006) 'Lexical processing and sentence context effects', in M.J. Traxler and M.A. Gernsbacher (eds) *Handbook of Psycholinguistics*, 2nd edn, London: Elsevier.

Morrish, L. and Sauntson, H. (2007) *New Perspectives on Language and Sexual Identity*, Houndmills: Palgrave.

Morrison, A. (2005) *Cross-cultural pragmatic study of refusals in English by speakers of German*, unpublished dissertation, Victoria University of Wellington.

Morrison, A. and Holmes, J. (2003) 'Eliciting refusals: a methodological challenge', *Te Reo*, 46: 47–66.

Morrow, P. (2006) 'Telling about problems and giving advice in an internet discussion forum: some discourse features', *Discourse Studies*, 8: 531–48.

Morsella, E. and Krauss, R. (2001) 'The role of gestures in spatial working memory and speech', *The American Journal of Psychology*, 117: 411–24.

Mortensen, C.D. (2006) *Human Conflict: Disagreement, Misunderstanding, and Problematic Talk*, Lanham, MD: Rowman and Littlefield.

Moskowitz, G.B. (2005) *Social Cognition: Understanding Self and Others*, New York, NY: Guilford Press.

Mounce, H.O. (1981) *Wittgenstein's Tractatus: An Introduction*, Oxford: Basil Blackwell.

Moyer, M.G. (2000) 'Negotiating agreement and disagreement in Spanish-English bilingual conversations with no', *International Journal of Bilingualism*, 4: 485–504.

Mukařovský, J. (1964) 'Standard language and poetic language', in P.L. Garvin (ed.) *A Prague School Reader on Aesthetics, Literary Structure and Style*, Washington, DC: Georgetown University Press.

Mulkern, A.E. (2003) *Cognitive status, discourse salience and information structure: evidence from Irish and Oromo*, unpublished thesis, University of Minnesota.

Mullany, L. (2007) *Gendered Discourses in the Professional Workplace*, Basingstoke: Palgrave Macmillan.

——(ed.) (2009) Special Issue: Politeness in Health Care Settings, *Journal of Politeness Research*, 5: 1–130.

Müller, F.E. (1996) 'Affiliating and disaffiliating with continuers: prosodic aspects of recipiency', in E. Couper-Kuhlen and M. Selting (eds) *Prosody in Interaction*, Cambridge: Cambridge University Press.

Müller, N. and Guendouzi, J.A. (2005) 'Order and disorder in conversation: encounters with dementia of the Alzheimer's type', *Clinical Linguistics and Phonetics*, 19: 393–404.

Munby, J. (1978) *Communicative Syllabus Design*, London: Cambridge University Press.

Mundorf, N. and Zillmann, D. (1991) 'Effects of story sequencing on affective reactions to broadcast news', *Journal of Broadcasting and Electronic Media*, 35: 197–211.

Muntigl, P., Weiss, G. and Wodak, R. (2000) *European Union Discourses on Un/Employment: An Interdisciplinary Approach to Employment Policy-Making and Organisational Change*, Amsterdam and Philadelphia, PA: John Benjamins.

Murphy, B. and Neu, J. (1996) 'My grade's too low: the speech act set of complaining', in S. M. Gass and J. Neu (eds) *Speech Acts Across Cultures: Challenges to Communication in a Second Language*, Berlin: Mouton de Gruyter.

Murphy, G. (1997) 'Polysemy and the creation of novel word meanings', in T. Ward, S. Smith and J. Vaid (eds) *Creative Thought: An Investigation of Conceptual Structures and Processes*, Washington, DC: American Psychological Association.

Murray, I.R. and Arnott, J.L. (1993) 'Toward the simulation of emotion in synthetic speech: a review of the literature on human vocal emotion', *Journal of the Acoustic Society of America*, 93: 1097–108.

——(1995) 'Implementation and testing of a system for producing emotion-by-rule in synthetic speech', *Speech Communication*, 16: 369–90.

Mushin, I. (2000) 'Evidentiality and deixis in narrative telling', *Journal of Pragmatics*, 32: 927–57.

Musloff, A. (2004) *Metaphor and Political Discourse: Analogical Reasoning in Debates about Europe*, Basingstoke: Palgrave Macmillan.

Myers, G. (1994) *Words in Ads*, London: Edward Arnold.

——(1995) 'From discovery to invention: the writing and rewriting of two patents', *Social Studies of Science*, 25: 57–105.

——(1996) 'Strategic vagueness in academic writing', in E. Ventola and A. Mauranen (eds) *Academic Writing: Intercultural and Textual Issues*, Amsterdam and Philadelphia, PA: John Benjamins.

——(1998) 'Displaying opinions: topics and disagreement in focus groups', *Language in Society*, 27: 85–111.

——(1999) 'Interaction in writing: principles and problems', in C. Candlin and K. Hyland (eds) *Writing: Texts, Processes and Practices*, London: Longman.

Myers, P.G. (1989) 'The pragmatics of politeness in scientific articles', *Applied Linguistics*, 10: 1–35.

——(1997) 'Hedging strategies in written academic discourse: strengthening the argument by weakening the claim', in R. Markkanen and H. Schröder (eds) *Hedging and Discourse: Approaches to the Analysis of a Pragmatic Phenomenon in Academic Text*, Berlin and New York: Walter de Gruyter.

Myers, P.S. (1999) *Right Hemisphere Damage: Disorders of Communication and Cognition*, San Diego, CA: Singular/Thompson.

Myers, P.S. and Linebaugh, C.W. (1981) 'Comprehension of idiomatic expressions by right-hemisphere-damaged adults', in R.H. Brookshire (ed.) *Clinical Aphasiology Conference*, Minneapolis, MN: BRK Publishers.

Myhill, J. (1998) 'A study of imperative usage in Biblical Hebrew and English', *Studies in Language*, 22: 391–446.

Nagel, T. (1974) 'What is it like to be a bat?', *The Philosophical Review*, 83: 435–50.

——(1986) *The View from Nowhere*, Oxford: Oxford University Press.

Nair-Venugopal, S. (2009) 'Malaysia', in F. Bargiela-Chiappini (ed.) *The Handbook of Business Discourse*, Edinburgh: Edinburgh University Press.

Nakabachi, K. (1996) 'Pragmatic transfer in complaints: strategies of complaining in English and Japanese by Japanese EFL speakers', *JACET Bulletin*, 27: 127–42.

Napoli, D.J. and Rando, E. (1978) 'Definites in *there*-sentences', *Language*, 54: 300–13.

Nariyama, S. (2001) 'Argument structure as another reference-tracking system with reference to ellipsis', *Australian Journal of Linguistics*, 21: 99–129.

——(2004) 'Subject ellipsis in English', *Journal of Pragmatics*, 36: 237–64.

Nash, W. (1989) 'Changing the guard at Elsinore', in R. Carter and P. Simpson (eds) *Language, Discourse and Literature*, London: Unwin Hyman/Routledge.

Neal, R.M. (1991) 'Connectionist learning of belief networks', *Artificial Intelligence*, 56: 71–113.

Neale, S. (1990) *Descriptions*, Cambridge, MA: MIT Press.

——(1992) 'Paul Grice and the philosophy of language', *Linguistics and Philosophy*, 15: 509–59.

——(2000) 'On being explicit', *Mind and Language*, 15: 284–94.

——(2005a) 'Pragmatism and binding', in Z. Szabo (ed.) *Semantics Versus Pragmatics*, Oxford: Oxford University Press.

——(ed.) (2005b) '100 years of "On Denoting"', *Mind*, 114: 809–1244.

Neary, D. (1990) 'Dementia of the frontal lobe type', *Journal of the American Geriatrics Society*, 38: 71–72.

Neary, D., Snowden, J., Mann, D., Northen, B., Goulding, P. and McDermott, M. (1990) 'Frontal lobe dementia and motor neuron disease', *Journal of Neurology, Neurosurgery, and Psychiatry*, 53: 23–32.

Neisser, U. (1967) *Cognitive Psychology*, Englewood Cliffs, NJ: Prentice-Hall.

Nelson, G.L., Al-Batal, M. and Echols, E. (1996) 'Arabic and English compliment responses: potential for pragmatic failure', *Applied Linguistics*, 17: 411–32.

Nelson, G.L., Carson, J., Al Batal, M. and El Bakary, W. (2002) 'Cross-cultural pragmatics: strategy use in Egyptian Arabic and American English refusals', *Applied Linguistics*, 23: 163–89.

Nelson, G.L., El-Bakary, W. and Al-Batal, M. (1993) 'Egyptian and American compliments: a cross-cultural study', *International Journal of Intercultural Relations*, 17: 293–313.

Nerlich, B. and Clarke, D.D. (1996) *Language, Action and Context*, Amsterdam: John Benjamins.

Nesi, H. and Basturkmen, H. (2006) 'Lexical bundles and discourse signalling in academic lectures', *International Journal of Corpus Linguistics*, 11: 283–304.

Nevile, M. (2004) *Beyond the Black Box: Talk-in-interaction in the Airline Cockpit*, Aldershot: Ashgate.

——(2006) 'Making sequentiality salient: *and*-prefacing in the talk of airline pilots', *Discourse Studies*, 8: 279–302.

Newbury, P. and Johnson, A. (2006) 'Suspects' resistance to constraining and coercive questioning strategies in the police interview', *International Journal of Speech, Language and the Law*, 13: 213–40.

Newell, A. (1990) *Unified Theories of Cognition*, Cambridge, MA: Harvard University Press.

Newell, A. and Simon, H.A. (1972) *Human Problem Solving*, Englewood Cliffs, NJ: Prentice-Hall.

——(1976) 'Computer science as empirical enquiry: symbols and search', *Communications of the Association for Computing Machinery*, 19: 113–26.

Newell, A.F. (1984) 'Do we know how to design communication aids?' in J.J. Presperin (ed.) *Proceedings of the Second Annual Conference on*

Rehabilitation Engineering, Bethesda, MD: Rehabilitation Engineers Society of North America.

Newmeyer, F.J. (1972) 'The insertion of idioms', in P.M. Peranteau, G.C. Phares and J.N. Levi (eds) *Papers from the eighth regional meeting of the Chicago Linguistics Society*, Chicago, IL: Chicago Linguistics Society.

Ng, S.K., Loong, C.S.F., He, A.P., Liu, J.H. and Weatherall, A. (2000) 'Communication correlates of individualism and collectivism: talk directed at one or more addressees in family conversations', *Journal of Language and Social Psychology*, 19: 26–45.

Nichols, S. and Stich, S. (2002) 'How to read your own mind: a cognitive theory of self-consciousness', in Q. Smith and A. Jokic (eds) *Consciousness: New Philosophical Essays*, Oxford: Oxford University Press.

Nickels, E.L. (2006) 'Interlanguage pragmatics and the effect of setting', in K. Bardovi-Harlig, J.C. Félix-Brasdefer and A.S. Omar (eds) *Pragmatics and Language Learning, Volume 11*, Honolulu, HI: University of Hawaii Press.

Nicolle, S. and Clark, B. (1999) 'Experimental pragmatics and what is said: a response to Gibbs and Moise', *Cognition*, 69: 337–54.

Ninio, A. (1983) 'A pragmatic approach to early language acquisition', paper presented at the Study Group on Crosscultural and Crosslinguistic Aspects of Native Language Acquisition, Institute for Advanced Studies, Hebrew University, Jerusalem, Israel.

——(1984) 'Functions of speech in mother-infant interaction', in L. Feagans, G.J. Garvey and R. Golinkoff (eds) *The Origins and Growth of Communication*, Norwood, NJ: Ablex.

Ninio, A. and Bruner, J.S. (1978) 'The achievement and antecedents of labelling', *Journal of Child Language*, 5: 1–15.

Ninio, A. and Goren, H. (1993) *PICA-100: Parental Interview on 100 Communicative Acts*, Jerusalem: Hebrew University.

Ninio, A. and Snow, C.E. (1996) *Pragmatic Development*, Boulder, CO: Westview Press.

Ninio, A. and Wheeler, P. (1984) 'A manual for classifying verbal communicative acts in mother-infant interaction', *Working Papers in Developmental Psychology*, 1, Jerusalem: The Martin and Vivian Levin Center, Hebrew University; reprinted in *Transcript Analysis* (1986), 3: 1–82.

Ninio, A., Snow, C.E., Pan, B.A. and Rollins, P.R. (1994) 'Classifying communicative acts in children's interactions', *Journal of Communication Disorders*, 27: 157–88.

Noens, I.L. and van Berckelaer-Onnes, I.A. (2005) 'Captured by details: sense-making, language and communication in autism', *Journal of Communication Disorders*, 38: 123–41.

Noguchi, H. and Den, Y. (1998) 'Prosody-based detection of the context of backchannel responses', paper presented at the *5th International Conference on Spoken Language Processing*, Sydney, Australia, November/December 1998.

Noh, E.-J. (1998) 'Echo questions: meta-representation and pragmatic enrichment', *Linguistics and Philosophy*, 21: 603–28.

——(2000) *Metarepresentation: A Relevance Theory Approach*, Amsterdam: John Benjamins.

Norbury, C.F. and Bishop, D.V. (2002) 'Inferential processing and story recall in children with communication problems: a comparison of specific language impairment, pragmatic language impairment and high-functioning autism', *International Journal of Language and Communication Disorders*, 37: 227–51.

Nord, C. (1997) *Translating as a Purposeful Activity: Functionalist Approaches Explained*, Manchester, UK: St Jerome Publishing.

Nordahl, H. (1999) 'Proverbes sans verbe: petite étude syntaxico-rhétorique sur les proverbes à ellipse verbale', in G. Boysen and J. Moestrup (eds) *Études de Linguistique et de Littérature Dédiées à Morten Nøjgaard*, Odense, Denmark: Odense University Press.

Norman, D.A. and Shallice, T. (1980) 'Attention to action: willed and automatic control of behavior', in R.J. Davidson, G.E. Schwartz and D. Shapiro (eds) *Consciousness and Self-Regulation, Vol. 4*, New York: Plenum Press.

Norment, N. (1994) 'Contrastive analyses of cohesive devices in Chinese and Chinese ESL in narrative and expository written texts', *Journal of the Chinese Language Teachers Association*, 29: 49–81.

Norrick, N.R. (1982) 'On the semantics of overstatement', in K. Detering, J. Schmidt-Radefeld and W. Sucharowski (eds) *Sprache Erkennen und Verstehen*, Tübingen: Niemeyer.

——(1984) 'Stock conversational witticisms', *Journal of Pragmatics*, 8: 195–209.

——(1985) *How Proverbs Mean*, Berlin: de Gruyter.

——(1989) 'How paradox means', *Poetics Today*, 10: 551–62.

——(1993) *Conversational Joking: Humor in Everyday Talk*, Bloomington, IN: Indiana University Press.

——(1994) 'Proverbial perlocutions: how to do things with proverbs', in W. Mieder (ed.) *Wise Words: Essays on the Proverb*, New York: Garland.

——(2001) 'Discourse markers in oral narrative', *Journal of Pragmatics*, 33: 849–78.

——(2004) 'Hyperbole, extreme case formulations', *Journal of Pragmatics*, 36: 1727–39.

——(2007) 'Proverbs as set phrases', in H. Burger, D. Dobrovolskij, P. Kühn and N. Norrick (eds) *Phraseology: An International Handbook of Contemporary Research*, vol. 28, 1, Berlin: de Gruyter.

Norris, J. and Ortega, L. (2000) 'Effectiveness of L2 instruction: a research synthesis and quantitative meta-analysis', *Language Learning*, 50: 417–528.

Northcott, J. (2001) 'Towards an ethnography of the MBA classroom: a consideration of the role of interactive lecturing styles within the context of one MBA programme', *English for Specific Purposes*, 20: 15–37.

Nöth, W. (1990) *Handbook of Semiotics*, Bloomington: Indiana University Press.

Noveck, I. (2001) 'When children are more logical than adults: experimental investigations of scalar implicature', *Cognition*, 78: 165–88.

——(2004) 'Pragmatic inferences related to logical terms', in I. Noveck and D. Sperber (eds) *Experimental Pragmatics*, Basingstoke: Palgrave Macmillan.

Noveck, I. and Posada, A. (2003) 'Characterizing the time course of an implicature: an evoked potentials study', *Brain and Language*, 85: 203–10.

Noveck, I. and Reboul, A. (2008) 'Experimental pragmatics: a Gricean turn in the study of language', *Trends in Cognitive Sciences*, 12: 425–31.

Noveck, I. and Sperber, D. (eds) (2004) *Experimental Pragmatics*, Houndmills: Palgrave Macmillan.

——(2007) 'The why and how of experimental pragmatics: the case of "scalar inferences"', in N. Burton-Roberts (ed.) *Advances in Pragmatics*, Basingstoke: Palgrave Macmillan.

Noveck, I., Bianco, M. and Castry, A. (2001) 'The costs and benefits of metaphor', *Metaphor and Symbol*, 16: 109–21.

Nunan, D. (1992) *Research Methods in Language Learning*, Cambridge: Cambridge University Press.

Nunberg, G. (1979) 'The non-uniqueness of semantic solutions: polysemy', *Linguistics and Philosophy*, 3: 143–84.

——(1993) 'Indexicality and deixis', *Linguistics and Philosophy*, 16: 1–44.

——(1995) 'Transfers of meaning', *Journal of Semantics*, 12: 109–32.

——(2004) 'The pragmatics of deferred interpretation', in L.R. Horn and G. Ward (eds) *The Handbook of Pragmatics*, Oxford: Blackwell.

Nunberg, G., Sag, I. and Wasow, T. (1994) 'Idioms', *Language*, 70: 491–538.

Nurmsoo, E. and Bloom, P. (2008) 'Preschoolers' perspective taking in word learning: do they blindly follow eye gaze?', *Association for Psychological Science*, 19: 211–15.

Nussbaum, M. (2001) *Upheavals of Thought: The Intelligence of Emotions*, Cambridge: Cambridge University Press.

Nystrand, M., Gamoran, A., Kachur, R. and Prendergast, C. (1997) *Opening Dialogue: Understanding the Dynamics of Language and Learning in the English Classroom*, New York: Teachers College Press.

O'Connor, J.D. and Arnold, G.F. (1961) *Intonation of Colloquial English*, London: Longman.

O'Halloran, K. (2004) *Multimodal Discourse Analysis: Systemic Functional Perspectives*, London: Continuum.

O'Hanlon, R. (2006) 'Australian hip hop: a sociolinguistic investigation', *Australian Journal of Linguistics*, 26: 193–209.

O'Keeffe, A. (2006) *Investigating Media Discourse*, London: Routledge.

O'Neil, D. and Chong, S. (2001) 'Preschool children's difficulty understanding the types of information obtained through the five senses', *Child Development*, 72: 803–15.

O'Neill, D.K. (2007) 'The language use inventory for young children: a parent-report measure of pragmatic language development for 18- to 47-month-old children', *Journal of Speech, Language, and Hearing Research*, 50: 214–28.

Oakhill, J. and Garnham, A. (1988) *Becoming a Skilled Reader*, Oxford: Blackwell.

Oaksford, M. and Chater, N. (1998) *Rationality in an Uncertain World*, Hove: Psychology Press.

Obeng, S.G. (1999) 'Apologies in Akan discourse', *Journal of Pragmatics*, 31: 709–34.

Ochs, E. (1979) 'Transcription as theory', in E. Ochs and B.B. Schiefelin (eds) *Developmental Pragmatics*, New York: Academic Press.

——(1988) *Culture and Language Development: Language Acquisition and Language Socialization in a Samoan Village*, Cambridge: Cambridge University Press.

——(1992) 'Indexing gender', in A. Duranti and C. Goodwin (eds) *Rethinking Context: Language as an Interactive Phenomenon*, Cambridge: Cambridge University Press.

——(1996) 'Linguistic resources for socializing humanity', in J.J. Gumperz and S.C. Levinson (eds) *Rethinking Linguistic Relativity*, Cambridge: Cambridge University Press.

Ochs, E., Schegloff, E.A. and Thompson, S.A. (eds) (1996) *Interaction and Grammar*, Cambridge: Cambridge University Press.

Ochs, E., Taylor, C., Rudolph, D. and Smith, R. (1992) 'Storytelling and a theory-building activity', *Discourse Processes*, 15: 37–72.

Odlin, T. (1989) *Language Transfer: Cross-Linguistic Influence in Language Learning*, Cambridge: Cambridge University Press.

Oelschlaeger, M. and Damico, J. (2000) 'Partnership in conversation: a study of word search strategies', *Journal of Communication Disorders*, 33: 205–23.

Oesterle, J. (1962) *Aristotle: On Interpretation. Commentary by St. Thomas and Cajetan*, Milwaukee, WI: Marquette University Press.

Ogden, C.K. and Richards, I.A. (1923) *The Meaning of Meaning: A Study of the Influence of Language Upon Thought and of the Science of Symbolism*, London: Routledge and Kegan Paul.

Ogden, R. (2006) 'Phonetics and social action in agreements and disagreements', *Journal of Pragmatics*, 38: 1752–75.

Ogiermann, E. (2007) 'Gender-based differences in English apology realizations', in B. Kraft and R. Geluykens (eds) *Cross-Cultural Pragmatics and Interlanguage English*, Munich: Lincom Europa.

Ohmann, R. (1964) 'Generative grammars and the concept of literary style', *Word*, 20: 423–39.

Ohta, A.S. (1995) 'Applying sociocultural theory to an analysis of learner discourse: learner-learner collaborative interaction in the zone of proximal development', *Issues in Applied Linguistics*, 6: 93–121.

——(2005) 'Interlanguage pragmatics in the zone of proximal development', *System*, 33: 503–17.

Okada, M. (2006) 'Speaker's sex or discourse activities? A micro-discourse-based account of use of nonparticle questions in Japanese', *Language in Society*, 35: 341–65.

Okamoto, S. (1993) 'Nominal repetitive constructions in Japanese: the tautology controversy revisited', *Journal of Pragmatics*, 20: 433–66.

Okamura, K. and Wei, L. (2000) 'The concept of self and apology strategies in two cultures', *Journal of Asia Pacific Communication*, 10: 1–24.

Oktoprimasakti, F. (2006) 'Direct and indirect strategies of refusing among Indonesians', *Direct and Indirect Strategies of Refusing*, 10: 103–16.

Olivecrona, K. (1971) *Law as Fact*, London: Stevens.

Olsen, M. (1986) *Some problematic issues in the study of intonation and sentence stress*, Ph.D. dissertation, University of Illinois.

Olsen, T. (1978) *Silences*, New York: Delta/Seymour Lawrence.

Olshtain, E. (1983) 'Sociocultural competence and language transfer: the case of Apology', in S. Gass and L. Selinker (eds) *Language Transfer in Language Learning*, Rowley, MA: Newbury House.

——(1989) 'Apologies across languages', in S. Blum-Kulka, J. House and G. Kasper (eds) *Cross-cultural Pragmatics: Requests and Apologies*, Norwood, NJ: Ablex.

Olshtain, E. and Cohen, A. (1983) 'Apology: a speech act set', in N. Wolfson and E. Judd (eds) *Sociolinguistics and Language Acquisition*, Rowley, MA: Newbury.

Olshtain, E. and Weinbach, L. (1987) 'Complaints: a study of speech act behaviour among native and non-native speakers of Hebrew', in J. Verschueren and P. Bertalucci (eds) *The Pragmatic Perspective*, Philadelphia, PA: John Benjamins.

——(1993) 'Interlanguage features of the speech act of complaining', in G. Kasper and S. Blum-Kulka (eds) *Interlanguage Pragmatics*, Oxford: Oxford University Press.

Onishi, K.H. and Baillargeon, R. (2005) 'Do 15-month-old infants understand false beliefs?', *Science*, 308: 255–58.

Orange, J.B., Lubinski, R.B. and Higginbotham, D.J. (1996) 'Conversational repair by individuals with dementia of the Alzheimer's type', *Journal of Speech and Hearing Research*, 39: 881–93.

Orange, J.B., Kertesz, A. and Peacock, J. (1998a) 'Pragmatics in frontal lobe dementia and primary progressive aphasia', *Journal of Neurolinguistics*, 11: 153–77.

Orange, J.B., VanGennep, K.M., Miller, L. and Johnson, A. (1998b) 'Resolution of communication breakdown in dementia of the Alzheimer's type: a longitudinal study', *Journal of Applied Communication Research*, 26: 120–38.

Origgi, G. and Sperber, D. (2000) 'Evolution, communication and the proper function of language', in P. Carruthers and A. Chamberlain (eds) *Evolution and the Human Mind: Modularity, Language and Meta-Cognition*, Cambridge: Cambridge University Press.

Ortony, A. (1979a) 'Beyond literal simile', *Psychological Review*, 86: 161–80.

——(1979b) 'The role of similarity in similes and metaphors', in A. Ortony (ed.) *Metaphor and Thought*, Cambridge: Cambridge University Press.

Osborne, J. ([[1960] 1983) *Look Back in Anger*, London: Faber and Faber.

Ostermann, A.C. (2003) 'Communities of practice at work: gender, facework and the power of habitus at an all-female police station and a feminist crisis intervention center in Brazil', *Discourse and Society*, 14: 473–505.

Ostertag, G. (ed.) (1998) *Definite Descriptions: A Reader*, London: MIT Press.

Osvaldsson, K. (2004) 'On laughter and disagreement in multiparty assessment talk', *Text*, 24: 517–45.

Ouellette, M. (2001) '"That's too bad": hedges and indirect complaints in "troubles-talk" narrative', *Working Papers in Educational Linguistics*, 17: 107–26.

Overstreet, M. and Yule, G. (2001) 'Formulaic disclaimers', *Journal of Pragmatics*, 33: 45–60.

Oyama, S. (1978) 'The sensitive period and comprehension of speech', *Working Papers on Bilingualism*, 16: 1–17.

Ozonoff, S. and Miller, J. (1996) 'An exploration of right-hemisphere contributions to the pragmatic impairments of autism', *Brain and Language*, 52: 411–34.

Ozyurek, A. (2002) 'Do speakers design their cospeech gestures for their addressees? The effects of addressee location on representational gestures', *Journal of Memory and Language*, 46: 688–704.

Paek, T. and Horvitz, E. (2000) 'Conversation as decision making under uncertainty', *Proceedings of the Sixteenth Conference on Uncertainty in Artificial Intelligence*, San Francisco, CA: Morgan Kaufmann Publishers.

Page, R.E. (2006) *Literary and Linguistic Approaches to Feminist Narratology*, Basingstoke, UK: Palgrave Macmillan.

Paivio, A. (1986) *Mental Representations: A Dual Coding Approach*, Oxford: Oxford University Press.

Pakkala-Weckström, M. (2005) *The Dialogue of Love, Marriage and Maistrie in Chaucer's Canterbury Tales*, Mémoires de la Société Néophilologique de Helsinki 67, Helsinki, Finland: Société Néophilologique.

Palmer, F. (1986) *Mood and Modality*, Cambridge: Cambridge University Press.

——(1990) *Modality and the English Modals*, London and New York: Longman.

Panagl, O. and Wodak, R. (eds) (2004) *Text and Kontext*, Würzburg, Germany: Königshausen and Neumann.

Panizza, D. and Chierchia, G. (2008) 'Two experiments on the interpretation of numerals',

paper presented at the *30th Annual Convention of the German Society of Linguistics (DGfS)*, Workshop 9 on Experimental Pragmatics/Semantics, Bamberg, February 2008.

Papafragou, A. (2000) *Modality: Issues in the Semantics–Pragmatics Interface*, Amsterdam: Elsevier.

——(2006) 'Epistemic modality and truth conditions', *Lingua*, 116: 1688–702.

Papafragou, A. and Musolino, J. (2003) 'Scalar implicatures: experiments at the semantics-pragmatics interface', *Cognition*, 86: 253–82.

Papafragou, A., Li, P., Choi, Y. and Han, C. (2007) 'Evidentiality in language and cognition', *Cognition*, 103: 253–99.

Papineau, D. (1987) *Reality and Representation*, Oxford: Basil Blackwell.

Parikh, P. (2001) *The Use of Language*, Stanford, CA: CSLI.

Park, Y.-Y. (2002) 'Recognition and identification in Japanese and Korean telephone conversation openings', in K.K. Luke and Th.-S. Pavlidou (eds) *Telephone Calls: Unity and Diversity in Conversational Structure across Languages and Cultures*, Amsterdam and Philadelphia: John Benjamins.

Parker, A. and Sedgwick, E.K. (eds) (1995) *Performativity and Performance*, New York: Routledge.

Parkinson, G.M. (2006) 'Pragmatic difficulties in children with autism associated with childhood epilepsy', *Pediatric Rehabilitation*, 9: 229–46.

Partee, B.H. (1984) 'Nominal and temporal anaphora', *Linguistics and Philosophy*, 12: 683–721.

——(1991) 'Topic, focus and quantification', in S. Moore and A. Wyner (eds) *Proceedings of Semantic and Linguistic Theory (SALT) 1*, Ithaca, NY: CLC Publications.

——(1995) 'Quantificational structures and compositionality', in E. Bach, E. Jelinek, A. Kratzer and B.H. Partee (eds) *Quantification in Natural Languages*, Dordrecht: Kluwer.

Partington, A. (1998) *Patterns and Meanings: Using Corpora for English Language Research and Teaching*, Amsterdam: John Benjamins.

——(2007) 'Irony and reversal of evaluation', *Journal of Pragmatics*, 39: 1547–69.

Passmore, J. (1966) *A Hundred Years of Philosophy*, London: Duckworth.

Pateman, T. (1983) 'How is understanding an advertisement possible?', in H. Davis and P. Walton (eds) *Language, Image, Media*, Oxford: Basil Blackwell.

Patkowski, M. (1980) 'The sensitive period for the acquisition of syntax in a second language', *Language Learning*, 30: 449–72.

Paul, H. (1880) *Prinzipien der Sprachgeschichte*, Tübingen: Niemeyer.

——(1889) *Principles of the History of Language*, trans. H.A. Strong, London: Macmillan.

Paul, R. and Cohen, D.J. (1985) 'Comprehension of indirect requests in adults with autistic disorders and mental retardation', *Journal of Speech and Hearing Research*, 28: 475–79.

Pavlidou, Th.-S. (1994) 'Contrasting German–Greek politeness and the consequences', *Journal of Pragmatics*, 21: 487–511.

——(1997) 'The last five turns: preliminary remarks on closings in Greek and German telephone calls', *International Journal of the Sociology of Language*, 126: 145–62.

——(2002) 'Moving towards closing: Greek telephone calls between familiars', in K.K. Luke and Th.-S. Pavlidou (eds) *Telephone Calls: Unity and Diversity in Conversational Structure across Languages and Cultures*, Amsterdam and Philadelphia, PA: John Benjamins.

Pavy, H. (1968) 'Verbal behavior in schizophrenia: a review of recent studies', *Psychological Bulletin*, 70: 164–78.

Payà, M. (2003a) 'Prosody and pragmatics in parenthetical insertions in Catalan', *Catalan Journal of Linguistics*, 2: 207–27.

——(2003b) 'Politeness strategies in spoken Catalan: when prosodic and non prosodic elements don't match', paper presented at the *6th NWCL International Conference: Prosody and Pragmatics*, Preston, UK, November 2003.

Peach, R.K. and Schaude, B.A. (1986) 'Reformulating the notion of "preserved" syntax following closed head injury', paper presented at the *Annual Convention of the American Speech-Language-Hearing Association*, Detroit, MI, November 1986.

Pearl, J. (1988) *Probabilistic Reasoning in Intelligent Systems: Networks of Plausible Inference*, San Mateo, CA: Morgan Kaufmann.

Pears, D. (1987) *The False Prison: A Study of the Development of Wittgenstein's Philosophy*, volume 1, Oxford: Clarendon Press.

——(1988) *The False Prison: A Study of the Development of Wittgenstein's Philosophy*, volume 2, Oxford: Clarendon Press.

Pederson, E., Danziger, E., Levinson, S.C., Kita, S., Senft, G. and Wilkins, D. (1998) 'Semantic typology and spatial conceptualization', *Language*, 74: 557–89.

Peirce, C.S. (1931–58) *The Collected Papers of Charles Sanders Peirce*, ed. C. Hartshorne and P. Weiss (vols 1–6), A. Burks (vols 7–8), Cambridge, MA: Harvard University Press.

——(1992a) *Reasoning and the Logic of Things: The Cambridge Conference Lectures of 1898*, edited by K.L. Ketner, Cambridge, MA: Harvard University Press.

——(1992b) *The Essential Peirce, Selected Philosophical Writings, Volume 1 (1867–1893)*, ed. N. Houser and C. Kloesel, Bloomington, IN: Indiana University Press.

——(1998) *The Essential Peirce, Selected Philosophical Writings, Volume 2 (1893–1913)*, ed. the Peirce Edition Project, Bloomington, IN: Indiana University Press.

Pelczar, M.W. (2004) 'The indispensability of *Farbung*', *Synthese*, 138: 49–77.

——(2007) 'Forms and objects of thought', *Linguistics and Philosophy*, 30: 97–122.

Peleg, O. and Eviatar, Z. (2008) 'Hemispheric sensitivities to lexical and contextual information: evidence from lexical ambiguity resolution', *Brain and Language*, 105: 71–82.

Peleg, O., Giora, R. and Fein, O. (2004) 'Contextual strength: the whens and hows of context effects', in I.A. Noveck and D. Sperber (eds) *Experimental Pragmatics*, London: Palgrave Macmillan.

Pell, M.D. (2002) 'Surveying emotional prosody in the brain', in B. Bel and I. Marlien (eds) *Proceedings of the First International Conference on Speech Prosody*. Online. Available www.isca-speech.org/archive/sp2002/sp02_077.pdf (accessed 21 January 2009).

——(2006) 'Judging emotion and attitudes from prosody following brain damage', *Progress in Brain Research*, 156: 303–17.

——(2007) 'Reduced sensitivity to prosodic attitudes in adults with focal right hemisphere brain damage', *Brain and Language*, 101: 64–79.

Penman, R. (1990) 'Facework and politeness: multiple goals in courtroom discourse', *Journal of Language and Social Psychology*, 9: 15–39.

Penn, C., Jones, D. and Joffe, V. (1997) 'Hierarchical discourse therapy: a method for the mild patient', *Aphasiology*, 11: 601–32.

Peregrin, J. (2001) *Meaning and Structure*, Aldershot: Ashgate.

——(2008) 'Semantics without meaning?', in R. Schantz (ed.) *Prospects of Meaning*, Berlin: de Gruyter.

Perelman, Ch. (1979) *The New Rhetoric and the Humanities: Essays on Rhetoric and its Applications*, Dordrecht: Reidel.

——(1982) *The Realm of Rhetoric*, trans. W. Kluback, Notre Dame, IN: University of Notre Dame Press.

Perelman, Ch. and Olbrechts-Tyteca, L. (1958) *La Nouvelle Rhétorique: Traité de l'Argumentation*, Brussels: University of Brussels.

——(1969) *The New Rhetoric: A Treatise on Argumentation*, trans. J. Wilkinson and P. Weaver, Notre Dame, IN: University of Notre Dame Press.

Perez de Ayala, S. (2001) 'FTAs and Erskine May: conflicting need? Politeness in Question Time', *Journal of Pragmatics*, 33: 143–70.

Perfetti, C. (1985) *Reading Ability*, New York: Oxford University Press.

Perkins, L. (1995) 'Applying conversation analysis to aphasia: clinical implications and analytic issues', *European Journal of Disorders of Communication*, 30: 372–83.

Perkins, L., Crisp, J. and Walshaw, D. (1999) 'Exploring conversation analysis as an assessment tool for aphasia', *Aphasiology*, 13: 259–81.

Perkins, L., Whitworth, A. and Lesser, R. (1997) *Conversation Analysis Profile for People with Cognitive Impairment*, London: Whurr Publishers Ltd.

Perkins, M.R. (1998) 'Is pragmatics epiphenomenal? Evidence from communication disorders', *Journal of Pragmatics*, 29: 291–311.

——(2005) (ed.) Special Issue: Clinical Pragmatics – An Emergentist Perspective, *Clinical Linguistics and Phonetics*, 19: 363–68.

Perner, J. (1991) *Understanding the Representational Mind*, Cambridge, MA: MIT Press.

Perner, J. and Ruffman, T. (2005) 'Infants' insight into the mind: how deep?', *Science*, 308: 214–16.

Perner, J. and Wimmer, H. (1985) '"John thinks that Mary thinks that … " Attribution of second-order beliefs by 5- to 10-year-old children', *Journal of Experimental Child Psychology*, 39: 437–71.

Perner, J., Leekam, S.R. and Wimmer, H. (1987) 'Three-year-olds' difficulty with false belief: the case of conceptual deficit', *British Journal of Developmental Psychology*, 5: 125–37.

Perry, J. (1977) 'Frege on demonstratives', *The Philosophical Review*, 86: 474–97.

——(1979) 'The problem of the essential indexical', *Noûs*, 13: 3–21.

Pesetsky, D. (1987) 'Wh-in-situ: movement and unselective binding', in E. Reuland and A. ter Meulen (eds) *The Representation of (In)definites*, Cambridge, MA: MIT Press.

——(2000) *Phrasal Movement and Its Kin*, Cambridge, MA: MIT Press.

Peters, J. (2006) 'Syntactic and prosodic parenthesis', *Proceedings of the International Conference on Speech Prosody*, 2–5 May 2006, Dresden, Germany: TUD Press.

Peterson, C. and McCabe, A. (1983) *Developmental Psycholinguistics: Three Ways of Looking at a Child's Narrative*, New York: Plenum Press.

Peterson, P. (1999) 'On the boundaries of syntax', in P. Collins and D. Lee (eds) *The Clause in English*, Amsterdam: John Benjamins.

Petraki, E. (2005) 'Disagreement and opposition in multigenerational interviews with Greek-Australian mothers and daughters', *Text*, 25: 269–303.

Pexman, P.M. and Zvaigzne, T.M. (2004) 'Does irony go better with friends?', *Metaphor and Symbol*, 19: 143–63.

Pexman, P.M., Ferretti, T. and Katz, N.A. (2000) 'Discourse factors that influence irony detection during on-line reading', *Discourse Processes*, 29: 201–22.

Phelps-Terasaki, D. and Phelps-Gunn, T. (1992) *Test of Pragmatic Language*, San Antonio, TX: The Psychological Corporation.

Philips, S. (1998) *Ideology in the Language of Judges: How Judges Practice Law, Politics and Courtroom Control*, New York: Oxford University Press.

——(2001) 'Power' in A. Duranti (ed.) *Key Terms in Language and Culture*, Oxford: Blackwell.

Phillips, W., Gómez, J.C., Baron-Cohen, S., Laá, V. and Rivière, A. (1995) 'Treating people as objects, agents, or "subjects": how young children with and without autism make requests', *Journal of Child Psychology and Psychiatry*, 36: 1383–98.

Piatelli-Palmarini, M. (1989) 'Evolution, selection and cognition: from "learning" to parameter setting in biology and in the study of language', *Cognition*, 31: 1–44.

Pica, T. (1983) 'Adult acquisition of English as a second language under different conditions of exposure', *Language Learning*, 33: 465–97.

Picard, M. ([1952] 1989) *The World of Silence*, trans. S. Godman, Chicago: Regnery.

Pickering, L., Corduas, M., Eisterhold, J., Seifried, B., Eggleston, A. and Attardo, S. (to appear) 'Prosodic markers of saliency in humorous narratives', *Discourse Processes*.

Pickering, M.S. and Garrod, S. (2004) 'Toward a mechanistic psychology of dialogue', *Behavioral and Brain Sciences*, 27: 169–90.

Pierce, K., Müller, R.-A., Ambrose, J., Allen, G. and Courchesne, E. (2001) 'Face processing occurs outside the fusiform "face area" in autism: evidence from functional MRI', *Brain*, 124: 2059–73.

Pierrehumbert, J. (1980) *The phonology and phonetics of English intonation*, unpublished thesis,
Massachusetts Institute of Technology.

Pietroski, P.M. (2005) *Events and Semantic
Architecture*, Oxford: Oxford University Press.

Pijper, J.R. de (1997) 'High-quality message-to-
speech generation in a practical application',
in J. van Santen, R. Sproat, J. Olive and J.
Hirschberg (eds) *Progress in Speech Synthesis*,
New York: Springer.

Pilkington, A. (2000) *Poetic Effects: A Relevance
Theory Perspective*, Amsterdam and Philadelphia:
John Benjamins.

Pillow, B. (1989) 'Early understanding of perception as a source of knowledge', *Journal of
Experimental Child Psychology*, 47: 116–29.

——(2002) 'Children's and adults' evaluation of
the certainty of deductive inferences, inductive
inferences, and guesses', *Child Development*, 73:
779–92.

Pinker, S. (1989) *Learnability and Cognition: The
Acquisition of Argument Structure*, Cambridge,
MA: MIT Press.

——(1997) *How the Mind Works*, Harmondsworth,
UK: Penguin.

Pinker, S. and Bloom, P. (1990) 'Natural language and natural selection', *Behavioral and
Brain Sciences*, 13: 707–84.

Pinker, S., Nowak, M.A. and Lee, J.J. (2008) 'The
logic of indirect speech', *Proceedings of the National
Academy of Sciences of the USA*, 105: 833–38.

Pinto, D.S. (1995) *A percepção da loucura: análise do
discurso de pacientes internadas em uma instituição
psiquiátrica*, unpublished thesis, Federal University of Rio de Janeiro.

——(2000) *A construção da referência no discurso de
uma paciente psiquiátrica: análise lingüística para
distúrbios de pensamento, fala e comunicação*,
unpublished thesis, Federal University of Rio
de Janeiro.

Pirie, S. (1997) 'The use of talk in mathematics',
in B. Davies and D. Corson (eds) *Encyclopedia
of Language and Education, Volume 3: Oral Discourse and Education*, London: Kluwer.

Pisoni, D.B. and Remez, R.E. (2005) *Handbook of
Speech Perception*, Oxford: Blackwell.

Pitcher, G. (ed.) (1964) *Truth*, Englewood Cliffs,
NJ: Prentice Hall.

——(ed.) (1966) *Wittgenstein: The Philosophical
Investigations*, London: Macmillan.

Pitts, A. (2005) *Assessing the evidence for intuitions about
what is said*, unpublished manuscript, University of Cambridge.

Pizziconi, B. (2003) 'Re-examining politeness,
face and the Japanese language', *Journal of
Pragmatics*, 35: 1471–506.

Place, U.T. (1956) 'Is consciousness a brain
process?', *British Journal of Psychology*, 47: 44–50.

Placencia, M.E. (1992) 'Politeness in mediated
telephone conversations in Ecuadorian
Spanish and British English', *Language Learning
Journal*, 6: 80–82.

——(1997) 'Opening up closings: the Ecuadorian
way', *Text*, 17: 53–81.

Plato (1990) *Gorgias*, Oxford: Oxford University
Press.

Polinsky, M. (1997) 'American Russian: lan-
guage loss meets language acquisition', in W.
Browne, E. Dornsich, N. Kondrashova and
D. Zec (eds) *Proceedings of the Annual Workshop
on Formal Approaches to Slavic Linguistics: The
Cornell Meeting 1995*, Ann Arbor, MI: Michigan
Slavic Publications.

Politzer, G. (1990) 'Characterizing spontaneous
inference', *Behavioral and Brain Sciences*, 13:
177–78.

Pollack, M.E. (1990) 'Plans as complex mental
attitudes', in P.R. Cohen, J. Morgan and M.
E. Pollack (eds) *Intentions in Communication*,
Cambridge, MA: MIT Press.

Pollard, C.M. and Sag, I.A. (1994) *Head-Driven
Phrase Structure Grammar*, Chicago, IL: University of Chicago Press.

Pollock, K. (2007) 'Maintaining face in the presentation of depression: constraining the
therapeutic potential of the consultation',
Health, 11: 163–80.

Pomerantz, A. (1978) 'Compliment responses:
notes on the co-operation of multiple constraints', in J. Schenkein (ed.) *Studies in the
Organization of Conversational Interaction*, New
York: Academic Press.

——(1984) 'Agreeing and disagreeing with
assessments: some features of preferred/
dispreferred turn shapes', in J.M. Atkinson
and J. Heritage (eds) *Structures of Social Action:
Studies in Conversation Analysis*, Cambridge and
New York: Cambridge University Press.

——(1986) 'Extreme case formulations: a way of
legitimizing claims', *Human Studies*, 9: 219–29.

Poncini, G. (2004) *Discursive Strategies in Multicultural Business Meetings*, Bern, Switzerland:
Peter Lang.

Poole, D. (1992) 'Language socialization in the
second language classroom', *Language Learning*,
42: 593–616.

Poole, D.A. and Lindsay, D.S. (2002) 'Reducing
child witnesses' false reports of misinformation from parents', *Journal of Experimental Child
Psychology*, 81: 117–40.

Pope, E.N. (1976) *Questions and Answers in English*,
The Hague: Mouton.

Porter, J.A. (1979) *The Drama of Speech Acts: Shakespeare's Lancastrian Tetralogy*, Berkeley, CA: University of California Press.

Potts, C. (2002) 'The syntax and semantics of *as*-parentheticals', *Natural Language and Linguistic Theory*, 20: 623–89.

——(2005) *The Logic of Conventional Implicatures*, Oxford: Oxford University Press.

Pouscoulous, N., Noveck, I., Politzer, G. and Bastide, A. (2007) 'Processing costs and implicature development', *Language Acquisition*, 14: 347–75.

Poutsma, H. (1928) *A Grammar of Late Modern English*, Gröningen, Holland: P. Noordhoof.

Povinelli, D.J. and Vonk, J. (2003) 'Chimpanzee minds: suspiciously human?', *Trends in Cognitive Science*, 7: 157–60.

Powell, G. (2001) 'The referential-attributive distinction: a cognitive account', *Pragmatics and Cognition*, 9: 69–98.

——(2002) 'Underdetermination and the principles of semantic theory', *Proceedings of the Aristotelian Society*, 102: 271–78.

Pratt, C. and Bryant, P. (1990) 'Young children understand that looking leads to knowing (so long as they are looking into a single barrel)', *Child Development*, 61: 973–82.

Pratt, M.L. (1977) *Toward a Speech Act Theory of Literary Discourse*, Bloomington, IN: Indiana University Press.

Predelli, S. (1998) 'Utterance, interpretation and the logic of indexicals', *Mind and Language*, 13: 400–14.

——(2001) 'Names and character', *Philosophical Studies*, 103: 145–63.

——(2005) *Contexts: Meaning, Truth and the Use of Language*, Oxford: Oxford University Press.

Preissler, M.A. and Carey, S. (2005) 'The role of inferences about referential intent in word learning: evidence from autism', *Cognition*, 97: B13–23.

Premack, D. and Premack, A.J. (1994) 'Why animals have neither culture nor history', in T. Ingold (ed.) *Companion Encyclopedia of Anthropology*, London: Routledge.

Premack, D. and Woodruff, D. (1978) 'Does the chimpanzee have a theory of mind?', *Behavior and Brain Sciences*, 1: 515–26.

Preminger, A. (ed.) (1974) *Princeton Encyclopedia of Poetry and Poetics*, Princeton, NJ: Princeton University Press.

Preyer, G. and Peter, G. (eds) (2005) *Contextualism in Philosophy: Knowledge, Meaning and Truth*, Oxford: Oxford University Press.

——(eds) (2007) *Context-Sensitivity and Semantic Minimalism: New Essays on Semantics and Pragmatics*, Oxford: Clarendon Press.

Priego-Valverde, B. (2003) *L'Humour dans la Conversation Familière: Description et Analyse Linguistiques*, Paris: L'Harmattan.

Prince, E.F. (1978) 'A comparison of WH-clefts and *it*-clefts in discourse', *Language*, 54: 883–906.

——(1981a) 'On the inferencing of indefinite-*this* NPs', in A.K. Joshi, B.L. Webber and I. Sag (eds) *Elements of Discourse Understanding*, Cambridge: Cambridge University Press.

——(1981b) 'Toward a taxonomy of given and new information', in P. Cole (ed.) *Radical Pragmatics*, New York: Academic Press.

——(1981c) 'Topicalization, focus-movement, and Yiddish-movement: a pragmatic differentiation', in D. Alford (ed.) *Proceedings of the 7th Annual Meeting of the Berkeley Linguistics Society*, Berkeley, CA: Berkeley Linguistic Society.

——(1984) 'Topicalization and left-dislocation: a functional analysis', in S.J. White and V. Teller (eds) *Discourses in Reading and Linguistics*, Annals of the New York Academy of Sciences, 433, New York: New York Academy of Sciences.

——(1992) 'The ZPG letter: subjects, definiteness, and information status', in S.A. Thompson and W. Mann (eds) *Discourse Description: Diverse Linguistic Analyses of a Fund-Raising Text*, Amsterdam: John Benjamins.

——(1998) 'On the limits of syntax, with reference to left dislocation and topicalization', in P. Culicover and L. McNally (eds) *Syntax and Semantics 29: The Limits of Syntax*, New York: Academic Press.

Prince, E.F., Frader, J. and Bosk, C. (1982) 'On hedging in physician-physician Discourse', in R.J. DiPietro (ed.) *Linguistics and the Professions*, Norwood, NJ: Ablex.

Principe, G.F. and Ceci, S.J. (2002) '"I saw it with my own ears": the effects of peer conversations on preschoolers' reports of nonexperienced events', *Journal of Experimental Child Psychology*, 83: 1–25.

Prinz, J. (2006) 'Is the mind really modular?', in R. Stainton (ed.) *Contemporary Debates in Cognitive Science*, Oxford: Blackwell.

Prinz, P. and Werner, F. (1987) *The Pragmatics Screening Test*, London: The Psychological Corporation.

Prizant, B.M. and Duchan, J.F. (1981) 'The functions of immediate echolalia in autistic children', *Journal of Speech and Hearing Disorders*, 46: 241–49.

Prizant, B.M. and Rydell, P.J. (1984) 'Analysis of functions of delayed echolalia in autistic children', *Journal of Speech and Hearing Research*, 27: 183–92.

Prucha, J. (1983) *Pragmalinguistics: East European Tradition*, Amsterdam: John Benjamins.

Pruden, S.M., Hirsh-Pasek, K., Golinkoff, R.M. and Hennon, E.A. (2006) 'The birth of words: ten-month-olds learn words through perceptual salience', *Child Development*, 77: 266–80.

Prutting, C. and Kirchner, D. (1987) 'A clinical appraisal of the pragmatic aspects of language', *Journal of Speech and Hearing Disorders*, 52: 105–19.

Psathas, G. (1991) 'The structure of direction-giving in interaction', in D. Boden and D.H. Zimmerman (eds) *Talk and Social Structure: Studies in Ethnomethodology and Conversation Analysis*, Cambridge: Polity Press.

Psathas, G. and Anderson, T. (1990) 'The "practices" of transcription in conversation analysis', *Semiotica*, 78: 75–99.

Pullin, G. (2006a) 'Hand-ear coordination in the control of emotionally expressive speech synthesis', poster presented at Workshop on Haptic and Audio Interaction Design, Glasgow, August/September 2006. Online. Available: www.computing.dundee.ac.uk/ac_research/publicationssearch.asp?person = 45 (accessed 28 August 2007).

——(2006b) '17 different ways to say "yes"', poster presented at Meeting of the British Association of Academic Phoneticians, Edinburgh, April 2006. Online. Available: www.computing.dundee.ac.uk/ac_research/publicationssearch.asp?person = 245 (accessed 28 August 2007).

Pulvermüller, F. and Schumann, J. (1994) 'Neurobiological mechanisms of language acquisition', *Language Learning*, 44: 681–734.

Pustejovsky, J. (1992) 'The syntax of event structure', in B. Levin and S. Pinker (eds) *Lexical and Conceptual Semantics*, Oxford: Blackwell.

——(1995) *The Generative Lexicon*, Cambridge, MA: MIT Press.

Pustejovsky, J. and Anick, P. (1988) 'On the semantic interpretation of nominals', in D. Vargha (ed.) *Proceedings of the 12th Conference on Computational Linguistics*, Morristown, NJ: Association for Computational Linguistics.

Pustejovsky, J. and Boguraev, B. (1993) 'Lexical knowledge representation and natural language processing', *Artificial Intelligence*, 63: 193–223.

——(1995) 'Lexical semantics in context', *Journal of Semantics*, 12: 133–62.

Putnam, H. (1967) 'The nature of mental states', in H. Putnam (ed.) (1975) *Mind, Language and Reality: Philosophical Papers Volume II*, Cambridge: Cambridge University Press.

——(1975) 'The meaning of "meaning"', in K. Gunderson (ed.) *Language, Mind and Knowledge*, Minneapolis, MN: University of Minnesota Press.

——(1993) 'Meaning and reference', in A.W. Moore (ed.) *Meaning and Reference*, New York: Oxford University Press.

——(1994) 'The importance of being Austin: the need for a "second naiveté"', *Journal of Philosophy*, 91: 466–87.

Pylyshyn, Z.W. (1973) 'What the mind's eye tells the mind's brain', *Psychological Bulletin*, 80: 1–24.

——(1984) *Computation and Cognition*, Cambridge, MA: MIT Press.

——(1991) 'The role of cognitive architectures in theories of cognition', in K. VanLehn (ed.) *Architectures for Intelligence*, Hillsdale, NJ: Lawrence Erlbaum Associates.

——(2003) *Seeing and Visualizing: It's Not What You Think*, Cambridge, MA: Harvard University Press.

Quigley, A. (1976) *The Pinter Problem*, Princeton, NJ: Princeton University Press.

Quillian, M.R. (1968) 'Semantic memory', in M.L. Minsky (ed.) *Semantic Information Processing*, Cambridge, MA: MIT Press.

Quine, W.V.O. (1940) *Mathematical Logic*, Cambridge, MA: Harvard University Press.

——(1956) 'Quantifiers and propositional attitudes', *Journal of Philosophy*, 53: 177–87; reprinted in A. Marras (ed.) (1972) *Intentionality, Mind and Language*, Urbana, IL: University of Illinois Press.

——(1960) *Word and Object*, Cambridge, MA: MIT Press.

Quintilian (1943) *Institutio Oratoria*, trans. H.E. Butler, London: William Heinemann.

Quirk, R., Greenbaum, S., Leech, G. and Svartvik, J. (1985) *A Comprehensive Grammar of the English Language*, London: Longman.

Ragin, A.B. and Oltmanns, T.F. (1986) 'Lexical cohesion and formal thought disorders during and after psychotic episodes', *Journal of Abnormal Psychology*, 95: 181–83.

Rampton, B. (2006) *Language in Late Modernity: Interaction in an Urban School*,

Random House (1999) *Random House Webster's College Dictionary*, 2nd edn, New York: Random House.

Rao, A. and Georgeff, M. (1992) 'An abstract architecture for rational agents', in B. Nebel, C. Rich and W. Swartout (eds) *Proceedings of KR 92: The 3rd International Conference on Knowledge Representation and Reasoning*, San Mateo, CA: Morgan Kaufmann.

Rapin, I. (1996) 'Developmental language disorders: a clinical update', *Journal of Child Psychology and Psychiatry*, 37: 643–55.

Rapin, I. and Allen, D.A. (1983) 'Developmental language disorders: nosological considerations', in U. Kirk (ed.) *Neuropsychology of Language, Reading and Spelling*, New York: Academic Press.

——(1998) 'The semantic-pragmatic deficit disorder: classification issues', *International Journal of Language and Communication Disorders*, 33: 82–87.

Raskin, V. (1985) *Semantic Mechanisms of Humor*, Dordrecht, Boston, MA and Lancaster: D. Reidel.

Rastle, K. (2007) 'Visual word recognition', in M. G. Gaskell (ed.) *The Oxford Handbook of Psycholinguistics*, Oxford: Oxford University Press.

Recanati, F. (1989) 'The pragmatics of what is said', *Mind and Language*, 4: 295–329.

——(1991) 'The pragmatics of what is said', in S. Davis (ed.) *Pragmatics: A Reader*, New York: Oxford University Press.

——(1993) *Direct Reference: From Language to Thought*, Oxford: Blackwell.

——(1995) 'The alleged priority of literal interpretation', *Cognitive Science*, 19: 207–32.

——(1996) 'Domains of discourse', *Linguistics and Philosophy*, 21: 95–115.

——(2000) *Oratio Obliqua, Oratio Recta: The Semantics of Metarepresentation*, Cambridge, MA: MIT Press.

——(2001a) 'Literal/nonliteral', *Midwest Studies in Philosophy*, 25: 264–74.

——(2001b) 'Open quotation', *Mind*, 110: 637–87.

——(2001c) 'What is said', *Synthese*, 128: 75–91.

——(2002a) 'Does linguistic communication rest on inference?', *Mind and Language*, 17: 105–26.

——(2002b) 'Unarticulated constituents', *Linguistics and Philosophy*, 25: 299–345.

——(2003) 'Embedded implicatures', *Philosophical Perspectives*, 17: 299–332.

——(2004a) 'Pragmatics and semantics', in L.R. Horn and G. Ward (eds) *The Handbook of Pragmatics*, Oxford: Blackwell.

——(2004b) *Literal Meaning*, Cambridge: Cambridge University Press.

——(2004c) '"What is said" and the semantics/pragmatics distinction', in C. Bianchi (ed.) *The Semantics/Pragmatics Distinction*, Stanford, CA: CSLI Publications.

——(2005) 'Literalism and contextualism: some varieties', in G. Preyer and G. Peter (eds) *Contextualism in Philosophy: Knowledge, Meaning, and Truth*, Oxford: Clarendon Press.

——(2007) 'Reply to Carston 2007', in M.J. Frápolli (ed.) *Saying, Meaning and Referring: Essays on François Recanati's Philosophy of Language*, Basingstoke: Palgrave Macmillan.

Rees-Miller, J. (2000) 'Power, severity, and context in disagreement', *Journal of Pragmatics*, 32: 1087–111.

Reeves, A., Bowl, R., Wheeler, S. and Guthrie, E. (2004) 'The hardest words: exploring the dialogue of suicide in the counselling process – a discourse analysis', *Counselling and Psychotherapy Research*, 4: 62–71.

Reichenbach, H. (1947) *Elements of Symbolic Logic*, Berkeley, CA: University of California Press.

Reimer, M. (1991) 'Do demonstrations have semantic significance?', *Analysis*, 51: 177–83.

Reimer, M. and Bezuidenhout, A. (eds) (2004) *Descriptions and Beyond*, Oxford: Clarendon Press.

Reinhart, T. (1981) 'Pragmatics and linguistics: an analysis of sentence topics', *Philosophica*, 27: 53–94.

——(1983a) 'Coreference and bound anaphora: a restatement of the anaphora questions', *Linguistics and Philosophy*, 6: 47–88.

——(1983b) *Anaphora and Semantic Interpretation*, London: Croom Helm.

——(1995) 'Interface strategies', *OTS Working Papers in Linguistics*, 55–109.

——(1997) 'Quantifier scope: how labor is divided between QR and choice functions', *Linguistics and Philosophy*, 20: 335–97.

——(2004) 'The processing cost of reference set computation: acquisition of stress shift and focus', *Language Acquisition*, 12: 109–55.

Reinhart, T. and Reuland, E. (1993) 'Reflexivity', *Linguistic Inquiry*, 24: 657–720.

Reinsch, N.L. Jr (2009) 'Management communication', in F. Bargiela-Chiappini (ed.) *The Handbook of Business Discourse*, Edinburgh: Edinburgh University Press.

Reisigl, M. (2008) *Nationale Rhetorik in Fest- und Gedenkreden*, Tübingen: Stauffenberg Verlag.

Reisigl, M. and Wodak, R. (2001) *Discourse and Discrimination*, London: Routledge.

Reiter, R. (1980) 'A logic for default reasoning', *Artificial Intelligence*, 13: 81–132.

——(2001) *Logic in Action: Logical Foundations for Specifying and Implementing Dynamical Systems*, Cambridge, MA: MIT Press.

Rescher, N. (1976) *Plausible Reasoning: An Introduction to the Theory and Practice of Plausible Inference*, Assen and Amsterdam: Van Gorcum.

Ribeiro, B.T. (1993) 'Framing in psychotic discourse', in D. Tannen, D. (ed.) *Framing in Discourse*. NY: Oxford University Press.

——(1994) *Coherence in Psychotic Discourse*, New York: Oxford University Press.

——(2000) 'Listening to narratives in psychiatric interviews', in M. Coulthard, J. Cotterill and F. Rock (eds) *Dialogue Analysis VII: Working with Dialogue*, Tübingen: Max Niemeyer Verlag.

Ribeiro, B.T. and Cabral Bastos, L. (2005) 'Telling stories in two psychiatric interviews: a discussion on frame and narrative', *AILA Review*, 18: 58–75.

Ribeiro, B.T. and Pinto, D.S. (2005) 'Medical discourse, psychiatric interview', in K. Brown (ed.) *The Encyclopedia of Language and Linguistics*, 2nd edn, Oxford: Elsevier.

Ricento, T. (2000) *Ideology, Politics and Language Policies*, Amsterdam: John Benjamins.

Richard, M. (1990) *Propositional Attitudes: An Essay on Thoughts and How We Ascribe Them*, Cambridge: Cambridge University Press.

——(1995) 'Defective contexts, accommodation, and normalization', *Canadian Journal of Philosophy*, 25: 551–70.

——(2004) 'Contextualism and relativism', *Philosophical Studies*, 119: 215–42.

Richards, D.A.J. (1971) *A Theory of Reasons for Actions*, Oxford: Oxford University Press.

Richards, K. (2006a) 'Being the teacher: identity and classroom conversation', *Applied Linguistics*, 27: 51–77.

——(2006b) *Language and Professional Identity: Aspects of Collaborative Interaction*, New York: Palgrave Macmillan.

Riddiford, N. (2007) 'Making requests appropriately in a second language: does instruction help to develop pragmatic proficiency?' *The TESOLANZ Journal*, 15: 88–102.

Rieber, S. (1997) 'Conventional implicatures as tacit performatives', *Linguistics and Philosophy*, 20: 51–72.

Rinaldi, M.C., Marangolo, P. and Baldassarri, F. (2004) 'Metaphor comprehension in right brain-damaged patients with visuo-verbal and verbal material: a dissociation (re)considered', *Cortex*, 40: 479–90.

Rinaldi, W. (2000) 'Pragmatic comprehension in secondary school-aged students with specific developmental language disorder', *International Journal of Language and Communication Disorders*, 35: 1–29.

Ring, M. (1991) '"Bring me a slab!": meaning, speakers, and practices', in R.L. Arrington and H.-J. Glock (eds) *Wittgenstein's Philosophical Investigations: Text and Context*, London: Routledge.

Rintell, E. (1979) 'Getting your speech act together: the pragmatic ability of second language learners', *Working Papers on Bilingualism*, 17: 97–106.

Ripich, D.N. and Terrell, B. (1988) 'Patterns of discourse cohesion and coherence in Alzheimer's disease', *Journal of Speech and Hearing Disorders*, 53: 8–15.

Ripich, D.N. and Wykle, M.L. (1996) *Alzheimer's Disease Communication Guide: The FOCUSED Program for Caregivers*, San Antonio, TX: The Psychological Corporation.

Ripich, D.N., Ziol, E., Fritsch, T. and Durand, E.J. (1999) 'Training Alzheimer's disease caregivers for successful communication', *Clinical Gerontologist*, 21: 37–56.

Rips, L. (1994) *The Psychology of Proof: Deductive Reasoning in Human Thinking*, Cambridge, MA: MIT Press.

Rips, L., Shoben, J. and Smith, E. (1973) 'Semantic distance and the verification of semantic relations', *Journal of Verbal Learning and Verbal Behaviour*, 12: 1–20.

Risjord, M. (1996) 'Meaning, belief, and language acquisition', *Philosophical Psychology*, 9: 465–75.

Rizzolatti, G., Sinigaglia, C. and Anderson, F. (2008) *Mirrors in the Brain: How Our Minds Share Actions, Emotions, and Experience*, Oxford: Oxford University Press.

Roberts, C. (1995) 'Domain restriction in dynamic semantics', in E. Bach, E. Jelinek, A. Kratzer and B.H. Partee (eds) *Quantification in Natural Languages*, Dordrecht: Kluwer.

——(1996) 'Information structure: towards an integrated formal theory of pragmatics', in J.H. Yoon and A. Kathol (eds) *OSU Working Papers in Linguistics*, volume 49: Papers in Semantics, Columbus, OH: The Ohio State University Department of Linguistics.

——(2002) 'Demonstratives as definites', in K. van Deemter and R. Kibble (eds) *Information Sharing*, Stanford, CA: CSLI Publications.

——(2003) 'Uniqueness in definite noun phrases', *Linguistics and Philosophy*, 26: 287–350.

Roberts, C. and Campbell, S. (2005) 'Fitting stories into boxes: rhetorical and textual constraints on candidate's performances in British job interviews', *Journal of Applied Linguistics*, 2: 45–73.

Roberts, C., Davies, E. and Jupp, T. (1992) *Language and Discrimination: A Study of Communication in Multi-Ethnic Workplaces*, London: Longman.

Roberts, K.P. (2002) 'Children's ability to distinguish between memories from multiple sources: implications for the quality and accuracy of eyewitness statements', *Developmental Review*, 22: 403–35.

Roberts, R. and Kreuz, R. (1994) 'Why do people use figurative language?', *Psychological Science*, 5: 159–63.

Robinson, D. (2003) *Performative Linguistics: Speaking and Translating as Doing Things with Words*, London and New York: Routledge.

——(2005) *Introducing Performative Pragmatics*, London and New York: Routledge.

Robinson, E.J. and Whitcombe, E. (2003) 'Children's suggestibility in relation to their understanding of sources of knowledge', *Child Development*, 74: 48–62.

Robinson, E.J., Mitchell, P. and Nye, R. (1995) 'Young children's treating of utterances as unreliable sources of knowledge', *Journal of Child Language*, 22: 663–85.

Robinson, J.D. (2006) 'Managing trouble responsibility and relationships during conversational repair', *Communication Monographs*, 73: 137–61.

Robinson, M. (1992) 'Introspective methodology in interlanguage pragmatics research', in G. Kasper (ed.) *Pragmatics of Japanese as Native and Target Language*, Honolulu, HI: Second Language Teaching and Curriculum Center, University of Hawaii at Manoa.

Rochester, S.R. and Martin, J.R. (1979) *Crazy Talk: A Study of the Discourse of Schizophrenic Speakers*, New York: Plenum.

Rock, F. (2007) *Communicating Rights: The Language of Arrest and Detention*, Basingstoke: Palgrave.

Rockwell, P. (2004) 'Differences in participants' estimates and identification of their own and their partners' sarcastic utterances', *Journal of Diplomatic Language*. Online. Available: www.jdlonline.org/I4Rockwell1.html (accessed 3 December 2007).

Rodriguez-Ferrera, S., McCarthy, R.A. and McKenna, P.J. (2001) 'Language in schizophrenia and its relationship to formal thought disorder', *Psychological Medicine*, 31: 197–205.

Rogoff, B. and Lave, J. (eds) (1984) *Everyday Cognition*, Cambridge, MA: Harvard University Press.

Rohde, H. (2006) 'Rhetorical questions as redundant interrogatives', *San Diego Linguistics Papers*, 2: 134–66.

Rollins, P.R. and Snow, C.E. (1998) 'Shared attention and grammatical development in typical children and children with autism', *Journal of Child Language*, 25: 653–73.

Romero, E. and Soria, B. (eds) (to appear) *Explicit Communication: Robyn Carston's Pragmatics*, London: Palgrave Macmillan.

Romney, A.K. and D'Andrade, R.G. (eds) (1964) *Transcultural Studies in Cognition*, American Anthropologist, volume 66, Washington, DC: American Anthropological Association.

Rooryck, J. (2001) 'Evidentiality', *Glot International*, 5: 123–33 (part I), 161–68 (part II).

Rooth, M. (1985) *Association with focus*, Ph.D. dissertation, University of Massachusetts, Amherst.

——(1992) 'A theory of focus interpretation', *Natural Language Semantics*, 1: 75–116.

——(1995) 'Indefinites, adverbs of quantification, and focus semantics', in G.N. Carlson and F.J. Pelletier (eds) *The Generic Book*, Chicago, IL: University of Chicago Press.

Rorty, R. (1979) *Philosophy and the Mirror of Nature*, Princeton, NJ: Princeton University Press.

Rosch, E. (1975) 'Cognitive reference points', *Cognitive Psychology*, 7: 532–47.

Rose, K.R. (2001) 'Compliments and compliment responses in film: implications for pragmatics research and language teaching', *IRAL*, 39: 309–26.

Rose, K.R. and Ng, C.K.F. (1999) 'Inductive and deductive approaches to teaching compliments and compliment responses', *Perspectives*, 11: 124–69.

Rosenfeld, H.M. (1966) 'Instrumental affiliative functions of facial and gestural expressions', *Journal of Personality and Social Psychology*, 4: 65–72.

Rosenthal, D.M. (1997) 'A theory of consciousness', in N. Block, O. Flanagan and G. Guzeldere (eds) *The Nature of Consciousness: Philosophical Debates*, Cambridge, MA: MIT Press.

Rosier-Catach, I. (1994) *La Parole Efficace: Signe, Rituel, Sacré*, Paris: Seuil.

——(2004) *La Parole Comme Acte: Sur la Grammaire et la Sémantique au XIIIe Siècle*, Paris: Vrin.

Ross, J.R. (1973) 'Slifting', in M. Gross, M. Halle and M.-P. Schützenberger (eds) *The Formal Analysis of Natural Languages. Proceedings of the First International Conference*, The Hague: Mouton.

——(1975) 'Where to do things with words', in P. Cole and J. Morgan (eds) *Syntax and Semantics 3: Speech Acts*, New York: Academic Press.

Rothschild, D. and Segal, G. (to appear) 'Indexical predicates', *Mind and Language*.

Rounds, P.L. (1987) 'Multifunctional personal pronoun use in an educational setting', *English for Specific Purposes*, 6: 13–29.

Röver, C. (2005) *Testing ESL Pragmatics*, Frankfurt am Main: Lang.

Rowan, L.E., Leonard, L.B., Chapman, K. and Weiss, A.L. (1983) 'Performative and presuppositional skills in language-disordered and normal children', *Journal of Speech and Hearing Research*, 26: 97–106.

Roy, C. (2000) *Interpreting as a Discourse Process*, Oxford: Oxford University Press.

Rubin, J. (1983) 'How to tell when someone is saying "no" revisited', in N. Wolfson and E. Judd (eds) *Sociolinguistics and Language Acquisition*, Rowley, MA: Newbury House.

Rude, S., Gortner, E. and Pennebaker, J. (2004) 'Language use of depressed and depression-vulnerable college students', *Cognition and Emotion*, 18: 1121–33.

Rudrum, D. (2005) 'From narrative representation to narrative use: towards the limits of definition', *Narrative*, 13: 195–204.

Ruhi, S. (2002) 'Complimenting women in Turkish: gender identity and otherness', in A. Duszak (ed.) *Us and Others: Social Identities Across Languages, Discourses and Cultures*, Amsterdam and Philadelphia, PA: John Benjamins.

Rumelhart, D.E. (1975) 'Notes on a schema for stories', in D.G. Bobrow and A. Collins (eds) *Representation and Understanding*, New York: Academic Press.

Rumelhart, D.E., McClelland, J.L. and the PDP Research Group (1986) *Parallel Distributed Processing: Explorations in the Microstructure of Cognition, Vol. 1: Foundations*, Cambridge, MA: MIT Press.

Russell, B. (1905) 'On denoting', *Mind*, 14: 479–93; reprinted in A.P. Martinich (ed.) (1996) *The Philosophy of Language*, Oxford: Oxford University Press.

——([1918] 2004) 'Knowledge by acquaintance and knowledge by description', in *Mysticism and Logic*, Mineola, NY: Dover Publications.

——(1919) *Introduction to Mathematical Philosophy*, London: Allen and Unwin.

——(1946) *History of Western Philosophy and its Connection with Political and Social Circumstances from the Earliest Times to the Present Day*, London: George Allen and Unwin Ltd.

——(2006) 'Against grammatical computation of scalar implicatures', *Journal of Semantics*, 23: 361–82.

Russell, J. (ed.) (1998) *Autism as an Executive Disorder*, Oxford: Oxford University Press.

Russell, S. and Norvig, P. (2003) *Artificial Intelligence: A Modern Approach*, Upper Saddle River, NJ: Prentice Hall.

Russon, A.E., Vasey, P.L., and Gauther, C. (2002) 'Seeing with the mind's eye: eye-covering play in orangutans and Japanese macaques', in R.W. Mitchell (ed.) *Pretending and Imagination in Animals and Children*, Cambridge: Cambridge University Press.

Rutter, D.R. (1985) 'Language in schizophrenia: the structure of monologues and Conversations', *British Journal of Psychiatry*, 146: 399–404.

Ruys, E.G. (1992) *The scope of indefinites*, Ph.D. dissertation, Utrecht University.

Ryan, M-L. (2006) 'Semantics, pragmatics and narrativity: a response to David Rudrum', *Narrative*, 14: 188–96.

Ryder, N. and Leinonen, E. (2003) 'The use of context in question answering by three, four and five year old children', *Journal of Psycholinguistic Research*, 3: 397–414.

Ryder, N., Leinonen, E. and Schulz, J. (2008) 'Cognitive approach to assessing pragmatic language comprehension in children with specific language impairment', *International Journal of Language and Communication Disorders*, 43: 427–47.

Rydgren, J. (ed.) (2005) *Moments of Exclusion*, New York: Nova.

Sabbagh, M.A. (1999) 'Communicative intentions and language: evidence from right-hemisphere damage and autism', *Brain and Language*, 70: 29–69.

Sacks, H. ([1963] 1995) *Lectures on Conversation*, vols I and II, ed. G. Jefferson, Oxford: Blackwell.

——(1974) 'An analysis of the course of a joke's telling in conversation', in J. Sherzer and R. Bauman (eds) *Explorations in the Ethnography of Speaking*, London: Cambridge University Press.

——(1987) 'On the preferences for agreement and contiguity in sequences in conversations', in G. Button and R. Lee (eds) *Talk and Social Organization*, Philadelphia, PA: Multilingual Matters.

——(1992) *Lectures on Conversation*, vols I and II, ed. G. Jefferson, Oxford: Blackwell.

——(2004) 'An initial characterization of the organization of speaker turn-taking in conversation', in G.H. Lerner (ed.) *Conversation Analysis: Studies from the First Generation*, Amsterdam and Philadelphia, PA: John Benjamins.

Sacks, H., Schegloff, E.A. and Jefferson, G. (1974) 'A simplest systematics for the organization of turn taking for conversation', *Language*, 50: 696–735.

Sadek, M.D. and de Mori, R. (1998) 'Dialogue systems', in R. de Mori (ed.) *Spoken Dialogues with Computers*, London: Academic Press.

Sadock, J.M. (1971) 'Queclaratives', *Proceedings from the 7th Regional Meeting of the Chicago Linguistic Society*, Chicago, IL: Chicago Linguistic Society.

——(1974) 'Some covert illocutionary acts in English', in J.M. Sadock (ed.) *Toward a Linguistic Theory of Speech Acts*, New York and London: Academic Press.

——(1978) 'On testing for conversational impli-
cature', in P. Cole (ed.) *Syntax and Semantics,
Volume 9: Pragmatics*, New York: Academic
Press.

——(1984) 'Whither radical pragmatics?', in D.
Schiffrin (ed) *Meaning, Form, and Use in Context:
Linguistic Applications*, Washington, DC:
Georgetown University Press.

Saeki, M. and O'Keefe, B.J. (1994) 'Refusals
and rejections: designing messages to serve
multiple goals', *Human Communication Research*,
21: 67–102.

Saffran, J.R., Werker, J. and Werner, L. (2006)
'The infant's auditory world: hearing, speech,
and the beginnings of language', in R. Siegler
and D. Kuhns (eds) *Handbook of Child Development*,
New York: Wiley.

Sajavaara, K. and Lehtonen, J. (1997) 'The
silent Finn revisited', in A. Jaworski (ed.)
Silence: Interdisciplinary Perspectives, Berlin: Mouton
de Gruyter.

Saka, P. (1998) 'Quotation and the use-mention
distinction', *Mind*, 107: 113–35.

Sakakibara, S. (1995) *The pragmatics and distribution of the Japanese reflexive pronoun* zibun, Ph.D.
dissertation, University of Illinois.

Salager-Meyer, F. (1994) 'Hedges and textual
communicative function in medical English
written discourse', *English for Specific Purposes*,
13: 149–70.

——(1997) 'I think that perhaps you should: a
study of hedges in written scientific discourse', in T. Miller (ed) *Functional Approaches to
Written Text: Classroom Applications*, Washington,
DC: United Information Agency.

Saldert, C. and Ahlsen, E. (2007) 'Inference in
right hemisphere damaged individuals' comprehension: the role of sustained attention',
Clinical Linguistics and Phonetics, 21: 637–55.

Salmon, N. (1986) *Frege's Puzzle*, Cambridge,
MA: MIT Press.

——(2002) 'Demonstrating and necessity', *The
Philosophical Review*, 111: 497–537.

Salmon, V. ([1967] 1987) 'Elizabethan collo-
quial English in the Falstaff plays', in V.
Salmon and E. Burness (eds) *A Reader in the
Language of Shakespearean Drama*, Amsterdam:
John Benjamins.

Saltmarsh, R. and Mitchell, P. (1998) 'Young
children's difficulty acknowledging false
belief: realism and deception', *Journal of
Experimental Child Psychology*, 69: 3–21.

Samuels, R. (2006) 'Is the human mind massively modular?', in R. Stainton (ed.) *Contemporary Debates in Cognitive Science*, Oxford:
Blackwell.

Samuels, R., Stich, S. and Tremoulet, P. (1999)
'Rethinking rationality: from bleak implications to Darwinian modules', in E. Lepore
and Z. Pylyshyn (eds) *What is Cognitive Science?*
Oxford: Blackwell.

Sanders, T.J.M., Spooren, W.P.M. and Noord-
man, L.G.M. (1993) 'Coherence relations in
a cognitive theory of discourse representation',
Cognitive Linguistics, 4: 93–133.

Sandra, D. (1998) 'What linguists can and can't
tell you about the human mind: a reply to
Croft', *Cognitive Linguistics*, 9: 361–478.

Sanford, A.J. and Garrod, S.C. (1981) *Understanding Written Language: Explorations of Comprehension Beyond the Sentence*, Chichester: John
Wiley.

Santo Pietro, M.J. and Ostuni, E. (2003) *Success-
ful Communication with Alzheimer's Patients: An In-
Service Training Manual*, 2nd edn, Boston, MA:
Butterworth-Heinemann.

Sapir, E. (1921) *Language*, New York: Harcourt
Brace.

Sarangi, S. and Roberts, C. (1999) 'The
dynamics of interactional and institutional
orders', in S. Sarangi and C. Roberts (eds)
*Talk, Work and Institutional Order: Discourse in
Medical, Mediation and Management Settings*,
Berlin: Mouton de Gruyter.

Sarangi, S. and Slembrouck, S. (1996) *Language,
Bureaucracy and Social Control*, London: Longman.

Sasaki, M. (1998) 'Investigating EFL students'
production of speech acts: a comparison of
production questionnaires and role plays',
Journal of Pragmatics, 30: 457–84.

Sauerland, U. (2004) 'Scalar implicatures in
complex sentences', *Linguistics and Philosophy*,
27: 367–91.

Sauerland, U. and Yatsushiro, K. (eds) (to
appear) *Semantics and Pragmatics: From
Experiment to Theory*, Basingstoke: Palgrave
Macmillan.

Saul, J. (2001) 'Critical study of Davis (1998)',
Noûs, 35: 630–41.

——(2002a) 'Speaker meaning, what is said and
what is implicated', *Noûs*, 36: 228–48.

——(2002b) 'What is said and psychological
reality: Grice's project and relevance theorists' criticisms', *Linguistics and Philosophy*, 25:
347–72.

——(2006) *Lying, misleading, and accidental falsehood:
the role of what is said*, unpublished manuscript,
University of Sheffield.

Sauntson, H. (2007) 'Girls' and boys' use of
acknowledging moves in pupil group classroom discussions', *Language and Education*, 21:
304–27.

Saussure, F. de (1916) *Cours de Linguistique Générale*, ed. C. Bally and A. Sechehaye, Paris: Payot.

Savickiene, I. and Dressler, W.U. (eds) (2007) *The Acquisition of Diminutives: A Cross-Linguistic Perspective*, Amsterdam: Benjamins.

Saville-Troike, M. (1985) 'The place of silence in an integrated theory of communication', in D. Tannen and M. Saville-Troike (eds) *Perspectives of Silence*, Norwood, NJ: Ablex.

——(2003) *The Ethnography of Communication*, Oxford: Blackwell.

Savundranayagam, M.Y., Hummert, M.L. and Montgomery, R.J.V. (2005) 'Investigating the effects of communication problems on caregiver burden', *The Journals of Gerontology Series B: Psychological Sciences and Social Sciences*, 60: S48–S55.

Sbisà, M. (2006) 'Communicating citizenship in verbal interaction. Principles of a speech act oriented discourse analysis', in H. Hausendorf and A. Bora (eds) *Analysing Citizenship Talk*, Amsterdam: John Benjamins.

Scarcella, R. (1979) 'On speaking politely in a second language', in C.A. Yorio, K. Peters and J. Schachter (eds) *On TESOL '79: The Learner in Focus*, Washington, DC: Teachers of English to Speakers of Other Languages.

——(1983) 'Discourse accent in second language performance', in S.M. Gass and L. Selinker (eds) *Language Transfer in Language Learning*, Rowley, MA: Newbury House.

Scardamalia, M. and Bereiter, C. (1987) 'Knowledge telling and knowledge transforming in written composition', in S. Rosenberg (ed.) *Advances in Applied Psycholinguistics*, vol. 2, Cambridge: Cambridge University Press.

Schachter, J. (1990) 'On the issue of completeness in second language acquisition', *Second Language Research*, 6: 93–124.

Schaeffer, J. (2000) *The Acquisition of Direct Object Scrambling and Clitic Placement*, Amsterdam and Philadelphia, PA: John Benjamins.

Schaeffer, J. and Matthewson, L. (2005) 'Grammar and pragmatics in the acquisition of article systems', *Natural Language and Linguistic Theory*, 23: 53–101.

Schafer, R. and de Villiers, J. (2000) 'Imagining articles: what *a* and *the* can tell us about the emergence of DP', in S.C. Howell, S.A. Fish and T. Keith-Lucas (eds) *Proceedings of the Boston University Conference on Language Development*, Somerville, MA: Cascadilla Press.

Schank, R.C. (1980) 'Language and memory', *Cognitive Science*, 3: 243–84.

Schank, R.C. and Abelson, R.P. (1977) *Scripts, Plans, Goals and Understanding*, Hillsdale, NJ: Erlbaum.

Scharten, R. (1997) *Exhaustive interpretation: a discourse-semantic analysis*, unpublished thesis, Katholieke Universiteit Nijmegen, Holland.

Schauer, G.A. (2006) 'Pragmatic awareness in ESL and EFL contexts: contrast and Development', *Language Learning*, 56: 269–318.

Schegloff, E.A. (1968) 'Sequencing in conversational openings', *American Anthropologist*, 70: 1075–95.

Schegloff, E.A. (1972) 'Notes on a conversational practice: formulating place', in D. Sudnow (ed.) *Studies in Social Interaction*, New York: Free Press.

——(1979a) 'Identification and recognition in telephone conversation openings,' in G. Psathas (ed.) *Everyday Language: Studies in Ethnomethodology*, New York: Irvington Publishers.

——(1979b) 'The relevance of repair to syntax-for-conversation', in T. Givon (ed.) *Syntax and Semantics 12: Discourse and Syntax*, New York: Academic Press.

——(1980) 'Preliminaries to preliminaries: "Can I ask you a question?"', *Sociological Inquiry*, 50: 104–52.

——(1982) 'Discourse as an interactional achievement: some uses of "uh huh" and other things that come between sentences', in D. Tannen (ed.) *Analyzing Discourse: Text and Talk*, Washington, DC: Georgetown University Press.

——(1986) 'The routine as achievement', *Human Studies*, 9: 111–51.

——(1987) 'Recycled turn beginnings: a precise repair mechanism in conversation's turn-taking organization', in G. Button and J.R.E. Lee (eds) *Talk and Social Organisation*, Clevedon, UK: Multilingual Matters.

——(1992) 'Repair after next turn: the last structurally provided defense of intersubjectivity in conversation', *American Journal of Sociology*, 98: 1295–345.

——(1993) 'Telephone conversation', in R.E. Asher (ed.) *Encyclopedia of Language and Linguistics*, vol. 9, Oxford: Pergamon Press.

——(1996) 'Turn organization: one intersection of grammar and interaction', in E. Ochs, E. A. Schegloff and S.A. Thompson (eds) *Interaction and Grammar*, Cambridge: Cambridge University Press.

——(1997a) 'Third turn repair', in G.R. Guy, C. Feagin, D. Schiffrin and J. Baugh (eds) *Towards a Social Science of Language 2*, Amsterdam and Philadelphia, PA: John Benjamins.

——(1997b) 'Practices and actions: boundary cases of other-initiated repair', *Discourse Processes*, 23: 499–545.

——(1998) 'Reflections on studying prosody in talk-in-interaction', *Language and Speech*, 41: 235–63.

——(2000) 'Overlapping talk and the organization of turn-taking for conversation', *Language in Society*, 29: 1–63.

——(2002) 'Reflections on research on telephone conversations: issues of cross-cultural scope and scholarly exchange, interactional import and consequences', in K.K. Luke and Th.-S. Pavlidou (eds) *Telephone Calls: Unity and Diversity in Conversational Structure across Languages and Cultures*, Amsterdam and Philadelphia, PA: John Benjamins.

——(2004) 'On dispensability', *Research on Language and Social Interaction*, 37: 95–149.

——(2007) *Sequence Organization in Interaction: A Primer in Conversation Analysis*, vol. 1, Cambridge: Cambridge University Press.

Schegloff, E.A. and Sacks, H. (1973) 'Opening up closings', *Semiotica*, 8: 289–327.

Schegloff, E.A., Jefferson, G. and Sacks, H. (1977) 'The preference for self-correction in the organization of repair in conversation', *Language*, 53: 361–82.

Schelletter, C. and Leinonen, E. (2003) 'Normal and language-impaired children's use of reference: syntactic versus pragmatic processing', *Clinical Linguistics and Phonetics*, 17: 335–43.

Schelling, T. (1960) *The Strategy of Conflict*, Cambridge, MA: Harvard University Press.

Scherer, K.R. (1986) 'Vocal affect expression: a review and a model for future research', *Psychological Bulletin*, 99: 143–65.

——(2000) 'A cross-cultural investigation of emotion inferences from voice and speech: implications for speech technology', paper presented at the 6th International Conference on Spoken Language Processing, Beijing, China, October 2000. Online. Available: www.unige.ch/fapse/emotion/publications/pdf/icspl00_crosscul.pdf (accessed 26 August 2008).

Scheurweghs, G. (1959) *Present-Day English Syntax: A Survey of Sentence Patterns*, London: Longmans.

Schiappa, E. (1999) *The Beginnings of Rhetorical Theory in Classical Greece*, New Haven, CT: Yale University Press.

Schieffelin, B. (1990) *The Give and Take of Everyday Life: Language Socialization of Kaluli Children*, Cambridge: Cambridge University Press.

Schiffer, S.R. (1972) *Meaning*, Oxford: Clarendon Press.

——(1987) *Remnants of Meaning*, London: MIT Press.

——(1992) 'Belief ascription', *Journal of Philosophy*, 89: 499–521.

——(1996) 'The hidden-indexical theory's logical-form problem: a rejoinder', *Analysis*, 56: 92–97.

——(2003) *The Things We Mean*, Oxford: Clarendon Press.

Schiffrin, D. (1987) *Discourse Markers: Studies in Interactional Sociolinguistics 5*, Cambridge: Cambridge University Press.

——(1989) 'Conversation analysis', in F.J. Newmeyer (ed.) *Linguistics: The Cambridge Survey: Volume 4, Language: The Socio-Cultural Context*, Cambridge: Cambridge University Press.

——(1994) *Approaches to Discourse*, Oxford: Blackwell.

——(1996) 'Narrative as self portrait: sociolinguistic constructions of identity', *Language in Society*, 25: 167–203.

——(1997) 'The transformation of experience, identity, and context', in G. Guy, C. Feagin and D. Schiffrin (eds) *Towards a Social Science of Language, II: Social Interaction and Discourse Structures*, Amsterdam: John Benjamins.

Schiffrin, D., Tannen, D. and Hamilton, H.E. (eds) (2001) *The Handbook of Discourse Analysis*, Oxford: Blackwell.

Schilling-Estes, N. (2004) 'Constructing ethnicity in interaction', *Journal of Sociolinguistics*, 8: 163–95.

Schlanger, P. and Schlanger, B. (1970) 'Adapting role playing activities with aphasic patients', *Journal of Speech and Hearing Disorders*, 35: 229–35.

Schlenker, P. (2004) 'Context of thought and context of utterance: a note on free indirect discourse and the historical present', *Mind and Language*, 19: 279–304.

Schlieben-Lange, B. (1983) *Tradition des Sprechens: Elemente einer Pragmatischen Sprachgeschichtsschreibung*, Stuttgart: Kohlhammer.

Schmerling, S.F. (1976) *Aspects of English Sentence Stress*, Austin, TX: University of Texas Press.

Schmidt, R. (1983) 'Interaction, acculturation and the acquisition of communicative competence', in N. Wolfson and E. Judd (eds) *Sociolinguistics and Second Language Acquisition*, Rowley, MA: Newbury House.

Schmitt, N. (2002) *An Introduction to Applied Linguistics*, London: Arnold.

Schmitz-Berning, C. (2000) *Vokabular des Nationalsozialismus*, Berlin: de Gruyter.

Schnädelbach, H. (1992) *Zur Rehabilitierung des Animal Rationale*, Frankfurt: Suhrkamp.

Schneider, K.P. (1988) *Small Talk: Analyzing Phatic Discourse*, Marburg, Germany: Hitzeroth.
——(2001) 'Pragmatics meets dialectology: investigating regional variation in language use', paper presented at the *International Workshop, New Orientations in the Study of Regionalism*, University of Bonn, Germany, July 2001.

Schneider, K.P. and Barron, A. (2005a) 'Variational pragmatics: contours of a new discipline', paper presented at the *9th International Pragmatics Conference*, Riva del Garda, July 2005.
——(2005b) 'Variational Pragmatics', symposium at the *9th International Pragmatics Conference*, Riva del Garda, July 2005.

Schneider, S. (2007a) *Reduced Parenthetical Clauses as Mitigators: A Corpus Study of Spoken French, Italian and Spanish*, Amsterdam: John Benjamins.
——(2007b) 'Reduced parenthetical clauses in Romance languages: a pragmatic typology', in N. Dehé and Y. Kavalova (eds) *Parentheticals*, Amsterdam: John Benjamins.

Schneiderman, E.I., Murasugi, K.G. and Saddy, J.D. (1992) 'Story arrangement ability in right brain-damaged patients', *Brain and Language*, 43: 107–20.

Schön, A. (1987) 'Silence in the myth: psychoanalytical observations', in M.G. Ciani (ed.) *The Regions of Silence: Studies on the Difficulty of Communicating*, Amsterdam: J.C. Gieben.

Schourup, L. (1985) *Common Discourse Particles in English Conversation*, New York: Garland Publishing.
——(1999) 'Discourse markers', *Lingua*, 107: 227–65.

Schubert, L.K. and Pelletier, F.J. (1987) 'Problems in the representation of the logical form of generics, plurals and mass nouns', in E. Lepore (ed.) *New Directions in Semantics*, London: Academic Press.

Schubert, L.K. and Pelletier, F.J. (1989) 'Generically speaking; or, using discourse representation theory to interpret generics', in G. Chierchia, B. Partee and R. Turner (eds) *Properties Types and Meaning, Volume 2: Semantic Issues*, Dordrecht: Kluwer.

Schulz, P., Roeper, T. and Pearson, B.Z. (2005) 'The acquisition of the semantics of exhaustive wh-questions from a cross-linguistic perspective', symposium presented at the *Triennial Meeting of the International Association for the Study of Child Language (IASCL)*, Berlin, July 2005.

Schumann, J.H. (1978) 'The acculturation model for second language acquisition', in R.C. Gringas (ed.) *Second Language Acquisition and Foreign Language Teaching*, Arlington, VA: Center for Applied Linguistics.

Schwartz, B.D. (1992) 'Testing between UG-based and problem-solving models of L2A: developmental sequence data', *Language Acquisition*, 2: 1–19.
——(1998) 'The second language instinct', *Lingua*, 106: 133–60.
——(2003) 'Child L2 acquisition: paving the way', in B. Beachley, A. Brown and F. Conlin (eds) *Proceedings of the 27th Annual Boston University Conference on Language Development*, Somerville, MA: Cascadilla Press.

Schwartz, B.D. and Sprouse, R.A. (1994) 'Word order and nominative case in non-native language acquisition: a longitudinal study of (L1 Turkish) German interlanguage', in T. Hoekstra and B.D. Schwartz (eds) *Language Acquisition Studies in Generative Grammar: Papers in Honor of Kenneth Wexler from the 1991 GLOW Workshops*, Amsterdam: John Benjamins.
——(1996) 'L2 cognitive states and the full transfer/full access model', *Second Language Research*, 12: 40–72.

Schwarz, B. (2001) 'Two kinds of long-distance indefinites', in R. van Rooy and M. Stokhof (eds) *Proceedings of the Thirteenth Amsterdam Colloquium*, Amsterdam: Institute for Language, Logic and Information, University of Amsterdam.

Schwarz, F. (2005) 'Presuppositions in processing – a case study of German *auch*', paper presented at Sinn und Bedeutung 10, Humboldt University, Berlin, October 2005.

Schwarzschild, R. (1999) 'GIVENness, AvoidF and other constraints on the placement of accent', *Natural Language Semantics*, 7: 141–77.
——(2002) 'Singleton indefinites', *Journal of Semantics*, 19: 289–314.

Schwenter, S.A. (2005) 'The pragmatics of negation in Brazilian Portuguese', *Lingua*, 115: 1427–56.

Schwoebel, J., Dews, S., Winner, E. and Srinivas, K. (2000) 'Obligatory processing of the literal meaning of ironic utterances: further evidence', *Metaphor and Symbol*, 15: 47–61.

Scollon, R. (2005) 'Lighting the stove: why habitus isn't enough for critical discourse analysis', in R. Wodak and P. Chilton (eds) *A New Agenda in (Critical) Discourse Analysis*, Amsterdam: John Benjamins.

Scollon, R. and Wong-Scollon, S. (2003) *Discourses in Place: Language in the Material World*, London: Routledge.

Scott, M. (2004) *WordSmith Tools Version 4*, Oxford: Oxford University Press.

Scott, M. and Tribble, C. (2006) *Textual Patterns: Key Words and Corpus Analysis in Language Education*, Amsterdam: John Benjamins.

Scott, S. (2002) 'Linguistic feature variation within disagreement: an empirical investigation', *Text*, 22: 301–28.

Scott-Phillips, T.C. (2008) 'Defining biological communication', *Journal of Evolutionary Biology*, 21: 387–95.

Seale, C., Ziebland, S. and Charteris-Black, J. (2006) 'Gender, cancer experience and internet use: a comparative keyword analysis of interviews and online cancer support groups', *Social Science and Medicine*, 62: 2577–90.

Searle, J.R. (1965) 'What is a speech act?', in M. Black (ed.) *Philosophy in America*, London: Allen and Unwin.

——(1969) *Speech Acts: An Essay in the Philosophy of Language*, Cambridge: Cambridge University Press.

——(1975a) 'A taxonomy of illocutionary acts', in K. Gunderson (ed.) *Language, Mind and Knowledge*, Minnesota Studies in the Philosophy of Science, vol. VII, Minneapolis, MN: University of Minnesota Press; reprinted in *Expression and Meaning* (1979), Cambridge: Cambridge University Press.

——(1975b) 'Indirect speech acts', in P. Cole and J.L. Morgan (eds) *Syntax and Semantics, Vol. 3: Speech Acts*, New York: Academic Press.

——(1976) 'A classification of illocutionary acts', *Language in Society*, 5: 1–23.

——(1977) 'Reiterating the differences: a reply to Derrida', *Glyph*, 1: 198–208.

——(1978) 'Literal meaning', *Erkenntnis*, 13: 207–24.

——(1979a) 'Metaphor', in A. Ortony (ed.) *Metaphor and Thought*, Cambridge: Cambridge University Press; reprinted in A.P. Martinich (ed.) (1990) *The Philosophy of Language*, 2nd edn, New York: Oxford University Press.

——(1979b) *Expression and Meaning: Studies in the Theory of Speech Acts*, Cambridge: Cambridge University Press.

——(1980) 'Minds, brains, and programs', *Behavioral and Brain Sciences*, 3: 417–56; reprinted in J. Haugeland (ed.) (1981) *Mind Design*, Cambridge, MA: MIT Press.

——(1983) *Intentionality*, Cambridge: Cambridge University Press.

——(1987) 'Empiricism, indeterminacy and the first person', *Journal of Philosophy*, 84: 123–46.

——(1990a) 'Consciousness, explanatory inversion, and cognitive science', *The Behavioral and Brain Sciences*, 13: 585–642.

——(1990b) 'Collective intentions and actions', in P. Cohen, J. Morgan and M.E. Pollack (eds) *Intentions in Communication*, Cambridge, MA: MIT Press.

——(1992) *The Rediscovery of the Mind*, Cambridge, MA: MIT Press.

——(1995) *The Construction of Social Reality*, London: Penguin.

——(2001) *Rationality in Action*, Cambridge: Cambridge University Press.

Searle, J.R. and Vanderveken, D. (1985) *Foundations of Illocutionary Logic*, Cambridge: Cambridge University Press.

Sebeok, T.A. (2002) *Global Semiotics*, Bloomington, IN: Indiana University Press.

Sedivy, J.C., Tanenhaus, M.K., Chambers, C. G. and Carlson, G.N. (1999) 'Achieving incremental semantic interpretation through contextual representation', *Cognition*, 71: 109–47.

Seedhouse, P. (2004) *The Interactional Architecture of the Language Classroom: A Conversation Analysis Perspective*, Oxford: Blackwell.

Segal, G. (1996) 'The modularity of theory of mind', in P. Carruthers and P.K. Smith (eds) *Theories of Theory of Mind*, Cambridge: Cambridge University Press.

Seitel, P. (1969) 'Proverbs: a social use of metaphor', *Genre*, 2: 143–61.

Selkirk, E.O. (1984) *Phonology and Syntax: The Relationship between Sound and Structure*, Cambridge, MA: MIT Press.

Sell, R.D. (ed.) (1991) *Literary Pragmatics*, London: Routledge.

——(1994) 'Postdisciplinary philology: culturally relativistic pragmatics', in F. Fernández, M. Fuster and J. José Calvo (eds) *English Historical Linguistics 1992. Papers from the Seventh International Conference on English Historical Linguistics Valencia, 22–26 September 1992*, Amsterdam: John Benjamins.

——(1998) 'Literary pragmatics', in J. Mey (ed.) *A Concise Encyclopedia of Pragmatics*, Oxford: Elsevier Science.

Sellars, W. (1949) 'Language, rules and behavior', in S. Hook (ed.) *John Dewey: Philosopher of Science and Freedom*, New York: Dial Press.

——(1953) 'Inference and meaning', *Mind*, 62: 313–38.

——(1954) 'Some reflections on language games', *Philosophy of Science*, 21: 204–28.

——(1969) 'Language as thought and as communication', *Philosophy and Phenomenological Research*, 29: 506–27.

——(1974) 'Meaning as functional classification', *Synthèse*, 27: 417–37.

——(1992) *Science and Metaphysics*, Atascadero, CA: Ridgeview.

Selting, M. (1996) 'On the interplay of syntax and prosody in the constitution of turn-constructional units and turns in conversation', *Pragmatics*, 6: 357–88.

——(2005) 'Syntax and prosody as methods for the construction and identification of turn-constructional units in conversation', in A. Hakulinen and M. Selting (eds) *Syntax and Lexis in Conversation*, Amsterdam: John Benjamins.

——(2008) 'Linguistic resources for the management of interaction', in G. Antos and E. Ventola (eds) *Handbook of Interpersonal Communication*, Berlin: Mouton de Gruyter.

Selting, M. and Couper-Kuhlen, E. (eds) (2001) *Studies in Interactional Linguistics*, Amsterdam and Philadelphia: John Benjamins.

Semino, E. (1997) *Language and World Creation in Poems and Other Texts*, London: Longman.

——(2002) 'A cognitive stylistic approach to mind style in narrative fiction', in E. Semino and J. Culpeper (eds), *Cognitive Stylistics: Language and Cognition in Text Analysis*, Amsterdam: John Benjamins.

Semino, E. (2006) 'Blending and characters' mental functioning in Virginia Woolf's *Lappin and Lapinova*', *Language and Literature*, 15: 55–72.

Semino, E. and Culpeper, J. (eds) (2002) *Cognitive Stylistics: Language and Cognition in Text Analysis*, Amsterdam: John Benjamins.

Semino, E. and Short, M. (2004) *Corpus Stylistics: Speech, Writing and Thought Presentation in a Corpus of English Writing*, London: Routledge.

Senft, G. (2007) 'Bronislaw Malinowski and linguistic pragmatics', *Lodz Papers in Pragmatics*, 3: 79–96.

Serratrice, L., Sorace, A. and Paoli, S. (2004) 'Crosslinguistic influence at the syntax-pragmatics interface: subjects and objects in English-Italian bilingual and monolingual acquisition', *Bilingualism: Language and Cognition*, 7: 183–205.

Sgall, P., Hajičová, E. and Benešová, E. (1973) *Topic, Focus, and Generative Semantics*, Kronberg, Gemany: Scriptor Verlag.

Sgall, P., Hajičová, E. and Panevová, J. (1986) *The Meaning of the Sentence in its Semantic and Pragmatic Aspects*, Dordrecht: Reidel.

Shaffer, B. (2004) 'Information ordering and speaker subjectivity: modality in ASL', *Cognitive Linguistics*, 15: 175–95.

Shallice, T. (1988) *From Neuropsychology to Mental Structure*, Cambridge: Cambridge University Press.

Shallice, T. and Warrington, E.K. (1970) 'Independent functioning of verbal memory stores: a neuropsychological study', *Neuropsychologia*, 15: 729–35.

Shamay-Tsoory, S.G., Tomer, R. and Aharon-Peretz, J. (2005a) 'The neuroanatomical basis of understanding sarcasm and its relationship to social cognition', *Neuropsychology*, 19: 288–300.

Shamay-Tsoory, S.G., Tomer, R., Berger, B.D., Goldsher, D. and Aharon-Peretz, J. (2005b) 'Impaired "affective theory of mind" is associated with right ventromedial prefrontal damage', *Cognitive and Behavioural Neurology*, 18: 55–67.

Shannon, C.E. and Weaver, W. (1949) *The Mathematical Theory of Communication*, Urbana: University of Illinois Press.

Sharifian, F. (2005) 'The Persian cultural schema of shekasteh-nafsi: a study of compliment responses in Persian and Anglo-Australian speakers', *Pragmatics and Cognition*, 13: 337–61.

Sharvy, R. (1980) 'A more general theory of definite descriptions', *Philosophical Review*, 89: 607–24.

Shatz, M. (1983) 'Communication', in J. Flavell and E. Markman (eds) *Handbook of Child Psychology, Volume 3, Cognitive Development*, New York: Wiley.

Shepard, R.N. (1980) *Internal Representations: Studies in Perception, Imagery, and Cognition*, Montgomery, VT: Bradford.

Shiffrin, D. (1980) 'Meta-talk: organizational and evaluative brackets in discourse', *Sociological Inquiry*, 50: 199–236.

Shimpi, P.M. and Huttenlocher, J. (2007) 'Redirective labels and early vocabulary development', *Journal of Child Language*, 34: 845–59.

Shohamy, E. (2006) *Language Policy: Hidden Agendas and New Approaches*, London: Routledge.

Shore, B. (1996) *Culture in Mind: Cognition, Culture, and the Problem of Meaning*, Oxford: Oxford University Press.

Short, M. (1989a) 'Discourse analysis and the analysis of drama', in R. Carter and P. Simpson (eds) *Language, Discourse and Literature*, London: Unwin Hyman.

——(ed.) (1989b) *Reading, Analysing and Teaching Literature*, London: Longman.

——(1996) *Exploring the Language of Poems, Plays and Prose*, London: Longman.

Short, M. and van Peer, W. (1989) 'Accident! Stylisticians evaluate', in M. Short (ed.) *Reading, Analysing and Teaching Literature*, London: Longman.

Short, M., Freeman, D.C., van Peer, W. and Simpson, P. (1998) 'Stylistics, criticism and mythrepresentation again: squaring the circle with Ray Mackay's subjective solution to all problems', *Language and Literature*, 7: 39–50.

Short, T.L. (2007) *Peirce's Theory of Signs*, Cambridge: Cambridge University Press.

Shriberg, E., Bates, R., Stolcke, A., Taylor, P., Jurafsky, D., Ries, K., Coccaro, N., Martin, R., Meteer, M. and Van Ess-Dykema, C. (1998) 'Can prosody aid the automatic classification of dialog acts in conversational speech?', *Language and Speech*, 41: 443–92.

Shulman, B. (1985) *Test of Pragmatic Skills*, Arizona: Communication Skill Builders.

Shuy, R.W. (1993) *Language Crimes*, Oxford: Blackwell.

——(1997) 'Discourse clues to coded language in an impeachment hearing: towards a social science of language', in G.R. Guy, C. Feagin, D. Schiffrin and J. Baugh (eds) *Papers in Honor of William Labov, Volume 2: Social Interaction and Discourse Structures*, Amsterdam: John Benjamins.

——(1998) *The Language of Confession, Interrogation and Deception*, Thousand Oaks, CA: Sage.

Sidelle, A. (1991) 'The answering machine paradox', *Canadian Journal of Philosophy*, 21: 525–39.

Siegal, M.E.A. (1995) 'Individual differences and study abroad: women learning Japanese in Japan', in B.F. Freed (ed.) *Second Language Acquisition in a Study Abroad Context*, Amsterdam: John Benjamins.

——(1996) 'The role of learner subjectivity in second language sociolinguistic competency: Western women learning Japanese', *Applied Linguistics*, 17: 356–82.

——(2002) '*Like*: the discourse particle and semantics', *Journal of Semantics*, 19: 35–71.

Siegal, M., Carrington, J. and Radel, M. (1996) 'Theory of mind and pragmatic understanding following right hemisphere damage', *Brain and Language*, 53: 40–50.

Sierz, A. (2001) *In-Yer-Face Theatre: British Drama Today*, London: Faber and Faber.

Sifianou, M. (1989) 'On the telephone again! Differences in telephone behaviour: England versus Greece', *Language in Society*, 18: 527–44.

——(1997) 'Silence and politeness', in A. Jaworski (ed.) *Silence: Interdisciplinary Perspectives*, Berlin: Mouton de Gruyter.

——(2002) 'On the telephone again! Telephone call openings in Greek', in K.K. Luke and Th.-S. Pavlidou (eds) *Telephone Calls: Unity and Diversity in Conversational Structure across Languages and Cultures*, Amsterdam and Philadelphia: John Benjamins.

Sifianou, M. and Antonopoulou, E. (2005) 'Politeness in Greece', in L. Hickey and M. Stewart (eds) *Politeness in Europe*, Clevedon: Multilingual Matters.

Silverstein, M. (1976) 'Shifters, linguistic categories, and cultural description', in K. Basso and H.A. Selby (eds) *Meaning in Anthropology*, Albuquerque, NM: University of New Mexico Press.

——(1996) 'Indexical order and the dialectics of sociolinguistic life', *Language and Communication*, 23: 193–229.

——(2003) 'Indexical order and the dialectics of sociolinguistic life', *Language and Communication*, 23: 193–229.

——(2004) '"Cultural" concepts and the language culture nexus', *Current Anthropology*, 45: 621–52.

Silverstein, M. and Urban, G. (1996) *Natural Histories of Discourse*, Chicago, IL: University of Chicago Press.

Simmons-Mackie, N., Elman, R., Holland, H. and Damico, J.S. (2007) 'Management of discourse in group therapy for aphasia', *Topics in Language Disorders*, 27: 5–23.

Simon, H.A. (1956) 'Rational choice and the structure of environments', *Psychological Review*, 63: 129–38.

——(1981) *The Sciences of the Artificial*, Cambridge, MA: MIT Press.

Simpson, D.M. and Davis, G.C. (1985) 'Measuring thought disorder with clinical rating scales in schizophrenic and non schizophrenic patients', *Psychiatric Research*, 15: 313–18.

Simpson, G.B. (1994) 'Context and the processing of ambiguous words', in M.A. Gernsbacher (ed.) *Handbook of Psycholinguistics*, San Diego, CA: Academic Press.

Simpson, P. (1990) 'Modality in literary-critical discourse', in W. Nash (ed.) *The Writing Scholar: Studies in Academic Discourse*, Newbury Park, CA: Sage.

——(1993) *Language, Ideology and Point of View*, London: Routledge.

——(1998) 'Studying discourses of incongruity', in J. Culpeper, M. Short and P. Verdonk (eds) *Exploring the Language of Drama: From Text to Context*, London: Routledge.

Simpson, R.C. and Mendis, D. (2003) 'A corpus-based study of idioms in academic speech', *TESOL Quarterly*, 37: 419–41.

Sinclair, J. McH. (ed.) (1987a) *Collins COBUILD English Language Dictionary*, London: Collins.

——(1987b) 'Collocation: a progress report', in R. Steele and T. Threadgold (eds) *Language*

Topics: Essays in Honour of Michael Halliday, Amsterdam: John Benjamins.

——(1987c) *Looking Up: An Account of the COBUILD Project in Lexical Computing*, London: Collins.

——(1991) *Corpus, Concordance, Collocation*, Oxford: Oxford University Press.

——(1996) 'The search for units of meaning', *Textus IX*, 1: 75–106.

——(1998) 'The lexical item', in. E. Weigand (ed.) *Contrastive Lexical Semantics*, Amsterdam: John Benjamins.

——(2004a) *Trust the Text*, Routledge: London.

——(2004b) *English Collocation Studies*, London: Continuum.

——(2005) 'Corpus and text – basic principles', in M. Wynne (ed.) *Developing Linguistic Corpora: A Guide to Good Practice*, Oxford: Oxbow Books. Online. Available: http://ahds.ac.uk/linguistic-corpora (accessed 14 May 2008).

Sinclair, J. McH. and Brazil, D. (1982) *Teacher Talk*, Oxford: Oxford University Press.

Sinclair, J. McH. and Coulthard, M. (1975) *Towards an Analysis of Discourse: The English Used by Teachers and Students*, Oxford: Oxford University Press.

Sinclair, J. McH. and Mauranen, A. (2006) *Linear Unit Grammar*, Amsterdam: John Benjamins.

Sinclair, J. McH., Ashby, M., Coulthard, M. and Forsyth, I. (1972) *The English Used by Teachers and Pupils: Final Report to the Social Science Research Council for the Period September 1970 to August 1972*, Birmingham: University of Birmingham.

Sinclair, J. McH., Jones, S. and Daley, R. (1970) *English Lexical Studies*, Birmingham: Department of English, University of Birmingham.

Singer, M. (1994) 'Discourse inference processes', in M.A. Gernsbacher (ed.) *Handbook of Psycholinguistics*, San Diego, CA: Academic Press.

Singh, G. (1973) 'Wit, understatement and irony: Montale's sixth book of poems', *Books Abroad*, 47: 507–10.

Singleton, D. and Lengyel, Z. (eds) (1995) *The Age Factor in Second Language Acquisition: A Critical Look at the Critical Period Hypothesis*, Philadelphia, PA: Multilingual Matters.

Sitta, H. (ed.) (1980) *Ansätze zu einer Pragmatischen Sprachgeschichte. Züricher Kolloquium 1978*, Tübingen: Niemeyer.

Skaffari, J., Peikola, M., Carroll, R., Hiltunen, R. and Wårvik, B. (eds) (2005) *Opening Windows on Texts and Discourses of the Past*, Amsterdam and Philadelphia, PA: John Benjamins.

Skarakis, E. and Greenfield, P.M. (1982) 'The role of new and old information in the verbal expression of language-disordered children', *Journal of Speech and Hearing Research*, 25: 462–67.

Skjei, E. (1985) 'A comment on performative, subject, and proposition in Habermas's theory of communication', *Inquiry*, 28: 87–104.

Slabakova, R. (2006) 'Is there a critical period for semantics?', *Second Language Research*, 22: 1–37.

Slobin, D.I. (1996) 'From "thought and language" to "thinking for speaking"', in J.J. Gumperz and S.C. Levinson (eds) *Rethinking Linguistic Relativity*, Cambridge: Cambridge University Press.

Small, J.A. and Perry, J. (2005) 'Do you remember? How caregivers question their spouses who have Alzheimer's Disease and the impact on communication', *Journal of Speech, Language, and Hearing Research*, 48: 125–36.

Small, J.A., Geldart, K. and Gutman, G. (2000) 'Communication between individuals with dementia and their caregivers during activities of daily living', *American Journal of Alzheimer's Disease and Other Dementias*, 15: 291–302.

Small, J.A., Perry, J. and Lewis, J. (2005) 'Perceptions of family caregivers' psychosocial behavior when communicating with spouses who have Alzheimer's disease', *American Journal of Alzheimer's Disease and Other Dementias*, 20: 281–89.

Smart, J.J.C. (1959) 'Sensations and brain processes', *Philosophical Review*, 68: 141–56.

Smith, B.C. (1991) 'The owl and the electric encyclopedia', *Artificial Intelligence*, 47: 251–88; reprinted in D. Kirsh (ed.) (1992) *Foundations of Artificial Intelligence*, Cambridge, MA: MIT Press.

Smith, B.R. and Leinonen, E. (1992) *Clinical Pragmatics*, London: Chapman Hall.

Smith, D. (1987) *The Everyday World as Problematic: A Feminist Sociology*, Boston, MA: Northeastern University Press.

Smith, L. (1998) 'Predicting communicative competence at 2 and 3 years from pragmatic skills at 10 months', *International Journal of Language and Communication Disorders*, 33: 127–48.

Smith, Q. (1989) 'The multiple uses of indexicals', *Synthese*, 78: 167–91.

Smolensky, P. (1988) 'On the proper treatment of connectionism', *Behavioral and Brain Sciences*, 11: 1–23.

——(1996) 'On the comprehension/production dilemma in child language', *Linguistic Inquiry*, 27: 720–31.

Snow, C.E. (1999) 'Social perspectives on the emergence of language', in B. MacWhinney (ed.) *Emergence of Language*, Hillsdale, NJ: Lawrence Erlbaum Associates.

Snow, C.E., Pan, B., Imbens-Bailey, A. and Herman, J. (1996) 'Learning how to say what one means: a longitudinal study of children's speech act use', *Social Development*, 5: 56–84.

Snow, P., Lambier, J., Parson, C., Mooney, L., Couch, D. and Russell, J. (1987) 'Conversational skill following closed head injury: some preliminary findings', in C. Field, A. Kneebon and M.W. Reid (eds) *Brain Impairment: Proceedings of the Eleventh Annual Brain Impairment Conference*, Richmond, Victoria: Australian Society for the Study of Brain Impairment.

Snowden, J.S., Goulding, P. and Neary, D. (1989) 'Semantic dementia: a form of circumscribed cerebral atrophy', *Behavioral Neurology*, 2: 167–82.

Snowden, J.S., Griffiths, H.L. and Neary, D. (1995) 'Autobiographical experience and word meaning', *Memory*, 3: 225–46.

——(1996) 'Semantic-episodic memory interactions in semantic dementia: implications for retrograde memory function', *Cognitive Neuropsychology*, 13: 1101–37.

Snowdon, P. (1990) 'The objects of perceptual experience', *Proceedings of the Aristotelian Society*, Supplement 64: 121–50.

Soames, S. (1982) 'How presuppositions are inherited: a solution to the projection problem', *Linguistic Inquiry*, 13: 483–545.

——(1984) 'Linguistics and psychology', *Linguistics and Philosophy*, 7: 155–79.

——(1985) 'Semantics and psychology', in J. Katz (ed.) *The Philosophy of Linguistics*, Oxford: Oxford University Press.

——(1987) 'Direct reference, propositional attitudes, and semantic content', *Philosophical Topics*, 15: 44–87; reprinted in N. Salmon and S. Soames (eds) (1988) *Propositions and Attitudes*, Oxford: Oxford University Press.

——(1995) 'Beyond singular propositions?', *Canadian Journal of Philosophy*, 25: 515–49.

——(2002) *Beyond Rigidity*, Oxford: Oxford University Press.

——(2003a) *Philosophical Analysis in the Twentieth Century. Volume 1: The Dawn of Analysis*, Princeton, NJ: Princeton University Press.

——(2003b) *Philosophical Analysis in the Twentieth Century. Volume 2: The Age of Meaning*, Princeton, NJ: Princeton University Press.

——(to appear) 'The gap between meaning and assertion: why what we literally say often differs from what our words literally mean', in M. Hackl and R. Thornton (eds) *Asserting, Meaning, and Implying*, Oxford: Oxford University Press.

Sobkowiak, W. (1997) 'Silence and markedness theory', in A. Jaworski (ed.) *Silence: Interdisciplinary Perspectives*, Berlin: Mouton de Gruyter.

Song, H. and Fisher, C. (2007) 'Discourse prominence effects on 2.5-year-old children's interpretation of pronouns', *Lingua*, 117: 1959–87.

Sorace, A. (2003) 'Near-nativeness', in C. Doughty and M. Long (eds) *Handbook of Second Language Acquisition*, Oxford: Blackwell.

——(2005) 'Syntactic optionality at interfaces', in L. Cornips and K. Corrigan (eds) *Syntax and Variation: Reconciling the Biological and the Social*, Amsterdam: John Benjamins.

Sørensen, H.S. (1961) 'An analysis of linguistic signs occurring in *Suppositio Materialis* or the meaning of quotation marks and their phonetic equivalents', *Lingua*, 10: 174–89.

Soroker, N., Kasher, A., Giora, R., Batori, G., Corn, C., Gil, M. and Zaidel, E. (2005) 'Processing of basic speech acts following localized brain damage: a new light on the neuroanatomy of language', *Brain and Cognition*, 57: 214–17.

Southgate, V., Chevallier, C. and Csibra, G. (to appear) 'Sensitivity to communicative relevance tells young children what to imitate', *Developmental Science*.

Southgate, V., Senju, A. and Csibra, G. (2007) 'Action anticipation through attribution offalse belief by 2-year-olds', *Psychological Science*, 18: 587–92.

Speirs, J. (1998) 'The use of face work and politeness theory', *Qualitative Health Research*, 8: 25–47.

Spencer-Oatey, H. (2000) 'Rapport management: a framework for analysis', in H. Spencer-Oatey (ed.) *Culturally Speaking: Managing Rapport through Talk across Cultures*, London: Continuum.

——(2002) 'Managing rapport in talk: using rapport sensitive incidents to explore the motivational concerns underlying the management of relations', *Journal of Pragmatics*, 34: 529–45.

——(2005) '(Im)Politeness, face and perceptions of rapport: unpackaging their bases and interrelationships', *Journal of Politeness Research*, 1: 95–120.

Spencer-Oatey, H. and Jiang, W.Y. (2003) 'Explaining cross-cultural pragmatic findings: moving from politeness maxims to sociopragmatic interactional principles (SIPs)', *Journal of Pragmatics*, 35: 10–11.

Spencer-Oatey, H. and Ng, P. (2001) 'Reconsidering Chinese modesty: Hong Kong and Mainland Chinese evaluative judgments of compliment responses', *Journal of Asian Pacific Communication*, 11: 181–201.

Sperber, D. (1984) 'Verbal irony: pretense or echoic mention?' *Journal of Experimental Psychology: General*, 113: 130–36.

——(1987) *On Anthropological Knowledge*, Cambridge: Cambridge University Press.

——(1990) 'The evolution of the language faculty: a paradox and its solution', *Behavioral and Brain Sciences*, 13: 756–58.

——(1994) 'Understanding verbal understanding', in J. Khalfa (ed.) *What is Intelligence?* Cambridge: Cambridge University Press.

——(1996a) 'Mental modularity and cultural diversity', in D. Sperber, *Explaining Culture: A Naturalistic Approach*, Oxford: Blackwell.

——(1996b) *Explaining Culture: A Naturalistic Approach*, London: Blackwell.

——(1997) 'Intuitive and reflective beliefs', *Mind and Language*, 12: 67–83.

——(2000) 'Metarepresentation in an evolutionary perspective', in D. Sperber (ed.) *Metarepresentations: A Multidisciplinary Perspective*, New York: Oxford University Press.

——(2001a) 'An evolutionary perspective on testimony and argumentation', *Philosophical Topics*, 29: 401–13.

——(2001b) 'In defence of massive modularity', in E. Dupoux (ed.) *Language, Brain, and Cognitive Development. Essays in Honor of Jacques Mehler*, Cambridge, MA: MIT Press.

——(2005) 'Modularity and relevance: how can a massively modular mind be flexible and context-sensitive?', in P. Carruthers, S. Laurence and S. Stich (eds) *The Innate Mind: Structure and Content*, New York: Oxford University Press.

——(2007) 'Seedless grapes: nature and culture', in S. Laurence and E. Margolis (eds) *Creations of the Mind: Theories of Artifacts and their Representation*, Oxford: Oxford University Press.

Sperber, D. and Origgi, G. (2005) 'Pourquoi parler, comment comprendre?', in J.-M. Hombert (ed.) *L'Origine de l'Homme, du Langage et des Langues*, Paris: Fayard.

Sperber, D. and Wilson, D. (1981) 'Irony and the use/mention distinction', in P. Cole (ed.) *Radical Pragmatics*, New York: Academic Press.

——(1986) 'Loose talk', *Proceedings of the Aristotelian Society*, 86: 153–71.

——([1986] 1995) *Relevance: Communication and Cognition*, Oxford: Blackwell.

——(1987a) 'Précis of *Relevance: Communication and Cognition*', *Behavioral and Brain Sciences*, 10: 697–710; reprinted in A. Kasher (ed.) (1998) *Pragmatics: Critical Concepts*, vol. V, London: Routledge.

——(1987b) 'Presumptions of relevance', *Behavioral and Brain Sciences*, 10: 736–53.

——(1990a) 'Rhetoric and relevance', in J. Bender and D. Wellbery (eds) *The Ends of Rhetoric: History, Theory, Practice*, Stanford, CA: Stanford University Press.

——(1990b) 'Spontaneous deduction and mutual knowledge', *Behavioral and Brain Sciences*, 13: 179–84.

——(1996) 'Fodor's frame problem and relevance theory: a reply to Chiappe and Kukla', *Behavioral and Brain Sciences*, 19: 530–32.

——(1998a) 'Irony and relevance: a reply to Seto, Hamamoto and Yamanashi', in R. Carston and S. Uchida (eds) *Relevance Theory: Applications and Implications*, Amsterdam: John Benjamins.

——(1998b) 'The mapping between the mental and the public lexicon', in P. Carruthers and J. Boucher (eds) *Language and Thought: Interdisciplinary Themes*, Cambridge: Cambridge University Press.

——(2002) 'Pragmatics, modularity and mindreading', *Mind and Language*, 17: 3–23.

——(2008) 'A deflationary account of metaphor', in R.W. Gibbs (ed.) *The Cambridge Handbook of Metaphor and Thought*, Cambridge: Cambridge University Press.

Sperber, D., Cara, F. and Girotto, V. (1995) 'Relevance theory explains the selection task', *Cognition*, 57: 31–95.

Sperling, G. (1960) 'The information available in brief visual presentations', *Psychological Monographs*, 74: 1–29.

Spitzbardt, H. (1963) 'Overstatement and understatement in British and American English', *Philologica Pragensia*, 6: 277–86.

Spitzer, L. (1948) *Linguistics and Literary History*, Princeton, NJ: Princeton University Press.

Spitzer, M., Braun, U. and Maier, S. (1993) 'Indirect semantic priming in schizophrenic patients', *Schizophrenia Research*, 11: 71–80.

Spivey, M.J. and Tanenhaus, M.K. (1998) 'Syntactic ambiguity resolution in discourse: modeling the effects of referential context and lexical frequency', *Journal of Experimental Psychology: Learning, Memory, and Cognition*, 24: 1521–43.

Spolsky, B. (ed.) (2004) *Language Policy*, Cambridge: Cambridge University Press.

Spradley, J. (ed.) (1972) *Culture and Cognition: Rules, Maps, and Plans*, San Francisco, CA: Chandler.

Stainton, R. (1994) 'Using non-sentences: an application of relevance theory', *Pragmatics and Cognition*, 2: 269–84.

——(1997) 'Utterance meaning and syntactic ellipsis', *Pragmatics and Cognition*, 5: 51–78.

——(2005) 'In defense of non-sentential assertion', in Z. Szabo (ed.) *Semantics Versus Pragmatics*, Oxford: Oxford University Press.

——(2006) *Words and Thoughts: Subsentences, Ellipsis, and the Philosophy of Language*, Oxford: Oxford University Press.

Stalnaker, R.C. (1970) 'Pragmatics', *Synthese*, 22: 272–89; reprinted in *Context and Content* (1999), Oxford: Oxford University Press.

——(1972) 'Pragmatics', in D. Davidson and G. Harman (eds) *Semantics of Natural Language*, Dordrecht: Reidel.

——(1973) 'Presuppositions', *Journal of Philosophical Logic*, 2: 447–57.

——(1974) 'Pragmatic presuppositions', in M.K. Munitz and P. Unger (eds) *Semantics in Philosophy*, New York: New York University Press.

——(1978) 'Assertion', in P. Cole and J.L. Morgan (eds) *Syntax and Semantics, Volume 9: Pragmatics*, New York: Academic Press.

——(1998) *Context and Content*, Oxford: Oxford University Press.

Stanley, J. (2000) 'Context and logical form', *Linguistics and Philosophy*, 23: 391–434.

——(2002) 'Making it articulated', *Mind and Language*, 17: 149–68.

——(2005) 'Semantics in context', in G. Preyer and G. Peter (eds) *Contextualism in Philosophy: Knowledge, Meaning, and Truth*, Oxford: Oxford University Press.

Stanley, J. and Szabo, Z. (2000) 'On quantifier domain restriction', *Mind and Language*, 15: 219–61.

Stedman Jones, G. (1983) *Languages of Class: Studies in English Working Class History 1832–1982*, Cambridge: Cambridge University Press.

Steen, G. (1994) *Understanding Metaphor in Literature: An Empirical Approach*, London: Longman.

Stein, D. (1985) 'Perspectives in historical pragmatics', *Folia Linguistica Historica*, 6: 347–55.

——(1992) *Cooperating with Written Texts: The Pragmatics and Comprehension of Written Texts*, Berlin and New York: Mouton de Gruyter.

Steiner, G. (1967) *Language and Silence*, London: Faber and Faber.

Stemmer, B. and Schönle, P.W. (2000) 'Neuropragmatics in the 21st century', *Brain and Language*, 71: 233–36.

Stemmer, B., Giroux, F. and Joanette, Y. (1994) 'Production and evaluation of requests by right hemisphere brain-damaged individuals', *Brain and Language*, 47: 1–31.

Stenström, A.-B. (1994) *An Introduction to Spoken Interaction*, Harlow: Longman.

Stern, D.N. (1985) *The Interpersonal World of the Infant*, New York: Basic Books.

Stern, J. (2000) *Metaphor in Context*, Cambridge, MA: MIT Press.

Sternberger, D., Storz, G. and Süskind, W.E. (1957) *Aus dem Wörterbuch des Unmenschen*, Hamburg: Claassen Verlag.

Stetter, C. (1991) 'Text und Struktur: hat die Sprechakttheorie eine Historische Dimension?', in D. Busse (ed.) *Diachrone Semantik und Pragmatik: Untersuchungen zur Erklärung und Beschreibung des Sprachwandels*, Tübingen, Germany: Max Niemeyer Verlag.

Stevens, P.B. (1993) 'The pragmatics of "no!": some strategies in English and Arabic', *Issues and Developments in English and Applied Linguistics (IDEAL)*, 6: 87–112.

Stewart, M. (2005) '"I'm just going to wash you down": sanitizing the vaginal examination', *Journal of Advanced Nursing*, 5: 587–94.

Stirman, S. and Pennebaker, J. (2001) 'Word use in the poetry of suicidal and non-suicidal poets', *Psychosomatic Medicine*, 63: 517–22.

Stivale, C.I. (1996) 'Spam: heteroglossia and harassment in cyberspace', in D. Porter (ed.) *Internet Culture*, London and New York: Routledge.

Stockwell, P. (2002) *Cognitive Poetics: An Introduction*, London: Routledge.

Stokoe, E. and Edwards, D. (2008) '"Did you have permission to smash your neighbour's door?" Silly questions and their answers in police-suspect interrogations', *Discourse Studies*, 10: 89–111.

Storto, G. and Tanenhaus, M. (2005) 'Are scalar implicatures computed online?', in E. Maier, C. Bary and J. Huitink (eds) *Proceedings of SuB9*. Online. Available: http://ncs.ruhosting.nl/sub9 (accessed 21 November 2008).

Stout, C.E., Yorkston, K.M. and Pimental, J.I. (2000) 'Discourse production following mild, moderate, and severe traumatic brain injury: a comparison of two tasks', *Journal of Medical Speech-Language Pathology*, 8: 15–25.

Stratta, P., Riccardi, I., Mirabilio, D., Di Tommaso, S., Tomassini, A. and Rossi, A. (2007) 'Exploration of irony appreciation in schizophrenia: a replication study on an Italian sample', *European Archives of Psychiatry and Clinical Neuroscience*, 257: 337–39.

Strauss, C. and Quinn, N. (1997) *A Cognitive Theory of Cultural Meaning*, Cambridge: Cambridge University Press.

Strawson, G. (2005) 'Intentionality and experience: terminological preliminaries', in D.W. Smith and A.L. Thomasson (eds) *Phenomenology and Philosophy of Mind*, Oxford: Clarendon Press.

Strawson, P.F. (1950a) 'On referring', *Mind*, 59: 320–44.

——(1950b) 'Truth', *Proceedings of the Aristotelian Society*, Supplement 24: 129–56.

——(1952) *Introduction to Logical Theory*, London: Methuen.

——(1956) 'On referring', in A. Flew (ed.) *Essays in Conceptual Analysis*, London: Macmillan and Co.; reprinted in A.P. Martinich (ed.) (1990) *The Philosophy of Language*, 2nd edn, New York: Oxford University Press.

——(1964a) 'Intention and convention in speech acts', *Philosophical Review*, 73: 439–60.

——(1964b) 'Identifying reference and truth values', *Theoria*, 30: 96–118; reprinted in D.D. Steinberg and L.A. Jakobovits (eds) *Semantics: An Interdisciplinary Reader in Linguistics, Philosophy, and Psychology*, Cambridge: Cambridge University Press.

——(1974) *Subject and Predicate in Logic and Grammar*, London: Methuen.

Streeck, J. (1980) 'Speech acts in interaction: a critique of Searle', *Discourse Processes*, 3: 133–54.

Street, B. (2003) 'What's "new" in new literacy studies? Critical approaches to literacy in theory and practice', *Current Issues in Comparative Education*, 5 (2). Online. Available: www.tc.columbia.edu/cice/Archives/5.2/52street.pdf (accessed 8 July 2008).

Stroll, A. (2002) *Wittgenstein*, Oxford: Oneworld Publications.

Strong, C. (1998) *The Strong Narrative Assessment Procedure*, Eau Claire, WI: Thinking Publications.

Struchen, M. (2005) 'Social communication intervention', in W.M. High, A.M. Sander, M. Struchen and K.A. Hart (eds) *Rehabilitation for Traumatic Brain Injury*, New York: Oxford University Press.

Stubbe, M., Lane, C., Hilder, J., Vine, E., Vine, B., Holmes, J., Marra, M. and Weatherall, A. (2003) 'Multiple discourse analyses of a workplace interaction', *Discourse Studies*, 5: 351–88.

Stubbs, M. (1976) *Language, Schools and Classrooms*, London: Methuen.

——(1983a) *Language, Schools and Classrooms*, London: Methuen.

——(1983b) *Discourse Analysis*, Chicago, IL: University of Chicago Press.

——(1995) 'Corpus evidence for norms of lexical collocation', in G. Cook and B. Seidlhofer (eds) *Principle and Practice in Applied Linguistics. Studies in Honour of H.G. Widdowson*, Oxford: Oxford University Press.

——(1996) *Text and Corpus Analysis: Computer-Assisted Studies of Language and Culture*, Oxford: Blackwell.

——(2001) *Words and Phrases*, Oxford: Blackwell.

——(2005) 'Conrad in the computer: examples of quantitative stylistic methods', *Language and Literature*, 14: 5–24.

Suddendorf, T. and Whiten, A. (2001) 'Mental evolution and development: evidence for secondary representation in children, great apes and other animals', *Psychological Bulletin*, 127: 629–50.

Sudnow, D. (1978) *Ways of the Hand: The Organization of Improvised Conduct*, London: Routledge and Kegan Paul.

Suler, J. (2004) 'The online disinhibition effect', *CyberPsychology and Behavior*, 7: 321–26.

Sullivan, H.S. (1964) 'The Language of schizophrenia', in J. S. Kasanin (ed.) *Language and Thought in Schizophrenia*, New York: Norton.

Sullivan, K. and Lindgren, E. (2006) *Computer Key-Stroke Logging and Writing: Methods and Applications*, London: Elsevier.

Sullivan, K. and Winner, E. (1991) 'When 3-year-olds understand ignorance, false belief and representational change', *British Journal of Developmental Psychology*, 9: 159–71.

Sun, H. (2004) 'Opening moves in informal Chinese telephone conversations', *Journal of Pragmatics*, 36: 1429–65.

Sunderland, J. (2004) *Gendered Discourses*, Basingstoke, UK: Palgrave.

Surian, L. and Siegal, M. (2001) 'Sources of performance on theory of mind tasks in right hemisphere-damaged patients', *Brain and Language*, 78: 224–32.

Surian, L., Baron-Cohen, S. and Van der Lely, H. (1996) 'Are children with autism deaf to Gricean maxims?', *Cognitive Neuropsychiatry*, 1: 55–71.

Sussman, R., Klein, N., Carlson, G. and Tanenhaus, M. (2006) 'Weak definites: evidence for a new class of definite NP interpretation', poster presented at the *Nineteenth Annual CUNY Conference on Human Sentence Processing*, New York, March 2006.

Suszczynska, M. (1999) 'Apologizing in English, Polish and Hungarian: different languages, different strategies', *Journal of Pragmatics*, 31: 1053–65.

Suzuki, L. and Calzo, J. (2004) 'The search for peer advice in cyberspace: an examination of online teen bulletin boards about health and sexuality', *Applied Developmental Psychology*, 25: 685–98.

Svartvik, J. (1968) *The Evans Statements: A Case for Forensic Linguistics*, Göteborg: University of Gothenburg Press.

——(ed.) (1992) *Directions in Corpus Linguistics*, Trends in Linguistics, 65, Berlin: Mouton de Gruyter.

Swales, J. (1990) *Genre Analysis*, Cambridge: Cambridge University Press.

——(2000) 'Languages for specific purposes', *Annual Review of Applied Linguistics*, 20: 59–76.

——(2004) *Research Genres*, Cambridge: Cambridge University Press.

Swales, J. and Malczewski, B. (2001) 'Discourse management and new episode flags in MICASE', in R.C. Simpson and J.M. Swales (eds) *Corpus Linguistics in North America: Selections from the 1999 Symposium*, Michigan: University of Michigan Press.

Swan, M. (1995) *Practical English Usage*, Oxford: Oxford University Press.

Swann, J. (1992) *Girls, Boys and Language*, Oxford: Blackwell.

Swart, H. d. (2006) 'Marking and interpretation of negation: a bi-directional OT approach', in R. Zanuttini, H. Campos, E. Herburger and P.H. Portner (eds) *Crosslinguistic Research in Syntax and Semantics: Negation, Tense and Clausal Architecture*, Washington, DC: Georgetown University Press.

Sweetser, E. (1990) *From Etymology to Pragmatics*, Cambridge: Cambridge University Press.

——(2006) 'Whose rhyme is whose reason? Sound and sense in *Cyrano de Bergerac*', *Language and Literature*, 15: 29–54.

Swinney, D. (1979) 'Lexical access during sentence comprehension: (re)consideration of context effects', *Journal of Verbal Learning and Verbal Behavior*, 5: 219–27.

Sysoeva, A. and Jaszczolt, K. (2007) 'Composing utterance meaning: an interface between pragmatics and psychology', paper presented at the 10th International Pragmatics Conference, Göteborg, July 2007.

Szabó, Z.G. (2001) 'Adjectives in context', in I. Kenesei and R.M. Harnish (eds) *Perspectives on Semantics, Pragmatics, and Discourse, A Festshrift for Ferenc Kiefer*, Amsterdam: John Benjamins.

——(ed.) (2005) *Semantics Versus Pragmatics*, Oxford: Clarendon Press.

Szatmari, P. (2004) *A Mind Apart*, New York: Guilford Press.

Szczepek Reed, B. (2004) 'Turn-final intonation in English', in E. Couper-Kuhlen and C.E. Ford (eds) *Sound Patterns in Interaction*, Amsterdam: John Benjamins.

Szuchewicz, B. (1997) 'Silence in ritual communication', in A. Jaworski (ed.) *Silence: Interdisciplinary Perspectives*, Berlin: Mouton de Gruyter.

Taavitsainen, I. and Jucker, A.H. (eds) (2003) *Diachronic Perspectives on Address Term Systems*, Amsterdam and Philadelphia, PA: John Benjamins.

——(2007) 'Speech acts and speech act verbs in the history of English', in S.M. Fitzmaurice and I. Taavitsainen (eds) *Methodological Issues in Historical Pragmatics*, Berlin: Mouton de Gruyter.

Tager-Flusberg, H. (1981) 'On the nature of linguistic functioning in early infantile autism', *Journal of Autism and Developmental Disorders*, 11: 45–56.

Tagliamonte, S. and D'Arcy, A. (2004) '"He's like she's like." The quotative system in Canadian youth', *Journal of Sociolinguistics*, 8: 493–54.

Taglicht, J. (1984) *Message and Emphasis: On Focus and Scope in English*, London and New York: Longman.

——(1998) 'Constraints on intonational phrasing in English', *Journal of Linguistics*, 34: 181–211.

Taguchi, N. (2007a) 'Development of speed and accuracy in pragmatic comprehension in English as a foreign language', *TESOL Quarterly*, 41: 318–38.

——(2007b) 'Task difficulty in oral speech act production', *Applied Linguistics*, 28: 113–35.

Takahashi, H. (1994) 'English imperatives and speaker commitment', *Language Sciences*, 16: 371–85.

Takahashi, M. and Beebe, L.M. (1987) 'The development of pragmatic competence by Japanese learners of English', *JALT Journal*, 8: 131–55.

Takahashi, S. (1996) 'Pragmatic transferability', *Studies in Second Language Acquisition*, 18: 189–223.

——(2001) 'The role of input enhancement in developing interlanguage pragmatic competence', in K. Rose and G. Kasper (eds) *Pragmatics in Language Teaching*, New York: Cambridge University Press.

——(2005) 'Pragmalinguistic awareness: is it related to motivation and proficiency?', *Applied Linguistics*, 26: 90–120.

Takahashi, S. and Roitblat, H. (1994) 'Comprehension process of second language indirect requests', *Applied Psycholinguistics*, 15: 475–506.

Takimoto, M. (2006) 'The effects of explicit feedback on the development of pragmatic proficiency', *Language Teaching Research*, 10: 393–417.

Talberg, I.-M. (2001) 'Deictic disturbances after right hemisphere stroke', *Journal of Pragmatics*, 33: 1309–27.

Talbot, M. (2007) *Media Discourse: Representation and Interaction*, Edinburgh: Edinburgh University Press.

Taleghani-Nikazm, C. (2002a) 'A conversation-analytic study of telephone conversation opening between native and nonnative speakers', *Journal of Pragmatics*, 34: 1807–32.

——(2002b) 'Telephone conversation openings in Persian', in K.K. Luke and Th.-S. Pavlidou (eds) *Telephone Calls: Unity and Diversity in Conversational Structure across Languages and Cultures*, Amsterdam and Philadelphia, PA: John Benjamins.

Talmy, L. (2000) *Toward a Cognitive Semantics*, Cambridge, MA: MIT Press.

Tan, P.K.W. (1993) *A Stylistics of Drama: With Special Focus on Stoppard's "Travesties"*, Singapore: Singapore University Press.

Tanaka, H. (1999) *Turn-Taking in Japanese Conversation: A Study in Grammar and Interaction*, Amsterdam: John Benjamins.

——(2000) *Turn-Taking in Japanese Conversation*, Amsterdam: John Benjamins.

Tanaka, K. (1994) *Advertising Language: A Pragmatic Approach to Advertising in Britain and Japan*, London and New York: Routledge.

Tanaka, N., Spencer-Oatey, H. and Cray, E. (2000) '"It's not my fault": Japanese and English responses to unfounded accusations', in H. Spencer-Oatey (ed.) *Culturally Speaking*, London: Continuum.

Tanck, S. (2002) *Speech Act Sets of Refusal and Complaint: A Comparison of Native and Non-Native English Speakers' Production*. Online. Available www.american.edu/tesol/wptanck.pdf (accessed 8 April 2008).

Tanenhaus, M.K., Spivey-Knowlton, M.J., Eberhard, K.M. and Sedivy, J.E. (1995) 'Integration of visual and linguistic information in spoken language comprehension', *Science*, 268: 1632–34.

Tannen, D. (1984a) *Conversational Style: Analyzing Talk Among Friends*, Norwood, NJ: Ablex.

——(1984b) 'The pragmatics of cross-cultural communication', *Pragmatics*, 5: 189–95.

——(1993) *Framing in Discourse*, New York: Oxford University Press.

Tannen, D. and Saville-Troike, M. (eds) (1985) *Perspectives of Silence*, Norwood, NJ: Ablex.

Tarski, A. (1935) 'Der Wahrheitsbegriff in den formalisierten Sprachen', *Studia Philosophica* I, 261–405; trans. J.H. Woodger 'The concept of truth in formalized languages', in A. Tarski

——(1956) *Logic, Semantics, Metamathematics*, Oxford: Clarendon Press.

——(1944) 'The semantic conception of truth', *Philosophy and Phenomenological Research*, 4: 341–75; reprinted in A.P. Martinich (ed.) (1990) *The Philosophy of Language*, 2nd edn, New York: Oxford University Press.

——(1956) *Logic, Semantics, Metamathematics. Papers from 1923 to 1938*, trans. J.H. Woodger, Oxford: Oxford University Press.

——(1983) *Logic, Semantics, Metamathematics. Papers from 1923 to 1938*, trans. J.H. Woodger, Indianapolis, IN: Hackett Publishing Company.

Tateyama, Y. (2001) 'Explicit and implicit teaching of pragmatic routines: Japanese sumimasen', in K.R. Rose and G. Kasper (eds) *Pragmatics in Language Teaching*, New York: Cambridge University Press.

Taylor, A. (1962) *The Proverb and Index to 'The Proverb'*, Hatboro, PA: Folklore Associates and Copenhagen: Rosenkilde and Bagger.

Taylor, J. (2002) *Cognitive Grammar*, Oxford: Oxford University Press.

Taylor, K. (2001) 'Sex, breakfast, and descriptus interuptus', *Synthese*, 128: 45–61.

Taylor, M.A., Reed, R. and Berenbaum, S. (1994) 'Patterns of speech disorders in schizophrenia and mania', *The Journal of Nervous and Mental Disease*, 182: 319–26.

Taylor, T.J. (1992) *Mutual Misunderstanding: Scepticism and the Theorizing of Language and Interpretation*, London: Routledge.

ten Have, P. (2002) 'The notion of member is the heart of the matter: on the role of membership knowledge in ethnomethodological inquiry', *Forum Qualitative Sozialforschung/ Forum: Qualitative Social Research*, 3. Online. Available: www.qualitative-research.net/fqs/ fqs-eng.htm (accessed 18 February 2008).

——(2007) *Doing Conversation Analysis: A Practical Guide*, 2nd edn, London: Sage.

Tenny, C. and Pustejovsky, J. (eds) (2000) *Events as Grammatical Objects: The Converging Perspectives of Lexical Semantics and Syntax*, Stanford, CA: Centre for the Study of Language and Information.

Tényi, T., Herold, R., Szili, I.M. and Trixler, M. (2002) 'Schizophrenics show a failure in the decoding of violations of conversational implicatures', *Psychopathology*, 35: 25–27.

Tepperman, J., Traum, D. and Narayanan, S. (2006) '"Yeah right": sarcasm recognition for spoken dialogue systems', paper presented at the 9th International Conference on Spoken Language Processing, Pittsburgh, PA,

September 2006. Online. Available: http://sail.usc.edu/publications/teppermann_sarcasm_ICSLP06.pdf (accessed 26 August 2008).

Terasaki, A.K. (2004) 'Pre-announcement sequences in conversation', in G.H. Lerner (ed.) *Conversation Analysis: Studies from the First Generation*, Amsterdam and Philadelphia, PA: John Benjamins.

Terkourafi, M. (2005) 'Beyond the micro-level in politeness research', *Journal of Politeness Research*, 1: 237–62.

Teubert, W. (2005) 'My version of corpus linguistics', *International Journal of Corpus Linguistics*, 10: 1–13.

Teubert, W. and Krishnamurthy, R. (2007) 'General introduction', in W. Teubert and R. Krishnamurthy (eds) *Corpus Linguistics: Critical Concepts in Linguistics*, London and New York: Routledge.

Thagard, P. (1996) *Mind: Introduction to Cognitive Science*, London: MIT Press.

Thayer, H.S. (1968) *Meaning and Action: A Critical History of Pragmatism*, New York: Bobbs-Merrill.

Thiessen, E.D., Hill, E. and Saffran, J.R. (2005) 'Infant-directed speech facilitates word segmentation', *Infancy*, 7: 53–71.

Thoma, P. and Daum, I. (2006) 'Neurocognitive mechanisms of figurative language processing: evidence from clinical dysfunctions', *Neuroscience and Biobehavioral Reviews*, 30: 1182–205.

Thomas, J. (1983) 'Cross-cultural *pragmatic* failure', *Applied Linguistics*, 4: 91–112.

——(1995) *Meaning in Interaction: An Introduction to Pragmatics*, London: Longman.

Thomas, M. (1989) 'The acquisition of English articles by first- and second-language learners', *Applied Psycholinguistics*, 10: 335–55.

Thomas, P. (1995) 'Thought disorder or communication disorder? Linguistic science provides a new approach', *British Journal of Psychiatry*, 166: 287–90.

Thomas, P., Kearney, G. and Napier, E. (1996) 'Speech and language in first onset psychosis: differences between people with schizophrenia, mania and controls', *British Journal of Psychiatry*, 168: 337–43.

Thomas, P., King, K., Fraser, W.I. and Kendell, R.E. (1990) 'Linguistic performance in schizophrenia: a comparison of acute and chronic patients', *British Journal of Psychiatry*, 156: 204–10.

Thomason, R.H. (1990) 'Accommodation, meaning, and implicature: interdisciplinary foundations for pragmatics', in P.R. Cohen, J. Morgan and M.E. Pollack (eds) *Intentions in Communication*, Cambridge, MA: MIT Press.

——(1997) 'Nonmonotonicity in linguistics', in J. van Benthem and A. ter Meulen (eds) *Handbook of Logic and Language*, Oxford: Elsevier Science.

Thompson, J. (1982) 'Universal pragmatics', in J. Thompson and D. Held (eds) *Habermas: Critical Debates*, Cambridge, MA: MIT Press.

Thompson, L.A. and Massaro, D.W. (1986) 'Evaluation and integration of speech and pointing gestures during referential understanding', *Journal of Experimental Child Psychology*, 42: 144–68.

Thompson, L.A., Driscoll, D. and Markson, L. (1998) 'Memory for visual-spoken language in children and adults', *Journal of Nonverbal Behavior*, 22: 167–87.

Thompson, S.A. and Mulac, A. (1991) 'A quantitative perspective on the grammaticization of epistemic parentheticals in English', in E. Traugott and B. Heine (eds) *Approaches to Grammaticalization. Volume 2: Types of Grammatical Markers*, Amsterdam: John Benjamins.

Thomson, J.J. (1977) *Acts and Other Events*, Ithaca, NY: Cornell University Press.

Thornborrow, J. (2002) *Power Talk: Language and Interaction in Institutional Discourse*, London: Longman.

Thorne, J.P. (1965) 'Stylistics and generative grammars', *Journal of Linguistics*, 1: 49–59.

Thurstun, J. and Candlin, C. (1998) 'Concordancing and the teaching of the vocabulary of academic English', *English for Specific Purposes*, 17: 267–80.

Tian, D. (2007) 'US and NATO apologies for the Chinese Embassy bombing: a categorical analysis', *International Journal of Communication*, 1: 360–76.

Tiersma, P.M. (1999) *Legal Language*, Chicago: University of Chicago Press.

Tiersma, P.M. and Solan, L. (2002) 'The linguist on the witness stand: forensic linguistics in American courts', *Language*, 78: 221–39.

Tirassa, M. (1999) 'Communicative competence and the architecture of the mind/brain', *Brain and Language*, 68: 419–41.

Tirassa, M. and Bosco, F.M. (2008) 'On the nature and role of intersubjectivity in communication', in F. Morganti, A. Carassa and G. Riva (eds) *Enacting Intersubjectivity: A Cognitive and Social Perspective to the Study of Interactions*, Amsterdam: IOS Press.

Tirassa, M., Bosco, F.M. and Colle, L. (2006a) 'Rethinking the ontogeny of mindreading', *Consciousness and Cognition*, 15: 197–217.

——(2006b) 'Sharedness and privateness in human early social life', *Cognitive Systems Research*, 7: 128–39.

Tirassa, M., Carassa, A. and Geminiani, G. (2000) 'A theoretical framework for the study of spatial cognition', in S. Ó Nualláin (ed.) *Spatial Cognition: Foundations and Applications*, Amsterdam and Philadelphia, PA: Benjamins.

Tocalli-Beller, A. (2003) 'Cognitive conflict, disagreement and repetition in collaborative groups: affective and social dimensions from an insider's perspective', *The Canadian Modern Language Review/La Revue Canadienne des Langues Vivantes*, 60: 143–71.

Todd, R.W., Khongput, S. and Darasawang, P. (2007) 'Coherence, cohesion and comments on students' academic essays', *Assessing Writing*, 12: 10–25.

Todman, J. (2000) 'Rate and quality of conversations using a text-storage AAC system: a training study', *Augmentative and Alternative Communication*, 16: 164–79.

——(2001) 'Availability and accessibility in whole utterance-based devices', *Perspectives on Augmentative and Alternative Communication*, 10: 8–11.

Todman, J. and Alm, N. (2003) 'Modelling conversational pragmatics in communication aids', *Journal of Pragmatics*, 35: 523–38.

Todman, J. and Rzepecka, H. (2003) 'Effect of pre-utterance pause length on perceptions of communicative competence in AAC-aided social conversations', *Augmentative and Alternative Communication*, 19: 222–34.

Togher, L., McDonald, S., Code, C. and Grant, S. (2004) 'Training communication partners of people with traumatic brain injury: a randomized controlled trial', *Aphasiology*, 18: 313–35.

Tognini-Bonelli, E. (2001) *Corpus Linguistics at Work*, Amsterdam and Philadelphia: John Benjamins.

Tolman, E.C. (1948) 'Cognitive maps in rats and men', *The Psychological Review*, 55: 189–208.

Tomasello, M. (1999) *The Cultural Origins of Human Cognition*, London and Cambridge, MA: Harvard University Press.

——(2001) 'Perceiving intentions and learning words in the second year of life', in M. Bowerman and S.C. Levinson (eds) *Language Acquisition and Conceptual Development*, Cambridge: Cambridge University Press.

——(2003) *Constructing a Language: A Usage-Based Theory of Language Acquisition*, Cambridge, MA: Harvard University Press.

——(2008) *Origins of Human Communication*, Cambridge, MA: MIT Press.

Tomasello, M. and Call, J. (1997) *Primate Cognition*, Oxford: Oxford University Press.

Tomasello, M. and Carpenter, M. (2007) 'Shared intentionality', *Developmental Science*, 10: 121–25.

Tomasello, M. and Haberl, K. (2003) 'Understanding attention: 12- and 18-month-olds know what's new for other persons', *Developmental Psychology*, 39: 906–12.

Tomasello, M., Carpenter, M. and Liszkowski, U. (2007) 'A new look at infant pointing', *Child Development*, 78: 705–22.

Tomasello, M., Carpenter, M., Call, J., Behne, T. and Moll, H. (2005) 'Understanding and sharing intentions: the origins of cultural cognition', *Behavioral and Brain Sciences*, 28: 675–91.

Tompkins, C.A. (1995) *Right Hemisphere Communication Disorders: Theory and Management*, San Diego, CA: Singular Publishing Group.

Tompkins, C.A. and Mateer, C.A. (1985) 'Right hemisphere appreciation of prosodic and linguistic indications of implicit attitude', *Brain and Language*, 24: 185–203.

Tompkins, C.A., Bloise, C.G., Timko, M.L. and Baumgaertner, A. (1994) 'Working memory and inference revision in brain-damaged and normally aging adults', *Journal of Speech and Hearing Research*, 37: 896–912.

Tompkins, C.A., Fassbinder, W., Lehman Blake, M., Baumgaertner, A. and Jayaram, N. (2004) 'Inference generation during text comprehension by adults with right hemisphere brain damage: activation failure versus multiple activation', *Journal of Speech, Language and Hearing Research*, 47: 1380–95.

Toolan, M. (ed.) (1992) *Language, Text and Context*, London: Routledge.

——(1996) 'Stylistics and its discontents; or, getting off the Fish "hook"', in J.-J. Weber (ed.) *The Stylistics Reader: From Roman Jakobson to the Present*, London: Arnold.

——(2001) *Narrative: A Critical Linguistic Introduction*, London: Routledge.

Torfing, J. (1999) *New Theories of Discourse: Laclau, Mouffe, Žižek*, Oxford: Blackwell.

Tottie, G. (1991) *Negation in Speech and Writing*, New York: Academic Press.

Toulmin, S. (1958) *The Uses of Argument*, Cambridge: Cambridge University Press.

Tracy, J.I. (1998) 'Language abnormalities in psychosis: evidence for the interaction between cognitive and linguistic mechanisms', in B. Stemmer and H.A. Whitaker (eds) *Handbook of Neurolinguistics*, San Diego, CA: Academic Press.

Traugott, E.C. (1982) 'From propositional to textual and expressive meanings: some semantic-pragmatic aspects of grammaticalization', in W.P. Lehmann and Y. Malkiel (eds) *Perspectives on Historical Linguistics*, Amsterdam: John Benjamins.

——(1989) 'On the rise of epistemic meanings in English: an example of subjectification in semantic change', *Language*, 57: 33–65.

——(1991) 'English speech act verbs: a historical perspective', in L.R. Waugh and S. Rudy (eds) *New Vistas in Grammar: Invariance and Variation*, Amsterdam: Benjamins.

——(1995) 'Subjectification in grammaticalization', in D. Stein and S. Wright (eds) *Subjectivity and Subjectivisation in Language*, Cambridge: Cambridge University Press.

——(1999) 'The role of pragmatics in semantic change', in J. Verschueren (ed.) *Pragmatics in 1998: Selected Papers from the 6th International Pragmatics Conference*, volume II, Antwerp: International Pragmatics Association.

——(2003) 'From subjectification to inter-subjectification', in R. Hickey (ed.) *Motives for Language Change*, Cambridge: Cambridge University Press.

——(2004) 'Historical pragmatics', in L.R. Horn and G. Ward (eds) *The Handbook of Pragmatics*, Oxford: Blackwell.

Traugott, E.C. and Dasher, R.B. (2002) *Regularity in Semantic Change*, Cambridge: Cambridge University Press.

Traum, D.R. (1994) *A computational theory of grounding in natural language conversation*, unpublished thesis, University of Rochester.

Traum, D.R. and Allen, J.F. (1994) 'Discourse obligations in dialogue processing', *Proceedings of the 32nd Annual Meeting of the Association for Computational Linguistics (ACL-94)*, Morristown, NJ: Association for Computational Linguistics.

Traum, D.R. and Larsson, S. (2003) 'The information state approach to dialogue management', in J. van Kuppevelt and R. Smith (eds) *Current and New Directions in Discourse and Dialogue*, Dordrecht: Kluwer.

Traverso, V. (2002) 'Transcription et traduction des interactions en langue étrangère', *Cahiers de Praxématique*, 39: 77–99.

Travis, C. (1981) *The True and the False: The Domain of the Pragmatic*, Amsterdam: John Benjamins.

——(1985) 'On what is strictly speaking true', *Canadian Journal of Philosophy*, 15: 187–229.

——(1989) *The Uses of Sense*, Oxford: Oxford University Press.

——(1997) 'Pragmatics', in B. Hale and C. Wright (eds) *A Companion to the Philosophy of Language*, Oxford: Blackwell Publishing.

Traxler, M., McElree, B., Williams, R. and Pickering, M. (2005) 'Context effects in coercion: evidence from eye movements', *Journal of Memory and Language*, 53: 1–25.

Trevarthen, C.B. (1977) 'Descriptive analyses of infant communication behavior', in H.R. Schaffer (ed.) *Studies in Mother-Infant Interaction: The Loch Lomond Symposium*, London: Academic Press.

——(1979) 'Instincts for human understanding and for cultural cooperation: their development in infancy', in M. von Cranach, K. Foppa, B. Lepenies and D. Ploog (eds) *Human Ethology: Claims and Limits of a New Discipline*, Cambridge: Cambridge University Press.

——(1998) 'The concept and foundations of infant intersubjectivity', in S. Bråten (ed.) *Intersubjective Communication and Emotion in Early Ontogeny*, Cambridge: Cambridge University Press.

Trevarthen, C.B. and Aitken, K. (2001) 'Infant intersubjectivity: research, theory, and clinical applications', *Journal of Child Psychology and Psychiatry*, 42: 3–48.

Tribble, C. (2008) 'Book review. From corpus to classroom: language use and language teaching', *ELT Journal*, 62: 213–16.

Trinch, S. (2001) 'The advocate as gatekeeper: the limits of politeness in protective order interviews with Latina survivors of domestic abuse', *Journal of Sociolinguistics*, 5: 475–506.

Trosborg, A. (1995a) 'Statutes and contracts: an analysis of legal speech acts in the English language of the law', *Journal of Pragmatics*, 25: 31–53.

——(1995b) *Interlanguage Pragmatics: Requests, Complaints, Apologies*, Berlin: Mouton de Gruyter.

Trudgill, P. (1974) *The Social Differentiation of English in Norwich*, Cambridge: Cambridge University Press.

Tryggvason, M.T. (2006) 'Communicative behavior in family conversation: comparison of amount of talk in Finnish, Swedish-Finnish, and Swedish families', *Journal of Pragmatics*, 38: 1795–810.

Tsimpli, I. and Dimitrakopoulou, M. (2007) 'The interpretability hypothesis: evidence from wh-interrogatives in second language acquisition', *Second Language Research*, 23: 215–42.

Tsohatzidis, S.L. (1994) 'Speaker meaning, sentence meaning and metaphor', in S.L. Tsohatzidis (ed.) *Foundations of Speech Act*

Theory: Philosophical and Linguistic Perspectives, London: Routledge.

Tsui, A.B.M. (1991) 'Sequencing rules and coherence in discourse', *Journal of Pragmatics*, 15: 111–29.

——(1995) *Introducing Classroom Interaction*, Harmondsworth: Penguin.

Tsuji, H. (2002) 'Young children expressing their communicative intents: a preliminary study of the interactions between Japanese children and their caregivers', *Educate*, 2: 72–84.

Tsur, R. (1992) *Toward a Theory of Cognitive Poetics*, Amsterdam: Elsevier (North Holland) Science Publishers.

Tucker, F.M. and Hanlon, R.E. (1998) 'Effects of mild traumatic brain injury on narrative discourse production', *Brain Injury*, 12: 783–92.

Tucker, G.J. and Rosenberg, S.D. (1975) 'Computer content analysis of schizophrenic speech: a preliminary report', *American Journal of Psychiatry*, 132: 611–16.

Tugendhat, E. (1985) 'J. Habermas on communicative action', in G. Seebass and R. Tuomela (eds) *Social Action*, Dordrecht: Reidel.

Tully, J. (ed.) (1988) *Meaning and Context: Quentin Skinner and His Critics*, Princeton, NJ: Princeton University Press.

Tuomela, R. (1995) *The Importance of Us*, Stanford, CA: Stanford University Press.

——(2005) 'We-intentions revisited', *Philosophical Studies*, 125: 327–69.

Turing, A.M. (1936) 'On computable numbers, with an application to the Entscheidungs problem', *Proceedings of the London Mathematical Society, Second Series*, 42: 230–65.

——(1950) 'Computing machinery and intelligence', *Mind*, 59: 433–60.

Turnbull, W. (2001) 'An appraisal of pragmatic elicitation techniques for the social psychological study of talk: the case of request refusals', *Pragmatics*, 11: 31–61.

Tversky, A. and Kahneman, D. (1974) 'Judgment under uncertainty: heuristics and biases', *Science*, 185: 1124–31.

Tyler, A. (1994) 'The role of repetition in perceptions of discourse coherence', *Journal of Pragmatics*, 21: 671–88.

Tyler, A. and Evans, V. (2003) *The Semantics of English Prepositions: Spatial Scenes, Embodied Meaning and Cognition*, Cambridge: Cambridge University Press.

Tyler, S.A. (ed.) (1969) *Cognitive Anthropology*, New York: Holt, Rinehart and Winston.

Uchiyama, H., Seki, A., Kageyama, H., Saito, D.N., Koeda, T., Ohno, K. and Sadato, N. (2006) 'Neural substrates of sarcasm: a functional magnetic-resonance imaging study', *Brain Research*, 1124: 100–10.

Ueda, K. (1972) 'Sixteen ways to say "no" in Japan', in J. Condon and M. Saito (eds) *Intercultural Encounters with Japan: Communication – Contact and Conflict*, Tokyo: The Simul Press.

Unger, C. (2006) *Genre, Relevance and Global Coherence*, Basingstoke, UK: Palgrave Macmillan.

Unger, P. (1995) 'Contextual analysis in ethics', *Philosophy and Phenomenological Research*, 55: 1–26.

Unsworth, S. (2005) *Child L2, adult L2, child L1, differences and similarities: a study on the acquisition of direct object scrambling in Dutch*, Ph.D. dissertation, Utrecht University.

——(2007) 'L1 and L2 acquisition between sentence and discourse: comparing production and comprehension in child Dutch', *Lingua*, 117: 1930–58.

Urbanová, L. (1999) 'On vagueness in authentic English conversation', *Anglica*, 25: 99–107.

Urmson, J.O. (1952) 'Parenthetical verbs', *Mind*, LXI: 480–96; reprinted in C. Caton (ed.) (1963) *Philosophy and Ordinary Language*, Urbana: University of Illinois Press.

——(1977) 'Performative utterances', *Midwest Studies in Philosophy*, 2: 120–27.

Utsumi, A. (2000) 'Verbal irony as implicit display of ironic environment: distinguishing ironic utterances from nonirony', *Journal of Pragmatics*, 32: 1777–807.

Vainikka, A. and Young-Scholten, M. (1994) 'Direct access to X'-theory: evidence from Korean and Turkish adults learning German', in T. Hoekstra and B.D. Schwartz (eds) *Language Acquisition Studies in Generative Grammar: Papers in Honor of Kenneth Wexler from the 1991 GLOW Workshops*, Amsterdam: John Benjamins.

——(1996) 'Gradual development of L2 phrase structure', *Second Language Research*, 12: 7–39

Valentine, T.M. (1994) 'When "no" means "yes": agreeing and disagreeing in Indian English discourse', paper presented at the International Conference on World Englishes Today, Urbana, IL, 31 March–2 April 1994.

Vallana, M., Bosco, F.M., Angeleri, R., Sacco, K., Bara, B.G. and Colle, L. (2007) 'Communicative ability in schizophrenic patients: executive function, theory of mind and mental representations', in D. McNamara and G. Trafton (eds) *Proceedings of the 29th Annual Conference of the Cognitive Science Society*, Nashville, TN: Cognitive Science Society.

Vallance, D.D., Im, N. and Cohen, N.J. (1999) 'Discourse deficits associated with psychiatric disorders and with language impairments in children', *Journal of Child Psychology and Psychiatry and Allied Disciplines*, 40: 693–704.

Vallduví, E. (1992) *The Informational Component*, New York and London: Garland.

Vallduví, E. and Vilkuna, M. (1998) 'On rheme and kontrast', in P. Cullicover and L. McNally (eds) *Syntax and Semantics*, vol. 29, New York: Academic Press.

van der Henst, J.-B. and Sperber, D. (2004) 'Testing the cognitive and communicative principles of relevance', in I. Noveck and D. Sperber (eds) *Experimental Pragmatics*, Basingstoke: Palgrave Macmillan.

van der Henst, J.-B., Politzer, G. and Sperber, D. (2002a) 'When is a conclusion worth deriving? A relevance-based analysis of indeterminate relational problems', *Thinking and Reasoning*, 8: 1–20.

van der Henst, J.-B., Carles, L. and Sperber, D. (2002b) 'Truthfulness and relevance in telling the time', *Mind and Language*, 17: 457–66.

Van der Sandt, R. (1992) 'Presupposition projection as anaphora resolution', *Journal of Semantics*, 9: 333–77.

van der Wal, S. (1996) *Negative polarity items and negation: tandem acquisition*, unpublished thesis, University of Groningen.

van der Wouden, T. (1996) 'Litotes and downward monotonicity', in H. Wansing (ed.) *Negation: A Notion in Focus*, Berlin: Walter de Gruyter.

——(1997) *Negative Contexts: Collocation, Polarity, and Double Negation*, London: Routledge.

van Dijk, T.A. (1984) *Prejudice in Discourse*, Amsterdam: John Benjamins.

——(1988) *News as Discourse*, Hillsdale, NJ: Erlbaum.

——(1991) *Racism and the Press*, London: Routledge.

——(1993) *Elite Discourse and Racism*, Newbury Park, CA: Sage.

——(1998a) 'Principles of critical discourse analysis', in J. Cheshire and P. Trudgill (eds) *The Sociolinguistics Reader. Volume 2: Gender and Discourse*, London: Arnold.

——(1998b) 'Opinions and ideologies in the press', in A. Bell and P. Garrett (eds) *Approaches to Media Discourse*, Oxford: Blackwell.

——(2006) 'Discourse and manipulation', *Discourse and Society*, 17: 359–83.

van Dijk, T.A. and Kintsch, W. (1983) *Strategies of Discourse Comprehension*, New York: Academic Press.

van Eemeren, F.H. and Grootendorst, R. (1984) *Speech Acts in Argumentative Discussions: A Theoretical Model for the Analysis of Discussions Directed Towards Solving Conflicts of Opinion*, Dordrecht: Foris Publications.

——(1992) *Argumentation, Communication, and Fallacies: A Pragma-Dialectical Perspective*, Hillsdale, NJ: Lawrence Erlbaum Associates.

——(1995) 'The pragma-dialectical approach to fallacies', in H.V. Hansen and R.C. Pinto (eds) *Fallacies: Classical and Contemporary Readings*, University Park, PA: Pennsylvania State University Press.

——(1996) 'Developments in argumentation theory', in J. van Benthem, F.H. van Eemeren, R. Grootendorst and F. Veltman (eds) *Logic and Argumentation*, Amsterdam: Royal Netherlands Academy of Arts and Sciences.

——(2004) *A Systematic Theory of Argumentation: The Pragma-Dialectical Approach*, Cambridge: Cambridge University Press.

van Geenhoven, V. (1996) *Semantic incorporation and indefinite descriptions: semantic and syntactic aspects of noun incorporation in West Greenlandic*, Ph.D. dissertation, University of Tubingen.

van Gompel, R.P.G. and Pickering, M.J. (2007) 'Syntactic parsing', in M.G. Gaskell (ed.) *The Oxford Handbook of Psycholinguistics*, Oxford: Oxford University Press.

Van Lancker, D.R. and Kempler, D. (1987) 'Comprehension of familiar phrases by left- but not by right-hemisphere damaged patients', *Brain and Language*, 32: 265–77.

Van Leer, E. and Turkstra, L. (1999) 'The effect of elicitation task on discourse coherence and cohesion in adolescents with brain injury', *Journal of Communication Disorders*, 32: 327–49.

Van Linder, B., van der Hoek, W. and Meyer, J.-J. (1995) 'Actions that make you change your mind', in A. Laux and H. Wansing (eds) *Knowledge and Belief in Philosophy and Artificial Intelligence*, Berlin: Akadamie Verlag.

——(2002) 'Formalising abilities and opportunities of agents', in J.-J. Meyer and J. Treur (eds) *Agent-Based Defeasible Control in Dynamic Environments: Handbook of Defeasible Reasoning and Uncertainty Management Systems*, Dordrecht: Kluwer.

van Peer, W. (1986) *Stylistics and Psychology*, London: Croom Helm.

van Rooy, R. (2003) 'Questioning to resolve decision problems', *Linguistics and Philosophy*, 26: 727–63.

——(2004) 'Signalling games select Horn strategies', *Linguistics and Philosophy*, 27: 493–527.

Vance, M. and Wells, B. (1994) 'The wrong end of the stick: language-impaired children's understanding of non-literal language', *Child Language Teaching and Therapy*, 10: 23–46.

Vande Kopple, W.J. (1985) 'Some exploratory discourse on metadiscourse', *College Composition and Communication*, 36: 82–93.

Vandepitte, S. (1989) 'A pragmatic function of intonation', *Lingua*, 79: 265–97.

Vanderveken, D. (1990) *Meaning and Speech Acts, vol. I, Principles of Language Use*, Cambridge: Cambridge University Press.

——(2002) 'Universal grammar and speech act theory', in D. Vanderveken and S. Kubo (eds) *Essays in Speech Act Theory*, Amsterdam: John Benjamins.

Vanhalle, C., Lemieux, S., Joubert, S., Goulet, P., Ska, B. and Joanette, Y. (2000) 'Processing of speech acts by right hemisphere brain-damaged patients: an ecological approach', *Aphasiology*, 11: 1127–42.

Varela, F.J. (1996) 'A science of consciousness as if experience mattered', in S.R. Hameroff, A. W. Kaszniak and A.C. Scott (eds) *Toward a Science of Consciousness: The First Tucson Discussions and Debates*, Cambridge, MA: MIT Press.

Varela, F.J., Thompson, E. and Rosch, E. (1991) *The Embodied Mind: Cognitive Science and Human Experience*, Cambridge, MA: MIT Press.

Varttala, T. (2001) *Hedging in Scientifically Oriented Discourse: Exploring Variation According to Discipline and Intended Audience*, Tampere, Finland: University of Tampere.

Vega Moreno, R. (2007) *Creativity and Convention: The Pragmatics of Everyday Figurative Speech*, Amsterdam: John Benjamins.

Velasco-Sacristan, M. and Fuertes-Olivera, P.A. (2006) 'Towards a critical cognitive-pragmatic approach to gender metaphors in advertising English', *Journal of Pragmatics*, 38: 1982–2002.

Vella, A. (2007) 'The phonetics and phonology of wh-question intonation in Maltese', paper presented at the 16th International Congress of Phonetic Sciences, Saarbrücken, Germany, August 2007. Online. Available: www.icphs 2007.de/conference/Papers/1677/1677.pdf (accessed 26 August 2008).

Velleman, J.D. (1989) *Practical Reflection*, Princeton, NJ: Princeton University Press.

Veltman, F. (1996) 'Defaults in update semantics', *Journal of Philosophical Logic*, 25: 221–61.

——(2000) *The Possibility of Practical Reason*, Oxford: Clarendon Press.

Venuti, L. (ed.) (1992) *Rethinking Translation: Discourse, Subjectivity, Ideology*, London: Routledge.

Vera, A.H. and Simon, H.A. (1993) 'Situated action: a symbolic interpretation', *Cognitive Science*, 17: 7–133.

Verdonk, P. (2002) *Stylistics*, Oxford: Oxford University Press.

Vermeerbergen, M., Leeson, L. and Crasborn, O. (eds) (2007) *Simultaneity in Signed Languages: Form and Function*, Amsterdam and Philadelphia, PA: John Benjamins.

Verschueren, J. (1987) 'Pragmatics as a theory of linguistic adaptation', Working Documents 1, Antwerp: International Pragmatics Association.

——(1995) 'The pragmatic perspective', in J. Verschueren, J.O.H. Östman, J. Blommaert and C. Bulcaen (eds) *Handbook of Pragmatics*, Amsterdam: John Benjamins.

——(1999) *Understanding Pragmatics*, London: Arnold.

——(2004) 'Notes on the role of metapragmatic awareness in language use', in A. Jaworski, N. Coupland and D. Galasinski (eds) *Metalanguage: Social and Ideological Perspectives*, Berlin and New York: Mouton de Gruyter.

Verschueren, J., Östman, J.O.H., Blommaert, J. and Bulcaen, C. (eds) (1995) *Handbook of Pragmatics*, Amsterdam: John Benjamins.

Vestergaard, T. and Schrøder, K. (1986) *The Language of Advertising*, Oxford: Basil Blackwell.

Vincente, B. (2002) 'What pragmatics can tell us about (literal) meaning: a critical note on Bach's theory of impliciture', *Journal of Pragmatics*, 32: 403–21.

Vine, B. (2004) *Getting Things Done at Work: The Discourse of Power in Workplace Interaction*, Amsterdam: John Benjamins.

Vision, G. (1985) 'I am here now', *Analysis*, 45: 198–99.

Vivanco, V. (2005) 'The absence of connectives and the maintenance of coherence in publicity texts', *Journal of Pragmatics*, 37: 1233–49.

Volden, J. (2004) 'Conversational repair in speakers with autism spectrum disorder', *International Journal of Language and Communication Disorders*, 39: 171–89.

Volden, J. and Lord, C. (1991) 'Neologisms and idiosyncratic language in autistic speakers', *Journal of Autism and Developmental Disorders*, 21: 109–30.

Volterra, V. and Antinucci, F. (1979) 'Negation in child language: a pragmatic study', in E. Ochs and B. Schieffelin (eds) *Developmental Pragmatics*, New York: Academic Press.

Von Eckardt, B. (2001) 'Multidisciplinarity and cognitive science', *Cognitive Science*, 25: 453–70.

von Fintel, K. (1994) *Restrictions on quantifier domains*, Ph.D. dissertation, University of Massachusetts, Amherst.

——(1999) 'NPI licensing, Strawson entailment, and context dependency', *Journal of Semantics*, 16: 97–148.

von Fintel, K. and Matthewson, L. (2008) 'Universals in semantics', *The Linguistic Review*, 25: 139–201.

von Heusinger, K. (2002) 'Specificity and definiteness in sentence and discourse structure', *Journal of Semantics*, 19: 245–74.

von Heusinger, K. and Turner, K. (2006) '(By way of an) introduction: a first dialogue on the semantics-pragmatics interface', in K. von Heusinger and K. Turner (eds) *Where Semantics Meets Pragmatics*, Oxford: Elsevier.

Vonk, F.J.M. (1992) 'Zur Geschichtsschreibung der Sprechakttheorie: der Fall Reinach', in A. Ahlqvist (ed.) *Diversions of Galway*, Amsterdam and Philadelphia, PA: John Benjamins.

Vosniadou, S. (1987) 'Children and metaphors', *Child Development*, 58: 870–85.

Vouloumanos, A. and Werker, J.F. (2004) 'Tuned to the signal: the privileged status of speech for young infants', *Developmental Science*, 7: 270–76.

Vries, M. de (2005) 'Coordination and syntactic hierarchy', *Studia Linguistica*, 59: 83–105.

——(2007) 'Invisible constituents? Parentheses as B-merged adverbial phrases', in N. Dehé and Y. Kavalova (eds) *Parentheticals*, Amsterdam: John Benjamins.

Vu, H., Kellas, G. and Paul, S.T. (1998) 'Sources of sentence constraint in lexical ambiguity resolution', *Memory and Cognition*, 26: 979–1001.

Vu, H., Kellas, G., Metcalf, K. and Herman, R. (2000) 'The influence of global discourse on lexical ambiguity resolution', *Memory and Cognition*, 28: 236–52.

Wadensjö, C. (1998) *Interpreting as Interaction*, London: Longman.

Wajnryb, R. (2001) *Silence: How Tragedy Shapes Talk*, Crow's Nest, NSW: Allen and Unwin.

Wakusawa, K., Sugiura, M., Sassa, Y., Jeong, H., Horie, K., Sato, S., Yokoyama, H., Tsuchiya, S., Inuma, K. and Kawashima, R. (2007) 'Comprehension of implicit meanings in social situations involving irony: a functional MRI study', *Neuroimage*, 37: 1417–26.

Wales, K. (2001) *A Dictionary of Stylistics*, London: Longman.

Walker, G. (2003) 'Doing a rushthrough – a phonetic resource for holding the turn in everyday conversation', paper presented at the 15th International Congress of Phonetic Sciences, Barcelona, August 2003.

Walker, M.A. (1989) 'Evaluating discourse processing algorithms', *Proceedings of the 27th Annual Meeting of the Association for Computational Linguistics (ACL-89)*, Morristown, NJ: Association for Computational Linguistics.

Walker, M.A., Joshi, A.K. and Prince, E. (eds) (1998) *Centering in Discourse*, Oxford: Oxford University Press.

Walker, T. (2007) *Thou and You in Early Modern English Dialogues: Trials, Depositions, and Drama Comedy*, Amsterdam and Philadelphia, PA: John Benjamins.

Walkinshaw, I. (2007) 'Power and disagreement: insights into Japanese learners of English', *RELC Journal*, 38: 278–301.

Wallace, P. (1999) *The Psychology of the Internet*, Cambridge: Cambridge University Press.

Walsh, R. (2003) 'The pragmatics of narrative fictionality', in J. Phelan and P.J. Rabinowitz (eds) *A Companion to Narrative Theory*, Malden, MA: Blackwell.

Walsh, S. (2006) *Investigating Classroom Discourse*, London: Routledge.

Walter, H., Adenzato, M., Ciaramidaro, A., Enrici, I., Pia, L. and Bara, B.G. (2004) 'Understanding intentions in social interaction: the role of the anterior paracingulate cortex', *Journal of Cognitive Neuroscience*, 16: 1854–63.

Walters, J. (1979) 'The perception of politeness in English and Spanish', in C. Yorio, K. Perkins and J. Schachter (eds) *On TESOL '79: The Learner in Focus*, Washington, DC: Teachers of English to Speakers of Other Languages.

——(1980) 'Grammar, meaning, and sociological appropriateness in second language acquisition', *Canadian Journal of Psychology/Revue Canadienne de Psychologie*, 34: 337–45.

Walton, D.N. (1985) 'Are circular arguments necessarily vicious?', *American Philosophical Quarterly*, 22: 263–74.

——(1992) 'Nonfallacious arguments from ignorance', *American Philosophical Quarterly*, 29: 381–87.

——(1995) *A Pragmatic Theory of Fallacy*, Tuscaloosa, AL: University of Alabama Press.

Wang, A.T., Lee, S.S., Sigman, M. and Dapretto, M. (2006) 'Neural basis of irony comprehension in children with autism: the role of prosody and context', *Brain*, 129: 932–43.

Ward, G. (1988) *The Semantics and Pragmatics of Preposing*, Outstanding Dissertations in Linguistics, New York: Garland.

——(2004) 'Equatives and deferred reference', *Language*, 80: 262–89.

Ward, G. and Birner, B. (2004) 'Information structure and non-canonical syntax', in L.R. Horn and G. Ward (eds) *Handbook of Pragmatics*, Oxford: Blackwell.

Ward, G. and Hirschberg, J. (1991) 'A pragmatic analysis of tautological utterances', *Journal of Pragmatics*, 15: 507–20.

Ward, G. and Horn, L.R. (1999) 'Phatic communication and pragmatic theory: a reply', *Journal of Linguistics*, 35: 555–64.

Ward, N. and Tsukahara, W. (2000) 'Prosodic features which cue back-channel responses in English and Japanese', *Journal of Pragmatics*, 32: 1177–207.

Warnock, G.J. (1973) 'Saturday mornings', in I. Berlin, L.W. Forguson, D.F. Pears, G. Pitcher, J.R. Searle, P.F. Strawson and G.J. Warnock, *Essays on J.L. Austin*, Oxford: Clarendon Press.

——(1989) *J.L. Austin*, London: Routledge.

Warren, M. (2006) *Features of Naturalness in Conversation*, Amsterdam: John Benjamins.

——(2007) '{/[OH] not a <^ LOT>}': discourse intonation and vague language', in J. Cutting (ed.) *Vague Language Explored*, London: Palgrave Macmillan.

Warrington, E. (1975) 'The selective impairment of semantic memory', *Quarterly Journal of Experimental Psychology*, 27: 635–57.

Washington, C. (1992) 'Identity theory of quotation', *The Journal of Philosophy*, 89: 582–605.

Wason, P.C. (1965) 'The contexts of plausible denial', *Journal of Verbal Learning and Verbal Behavior*, 4: 7–11.

——(1966) 'Reasoning', in B.M. Foss (ed.) *New Horizons in Psychology*, Harmondsworth: Penguin Books.

Wason, P.C. and Evans, J.S. (1975) 'Dual processes in reasoning?', *Cognition*, 3: 141–54.

Watson, C.M., Chenery, H.J. and Carter, M.S. (1999) 'An analysis of trouble and repair in the natural conversations of people with dementia of the Alzheimer's type', *Aphasiology*, 13: 195–218.

Watson, D. and Gibson, E. (2004) 'The relationship between intonational phrasing and syntactic structure in language production', *Language and Cognitive Processes*, 19: 713–55.

Watson, D., Gunlogson, C. and Tanenhaus, M. K. (2006) 'Online methods for the investigation of prosody', in S. Sudhoff, D. Lenertov, R. Meyer, S. Pappert, P. Augurzky, I. Mleinek, N. Richter and J. Schlieer (eds) *Methods in Empirical Prosody Research*, New York: Walter de Gruyter.

Watt, D. (2002) '"I don't speak with a Geordie accent, I speak, like, the Northern accent": contact-induced levelling in the Tyneside vowel system', *Journal of Sociolinguistics*, 6: 44–63.

Watt, R.J.C. (2004) *Concordance Version 3.2*. Online. Available: www.concordancesoftware.co.uk (accessed 14 May 2008).

Watts, R.J. (2003) *Politeness*, Cambridge: Cambridge University Press.

——(2005) 'Linguistic politeness research: quo vadis?', in R.J. Watts, S. Ide and K. Ehlich (eds) *Politeness in Language: Studies in its History, Theory and Practice*, 2nd edn, Berlin: Mouton de Gruyter.

Waxman, S.R., Lynch, E.B., Casey, K.L. and Baer, L. (1997) 'Setters and samoyeds: the emergence of subordinate level categories as a basis for inductive inference in preschool-age children', *Developmental Psychology*, 33: 1074–90.

Wearing, C. (2006) 'Metaphor and what is said', *Mind and Language*, 21: 310–32.

Weber, J.-J. (1992) *Critical Analysis of Fiction*, Amsterdam: Rodopi.

Weber, M. (1978) *Economy and Society: An Outline of Interpretative Sociology*, Berkeley, CA: University of California Press.

Weigand, E. (1999) 'Misunderstanding: the standard case', *Journal of Pragmatics*, 31: 763–85.

Weijts, W., Houtkoop, H. and Mullen, P. (1993) 'Talking delicacy: speaking about sexuality during gynaecological consultations', *Sociology of Heath and Illness*, 15: 295–314.

Weiner, M. (2006) 'Are all conversational implicatures cancellable?', *Analysis*, 66: 127–30.

Weinreich, U. (1964) '*Webster's Third*: a critique of its semantics', *International Journal of American Linguistics*, 30: 405–9.

Weinstein, E.A. (1964) 'Affections of speech with lesions of the non-dominant hemisphere', *Association for Research in Nervous and Mental Disease*, 42: 220–28.

Weisbrod, M., Maier, S., Harig, S., Himmelsbach, U. and Spitzer, M. (1998) 'Lateralised semantic and indirect semantic priming effects in people with schizophrenia', *British Journal of Psychiatry*, 172: 142–46.

Welker, K. (1994) *Plans in the common ground: toward a generative account of conversational implicature*, unpublished thesis, Ohio State University.

Wellman, H.M. and Bartsch, K. (1988) 'Young children's reasoning about beliefs', *Cognition*, 30: 239–77.

Wellman, H.M., Cross, D. and Watson, J. (2001) 'Meta-analysis of theory-of-mind development: the truth about false belief', *Child Development*, 72: 655–84.

Wellmer, A. (1992) 'What is a pragmatic theory of meaning?', in A. Honneth, T. McCarthy, C. Offe and A. Wellmer (eds) *Philosophical Interventions in the Unfinished Project of Enlightenment*, Cambridge, MA: MIT Press.

Wells, B. and Corrin, J. (2004) 'Prosodic resources, turn-taking and overlap in children's talk-in-interaction', in E. Couper-Kuhlen and

C.E. Ford (eds) *Sound Patterns in Interaction*, Amsterdam: John Benjamins.

Wells, B. and Peppe, S. (1996) 'Ending up in Ulster', in E. Couper-Kuhlen and M. Selting (eds) *Prosody in Interaction*, Cambridge: Cambridge University Press.

Wells, G. (1986) *The Meaning Makers: Children Learning Language and Using Language to Learn*, London: Hodder and Stoughton.

——(1999) *Dialogic Inquiry: Toward a Sociocultural Practice and Theory of Education*, Cambridge: Cambridge University Press.

Wells, J.C. (2006) *English Intonation: An Introduction*, Cambridge: Cambridge University Press.

Wenger, E. (1998) *Communities of Practice: Learning, Meaning, and Identity*, Cambridge: Cambridge University Press.

Werhane, P.H. (1992) *Skepticism, Rules, and Private Languages*, London: Humanities Press.

Werlich, E. (1976) *A Text Grammar of English*, Heidelberg: Quelle and Meyer.

Werner, H. and Kaplan, B. (1963) *Symbol Formation: An Organismic Developmental Approach to Language and the Expression of Thought*, New York: John Wiley.

Wernick, A. (1991) *Promotional Culture*, London: Sage.

Werth, P. (1999) *Text Worlds: Representing Conceptual Space in Discourse*, London: Longman.

Wesker, A. (1964) *Chicken Soup with Barley*, Harmondsworth: Penguin Books.

West, C. (1984) *Routine Complications: Troubles in Talk between Doctors and Patients*, Bloomington, IN: Indiana University Press.

West, C. and Zimmerman, D. (1987) 'Doing gender', *Gender and Society*, 1: 125–51.

Westbury, C. and Wilensky, U. (1998) *Knowledge Representation in Cognitive Science: Implications for Education*, internal document commissioned by the Planning Office of the Ministry of Education, Government of Peru.

Westerståhl, D. (1984) 'Determiners and context sets', in J. van Benthem and A. ter Meulen (eds) *Generalized Quantifiers in Natural Language*, Dordrecht: Foris.

——(1985) 'Determiners and context sets', in J. van Benthem and A. ter Meulen (eds) *Generalized Quantifiers in Natural Language*, Dordrecht: Foris Publications.

Wetherby, A.M. and Prizant, B.M. (1998) 'Communicative, social/affective, and symbolic profiles of young children with autism and pervasive developmental disorders', *American Journal of Speech-Language Pathology*, 7: 79–91.

Wetherby, A.M. and Prutting, C.A. (1984) 'Profiles of communicative and cognitive-social abilities in autistic children', *Journal of Speech and Hearing Research*, 27: 364–77.

Wetherby, A.M., Cain, D., Yonclas, D. and Walker, V. (1988) 'Analysis of intentional communication of normal children from the prelinguistic to multi-word stage', *Journal of Speech and Hearing Research*, 31: 240–52.

Wexler, K. (to appear) 'Maximal trouble: cues don't explain learning', in E. Gibson and N. Pearlmutter (eds) *The Processing and Acquisition of Reference*, Cambridge, MA: MIT Press.

Weylman, S.T., Brownell, H.H., Roman, M. and Gardner, H. (1989) 'Appreciation of indirect requests by left- and right-brain-damaged patients: the effects of verbal context and conventionality of wording', *Brain and Language*, 36: 580–91.

Wharton, T. (2003a) 'Interjections, language and the "showing"/"saying" continuum', *Pragmatics and Cognition*, 11: 39–91.

——(2003b) 'Natural pragmatics and natural codes', *Mind and Language*, 18: 447–77.

——(2006) 'The evolution of pragmatics', in K. Brown (ed.) *Encyclopaedia of Language and Linguistics*, Oxford: Elsevier.

——(2009) *Pragmatics and Non-Verbal Communication*, Cambridge: Cambridge University Press.

White, H. (1973) *Metahistory: The Historical Imagination in Nineteenth-Century Europe*, Baltimore, MD: Johns Hopkins University Press.

White, L. (1991) 'Adverb placement in second language acquisition: some effects of positive and negative evidence in the classroom', *Second Language Research*, 7: 133–61.

——(2003) *Second Language Acquisition and Universal Grammar*, Cambridge: Cambridge University Press.

White, L. and Genesee, F. (1996) 'How native is near-native? The issue of ultimate attainment in second language acquisition', *Second Language Research*, 12: 238–65.

White, R. (1993) 'Saying please', *ELT Journal*, 47: 193–202.

——(1996) *The Structure of Metaphor: The Way the Language of Metaphor Works*, Oxford: Blackwell.

Whiten, A. (ed.) (1991) *Natural Theories of Mind: Evolution, Development, and Simulation of Everyday Mindreading*, Cambridge, MA: Blackwell.

——(1996) 'Imitation, pretense and mindreading: secondary representation in comparative primatology and developmental psychology?', in A.E. Russon, K.A. Bard and S.T. Parker (eds) *Reaching into Thought: The Minds of the Great Apes*, Cambridge: Cambridge University Press.

Whiten, A. and Byrne, R. (1988a) 'Taking (Machiavellian) intelligence apart: editorial', in R. Byrne and A. Whiten (eds) *Machiavellian Intelligence: Social Expertise and the Evolution of Intellect in Monkeys, Apes and Humans*, Oxford: Clarendon Press.

——(1988b) 'Tactical deception in primates', *Behavioral and Brain Sciences*, 11: 233–73.

——(1991) 'The emergence of metarepresentation in human ontogeny and primate phylogeny', in A. Whiten (ed.) *Natural Theories of Mind: Evolution, Development and Simulation of Everyday Mindreading*, Oxford: Blackwell.

Whitworth, A., Lesser, R. and McKeith, I. (1999) 'Profiling conversation in Parkinson's disease with cognitive impairment', *Aphasiology*, 13: 407–25.

Whitworth, A., Perkins, L. and Lesser, R. (1997) *Conversation Analysis Profile for People with Aphasia*, London: Whurr Publishers Ltd.

Whorf, B.L. (1956a) 'Selected writings of Benjamin Lee Whorf', in J. Carroll (ed.) *Language, Thought and Reality*, Cambridge, MA: MIT Press.

——(1956b) *Language, Thought and Reality: Selected Writings*, Cambridge, MA: MIT Press.

Wichmann, A. (2000) *Intonation in Text and Discourse*, London: Longman.

——(2001) 'Spoken parentheticals', in K. Aijmer (ed.) *A Wealth of English*, Göteborg: Acta Universitatis Gothoburgensis.

——(2002) 'Attitudinal intonation and the inferential process', in B. Bell and I. Marlien (eds) *Proceedings Speech Prosody 2002*, Aix-en-Provence, France, 11–15.

——(2004) 'The intonation of *please*-requests: a corpus-based study', *Journal of Pragmatics*, 36: 1521–49.

Wichmann, A., House, J. and Rietveld, T. (2000) 'Discourse effects on f0 peak timing in English', in A. Botinis (ed.) *Intonation: Analysis, Modelling and Technology*, Dordrecht: Kluwer.

Wichmann, A., Simon-Vandenbergen, A.-M. and Aijmer, K. (to appear) 'How prosody reflects semantic change: a synchronic case study of *of course*', in H. Cuyckens, K. Davidse and L. Vandelanotte (eds) *Subjectification, Intersubjectification and Grammaticalization*, Berlin: Mouton de Gruyter.

Widdowson, H.G. (1984) *Explorations in Applied Linguistics 2*, Oxford: Oxford University Press.

——(1992) *Practical Stylistics*, Oxford: Oxford University Press.

Widjaja, C.S. (1997) 'A study of date refusals: Taiwanese females vs. American females', *University of Hawaii Working Papers in ESL*, 15: 1–43.

Wieland, M. (1995) 'Complimenting behavior in French/American cross-cultural dinner conversations', *French Review*, 68: 796–812.

Wiener, N. (1948) *Cybernetics: Or the Control and Communication in the Animal and the Machine*, Cambridge, MA: MIT Press.

Wierzbicka, A. (1985) 'Different cultures, different languages, different speech acts', *Journal of Pragmatics*, 9: 145–78.

——(1986a) 'Precision in vagueness: the semantics of English "approximatives"', *Journal of Pragmatics*, 10: 597–613.

——(1986b) 'The semantics of "internal dative" in English', *Quaderni di Semantica*, 7: 121–35.

——(1987) 'Boys will be boys: radical pragmatics vs. radical semantics', *Language*, 63: 95–114.

——(1988) 'Boys will be boys: a rejoinder to Bruce Fraser', *Journal of Pragmatics*, 12: 221–24.

——(1991) *Cross-Cultural Pragmatics: The Semantics of Human Interaction*, Berlin: Mouton de Gruyter.

——(1996) 'Japanese cultural scripts: cultural psychology and "cultural grammar"', *Ethos*, 24: 527–55.

——(1997) *Understanding Cultures Through their Keywords*, Oxford: Oxford University Press.

——(1998) 'German "cultural scripts": public signs as a key to social attitudes and cultural values', *Discourse and Society*, 9: 241–82.

——(2002) 'Russian cultural scripts: the theory of cultural scripts and its applications', *Ethos*, 30: 401–32.

——(2003) *Cross-Cultural Pragmatics*, 2nd edn, Berlin: Mouton de Gruyter.

——(2006a) 'Anglo scripts against "putting pressure" on other people, and their linguistic manifestations', in C. Goddard (ed.) *Ethnopragmatics: Understanding Discourse in Cultural Context*, Berlin: Mouton de Gruyter.

——(2006b) *English: Meaning and Culture*, New York: Oxford University Press.

——(2008) 'A conceptual basis for intercultural pragmatics and world-wide Understanding', in M. Pütz and J. Neff-van Aertselaer (eds) *Developing Contrastive Pragmatics: Interlanguage and Cross-Cultural Perspectives*, Berlin: Mouton de Gruyter.

Wilbur, R. (1997) 'A prosodic/pragmatic explanation for word order variation in ASL with typological implications', in M. Verspoor, K. D. Lee and E. Sweetser (eds) *Lexical and Syntactical Constructions and the Construction of Meaning*, Amsterdam: John Benjamins.

Wilcock, G. (1999) 'Lexicalization of context', in G. Webelhuth, J.-P. Koenig and A. Kathol (eds) *Lexical and Constructional Aspects of Linguistic Explanation*, Stanford, CA: CSLI Publications.

Wilcox, J. and Webster, E.J. (1980) 'Early discourse behavior: an analysis of children's responses to listener feed-back', *Child Development,* 51: 1120–25.

Wildner-Bassett, M. (1984) *Improving Pragmatic Aspects of Learners' Interlanguage,* Tübingen, Germany: Narr.

Wilkins, D.P. (1976) *Notional Syllabuses: A Taxonomy and its Relevance to Foreign Language Curriculum Development,* London: Oxford University Press.

——(1994) 'Applied linguistics', in R.E. Asher and J.M.Y. Simpson (eds) *The Encyclopedia of Language and Linguistics,* Oxford: Pergamon Press.

Williams, D. (1992) *Nobody Nowhere: The Remarkable Autobiography of an Autistic Girl,* London: Jessica Kingsley.

——(1994) *Somebody Somewhere,* London: Jessica Kingsley.

——(1999) *Like Colour to the Blind,* London: Jessica Kingsley.

Williams, E. (1997) 'Blocking and anaphora', *Linguistic Inquiry,* 28: 577–628.

Williams, G. and Morris, D. (2000) *Language Planning and Language Use,* Cardiff: University of Wales Press.

Williamson, T. (2000) *Knowledge and Its Limits,* Oxford: Oxford University Press.

Willis, J. (1992) 'Inner and outer: spoken discourse in the language classroom', in M. Coulthard (ed.) *Advances in Spoken Discourse Analysis,* London: Routledge.

Wilson, B. (1998) *Wittgenstein's Philosophical Investigations: A Guide,* Edinburgh: Edinburgh University Press.

Wilson, D. (1975) *Presuppositions and Non-Truth-Conditional Semantics,* London: Academic Press.

——(2000) 'Metarepresentation in linguistic communication', in D. Sperber (ed.) *Metarepresentation in an Evolutionary Perspective,* Oxford: Oxford University Press.

——(2003) 'Relevance and lexical pragmatics', *Italian Journal of Linguistics / Rivista di Linguistica,* 15: 273–91.

——(2005) 'New directions for research on pragmatics and modularity', *Lingua,* 115: 1129–46.

——(2006) 'The pragmatics of verbal irony: echo or pretence?', *Lingua,* 116: 1722–43.

Wilson, D. and Carston, R. (2006) 'Metaphor, relevance and the "emergent property" issue', *Mind and Language* 21: 404–33.

——(2007a) 'A unitary approach to lexical pragmatics: relevance, inference and ad hoc concepts', in N. Burton-Roberts (ed.) *Advances in Pragmatics,* Basingstoke: Palgrave Macmillan.

——(2007b) 'Metaphor and the "emergent property" problem: a relevance-theoretic approach', in E. Camp (ed.) *The Baltic International Yearbook of Cognition, Logic and Communication. Vol. 3: A Figure of Speech.* Online. Available: http://thebalticyearbook.org/journals/baltic/article/view/23/22 (accessed 24 November 2008).

Wilson, D. and Sperber, D. (1981) 'On Grice's theory of conversation', in P. Werth (ed.) *Conversation and Discourse,* London: Croom Helm; reprinted in A. Kasher (ed.) (1998) *Pragmatics: Critical Concepts,* vol. IV, London: Routledge.

——(1988) 'Mood and the analysis of non-declarative sentences', in J. Dancy, J. Moravcsik and C. Taylor (eds) *Human Agency: Language, Duty and Value,* Stanford, CA: Stanford University Press; reprinted in A. Kasher (ed.) (1998) *Pragmatics: Critical Concepts,* vol. II, London: Routledge.

——(1992) 'On verbal irony', *Lingua,* 87: 53–76.

——(1993) 'Linguistic form and relevance', *Lingua,* 90: 1–25.

——(1998) 'Pragmatics and time', in R. Carston and S. Uchida (eds) *Relevance Theory: Applications and Implications,* Amsterdam: John Benjamins.

——(2002) 'Truthfulness and relevance', *Mind and Language,* 111: 583–632.

——(2004) 'Relevance theory', in L.R. Horn and G. Ward (eds) *Handbook of Pragmatics,* Oxford: Blackwell.

——(2007) 'On verbal irony', in R. Gibbs and H. Colston (eds) *Irony in Language and Thought: A Cognitive Science Reader,* New York: Lawrence Erlbaum Associates.

Wilson, D. and Wharton, T. (2006) 'Relevance and prosody', *Journal of Pragmatics,* 38: 1559–79.

Wilson, J. (1990) *Politically Speaking: The Pragmatic Analysis of Political Language,* Oxford: Blackwell.

Wilss, W. (1996) *Knowledge and Skills in Translator Behavior,* Amsterdam: John Benjamins.

Wimmer, H. and Perner, J. (1983) 'Beliefs about beliefs: representation and constraining function of wrong beliefs in young children's understanding of deception', *Cognition,* 13: 103–28.

Winner, E. (1988) *The Point of Words: Children's Understanding of Metaphor and Irony,* Cambridge, MA: Harvard University Press.

Winner, E. and Gardner, H. (1977) 'The comprehension of metaphor in brain-damaged patients', *Brain,* 100: 717–29.

Winner, E. and Leekam, S. (1991) 'Distinguishing irony from deception: understanding the speaker's second-order intention', *British Journal of Developmental Psychology,* 9: 257–70.

Winner, E., Brownell, H., Happe, F., Blum, A. and Pincus, D. (1998) 'Distinguishing lies from jokes: theory of mind deficits and discourse interpretation in right hemisphere brain-damaged patients', *Brain and Language*, 62: 89–106.

Winner, E., Levy, J., Kaplan, J. and Rosenblatt, E. (1988) 'Children's understanding of nonliteral language', *Journal of Aesthetic Education*, 22: 51–63.

Winner, E., Windmueller, G., Rosenblatt, E. and Bosco, L. (1987) 'Making sense of literal and nonliteral falsehood', *Metaphor and Symbolic Activity*, 2: 13–32.

Winograd, T. (1972) *Understanding Natural Language*, San Diego, CA: Academic Press.

Winograd, T. and Flores, F. (1986) *Understanding Computers and Cognition: A New Foundation for Design*, Norwood, NJ: Ablex.

Winston, E.A. (1995) 'Spatial mapping in comparative discourse frames', in K. Emmorey and J.S. Reilly (eds) *Language, Gesture, and Space*, Hillsdale, NJ: Lawrence Erlbaum.

Winston, P.H. (ed.) (1975) *The Psychology of Computer Vision*, New York: McGraw-Hill.

Winter, Y. (1997) 'Choice functions and the scopal semantics of indefinites', *Linguistics and Philosophy*, 20: 399–467.

Withers, S. (1997) 'Silence and communication in art', in A. Jaworski (ed.) *Silence: Interdisciplinary Perspectives*, Berlin: Mouton de Gruyter.

Wittgenstein, L. ([1922] 1974) *Tractatus Logico-Philosophicus*, London: Routledge and Kegan Paul.

——([1953a] 1963) *Philosophical Investigations*, trans. G.E.M. Anscombe, Oxford: Basil Blackwell.

——(1953b) *The Blue and Brown Books*, New York: Harper and Row.

——(1958) *Philosophical Investigations*, Oxford: Blackwell.

Wodak, R. (1996) *Disorders of Discourse*, London: Longman.

——(2005) 'Discourse analysis (Foucault)', in D. Herman, M. Jahn and M.-L. Ryan (eds) *Routledge Encyclopedia of Narrative Theory*, London: Routledge.

——(2008) 'Introduction: discourse, text and context', in R. Wodak and M. Krzyżanowski (eds) *Qualitative Discourse Analysis in the Social Sciences*, Basingstoke: Palgrave Macmillan.

——(2009) *Politics as Usual: The Discursive Construction and Representation of Politics in Action*, Basingstoke: Palgrave Macmillan.

Wodak, R. and Chilton, P. (2005) *A New Agenda in (Critical) Discourse Analysis*, Amsterdam: John Benjamins.

Wodak, R. and de Cillia, R. (2006) 'Politics and language: overview', in K. Brown (ed.) *Encyclopedia of Language and Linguistics*, Oxford: Elsevier.

——(2007) 'Commemorating the past: the discursive construction of official narratives about the rebirth of the second Austrian republic', *Discourse and Commmunication*, 1: 337–63.

Wodak, R. and Kirsch, P. (eds) (1995) *Totalitäre Sprachen: Langue de Bois*, Vienna: Passagen Verlag.

Wodak, R. and Pelinka, A. (eds) (2002) *The Haider Phenomenon in Austria*, New Brunswick, NJ: Transaction Press.

Wodak, R. and Van de Craen, P. (eds) (1987) *Neurotic and Psychotic Language Behaviour*, Philadelphia, PA: Elevedon.

Wodak, R. and van Dijk, T.A. (eds) (2000) *Racism at the Top*, Klagenfurt, Austria: Drava.

Wodak, R. and Weiss, G. (2007) 'Analyzing European Union discourses: theories and applications', in R. Wodak and P. Chilton (eds) *A New Agenda in (Critical) Discourse Analysis*, Amsterdam: John Benjamins.

Wolfram, W. and Schilling-Estes, N. (2006) *American English: Dialects and Variation*, Malden, MA: Blackwell.

Wolfram, W. and Shuy, R. (1974) *The Study of Social Dialects in American English*, New York: Prentice-Hall.

Wolfson, N. (1980) 'The compliment as a social strategy', *Papers in Linguistics*, 13: 391–410.

——(1981) 'Compliments in cross-cultural perspective', *TESOL Quarterly*, 15: 117–24.

——(1983) 'An empirically based analysis of complimenting in American English', in N. Wolfson and E. Judd (eds) *Sociolinguistics and Language Acquisition*, Cambridge, MA: Newbury House.

——(1984) 'Pretty is as pretty does: a speech act view of sex roles', *Applied Linguistics*, 5: 236–44.

——(1989) 'The social dynamics of native and nonnative variation in complimenting behaviour', in M. Eisenstein (ed.) *The Dynamic Interlanguage: Empirical Studies in Second Language Variation*, New York: Plenum Press.

Wolfson, N., Marmor, T. and Jones, S. (1989) 'Problems in the comparison of speech acts across cultures', in S. Blum-Kulka, J. House and G. Kasper (eds) *Cross-Cultural Pragmatics: Requests and Apologies*, Norwood, NJ: Ablex.

Wolter, L. (2006) *That's that: the semantics and pragmatics of demonstrative noun phrases*, Ph.D. dissertation, University of California, Santa Cruz.

Wong, J. (2004) 'Cultural scripts, ways of speaking and perceptions of personal autonomy:

Anglo English vs. Singapore English', *Intercultural Pragmatics*, 1: 231–48.

Wood, A.W. (1985) 'Habermas's defence of rationalism', *New German Critique*, 35: 145–64.

Wood, J.N., Glynn, D.D., Phillips, B.C. and Hauser, M.D. (2007) 'The perception of rational, goal-directed action in nonhuman primates', *Science*, 317: 1402–5.

Wood, L. (1933) 'The paradox of negative judgment', *Philosophical Review*, 42: 412–23.

Woodfield, A. (1994) 'Intentionality', in R.E. Asher (ed.) *The Encyclopedia of Language and Linguistics*, Oxford: Pergamon Press.

Woods, J. (1991) 'Pragma-dialectics: a radical departure in fallacy theory', *Communication and Cognition*, 24: 43–54.

——(1995) 'Appeal to force', in H.V. Hansen and R.C. Pinto (eds) *Fallacies: Classical and Contemporary Readings*, Pennsylvania: The Pennsylvania State University Press.

——(2004) *The Death of Argument: Fallacies in Agent-Based Reasoning*, Dordrecht and Boston, MA: Kluwer.

Woods, J. and Walton, D. (2007) *Fallacies: Selected Papers 1972–1982*, 2nd edn, London: College Publications.

Woods, W.A. (1975) 'What's in a link: foundations for semantic networks', in D.G. Bobrow and A. Collins (eds) *Representation and Understanding*, New York: Academic Press.

Woodward, A.L. (2000) 'Constraining the problem space in early word learning', in R. Golinkoff, K. Hirsh-Pasek, N. Bloom, G. Hollich, L. Smith, A.L. Woodward, L. Akhtar, M. Tomasello and G. Hollich (eds) *Becoming a Word Learner: A Debate on Lexical Acquisition*, Oxford: Oxford University Press.

Wooffitt, R. (2005) *Conversation Analysis and Discourse Analysis: A Comparative and Critical Introduction*, London: Sage.

Woolls, D. (2003) 'Better tools for the trade and how to use them', *Forensic Linguistics*, 10: 102–12.

Woolls, D. and Coulthard, M. (1998) 'Tools for the trade', *Forensic Linguistics*, 5: 33–57.

Wootton, A.J. (1981) 'Conversation analysis', in P.G. French and M. Maclure (eds) *Adult-Child Conversation: Studies in Structure and Process*, London: Croom Helm.

——(1989) 'Remarks on the methodology of conversation analysis', in D. Roger and P. Bull (eds) *Conversation*, Clevedon: Multilingual Matters.

Worrall, L. and Yiu, E. (2000) 'Effectiveness of functional communication therapy by volunteers for people with aphasia following stroke', *Aphasiology*, 14: 911–24.

Worster, D. (1996) 'How to do things with salesmen', in L. Kane (ed.) *David Mamet's Glengarry Glen Ross: Text and Performance*, New York and London: Garland Publishing.

Wortham, S. (2000) 'Interactional positioning and narrative self-construction', *Narrative Inquiry*, 10: 157–84.

——(2006) *The Joint Emergence of Social Identification and Academic Learning*, Cambridge: Cambridge University Press.

Wouk, F. (2006) 'The language of apologising in Lombok, Indonesia', *Journal of Pragmatics*, 38: 1457–86.

Wray, A. (2002a) *Formulaic Language and the Lexicon*, Cambridge: Cambridge University Press.

——(2002b) 'Formulaic language in computer-supported communication: theory meets reality', *Language Awareness*, 11: 114–31.

Wray, A. and Perkins, M. (2000) 'The functions of formulaic language: an integrated model', *Language and Communication*, 20: 1–28.

Wright, S. (2003) *Language Policy and Language Planning: From Nationalism to Globalization*, London: Palgrave Macmillan.

——(2004) *Language Policy and Language Planning: From Nationalism to Globalisation*, Basingstoke: Palgrave Macmillan.

Wrobel, J. (1990) *Language and Schizophrenia*, Philadelphia: John Benjamins.

Wu, S. and Keysar, B. (2007) 'The effect of culture on perspective taking', *Psychological Science*, 18: 600–606.

Xu, F. (2007) 'Sortal concepts, object individuation, and language', *Trends In Cognitive Science*, 11: 400–406.

Yamada, M. (2003) *The Pragmatics of Negation*, Tokyo: Hituzi Syobo.

Yamashita, S.O. (1996) *Six Measures of JSL Pragmatics*, Honolulu, HI: Second Language Teaching and Curriculum Center, University of Hawaii at Manoa.

Yamayaki, J. (2004) 'Crafting the apology: Japanese apologies to North Korea in 1990', *Asian Journal of Communication*, 14: 150–73.

Yang, L.-C. (2004) 'Duration and pauses as cues to discourse boundaries in speech', paper presented at Speech Prosody 2004, Nara, Japan, March 2004. Online. Available: www.isca-speech.org/archive/sp2004/sp04_267.pdf (accessed 25 September 2008).

Ye, L. (1995) 'Complimenting in Mandarin Chinese', in G. Kasper (ed.) *Pragmatics of Chinese as Native and Target Language*, Honolulu, HI: Second Language Teaching and Curriculum Centre, University of Hawaii at Manoa.

Yi, Y. (2002) 'Compliments in Kunming Chinese', *Pragmatics*, 12: 183–225.

Ylanne-McEwen, V. (1993) 'Complimenting behaviour: a cross-cultural investigation', *Journal of Multilingual and Multicultural Development*, 14: 499–508.

Yli-Vakkuri, V. (2005) 'Politeness in Finland', in L. Hickey and M. Stewart (eds) *Politeness in Europe*, Clevedon: Multilingual Matters.

Ylvisaker, M. (2006) 'Self-coaching: a context-sensitive, person-centred approach to social communication after traumatic brain injury', *Brain Impairment*, 7: 246–58.

Ylvisaker, M. and Szekeres, S.F. (1989) 'Meta-cognitive and executive impairments in head-injured children and adults', *Topics in Language Disorders*, 9: 34–49.

Ylvisaker, M., Szekeres, S.F. and Feeney, T. (2001) 'Communication disorders associated with traumatic brain injury', in R. Chapey (ed.) *Language Intervention Strategies in Aphasia and Related Neurogenic Communication Disorders*, Philadelphia, PA: Lippincott, Williams and Wilkins.

Yngve, V. (1970) 'On getting a word in edgewise', in M.A. Campbell (ed.) *Papers from the Sixth Regional Meeting of the Chicago Linguistic Society*, Chicago, IL: Chicago Linguistic Society.

Young, E.C., Diehl, J.J., Morris, D., Hyman, S. L. and Bennetto, L. (2005) 'The use of two language tests to identify pragmatic language problems in children with autism spectrum disorders', *Language, Speech and Hearing Services in Schools*, 36: 62–72.

Youse, K.M. (2005) *Attentional deficits and conversational discourse in closed-head injury*, unpublished thesis, University of Connecticut.

Yu, M.C. (2003) 'On the universality of face: evidence from Chinese compliment response behavior', *Journal of Pragmatics*, 35: 1679–710.

Yuan, Y. (1998) *Sociolinguistic dimensions of the compliment event in the southwestern Mandarin spoken in Kunming, China*, unpublished thesis, Indiana University.

Yuill, N. and Oakhill, J. (1992) *Children's Problems in Text Comprehension*, Cambridge: Cambridge University Press.

Yus, F. (2003) 'Humor and the search for relevance', *Journal of Pragmatics*, 35: 1295–331.

——(2008) *Relevance Theory Online Bibliography*. Online. Available: www.ua.es/personal/francisco.yus/rt.html (accessed 3 March 2008).

Zachry, M. (2009) 'Rhetorical analysis', in F. Bargiela-Chiappini (ed.) *The Handbook of Business Discourse*, Edinburgh: Edinburgh University Press.

Zaenen, A. (ed.) (1982) *Subjects and Other Subjects: Proceedings of the Harvard Conference on Grammatical Relations*, Bloomington, IN: Indiana University Linguistics Club.

Zahn, C. (1984) 'A reexamination of conversational repair', *Communication Monographs*, 51: 56–66.

Zaidel, E., Kasher, A., Soroker, N. and Batori, G. (2002) 'Effects of right and left hemisphere damage on performance of the "right hemisphere communication battery"', *Brain and Language*, 80: 510–35.

Zaidel, E., Kasher, A., Soroker, N., Batori, G., Giora, R. and Graves, D. (2000) 'Hemispheric contributions to pragmatics', *Brain and Cognition*, 43: 438–43.

Zajdman, A. (1991) 'Contextualization of canned jokes in discourse', *HUMOR: International Journal of Humor Research*, 4: 23–40.

Zeevat, H. (2001) 'The asymmetry of optimality theoretic syntax and semantics', *Journal of Semantics*, 17: 243–62.

——(2003) 'Particles: presupposition triggers, context markers or speech act markers', in R. Blutner and H. Zeevat (eds) *Optimality Theory and Pragmatics*, New York: Palgrave Macmillan.

——(2006) 'Freezing and marking', *Linguistics*, 44: 1095–111.

——(2008) 'Discourse structure in optimality theoretic pragmatics', in C. Sidner, J. Harpur, A. Benz and P. Kühnlein (eds) *Proceedings of the 2nd Workshop on Constraints in Discourse*, Amsterdam and Philadelphia, PA: John Benjamins.

Zeevat, H. and Jäger, G. (2002) 'A statistical reinterpretation of harmonic alignment', in D. de Jongh, M. Nilsenova and H. Zeevat (eds) *Proceedings of the 4th Tbilisi Symposium on Logic, Language and Linguistics*, Tiblisi and Amsterdam: ILLC/ICLC.

Žegarac, V. (1998) 'What is phatic communication?', in V. Rouchota and A. Jucker (eds) *Current Issues in Relevance Theory*, Amsterdam: John Benjamins.

Žegarac, V. and Clark, B. (1999a) 'Phatic interpretations and phatic communication', *Journal of Linguistics*, 35: 321–46.

——(1999b) 'A reply to Ward and Horn', *Journal of Linguistics*, 35: 565–77.

Žegarac, V. and Pennington, M. (2000) 'Pragmatic transfer in intercultural communication', in H. Spencer-Oatey (ed.) *Culturally Speaking: Managing Rapport through Talk across Cultures*, London: Continuum.

Zeldovich, G. (2005) 'Russian "Chto bylo, to bylo", Polish "Co bylo, to bylo": are the rules of pragmatics language-specific?', *Studies in Polish Linguistics*, 2: 49–59.

Zhang, H. (2001) 'Culture and apology: "The Hainan Island incident"', *World Englishes*, 20: 383–91.

Zhang, J.Y., Toth, A.R., Collins-Thompson, K. and Black, A.W. (2004) 'Prominence prediction for supersentential prosodic modeling based on a new database', in A.W. Black and K. Lenzo (eds) *Proceedings of the Fifth International Speech Communication Association Speech Synthesis Workshop*, Pittsburg, PA: ISCA.

Zhang, Y.-Y. (1995) 'Indirectness in Chinese requesting', in G. Kasper (ed.) *Pragmatics of Chinese as Native and Target Language*, Manoa, HI: University of Hawaii Press.

Zhou, J. (2002) *Pragmatic Development of Mandarin-Speaking Children from 14 Months to 32 Months*, Nanjing, China: Nanjing Normal University Press.

Zhu, Y. and Li, L. (2009) 'China', in F. Bargiela-Chiappini (ed.) *The Handbook of Business Discourse*, Edinburgh: Edinburgh University Press.

Zipf, G.K. (1949) *Human Behavior and the Principle of Least Effort*, Cambridge: Addison-Wesley.

Ziv, Y. (1976) *On the communicative effect of relative clause extraposition in English*, Ph.D. dissertation, University of Illinois.

——(2002) 'This, *I believe*, is a processing instruction: discourse linking via parentheticals', in Y.N. Falk (ed.) *Proceedings of Israel Association for Theoretical Linguistics* 18, Bar Ilan University.

Zorn, R. (ed.) (1972) *Machiavelli, Nicolo: Der Fürst. 'Il Principe'*, Stuttgart: Klett.

Zwarts, J. (2003) 'Lexical competition: "round" in English and Dutch', in P. Dekker and R. van Rooy (eds) *Proceedings of the Fourteenth Amsterdam Colloquium*, Amsterdam: ILLC.

——(2006) 'Om en rond: een semantische vergelijking', *Nederlandse Taalkunde*, 11: 101–23.

Zwarts, L.R. (1995) 'Nonveridical contexts', *Linguistic Analysis*, 25: 286–312.

Zwicky, A. and Sadock, J. (1975) 'Ambiguity tests and how to fail them', in J.P. Kimball (ed.) *Syntax and Semantics*, vol. 4, New York: Academic Press.

Zwicky, A.M. (1974) 'Hey, whatsyourname!', in M.W. LaGaly (ed.) *Papers from the Tenth Regional Meeting of the Chicago Linguistic Society*, Chicago, IL: University of Chicago Press.

Index

abduction **1–3**; computational pragmatics and 72; conjectural nature of 1; inference and 218; pragmatics and 343; utterance interpretation and 486

academic discourse **3–5**; disciplinary differences in 4–5; hedges and 186; interactiveness in 4

advertising: cohesion in 5–6; given and new information, concepts of 6; historical pragmatics and 190; pragmatics of **5–7**; relevance, concept of 7; semiotics and 432

Aitchison, Jean 243

Alzheimer's Association 105–6

Alzheimer's disease (AD) 42, 105, 106, 293, 343, 344

ambiguity **7–9**; in academic discourse 4; Austin on 29; context and 75; contextual plasticity of words 8; demonstratives and 108; disambiguation and 113; discourse markers and 127; ellipsis and 143; identification of 8; indefiniteness and 214; in internet language 236; lexical ambiguity 8; negation, pragmatics and 288; post-Gricean pragmatics and 334; propositional attitudes and 359; prosody, pragmatics and 360; psycholinguistics and 367; reference and 388; relevance theory and 396; semantics-pragmatics interface and 429; specificity and 450; translation, pragmatics and 475; vagueness and 487; what is said and 489

American National Corpus (ANC) 88

American Psychiatric Association (APA) 105–6

anaphora, pragmatics of **9–13**, 342; deixis, language and 104; formal pragmatics and 168; narrative discourse and 284; neo-Gricean account 12; neo-Gricean pragmatics and 289; pragmatic approach to anaphora 11–13; pragmatic nature of anaphora 9–11;

semantics and 426; syntax-pragmatics interface and 462

Angell, James 281

Anglo-American tradition **13**; pragmatics and 341

animal communication: communication and 60; knowledge in 243; misunderstanding 270; non-verbal communication, pragmatics and 296; pragmatics of **15–17**; psycholinguistics and 365

Anscombe, Elizabeth 304

Apel, Karl Otto 192

Aphasia Treatment Program 392

apologies **17–19**; complaints and 68, 70; cross-cultural pragmatics and 90; definition of 17–18; disagreement and 112; historical pragmatics and 192; pragmatics and 344; refusals and 389; semantic formulas for 17; societal pragmatics and 446; speech act type and 457; translation, pragmatics and 475

applied linguistics **19–21**; functionality in 20; interlanguage pragmatics and 234; second language acquisition and 420

approximation in lexical pragmatics 247

approximators 186

argumentation theory **21–23**; fallacy theory and 163; hedges and 187

argumentum ad hominem, fallacy of 338

Aristotle 87, 133, 193, 227, 287, 422; analytics, argumentation theory and 21; *De Interpretatione* 80; politics, political discourse and 330; *Prior Analytics* 1; refutations, sophistical 164; *Rhetoric* 403–4; systematic logic foundation of 163

artificial intelligence **23–25**; cognitive anthropology and 44; cognitive science and 56; context and 75; formal pragmatics and 169; knowledge in 242; Markov Decision